APPLIED SPORT PSYCHOLOGY

SIXTH EDITION

APPLIED SPORT PSYCHOLOGY

PERSONAL GROWTH TO PEAK PERFORMANCE

Jean M. Williams, Editor
University of Arizona, Emeritus

McGraw Hill

Boston   Burr Ridge, IL   Dubuque, IA   Madison, WI   New York   San Francisco   St. Louis
Bangkok   Bogotá   Caracas   Kuala Lumpur   Lisbon   London   Madrid   Mexico City
Milan   Montreal   New Delhi   Santiago   Seoul   Singapore   Sydney   Taipei   Toronto

The McGraw·Hill Companies

APPLIED SPORT PSYCHOLOGY, SIXTH EDITION
International Edition 2010

Exclusive rights by McGraw-Hill Education (Asia), for manufacture and export. This book cannot be re-exported from the country to which it is sold by McGraw-Hill. This International Edition is not to be sold or purchased in North America and contains content that is different from its North American version.

Published by McGraw-Hill, an imprint of The McGraw-Hill Companies, Inc., 1221 Avenue of the Americas, New York, NY 10020. Copyright © 2010, 2006, 2001, 1998, 1993, 1986 by The McGraw-Hill Companies, Inc. All rights reserved. No part of this publication may be reproduced or distributed in any form or by any means, or stored in a database or retrieval system, without the prior written consent of The McGraw-Hill Companies, Inc., including, but not limited to, in any network or other electronic storage or transmission, or broadcast for distance learning.
Some ancillaries, including electronic and print components, may not be available to customers outside the United States.

10 09 08 07 06 05 04 03 02
20 15 14 13 12 11 10
CTP BJE

The Internet addresses listed in the text were accurate at the time of publication. The inclusion of a Web site does not indicate an endorsement by the authors of McGraw-Hill, and McGraw-Hill does not guarantee the accuracy of the information presented at these sites.

When ordering this title, use ISBN 978-007-126798-4 or MHID 007-126798-0

Printed in Singapore

AS EDITOR, I DEDICATE THIS SIXTH EDITION TO ALL THE CONTRIBUTORS WHO PARTICIPATED IN THIS PROJECT AND THUS SHARED THEIR VAST EXPERTISE WITH THE READERS. THE HIGH ACCEPTANCE GIVEN TO EARLIER EDITIONS OF THIS BOOK, AND THE FACT THAT WE ARE GOING INTO OUR SIXTH EDITION 25 YEARS LATER, IS DUE PRIMARILY TO THEIR EFFORTS, AND I AM GREATLY INDEBTED TO THEM. WHATEVER CONTRIBUTION THIS BOOK CONTINUES TO MAKE TO APPLIED SPORT AND EXERCISE PSYCHOLOGY WILL BE IN LARGE MEASURE A CONSEQUENCE OF THEIR EFFORTS.

BRIEF CONTENTS

CONTENTS

Coaches and athletes have turned to applied sport psychology to gain a competitive edge—to learn, among other things, ways to manage competitive stress, control concentration, improve confidence, increase communication skills, and promote team harmony.

The first edition of *Applied Sport Psychology: Personal Growth to Peak Performance,* which was published 25 years ago, was one of the first books written specifically to introduce coaches and sport psychologists to psychological theories and techniques that could be used to enhance the performance and personal growth of sport participants from youth sport to elite levels. The book focused primarily on three dimensions: (1) techniques for developing and refining psychological skills to enhance performance and personal growth, (2) suggestions for establishing a learning and social environment that would enhance the effectiveness of coaches and maximize the skill and personal growth of athletes, and (3) special issues such as staleness and burnout, psychology of injury and injury rehabilitation, and retirement from athletics.

Later editions had the same focus but were expanded to cover more topics and to add a physical activity focus. New chapters were added on motivation, training youth sport coaches, improving communication, referring athletes for professional counseling, drug abuse in sport, and exercise psychology. The last chapter reflected the growing importance to applied sport psychology of understanding the psychological benefits and risks of exercise and the psychological and behavioral principles for enhancing exercise adoption and adherence.

The same important topics, focus, and organizational structure have been retained for this sixth edition, but the revision reflects the latest research, practice, and anecdotal examples in applied sport psychology. Many new exercises and case studies have been added in order to help students think more critically and to apply the content to real-world situations. In addition, a chapter has been added on gender and cultural considerations to reflect the importance of sport psychology researchers and practitioners having cultural competence.

Applied Sport Psychology is particularly well suited as a text for classes in applied sport psychology and psychology of coaching. The book is also a valuable reference for practicing coaches, sport psychologists, and psychologists. Here are some of the reasons the sixth edition continues to be exceptionally well suited for these classes and individuals.

Written Specifically for Sport Psychologists and Coaches

Approximately 400 books have been published on mental skills for peak performance, but most of these books continue to be written primarily for the sport participant. Their coverage is not comprehensive enough for the sport psychologist or coach who need to understand the rationale behind the psychological constructs and must know how to make application across a wide variety of situations and sport participants. Books written for sport psychologists and coaches are typically general textbooks that attempt to cover the entire field of sport psychology. Thus their coverage of applied issues—and particularly psychological interventions for enhancing sport performance, personal growth, and exercise participation—is superficial compared to the in-depth coverage this text provides. Other applied textbooks do not have the comprehensive coverage of this book, the expertise of the diverse contributors, or as clear a presentation of the theories and research that provide the foundation for application.

Based on the Latest Research and Practice

The knowledge and experiential base in applied sport psychology, particularly for science-based interventions, has greatly expanded since the initial publication of this book. Each new edition has reflected the latest research and cutting-edge practice in applied sport psychology. Although the primary focus of the sixth edition continues to be on application, each chapter provides theoretical and research foundations when appropriate. When using the book as a textbook for a graduate course, the instructor may want to supplement it with readings from the research studies cited by the contributors.

Comprehensive Coverage of Topics

No other text in applied sport psychology encompasses the comprehensive approach taken here. The first chapter discusses the past, present, and future of sport psychology. The remainder of the book is divided into four parts.

Part One covers learning, feedback, motivation, leadership, and social interactions that result in group cohesion and the development of effective groups and communication. For clarity and simplicity, some of these chapters have been written in the vernacular of the coach. These chapters are not only useful for coaches, however. Sport psychologists frequently find it necessary to work with coaches in areas such as improving communication skills, building team rapport, and fostering more effective leadership behaviors. Also, the same principles of learning, motivation, and social interaction that help to increase a coach's effectiveness apply to the sport psychologist teaching mental skills and interacting with athletes. Thus the knowledge and insight gained from reading the chapters in Part Two are as appropriate for current and prospective sport psychologists as they are for coaches.

Part Two of the book discusses mental training for enhancing performance. This section begins with a chapter on the psychological characteristics of peak performance; other chapters discuss identifying ideal performance states, setting and achieving goals, managing stress and energy levels, training in imagery, identifying optimal concentration and learning how to control it, and building confidence. Part Three deals with implementing training programs. The first chapter provides suggestions for integrating and implementating a psychological skills training program. The second chapter provides guidance on how to conduct sport psychology training programs with coaches. The final chapter, which is new to this edition, deals with gender and cultural considerations, including suggestions for achieving cultural competence.

Part Four focuses on enhancing health and wellness. It contains chapters that address when sport competitors should be referred for professional counseling, causes and cures for drug abuse in sport, the occurrence and prevention of burnout, injury risk and rehabilitation, termination from sport competition, and the psychological benefits of exercise as well as interventions to increase exercise adoption and adherence. No sport psychology book has dealt with all of these issues, even though they are crucial to sport performance, personal development, and the enhancement of sport and exercise participation and benefits.

The appropriateness of these chapters for certain courses will depend on the students' backgrounds and interests. The book was planned to provide complete coverage of psychological theories, techniques, and issues relevant to enhancing personal growth, sport performance, and exercise participation. Instructors may select those chapters that are appropriate for their courses. For example, Chapters 2 and 3 concern motor skills learning and principles of reinforcement and feedback; this material might be redundant if students already have a thorough background in motor learning. Chapter 24, on termination from sport competition, may interest only individuals who work with athletes who are nearing retirement or dropping out of sport competition.

Written by Leading Experts in Sport Psychology

The contributors to this volume are leading scholars and practitioners in sport and exercise psychology. They work with sport participants from youth sport to Olympic and professional levels, and many have illustrious backgrounds as elite athletes or coaches.

Integrated Organization and Writing Style

The book has the major advantage of drawing on the diverse expertise and perspectives of 46 contributors, but it avoids the common disadvantage of disparate coverage and diverse writing styles frequently found in edited textbooks. The content and sequencing of chapters have been carefully coordinated to ensure comprehensive coverage and progressive development of concepts while eliminating undesirable overlap and inconsistency in terminology. Writing focus, styles, and organization have been standardized as much as possible. In addition, many of the chapters in this edition have been rewritten for even greater clarity and succinctness. Each chapter cites appropriate research and theory, applies this work to the world of sport and/or exercise, and provides examples and intervention exercises whenever appropriate. Each chapter also begins with an introduction that highlights the content of the chapter and ends with a conclusion or summary of the major psychological constructs and skills and study questions for students.

Application Examples and Teaching Resources

The numerous examples given throughout the book greatly facilitate the translation of psychological theory and constructs into everyday practice. Many of the examples involve well-known professional and amateur sportspeople. The examples cut across more than 40 sports and provide important anecdotal evidence that can be used to motivate individuals to develop psychological and behavioral skills for their sport and exercise participation. These real-life examples are frequently supplemented with hypothetical examples, exercises, and case studies created by the contributors to clarify appropriate applications.

In addition, McGraw-Hill's Instructors Website for this book supplements the text student-learning experiences with other exercises that are either general or specific to a given chapter. To further provide an optimal learning environment for students, the website contains for each chapter lecture PowerPoints, an objective test bank, and an annotated list of audiovisual resources such as videotapes, CD-ROMs, DVDs, and audiotapes. The Instructors Website can be found at http://www.mhhe.com/williams6e

Applied Sport Psychology Provides Many Benefits

The rewards are many for those who choose to dedicate themselves to the pursuit of excellence and personal growth through use of the theories and techniques of applied sport and exercise psychology. Coaches and sport participants acknowledge the importance of mental factors in sport development and performance, yet the time individuals actually spend practicing mental skills belies this view. In publishing this book, we have made a serious effort to help abolish that inconsistency by supplying not only the necessary knowledge to improve performance, but also the knowledge to improve the psychological climate of a sports program. The benefits that can be derived from this text will arise not just in sport performance but in overall performance outside of sport and, perhaps most important, in general personal growth and increased physical and mental health.

Acknowledgments

We wish to thank John Bartholomew, University of Texas at Austin, David Furst, San Jose State University, Tony Quinn, Saint Mary's University,

Winona, Minnesota, and Kristin Kaltenbach, Arizona State University, for their insightful reviews of the fifth edition.

We are also indebted to the fine editorial staff at McGraw-Hill, most particularly Phil Butcher, for his support and skill. In addition, we thank Marley Magaziner, our developmental editor, for her efficiency and thoroughness during the development of this edition. Finally, we would like to thank Jill Eccher, our free-lance production editor, and Ginger Rodriguez, the freelance copyeditor, for their attention to detail and guidance during the production process.

Jean M. Williams

Jean M. Williams is a professor emeritus at the University of Arizona. She taught courses in stress and coping and psychology of excellence and did consulting with intercollegiate athletes and coaches and with top amateur and professional athletes. Earlier in her career she coached nationally ranked fencing teams. Dr. Williams has published eight books (seven edited) and more than 100 research articles and book chapters. She is a past president, fellow, and certified consultant in the Association of Applied Sport Psychology and a fellow in the American Academy of Kinesiology and Physical Education.

Mark B. Andersen is a registered psychologist and professor at Victoria University, Melbourne, Australia. He teaches in the School of Sport and Exercise Science and coordinates the master and doctorate of applied psychology degrees (sport emphasis) in the School of Psychology. He teaches research design, rehabilitation, and the professional practice of psychology. He currently sits on four editorial boards. He has published five books, more than 140 journal articles and book chapters, and has made over 100 national and international conference presentations. Dr. Andersen has worked for many years counseling athletes ranging from 12-year-old juniors to American and Australian Olympians.

Mark H. Anshel is a professor in the Department of Health and Human Performance, with a joint appointment in the Department of Psychology at Middle Tennessee State University. His academic degrees include a BS in physical education (Illinois State University), and an MA (McGill University) and PhD (Florida State University) in motor behavior/sport psychology. He is the author of *Sport Psychology: From Theory to Practice* (4th ed.), *Applied Exercise Psychology,* and *Concepts in Fitness: A Balanced Approach to Good Health.* He has authored numerous book chapters and articles in scientific journals. Dr. Anshel is a Fellow with the American Psychological Association (Div. 47).

Shawn M. Arent is an assistant professor and Director of the Human Performance Laboratory in the Department of Exercise Science at Rutgers University. He completed his doctorate in exercise science at Arizona State University. His research focuses on the mechanisms underlying physiological and behavioral responses to sport and exercise. He received a national award for his work on the arousal-performance relationship. Dr. Arent is on the national staff for the U.S. Soccer Federation and is a performance consultant for various college and professional coaches and athletes. He is also a Certified Strength and Conditioning Specialist with the NSCA.

Linda K. Bunker is professor emeritus at the University of Virginia. She has worked extensively with professional golfers and tennis players. Dr. Bunker was selected as the 2000–2001 Alliance Scholar for the AAHPERD. She has written more than 100 articles and authored 15 books, including *Motivating Kids Through Play, Parenting Your Super-star, Golf: Steps to Success,* and *Mind Mastery for Winning Golf.* She was on the Advisory Board of the Womens Sports Foundation, *SHAPE* magazine, and the Melpomene Institute and was a nationally ranked tennis player and four-sport athlete at the University of Illinois.

Shauna M. Burke is an Assistant Professor in the Bachelor of Health Sciences Program at the University of Western Ontario. Her research area is the psychology of sport and exercise with a primary focus on group dynamics and physical activity. In addition to presentations at national and international scientific and professional conferences, Shauna has published her research in a number of peer-reviewed journals including *Journal of Applied Sport Psychology, Small Group Research, Psychology of Sport and Exercise,* and *Sport and Exercise Psychology Review.* Shauna also serves as a Digest Compiler for the *Journal of Sport and Exercise Psychology.*

Albert V. Carron received an EdD from the University of California, Berkeley in 1967 after undergraduate and masters degrees from the University of Alberta, Edmonton. He has taught at the University of Western Ontario for 34 years. Dr. Carron has been an author or co-author of a number of books and monographs, chapters in edited texts, and refereed publications. Professionally, he is a Fellow in the American Association of Applied Sport Psychology, and the Canadian Society for Psychomotor Learning and Sport Psychology.

Heather O'Neal Chambliss received her MA in Counseling from Louisiana Tech University and PhD in Exercise Psychology from the University of Georgia. Dr. Chambliss was a research scientist at The Cooper Institute in Dallas, TX where she was Project Director of a NIMH-funded trial examining exercise as an anti-depressant treatment and was co-chair of the CI Physical Activity and Mental Health Conference. Her interests include exercise and mental health and health behavior change. Dr. Chambliss is a fellow of the American College of Sports Medicine and serves on the ACSM Behavioral Strategies Committee.

Cheryl Coker is a professor in the Department of Human Performance, Dance and Recreation at New Mexico State University. She has coached at the Division I level in both track and field and strength and conditioning and continues to consult with several teams. This coaching experience together with her experiences as an international competitor in track and field have contributed to her research examining skill acquisition. In addition to numerous publications and presentations on coaching and motor behavior,

Dr. Coker is the author of *Motor Learning and Control for Practitioners.*

Paul W. Dennis is the development coach for the Toronto Maple Leafs of the National Hockey League, a position that requires technical and applied sport psychology expertise. He has previously consulted with the NBA's Toronto Raptors and MLS's Toronto FC. In 2002 and 2003, he was the sports psychologist to Canada's World Junior hockey team. He is currently an adjunct professor at Toronto's York University and the University of Toronto, where he teaches sport psychology courses. He received his doctorate from the University of Western Ontario under the supervision of Dr. Albert V. Carron.

Rod K. Dishman is a professor of exercise science and an adjunct professor of psychology at the University of Georgia. He advises graduate students studying behavioral neuroscience and interventions to increase physical activity. Dr. Dishman received his PhD at the University of Wisconsin, Madison and has focused his research on neurobiological aspects of the mental health outcomes associated with physical activity and on the behavioral determinants of physical activity. He is a fellow of the American College of Sports Medicine, the American Psychological Association, and the AAKPE. He has served as a consultant on exercise for the National Institutes of Health and the Sports Medicine Council for the USOC.

Joan L. Duda is a professor of sports psychology in the School of Sport and Exercise Sciences at The University of Birmingham, UK. She is past president of the AASP and has been a member of the executive boards of several professional organizations in the field. Professor Duda has published extensively on motivational processes in the physical domain and the psychological and emotional dimensions of sport, exercise, and dance. She also has been a mental skills consultant for over 25 years, working with athletes/dancers, coaches, and parents from the grassroots to the Olympic and professional levels.

Mark A. Eys received his PhD and Master's from The University of Western Ontario. He is currently an Associate Professor at Laurentian University in the School of Human Kinetics, and his research interests include group dynamics in sport and exercise with specific interests in cohesion and individual roles within a group environment. Dr. Eys is an active member of professional associations (e.g., AAASP, NASPSPA, and SCAPPS) and is an Early Researcher Award recipient from the Ministry of Research and Innovation (Province of Ontario). He is a former intercollegiate basketball player and has coached soccer at the club and university levels.

Mark G. Fischman is a Wayne T. Smith Distinguished Professor in the Department of Kinesiology at Auburn University. His doctorate is in motor learning from the Pennsylvania State University. Dr. Fischman conducts research on factors that constrain grip selection in humans, and divided attention. Dr. Fischman is a past president of NASPSPA, a fellow of the American Academy of Kinesiology and Physical Education, and the Research Consortium of AAHPERD. He will begin a three-year term as Editor-in-Chief of the *Research Quarterly for Exercise and Sport* in September, 2009. Dr. Fischman was a collegiate swimmer and has coached collegiate and age-group swimming.

Diane L. Gill is a professor in the Department of Exercise and Sport Science at the University of North Carolina at Greensboro. Her research emphasizes social psychology, with a focus on physical activity and psychological well-being. Her publications include the text, *Psychological Dynamics of Sport and Exercise,* and over 100 journal articles, and she has presented over 100 scholarly papers at national and international conferences. She is former editor of the *Journal of Sport and Exercise Psychology,* and former president of APA Division 47, the North American Society for the Psychology of Sport and Physical Activity, and the Research Consortium of AAHPERD.

Kate Goodger recently completed her PhD at Loughborough University in the U.K. in athlete burnout. She is an accredited sport psychologist with the British Association of Sport and Exercise Sciences and a practicing consultant with the English Institute of Sport (EIS). Kate works with Lottery Funded World Class athletes in Canoeing (Flatwater and Slalom) and Curling, and supported Team GB as a Holding Camp Psychologist for the British Olympic Association in Macau ahead of the Beijing 2008 Olympics. She continues her research interests as the research coordinator for the EIS Performance Psychology team.

Trish Gorely is a faculty member in the School of Sport and Exercise Sciences at Loughborough University. She received a master's degree and doctorate in sport and exercise psychology from The University of Western Australia. She has research interests in commitment, and physical activity and health. Dr. Gorely plays golf and racquet sports in her leisure time.

Daniel Gould is the director of the Institute for the Study of Youth Sports and a professor at Michigan State University. His research focuses on competitive stress and coping, positive youth development through sport, and the effectiveness of psychological skills training interventions. He is also involved in coaching education and children's sports. Dr. Gould has been a consultant to elite international athletes in a wide variety of sports. Formerly a wrestler and football and baseball player, he remains an avid fitness enthusiast. Dr. Gould was the founding co-editor of *The Sport Psychologist.* He served as president of the AASP and held leadership positions with numerous organizations such as U.S.A. Wrestling and the U.S. Olympic Committee.

Christy Greenleaf received her undergraduate degree in psychology from Bowling Green State University, her master's degree in sport studies from Miami University (Ohio), and her doctoral degree in exercise and sport science from UNC-Greensboro. She is an associate professor in the Department of Kinesiology, Health Promotion, and Recreation at the University of North Texas. She is also a member of the university's Center for Sport Psychology and Performance

Excellence. Dr. Greenleaf's research focuses on physical activity, body image, and eating attitudes within exercise and sport contexts. Dr. Greenleaf is a competitive member of an adult synchronized skating team.

Chris Harwood is a senior lecturer in the School of Sport and Exercise Sciences at Loughborough University. He received both his master's and doctoral degrees from Loughborough, and was awarded the AAASP doctoral dissertation award in 1998 for his applied research in achievement motivation. An active practitioner who is both chartered and accredited by the British Psychological Society and the British Association of Sport and Exercise Sciences, his applied work centers on coach, parent, and athlete education in high performance environments. He is currently serving as Vice-President of the European Federation of Sport Psychology (FEPSAC). Dr. Harwood plays tennis for a regional men's team and is a keen golfer and runner.

Thelma Sternberg Horn is an associate professor in the Department of Kinesiology and Health at Miami University (Ohio). Her research interests are focused on the social psychological factors that influence the psychosocial development of children, adolescents, and young adults in sport and physical activity settings. Dr. Horn is a former editor of the *Journal of Sport and Exercise Psychology,* and the third edition of her edited text, *Advances in Sport Psychology,* has just been published. She has coached at both interscholastic and intercollegiate levels and continues to work as a consultant with coaches in youth sport and interscholastic programs.

Cindra S. Kamphoff, PhD, is an assistant professor in the Department of Human Performance at the Minnesota State University, Mankato. She received her PhD from the University of North Carolina at Greensboro. Her research has focused on gender and cultural diversity, including projects on women's issues in coaching, cultural competence, and diversity content in AASP conference programs. She received the 2006 NASPE

Sport and Exercise Psychology Academy Dissertation Award. She is an active member of AAHPERD and AASP, and has presented over 30 papers at national and international conferences. She works regularly as a consultant teaching mental skills to athletes.

Vikki Krane is a professor with the School of Human Movement, Sport, and Leisure Studies at Bowling Green State University. She is a former editor of *The Sport Psychologist* and the *Women in Sport and Physical Activity Journal.* Dr. Krane is on the editorial boards of the *Journal of Applied Sport Psychology, The Sport Psychologist,* and *Qualitative Research in Sport & Exercise.* Dr. Krane is a fellow of AASP and a certified consultant. She has consulted with a variety of athletes, including high school, rising elite adolescents, and college athletes.

Francisco (Paco) Labrador received a bachelor's degree in psychology and exercise science from Hiram College in Ohio and a master's degree in sport studies from Miami University. Mr. Labrador has just completed his sixth season as the head volleyball coach of the women's intercollegiate team at Wittenberg University in Ohio. His team has reached the Final Four of the NCAA Division III national tournament during three of his six years as head coach. Mr. Labrador has also served as an assistant coach at both Miami University and at Hiram College.

Daniel M. Landers is a regents' Professor Emeritus of Kinesiology at Arizona State University. He was founding editor of the *Journal of Sport and Exercise Psychology,* and has served as president of several sport psychology research societies. He received several national-level research awards, including the NASPSPA Distinguished Scholar Award and the NASPE Hall of Fame Award for Sport Psychology. His research has focused on the arousal-performance relationship and the effect of exercise on mental health variables. He has served as a sport psychologist for collegiate teams, professional teams, and national Olympic teams in the U.S., Canada, and Korea.

David Lavallee is a Professor and Head of Department of Sport and Exercise Science at Aberystwyth University in Wales. He received a master's degree in counseling psychology from Harvard University and doctorate in sport and exercise psychology from The University of Western Australia. Professor Lavallee is Founding Editor of *Sport & Exercise Psychology Review,* Associate Editor of *The Psychologist* and *International Review of Sport and Exercise Psychology,* and on the Editorial Board of *Psychology of Sport and Exercise* and *Qualitative Research in Sport and Exercise.* He is also a former All-American soccer player.

Curt L. Lox is a professor of kinesiology and health education and an associate dean in the School of Education at Southern Illinois University Edwardsville. His research interests center broadly around the psychological and emotional aspects of exercise in special populations. Dr. Lox has coached at the youth and high school levels and continues to serve as a sport psychology consultant to players and coaches at the interscholastic, intercollegiate, and professional levels in the greater St. Louis area. He is also coauthor of an exercise psychology text titled *The Psychology of Exercise: Integrating Theory and Practice.*

Betty L. Mann received her doctorate from Springfield College, where she is a Professor of Physical Education. In August 2008, she retired from the position of Associate Vice President for Graduate Education and Research. Previous to serving in this capacity, she was Associate Dean, Graduate School with primary responsibility for coordinating physical education programs. Her areas of expertise are sport psychology, sport law, and administration. Dr. Mann has made presentations on leadership and legal issues and has written articles about the topics. She has coached women's basketball at the college and high school levels and taught middle school physical education.

Jennifer K. Mead is currently an instructor of research and statistics in the Department of Health, Physical Education, and Recreation at Springfield College. She is also completing her PhD in Physical Education with a specialization in sport and exercise psychology. Her research interests include coaching and leadership education within sport and exercise settings. Jennifer has coached at the youth, high school, and intercollegiate level. Additionally, she has competed as a member of the United States National Soccer Team, as a professional soccer player in the WUSA, and as a basketball and soccer student-athlete at Providence College and George Mason University.

Mimi C. Murray is a professor of physical education at Springfield College. Dr. Murray has been a very successful gymnastics coach. Her teams at Springfield College won three Division I National Championships and were undefeated in dual meet competition. As a sport psychology consultant, Dr. Murray has published many articles and lectured throughout the world and has worked with Olympic, professional, and collegiate athletes. She is listed on the U.S.O.C Sport Psychology Registry, is past president of the National Association for Girls and Women in Sport (NAGWS), AAHPERD, and International Council For Health, Physical Education, Recreation, Sport, & Dance (ICHPER-SD).

Robert M. Nideffer has been a professor on the faculties of the University of Rochester, the California School of Professional Psychology, and San Diego State University. He has been involved in sport psychology since 1969 and is the founder of Enhanced Performance Systems. Dr. Nideffer has published extensively in the sport psychology and stress management areas, with 15 books and more than 100 articles to his credit. He has worked with Olympic-level and professional athletes in a wide variety of sports and has been a member of policy-setting committees in the United States, Canada, and Australia.

Erik Peper, PhD, Professor of Holistic Health Studies at San Francisco State University, is president of the Biofeedback Foundation of Europe, past president of the Association for

Applied Psychophysiology. He was the behavioral scientist for the United States Rhythmic Gymnastic team. He received the 2004 California Governor's Safety Award for his work on Healthy Computing. He is an author of scientific articles and books. His most recent co-authored books are *Biofeedback Mastery, Muscle Biofeedback at the Computer*, and *Make Health Happen*. He co-produces weekly Healthy Computing Email Tips. His research interests focus on biofeedback and self-regulation, psychophysiology of health and healing.

Kenneth Ravizza is a professor at California State University at Fullerton. His research examines the nature of peak performance in a variety of domains. He has developed and implemented performance-enhancement programs for business groups, health care and school staffs, cancer patients, police officers, and physicians. He has worked with his university's baseball, softball, and gymnastics teams; with Olympic athletes such as U.S. baseball, water polo, softball, and figure skaters; and with professional teams such as the Anaheim Angels and New York Jets. He also has consulted with numerous athletic departments in the area of coaching effectiveness (UCLA, Texas, L.S.U., Harvard). Ken enjoys working in his garden to recharge himself.

Marc-Simon Sagal is Managing Partner at Winning Mind LLC. He consults regularly with Olympic and professional athletes from around the world and has worked with a variety of organizations and corporations. Marc is widely published in the area of performance psychology, and co-authored the book *Assessment in Sport Psychology* with Dr. Robert Nideffer. Additionally, Marc played a key role in the development of the Athlete's Competitive Edge system, the world's first web-based, sport-psychological assessment and training program. Marc is a former professional soccer player and currently serves as an adjunct professor at San Diego State University.

Carrie B. Scherzer is an assistant professor of psychology at the State University of New York College at Potsdam. She completed her doctorate at the University of Arizona in clinical psychology, with an emphasis in sport psychology. Dr. Scherzer received her BA in psychology (Honours) from Concordia University and her MS in athletic counseling at Springfield College. Her research interests include rehabilitation from injury, eating disorders, and professional training and development. She is a Certified Consultant of the AASP and a member of the graduate training committee. She has done performance enhancement, injury rehabilitation, and academic counseling with intercollegiate athletes.

Ronald E. Smith is Professor of Psychology and Director of Clinical Training at the University of Washington. He received his PhD in clinical psychology from Southern Illinois University. Dr. Smith is a past president of the Association of Applied Sport Psychology. His major research interests are in personality, stress and coping, and sport psychology research and interventions for coaches, parents, and athletes. He has contributed several widely-used sport psychology measurement tools, including the Coaching Behavior Assessment System, the Sport Anxiety Scale, the Athletic Coping Skills Inventory, and recently-developed child-appropriate measures of motivational climate and achievement goal orientations.

Frank L. Smoll is a professor of psychology at the University of Washington. His research focuses on coaching behaviors in youth sports and on the psychological effects of competition. He has published more than 130 scientific articles and book chapters, and he is co-author of 19 books and manuals on children's athletics. Dr. Smoll is a fellow of the APA, the AAKPE, and the AASP. He is a certified sport consultant and was the recipient of AASP's Distinguished Professional Practice Award. Dr. Smoll has extensive experience in conducting psychologically oriented coaching clinics and workshops for parents of young athletes.

Bill Straub is a retired professor of sport psychology and sport biomechanics. Most recently he has taught sport psychology classes part-time at Binghamton and Syracuse Universities. In addition, he does sport psychology consulting work with high school, and college and university teams. Unusual for a sport psychologist, Straub is an avid videographer. His Sport Science International company specializes in sport video production. He makes recruiting tapes for high school athletes, and college and university teams. Bill received his PhD from the University of Wisconsin, Madison and has earned master's degrees in education (State University of New York, Albany) and psychology (New School for Social Research).

Jim Taylor has worked with junior-elite, collegiate, world-class, and professional athletes for 23 years. His consulting practice focuses on sports performance, parenting, and corporate training. He received his bachelor's degree from Middlebury College and earned his MA and PhD in psychology from the University of Colorado. Dr. Taylor is the author of 10 books, has published over 500 popular and scholarly articles, and has given more than 600 workshops throughout North America, Europe, and the Middle East. He competed internationally as an alpine ski racer, holds a second degree black belt in karate, and is a marathon runner and Ironman triathlete.

David Tod teaches in the Department of Sport and Exercise Science, Aberystwyth University, UK. He received his doctorate from Victoria University in 2006. His research interests include the training and supervision of practitioners, and the psychological factors associated with strength training and performance. David is on the editorial boards of the *Qualitative Journal in Sport and Exercise* and *The Sport and Exercise Scientist*. Since 1993, David has provided applied sport psychology services to a range of athletes from juniors to Olympians across a variety of sports. To stay fit, David participates in Ballroom and Latin American dance competitions.

Darren Treasure is currently a high performance sport consultant. His current clients include Nike, the University of California, Berkeley

and the NCAA. He previously held faculty positions at Arizona State University, Southern Illinois University, and the University of Illinois. Darren has published over 50 scientific articles and book chapters on motivation and the psychology of peak performance and is actively involved in research with various groups around the world. Dr. Treasure is the author of the National Federation of State High School Associations recently launched Coach Education Program.

Robin S. Vealey is a professor in the Department of Kinesiology and Health at Miami University. She has authored two books: *Coaching for the Inner Edge* and *Competitive Anxiety in Sport*. She has served as a sport psychology consultant for the U.S. Ski Team, U.S. Field Hockey, elite golfers, and many college athletes and teams. Dr. Vealey is a fellow, certified consultant, and past president of the Association of Applied Sport Psychology and former editor of *The Sport Psychologist*. A former collegiate basketball player and coach, she now enjoys the mental challenge of golf.

Robert S. Weinberg is a professor in the Department of Kinesiology and Health at Miami University. He has published over 140 journal articles as well as 8 books and 30 book chapters. He was editor-in-chief of the *Journal of Applied Sport Psychology* and served as president of AASP and NASPSPA and chair of the AAHPERD Sport Psychology Academy. He is a certified consultant of AASP and a member of the U.S. Olympic Committee's Sport Psychology Registry. He has worked extensively with young athletes developing psychological skills. He has been a varsity athlete and coach in tennis, football, and basketball.

Vietta E. "Sue" Wilson is a retired professor of York University, where she taught sport psychology, coaching, and self-regulation courses. She is certified (BCIA) in biofeedback and neurofeedback. She has worked with a variety of sports and from novice athletes to Olympic and world champions. Her BF/NF Performance Enhancement Suite is used worldwide for the assessment and training of athletes with Sue providing training via hands-on seminars or delivered via the web. She was an athlete and coach in three sports, taught for the Canadian Coaching Association, and remains physically active.

David Yukelson is Director of sport psychology services for the Penn State University Athletic Department. He provides counseling and support to coaches and athletes in the areas of mental training techniques for managing concentration and confidence under pressure, leadership effectiveness, communication and team cohesion, coping skill strategies for handling multiple demands and stress effectively, and issues pertaining to the personal development of intercollegiate student-athletes. He is a past president, fellow, and certified consultant in the Association of Applied Sport Psychology

(AASP), has published numerous articles in professional refereed journals, and is a frequent invited speaker at national and international conferences.

Nate Zinsser is director of the Performance Enhancement Program at the United States Military Academy, and is responsible for a sport psychology curriculum currently being implemented throughout the U.S. Army. Dr. Zinsser is the author of *Dear Dr Psych*, the first sport psychology guidebook for youth sport participants, and he contributed a sport psychology advice column to *Sports Illustrated for Kids* for 5 years. His formal training in sport psychology from the University of Virginia is complemented by his experience as a state wrestling champion, world-class mountaineer, and third degree black belt in karate.

Sport Psychology: Past, Present, Future

Jean M. Williams, *University of Arizona, Emeritus*
William F. Straub, *Sport Science International*

Within the past 35–40 years, the academic community and the public have recognized a new field of study called sport psychology. Sport psychologists study motivation, personality, violence, leadership, group dynamics, exercise and psychological well being, thoughts and feelings of athletes, and many other dimensions of participation in sport and physical activity. Among other functions, modern-day sport psychologists teach sport psychology classes, conduct research, and work with athletes, coaches, and exercise participants to help improve performance and enhance the quality of the sport and exercise experience.

Coaches showed interest in the psychological aspects of athletic competition even before there was a science called sport psychology. For example, in the 1920s Knute Rockne, the football coach of the fighting Irish of Notre Dame, popularized the pep talk by making it an important part of his coaching. We should note, however, that Rockne did not attempt to psych up his team for every contest. Coaching interest in contemporary sport psychology also involves more than a mere concern for psyching up athletes for competition.

Applied sport psychology is concerned with the psychological factors that influence participation and performance in sport and exercise, the psychological effects derived from participation, and theories and interventions that can be used to enhance performance, participation, and personal growth. Applied sport psychology has grown tremendously in recent years, as evidenced by the number of coaches and athletes now looking to sport psychology for a competitive edge. These individuals have turned to various psychological training programs to learn, among other things, ways to manage competitive stress, control concentration, improve confidence, and increase communication skills and team harmony.

One goal of psychological interventions is to learn to consistently create the ideal mental climate that enables athletes to perform at their best. An additional goal, for exercise psychologists, is to use interventions to enhance physical and mental health by increasing exercise participation. In addition to these two broad goals, there are many specific intervention goals. What follows are a few situations that identify the diverse circumstances under which individuals might turn to the field of sport psychology for help.

When to use sport psychology

Val is only a third-year coach but already has the reputation of coaching players with excellent physical fundamentals and conditioning. Her team's poor play comes more from mental lapses and from not handling pressure. Val's goal this season is to increase her players' mental toughness.

Tim is a student athletic trainer. After taking a sport psychology workshop, he recognizes that he could be more effective in helping his injured athletes heal and be ready mentally to return to play if he incorporated psychological skills into their injury rehabilitation program.

Matt is a sport psychology consultant who was just hired by a professional team that rarely plays up to its potential because of internal dissention and too much concern with personal stats. His task is to help resolve the conflicts and enhance cohesiveness and team play.

Andrew is a fitness trainer at a health resort. Most of the guests either have led sedentary lives or have started exercise programs but quit within a few months. Andrew's job is to help the guests set fitness goals and plan strategies that will achieve those goals.

Brian arrives as a new wrestling coach at a major university. He discovers that some of his wrestlers are on steroids and others have eating disorders. What should he do?

Jennifer is a recreational golfer who has played for over 20 years. She loves golf but has become quite frustrated with her putting. Her normally excellent putting game has gone into a 2-year slump. She knows it's mental but can't seem to correct it.

Kimberly is a first-year physical education teacher who is having difficulty motivating many of her students to actively participate in class. How can she improve her teaching?

The authors of subsequent chapters will present psychological principles and interventions that can be used to enhance performance, personal growth, and health. These principles and interventions provide the foundation for effectively dealing with the preceding situations as well as many others that athletes, coaches, sport psychology consultants, athletic trainers, fitness trainers, and physical educators might encounter.

But, first, in this chapter we will provide a brief overview of the past, present, and future of sport psychology, with primary emphasis on sport psychology practices in North America and the role Eastern Europe played in the early development and use of sport psychology to enhance performance. The coverage is not all-inclusive but selective to the focus of the book. For a more comprehensive historical overview see Landers (1995) and Vealey (2006).

History of Sport Psychology

According to Mahoney (1989), sport psychology's conceptual roots lie in antiquity. For example, in early Greek and Asian cultures the interdependence of mind and body was not only acknowledged but emphasized as central to both performance and personal development. In the last 40 years, however, most of the scientific foundation of modern sport psychology developed. The roots for the emergence and acceptance of sport psychology as a discipline lie largely within the domain of kinesiology (the study of physical activity), but developments within the discipline of psychology also played a major role in its evolution and psychologists conducted some of the early influential sport psychology investigations.

Coleman Griffith, a psychologist considered by many to be the father of sport psychology in North America, was the first person to research sport psychology over an extended period of time and then to apply it to enhance the performance of athletes and coaches (Gould & Pick, 1995). Griffith was hired by the University of Illinois in 1925 to help coaches improve the performance of their players. He wrote two books, *Psychology of Coaching* (1926) and *Psychology of Athletics* (1928); established the first sport psychology laboratory in North America; published over 40 articles (half dealt with sport psychology); and taught the first courses in sport psychology. (We should also credit Carl Diem in Berlin and A. Z. Puni in Leningrad (now St. Petersburg) for establishing sport psychology laboratories in Europe about this same time period.) Griffith also corresponded with Notre Dame coach Rockne about psychological and motivational aspects of coaching, and he was hired in 1938 to improve the performance of the Chicago Cubs baseball team.

Another pioneer practitioner and researcher from this historical era was Dorothy Yates (Kornspan & MacCracken, 2001). She taught at Stanford and San Jose State College and had a private practice in psychology. Yates wrote two books (1932, 1957) and a research article (1943) describing her mental training interventions with boxers and aviators. The intervention focused on mental preparation, particularly a relaxation set-method. Because of her success she was asked in 1942 to develop a psychology course at San Jose State for athletes and aviators. Some of her students became aviators flying during World War II, and letters from them testified to the effectiveness of her work and teaching.

Unfortunately, the pioneering efforts in sport psychology by Griffith and Yates were not followed in any systematic way, and therefore no recognizable discipline of sport and exercise psychology was established in the 1930s and 1940s (Vealey, 2006). In fact, up until the mid-1960s, very little writing occurred in sport psychology except for one book and occasional research studies that were, according to Landers (1995), typically atheoretical, unsystematic, and laboratory-based. The book, *Psychology of Coaching* (1951), was written by John Lawther, a psychologist who also headed the Pennsylvania State University basketball team. Coaches were particularly interested in Lawther's treatment of such topics as motivation, team cohesion, personality, feelings and emotions, and handling athletes.

1965–1979: Birth of Sport Psychology and Supporting Organizations

During the 1960s, two San Jose State University clinical psychologists, Bruce Ogilvie and Tom Tutko (1966), created considerable interest in sport psychology with their research and the book that resulted, *Problem Athletes and How to Handle Them*. According to Ogilvie, this book "moved the coaching world off dead center." After extensively researching the personality of athletes, Ogilvie and Tutko developed the controversial Athletic Motivation Inventory, which they claimed predicted success and problems in athletes. In actuality, sport is so complex that no inventory can predict performance, let alone one based on trait personality theory. For example, they advised one football team not to draft a highly successful college player because he did not mentally have what it would take to make it in the pros. He went to another team and earned the Rookie of the Year award. Despite legitimate criticism of their prediction claims (see Fisher, Ryan, & Martens, 1976), Ogilvie and Tutko's considerable consulting with college and professional teams did much to foster public interest in applied sport psychology. Because of Ogilvie's numerous contributions in the 60s, and later, many in the field have called him the father of applied sport psychology in North America.

Establishment of professional organizations. The 1960s also witnessed the first attempts to bring together groups of individuals interested in sport psychology. Sport psychology first organized on the international level with the formation in Rome in 1965 of the International Society of Sport Psychology (ISSP). More than 400 attendees representing 27 countries came to Rome. Dr. Ferruccio Antonelli, an Italian psychiatrist, was elected the first president of the organization and provided leadership during the early years. The ISSP publishes the *International Journal of Sport Psychology* (first published in 1970) and hosts worldwide meetings.

The second meeting of ISSP was hosted in 1968 at Washington, DC, by the newly formed North American Society for the Psychology of

Sport and Physical Activity (NASPSPA). The first annual meeting of NASPSPA was held in 1967 prior to the American Alliance for Health, Physical Education, Recreation and Dance (AAHPERD) conference in Las Vegas, Nevada. Dr. Arthur Slatter-Hammel of Indiana University was the first president. NASPSPA hosts annual meetings that focus on research in the subareas of motor learning and control, motor development, and sport and exercise psychology.

The late 1960s also saw the formation of the Canadian Society for Psychomotor Learning and Sport Psychology, also referred to as SCAPPS to reflect the French translation of the name. Founded by Robert Wilberg at the University of Alberta in 1969, SCAPPS was initially under the auspices of the Canadian Association for Health, Physical Education and Recreation, but it became independent in 1977. The members and leaders of NASPSPA and SCAPPS were extremely influential in building the research base in sport psychology and gaining acceptance of the field. During this same time period, the equivalent can be said within Europe for sport psychologists

who, in 1969, created the European Federation of Sport Psychology (FEPSAC—the acronym reflects the French translation of the name) and elected Ema Geron (then from Bulgaria, now Israel) as its first president.

Sport psychology's organizational growth continued in the 1970s, when it was added to the conference programs of the American College of Sports Medicine (ACSM) and AAHPERD. The Sport Psychology Academy (SPA), formed within AAHPERD in 1975, was the first group for which a major goal was to bridge the gap between the researcher and practitioner by providing an opportunity for sport psychologists to share their research and expertise with coaches and physical education teachers.

Recognition through knowledge base. In the decade of the 1970s, sport psychology in North America began to flourish and to receive recognition within kinesiology as a subdiscipline separate from motor learning. Systematic research by ever-increasing numbers of sport psychologists played a major role in this coming of age. In

Table 1-1   **Timeline for the Establishment of Professional Organizations and Journals***

1965	International Society for Psychology of Sport (ISSP)
1967	North American Society for the Psychology of Sport and Physical Activity (NASPSPA)
1969	Canadian Society for Psychomotor Learning and Sport Psychology (SCAPPS)
1969	European Federation of Sport Psychology (FEPSAC)
1970	*International Journal of Sport Psychology* (ISSP)
1975	Sport Psychology Academy (SPA) added to AAHPERD
1979	*Journal of Sport and Exercise Psychology* (NASPSPA) (its name was *Journal of Sport Psychology* prior to 1988)
1985	Association for Applied Sport Psychology (AASP) (its name was the Association for the Advancement of Applied Sport Psychology prior to 2006)
1987	Division 47 (Exercise and Sport Psychology) of the American Psychological Association (APA)
1987	*The Sport Psychologist*
1989	*Journal of Applied Sport Psychology* (AASP)
2000	*Psychology of Sport and Exercise* (FEPSAC)
2003	*International Journal of Sport and Exercise Psychology*
2007	*Journal of Clinical Sport Psychology*

*Initials in parenthesis after journals indicate sponsoring organization

fact, the primary goal of sport psychologists in the 1970s was to gain acceptance for the field by advancing the knowledge base through experimental research (largely lab-based). Although no agreement existed as to an appropriate knowledge base for the field, and research topics were diverse and involved many target populations, most of the scholarship in this era was directed toward social psychological research (e.g., personality, social facilitation, achievement motivation, competitive anxiety, team cohesion, coach behaviors, coach–athlete relations).

The earlier interest in personality research declined in the mid-70s because of heated debates about the validity of personality traits and the inventories used to assess them, most of which came from mainstream psychology. Many sport psychologists continued to believe that internal mechanisms (i.e., traits) govern behavior, but these psychologists also became concerned about the influence of environmental variables. The **interactionism paradigm,** which considers person and environmental variables and their potential interaction, surfaced and gained considerable credibility. Although not as extensive, research also began to focus on two other areas in the 70s: the study of women in sport from a feminist perspective, largely due to a conference hosted by Dorothy Harris (1972) and a book published by Carole Oglesby (1978), and exercise psychology, largely through Bill Morgan's research into exercise, fitness, and well-being. The growing volume of quality research in the 70s led in 1979 to the establishment of the *Journal of Sport Psychology*.

Discouragement of applied work. In addition, we should mention that applied work was discouraged during the 70s. Some of the negativity towards premature application came from the bad publicity stemming from Arnold Mandel's work with the San Diego Chargers. Mandel was a psychiatrist who was hired in 1973 to enhance performance, but an offshoot of his work was the discovery that many of the professional football players were taking steroids and "speed" purchased on the street. Mandel wrote them prescriptions for the drugs in an effort to get them off uncontrolled substances. Management

would not acknowledge the drug problem, let alone try to help him resolve it. The end result was that, by court order, Mandel was banned from further contact with players and not even allowed within a certain geographical radius of the stadium! See Mandel's book, *The Nightmare Season* (1976), for an interesting description of his work with the Chargers.

Instead of forays into application, many in the field felt that sport psychology would be better served by first developing a research base upon which intervention work might be based. This goal influenced some of the research during the 70s, but provided an even greater influence on research in the 80s (which continues today). It also contributed to the emphasis within sport psychology research in the late 1970s and early 1980s on a more cognitive focus (see the next section) as this inquiry is particularly relevant to applied concerns.

The 1980s: Increased Research, Professional Growth, and Acceptance

In the 1980s, the emphasis on scientific credibility, including the development of a sufficient scholarly foundation to justify the practice of sport psychology, grew tremendously. That, in turn, led to consulting with athletes and to recognizing and addressing important professional issues.

Research. Examining the cognitive perspective became a dominant theme in the 1980s. Some of this research was driven by cognitive theories from psychology and the desire to test their applicability within a sport and exercise setting (e.g., self-efficacy, motivational orientations, competence motivation, outcome attributions) and some by topics of relevance to potential performance enhancement interventions (e.g., athletes' thoughts, images, and attention control). The 1983 New York City Marathon provides an excellent example of how inner dialogue can influence performance. Geoff Smith, an Englishman, led for most of the race. Within approximately 300 meters of the finish line, Rod Dixon, a New Zealander, passed Smith and won the race. Morgan (1984) indicated that Dixon's success may have been aided by his cognitive strategy. According to newspaper reports, Dixon stated, "With a mile to go I was thinking, 'A miler's kick does the trick,' and 'I've got to go, I've got to go.'" In contrast, Smith is reported to have said, "My legs have gone." Later Smith noted, "I was just running from memory. I thought I was going to stumble and collapse." In fact, he did collapse at the finish line. Since then, sport psychologists have developed techniques to train athletes to think more productively by focusing on what they want to happen as opposed to what they do *not* want to happen. Perhaps the results of the marathon would have differed had Smith been exposed to these interventions.

The interest in cognitive sport psychology paralleled an increase in field research. This influence partly came from a 1979 article, "About Smocks and Jocks," by Rainer Martens. In it he chided the field for largely conducting laboratory-based research when more relevant questions and results would result from field research. His chastisement had the desired effect: more field research, which spurred more and better applied questions and results. Field research has been conducted on topics such as identifying coaching behaviors most effective in promoting learning and personal growth; discovering ways to enhance team harmony and coach–athlete communications; learning how to set and use goals; determining psychological characteristics of successful performers; and developing psychological and behavioral interventions for enhancing performance, personal growth, and exercise participation.

In addition to the cognitive focus and field research, two other important research developments occurred during the 1980s. One was better documentation of the effectiveness of psychological interventions at enhancing performance (see the meta-analysis by Greenspan and Feltz, 1989, for examples of research documentation from this era). The second was increased attention to exercise and health psychology issues such as the psychological effects of exercise and overtraining, factors influencing participation in and adherence to exercise programs, exercise addiction, the relationship of exercise to stress reactivity, and psychology of injury and injury

rehabilitation (see Chapters 23 and 25). The end result was the establishment during the 80s of a distinct knowledge base for exercise and health psychology and for applied work to enhance the performance of athletes.

Journals. Perhaps the best reflection of the quality and volume of work in any academic area is the number of research journals devoted strictly to the discipline. In addition to the two sport psychology journals started in the 1970s, two more journals were added in the 1980s: *The Sport Psychologist* in 1987 and the *Journal of Applied Sport Psychology* in 1989, both of which are devoted exclusively to applied sport psychology. To reflect the growing knowledge base within exercise psychology, *JSP* changed its name to the *Journal of Sport and Exercise Psychology* in 1988. Three more sport psychology journals were added starting in 2000 (see Table 1-1 on page 4).

Use by USOC and others of sport psychology professionals. Considerable growth and recognition of the value of sport psychology interventions occurred because of publicity stemming from sport psychology professionals working with athletes, particularly Olympic athletes. In 1983, the USOC established an official Sport Psychology Committee and a registry of qualified sport psychologists and in 1985, the USOC hired Shane Murphy, its first fulltime sport psychologist. As a result of the USOC's development of its sport psychology program, sport psychologists played an increasingly prominent and visible role in the 1984 and 1988 Olympics (see Suinn, 1985, and *The Sport Psychologist,* no. 4, 1989). Television and written coverage of various sport psychology topics and interventions with Olympic athletes also created considerable interest among professionals and laypersons. Involvement by sport psychologists in the Olympic movement and on the professional level (see *The Sport Psychologist,* no. 4, 1990) and intercollegiate level continues to grow.

Professional issues. The growing use of sport psychology practitioners during the 1980s led to important professional issues such as, "Is there an adequate scientific base for the practice of sport psychology? What kinds of services should be offered? Who is qualified to provide these services?" Almost 20 studies debating these issues were published in sport psychology journals during the 80s. In reference to the second question, an article by Danish and Hale (1981) was particularly influential. They advocated a human development and educational approach (e.g., teaching mental skills) for sport psychology interventions as opposed to the clinical and remedial model of correcting problems typically found in clinical psychology. This early clarification and distinction stemmed partly from tensions between sport psychologists trained in kinesiology-based versus clinical psychology–based programs. It is still relevant today, but less so as evidenced by the creation in 2007 of the *Journal of Clinical Sport Psychology.*

Formation of AASP and APA Division 47.   One important applied development during the 1980s was the formation in 1985 of the Association for Applied Sport Psychology (AASP, the name was the Association for the Advancement of Applied Sport Psychology prior to 2006). John Silva, a University of North Carolina sport psychologist, played the primary role in forming AASP and served as its first president. The purpose of AASP is to promote applied research in the areas of social, health, and performance enhancement psychology; the appropriate application of these research findings; and the examination of professional issues such as ethical standards, qualifications for becoming a sport psychologist, and certification of sport psychologists. Another objective is to promote the field of sport psychology within mainstream psychology. Prior to this time relatively few people from psychology were involved in sport psychology. AASP has clearly met this last objective—approximately 35% of its more than 1,200 members declare psychology as their primary area of specialization and another third list a combination of psychology and sport science.

Additional support for the growing recognition of sport psychology within mainstream psychology comes from the American Psychological Association (APA). In 1987 the APA officially recognized a sport and exercise psychology division, Division 47. Bill Morgan, a University of Wisconsin sport psychologist, served as the first president. Division 47 provides APA members with an opportunity to share research and address relevant sport psychology issues.

1990–2009: Progress in Research, Application, and Professional Issues

The last 20 years have been characterized by exciting growth and diversification in knowledge and practice of sport psychology and considerable progress regarding professional issues in sport psychology.

Intervention Research.   Particularly impressive, and relevant to this book, is the continued research into the effectiveness of interventions to enhance the performance of athletes and to increase the physical activity levels of all types of individuals. For a quantitative review of these intervention studies, see the meta-analysis of Meyers, Whelan, and Murphy (1996) and Dishman and Buckworth (1996). Intervention advances since the publication of these meta-analyses can be found in Chapters 9 to 18 and 25 in this book. Although more research is needed, the findings from this era should quiet critics who have questioned whether sufficient knowledge exists to justify ethical delivery of sport psychology services. For example, when this book was first published in 1986, Jean Williams, the editor, was criticized by several prominent colleagues because she had envisioned a book to promote applied sport psychology by exposing current and future coaches and sport psychologists to psychological theories and interventions they could use to enhance the performance and personal growth of athletes. One colleague even called her a charlatan!

Diversifying research.   In her overview of the historical development of sport and exercise psychology, Vealey (2006) describes 1993–2005 as a time of emerging diversity in methods, paradigms, and epistemology. For examples, she cites hermeneutic or interpretive approaches, feminist epistemology and methodology using gender as a dependent variable, a pragmatic research philosophy, an ecological meta-theoretical approach, and use of single-subject designs and qualitative methods. As Vealey notes, the use and promotion of such diverse approaches is promising because it leads to multiple ways to ask and address different questions.

Two of the preceding advances are particularly important. The use of single-subject designs has been particularly beneficial to intervention research (and practice) because it allows personalizing interventions based on qualities of the individual and it avoids the masking effect that sometimes occurs with nomothetic (group means) comparisons. Qualitative studies are also noteworthy. They have the potential to add greatly to knowledge in applied sport psychology because rather than statistically analyzing numbers or ratings, they involve researchers looking for trends and patterns in what people say and how they act. Before the 1990s, research consisted almost exclusively of quantitative paradigms, but during the 90s qualitative data collection techniques such as interviews, observation, and open-ended questions increased to approximately 1 of 7 published studies in three sport psychology journals (Culver, Gilbert, & Trudel, 2003). Much of this growth can be attributed to Tara Scanlan's work and promotion efforts (Scanlan, Ravizza, & Stein, 1989; Scanlan, Stein, & Ravizza, 1989). She also was instrumental in using and advocating the mixed methods approach (combining qualitative and quantitative research methods in a single study or across a line of research) (Scanlan, Russell, Beals, & Scanlan, 2003).

Another indicator of diversity in the field during this era (1990–2009) was the call for more research into the influence of culture on psychological processes and behavior. It began in 1990 when Duda and Allison called the field of sport psychology to task for its failure to consider variability among different cultural groups, thus diminishing the importance of nondominant group experiences and producing potentially biased and distorted theoretical understandings. The recognition of this problem and call for its

correction has only grown over this era (e.g., Gill, 2004; Ram, Starek, & Johnson, 2004, Si & Lee, 2007). Although some progress has been made (see Chapter 19 and Peters & Williams, 2009, for a summary of publication figures), considerably more is needed.

Sport psychology books.   Another reflection of the increase in knowledge in sport psychology and its application comes from the tremendous growth in the number of books dealing with applied sport psychology. In a 1991 critique of psychological skills training books in applied sport psychology, Sachs identified 48 books. The list had grown to 187 books by 1998 (Sachs & Kornspan, 1998), 282 by 2004 (Burke, Sachs, & Gomer, 2004), and 391 in 2008 (Burke, Sachs, Fry, & Schweghhardt, 2008).

Training of sport psychology consultants.   What is the necessary minimum curriculum to produce the scholarly competencies and practitioner skills for the would-be sport psychology consultant? Answering that question, and then monitoring the impact on graduate programs, the training of graduate students, and the use of sport psychology consultants has been a major professional focus during this era. In 1991 AASP established a curricular model for individuals to become certified to provide services such as performance enhancement interventions for athletes. AASP's standards encompass 14 criteria, including a doctoral degree from an accredited institution and training that bridges the disciplines of psychology (e.g., basic skills in counseling, psychopathology, and its assessment) and kinesiology (e.g., physiological bases of sport or biomechanics; historical, philosophical, social, or motor behavior bases of sport). Also required is knowledge of sport psychology (equivalent to three courses), training in professional ethics and standards, and a supervised practicum with a qualified professional. Two changes have occurred since 1991. In 2004 the required number of supervision hours was increased to 400, and in 2002 AASP approved a process for certifying individuals with a Master's degree. See AASP's Web site (http://www.appliedsportpsych.org) for the specific criteria and process for becoming a certified consultant.

Tracking surveys of graduates with a specialization in sport psychology from 1989 to 1994 (Andersen, Williams, Aldridge, & Taylor, 1997) and 1994 to 1999 (Williams & Scherzer, 2003) show that a high percentage of Master's and doctoral degrees met the 14 certification criteria if consulting with athletes was one of their career goals. One disturbing finding, however, was that the doctoral graduates from 1994 to 1999 were less prepared to meet the criteria than those from 1989 to 1994. Whether good or bad, it appears that this curricular model has influenced the program of study of most graduate students in the United States who have an interest in consulting. Another indication of the acceptance of AASP's certification standards is that, starting in 1996, the USOC requires consultants who wish to work with Olympic programs to be AASP-certified. Unfortunately, it is unlikely that other consumers are equally aware of the importance of picking qualified consultants.

Ethical standards. Another professional issue in which progress occurred in the 1990s is setting standards for ethical behavior. Although the growth in applied sport psychology led to a tremendous boon for individuals interested in consulting, negative by-products resulted, such as unqualified individuals providing services and unethical practitioners promising more than they could deliver. These concerns and others led the AASP to approve ethical standards and guidelines for sport psychologists in 1994 and 1996 (see Burke et al., 2008, for a copy). Individuals certified by AASP have to agree to observe these ethical standards.

Consulting job market. Growth has occurred over the last 20 years in consulting opportunities for applied sport psychologists. For example, of the 1994 to 1999 graduates in the Williams and Scherer (2003) tracking study, 52% of the doctoral graduates and 41% of the Master's graduates indicated that they did some paid sport psychology consulting. In most of the cases, the work was part time rather than full time. Only 13 (12%) of the doctoral graduates and 7 (5%) of the

Master's graduates held a full-time position doing performance enhancement consulting. Some of this consulting occurred in domains outside of sport such as music, business, and health (e.g., injury rehabilitation in medical centers). When asked about the ease or difficulty in finding paid consulting work, almost equal numbers of the doctoral graduates responded very easy or moderately easy, moderately difficult, very difficult, or did not seek such work. Although progress has occurred since these graduates were surveyed in 1989 to 1994, it is still unrealistic to expect to find full-time work doing sport psychology consulting. For example, of 51 (53% of the sample) NCAA Division I universities that provide sport psychology services, only 7 (14%) of the athletic departments employed a full-time sport psychology consultant (Voight & Callaghan, 2001).

Academic job market. The 1990s have shown a tremendous growth in academic positions. For example, the graduate tracking studies found that 54 of the 92 doctoral respondents from 1989 to 1994 obtained positions in kinesiology departments (Andersen et al., 1997) compared to a figure of 66 of 107 for the 1994 to 1999 graduates (Williams & Scherzer, 2003). In contrast, an even earlier study of doctoral graduates in kinesiology from 1984 to 1989 found that only 23 of the 34 respondents obtained positions in colleges or universities (Waite & Pettit, 1993). From 1989 to 1999, academic appointments in psychology departments dropped from 12 to 5 over the two 5-year time spans, but part of this drop was a reflection of fewer graduates from psychology departments (12 versus 20). When the 1994 to 1999 graduates were asked if they held a replacement or new academic position, 19 indicated new positions (16 in kinesiology and 3 in psychology departments). All the new positions, except for two in kinesiology, were described as having a primary emphasis in sport psychology. As promising as this growth appears, enthusiasm should be tempered by the fact that we do not know how many sport psychology positions were lost over this time span. We also, unfortunately, have no information on what has happened since 1999.

Growth in exercise psychology. Another important development during the last 20 years is that exercise psychology has become a highly viable area of specialization, particularly within the academic community. Although the content within this domain is meritorious in its own right and grew tremendously during this era, much of the growth has been driven by widespread grant support. For example, funding opportunities have occurred because of recent attention to the exercise goals in Healthy People 2000 and the position statements from the ACSM and Centers for Disease Control on the importance of exercise in reducing risk of disease and all-cause mortality.

History of Sport Psychology in Eastern Europe

Sport psychology in the former Iron Curtain countries of Eastern Europe is of particular importance to people interested in peak performance. These nations have a long history of giving a great deal of attention to the applied aspects of sport psychology—more specifically, to enhancing elite athletes' performance through applied research and direct intervention. As a consequence of this emphasis, sport psychologists in Eastern Europe played an active role in the selection, training, and competitive preparation of athletes.

Before the breakup of the Soviet Union and the fall of communist control, sport psychology in Eastern Europe was a highly esteemed field of academic and professional concern that received considerable state support and acceptance. In some nations, sport psychologists were even awarded the title of academician, a title that elevated the recipient to the level of a national hero. This high esteem occurred because the countries perceived sport excellence as an important propaganda tool in advancing the communist political system, and sport psychologists were viewed as central figures in facilitating the athlete's quest for excellence.

Vanek and Cratty (1970) reported that the first interest in sport psychology in Eastern Europe can be traced to a physician, Dr. P. F. Lesgaft, who in 1901 described the possible psychological benefits of physical activity. The first research articles were published by Puni and Rudik in the early 1920s. The Institutes for Physical Culture in Moscow and Leningrad also were established in the early 1920s, and the beginning of sport psychology can be traced to them.

Garfield and Bennett (1984) reported that "the extensive investment in athletic research in the communist countries began early in the 1950s as part of the Soviet space program" (p. 13). Russian scientists successfully explored the possibility of using ancient yogic techniques to teach cosmonauts to control psychophysiological processes while in space. These techniques were called **self-regulation training** or **psychic self-regulation** and were used to voluntarily control such bodily functions as heart rate, temperature, and muscle tension, as well as emotional reactions to stressful situations such as zero gravity. Nearly 20 years passed before these methods were systematically applied to the Soviet and East German sport programs. According to Kurt Tittel, then director of the Leipzig Institute of Sports (a 14-acre sport laboratory that during the 1970s employed 900 people, over half of whom were scientists), new training methods similar to psychic self-regulation were responsible for the impressive victories by East German and Soviet athletes during the 1976 Olympics (Garfield & Bennett, 1984).

Salmela (1984) reported that sport psychology research in Eastern European countries was more limited in scope than in North America because of greater governmental control. Rather narrowly focused 5-year research plans were determined by the state with the advice of its sport psychologists. All sport psychology researchers within the country were required to coordinate and streamline their research efforts to accomplish the stated research objective. Salmela (1981) also indicated that this research focus tended to be of a field variety and applied primarily toward top-level achievement in sport. This focus is not surprising considering each state's heavy emphasis on sport excellence and the easy access by sport psychologists to elite athletes. Most of the Eastern European sport institutes where the athletes were trained had teams of sport psychologists. For example, on a visit to a major sport institute in Bucharest, Romania, Salmela (1984) reported meeting with a team of eight sport psychologists. A sport psychology faculty of that size is considered normal for that type of sport institute. In contrast, at that time in North America one or two people were normal.

Although most North American sport psychologists would find government-dictated research endeavors abhorrent, a large-scale, unified approach to a particular research topic does have advantages. Salmela (1984) cited one positive example: all Eastern European countries successfully implemented as many as 30 hours of training in self-control for all elite athletes.

The exact training techniques the Eastern European sport psychologists employed remain vague; however, a book by a Russian sport psychologist indicates that autogenic training, visualization, and autoconditioning (self-hypnosis) were key components (Raiport, 1988). Because of its government-funded research and widespread integration of sophisticated mental training programs with rigorous physical training, many authorities believed Eastern Europe was ahead of North America and the rest of the world in the development and application of applied sport psychology. Whatever gap initially existed has closed. As communist control in Eastern Europe ended and the Soviet Union broke up in the late 1980s and 1990s, the status of sport and sport psychology in Eastern Europe changed. With the considerable decline in state support, many sport psychology consultants who worked with elite athletes either lost their positions or moved to other countries. Another consequence of these changes is that interests among the remaining sport psychologists became broader (including, for example, noncompetition) (Kantor & Ryzonkin, 1993).

Future Directions in North American Applied Sport Psychology

Exciting challenges remain for applied sport psychology, both in terms of expanding its scientific foundation and professional practice and in dealing with professional issues. Vealey (2006) offers some good future directions for research. In line with the diversifying research theme identified earlier, she advocates that questions and methods be even more inclusive and diverse, which requires taking a problem-focused approach to scholarship and avoiding the traps of traditional insular paradigms. Further, she suggests asking questions such as, "How can we induce social-structural change in sport and exercise to enhance the psychological and physical well-being of participants? How do social-cultural factors influence mental processes and behavior related to sport and exercise psychology? . . . What types of sport experiences influence positive and negative psychological outcomes for participants?" (pp. 148–150).

To elaborate on Vealey's diversity comments and second question, we hope the addition of a chapter on gender and cultural diversity in this sixth edition will encourage more scholarship on diversity issues and greater emphasis on cultural competencies in professional practice. In this millennium we need to assure that practitioners are multiculturally competent, and that requires a multicultural research base from which to develop multicultural training (Peters & Williams, 2009).

When it comes to interventions, Vealey advocates the inclusion of a cultural praxis approach (Ryba & Wright, 2005). For example, interventions should be designed as tools for individual empowerment and social justice and they should help athletes understand how problematic subcultures may have enculturated negative self-perceptions and unhealthy behaviors. In other words, sport psychology interventions should do more than help athletes perform better.

We offer a few additional observations, suggestions, and predictions. One certainty in this new millennium is that both knowledge and interest in applied sport psychology will continue to grow and even larger numbers of individuals will seek the services of a sport psychology consultant or express interest in becoming a sport psychologist. The appropriate training of these future sport psychologists will depend on their career goals. For those who aspire to do consulting work, we believe AASP's certified consultant requirements will remain the dominant curricular model for their training and efforts will continue to increase flexibility in meeting the requirements. Because of a tremendous growth in the knowledge base within sport and exercise psychology, we predict even greater specialization in the training of future students. The growth in specialization will particularly continue within health and exercise psychology, driven largely by ever-increasing opportunities in external research funding and the resulting potential for academic positions.

The tracking studies of graduate students indicate that more career opportunities are needed for sport psychologists. We are hopeful the academic job market will expand, but it must be supplemented by greater growth in consulting and nontraditional career options. The most consulting opportunities in the future, including full-time ones, will probably come from applied sport psychologists who recognize the potential for using their training in sport psychology not just in sport settings but also to enhance performance in domains such as the performing arts, music, business, and the military. For example, Gould (2002) noted that the 2001 American Psychological Association Convention contained many sessions on corporate "coaching," that is, helping businesspersons achieve performance excellence. With only minimal additional training and preparation, who is better qualified than sport psychology consultants to do such coaching? (See the December 2002 issue of the *Journal of Applied Sport Psychology,* which was devoted to moving beyond the psychology of athletic excellence, for articles regarding these types of consulting.)

Other less traditional realms for future career growth are areas such as youth life-skills development through sport, injury prevention and rehabilitation (e.g., hospitals, sports medicine, and physical therapy centers), exercise and wellness promotion (e.g., insurance companies, employee wellness programs, medical centers, and treatment centers for substance abuse), and the military. Good examples of programs in youth life-skills development are The First Tee (Petlichkoff, 2004; http://www.thefirst-tee.org) and Play It Smart (Petitpas, Van Raalte, Cornelius, & Presbrey, 2004; http://playitsmart. footballfoundation.com).

Particularly exciting are the new career opportunities in the military. Most recently, the United States Army has recognized the relevance of performance enhancement skills in military settings. From 2006 to 2008, the Army established nine Army Centers for Enhanced Performance (ACEPs) at selected locations on a pilot basis. An additional 20 centers are proposed with three additional locations likely in support of combat operations overseas, bringing the total number of centers to 32. As of June 2008, the ACEP program employed a total of 65 people, 35 of whom possess degrees in performance enhancement, sport psychology, or related fields of study. If it continues to expand at its current rate and increases in size as projected, the ACEP program will ultimately have approximately 650 employees, with approximately 400 of those positions requiring postgraduate degrees in performance psychology, sport psychology, or related fields of study, as well as AASP certification.

In the future, we anticipate even greater acceptance of sport psychology within mainstream psychology. One continuing impetus comes from what sport psychology has to offer in response to the call for more emphasis on studying positive psychology, which seeks to understand positive emotion and build one's strengths and virtues (Seligman & Csikszentmihalyi, 2000). The field of sport psychology has been doing this since its inception! Greater acceptance will result in more research and professional practice cross-fertilization, and more sport psychology and psychology of excellence course offerings in psychology departments, but probably no appreciable increases in sport psychology appointments within psychology departments.

In conclusion, as great as the growth of applied sport psychology has been, the future looks even brighter. We are confident that the field of applied sport psychology has much to offer you, the reader of this book. We are hopeful that you will use the content in this book to enhance your own performance and personal growth.

Summary

Applied sport psychology is concerned with the psychological factors that influence participation and performance in sport and exercise, the psychological effects derived from participation, and theories and interventions that can be used to enhance performance, participation, and personal growth. Today many athletes and coaches look to sport psychology for a competitive edge by seeking psychological training programs to learn, among other things, ways to manage competitive stress, control concentration, improve confidence, and increase communication skills and team harmony.

Although the roots of sport psychology are older, it was not until the 1960s that groups of individuals got together to form sport psychology associations. During the 1970s, sport psychology began to flourish and gain acceptance as a separate subdiscipline within kinesiology, largely through a concerted research effort to develop the knowledge base, with most of the scholarship directed toward social psychological research. A few individuals did applied work, but such work was discouraged because of an inadequate knowledge base for interventions.

During the 1980s, examining the cognitive perspective became a dominant theme and a shift occurred from primarily laboratory to field research. Additionally, a distinct knowledge base was developed for exercise and health psychology and for applied work to enhance the performance of athletes. The growing use of sport psychology practitioners to enhance the performance and personal growth of athletes led to examining important professional issues such as what kinds of services should be offered and who is qualified to provide these services. The growth in applied sport psychology resulted in the formation of an additional sport psychology organization and two journals. Establishment of a sport and exercise psychology division within the APA exemplified increasing acceptance of sport psychology within mainstream psychology.

The last 20 years saw a tremendous growth in knowledge and increased career opportunities in academia and consulting, including performance enhancement work with nonsport populations such as performing artists and businesspeople. Exercise psychology became an even stronger specialization area. Great strides were made in addressing critical professional issues such as trying to identify minimal standards for training and certifying sport psychologists and establishing a code of ethics. During this same time, sport psychology became more acceptable to mainstream psychology, and an increasing number of psychologists became active in sport psychology. It was also a time of emerging diversity in research topics, methods, paradigms, and epistemology.

Sport psychology in Eastern Europe has a long history of devoting a great deal of attention to enhancing the performance of elite athletes through applied research and direct intervention. Sport psychologists in these countries were viewed as central figures in facilitating an athlete's quest for excellence and were held in great esteem because of their propaganda role in advancing the communist political system. With the breakup of communist party control in Eastern Europe and the reduction in governmental support, most sport psychology consultants lost their positions or moved to other countries.

Challenges remain for applied sport psychology, both in terms of expanding its scientific foundation and professional practice and in dealing with professional issues, but one certainty is that both knowledge and interest in sport psychology will continue to grow. A key future challenge will be growing the job market at a rate that parallels the increasing number of individuals interested in becoming a sport psychologist and then ensuring that these individuals are appropriately trained for the job market. We anticipate the academic job market will remain strong, particularly for individuals specializing in exercise psychology, but it must be supplemented by greater growth in consulting and nontraditional career options. As great as the growth of applied sport psychology has been, the future looks even brighter.

Study Questions

1. Define what is meant by applied sport psychology and when it might be used.

2. How are sport psychologists trained and what do they do?

3. Briefly describe the development of sport psychology in North America.

4. Contrast the development of sport psychology in Eastern Europe to that in North America.

5. If you conducted a really good study that might be publishable or given as a talk, what journals and organizations would you want to check out?

6. What progress has been made on the professional issues identified in this chapter?

7. What are some of the concerns and questions that sport psychologists must address in the future?

8. What relationship does sport psychology have to the call for psychologists to put more emphasis on positive psychology?

9. Describe some of the traditional and nontraditional job opportunities that sport psychology professionals might pursue.

References

Andersen, M. B., Williams, J. M., Aldridge, T., & Taylor, T. (1997). Tracking the training and careers of graduates of advanced degree programs in sport psychology, 1989 to 1994. *The Sport Psychologist, 11*, 326–344.

Burke, K. L., Sachs, M. L., & Gomer, S. (Eds.). (2004). *Directory of graduate programs in applied sport psychology* (7th ed.). Morgantown, WV: Fitness Information Technology.

Burke, K. L., Sachs, M. L., Fry, S., & Schwehhardt, S. (Eds.). (2008). *Directory of graduate programs in applied sport psychology* (9th ed.). Morgantown, WV: Fitness Information Technology.

Culver, D. M., Gilbert, W. D., & Trudel, P. (2003). A decade of qualitative research in sport psychology journals: 1990–1999. *The Sport Psychologist, 17*, 1–15.

Dishman, R. K., & Buckworth, J. (1996). Increasing physical activity. A quantitative synthesis. *Medicine and Science in Sports and Exercise, 28,* 706–719.

Duda, J. L., & Allison, M. T. (1990). Cross-cultural analysis in exercise and sport psychology: A void in the field. *Journal of Sport & Exercise Psychology, 12,* 114–131.

Garfield, C. A., & Bennett, H. Z. (1984). *Peak performance.* Los Angeles: Tarcher.

Gill, D. L. (2004). Gender and cultural diversity across the lifespan. In Weiss, M. R. (Ed.), *Developmental sport and exercise psychology: A lifespan perspective* (pp. 475–501).

Gould, D. (2002). Sport psychology in the new millennium: The psychology of athletic excellence and beyond. *Journal of Applied Sport Psychology, 14,* 137–139.

Gould, D., & Pick, S. (1995). Sport psychology: The Griffith era, 1920–1940. *The Sport Psychologist, 9,* 391–405.

Greenspan, M. J., & Feltz, D. L. (1989). Psychological interventions with athletes in competitive situations: A review. *The Sport Psychologist, 3,* 219–236.

Griffith, C. R. (1926). *Psychology of coaching.* New York: Scribner.

Griffith, C. R. (1928). *Psychology of athletics.* New York: Scribner.

Harris, D. V. (Ed.). (1972). *Women in sport: A national research conference.* State College, PA: Pennsylvania State University.

Kantor, E., & Ryzonkin, J. (1993). Sport psychology in the former USSR. In R. N. Singer, M. Murphey, & L. K. Tennant (Eds.), *Handbook of research on sport psychology* (pp. 46–49). New York: Macmillan.

Kornspan, A. S., & MacCracken, M. J. Psychology applied to sport in the 1940s: The work of Dorothy Hazeltine Yates. *The Sport Psychologist, 15,* 342–345.

Landers, D. M. (1995). Sport psychology: The formative years, 1950–1980. *The Sport Psychologist, 9,* 406–417.

Lawther, J. D. (1951). *Psychology of coaching.* Englewood Cliffs, NJ: Prentice Hall.

Mahoney, M. J. (1989). Sport psychology. In I. Cohen (Ed.), *The G. Stanley Hall lecture series* Vol. 9 (pp. 97–134). Washington, DC: American Psychological Association.

Martens, R. (1979). About smocks and jocks. *Journal of Sport Psychology, 1,* 94–99.

Meyers, A. W., Whelan, J. P., & Murphy, S. M. (1996). Cognitive behavioral strategies in athletic performance enhancement. In M. Hersen, R. M. Eisler, & P. M. Miller (Eds.), *Progress in behavior modification, 30* (pp. 137–164). Pacific Grove, CA: Brooks/Cole.

Morgan, W. P. (1984). Mind over matter. In W. F. Straub & J. M. Williams (Eds.), *Cognitive sport psychology* (pp. 311–316). Lansing, NY: Sport Science International.

Ogilvie, B., & Tutko, T. (1966). *Problem athletes and how to handle them.* London: Pelham.

Oglesby, C. A. (1978). *Women in sport: From myth to reality.* Philadelphia: Lea & Febiger.

Peters, H. J., & Williams, J. M. (2009). Implications of neglecting culture in sport psychology research and practice. In R. Schinke & S. Hanrahan (Eds.), *Cultural sport psychology: From theory to practice.* Champaign, IL: Human Kinetics.

Petitpas, A. J., Van Raalte, J. L., Cornelius, A., & Presbrey, J. (2004). A life skills development program for high school student-athletes. *The Journal of Primary Prevention, 24,* 325–334.

Petlichkoff, L. M. (2004). Self-regulation skills in children and adolescents. In M. R. Weiss (Ed.), *Developmental sport and exercise psychology: A lifespan perspective* (pp. 273–292). Morgantown, WV: Fitness Information Technology, Inc.

Raiport, G. (1988). *Red gold: Peak performance techniques of the Russian and East German Olympic victors.* New York: Tarcher.

Ram, N., Starek, J., & Johnson, J. (2004). Race, ethnicity, and sexual orientation: Still a void in sport and exercise psychology? *Journal of Sport & Exercise Psychology, 26,* 250–268.

Ryba, T. V., & Wright, H. K. (2005). From mental game to cultural praxis: A cultural studies model's implications for the future of sport psychology. *Quest, 57,* 192–212.

Sachs, M. L. (1991). Reading list in applied sport psychology: Psychological skills training. *The Sport Psychologist, 5,* 88–91.

Sachs, M. L., Burke, K. L., & Gomer, S. (Eds.). (1998). *Directory of graduate programs in applied sport psychology* (5th ed.). Morgantown, WV: Fitness Information Technology.

Sachs, M. L., & Kornspan, A. S. (1998). Reading list in applied sport psychology: Psychological skills training. In M. L. Sachs, K. L. Burke, & S. Gomer (Eds.), *Directory of graduate programs in applied sport psychology* (5th ed.) (pp. 264–274). Morgantown, WV: Fitness Information Technology.

Salmela, J. H. (1981). *The world sport psychology sourcebook.* Ithaca, NY: Mouvement Publications.

Salmela, J. H. (1984). Comparative sport psychology. In J. M. Silva III & R. A. Weinberg (Eds.), *Psychological foundations of sport* (pp. 23–24). Champaign, IL: Human Kinetics.

Scanlan, T.K., Ravizza, K., & Stein, G.L. (1989). An in-depth study of former elite figure skaters: I. Introduction to the project. *Journal of Sport & Exercise Psychology,* 11, 54–64.

Scanlan, T.K., Stein, G.L., & Ravizza, K. (1989). An in-depth study of former elite figure skaters: II. Sources of enjoyment. *Journal of Sport & Exercise Psychology,* 11, 65–83.

Seligman, M., & Csikszentmihalyi, M. (2000). Positive psychology: An introduction. *American Psychologist, 55,* 5–14.

Si, G., & Lee, H. (2007). Cross-cultural issues in sport psychology research. In S. Jowette, & D. Lavallee (Eds.), *Social psychology in sport.* Champaign, IL: Human Kinetics.

Suinn, R. M. (1985). The 1984 Olympics and sport psychology. *Journal of Sport Psychology, 7,* 321–329.

U.S. Olympic Committee. (1983). U.S. Olympic Committee establishes guidelines for sport psychology services. *Journal of Sport Psychology, 5,* 4–7.

Vanek, M., & Cratty, B. J. (1970). *Psychology and the superior athlete.* New York: Macmillan.

Voight, M., & Callaghan, J. (2001). The use of sport psychology services at NCAA Division I universities from 1998–1999. *The Sport Psychologist, 15,* 91–102.

Vealey, R. S. (2006). Smocks and jocks outside the box: The paradigmatic evolution of sport and exercise psychology. *Quest, 58,* 128–159.

Waite, B. T., & Pettit, M. E. (1993). Work experiences of graduates from doctoral programs in sport psychology. *Journal of Applied Sport Psychology, 5,* 234–250.

Williams, J. M., & Scherzer, C. B. (2003). Tracking the training and careers of graduates of advanced degree programs in sport psychology, 1994 to 1999. *Journal of Applied Sport Psychology, 15,* 335–353.

Yates, D. H. (1932). *Psychological racketeers.* Boston: Badger.

Yates, D. H. (1943). A practical method of using set. *Journal of Applied Psychology, 27,* 512–519.

Yates, D. H. (1957). *Psychology you can use.* New York: Crowell.

Learning, Motivation, and Social Interaction

Motor Skill Learning for Effective Coaching and Performance

Cheryl A. Coker, *New Mexico State University*
Mark G. Fischman, *Auburn University*

It's not necessarily the amount of time you spend at practice that counts; it's what you put into the practice.

—Eric Lindros

Effective coaching depends on many factors. Coaches must have excellent knowledge of their sport, be innovative strategists, skilled motivators, and effective personal counselors. However, at the core of successful coaching is an understanding of the motor learning process. First and foremost, effective coaches must be good teachers. Most sports comprise a diverse array of complex motor skills. Athletes enter the sporting arena with different abilities and prior experiences. The coach must understand both how the novice performer acquires brand-new skills and how the experienced athlete maintains, and possibly improves peak performance on well-learned skills. This understanding will enable the coach to structure effective practices and to provide clear, effective feedback to the athlete about performance errors. For the sport psychologist, this understanding serves as the basis for a more comprehensive assessment of athlete behavior

and of potential intervention strategies that will enhance performance.

Motor Learning Defined

Motor skill learning should be understood as a set of internal processes, associated with practice or experience, leading to relatively permanent changes in the capability for skilled movement behavior. **Capability** means that once a skill has been learned, the potential, or likelihood, for exhibiting skilled performance is quite high, although we realize that even highly skilled athletes do occasionally make errors. Because motor learning is internal, taking place within the athlete's central nervous system, we cannot observe learning directly. We can, however, monitor an athlete's *performance*, which is observable behavior, and draw an inference about learning. For example, a beginning swimmer's first attempts at the butterfly stroke will likely proceed in an awkward, step-by-step manner. As the swimmer practices, form, timing, and coordination improve. By monitoring these changes in performance, we infer that the swimmer is learning. It is also important that the changes in performance are relatively permanent; that is, the athlete should be able to demonstrate the skill repeatedly, even after a period of no practice.

Phases of Motor Skill Learning

As athletes progress from the novice stage to an advanced level, they go through different phases or steps. These phases commonly are characterized by the goal of the athlete in each (Gentile, 2000), as well as their behavioral tendencies (Fitts & Posner, 1967). Such information is useful, as it provides the coach a basis from which to make informed decisions that will optimize the learning of his or her athletes. It would, however, be misleading to think of these phases as distinct because, as learning progresses, one phase blends gradually into another so that no clear transition between them is evident (Christina & Corcos, 1988; Fitts & Posner, 1967). Thus, the phases of learning should be thought of as a continuum, with some overlap occurring between them (see Figure 2-1). Coaches should also be aware that an athlete can be in one stage for a given skill and in a different stage for another skill. For example, a soccer player may be in the autonomous stage

for dribbling but the cognitive stage for heading the ball because it is being introduced for the first time. Finally, it would also be misleading to think of these stages as age dependent. Landon Shuffett, a seventh grader and recognized professional billiards player, would be considered highly proficient, yet adults who have skied all of their lives become novices when introduced to snowboarding for the first time!

The Cognitive Phase

In the cognitive or beginning phase of skill learning, athletes focus on gaining an understanding of how the skill is to be performed. The coach or instructor assists the athlete in this process by describing the skill's key elements. In addition, he or she will typically provide demonstrations, films, charts, or other visual cues to help the learners "picture" the new skill.

Based on the explanation and demonstrations provided by the coach, athletes begin to develop a **motor program** for that skill. A motor program is an abstract, internal representation of the skill, similar to a computer program that contains a set of instructions to guide the movement. At first the motor program may be very crude, containing just enough details to allow the athletes to make a "ballpark" response. There also are likely to be errors in the program. However, with practice and feedback, both from the athlete's sensory systems and from the coach, the motor program is revised and refined so that it gradually becomes more effective at controlling performance.

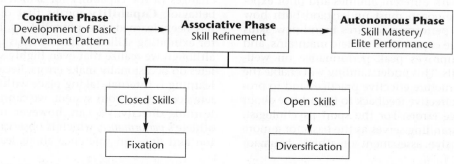

Figure 2-1 **Stages of learning**

Much conscious attention is directed toward the details of the movement in this phase and athletes are unable to attend to external events such as the positions of teammates or movements of defensive players. The movements produced in this phase will lack synchronization and appear choppy and deliberate. This phase is also characterized by inconsistency, and the production of numerous errors that are typically gross in nature. Athletes will be highly dependent on the coach at this point as they lack the capability to determine the specific cause of an error and its subsequent correction. Finally, the dominant sensory system in this phase is *vision* as is evident when a beginner learns to dribble a basketball, intently watching both the hand and the ball.

Role of the coach.   The role of the coach during the cognitive phase is to facilitate the athlete's development of a basic movement pattern by clearly communicating the critical aspects of the skill through verbal instructions and demonstrations. There is much truth in the saying "a picture is worth a thousand words," and a demonstration will help learners create a reference image of the skill so that practice can begin. However, a correctly performed demonstration does not necessarily ensure that the athletes' attention was focused on the most important part of the demonstration. Verbal cues should be used to direct athletes' attention in conjunction with the demonstration (e.g. Janelle, Champenoy, Coombes, & Mousseau, 2003). The coach must tell the athletes *specifically* what to look for, whether it be the pattern of racket movement in a looped tennis back-swing, the position of the recovery elbow in the freestyle, or the entire pattern of coordination in a baseball swing. Magill (2004) further recommends that those cues be short and concise rather than providing "continuous verbal commentary while demonstrating the skill" (p. 259) to avoid overloading the athlete with information.

Studies have also compared the use of expert versus novice models who exhibit errors in their performance using a variety of tasks including tennis (Hebert & Landin, 1994) and weight lifting (McCullagh & Meyer, 1997). Results suggest that observing a learning model can be as effective as observing a skilled model, provided that the observer has access to the feedback given to the model. Psychological benefits may also be derived from watching a learning model in terms of improved self-esteem and self-efficacy. (For a review on observational learning, see Horn & Williams, 2004; McCullagh & Weiss, 2001.)

Once athletes have been exposed to several demonstrations, they must be afforded the opportunity to practice the skill. Accordingly, the role of the coach also entails the design of practice experiences for initial motor program development. This practice should allow for numerous repetitions (blocked practice) in which the athletes can allocate their undivided attention to the details of the movement itself to encourage the discovery of effective performance strategies. Furthermore, the provision of feedback is important in this phase to reinforce, motivate, and guide athletes in modifying their performance.

Duration of the cognitive phase.   The cognitive phase of learning is a relatively short period in the overall learning process. It may last only a few minutes or it may involve a longer period if the skill is complex. The cognitive phase is complete when the athletes can reasonably execute the skill the way it was demonstrated (Christina & Corcos, 1988).

The Associative Phase

The focus of the associative or intermediate phase of skill learning is refinement. Through practice, the learner moves from having a general idea of how to execute the movement to being able to perform the skill both accurately and consistently. The coach's role during this phase shifts to one that mainly involves planning and implementing effective practice conditions as well as providing feedback for skill enhancement.

During the associative phase of learning, the motor program is further developed and athletes gradually eliminate extraneous movements and make fewer, less gross errors. They improve their speed, accuracy, coordination, and consistency. Movements will become more automated and less attention is allocated to the physical execution of the skill and can now be devoted to other aspects of the environment, such as planning strategy. Visual control of movement is gradually replaced by **proprioceptive control,** or "feel" and dribbling a basketball can now be effectively performed without looking at the ball or hand and probably even with the eyes closed. Were proprioceptive cues not available during the early phases of learning? Yes, they were available but it takes many practice trials before athletes come to associate the feel of their movements with the outcomes that these movements produce. Schmidt (1975) referred to the generation of "expected sensory consequences," meaning that we expect our movements to feel a certain way, and we can use such sensory feedback to evaluate the correctness of our movements. In other words, using this information, the athlete not only learns to identify the cause of performance errors but, over time, will also develop the capability to generate strategies for their correction.

Another aspect of vision that changes with increases in skill is visual search patterns, or what the athlete actually monitors in the environment. Research shows that there are marked differences in visual search strategies between beginners and experts. For example, expert soccer players were found to fixate more often on the knee and hip regions of their opponents than did novice players, suggesting that the information in these areas was important in anticipating the opponents' next move (Nagano, Kato, & Fukada, 2004). Also in soccer, as a kicker approached the ball, the focus of experienced goalkeepers progressed from the kicker's head to the nonkicking foot, then the kicking foot and finally to the ball, whereas novices focused more on the trunk, arms, and hips (Savelsbergh, Williams, van der Kamp, & Ward, 2002). Furthermore, the experienced goalkeepers directed their attention toward the ball more than twice the time of novices. Finally, comparisons between elite and near-elite athletes revealed differences in gaze behaviors of Team Canada ice hockey players who displayed exceptional defensive abilities and those known for making tactical errors during games (Martell & Vickers, 2004). In soccer, Savelsbergh, van der Kamp, Williams, and Ward (2005) found differences between successful and less successful

expert goalkeepers in stopping a penalty kick. The successful experts more accurately predicted the height and direction of the kick, waited longer to initiate their response and spent more time fixated on the nonkicking leg than did their less successful counterparts. The knowledge gained through these studies provides invaluable information to coaches that have important implications for designing training programs to improve anticipation, selective attention, and decision-making skills. (For a comprehensive resource on decision training refer to Vickers, 2007.)

The role of the coach. During the associative phase, the coach must design effective practices to optimize skill refinement. Understanding the nature of the skill is the first step to accomplishing this objective. A skill can be categorized as falling on a continuum between being closed and open according to the predictability of the environment in which that skill is performed. Closed skills are those performed in a relatively stable, predictable environment such as bowling, target archery, free throw shooting, and tennis serving. Successful performance of such skills requires that the athlete be able to consistently and accurately replicate the movement pattern (*fixation*), and practice should reflect this objective. Some closed skills, however, involve intertrial variability. For example, each time a putt is attempted in a round of golf, it is from a different position in relation to the hole. For these types of skills, consistency in technique is important, but the performer also must be able to utilize that technique in a variety of situations. Accordingly, the athlete should practice on different greens, a variety of slopes, and from different locations and distances from the hole. Open skills are those in which the environment is changing and unpredictable. Examples include returning a punt in football, executing a breakaway in field hockey or soccer, and driving through heavy rush-hour traffic. Because the performer must constantly conform his or her actions to those of the environment, the objective of practice is to *diversify* the movement pattern or teach the athlete to be able to quickly adapt to the demands of the performance situation. Practice should therefore be gamelike so that the athlete becomes better at anticipating changes in the environment.

As indicated earlier, athletes in the associative phase are increasingly able to direct their attention toward aspects of the performance environment. Given the nature of open skills, learning where to direct one's attention to locate appropriate cues is critical to successful performance. Research has shown that anticipatory skills can be acquired and enhanced through specific training in visual search strategies (Abernethy, Wood, & Parks, 1999; Raab, Masters, & Maxwell, 2005). By directing athletes to focus on the areas in which the critical cues for performance occur and providing a variety of practice experiences in which athletes must identify and respond to those cues, coaches can assist athletes in developing effective visual search strategies (Magill, 1998).

Finally, the provision of effective feedback continues to be an important role of the coach throughout this phase. That feedback not only should guide the athletes in correcting movement errors but should help them develop their error detection and correction capabilities by teaching them to relate the feelings associated with a movement to the resulting performance outcome.

Duration of the associative phase.   The associative phase of skill learning is a much longer period than the cognitive phase, ranging from perhaps a few hours for learning simple skills to several years for mastering complex ones. In fact, not all learners will transition to the final stage of learning as it represents the highest level of skill proficiency.

The Autonomous Phase

The autonomous or advanced phase of learning emerges when the learner can perform the skill at a maximal level of proficiency. As the term implies, performance is quite automatic; the learner seems to require very little conscious thought or attention to the details of movement. In fact, asking highly skilled performers to consciously focus on their movements will seriously disrupt performance, especially in high-speed activities such as performing a routine on the uneven bars in gymnastics or executing a dodge and kick for a goal in soccer.

Automatic Behavior

To experience what happens when elite athletes consciously focus on their movements, perform the following:

Everyone has a natural walking pace. Determine your natural pace by walking across the room several times. Describe your thought process during this activity as well as what happened to your gait. (From Coker, 2004; p. 107)

In the autonomous phase, the athletes' motor program for generating the correct movements is highly developed and well established in memory. Free from having to concentrate on executing the skill, they can concentrate on other things besides technique. For example, the NBA's Jason Kidd can dribble down court at full speed on a fast break and does this without looking at the ball and while planning the best strategy for getting the ball to the basket. During such a play, he considers the position and movements of his opponents and teammates and whether to pass, drive to the basket, pull up short and shoot or set up a new play. Kidd does all this while dribbling the ball at full speed, giving no thought to the mechanics of dribbling.

Progressing from the cognitive through the associative and arriving at the autonomous phase of learning requires an amount of practice and a period of time that depends on the abilities of the individual, the complexity of the task itself, the learner's prior movement experiences, and the efficiency of the learning environment. Certainly high-speed dribbling requires more time and practice to master than does a vertical jump or a simple forward roll. In fact, some speculate that it requires a minimum of 10 years and over a million repetitions to produce high-level performance in major sports such as football, basketball, baseball, and gymnastics (Ericsson, Krampe, & Tesch-Römer, 1993).

Role of the coach.   Instruction during the autonomous phase of learning basically serves two purposes: first, to help athletes maintain their level of skill, and, second, to motivate the athletes to want to continue to improve. Once a consistently high level of skill is achieved, it must be maintained not only during a single season but also from season to season. Recall that our definition of motor learning referred to changes in the capability for skilled behavior that are relatively permanent. Also, it would be a mistake to assume that learning has ended in the autonomous phase and that performance cannot be improved. Although the level of competence an athlete may achieve in a skill has certain limits, and performance may be approaching some arbitrary standard of perfection, the progression to this point usually occurs so gradually that it is rarely possible to claim that athletes have reached their highest level of achievement (Christina & Corcos, 1988; Ericsson, 1996). However, because of the difficulty in improving performance as one approaches the highest levels of skill, even though practice continues, athletes may lose motivation to strive for improvement. Thus, the role of the coach as a motivator becomes very important during this phase of learning. The use of goal setting and reinforcement can help skilled athletes maintain motivation. These topics will be discussed in detail in later chapters.

Error correction and the learning process. An understanding of the motor learning process and the phases of skill learning is not only important for teaching new skills to novice athletes but also when a coach desires to *change* a highly skilled athlete's well-learned technique (see Table 2-1). Making a minor change in technique, such as widening a baseball player's batting stance, is simple and can usually be accomplished easily. Having a tennis player change from an Eastern forehand grip to the continental grip also should be accomplished with little difficulty. This is because changes such as these require very little relearning. However, when you ask athletes to make a major change in technique, such as going from a two-hand backhand in tennis to a one-hand backhand, you are essentially asking them to return to the cognitive phase of learning and progress

through the associative to the autonomous phases again. When you consider that it may have taken years of practice to perfect the motor program for the original technique, you realize that learning the new technique will require a great deal of time. Thus, major changes in technique should probably be undertaken during the off-season. Furthermore, when athletes are in the process of relearning a skill, performance initially will suffer. This can be very discouraging, and athletes may hold the coach responsible. The coach should be prepared to accept this responsibility and take some of the pressure off the athletes by providing much encouragement. Ultimately, when relearning is accomplished, performance should be better than it was with the old technique.

Practice Considerations

Often considered the single most important factor in the control of learning is **practice.** In general, the greater the number of practice trials, the better the learning. Current knowledge suggests that the necessary conditions for reaching international-level performance in many different domains is at least 10 years of effortful practice under optimal training conditions (Ericsson, 1996, 2003; Ericsson et al., 1993). Such conditions require a well-defined task of appropriate difficulty for the athlete, information feedback, and sufficient opportunities for repetition and correction of errors. Ericsson and his colleagues use the term *deliberate practice* to characterize training activities that contain all of these elements.

Deliberate practice by itself, however, is not enough to enable athletes to learn a skill correctly. For practice to be effective, the athletes must be motivated to learn. The old adage "practice makes perfect" is not necessarily true; athletes must practice with the *intent* to improve. This means that skill learning involves more than simply going through the motions physically. Without the goal to constantly improve the level of performance, practice can lead to a mediocre level of proficiency or, worse, a deterioration of skill.

Table 2-1 **Performer Characteristics and Role of the Coach for Each Stage of Learning**

Stage of Learning	Performer Characteristics	Role of the Coach
Cognitive	High degree of cognitive activity	Motivate to want to learn the skill
	Use of self-talk	Provide verbal instructions and demonstrations to help learners gain a basic understanding of the skill
	Development of initial motor program	
	Much conscious attention to details of movement	Design experience for initial development of motor program
	Inability to attend to external events	Assist learner by providing feedback regarding errors and prescribing corrections
	Lack synchronization and appear choppy and deliberate	
	Inconsistent	Encourage
	Production of numerous errors	
	Errors are large	
	Lack capability to determine specific cause of errors and subsequent corrections	
	Vision is the dominant sensory system	
Associative	Fewer errors	Plan and implement appropriate practice opportunities (fixation vs. diversification)
	Improvements in speed, accuracy, coordination, and consistency	
	Attend less to physical execution of skill	Teach visual search strategies
	Can devote attention to environment	Continue to provide feedback to reinforce, motivate, and correct performance
	Proprioceptive control replaces visual	
	Refining motor program	Help athletes to develop error detection and correction capabilities
	Developing capability to identify errors and generate strategies for their correction	
Autonomous	Highly proficient	Continue to plan appropriate practice opportunities
	Performance is automatic	
	Focus completely directed to environment and decision making	Provide feedback when needed
		Motivate

Teaching Several Skills: Blocked versus Random Practice

In most sports, athletes are challenged to learn a variety of different skills. Swimmers, for example, must learn four competitive strokes, along with starts and turns. Gymnasts must learn many routines on several pieces of equipment. Tennis players must learn forehand and backhand ground strokes, several different serves, net play, and appropriate strategies. Golfers are charged with learning to hit many different clubs over a variety of distances and often through various obstacles. Novice athletes have to learn the many skills of their sport before the first competition. Experienced athletes have to practice these many skills in order to maintain peak performance.

Considering the large number of skills most sports comprise and the often-restricted practice time available, coaches are forced to teach more than one skill in a week; often, several skills must be taught in a single practice session. How can a coach sequence the practice of several tasks during the practice period to maximize learning?

Suppose that an age group swim team practices four times a week for an hour per session. The coach would like to devote 2 weeks to teaching the four competitive strokes: butterfly, backstroke, breast-stroke, and freestyle. A commonsense approach to scheduling would be to practice the butterfly for two sessions, then the backstroke for two sessions, and so on until all four strokes are completed. This schedule of practice is called **blocked practice,** where all the trials of a given task are completed before moving on to the next task. Note that the order in which the strokes are practiced could be arbitrary as long as practice on one stroke is completed before beginning practice on the next stroke. Intuitively, blocked practice seems to make sense because it allows the swimmers to concentrate on one stroke at a time without worrying about interference from the other strokes.

An alternative approach to scheduling would be to practice all four strokes within each practice period but to do so in a random order so that the swimmers never practice the same stroke on two consecutive trials. This is called a **random practice** schedule. It is important to note that, at the end of the 2-week period, both practice schedules would have provided the same amount of practice on each of the four strokes.

Which of these practice schedules might produce more efficient learning in our swimmers? At first glance, the obvious answer would be blocked practice as it would appear that random practice would present a more difficult environment for the athlete because of the constant switching between tasks. Indeed, if we plotted the swimmers' performance of the four strokes over the 2-week learning period, we would probably find better performance under blocked practice. However, a sizable body of research seems to contradict this intuitive view about practice. The results of many laboratory-based experiments indicate that blocked practice produces better

acquisition performance than random practice, but poorer long-term learning, as measured by delayed retention and **transfer,** the application of the practiced skill in a new situation (e.g. Li & Wright, 2000; Shea & Morgan, 1979). Studies using more real-world sport skills, such as learning different badminton serves (Goode & Magill, 1986; Wrisberg & Liu, 1991), forehand and backhand ground strokes in tennis (Hebert, Landin & Solmon, 1996), and different snowboarding skills (Smith, 2002) lend additional support to this notion. This phenomenon is known as the **contextual interference** effect, based on the early work of Battig (1966). (For reviews on contextual interference see Barreiros, Figueiredo, & Godinho, 2007; Brady, 2004, 2008.)

Essentially, contextual interference proposes that making the practice environment more difficult for the learner, as with random practice, leads to better learning, even though performance during acquisition is depressed. This is certainly a counterintuitive idea. Attempts to explain why random practice is more effective than blocked practice for learning suggest two possible mechanisms. First, when several tasks are present in the athletes' working memory at the same time, they have to use more elaborate processing strategies to keep the tasks distinct. The more effortful processing produces better memory representations for the tasks (Shea & Zimny, 1983, 1988). Second, when athletes practice a task on Trial 1 but do not repeat that task until several trials later, there may be some forgetting of the "solution" to the task. Consequently, the athletes are forced to go through more solution generations with random practice, which ultimately leads to better retrieval (Lee & Magill, 1983).

Although the research on contextual interference discussed thus far implies that a random practice schedule would optimize learning, one additional factor should be considered. Evidence exists indicating that during the initial stage of skill acquisition, when the learner is getting the idea of the movement, blocked practice conditions may be more beneficial than random practice (e.g. Landin & Hebert, 1997). However, once the basic movement pattern is acquired, the amount of contextual interference must be increased. Aside from doing so through random practice, Landin and

Practice Strategy	Time	Session 1	Session 2	Session 3	Session 4	Session 5	Session 6	Session 7	Session 8
Blocked Practice	40 min	FLY	FLY	BK	BK	BR	BR	FR	FR
Repeated Blocked Practice	5 min 5 min 5 min 5 min × 2	FLY BK BR FR	FLY BK BR FR	FLY BK BR FR	FLY BK BR FR	FLY BK BR FR	FLY BK BR FR	FLY BK BR FR	FLY BK BR FR
Random Practice	40 min	FLY BK BR FR BR FR BK FLY BR FR FLY BK Etc.	FLY BR FR BK BR FR BR FLY BK BR FLY FR Etc.	BK BR FR BK FR FLY BR FR BK BR FR FLY Etc.	FR BR FLY BK BR FLY FR BR BK FLY BR Etc.	BK BR FR BR FLY BR FR BK BR FR FLY Etc.	FLY BK FR BR FR BR FLY BK BR FLY FR Etc.	FR BR FLY BK FLY FR FR FR BK FLY BR Etc.	FLY BK BR FR BR FR BK FLY BR FR FLY BK Etc.

Figure 2-2 **Three practice variations for practicing swimming strokes**
(**FLY** = butterfly; **BK** = backstroke; **BR** = breaststroke; **FR** = freestyle)

Hebert (1997) propose the use of a third approach to scheduling, **repeated blocked practice,** which may combine the advantages of both blocked and random practice. Using the swimming example, rather than practicing the butterfly for two sessions followed by the backstroke for two sessions and so on until all four strokes are completed (blocked practice) or practicing all four strokes within each practice period where the same stroke is never practiced consecutively (random practice), repeated blocked practice would be organized such that several successive trials of each stroke are performed with the rotation repeated throughout the practice period. Figure 2-2 shows sample practice variations for all three strategies.

Although Keller, Li, Weiss, and Relyea found support for repeated blocked practice (2006) in pistol shooting skills, more field-based research in a variety of sports is needed before we can be truly confident about the learning benefits of both repeated blocked and random practice. Nevertheless, the available research should

encourage coaches to at least think about some of their deeply rooted traditional practice methods.

Teaching Several Variations of a Skill: Variable Practice

In the preceding discussion, the coach's goal was to teach several *different* tasks. There also are times, however, when only a single task is to be learned during a practice session, such as shooting a jump shot, kicking a field goal, or fielding a ground ball. How should the coach structure practice for these situations to maximize learning?

Consider the task of fielding a ground ball and throwing to first base. This task essentially involves perceiving a stimulus (the ground ball), moving the body in front of the ball, fielding it, and making an accurate throw. Coach A believes the best way to learn this task would be to practice under **constant** conditions. She will give her shortstop 100 ground balls to field, but each one will be thrown by a pitching machine, have constant velocity, come to the same spot on the field, and have exactly the same bounce and roll characteristics. Coach A feels that this type of practice will allow her shortstop to master the fundamentals of fielding and to "groove" her response.

Coach B adopts a **variable** practice approach. She also will give her shortstop 100 balls to field, but each one will be hit by a batter, possess different bounce and roll characteristics, and go to different spots on the field, forcing the player to move to multiple locations and adapt to the ever-changing demands presented. Coach B reasons that in the real game no two ground balls are exactly alike, so variability of practice would be more likely to produce the specific skills needed by a shortstop. This type of drill more realistically simulates actual game conditions. It is also possible that in an actual game a shortstop will have to field a ball that is slightly different from any of the 100 variations experienced during practice.

The variable practice approach adopted by Coach B has been shown to result in better learning than the constant conditions offered by Coach A's practice (e.g., Douvis, 2005; Shoenfelt, Snyder, Maue, McDowell, & Woolard, 2002). Coach B's shortstop would be more likely to experience success when faced with a "novel" fielding situation than Coach A's shortstop because of all the practice with similar versions of the task. What is actually being learned through variable practice is more than simply the specific actions practiced. The shortstop develops a general capability to produce fielding responses, a capability that enhances generalizability, allowing athletes to transfer their learning to actions not specifically experienced in practice. According to schema theory (Schmidt, 1975), variable practice allows the learner to discover relationships among environment conditions (her location on the field, speed and bounce characteristics of the ball, distance from first base); what she "told" her muscles to produce (how fast to move, where to put her glove, how hard to throw); and the outcomes that these movements produced (missed/caught the ball, threw too far or too short). Through

variable practice, the athlete's understanding of these relationships becomes stronger, and she develops a schema or rule that relates the initial environment conditions, such as distance of the throw, to the force and trajectory requirements that must be selected to produce a correct throw. When the shortstop is called on to execute a "new" fielding response, one that she has never experienced before, her variable practice experiences allow her to better estimate the response specifications needed by her motor program to produce the new response. The athlete who has experienced only one version of the task, through constant practice, may be able to execute that version very well but will be limited in developing a repertoire of responses that may be needed in the criterion activity.

Before we leave the topic of variable practice, a word of caution may be in order. As discussed with blocked and random practice, the skill level of the athlete should be considered prior to deciding whether to employ constant or variable practice. When athletes have no prior experience in an activity, then it may be advantageous to begin with constant practice at one version of the task, shooting a jump shot from one spot on the court, for example, before introducing variable practice. Initial constant practice will allow the pure beginner to master the basics of the skill and pass through the cognitive phase of learning. Once this is accomplished, however, variable practice should be introduced to develop the schemas needed in the actual sport.

Whole versus Part Practice

Many of the sport skills an athlete must learn are quite complex, such as a floor exercise routine in gymnastics, a reverse lay-up in basketball, or a forward double somersault with two twists in diving. Even a relatively simple skill, such as a 2-foot putt in golf, may seem very complex to the beginner. A coach must decide whether to present all aspects of such skills to the athlete at once for practice or to divide the skill into smaller, meaningful units that can be practiced separately and then combined into the whole skill.

The **whole** method requires that the athletes practice the activity or skill in its entirety, as a single unit. The **part** method requires that the athletes practice each component of the activity or skill separately and then combine the parts into the whole skill. Between these two extremes are two variations. In the first, the **progressive-part** method, the first two parts of a skill are practiced separately and then combined and practiced as a unit. The third part is practiced separately next and then combined with the first two, and so on until the skill is performed in its entirety. The second variation is known as the **repetitive-part** method. Using this method, the first part is practiced independently. Once a level of proficiency is obtained, the second is immediately added to it and the two parts are practiced together. The pattern continues until all parts have been integrated. Figure 2.3 illustrates each part method using bowling.

Both the whole and part methods of practice offer distinct advantages. The part method of practice is of greatest value when a skill is very complex and involves separate, independently performed parts. For example, a gymnastics floor exercise routine is suited to the part method of practice because each individual trick can be practiced independently. Also, using this method, the gymnast can devote more practice time to particularly difficult tricks in the routine without practicing the easier ones, thus making practice more efficient. However, the successful gymnastics routine is more than a series of well-executed individual movements. The transitions between individual elements must be executed smoothly so that the entire performance "flows" as a coherent unit. Most serial activities of reasonably long duration are characterized by an inherent timing or rhythmic structure among certain components. The coach must be careful to identify the components within the routine that go together and have the athletes practice them as a unit so as not to disrupt the essential timing.

The undue adherence to the part method can also result in the development of a series of well-learned components that are disconnected and are performed in a disjointed and segmented fashion when combined into a whole. Learning a skill through the part method therefore requires both learning the individual parts and *connecting* them into a cohesive unit. By demonstrating the whole skill before breaking it down for part practice and explaining how the parts are associated, coaches can facilitate the athletes' understanding of how the parts fit into the whole.

The decision to practice a motor skill as a whole or by parts should be based on the nature of the skill *and* the nature of the learner. Christina and Corcos (1988) provide several excellent suggestions for how to do this. In general, the whole method is favored if (a) the skill

Part-Whole	Progressive Part	Repetitive Part
• Approach • Push Away • Pendulum Swing • Delivery • Approach + Push Away + Pendulum Swing + Delivery	• Approach • Push Away • Approach + Push Away • Pendulum Swing • Approach + Push Away + Pendulum Swing • Delivery • Approach + Push Away + Pendulum Swing + Delivery	• Approach • Approach + Push Away • Approach + Push Away + Pendulum Swing • Approach + Push Away + Pendulum Swing + Delivery

Figure 2-3 **Illustration of part practice techniques using bowling**

is not too complicated and can be understood in a meaningful way; (b) the skill is not too dangerous and can be practiced with a reasonable degree of success (many gymnastics and diving routines, certain wrestling maneuvers, and pole vaulting, for example, because of the potential for injury, lend themselves to part practice); (c) the athlete is capable, highly motivated, and has an extensive background in various sports; and (d) the athletes' attention span is long enough to deal with the whole. Skills with components that are highly interdependent also are best served by whole practice.

There also are times when parts of an activity should be practiced separately. For example, when one particular skill or phase of the overall activity is causing difficulty, such as a tennis player having problems tossing the ball accurately and consistently, concentration and practice on this particular component are appropriate for a time. This allows additional practice where it is most needed. However, too much part practice on an isolated component can cause it to become disconnected from the surrounding components. The coach should seek to integrate the troublesome part back into the whole skill as quickly as possible.

Feedback: Its Functions and Use in Skill Learning and Performance

Chen (2001) suggests that feedback is the most critical form of guidance that a coach can provide an athlete. After all, if people do not know how they are doing, there is no reason for them to change their behavior. Furthermore, if they arbitrarily make a change, there is no assurance that it will be in the right direction (For a review of research on feedback and motor learning, see Magill, 2001; and Wulf & Shea, 2004.)

Kinds of Feedback

Information available to athletes about their movements can be of two types: intrinsic feedback and augmented feedback. **Intrinsic feedback** is information athletes receive as a natural

consequence of moving; it is provided by the athletes' own sensory systems. For example, when basketball players shoot the ball, they can *feel* the proprioceptive sensations coming from their muscles, joints, and tendons. They can *hear* the sound of the ball hitting the rim, or perhaps swishing through the net. Finally, they can *see* whether the ball went into the basket or not. All these sensations provide the athletes with information about the outcome of their shot in terms of achieving the environmental goal. In many sports, information about the success in achieving some goal is readily apparent to performers intrinsically. For example, it is easy to see where the arrow lands in the archery target, whether one clears the bar in the high jump, how many pins are knocked down in bowling, or whether the tennis ball lands in the service area. In these activities it is not necessary for anyone to provide information as to the results of the performances. This information is clearly evident to the athlete.

Augmented feedback is information athletes receive that is not a natural consequence of executing a response. It must be provided by some external source such as a coach, teammate, stopwatch, judge's score, videotape replay, and so on. Augmented feedback is supplied beyond intrinsic feedback and supplements the information naturally available. It can provide information about the outcome of the performance or about the movement pattern that the athletes have just made.

In many sports the performers have no clear idea of how well they are doing. In track, the runner does not know his or her time in a 400-meter trial run until informed by another person or a clock. Neither does the long jumper know the distance of the jump until a measure is taken and reported by an official. Gymnasts, divers, and figure skaters have minimal information about the quality of their performance until they receive the judges' score or are informed by the coach or other observers.

The augmented feedback a coach gives athletes should not be redundant with the intrinsic feedback the athletes have already obtained. It is absurd for a football coach to tell a receiver, "You dropped the ball." The athlete knows this.

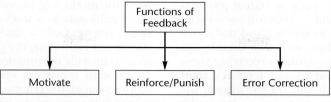

Figure 2-4 **Functions of feedback**

Feedback should provide specific information directed at correcting errors or reinforcing correct performance. For example, a bowler sees that the ball is repeatedly veering off into the left gutter but has no idea of what is causing it. A coach may be able to point out that during the follow-through the arm is pulling across the left shoulder, therefore pulling the ball off to the left. Consequently, focusing the athlete's attention on executing a follow-through that is straight past the visual line may correct the problem.

Functions of Feedback

Feedback serves at least three important functions in skill learning and performance: (a) motivation, (b) reinforcement or punishment, and (c) error correction information (see Figure 2-4).

Feedback as motivation. How hard would you try or how long would you persist at learning a task in which you had no idea how well you were performing? Feedback can play a powerful role in energizing and directing athletes' behavior in a particular task. A casual comment from a coach, such as "You're doing great, Jason, only two more repeats to go!" can help Jason get through a grueling practice and perhaps put out even a little more effort. Notice that this comment is of a general nature in that it did not convey specific information about Jason's performance. Nevertheless, the extra effort such feedback can cause athletes to bring to the task can only benefit them in terms of increased performance.

Feedback also can influence motivation in terms of goal setting and goal evaluation. Most athletes, with the help of their coaches, set performance goals for themselves, both immediate and long range. Feedback (intrinsic or augmented) informs the athletes about their progress toward those goals. If the feedback indicates that the athletes are improving, it may be very satisfying to them, causing them to try to improve present performance until the goal is achieved. If the feedback indicates that very little or no improvement is occurring, it may either lower the athletes' incentive to keep trying to learn the skill or reveal that the original goals were unrealistic and need to be adjusted.

Feedback as reinforcement or punishment. **Reinforcement** is any event that *increases* the likelihood that a specific action will occur again under similar circumstances. **Punishment** is just the opposite; it is any event that *decreases* the likelihood that a specific action will occur again. The reinforcing and punishing properties of feedback operate according to Thorndike's (1927) empirical **law of effect,** which essentially says that actions followed by rewarding consequences tend to be repeated, whereas actions followed by unpleasant, or punishing, consequences tend *not* to be repeated.

An example of intrinsic feedback that may serve as positive reinforcement is the satisfaction of seeing your tennis serve go untouched for an ace because you served it exactly where you wanted to and sensing (via proprioception) that your body moved just as you intended it to move when executing the serve. To experience these rewarding sensations again you will try to perform the serve in the same way in the future under similar conditions.

Examples of augmented feedback that may serve as reinforcement are compliments or praise from the coach, such as "Great job boxing him out," "Nice shot," "Your form was excellent that time," "Way to hustle," and nonverbal types of communication, such as a thumbs up, a smile, or a high five. Athletes receiving these kinds of rewarding augmented feedback right after performing a skill will try to perform the skill in the same way in the future under similar circumstances.

Based on the preceding discussion, it should be easy to see how intrinsic and augmented feedback also can operate as punishment. When Hilary lands on her back following a dive, her pain receptors provide powerful feedback that an error occurred. She may or may not know precisely what was wrong, but she knows she must change something on her next attempt to avoid this unpleasant experience. Intrinsic feedback does not necessarily have to be associated with physical pain to be offensive. When Mike attempts a field goal, seeing the ball veer off wide to the left and feeling the sensations associated with that kick also should be unpleasant and cause Mike to modify his next attempt. Essentially, athletes will try to avoid punishing feedback by learning not to perform the response being punished.

In the preceding examples, augmented feedback from coaches, such as verbally expressing disapproval of the incorrect performance or nonverbally expressing disapproval (shake of the head, scowl), also could serve as punishment to stop athletes from repeating their errors. It is important to note, however, that if a coach elects to use augmented feedback as punishment, the undesirable behavior, the performance error, should be the focus, not the athlete. The coach should praise sincere effort and any part of the skill that was performed correctly, thereby reinforcing these desirable aspects of the performance.

Feedback as error correction information. There is little doubt that the most important component of feedback for motor skill learning is the information it provides about patterns of movement, specifically, errors in the movement pattern. This feedback about errors, prescribing ways for modifying performance, is the reason the coach's role as a teacher is so important for skill learning. Only a skilled teacher can know the correct technique, the proper movement pattern, to provide information feedback.

In some sports, because of the nature of the scoring system, the criterion for successful performance *is* the movement pattern itself. Examples include diving, figure skating, gymnastics, and synchronized swimming. Because it is impossible to receive a high score in these sports without producing technically correct patterns of movement, the coach's augmented feedback must be directed at helping the athletes achieve the correct mechanics. In other sports, however, successful performance outcomes are possible even in the absence of textbook-perfect movement patterns. For example, it does not matter how a basketball player shoots the free throw as long as the ball goes into the basket, how a runner swings her arms as long as she crosses the finish line first, or how a golfer grips the club as long as the result is a 250-yard drive straight down the fairway. Nevertheless, the probability of producing successful performance outcomes is greater when athletes use proper mechanics than when they use improper mechanics. Therefore, coaches should teach and reinforce the use of correct fundamental movement patterns in *all* sports.

How does information feedback operate in skill learning? What does information about errors cause the learner to do? First and foremost, giving information helps to guide the learners toward the movement goal (Salmoni, Schmidt, & Walter, 1984). This guidance is very important during the early stages of learning, when performance errors are quite large and tend to occur often. Continued use of augmented feedback from the coach helps keep errors to a minimum and allows them to be corrected quickly, thus bringing performance close to the goal and helping to maintain it there. Although this would seem to be good for learning, studies have shown that the guidance properties of feedback may cause learners to become too dependent on the feedback, using it as a "crutch," so that performance can be maintained only when the feedback is present (e.g. Butki & Hoffman, 2003;

Schmidt, Young, Swinnen, & Shapiro, 1989). When the feedback is withdrawn, as it must be during actual competition, the athletes may have trouble performing. The constant provision of augmented feedback also may distract athletes from processing their own sensory feedback. If the athletes know that the coach will give feedback on every practice attempt, they simply have to wait for it, without attending to the rich sources of intrinsic feedback that can be important for learning. A strategy that may help athletes focus more on intrinsic feedback is to have them subjectively estimate, or guess, their error following a particular performance before providing augmented feedback.

The practical implications here seem clear. A high frequency of augmented feedback is important during the early stage of learning to bring performance close to the goal. As proficiency increases, augmented feedback should gradually become less and less frequent so that the athlete learns to become less dependent on it for successful performance (Winstein & Schmidt, 1990). When a high degree of proficiency is attained, the athletes need only an occasional dose of information feedback to be certain that performance is correct. This method, whereby augmented feedback is gradually reduced as performance improves, is called *faded feedback* (Winstein & Schmidt, 1990).

Another method for reducing the frequency of augmented feedback is *bandwidth feedback* (e.g. Butler & Fischman, 1996; Butler, Reeve, & Fischman, 1996), in which the coach identifies an acceptable error tolerance, or "bandwidth," and provides feedback only when the athlete's performance falls outside this acceptable range. Early in learning, the athlete's performances are more likely to fall outside the bandwidth, and so the coach would provide feedback more frequently. As performance improves and more responses start to fall inside the bandwidth, the frequency of feedback is reduced. This method appears to have a great deal of merit because it is based on the athlete's actual performance rather than some arbitrary, fixed schedule. Earlier studies of bandwidth feedback relied mainly on laboratory-type tasks, but recent work by Smith, Taylor, and Withers (1997) and Chambers and Vickers (2006) showed that the method can be successfully applied to learning a golf chip shot and to the development of swimming technique and speed.

Learner-regulated feedback, in which augmented feedback is only provided to the athlete when he or she requests it, is an alternative strategy that has recently been shown to be effective (Chen, 2001; Chen, Kaufman, & Chung, 2001; Chiviacowsky & Wulf, 2002, 2005; Janelle, Barba, Frehlich, Tennant, & Cauraugh, 1997; Janelle, Kim, & Singer, 1995). Because athletes control when augmented feedback is given, feedback frequency is individualized. Moreover, the athlete is thought to benefit by becoming actively engaged in the learning process.

Diagnosing and Correcting Errors

Providing timely and effective feedback to athletes is not a simple matter. First, prescribing modifications for skill improvement is dependent on the coach's capability to accurately identify performance errors. Second, even when the movement faults are obvious to the coach and the appropriate corrective responses are clear, transmitting this information to learners so that they can comprehend and use it is not always easy. Frequently, the athletes are unable to translate the verbiage into meaningful movement behavior. At other times they simply may not believe or accept what they are being told. Consequently, the following sections offer strategies for both analyzing a skill and providing the athlete with augmented feedback.

Analyzing the Skill

Before giving augmented feedback designed to correct errors in performance, the coach should first do a careful, thorough analysis of the athlete's technique. Christina and Corcos (1988) advocate a three-step process for analyzing skill technique. The first step is to compare the athlete's technique with correct technique. The key here is to focus on the basic movement pattern rather than on small idiosyncrasies in individual style. The coach asks, "Is this athlete's technique fundamentally sound?" It may take several observations of the skill to evaluate the seriousness of observed errors, and the coach should avoid the mistake of offering feedback too quickly. Errors in technique should be corrected if they will substantially improve performance or increase safety.

The second step in analyzing technique is to select which error to correct. With beginners especially, several performance errors are probably occurring simultaneously. If the coach tried to give feedback about every error observed, the athlete would likely be overloaded with too much information, resulting in very little correction on the next trial. Consequently, only one error should be addressed at a time.

Given multiple errors, where does one begin? The coach should try to identify the error that is most fundamental or critical and give feedback only about it. Very often, one error is the cause of other errors, and if this critical error can be corrected, others may be eliminated. When the fundamental aspect is mastered, then attention can be devoted to the next most important error. When multiple errors seem unrelated, a good strategy is to select the one that is easiest to learn and leads to the greatest improvement. The benefits here may be twofold. First, the athlete's respect for the coach's knowledge may be enhanced, and, second, improved performance will contribute to the athlete's motivation to continue learning the skill. Finally, a third strategy is to identify the critical error that occurs earliest in the sequence. For example, in diving, if the approach on the board is incorrect, the takeoff, the dive itself, and the entry will likely be adversely affected. By correcting the faulty approach, the errors that emerged later in the sequence as a consequence are likely to be eliminated. (For more information on these and other strategies, see Knudson and Morrison, 2002).

The final step in analyzing technique is to determine the cause of the error and what the athlete must do to correct it. Causes of errors can range from the relatively simple, such as forgetting to concentrate on some aspect of the skill,

to the very difficult, such as a subtle change in mechanics. If the coach determines that forgetting is the cause of an error, then the correction is a simple reminder. "Square up your racket to the net" may be all a young tennis player needs to correct a short volley. Determining the cause of a nonpropulsive breaststroke kick may be more difficult, however, because the problem may lie in poor body position, incorrect timing, position of the ankle, and so on. Further analysis, perhaps through filming, may be necessary.

If the coach cannot isolate the cause of an error or is uncertain about how to correct it, he or she should not experiment with random suggestions. If the hasty suggestions do not lead to improved performance, athletes may come to doubt their coach's ability, as well as experience a great deal of frustration. Coaches should think through the situation carefully and watch the performance many times before prescribing modifications.

Providing Augmented Feedback

Once the coach has completed the analysis, a positive approach to correcting the identified performance error(s) is advocated (Christina & Corcos, 1988; Martens, 2004). To confirm the athlete's progress, effort and any parts of the technique that were correct should be reinforced. Coaches should be specific when conveying what aspects of the performance were correct and only reinforce real progress or they could lose credibility (Rink, 2006). To facilitate skill acquisition, the coach should give simple, precise, error correction information. Adhere to the "KISS" principle—"Keep It Short and Simple." Feedback must provide sufficient information to benefit the athletes, but it must not provide too much or it may become confusing. Also, the coach should be sure to verify the athletes' understanding of the feedback by asking them to repeat it and explain how they will attempt to make the correction. Finally, the coach should motivate the athlete to incorporate the prescribed modifications. Notice that this approach simply takes advantage of the three functions of feedback, with error correction information sandwiched between reinforcement and motivation. The following is an example: "Good, Susan. You are rotating your head to the side much better now. Remember to blow all of your air out underwater though *before* you turn to breathe. You'll be able to get more air and swim a greater distance before running out of breath."

A teacher or coach who can provide accurate and understandable feedback is important to athletes at all levels of the performance scale, from novice to elite. Clearly, the beginner in any sport needs early and consistent instruction as well as regular feedback. What is not as often understood is that performers at average and even advanced levels also need effective feedback. Major league pitchers at the peak of their careers sometimes run into slumps that are not attributable to any physical or emotional problem they can detect. At this point, the pitching coach must set aside a period to work with such pitchers and attempt to determine what they are doing differently and how the problem can be corrected. At this high level of performance, problems are usually very subtle; errors in technique are so slight that only a highly skilled coach, who is thoroughly familiar with the particular player, can detect them and prescribe appropriate modifications for their correction.

Summary

This chapter has focused on one of the most important roles of a coach, that of a teacher of motor skills. The motor learning process is incredibly complex, and we have attempted to provide a basic understanding of that process. We began by defining the term *motor learning* and then describing a three-phase model of motor skill learning consisting of the cognitive (beginning), associative (intermediate), and autonomous (advanced) phases. Understanding the phases of learning is important both for teaching novice athletes a brand-new skill and for changing well-learned techniques of highly skilled athletes.

Practice and feedback are two of the most important determinants of motor learning and performance, and we have provided some guidelines for structuring effective practice sessions and for providing effective feedback to learners. In some instances, current research findings run counter to some of our long-held beliefs about practice and feedback.

Study Questions

1. Define the term *motor learning* and explain why learning must remain an inference based on performance.

2. Briefly describe Fitts and Posner's three phases of motor skill learning.

3. What are the important points to remember when demonstrating a new skill for learners?

4. How is proprioception, or "feel," important in motor performance?

5. What are the effects of asking highly skilled performers to consciously attend to their movements?

6. Explain why the coach's role as motivator is so important during the autonomous phase of learning.

7. Describe how a coach should proceed to change a highly skilled athlete's well-learned technique.

8. How could one use blocked practice to teach several skills? Random practice? Which would be more effective and why?

9. Give an example of how a coach could use variable practice to teach several variations of a skill.

10. What are schemas, and how does variable practice contribute to their development?

11. What general guidelines should a coach consider in deciding to use the whole method versus the part method of practice?

12. What are the two major types of feedback? Give three examples of each type.

References

Abernethy, B., Wood, J. M., & Parks, S. (1999). Can anticipatory skills of experts be learned by novices? *Research Quarterly for Exercise and Sport, 70,* 313–318.

Barreiros, J., Figueiredo, T., & Godinho, M. (2007). The contextual interference effect in applied settings. *European Physical Education Review, 12,* 195-208.

Battig, W. F. (1966). Facilitation and interference. In E. A. Bilodeau (Ed.), *Acquisition of skill* (pp. 215–244). New York: Academic Press.

Brady, F. (2004). Contextual interference: A meta-analytic study. *Perceptual and Motor Skills, 99,* 116–126.

Brady, F. (2008). The contextual interference effect in sport skills. *Perceptual and Motor Skills, 106,* 461–472.

Butki, B. D., & Hoffman, S. J. (2003). Effects of reducing frequency of intrinsic knowledge of results on the learning of a motor skill. *Perceptual and Motor Skills, 97,* 569–580.

Butler, M. S., & Fischman, M. G. (1996). Effects of bandwidth feedback on delayed retention of a movement timing task. *Perceptual and Motor Skills, 82,* 527–530.

Butler, M. S., Reeve, T. G., & Fischman, M. G. (1996). Effects of the instructional set in the bandwidth feedback paradigm on motor skill acquisition. *Research Quarterly for Exercise and Sport, 67,* 355–359.

Chambers, K. L., & Vickers, J. N. (2006) The effect of bandwidth feedback and questioning on competitive swim performance. *The Sport Psychologist, 20,* 184–197.

Chen, D. D. (2001). Trends in augmented research and tips for the practitioner. *Journal of Physical Education, Recreation, and Dance, 72*(1), 32–36.

Chen, D. D., Kaufman, D., & Chung, M. W. (2001). Emergent patterns of feedback strategies in performing a closed motor skill. *Perceptual and Motor Skills, 93,* 197–204.

Chiviacowsky, S., & Wulf, G. (2002). Self-controlled feedback: Does it enhance learning because performers get feedback when they need it? *Research Quarterly for Exercise and Sport, 73,* 408–415.

Chiviacowsky, S., & Wulf, G. (2005). Self-controlled feedback is effective if it is based on the learner's performance. *Research Quarterly for Exercise and Sport, 76,* 42–48.

Christina, R. W., & Corcos, D. M. (1988). *Coaches' guide to teaching sport skills*. Champaign, IL: Human Kinetics.

Coker, C. A. (2004). *Motor learning and control for practitioners*. St. Louis, MO: McGraw-Hill.

Coker, C. A. (2006). To break it down or not break it down: That is the question. *Teaching Elementary Physical Education, 17,* 27–28.

Douvis, S. (2005). Variable practice in learning the forehand drive in tennis. *Perceptual and Motor Skills, 101,* 531–545.

Ericsson, K. A. (2003). Development of elite performance and deliberate practice: An update from the perspective of the expert performance approach. In J. L. Starkes & K. A. Ericsson (Eds.), *Expert performance in sports: Advances in research on sport expertise* (pp. 49–83). Champaign, IL: Human Kinetics.

Ericsson, K. A. (1996). The acquisition of expert performance: An introduction to some of the issues. In K. A. Ericsson (Ed.), *The road to excellence: The acquisition of expert performance in the arts and sciences, sports, and games* (pp. 1–50). Mahwah, NJ: Erlbaum.

Ericsson, K. A., Krampe, R. T., & Tesch-Römer, C. (1993). The role of deliberate practice in the acquisition of expert performance. *Psychological Review, 100,* 363–406.

Fitts, P. M., & Posner, M. I. (1967). *Human performance*. Pacific Grove, CA: Brooks/Cole.

Gentile, A. M. (2000). Skill acquisition: Action, movement, and the neuromotor processes. In J. H. Carr, R. B. Shepard, J. Gordon, A. M. Gentile, & J. M. Hind (Eds.), *Movement science: Foundations for physical therapy in rehabilitation* (pp. 111–187). Rockville, MD: Aspen.

Goode, S., & Magill, R. A. (1986). Contextual interference effects in learning three badminton serves. *Research Quarterly for Exercise and Sport, 57,* 308–314.

Hebert, E. P., & Landin, D. (1994). Effects of a learning model and augmented feedback on tennis skill acquisition. *Research Quarterly for Exercise and Sport, 65,* 250–257.

Hebert, E. P., Landin, D., & Solmon, M. A. (1996). Practice schedule effects on the performance and learning of low- and high-skilled students: An applied study. *Research Quarterly for Exercise and Sport, 67,* 52–58.

Horn, R. R., & Williams, A. M. (2004). Observational learning: Is it time we took another look? In A.M. Williams & N.J. Hodges (Eds.), *Skill acquisition in sport: Research, theory and practice* (pp. 175–206). London: Rutledge.

Janelle, C. M., Barba, D. A., Frehlich, S. G., Tennant, L. K., & Cauraugh, J. H. (1997). Maximizing performance feedback effectiveness through videotape replay and a self-controlled learning environment. *Research Quarterly for Exercise and Sport, 68,* 269–279.

Janelle, C. M., Champenoy, J. D., Coombes, S. A. & Mousseau, M. B. (2003). Mechanisms of attentional cueing during observational learning to facilitate motor skill acquisition. *Journal of Sports Sciences, 21,* 825–838.

Janelle, C. M., Kim, J., & Singer, R. N. (1995). Subject-controlled feedback and learning a closed skill. *Perceptual and Motor Skills, 81,* 627–634.

Keller, G. J., Yuhua, L., Weiss, L. W. & Relyea, G. E. (2006). Contextual interference effect on acquisition and retention of pistol shooting skills. *Perceptual and Motor Skills, 103,* 241–252.

Knudson D. V., & Morrison, C. S. (2002). *Qualitative analysis of human movement.* Champaign, IL: Human Kinetics.

Landin, D., & Hebert, E. P. (1997). A comparison of three practice schedules along the contextual interference continuum. *Research Quarterly for Exercise and Sport, 68,* 357–361.

Lee, T. D., & Magill, R. A. (1983). The locus of contextual interference in motor-skill acquisition. *Journal of Experimental Psychology: Learning, Memory, and Cognition, 9,* 730–746.

Li, Y., & Wright, D. L. (2000). An assessment of the attention demands of random and blocked practice. *Quarterly Journal of Experimental Psychology, 53A,* 591–606.

Magill, R. A. (2004). Motor learning and control: Concepts and applications. *Motor learning: Concepts and applications.* St. Louis, MO: McGraw-Hill.

Magill, R. A. (2001). Augmented feedback in motor skill acquisition. In R. N. Singer, H. A. Hausenblaus, & C. M. Janelle (Eds.), *Handbook of research on sport psychology* (pp. 86–114). New York: John Wiley & Sons.

Magill, R. A. (1998). Knowledge is more than we talk about: Implicit learning in motor skill acquisition. *Research Quarterly for Exercise and Sport, 69,* 104–110.

Martell, S. G., & Vickers, J. N. (2004). Gaze characteristics of elite and near-elite ice hockey players. *Human Movement Science, 22,* 689–712.

Martens, R. (2004). *Successful coaching.* Champaign, IL: Human Kinetics.

McCullagh, P., & Meyer, K. N. (1997). Learning versus correct models: Influence of model type on the learning of a free-weight squat lift. *Research Quarterly for Exercise and Sport, 68,* 56–61.

McCullagh, P., & Weiss, M. R. (2001). Modelling: Considerations for motor skill performance and psychological responses. In R. N. Singer, H. A. Hausenblas & C. M. Janelle (Eds.), *Handbook of sport psychology* (pp. 205–238). New York: Wiley.

Nagano, T., Kato, T., & Fukuda, T. (2004). Visual search stratedies of soccer players in one-on-one defense situations on the field. *Perceptual and Motor Skills, 99,* 968–974.

Raab, M., Masters, R. S. W., & Maxwell, J. P. (2005). Improving the 'how' and 'what' decisions of elite table tennis players. *Human Movement Science, 24,* 326–344.

Rink, J. E. (2006) *Teaching physical education for learning.* San Francisco, CA: McGraw-Hill.

Salmoni, A. W., Schmidt, R. A., & Walter, C. B. (1984). Knowledge of results and motor learning: A review and critical reappraisal. *Psychological Bulletin, 95,* 355–386.

Savelsbergh, G. J. P., van der Kamp, J., Williams, A. M., & Ward, P. (2005). Anticipation and visual search behavior in expert soccer goalkeepers, *Ergonomics, 48,* 1686–1697.

Savelsbergh, G. J. P., Williams, A. M., van der Kamp, J., & Ward, P. (2002). Visual search, anticipation and expertise in soccer goal keepers, *Journal of Sport Sciences, 200,* 279–287.

Schmidt, R. A. (1975). A schema theory of discrete motor skill learning. *Psychological Review, 82,* 225–260.

Schmidt, R. A., Young, D. E., Swinnen, S., & Shapiro, D. C. (1989). Summary knowledge of results for skill acquisition: Support for the guidance hypothesis. *Journal of Experimental Psychology: Learning, Memory, and Cognition, 15,* 352–359.

Shea, J. B., & Morgan, R. L. (1979). Contextual interference effects on the acquisition, retention, and transfer of a motor skill. *Journal of Experimental Psychology: Human Learning and Memory, 5,* 179–187.

Shea, J. B., & Zimny, S. T. (1983). Context effects in memory and learning movement information. In R. A. Magill (Ed.), *Memory and control of action* (pp. 345–366). Amsterdam: North-Holland.

Shea, J. B., & Zimny, S. T. (1988). Knowledge incorporation in motor representation. In O. G. Meijer & K. Roth (Eds.), *Complex movement behaviour: "The" motor-action controversy* (pp. 289–314). Amsterdam: Elsevier Science Publishers B.V.

Shoenfelt, E. L., Snyder, L. A., Maue, A. E., McDowell, C. P., & Woolard, C. D. (2002). Comparison of constant and variable practice conditions on free throw shooting. *Perceptual and Motor Skills, 94,* 1113–1123.

Smith, P. J. K. (2002). Applying contextual interference to snowboarding skills. *Perceptual and Motor Skills, 95,* 999–1005.

Smith, P. J. K., Taylor, S. J., & Withers, K. (1997). Applying bandwidth feedback scheduling to a golf shot. *Research Quarterly for Exercise and Sport, 68,* 215–221.

Thorndike, E. L. (1927). The law of effect. *American Journal of Psychology, 39,* 212–222.

Vickers, J. N. (2007). *Perception, cognition and decision training: The quiet eye in action.* Champaign, IL: Human Kinetics.

Winstein, C. J., & Schmidt, R. A. (1990). Reduced frequency of knowledge of results enhances motor skill learning. *Journal of Experimental Psychology: Learning, Memory, and Cognition, 16,* 677–691.

Wrisberg, C. A., & Liu, Z. (1991). The effect of contextual variety on the practice, retention, and transfer of an applied motor skill. *Research Quarterly for Exercise and Sport, 62,* 406–412

Wulf, G., & Shea, C. H. (2004). Understanding the role of feedback: The good, the bad and the ugly. In A. M. Williams & N. J. Hodges (Eds.), *Skill acquisition in sport: Research, theory and practice* (pp. 121–144). London: Rutledge.

A Positive Approach to Coaching Effectiveness and Performance Enhancement

Ronald E. Smith, *University of Washington*

I try never to plant a negative seed. I try to make every comment a positive comment. There's a lot of evidence to support positive management.

—Jimmy Johnson, Former College and Professional Football Coach

To really win, you have to get every player to go beyond his capabilities. He must feel great about himself. . . .
He must feel that his coaches or supervisors have total confidence in his ability, and he must feel that his weaknesses are small and his strengths are much bigger. You do that by positive reinforcement, making sure that no one thinks negatively at any time.

—Rick Pitino, Basketball Coach, University of Louisville

If a pitcher throws one good pitch during the whole morning, you have something to work on. Let him know it. That will give him all the incentive he needs. He too sees that he can do a certain thing. He may not know exactly how he did it. He has to find that out from his own study.

—The late Branch Rickey, Legendary Baseball Executive

Much of human interaction consists of attempts to influence the behavior of other people. Influence attempts occur constantly in virtually every life setting. Sometimes the attempts are directed at influencing attitudes, motives, values, or emotions. At other times social interactions or task performance are the targets of influence attempts.

Sport is a setting where all of these targets of influence—thoughts, emotions, motivational factors, and behaviors—are relevant. Influence attempts occur constantly as athletes interact with teammates, opponents, officials, and their coaches. In the discussion to follow I will focus on influence attempts directed by coaches to their athletes and provide a conceptual framework to which other topics in this book, such as motivational processes (Chapter 4), goal setting (Chapter 11), and intervention programs directed toward coaches (Chapter 18), may be related. My focus will be primarily on enhancing sport performance, although, as you'll see, this goal is intimately related to the psychosocial climate created by interactions among coaches and athletes.

Coaches try to influence their players in many important ways. One of their most important goals is to create a good learning situation where athletes can acquire the technical skills needed to succeed as individuals and as a team. Another priority for most coaches is to create a social environment where the participants can experience positive interactions with one another. This is certainly a key factor in building team cohesion, in making athletes more receptive to technical instruction, and in fostering a supportive environment where athletes can develop teamwork, dedication, "mental toughness," and other valued traits. Indeed, virtually everything coaches do can be viewed as attempts to increase certain desired behaviors and to decrease undesirable behaviors.

The "psychology of coaching" essentially may be regarded as a set of strategies designed to increase a coach's ability to influence the behavior of others more effectively. It is often said that stripped of its jargon and complexities psychology is basically the application of common sense. I believe the basic principles of learning discussed in this chapter—positive (as opposed to aversive) control, reinforcement, and performance feedback—make good sense. But more important, they have been shown in many scientific studies to be among the most effective ways to increase motivation, morale, enjoyment of the athletic situation, and performance (Smith, Smoll, & Christensen, 1996).

The ABCs of Behavior Control

To understand what motivates people and controls their behavior, we must take into account the relations between people and their environment. In psychology one influential approach to this task is the study of **operant conditioning,** which considers in part the manner in which our behaviors are influenced by their consequences (Martin & Pear, 2007).

The operant analysis of behavior involves the study of relations between three kinds of events: **antecedents** (A), or environmental stimuli; behaviors (B) in which the person engages; and consequences (C) that follow the behaviors and either strengthen or weaken them. The relations that exist among these "if, then" elements are called **contingencies.** The ABCs of contingencies can be expressed in the following way:

IF antecedent stimuli (A) are present

AND behavior (B) is enacted,

THEN a particular consequence (C) will occur.

Two aspects of these relations are of interest. The first is the relation between antecedents and behaviors (A and B); the second is the contingency between behavior and its consequences (B and C).

Antecedents: Stimulus Control of Behavior

Through experience we learn which behaviors have which consequences under which conditions. Antecedents that signal the likely consequences of particular behaviors in given situations are known as **discriminative stimuli.** These signals help guide our behavior so that it is "appropriate" and most likely will lead to positive consequences. Much skill learning in sports involves learning to "read" the environment and respond appropriately. Thus, a basketball player learns how to set up the offense when the opponent switches from one defense to another. The same player also may learn that it is not a good idea to crack jokes in the presence of the coach after a tough loss. When antecedents are influential in governing a behavior, that behavior is said to be under **stimulus control.**

With experience in sports, many behaviors come under stimulus control, and we react automatically and mindlessly to changing stimulus conditions. The same thing occurs in the realm of social behaviors.

Response Consequences

The key feature in operant conditioning is what happens after a response is made. Psychologists have done a great deal of research on how different types of consequences affect behavior. In general, consequences always involve either the presentation, the nonoccurrence, or the removal of a positive or an unpleasant or aversive stimulus. For example, in the coach–athlete interaction a positive stimulus may be a word of praise or a smile, and an aversive stimulus may be a critical comment made by the coach.

Figure 3-1 shows five basic response consequences that result from the presentation or removal of positive or aversive stimuli in response to a given behavior. Presentation of a positive (rewarding) stimulus is called **positive reinforcement,** and it increases the likelihood that the behavior will occur in the future under the same conditions. **Negative reinforcement** involves *removal or avoidance* of aversive stimuli, the effect being a strengthening of the behavior that results in successful escape or avoidance. For example, an athlete may drop out of a sport program to escape an abusive coach, or a gymnast who has been injured may avoid performing a particular routine because of anxiety concerning possible reinjury. In the latter case the avoidance response may become stronger over time because each time it occurs it is negatively reinforced by anxiety reduction.

Removal of a positive stimulus that has in the past followed the behavior results in **extinction,** reducing the likelihood of the behavior. Extinction of operant behaviors occurs when reinforcement stops. Thus, if an athlete stops getting attention for inappropriate comments, that behavior is likely to decrease. When previously reinforced behaviors no longer "pay off," we are likely to abandon them and replace them with more successful ones.

Other consequences involve either presentation or removal of unpleasant, aversive stimuli, as the two forms of punishment illustrate. **Aversive punishment** entails the *presentation* of aversive stimuli, with the effect of suppressing the behavior. Thus, a coach who harshly criticizes an athlete for being late for practice will probably find a marked reduction in tardiness in the future. Another form of punishment, known as **response cost,** involves *removal of a positive event,* as when an athlete is benched after performing poorly. Here is another example of response cost punishment:

> The legendary baseball umpire Bill Klem once called a batter out on a close third strike. The enraged batter flung his bat high into the air and whirled around to argue the call. Klem whipped off his mask, fixed the batter with a steely gaze, and said, "If that bat comes down, it'll cost you 100 bucks." (Smith, 1993, p. 280)

	Present	**Remove**
Positive Stimuli	Positive reinforcement *(strengthens behavior)*	Extinction *(weakens behavior)* Response cost punishment *(weakens behavior)*
Aversive Stimuli	Punishment *(suppresses/weakens behavior)*	Negative reinforcement *(strengthens behavior)*

Figure 3-1 **Five basic response consequences created by the presentation or removal of positive or negative stimuli and their effects on behavior**

The term *negative reinforcement* is sometimes confused with punishment, but the two are clearly different. Punishment reduces the likelihood of a behavior, whereas negative reinforcement, like positive reinforcement, strengthens the behavior.

Positive and Aversive Approaches to Influencing Behavior

As our cursory examination of response consequences and their influence on behavior suggests, two basic approaches can influence the behavior of others. Psychologists refer to these as **positive control** and **aversive control** (Sarafino, 2004). Both forms of control are based on the fact that behavior is strongly influenced by the consequences it produces. Positive reinforcement and punishment are the respective cornerstones of positive and aversive control of behavior. Positive and aversive control, in turn, underlie the *positive approach* and the *negative approach* to coaching (see Chapters 4 and 5 of this volume, and Smith & Smoll, 2001).

The positive approach is designed to strengthen desired behaviors by motivating players to perform them and by reinforcing the behaviors when they occur. The second approach, the negative approach, involves attempts to eliminate unwanted behaviors through punishment and criticism. The motivating factor in this approach is fear. Observational studies of coaches indicate that most coaches use a combination of positive and aversive control (Smith, Zane, Smoll, & Coppel, 1983).

In our society, aversive control through punishment is perhaps the most widespread means of controlling behavior. Our system of laws is backed up by threats of punishment. Similarly, fear of failure is one means of promoting school achievement, social development, and other desired behaviors. The reason punishment is the glue that holds so much of our society's fabric together is that, for the most part, it seems to work. It is the fastest way to bring behavior under control (Zirpoli, 2004). In sports it finds one mode of expression in the negative approach to coaching.

Frequently in sport we hear the statement, "The team that makes the fewest mistakes will win"—and, indeed, this is usually the case. Many coaches, therefore, develop coaching tactics oriented toward eliminating mistakes. The most natural approach is to use aversive control. To get rid of mistakes, we simply punish and criticize athletes who make them. The assumption is that if we make players fearful enough of making mistakes they are more likely to perform well. We do not have to look far to find examples of highly successful coaches who are "screamers" and whose teams seem to perform like well-oiled machines. Other less experienced coaches may conclude that this is the most effective way to train athletes. They too adopt this aspect of the successful coaches' behavior, perhaps to the exclusion of other teaching techniques that probably are the screamers' true keys to success.

Negative Side Effects of Punishment

There is clear evidence that punishment and criticism can decrease unwanted behaviors. Unfortunately, the evidence is equally compelling that punishment has certain undesirable side effects that can actually interfere with what a coach is trying to accomplish (Maag, 2003). First, punishment works by arousing fear. If used excessively, punishment promotes the development of fear of failure, and this is undoubtedly the least desirable form of athletic motivation. If it becomes the predominant motive for athletic performance, it not only decreases enjoyment of the activity but also increases the likelihood of failure. The athlete with a high fear of failure is motivated not by a positive desire to achieve and enjoy "the thrill of victory" but by a dread of "the agony of defeat." Athletic competition is transformed from a challenge into a threat. Because high anxiety disrupts motor performance and interferes with thinking, the high fear of failure athlete is prone to "choke" under pressure because he or she is concentrating more on the feared consequences of mistakes or failure than on what needs to be done in a positive sense. Research has shown that athletes having high fear of failure not only perform more poorly in competition but also are at greater risk for injury, enjoy the sport experience less, and are more likely to drop out (Smith, Smoll, & Passer, 2002). The research literature also shows that the quickest and most effective way to develop fear of failure is by punishing people when they fail (Petri & Govern, 2004). Thus, coaches who create fear of failure through the use of punishment may, ironically, increase the likelihood that their athletes will make the very mistakes they are trying to prevent. Moreover, high levels of fear may have a generally depressing effect on behavior and make athletes afraid to take risks of any kind.

Punishment has other potential side effects that most coaches wish to avoid. A predominance of aversive control makes for an unpleasant teaching situation. It arouses resentment and hostility, which may be masked by the power differential that exists between coach and athlete. It may produce a kind of cohesion among players based on their mutual hatred for the coach, but most coaches would prefer other bases for team cohesion. It is even possible that players may consciously or subconsciously act in ways that sabotage what the coach is trying to accomplish. Moreover, coaches occupy a role that athletes admire, and they should not overlook their importance as models for young people who are developing socially. The abusive screamer is certainly not exhibiting the kind of behavior that will contribute to the personal growth of athletes who emulate the coach.

Does this mean coaches should avoid all criticism and punishment of their athletes? Not at all. Sometimes these behaviors are necessary for instructional or disciplinary purposes, but they should be used sparingly and with a full appreciation for their potential negative side effects. The negative approach should never be the primary approach to athletes. This is particularly the case where child athletes are concerned, but it also applies at higher competitive levels, including professional sports (Smith & Johnson, 1990).

Although abusive coaches may enjoy success and may even be admired by some of their players, they run the risk of losing other players who could contribute to the team's success and who could profit personally from an athletic experience. Those who succeed through the use of aversive control usually do so because (a) they are also able to communicate caring for their players as people, so athletes don't take the abuse personally; (b) they have very talented athletes; (c) they recruit thick-skinned athletes who are less affected by aversive feedback; or (d) they are such skilled teachers and strategists that these abilities overshadow their negative approach. In other words, such coaches win in spite of, not because of, the negative approach they espouse.

The second form of punishment, response cost, involves depriving people of something they value. This form of punishment has two distinct advantages over aversive punishment. First, even though response cost may arouse temporary frustration or anger, it does not create the kind of fear that aversive punishment does (Sarafino, 2004). It is therefore less likely to cause avoidance of the punisher or the punishing situation, and it may actually increase the attractiveness of the withdrawn reinforcer (which can then be used to reinforce desired alternative behaviors). Second, the punisher is not modeling abusive aggression, so there is less opportunity for learning aggression through imitation. For these reasons, the response cost procedure is a preferred alternative to aversive punishment. In using such punishment, it is useful to verbalize the contingency in a matter of fact fashion, without expressing anger, for example, "I don't like to do this, but because you were late for practice, it automatically means you get less playing time during our next game."

The Positive Alternative

Fortunately, there is an alternative to the negative approach. As a means of influencing behavior, it can accomplish everything aversive control does and much more—without the harmful side effects. The positive approach is aimed at strengthening desired behaviors through the use of encouragement, positive reinforcement, and sound technical instruction carried out within a supportive atmosphere. From this point of view the best way to eliminate mistakes is not to try to stamp them out with punishment but to strengthen the correct or desired behaviors. The motivational force at work here is a positive desire to achieve rather than a negative fear of failure. Mistakes are seen not as totally negative occurrences but as, in the words of John Wooden, "stepping stones to achievement" that provide the information needed to improve performance. The positive approach, through its emphasis on improving rather than on "not screwing up," fosters a more positive learning environment and tends to promote more positive relationships among coaches and athletes. Research has clearly shown that athletes like positive coaches better, enjoy their athletic experience more and report higher team cohesion when playing for them, and perform at a higher level when positive control techniques are used (Martin & Hyrcaiko, 1983). Even negative control procedures work more effectively if they occur within a context of positive interactions. Thus, Jimmy Johnson, a highly successful former college and professional football coach, once noted, "We rely ninety percent on positive reinforcement, so when we do use punishment, it really makes an impact" (*Orlando Sentinel,* July 24, 1996, p. C2).

The cornerstone of the positive approach is the skillful use of positive reinforcement to increase motivation and to strengthen desired behaviors. Another highly effective technique is the use of performance feedback. Let's discuss these specific techniques.

Positive Reinforcement: Getting Good Things to Happen

As noted earlier, positive reinforcement is any consequence that increases the likelihood of a behavior that it follows. For our present purposes, positive reinforcement can be viewed as related to the more familiar concept of "reward,"

as long as we keep in mind that a consequence that may be rewarding from the perspective of one person may not function as a reinforcer for another person who is not motivated by that consequence. Thus, a compliment from a coach her athletes despise may have no positive impact on their behavior. (Likewise, rat food is a highly effective reinforcer for the white rat, but notoriously ineffective for children.) Reinforcement can take many possible forms: verbal compliments, smiles or other nonverbal behaviors that convey approval, increased privileges, awards, and so on.

The effective use of reinforcement to strengthen behavior requires that a coach (a) find a reinforcer that works for a particular athlete, (b) make the occurrence of reinforcement dependent on performance of the desired behavior, and (c) make sure the athlete understands why the reinforcement is being given. The relations between behaviors and their consequences are termed **reinforcement contingencies.**

Choosing Effective Reinforcers

Choosing a reinforcer is not usually difficult, but in some instances the coach's ingenuity and sensitivity to the needs of individual athletes may be tested. Potential reinforcers include social behaviors such as verbal praise, smiles, nonverbal signs such as applause, or physical contact such as a pat on the back. They also include the opportunity to engage in certain activities (such as extra batting practice) or to play with a particular piece of equipment.

Social reinforcers are most frequently employed in athletics, but even here the coach must decide what is most likely to be effective with each athlete. One athlete might find praise given in the presence of others highly reinforcing, whereas another might find it embarrassing. The best way for a coach to find an effective reinforcer is to get to know each athlete's likes and dislikes. In some instances a coach may elect to praise an entire unit or group of athletes; at other times reinforcement may be directed at one athlete. If at all possible, it is a good idea to use a variety of reinforcers and vary what one says and does so that the coach does not begin to sound like a broken record. In the final analysis the acid test of one's choice of reinforcer is whether it affects behavior in the desired manner.

The effectiveness of verbal reinforcement can be increased by combining it with a specific description of the desirable behavior the athlete just performed. For example, a coach might say, "Way to go, Bob. Your head stayed right down on the ball on that swing." In this way the power of the reinforcement is combined with an instructional reminder of what the athlete should do. This also cues the athlete to what the coach wants him to concentrate on.

Selecting and Reinforcing Target Behaviors

Systematic use of reinforcement forces coaches to be specific in their own minds about exactly which behaviors they want to reinforce in a given athlete at a particular time. Obviously, they will not want to reinforce everything an athlete does correctly, lest the power of the reinforcer be diluted. The most effective use of "reward power" is to strengthen skills an athlete is just beginning to master. In many instances complex skills can be broken down into their component subskills, and coaches can concentrate on one of these subskills at a time until it is mastered. For example, a football coach might choose to concentrate entirely on the pattern run by a pass receiver, with no concern about whether or not the pass is completed. This is where a coach's knowledge of the sport and of the mastery levels of individual athletes is crucial. Athletes can enjoy lots of support and reinforcement long before they have completely mastered the entire skill if coaches are attentive to their instructional needs and progress. Such reinforcement will help to keep motivation and interest at its maximum.

Shaping

We have all marveled at the complex behaviors performed by animals in circuses, at amusement parks, and in the movies. These behavioral feats are brought about by the use of a positive reinforcement procedure known as **shaping.** At the beginning of training the animal was incapable of anything even approximating the desired behavior. The trainer chose some behavior the animal was already performing and began reinforcing that behavior. Then, over time, the requirements for reinforcement were gradually altered so that the animal had to perform acts that more and more closely resembled the final desired behavior until that behavior had been "shaped" by the systematic application of reinforcement.

The products of operant conditioning go far beyond rats pressing bars and pigeons pecking discs in Skinner boxes, and even beyond the feats performed by trained animals. Humans also learn many complex behaviors through shaping, including athletic skills. To use shaping effectively, start with what the athlete is currently capable of doing, and then gradually require a more skillful level of performance before reinforcement is given. It is important that the shift in demands be realistic and that the steps be small enough so that the athlete can master them and be reinforced. For example, a youth softball coach may at first praise novice infielders whenever they stop a ball (with any part of their anatomy). As proficiency increases, however, she may require that the players field the ball in the correct position, and later that they field the ball cleanly in the correct position and make an accurate throw. Used correctly, shaping is one of the most powerful of all the positive control techniques.

An Example of a Successful Positive Reinforcement Program

A comprehensive review of research on the effectiveness of behavioral techniques for enhancing sport performance revealed a consistently high success rate for the systematic use of positive reinforcement techniques (Smith et al., 1996). Let us consider an example from youth sports that involved the use of shaping as well.

The systematic use of positive reinforcement to improve the performance of a youth football team's offensive backfield was described by Judi Komaki and Fred Barnett (1977). The coach selected three different offensive plays. Each of the plays was broken down into five stages judged to be crucial to the execution of the play and was presented to the players accordingly. For example, one of the plays included the following stages: (1) quarterback-center exchange; (2) quarterback spin and pitch; (3) right halfback and fullback lead blocking; (4) left halfback route; and (5) quarterback block. Breaking down the play in this manner allowed the coach to respond to the elements that were run correctly, give specific feedback to the players about their execution of each of the five stages, and gradually shape their learning of the entire play.

During the first phase of the experiment, data were carefully collected on how often the stages of each play were executed correctly. Then the coach began to systematically apply reinforcement procedures to Play A. Each time the play was run in practice, the coach checked off which of the elements had been successfully executed and praised the players for the stages that were run successfully. Reinforcement was not applied when Plays B and C were run. After a period of time, the reinforcement procedure was shifted to Play B only, and later to Play C only. Applying the technique to only one play at a time permitted a determination of the specific effects of reinforcement on the performance of each of them.

A comparison of the percentage of stages executed correctly before and after introduction of the reinforcement procedure indicated that performance increased for all three plays, but only after reinforcement was introduced. The level of performance for Play A improved from 61.7% to 81.5% when reinforcement was applied, but execution of B and C did not improve until reinforcement was also applied to them. When this occurred, execution of play B improved from 54.4% to 82%, and execution of Play C improved from 65.5% to 79.8%. Clearly, the systematic use of reinforcement led to a substantial improvement in performance. Other studies have shown similar performance improvement in gymnastics, swimming, baseball, golf, and tennis (see Martin & Hyrcaiko, 1983).

Schedules and Timing of Reinforcement

One of the most frequently asked questions is how often and how consistently reinforcement should be given. Fortunately, a great deal of research has been done concerning the effects of so-called **schedules of reinforcement** on behavior change. Reinforcement schedules refer to the pattern and frequency with which reinforcement is administered. Although there are many different kinds of schedules, the most important distinction is between continuous and partial schedules. On a continuous schedule, *every* correct response is reinforced. On partial schedules, some proportion of correct responses are reinforced and some are not.

During the initial stages of training, reinforcement is best given on a continuous schedule. Frequent reinforcement not only helps strengthen the desired response but also provides the athlete with frequent feedback about how well he or she is doing. Once the behavior is learned, however, reinforcement should be shifted to a partial schedule. Research has shown that behaviors reinforced on partial schedules persist much longer in the absence of reinforcement than do those that have been reinforced only on a continuous schedule (Skinner, 1969). For example, people will put a great many coins into slot machines, which operate on partial schedules. In contrast, they are unlikely to persist long in putting coins into soft drink machines that do not deliver because these machines normally operate on a continuous schedule. Thus, the key principle in using schedules is to start with continuous reinforcement until the behavior is mastered, then to shift gradually to partial reinforcement to maintain a high level of motivation and performance (Martin & Pear, 2007).

The timing of reinforcement is another important consideration. Other things being equal, the sooner after a response that reinforcement occurs, the stronger are its effects on behavior. Thus, whenever possible, try to reinforce a desired behavior as soon as it occurs. If this is not possible, however, try to find an opportunity to praise the athlete later on.

Reinforcing Effort and Other Desirable Behaviors

To this point, I have discussed the use of reinforcement to strengthen skills. It is important to realize, however, that reinforcement can be used to strengthen other desirable behaviors as well. For example, the positive approach can be used to reduce the likelihood of disciplinary problems by reinforcing compliance with team rules. There is no reason a coach should not recognize and reinforce exemplary conduct on the part of particular athletes or the team as a whole. One of the most effective ways of avoiding disciplinary problems is by strengthening the opposite (desired) behaviors through reinforcement (Smith & Smoll, 2001).

Similarly, instances of teamwork and of athletes' support and encouragement of one another should be acknowledged and reinforced from time to time. Doing so not only strengthens these desirable behaviors but also creates an atmosphere in which the coach is actually serving as a positive model by supporting them. Research has shown that the best predictor of liking for the coach and desire to play for him or her in the future is not the won-lost record of the team but how consistently the coach applies the positive approach and avoids the use of punishment (Smith & Smoll, 1991).

I have saved one of the most important points of all until last. It's easy to praise an athlete who has just made a great play. It is less natural to reinforce an athlete who tried but failed. A good principle is to reinforce effort as much as results. After all, the only thing athletes have complete control over is the amount of effort they make; they have only limited control over the outcome of their efforts. Coaches have a right to demand total effort, and this is perhaps

the most important thing of all for them to reinforce. If athletes have had good technical instruction, are free from self-defeating fear of failure, and are giving maximum effort (all of which should be promoted by the use of the positive approach), then performance and winning will take care of themselves within the limits of the athletes' ability. John Wooden, the legendary "Wizard of Westwood," placed great emphasis on this concept:

> You cannot find a player who ever played for me at UCLA that can tell you he ever heard me mention "winning" a basketball game. He might say I inferred a little here and there, but I never mentioned winning. Yet the last thing that I told my players, just prior to tipoff, before we would go on the floor was, "When the game is over, I want your head up—and I know of only one way for your head to be up—and that's for you to know that you did your best. . . . This means to do the best YOU can do. That's the best; no one can do more. . . . You made that effort. (personal communication, 1975)

Reinforcement and Intrinsic Motivation

Motivation theorists make an important distinction between **intrinsic motivation** and **extrinsic motivation** (see Chapter 4). When people are motivated to perform an activity for its own sake, for "the love of the game," they are said to be **intrinsically motivated.** When they perform the activity only to obtain some external reward, they are **extrinsically motivated.**

Can positive reinforcements like trophies and money undermine intrinsic motivation? Under some circumstances, yes. If external rewards are suddenly introduced for performance of a behavior that is intrinsically rewarding, a person may come to attribute his or her performance to the extrinsic reward and cease performing the behavior if the external reward is withdrawn. Thus, in one study children who loved drawing with pens were offered external reinforcement (a "good player" award) for drawing with the pens. Later, when the good player award was withdrawn, the children showed a sharp decrease in their tendency to draw with the pens (Lepper & Greene, 1978).

Most of us would like athletes to be intrinsically motivated to participate in athletics. Is it possible that the positive approach, with its emphasis on reinforcement from the coach, could undermine their love of the game for its own sake?

It now appears that if extrinsic reinforcement is given to acknowledge a specific level of performance, it is unlikely to undermine intrinsic motivation (Deci, Koestner, & Ryan, 1999). Rather, it provides important information to an athlete that she has met a standard of excellence and thereby provides a basis for positive self-reinforcement by the athlete. Positive internal self-evaluations can strengthen behavior and also maintain and even increase intrinsic motivation (Cervone, 1992). Thus, it is a good idea for coaches to instill self-pride in their athletes with statements like "Great job! You ought to feel proud of yourself for that effort." There is considerable evidence that standards for self-reinforcement are often adopted from other people, and a coach can be an influential source of standards of excellence that athletes can internalize, particularly if the coach has developed a strong positive relationship with them.

Positive Reinforcement and Motivational Climate

Positive reinforcement can be applied to virtually any behavior. For example, we could choose to reinforce effort, persistence, and improvement, or we could give reinforcement only when an athlete is outperforming others, both teammates and opponents. The positive approach described earlier has emphasized reinforcement for effort, improvement, and meeting internal standards of performance. This approach is designed to foster a *mastery (task)-oriented motivational climate,* in which athletes will feel successful and competent when they have learned something new, witnessed skill improvement, mastered the task at hand, or given their best effort. Importantly, even if athletes perceive themselves as possessing lower ability than others, they can still feel competent and successful if focused on mastery-oriented achievement goals (Nicholls, 1989).

By contrast, when young athletes are in a state of *ego involvement,* their definitions of personal success and demonstrated competence are *other-referenced.* The goal here is to show that one is superior to relevant others (approach ego orientation), or to avoid appearing inferior to others (avoidance ego orientation). When coaches make reinforcement contingent on outperforming others or winning, punish unsuccessful performance, and fail to attend to effort or to developing personal goals for improvement, they can easily create an **ego-oriented motivational climate.**

Research in both educational and sport settings reveal that the motivational climate created by teachers and coaches has strong effects on achievement goals, standards of success, and behavior. Research in the educational domain indicates that children are more likely to invest in learning, develop intrinsic motivation, and adopt adaptive achievement strategies in mastery (task)-involving environments, in which the emphasis in on learning, personal improvement, and developing new skills rather than on interpersonal evaluation and social comparison with others. By contrast, maladaptive achievement strategies, fear of failure, and motivational problems tend to occur in ego-involving motivational climates, in which mistakes are punished, children with greater ability receive more encouragement and rewards, and social comparison is emphasized (Ames, 1992). As described in the next chapter, similar findings have been reported in the sport environment, and we can safely conclude that a mastery motivational climate is greatly preferable to an ego-oriented one (McArdle & Duda, 2002). As John Wooden and other progressive coaches have recognized, focusing on effort, preparation, and dedication to personal improvement pays dividends not only in performance but also in the development of healthy attitudes and values concerning sport participation. Especially noteworthy is the fact that athletes report greater enjoyment of their sport experience when coaches create a mastery motivational climate. One recent study revealed that the extent to which coaches created a mastery environment was 10 times more important than was the team's won-lost record in accounting for how much young athletes liked their coach (Cumming, Smoll, Smith, & Grossbard, 2007). Knowing what to reinforce is a key to creating such a climate.

Other research has shown that training coaches to create a mastery climate has notable positive effects on young athletes. In response to a decreased emphasis on winning, such athletes exhibited significant decreases in performance anxiety over the course of the season, whereas athletes' trait anxiety increased over the course of the season in a control condition whose coaches did not receive the Mastery Approach to Coaching intervention (Smith, Smoll, & Cumming, 2007). Athletes also showed salutary changes in their achievement goals, defining success in terms of personal improvement and fun rather than winning or besting others (Smoll, Smith, & Cumming, 2007).

Performance Feedback

Positive reinforcement serves not only as a reward for desirable behavior but also as a form of performance feedback. In other words, providing knowledge of results communicates the message that performance has met or exceeded the coach's standards. When it is possible to measure desired and undesired behaviors objectively, the coach can utilize the highly effective tool of performance feedback to increase motivation and performance.

In recent years, there has been a surge of interest in objective feedback as a technology for improving job performance in business, industry, and other settings (Huberman & O'Brien, 1999; Latham & Seijts, 1999; Tauer & Harackiewicz, 1999). The evidence indicates that performance feedback is a highly effective tool. One review of 18 studies carried out in a variety of job settings found increases in objective performance indicators averaging 53% after systematic performance feedback procedures were instituted (Kopelman, 1982–83). Specific work behaviors improved an average of 78%, and overall productivity an average of 16%. These increases were recorded over intervals ranging from 8 weeks to 4 years.

Performance feedback is a prominent feature of what many successful coaches do. For example, psychologists Ronald Gallimore and Roland Tharp (2004) charted all of John Wooden's behaviors during 15 practice sessions. They found that 75% of Wooden's comments to his players contained instructional feedback. Most of his comments were specific statements of what to do and how the players were or were not doing it. Indeed, Wooden was five times more likely to inform than to merely praise or reprimand.

How Feedback Motivates

Objective feedback is so consistently effective in motivating increased performance for a variety of reasons. For one thing, feedback can correct misconceptions. Athletes, like other people, often have distorted perceptions of their own behavior. Objective evidence in the form of statistics or numbers can help correct such misconceptions and may motivate corrective action. For example, it can be a sobering experience for a basketball player who fancies himself a great ball handler to learn that he has more turnovers than assists. Performance feedback can have powerful informational effects that can help enhance behavior (Latham & Seijts, 1999).

Feedback also creates internal consequences by stimulating athletes to experience positive (or negative) feelings about themselves, depending on how well they performed in relation to their standards of performance. An athlete who is dissatisfied with his or her level of performance may not only be motivated to improve but will experience feelings of self-satisfaction that function as positive reinforcement when subsequent feedback indicates improvement.

Such self-administered reinforcement can be even more important than external reinforcement from the coach in bringing about improved performance (Cervone, 1992). Promoting self-motivation in athletes also reduces the need for coaches to reinforce or punish. When feedback is public, as in posting statistics, the actual or anticipated reactions of others to one's performance level can serve as an additional motivator of increased effort and performance. Improvement is also likely to result in reinforcement from teammates.

A final motivational function of objective feedback is in relation to formal goal-setting programs. Because goal setting is discussed in detail in Chapter 11, I will simply point out that successful goal-setting programs provide clear feedback that informs workers as to their performance in relation to the goal (Locke & Latham, 1990). Without such feedback, goal setting does not improve performance, and without clear and specific goals that are either assigned by others or set internally, performance feedback has little effect on performance. For example, in a study by Albert Bandura and Daniel Cervone (1983) participants engaged in a strenuous aerobic task on an arm-powered exercise bicycle. Four experimental conditions were created by the presence/absence of challenging assigned goals and the presence/absence of performance feedback. Over the three performance periods, those who had both assigned goals and feedback improved their level of performance 59%. In contrast, those who had only goals without feedback or received only feedback improved from 20% to 25%, no more than the group that received neither goals or feedback. The presence of both challenging goals and performance feedback provided a powerful motivational boost to task performance.

Performance feedback can also result in increases in self-efficacy, the belief that one is capable of successful behavior (Cervone, 1992). In one study, participants performed an athletic task, in this case, the hurdles. Performance feedback contributed to subsequent self-efficacy, choice of more difficult hurdles, and performance (Escarti & Guzman, 1999).

Instructional Benefits of Feedback

Feedback has not only motivational but also instructional effects (see Chapter 2, this volume). It helps direct behavior. Objective performance feedback provides information about (a) the specific behaviors that should be performed, (b) the levels of proficiency that should be achieved in each of the skills, and (c) the athlete's current level of proficiency in these activities. This instructional function of feedback can be especially valuable when execution of a given skill is broken down into its stages or components, as was done in the football study described earlier. When the skill is a highly complex one, such as hitting a baseball, objective feedback on how frequently a hitter executes each of the essentials (keeping the bat in the correct position, shifting one's weight correctly, striding with the hips closed, keeping one's head down during the swing, and so on) can be very valuable in pinpointing areas of strength and weakness so that attention can be directed toward correcting mistakes. The information provided by subsequent objective feedback allows both coach and athlete to monitor progress in a more useful fashion than by depending on a more global measure of proficiency, such as batting average.

The foregoing discussion suggests a number of principles for giving effective feedback to athletes. Feedback should be contingent on what the athlete has just done, and it should be framed so that it can help the athlete continue to improve. The athlete is provided with feedback both on correct aspects of performance and on errors that were made. However, the athlete should then be told very specifically how to correct the error and encouraged to attempt the change. Expressions of confidence that with effort and time correct performance will result are likely to help maintain or even increase the athlete's own self-efficacy (Bandura, 1997).

Sometimes coaches need to give feedback that focuses on unfavorable aspects of performance. Such feedback is not always welcomed by the athlete. Indeed, much research in business organizations has shown that such feedback often results in negative emotional reactions and can actually create resistance to changing the problematic behavior. One study of factors that help counteract these negative reactions to unfavorable feedback showed that employees were more motivated to improve their job performance when the source of the corrective feedback was viewed as credible, the feedback was specific and of high quality, and the feedback was delivered in a considerate, supportive manner (Steelman & Rutkowski, 2004). When coaches can communicate to athletes that the corrective feedback is intended to help them achieve their own performance goals, athletes are more likely to be receptive to it and utilize it in the intended manner.

Implementing a Performance Measurement and Feedback System

As in the application of positive reinforcement, a successful feedback program requires that coaches identify specific and measurable behaviors or consequences—something that can be counted. The performance measures can be fairly global (e.g., number of rebounds per minute) or more specific and dealing with subskills (e.g., percentage of rebound plays in which the opponent is boxed out). Because successful execution does not always result in a successful outcome, it is sometimes preferable to use a measure of successful execution. For example, some baseball coaches keep statistics on the percentage of times the batter hits either a line drive or a hard ground ball in preference to batting average. In other words, select the specific behaviors you want to track, and then develop a system for measuring them. At this stage it is important to communicate with players so they are in agreement with the coach that the behaviors are important ones. A coach should try to elicit suggestions from the athletes so that they feel a sense of involvement in the program.

In many instances, coaches can choose between measuring a desired behavior or its undesirable counterpart. In line with the positive approach to coaching, I strongly recommend choosing the correct behavior for feedback rather than the mistake (or, at the very least, presenting both). This puts a coach in the position of reinforcing improvement rather than punishing or criticizing mistakes. It also focuses players' attention on what they should do rather than on what they should *not* do.

The measurement and feedback system coaches choose is limited only by their own ingenuity and awareness of the specific behaviors they want to promote. Some coaches have developed "total performance indexes" that include a variety of behaviors. For example, college basketball coach Lute Olson devised an index in which negative behaviors such as turnovers, missed free throws, and defensive mistakes were subtracted from positive behaviors such as points scored, rebounds, and assists. Most college and professional football coaches have highly detailed performance feedback systems that chart the percentage of plays during games and scrimmages in which each player successfully carries out his specific assignment. The measures are derived from game films and posted after every game and scrimmage. Such statistics also can provide an objective basis for selecting starters and allocating playing time.

Finally, it is important to note that performance feedback measures can be derived not only for individual players but also for subgroups or even for the team as a whole. Such measures can help to promote team cohesion by emphasizing the importance of teamwork and by providing a specific measure of group performance.

Positive reinforcement and performance feedback techniques can be applied to sports in many ways. Given the success they have enjoyed in a wide variety of performance settings, these strategies have the potential to increase coaching effectiveness at all competitive levels, from children's programs to the demanding and exacting realm of elite and professional sports. Table 3-1 presents some practical guidelines based on the positive approach emphasized in this chapter.

Table 3-1 **Getting Positive Things to Happen: Some Practical Guidelines**

Administering positive reinforcement

1. Be liberal with reinforcement, particularly in the early stages of learning.
2. Have realistic expectations and consistently reinforce compliance with your standards.
3. Try to reinforce desired behaviors as soon as they occur.
4. Reinforce effort and perseverance, not just results.
5. Pair reinforcement with a statement of what the athlete did correctly (e.g., "Way to go, you blocked out really well").
6. Verbally reinforce compliance with team rules to help prevent disruptive behavior.
7. Help athletes set positive, individualized, behavioral performance goals. Use written or statistical performance feedback to track improvement and stimulate self-reinforcement processes in athletes.

Reacting to mistakes

1. Regard mistakes as learning opportunities.
2. Ask the athlete what should have been done instead to reinforce the performance principle.
3. If the athlete knows how to correct the mistake, give encouragement. If not, demonstrate.
4. The "positive sandwich" is an excellent way to combine instruction with encouragement and reinforcement. First, find something the athlete did right and reinforce it (e.g., "You did a good job of getting to that fly ball"). Then tell the athlete how to correct the mistake, emphasizing the good things that will happen as a result (e.g., "Now, if you catch the ball with both hands, you'll hang onto it and make that play"). Finally, end with an encouraging statement (e.g., "Keep working on this and you're going to be a good fielder").
5. Restrict criticism to behaviors that are in the athlete's control, such as lack of effort.
6. Avoid aversive punishment as much as possible. It builds fear of failure, the athlete's worse enemy. Response cost is a more desirable alternative if punishment is used.

Source: Adapted with permission from Smith, R. E., & Smoll, F. L. (2002). *Way to go, Coach! A scientifically proven approach to coaching effectiveness* (2nd ed.). Portola Valley, CA: Warde Publishers.

Summary

In this chapter I have focused on some of the advantages of a positive approach to coaching that uses reinforcement (a) to strengthen desired behaviors and (b) to promote the development of a positive motivation for success rather than fear of failure. Objective performance feedback on specific aspects of performance is a highly successful motivational and instructional technique. Both systematic reinforcement and objective feedback require that the coach identify specific behaviors that are important to individual and team success. This is in itself a highly desirable practice because it focuses both coach and player attention on exactly what needs to be mastered and executed. It also promotes goal setting based on specific behaviors rather than on more general goals that are difficult to measure. Systematic use of positive reinforcement and objective feedback has yielded impressive results in many performance settings, including sports, and their utilization is appropriate at all competitive levels of athletics.

Study Questions

1. In what ways can coaching be viewed as attempts to influence behavior?
2. What are the ABCs of behavior control within an operant conditioning analysis of behavior?
3. Define the four basic consequences created by the presentation or removal of positive or aversive stimuli, and explain their effects on behavior.
4. Differentiate between negative reinforcement and punishment.
5. Define positive reinforcement and contrast it with punishment in terms of its effects on behavior and the motivational factors that underlie its effectiveness.
6. What are the direct effects and undesirable side effects of punishment? Distinguish between aversive punishment and response cost. How can we explain the fact that highly punitive coaches are sometimes very successful in eliciting high levels of athlete performance?
7. What are reinforcement contingencies, and how are they applied in shaping?
8. Summarize the schedules of reinforcement described in the text, as well as their effects on performance.
9. What is the importance of reinforcing effort rather than focusing entirely on outcome?
10. How can the positive approach be used to reduce disciplinary problems?
11. Differentiate between intrinsic and extrinsic motivation. Under what conditions can intrinsic motivation be undermined by positive reinforcement, and what can be done to reduce this danger?
12. How would you use positive reinforcement to create (a) a task-oriented motivational climate and (b) an ego-oriented motivational climate?
13. What are the effects of performance feedback on task performance, and what are the mechanisms whereby feedback is assumed to motivate behavior? What is the instructional value of feedback?
14. What are some of the key principles in implementing a performance feedback program? How are these related to the positive approach to coaching?

References

Ames, C. (1992). Achievement goals and adaptive motivational patterns: The role of the environment. In G. C. Roberts (Ed.), *Motivation in sport and exercise* (pp. 161–176). Champaign, IL: Human Kinetics.

Bandura, A. (1997). *Self-efficacy: The exercise of control.* New York: Freeman.

Bandura, A., & Cervone, D. (1983). Self-evaluative and self-efficacy mechanisms governing the motivational effects of goal systems. *Journal of Personality and Social Psychology, 45,* 1017–1028.

Cervone, D. (1992). The role of self-referent cognitions in goal setting, motivation, and performance. In M. Rabinowitz (Ed.), *Applied cognition* (pp. 79–96). New York: Ablex.

Cumming, S. P., Smoll, F. L., Smith, R. E., & Grossbard, J. R. (2007). Is winning everything? The relative contributions of motivational climate and won-lost percentage in youth sports. *Journal of Applied Sport Psychology, 19,* 322–336.

Deci, E. L., Koestner, R., & Ryan, R. M. (1999). A meta-analytic review of experiments examining the effects of extrinsic rewards on intrinsic motivation. *Psychological Bulletin, 125,* 627–668.

Escarti, A., & Guzman, J. F. (1999). Effects of feedback on self-efficacy, performance, and choice on an athletic task. *Journal of Applied Sport Psychology, 11,* 83–96.

Gallimore, R., & Tharp, R. (2004). What a coach can teach a teacher, 1975–2004: Reflections and reanalysis of John Wooden's teaching practices. *The Sport Psychologist, 18,* 119–137.

Huberman, W. L., & O'Brien, R. M. (1999). Improving therapist and patient performance in chronic psychiatric group homes through goal-setting, feedback, and positive reinforcement. *Journal of Organizational Behavior Management, 19,* 13–36.

Komaki, J., & Barnett, F. T. (1977). A behavioral approach to coaching football: Improving the play execution of an offensive backfield on a youth football team. *Journal of Applied Behavior Analysis, 10,* 657–664.

Kopelman, R. E. (1982–83). Improving productivity through objective feedback: A review of the evidence. *National Productivity Review, 24,* 43–55.

Latham, G. P., & Seijts, G. H. (1999). The effects of proximal and distal goals on performance of a moderately complex task. *Journal of Organizational Behavior, 20,* 421–429.

Lepper, M. R., & Greene, D. (1978). *The hidden costs of reward: New perspectives on the psychology of motivation.* Hillsdale, NJ: Erlbaum.

Locke, E. A., & Latham, G. P. (1990). *A theory of goal setting and task performance.* Englewood Cliffs, NJ: Prentice Hall.

Maag, J. W. (2003). *Behavior management: From theoretical implications to practical applications.* Pacific Grove, CA: Wadsworth.

Martin, G. L., & Hyrcaiko, D. (1983). *Behavior modification and coaching: Principles, procedures, and research.* Springfield, IL: Charles C. Thomas.

Martin, G., & Pear, J. (2007). *Behavior modification: What it is and how to do it* (7th ed.). Englewood Cliffs, NJ: Prentice Hall.

McArdle, S., & Duda, J. K. (2002). Implications of the motivational climate in youth sports. In F. L. Smoll & R. E. Smith (Eds.), *Children and youth in sport: A biosocial perspective* (2nd ed.). Dubuque, IA: Kendall/Hunt.

Petri, H. L., & Govern, J. (2004). *Motivation: Theory, research, and applications* (5th ed.). Belmont, CA: Wadsworth/Thomson Learning.

Sarafino, E. P. (2004). *Behavior modification: Principles of behavior change.* Long Grove, IL: Waveland Press.

Skinner, B. F. (1969). *Contingencies of reinforcement: A theoretical analysis.* New York: Appleton-Century-Crofts.

Smith, R. E. (1993). *Psychology.* Minneapolis, MN: West.

Smith, R. E., & Johnson, J. (1990). An organizational empowerment approach to consultation in professional baseball. *The Sport Psychologist, 4,* 347–357.

Smith, R. E., & Smoll, F. L. (1991). Behavioral research and intervention in youth sports. *Behavior Therapy, 22,* 329–344.

Smith, R. E., & Smoll, F. L. (2001). *Way to go, Coach: A scientifically-proven approach to coaching effectiveness* (2nd ed.). Portola Valley, CA: Warde Publishers.

Smith, R. E., & Smoll, F. L. (1997). Athletic performance anxiety. In H. Leitenberg (Ed.), *Handbook of social and evaluation anxiety* (pp. 417–454). New York: Plenum.

Smith, R. E., Smoll, F. L., & Christensen, D. S. (1996). Behavioral assessment and interventions in youth sports. *Behavior Modification, 20,* 3–44.

Smith, R. E., Smoll, F. L., & Cumming, S. P. (2007). Effects of a motivational climate intervention for coaches on children's sport performance anxiety. *Journal of Sport & Exercise Psychology, 29,* 39–59.

Smith, R. E., Smoll, F. L., & Passer, M. W. (2002). Sport performance anxiety in young athletes. In F. L. Smoll & R. E. Smith (Eds.), *Children and youth in sport: A biosocial perspective* (2nd ed.). Dubuque, IA: Kendall/Hunt.

Smith, R. E., Zane, N. S., Smoll, F. L., & Coppel, D. B. (1983). Behavioral assessment in youth sports: Coaching behaviors and children's attitudes. *Medicine and Science in Sports and Exercise, 15,* 208–214.

Smoll, F. L., Smith, R. E., & Cumming, S. P. (2007). Effects of a psychoeducational intervention for coaches on changes in child athletes' achievement goal orientations. *Journal of Clinical Sport Psychology, 1,* 23–46.

Steelman, L. A., & Rutkowski, K. A. (2004). Moderators of employee reactions to negative feedback. *Journal of Managerial Psychology, 19,* 6–18.

Tauer, J. M., & Harackiewicz, J. M. (1999). Winning isn't everything: Competition, achievement orientation, and intrinsic motivation. *Journal of Experimental Social Psychology, 35,* 209–238.

Zirpoli, T. J. (2004). *Behavior management: Applications for teachers.* Upper Saddle River, NJ: Prentice Hall.

Motivational Processes and the Facilitation of Quality Engagement in Sport

Joan L. Duda, *The University of Birmingham*
Darren C. Treasure, *Competitive Advantage International*

I've always believed that if you put in the work, the results will come. I don't do things halfheartedly. Because I know if I do, then I can expect half-hearted results. That's why I approached practices the same way I approached games. You can't turn it on and off like a faucet. I couldn't dog it during practice and then, when I need that extra push late in the game, expect it to be there.

　　　　　　—Michael Jordan, National Basketball Association MVP 1988, 1991, 1993, 1996, and 1998

The principle is competing against yourself. It's about self-improvement, about being better than you were the day before.

　　　　　　　　　　　　　　　　　　　　　　—Steve Young, VP Super Bowl XXIX

Michael Jordan and Steve Young speak to the very essence of why understanding motivation is of such interest to coaches, parents, sport psychologists, and athletes alike. Motivation is the foundation of sport performance and achievement. Without it, even the most talented athlete is unlikely to reach his or her full potential. Motivation is also pertinent to how the athlete experiences and responds to sport. Whether or not sport contributes positively or negatively to athletes' welfare is linked to motivation-related factors. In spite of its significance in the athletic milieu, however, motivation is one of the most misunderstood psychological constructs among sport participants and practitioners.

What is motivation, and how does an athlete or his or her coach optimize it? Some think that whether an athlete is high or low in motivation is somehow inherent in the athlete's personality—a relatively unchangeable characteristic of the person. Others believe coaches "motivate" athletes, perhaps in their pre-game "pep talks" or in the techniques they use in practice to foster their athletes' focus and intensity. There is, perhaps, some truth in each of these perspectives. However, sport motivation is more complex and multifaceted than either.

Contemporary research shows motivation to be dependent both on some malleable, psychological tendencies of the athletes themselves *and* on aspects of the social environments in which they develop, train, and compete. In particular, variations in motivation are held to be a function of the diverse ways in which athletes *interpret* their sport-related experiences. These different ways of interpreting sport stem from individual dispositional differences between athletes and situational dynamics.

How do we decide if an athlete is motivated? Is good or poor performance the best or only indicator? In general, researchers suggest that motivation is inferred from variability in **behavioral patterns.** For example, John, a club tennis player, seeks out opponents who really challenge his game. Whether practicing or competing, John tries his hardest to get to every shot and to hit it well, even when down love–40 in a game or behind 1–5 in a set. John maximizes the tennis talent that he has. When an athlete such as John tries hard, seeks out challenge, persists in the face of adversity, and performs up to his ability level on a reasonably consistent basis, we typically conclude that this person is highly motivated. In contrast, if John were to hold back in training or a match and not give his best effort, prefer to play opponents or work on drills that are too easy or way beyond his capabilities, regularly experience performance impairment or fail to live up to his potential, and contemplate dropping out or actually quitting tennis, we infer that motivational problems abound.

A number of factors need to be considered before we can determine the degree to and way in which the participant is motivated. It is important to take into account how much motivation the individual has (i.e., the *quantity* of motivation) as well as the *quality* of that motivation (Duda, 2001, 2005). Typically, the quantity of motivation is reflected in how "into" her or his sport the athlete is at the present time and how well she or he is currently performing. The quality of motivation is inferred by the athlete's

sustained and positive engagement in the sport. This includes both the athlete's accomplishments and the degree of enjoyment and psychological and physical benefits associated with sport involvement. Variability in the quantity and quality of sport motivation are intricately linked with how athletes *think* before, during, and after their engagement in sport.

What thoughts appear critical to variations in motivation? Researchers (e.g., Ryan & Deci, 2002) have shown that individuals feel and act more motivated when they think they have the competence to meet the demands of the task at hand and believe they have some control, or autonomy, in regard to their participation. The assumption that perceptions of ability and autonomy are critical to motivational patterns is fundamental to a number of popular contemporary theories of motivated behavior. Three of those theoretical frameworks, which have provided a foundation for research and practice on sport motivation, will be reviewed here. These are (1) self-efficacy or social cognitive theory, (2) the achievement goal frameworks, and (3) self-determination theory.

Believing That One Can: The Construct of Self-Efficacy

I don't even think about the prospect of not winning—it never occurs to me. I really am that confident.

> —Daley Thompson, 1984 and 1988
> Olympic decathlon champion

Negative thoughts lead to a negative performance; the connection is as straightforward as that.

> —Sally Gunnell, Olympic gold medalist,
> world record holder, and world champion
> 400 meter hurdler

Although not exactly synonymous with the concept of self-efficacy, the words of Daley Thompson, one of the world's greatest ever athletes, are a clear testament to the "power of positive thinking." The words of Sally Gunnell also provide insight into the effect of negative thinking—namely, that if you don't think you can do it you won't.

Positive thinking is thought to be a very important antecedent of positive behavioral patterns, especially in challenging, achievement-oriented contexts such as competitive sport. Athletes think positively when they believe they can do something effectively, that is, when they think in a self-efficacious manner. (See Chapter 17 for a more complete discussion of positive versus negative thinking.) **Self-efficacy** is defined as a person's judgment about her or his capability to successfully perform a particular task (Bandura, 1986). Such judgments relate to the *level* of performance expected, the *strength* or certainty of those attainment beliefs, and the *generality* of those beliefs to other related tasks or domains. Bandura (1997) refined the definition of self-efficacy to encompass those beliefs regarding individuals' capabilities to produce performances that will lead to anticipated outcomes, and the term **self-regulatory efficacy** now encompasses a social cognitive approach that articulates the role cognition plays in performance above and beyond simple behavioral or skill beliefs.

Bandura (1986) has argued that (1) our efficacy beliefs mediate subsequent thought patterns, affective responses, and action and that (2) self-efficacy is positively related to positive motivational patterns. In general, sport research has shown that self-efficacy is a positive predictor of motor skill acquisition, execution, and competitive sport performance (Bandura, 1997; Feltz, Short, & Sullivan, 2007; Treasure, Monson, & Lox, 1996). Self-efficacy is one among a variety of mechanisms that is associated with higher performance. Athletes with high self-efficacy are more likely to try harder, choose challenging tasks, experience positive emotions, and be less anxious. The influence of self-efficacy on performance and other achievement-related behaviors also seems to be intertwined with the goal-setting process (see Chapter 13). That is, although self-efficacy may directly relate to variations in performance, its impact may be because of its effect on athletes' personal goal setting and the development and employment of self-regulation skills (Feltz, et al., 2007; Schunk, 1995).

It is interesting to note, however, that previous performance tends to be a better predictor of subsequent pretask self-efficacy than efficacy judgments are of ensuing performance (Feltz, et al., 2007). The athlete's incentives (whether intrinsic or extrinsic) to try to turn that self-efficacy into reality have an impact on the predictive utility of those initial task-specific confidence judgments. Further, if high performance is defined with respect to successful competitive outcomes, the athlete has relatively less control over achieving those outcomes than if the performance standard is self-referenced. That is, high self-efficacy does not always translate into a win. It does increase the probability, however, that the athlete will do well in terms of the facets of performance within her or his personal control which could contribute to winning. Coaches, sport psychologists, and athletes themselves would be wise to optimize efficacy judgments prior to the athletes' engagement in training or competitive-related activities. In other words, it is important for athletes to think (and act!) confidently if they want to perform optimally.

Implications for Practice

How do we increase an athlete's self-efficacy? Thankfully, existing theoretical frameworks and sport research provide some insight into the antecedents of task-specific confidence in the sport domain. Six key determinants of self-efficacy are emphasized (e.g., Bandura, 1997; Feltz et al., 2007) (Figure 4-1):

1. The most influential determinant of self-efficacy is *past performance*. Especially when the task is difficult, we tend to feel more confident about performing a particular task when we have demonstrated mastery of that activity before—success breeds success. Therefore, when learning a new aspect of technique or strategy or gaining experience in sport competitions, it is important for athletes to accumulate progressively more demanding accomplishments to build their sense of competence. Breaking down the task into manageable "chunks" or decreasing the difficulty of early-in-the-season opponents are two ways of increasing the probability of initial positive performance and, thus, fostering athletes' self-efficacy.

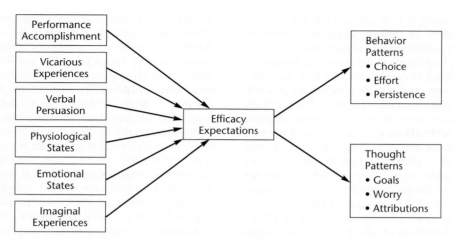

Figure 4-1 **The relationship between sources of self-efficacy, efficacy expectations, and behavior and thought patterns**
Source: Adapted from Feltz, 1988.

2. Another antecedent of athletes' efficacy judgments is *vicarious experience* (Bandura, 1986). For example, watching someone else successfully perform the activity, especially if this person is deemed to be similar to the athlete in question, can facilitate self-efficacy. This is a more salient source of efficacy information among younger athletes and those who have had limited experience with the task at hand. By watching or modeling others, athletes can learn how to do things. Also, if done in an informative rather than a comparative manner, coaches can use vicarious experiences to help athletes believe that "if he or she can do it, so can I!" Participation modeling, where the athlete engages in the task while observing someone else do it (and, thus, works his or her way through the activity), can be particularly appropriate for efficacy building (Feltz, et al., 2007).

3. It is important to remember that our heads are attached to our bodies (and vice versa!). With respect to formulating efficacy judgments, athletes also may look to their *physiological state* in deciding whether they can successfully meet specific task demands. More specifically, athletes appraise their physiological condition—state of autonomic arousal, fear,

pain, fatigue, and so on—and make judgments as to their readiness to "rise to the occasion." By mastering techniques such as progressive muscle relaxation and deep breathing, which help them modify physiological conditions such as the heightened muscle tension, heart rate, and respiration rate associated with stress (Chapter 15), athletes can facilitate their pre-performance self-efficacy. Similarly, for those athletes who have difficulty "getting up" for competition, energizing strategies may be effective in increasing arousal levels that will, for example, enhance perceptions of precompetition self-efficacy.

4. *Verbal persuasion* from coaches, sport psychologists, and significant others is another antecedent of self-efficacy. This can be in the form of feedback ("Here's how to do this"; "You did this correctly") or motivational ("Come on, you can do it!") statements. If the person conveying the efficacy-enhancing information is considered credible and knowledgeable, the verbal persuasion is likely to be more influential. Athletes also often employ verbal persuasion (or positive self-talk, see Chapter 17) to help themselves feel efficacious about what they are about to do. As there is a tendency to act according to how we think, positive self- and task-related statements made by athletes can increase their self-efficacy, too.

5. Similar to a consideration of their physiological state, athletes also appraise their *emotional state,* or mood, prior to performing when they decide on their level of confidence (Maddux, 1995). Consequently, emotional control techniques should be helpful in enhancing task-specific confidence among athletes who find themselves being debilitated by anger, frustration, and other negative mood states. Our thoughts can precipitate different emotional responses, and cognitive interventions such as "negative thought stopping" (see Chapter 17) can also result in higher efficacy judgments among sport competitors, not only decreasing negative mood states but also, and perhaps more significantly, increasing positive mood states (Treasure et al., 1996).

6. Finally, *imaginal experiences* are assumed to have an impact on task-specific self-confidence (Maddux, 1995). If athletes go through the demands of a sport activity in their minds before performing, those demands might not seem so daunting or unfamiliar, and the athletes' perceptions of their ability to meet those demands should be increased. Seeing (and feeling) yourself doing something successfully before actually doing it can also enhance your perceptions of ability (see Chapter 16 on imagery in sport).

Keep in mind that these critical antecedents to self-efficacy can be interdependent. For example, an athlete can use imagery to help reduce over-activation (e.g., imaging a peaceful setting to diminish one's muscular tension or high heart rate) or to attenuate the cognitive anxiety associated with an upcoming competition. In this way imaginal strategies are employed to influence the physiological and emotional states that subsequently feed an athlete's preperformance efficacy judgments.

It is beyond the scope of the present chapter to go into depth regarding these constructs and their correlates, but sport researchers have also considered perceptions of task-specific confidence

in terms of teams and team leaders (i.e., coaches). *Collective efficacy* captures the degree of confidence team members have in their collective abilities to do what is necessary (e.g., play effective defense) to reach team goals (Feltz, et al., 2007). Perceptions of collective efficacy share many of the same antecedents as self-efficacy (Bandura, 1997), but these sources of confidence center on the team as a whole (e.g., previous team performance, verbal persuasion by the coach or spectators directed toward the team). According to Feltz and colleagues (Feltz, Chase, Moritz, & Sullivan, 1999, p. 765), *coaching efficacy* relates to the degree "to which coaches believe they have the capacity to affect the learning and performance of their athletes." Assumed to be multidimensional, overall coaching efficacy is held to be a function of coaches' judgments regarding their ability to teach and implement strategy, effectively motivate their athletes, diagnose and provide proper instruction regarding sport skills, and promote "character" and psychosocial maturity in their players. Previous coaching-related success, coaching experience and preparation, and the perceived skill and efficacy of one's athletes have been proposed as important antecedents of coaching efficacy (Feltz, et al., 2007).

Achievement Goals: The Importance of How We Judge Our Competence

> *I never played to get into the Hall of Fame. I only tried to be the best that I could be.*
>
> —*Walter Payton, member of the National Football League Hall of Fame*

Maintaining confidence is certainly important to exhibiting optimal motivated behaviors in sport settings. However, anyone with experience with training and competing in sport has witnessed athletes whose judgments of self-efficacy are more fragile than those of other athletes. We also have observed that not every competitor who has experienced setbacks (performance failure, losses) and is not feeling especially confident exhibits problems regarding the quantity or quality of his or her motivation. Why might that be so? Our contemporary understanding of sport motivation recognizes that adaptive versus problematic motivational patterns are not merely a function of whether an athlete has high or low self-efficacy. Rather, we need to also consider the criteria that athletes use to decide whether they are able or not. That is, how does the athlete define demonstrated competence?

Thus, another area of research that may assist athletes, coaches, and sport psychologists in understanding and enhancing motivation in sport is based on achievement goal frameworks. These frameworks assume that differences in goal perspectives, or the ways in which individuals judge their competence and perceive success, are the critical antecedents to variations in the direction and intensity of behavior. These models of motivation, similar to self-efficacy theory (Bandura, 1986), assume that perceptions of competence (how able we think we are) do relate to motivational patterns. However, achievement goal frameworks also state that how we decide whether we have been able or not is essential to the prediction of the quantity and quality of our motivation (Duda, 2001).

Fundamental to achievement goal models is that there are, at least, two central achievement goal perspectives (task and ego) that govern the way athletes think about achievement and guide subsequent decision making and action (Nicholls, 1989). According to Nicholls (1989), task and ego goal states entail distinct ways of processing an activity and can fluctuate throughout the course of an event. When task involved, an athlete's main purposes are to gain skill or knowledge, to exhibit effort, to perform at one's best, and to experience personal improvement. This athlete is focused on what he or she is doing and is thinking primarily about how to accomplish the task. If such purposes are achieved, the individual feels competent and successful. When ego-involved, athletes are preoccupied with the adequacy of their ability and the demonstration of superior competence compared to others. Perceptions of competence and subjective achievement, in this case, entail social comparisons with others. High ability is demonstrated for the ego-involved athlete when his or her performance is perceived to exceed that of others or to be equivalent with less effort exerted. The athlete's focus is on whether he or she is good enough (if confidence is low) and how to prove (rather than improve) his or her high level of competence (if confidence is high).

When task involvement is manifested, it is assumed that the athlete will think, act, and feel in a motivated manner regardless of his or her level of perceived ability. Ego involvement, too, can correspond to positive achievement patterns (e.g., high performance, or persistence) as long as the athlete is quite certain that her or his ability is high. When an athlete is ego-involved and thinks the possibility of demonstrating superior competence is "slim to none," the achievement-related cognitions, emotions, and behaviors displayed are far less than optimal. That is, the quantity and, in particular, the quality of motivation is diminished.

Achievement goal theory states that an individual's goal perspective state—task or ego involvement—is the result of both individual differences and situational factors. With respect to the former, an athlete's proneness for task and ego involvement is thought to be captured by his or her dispositional task and ego goal orientations. We will first discuss the nature and implications of these goal orientations in the athletic domain.

Significance of Goal Orientations

Achievement goal orientations are not bipolar opposites (Nicholls, 1989). Rather, they are independent dimensions. As a result, an athlete can be high ego/low task, high task/low ego, high task/high ego, or low task/low ego. From both a theoretical and applied perspective, it is important to consider athletes' degree of proneness for both task and ego goals to get a more complete view of their motivational processes.

Findings from studies involving male and female athletes from a variety of competitive levels and age groups show that an adaptive achievement profile is one of high task and high ego orientation (Duda, 2001). But why might this be the case? Some researchers have suggested that a high task orientation might, to some degree, insulate highly ego-oriented individuals from the negative consequences of low perceived ability when they are performing poorly and, thus, be motivationally advantageous in the long run (Nicholls, 1989). Athletes who are high in both task and ego orientation have multiple sources of subjective success and perceived competence. They have the flexibility of focusing on either task or ego goals at different times in their training or competitions to enhance their motivation (Duda, 2001). We should note that there are some questions regarding whether a high-task/high-ego orientation profile is most adaptive when the focus is on indexes of the *quality* of motivation (Duda, 2001). For example, research examining the subjective well-being and moral functioning of athletes suggests that high-task/high-ego participants can be similar to their low-task/high-ego counterparts in views about and responses to sport (Reinboth & Duda, 2004).

In general, a significant body of research has revealed that task and ego goal orientations are associated with qualitatively different behavioral, cognitive, and affective patterns in sport that are likely to have an impact not only on short-term performance but also on the quantity and quality of long-term participation. Researchers have found a task orientation to be related to positive motivational outcomes—for example, the belief that effort is a cause of success, the use of problem-solving and adaptive learning strategies, enjoyment, satisfaction, and intrinsic interest (Duda, 2001, 2005; Roberts, Treasure, & Kavussanu, 1997). Previous work has also revealed a task orientation to be associated with the belief that one's level of physical ability is changeable or malleable (Sarrazin, Biddle, Famose, Cury, Fox, & Durand, 1996). This is very important in the context of sport, because elite level performers usually reach their potential only after years of training. If an athlete believed this commitment to training was not going to lead to increases in ability (i.e., given that he or she holds the view that sport ability is "fixed"), it is unlikely that the athlete would be optimally motivated to train over time.

In contrast, an ego orientation has been found to be associated with boredom, the belief

that deception is a cause of success, and reported anxiety (Duda, 2001; Roberts, et al., 1997). Ego orientation also has been found to be related to the belief that ability is an important determinant of success and the idea that sport competence is stable and a "gift" (Sarrazin et al., 1996). Such a belief system may lead an athlete who is questioning his or her ability not to be as motivated or committed to long-term training. These individuals believe that ultimately "You've either got it or you haven't," and the possession of "it" is deemed a prerequisite to sport achievement.

Achievement goal models state that individuals in a state of ego involvement who have high perceptions of perceived ability are likely to respond in a fashion similar to competitors who are task involved, regardless of whether their perceived competence is high or low. This has led a number of leading sport psychology researchers to contend that a high ego orientation may not be detrimental to performance. Indeed, it has been argued that it is hard to see how an individual could succeed, particularly at the elite level, without having a strong ego orientation. The assumption here is that elite athletes are primarily motivated by winning and outperforming others.

Although we would agree that all elite level athletes perceive success in an ego-involving fashion at certain times, we would caution those who want to *promote* ego orientation. Indeed, high levels of ego orientation may not be motivating at the elite level of sport as even these athletes sometimes doubt their ability (e.g., due to injury, during a performance slump). At such times, a predominant ego orientation coupled especially with moderate or low task orientation puts individuals at jeopardy for feeling incompetent because their focus is primarily on their performance compared to others (Duda, 2001; Nicholls, 1989). Because of the social comparative nature of sport and the high demands placed on competitors, both in training and competition, athletes (particularly those who are elite) are involved in an activity that is designed to challenge the adequacy of their perceived ability on a day-to-day basis.

Pertinent to any debate of the advantages or disadvantages of an ego orientation in sport are contemporary extensions of achievement goal models (e.g., Elliot, 1999; Elliot & McGregor, 2001). That is, recently some researchers have called for a reconsideration of dichotomous task/ego approaches to achievement goals and have instead advocated consideration of approach and avoidance aspects of an ego goal focus. An athlete would be considered ego-approach oriented when he or she is preoccupied with demonstrating superior ability compared to others. In contrast, an athlete emphasizing an ego-avoidance goal would be most concerned about not revealing his or her inferiority. For this athlete, the most important thing is to avoid showing that he or she does not possess adequate levels of ability. Central to this elaboration of the two-goal model of achievement goals (Nicholls, 1989) is the assumption that an ego approach goal orientation would positively relate to achievement striving, whereas an ego avoidance goal emphasis would be coupled with negative motivational outcomes.

Drawing from the existent research and similar to the findings of studies based on the dichotomous goal models, results regarding the presumed positive implications of ego-approach goals in sport-related settings have been equivocal (Adie, Duda, & Ntoumanis, 2008; Nien & Duda, 2008). Our understanding of the nature, antecedents, and consequences of ego-avoidance goals, especially in contrast to an ego-approach goal perspective, is still in its infancy (Duda, 2005). An ego-avoidance perspective on sport achievement has been linked to greater fear of failure, stronger beliefs that sport ability is fixed or unchangeable, perceptions of an ego-involving climate, heightened anxiety, lower intrinsic motivation, and greater amotivation (Conroy, et al., 2003, 2006; Cury, DaFonseca, Rufo, Peres, & Sarrazin, 2003; Morris & Kavussanu, 2006; Nien & Duda, 2008, in press).

Regardless of skill level, or whether their ego goal focus is approach or avoidance oriented, those who are particularly concerned about how they are doing compared to others (ego-involved athletes) are likely to become prime candidates for questioning their competence. This might be a regular occurrence for those of us who are less talented but could strike *any* athlete at *any* time. It is

important at this point to remember that we are discussing *perceived* ability here, not *actual* ability. Although actual ability may not be altered during a game of tennis or a round of golf, athletes' perceptions of ability can and do change, often in a relatively short period of time, and are seldom stable over a long period of time. Indeed, recent lab-based research by Nien and Duda (2006) found that (in contrast to those focused on a task goal), the performance and affective responses of study participants who emphasized ego-approach goals were no different than what was observed for participants geared toward ego-avoidance goals following competitive losses in cycling races. Whether approach or avoidance-oriented, centering on ego goals translated into negative processes and outcomes when coupled with failure to demonstrate superiority. Such findings are not surprising when one considers that sport studies to date have found a strong positive correlation between ego approach and ego avoidance goal emphases (e.g., Nien & Duda, 2008). Moreover, aligned with theoretical expecations (Elliot, 1999), both ego-approach and ego-avoidance goals have been found to be tied to fear of failure in the sport domain (Nien & Duda, 2008).

How can ego involvement set the stage for performance impairment? Nicholls (1989) has suggested that the negative relationship between ego involvement and performance is instigated by the expectation an individual holds about looking incompetent. This expectation of looking low in ability can result in a decrease in performance in a number of ways. First, in an attempt to protect one's perceptions of competence, it may cause an athlete to select sport tasks that are too easy or too difficult. Although choosing to engage in less challenging tasks prevents the unhappy prospect of making errors and appearing to be less able, it simultaneously hinders an individual from developing a variety of sport skills to the maximum. Likewise, selecting tasks that are much too hard provides the athlete with a ready-made justification for the unsuccessful outcome as he or she is able to state, "I failed, but so did everyone else." This strategy, however, will be costly for the athlete in terms of maintaining or enhancing his or her skill development over time.

Second, the expectation of looking incompetent can result in a lack of trying when failure is looming and when it looks like one will appear less able compared to others. For example, athletes who back off at the end of a race because the outcome is already determined (i.e., they won't be the winner) and coast to the finish line or athletes who begin to engage in inappropriate achievement strategies or unsportspersonlike behavior when it looks like they will not be the best on that day are unlikely to ever reach their full potential.

Finally, if the expectation of demonstrating low ability becomes chronic, it may lead to regular and high levels of anxiety and, eventually, a devaluing of, and loss of interest in, the activity. If this chain of events occurs, it is likely that these athletes may find themselves in a state of amotivation (Vallerand, 2001). At the very least, if such high ego approach-oriented athletes stay in sport, we might expect them to become strongly ego avoidance goal-oriented over time (Duda, 2005).

Elliot and colleagues (Elliot & McGregor, 2001) have also distinguished between the approach and avoidance facets of task (or mastery-based) goals. This distinction has led to what is termed the 2×2 achievement goal framework. A task (or mastery) approach goal entails a focus on the development of personal competence and realization of task mastery. A task (or mastery) avoidance goal, on the other hand, centers on the avoidance of demonstrating self-referenced incompetence. To date, sport studies grounded in the 2×2 achievement goal model have pointed to the same advantages of a task approach goal as has been revealed in the multitude of studies based on dichotomous achievement goal frameworks (Duda, 2001, 2005; Dweck, 1999; Nicholls, 1989). Task approach goals have been found to correspond positively to perceptions of a task-involving climate, intrinsic motivation, and the belief that sport competence is an attribute that can be enhanced through training. Consonant with the predictions emanating from the 2×2 achievement goal model (Elliot & McGregor, 2001), task avoidance goals have been linked to

negative processes and outcomes such as amotivation, self-handicapping, fear of failure and anxiety (Nien & Duda, 2008).

Significance of the Sport Context

A key variable in determining the motivation of athletes is situational and relates to the salience of task- and ego-involving cues in the achievement context. The focus here is on how the *perceived* structure of the environment, often referred to as the **motivational climate** (Ames, 1992; Duda & Balaguer, 2007), can make it more or less likely that a particular goal state is manifested in training or competition. This perception of the motivational climate affects the achievement patterns of individuals through their view of what goals are reinforced in that setting (Treasure, 2001). In essence, perceptions of the goal perspectives emphasized in these social environments are assumed to be predictive of variability in motivational processes.

Sport research has shown that a perceived task-involving setting is characterized by the athletes' view that the coach does reinforce high effort, cooperation among team members, as well as learning and improvement, and the perception that everyone on the team (regardless of ability level) contributes to the team's achievements (Newton, Duda, & Zin, 1999). A perceived ego-involving team climate, in contrast, is marked by athletes perceiving that the coach punishes their mistakes, fosters rivalry among team members, and gives much of his or her attention to the most talented athletes on the team.

Research has shown a perceived task-involving climate to be associated with more adaptive motivational and affective patterns than perceptions of a performance or ego-involving climate in sport (Duda & Balaguer, 2007). For example, perceptions of task-involving coach-created environments have corresponded to greater enjoyment, more adaptive coping strategies, perceived competence, greater team cohesion and more positive peer relationships, and higher levels of moral functioning. Studies have also shown perceptions of a task involving climate to be negatively related to claimed self-handicapping behavior in elite level sport (e.g., Kuczka & Treasure, 2005). Self-handicapping is evident when athletes, who might be concerned about not performing well, "set the stage" to provide an excuse or "scapegoat" to explain their poor subsequent performance. In so doing, failure could be attributed to the "handicap" rather than any inadequacy in personal ability. Such a strategy also allows athletes to save face in front of others.

In contrast, perceptions of an ego-involving motivational climate have been linked to greater anxiety and performance-related worry, dropping out of sport, greater peer conflict, greater self-handicapping, and lower levels of moral functioning (Duda & Balaguer, 2007). Other work has found perceptions of an ego-involving climate to positively predict indexes of physical ill-being among athletes (e.g., reported physical exhaustion and symptoms; Reinboth & Duda, 2004). Moreover, the degree to which the sport environment is deemed ego-involving appears to have implications for athletes' level of self-esteem and the degree to which their self-worth is tied to athletic performance (Reinboth & Duda, 2004). When athletes train and compete in a highly ego-involving motivational climate and have some doubts about their sport competence, they also are more likely to question their worth as a person overall. When a highly ego-involving atmosphere is deemed to be operating on a team, athletes also perceive their coach to provide less social support and positive feedback and be more punishment oriented (Duda & Balaguer, 2007).

One of the key elements of achievement goal theory is that dispositional goal orientations and perceptions of the climate are considered two independent dimensions of motivation that interact to affect behavior (Nicholls, 1989). Specifically, the theory calls for examination of a Person X Situation interaction effect. For example, let us consider a basketball player with a predominantly ego-oriented goal orientation (high ego/low task) who finds herself in a situation where the task- and ego-involving cues are vague or weak. In this case it is likely that the athlete's goal orientation will be most predictive of her goal state. In a situation in which the cues are in favor of an ego-involving climate, it is likely that

these perceptions will complement the athlete's goal orientation in predicting a strong state of ego involvement. For a state of task involvement to emerge for this basketball player, the perceptions of a task-involving climate would have to be extremely strong. The stronger the goal orientation, the less probable it is to be overridden by situational cues and the stronger the situational cues must be. Alternatively, the weaker the disposition, the more easily it may be altered by situational cues (Newton & Duda, 1999).

Consideration of situational criteria would not be complete, particularly in the context of youth sport, without taking into account the influence peers (Vazou, Ntoumanis, & Duda, 2007) and parents (White, 1996) have in the development of children's and adolescents' achievement motivation. The majority of the work on the motivational climates created by such significant others in the sport setting has concentrated on parental influences. This research points to the benefits of task-involving parents and the negative implications of an ego-involving parental climate (Duda, 2001).

Implications for Practice

The existent research establishing links between task and ego goals (whether dispositional or situational in nature or approach or avoidance centred) and various motivational patterns has contributed to our understanding of motivational processes in sport. But how do we enhance motivation based on the research grounded in achievement goal frameworks? According to theoretical predictions and existing empirical findings, high ego/low task athletes are the most susceptible to motivational difficulties. The evidence suggests that a sport psychology consultant should try to enhance the dispositional task goal orientation for these athletes, perhaps by introducing process or performance centered goal-setting (see Chapter 11) and/or self-regulation techniques (Duda, Cumming, & Balaguer, 2005; Schunk, 1995; see Chapter 13). We should consider implementing strategies that encourage athletes to focus on gains in skill or knowledge, monitoring effort levels, and self-referenced criteria for success. It may be very difficult in the ego-involving milieu of sport to reduce an athlete's ego orientation, and it is likely that many athletes and coaches will be unwilling to moderate what they believe is a vital ingredient in developing motivation in sport—namely, focusing on winning and being superior. A high ego orientation is not necessarily detrimental to achievement striving (at least from a quantity of motivation perspective; Duda, 2001), but it is especially problematic when coupled with low task orientation and low perceived competence, and/or grounded in a fear of looking incompetent. All in all, techniques designed to increase task orientation are likely to be more readily accepted by practitioners in the sport world and probably will be a more effective strategy for an applied sport psychologist to pursue.

Focusing on the individual to enhance the quality of motivation by affecting his or her dispositional goal orientations may seem a viable option, but practically speaking this strategy may be most suitable for an elite athlete who has access to a sport psychologist on a regular basis. Concentrating on individual change in dispositional tendencies may not be the most efficient and feasible alternative for a team or, especially, in the youth sport setting where the goal should be the development of *all* players rather than the performance of a select few. However, in a relatively short period of time, a coach may be able to structure a context in such a way as to influence athletes' recognition that they participate in a more task-involving motivational climate. In so doing, the coach can have a positive impact on the quality of athletes' sport participation.

In addition to coaches, particularly youth coaches, interventions designed to enhance motivation should target the attitudes and behaviors of Moms and Dads and other significant people in the athletes' lives. By making certain types of goals and performance feedback salient, a parent can influence young athletes' views about themselves, perceptions of the sport activity per se, and the criteria they use to evaluate success and failure. For example, when a young sport participant returns from a weekly tennis game and a parent asks, "Did you win?" the athlete receives a rather clear message as to what the parent considers most important. This message may counter or compromise the efforts of a coach or sport psychologist to enhance task involvement. We would suggest, therefore, that any intervention designed to promote task involvement in sport recognize the role parents and other significant adults (e.g., league officials) and peers (Vazou et al., 2007) may play in determining a young athlete's views on how to define sport success and the manner in which he or she tends to judge demonstrated competence.

By emphasizing certain cues, rewards, and performance expectations, a coach, parent, peer or teammate, or sport psychologist can encourage a particular goal state and in so doing affect the way an athlete perceives and responds to the sport. For the remaining discussion, the focus will be on intervention strategies relevant to adults in contrast to potential peer or teammate influences.

To enhance motivation, coaches, parents and sport psychologists should critically evaluate what they do and how they do it in terms of task and ego goals. For example, how do you define sport success for your players or children? Is it in terms of development and effort, or winning and losing? As a coach, do you design practice sessions that optimally challenge your players, or do you repeat well-learned skills that may delay or stifle development even though they increase the probability of winning? How do you evaluate performance? What behaviors do you consider desirable? Do you congratulate players and your children when they win and outperform others or when they try hard and improve? How do you react when the team, your athlete, or your child loses? If you feel that you coach, parent, or consult in a task-involving manner, then you are probably fostering the quality of athletes' motivation and promoting adaptive beliefs and positive achievement strategies. If your style of coaching, parenting, or consulting is ego-involving, you may be setting up more mature athletes or children, even those who are currently the most successful, for motivational difficulties in the future.

To assist the coach, parent, or sport psychologist in modifying the motivation-related atmosphere being created for athletes, Table 4-1

Table 4-1   **Description of TARGET Structures and Strategies That Enhance Task Involvement**

TARGET Structure	Strategies
Task. What athletes are asked to learn and what tasks they are given to complete (e.g., training activities, structure of practice conditions).	Provide the athlete with a variety of moderately demanding tasks that emphasize individual challenge and active involvement.
	Assist athletes in goal setting.
	Create a developmentally appropriate training environment by individualizing the demands of the tasks set.
Authority. The kind and frequency of participation in the decision-making process (e.g., athlete involvement in decisions concerning training, the setting and enforcing of rules).	Encourage participation by your athletes in the decision-making process.
	Develop opportunities for leadership roles.
	Get athletes to take responsibility for their own sport development by teaching self-management and self-monitoring skills.
Recognition. Procedures and practices used to motivate and recognize athletes for their progress and achievement (e.g., reasons for recognition, distribution of rewards, and opportunities for rewards).	Use private meetings between coach and athlete to focus on individual progress.
	Recognize individual progress, effort, and improvement.
	Ensure equal opportunities for rewards to all.
Grouping. How athletes are brought together or kept apart in training and competition (e.g., the way in-groups are created during practice).	Use flexible and mixed ability grouping arrangements.
	Provide multiple grouping arrangements (i.e., individual, small group, and large group activities).
	Emphasize cooperative solutions to training problems set.
Evaluation. Standards set for athletes' learning and performance and the procedures for monitoring and judging attainment of these standards.	Develop evaluation criteria based on effort, improvement, persistence, and progress toward individual goals.
	Involve athletes in self-evaluation.
	Make evaluation meaningful. Be consistent.
Timing. Appropriateness of the time demands placed on learning and performance (e.g., pace of learning and development, management of time and training schedule).	Training programs should recognize that athletes, even at the elite level, do not train, learn, or develop at the same rate.
	Provide sufficient time before moving on to the next stage in skill development.
	Spend equal time with all athletes.
	Assist athletes in establishing training and competition schedules.

lists some suggestions on how to develop a task-involving motivational climate (Duda & Balaguer, 2007; Treasure, 2001). These suggestions have been organized around the task, authority, recognition, grouping, evaluation, and timing (TARGET) situational structures Epstein (1989) has argued make up the "basic building blocks" of the achievement environment.

Doing It for the Joy: The Determinants of Intrinsic Motivation and Self-Determination

I love golf as much for its frankness as for those rare occasions when it rewards a wink with a smile.

—*Tiger Woods*

Sport is an achievement activity. Therefore, knowing how competent athletes perceive themselves and being aware of the criteria by which these athletes define their competence is relevant to their motivation in sport. Also relevant to motivational patterns are the reasons why athletes decide to participate in their selected sport activity.

When athletes are **intrinsically motivated,** they participate in sport for its own sake. That is, the motivation for sport engagement primarily revolves around the inherent pleasure of doing the activity. Someone or something else does not instigate athletes' sport participation in this case. Rather, they play sport out of personal choice. The motivation literature suggests that in various achievement activities, including sport, intrinsic motivation is associated with positive affect and maximal engagement.

Self-determination theory (SDT; Ryan & Deci, 2002) has become a very popular approach to understanding motivation and behavior in sport. Fundamentally, SDT distinguishes between behaviors that individuals perform freely or autonomously and those that they pursue for more or less extrinsic reasons. The theory examines why an individual acts (i.e., the level that

their motivation is more or less self-determined), how various types of motivation lead to different outcomes, and what social conditions support or undermine optimal functioning and well-being via the satisfaction of basic psychological needs.

There are different types of intrinsic and extrinsic motivation, and according to Deci and Ryan (2002) they vary along a self-determination continuum (Figure 4-2). We will start by describing the least self-determined types of motivation and move toward a portrayal of more autonomous motivational regulations (Vallerand, 2001). First are those athletes characterized by **amotivation.** These athletes have no sense of personal control with respect to their sport engagement, and there are no extrinsic (or intrinsic) reasons for doing the activity. Amotivated athletes are no longer sure of why they are playing their sport.

Next on the continuum come three forms of extrinsic motivation, with the least autonomous being **external regulation.** In this case, behavior is performed to satisfy an external demand or stems from the external rewards an athlete expects to secure. For example, an athlete might say "I'm going to practice today but only because my scholarship depends on it." With the second form of extrinsic motivation, **introjected regulation,** athletes participate because they feel they *have* to play sport. Such motivation is still extrinsic in nature; it only replaces the external source of control with an internalized contingency. For example, "I'm going to practice today because I can't deal with the guilt I will feel if I miss." With the third type of extrinsic motivation, **identified regulation,** behavior is undertaken out of free choice but as a means to an end, with the athlete often not considering the behavior itself pleasurable. For example, an athlete who wants to improve his fitness level chooses not to miss any sessions during off-season conditioning and preseason training, even though the activity is very demanding and unpleasant. At the opposite end of the self-determination continuum is the classic state of **intrinsic motivation,** in which an athlete participates in an activity for its inherent satisfactions. It is highly autonomous and represents the quintessential state of self-determination (Ryan & Deci, 2002).

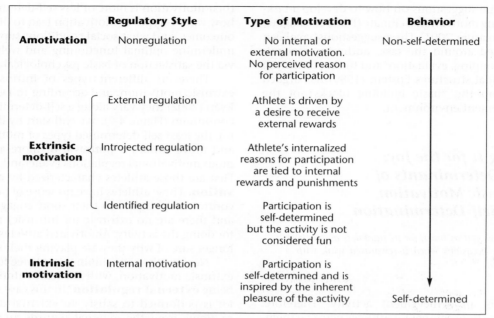

	Regulatory Style	Type of Motivation	Behavior
Amotivation	Nonregulation	No internal or external motivation. No perceived reason for participation	Non-self-determined
Extrinsic motivation	External regulation	Athlete is driven by a desire to receive external rewards	
	Introjected regulation	Athlete's internalized reasons for participation are tied to internal rewards and punishments	
	Identified regulation	Participation is self-determined but the activity is not considered fun	
Intrinsic motivation	Internal motivation	Participation is self-determined and is inspired by the inherent pleasure of the activity	Self-determined

Figure 4-2 The self-determination continuum
Source: Deci & Ryan, 1985, 1992. With kind permission of Springer Science and Business Media.

Results of a recent qualitative study by Mallett and Hanrahan (2004) with elite Australian track and field athletes offers support for Deci and Ryan's (1985) multidimensional conceptualization of extrinsic motivation. Mallett and Hanrahan found that in addition to excitement, enjoyment, a love for competing at the highest level, and a sense of relatedness with fellow athletes, less self-determined motives for participation emerged. Specifically, these elite level athletes identified money and social recognition as motives while others spoke to the job aspect of the sport. The data showed, however, that the athletes had successfully managed to internalize and integrate the more self-determined extrinsic motivation regulations into their personal values as elite level performers. This is an important finding as motivation-related differences between athletes who engage in sport for more or less self-determined reasons are likely to be great.

A fundamental tenet of self-determination theory is that individuals engaged in an activity by choice will experience better consequences than those whose participation is less autonomous. Research has found a positive relationship between autonomous motivation and higher levels of task perseverance and psychological well-being and found it to be negatively related to feelings of stress, anxiety, and self-criticism in sport (e.g., Gagné, Ryan, & Bargmann, 2003; Krane, Greenleaf, & Snow, 1997). Consistent with this line of inquiry, recent studies have suggested that SDT may provide a useful framework to understand burnout in sport. In a sample of elite level swimmers, Lemyre, Treasure, and Roberts (2006) found that over the course of a competitive swimming season, susceptibility to burnout was more likely to occur when an athlete's reasons for participating shift to a more extrinsic motivation regulation representing a loss of autonomy. Aligned with the findings of

Lemyre and colleagues, a study by Cresswell and Eklund (2005) on burnout among top amateur rugby union players showed intrinsic motivation to be negatively associated, amotivation positively associated, and extrinsic regulation not related to reported burnout.

According to SDT, whether or not an athlete has more or less self-determined reasons for engaging in sport is dependent on his or her degree of basic need satisfaction. More specifically, Deci and Ryan (2002; Ryan & Deci, 2002) propose that all of us, athletes and nonathletes alike, need to feel competent (i.e., feel sufficiently efficacious to interact effectively with the environment), autonomous (i.e., perceive we are acting according to our own volition and have options and choices), and connected with others (i.e., view relationships with important individuals as being supportive and respectful) within our various life domains. When the sport environment meets these three basic needs, we expect to witness greater self determination, investment, as well as well-being in the athletic setting (Reinboth, Duda, & Ntoumanis, 2004). However, if one or more of the needs are not satisfied, ill-being and poor functioning are hypothesized to occur.

Understanding the social contexts that facilitate athletes' motivation, performance, and well-being via the satisfaction of these needs is an important line of inquiry. To this end, research in youth (e.g., Reinboth, et al., 2004; Sarrazin et al., 2002) and amateur as well as elite sport (e.g., Adie, Duda & Ntoumanis, in press; Balaguer, Castillo, & Duda, 2008; Reinboth & Duda, 2006; Treasure, Lemyre, Kuczka, & Standage, 2007) has shown that perceptions of autonomy support (and the degree of involvement or social support offered) from the coach positively predict the satisfaction of the participants' needs for competence, relatedness, and autonomy. The satisfaction of these needs hold implications for indexes of athletes' psychological, emotional, and physical health. In terms of parental support, Gagné and associates (2003) found, in a sample of 33 female subelite gymnasts between the ages of 7 and 18 years, that perceptions of both coach and parent autonomy support and involvement influenced the quality of the gymnasts' motivation in training. Specifically, the more the gymnasts perceived their parents and coaches to be autonomy supportive and involved, the more autonomously motivated the gymnasts were. Not surprisingly, parental involvement, parental autonomy support, and autonomous motivation had effects upon the athletes' practice attendance, which supports the assertion that autonomous forms of motivation not only influence the quality of an athlete's experiences, but also his or her behavior.

Intrinsic Motivation in the Often Extrinsic World of Sport

At all competitive levels, some athletes play sport for intrinsic reasons. The sources of that intrinsic interest may vary. It may be the continuous learning that sport affords, the possibility of personal accomplishment and mastery, or the opportunity to experience pleasant sensations whether they be sensory or aesthetic (Vallerand, 2001). All in all, intrinsically motivated athletes find sport pleasurable in and of itself and are maximally motivated both quantitatively and qualitatively. Indeed, we would argue that it is most unlikely that athletes, even multimillionaires, would be able to sustain high levels of motivation and commitment throughout their careers if they did not have high levels of intrinsic motivation for engaging in their sport, particularly during periods of adversity, duress, and poor performance.

From youth sport onward, competitive athletics is dominated by extrinsic reinforcements. One can win medals and trophies. Fame and fortune may be the consequences of sport involvement for some. Talented college athletes in the United States may be rewarded with scholarships. Athletes at the professional level are paid for their sport achievements. An interesting question, therefore, is, What is the effect of extrinsic rewards on intrinsic motivation? The answer to this question is, "It depends." Athletes who are intrinsically motivated and receive extrinsic rewards are not necessarily more motivated. Indeed, research has indicated that extrinsic rewards can diminish intrinsic interest

(Deci & Ryan, 1985). Rewards, however, also can foster intrinsic motivation. What seems to be critical in sport is to consider how extrinsic reinforcements are interpreted by individual athletes. That is, what do these rewards mean to the athlete?

Extrinsic rewards have a *controlling* aspect. The use of extrinsic reinforcements by coaches and parents can provide athletes with a sense of "who is pulling the strings" in terms of their sport involvement. Rewards are detrimental to intrinsic motivation when they take away from athletes' sense of self-determination. Consider how a coach might refer to an intercollegiate athlete's scholarship and the resulting impact on that athlete's intrinsic interest in the sport. Perhaps, during the recruitment process, the coach repeatedly used the scholarship to coax the athlete to come play for his or her team. In this case the athlete's decision to play for this coach might be more likely to be perceived as contingent on this external reward rather than being self-determined. When that athlete performs poorly, if the coach says, "How can you play like that? We're paying you to perform!", the athlete might think of his or her participation as more like work and less like an inherently enjoyable activity, which may lead to motivational difficulties.

It is important to keep in mind that sometimes rewards inform us about our level of competence and worth. When receiving the reward is contingent on personally controllable aspects of performance and an athlete obtains the reward, this should increase his or her perceived ability while not undermining self-determination. As a result, it should foster intrinsic motivation. The social environment that surrounds athletes (which is created by coaches, parents, sport psychologists, peers, the media, and fans) has a huge impact on the meaning of extrinsic rewards. Whether extrinsic reinforcements are likely to be viewed as controlling or informational regarding one's ability is a function of characteristics of these environments. In sport situations that allow athletes little autonomy, the rewards are more likely to be interpreted in a controlling manner.

Implications for Practice

The literature on intrinsic motivation and self-determination in sport provides another rationale for cultivating perceived competence as well as perceived personal control among sport participants. In essence, this research indicates that perceived adequate ability and autonomy are the fuel that fire athletes' intrinsic motivation. Caution in the use (and especially the *overuse*) of extrinsic reinforcements in athletic settings is required. Extrinsic rewards must be salient to the athletes to have any influence, positive or negative, and should be used sparingly so that athletes are less likely to construct a behavior–reward contingency (i.e., "If I do this, I will get that"). This can promote an external locus of control in the athlete's sport involvement. The goals cooperatively set between coach, sport psychologist, and athlete (see Chapter 13) should be performance rather than primarily outcome based and more task-involving. They also should be realistic, that is, optimally challenging with the exertion of effort. Achieving these goals will enhance perceptions of competence and are more within the athlete's personal control than goals tied to competitive outcomes.

Finally, coaches and other significant people in athletes' lives can foster their self-determination (Reinboth et al., 2004) in other ways. We have already discussed the motivational significance of a task- versus ego-involving sport environment. Drawing from the SDT literature, it is important to try to make the athletic environment as *autonomy supportive* as possible. Considering the athletes' perspective and allowing them to make choices in training and competition events should cultivate a greater sense of personal autonomy. SDT and related research also points to the relevance of *socially supportive* sport environments (Reinboth et al., 2004). Socially supportive coaches are there to assist athletes when they need help and convey that they care about their athletes as people rather than only as sport performers. Committed and compatible coach–athlete relationships (Olympiou, Jowett, & Duda, in press) and the fostering of positive social exchanges between and cooperation among team members should also lead to an enhanced sense of relatedness and social support.

Summary

Based on both anecdotal and scientific evidence, we know that elevated (or the quantity of) motivation is relevant to sport participation. Research and the wisdom gleaned from practice also suggest that motivational factors are fundamental to maximizing that involvement in terms of its quality. Sport allows for achievement, satisfaction, enjoyment, and interest, and athletes have an opportunity to develop in body, mind, and spirit. Motivation is a key ingredient in athletes' success, and we need to recognize that the quantity *and* quality of athletes' motivation is inferred from a constellation of behaviors, emotions, and cognitive variables—not from competitive sport performance alone. Indeed, indexes of athletes' mental and physical welfare and other indicators of optimal functioning (e.g., the ability to stay focused, enjoyment of one's sport) should be taken into account when we evaluate whether they are optimally motivated or not (Duda, 2001).

Athletes are more likely to exhibit an adaptive form of motivation when they perceive they have the necessary capabilities to match the psychological and physical challenges of the sport in question, have a sense of personal autonomy, and feel connected to others in regard to their sport involvement. Motivation deficits appear when an athlete doesn't think he or she "has what it takes," perceives him or herself to be like "a pawn on a chessboard," and/or feels disenfranchised from or not respected by relevant others in the sport setting. In other words, understanding variations in sport motivation implies that we pay attention to athletes' thoughts regarding issues of competence, personal control, and connectedness to others.

With respect to feeling competent, a number of elements contribute to athletes' perceived self-efficacy. For example, by providing effective models, "setting the stage" for success when athletes are learning a new skill or starting the competitive season, and efficacy-building verbal persuasion, coaches and sport psychologists can augment the confidence level of their athletes. Through learning and mastering psychological skills (e.g., arousal regulation, imagery), athletes make it more likely that their self-efficacy is elevated and more resistant to vacillation.

When sport participants feel competent and in charge of their own destiny, their motivation to participate is more likely to be more internalized. When athletes play sport for the love of the game and other self-determined reasons, they do not need external rewards to encourage or legitimize their involvement. As a consequence, coaches, sport psychologists, and other significant social agents in athletes' lives need to be careful when considering the use of extrinsic reinforcements as a means to increase motivation. These reinforcements can become the primary incentive for participation and diminish intrinsic interest. External reward contingencies can lead to self-determination if they inform athletes about their gains in competence, are not employed in overabundance, and are provided in an autonomy-supportive manner. Otherwise, they may cause more harm than good. For optimal engagement in sport, we would like athletes to primarily participate because they like and/or value sport rather than because of extrinsic rewards or a sense of guilt or compulsion.

Notwithstanding the importance of athletes' sense of autonomy and relatedness to others, perceptions of competence are a significant predictor of adaptive, more self-determined motivational patterns among athletes. However, research on achievement goals has indicated that how athletes judge their competence level is also critical to motivational processes and outcomes. A focus on task involvement in the athletic setting has several advantages, including that the source of subjective success is more within the athlete's direct influence and is less likely to result in feelings of incompetence. Defining sport competence in terms of self-referenced effort or task mastery criteria repeatedly stokes the motivation fire.

An emphasis on ego involvement can advance an athlete's desire to excel too, but it can also have its motivational costs. First, a strong ego focus, whether approach or avoidance oriented, means that others are individuals to be surpassed or from whom an athlete should hide his or her inadequacies. Opponents and teammates become primarily reference points for feeling more or less competent, rather than cohorts with whom we learn, collaborate to improve individually and collectively, or cooperate in competition. Thus, an emphasis on ego goals can jeopardize an athlete's sense of connectedness in the sport environment.

Second, when aiming to reach ego-centered goals, the criteria for success (showing superiority or avoiding the demonstration of inferiority) are less within the athlete's control. This means that maintaining an autonomous perspective on sport achievement is endangered when the athlete's inclination is toward ego-approach or ego-avoidance goals. The criteria underlying success, in both cases, are external to the athlete and her or his performance.

Finally, no matter the degree of athletic prowess or the competitive level of the athlete, emphasizing ego goals can prove detrimental if that individual's confidence starts to waiver and he or she possesses a weak task orientation. In this instance, the athlete desperately wants to be the best, fears he or she will not be, and has no other meaningful way of redefining his or her goals and sense of competence to feel good about the performance. Because the world of sport is competitive, challenging, and conducive to competence questioning, coaches, parents, and sport psychologists should encourage task involvement in an attempt to optimize sport motivation.

Study Questions

1. What are the behavioral characteristics that reflect whether an athlete's motivation is high or low?

2. What is the difference between the quantity and quality of motivation among athletes?

3. What is self-efficacy, and why is it supposed to affect motivation?

4. Provide examples for each of the six antecedents of self-efficacy in a sport setting.

5. How do task- and ego-involved athletes differ in the way they judge their competence and perceive success in sport?

6. What are the distinctions between and consequences of being more ego-approach or ego-avoidance goal-oriented?

7. Define and give an example of a task (or mastery) approach and task avoidance goal focus.

8. Illustrate how being primarily oriented to ego goals can set the stage for performance impairment and motivational difficulties.

9. What do we mean when we say that an athlete is intrinsically motivated in contrast to extrinsically motivated?

10. Describe the process by which external rewards can influence the intrinsic motivation of athletes.

11. What are ways in which we can make a sport environment more autonomy supportive?

References

Adie, J., Duda, J. L., & Ntoumanis, N. (2008). Achievement goals, competition appraisals and the psychological and emotional welfare of sport participants. *Journal of Sport and Exercise Psychology,30, 302–322.*

Adie, J., Duda, J. L., & Ntoumanis, N. (in press). Environmental support factors, basic need satisfaction and well-being among adult team sport participants: Tests of mediation and gender invariance. *Motivation and Emotion, 32, 189–199.*

Ames, C. (1992). Achievement goals, motivational climate, and motivational processes. In G. C. Roberts (Ed.), *Motivation in sport and exercise* (pp. 161–176). Champaign, IL: Human Kinetics.

Balaguer, I., Castillo, I., & Duda, J. L. (2008). Apoyo a la autonomia satisfacción de las necesidades, motivation, y bienestar en deportistas de competición: Un analysis de la teoria de la autodeterminación (Autonomy support, needs satisfaction, motivation and well-being in competitive athletes: A test of Self-Determination Theory). *Revista de Psicología del Deporte, 17, 123–139.*

Bandura, A. (1986). *Social foundations of thought and action: A social cognitive theory.* Englewood Cliffs, NJ: Prentice Hall.

Bandura, A. (1997). *Self-efficacy. The exercise of control.* New York: W. H. Freeman.

Conroy, D. E., Elliot, A. J., & Hofer, S. M. (2003). A 2 × 2 achievement goals questionnaire for sport: Evidence for factorial invariance, temporal stability, and external validity. *Journal of Sport and Exercise Psychology, 25, 456–476.*

Conroy, D. E., Kaye, M. P., & Coatsworth, J. D. (2006). Coaching climates and the destructive effects of mastery avoidance achievement goals on situational motivation. *Journal of Sport and Exercise Psychology, 28, 69–92.*

Cresswell, S. L., & Eklund, R. C. (2005). Motivation and burnout among top amateur rugby players. *Medicine and Science in Sports and Exercise, 37, 469–477.*

Cury, F., Da Fonseca, D., Rufo, M., Peres, C., & Sarrazin, P. (2003). The trichotomous model and investment in learning to prepare a sport test: A mediational analysis. *British Journal of Educational Psychology, 73, 529–543.*

Deci, E. L., & Ryan, R. M. (1985). *Intrinsic motivation and self-determination in human behavior.* New York: Plenum.

Deci, E. L., & Ryan, R. M. (2002). (Eds.). *Handbook of self-determination research.* Rochester, NY: University of Rochester Press.

Duda, J. L. (2001). Goal perspective research in sport: Pushing the boundaries and clarifying some misunderstandings. In G. C. Roberts (Ed.), *Advances in motivation in sport and exercise* (pp. 129–182). Champaign, IL: Human Kinetics.

Duda, J. L. (2005). Motivation in sport: The relevance of competence and achievement goals. In A. J. Elliot & C. S. Dweck (Eds.), *Handbook of competence and motivation* (pp. 318–335). New York: Guildford Publications.

Duda, J.L. & & Balaguer, I. (2007). The coach-created motivational climate. In S. Jowett & D. Lavalee (Eds.), *Social psychology of sport* (pp. 117–130). Champaign, IL: Human Kinetics.

Duda, J. L., Cumming, J., & Balaguer, I. (2005). Enhancing athletes' self regulation, task involvement, and self determination via psychological skills training. In D. Hackfort, J. Duda, & R. Lider (Eds.), *Handbook of applied sport psychology research* (pp. 159–181). Morgantown, WV: Fitness Information Technology.

Dweck, C. S. (1999). *Self-theories and goals: Their role in motivation, personality, and development.* Philadelphia, PA: Taylor & Francis.

Elliot, A. J. (1999). Approach and avoidance motivation and achievement goals. *Educational Psychologist, 34,* 169–189.

Elliot, A. J., & McGregor, H. A. (2001). A 2 × 2 achievement goal framework. *Journal of Personality and Social Psychology, 80,* 501–519.

Epstein, J. (1989). Family structures and student motivation: A developmental perspective. In C. Ames & R. Ames (Eds.), *Research on motivation in education: Vol. 3* (pp. 259–295). New York: Academic Press.

Feltz, D. L., Chase, M. A., Moritz, S. E., & Sullivan, P. J. (1999). Development of the multidimensional coaching efficacy scale. *Journal of Educational Psychology, 91,* 765–776.

Feltz, D. L., Short, S., & Sullivan, P. J. (2007). *Self-efficacy in sport: Research strategies for working with athletes, teams and coaches.* Champaign, IL: Human Kinetics.

Gagne, M., Ryan, R. M., & Bargmann, K. (2003). Autonomy support and need satisfaction in the motivation and well-being of gymnasts. *Journal of Applied Sport Psychology, 15,* 372–390.

Krane, V., Greenleaf, C. A., & Snow, J. (1997). Reaching for gold and the practice of glory: A motivational case study of an elite gymnast. *The Sport Psychologist, 11,* 53–71.

Kuczka, K., & Treasure, D. C. (2005). Self-handicapping in competitive sport: Influence of the motivational climate, self-efficacy and perceived importance. *Psychology of Sport and Exercise, 6,* 539–550.

Lemyre, P-N., Treasure, D. C., & Roberts, G. C. (2006). Influence of variability of motivation and affect on elite athlete burnout susceptibility. *Journal of Sport and Exercise Psychology, 28,* 32–48.

Maddux, J. E. (1995). Self-efficacy theory: An introduction. In J. E. Maddux (Ed.), *Self-efficacy, adaptation, and adjustment* (pp. 3–33). New York: Plenum.

Mallett, C. J., & Hanrahan, S. J. (2004). Elite athletes: Why does the 'fire' burn so brightly? *Psychology of Sport and Exercise, 5,* 183–200.

Morris, R., & Kavussanu, M. Antecedents of approach-avoidance goals in sport. *Journal of Sport Sciences, 26,* 465–476.

Newton, M., & Duda, J. L. (1999). The interaction of motivational climate, dispositional goal orientation and perceived ability in predicting indices of motivation. *International Journal of Sport Psychology, 30,* 63–82.

Newton, M. L., Duda, J. L., & Yin, Z. (2000). Examination of the psychometric properties of the perceived motivational climate in sport questionnaire-2 in a sample of female athletes. *Journal of Sports Sciences, 18*, 275–290.

Nicholls, J. (1989). *The competitive ethos and democratic education.* Cambridge, MA: Harvard University Press.

Olympiou, A., Jowett, S., & Duda, J. L. (2008). The psychological interface between the coach-created motivational climate and the coach-athlete relationship in team sports. *The Sport Psychologist, 22, 423–438.*

Nien, C-L. & Duda, J. L. (2006) The effect of situationally-emphasised achievement goals and win/loss on engagement in a cycle ergometer task. Presented at Annual Conference of the British Association of Sport and Exercise Sciences, Wolverhampton, UK. ISSN 0264-0414 print /ISSN1466-447X online.

Nien, C., & Duda, J. L. (2008). Antecedents and consequences of approach and avoidance achievement goals: A test of gender invariance. *Psychology of Sport and Exercise, 9*, 352–372.

Nien, C., & Duda, J. L. (in press). Construct validity of multiple achievement goals: A multitrait-multimethod approach. *International Journal of Sport and Exercise Psychology.*

Reinboth, M., & Duda, J. L. (2004). Relationship of the perceived motivational climate and perceptions of ability to psychological and physical well-being in team sports. *The Sport Psychologist, 18*, 237–251.

Reinboth, M., Duda, J. L., & Ntoumanis, N. (2004). Dimensions of coaching behavior, need satisfaction, and the psychological and physical welfare of young athletes. *Motivation and Emotion, 28*, 297–313.

Reinboth, M., & Duda, J. L. (2006). Perceived motivational climate, need satisfaction and indices of well-being in team sports: A longitudinal perspective. *Psychology of Sport and Exercise, 7*, 269–286.

Roberts, G. C., Treasure, D. C., & Kavussanu, M. (1997). Motivation in physical activity contexts: An achievement goal perspective. In M. L. Maehr & P. R. Pintrich (Eds.), *Advances in motivation and achievement. Vol. 10* (pp. 413–447). Greenwich, CT: JAI Press.

Ryan, R. M., & Deci, E. L. (2002). An overview of self-determination theory: An organismic-dialectical perspective. In E. L. Deci & R. M. Ryan (Eds.), *Handbook of self-determination research* (pp. 3–33). Rochester, NY: University of Rochester Press.

Ryan, R. M., & Deci, E. L. (2007). Active human nature: Self-determination theory and the promotion and maintenance of sport, exercise and health. In M. S. Haggar and N. L. D. Chatzisarantis (Eds.) *Intrinsic motivation and self-determination in exercise and sport,* (pp. 1–20). Champaign, IL: Human Kinetics.

Sarrazin, P., Biddle, S. J. H., Famose, J.-P., Cury, F., Fox, K. R., & Durand, M. (1996). Goal orientations and conceptions of sport ability in children: A social cognitive approach. *British Journal of Social Psychology, 35*, 399–414.

Sarrazin, P., Vallerand, R. J., Guillet, E., Pelletier, L. G., & Cury, F. (2002). Motivation and dropout in female handballers: A 21-month prospective study. *European Journal of Social Psychology, 32*, 395–418.

Schunk, D. H. (1995). Self-efficacy, motivation, and performance. *Journal of Applied Sport Psychology, 7*, 112–137.

Treasure, D. C. (2001). Enhancing young people's motivation in physical activity. In G. C. Roberts (Ed.), *Advances in motivation in sport and exercise* (pp. 79–100). Champaign, IL: Human Kinetics.

Treasure, D. C., Lemyre, P. N., Kuczka, K. K., & Standage, M. (2007). Motivation in elite level sport: A self-determination perspective. In M. S. Haggar and N. L. D. Chatzisarantis (Eds.) *Intrinsic motivation and self-determination in exercise and sport,* (pp. 153–166). Champaign, IL: Human Kinetics.

Treasure, D. C., Monson, J., & Lox, C. (1996). Relationship between self-efficacy, wrestling performance, and affect prior to competition. *The Sport Psychologist, 10*, 73–83.

Vallerand, R. (2001). A hierarchical model of intrinsic and extrinsic motivation in sport and exercise. In G. C. Roberts (Ed.), *Advances in motivation in sport and exercise* (pp. 263–320). Champaign, IL: Human Kinetics.

Vazou, S., Ntoumanis, N., & Duda, J. L. (2007). Perceptions of peer motivational climate in youth sport: Measurement development and implications for practice. In S. Jowett & D. Lavalee (Eds.), *Social psychology of sport* (pp. 145–156). Champaign, IL: Human Kinetics.

White, S. A. (1996). Goal orientation and perceptions of the motivational climate initiated by parents. *Pediatric Exercise Science, 8*, 122–129.

The Self-Fulfilling Prophecy Theory: When Coaches' Expectations Become Reality

Thelma Sternberg Horn, *Miami University*
Curt L. Lox, *Southern Illinois University*
Francisco Labrador, *Wittenberg University*

I couldn't believe it! This kid came to the first day of Little League draft tryouts with bright purple and spiked hair! Me and all of the other coaches . . . none of us wanted him on our team. But, in the last round of draft picks, I got stuck with him. The funny thing is that by the end of the season, he turned out to be our team's Most Valuable Player! Once you got past the purple hair, the kid was a real solid baseball player.

—*Coach of a Little League Baseball Team*

In 1968 Rosenthal and Jacobson published the results of an experiment they had conducted with teachers and students in 18 elementary school classrooms. This research study, which was appropriately titled "Pygmalion in the Classroom," had been designed to determine whether the academic progress of students could actually be affected by their teachers' expectations or beliefs concerning their intellectual abilities. To investigate this issue, Rosenthal and Jacobson informed the sample of teachers that certain children in each of their classes had been identified, via scores on a standardized test of academic ability, as latent achievers or "late bloomers" who

could be expected to show big gains in academic achievement over the coming school year.

In actuality, the identified children had been selected at random from the total group, and there was no reason to expect that they would show any greater academic progress than their classmates. At the end of the school year, however, many of the targeted children, especially those in the lower elementary grades, had made greater gains intellectually than had children who were not so identified. Rosenthal and Jacobson concluded that the false information given to the teachers had led them to hold higher expectations for the targeted children and then to act in ways that would stimulate better performance from those students. Thus, the authors were suggesting that the teachers' expectations served as self-fulfilling prophecies by initiating a series of events that ultimately caused the expectations to be fulfilled.

The publication of this study elicited considerable interest among other researchers, some of whom responded with criticism of the Pygmalion study for a variety of methodological and statistical flaws (Elashoff & Snow, 1971; Thorndike, 1968). The ensuing controversy concerning the legitimacy of the self-fulfilling prophecy phenomenon stimulated an impressive amount of research during the next several decades. Although most of these investigations were oriented toward the study of expectancy effects in the academic classroom, some of them were conducted in physical education classrooms or in competitive sport contexts (e.g., Cousineau & Luke, 1990; Horn, 1984; Martinek, 1988; Papaioannou, 1995; Rejeski, Darracott, & Hutslar, 1979; Sinclair & Vealey, 1989; Solomon, 2001; Solomon & Kosmitzki, 1996; Solomon, DiMarco, Ohlson, & Reece, 1998; Solomon, Golden, Ciapponi, & Martin, 1998; Solomon, Striegel et al., 1996; Solomon, Wiegardt et al., 1996; Trouilloud, Sarrazin, Martinek, & Guillet, 2002; Trouilloud, Sarrazin, Bressoux, & Bois, 2006). Several excellent reviews of this literature have been compiled (e.g., Brophy, 1983; Good & Brophy, 2000; Harris & Rosenthal, 1985; Jussim & Harber, 2005; Martinek, 1989). Based on a thorough examination of the expectancy research, the authors of these reviews have generally concluded that teachers' expectations certainly do have the potential to affect the academic progress of individual students. However, these writers also caution that the overall effects of teacher expectations on student learning and performance appear to be relatively small, with effect sizes ranging from .1 to .3. Despite this relatively small effect size, there does appear to be considerable variability between teachers (and, by extension, coaches) in the degree to which their expectations can and do affect their own behavior as well as the learning and performance of their student-athletes. Several recent studies

(e.g., Jussim, Eccles, & Madon, 1996; Kuklinski & Weinstein, 2001; Trouilloud et al., 2006) have found, for example, that under some conditions (i.e., in some instructional situations) the impact of teachers' expectations on student learning and performance is much more powerful than the average effect size would suggest. Thus, although many teachers and coaches are not Pygmalion-prone (i.e., they do not allow their expectations to affect the performance or the achievement of their students and athletes), there certainly does appear to be a subset of teachers and coaches who exhibit expectancy biases in educational and sport settings.

Such variation among teachers and coaches implies that those who are aware of and understand the self-fulfilling prophecy phenomenon can avoid becoming Pygmalion-type coaches or teachers. Therefore, it is the purpose of this chapter to present coaches with information concerning the expectation–performance process. In the following pages, we will examine how coaches' expectations or judgments of their athletes can influence the athletes' performance and behavior and how such expectancy effects can be particularly negative for selected athletes. The chapter will conclude with a discussion of ways coaches can individualize their interactions with athletes to avoid behaving in expectancy-biased ways and thus facilitate the performance of all athletes.

The Expectation–Performance Process

According to the self-fulfilling prophecy theory, the expectations coaches form about the ability of individual athletes can serve as prophecies that dictate or determine the level of achievement each athlete will ultimately reach. Several researchers who have studied the self-fulfilling prophecy phenomenon in educational contexts (e.g., Brophy, 1983; Harris & Rosenthal, 1985; Jussim, 1986) have proposed a sequence of steps to explain how the expectation–performance connection is accomplished. These models or sequences of events can be adapted to describe how the self-fulfilling prophecy phenomenon can also occur in sport settings.

Step 1: The coach develops an expectation for each athlete that predicts the level of performance and type of behavior that athlete will exhibit over the course of the year.

Step 2: The coach's expectations influence his or her treatment of individual athletes. That is, the coach's behavior toward each athlete differs according to the coach's belief concerning the athlete's competence.

Step 3: The way in which the coach treats each athlete affects the athlete's performance and rate of learning. In addition, differential communication tells each athlete how competent the coach thinks he or she is. This information affects the athlete's self-concept, achievement motivation, and level of aspiration.

Step 4: The athlete's behavior and performance conform to the coach's expectations. This behavioral conformity reinforces the coach's original expectation, and the process continues.

We will now examine each of these steps in detail.

Step 1: Coaches Form Expectations

At the beginning of an athletic season most coaches form expectations for each athlete on their teams. These expectations are really initial judgments or assessments regarding the physical competence or sport potential of each athlete and are based on certain pieces of information available to the coach. In particular, the research indicates that teachers and coaches most often use three types, or categories, of information.

The first category contains what we can label as **person cues** and includes such informational items as the individual's socioeconomic status,

racial or ethnic group, family background, gender, physical attractiveness, body size, physique, and style of dress. The exclusive use of any or all of these person cues to form judgments about an athlete's physical competence would certainly lead to inaccurate and very stereotypic expectations (see the last section of this chapter). Fortunately, according to the research on expectancy effects, not all coaches form their expectations solely on demographic or physical appearance cues; they also use behaviorally based information. Thus, many coaches use additional **performance information** such as the athlete's scores on certain physical skills tests, the athlete's past performance achievements (e.g., previous season statistics or related sport accomplishments), as well as other teachers' or coaches' comments concerning the athlete's performance and behavior. Coaches also base initial impressions of athletes on observation of their behavior in practice or tryout situations (e.g., observation of the player's motivation, work ethic, enthusiasm, pleasantness, response to criticism, interaction with teammates).

A third and more recently identified category of information sources that coaches can and do use to evaluate their athletes' performance potential includes **psychological characteristics.** Specifically, Solomon (e.g., 2001; Becker & Solomon, 2005) has conducted a series of research studies showing that coaches' preseason expectations for their athletes' sport potential are based not only on coaches' perceptions of their athletes' physical competencies (e.g., strength, athleticism) but also on coaches' estimates of athletes' psychological abilities (e.g., coachability, role acceptance, self-discipline, maturity). In fact, Solomon's research has suggested that college coaches are very prone to using their perceptions of players' psychological characteristics to form expectations about individual athletes' performance ability.

Although the initial expectations formed by most coaches are based on information from a variety of sources, individual coaches probably differ in regard to the weight they assign to each source. That is, some coaches may particularly value the comments of other coaches in evaluating an athlete during recruitment or at the beginning of the season, whereas other coaches may place greater emphasis on the player's physical attributes (e.g., speed, size, strength, body build). Therefore, two coaches could form very different sets of expectations for the same athlete on the basis of what sources of information each valued most.

Exercise:

Assume that you have just been appointed to be the new varsity coach for a high school soccer team. Because you are new to the school, you know very little about the players who will try out for your team. However, your assistant coach has been in the program for several years and knows all of the players. Team tryout days arrive, and you realize that you will have to make some difficult cuts. How much will you rely on your own observation of the players' performance and behavior during tryouts rather than on the feedback provided by your assistant coach based on her or his years of work with these players?

It obviously follows, then, that a coach's initial judgment of an athlete may be either accurate or inaccurate depending on the sources of information used. Accurate assessments of a player's competence generally pose no problem as they usually do not adversely affect the player's subsequent performance. However, inaccurate expectations (i.e., expectations that are either too high or too low) that are *also* inflexible can be very disruptive for athletes and can interfere with their optimal athletic progress. Consider, for example, the coach who misjudges a particular athlete at the beginning of the season and falsely believes that individual to be less competent than he or she really is. If the coach's expectation or judgment is flexible (i.e., changes when the athlete demonstrates better performance than expected), then the initial false expectation does not cause a problem. In contrast, a coach who

is very inflexible and resistant to modifying her or his initial beliefs may well "see" only what she or he expects to see from that player. That is, all evidence of skill errors by the athlete will reinforce the coach's belief that the athlete is incompetent, and the coach will either ignore all skill success or simply consider it to be "lucky" and not indicative of the athlete's sport skill. Solomon and her colleagues (e.g., Solomon & Kosmitzki, 1996; Solomon, Golden et al., 1998) have recently referred to this characteristic of coaches as "perceptual flexibility" or, by extension, "perceptual inflexibility." Coaches who develop expectations of players at the beginning of the season that are not flexible or fluid tend to perceive individual athletes' performance and behavior from a very rigid perspective. That is, these coaches will perceive in their athletes' performance and behavior exactly what they expect to see. This type of situation is illustrated in Example 1. In this example the coach's initial expectations or judgments concerning the relative basketball ability of both Chris and Robert are formed on the basis of information provided by a colleague. These initial expectations, which may *not* be accurate, cause the coach to *perceive* the two players' performance differently. Such differential perceptions, in turn, affect the way the coach reacts or responds to that player. This type of situation leads to the second step in the sequence of events composing the self-fulfilling prophecy phenomenon.

Step 2: Coaches' Expectations Affect Their Behavior

The expectations that coaches typically form for each athlete at the beginning of an athletic season do not necessarily or automatically act as self-fulfilling prophecies. Expectations do, however, have the potential for doing so if they affect the coaches' treatment of their athletes.

Much of the research on the self-fulfilling prophecy phenomenon in competitive sport situations has focused on this issue by asking the crucial question, "Do coaches treat athletes they believe have high ability (i.e., high-expectancy individuals) differently from athletes they believe

Example 1

The new coach of a junior high basketball team is informed by the principal that the team has two point guards returning from last year. The first player, Chris, is described as a talented athlete, and the other player, Robert, is portrayed as having been a member of last year's squad "only because he was the coach's son." At practice the first day, Robert dribbles fast up the court but then loses control of the ball. The coach, who has developed the expectation that Robert is not a talented athlete, sees this error as proof of Robert's lack of innate basketball ability. Thus, the coach responds by telling Robert to slow down. Moments later, Chris also mishandles the ball during the same dribbling drill. The coach, who believes Chris to be an excellent dribbler, assumes that the error occurred because the basketball is either worn and slippery or overinflated (and thus difficult to dribble). Based on this perception, the coach orders that the ball not be used again and that Chris should get another ball and try again.

to each athlete, and (c) the frequency and type of performance feedback given to each athlete.

In the first behavioral category, **frequency and quality of coach–athlete interactions,** a Pygmalion-prone coach typically shows fewer tendencies to initiate interpersonal contact (either of a social or a skill-related nature) with athletes he or she believes to be less skilled. As a result, the coach spends significantly more time with athletes who are highly skilled (see Example 2). In addition, the quality of coach–athlete interactions may also differ, with high-expectancy players being shown more warmth and positive affect (e.g., smiling, head nodding, and personal contact) than their low-expectancy teammates.

Perhaps of greater consequence is the differential treatment that high- and low-expectancy players may receive in regard to the **quantity and quality of instruction.** If a coach firmly believes certain players on her or his team do not have the requisite athletic competencies to be successful (i.e., the low-expectancy players), that coach may, first of all, reduce the amount of material or skills those players are expected to learn, thus establishing a lower standard of performance for them. Second, the coach may allow

have low ability (i.e., low-expectancy individuals)?" Generally this question has been studied by observing and recording the type, frequency, and quality of instructional behavior coaches exhibit toward individual athletes. Again, the overall conclusion from this research (see studies by Horn, 1984; Rejeski et al., 1979; Sinclair & Vealey, 1989; Solomon & Kosmitzki, 1996; Solomon, DiMarco et al., 1998; Solomon, Golden et al., 1998; Solomon, Striegel et al., 1996) indicates that *some* coaches do indeed show differential instructional behaviors to these two groups of athletes. Applying the results of this research to any specific athletic setting, we could expect the Pygmalion-type coach to show differential behavior to high- and low-expectancy athletes in regard to (a) the frequency and quality of interactions the coach has with the individual athletes, (b) the quantity and quality of instruction given

Example 2

Ashton and Kari, who are teammates on their school's varsity basketball team, stay after practice to play a game of one-on-one. Their coach comes over to watch. When Ashton (a high-expectancy athlete) executes a successful fake and drive, the coach responds with approval but also stops the game to provide Ashton with further instruction (i.e., what she should do in a similar situation if the weak side defender had moved across the key). Later when Kari (a low-expectancy player) executes the same successful fake and drive, the coach responds with approval only ("Good move, Kari") but then goes on to show Ashton how she should have prevented or defended against such an offensive move.

the low-expectancy players less time in practice drills. As a result, these athletes may spend relatively more practice time in non-skill-related activities such as shagging balls, waiting in line, and keeping score. Finally, the coach may be less persistent in helping low-expectancy athletes learn a difficult skill. The Pygmalion-prone coach tends to give up on a low-expectancy player who fails after two or three attempts to learn a new skill but will persist in working with a high-expectancy player who is having the same difficulty (see Example 3).

In addition to differences in the quality of instruction, researchers have also found differences in the **type and frequency of feedback** that coaches give to high- and low-expectancy players. One of the primary ways coaches respond differently to individual athletes is in their use of praise and criticism. Some researchers investigating expectancy issues in the physical education or sport setting (e.g., Martinek & Johnson, 1979; Martinek & Karper, 1982; Rejeski et al., 1979; Solomon, DiMarco et al., 1998; Solomon, Striegel et al., 1996) have found that teachers and coaches give high-expectancy students and athletes more reinforcement and praise after a successful performance than they do low-expectancy individuals. In contrast, other researchers have found that low-expectancy students and athletes are the ones who receive proportionately more reinforcement (Horn, 1984; Martinek, 1988). However, as Horn noted in her discussion, the higher frequency of reinforcement or praise given by coaches and teachers to these low-expectancy individuals may actually be qualitatively suspect because the reinforcement is often given inappropriately (i.e., given for a mediocre performance or for success at a very easy task) (see Example 4). Therefore, it appears that Pygmalion-prone coaches may (a) provide low-expectancy athletes with less frequent reinforcement and (b) give them less appropriate and less beneficial feedback after successful performances.

Observation of teachers' and coaches' feedback also has revealed differences in the amount of corrective or technical instruction given. In the sport setting such differential treatment may be especially evident in the feedback coaches provide their athletes following a performance. As illustrated in Example 5, high-expectancy performers receive informational and corrective feedback that tells them how to improve their performance. In contrast, low-expectancy performers receive a positive communication from the coach but no accompanying technical information to tell them what they can do to improve their performance. These differences in feedback responses may well be due to the different expectations the coach holds for the various athletes. For example, because the coach fully expects Jared's performance to improve, he is more apt

Example 3

During a practice scrimmage, Ashton (the high-expectancy player in Example 2) is having problems running a particularly difficult offensive pattern. The coach stops the team drill and spends 3 or 4 minutes helping Ashton learn the pattern. When Kari (the low-expectancy athlete) later evidences the same difficulty, the coach removes her from the scrimmage team by saying to another player, "Joci, come here and take Kari's place. Let's see if you can run this play."

Example 4

During the course of a varsity volleyball match, a hitter approaches the net for a spike. Seeing her opponents put up a single block, she reaches out to "tip" the ball around the block. No point is scored, but the ball is kept in play. The athlete, who is a high-expectancy player, is told by her coach, "OK, Keisha, at least you kept the ball in play. But next time you go up against a single block, hit the ball. Your spike is good enough to get it through that block." If, however, a low-expectancy player executes the same play, the Pygmalion-type coach might respond with approval only: "Great work, Kara, you kept the ball away from the block. That was smart."

Example 5

Jared and Charlie have both joined an age-group swimming team. Although both swimmers begin the season at the same level of performance, their coach has very high expectations for Jared's improvement and ultimate success because of his "natural" physical attributes. The coach does not have the same high expectations for Charlie. At the first meet of the season, both swimmers take fifth place in their respective events. The coach responds to Jared's performance by telling him that he can considerably reduce his time if he improves his technique on the turns. The coach concludes with the comment, "We'll work on those turns all next week so you'll be ready for the next meet." In contrast, the coach responds to Charlie's fifth place performance by saying, "Good job, Charlie. Hang in there."

to provide Jared with technical information to help him achieve skill success. However, the low expectations the coach holds for Charlie lead the coach to believe that corrective instruction may be fruitless and certainly not useful for Charlie.

Finally, coaches may also differ in the type of attribution they use to explain the cause of the high- and low-expectancy athletes' successful or unsuccessful performances. Although this aspect of performance feedback has received very little research attention, we certainly might speculate that a coach's beliefs concerning the competence or incompetence of selected players on his or her team would induce that coach to verbalize different attributions for the athletes' performance outcome. For instance, the coach in Example 6 holds different perceptions or expectations concerning the physical competence of Jonathan (a high-expectancy player) and P.J. (a low-expectancy player). These expectations lead the coach to attribute these players' performance to different causes. When P.J. reaches first base safely, the coach immediately, and in this case verbally, attributes that success to the opposing team's error (i.e., a lucky break for P.J.). In comparison, the coach verbally attributes the same

Example 6

During a baseball game, P.J. (a low-expectancy athlete) hits a pitched ball sharply toward the left side of the infield. The shortstop makes a nice backhanded move for the ball and fields it. Although he then slightly mishandles it, he does throw it hard to first for a close play, with the runner (P.J.) being called safe. The coach comments, "What a break, P.J.! We were lucky he [the shortstop] bobbled it, or you would have been out." However, in a similar situation with Jonathan (a high-expectancy player) as the batter/runner, the coach responds to the same performance by exclaiming, "Way to hit the hole, Jonathan, and great speed! You beat the throw again!"

performance by Jonathan to Jonathan's ability (i.e., his batting prowess and speed). Similarly, the coach's response to these athletes' performance errors may also be affected by the coach's judgment of each player's ability. In Example 7 the coach attributes Jonathan's lack of success in stealing a base to poor positioning and thus suggests that the performance can be corrected. The coach attributes a similar failure by P.J. to P.J.'s lack of ability (i.e., his lack of speed).

Example 7

Later in the game described in Example 6, Jonathan (the high-expectancy player) attempts to steal second without the coach's giving a steal sign. Jonathan is easily thrown out. As he reaches the dugout, the coach tells him, "Good try, Jonathan. That would have been a good pitch to steal on, but you didn't have a big enough lead to go. Next time, you should . . . ." When P.J. (the low-expectancy player) attempts the same performance, the coach angrily responds, "What are you doing out there? I didn't tell you to go . . . you're too slow to steal second, especially on that catcher."

As the previous examples illustrate, coaches may indeed treat their high- and low-expectancy athletes differently. However, we need to exercise caution in regard to these observed differential coaching behaviors. That is, we must not jump to the conclusion that it is essential for coaches to treat all athletes on their teams in exactly the same way. Because athletes differ in their skills as well as in their personalities, coaches are well advised to individualize their instructional behavior to accommodate the uniquenesses of each athlete. Therefore, it is important at this point to emphasize that observable differences in a coach's behavior toward individual athletes on his or her team do not automatically imply that the coach is acting in a biased manner and that the athletes' progress will be impeded. If the differences in the coach's behavior are designed to and actually do facilitate the performance and achievement of *each* athlete, then such differential coaching behavior is appropriate. However, if the differential treatment an athlete or a group of athletes *consistently* receives from their coach in practices and games limits the athletes' ability or opportunity to learn, then such differential coaching behavior is dysfunctional, and the coach's expectations may be serving as self-fulfilling prophecies.

Step 3: Coaches' Behavior Affects Athletes' Performance and Behavior

The third step in the sequence of events in the self-fulfilling prophecy phenomenon occurs when a coach's expectancy-biased treatment of an individual athlete affects that athlete's performance and psychological growth. It is easy to understand how the biased behavior described in the preceding section is likely to maximize the athletic progress of high-expectancy athletes while limiting the achievements of their low-expectancy teammates. Players who are *consistently* given less effective and less intensive instruction or who are allowed less active time in practice drills will not show the same degree of skill improvement as their teammates who are given optimal learning opportunities. In Examples 2 and 3, Ashton and Kari are obviously not

being given the same quality of instruction. If this instructional behavior is typical of the treatment these athletes receive from their coach over the season, we might well anticipate that after a certain period of time Ashton's basketball skills will be considerably better than Kari's. Their coach will attribute these skill differences to what she believes to be the innate differences in Ashton's and Kari's basic athletic talent. Given the observed variation in the coach's instructional behavior toward these two athletes, it is equally likely that the coach's original expectation or judgment concerning each athlete's sport potential actually *determined,* rather than just *predicted,* the level of achievement that Ashton and Kari reached. The coach's expectations, then, served as self-fulfilling prophecies by setting in motion a series of events (i.e., consistent differences in the quality of instruction) that ultimately caused the original expectations to be fulfilled.

In addition to the negative effects that a coach's biased instructional behavior has on an athlete's rate of learning and level of achievement, such behavior can also affect the athlete's psychological growth. Recent research in sport psychology has demonstrated that the type of instructional behaviors a coach exhibits in games and in practices is correlated with, and can actually cause, changes in athletes' self-concept, perceived competence, intrinsic motivation, and level of competitive trait anxiety over a season (see reviews of this work by Chelladurai, 2007; Duda & Balaguer, 2007; Horn, 2008; and Mageau & Vallerand, 2003). This association between coaches' behavior and changes in athletes' self-perceptions, intrinsic motivation, and anxiety is quite consistent with several developmental, cognitive, and social psychological theories (e.g., Bandura, 1997; Eccles, 2005; Harter, 1999; Ryan & Deci, 2000; Vallerand, 2007; Weiner, 1992) that suggest that the evaluation or feedback adults provide is an important source of information that children and adolescents use to determine how competent or incompetent they are.

In the athletic setting, then, the type of feedback coaches give to individual athletes may affect the athletes' self-perceptions (e.g., their self-confidence, self-efficacy, and anxiety) by communicating to the athletes how competent or skilled the coach thinks they are. Occasionally, of course, the coach communicates this evaluative information directly to the athletes. More commonly, however, coaches communicate their judgments or beliefs concerning the athletes' abilities in more subtle or indirect ways. Specifically, the coach's reinforcement patterns (i.e., the level of performance or type of behavior the coach rewards) provide athletes with information that tells them how skilled the coach thinks they are. In Example 4, Keisha and Kara have demonstrated the same level of performance, but each receives a different response from the coach. This differential feedback may be communicating to these athletes what standard of performance each is expected to achieve. Kara, who is clearly reinforced for that level of performance, may be receiving information telling her that she is at the maximum level she is capable of achieving. Keisha, however, is led to believe her performance, although acceptable, can and should be improved because she has the requisite skills to perform at a higher level.

Correspondingly, the amount and frequency of corrective instruction a coach provides after a skill error may also tell each athlete how competent or skillful the coach thinks he or she is. In Example 5, for instance, the coach responds to Jared's fifth-place performance with corrective feedback, thus overtly telling him that his performance can be improved with effort and covertly supplying him with the perception that he is capable of a higher level of skill. In contrast, although the coach gives Charlie a positive and encouraging response for a similar level of performance, the coach does not provide Charlie with the additional information to tell him that he can improve his performance and that he is capable of achieving at a higher level. Thus, the coach has indirectly communicated his expectations or judgments concerning each athlete's level of ability. In summary, then, the evaluative feedback coaches give to individual athletes is indeed providing the athletes with information concerning their competence. Certainly the differential feedback that low- and high-expectancy athletes receive from Pygmalion-prone coaches

may affect the athletes' perceptions or beliefs concerning their own skill competence.

Similarly, there is reason to believe that the differential feedback received by high- and low-expectancy athletes would also affect these athletes' levels of anxiety in sport contexts. Specifically, researchers (e.g., Smith, Smoll, & Barnett, 1995) have found that athletes who receive higher frequencies of technically instructive and corrective feedback, delivered by coaches in a positive and encouraging way, may have fewer problems with performance anxiety in sport contexts than do athletes who receive punishment-oriented or no corrective feedback. Thus, the differential type of feedback that high- and low-expectancy athletes receive from their coaches not only may affect the athletes' perceptions of their sport ability but also may have an effect on the degree of anxiety they will experience in performance situations.

Finally, as noted in the previous section, coaches also may affect their athletes' self-perceptions by the attributions they make for their athletes' performance. Such attributions provide each athlete with information concerning his or her competence. When a coach attributes an athlete's successful performance to the athlete's innate ability (e.g., Example 6) the athlete develops a high expectancy for future success and a positive attitude toward the sport activity. In contrast, when a coach attributes successful performance to luck, the attribution does not encourage an athlete to believe that he or she can attain the same performance in the future and provides the athlete with no information concerning personal competence. Similarly, a coach who attributes an athlete's skill error to lack of effort, lack of practice, or some other athlete-controlled factor will do more to facilitate future motivation, decrease feelings of helplessness, and encourage a positive attitude than attributing the athlete's failure to lack of ability. In Example 7, Jonathan's performance failure is attributed by his coach to incorrect skill execution (a controllable and correctable error), whereas P.J.'s failure is attributed to his lack of speed (a less controllable and less correctable cause). The differential messages carried via these coaching communications may affect each athlete's future performance and motivation.

Step 4: The Athlete's Performance Conforms to the Coach's Expectations

The final step in the chain of events in the self-fulfilling prophecy phenomenon occurs when the athlete's performance and behavior conform to the coach's original expectation. This behavioral conformity is, in itself, a very important component in the chain of events because it reinforces for the coach that his or her initial judgment of the athlete was accurate. This confirms for the Pygmalion-prone coach that he or she is a very astute judge of sport potential and can recognize true athletic talent at the beginning of the season. Unfortunately, such "success" may reinforce or intensify the coach's Pygmalion tendencies.

As a final point in regard to the self-fulfilling prophecy process, it is important to recognize that *not* all athletes allow their coach's behavior or expectations to affect their performance or psychological responses. Just as all coaches are not Pygmalion prone, so, too, all athletes are not susceptible to the self-fulfilling prophecy. Earlier research in the coaching effectiveness area (as summarized by Horn, 2008) has suggested that the self-perceptions of some athletes are more easily affected by their coach's evaluative feedback than the self-perceptions of their teammates are. It is likely that individuals who tend to be very dependent on their coach's feedback to provide them with information concerning their competence would be most easily "molded" by their coach's expectations. In contrast, those athletes who are resistant to the Pygmalion process may not use the coach's feedback as a sole source of information to tell them how competent they are. If these resistant athletes do receive biased feedback from a coach, they may respond by discounting that information and using other informational sources (e.g., feedback from peers, parents, or other adults) to form their perceptions of how competent or skilled they are. Research from the educational psychology literature (e.g., Madon, Jussim, & Eccles, 1997) has suggested that high-achieving students in academic classrooms are almost completely invulnerable to negative teacher perceptions/expectations, whereas their lower-achieving classmates are very susceptible to their teachers' expectations (i.e., their academic achievement over the school year was significantly predicted by their teachers' initial expectations of their academic potential). Assuming that such interindividual variability in susceptibility to adult expectations also occurs in the athletic setting, it would be reasonable to believe that there are some athletes (perhaps the higher-achieving ones) who will be resistant to their coaches' expectations. Thus, even if a coach shows biased treatment of an individual athlete, the self-fulfilling prophecy process will short-circuit if the athlete is resistant to the coach's bias. It is important to note, then, that all four steps in the sequence are essential if the self-fulfilling prophecy phenomenon is to occur in the athletic setting.

Sport Applications

The research and theory detailed in the previous pages describe the processes by which coaches' expectations and behavior can affect the performance and psychological growth of individual athletes on their team. Some of this information is based on research work that has been conducted in the academic classroom and that is then applied to the sport domain. Although these two instructional contexts certainly have many similarities, some factors make each domain unique. This section discusses four expectancy-related issues that are particularly relevant to the sport context.

Expectancy Effects in Youth Sport Programs

Although Pygmalion-prone coaches can almost certainly be found at any level within the sport system (e.g., from youth sports through the professional level), the negative effects of a coach's expectancy-biased behavior may be particularly devastating at the younger age levels for three reasons. First, because children's initial experience with any particular sport is typically through a youth sport program, their interest in and enjoyment of that particular activity is being formed. Ineffective or expectancy-biased feedback from the coach during these early years may cause children to develop extremely negative feelings about that activity and subsequently to discontinue participation before they have had an opportunity to learn the skills.

Second, a series of research studies recently conducted with children ranging in age from 8 to 18 years (see summary of this research by Horn, 2004) shows that the self-perceptions of younger children (those under the age of 10) are based, to a large extent, on the feedback of significant adults. That is, these children are very much apt to evaluate how "good" or "bad" they are at a sport or physical activity based on what their parents, coaches, or teachers say to them. For example, a child in this age range is apt to say, "I know that I am a good runner because my mom says I am" or "I don't think that I'm a very good soccer player because my coach is always yelling at me." Thus, for children under 10, the feedback of a coach can have significant effects on the child's self-esteem and self-confidence in that sport.

Third, based on research information obtained from the motor development literature (e.g., Thomas, Gallagher, & Thomas, 2001), children in the early and midchildhood years (4 to 10 years) should be acquiring a variety of fundamental motor and sport-specific skills. Specifically, children should be learning to throw, catch, kick, jump, and run using mature and efficient movement patterns. In addition, this is a good time for children to learn some fundamental sport-specific skills (e.g., dribbling, passing, trapping). If children do not acquire these fundamental motor and sport skills during the formative years, it will be difficult for them to participate with any degree of skill in the more competitive sport programs available to children after the age of 10 years. Because Pygmalion-prone coaches tend to act in ways that impede the skill progress of their low-expectancy players, these children will be prevented from learning the necessary fundamental motor and sport

skills. This, in turn, serves as a limiting factor in regard to their subsequent participation in the more advanced sport programs. Thus, again, the negative effects of a coach's expectancy-biased behavior may be particularly devastating in the early and midchildhood years.

Maturational Rates and the Sport Expectancy Process

A second expectancy issue, which is related to the first, is that children vary considerably in the rate at which they grow and mature. Children who mature early will reach full physical maturation 2 to 3 years earlier than children who mature at a more average rate. Furthermore, children who mature late will not reach full physical maturation until 2 or 3 years later than their average maturing peers and 4 to 5 years later than the early maturing child. As a result, within any given chronological age group, there will likely be considerable variation in children's physical status. Such differences in maturational rates may be a factor that not only affects children's and adolescents' performance and behavior in sport situations but also causes coaches to hold differential expectancies for individual athletes.

On a seventh-grade basketball team, for example, all boys may be between 12 and 13 years old chronologically, but they may differ in terms of their biological and physical status. The early maturing 12-year-old boy may be at a stage of physical development comparable to that of the average 14- or 15-year-old boy. In contrast, a late maturing 12-year-old may be at a stage of development comparable to that of a 9- or 10-year-old boy. Given such obvious differences in rate of maturation, the early maturer's physical and motor abilities are likely to be superior to those of the late maturer. It is important to know, however, that the late maturing boy's disadvantage is only temporary—he will eventually catch up to and may even surpass his early maturing peers in physical size and athletic performance. Unfortunately, however, because the late maturing boy in many youth sport programs is falsely diagnosed by unwitting coaches to be a low-expectancy athlete (i.e., a child who is not now and never will be physically competent), that child may not receive optimal instruction, adequate playing time, or effective performance feedback and may even, in fact, be cut from the program. Thus, even though the late maturing boy could develop into a proficient athlete, he may be inhibited from doing so because of expectancy-biased coaching behaviors. Therefore, we should consider late maturing boys to be at an especially high risk for negative expectancy effects.

A more complicated pattern of expectancy bias may occur for girls in sport. Although early maturing girls may have the same advantages as early maturing boys during the childhood years (before the age of 12), the reverse may be true after this age. That is, early maturing girls could begin experiencing the effects of a negative expectancy bias on the part of their coaches around or after the time that these girls reach puberty. This could occur because some of the physical changes that girls experience as they reach puberty (e.g., breast development, menarche, increase in hip width, increase in body fat) are typically not perceived in our society as conducive to sport proficiency. Thus, some coaches may perceive or believe that these physical changes, which occur at an earlier age for the early maturing girls, will be detrimental to their sport proficiency and performance. In addition, gender-biased coaches may believe girls who are becoming more "womanly" in appearance may no longer be interested in sport, because such gender-biased individuals still perceive participation in sport as antithetical to femininity. Thus, early maturing girls (i.e., girls who reach puberty earlier than their female peers) may suddenly be seen by gender-biased coaches as less physically competent and less interested in sport participation.

This argument is consistent with the biosocial hypothesis developed by Malina (1994, 2002) to explain the correlational relationship that links girls' participation in intensive sport training with a delay in age of menarche. As Malina suggests, coaches may use a linear body build (narrow hips, flat chest, relatively low body fat), which is more typical of a late rather than an early maturing girl, to select athletes into particular sport programs such as gymnastics, dance, track, volleyball, swimming, and diving. Thus, early maturing girls who no longer exhibit a linear build may either be cut from sport programs once they reach puberty or be socialized out of sport (i.e., be encouraged to turn to more feminine activities). It is the early maturing girl, then, who may be at especially high risk for negative expectancy effects once she reaches (early) puberty.

Another issue relating to maturation and expectancy effects in the sport setting concerns the concept of "developmental vulnerability." Specifically, recent research in the educational setting (e.g., Rudolph, Lambert, Clark, & Kurlakowsky, 2001; Valeski & Stipek, 2001) has indicated that children and adolescents may be more susceptible to socioenvironmental factors at particular times in their educational careers. These particularly vulnerable times appear to be at important transition points (e.g., from kindergarten to first grade and from elementary to middle or junior high school). The increased vulnerability of children and adolescents to experience academic or psychological problems at these time points is likely because of the uncertainty, unfamiliarity, or novelty that are characteristic of a new achievement situation as well as the increased demands that are placed on them in the new (higher level) achievement context (see arguments on this point by Eccles, Wigfield, & Schiefele, 1998 and Jussim & Harber, 2005). Applying this concept to expectancy effects in the sport setting, we might hypothesize that individual children may be more susceptible to their coaches' expectancy-biased behavior when such children make transitions from the recreational to the more select or competitive level (i.e., from sport programs in which everyone makes the team to programs where tryouts are held and only select players make the team). Similarly, transitions from middle school or junior high programs to high school sport programs, and, eventually, from junior varsity to varsity programs, may result in greater susceptibility of children/adolescents to their coaches' expectancy-biased behavior.

Exercise

You have just been appointed director of an age-group youth sport program for a particular sport. This program provides nonschool competitive sport opportunities for children from ages 8 to 16 years. The previous director of this program had used an ability tracking system. That is, at each age level, children had been assigned, based on a tryout system, into one of three ability-differential teams: (a) a high competitive, travel-oriented team comprised of the best athletes at that age level; (b) a moderate-level competitive team that competed at the local or regional level; and (c) a low competitive team that was open to all those who tried out and that was primarily instructional in nature. Will you continue this practice of ability tracking children/adolescents at each age group? What are the arguments for and against such a practice? Should your decision on this issue be different for different age groups?

Sport Stereotypes and the Expectancy Process

A third expectancy issue concerns selected stereotypes that are related to the performance and behavior of individuals in sport situations. The two most pervasive stereotypes in the sport setting are those concerning ethnicity and gender. In regard to ethnicity, it is commonly believed that African American individuals are "naturally" gifted in particular sports and physical activities (e.g., basketball, sprinting events). Although this may initially appear to be a positive stereotype, it has certain negative ramifications for those African American children who are not "as good as they are supposed to be." Coaches may perceive an African American child who, for example, does not score *higher* than his Euro-American (white) peers on a series of sport skills tests as either lazy or "untalented." That is, even though he may have performed as well as his Euro-American peers, he is perceived by the

Pygmalion-prone coach to be less than adequate. Such perceptions may be reflected in the fact that African American athletes in some programs must either make the starting lineup or be cut from the team (i.e., they will not make the team unless they are significantly more talented than the other athletes). Thus, African American children may be held to a higher standard of performance in these sports because of the stereotypes concerning their physical prowess.

Another aspect of ethnically biased stereotypes involves perceptions concerning athletes' mental capabilities. Specifically, although African American athletes are perceived to be very competent in regard to physical capabilities (e.g., speed, reaction time, strength), Euro-American athletes are perceived to be better in regard to mental capabilities (i.e., they are believed to be better decision makers and leaders). Pygmalion-prone coaches who subscribe to such ethnic stereotypes will act in ways that reflect these biased beliefs. Thus, African American athletes may not be considered for sport leadership or decision-making positions (e.g., football quarterback, basketball point guard, volleyball setter, baseball catcher). Even if they are given the opportunity to practice or play at such positions, their "mistakes" will be perceived as evidence of their innate inability to perform well in these roles rather than as an indicator that they may need more instruction or practice to acquire the necessary skills.

The situations described in the previous paragraphs only illustrate *some* of the ethnicity-related stereotypes that abound in the sport context. There are certainly many more (see, for example, Brooks & Althouse, 2000). The examples given in the previous paragraphs show that expectations based on ethnicity are not accurate and certainly can inhibit the progress of individual athletes or groups of athletes. Support for this idea is evident in the educational psychology literature where researchers (e.g., Jussim et al., 1996) have found that teacher expectations or teacher stereotypes have greater effects on the academic achievement of African American students and students from lower socioeconomic backgrounds than they do on children who are not from these two backgrounds. Other support for the effect of negative racial stereotypes on academic and athletic performance comes from the work of Steele (1997; Steele & Aronson, 1995), Stone (2002; Stone, Perry, & Darley, 1997; Stone, Lynch, Sjomeling, & Darley, 1999), and Beilock (Beilock & McConnell, 2004).

In regard to gender stereotypes, it is commonly believed that females are less physically capable than males. Although these beliefs are based to some extent on research showing that postpubertal males and females do differ on selected physical characteristics (e.g., height, body composition, limb length) (Malina, 1994, 2002; Ransdell, 2002), they also are based on inaccurate stereotypes concerning the performance and behavior of females. In particular, the available research indicates that there are very few physiological or biological differences between boys and girls prior to puberty (particularly before 10 years of age) (Malina, 1994, 2002). Despite these research findings, many teachers, coaches, and parents continue to believe that girls from early childhood on are not "naturally talented" in the physical activity area. Because of such stereotyped beliefs, girls in coeducational youth sport programs may be more apt to be treated as low-expectancy athletes. That is, their coaches may give them less instruction in practice and less playing time in games. When they do play in games, they may be relegated to positions where they are inactive for large amounts of time. (For interesting detail regarding gendered behavior in children's sport contexts, see recent observational studies by Landers & Fine, 1996, and Messner, 2000.) Even on all-girl teams, a coach's stereotyped belief that girls are not and cannot be physically competent may cause her or him to establish lower standards of performance for them and to give greater amounts of inappropriate praise (i.e., to accept and praise mediocre performance accomplishments). Again, such expectancy-biased behavior is particularly negative during the childhood years because girls may then be less apt to develop the necessary fundamental motor and sport skills. As indicated earlier in this section, failure to acquire these skills during the childhood years serves as

an inhibitor of sport performance in the post-pubertal years. Thus, as several researchers and writers have suggested, any differences that are observed in the physical performance capabilities of postpubertal males and females may be due as much to inadequate instruction, participation, and training during the childhood years as to actual physiological or biological differences between males and females (Smoll & Schutz, 1990; Thomas & French, 1985). Furthermore, even if there are post-pubertal gender differences in strength, speed, power, and endurance, this does not necessarily mean that all girls are less strong or less fast than all boys. Thus, coaches who develop expectations concerning the physical competencies of children and adolescents based solely or primarily on gender ignore the reality that there is as much (or more) variation within each gender as there is between genders. Thus, coaches' expectations should be based to a greater extent on characteristics specific to each individual child rather than on the ethnic group or biological gender to which that child belongs.

The information provided in this section clearly indicates that selected children may be more apt to be perceived as low-expectancy athletes by their coaches than are other children. The specific concern here is that because such expectancies are based either on inaccurate stereotypes (e.g., ethnicity and gender) or on coaches' lack of knowledge concerning the physical growth and maturation process, these expectancies have the potential to seriously inhibit children's sport development. Thus, we need to consider such children as at greater risk for negative expectancy effects than their peers.

Coaches' Personal Characteristics, Their Leadership Styles, and the Sport Expectancy Process

As noted earlier in this chapter, the research conducted to date suggests that not all coaches are expectancy biased. Given this variability in coaches' tendency to be Pygmalion prone, it would seem to be of interest to determine what types of coaches are most apt to fall into this category. That is, what characteristics distinguish those coaches who act in expectancy-biased ways from coaches who do not do so?

Many characteristics of coaches could be investigated as possible correlates or predictors of expectancy-biased behavior. Based on the research concerning gender stereotypes in sport settings (see, for example, Griffin, 1998; Harry, 1995; Krane, 1996; and Messner, 1992), it might be hypothesized that coaches of male athletes who hold strong gender-stereotyped and homophobic beliefs would act very positively toward the players on their team who "fit" the masculine stereotype (i.e., those who have broad shoulders, high muscle mass, and who act in aggressive ways) while acting less positively toward the players who do not "fit" this masculine stereotype (i.e., players who have a more linear body shape and lower amounts of muscle mass, and who do not exhibit aggressive behaviors). Similarly, gender-biased and homophobic coaches of female athletes might act more positively to the athletes on their team who conform to the "feminine" ideal (i.e., female athletes who have longer hair, have boyfriends, wear makeup off the court) than to those athletes who do not conform to this image.

From the cognitive psychology (e.g., Skinner, 1996) theoretical literature as well as from the teacher education research literature (e.g., Cooper, 1979; Guskey, 1981), it appears that we might want to examine individual coaches' perceptions or locus of control with regard to their job responsibilities. That is, coaches may differ in how much they perceive that they personally can control the performance outcomes their teams can achieve. Coaches who possess an external locus of control would believe that the degree to which their teams will be successful over a season (i.e., have a high win–loss record) will be a function of external factors (e.g., "Do I have good athletes this year?" "Will we have any significant injuries?"). In contrast, coaches with an internal perception or locus of control might believe that a successful season would be, at least in large part, under their own personal control (i.e., "if I design my practices well," "if I work hard to teach my athletes the basic skills," "if I choose and implement the right offensive and defensive strategies," "if I maximize my athletes' level of conditioning"). Based on these different perceptions or beliefs on the part of the coaches, their behaviors toward and with their athletes might differ. Because coaches with an internal perception of control have a stronger belief that they can personally affect the degree to which their athletes can learn skills, such coaches might be more apt to persist in their efforts to teach all athletes the basic skills and to spend extra time with those who need more help or more repetitions. In contrast, coaches who generally believe successful outcomes are not under their own control but, rather, are more dependent on the athletes themselves may be more apt to give up on individual athletes who cannot perform the skills the right way the first time and focus all of their practice time and attention on the higher-skilled athletes. Thus, we might well find that coaches who have such an external perception or locus of control with regard to seasonal outcomes also would tend to be Pygmalion-prone coaches (i.e., act in expectancy-biased ways).

Exercise:

As a college coach, your philosophy is that you want to be as fair as possible to all athletes on your team and to provide all of them with equal opportunities. How do you balance this coaching philosophy of equity for all with the pressure you feel from the university and the fans to train and play only the best athletes so that you can win games? Would your answer to this question be different if you were a high school varsity coach? A high school junior varsity coach? A junior high school coach?

A more recent concept that certainly may be related to coaches' perceptions of control concerns their implicit theories regarding individuals' traits or abilities. This concept was introduced by Carol Dweck and her colleagues (e.g., Chiu, Hong, & Dweck, 1997; Erdley & Dweck, 1993; Levy, Stroessner, & Dweck, 1998) to describe two types of individuals. Entity theorists are those individuals who believe that people's traits and abilities are fixed. In contrast, incremental theorists are those individuals who believe that traits and abilities are malleable (i.e., that abilities can be changed or improved over time or with effort). In a series of experiments, Dweck and her colleagues have shown that these two types of theorists differ in their perceptions and beliefs about others. Specifically, entity theorists, as compared to incremental theorists, (a) made more extreme judgments about others' traits and abilities based on a small sample of their behavior; (b) believed more strongly that individuals will show a high degree of consistency in their behavior over time; (c) showed a lesser tendency to adjust their initial trait judgments of another person even when exposed to information that was contrary to their initial trait judgment of that individual; and (d) more strongly agreed with societal stereotypes regarding particular ethnic and occupational groups. In contrast, incremental theorists viewed people's behavior as varying across time and contexts. Thus, for incremental theorists, the initial information they received about a person's characteristics or traits served as only tentative or provisional descriptors of their future performance and behavior. Assuming that coaches also can be identified or categorized as either entity or incremental theorists, it would follow that such a global perspective or worldview regarding the fixedness or malleability of athletes' traits or abilities would predict the degree to which coaches would exhibit expectancy-biased behavior. Coaches who adhere to an entity perspective (i.e., that an athlete's traits and abilities are fixed) should be more apt to be Pygmalion prone whereas coaches who adhere to an incremental perspective (i.e., that an athlete's traits and abilities are malleable) should be less at risk for developing and exhibiting Pygmalion-prone behaviors.

From a somewhat different perspective, we could also look at the research on coaches' leadership styles to identify possible predictors of Pygmalion-prone behaviors. Based on the sport research conducted to date on the topic of leadership styles in coaches (see Chelladurai, 2007; Horn, 2008, and Mageau & Vallerand, 2003), it

is clear that coaches do differ in the type of leadership styles they employ in sport contexts. An examination of some of these leadership styles may reveal possible links to the expectancy-bias process. For example, a highly autocratic coaching style might be associated with a tendency to act in expectancy-biased ways. As Chelladurai explains (2007), coaches who exhibit an autocratic leadership style tend to stress their own personal authority in working with athletes. These coaches are the source of all rules, and they make all decisions. They also demand strict compliance from their athletes in following these rules. Of necessity, autocratic coaches also tend to separate themselves from their athletes. That is, they remain emotionally distant or aloof from players on their team. In contrast, coaches who exhibit a democratic leadership style encourage and solicit the participation of their athletes in making decisions pertaining to group goals, practice methods, game tactics, and strategies. Such coaches also tend to interact more frequently with individual athletes to solicit their opinions and feedback regarding team rules, practices, and games. Given such contrasting styles, it would seem reasonable to hypothesize that coaches who adopt a more autocratic leadership style would be more apt to act in expectancy-biased ways than would coaches who adopt a more democratic style. Trouilloud et al. (2006) recently demonstrated initial support for this link in their research with teachers and students in physical education classes.

From a related perspective, we can contrast coaches who create a more **mastery-oriented** team climate with coaches who create a more **performance-oriented** team climate. Based on the work of several researchers and writers (see reviews by Ames, 1992; Duda & Balaguer, 2007; Ntoumanis & Biddle, 1999), we can describe coaches who create a performance-oriented climate as those who place heavy emphasis in practices and games on performance outcomes (e.g., winning or losing). Such coaches also create a team environment that encourages between-player rivalries (e.g., coaches try to motivate athletes to outperform each other) and focuses attention on a limited number of players (e.g., only the "stars" get attention from the coach). In addition, in this type of team climate, player mistakes are perceived as extremely negative and deserving of punishment. In contrast, coaches who create a mastery-oriented team climate place greatest emphasis in practices on the development of individual players' skills (e.g., reinforcement and rewards given to all individuals who work hard and who show improvement in skills). Such coaches also view player mistakes as part of the learning process and distribute their time and attention to all players on the team and not just the "stars." Again, based on behavioral differences between these two contrasting leadership styles, we could hypothesize that performance-oriented coaches would be more apt to exhibit expectancy-biased behaviors than would mastery-oriented coaches (see corresponding research on this hypothesized link by Papaioannou, 1995 in the physical education context).

As the comments in this section indicate, certain coaching characteristics, attitudes, beliefs, and leadership styles may be more conducive than others to the occurrence of expectancy effects in the sport setting. A summary of these personal factors is provided in Table 5-1. Coaches who adopt, assume, or exemplify the characteristics, beliefs, attitudes, and behaviors descriptive

Table 5-1 Characteristics, Attitudes, Beliefs, and Behaviors of Pygmalion-Prone and Non-Pygmalion-Prone Coaches

	Pygmalion-Prone Coach	Non-Pygmalion-Prone Coach
Beliefs about Athletic Ability	"Good athletes are just born that way."	"Athletic ability is something that can be developed through practice and good training."
Beliefs about Coaching Success	"I can be a successful coach if I recruit or get good athletes." "If my team does not have a successful season, it's because I did not have good athletes, or because my athletes did not do what they could or should have done to be successful. I don't have to change any of my strategies or behaviors next season. I just need to get better athletes or more cooperative athletes."	"I can be a successful coach if I work hard to design and conduct good practices and institute the right game strategies and tactics." "If my team does not have a successful season, I will consider the possibility that I could or should have done something differently. I will likely change some of my strategies, behaviors, and tactics next season in an effort to improve my coaching effectiveness."
Stereotypic Beliefs	The Pygmalion-prone coach holds stereotypic beliefs regarding gender, race/ethnicity, country of origin, and socioeconomic status. These stereotypic beliefs affect or determine the coach's attitude toward, and behaviors with, individual athletes.	The non-Pygmalion-prone coach does not subscribe to stereotypic beliefs regarding gender, race/ethnicity, country of origin, or socioeconomic status. The coach's behaviors toward and with athletes are individualized.
Preseason Expectations	This coach tends to form preseason expectations for individual athletes based on "person" cues (e.g., race/ethnicity, gender, body size, and appearance).	This coach forms preseason expectations for individual athletes based primarily on performance-related information sources (i.e., how athletes perform in drills, scrimmages, and other performance contexts).

(continued)

Table 5-1 **Characteristics, Attitudes, Beliefs, and Behaviors of Pygmalion-Prone and Non-Pygmalion-Prone Coaches (*Continued*)**

	Pygmalion-Prone Coach	Non-Pygmalion-Prone Coach
Perceptual Flexibility	This coach's preseason expectations are rigid and fixed. Thus, coach sees in each athlete's performance and behavior in practices and games exactly what he or she expected to see.	This coach's preseason expectations are fluid and flexible. Thus, expectations for individual athletes may change as the athlete's performance and behavior in practices and games provide new information for the coach to use in evaluating that athlete.
Leadership Style	This coach exhibits an autocratic or controlling leadership style. Source of power lies within the coach. Athletes are not consulted about any team decisions, rules, strategies, or practices. Coach is central source of authority, and he or she conveys the attitude that "it's my way or the highway."	This coach exhibits a democratic or autonomous leadership style. Although coach is clearly the team leader, he or she regularly consults with athletes regarding team decisions, team rules, strategies, practices, etc. Coach encourages athletes to take personal responsibility for their own behaviors, motivation levels, training, etc.
Team Climate	This coach creates a climate in practices and games that is performance-oriented or ego-involving. In this climate, player mistakes are punished; better players receive more attention, encouragement, and rewards; and intrateam rivalry is encouraged.	This coach creates a team climate in practices and games that is mastery-oriented or task-involving. In this climate, each team member is perceived to be a valuable contributor, emphasis is placed on individual effort and skill improvement, and mistakes are viewed as opportunities to learn and improve.

of the Pygmalion-prone coach may certainly be at risk for undermining the performance and behavior of individual athletes on their team.

Exercise:

As a head coach, you know there are a number of ways to select team captains. You can let members of your team vote on who they want to be their captain(s). You can pick the captain(s) yourself with no input from your athletes. Or, you can use a combination of these methods. Using information from this chapter about the differing types of coaches' leadership styles, discuss the positive and negative effects of these different ways to select team captains.

Behavioral Recommendations for Coaches

The information on how coaches' expectations and behavior can affect the performance and psychological growth of individual athletes on their team can and should be used to promote positive coach–athlete interactions. Therefore, the following recommendations can help coaches and prospective coaches evaluate and perhaps modify their own behavior in the athletic setting.

1. *Coaches should determine what sources of information they use to form preseason or early season expectations for each athlete.* Performance-based information sources are generally more reliable and accurate predictors or indicators of an individual's physical competence than are person cues such as the

athlete's gender, ethnic background, socio-economic status, or physical appearance.

2. *Coaches should realize that their initial assessments of an athlete's competence may be inaccurate and thus need to be revised continually as the season progresses.* As the research literature in the motor learning area suggests, individuals do not always learn or progress at the same rate. Some individuals may show rapid progress early in the season but then slow down or even plateau toward the middle and end of the season. Other athletes may start slowly but then evidence a rapid increase in performance during the latter part of the season. Given such inter-individual variation in learning and performance rates, it is obvious that expectations based on initial assessments of an athlete's capabilities may soon become inaccurate. Thus, coaches at all levels of play should maintain a certain degree of flexibility with regard to their expectations or judgments concerning individual athletes' abilities.

3. During practices, *coaches should keep a running count of the amount of time each athlete spends in non-skill-related activities* (e.g., shagging balls, waiting in line, sitting out of a scrimmage or drill). Certainly it is advisable for coaches to ask a friend or another coach to observe their practices and record the amount of time a starter (usually a high-expectancy athlete) and a nonstarter (usually a low-expectancy athlete) spend in practice drills.

4. *Coaches should design instructional activities or drills that provide all athletes with an opportunity to improve their skills.* In planning practice activities, the Pygmalion-type coach typically uses skill drills that are most appropriate for the highly skilled players. When the less skilled athletes cannot keep up, the coach then gives up on these

athletes because he or she believes their failure is inevitable because of low skill abilities. The more effective coach, upon finding that his or her less skilled players cannot master the skill, will implement instructional activities designed to help them ultimately achieve success (e.g., break the skill down into component parts, employ performance aids, or ask the athlete to stay a few minutes extra after practice for more intensive work).

5. As a general rule, *coaches should respond to skill errors with corrective instruction* that tells each athlete what she or he can do to improve the skill performance. Also, praise and criticism should be given contingent to or consistent with the level of performance that was exhibited.

6. *Coaches should emphasize skill improvement as a means of evaluating and reinforcing individual athletes* rather than using absolute performance scores or levels of skill achievement. To the degree that a coach conveys the attitude that *all* athletes can *improve* their skill performance, no matter what their present level, then positive expectations can be communicated to each athlete.

7. *Coaches should interact frequently with all athletes on their team to solicit information concerning athletes' perceptions, opinions, and attitudes regarding team rules and practice organization.* Such individual coach–athlete interactions should allow each athlete to feel like a valued member of the team no matter what his or her level of skill is.

8. *Coaches should try to create a mastery-oriented climate in team practices.* Such a climate is most conducive to the development of skill in all players and to the maintenance of a team-oriented attitude.

Summary

Coaches' preseason judgments of individual athletes can serve as self-fulfilling prophecies by initiating a series of events that cause the coaches' initial expectations to become reality. This self-fulfilling prophecy phenomenon can be most detrimental when a coach forms an initial expectation that is inaccurate and underestimates an athlete's true ability. The coach's biased judgment of the athlete's sport potential, in turn, causes the coach to provide that player with less frequent and less effective instruction. Not only does such biased coaching behavior ultimately interfere with the athlete's opportunity to learn, but it also has a negative effect on his or her motivation and self-confidence. When the athlete subsequently exhibits an inability to perform well and a lack of motivation in practice situations, the coach's original but false judgment of incompetence is fulfilled.

Fortunately, the research that has been conducted in academic classrooms as well as in physical activity settings shows that all coaches are not Pygmalion prone. That is, some coaches do not allow their preseason judgments of individual athletes to affect the quality of their interaction with those players. It seems likely that coaches who are made aware of the effects that their expectations may have on athletes and who are trained to monitor their own instructional behavior may become more effective in working with individual athletes. The results of this research demonstrate that it is important that researchers and coaches more closely examine coaching behavior as one of the major factors that affect the performance and psychological growth of young athletes.

Study Questions

1. Identify and briefly describe the four steps in the expectation–performance process.

2. What sources of information might coaches use to form initial expectations for individual athletes on their team?

3. A coach's initial expectations for an individual athlete can vary along two dimensions (accuracy and flexibility). Briefly describe the consequences of the four possible combinations.

4. Do all coaches show expectancy-biased behavior? Explain what is meant by the term *Pygmalion-prone* coach.

5. Explain what the term *late maturing child* means, and then explain why late maturing boys may be at an especially high risk for negative expectancy effects.

6. Explain why early maturing girls may be at greater risk for negative expectancy effects once they reach puberty.

7. Describe the stereotypes in the sport setting associated with ethnicity. Explain how such stereotypes may affect selected groups of athletes.

8. Define the terms *entity theorist* and *incremental theorist*. Explain why coaches who adhere to an entity theorist perspective of athletic ability might be more apt to be Pygmalion prone in their interactions with individual athletes.

9. Compare and contrast the behaviors of an autocratic and a democratic coach.

10. Explain how a mastery-oriented team climate differs from a performance-oriented one.

References

Ames, C. (1992). Achievement goals, motivational climate, and motivational processes. In G. C. Roberts (Ed.), *Motivation in sport and exercise* (pp. 161–176). Champaign, IL: Human Kinetics.

Bandura, A. (1997). *Self-efficacy: The exercise of control.* New York: Freeman.

Becker, A. J. & Solomon, G. B. (2005). Expectancy information and coaching effectiveness in intercollegiate basketball. *The Sport Psychologist, 19,* 251–266.

Beilock, S. L. & McConnell, A. R. (2004). Stereotype threat and sport: Can athletic performance be threatened? *Journal of Sport and Exercise Psychology, 26,* 597–609.

Brooks, D., & Althouse, R. (Eds.). (2000). *Racism in college athletics: The African-American athlete's experience* (2nd ed.). Morgantown, WV: Fitness Information Technology.

Brophy, J. (1983). Research on the self-fulfilling prophecy and teacher expectations. *Journal of Educational Psychology, 75,* 631–661.

Chelladurai, P. (2007). Leadership in sports. In G. Tenenbaum & R. C. Eklund (Eds.), *Handbook of sport psychology* (3rd ed.) (pp. 113–135). New York: John Wiley.

Chiu, C., Hong, Y., & Dweck, C. S. (1997). Lay dispositionism and implicit theories of personality. *Journal of Personality and Social Psychology, 73,* 19–30.

Cooper, H. M. (1979). Pygmalion grows up: A model for teacher expectancy communication and performance influence. *Review of Educational Research, 49,* 389–410.

Cousineau, W. J., & Luke, M. D. (1990). Relationships between teacher expectations and academic learning time in sixth grade physical education basketball classes. *Journal of Teaching in Physical Education, 9,* 262–271.

Duda, J. L. & Balaguer, I. (2007). Coach-created motivational climate. In S. Jowett & D. Lavalee (Eds.), *Social psychology in sport* (pp. 117–130). Champaign, IL: Human Kinetics.

Eccles, J. S. (2005). Subjective task value and the Eccles et al. model of achievement-related choices. In A. J. Elliott & C. S. Dweck (Eds.), *Handbook of competence and motivation* (pp. 105–121). New York: Guilford Press.

Eccles, J. S., Wigfield, A., & Schiefele, U. (1998). Motivation to succeed. In W. Damon (Series Ed.) & N. Eisenberg (Vol. Ed.), *Handbook of child psychology: Vol 3. Social, emotional and personality development* (5th ed., pp. 1017–1094). New York: John Wiley & Sons.

Elashoff, J., & Snow, R. (1971). *Pygmalion reconsidered.* Worthington, OH: Jones.

Erdley, C. A., & Dweck, C. S. (1993). Children's implicit personality theories as predictors of their social judgments. *Child Development, 64,* 863–878.

Good, T. L. & Brophy, J. E. (2000). *Looking in classrooms* (8th ed.). New York: Longman.

Griffin, P. (1998). *Strong women, deep closets: Lesbians and homophobia in sport.* Champaign, IL: Human Kinetics.

Guskey, T. (1981). Measurement of the responsibility teachers assume for academic successes and failures in the classroom. *Journal of Teacher Education, 32,* 44–51.

Harris, M., & Rosenthal, R. (1985). Mediation of interpersonal expectancy effects: 31 meta-analyses. *Psychological Bulletin, 97,* 363–386.

Harry, J. (1995). Sports ideology, attitudes toward women, and anti-homosexual attitudes. *Sex Roles, 32,* 109–116.

Harter, S. (1999). *The construction of the self: A developmental perspective.* New York: Guilford Press.

Horn, T. S. (1984). Expectancy effects in the interscholastic athletic setting: Methodological considerations. *Journal of Sport Psychology, 6,* 60–76.

Horn, T. S. (2008). Coaching effectiveness in the sport domain. In T. S. Horn (Ed.), *Advances in sport psychology* (3rd ed.) (pp. 237–267). Champaign, IL: Human Kinetics.

Horn, T. S. (2004). Developmental perspectives on self-perceptions in children and adolescents. In M. R. Weiss (Ed.), *Developmental sport and exercise psychology: A lifespan perspective* (pp. 101–141). Morgantown, WV: Fitness Information Technology.

Jussim, L. (1986). Self-fulfilling prophecies: A theoretical and integrative review. *Psychological Review, 93,* 429–445.

Jussim, L. & Harber, D. (2005). Teacher expectations and self-fulfilling prophecies: Knowns, unknowns, resolved and unresolved controversies. *Personality and Social Psychology Review, 9,* 131–155.

Jussim, L., Eccles, J., & Madon, S. (1996). Social perception, social stereotypes, and teacher expectations: Accuracy and the quest for the powerful self-fulfilling prophecy. In M. P. Zanna (Ed.), *Advances in experimental social psychology, Vol. 28* (pp. 281–388). San Diego, CA: Academic Press.

Krane, V. (1996). Lesbians in sport: Toward acknowledgement, understanding, and theory. *Journal of Sport and Exercise Psychology, 18,* 237–246.

Kuklinski, M. R. & Weinstein, R. S. (2001). Classroom and developmental differences in a path model of teacher expectancy effects. *Child Development, 72,* 1554–1578.

Landers, M. A., & Fine, G. A. (1996). Learning life's lessons in tee ball: The reinforcement of gender and status in kindergarten sport. *Sociology of Sport Journal, 13,* 87–93.

Levy, S. R., Stroessner, S. J., & Dweck, C. S. (1998). Stereotype formation and endorsement: The role of implicit theories. *Journal of Personality and Social Psychology, 74,* 1421–1436.

Madon, S., Jussim, L., & Eccles, J. (1997). In search of the powerful self-fulfilling prophecy. *Journal of Personality and Social Psychology, 72,* 791–809.

Mageau, G. & Vallerand, R. J. (2003). The coach–athlete relationship: A motivationai model. *Journal of Sports Sciences, 21,* 883–904.

Malina, R. M. (1994). Physical growth and biological maturation of young athletes. In J. O. Holloszy (Ed.), *Exercise and sport science reviews, Vol. 22* (pp. 388–433). Baltimore, MD: Williams & Wilkins.

Malina, R. M. (2002). The young athlete: Biological growth and maturation in a biocultural context. In F. L. Smoll & R. E. Smith (Eds.), *Children and youth in sport: A biopsychosocial perspective* (2nd ed.) (pp. 261–292). Dubuque, IA: Kendall/Hunt.

Martinek, T. (1988). Confirmation of a teacher expectancy model: Student perceptions and causal attributions of teaching behaviors. *Research Quarterly for Exercise and Sport, 59,* 118–126.

Martinek, T. (1989). Children's perceptions of teaching behaviors: An attributional model for explaining teacher expectancy effects. *Journal of Teaching in Physical Education, 8,* 318–328.

Martinek, T., & Johnson, S. (1979). Teacher expectations: Effects on dyadic interactions and self-concept in elementary age children. *Research Quarterly, 50,* 60–70.

Martinek, T., & Karper, W. B. (1982). Canonical relationships among motor ability, expression of effort, teacher expectations, and dyadic interactions in elementary age children. *Journal of Teaching in Physical Education, 1,* 26–39.

Messner, M. A. (1992). *Power at play: Sports and the problem of masculinity.* Boston: Beacon Press.

Messner, M. A. (2000). Barbie girls versus sea monsters: Children constructing gender. *Gender and Society, 14,* 765–784.

Ntoumanis, N., & Biddle, S. J. H. (1999). A review of motivational climate in physical activity. *Journal of Sports Science, 17,* 643–665.

Papaioannou, A. (1995). Differential perceptual and motivational patterns when different goals are adopted. *Journal of Sport and Exercise Psychology, 17,* 18–34.

Ransdell, L. B. (2002). The maturing young female athlete: Biophysical considerations. In F. L. Smoll & R. E. Smith (Eds.), *Children and youth in sport: A biopsychosocial perspective* (2nd ed.) (pp. 311–338). Dubuque, IA: Kendall/Hunt.

Rejeski, W., Darracott, C., & Hutslar, S. (1979). Pygmalion in youth sports: A field study. *Journal of Sport Psychology, 1,* 311–319.

Rosenthal, R., & Jacobson, L. (1968). *Pygmalion in the classroom: Teacher expectations and pupils' intellectual development.* New York: Holt, Rinehart & Winston.

Rudolph, K. D., Lambert, S. F., Clark, A. G., & Kurlakowsky, K. D. (2001). Negotiating the transition to middle school: The role of self-regulatory processes. *Child Development, 72,* 929–946.

Ryan, R. M., & Deci, E. L. (2000). Self-determination theory and the facilitation of intrinsic motivation, social development, and well-being. *American Psychologist, 55,* 68–78.

Sinclair, D. A., & Vealey, R. S. (1989). Effects of coaches' expectations and feedback on the self-perceptions of athletes. *Journal of Sport Behavior, 12,* 77–91.

Skinner, E. A. (1996). A guide to constructs of control. *Journal of Personality and Social Psychology, 71,* 549–570.

Smith, R. E., Smoll, F. L., & Barnett, N. P. (1995). Reduction of children's sport anxiety through social support and stress-reduction training for coaches. *Journal of Applied Developmental Psychology, 16,* 125–142.

Smoll, F. L., & Schutz, R. W. (1990). Quantifying gender differences in physical performance: A developmental perspective. *Developmental Psychology, 26,* 360–369.

Solomon, G. B. (2001). Performance and personality impression cues as predictors of athletic performance: An extension of expectancy theory. *International Journal of Sport Psychology, 32,* 88–100.

Solomon, G. B., DiMarco, A. M., Ohlson, C. J., & Reece, S. D. (1998). Expectations and coaching experience: Is more better? *Journal of Sport Behavior, 21,* 444–455.

Solomon, G. B., Golden, A. J., Ciapponi, T. M., & Martin, A. D. (1998). Coach expectations and differential feedback: Perceptual flexibility revised. *Journal of Sport Behavior, 21,* 298–310.

Solomon, G. B., & Kosmitzki, C. (1996). Perceptual flexibility and differential feedback among intercollegiate basketball coaches. *Journal of Sport Behavior, 19,* 163–176.

Solomon, G. B., Striegel, D. A., Eliot, J. F., Heon, S. N., Maas, J. L., & Wayda, V. K. (1996). The self-fulfilling prophecy in college basketball: Implications for effective coaching. *Journal of Applied Sport Psychology, 8,* 44–59.

Solomon, G. B., Wiegardt, P. A., Yusuf, F. R., Kosmitzki, C., Williams, J., Stevens, C. E., & Wayda, V. K. (1996). Expectancies and ethnicity: The self-fulfilling prophecy in college basketball. *Journal of Sport and Exercise Psychology, 18,* 83–88.

Steele, C. M. (1997). A threat in the air. How stereotypes shape intellectual identity and performance. *American Psychologist, 52,* 613–629.

Steele, C. M., & Aronson, J. (1995). Stereotype threat and the intellectual test performance of African-Americans. *Journal of Personality and Social Psychology, 69,* 797–784.

Stone, J. (2002). Battling doubt by avoiding practice: The effects of stereotype threat on self-handicapping in white athletes. *Personality and Social Psychology Bulletin, 28,* 1667–1678.

Stone, J., Lynch, C. I., Sjomeling, M., & Darley, J. M. (1999). Stereotype threat effects on black and white athletic performance. *Journal of Personality and Social Psychology, 77,* 1213–1227.

Stone, J., Perry, Z. W., & Darley, J. M. (1997). "White men can't jump": Evidence for the perceptual confirmation of racial stereotypes following a basketball game. *Basic and Applied Social Psychology, 19,* 291–306.

Thomas, J. R., & French, K. E. (1985). Gender differences across age in motor performance: A meta-analysis. *Psychological Bulletin, 98,* 260–282.

Thomas, K. T., Gallagher, J. D., & Thomas, J. R. (2001). Motor development and skill acquisition during childhood and adolescence. In R. N. Singer, H. A. Hausenblas, & C. M. Janelle, *Handbook of sport psychology,* (2nd ed.) (pp. 20–52). New York: John Wiley & Sons.

Thorndike, R. (1968). Review of Pygmalion in the classroom. *American Educational Research Journal, 5,* 708–711.

Trouilloud, D. O., Sarrazin, P. G., Martinek, T. J., & Guillet, E. (2002). The influence of teacher expectations on student achievement in physical education classes: Pygmalion revisited. *European Journal of Sport Psychology, 32,* 591–607.

Trouilloud, D., Sarrazin, P., Bressoux, P., & Bois, J (2006). Relation between teachers' early expectations and students later perceived competence in physical education classes: Autonomy-supportive climate as a moderator. *Journal of Educational Psychology, 98,* 75–86.

Valeski, T. N., & Stipek, D. J. (2001). Young children's feelings about school. *Child Development, 72,* 1198–1213.

Vallerand, R.J. (2007). Intrinsic and extrinsic motivation in sport and physical activity: A review and a look at the future. In G. Tenenbaum & R. C. Eklund (Eds.), *Handbook of sport psychology* (3rd ed.) (pp. 59–83). New York: John Wiley.

Weiner, B. (1992). *Human motivation: Metaphors, theories, and research.* Newbury Park, CA: Sage.

Leadership Effectiveness and Decision Making in Coaches

Mimi C. Murray, *Springfield College*
Betty L. Mann, *Springfield College*
Jennifer K. Mead, *Springfield College*

Having great leadership is a big key to success. Our team will go as far as our leaders are willing to take us.

—Mike Candrea, University of Arizona and U.S.A. Olympic team softball coach

Sure, I listen to the players when they talk to me and make suggestions, just as Coach Smith (former head basketball coach at University of North Carolina) did. But when it's time to make a decision for the good of the team, like Coach Smith, I'm a benevolent dictator. Great leaders know what it means to make tough decisions, even if they sometimes aren't popular with the people they're leading.

—Roy Williams, head basketball coach at the University of North Carolina

In every great group, "there is one person who acts as maestro, organizing the genius of the others. He or she is a pragmatist dreamer, a person with an original but attainable vision. Ironically, the leader is able to realize his or her dream only if the others are free to do exceptional work . . . like [a] great conductor, [the leader] may not be able to play Mozart's First Violin Concerto, but he or she has a profound understanding of the work and can create the environment to realize it" (Bennis & Biederman, 1997, pp. 199–200).

Socal scientists, behavioral psychologists, and researchers in organizational and business management have studied leadership for many decades. With hundreds of definitions of leadership and thousands of empirical investigations of leaders, there is still no universally accepted definition of leadership or consensus on the specific qualities, skills, and behaviors that distinguish successful leaders from less successful leaders. Nevertheless, meaningful theories and practical knowledge exists from organizational, educational, and sport settings regarding leadership effectiveness.

When people are asked to identify a famous leader in sport, names like Lombardi, Bryant, Stagg, Torre, Holtz, Walsh, Smith, Carroll, Auerbach, Belichick, Stringer, Jackson, Wooden, Riley,

Summitt, or Robinson probably will appear among those listed. By the nature of their assigned title, referent power, and position of authority, coaches are granted the title of "leader." As such, they are expected to demonstrate the skills, attributes, and behaviors of a leader. They also are expected to develop leadership within their team, such as team captains. Thus coaching effectiveness can be maximized through understanding the concepts of leadership.

Although sport psychology consultants rarely serve in a direct leadership capacity, it is not uncommon for them to serve as a resource for providing education and guidance regarding the identification and development of effective leadership skills and behaviors—for both coaches and athletes. When providing this supporting role with athletes, the sport psychology consultant must be sure to defer to the vision and preferences of the head coach. Although this chapter is often written in the lexicon of the coach and may initially appear to be aimed exclusively at coaches, this is not the case. Knowledge of the basic principles of leadership presented in this chapter will help individuals in sport psychology deal more effectively with athletes; it will also help them to more fully understand effective coach–athlete communications, help coaches to become more effective leaders, and help coaches develop player leadership within a team. This chapter describes several approaches to leadership and relates these theoretical frameworks to dimensions of leadership behavior in sports, including decision making in coaching.

What Is Leadership?

To enhance leadership effectiveness, we must begin by defining and understanding leadership. Most accepted definitions of leadership have historically included some reference to the behaviors, traits, or abilities associated with the task of guiding or moving other people in a given direction. Noted leadership scholars (Barrow, 1977; Stogdill, 1974) define leadership as the behavioral process of influencing the activities of an organized group toward specific goals and the achievement

of those goals. Others simply define leadership as the process whereby an individual influences others to do what he or she wants them to do. But leadership is often far more complex than the latter definition implies. Leadership should be viewed as the art and the science of influencing others through credibility, capability, and commitment. Individuals attempting to understand leader–follower interaction should not only pay attention to *why* and *how* leader and individual followers interact, but also commit to understanding from *where* a leader's behavior originates.

Leadership Theories and Implications

Leadership researchers have attempted to identify personal qualities and behaviors that are most likely to result in effective leadership. Additionally, researchers seek to determine the influence that specific situational factors may have on these variables. Over the past several decades, leadership researchers have investigated trait, behavioral, situational, relational, transformational, and authentic theories of leadership, as well as cognitive frameworks for viewing leadership. Each of these theories is discussed in this chapter. Current sport leadership models have been developed by integrating components of many of these theories (see Chelladurai & Carron, 1978; Chelladurai & Saleh, 1978, 1980; Chelladurai, 1990, 2007; Smoll & Smith, 1989; Horn, 2008). As an example, we will briefly describe Chelladurai's multidimensional model of leadership development (Chelladurai & Carron, 1978; Chelladurai & Saleh, 1978, 1980; Chelladurai, 1990, 2007), as well as a coaching model developed by Côté and colleagues (1995).

Trait Approach

Assessing personality characteristics and traits to determine whether effective leaders have similar qualities takes the same approach as trying to understand why certain people are successful athletes. Researchers using the trait approach to examine leadership effectiveness have attempted to identify and describe a universal personality for leadership success. This approach has also been referred to as the great-person (man) theory of leadership. More accurate and valuable insights will come from thinking of these significant qualities or traits as **dispositional.** *Dispositional* means that behavior associated with a given trait can vary from situation to situation, but individuals tend to keep the same relative position. For example, the most assertive individual will respond with the highest level of assertiveness, but that level will vary across situations.

Hendry (1972, 1974) described the stereotypical coach/physical educator as someone who is inflexible, domineering, and emotionally inhibited, as well as someone who needs to be in control. Sage (1975) did not concur with these findings, which seemingly indicate that coaches are highly authoritarian, dogmatic, and manipulative. Sage based his reservations on the small number of samples and the sampling techniques employed in Hendry's work.

Coaches who possess an authoritarian personality profile may demonstrate ineffective coping skills with regard to ambiguity and avoidance of unstructured situations due to perceptions of such situations as being psychologically threatening. Authoritarian coaches may fail to adapt to new situations and challenges, even when existing methods fail to achieve stated goals and objectives. According to Triandis (1971), authoritarians typically avoid introspection, approve of severe punishment, and tend to hold strong prejudices. In a study of attitudes of coaches and athletic directors, Maier and Laurakis (1981) revealed that males who were identified as having an authoritarian leadership style were also more concerned with winning at the expense of fair play or sportsmanship, had negative attitudes about women, admired traditional male roles, and were opposed to gender equity.

In his book, *On Leadership,* John Gardner (1990) identified the following attributes or qualities of effective leaders that appear to be transferrable from leadership in one situation to leadership in another:

- Physical vitality and stamina
- Intelligence and action orientation

- Eagerness to accept responsibility
- Task competence
- Understanding of followers and their needs
- Skill in dealing with people
- Need for achievement
- Capacity to motivate people
- Courage and resolution
- Trustworthiness
- Decisiveness
- Self-confidence
- Assertiveness
- Adaptability/flexibility

While lists of leadership attributes, such as the one presented by Gardner, present a possible and even likely description of effective leaders, it would be impossible for lists of this type to be inclusive. Effective leadership extends well beyond a mere checklist of traits. Furthermore, is it not possible for an individual to have all of these attributes and still be an ineffective leader?

The collective results of research related to leadership personality characteristics and traits have been equivocal. No readily identifiable personality traits have been found to relate to leadership status or leadership effectiveness in *all* situations. Overall, the trait approach does little to explain differences in the leadership style of successful and unsuccessful coaches. Given the limited support for the use of trait theories to predict leadership effectiveness, researchers have directed their efforts toward examining characteristic behaviors of effective leaders rather than assessing their distinguishing personality traits.

Recently, Zaccaro (2007) has proposed that researchers consider revisiting the study of leadership traits. He argues that the movement away from using trait-based approaches to examine and understand leadership effectiveness was not based upon empirical evidence. Additionally, he identifies a significant body of empirical evidence that supports traits as the precursors of effective leadership. The integration of a combination of traits and attributes, he argues, as opposed to independent traits may ultimately predict effective leadership. Finally, Zaccaro recommends that leadership researchers examine the integrated role of situational factors and both proximal and distal influences of traits in the development of leaders.

Behavioral Theories

The behavioral approach examines the behaviors of leaders and their relationship to the productivity and satisfaction of group members. The concern with leadership behaviors first emerged in business management areas, as did the factor/trait approach to studying leadership. The majority of early studies of the behaviors of leaders were conducted by researchers at The Ohio State University (Halpin, 1957; Halpin & Winer, 1957). From these initial studies, two leader behavior characteristics emerged that related to group effectiveness: consideration and initiating structure. *Consideration* in work relationships involves mutual trust and respect for and attention to the feelings and ideas of others. Leaders identified as having high consideration behaviors demonstrated effective communication and rapport with others. *Initiating structure* is reflected in behaviors that serve to define and structure individual roles toward goal attainment. Leaders who were identified as behaving with high initiating structure were active in directing group activities, communicating, scheduling, and experimenting with new ideas.

Further studies related to the leader behaviors associated with organizational effectiveness were conducted at the University of Michigan (Blake & Mouton, 1964, 1978). These researchers described a leader as being either production centered with high reported initiating structure behaviors or employee centered with high reported consideration behaviors (Stogdill, 1974). Subsequent research has revealed that leaders' behaviors can be both employee centered and production centered. More importantly, the most effective leaders tend to score high on both behaviors.

Additional researchers have examined sport leadership from a behavioral perspective. According to Hoffman (2003), athletes reported work ethic, knowledge, and preparation as the most important coaching behaviors. Neil and Kirby (1985) revealed that less skilled and younger rowers preferred coaches who demonstrated person-oriented behaviors. Weiss and Friedrichs (1986) found that coaches of losing basketball teams reported high social support scores, indicating that social support does not always lead to successful performances. Whether winning or losing, athletes who played for coaches who provided encouragement and instruction reported higher perceptions of competence in their abilities, identified themselves as being successful, and gave more effort (Black & Weiss, 1992). Interestingly, Feltz, Chase, Moritz, and Sullivan (1999) found that confident coaches used praise and encouragement more frequently than less confident coaches. In an examination of perceived leadership behaviors of both coaches and athletes, Loughead and Hardy (2005) revealed that peer leaders exhibited social support, positive feedback, and democratic decision-making style leadership behaviors to a greater degree than coaches. Conversely, coaches were perceived as exhibiting training and instruction and autocratic behaviors to a greater extent than peer leaders.

Although behavioral theories have been and continue to be used extensively to understand leadership in sport settings, the literature offers enough inconsistencies to suggest that leadership is far more complex than traits or behaviors alone can explain. Theorists subsequently began to examine effective leadership through an interactive lens, considering both situational and individual factors in their description of leadership.

Situational Theories

In their examination of effective leadership, researchers eventually began to consider the factors that make each situation unique. Situational factors include the characteristics of followers, the organizational situation, and the demands of the situation. Of particular interest to those individuals working within sport are the interactions between coaches (leaders) and athletes (followers) in specific sport situations.

In his contingency model, Fiedler (1967) argued that leadership behavior or leader–member relations, the task structure, and the leader's position relative to authority and power interact to affect group performance and satisfaction. Fiedler proposed that the style of a leader is a product of his or her own needs and personality. He also suggests that leadership style is a stable and well-established personality characteristic. According to Fiedler, leadership behaviors can be placed in one of two categories: people-centered or task-centered. In the case of an inflexible leader in a nonproductive organizational setting, Fiedler proposed that the situation should change or the leader should be replaced. If one accepts this theory, then leadership style can be generalized to any situation. Accordingly, leadership can be improved in a given situation in one of two ways. First, the leader's personality would be altered to suit the situation—not an easy task even if the leader wishes to make a change. The second recommendation is to change the situation, including the organizational structure, so that it is more compatible with the leader's personality. According to Fiedler's model, personalities and situations should be matched and congruent for maximum leadership effectiveness.

The application of Fiedler's model to sport might imply that a coach who is successful in one situation may not be so in another similar situation. We can attempt to apply the contingency model to the cases of Pete Carroll, John Calipari, and Rick Pitino, three coaches who made well-publicized moves between the intercollegiate and professional coaching ranks. Carroll, Calipari, and Pitino all experienced tremendous success coaching athletes, in the same sport, at one level, but not both. Why did these coaches not experience the same level of success at both levels? Using the contingency model, we could speculate that the coaching styles of Carroll, Calipari, and Pitino, based upon their own unique personalities and needs, were better matched with an intercollegiate coaching situation. Conversely, there are examples of successful coaches in sport who have been successful moving from one team to another. Rutgers University's head women's basketball coach, C. Vivian Stringer,

has experienced tremendous success in three unique coaching situations: Cheyney State, the University of Iowa, and Rutgers University. Similarly, Phil Jackson left an extremely successful Chicago Bulls coaching experience to experience more success as the coach of the Los Angeles Lakers. Jackson is known to have incorporated his Zen philosophy in his approach to coaching in both situations (Jackson & Rosen, 2001). Both with the Bulls and the Lakers, Jackson was coaching athletes who were arguably among the most talented athletes ever to play in the NBA. Are the common denominators in each situation Stringer's or Jackson's coaching style? Might the similar level of athlete in each situation have been an equally strong component of the success both of these coaches?

In other situation-specific theories, the focus is on the *behaviors* of leaders in a given situation and how these behaviors affect followers. Two situation-specific theories that will be briefly mentioned here are the life-cycle and path-goal theories. Hersey and Blanchard (1969, 1977, 1982) proposed that effective leaders can and should adjust their leadership style to respond to the **life-cycle** needs of their followers and to the environment. Hersey and Blanchard (1982) suggested that an appropriate leadership style for a specific situation is determined by the maturity of the followers. Thus, the emphasis is on the follower and not the leader. Maturity is defined as "the ability and willingness of people to take responsibility for directing their own behavior" (Hersey & Blanchard, 1982, p. 151). The behavior of the leader in relation to the followers is based on three variables: (1) the amount of guidance and direction a leader gives, or initiating behavior; (2) the amount of socioemotional support a leader-gives, or consideration behavior; and (3) the maturity level of the followers as they perform a task. Case (1984) illustrated the importance of adapting leadership style to the needs of the followers within a particular situation by asking us to consider differences in leadership style that would be appropriate when coaching 9-year-old soccer players as compared to Division I collegiate soccer players. The experience, maturity, and skill level of the players may influence the leadership styles that would be most effective within the specific environment.

In the **path-goal theory** the leader is viewed as a facilitator who helps others achieve their goals (House, 1971). As the term implies, the leader provides a path by which the followers can reach their goals. The specific characteristics of each situation should determine the leader behaviors that may most effectively aid the follower. For example, a swim coach who determines that her athlete wants to qualify for a regional championship would provide the appropriate and specific conditioning program to help her decrease her time to meet her qualifying goal. Neither the life-cycle theory nor the path-goal theory have been applied to any great extent in sport. The results of the few studies that have done so are contradictory and inconclusive (Carron, 1984; Chelladurai & Carron, 1978; Chelladurai & Saleh, 1978; Von Strache, 1979).

There appear to be no direct and simple answers to the question, "Is group effectiveness caused by how a leader behaves, or does the leader behave in a certain way because of the group's performance?" It would be extremely difficult and unwise to assume any cause–effect relationships on the basis of the limited and somewhat contradictory research evidence available. With situation at the center of the equation, flexibility would appear to be an ideal approach to coaching because of the situational diversity in sport.

Relational Models of Leadership

In 1975, Graen and Cashman proposed the leader–member exchange (LMX) theory, which was originally referred to as the vertical-dyad linkage. The LMX model is grounded in role theory, which suggests that members of a group take on specific roles or sets of behaviors that are expected of position holders. According to Yukl (1998), the LMX model can be used to describe the relationship between a leader and a follower as they influence each other and negotiate the follower's role within the group. Relational models of this type serve to provide a method for examining the effect that the *quality* of the relationship between a leader and an individual follower may have on individual performance and satisfaction.

Due to time restraints and various pressures, leaders may develop close relationships, which consist of increased latitude, with a limited number of individual followers. Followers with increased latitude are empowered by the leader and can be labeled the "high-quality LMX" group. High-quality LMX group members may receive material benefits (e.g., privileges) and psychological benefits (e.g., trust, confidence, respect). Individuals receiving relatively less latitude are considered the "low-quality LMX" group. Leader–athlete relationships and exchanges with individuals in the low-quality LMX group are considerably more limited and may reflect the minimum contracted exchange that is required of a coach. Dienesch and Linden (1986) proposed that high-quality LMX group members might become advisors or assistants to the leader. Members of the low-quality LMX group have less influence and are required to comply with the leader's directions and role expectations. Graen and Cashman (1975) identified compatibility, competence, and dependability as the primary determinants of high-quality or low-quality LMX group membership. The quality of social exchange relationships has been found to have an impact on the experiences of followers (Gerstner & Day, 1997; Graen & Uhl-Bien, 1995).

In a study involving summer basketball camp attendees, Case (1998) operationalized starters as members of the high-quality LMX and non-starters as members of the low-quality LMX group. Traditionally, we have assumed that individual team members' perceptions of leadership are consistent and standard; however, the results of this study contradicted that assumption. High-quality LMX group members, or starters, had higher performance levels, scoring significantly higher on the LMX Scale (Graen & Cashman, 1975) than the low-quality LMX group non-starters. Based upon these findings, Case (1998) recommended that coaches should increase their awareness that there is typically considerable variance in their exchanges with individual group members.

A limitation in the use of the LMX model (Hogg & Martin, 2003; Hogg, Martin, & Weedon, 2003) is that it primarily focuses on the dyadic leader–member relationships and fails to consider the fact that these exchanges commonly occur in a team context. When LMX relationships occur within a climate of group social comparisons, concerns of fairness will, undoubtedly, arise as individuals evaluate not only their own LMX relationship but also the LMX relationships of other group members (Hogg et al., 2005). In both individual and team sport settings, athlete satisfaction and performance may be enhanced through increasing the coach's awareness and monitoring of the exchanges between coaches and athletes. Specifically, in a team-sport setting, LMX exchanges may not only influence individual athlete's satisfaction and performance, but will most likely effect the performance and satisfaction of the group as a whole.

Transformational Leadership

Since the 1980s, transformational leadership paradigms have become the focus of the study of leadership. In *The Next American Frontier* (1983), author Robert Reich describes leadership as being flexible, adaptive, organic systems of management in which the worker is viewed as a vital resource. He presents this view in contrast to the traditional view of management as being bureaucratic, top-heavy, and authoritarian. The transformational model of leadership has been proposed as one that effectively incorporates the follower as an essential element in understanding effective leadership. Not only are followers essential to understanding effective leadership, they should also be affected by leadership.

Transformational leadership involves the *transformation* of individuals from their current selves into their possible selves. According to Seltzer and Bass (1990), transformational leadership occurs when "leaders broaden and elevate the interests of their followers, when they generate awareness and acceptance among their followers of the purposes and mission of the group, and when they move their followers to transcend their own self-interests for the good of the group" (pp. 693–694).

Guiding the transformational leader is his or her vision. Vision is considered to be the "key to leadership, and leadership is the key to organizational success" (Nanus, 1992, p. 7). In a description of the unique purpose of leaders, Kouzes and Posner (1987) referred to leaders as "pioneers" who "guide us to new and often unfamiliar destinations" (p. 32). To be most effective a leader should begin by adopting a vision that aligns the stated objectives of an organization, the needs and abilities of a specific group of individuals, and their own individual values. Once clarified, that vision should be communicated to others through both words and actions. Bennis and Nanus (1989) describe a leaders as individuals who "acquire and wear their visions like clothes" (p. 46). Finally, leaders must convince others to become committed to their vision (Nanus, 1992). Charisma is a quality that has often been associated with leaders who inspire others to work to achieve a shared vision. Leaders must exhibit a sustained commitment to their vision through both thoughts and actions.

In sport, the core element of a coach's vision typically includes winning as the ultimate goal. This type of narrow visionary focus leads many coaches to fail to properly emphasize broad visionary goals that involve the pursuit of positive growth and development of athletes. In addition to narrow goals of winning, a more broadly defined and communicated vision may lead to more broadly defined successes.

The influence of the leader on his or her associates or followers is critical to understanding the distinction between transformational theory and previous theories that some have described as transactional theories (Bass & Avolio, 1995; Burns, 1978). Transactional theories, according to Bass and Avolio (1995), may be more closely associated with management than leadership. Doherty and Danylchuk (1996) further explained that transactional leadership involves a leader–worker "exchange relationship in which rewards are provided or punishment is withheld, in return for performance" (p. 295). Transformational leaders, by contrast, influence others by their ability to inspire, to empower, and to intellectually stimulate others to achieve beyond expectations toward the fulfillment of higher order needs (Bass & Avolio, 1995).

A limited number of studies have been conducted in which the transformational or transitional leader behaviors of sport leaders are examined (Weese, 1995; Weese & Bourner, 1995; Prujin & Boucher, 1995). Utilizing a transformational/transactional model (Bass, 1985), Doherty and Danylchuk (1996) examined the leadership of intercollegiate athletics administrators. The results of the study reveal a profile of predominantly transformational as opposed to transactional or managerial behavior. Leader-centered behavior was used more often than follower-centered behavior by the participants. Satisfaction of coaches with their respective administrators was positively associated with transformational leadership and contingent reward behavior. Negative relationships were found for management-by-exception, passive, and nonleader behavior. While satisfaction with leader behavior has been examined using transformational leadership theory, few researchers have examined the influence of transformational leadership on sport performance. In 2001, Charbonneau, Barling, and Kelloway described the moderating role of intrinsic motivation in the relationship between coaches' transformational leadership behaviors and university students' sports performance. Zacharatos, Barling, and Kelloway (2000) identified the influential role of transformational peer leadership behaviors on subjective sport performance outcomes, as well as satisfaction.

Cognitive Framework for Understanding Leader Behavior

Howard Gardner (1995), in his book *Leading Minds: An Anatomy of Leadership,* provides a highly original framework of leadership that emphasizes that the nature and processes of leadership can be understood through examining the minds of leaders and their followers. This innovative approach contains traditional ideas of how to judge great leaders, such as the great person theory; however, it considers the mind of the leader, not the personality. This cognitive approach to the thinking of great leaders and how their ideas developed is the antithesis of the behavioral approach, which focuses only on leaders' actions.

As an approach to discerning effective leadership, the needs and demands of the audience or followers as well as the nature of the times are essential factors. For example, Lou Holtz, former Notre Dame and South Carolina head football coach, observed that "the difference between athletes now and 25 years ago is that today everybody wants to talk about his [her] rights and privileges, whereas 25 years ago people talked about their obligations and responsibilities." As leaders, we need to be cognizant of the characteristics of those growing up in the millennial age. Leadership can best be understood, then, with a cognitive, cultural, and contextual appreciation. According to Gardner (1995), the previously described models of leadership have been unable to adequately explain the leadership phenomena. He suggests that the missing link is adequate understanding of the cognitive processes, or thoughts, of effective leaders.

In applying the cognitive framework, Gardner (1995) introduces six constants of leadership: the story, the audience, the organization, the embodiment, direct and indirect leadership, and the issue of expertise. Each constant explains leadership as a cognitive enterprise, which is a dynamic process between and within the minds of the leader and the followers.

The story.   Great leaders achieve power through the stories they relate. In these stories the leader is able to put words and symbols to the longings and needs of others. This central story or message should become the leader's central mission and should address the sense of the individual as well as the group. Martin Luther King's story was built on religion and history and was well circulated, yet he was able to synthesize and present this message in a new and fresh way, a way by which many were able to hear, learn, and grow. His message was inclusionary. Other leaders have capitalized on exclusionary stories, for example, Hitler, by attempting to exclude all but white Aryans from his Nazi Germany.

Gardner divides leaders into three types according to the stories they relate: the ordinary leader, the innovative leader, and the visionary leader. The "ordinary leader" is one who relates a traditional story of his or her group as effectively as possible. An ordinary leader from politics is Gerald Ford; from sport, Vince Lombardi might be considered an ordinary leader in that his football strategy was based on a team steeped in sound fundamentals.

Gardner's "innovative leader" takes a latent story of his or her group and brings new attention as well as a new twist to it. Bill Bowerman, former track and field coach at the University of Oregon and co-founder of Nike, was an innovative leader in sport. Not only did Bowerman work tirelessly to reduce the weight and drag of his athletes' track shoes in order to improve their performance, he also led a movement to widen the track from six to eight lanes. Bill Walsh, the three-time Super Bowl Champion former coach of the San Francisco 49ers, is also known as the innovator of the now ubiquitous West Coast offense.

The audience. The relationship between the leader and the audience or the followers is an elusive, mysterious, complex, and very interactive one. The interaction occurs between the desires of the audience and the leader's story. It seems the leader's best chances for success rest in a steadfast concentration on the same core message, flexibility in presentation of the story, and the audience's openness to comprehending the message.

The organization. Although leaders can share their stories with eager and receptive audiences so that bonding occurs between the leader and audience, an organizational or institutional basis is required if the story is to endure. Certainly, the early visionary religious leaders embodied their stories, and their stories resonated with the resulting bonding with their followers. Would these stories or religions have endured without a strong religious institutionalization? Would basketball still be played had it not been initially embraced by the YMCA leaders who graduated

from Springfield College and spread the "word" of basketball throughout the world? A strong and viable institution or organization is essential for effective leadership. Could this also explain the popularity and success of intercollegiate sport, housed within U.S. colleges and universities and in large degree controlled by their national organizations such as the National Collegiate Athletic Association (NCAA)?

Direct and indirect leadership. Leaders seem to exert their influence in either a direct or indirect way (Gardner, 1995). Winston Churchill is an example of a leader whose influence was direct, whereas Einstein (*Time* magazine's "Person of the Century"), through the ideas he developed and the presentation of his thoughts as a theory, is an example of an indirect leader. In sport, basketball coach John Wooden is an example of a leader who has been influential in both direct and indirect ways. His thoughts and influence on his players, other coaches, and administrators were direct; and his "pyramid of success," a formalized collection of life's principles, building blocks for both personal and professional achievement, will endure as an indirect approach to effective coaching and will continue to influence others indirectly in the future.

The embodiment. The leader should in some way embody the story. If the leader's story and life are inconsistent or the leader appears hypocritical, the story becomes unconvincing. Consider the conduct of the former executives from Enron and Tyco. These leaders were the antithesis of their stories.

The issue of expertise. Individuals who aspire to be effective leaders will be perceived as credible if their work is of a high quality. Coaches at some levels of competition can and do remain technically competent, but today those at the elite level will find it exceedingly difficult to remain technically competent in all of the areas or domains that can affect athlete performance. Hence, astute leaders will form a support team of knowledgeable people such as experts in the areas of conditioning and strength training, sports medicine, athletic training, nutrition, and, of course, sport psychology. This is an approach of strength. Furthermore, in such situations, there is no doubt who the head coach is and who is responsible.

Leadership effectiveness may depend on a workable match between the leader's style and situational variables, and we may better understand the nature of leadership by examining the cognitive processes of leaders and followers. Goleman (1998) described emotional intelligence as a common denominator among effective leaders. In their ability model, Mayer and Salovey (1997) described emotional intelligence as a defined set of abilities: (a) the ability to perceive and express emotions; (b) the ability to assimilate emotions in thought; (c) the ability to understand and analyze emotions; and (d) the ability to regulate emotions. Due to its basis in skill learning and mastery, Meyer and Fletcher (2007) have recommended the use of the ability model in sport domains. Goleman (1998) identified five components of emotional intelligence:

> *Self-awareness* is "the ability to recognize and understand your moods, emotions, and drives and their effect on others." A person who is highly self-aware has self-confidence and is willing to candidly and realistically assess his or her capabilities.
>
> *Self-regulation* is "the ability to control or redirect disruptive impulses and moods . . . and the propensity to think before acting." Trustworthiness, integrity, and openness to change are hallmarks of a person who exhibits self-regulation.
>
> *Social skill* is "proficiency in managing relationships and building networks . . . finding common ground and building rapport." Individuals with good social skills are persuasive and effective in leading change. Appropriate social skills are key ingredients of effective managerial and leader effectiveness.
>
> *Motivation* is a passion to work for reasons that go beyond money or status and "a propensity to pursue goals with energy and

persistence." The motivation component of emotional intelligence is associated with a strong drive to achieve, optimism, and organizational commitment.

> *Empathy* is "the ability to understand the emotional makeup of other people. . . and skill in treating people according to their emotional reactions." A person who exhibits empathy is likely to possess cross-cultural sensitivity and is able to build and retain talent (p. 95).

By definition leaders work with and influence others. A successful leader realizes the importance of getting along with others, communicating his or her passion and vision to others, and doing so in a trusting, respectful, fair, transparent, and caring manner. Sport leaders have a responsibility to promote such behaviors by teaching, enforcing, advocating, and modeling ethical principles (Arizona Sport Summit Accord, 1999).

Authentic Leadership

While the shelves of the business section in any bookstore may indicate otherwise, as a coach or sport psychology consultant, you have undoubtedly come to realize that there is no simple "recipe" for leadership. Like any skill in sport, leadership cannot be granted to another via the wave of a magic wand. Developing as a leader is, and should be, a lifelong journey that requires a significant commitment and effort. At the foundation of that development should be an increased understanding of the authentic self. It would be misguided to attempt to facilitate the development of effective leadership by merely matching a set of skills, behaviors, or concepts of leadership to a given situation or context without first committing time and effort to understanding the strengths, values, abilities, and purposes of the individual. If this step isn't taken, how will you know what is being matched?

In 2007, Avolio acknowledged that leadership research has been devoted to "determining what causes leaders to emerge and be effective," and that "relatively little effort has been devoted to systematically explaining how such leaders and leadership develop (pp. 29–30). Several researchers have collaborated to propose an integrated model describing authentic leaders, as well as authentic followers in group and organizational settings (Luthans & Avolio, 2003; Gardner, Avolio, Luthans, May, & Walumba, 2005; Avolio & Luthans, 2006).

Authenticity is a concept that has been borrowed from the positive psychology movement of the past decade. Historically, authenticity is a quality that has been identified and celebrated in leaders within sport. Examples of authenticity may include Stagg, Wooden, Summit, and Belichick. Kernis (2003) defined authenticity as "the unobstructed operation of one's true, or core, self in one's daily enterprise" (p. 1). Authentic leadership not only involves the authenticity of the leader, but also the authentic relations between the leader and his or her followers. According to Gardner et al. (2005), authentic leadership relationships are characterized by the following: "(a) transparency, openness, and trust, (b) guidance toward worthy objectives, and (c) an emphasis on follower development" (p. 345). Leader authenticity is achieved through self-awareness, self-acceptance, and authentic actions and relationships (Gardner et al., 2005).

In recent years, the direction of leadership research has shifted toward development of leader authenticity. Theories related to authentic leadership development have yet to be utilized as a framework for the examination of leadership in sport settings. We suggest that authentic leadership development is an appropriate practical approach for meeting Vealey's (2005) triad of objectives for sport psychology: optimal performance, optimal development, and optimal experience for athletes. As such, we suggest that efforts to develop positive and effective sport leaders should have, as a foundation, the "root construct" of authenticity (Avolio & Gardner, 2005; George, 2003, 2007). We believe that any individual who aspires to lead, or who is expected to lead, should begin by directing their efforts toward being able to confidently respond to the question posed by Goffee and Jones (2006) in the title of their book: *Why Should Anyone Be Led by You?*

In a working model of coaching effectiveness, Horn (2008) presents elements that are consistent with existing multidimensional models used to examine effective leadership (Chelladurai & Carron, 1978; Chelladurai & Saleh, 1978, 1980; Chelladurai, 1990, 2007; Smoll and Smith, 1989). Additionally, Horn draws from developmental and social-cognitive theory as sources from which to increase understanding of coaching effectiveness. While the antecedents and consequences of coaching behaviors are similar to existing models, Horn incorporates a coach's expectancies, values, goals, and beliefs into her model in a mediating role between traditional antecedents of leader behavior and actual behavior. Consistent with authentic leadership development theory (Avolio & Gardner, 2005; George, 2003, 2007), increasing and clarifying a coach's awareness and understanding of their values, beliefs, and goals is a fertile venue for sport psychology interventions that seek to positively influence leadership behavior.

Exercise: Leading Authentically

Don't compromise yourself. You are all you've got.

—Janis Joplin

As you develop your vision as a leader, use this exercise to guide the alignment of your authentic values with that vision. Close your eyes and imagine that your life is a house. For each role in your life, imagine that there is a room in this house. There is a room for you as a member of your family, as a friend, as a student, as a coach, as an athlete, as a partner or spouse, as a parent, as a child, as a member of your church community, as an employee, and as a leader. In his book True North *(2007), Bill George posed the following hypothetical question with regard to your values within this imaginary house: What values remain consistent and do not change as you move from room to room in your house? If all of the walls were knocked down, who would you be? What values would remain constant? Some other questions to ask include the following:*

- *Have you created a vision for your team's success that is in conflict with your core values as an individual?*
- *Does your leadership behavior reflect your authentic strengths and values?*
- *Do you create opportunities for your athletes and for your staff to uncover and develop their own authentic strengths and values?*
- *Does your behavior as a leader allow others to be authentic and true to their strengths and values?*

Multidimensional Models of Leadership in Sport

Chelladurai (Chelladurai & Carron, 1978; Chelladurai & Saleh, 1978, 1980; Chelladurai, 1990, 2007) developed a multidimensional model of leadership (MML) behavior to identify and describe the behavior of leaders in specific sport situations. The MML consists of antecedents of leader behavior, leader behaviors, and consequences of leader behavior. Antecedent factors that influence leader behavior include situations, leader, and team member characteristics. The model examines leadership behavior from three perspectives: actual behavior exhibited by the coach, the type of behavior preferred by the athletes, and the type of leader behavior appropriate to or required in a given situation. Consequences of leader behavior are commonly determined through measurements of the overall satisfaction of athletes or objective group performance outcomes.

Chelladurai and Saleh (1978) developed the Leadership Scale for Sports (LSS) to assess the following dimensions of a coach's leadership style: decision making, motivational tendencies, and instructional behavior in sport settings. The LSS represents five dimensions of leader behavior in sport: training and instruction, democratic behavior, autocratic behavior, social support, and positive feedback. Using the LSS, researchers have identified the following behaviors of coaches as being most desired by athletes: training for competitiveness, providing social support, and providing rewards (Chelladurai & Riemer, 1998). Effective leadership is achieved when congruence exists among all three dimensions of leader behavior: required, actual, and preferred (Chelladurai & Riemer, 1998). Chelladurai (2007) has recently added feedback loops to his description of the MML. A coaches' behavior may be influenced by feedback he or she receives through interpretation of the influential role specific past behaviors may have played in performance outcomes.

Through qualitative methods, Côté and colleagues (1995) have created a model to describe the behavioral and cognitive aspects of effective coaching. The Coaching Model (CM; Côté et al., 1995) represents a coach's knowledge in the following six components: training, organization, competition, an athlete's personal characteristics and development, a coach's personal characteristics, and various contextual factors to create a "vision" or image of an athlete's or team's potential. Using the CM, a coach can identify and develop specific and effective coaching behaviors that will provide an optimal setting in which to prepare for training and competition. An optimal performance environment can be created through the transformation of a coach's vision of an athlete's or team's potential into a tangible mission statement to guide long- and short-term planning and organization (Desjardins, 1996).

Through interviews with five expert Canadian coaches, Vallee and Bloom (2005) conducted an investigation of factors contributing to the development of successful team sport programs. The researchers identified four variables in the leadership style of expert coaches that contributed to a turnaround from an unsuccessful program to a championship level program. They developed a holistic model to describe the coaches' success that included the following: a coach's leadership attributes, a coach's desire to foster individual growth, a coach's organizational skills, and a coach's vision.

Vallee and Bloom (2005, p. 195) offered the following suggestions for individuals trying to build successful sport programs:

- Coaches should realize that investing in the personal development of their athletes may lead to better long-term results than solely aiming to win at all costs.

- Athlete empowerment may lead to a better coach–athlete relationship.

- Coaches should utilize a broad range of characteristics to reach their athletes' preferred behavior.

- Coaches should possess strong organizational skills to help them balance the multitude of noncoaching administrative and managerial tasks.

- When coaching a new team, coaches should begin by creating a vision that includes the goals and directions for their program.

Decision Making in Coaches

Various leadership styles have been attributed to coaches in sport settings. Autocratic and democratic are two terms you may have heard used, or you may have used yourself, to describe a coach. The autocratic label is often associated with an authoritarian coach who has absolute control and makes all final decisions with little or no input from the group. Conversely, the participative or democratic coach is described as one who relinquishes control to become a part of the group and allows input and involvement of group members when decisions that affect the group are made. Finally, a permissive or laissez-faire coach is one who demonstrates no decision-making style at all. While this style may be appropriate in certain coaching situations, such as determining which color hair ribbon to wear for a specific game, it is generally not an effective leadership practice.

Labels such as autocratic and democratic are often used as absolutes when describing coaches. But such labels are often misleading and inaccurate. Vealey (2005) describes a distinction between a democratic or autocratic process and a democratic or autocratic decision. Within a democratic process, specific situations call for an autocratic decision. As Chelladurai and Queck (1995) and Chelladurai, Haggerty, and Baxter (1989) demonstrated, athletes participating on intercollegiate athletic teams preferred coaches who made decisions autocratically. This does not, however, indicate that they would prefer their overall intercollegiate athletic experience to be completely autocratic.

New England Patriots head coach, Bill Belichick, is an example of a coach who is perceived as running an organization that few would describe as democratic in nature. From the outside, group members do not appear to be consulted about game-related decisions; Belichick appears to be in complete control of all decisions related to the team. One may ask, why then has Belichick surrounded himself with such knowledgeable assistant coaches and experienced veteran NFL athletes? If his style were purely autocratic, why would he create such an information-dense net around himself?

To answer this hypothetical question, we must more closely examine the processes involved in making decisions. Decision making is considered to be an interactive process that is both cognitive and social in nature. Cognitively, the process of making a decision consists of optimal and objective use of available information. The cognitive process involved in Belichick's decision making style requires not only his own knowledge, but also the information contained in the human net of experience and information that surrounds him. The social component of the decision making process involves *who* makes a decision and *how* the ultimate decision is made. Undoubtedly, a coach will make most final decisions although this process frequently involves several other group members. While viewing decision making as an interactive process allows for a more comprehensive examination of the construct, it also increases the complexity involved in applying the information within a dynamic sport setting.

Few, if any, elite coaches make 100% of all decisions without input from another member of a group. Coaches may not consult others in every scenario. Nonetheless several situations call for broad participation in decision making. In their normative model of decision styles in coaching, Chelladurai and Haggerty (1978) indicated that the following seven attributes should be considered when determining the situational appropriateness of a given style of decision making:

1. *Time pressure.* Sport is a unique setting in which game performance may be impacted by the speed with which a decision occurs. In most sports there are shot clocks, play clocks, or timers that typically require a coach to make critical decisions with little or no input from other group members.

2. *Decision quality required.* The instrumentality of decision making in attaining the overall goals and objectives of the group should be considered. For example, the warm-up music played before a game may have less influence on the overall outcome of a game than deciding which defense the team will run when the game begins.

3. *Information location.* The appropriate source of information is required to make a high-quality decision. For example, an assistant football coach who was a former kicker and works daily with the team's kicker may be the best source of information when a head coach is making a decision about whether to attempt a field goal. Likewise, the former kicker, who has never played any other position or worked with any other team members, may not be the best source of information when calling a play on third down and long.

4. *Problem complexity.* Decisions that involve a greater a level of complexity, in terms of options, sequence of options, consequences, and relative abilities of athletes, typically are best made without consulting with the group. An example of this type of problem can be found when a coach calls a 20-second timeout in the final minute of a basketball game in which a play must be called while considering the score, the possession arrow, the foul situation, and the relative abilities

of the players on the court. In this situation, a quality coach would be unlikely to consult the group about what they would like to do on the court.

5. *Group integration.* The quality of relationships within the team, as well as balance in terms of ability and experience, should be considered when determining how to approach making decisions. A coach who has been appointed to coach a youth all-star team that has never played together would probably benefit from making game-related decisions with limited input from the whole group.

6. *Group acceptance.* Acceptance of a decision by the group will influence the outcome of a decision. For example, a high school coach's decision to appoint a freshman as captain on a varsity team may be ineffective if the group does not accept this decision as in the best interest of the team.

7. *Coach's power.* The power the coach has over a group may affect acceptance of and compliance with a decision. For example, a team is likely to accept a coach's decision to add an optional, additional hour of practice if the athletes admire and respect the coach's knowledge and experience. They may also comply with a coach's decision to add the optional, extra hour of practice if they perceive that the coach will punish them if they do not.

Various styles of decision making can be used as an effective means of enhancing the positive outcomes associated with sport participation. Coaches who use a democratic or participative style of decision making may enhance their team's feelings of ownership, self-worth, and self-confidence. Depending on the nature of the decision being made, coaches may also facilitate the development of problem-solving skills in their athletes. Likewise, a coach who effectively uses an autocratic style of decision making in times of stress will minimize athletes' stress and increase the likelihood of successful performance outcomes.

Evaluating Leadership

Interestingly, often the coach's and the athletes' perceptions of the coach's behaviors are very different (Kenow & Williams, 1992; Smith, Smoll, & Curtis, 1978). In 1992, Kenow and Williams reported that coaches rated their own behaviors more positively than athletes rated the coach's behaviors.

In addition, coaches should be aware of gender differences in preferred leadership behavior. Riemer and Toon (2001) used Riemer and Chelladurai's (1998) Athlete Satisfaction Scale and found that females preferred positive feedback behavior from the coach whereas males preferred more autocratic behavior. The researchers further suggested coaches of individual sport athletes should avoid autocratic behaviors if athlete satisfaction is to be maximized. Female athletes reported a preference for social support behavior from male coaches, but did not report the same preference from female coaches.

In a study by Martin, Jackson, Richardson, and Weiller (1999), children were asked what they thought was the most important duty of a coach. The adolescents, aged 10–18, rated skill instruction and positive feedback as most important. They also rated democratic behavior higher than autocratic behavior. Furthermore, females more than males preferred democratic coaching styles. Females also preferred social support. Ratings by parents were similar to those of their children.

Leadership in terms of influencing others to maintain programs of physical activity was studied by Fox, Rejeski, and Gauvin (2000). They found that participants were more likely to enjoy and to continue to participate in physical activity when the leader demonstrated personal interest in them and when the participants were able to positively interact with each other, thus demonstrating the efficacy of social support.

A coach must not expect any more from an athlete than what the coach is willing to give or be. Athletes are likely to emulate the coach's behavior. This means that the coach should be committed to exemplifying as well as enforcing the rules for the players. For example, if there is a punctuality rule, then the coach should abide by it, too.

Control of emotions is another expectation that most coaches have for their athletes. This is a worthy expectation, for people cannot function maximally in terms of physical performance or interpersonal relations if they lose emotional control. Decision making, information processing, speed and coordination, objectivity, reasonableness, and the acuity of the senses are just a few of the factors that are adversely affected by loss of emotional control. Coaches who lose emotional control are not performing at their optimal level, and they are also presenting negative role modeling. If coaches can misbehave on the sidelines, why can't athletes misbehave on the sidelines or lose their tempers while performing? In particular, athletes with higher anxiety and less confidence have been found to rate coaching behaviors more negatively when they perceive their coach to lack emotional control (Kenow & Williams, 1992, 1999). The athletes also felt that such behavior made them nervous and contributed to their not playing well.

Planning and commitment are also behaviors coaches expect from their athletes. In an interview with Rapaport (1993), Bill Walsh, who coached the San Francisco 49ers, stressed the importance of precise, "minute-by-minute," well-planned, and tightly structured practices. "It's all in the way you prepare" (p. 115); ". . . you need to have a plan for every scenario" (p. 113), he claimed. Bill Walsh set a standard of competence and excellence for his players and believed that "those coaches who are most successful are the ones that have demonstrated the greatest commitment to their players" (p. 112). Preparation begins with setting goals and identifying the skills and strategies needed to compete successfully.

Goal setting is appropriate and important for athletes, as well as for coaches and sport psychology consultants. The emphasis should be on short-range goals. Setting goals is only the beginning. Goals can be used to plan practices and psychological interventions down to the smallest detail. Such practices are extremely positive ways for a coach or sport leader to facilitate teaching and learning. For example, during games, Bear Bryant carried reminders on a piece of paper.

Among the things that he had written down were "Don't forget—use timeouts intelligently—double timeouts—run clock down last play—ORDERLY BENCH." (For detailed information on how to set effective goals and what strategies help to achieve these goals, see Chapter 13.)

In summary, exhibiting conduct that exemplifies the behavior expected from athletes, balancing the cost–benefit reinforcement ratio for complying with the leader's wishes, complete planning, and total commitment are specific behaviors leaders may use to improve their credibility and influence. Improvement in any of these areas can potentially increase one's effectiveness as a leader.

Feedback: Utilizing feedback

Leadership may be enhanced through effective use of feedback. Feedback should be sought from all directions, including peers, supervisors, athletes, friends, and significant others. All available sources of information should be pursued in an effort to complete the full leadership picture. An effective leader is one who lacks complacency and recognizes that growth as a leader and ability to adapt to change are contributing factors in the success of the program. Dale and Conant (2004) have recommended two methods through which to acquire information from which to develop your leadership: (1) allow the staff to provide you with feedback; and (2) allow athletes to evaluate your leadership and your program.

As a means of receiving feedback from your staff, Dale and Conant (2004) recommend the following:

The ideal situation would be for you to provide them the opportunity to provide feedback in a one-on-one manner . . . If you have individual conversations with the staff, it is important to conduct these meetings someplace other than your office . . . This will put them more at ease

and they will be more willing to be honest with you . . . It is necessary for you to take the feedback, learn from it, change those areas you feel will help the team and avoid holding grudges against your staff. If you hold grudges, no one will be honest with you in the future (p. 136).

When seeking feedback from your athletes, Dale and Conant (2004) recommend that you create a form that includes specific aspects of your coaching. Examples of areas that you may ask about include "knowledge of the sport, organization of practice, game coaching, respect of players, ability to teach skills, pride in your work, ability to communicate effectively, willingness to listen, consistency in areas such as discipline of athletes, and your disposition on a daily basis" (p. 48). Additionally, questions that indicate whether your athletes perceive your behaviors as authentic and truthful may inform your future actions.

It is recommended that athletes be allowed to provide feedback to each coach with whom they interact on a regular basis. Feedback from athletes should be anonymous to allow for honesty. Receiving feedback from those you lead may sting if you are not confident in yourself as a leader. Some feedback that is less than comfortable to hear may be the price you may have to pay for a growth opportunity. Once you have a full range of feedback about your leadership, you will be able to utilize this information to evaluate your leadership and make changes where appropriate.

Leading Ethically

Most individuals would agree that leaders in sport have a moral responsibility and obligation to promote ethical behavior in all situations. Unfortunately, the American values demonstrated, reinforced, and learned in sport are not all positive or praiseworthy. The most pervasive and potentially immoral value in sport and in society is that of "win at any cost." Such a costly attitude can be noted in the rampant use in sport of performance-enhancing drugs, violence, cheating, and practices that keep athletes eligible but fail to educate them. The unethical behaviors that emanate from this doctrine are destructive for athletes, coaches, spectators, educators, and, ultimately, society.

Granted, it is awful to lose. Anyone who competes has felt the sting. Vince Lombardi, reflecting later on his quote, "Winning isn't everything, it's the only thing," said, "I wish to hell I'd never said the damn thing. I meant having a goal. . . . I sure as hell didn't mean for people to crush human values and morality" (Michener, 1976, p. 432). Dramatic ethical and moral changes could be made in sport, and thus in society, through ethical leadership. Ethical leadership should insist that all in sport follow the letter and spirit of the rules and cease and desist from valuing the cheater, the "get away with whatever you can" ethic. Character should be the basis for our personal and social ethics. Virtue—doing the right thing—should be our goal in sport. James Naismith, the inventor of basketball mentioned earlier, had one goal in life, to "do good." How simple, and yet how profound.

John Wooden suggested that "if you know in your heart that you've made the effort to do the best of which you are capable, that's not failure, that's success. And I want each individual to feel that. It doesn't matter if it's in business or in the classroom or on the athletic field." An ethical leader should be concerned with equity and fairness in sport. Just as social issues, such as racism and sexism, are prevalent in our society, so too are they present in sport. It should be a goal of leaders in sport to provide equitable opportunities for all athletes.

If we help to develop virtuous leaders (e.g., coaches, sport psychology consultants, administrators, parents) who demand, expect, reward, and practice virtue, we will be contributing through sport to a better world. As Sophocles claimed, "I would prefer to fail with honor than to win by cheating." The Arizona Sports Summit Accord, which almost 50 sports leaders adopted on May 25, 1999, emphasizes "the ethical and character-building aspects of athletic competition—with the hope that the framework of principles and values set forth will be adopted and practiced widely" (Arizona Sport Summit Accord, 1999).

Developing Leadership within the Team

In identifying leaders within a team, a coach should be attuned to functional leadership that arises spontaneously in a climate of trust. Such a climate is present when coaches accept the uniqueness of each team member—including what might appear as deviant behavior, provided this behavior does not have a negative impact on the effectiveness of the team or the satisfaction of its members. Leadership within a team should go to the most competent. Natural leaders will usually surface if there is a climate of acceptance and if athletes are encouraged to provide input and leadership. A coach can help certain athletes demonstrate or develop their leadership abilities by giving those individuals responsibilities, small at first, and then positively reinforcing their successful attempts at leadership. In a qualitative study of six leader–athletes, Wright and Côté (2003) indicated that leadership development in sport focused on high skill, strong work ethic, sport knowledge, and good people skills. Leader–member exchange theory supports these suggestions.

Human relations within a team can be improved if everyone is aware of expectations, if the rules and regulations are clearly stated, if team procedures are well written and available, and if responsibilities that do not overlap are clearly defined. Here are some suggestions for building effective team leaders:

- Identify potential leaders and provide opportunities for leadership within the team.

- Use these athlete leaders, as well as leaders such as athletic trainers, managers, and assistant coaches, wisely by delegating authority and responsibility to them.

- Deal with all athletes and assistant leaders as individuals.
- Keep communication open and direct rather than having team leaders serve as a buffer between the coach and other athletes.

Developing Morale within the Team

Morale is an elusive quality, like charisma. Morale is a feeling within each team member that is generated by a sense of caring and belonging that is communicated within the team. Positive morale includes awareness that each individual on the team is important and the knowledge that hard work and sacrifices are recognized and appreciated. These two behaviors generate an ambiance that causes an increase in loyalty and productiveness.

Morale may determine motivation, which directs energy in either acceptable or unacceptable ways on the team. When morale is positive, it is worth more than anything money can buy. The reverse is true too. Morale can be enhanced if the leaders' behavior tells the truth. Coaches should not try to fool athletes. They should "walk the talk, walk the walk." Positive morale cannot be purchased; therefore, material incentives are not the answer. Leaders at every level are responsible for morale, from the equipment manager, to the trainer, assistant coaches, and head coach.

Further, morale is based on trust. If the players don't believe that the coach or director of athletics is working in their best interests, morale declines. Morale is resistant to change, so once trust is established the players are more tolerant of setbacks. Negative morale is also resistant to change. Without trust, it is very hard for players to move beyond defensive postures, and defensiveness impedes creativity, innovation, decision making, and productivity.

Morale is highly contagious. It is often communicated by the coach's or institution's attitude toward the team members as people. Both positive and negative information spreads like wildfire,

horizontally. Player-to-player communication consistently reinforces positive or negative perceptions of the team, its management, and management's motives. Influencing player-to-player communication must be a primary goal of any team effort if one wishes to build positive morale.

Positive morale can create a strong emotional bond to and within the team. When morale is low, player departure or disgruntlement increases. To increase positive morale, basic player security is required. Either too much security (intolerance or laziness is tolerated) or too little ("will I be next?") affects morale. Positive morale necessitates that competency is valued. Often low morale occurs when playing or starting time is based on player longevity or "who you know" or school or team politics rather than skill level. When players see this, even the most dedicated become negative or cynical.

How can a coach or athletics director assess team morale? Looking and listening informally to the following types of communication can help:

- *Humor.* Is it filled with anger, hostility, deep cynicism, or excessive sarcasm? Is there no humor at all? Look for upbeat humor that indicates athletes are laughing at the funny side of life.
- *The grapevine.* When morale is positive, the talk on the informal communication network is about the "comings and goings and doings" of people players know. When morale is low, the talk is strong and defensive: "What's the coach or A.D. going to do now?"
- *Griping and complaints.* This exists no matter how high morale is, but it typically is not serious.
- *Coach/administrator responsiveness.* Communication is usually pretty good from the top down, but what about bottom up? Are players listened to?

Coaches can boost morale when they make the environment an emotionally secure one in which a sense of caring and appreciation are communicated. Players feel a sense of belonging to something good. A positive sense of self-esteem is validated, and appreciation is expressed in positive, personally validating ways for the athletes. Further, they also feel free to change and grow. Savvy coaches can build healthy relationships within a team. Enhanced morale results in fewer player problems, a more upbeat attitude, and better performance—a win-win situation for all.

We would like to suggest 10 qualities for effective leadership that offer only positive benefits for those who employ them. They are symbolic derivatives of the original "magic words," please and thank you. They are effective and help others work better. They are fundamental to human relationships.

1. *Trust* is given as a gift, although once given it must be nurtured because it is so fragile it can be broken by one lie. When we trust others, they trust us. As a leader, "dig into the problem, not the person."

2. *Fairness* is like beauty, for it is often "in the eye of the beholder." Whether or not fairness is achieved or perceived, it must be our goal. Athletes will accept a coach's actions even if they disagree with them, as long as they believe the coach acted out of the principle of fairness.

3. *Generosity* is forgiving past grievances or mistakes. It is giving the benefit of the doubt. It involves providing opportunities for others to shine. It is demonstrated by speaking more often of "we" than "I."

4. *Respect* is showing and treating others with esteem, consideration, and regard.

5. *Consideration* is demonstrating concern for others as individuals. In current society the stress and pressure to succeed are high. There are ways of dealing with stress that avoid acting disrespectfully toward others.

6. *Gratefulness* is appreciating and being thankful for everything. Although many athletes demonstrate a sense of entitlement, we are not entitled to anything in this world. Entitlements are gifts from others; therefore, take no one or no pleasure for granted. Grateful leaders see opportunities where the entitled see problems and despair.

7. *Dignity* is carrying oneself with pride and self-respect. It shines through at all times, especially during trying times. Leaders with dignity look the part. If we don't recognize our own dignity and that of others, our respect is lost. Dignity is something we have and do not want damaged, whereas respect is something we give to others. Coaches who forget their own dignity find that others lose regard for them. Coaches who snivel, whine, make excuses for poor performance (such as blaming others), or seek special privileges compromise their respect. Coaches and leaders need to find ways to help others preserve their dignity as well. The "isms" are ways we prevent giving respect, which takes dignity away from those who may be different.

8. *Integrity* is to be integrated psychologically, spiritually, intellectually, ethically, and socially. Leaders with integrity don't speak out of both sides of their mouths. Having integrity has potential benefits as well as pain for the leader. The positive side of having integrity is that the leader has predictable values that athletes can rely on. The painful part of having integrity is that holding to a core principle can cost one personally. Integrity does not mean rigidity; it means holding dear to various parts of your life, to yourself.

9. *Caring candor* is giving feedback that shows you are concerned about the person, especially if the feedback is critical. When using caring candor, the coach does not hang a person and then give them a fair trial. Caring candor is descriptive rather than punitive, so it is not *brutal* honesty. Coaches who lose their tempers do not motivate others. Athletes want no part of coaches who invade their space and scream and carry on in what amounts to tantrums. Tantrums are selfish and self-centered. Today there are few successful bullies.

10. *Responsiveness* is being dependable. It is reacting easily or readily to suggestion or appeal, or closing the communication gap. Coaches who are unresponsive might be procrastinators, or they might say "yes," but lack follow-through. Responsive leaders are on time, make calls and decisions, write reports, do the paperwork, confront when necessary, pay compliments, and do more than what is required or expected. When a coach makes a commitment, it is to be honored.

In the 21st century, leadership will be through persuasion and goodwill; it will replace leadership through power and intimidation. These qualities are not intended to manipulate others. They are basic humanistic contentions about dignity and worth of others.

Because of the significant role coaches play in the skill and personal development of their athletes, their influence, power, and effect cannot be negated. Being a good leader involves an appreciation of leadership theory and knowledge of how a leader can maximize influence and followership through positive role modeling, planning, preparation, and being true to oneself. Leaders must accept their athletes' individuality as well as their own.

Leadership theory, as well as coaching experience, offer specific ideas of what coaches, athletic directors, and sport psychology consultants who are responsible professionals and successful leaders should do:

- Master and apply current knowledge of sport physiology, psychology, and biomechanics.

- Develop interpersonal skills including the communication skills of speaking, writing, observing, understanding defensive mechanisms, motivating, and listening. Of all the communication skills, coaches are generally the weakest at listening. Interpersonal interactions are critical to sport success, and communication is the key (Mancini & Agnew, 1978). See Chapter 9 for a discussion of effective communication skills.

- Eliminate all sexist, ageist, heterosexist, racist, ableist, and dehumanizing language.

- Eliminate any attitude that involves the humiliation of losers and the glorification of winners.

- Encourage the athletes to view the opponent as a challenge and not an enemy.

- Understand the effects of social reinforcement on individual performance.

- Control one's own arousal level and be an example for the athletes of the emotionality needed for successful performance.

- Help athletes set their *own* goals. Emphasize the process (participation and playing as well as possible) and not the outcome (winning). This is an important concept because goals should be something that an individual can accomplish or control. Athletes can control their own performance but not the opponents'.

- Live in the present. Do *not* constantly remind athletes of past winners or of the potential for team success two years hence.

- Provide opportunities for success through well-planned practices, good game conditions, sensible scheduling, and a pleasant atmosphere. The administrative aspects of a coach's job cannot be overlooked. Planning, preparation, and budgeting are important functions that affect leadership performance.

- A coach must be a teacher, a leader, and an administrator.

- Be rational and humanistic.

Summary

Successful coaches create environments in which trust, respect, and consideration grow and flourish. When these aspects are present in daily interactions with others, organizations, teams, students, players, and colleagues have a high quality of life, resulting in greater productivity and service. This makes work much more manageable and enjoyable. An effort should be made to keep our teams, schools, organizations, disciplines, and professions safe from pollutants such as fear, selfishness, bigotry, abuse, deceit, and prejudice.

We propose that the future direction of research related to leadership effectiveness and development in sport should involve a closer examination of the authenticity of effective leaders. Additionally, we propose that future researchers consider applying the existing descriptive models of leadership behaviors to address the gap in the sport literature related to strategies for developing individual leaders in and through sport. As coaches and sport psychology consultants, we should commit to leadership in sport that is dedicated to the ethics and morality of positive growth for all athletes.

Study Questions

1. Why is leadership of particular interest to sport psychology consultants?
2. Describe the authoritarian personality profile.
3. Distinguish between the trait and behavioral leadership theories.
4. Is there a difference in expectations between what coaches and athletes prefer for leadership in the sport environment?
5. Describe in detail one situational theory. How do situational theories differ from trait and behavioral theories?
6. Explain the 10 suggested qualities for successful leadership.
7. Describe the various styles of decision making.
8. What situational attributes may influence the manner in which a decision is made.
9. List four suggestions for building effective team leaders.
10. Identify factors, traits, and behaviors that you believe are important for the effective leader.
11. Describe the behaviors of a transformational leader.
12. Discuss ways in which various theories of leadership are related or integrated.
13. Discuss the benefits of various styles of decision making.
14. Identify ways to foster and model ethical behavior.
15. Discuss Howard Gardner's cognitive framework for leadership and how it might be developed.
16. Discuss "authenticity" and leadership.

References

Arizona Sport Summit Accord. (1999). Pursuing victory with honor [Online]. Available at http://www.charactercounts.org

Avolio, B. J., & Gardner, W. L. (2005). Authentic leadership development: Getting to the root of positive forms of leadership. *Leadership Quarterly, 16*, 315–338.

Avolio, B. J., & Luthans, F. (2006). *The high impact leader: Moments that matter in authentic leadership development.* New York: McGraw-Hill.

Barrow, J. C. (1977). The variables of leadership: A review and conceptual framework. *Academy of Management Review, 2*, 233–251.

Bass, B., & Avolio, B. (1995). *MLQ: Multifactor Leadership Questionnaire.* Palo Alto, CA: Mind Garden.

Bennis, W., & Biederman, P. W. (1997). *Organizing genius: The secrets of creative collaboration.* Reading, MA: Addison-Wesley.

Bennis, W. G., & Nanus, B. (1985). *Leaders: The strategies for taking charge.* New York: Harper & Row.

Blake, R. R., & Mouton, J. S. (1964). *The managerial grid.* Houston, TX: Gulf.

Blake, R. R., & Mouton, J. S. (1978). *The new managerial grid.* Houston, TX: Gulf.

Black, S. J., & Weiss, M. R. (1992). The relationship among perceived coaching behaviors, perceptions of ability, and motivation in competitive age-group swimmers. *Journal of Sport and Exercise Psychology, 14*, 309–325.

Burns, J. M. (1978). *Leadership.* New York: Harper & Row.

Carron, A. V. (1984). *Motivation: Implications for coaching and teaching.* London, ON: Sports Dynamics.

Case, R. (1984). Leadership behavior in sport: A field test of situational leadership theory. *International Journal of Sport Psychology, 18*, 256–268.

Case, R. (1998). Leader member exchange theory and sport: Possible applications. *Journal of Sport Behavior, 21*, 387–93.

Charbonneau, D., Barling, J., & Kelloway, E. K. (2001). Transformational leadership and sports performance: The mediating role of intrinsic motivation. *Journal of Applied Social Psychology, 31*, 1521–1534.

Chelladurai, P. (1990). Leadership in sports: A review. *International Journal of Sport Psychology, 21*, 328–354.

Chelladurai, P. (2007). Leadership in sports. In G. Tenenbaum & R. C. Eklund (Eds.), *Handbook of sport psychology* (3rd ed.) (pp. 113–135). Morgantown, WV: Fitness Information Technology.

Chelladurai, P., & Carron, A. V. (1978). *Leadership.* Canadian Association for Health, Physical Education and Recreation, Sociology of Sport Monograph Series. Ottawa, Ontario.

Chelladurai, P. & Haggerty, T. R. (1978). A normative model of decision styles in coaching. *Athletic Administrator, 13*, 6–9.

Chelladurai, P., Haggerty, T. R., & Baxter, P. R. (1989). Decision style choices of university basketball coaches and players. *Journal of Sport and Exercise Psychology, 11,* 201–215.

Chelladurai, P., & Quek, C. B. (1995). Decision style choices of high school basketball coaches: The effects of situational and coach characteristics. *Journal of Sport Behavior, 18,* 91–108.

Chelladurai, P., & Riemer, H. A. (1998). In J. L. Duda (Ed.), *Advances in sport and exercise psychology* (pp. 227–253). Morgantown, WV: Fitness Information Technology.

Chelladurai, P., & Saleh, S. (1978). Preferred leadership in sport. *Canadian Journal of Applied Sport Sciences, 3,* 85–97.

Chelladurai, P., & Saleh, S. (1980). Dimensions of leader behaviors in sports: Development of a leadership scale. *Journal of Sport Psychology, 2,* 34–45.

Côté, J., Salmela, J., Trudel, P., Baria, A., & Russell, S. (1995). The coaching model: A grounded assessment for expert gymnastic coaches' knowledge. *Journal of Sport and Exercise Psychology, 17,* 1–17.

Dale, G., & Conant, S. (2004). *101 teambuilding activities: Ideas every coach can use to enhance teamwork, communication, and trust.* Durham, NC: Excellence in Performance.

Desjardins, G., Jr. (1996). The mission. In J. H. Salmela (Ed.), *Great job coach! Getting the edge from proven winners* (pp. 69–100). Ottawa, ON: Potentium.

Dienesch, R. M., & Linden, R. C. (1986). Leader–member exchange model of leadership: A critique and further development. *Academy of Management Journal, 11,* 618–634.

Doherty, A. J., & Danylchuk, K. E. (1996). Transformational and transactional leadership in interuniversity athletics management. *Journal of Sport Management, 10* (3), 292–309.

Feltz, D. L., Chase, M. A., Moritz, S. E., & Sullivan, P. J. (1999). A conceptual model of coaching efficacy: Preliminary investigation and instrument development. *Journal of Educational Psychology, 91,* 765–776.

Fiedler, F. (1967). *A theory of leadership effectiveness.* New York: McGraw-Hill.

Fox, L. D., Rejeski, W. J., & Gauvin, L. (2000). Effects of leadership style and group dynamics on enjoyment of physical activity. *American Journal of Health Promotion, 14* (5), 277–283.

Gardner, H. (1995). *Leading minds: An anatomy of leadership.* New York: Basic Books.

Gardner, J. W. (1990). *On leadership.* New York: The Free Press.

Gardner, W. L., Avolio, B. J., Luthans, F., May, D. R., & Walumba, F. O. (2005). "Can you see the real me?" A self-based model of authentic leader and follower development. *Leadership Quarterly, 16,* 343-372.

George, B. (2003). *Authentic leadership.* San Francisco: Jossey-Bass.

George, B., (with) Simms, P. (2007). *True north: Discover your authentic leadership.* San Francisco, CA: Jossey-Bass.

Gestner, C. R., & Day, D. V. (1997). Meta-analytic review of leader–member exchange theory: Correlates and construct issues. *Journal of Applied Psychology, 82,* 827–844.

Goffee, R., & Jones, G. (2006). *Why should anyone be led by you?* Boston, MA: Harvard Business School Press.

Goleman, D. (1998). What makes a leader? *Harvard Business Review, 76,* 93–102.

Graen, G., & Cashman, J. F. (1975). A role-making model of leadership in formal organizations: A developmental approach. In J. G. Hunt & L. L. Larson (Eds.), *Leadership frontiers* (pp. 143–165). Kent, OH: Kent State University Press.

Graen, G. B., & Uhl-Bien, M. (1995). Relationship-based approach to leadership: Development of leader-member exchange (LMX) theory of leadership over 25 years: Applying a multi-level multi-domain approach. *Leadership Quarterly, 6,* 219–247.

Halpin, A. W. (1957). *Manual for the leader behavior description questionnaire.* Columbus, OH: Bureau of Business Research.

Halpin, A. W., & Winer, B. J. (1957). A factorial study of leader behavior descriptions. In R. M. Stodgill & A. E. Coons (Eds.), *Leader behavior: Its description and measurement* (pp. 399–451). Columbus, OH: Bureau of Business Research.

Hendry, L. B. (1972). The coaching stereotype. In H. T. A. Whiting (Ed.), *Readings in sport psychology.* London: Kingston.

Hendry, L. (1974). Human factors in sport systems. *Human Factors, 16,* 528–544.

Hersey, P., & Blanchard, K. H. (1969). Life style theory of leadership. *Training and Development Journal, 23,* 26–34.

Hersey, P., & Blanchard, K. H. (1977). *Management of organizational behavior.* Englewood Cliffs, NJ: Prentice Hall.

Hershey, P. G., & Blanchard, K. (1982). Leadership style: Attitudes and behavior. *Training and Development Journal, 36* (5), 50–52.

Hogg, M. A., & Martin, R. (2003). Social identity analysis of leader-member relations: Reconciling self-categorization and leader–member exchange theories of leadership. In S. A. Haslam, D. van Knippenberg, M. J. Platow, & N. Ellemers (Eds.), *Social identity at work: Developing theory for organizational practice* (pp. 134–154). New York: Psychology Press.

Hogg, M. A., Martin, R., & Weedon, K. (2003). Leader–member relations and social identity. In D. van Knippenberg & M. A. Hogg (Eds.), *Leadership and power: Identity processes in group organizations* (pp. 18–33). London: Sage.

Hogg, M. A., Martin, R., Epitropaki, O., Mankad, A., Svensson, A., & Weeden, K. (2005). Effective leadership in salient groups: Revisiting leader–member exchange theory from the perspective of social identity theory of leadership. *Personality and Social Psychology Bulletin, 31* (7), 991–10041.

Horn, T. S. (2008). Coaching effectiveness in the sport domain. In T. S. Horn (Ed.), *Advances in sport psychology* (3rd ed.) (pp. 239–267). Champaign, IL: Human Kinetics.

House, R. J. (1971). A path–goal theory of leader effectiveness. *Administrative Science Quarterly, 16,* 321–338.

House, R. J. (1976). A 1976 theory of charismatic leadership. In J. G. Hunt & L. L. Larson (Eds.), *Leadership: The winning edge.* Carbondale: Southern Illinois University Press.

Jackson, P. & Rosen, C. (2001). *More than a game*. New York: Seven Stories Press.

Kaplan, E. (1983, January 30). The legend of Vince Lombardi. *Family Weekly*.

Kenow, L. J., & Williams, J. M. (1992). Relationship between anxiety, self-confidence, and evaluation of coaching behaviors. *The Sport Psychologist, 6*, 344–357.

Kenow, L., & Williams, J. (1999). Coach–athlete compatibility and athlete's perception of coaching behaviors. *Journal of Sport Behavior, 22*, 251–259.

Kernis, M. H. (2003). Toward an conceptualization of optimal self-esteem. *Psychological Inquiry, 14*, 1–26.

Kouzes, J. M., & Posner, B. Z. (1987). *The leadership challenge: How to get extraordinary things done in organizations*. San Francisco: Jossey-Bass.

Loughead, T. M., & Hardy, J. (2005). An examination of coach and peer leader behaviors in sport. *Psychology of Sport and Exercise, 6*, 303–313.

Luthans, F. & Avolio, B. J. (2003). Authentic leadership: A positive developmental approach. In K. S. Cameron, J. E. Dutton, and R. E. Quinn, (Eds.), *Positive organizational scholarship* (pp. 241–261). San Francisco, CA: Barrett-Koehler.

Maier, R., & Laurakis, D. (1981). Some personality correlates of attitudes about sports. *International Journal of Sport Psychology, 12*, 19–22.

Mancini, V., & Agnew, M. (1978). An analysis of teaching and coaching behaviors. In W. Straub, (Ed.), *Sport psychology: An analysis of athlete behavior*. Ithaca, NY: Movement Publications.

Martin, S. B., Jackson, A. W., Richardson, P. A., & Weiller, K. H. (1999). Coaching and preferences of adolescent youths and their parents. *Journal of Applied Sport Psychology, 11*, 247–262.

Mayer, J. D., & Salovey, P. (1997). What is emotional intelligence? In P. Salovey & D. Sluyter (Eds.), *Emotional development and emotional intelligence: Implications for educators* (pp. 3–31). New York: Basic Books.

Meyer, B. B., & Fletcher, T. B. (2007). Emotional intelligence: A theoretical overview and implications for research and professional practice in sport psychology. *Journal of Applied Sport Psychology, 19*, 1–15.

Michener, J. A. (1976). *Sports in America*. Greenwich, CT: Fawcett.

Naisbitt, J. (1984). *Megatrends*. New York: Warner Books.

Nanus, B. (1989). *The leader's edge: The seven keys to leadership in a turbulent world*. Chicago: Contemporary Books.

Nanus, B. (1992). *Visionary leadership: Creating a compelling sense of direction for your organization*. San Francisco: Josey-Bass.

Neil, G. I., & Kirby, S. L. (1985). Coaching styles and preferred leadership among rowers and paddlers. *Journal of Sport Behavior, 8*, 3–17.

Prujin, G. H. J., & Boucher, R. L. (1995). The relationship of transactional and transformational leadership to the organizational effectiveness of Dutch National Sport Organizations. *European Journal for Sport Management, 2*, 72–87.

Rapaport, R. (1993, January–February). To build a winning team: An interview with head coach Bill Walsh. *Harvard Business Review, 71* (1), 111–120.

Reich, R. (1983). *The next American frontier.* New York: Times Books.

Riemer, H. A., & Chelladurai, P. (1998). Development of the Athlete Satisfaction Questionnaire (ASQ). *Journal of Sport and Exercise Psychology, 20,* 127–156.

Riemer, H. A., & Toon, K. (2001). Leadership and satisfaction in tennis: Examination of congruence, gender, and ability. *Research Quarterly for Exercise and Sport, 72* (3), 243–256.

Sage, G. (1975). An occupational analysis of the college coach. In D. Ball & L. Loy (Eds.), *Sport and social order.* Reading, MA: Addison-Wesley.

Seltzer, J., & Bass, B. M. (1990). Transformational leadership: Beyond initiation and consideration. *Journal of Management, 16,* 693–703.

Smith, R. E., Smoll, F. L., & Curtis, B. (1978). Coaching behaviors in Little League Baseball. In F. L. Smoll & R. E. Smith (Eds.), *Psychological perspectives in youth sports* (pp. 173–201). Washington, DC: Hemisphere.

Smoll, F. L., & Smith R. E. (1989). Leadership behaviors in sport: A theoretical model and research paradigm. *Journal of Applied Social Psychology, 19,* 1522–1551.

Stogdill, R. (1974). *Handbook of leadership: A survey of theory and research.* New York: Free Press.

Triandis, H. C. (1971). *Attitude and attitude change.* New York: Wiley.

Vallee, C. N., & Bloom, G. A. (2005). Building a successful university program: Key and common elements of expert coaches. *Journal of Applied Sport Psychology, 17,* 179–196.

Vealey, R. S. (2005). *Coaching for the inner edge.* Morgantown, WV: Fitness Information Technology.

Von Strache, C. (1979). Players' perceptions of leadership qualities for coaches. *Research Quarterly, 50,* 679–686.

Weese, W. J. (1995). A synthesis of leadership theory and a prelude to the five "C" model. *European Journal of Sport Management, 2,* 59–71.

Weese, W. J., & Bourner, F. (1995). Effective leadership and organizational effectiveness in the Canadian Hockey League. *European Journal of Sport Management, 2,* 88–100.

Weiss, M. R., & Friedrichs, W. D. (1986). The influence of leader behaviors, coach attributes, and institutional variables on performance and satisfaction of collegiate basketball teams. *Journal of Sport Psychology, 8,* 332–346.

Wright, A., & Côté, J. (2003). A retrospective analysis of leadership development through sport. *The Sport Psychologist, 17,* 268–291.

Yukl, G. (1989). *Leadership in organizations* (2nd ed.). Englewood Cliffs, NJ: Prentice Hall.

Zaccaro, S. J. (2007). Trait-based perspectives of leadership. *American Psychologist, 62* (1), 6–16.

Zacharatos, A., Barling, J., & Kelloway, E. K. (2000). Development and effects of transformational leadership in adolescents. *Leadership Quarterly, 11,* 211–226.

CHAPTER

7

The Sport Team as an Effective Group

Mark A. Eys, *Laurentian University*
Shauna M. Burke, *The University of Western Ontario*
Albert V. Carron, *The University of Western Ontario*
Paul W. Dennis, *Toronto Maple Leafs Hockey Club*

I'm humiliated, not for the loss—I can always deal with wins and losses—but I'm disappointed because I had a job to do as a coach, to get us to understand how we're supposed to play as a team and act as a team, and I don't think we did that.

—*United States Men's Olympic Basketball Coach Larry Brown after losing to Puerto Rico in the preliminary rounds of the Athens 2004 Summer Games*

Membership and involvement in groups is a fundamental characteristic of our society. We band together in a large number and variety of groups for social reasons or to carry out more effectively some job or task. Thus, each of us interacts daily with numerous other people in group settings—in the family, at work, in social situations, on sport teams. The result is a reciprocal exchange of influence; we exert an influence on other people in groups, and, in turn, those groups and their members have an influence on us. The following two examples illustrate just how powerful this influence can be.

In January 1980, Tony Conigliaro, a former Boston Red Sox baseball player, was driving with his brother when he suffered a massive heart attack—he experienced "sudden death." At least 6 minutes passed before CPR was administered

and his heart was stimulated into activity. He remained in a coma for 4 days, and the prognosis for any significant recovery was bleak. A lack of oxygen to the brain for as few as 4 minutes can produce permanent brain damage. Also, people who are comatose for the length of time Conigliaro experienced are almost never able to walk, talk, or look after themselves totally again.

Conigliaro's family refused to believe the prognosis. They were at his side constantly, talking, encouraging, and providing love and affection. Slowly Conigliaro fought back, began to talk, and showed improvements that astounded his doctors. In fact, as Maximillian Kaulback, one of his doctors, stated, "This case is beyond science. . . . I wouldn't be surprised if someday it was proven that the input of the family in cases like this is significant" (as quoted in McCallum,

1982, p. 72). The incident is powerful and moving; it also illustrates the importance of the family's positive influence—its love, concern, and physical and emotional support. The second illustration, however, shows another side of group influence.

In August of 2003, members of a high school football team in Pennsylvania attended a preseason camp. During the week of practices and team bonding, three members of the team were subjected to the common practice of hazing, a process of humiliating new members of the group. However, in this instance, the actions of the more senior members not only humiliated the freshmen but caused two members to seek medical treatment for their injuries. As a result, a number of spiraling events occurred that included the suspension of the team, first-degree felony charges for the perpetrators, and a media frenzy around the small community. Wahl and Wertheim (2003) described the situation:

> As the hazing inquiry intensified and the severity of the acts became more apparent, investigators from the criminal justice system . . . confronted an impenetrable wall of silence. The victims had spoken, albeit reluctantly, but no other players were willing to provide firsthand accounts. Nuwer says this is typical behavior: "Until you get to be about 25 years old, loyalty to the group is more important than moral qualms. We're more likely to agree as a group that we should turn on this victim than we are to confront one another."

These anecdotes show the dramatic influence groups can have on their members. In the Conigliaro case the influence was a positive one, whereas in the hazing case the influence was negative and destructive. The fundamental question is how groups can come to exert such influence. From a coaching perspective, insight into this issue could produce possible prescriptions for the development of a positive, productive sport group—an effective, cohesive team. In this chapter, both the nature of groups and group cohesion are discussed, and some suggestions for the development of effective groups in sport settings are offered.

The Nature of Sport Groups

Definition

As Carron, Hausenblas, and Eys (2005) note, "every group is like all other groups, like some other groups, and like no other group" (p. 11). What this means, of course, is that every group not only contains characteristics that are common to every other group but they also possess characteristics that are unique to themselves. The uniqueness or diversity among groups has led group dynamics theoreticians to advance a variety of definitions in an attempt to portray what a group is. With regard to sport groups, Carron et al. defined a team as:

> a collection of two or more individuals who possess a common identity, have common goals and objectives, share a common fate, exhibit structured patterns of interaction and modes of communication, hold common perceptions about group structure, are personally and instrumentally interdependent, reciprocate interpersonal attraction, and consider themselves to be a group. (p. 13)

A university basketball team can be used to illustrate each of these definitional components. Such teams are typically composed of 12 athletes (i.e., two or more individuals), all of whom consider themselves to be members of a group representing the university in intercollegiate competitions (i.e., common identity). Every team has explicit or implicit short- and long-term goals such as, for instance, winning upcoming games or eventually winning the conference (i.e., common goals and objectives). Success or failure in the achievement of these goals is experienced by the team as a whole (i.e., common fate). To increase the chance for team success, the coaching staff implements and emphasizes team offensive plays and defensive formations (i.e., structured pattern of interaction). In the heat of game competition, the athletes (or coaching staff) communicate various offensive or defensive options using either nonverbal communications or coded verbal communications (i.e., structured modes of communication).

Over time, team positions become fixed, individual roles such as leadership become established, and common expectations for behavior develop (i.e., group structure). In order for the team to function effectively, team social gatherings and team competitions must be attended by a minimum quorum of athletes (i.e., personal and task interdependence). Because of the constant contact athletes have in a team context, friendships typically develop (i.e., interpersonal attraction). Finally, athletes on any team consider themselves to be members of that group (i.e., self-categorization).

It should be noted that the above characteristics are likely present *to some degree* on all sport teams. However, some characteristics will be more or less important than others and it is possible that others could be absent in certain contexts (e.g., it is not always a necessity for interpersonal attraction to be present for task-oriented groups to be successful; see Lenk, 1969). Regardless, on a sport team, coaches or leaders must facilitate the development of the sense of "we" and reduce the importance of "I." Associated with the development of a stronger sense of "we" is an increase in group cohesiveness.

Group Cohesion

Definition

Groups are dynamic, not static. They exhibit life and vitality, interaction, and activity. Their vitality may be reflected in many ways—some positive, others negative. For example, at times the group and its members may be in harmony; at other times, conflict and tension may predominate. Sometimes communication may be excellent between leaders and members, but at other times, it may be nonexistent. Also, commitment to the group's goals and purposes may vary over time. All these variations represent different behavioral manifestations of an underlying, fundamental group property that is referred to as "cohesiveness." Carron, Brawley, and Widmeyer (1998) proposed that cohesion is "a dynamic process which is reflected in the tendency for

a group to stick together and remain united in the pursuit of its instrumental objectives and/or for the satisfaction of member affective needs" (p. 213).

Cohesion has many dimensions or aspects—it is perceived in multiple ways by different groups and their members. It has been proposed (Brawley, Carron, & Widmeyer, 1987; Carron, Widmeyer, & Brawley, 1985; Widmeyer, Brawley, & Carron, 1985) that these multidimensional perceptions of the group are organized and integrated by individual members into two general categories (Figure 7-1). The first category, **group integration,** represents each individual's perceptions about the closeness, similarity, and bonding within the group as a total unit, set, or collection (i.e., it consists of "we" and/or "us" evaluations). The second, **individual attractions to the group,** represents each individual's personal attractions to the group, and more specifically, what personal motivations act to retain an individual in the group (i.e., consists of "I" and/or "me" evaluations). Both of these categories of perceptions about the degree of unity within the group are also assumed to be manifested in two principal ways: in relation to the group's *task* and in terms of the *social* aspects of the group. This conception of cohesiveness is depicted in Figure 7-1. As the figure

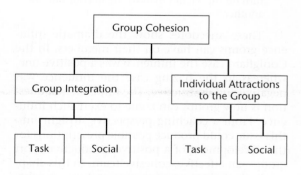

Figure 7-1 A conceptual model for group cohesiveness
Source: Brawley, Carron, and Widmeyer, 1987; Carron, Widmeyer, and Brawley, 1985; Widmeyer, Brawley, and Carron, 1985.

shows, cohesion within sport groups is considered to have four facets: individual attractions to the group–task, individual attractions to the group–social, group integration–task, and group integration–social.

The Correlates of Cohesiveness

Because cohesiveness is multidimensional, it is associated with a wide variety of correlates or factors. Carron et al. (2005) have provided a framework to discuss the main correlates of cohesion in sport teams. As Figure 7-2 shows, one general category is referred to as *environmental factors,* which are situational. Cohesiveness in sport teams is related to aspects of the social setting, the physical environment, and various structural characteristics of the group. Characteristics of individual team members are also associated with the nature and amount of cohesiveness that is present; the category *personal factors* represents these correlates. *Leadership factors,* the third general category, are an acknowledgment that decision styles, leader behaviors, and leader–member relations are also related to team cohesion. The fourth category, *team factors,* represents the group-based aspects that are associated with a stronger bond, a sense of "we," and a commitment to the collective. In the following sections,

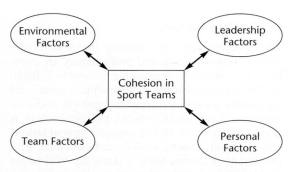

Figure 7-2 **A general framework for examining the correlates of cohesion in sport teams**
Source: Reprinted by permission from Carron and Hausenblas, 1998.

some of the main correlates within each general category are identified.

Developing a Team Concept: Correlates of Cohesion

Environmental Factors

Individuals who are in close **proximity,** who are physically close to each other, have a greater tendency to bond together. Physical proximity by itself is not always sufficient for producing cohesiveness, but being in close contact and having the opportunity for interaction and communication does hasten group development. Some situations in sport that ensure physical proximity among group members include having a specific team locker room, residence, or athletic therapy center. In youth sport situations, scheduling games that require the team to travel together in a bus or car is also beneficial. The important point is that group members should be placed in situations where interaction is inevitable.

A second situational factor associated with the development of cohesiveness is **distinctiveness.** As a set of individuals becomes more separate, more distinctive from others, feelings of oneness and unity increase. Traditionally, distinctiveness is achieved through team uniforms and mottos, by providing special privileges, or by demanding special sacrifices.

Many of the factors that make athletes distinct from the general population are taken for granted. These include year-round intensive training programs and reduced time for social activities or part-time employment. The coach should highlight such factors to develop a stronger feeling of commonality. Finally, emphasizing the sense of tradition and the history of the organization or team can contribute to the feeling of distinctiveness.

The team's **size** is also associated with the development of cohesiveness. Research by Widmeyer, Brawley, and Carron (1990) has shown that there is an inverted-U relationship between social cohesion and team size in intramural basketball teams. That is, moderate-sized groups showed the greatest cohesiveness, and larger and smaller groups exhibited the least. Interestingly, the results of this study also showed that task cohesiveness decreases with increasing group size. Widmeyer and colleagues felt that this decrease could be attributed to the fact that it is more difficult to obtain consensus and task commitment in larger groups. In research by Widmeyer and Williams (1991) using only the travel rosters of women's NCAA golf teams, social cohesion did not vary with team size, although increasing team size was associated with increasing task cohesion. However, they only tested the four to five competitors on the travel rosters who were actually involved in the competition. The maximum team size among the teams examined was 12. Consequently, it is possible that the responses from the seven to eight golfers who were not on the travel rosters might have substantially altered the profile of the team's cohesiveness.

Personal Factors

A number of personal factors have been shown to be associated with cohesion. Arguably the most important personal factor associated with the development of both task and social cohesion in sport teams is individual **satisfaction.** Satisfaction is derived from many sources (Widmeyer & Williams, 1991). The quality of the competition is one element; having opportunities for social interactions with teammates is another. In order to feel satisfied, athletes also need to feel that they are improving in skill. Satisfaction also results from the recognition of others—parents, coaches, teammates, fellow students, the public. And, of course, the athlete's relationship with his or her coach is yet another potential source of satisfaction or dissatisfaction. When these elements are satisfying, cohesiveness is enhanced.

Another personal factor that has been shown to be related to cohesion is **competitive state anxiety.** Prapavessis and Carron (1996) found that athletes who perceived their teams to be higher in task cohesion seemed to experience less cognitive anxiety. They suggested that this might be the case because members of more cohesive

teams could experience less pressure to (a) carry out the responsibilities of the group and (b) satisfy other members' expectations of themselves. In addition, Eys, Hardy, Carron, and Beauchamp (2003) extended the above work and found that those athletes who perceived greater task cohesion were more likely to view their symptoms of both cognitive (e.g., worry) and somatic (e.g., sweaty palms) anxiety as facilitative (i.e., beneficial) and necessary for their competition.

The degree to which athletes engage in **social loafing** is another personal factor related to cohesion. Social loafing reflects "the reduction in individual effort when people work in groups versus when they work alone" (Carron et al., 2005, p. 250). Individuals feel they can reduce their effort in a group for a number of reasons. These include the fact that once more people take part in a task it is easier to get lost in the crowd and, thus, not expend as much effort. However, McKnight, Williams, and Widmeyer (1991) found that individuals who were members of swimming relay teams that were high in task cohesion were less likely to be social loafers.

Finally, other personal factors that are related to increased cohesion include a tendency to assume greater responsibility for negative events and outcomes (Brawley, Carron, & Widmeyer, 1987), greater commitment to the team or organization (Widmeyer & Williams, 1991), and an increase in sacrifice behaviors (Carron et al., 2005).

Leadership Factors

The interrelationships among the coach, the athlete, cohesiveness, and performance are complex. In a mutiny, for example, cohesion is high, the leader–subordinate relationship is poor (and the leader is excluded from the group), and performance from an organizational perspective is poor. One example of the complex interrelationship between coach, athlete, cohesiveness, and performance comes from a study by Widmeyer and Williams (1991). They had golf coaches rate the importance they attached to task cohesion, the importance they attached to social cohesion, and the number of techniques they used to foster cohesiveness. These measures were not related to their athletes' perceptions of the amount of team cohesiveness. In short, in the Widmeyer and Williams study, coaches were not crucial to the development of group cohesion.

Another example of the complex relationship arises when a leader is on the fringe of the group from the perspective of cohesiveness—this can produce problems. The perceptions a group has about itself, about other groups, and about nongroup members often become distorted with increased group cohesiveness. The group tends to be very favorable in its perception of its own members and to overvalue its own contributions, importance, and performance. Also, the group tends to undervalue the contributions, importance, and performance of other groups or nongroup members. This turning inward can lead to some difficulties for a new, formally appointed leader such as a coach. The new leader may not be readily accepted, and any proposed changes to existing practices may be met with resistance (Jewell & Reitz, 1981).

This situation is often encountered in sport when a new coach replaces a highly popular, highly successful predecessor. The group makes constant comparisons between the two leaders' personalities, methods, and so on. And because a cohesive group tends to overvalue its own membership and undervalue outsiders, the new coach will encounter initial difficulties in being accepted.

When people have ownership over a decision, they tend to support that decision more strongly. Consequently, the coach's *decision style* can have an influence on the level of cohesiveness within the team. Team members engage in behaviors more persistently, with greater intensity, and for a longer duration when they have had an opportunity to participate in decision making. In short, as Westre and Weiss (1991) found when they examined the relationship between coaching behaviors and the perceptions of team cohesion by high school football players, coaches who are viewed as engaging in more democratic behaviors will be more likely to have teams with higher cohesion.

Team Factors

When a set of individuals is brought together with the intention of performing as a group, cohesion can be influenced by a number of structural characteristics that emerge as the group develops (e.g., roles and norms), processes that take place between group members (e.g., group goals, communication), and group performance outcomes that occur throughout the duration of its existence. The emergence of these factors is inevitable and essential if the set of individuals is to become a more cohesive group.

Roles. A role is a set of behaviors that are expected from the occupants of specific positions within the group. Thus, when we think of the "role of a coach," a number of expectations for behavior come to mind: instruct athletes; set up the team's offensive and defensive alignments; communicate with parents, media, and the general public; organize practices; and so on.

Within every group there are two general categories of roles, formal and informal (Mabry & Barnes, 1980). As the term suggests, **formal roles** are explicitly set out by the group or organization. Coach, team captain, and manager are examples of explicit leadership roles within a team. Spiker and setter in volleyball; forward, guard, and center in basketball; and scrum half and prop in rugby are examples of explicit performance roles. The sport team as an organization requires specific individuals to carry out each of these roles. Thus, individuals are trained or recruited for these roles, and specific expectations are held for their behavior. **Informal roles** evolve as a result of the interactions that take place among group members. Some examples of the informal roles that often emerge on a sport team are leader (vocal or "lead by example" leaders), task booster (spark plug), enforcer, mentor, social convener, cancer, distracter, team player, star player, and comedian (Cope, Eys, & Beauchamp, 2007). In the case of informal roles, it should be pointed out that these can have a positive (e.g., mentor) or negative (e.g., distracter) influence on the team.

A variety of elements associated with athletes' roles determine how effectively they can be performed. One element is the degree to which athletes understand, or do not understand, what constitutes their role. The term **role ambiguity** is often used to describe this element of role involvement and is defined as the lack of clear consistent information regarding one's role (Kahn, Wolfe, Quinn, Snoek, & Rosenthal, 1964). Beauchamp, Bray, Eys, and Carron (2002) noted that it is important for athletes to understand four aspects with regard to their role: (a) the scope of their responsibilities or generally what their role entails; (b) the behaviors that are necessary to successfully fulfill their role responsibilities; (c) how their role performance will be evaluated; and (d) what the consequences are should they not successfully fulfill their role responsibilities. In general, previous research has shown that athletes who understand their roles better are more satisfied (Eys, Carron, Bray, & Beauchamp, 2003), experience less anxiety (Beauchamp et al., 2003), and are likely to view their teams as more cohesive (Eys & Carron, 2001).

A National Hockey League coach once observed that the worst thing that could happen to a team was to have its "enforcer" score a few goals in successive games. The enforcer would then begin to see himself as and prefer the role of goal scorer, to the detriment of the team as a whole. The roles that individuals are expected to perform should be clearly spelled out.

A second element of role involvement that has been shown to be related to group cohesiveness is the degree to which athletes accept their role responsibilities (e.g., Bray, 1998). It is beneficial to set out any contingencies associated with role performance. "We plan to use you as a defensive specialist only. If you cannot or do not want to play this role, you will probably get very little playing time this year." Role acceptance is also enhanced when the coach minimizes the status differences among roles. Thus, the success of the total team and the importance of all roles for team success should be continually emphasized. When all group members perceive that their responsibilities are important and make a contribution to the common good, they more willingly accept and carry them out.

A number of interventions, although not empirically tested, could potentially improve role clarity and role acceptance. One very simple intervention that serves to open communication channels and clarify roles is to arrange for individual meetings between the athlete and his or her coach. Another method is to utilize an effective goal setting program. Goal setting serves four important functions: it (a) directs the individual's attention and actions toward appropriate behaviors; (b) mobilizes and increases effort toward the task; (c) increases persistence in the task; and (d) motivates the individual to develop strategies and action plans to accomplish the task (Locke, Shaw, Saari, & Latham, 1981). All of these contribute to role clarity and acceptance.

Finally, other elements of role involvement that are extremely important to the group environment and are likely contributors to the cohesiveness of sport teams include **role efficacy** (i.e., athletes' beliefs about their capabilities to carry out role responsibilities; Bray, Brawley, & Carron, 2002), **role conflict** (i.e., athletes' perceiving others to be sending incongruent expectations; Kahn et al., 1964), **role overload** (i.e., athletes' having too many role expectations and/or being unable to prioritize them appropriately), and **role satisfaction** (i.e., how happy athletes are with their given role on the team). The applied practitioner or coach should be conscious of these role elements when working with sport teams.

Norms. The presence of **norms** is also associated with increased cohesiveness (Gammage, Carron, & Estabrooks, 2001). A norm is a standard for behavior that is expected of members of the group. It may be task irrelevant or task relevant; in either case, a norm reflects the group's consensus about behaviors that are considered acceptable. The athletes' treatment of team managers (Gammage et al., 2001) or trainers is one example of a task-irrelevant norm. On one team the manager might be regarded and treated as little more than an unpaid servant; on another team he or she might be considered a member of the coaching staff. In both cases new team members quickly become aware of the standard of behavior considered acceptable in their interactions with the manager and begin to act accordingly.

In a sport setting, Munroe and her colleagues (1999) asked athletes to identify the types of norms that exist within their teams. What they found was that important norms existed in four different contexts. First, the two most important norms in the context of *competition* were that teammates put forth maximum effort toward the task and that they supported the other members of the team. These two norms also were the most relevant in the second context, *practice*. The third context for the existence of norms was the *off-season*. In this context the most relevant norms for members of sport teams were to continue training and development as well as maintaining contact with other group members. Finally, norms also were identified for social situations in which group members had expectations to attend social events (e.g., parties) and have respect for each other.

The relationship between the presence of group norms and the degree of group cohesiveness is circular. The development of norms contributes to the development of cohesiveness. With increased group cohesiveness there is also greater conformity to group standards for behavior and performance. A recently formed group has minimal influence over its members. But as the group develops and becomes more cohesive, adherence to norms for behavior increases. Failure to conform can lead to different sanctions or types of punishment. For example, the group can control the amount of interaction it permits members, their degree of involvement in decision making, and their accessibility to task and social rewards. Controlling the opportunity to interact and to influence the group is probably the most powerful sanction the group possesses. As a group increases in cohesiveness, its members place increasing value on social approval and the opportunities to interact with other group members. Therefore, they show an increasing tendency to adhere to the group norms and to give in to the group influence—even if that

influence is negative. Some examples of negative influence are the performance of deviant behavior (as in the case of the high school football team hazing incident) or the maintenance of an inappropriately low work quota (low standards for productivity).

One of the best-known, most heavily researched issues relating to task-relevant norms is the **norm for productivity.** One example of this occurs in industrial settings when the group establishes a level or rate of performance as acceptable and refuses to tolerate productivity above (rate busting) or below (malingering) that standard. Cohesion and the norm for productivity jointly influence group productivity and achievement. Traditionally it was assumed that there is a direct, positive relationship between cohesion and productivity: As the former increased, the latter was improved. Research in management science, psychology, and sport, however, has shown that the picture is not quite that simple. For example, when Stogdill (1972) reviewed 34 studies that had been carried out with a variety of different groups, he found that cohesiveness was positively related to performance in 12, negatively related in 11, and unrelated to performance in 11. According to Stogdill, the key factor that influences the relationship between cohesion and performance is the group's norm for productivity (Table 7-1). If group cohesiveness is high and the norm for productivity is high, performance will be positively affected (number 1). Conversely, if cohesion is high and the norm for productivity is low (number 4), performance will be low or negatively affected. When cohesiveness is low, groups with a high norm (number 2) will outperform groups with a low norm (number 3).

Another important aspect of group norms is their *stability*. It has been demonstrated experimentally that an arbitrary norm can persist for four or five generations after the original members have been removed from the group (Jacobs & Campbell, 1961). Thus, if a sport team develops negative norms, such as abusive behavior toward officials or other team members, a laissez-faire attitude toward training, or a reliance on

Table 7-1 **Interactive Effects of Group Cohesiveness and Group Norm for Productivity on Individual and Group Performance**

		Group Cohesion	
		High	**Low**
	High	Best performance (1)	Intermediate performance (2)
Group Norm for Productivity			
	Low	Worst performance (4)	Intermediate performance (3)

individual versus team goals, those norms could persist over a number of seasons unless steps are taken to eliminate them.

Establishing positive group norms is extremely important in sport teams, particularly if an inappropriate norm is in place. One technique that has been used successfully is to enlist the formal and informal leaders of the group as active agents. If group leaders (in addition to the coach) accept and adhere to specific standards, other group members soon follow.

In some instances the group leaders may be resistant to change. This poses a problem because on sport teams the formal and informal leaders are usually the most highly skilled. If this is the case, the coach must decide how important the new standard is to the long-term success of the organization. In the event that the new standard is considered to be very important, the coach may have to release the resistant team members.

Group processes. Another important team factor that influences the development of a team concept and task cohesion is the interactive processes that occur among the members. One process is the establishment of *group goals and rewards*. In most group activities, including track and field, swimming, baseball, and even basketball, hockey, and soccer, there is an opportunity for the gifted individual competitor to obtain special recognition and rewards. This is inevitable. However, to ensure that a concept

of unity develops, the coach must emphasize the group's goals and objectives as well as the rewards that will accrue to the group if these are achieved. Individual goals and rewards should be downplayed.

Communication is another group process associated with increased group cohesiveness, but the relationship is circular. As the level of communication relating to task and social issues increases, cohesiveness is enhanced. And as the group becomes more cohesive, communication also increases. Group members are more open with one another, they volunteer more, they talk more, and they listen better. In short, the exchange of task information and social pleasantries increases with cohesiveness.

Performance outcome. As has been the case with so many other factors, the relationship between cohesion and performance outcome is a circular one. More specifically, cohesiveness contributes to performance success, and performance success increases cohesiveness. In fact, Carron, Colman, Wheeler, and Stevens (2002) conducted a meta-analysis to examine a number of issues related to the cohesion–performance relationship. A number of issues arose from their results. First, *both* task and social cohesion were positively related to performance and the relationships were cyclical (as mentioned earlier). That is, the strength of the cohesion to performance relationship was as strong as performance to cohesion. Second, there was no significant difference between the strengths of the task cohesion–performance relationship (i.e., effect size = .61) and the social cohesion–performance relationship (i.e., effect size = .70) although the latter was slightly greater. Finally, these relationships existed equally for interactive (e.g., volleyball) and coaching (e.g., track and field) sports and were present across the spectrum of skill and competitive levels, but seemed to be stronger in female teams. Overall, performance success is an important team factor for developing cohesion. Consequently, if it is at all possible, a coach should try to avoid an excessively difficult schedule early in a season.

Team Building

> If everybody can find a way to put their personal agendas aside for the benefit of the team, ultimately they will gain for themselves in the long run. But I think what often happens is people think they have to take care of themselves first and the team second. Then the infrastructure breaks down and nobody's accountable. You have to sacrifice yourself for the good of the team, no matter what role you play on the team—whether you're playing 30 minutes or two minutes a game.
>
> —Mark Messier (as quoted in Miller, 2001, p. 152)

As this quote by Mark Messier illustrates, the importance of cohesion in sport teams is recognized even by those who are best known for their individual prowess. Because it is critical for group development, group maintenance, and the group's collective pursuit of its goals and objectives, cohesion has been identified as the most important small group variable (see Golembiewski, Hilles, & Kagno, 1974). Consequently, at the core of any team-building program is the expectation that the intervention will produce a more cohesive group.

Coaches, either alone or with the help of a sport psychologist, invariably seek ways to build an effective team. It's not enough for the coach

to proclaim to his or her charges, "Let's act like a team." Consequently, coaches or sport psychology specialists often engage in what is known as **team building.** As Carron and colleagues (2005) noted, team building can be defined as "team enhancement or team improvement for both task and social purposes" (p. 327). Thus, it would seem prudent for coaches and sport psychologists to implement certain strategies to foster team building so that athletes may have meaningful experiences that ultimately may lead to a greater sense of unity and cohesiveness.

However, sport is not the only physical activity domain in which team building has been shown to be effective. Research by Carron and Spink (1993) and Spink and Carron (1993) has shown that a team-building intervention program can have a substantial impact on perceptions of cohesiveness as well as on individual adherence behavior in an exercise context. In short, the group has a substantial stabilizing influence on its membership. Given that 50% of adults who initiate an exercise program drop out within the first 6 months (Dishman, 1994), this seems an important area for intervention. Thus, this chapter will conclude with suggestions for implementing a team-building protocol in both sport and exercise settings.

Owing to its distinct nature, the implementation of team-building interventions in sport and exercise settings is typically *indirect*. The coach/leader is generally the primary arbitrator of group goals, individual roles, and leadership style. As a consequence of this, all of the team-building interventions in these settings become more indirect as they must be filtered through the coach/leader in each instance.

One approach to team-building interventions adopted by Carron, Spink, and Prapavessis (Carron & Spink, 1993; Prapavessis, Carron, & Spink, 1996; Spink & Carron, 1993) involved the use of a four-stage process comprising an *introductory stage*, a *conceptual stage*, a *practical stage*, and an *intervention stage*. The purpose of the introductory stage was to provide the coach/leader with a brief overview of the general benefits of group cohesion. For example, in team building with sport teams, the relationship between perceptions of cohesiveness and enhanced team dynamics was discussed (Prapavessis et al., 1996). In team building with exercise groups, the introductory stage consisted of a discussion of the relationship between perceptions of cohesiveness and increased adherence to the exercise program (Carron & Spink, 1993).

The conceptual stage was used to accomplish three purposes: (a) to facilitate communication with the coaches/leaders about complex concepts (e.g., groups, cohesiveness); (b) to highlight the interrelatedness of various components of the team-building protocol; and (c) to identify the focus for possible interventions (Carron & Spink, 1993).

The purpose of the practical stage was to have coaches/leaders, in an interactive brainstorming session, generate as many specific strategies as possible to use for team building in their group. This was thought to be desirable for three reasons. First, coaches/leaders differ in personality and preferences; therefore, a strategy that might be effectively implemented by one coach/leader might not be by another. Second, groups differ, and coaches/leaders are the individuals most familiar with their groups. An intervention strategy that might be effective in one group might be ineffective in another. Finally, de Charms's (1976) origin-pawn research has shown that motivation is enhanced when individuals are given greater control over personal behavior. Thus, coaches and exercise leaders are likely to be motivated to employ various team-building strategies because they are given the opportunity to participate in the brainstorming session, and they have control over which strategies they use with their team or class.

Research by Carron and Spink (1993) and Spink and Carron (1993) in the exercise domain provides a good illustration of the type of activities characteristic of the practical stage. Carron and Spink encouraged fitness instructors to develop specific strategies to use in their classes. Table 7-2 contains examples of some of the specific team-building strategies identified by fitness leaders in the practical stage, as well as suggested strategies for coaches of sport teams.

In the intervention stage, the team-building protocols coaches or exercise leaders introduced and maintained in order to increase the level of task cohesiveness of the groups. One team-building intervention that was implemented in a sport setting used elite male soccer teams (Prapavessis et al., 1996). The coaches involved in the team-building intervention attended a workshop two weeks before the beginning of the season, at which the specific strategies for implementing a team-building program were established. Throughout the preseason and then during six weeks of the season, the coaches emphasized the team-building strategies. Perceptions of cohesiveness were assessed in the preseason and after eight weeks. No differences in cohesiveness were found, however, between the team-building, attention-placebo, and control conditions.

One possible explanation advanced to account for these results was that many sport coaches inevitably engage in team-building strategies on their own. That is, they establish goals and objectives, work to ensure conformity to group norms, facilitate role clarity and role acceptance, and so on. Also, in sport teams, cohesion is an inevitable by-product of group processes (e.g., communication), an evolving group structure (e.g., development of roles), and group outcomes (e.g., winning or losing). Thus, a team-building program in a sport team would most likely combine in an interactive way with ongoing concomitants of cohesion. The lack of research in sport on the impact of team building on cohesiveness makes it difficult to arrive at any definitive conclusions. Perhaps practitioners and researchers engaged in team building in sport might wish to consider the athletes' opinions on collective areas of concern (i.e., targets for team-building strategies). The applied example that follows highlights a protocol the Toronto Maple Leafs (of the National Hockey League) use to develop "team values" that enlisted and depended on the opinions of all team members. In addition, the inclusion of selected high-status members of the team (i.e., captains, co-captains) in implementing this team-building strategy was considered critical for its delivery.

Table 7-2 **Examples of Specific Team-Building Strategies for Coaches and Fitness Class Instructors**

Factor		Examples of Intervention Strategies
Distinctiveness	Sport[a]	Provide the team with unique identifiers (e.g., shirts, logos, mottos, etc.). Emphasize any unique traditions and/or history associated with the team.
	Exercise[b]	Have a group name. Make up a group T-shirt. Hand out neon headbands or shoelaces. Make up posters and slogans for the class.
Individual positions	Sport[a]	Create a team structure in which there is a clear differentiation in team positions and roles.
	Exercise[b]	Use three areas of the pool depending on fitness level. Have signs to label parts of the group. Use specific positions for low-, medium-, and high-impact exercisers. Let them pick their own spot and encourage them to remain in it throughout the year.
Group norms	Sport[c]	Show individual team members how the group's standards can contribute to more effective team performance and a greater sense of team unity. Point out to all team members how their individual contributions can contribute to the team's success. Reward those team members who adhere to the group's standards and sanction those who do not.
	Exercise[b]	Have members introduce each other to increase social aspects. Encourage members to become fitness friends. Establish a goal to lose weight together. Promote a smart work ethic as a group characteristic.
Individual sacrifices	Sport[a]	Encourage important team members to make sacrifices for the team (e.g., ask a veteran athlete to sit out in order to give a novice athlete more playing time).
	Exercise[b]	Use music in aqua fitness (some do not want music). Ask two or three people for a goal for the day. Ask regulars to help new people—fitness friends. Ask people who aren't concerned with weight loss to make a sacrifice for the group on some days (more aerobics) and people who are concerned with weight loss to make a sacrifice on other days (more mat work).
Interaction and communication	Sport[d]	Provide opportunities for athlete input; create an environment that fosters mutual trust and respect so that athletes will feel comfortable communicating.[e] Have all players identify (on paper) why they want their fellow players on the team, then create a summary sheet for each player.
	Exercise[b]	Use partner work and have them introduce themselves. Introduce the person on the right and left. Work in groups of five and take turns showing a move. Use more partner activities.

[a]Bull, Albinson, and Shambrook, 1996

[b]Adapted from Carron and Spink, 1991; Spink and Carron, 1991

[c]Zander, 1982

[d]Yukelson, 1984

[e]Munroe, Terry, and Carron, 2002

Example

Developing team values

In recent years, the Toronto Maple Leafs hockey team, a member of the National Hockey League, has engaged in several values-based team-building exercises. Values are beliefs that influence behavior and serve as guidelines to evaluate behavior (Crace & Hardy, 1997). A modified version of the Crace and Hardy intervention model was introduced to the Toronto Maple Leafs at the beginning of the 2005–2006 season. Although the model recommends that the players and coaches be introduced to the principles behind team-building interventions, it was felt that professional hockey players already had a clear understanding of what constitutes a functional team environment.

Thus, the session began with players divided into four groups of six, each table with a group leader who was one of the team's captains. The Player Development coach asked the leaders to discuss in their groups the important beliefs that would help guide their behavior and motivation for the upcoming season. After a 20-minute discussion, the group leaders reported three or four of their groups' most important beliefs. A general discussion ensued and the players collectively rank-ordered the beliefs. Following are the results:

Team Values Summary, 2005–2006 Season

1. *Team Toughness: Mentally and physically, never quit. Stick up for one another.*

2. *Team Speed: We must all take short shifts so we can wear down our opponents by the third period. We'll be able to win the close games if we can do this.*

3. *Team Defense: We can score, but in the past we've hung the goalies "out-to-dry." We need a commitment to play solid defense.*

4. *Work Ethic: On and off the ice strive towards your goal. Push yourself to be better.*

5. *Accountability: Being truthful and up front to your teammates. Don't make excuses. It has to be 24 players held accountable by each other and the coaches.*

6. *Respect: Respect must be earned. Respect each other's roles and what different players bring to the table, for example, goal scoring, checking, penalty killing.*

7. *Positive Attitude: We need to be more positive. No complaining about line combinations, defense partner and so on.*

8. *Loyalty: Don't cheat yourself or your teammates from your best effort. If you play 5 minutes or 20 minutes, work hard whenever you get the chance.*

9. *Leadership: There are 24 leaders in this dressing room, no passengers.*

10. *Commitment: Make the commitment to team concepts, systems, and off-ice conditioning.*

The 10 beliefs the players presented to the coaching staff were transformed into a plaque, and each player took ownership by signing his name to it. The plaque was mounted in the dressing room as a reminder of what the group valued as a team. Throughout the season, head coach Pat Quinn often referred to one of the values as a theme to begin his team meetings in preparation for an upcoming game. In addition, if the team was underachieving, he would target one of the belief statements. For example, if there was a lackluster effort after a period, the coach would refer to "loyalty," which the players had defined as not cheating themselves or their teammates from giving their best effort. The coach implied that they were letting each other down and not adhering to their own values. Such tactics would help motivate the players into giving a more concerted effort to achieve their goals.

Summary

Groups are dynamic, not static; they exhibit life and vitality, interaction, and activity. Athletic teams are simply a special type of group. One important implication of this is that they are therefore subject to change, to growth, to modification, and to improvement. The coach is probably in the best position to influence change in a positive direction. To do this efficiently and effectively, it is beneficial to draw on the wealth of research information that has been developed over a number of years in management science, social psychology, sociology, and physical education. Given the influence that groups have on their members, a knowledge of group structure, group dynamics, and group cohesiveness is essential for coaches. This understanding will provide an excellent base from which to weld athletes into a more effective team.

Study Questions

1. Using Carron's definition of a group, briefly describe the six features that characterize groups.

2. Define cohesiveness. What are the four specific facets of cohesion?

3. List the four factors that contribute to cohesiveness and give one specific example of each.

4. Discuss the relationship of team size to group cohesiveness.

5. Describe the environmental, personal, and leadership factors that contribute to the development of cohesiveness.

6. Four team factors related to cohesion are roles, norms, group processes, and performance outcome. Distinguish between each of these factors and describe how the factors might be manipulated or modified to enhance team cohesion.

7. Give at least one example (using a sport of your choice or an exercise class) of a strategy that a coach, fitness leader, or sport psychologist to enhance group cohesiveness using each of the following factors: (a) distinctiveness, (b) individual positions, (c) group norms, (d) individual sacrifices, and (e) interaction and communication.

References

Beauchamp, M. R., Bray, S. R., Eys, M. A., & Carron, A. V. (2002). Role ambiguity, role efficacy, and role performance: Multidimensional and mediational relationships within interdependent sport teams. *Group Dynamics: Theory, Research, and Practice, 6* (3), 229–242.

Beauchamp, M. R., Bray, S. R., Eys, M. A., & Carron, A. V. (2003). The effect of role ambiguity on competitive state anxiety. *Journal of Sport and Exercise Psychology, 25* (1), 77–92.

Brawley, L. R., Carron, A. V., & Widmeyer, W. N. (1987). Assessing the cohesion of teams: Validity of the Group Environment Questionnaire. *Journal of Sport Psychology, 9,* 275–294.

Bray, S. R. (1998). *Role efficacy within interdependent teams: Measurement development and tests of theory.* Unpublished doctoral thesis. University of Waterloo, Waterloo, Canada.

Bray, S. R., Brawley, L. R., & Carron, A. V. (2002). Efficacy for interdependent role functions: Evidence from the sport domain. *Small Group Research, 33,* 644–666.

Bull, S. J., Albinson, J. G., & Shambrook, C. J. (1996). *The mental game plan: Getting psyched for sport.* Eastborne, UK: Sports Dynamics.

Carron, A. V., Brawley, L. R., & Widmeyer, W. N. (1998). The measurement of cohesiveness in sport groups. In J. L. Duda (Ed.), *Advancements in sport and exercise psychology measurement* (pp. 213–226). Morgantown, WV: Fitness Information Technology.

Carron, A. V., Colman, M. M., Wheeler, J., & Stevens, D. (2002). Cohesion and performance in sport: A meta-analysis. *Journal of Sport and Exercise Psychology, 24,* 168–188.

Carron, A. V., Hausenblas, H. A., & Eys, M. A. (2005). *Group dynamics in sport* (3rd ed.). Morgantown, WV: Fitness Information Technology.

Carron, A. V., & Spink, K. S. (1991). *Team building in an exercise setting: Cohesion effects.* Paper presented at the Canadian Psychomotor Learning and Sport Psychology Conference, London, ON.

Carron, A. V., & Spink, K. S. (1993). Team building in an exercise setting. *The Sport Psychologist, 7,* 8–18.

Carron, A. V., Widmeyer, L. R., & Brawley, L. R. (1985). The development of an instrument to assess cohesion in sport teams: The Group Environment Questionnaire. *Journal of Sport Psychology, 7,* 244–266.

Cope, C., Eys, M. A., & Beauchamp, M. R. (2007). *Informal roles on sport teams.* Paper presented at the Association for Applied Sport Psychology Conference, Louisville, KY.

Crace, R. K., & Hardy, C. J. (1997). Individual values and the team building process. *Journal of Applied Sport Psychology, 9,* 41–60.

de Charms, R. (1976). *Enhancing motivation: Change in the classroom.* New York: Halstead.

Dishman, R. K. (1994). *Exercise adherence: Its impact on public health.* Champaign, IL: Human Kinetics.

Eys, M. A., & Carron, A. V. (2001). Role ambiguity, task cohesion, and task self-efficacy. *Small Group Research, 32,* 356–372.

Eys, M. A., Carron, A. V., Bray, S. R., & Beauchamp, M. R. (2003). Role ambiguity and athlete satisfaction. *Journal of Sports Sciences, 21,* 391–401.

Eys, M. A., Hardy, J., Carron, A. V., & Beauchamp, M. R. (2003). The relationship between task cohesion and competitive state anxiety. *Journal of Sport and Exercise Psychology, 25,* 66–76.

Gammage, K. L., Carron, A. V., & Estabrooks, P. A. (2001). Team cohesion and individual productivity: The influence of the norm for productivity and the identifiability of individual effort. *Small Group Research, 32,* 3–18.

Golembiewski, R. T., Hilles, R., & Kagno, M. S. (1974). A longitudinal study of flexi-time effects: Some consequences of an O.D. structural intervention. *Journal of Applied Behavioral Science, 10,* 485–500.

Jacobs, R. C., & Campbell, D. T. (1961). The perpetuation of an arbitrary tradition through several generations of a laboratory microculture. *Journal of Abnormal and Social Psychology, 62,* 649–658.

Jewell, L. N., & Reitz, H. J. (1981). *Group effectiveness in organizations.* Glenview, IL: Scott, Foresman.

Kahn, R. L., Wolfe, D. M., Quinn, R. P., Snoek, J. D., & Rosenthal, R. A. (1964). *Occupational stress: Studies in role conflict and ambiguity.* New York: Wiley.

Lenk, H. (1969). Top performance despite internal conflict: An antithesis to a functional proposition. In J. Loy & G. Kenyon (Eds.), *Sport, culture, and society: A reader on the sociology of sport.* Toronto, ON: MacMillan.

Locke, E. A., Shaw, K. N., Saari, L. M., & Latham, G. P. (1981). Goal setting and task performance: 1969–1980. *Psychological Bulletin, 90,* 125–152.

Mabry, E. A., & Barnes, R. E. (1980). *The dynamics of small group communication.* Englewood Cliffs, NJ: Prentice Hall.

McCallum, J. (1982). Faith, hope, and Tony C. *Sports Illustrated, 57,* 58–72.

McKnight, P., Williams, J. M., & Widmeyer, W. N. (1991, October). *The effects of cohesion and identifiability on reducing the likelihood of social loafing.* Presented at the Association for the Advancement of Applied Sport Psychology Annual Conference, Savannah, GA.

Miller, S. L. (2001). *The complete player: The psychology of winning hockey.* Toronto, ON: Soddart.

Munroe, K., Estabrooks, P., Dennis, P., & Carron, A. V. (1999). A phenomenological analysis of group norms in sport teams. *The Sport Psychologist, 13,* 171–182.

Munroe, K., Terry, P., & Carron, A. (2002). Cohesion and teamwork. In B. Hale & D. Collins (Eds.), *Rugby tough* (pp. 137–153). Champaign, IL: Human Kinetics.

Prapavessis, H., & Carron, A. V. (1996). The effect of group cohesion on competitive state anxiety. *Journal of Sport and Exercise Psychology, 18,* 64–74.

Prapavessis, H., Carron, A. V., & Spink, K. S. (1996). Team building in sport. *International Journal of Sport Psychology, 27,* 269–285.

Spink, K. S., & Carron, A. V. (1991, October). *Team building in an exercise setting: Adherence effects.* Paper presented at the Canadian Psychomotor Learning and Sport Psychology Conference, London, ON.

Spink, K. S., & Carron, A. V. (1993). The effects of team building on the adherence patterns of female exercise participants. *Journal of Sport and Exercise Psychology, 15,* 39–49.

Stogdill, R. M. (1972). Group productivity, drive and cohesiveness. *Organizational Behavior and Human Performance, 8,* 26–43.

Wahl, G., & Wertheim, L. J. (2003). A rite gone terribly wrong. *Sports Illustrated, 99* (24), 68.

Westre, K. R., & Weiss, M. R. (1991). The relationship between perceived coaching behaviors and group cohesion in high school football teams. *The Sport Psychologist, 5,* 41–54.

Widmeyer, W. N., Brawley, L. R., & Carron, A. V. (1985). *The measurement of cohesion in sport teams: The Group Environment Questionnaire.* London, ON: Sports Dynamics.

Widmeyer, W. N., Brawley, L. R., & Carron, A. V. (1990). The effects of group size in sport. *Journal of Exercise and Sport Psychology, 12,* 177–190.

Widmeyer, W. N., & Williams, J. M. (1991). Predicting cohesion in a coaching sport. *Small Group Research, 22,* 548–570.

Yukelson, D. P. (1984). Group motivation in sport teams. In J. M. Silva & R. S. Weinberg (Eds.), *Psychological foundations of sport.* Champaign, IL: Human Kinetics.

Communicating Effectively

David P. Yukelson, *The Pennsylvania State University*

I wish my coach was a little clearer with me. I wish I knew where I stood with her. I wish she believed in me more. Right now, I feel like I'm working really hard but nothing ever seems to be good enough. Anytime I go into my coach's office to talk, things get turned around and I'm always on the defensive. I wish the communication between us was better and more open.

—*Penn State University Student-Athlete*

In my work with intercollegiate student-athletes, I am often asked to address the topic of communication, particularly as it pertains to group cohesion, team dynamics, and interpersonal relationships. Effective communication is critical to the success of any team or organization and its members. It affects attitudes, motivation, expectations, emotional dispositions, and behaviors. The ability to express one's thoughts, feelings, and needs effectively, and reciprocally to be able to understand the thoughts, feelings, ideas, and needs of others, is central to good communication.

One day following a workshop on communication and team building, a football player came up to me and remarked that, to him, communication is what teamwork and group chemistry are all about. From a group perspective, it is tied to oneness of thought, synchronization of roles, and everyone being on the same page. He elaborated by saying, "If I can walk up to the line of scrimmage and know that the offensive tackle next to me is thinking the same thing I am, has internalized what needs to be done on this particular play, transmits to me a nonverbal signal indicating it's time to take care of business, then I know with great confidence, we are going to execute the upcoming play with precise timing, intensity, and cohesiveness." His remarks reminded me that there is much more to communication than meets the ear. From a global perspective, communication goes beyond talking and listening; rather, it's about connecting with people in a meaningful way.

Although coaches, athletes, and sport psychologists talk about the importance of effective communication, very little has been written about the subject, particularly as it pertains to sport (Anshel, 1997; Connelly & Rotella, 1991; Harris & Harris, 1984; Henschen & Miner, 1989; Martens, 1987, 2004; Orlick, 1986; Rosenfeld & Wilder, 1990; Vealey, 2005; Yukelson, 1997). Hence, the purpose of this chapter is to explore what effective communication is as it relates to sport, identify barriers to effective communication, and develop strategies for improving communication processes within athletic environments.

Communication Defined

Effective communication has been identified as a very important part of team success (Connelly & Rotella, 1991; Harris & Harris, 1984; Janssen & Dale, 2002; Krzyzewski, 2000; Martens, 2004; Orlick, 1986; Salmela, 1996). Unfortunately, consensus among researchers as to what the word *communication* means is equivocal. For instance, Dance and Larson (1976) surveyed a wide variety of diverse journals and publications in the literature and found 126 different definitions. According to the *American Heritage Dictionary* (1983), communication refers to an act of transmitting or exchanging information, knowledge, thoughts, and/or feelings by means of written or verbal messages. However, as we will come to learn in this chapter, the message transmitted is not always the message received.

Moving beyond a simplistic dictionary definition to a deeper and richer context, the philosopher and social theorist John Dewey notes that the word *communication* shares the same etiology or root as the word *community,* and is the result of people feeling engaged in shared projects and meaningful social interactions (Stuhr, 1997). At the core of this issue of community is the notion of engaged communication processes and connecting with people in a meaningful way. When an individual feels engaged in conversation, she or he feels the other person genuinely cares and is listening. The quote at the beginning of the chapter points to the importance of engagement and the athlete's desire to connect with her coach on a meaningful level.

Communication is a process that involves sending, receiving (encoding), and interpreting (decoding) messages through a variety of sensory modalities (Crocker, 1990; Harris & Harris, 1984). These messages can be verbal (as in written or spoken communication) or nonverbal (facial expressions, body language, body positioning) and can be distinguished in terms of content and emotion. The way a message is expressed will influence how the message is received and interpreted. Likewise, communication does not exist in a vacuum; rather, content and context interact to produce meaning in every communication episode (Clampitt, 2005).

Both person and situation variables influence this dynamic process. An individual's personality, upbringing, values, beliefs, personal mannerisms and style of communicating interact with a variety of situation-specific circumstances to influence the way messages are transmitted and received. Contextual factors come into play such as your relationship with the other person (e.g., the history you share, perceived level of trust, power and control issues), the environment you find yourself in (e.g., office, practice field, public or private setting), and the cultural context from which communication is to take place (e.g., learned rules and behaviors that are supposed to be followed). Although there are individual differences in the way people respond, understanding the dynamics that surround these contexts can attenuate misunderstanding and influence individuals' interpersonal effectiveness (Beebe, Beebe, & Redmond, 1996; Clampitt, 2005).

Other factors such as stress, selective attention, perceptual filtering, and psychological expectancies can all influence the way messages are expressed, received and interpreted (Henschen & Miner, 1989; Norman, 1976; Tubbs & Moss, 1987; Vealey, 2005). In the process of interpreting verbal and nonverbal messages, information may be lost or distorted (Henschen & Miner, 1989). Sometimes we think we hear a person say one thing when, in fact, he or she said something different. We then act on the basis of what we think the person said. Many communication problems are rooted in this kind of misunderstanding.

The following example provides an illustration of how communicating a compliment can be misinterpreted due to stress, selective filtering, or emotional mood states. During a practice, an athlete misses an offensive rebound, yet the coach compliments him for demonstrating good positioning, footwork, and intensity. Stressed over a variety of things going on in his life (e.g., two midterms, limited playing time the past two weeks, breaking up with his girlfriend), the athlete processes the compliment as an insult. For reasons not apparent to the coach, tension builds and tempers fly. Angry over the turn of events, the coach verbally denounces the athlete's reaction as stupid, mumbles to himself, "I can't control how he took it," and benches the athlete. Consequently, a wall is formed, communication blocked, and the intent of the message is never received.

Likewise, during the course of a long competitive season, coaches also are susceptible to heightened job stress and emotional mood swings (Dale & Weinberg, 1990; Smith, 1986), which in turn can have an adverse effect on their communication. I recall a situation midway through the course of a season; a coach was not happy with the way her team was playing. The pressure to win, coupled with increased travel demands and injuries to key personnel, resulted in the coach being extremely stressed. Frustrated and impatient toward the end of practice, the coach yelled and chastised a young, inexperienced freshman for making a mistake. The coach's comments were so demeaning and degrading, her tone of voice so penetrating and hurtful, her nonverbal body language so piercing that the athlete shut down and tuned out anything positive that was said thereafter. The whole situation was unfortunate because the athlete, talented yet low in self-confidence, began to fear failure, was scared to make a mistake, and never quite recovered for the rest of the season.

Practically speaking, it has been my experience that many interpersonal problems in teams result from individuals' lack of understanding of each other's needs and feelings. As Orlick astutely notes, "It is difficult to be responsive to another's needs or feelings when you do not know what they are" (Orlick, 2008, p. 283). Similarly, it is difficult to respect another person's perspective if you do not understand what it is or where it came from. Consequently, an important goal of interpersonal communication is to simply express oneself so the other person is in a better position to understand. This entails a process in which there is engaged mutual sharing.

These examples show how communication is an attitude that goes beyond the content of what is said. How one sends the message is just as important as what is said, especially in stressful situations (Henschen & Miner, 1989). Consequently, coaches and athletes must make certain the message conveyed is the message received. Tone of voice, facial expressions, body posture and spatial distance, and eye contact are some of the nonverbal cues that influence communication. A good rule of thumb is to become aware of how you come across to others and to make sure you say what you mean and mean what you say.

Communication in Sport

With regard to sport, much of what goes on in athletics revolves around communication. Research regarding communication in athletic settings has primarily emphasized the importance of leadership and communication styles as they relate to a number of variables, including motivation, team cohesion, expectations, coaching effectiveness, principles of feedback and reinforcement, and conflict resolution skills (Anshel, 1997; Carron & Hausenblas, 1998; Connelly & Rotella, 1991; Horn, 1985, 2008; Jowett & Chaundry, 2004; Martens, 1987; Orlick, 1986; Smith, Smoll, & Curtis, 1979). Although styles of communication vary from coach to coach, it is important to communicate in a manner consistent with one's own personality and coaching philosophy (Wooten, 1992). In terms of communication styles, Martens (1987) notes that clear, honest, and direct communication with no hidden agenda is what coaches should strive for in developing successful coach–athlete relationships. Furthermore, empathy, consistency, and responsiveness to individual differences have also been shown to be critical elements for effective communication in sport settings (Martens, 2004; Smith et al., 1979; Yukelson, 1997).

As noted earlier, communication is a dynamic process that involves mutual sharing. Mutual sharing implies reciprocal participation (e.g., two parties sharing thoughts, feelings, ideas, or information about a particular subject). Likewise, to truly understand or comprehend another individual's perspective, people need to be adept at the art of listening. In essence, mutual sharing leads to mutual understanding (through sharing, the other person is in a better position to truly understand). In the team context, if a group is to function effectively, its members must be able to communicate openly and honestly with one another about the efficiency of group functioning and the quality of interpersonal relationships (Yukelson, 1997). Effective communication is apparent when team members listen to one another and attempt to build on each other's strengths and contributions (Sullivan, 1993).

For coaches, the foundation for effective communication skills is having credibility in the eyes of their athletes, and having developed trust and respectful relationships (Orlick, 2008; Yukelson, 1984). Credibility is reflected in the athletes' attitudes about the trustworthiness of what you say and do (Martens, Christina, Harvey, & Sharkey, 1981; Vealey, 2005). Trust is linked to the concepts of honesty, integrity, authenticity, sincerity, and respect. Lack of honesty and betrayal of trust can lead to many interpersonal problems within a team including feelings of tension, anger, hostility, resentment, and jealousy (Tubbs & Moss, 1987). It is very difficult to regain someone's trust once it is broken.

Athletes seem to be motivated most by coaches for whom they have a lot of respect (Halliwell, 1989; Lynch, 2001). Respect is not often communicated directly in words; rather, it is demonstrated through actions, a sense of genuineness, sincerity, and social influence (Egan, 1994). Athletes will lose respect for their coaches if they feel betrayed or manipulated, or if they perceive that coaches are not listening. To illustrate the latter point, I remember a situation where a coach "heard through the grapevine" that a particular athlete violated a long-standing team rule. The coach, who liked to be in control of everything, failed to garner all the facts. She solicited information from other teammates as to what had happened, but never talked directly to the person in question. As a consequence, the athletes felt betrayed and angry, respect for the coach was shattered, and interpersonal relations among the athletes became strained. A good rule of thumb is to solicit all the facts before passing judgment and to treat people exactly the way you want to be treated! Putting yourself in the shoes of others and seeing things from their perspective (i.e., empathy) helps build credibility, trust, and mutual respect.

Coaches who are good communicators have credibility with their athletes. They establish open lines of communication; they are honest, fair, authentic, sincere, and consistent. They accept individuals for who they are, and they genuinely care about them as people outside of athletics. This values-based perspective is consistent with Janssen and Dale's (2002), qualititative research, which found that credible coaches were character based, competent, committed, caring, consistent, confidence builders, and good communicators.

Further, coaches who are good communicators explain, clarify, and individualize instruction to meet the athlete's needs and personality. They observe performance analytically and are able to help athletes improve performance by providing clear and constructive behavioral feedback in a nonthreatening manner (Smith, 1986; Martin & Hrycaiko, 1983). The following discussion between a coach and a fencer between competitive bouts highlights the point: "Kathy, you are too anxious on the strip. You are telegraphing messages to your opponent as to what your intentions are. Relax, see things develop, trust your decisions and actions, and when you see the window of opportunity open up, go for it!" The importance of giving constructive feedback in relation to goals an individual or team is striving to accomplish cannot be overstated.

Athletes react in various ways to how coaches communicate with them. They know the characteristics they like and dislike in coaches. In general, research in the area of youth sports indicates that young athletes like coaches who are knowledgeable and instructive, supportive and encouraging, enthusiastic and motivated, reliable, fair, and consistent (Martens, 2004; Martens et al., 1981; Smith, Smith, & Smoll, 1983). In contrast, young athletes dislike coaches who are judgmental, manipulative, capricious, indifferent, inconsistent, or constantly negative. Personally, I believe the same principles hold true for older athletes. My observation at the intercollegiate level has been that athletes seem to respond best to coaches who are open, honest, sincere, approachable, and caring. Most athletes do not mind being yelled at as long as they know the coach cares. One of our coaches at Penn State says that "creating players who respect you as a coach is a difficult task. You want the players to feel comfortable around you, but at the same time, realize you are the authority figure." He goes on to say, "Gaining trust is the first step toward building respect. A coach can gain trust with their athletes by being honest and approachable. I try to get my athletes to respect me by attempting to be fair in my decisions and truthful when giving assessment and advice. By listening to my athletes and taking into account suggestions they might have, I feel I establish some form of credibility with my athletes, and hopefully, they will think of me as a more understanding coach."

Again, from a philosophical perspective, this example points to the importance of engaging athletes in the communication processes, creating an atmosphere that reflects a community of caring. Athletes want to feel a sense of connection with their coach on a genuine and meaningful level. They expect to be treated with dignity and respect, and they should give the same back in return. Similarly, athletes (and people in general) want to know their role is valued and contributions appreciated. When the communication process is working properly, authentic sharing and active listening lead to mutual understanding, trust, and respect.

Communication and Groups

One of the most gratifying experiences a coach or athlete can have is to be a member of a team that gets along well and works together efficiently in a cohesive, harmonious, task-oriented manner (Orlick, 2008; Yukelson, 1984). Communication lies at the heart of group process. If a group is to function effectively, members must be able to communicate easily and efficiently with one another (Shaw, 1981). Because communication directly affects group solidarity, collective efficacy, and team performance (Zaccaro, Blair, Peterson, & Zazanis, 1995), I spend a great deal of time talking with teams about group process, team dynamics, and methods for improving harmonious team relations. Team building comes from a shared vision

of what the group is striving to achieve and is tied to commitment, individual and mutual accountability, collaboration, communication, and teamwork. A shared vision that has meaning and purpose creates synergistic empowerment. Likewise, in successful teams, coaches and athletes talk openly and honestly about interpersonal and task related issues that affect them directly, and everyone works together to develop a positive group atmosphere or team culture conducive for team success (Cannon-Bowers & Salas, 2001; Collins, 2001; Goleman, Boyatzis, & McKee, 2002; Janssen, 1999; Yukelson, 1997).

Unfortunately, not every group functions cohesively. Many interpersonal problems on teams stem from poor communication. Interpersonal conflict is often the result of misunderstanding or miscommunication of feelings. Henschen and Miner (1989) have identified five types of misunderstandings that often surface within groups: (1) a difference of opinion resolvable by common sense, (2) a clash of personalities in the group, (3) a conflict of task or social roles among group members, (4) a struggle for power between one or more individuals, and (5) a breakdown of communication between the leader and the group or among members of the group itself. Misunderstandings are also the result of inaccessibility to relevant information (not being privy to certain sources of information); inattentiveness (failing to listen, not paying attention, being distracted); lack of assertiveness (failure to speak up); or misperceiving someone's motives, intentions, or behavior (inference mind reading). Similarly, people are often afraid to express how they truly feel for fear of being ridiculed or rejected for saying what is truly on their minds (Orlick, 1986).

Several teams I have worked with have had their fair share of interpersonal communication problems and conflict. Problems have ranged from interpersonal jealousies within the team to power struggles, control issues, perceived injustices, and coach–athlete as well as athlete–athlete inequities. Learning how to express oneself in a constructive manner and to communicate effectively is an important initial step in preventing and solving problems.

It has been stated that the more open you can be with each other, the better are your chances of getting along and achieving both individual and team goals (Orlick, 1986). Thus, it is important for coaches and athletes to learn how to express their thoughts and feelings about various issues that affect them directly. Team building requires a group climate of openness in which airing problems and matters of concern is not just appropriate but encouraged. Orlick expounds by saying, "Harmony grows when you look for the good qualities in teammates and they look for yours, when you take the time to listen to others and they listen to you, when you respect their feelings and contributions and they respect yours, when you accept their differences and they accept yours, when you choose to help them and help you. Harmony and improved team performance is rooted in mutual trust and respect" (Orlick, 2008, p. 282).

Team Communication Dynamics

As already mentioned, many communication problems on teams are the result of misunderstanding or miscommunication between the coach and the team or among athletes themselves. Harris and Harris (1984) offer an interesting framework to examine communication processes in athletic teams. The framework consists of coach–team, coach–athlete, and athlete–athlete interactions.

Coach–team communications. From a coach–team perspective, group synergy and team chemistry are of vital importance. According to DePree (1989), group synergy comes from leaders (in this case coaches) sharing a vision of what could be if everyone puts his or her skills and resources together to achieve team goals and objectives. Individual and mutual accountability, passion and belief, and a genuine commitment to a common team goal are needed. Athletes unite behind common goals, so it is important to get athletes to think in terms of the philosophy, operating procedures, and values that govern the team (Yukelson, 1984). Similarly, group synergy requires homogenous attitudes and expectations

(e.g., unity of purpose) as well as shared ideals and covenants to live by (Riley, 1993; Walsh, 1998). In terms of shared ideals, it is important to obtain *consensus and commitment* from the team regarding team goals, operating procedures, rules of engagement, and normative behaviors including appropriate methods for achieving them (Carron & Hausenblas, 1998; Goleman et al., 2002; Martens, 1987). To this end, the coach should solicit input from team members regarding their perceptions of what needs to be done for everyone to come together and be an effective team (Janssen, 1999; Kouzes & Posner 1995; Yukelson, 1997). Everyone on the team must be on the same page, working together with a collective desire to be successful.

To achieve these ends, a coach may find these communication principles useful: impart, inspire, monitor, clarify, and reinforce.

- *Impart* relevant information regarding team rules, expectations, operating procedures, and goals the group is striving to achieve. Clarify the team's mission, outline strategies and action plans to reach team goals and objectives, and involve staff and athletes in decisions that affect them directly.

- *Inspire* athletes to reach for their best. Communicate with a sense of inspired enthusiasm. Be honest, direct, and sincere. Instill a sense of pride, passion, belief, and team spirit. Strive to make everyone on the team feel valued and significant.

- *Monitor the progress team is making.* Set up a goal-setting program (e.g., goal boards are often very helpful) and monitor, evaluate, and adjust goals as needed. Give athletes feedback on how they are doing in relation to individual and team goals, and challenge everyone involved to become better.

- *Clarify* how things are going. Talk openly about the commitment that is required to achieve team goals and what needs to be done to keep things on task. Challenge everyone to take responsibility for their own actions and to work with continued effort, purpose, and focus.

- *Reinforce* behavior that you want repeated. Catch people doing things right; provide lots of support, encouragement, and positive reinforcement; discipline athletes according to your coaching philosophy and team mission statement; and correct errors in a positive way.

Coach–athlete communications. As for coach–athlete lines of communication, coaches should build a psychological and social environment conducive to goal achievement and team success. They should take the time to get to know their athletes as unique goal-oriented individuals and find out what their strengths, interests, and needs are. The principles of transformational leadership and reciprocal influence are applicable here in the context of athletes and coaches working together to meet each other's needs and goals (Goleman et al., 2002; Martens, 1987; Yukelson, 1993). Coaches should be open, honest, and upfront with athletes about various decisions that affect them directly. Likewise, athletes need feedback as to where they stand and how they are progressing in relation to individual and team goals. Research indicates that *evaluative feedback* is an important part of communication and the goal-setting process (see Chapter 13 and Locke & Latham, 1990). Unfortunately, some coaches are not very good at giving feedback in a positive and supportive manner (Orlick, 2008). This can lead to motivation problems and performance inconsistencies. Similarly, many athletes have difficulty internalizing feedback for what it is and, as a consequence, take feedback personally as opposed to constructively. Developing strategies to improve coach–athlete communication processes can rectify many misunderstandings and hurt feelings.

Similarly, another area coaches should address with athletes is communication at the competition site (Orlick, 2008). Because of individual differences in the way athletes prepare and respond in competition, coaches should assess ahead of time what their athletes' needs and preferences are. Prior to competition, some athletes like to be left alone; others appreciate a word of encouragement or a task-oriented cue

that reminds them to concentrate and bring their best focus forward. The same holds true for postcompetition feedback. Some athletes are very emotional after competition and don't want to be disturbed; others want feedback immediately. Thus, a coach–athlete communication plan for competition helps to alleviate stress and possible misunderstandings that may arise.

In addition to providing tangible feedback about performance accomplishments, many athletes will seek out their coach to talk about things outside of sport that affect their lives and self-esteem. In intercollegiate settings, this might include concerns about various transition and adjustment issues, academic and time management problems, and ways to navigate interpersonal relationships. Thus, a coach is often asked to take on many mentoring roles (e.g., counselor, confidant, teacher, friend, role model, and sometimes substitute parent). For these reasons, it is important that lines of communication be open between athlete and coach and that a trusting relationship be established.

As for breakdowns in coach–athlete communications, many athletes do not feel confident approaching a coach if they do not trust or respect him or her. Although it is common for coaches to have a so-called open-door policy, many athletes find it difficult to walk through the door if they feel the coach is not going to listen to their concerns with genuine interest and openness, if they perceive a hidden agenda, or if they fear reprisal. Connelly and Rotella (1991) note that some athletes go so far as to "fake honesty"—tell coaches what they think they want to hear so the athletes don't have to deal with the situation at hand.

Likewise, situations often arise during the course of a season that can cause communication problems between the coach and athlete (e.g., frustration associated with losing, poor performance, lack of playing time, stress and fatigue, personality clashes, and injury, to name just a few). In situations like these, athletes often perceive the coach as being insensitive, unappreciative, unapproachable, or uninterested. As a result, it is not unusual for an athlete to feel apprehensive about approaching the coach.

Rather than clam up, athletes need to learn how to express themselves in an assertive manner. A practical technique I have found to be useful is to have athletes write down on a cue card three main points they would like to express to the coach. We then role-play and simulate potential scenarios. Athletes visualize themselves communicating their message in a confident and successful manner. This type of preparation helps to build confidence and desensitize athletes to situations they perceive to be stressful.

Communication is a two-way street; hence, both the coach and the athlete have a responsibility to make it work! In terms of coach–athlete communications, Anshel (1997), Janssen and Dale (2002), Lynch (2001), Orlick (2008), Martens (1987, 2004), Thompson (1993), and Vealey (2005) offer several practical cognitive-behavioral interpersonal techniques to facilitate improved relations. A summary of tips for improving coach–athlete communications follows. If these suggestions don't work, it might be appropriate for a sport psychologist to intervene.

- To communicate successfully, you must understand that each person with whom you communicate has had different experiences and perhaps even a different cultural upbringing than you have had. Hence, recognize individual differences in the way people respond. Do not assume that you (the communicator) and the other person(s) (the receiver) will interpret the information in the same manner.

- Use a style of communication that is comfortable for you. Whether you are laid back, animated, relaxed, vocal, or somewhere in between, communicate in a manner that is consistent with your personality and coaching philosophy.

- Characteristics of effective communication include being open, honest, sincere, genuine, and consistent. Sarcasm, ridicule, and degrading or demeaning comments are poor communication techniques and should be discouraged.

- Convey rationales as to why athletes should or should not do certain behaviors.

- Never underestimate the power of positive social influence techniques. Focus on being positive; catch people doing things correctly. Be generous with praise, encouragement, and positive reinforcement. The skillful use of positive reinforcement can increase motivation and strengthen a person's confidence and self-esteem (see Chapters 2 and 3).

- Work to improve nonverbal communication skills. Remember the axiom: "Your actions speak louder than words."

- Work on developing empathy skills. Put yourself in the other's shoes. Listen attentively to feelings and concerns. Collaborate to find appropriate solutions.

- Reduce uncertainty; be supportive. As a coach, you play a vital role in helping athletes feel worthy and important. Strive to create a supportive atmosphere in which athletes feel their efforts and contributions to the team are valued and appreciated.

- Recognize the importance of managing your own emotions. When coaches and athletes lose control of their emotions, frustration may distort or override the content of what gets heard.

- If you have an open-door policy, show athletes (and your assistants) that you are sincere about using it!

- Evaluate and monitor group process. Set aside time with the team to discuss openly how things are going (e.g., what is working, what is not, what you need more or less of from coaches, teammates, trainers, sport psychologist, support staff). This is an excellent way to open communication channels and show athletes you care about their feelings and opinions.

Athlete–athlete communications. As for athlete–athlete communication, it is important that teammates establish and maintain harmonious working relationships with each other. Ideally, they should show genuine support and care for each other both on and off the athletic field. In fact, some of the most cohesive teams I have ever been associated with had a special relationship off the field (i.e., a "bonding together feeling") that propelled them to be successful as a team during competitions. This was particularly evident during pressure situations within a competitive contest when they needed to trust each other most.

Along these lines, athletes can be a great source of support for one another; they often spend a lot of time together and share common experiences that are unique to their own peer subculture. In order for teams to get to know one another better and develop a sense of team camaraderie, I often employ team-building activities that promote personal disclosure through mutual sharing. For instance, I might have a team go around a circle discussing individual and team assets and strengths or a life event that significantly influenced them as a person or team (Yukelson, 1997). These team disclosures promote diversity and team cohesion and lend depth to understanding teammates. Recent qualitative research by Dunn & Holt (2004) as well as anecdotal accounts from coaches noting the benefits of using personal disclosure and mutual sharing team-building activities before major competitions has been documented in the literature (Cannon-Bowers & Salas, 2001; Dunn & Holt, 2004, Yukelson, Sullivan, Morett, & Dorenkott, 2003).

It takes a great deal of dedication, commitment, time, and discipline to excel in sport. In many cases, athletes can become encapsulated in their own athletic world; they don't have time for themselves and can take it out on each other. Unfortunately, if interpersonal relationships and team dynamics break down, the experience can be quite stressful.

Athletic teams are very much like families. Some degree of tension, frustration, and conflict is inevitable. At the intercollegiate level, several teams I have worked with have had their fair share of interpersonal communication problems and conflict. Problems have ranged from roommate problems (e.g., incompatibility, intolerance, general needs not being met), to interpersonal jealousies within the team, to coach–athlete inequities, to freshmen adjustment and other transition issues. Typically, the

underlying issues revolve around misunderstanding, insensitivity, distrust, betrayal, and athletes feeling, in general, like they are not being heard or listened to.

Likewise, in a multicultural athletic environment some degree of conflict or misunderstanding is unavoidable. When teammates come from different racial, ethnic, religious, or socioeconomic backgrounds, dissimilarities due to deeply rooted cultural systems often lead to intercultural misunderstandings (Schinke & Hanrahan, 2009; Tubbs & Moss, 1987). Because values, beliefs, relational roles, and attitudes in one culture are often different from those held in another, athletes need to learn to be tolerant, accepting, respecting, and understanding (Parham, 1996).

Learning how to communicate effectively is an important first step in developing satisfying interpersonal team relationships. Recognizing that it is difficult to be responsive to someone else's thoughts, feelings, ideas, and needs when you don't know what they are, here are some suggestions derived from Orlick (1986, 2008) and from my personal experiences to help you improve interpersonal communication processes within a team:

- Make sure everyone is pulling in the same direction (team comes first). Recognize that the more open you can be with each other, the better are your chances of getting along and achieving your goals.

- Discuss strategies for improving team harmony, including ways to support and help each other both on and off the athletic field.

- Listen to others; they will listen to you! Put yourself in the shoes of others; try to understand the other person's perspective.

- Learn how to give and receive feedback or criticism constructively. Listen to the *intent* of what is being said; avoid taking things personally.

- Learn how to tolerate each other better. Accept team members for who they are, including their flaws, personality quirks, idiosyncrasies, and funny little habits that make them unique.

- Avoid backstabbing and gossiping about teammates. Interpersonal cliques and petty jealousies will destroy team morale quickly.

- Keep confrontations private; deal with the person directly.

- Recognize that not all conflicts can be resolved, but most can be managed more effectively if both parties communicate.

Active Listening and Empathy

Whether you are a sport psychologist, coach, athlete, or friend, listening is an essential interpersonal skill to develop. Many of us have heard the axiom "listen to others and they will listen to you." It seems so simple, almost intuitive, but it has been my experience counseling coaches and athletes over the last 25 years that most communication problems in interpersonal relationships stem from lack of listening.

Rosenfeld and Wilder (1990) have identified three levels of listening, each representing a different degree of listening effectiveness. **Active listening** is the preferred mode of listening in which the listener is attuned, connected, and engaged and demonstrates a caring attitude and desire to truly understand what the other person has to say (Pietsch, 1974). The second level of listening is called **superficial** or **inattentive listening.** In this situation, listeners tune out quickly once they think they have enough information to decipher what the speaker's intent is. Although listeners at this level may grasp the basic meaning of the message, they often fail to comprehend the emotional feeling or underlying concepts of what is being communicated. Level three listening can be characterized as **arrogant listening.** Here, listeners seem to be more interested in what they have to say as opposed to what the other person is saying. These individuals often wait for pauses in the conversation so they can jump in and hear themselves speak.

By far the most useful tool for improving listening is active listening (Martens, 1987). When people talk about themselves, they do so in terms of experiences (things that happen to them), behaviors (what they do or fail to do), and

emotional affect (the feelings that accompany these experiences and behaviors) (Egan, 1994). Elements of good listening skills include attending physically and psychologically to the person you are communicating with (e.g., adopt a posture that indicates active involvement), listening to become more aware of what it is the person is really trying to say (both verbally and nonverbally), paraphrasing or clarifying to ensure your understanding is correct, and some form of summarizing statement to pull everything together in a respectful empathetic way (Corey, 1977; Egan, 1994). Along these lines, the acronym SOLER outlined in Egan (1994) has proven to be a very useful nonverbal technique facilitating the attending process: *Square* and face the speaker (adopt a posture that indicates involvement); espouse an *open* posture to communicate openness and availability to the speaker; *lean* toward the speaker (this connotes that you are interested in what he or she has to say); maintain good *eye* contact (this deepens your level of engagement); and *relax* your body position (being natural puts people at ease).

Reflective listening is one of the most powerful methods of demonstrating to the person you are working with that you are actively listening and striving to understand. Reflective listening can be thought of in relation to verbal communication as video feedback relates to physical skill instruction (Henschen & Miner, 1989). The skills of questioning, encouraging, paraphrasing, reflecting, and summarizing make up the basic listening sequence. The following reflective listening techniques (Egan, 1994; Ivey, 1983) may facilitate better communication between athlete and sport psychologist (or coach):

- *Questioning.* Use open-ended questions and statements that encourage the athlete to continue speaking. ("How are you feeling about the injury?" "Tell me more about what happened") As a general rule, avoid initial "why" questions. This may put the person you are talking with on the defensive. Wait until he or she has reached an appropriate comfort level.

- *Clarifying.* Make clear to the other person what you have heard. Clarifying does not mean "I agree with your opinion," but rather, it lets the speaker know someone cares enough to truly listen. Some good lead-ins include "What I hear you saying is . . ."; "I am not sure I quite understand, but it sounds as though you are angry with the coach because she benched you. Is that it?"

- *Encouraging.* Use a variety of verbal and non-verbal statements or mannerisms to prompt athletes to keep talking. These include head nods, gestures, a phrase such as "uh-huh," or the simple repetition of key words the athlete has uttered.

- *Paraphrasing.* Rephrase the athlete's main points to check whether you understand the message. Similar to reflective listening, paraphrasing involves using one's own words, in concise comments, to feed back to the athlete the essence of what has just been said.

- *Reflecting.* Let the person know you hear the content and feelings of what is being said. ("You're sad because . . ."; "You feel confident of your ability to play at this level but worry about getting in.")

- *Understanding.* Use empathy to keep the person you are dealing with focused on important issues. ("It must be hard for you to sit and watch teammates practice while you are recovering from arthroscopic knee surgery.")

- *Summarizing.* Pull together all the main ideas and feelings of what has been said. ("It sounds as if you have mixed feelings about the situation. On one hand, you have more time for yourself, but are also apprehensive about getting your starting job back.") Summaries may be used to begin or end a conversation, for transition to a new topic, or to provide clarity when dealing with lengthy or complex issues or statements.

The skills of attending and listening are not always sufficient in and of themselves to provide quality relationships with people. Of primary interest is the concept of **empathy.** Empathy is a special kind of understanding. In essence, it means putting yourself in the shoes of the other person, trying to understand and feel what the other person is experiencing from his or her own perspective.

Empathy is not the same thing as sympathy. Rather, it is an acquired skill that reflects an attitude of caring, concern, and genuine interest (Egan, 1994). Empathetic listeners reflect what they hear by restating ideas heard in their own words and by asking good probing questions (Ivey, 1983; Rosenfeld & Wilder, 1990). The following example gives two responses, one low and one high in empathy:

Athlete describes presenting problem: I really get mad when my coach criticizes me without letting me explain anything. I get angry not because he criticizes me, but because he does it in such a degrading way.

Sport psychologist (low empathy): "You don't like being criticized."

Sport psychologist (high empathy): "You get really mad when he criticizes you and his insulting manner makes you feel personally attacked."

It is important to remember that not all problems can be resolved and not all people want help. Listen to what the athlete is asking for, and respond accordingly. The following guidelines can help you become a more effective listener:

- *Focus* on the person who is talking. Be attentive, non-judgmental, supportive, and authentic.

- Be attuned to *body language* and listen for both *content* and *feelings*.

- Show that you *understand* what is being said by paraphrasing and summarizing main points.

- Set *goals* and develop concrete *action plans* based on what the individual is striving to achieve. Introduce role playing scenarios and coping rehearsal techniques to help the individual feel prepared and confident to take immediate action.

Assertiveness Training: The Need for Expression

At times athletes need to stand up for their rights and be able to express themselves in a forthright yet respectful manner. **Assertiveness** refers to the honest and straightforward expression of a person's thoughts and feelings in a socially appropriate way that does not violate or infringe on the rights of others (Connelly & Rotella, 1991; Lazarus, 1973).

Assertiveness is a learned social skill that takes time, practice, and patience to be perfected. Learning to assert oneself in a respectful and considerate manner comes easy for some, yet it is difficult for others. Reasons people have difficulty include lack of confidence (i.e., it takes courage to be assertive); vulnerability (i.e., risk of making oneself known has potential negative consequences); interpersonal concerns (e.g., being hesitant to speak up for fear of hurting someone's feelings); and lack of awareness (i.e., failure to learn how to be assertive) (Connelly, 1988; Connelly & Rotella, 1991; Egan, 1994). As an example, some freshmen may be afraid to speak up in team meetings for fear of looking bad in the eyes of upperclassmen. Likewise, some freshmen might feel intimidated by their coach and be hesitant to seek feedback or ask for help. Sociocultural upbringing and other socialization factors may also affect one's decision to be assertive. For example, it may be awkward for a newcomer of Asian or Latin American descent to feel comfortable speaking up, particularly to an authority figure.

The following approach, Greenberg's (1990) DESC formula, is a good example of how people can express themselves more assertively:

- *Describe* the situation as you see it; paint a verbal picture of the other person's behavior or the situation to which you are reacting: "What I see happening is this . . ."; "When my play is criticized, I feel. . . ."

- *Express* your feelings regarding the other person's behavior or the situation you have just described: "When you do this, it makes me feel like . . ."; "I get angry and frustrated when you talk behind my back."

- *Specify* what changes you would like to see take place: "I would prefer you give me feedback in a more constructive, less degrading manner"; "I would appreciate it if you did not talk behind my back."

- State the *consequences* to expect: "If you don't get off my case, I will ask coach to meet with us to straighten this situation out."

In terms of resolving team conflicts, Vealey (2005) offers an innovative communication strategy called the "Four Olves": invOLVE, resOLVE, absOLVE, and evOLVE. Making the group the target of change, begin by talking about what constitutes an effective team culture and the commitment required from each member to make it work; solicit input from team members during the season as problems or conflicts arise; collaborate and come up with collective solutions for problems discussed; hold them responsible and accountable for their actions; once the issue is resolved, move on free of any lingering repercussions (e.g., do not make them feel they are in the doghouse once things are resolved), and use each episode as an opportunity to learn and grow into a smarter, more experienced cohesive unit. Vealey goes on to note most people do not enjoy confrontations, but by communicating honestly and directly in a respectful manner, good things will occur.

The Sport Psychologist as a Skilled Helper

Throughout the chapter I have talked about the importance of coaches and athletes developing good listening and communication skills. Likewise, sport psychologists must develop good interpersonal communication skills to work effectively with coaches, athletes, and teams. For sport psychologists to do a good job, they must be able to develop rapport, listen attentively, speak the appropriate sport language, and earn the trust of both the coach and athlete and other personnel.

In my own day-to-day interactions I find myself working with a variety of people within the intercollegiate athletics hierarchy: student-athletes, coaches, parents, athletic administrators, academic counselors and support personnel, sports medicine doctors and athletics trainers, strength trainers, and alumni. These people have a wealth of information and experience to draw upon. They all have their own personality and comfort level from which they work and communicate. There are certain protocols to follow, appropriate chains of command to work through, written and unwritten rules and policies that can't be violated. But it is impossible to implement a thorough and effective applied sport psychology program if one is unable to gain the trust and support of key personnel at all levels of the athletics organization. This can be accomplished by establishing open lines of communication, by listening, gathering facts, being visible and observing as much as possible about the dynamics surrounding the team. Gaining entry and building trust takes time and patience.

The same communication principles presented for coaches and athletes apply to sport psychologists. With regard to individual consultations, the sport psychologist must be a skilled interviewer, adept at listening, good at probing, and able to individualize interventions based on the person's needs and concerns. Again, good communication skills are essential. Drawing from counseling theory, general communication skills sport psychologists need in order to be effective include genuineness (responding with honesty, sincerity, authenticity, and integrity); openness (accepting others as they are, nonjudgmentally, even if you don't agree with them); warmth (helping people feel at ease when expressing intimate thoughts and feelings); empathy (accepting, understanding, good listening skills); creativity and skill (helping athletes generate alternative ways of looking at problems); and trustworthyness (being able to maintain confidences) (Corey, 1977; Danish, D'Augelli, & Ginsberg, 1984; Egan, 1994; Ivey, 1983).

Summary

Communication is a multifaceted process that involves the transmission or exchange of thoughts, ideas, feelings, or information through verbal and nonverbal channels. Effective communication involves mutual sharing and mutual understanding. Its foundation is based on trust and mutual respect. Open lines of communication can help alleviate many problems that arise within sport environments.

Characteristics of effective and ineffective communication styles have been identified. An important aspect of communication is the need to be honest, sincere, direct, and consistent. Because messages transmitted are not always received and interpreted the same way, coaches, athletes, and sport psychologists must strive to be consistent in their verbal and nonverbal communications. Many times when incongruent messages are transmitted, the receiver can become confused as to the true meaning of the message, thus leaving the door open for miscommunication and misunderstanding.

Although much of this chapter has focused on coach–athlete communications, many of these principles carry over to the applied sport psychologist working in an athletics environment. The communication skills we teach coaches and athletes are the same skills we use as effective consultants. Gaining entry, building rapport, developing trust, and individualizing a mental skills training program based on the needs and desires of coaches and athletes all require good listening and communication skills.

Study Questions

1. Why is communication an important tool for a coach and sport psychologist to possess?

2. There is no true definition of *communication* in the literature. How would you define *communication* in sport?

3. What factors interfere with effective communication processes in sport?

4. Give some behavioral examples of verbal and nonverbal communication in sport.

5. What role does communication play in teaching mental skills to coaches and athletes?

6. As a sport psychologist, what are some things you would do to improve coach–athlete communications?

7. As a coach or sport psychologist, what would you do to intervene if interpersonal conflict arose among team members that resulted in disruption of group cohesion and team harmony?

8. The volleyball team at Nike University has a tendency to clam up when the going gets tough (i.e., communication breaks down; the team loses its intensity, enthusiasm, and focus in critical situations and fails to make appropriate adjustments to things that are going on during competition). How would you intervene as either a sport psychologist or coach to deal with this situation?

9. Why are active listening and empathy such important skills for a sport psychologist to develop in working with coaches and athletes?

10. What are some things you could do to become a better listener?

References

American heritage dictionary. (1983). New York: Dell.

Anderson, M. P. (1959). What is communication? *The Journal of Communication, 9,* 5.

Anshel, M. (1997). *Sport psychology: From theory to practice* (3rd ed.). Scottsdale, AZ: Gorsuch Scarisbrick.

Beebe, S. A., Beebe, S. J., & Redmond, M. V. (1996). *Interpersonal communication: Relating to others.* Boston: Allyn and Bacon.

Cannon-Bowers, J. A., & Salas, E. (2001). Reflections on shared cognition. *Journal of Organizational Behavior, 22,* 105–202.

Carron, A. V., & Hausenblas, H. A. (1998). *Group dynamics in sport* (2nd ed.). Morgantown, WV: Fitness Information Technology.

Clampitt, P. G. (2005). *Communicating for managerial effectiveness* (3rd ed.). Thousand Oaks, CA: Sage Publications.

Collins, J. (2001, January). Level 5 leadership: The triumph of humility and fierce resolve. *Harvard Business Review,* 65–76.

Connelly, D. (1988). Increasing intensity of play in nonassertive athletes. *The Sport Psychologist, 2,* 255–265.

Connelly, D., & Rotella, R. J. (1991). The social psychology of assertive communication: Issues in teaching assertiveness skills to athletes. *The Sport Psychologist, 5,* 73–87.

Corey, G. (1977). *Theory and practice of counseling and psychotherapy.* Pacific Grove, CA: Brooks/Cole.

Crocker, P. (1990). Facial and verbal congruency: Effects on perceived verbal and emotional feedback. *Canadian Journal of Sport Science, 15,* 17–22.

Dale, J., & Weinberg, R. (1990). Burnout in sport: A review and critique. *Journal of Applied Sport Psychology, 2,* 67–83.

Dance, F. E., & Larson, C. E. (1976). *The functions of human communication: A theoretical approach.* New York: Holt, Rinehart, and Winston.

Danish, S., D'Augelli, A. R., & Ginsberg, M. (1984). Life development intervention: Promotion of mental health through the development of competence. In S. Brown & R. Lent (Eds.), *Handbook of counseling psychology* (pp. 520–544). New York: John Wiley.

DePree, M. (1989). *Leadership is an art.* New York: Doubleday.

Dunn, J. G. H., & Holt, N. L. (2004). A qualitative investigation of a personal-disclosure mutual-sharing team building activity. *The Sport Psychologist, 18,* 363–380.

Egan, G. (1994). *The skilled helper: A problem management approach to helping* (5th ed.). Pacific Grove, CA: Brooks/Cole.

Goleman, D., Boyatzis, R., & McKee, A. (2002). *Primal leadership: Realizing the power of emotional intelligence.* Boston, MA: Harvard Business School Press.

Greenberg, J. S. (1990). *Coping with stress: A practical guide.* Dubuque, IA: William C Brown.

Halliwell, W. (1989). What sport psychologists can learn from coaches and athletes about the psychology of sport. *AAASP Newsletter,* p. 7.

Harris, D. V., & Harris, B. L. (1984). *Sports psychology: Mental skills for physical people.* Champaign, IL: Leisure Press.

Henschen, K., & Miner, J. (1989). *Team principles for coaches.* Ogden, UT: Educational Sport Services.

Horn, T. S. (1985). Coaches' feedback and changes in children's perceptions of their physical competence. *Journal of Educational Psychology, 77,* 174–186.

Horn, T.S. (2008). Coaching effectivenss in the sport domain. In T.S. Horn (Ed.), *Advances in Sport Psychology* (3rd ed.), (pp. 239–267). Champaign, IL: Human Kinetics.

Ivey, A. E. (1983). *Intentional interviewing and counseling.* Pacific Grove, CA: Brooks/Cole.

Janssen, J. (1999). *Championship team building.* Tucson, AZ: Winning the Mental Game.

Janssen, J., & Dale, G. (2002). *The seven secrets of successful coaches: How to unlock and unleash your team's full potential.* Cary, NC: Winning the Mental Game.

Jowett, S., & Chaundry, V. (2004). An investigation into the impact of coach leadership and coach–athlete relationship on group cohesion. *Group Dynamics: Theory, Research, and Practice, 8,* 302–311.

Kouzes, J. J., & Posner, B. Z. (1995). *The leadership challenge: How to keep getting extraordinary things done in organizations* (2nd ed.). San Francisco: Jossey-Bass.

Krzyzewski, M. (2000). *Leading with the heart.* New York: Warner Books.

Lazarus, A. A. (1973). On assertive behavior: A brief note. *Behavior Therapy, 4,* 697–699.

Locke, E. A., & Latham, G. P. (1990). *A theory of goal setting and task performance.* Englewood Cliffs, NJ: Prentice Hall.

Lynch, J. (2001). *Creative coaching.* Champaign, IL: Human Kinetics.

Martens, R. (1987). *Coaches guide to sport psychology.* Champaign, IL: Human Kinetics.

Martens, R. (2004). *Successful coaching* (3rd ed.). Champaign, IL: Human Kinetics.

Martens, R., Christina, R. W., Harvey, J. S., & Sharkey, B. J. (1981). *Coaching young athletes.* Champaign, IL: Human Kinetics.

Martin, G., & Hrycaiko, D. (1983). Effective behavioral coaching: What's it all about? *Journal of Sport Psychology, 5,* 8–20.

Norman, D. A. (1976). *Memory and attention: An introduction to human information processing.* New York: John Wiley and Sons.

Orlick, T. (1986). *Psyching for sport.* Champaign, IL: Human Kinetics.

Orlick, T. (2008). *In pursuit of excellence* (4th ed.). Champaign, IL: Human Kinetics.

Parham, W. D. (1996). Diversity within intercollegiate athletics: Current profile and welcomed opportunities. In E. F. Etzel, A. P. Ferrante, & J. W. Pinkney (Eds.), *Counseling college student-athletes* (pp. 27–54). Morgantown, WV: Fitness Information Technology.

Pietsch, W. V. (1974). *Human being: How to have a creative relationship instead of a power struggle.* New York: New American Library.

Riley, P. (1993). *The winner within.* New York: Putnam.

Rosenfeld, L., & Wilder, L. (1990). Communication fundamentals: Active listening. *Sport Psychology Training Bulletin, 1* (5), 1–8.

Salmela, J. H. (1996). *Great job coach.* Ottawa, ON: Potentium.

Schinke, R. & Hanrahan, S. (Eds.) (2009). *Cultural sport psychology: From theory to practice.* Champaign, IL: Human Kinetics.

Shaw, M. E. (1981). *Group dynamics: The psychology of small group behavior* (3rd ed.). New York: McGraw-Hill.

Smith, N. J., Smith, R. E., & Smoll, F. L. (1983). *Kidsports: A survival guide for parents.* Reading, MA: Addison-Wesley.

Smith, R. E. (1986). Toward a cognitive-affective model of athletic burnout. *The Journal of Sport Psychology, 8,* 36–50.

Smith, R. E., Smoll, F., & Curtis, B. (1979). Coach effectiveness training: A cognitive-behavioral approach to enhancing relationship skills in youth sport coaches. *Journal of Sport Psychology, 1,* 59–75.

Stuhr, J. (1997). *Genealogical pragmatism: Philosophy, experience, and community.* Albany: State University of New York.

Sullivan, P. A. (1993). Communication skills training for interactive sports. *The Sport Psychologist, 7,* 79–91.

Thompson, J. (1993). *Positive coaching: Building character and self-esteem through sports.* Dubuque, IA: William C. Brown.

Tubbs, S. L., & Moss, S. (1987). *Human communication* (5th ed.). New York: Random House.

Vealey, R. S. (2005). *Coaching for the inner edge.* Morgantown, WV: Fitness Information Technology.

Vernacchia, R. A., McGuire, R. T., & Cook, D. L. (1992). *Coaching mental excellence: It does matter whether you win or lose.* Dubuque, IA: William C. Brown and Benchmark.

Walsh, B. (1998). *Finding the winning edge.* Champaign, IL: Sports Publishing Inc.

Wenburg, J. R., & Wilmot, W. W. (1982). *The personal communication process.* Malabar, FL: Krieger Publishing.

Wooten, M. (1992). *Coaching basketball effectively.* Champaign, IL: Human Kinetics.

Yukelson, D. (1984). Group motivation in sport teams. In J. Silva & R. Weinberg (Eds.), *Psychological foundations in sport* (pp. 229–240). Champaign, IL: Human Kinetics.

Yukelson, D. (1997). Principles of effective team building interventions in sport: A direct service approach at Penn State University. *Journal of Applied Sport Psychology, 9,* 73–96.

Yukelson, D., Sullivan, B. A., Morett, C., & Dorenkott, B. (2003). *Coaches' perspectives on applying sport psychology into their coaching.* Invited symposium presented at the annual meeting of the Association for the Advancement of Applied Sport Psychology, Philadelphia, PA.

Zaccaro, S. J., Blair, V., Peterson, C., & Zazanis, M. (1995). Collective efficacy. In J. Maddox (Ed.), *Self-efficacy, adaptation, and adjustment* (pp. 305–328). New York: Plenum Press.

Mental Training for Performance Enhancement

Psychological Characteristics of Peak Performance

Vikki Krane, *Bowling Green State University*
Jean M. Williams, *University of Arizona*

Trying to articulate the zone is not easy because it's such an indescribable feeling. That moment doesn't happen often, and when it does happen, you feel like you're playing out of your head! You aren't feeling any tension or any pressure and physically your strokes are just flowing, every ball you hit is going in. Emotionally you're really calm. There's no strain involved. It's a euphoric feeling. The feeling that whatever you touch turns to gold. Whatever you do, whatever decision you make on the court, whatever stroke or shot you try, you know it's going to work.

—*Chris Evert, Tennis Champion*

Peak performances are those magic moments when an athlete puts it all together—both physically and mentally. The performance is exceptional, seemingly transcending ordinary levels of play. Privette defined **peak performance** as "behavior which exceeds one's average performance" (1982, p. 242) or "an episode of superior functioning" (1983, p. 1361). Competitively, these performances often result in a personal best. They are the ultimate high, the thrilling moment that athletes and coaches work for in their pursuit of excellence. Unfortunately, they also are relatively rare and, according to many athletes, nonvoluntary. But are they truly nonvoluntary? Can athletes be trained so that peak performances occur more frequently? If not to produce a peak performance, can athletes be

trained so they consistently play closer to their optimal level?

To answer these questions, it is first necessary to know if there are any common characteristics that identify peak performances. For example, is there an ideal body–mind state associated with peak performance? If so, is this ideal state similar from one athlete to another or one sport to another? More important, if common qualities are identified, can they be learned and developed?

It is safe to assume that peak performance is a consequence of both physical and mental factors. Mind and body cannot be separated. A precondition to peak performance is a certain level of physical conditioning and mastery of the necessary physical skills. While athletic and sport science communities long have been devoted to improving physical training programs, today emphasis is being placed on the psychological components of performance as well.

Obviously, the higher the level of physical skill and conditioning, the more potential control the athlete has over his or her performance. Yet, one must realize that peak performance is relative to each athlete's present level of ability. Peak performances are most likely to occur when athletes' skills match the demand or challenge of the situation (Csikszentmihalyi, 1990). Absolute skill level is not important; rather, it is important that the athlete has the skills to match the expected level of play. Thus, concern for enhancing peak performance is as relevant to coaches and sport psychologists who work with less skilled and youth sport athletes as it is to coaches and sport psychologists who work with professional or elite amateur athletes.

Overview of Peak Performance

The focus of this chapter is the mental side of peak performance and how the mind interacts with the body in ultimately producing performance. Most athletes and coaches will acknowledge that at least 40% to 90% of success in sports is due to mental factors. The higher the skill level, the more important the mental aspects become. In fact, on the elite competitive level, it is not uncommon to hear that the winner invariably comes down to who is the strongest athlete—mentally—on a given day! When describing his approach to golf, Tiger Woods (2001) stated, "it is a thinking man's (or woman's) game to a great degree. I believe my creative mind is my greatest weapon" (p. 255). When the physical, technical, and mental readiness of Olympic athletes was assessed, only mental readiness significantly predicted Olympic success (Orlick & Partington, 1988). Likewise, a study of professional baseball players (Smith & Christensen, 1995) showed psychological skills, but not physical skills, significantly predicted pitching performance. For predicting batting performance and which players would remain in professional baseball two and three

years later, psychological skills did as well as the physical skills

If the mental side of performance is so important to success, then perhaps an ideal internal psychological climate exists during peak performance. Before discussing the research supporting this premise, we must offer a caution. Do not think that the field of sport psychology has found all the answers. There is, however, a growing foundation for understanding the mental side of performance. As we identify an optimal psychological state for peak performance, we also provide a foundation for developing a mental skills training program. In fact, research now exists showing that psychological skills training can improve performance. This chapter, and the following chapters in this section, reflect the latest state of knowledge and the current thinking and practices of those involved in mental training for peak performance.

Psychological Characteristics During Peak Experiences in Sport

In early research in this area, athletes were interviewed and asked to describe their "greatest moment" in sport (Ravizza, 1977), how they felt when they were playing at their best (Loehr, 1984), or characteristics of the feelings they have at those moments when they are doing something extraordinarily well (Garfield & Bennett, 1984). Loehr compiled the following composite of athletes' interview statements:

> I felt like I could do almost anything, as if I were in complete control. I really felt confident and positive. [Regarding arousal,] I felt physically very relaxed, but really energized and pumped up. I experienced virtually no anxiety or fear, and the whole experience was enjoyable. I experienced a very real sense of calmness and quiet inside, and everything just seemed to flow automatically. . . . Even though I was really hustling, it was all very effortless. (Cited in Garfield & Bennett, 1984, pp. 37, 95)

Across these studies, the athletes gave surprisingly similar accounts. Common psychological characteristics associated with peak performances included

- Loss of fear—no fear of failure
- Total immersion in the activity
- Narrow focus of attention on the present
- Feeling in complete control
- Time/space disorientation (usually slowed down)
- Feeling that performance was automatic and effortless
- Control over emotion, thoughts, and arousal
- Highly self-confident
- Physically and mentally relaxed
- Highly energized

Garfield and Bennett summed up these feelings as "being in the cocoon" (feeling completely detached from the external environment and any potential distractions). According to Loehr (1984), athletes felt "it was like playing possessed, yet in complete control. Time itself seemed to slow down, so they never felt rushed. They played with profound intensity, total concentration and an enthusiasm that bordered on joy" (p. 67).

Privette and Bundrick (1997) further identified what they called the "peak performance dyad," which encompassed full focus on the activity and "self in process." They described it this way: "focusing fully on the relevant task of the game, whether narrowly on the placement of the ball or broadly over the entire field, while simultaneously being acutely aware of self as the doer, underlay peak performance" (p. 331). They concluded that peak performances are personally meaningful, rewarding, and fulfilling. Not surprisingly, athletes frequently associate this state with fun or enjoyment (Cohn, 1991).

Athletes described these qualities of peak performance similarly across sports, as well as across skill and competitive levels. For example, both Ravizza (1977) and Cohen (1991) noted that over 80% of the athletes in their studies reported experiencing these perceptions. Noteworthy, peak performance often was considered a temporary and involuntary phenomenon. However, as Loehr (1984) concluded, the probability of good performance could be substantially increased if the following combination of feelings could be triggered and maintained: high energy (challenge, inspiration, determination, intensity), fun and enjoyment, no pressure (low anxiety), optimism and positiveness, mental calmness, confidence, being very focused, and being in control.

Flow and Peak Performance

Often associated with peak performance is the psychological construct *flow,* defined as "the state in which people are so involved in an activity that nothing else seems to matter" (Csikszentmihalyi, 1990, p. 4). Csikszentmihalyi (1985) considers flow the basis of intrinsically motivated experiences or self-rewarding activity. This was evident in high-altitude rock climbers who reported that the possibility of experiencing flow motivated them to engage in this high-risk sport (Delle Fave, Bassi, & Massimini, 2003). Flow is not analogous to peak performance. One may be in flow and not necessarily be having a peak performance; however, when an athlete experiences peak performance, he or she appears to be in a flow state.

Jackson (1996) distinguished between flow and peak performance, suggesting that flow may be a precursor to, or the psychological process underlying, peak performance and it has been found to be positively related to performance (Jackson, Thomas, Marsh, & Smethurst, 2001). Nine dimensions of flow have been described (Csikszentmihalyi, 1990; Jackson, 2000). When athletes are in flow, they experience the following:

> The challenge of the situation matches the skills of the athlete, and these challenges and skills are at a personal high level.
>
> Awareness and action merge, the athlete "ceases to be aware of herself as separate from her action" (Jackson, 2000, p. 142).
>
> Goals are clear; "there is clarity about what one is to do" (Jackson, 2000, p. 142).

Unambiguous feedback indicates that what is being done is correct.

Total and complete concentration on the task at hand occurs.

There is a paradox of control, or the sense of being in complete control without actively attempting to be in control (also described as effortless and without fear of failure).

Loss of self-consciousness whereby one is aware of performing but is not concerned with self-evaluation.

Time seems to speed up or slow down.

The experience is autotelic—the activity is enjoyable and participation becomes its own reward.

Interviews with elite, international level athletes revealed psychological states that coincided with these characteristics of flow (Jackson 1992, 1996), which are very similar to those reported to accompany peak performances. Researchers also have examined the factors perceived by athletes to disrupt or facilitate flow. Interviews with elite figure skaters (Jackson, 1992) and college athletes (Russell, 2000) revealed the following factors interfered with flow: having physical problems or making mistakes, an inability to maintain their focus, a negative mental attitude, and a lack of audience response. Furthermore, interviews with elite athletes across a variety of sports (Jackson, 1992, 1995) showed that mental preparation that facilitated the likelihood of achieving flow included the following:

Having a positive attitude (confidence, positive thinking).

Following precompetitive plans and preparation.

Completing the optimal physical preparation prior to competition.

Attaining optimal arousal.

Achieving appropriate motivation to perform.

Being in tune with movements and performance—feeling good.

Being focused on the task.

Having optimal environmental and situational conditions.

Having positive team interactions or partner unity.

Enjoying what one is doing.

Studies employing flow questionnaires have found that athletes who experience flow, compared to those who do not, have higher preevent self-confidence (Catley & Duda, 1997; Stein, Kimiecik, Daniels, & Jackson, 1995), higher perceived ability, a task goal orientation, and lower anxiety (Jackson & Roberts, 1992; Jackson, Kimiecik, Ford, & Marsh, 1998). Additionally, intrinsic motivation (Kowal & Fortier, 2000) and athletic self-concept (Jackson, Thomas, Marsh, & Smethurst, 2000) have been found to be positively related to flow experiences. Jackson et al. (1998) concluded that high perceptions of one's athletic abilities appear to be crucial to the experience of flow. As they stated, "athletes who believe in their capabilities are probably more likely to experience a balance between challenge and skills, even when the challenge of a specific sport competition is relatively high" (p. 373).

When considering the characteristics of flow and the factors that facilitate or disrupt it, it seems that using psychological skills may enhance the likelihood of experiencing flow. Jackson et al. (2000) explored this notion in a study of competitors in surf life saving, orienteering, and road cycling. They found "the avoidance of negative thinking, combined with good emotional control, relaxation, appropriate activation levels, and, to a lesser extent, setting goals, use of imagery, and positive self-talk facilitated flow" (p. 148). In a rare intervention study aimed to enhance flow, Pates, Cummings, and Maynard (2002) tested the effect of a hypnosis intervention. Using an ideographic (i.e., individualized) design, five athletes were taught how to use hypnosis and applied this skill during a basketball shooting task (i.e., three-point shots). The hypnosis intervention consisted of relaxation, imagery, hypnotic induction and regression, and use of a trigger. The results showed that the intensity of flow experienced during the shooting task increased after learning to use hypnosis, as did performance.

These findings suggest that athletes can learn prerequisite skills that may enhance the likeliness of experiencing flow. Athletes who learn to be confident, focus their attention on the task at hand, control their anxiety, and have appropriate and challenging goals may experience flow and peak performance more often.

The Individualized Zone of Optimal Functioning

Another approach to examining psychological states during successful athletic performance focuses on performance-related emotions (Hanin, 2000a). The Individualized Zone of Optimal Functioning (IZOF) model (Hanin, 2000b) attempts to identify emotional patterns associated with individual athletes' successful performances. Hanin (1997) acknowledges that each athlete has her or his own unique emotional state in which successful performances are most likely. Optimal performance states can include both positive and negative emotions (Hanin, 2000b). This model includes four groups of emotional states: positive performance-enhancing, positive performance-impairing, negative performance-enhancing, and negative performance-impairing. For example, elite Finnish athletes described feeling energetic as a positive performance-enhancing emotion, whereas easygoing was considered a positive emotion that was performance-impairing (Hanin, 2000c). Tense and dissatisfied were described as negative performance-enhancing emotions, whereas feeling tired was considered negative and performance-impairing. To identify individuals' IZOFs, athletes complete an assessment identifying emotions related to their successful and unsuccessful performances. Different athletes may include different emotions in their profiles. This assessment results in identifying a range of

optimal and dysfunctional emotions, and an IZOF iceberg profile emerges. As Figure 9-1 shows, both positive and negative emotions considered performance-enhancing comprise the optimal zone, and performance-impairing emotions comprise the dysfunctional zones. Athletes whose emotional states are within their IZOF are more successful than athletes with emotional profiles out of their IZOFs (Hanin, 2000c). For example, successful junior soccer players had emotional profiles that were close to their optimal zones and outside of their dysfunctional zones (Syrja, Hanin, & Pesonen, 1995, as cited in Hanin, 2000c). The soccer players who had poor performances had emotional profiles outside of their optimal zones prior to competition, and they never entered their IZOFs once the match began. Similarly, successful international competitors in squash and badminton had emotions that were close to their optimal zones and outside of their dysfunctional zones (Syrja, Hanin, & Tarvonen, 1995, as cited in Hanin, 2000c).

Robazza and Bortoli (2003) compared the emotional profiles of elite athletes (who competed in major national or international championships) and nonelite athletes from a variety of sports. Their findings showed that the more elite athletes had a higher intensity of facilitating positive emotions than the less elite athletes. Prior to successful and less successful performances, the emotional profiles of elite competitors in blackbelt karate differed (Robazza, Bortoli, & Hanin, 2004). When these athletes compared their emotion scores at competition to their worst-ever emotion score, better performances were associated with larger differences (or greater distance from worst-ever emotions).

This research supports the conclusion that performance-enhancing and performance-impairing IZOFs can be identified for individual athletes. Interestingly, these patterns of optimal and dysfunctional emotions differed not only across athletes, but also across contexts. Elite Finnish cross-country skiers identified different IZOFs for races, intensive training, and technical training (Hanin & Syrja, 1997). Teaching athletes to maintain their emotional state within their performance-enhancing zones may increase the

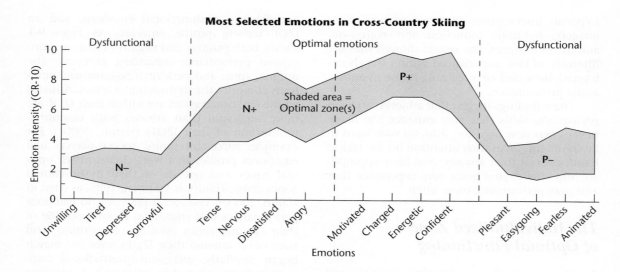

Most Selected Emotions in Cross-Country Skiing

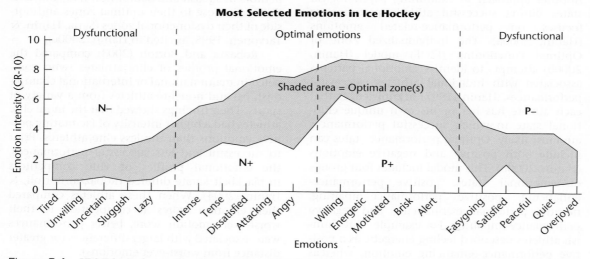

Most Selected Emotions in Ice Hockey

Figure 9-1   **IZOF-based-emotion iceberg profiles in cross-country skiing and ice hockey**
Source: Reprinted from Hanin, Y. L. (2000c). Successful and poor performance and emotions. In Y. L. Hanin (Ed.), *Emotions in sport* (p. 185). Champaign, IL: Human Kinetics.

likelihood of peak performance or assist athletes to perform more consistently.

Hanin extended the IZOF approach to include the "metaphor self-generation method" in which athletes develop a personally meaningful, symbolic image "that allows for understanding something unknown (or difficult to describe)" (Hanin & Stambulova, 2002, p. 397). Individual metaphor profiles revealed that when considering their best performances, athletes' metaphors were action-oriented and symbolized strength, power, and skill (e.g., "a tiger ready to pounce," "a well working pipeline"). Not surprisingly, when considering worst performances, athletes generated converse images reflecting weakness and lack of readiness (e.g., "an empty bottle," "a cow on the ice," "a sinking boat"). Notably, it was not unusual for athletes to describe negative images and unpleasant feelings preevent, even when describing best-ever performance. However, these negative feelings and images changed to productive feelings and images during the event. Additionally, Ruiz and Hanin (2004) found that these symbolic images remained relatively stable over a 5-month period. Yet the images also evolved and reflected new experiences. Ruiz and Hanin concluded that metaphors can both increase awareness of competitive emotions and be used to change dysfunctional images and beliefs.

Psychological Attributes and Skills of Successful and Less Successful Athletes

Although it is interesting to understand the psychological characteristics associated with peak performances, it may be considered even more important to know how athletes achieve these psychological states. Hence, a substantial amount of research has examined the psychological skills that successful athletes use, often by comparing more and less successful athletes with the goal of learning why some individuals outperform others.

Mahoney and Avener (1977) designed a questionnaire to assess various psychological factors such as confidence, concentration, anxiety, self-talk, and imagery. Researchers studying athletes in an array of sports (e.g., gymnastics, wrestling, tennis, racquetball, and diving) and across competitive levels (e.g., college, Olympic) have used this basic tool, or variations of it. Findings from these studies revealed consistent results across samples: The more successful athletes had high self-confidence and few self-doubts, used imagery more often, and controlled their anxiety better than the less successful athletes (e.g., Gould, Weiss, & Weinberg, 1981; Highlen & Bennett, 1979, 1983; Meyers, Cooke, Cullen, & Liles, 1979).

Using similar questionnaires, modified for golfers and ten-pin bowlers, researchers found that the more skilled athletes had better mental preparation, concentration, automaticity, commitment, competitiveness, confidence in their equipment and technique, interest in improving, and consistency (Thomas & Over, 1994; Thomas, Schlinker, & Over, 1996).

In an attempt to improve our ability to compare findings across studies, researchers have developed a variety of scales that measure psychological skills used by athletes. Mahoney, Gabriel, and Perkins (1987) developed the Psychological Skills Inventory for Sport (PSIS) that measures anxiety management, concentration, self-confidence, motivation, mental preparation, and team emphasis. Using this scale, they examined differences in use and effectiveness of psychological skills in elite, preelite, and collegiate athletes in a variety of sports. Elite athletes reported that they experienced fewer anxiety problems, had better concentration before and during competition, were more self-confident, used internal and kinesthetic imagery in their mental preparation, were more focused on individual rather than team performance, and were more highly motivated to do well than less elite athletes. Other studies using the PSIS found similar results. For example, highly skilled collegiate rodeo athletes (Meyers, LeUnes, & Bourgeois, 1996) and elite equestrian athletes (Meyers, Bourgeois, LeUnes, & Murray, 1998) reported better anxiety management, concentration, confidence, and motivation compared to their less skilled counterparts.

The Test of Performance Strategies (TOPS; Thomas, Murphy, & Hardy, 1999) was developed to assess the frequency with which athletes used goal setting, relaxation, activation, imagery, self-talk, attentional control, negative thinking, emotional control, and automaticity. Athletes rate how frequently they use the various skills in competitive and practice situations. Initial findings using this scale have shown that male international competitors scored higher on goal-setting, imagery, and activation compared to less elite athletes (Thomas et al., 1999). Female international athletes had higher self-talk, emotional control, goal-setting, imagery, activation, negative thinking, and relaxation compared to their less elite peers. College softball and baseball players who reported high use in both practice and competition of the mental skills assessed by the TOPS also revealed higher perceptions of success compared to the players who reported moderate or low use of the mental skills. (Frey, Laguna, & Ravizza, 2003).

The Ottawa Mental Skill Assessment Tool (Durand-Bush, Salmela, & Green-Demers, 2001) measures athletes' use of goal setting, stress reactions, fear control, relaxation, activation, focusing, refocusing, imagery, mental practice, and mental planning, as well as confidence and commitment. When this scale was administered to Canadian elite (national or international competitors) and competitive (college or provincial sport club) athletes, the elite athletes had higher scores on confidence, commitment, stress reactions, focusing, and refocusing compared to the competitive athletes.

Across a wide array of studies, it seems that regardless of how it is measured, elite and successful athletes consistently report using the following psychological skills, which likely contribute to their high-level performances:

Imagery

Attentional focusing

Maintaining concentration

Controlling anxiety and activation

Positive self-talk

Goal setting

Also, athletes who consider anxiety as facilitative or helpful to performance have been found to be more successful than athletes who interpret their anxiety negatively or as debilitative to performance (Hanton & Jones, 1999a; Jones & Swain, 1995; Jones, Swain, & Hardy, 1993). Subsequent research has shown that athletes who employed a facilitative interpretation of their anxiety also associated more positive emotional states with their athletic performance compared to the athletes who had a debilitative interpretation of anxiety (Mellalieu, Hanton, & Jones, 2003). In this study, elite athletes also reported

higher self-confidence and lower cognitive and somatic anxiety, and they interpreted their anxiety as less debilitating and unpleasant compared to the nonelite athletes. Further, nonelite swimmers' performance improved after participating in an intervention to redefine their anxiety as facilitative to performance (Hanton & Jones, 1999b).

More recently, Thomas, Hanton, and Maynard (2007) interviewed elite female field hockey players and found that "facilitators possess a refined repertoire of psychological skills that they can draw upon during the time preceding performance" (p. 394). More specifically, facilitators had refined imagery skills, used performance and process goals, and restructured negative thoughts. Debilitators attempted to implement psychological skills, yet they were unable to control the negative symptoms of cognitive and somatic anxiety.

Employing a different methodological approach, qualitative researchers examining peak performance have interviewed athletes to obtain a more detailed description of the athletes' perceptions and experiences than can be expressed through questionnaires. The explosion of qualitative research with Olympic and other elite athletes has greatly expanded our understanding of psychological attributes associated with peak performances. These studies have provided comprehensive assessment of Canadian Olympians (Orlick & Partington, 1988), U.S. Olympic teams (Gould, Eklund, & Jackson, 1992a, 1992b; Gould, Guinan, Greenleaf, Medbury, & Peterson, 1999; Greenleaf, Gould, & Dieffenbach, 2001) and professional athletes (McCaffrey & Orlick, 1989). Across these studies, a consistent pattern emerged of what Orlick and Partington (1988) called, "mental links to excellence." These athletes described

Total commitment.

Clearly defined goals.

High confidence.

A positive attitude.

Control of arousal levels and a facilitative interpretation of anxiety.

Daily imagery practice.

Well-developed concentration and focusing skills.

Well-honed practice and competition plans.

Distraction control strategies.

Postcompetition evaluation and continual refinement of their mental approach.

Emphasis on quality rather than quantity of practice.

Use of competition simulation.

Adding to the previous findings, Gould, Dieffenbach, and Moffett's (2002) interviews with Olympic champions also revealed that they had high optimism, high levels of dispositional hope (i.e., a sense of control in setting and achieving goals), high productive perfectionism (i.e., personal standards), and low unproductive perfectionism (i.e., concerns about mistakes, parental criticism and expectations, doubts). These champion athletes also possessed "sport intelligence," which Gould and colleagues identified as analyzing skills and performances, being innovative regarding technique, making good decisions, being a quick learner, being "a student of the sport," and "understanding the nature of elite sport" (p. 199).

In contrast to the preceding mental links to excellence, these qualitative researchers typically found that poor performances or failure to meet one's goals was associated with feeling listless, over- or underarousal, lacking concentration, irrelevant or negative thoughts, and worrying about losing (e.g., Eklund, 1994; Gould Eklund, & Jackson, 1992a). Perhaps one of the most salient differences between more and less successful performances is the extent to which athletes adhere to their mental preparation plans and precompetition routines and how well practiced and internalized their coping strategies were. Overall, successful athletes have highly developed techniques for coping with distractions, which act as "automatized buffers" that reduce the impact of negative unforeseen events or allow them to interpret these occurrences positively. Coping strategies often included using positive thinking; a narrow, specific focus of attention; and changing their environment (e.g., avoiding potential irritants, moving away from others). The less successful athletes departed from their normal routines, abandoned competitive plans when under pressure, lost competitive focus, and did not rigorously adhere to their mental preparation plans.

Edwards and colleagues' (Edwards, Kingston, Hardy, & Gould, 2002) qualitative study also sheds light on the mental links to poor performance. They interviewed eight elite male athletes about a "catastrophic performance." A drop in confidence was the most evident characteristic of these performances, followed by increases in cognitive anxiety, inferring their incapacitating effect on performance. These athletes also recalled feeling a loss of control as performance deteriorated and eventually resignation and withdrawal of effort.

Across all these quantitative and qualitative studies, there appear to be some commonalities in the psychological characteristics of more successful athletes. For successful athletes, the most consistent finding is that they are highly confident. Without exception, the research shows that elite and more successful athletes believed in themselves more than less successful athletes. They tended to be "psyched up" rather than "psyched out" by demanding competitive situations, such as the Olympics or World Championships. As Greenleaf, Gould, and Dieffenbach, (2001) described, successful Olympic athletes perceived the Games as a "time to shine." These athletes had numerous other commonalities and they also used a wide array of psychological skills. In particular, they used imagery and had well-developed plans for competition and for refocusing if distracted.

Overall, the successful athletes were less likely to be distracted and had a higher ability to rebound from mistakes. The psychological characteristics associated with successful elite athletic performance include the following:

High self-confidence.

Total commitment.

A strong performance focus.

The ability cope well with stress and distractions.

Good attention-focusing and refocusing skills.

An optimistic, positive attitude.

High personal standards.

Well-developed precompetition and competitive plans.

The ability to control emotions and remain appropriately activated.

A view of anxiety as beneficial.

The use of performance goals.

The use of imagery.

An interesting new theme that has emerged from recent studies with elite performers links peak performance with being creative, engaging in self-reflection, developing perspective, and having balance in one's life (Gould, Dieffenback, & Moffett, 2002). Comparable to Gould, Dieffenback, and Moffett's (2002) notion of sport intelligence, optimal performance appears to be related to training smart. Developing talent, according to Csikzentmihalyi et al. (1993), involves viewing difficult situations as challenging and enjoying the hardships inherent in perfecting skills. Being creative and reflective may allow athletes to view challenges more like a puzzle to complete rather than as a difficult situation. As Csikzentmihalyi et al. (1993) found with talented teenagers, creativity is associated with flow experiences, and flow is an enjoyable state. In all, enjoyment is one of the primary determinants of developing talent (Csikzentmihalyi et al., 1993). Part of enjoying sport excellence and being mentally tough is having balance in one's life. This new theme suggests that a broader view of psychological influences on peak performance may be appropriate.

A Profile of Mental Toughness

It seems that throughout this chapter we have been discussing what may be termed *mental toughness*. When discussing what it takes to be successful in sport, athletes often express that to have consistently strong athletic performances, they need to be mentally tough. Although athletes, coaches, and sport psychologists commonly use this term, mental toughness can be described in many different ways. In "What Is This Thing Called Mental Toughness," Jones, Hanton, and Connaughton (2002) asked 10 elite athletes (competitors from the Olympic and Commonwealth

Games) to come to a consensus definition of *Mental Toughness*. The following definition emerged:

> Mental toughness is having the natural or developed psychological edge that enables you to:
> Generally, cope better than your opponents with the many demands (competition, training, lifestyle) that sport places on a performer.
> Specifically, be more consistent and better than your opponents in remaining determined, focused, confident, and in control under pressure. (p.209)

These attributes were verified and extended in a subsequent study with "super-elite" athletes (Olympic and world champions) and coaches and sport psychologists who worked with super-elite athletes (Jones, Hanton, & Connaughton, 2007). The components these athletes added to the concept of mental toughness perhaps reflect the super-elites' greater insight into exceptional performance. Based on the resulting broader conception of mental toughness, Jones et al. proposed a mental toughness framework that contains two subcomponents: belief and focus. Mental toughness is composed of an unshakable belief that one can achieve her or his goals regardless of obstacles or setbacks. Through focus, mentally tough athletes prioritize their long-term sport goal over all other life goals, yet they also possess the ability to switch off this focus to maintain balance in their lives, which then contributes to their success.

Further, belief and focus interact with the sport context (i.e., training, competition, postcompetition). The super-elites expressed the importance of long-term goal setting, controlling the environment, and pushing oneself to the limit in training. During competitions, mentally tough athletes:

Have an "unshakable belief" (they know they can do anything they set their minds to do).

Stay focused.

Regulate performance (increase effort as necessary).

Cope well with pressure.

Are aware of, and control, their thoughts and feelings.

Control the environment (i.e., are not affected by things out of their control).

Postcompetition, these athletes are able to cope with both failure and success. They learn from their failures and use them to motivate themselves toward future success. Balancing competitive demands with other life priorities is another essential aspect of being mentally tough. See Crust (2007) for a recent review of mental toughness research in sport.

Bull, Shambrook, James, and Brooks (2005) have developed a framework of mental toughness that seems to integrate Hanin's metaphor concept with athletes' perceptions of mental toughness. Their four-level pyramid of mental toughness reflects a developmental approach to elite athlete performance (see Figure 9-2). At the base of the pyramid, the environment provides the foundation for developing mental toughness, which is illustrated with an image of a production line. Then athletes' tough character (i.e., fairly stable personality attributes such as independence, resilient confidence, competitiveness) is akin to the engine which is fueled

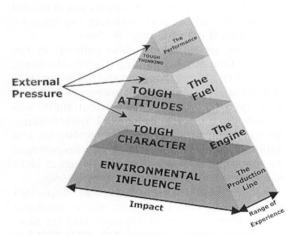

Figure 9-2   **The mental toughness pyramid**
In Bull, S. J., Shambrook, C. J., James, W., & Brooks, J. E. (2005). Towards an understanding of mental toughness in elite English cricketers. Journal of Applied Sport Psychology, 17, 209–227.

by athletes' tough attitudes (i.e., belief in preparation, "never say die," and "go the extra mile" mindsets), ultimately resulting in tough thinking leading to the performance.

Team, Coach, Family, and Organizational Influences on Peak Performance

To this point, we have emphasized factors within athletes that help or hinder peak performance. Another consideration is the effect that other people may have on high-level athletic performance, such as teammates, coaches, family members, and administrators. For example, Olympic athletes believed that team cohesion was an important contributor to their success (Gould, Greenleaf, Chung, & Guinan, 2002; Greenleaf et al., 2001). In particular, having a positive team leader and strong team chemistry were considered helpful while lacking trust and confidence in one's teammates interfered with optimal performance. Athletes on Olympic teams that achieved their team goals also described having positive social support from friends and family (Gould, Guinan, Greenleaf, Medbery, & Peterson, 1999). Conversely, members of less successful teams noted poor team cohesion and a lack of trust among team members. See Chapter 7 for a more complete discussion of cohesion and its role in performance.

Coaches also can be quite influential on athletes. Ideally, coaches help athletes learn the psychological, physical, and tactical skills needed to be successful. However, coaches may unintentionally interfere with success. U.S. Olympic athletes identified that coaches with strong commitment and those who implemented a clear performance plan assisted successful performances (Gould, Greenleaf, Chung, & Guinan, 2002; Gould, Guinan, Greenleaf, & Chung, 2002). Conversely, the following coach attributes hindered team success:

Inability to deal with crises.

Unrealistic expectations.

Overcoaching and excessive interactions with team members.

Inability to make decisive and fair decisions.

Inability to "keep it simple."

Coaches and athletes who were on teams that did not meet their Olympic expectations also believed that negative attitudes toward the coach and poor coach–athlete communications were at least partially to blame (Gould, Guinan, Greenleaf, & Chung, 2002).

Studies of US Olympic champions (Gould, Dieffenbach, & Moffett, 2002) and young Canadian national level athletes (Côté, 1999) uncovered the critical role that parents and family members played in athletes' support network. In these studies, families provided social and emotional support and encouragement and showed interest in the athletes' sport activity while exherting little pressure to win. Additionally, family members voiced their belief in the athlete's ability to succeed, encouraged a "can-do attitude," and created an "optimistic achievement oriented climate" (Gould, Dieffenbach, & Moffett, 2002; p. 200).

Another issue affecting athletes' ability to perform optimally is organizational stress, or concerns that arise because of the management of teams. Interviews with British Olympic and elite (i.e., international competitors) athletes revealed that they experienced concerns related to finances, travel, accommodations, team selection, coaching styles, and team atmosphere (Fletcher & Hanton, 2003; Woodman & Hardy, 2001). Some athletes overtly claimed that when faced with interpersonal or financial difficulties, they had less than ideal performances (Woodman & Hardy, 2001). Interviews with U.S. Olympic athletes corroborated these findings. U.S. athletes who competed at the Atlanta and Nagano games indicated that a wide range of variables influenced their performances, including transportation difficulties, housing problems, getting event tickets for family, media distractions, and team selection issues (Gould, Guinan, Greenleaf, & Chung, 2002; Greenleaf et al., 2001). All of these factors are aspects of organizational stress. In all,

it seems that team and environmental factors affect the likelihood of peak performance.

Conclusion: What It Takes to "Make It"

There seems to be a fairly strong consensus that to become a successful elite athlete takes commitment, dedication, mental toughness, and the ability to pursue a dream in a rational manner. When top coaches and scouts in the National Hockey League were asked what determines who does and does not make it at the professional level, they used words such as desire, determination, attitude, heart, and self-motivation (Orlick & Reed, cited in Orlick, 1980). Olympic coaches felt that athletes needed confidence, social support, and cohesive teams (Gould, Guinan, et al., 1999; Gould, Guinan, Greenleaf, & Chung, 2002) and needed to be able to maintain their composure, be prepared to cope with distractions, and have a sound competitive plan (Gould, Guinan, et al., 2002). All of these attributes may be developed or enhanced by using psychological skills. Gould, Guinan, et al. (2002) concluded that, according to Olympic coaches, "the role of psychological variables was perceived as especially salient and reinforces the need for psychological skills training" (p. 248).

Junior tennis coaches also believed in the need for mental skills training (Gould, Medberry, et al., 1999). They considered the following skills as particularly essential to the success of their athletes: enjoyment/fun, focus/concentration, self-confidence, and emotional control. These findings are consistent with studies of intercollegiate and national team coaches who also acknowledged the importance of athletes' psychological skills (Gould, Hodge, Peterson, & Giannini, 1989).

That mental preparation was important for success in elite level sport was a consistent theme across studies of Olympic athletes (e.g., Gould et al., 1999; Greenleaf et al., 2001; Orlick & Partington, 1988). The Canadian Olympians in Orlick and Partington's (1988) study believed that through psychological skills training they improved their performance level and learned to perform more consistently at their best. Many of the Olympic athletes interviewed by Orlick and Partington stated that they could have obtained their best performances much sooner had they strengthened their mental skills earlier in their athletic careers. As U.S. Olympic athletes who met or exceeded their goals pointed out, mental preparation was essential (Gould et al., 1999), whereas athletes on less successful teams felt that they did not spend enough time on mental preparation.

At this point, a word of caution is needed regarding the interpretation of the research summarized in this chapter. All of the studies presented were either descriptive or correlational. What this means is that they generated descriptions of successful athletic experiences or identified relationships between psychological skills and peak performances. Based on this type of research, we cannot make any conclusions about cause-and-effect relationships—we cannot say certain mental states cause peak performances;

we can only note that they are related. When considering the question, "Are the psychological differences between successful and less successful athletes critical to performance differences?" we cannot be absolutely sure. There seems to be a lot of evidence suggesting that psychological characteristics are associated with peak performances. Still, we do not know if athletes first learned the psychological skills necessary to achieve an ideal mental state or if they developed these characteristics by being consistently successful (that is, being successful leads to being confident of continued success) (Heyman, 1982). It also is plausible that athletes with certain psychological strengths are drawn to elite level sport. We may never know what causes an ideal mental state. However, given the weight of the evidence presented, it seems safe to assume that athletes use psychological skills in pursuit of their athletic goals and that they have consistent psychological profiles when they compete at elite levels.

Summary

This chapter began with the questions "Is there an ideal body–mind state associated with peak performance?" and "If so, is this ideal state similar from one athlete to another or one sport to another?" Across a wide range of sources, a certain psychological profile appears to be linked with successful athletic performance. Although there are individual variations, in most cases this general profile is depicted by the following characteristics:

High self-confidence and expectations of success.

Self-regulation of arousal (energized yet relaxed).

Feeling in control.

Total concentration.

Keen focus on the present task.

Viewing difficult situations as exciting and challenging.

Productive perfectionism (i.e., have high standards, yet flexibility to learn from mistakes).

Positive attitude and thoughts about performance.

Strong determination and commitment.

Mental states associated with poor performances include self-doubts, acting contrary to normal performance routines, focusing on distractions, concerns about the outcome or score, over- or underarousal, and lack of concentration.

This ideal performance state does not just happen. Top-level athletes have identified their own ideal performance state and have learned, intentionally or subconsciously, to create and maintain this state voluntarily so that their talents and physical skills thrive. Achieving one's own ideal internal psychological climate is not a simple task. As Orlick and Partington (1988) stated, "Mental readying is derived from a number of learned mental skills that must be continually practiced and refined for an athlete to perform to potential and on a consistent basis" (p. 129). Accordingly, elite athletes employ meticulous planning for competitive performances. Generally, this involves

Setting goals.

Using imagery.

Developing competition and refocusing plans.

Practicing coping skills so they become automatic.

Employing competitive simulation.

Successful athletes also have highly developed coping skills that they use to deal with the demands of practice and competition. They are quite diverse and typically encompass

Thought control strategies.

Arousal management techniques.

Interpreting anxiety as facilitative to performance.

Attention control.

Refocusing skills.

Successful athletes also have strong support networks that include their families, friends, teammates, and coaches. Having high team cohesion, good communication and relationships with coaches, and minimal organizational stress are associated with elite performances. Conversely, lacking team cohesion, trust, or confidence in one's teammates or coach hampers good performances. When coaches make poor decisions, have unrealistic expectations, or have poor coping or communication skills, they can interfere with athletes' optimal functioning. Problems with travel and accommodations, concerns about team selection, financial problems, and other administrative issues also may negatively affect athletes.

The commonalities in mental states and psychological skill use have led researchers and practitioners to conclude that the right psychological climate helps mobilize mental and physical reactions that are essential to performing at one's best. Conversely, things that create a negative mental climate will impede the likelihood that an athlete can perform optimally. Through teaching athletes to control unproductive mental states and enhance the productive ones, athletes will be more likely to create ideal performance states. Psychological skills are learned through knowledge and practice, just as physical skills and competitive strategies are learned. Some gifted athletes may perfect these mental states on their own, but most need to be taught specific training techniques.

The remaining chapters in this section of the book address specific psychological states associated with peak performance and, when appropriate, provide techniques for learning to create and maintain desirable mental and physiological states. Chapter 10 is unique in that its purpose is to help coaches and sport psychologists learn how to assist each athlete in identifying his or her own internal psychological climate for peak performance and to identify those factors that tend to enhance or detract from this ideal climate. Such awareness is the first step in mental skills training. In the chapters that follow, it becomes obvious that peak performance need not be a unique, temporary, involuntary experience. It is a product of the body and mind, and it can be trained. Just as improving physical skills, strategies, and conditioning increases the likelihood of peak performance, learning to control psychological readiness and the ideal mental climate for peak performance also enhances performance.

Study Questions

1. Define peak performance.

2. Think back to your own best sporting performance. What were the psychological states that you experienced? How does your experience compare to the descriptions about the psychological characteristics of peak performance in the research?

3. Summarize the psychological states typically associated with peak performances.

4. Define *flow* and describe its dimensions.

5. What are factors that will enhance and hinder flow experiences?

6. What is the Individualized Zone of Optimal Functioning (IZOF) model and how does it relate to peak performance?

7. Describe several metaphors you associate with successful and less successful performances.

8. What are the primary psychological characteristics that distinguish between more and less successful athletic performances?

9. Summarize the major psychological characteristics of elite athletes.

10. What are the primary psychological skills that elite athletes use? What is the association between these skills and peak performance?

11. Describe mental toughness and its relationship to performance.

12. Describe how athletes' relationships with their teammates may influence optimal performance.

13. What are things that coaches may do that will interfere with peak performance?

14. What is organizational stress and how might it influence athletes' performances?

15. If you were a coach or administrator, how would you minimize the problems faced by Olympic athletes who did not achieve their goals?

References

Bloom, B. S. (Ed.). (1985). *Developing talent in young people.* New York: Ballantine.

Bull, S. J., Shambrook, C. J., James, W., & Brooks, J. E. (2005). Towards an understanding of mental toughness in elite English cricketers. *Journal of Applied Sport Psychology, 17,* 209–227.

Catley, D., & Duda, J. L. (1997). Psychological antecedents of the frequency and intensity of flow in golfers. *International Journal of Sport Psychology, 28,* 309–322.

Cohn, P. J. (1991). An exploratory study on peak performance in golf. *The Sport Psychologist, 5,* 1–14.

Côté, J. (1999). The influence of the family in the development of talent. *The Sport Psychologist, 13,* 395–417.

Crust, L. (2007). Mental toughness in sport: A review. *International Journal of Sport and Exercise Psychology, 5,* 270–290.

Csikszentmihalyi, M. (1985). Emergent motivation and the evolution of the self. In D. Kleiber & M. Maehr (Eds.), *Advances in motivation and achievement,* Vol. 4 (pp. 93–119). Greenwich, CT: JAI.

Csikszentmihalyi, M. (1990). *Flow: The psychology of optimal experience.* New York: Harper & Row.

Csikszentmihalyi, M., Rathunde, K., & Whalen, S. (1993). *Talented teenagers: The roots of success and failure.* New York: Cambridge University Press.

Delle Fave, A., Bassi, M., & Massimini, F. (2003). Quality of experience and risk perception in high-altitude rock climbing. *Journal of Applied Sport Psychology, 15,* 82–98,

Durand-Bush, N., & Salmela, J. H. (2001). The development of talent in sport. In R. N. Singer, H. A. Hausenblas, & C. M. Janelle (Eds.), *Handbook of sport psychology* (pp. 269–289). New York: John Wiley & Sons.

Durand-Bush, N., & Salmela, J. H. (2002). The development and maintenance of expert athletic performance: Perceptions of world and Olympic champions. *Journal of Applied Sport Psychology, 14,* 154–171.

Durand-Bush, N., Salmela, J. H., & Green-Demers, I. (2001). The Ottawa Mental Skills Assessment Tool (OMSAT-3). *The Sport Psychologist, 15,* 1–19.

Edwards, T., Kingston, K., Hardy, L., & Gould, D. (2002). A qualitative analysis of catastrophic performances and the associated thoughts, feelings, and emotions. *The Sport Psychologist, 16,* 1–19.

Eklund, R. C. (1994). A season long investigation of competitive cognition in collegiate wrestlers. *Research Quarterly for Exercise and Sport, 65,* 169–183.

Fletcher, D., & Hanton, S. (2003). Sources of organizational stress in elite sports performers. *The Sport Psychologist, 17,* 175–195.

Frey, M., Laguna, P., & Ravizza, K. (2003). Collegiate athletes' mental skill use and perceptions of success: An exploration of the practice and competition settings. *Journal of Applied Sport Psychology, 15,* 115–128.

Garfield, C. A., & Bennett, H. Z. (1984). *Peak performance: Mental training techniques of the world's greatest athletes*. Los Angeles: Tarcher.

Gould, D., Dieffenbach, K., & Moffett, A. (2002). Psychological characteristics and their development in Olympic champions. *Journal of Applied Sport Psychology, 14*, 172–204.

Gould, D., Eklund, R. C., & Jackson, S. A. (1992a). 1988 U.S. Olympic wrestling excellence: I. Mental preparation, precompetitive cognition, and affect. *The Sport Psychologist, 6*, 358–382.

Gould, D., Eklund, R. C., & Jackson, S. A. (1992b). 1988 U.S. Olympic wrestling excellence: II. Thoughts and affect occurring during competition. *The Sport Psychologist, 6*, 383–402.

Gould, D., Greenleaf, C., Chung, Y., & Guinan, D. (2002). A survey of U.S. Atlanta and Nagano Olympians: Variables perceived to influence performance. *Research Quarterly for Exercise and Sport, 73*, 175–186.

Gould, D., Guinan, D., Greenleaf, C., & Chung, Y. (2002). A survey of U.S. Olympic coaches: Variables perceived to have influenced athlete performances and coach effectiveness. *The Sport Psychologist, 16*, 229–250.

Gould, D., Guinan, D., Greenleaf, C., Medbery, R., & Peterson, K. (1999). Factors affecting Olympic performance: Perceptions of athletes and coaches from more and less successful teams. *The Sport Psychologist, 13*, 371–394.

Gould, D., Hodge, K., Peterson, K., & Giannini, J. (1989). An exploratory examination of strategies used by elite coaches to enhance self-efficacy in athletes. *Journal of Sport and Exercise Psychology, 11*, 128–140.

Gould, D., Medberry, R., Damarjian, N., & Lauer, L. (1999). A survey of mental skills training knowledge, opinions, and practices of junior tennis coaches. *Journal of Applied Sport Psychology, 11*, 28–50.

Gould, D., Weiss, M., & Weinberg, R. (1981). Psychological characteristics of successful and nonsuccessful Big Ten wrestlers. *Journal of Sport Psychology, 3*, 69–81.

Greenleaf, C., Gould, D., & Dieffenbach, K. (2001). Factors influencing Olympic performance: Interviews with Atlanta and Nagano U.S. Olympians. *Journal of Applied Sport Psychology, 13*, 154–184.

Hanin, Y. L. (1997). Emotions and athletic performance: Individualized zones of optimal functioning model. *European Yearbook of Sport Psychology, 1*, 29–72.

Hanin, Y. L. (2000a). *Emotions in sport*. Champaign, IL: Human Kinetics.

Hanin, Y. L. (2000b). Individual zones of optimal functioning (IZOF) model: Emotion–performance relationships in sport. In Y. L. Hanin (Ed.), *Emotions in sport* (pp. 65–89). Champaign, IL: Human Kinetics.

Hanin, Y. L. (2000c). Successful and poor performance and emotions. In Y. L. Hanin (Ed.), *Emotions in sport* (pp. 157–187). Champaign, IL: Human Kinetics.

Hanin, Y. L., & Syrja, P. (1997). Optimal emotions in elite cross-country skiers. In E. Muller, H. Schwameder, E. Kornexl, & C. Raschner (Eds.), *Science and skiing* (pp. 408–419). London: SPON.

Hanin, Y.L., & Stambulova, N.B. (2002). Metaphoric description of performance states: An application of the IZOF model. *The Sport Psychologist, 16,* 396–415.

Hanton, S., & Jones, G. (1999a). The acquisition and development of cognitive skills and strategies: I. Training the butterflies to fly in formation. *The Sport Psychologist, 13,* 1–21.

Hanton, S., & Jones, G. (1999b). The acquisition and development of cognitive skills and strategies: II. Training the butterflies to fly in formation. *The Sport Psychologist, 13,* 22–41.

Heyman, S. R. (1982). Comparisons of successful and unsuccessful competitors: A reconsideration of methodological questions and data. *Journal of Sport Psychology, 4,* 295–300.

Highlen, P. S., & Bennett, B. B. (1979). Psychological characteristics of successful and non-successful elite wrestlers: An exploratory study. *Journal of Sport Psychology, 1,* 123–137.

Highlen, P. S., & Bennett, B. B. (1983). Elite divers and wrestlers: A comparison between open-and closed-skill athletes. *Journal of Sport Psychology, 5,* 390–409.

Jackson, S. A. (1992). Athletes in flow: A qualitative investigation of flow states in elite figure skaters. *Journal of Applied Sport Psychology, 4,* 161–180.

Jackson, S. A. (1995). Factors influencing the occurrence of flow states in elite athletes. *Journal of Applied Sport Psychology, 7,* 138–166.

Jackson, S. A. (1996). Toward a conceptual understanding of the flow experience in elite athletes. *Research Quarterly for Exercise and Sport, 67,* 76–90.

Jackson, S. A. (2000). Joy, fun, and flow state in sport. In Y. L. Hanin (Ed.), *Emotions in sport* (pp. 135–156). Champaign, IL: Human Kinetics.

Jackson, S. A., Kimiecik, J. C., Ford, S. K., & Marsh, H. W. (1998). Psychological correlates of flow in sport. *Journal of Sport & Exercise Psychology, 20,* 358–378.

Jackson, S. A., & Roberts, G. C. (1992). Positive performance states of athletes: Toward a conceptual understanding of peak performance. *The Sport Psychologist, 6,* 156–171.

Jackson, S., Thomas, P. R., March, H. W., & Smethurst, C. J. (2001). Relationships between flow, self-concept, psychological skills, and performance. *Journal of Applied Sport Psychology, 13,* 129–153.

Jones, G., Hanton, S., & Connaughton, D. (2002). What is this thing called mental toughness? An investigation of elite sport performers. *Journal of Applied Sport Psychology, 14,* 205–218.

Jones, G., Hanton, S., & Connaughton, D. (2007). A framework of mental toughness in the world's best performers. *The Sport Psychologist, 2,* 243–264.

Jones, G., & Swain, A. (1995). Predispositions to experience debilitative and facilitative anxiety in elite and non-elite performers. *The Sport Psychologist, 9,* 201–211.

Jones, J. G., Swain, A., & Hardy, L. (1993). Intensity and direction dimensions of competitive state anxiety and relationships with performance. *Journal of Sports Sciences, 11,* 525–532.

Kowal, J., & Fortier, M. S. (2000). Testing relationships from the hierarchical model of intrinsic and extrinsic motivation using flow as a motivational consequence. *Research Quarterly for Exercise and Sport, 71,* 171–181.

Loehr, J. E. (1984, March). How to overcome stress and play at your peak all the time. *Tennis,* 66–76.

Mahoney, M. J. (1989). Psychological predictors of elite and non-elite performance in Olympic weightlifting. *International Journal of Sport Psychology, 20,* 1–12.

Mahoney, M. J., & Avener, M. (1977). Psychology of the elite athlete: An exploratory study. *Cognitive Therapy and Research 1,* 135–142.

Mahoney, M. J., Gabriel, T. J., & Perkins, T. S. (1987). Psychological skills and exceptional athletic performance. *The Sport Psychologist, 1,* 181–199.

McCaffrey, N., & Orlick, T. (1989). Mental factors related to excellence among top professional golfers. *International Journal of Sport Psychology, 20,* 256–278.

Mellalieu, S. D., Hanton, S., & Jones, G. (2003). Emotional labeling and competitive anxiety in preparation and competition. *The Sport Psychologist, 17,* 157–174.

Meyers, M. C., Bourgeois, A. E., LeUnes, A., & Murray, N. G. (1998). Mood and psychological skills of elite and sub-elite equestrian athletes. *Journal of Sport Behavior, 22,* 399–409.

Meyers, A. W., Cooke, C. J., Cullen, J., & Liles, L. (1979). Psychological aspects of athletic competitors: A replication across sports. *Cognitive Therapy and Research, 3,* 361–366.

Meyers, M. C., LeUnes, A., & Bourgeois, A. E. (1996). Psychological skills assessments and athletic performance in collegiate rodeo athletes. *Journal of Sport Behavior, 19,* 132–146.

Miller, P. S., & Kerr, G. A. (2002). Conceptualizing excellence: Past, present, and future. *Journal of Applied Sport Psychology, 14,* 140–153.

Orlick, T. (1980). *In pursuit of excellence.* Champaign, IL: Human Kinetics.

Orlick, T., & Partington, J. (1988). Mental links to excellence. *The Sport Psychologist, 2,* 105–130.

Pates, J., Cummings, A., & Maynard, I. (2002). The effects of hypnosis on flow states and three-point shooting performance in basketball layers. *The Sport Psychologist, 16,* 34–47.

Privette, G. (1982). Peak performance in sports: A factorial topology. *International Journal of Sport Psychology, 13,* 242–249.

Privette, G. (1983). Peak experience, peak performance, and flow: A comparative analysis of positive human experiences. *Journal of Personality and Social Psychology, 45,* 1361–1368.

Privette, G., & Bundrick, C. M. (1997). Psychological processes of peak, average, and failing performance in sport. *International Journal of Sport Psychology, 28,* 323–334.

Ravizza, K. (1977). Peak experiences in sport. *Journal of Humanistic Psychology, 17,* 35–40.

Robazza, C., & Bortoli, L. (2003). Intensity, idiosyncratic content and functional impact of performance-related emotions in athletes. *Journal of Sport Sciences, 21,* 171–189.

Robazza, C., Bortoli, L., & Hanin, Y. (2004). Precompetition emotions, bodily symptoms, and task-specific qualities as predictors of performance in high level karate athletes. *Journal of Applied Sport Psychology, 15,* 151–165.

Ruiz, M. C., & Hann, Y. L. (2004). Metaphoric description and individualized emotion profiling of performance states in top karate athletes. *Journal of Applied Sport Psychology, 16,* 258–273.

Russell, W. D. (2000). An examination of flow state occurrence in college athletes. *Journal of Sport Behavior, 24,* 83–107.

Smith, R. E., & Christensen, D. S. (1995). Psychological skills as predictors of performance and survival in professional baseball. *Journal of Sport and Exercise Psychology, 17,* 399–415.

Stein, G. L., Kimiecik, J. C., Daniels, J. L., & Jackson, S. A. (1995). Psychological antecedents of flow in recreational sport. *Personality and Social Psychology Bulletin, 21,* 125–135.

Thomas, O., Hanton, S., & Maynard, I. (2007). Anxiety responses and psychological skill use during the time leading up to competition: Theory to practice I. *Journal of Applied Sport Psychology, 19,* 379–397.

Thomas, P. R., Murphy, S. M., & Hardy, L. (1999). Test of performance strategies: Development and preliminary validation of a comprehensive measure of athletes' psychological skills. *Journal of Sports Sciences, 17,* 697–711.

Thomas, P. R., & Over, R. (1994). Psychological and psychomotor skills associated with performance in golf. *The Sport Psychologist, 8,* 73–86.

Thomas, P. R., Schlinker, P. J., & Over, R. (1996). Psychological and psychomotor skills associated with prowess at ten-pin bowling. *Journal of Sports Sciences, 14,* 255–268.

Woodman, T., & Hardy, L. (2001). A case study of organizational stress in elite sport. *Journal of Applied Sport Psychology, 13,* 207–238.

Woods, T. (2001). *How I play golf.* New York: Warner Books.

10

Increasing Awareness for Sport Performance

Kenneth Ravizza, *California State University at Fullerton*

The end of the soccer game results in a critical penalty kick. Both teams have played hard and well and now it gets down to one player shooting the shot that determines the outcome. All too often, the coach's instruction is "Just relax" or "Concentrate," and frequently this results in even more perceived pressure by the athlete, because now the coach knows she is not relaxed or focused.

The underlying basis of psychological interventions for performance enhancement involves teaching athletes the importance of the recognition, or awareness, of the need to do something to gain control. Athletes will not be aware of the need to gain control unless they first identify their own ideal performance state (see Chapter 9) and can contrast that state with the present one. Thus, **awareness** is the first step to gaining control of any pressure situation. The athlete must "check in" and determine if his or her arousal level, emotional state, thought processes, and focus are where they need to be and, if not, adjust them to give the best opportunity for success. For example, the athlete must be aware of arousal level that is too low or too high and adjust it as needed to reach the optimal arousal level for performance. Then the athlete must attend to the appropriate focal points that will fine-tune or lock in his or her concentration. For example, a softball player

will only get two or three great pitches to hit in a game. The player must be fully focused on each pitch so that when the appropriate pitch comes she is ready to make solid contact. The lack of awareness demonstrated by many athletes is often a by-product of the sport socialization process, whereby the athlete is encouraged to follow orders and not to question the coach's authority. More and more, coaches are beginning to take a less dogmatic approach because they realize that dependence often results from a strictly authoritarian coaching style.

Furthermore, lack of awareness in athletes is almost always the result of excessive concern with achieving the end result. For example, the baseball player in the pressure situation focuses on the end result of getting a hit. Awareness and control are part of the process of skill execution—specifically, execution in the present moment. The anxiety lies in the end result. Thus, the field-goal kicker in football must focus on the key components of kicking such as wind, ground conditions, the opponents' alignment, getting proper distance, and his target. At this point the athlete is totally focused on the task at hand and is ready to react spontaneously to the situation with controlled intensity. This type of appropriate **focus of attention** is essential to maximize performance.

The athlete's challenge is to focus on basic skills even when the athlete's pulse rate may increase significantly. The situation can be perceived as speeded-up or out-of-the-usual perspective because of the perceived threat of the situation. This chapter does not suggest a multitude of performance changes; instead, it suggests that athletes be encouraged to become aware of their own ideal performance state and *routine behaviors* they are already using to achieve this state. The athlete performs many of the techniques we talk about in sport psychology instinctively. Awareness of these instinctive routines provides athletes with something to focus on to regain control. Sport psychology consultants have contributed to enhancing performance by providing a structure or consistent framework for the various mental skills athletes have often developed and practiced haphazardly.

This structure clarifies for athletes the fact that there is a relationship between the various things they do to maximize performance. When they can begin to understand that the imagery skills that are used for pregame preparation can also be used for concentration and relaxation training (as well as for academic studies), they have a better sense of control. **Control** is the key issue because an athlete's anxiety level tends to decrease with a feeling of control.

The purpose of this chapter is to discuss the importance of awareness in reaching peak performance in sport. Awareness, the first essential step in goal setting and self-regulation, will be discussed in relation to skill development and the management of performance stress and other psychological factors. Then, the final section will discuss specific methods athletes can use to develop heightened awareness.

The Importance of Awareness in Athletics

Peak performance is about compensating and adjusting. An athlete is not in the flow state most of the performance. I have found athletes to be in the "zone" 10–20% of the time. So, why are athletes so concerned with feeling just right and

surprised when they aren't? Lou Pinella, a veteran professional baseball manager, claimed, "A player must learn to feel comfortable being uncomfortable." "So what, deal with it!" is what I tell athletes. But this is only after they have practiced dealing with adversity in practice and recognizing that they have "something to go to" (mental skills) to get them refocused. In order to compensate and adjust, athletes must first be aware that they are not where they need to be. As athletes work on this ability to deal with adversity in practice, it only increases their confidence to know they don't have to feel great to perform well. For example, in one of the most high-performance fields, astronauts in training do not just have positive thoughts and use positive imagery. They practice dealing with adversity in the simulator so that, when adversity occurs, they are prepared to deal with it with confidence and focus.

Every sport requires athletes to execute basic skills. Athletes must stand alone and accept responsibility for their performance. During the off-season, individual responsibility is an even more crucial aspect since it is then that athletes must put in hours of isolated, rigorous training and self-coaching to develop and refine essential skills. Athletes must perform the skills, reflect on the feedback gained from the performance, make corrections and refinements, and then make the skills feel natural through a multitude of repetitions and refinements.

Athletes must recognize their strengths and weaknesses so they can maximize their strengths and correct their weaknesses. Goal setting can be used to facilitate performance enhancement. At first, athletes want to be told what their goals should be, but it is essential that they make the major contribution to establishing individual goals. This requires athletes to reflect on and evaluate past performance. The coach gains a great deal of insight about the athletes' awareness from this evaluation of perceived strengths and weaknesses. The goals should be **performance goals,** such as "I will be more consistent at the foul line by shooting 50 shots a day with the goal of hitting over 60% by the end of two weeks and 65% after one month." This is different from an **outcome goal,** such as "I want to improve my foul shooting." The goals should be as specific as possible and of various durations: short-term, intermediate, and long-range. (See Chapter 13 for additional guidelines for goal setting and strategies for achieving goals.)

A good way for a player to develop more awareness in this area is to have players write a scouting report on themselves. What is the opponent saying about them? Also, have them write about what they would like the opponent to say about them. Julie Wilhout, Loyola Marymount's women's basketball coach, uses this technique to help the players increase their awareness of where they need to direct their attention. Another practical way to remind players to have a mission for practice is to have them establish a routine. For example, when you put on your shoes, set two goals for today's practice or game, and when you take your shoes off, evaluate how you did. The athlete took 2 hours out of her life; what did she learn to get better? The reality is that each day we take a step toward our goal, or remain the same, or take a step back. Always remember, failure can be a step forward if you learn from it. Failure is positive feedback if you are aware of it and use the information to get better.

Goal setting requires awareness because the athlete first sets the goals, then strives to reach them, then proceeds to evaluate the performance feedback, and, finally, adjusts the goals appropriately (Harris & Harris, 1984; McClements & Botterill, 1979).

Awareness as It Relates to Skill Development

Athletes must learn the difference between merely performing skills and experiencing skills. For example, try this exercise. Raise your right arm over your head five times—one . . . two . . . three . . . four . . . five—and halt. Now deeply inhale as you slowly raise your right arm over your head. Breathe slowly and steadily as you feel the movement, experience the muscles involved, feel the gentle stretch through the different muscles, feel that extension all through the arm, and now slowly let the arm down.

The difference between just going through the motions and really experiencing the skills hinges on the awareness involved. Feldenkrais (1972), a movement specialist, offers the following analogy:

> A man without awareness is like a carriage whose passengers are the desires, with the muscles for horses, while the carriage itself is the skeleton. Awareness is the sleeping coachman. As long as the coachman remains asleep the carriage will be dragged aimlessly here and there. Each passenger seeks a different destination and the horses pull different ways. But when the coachman is wide awake and holds the reins the horses will pull and bring every passenger to his proper destination. (p. 54)

Like the coachman, athletes must gain control of muscles, emotions, and thoughts and integrate them into a smooth performance. When athletes are aware and focused on the sport experience, they exert more control over the situation. They recognize sooner when their balance is off, when too much tension is present in certain muscle groups, or when thoughts have become self-defeating. Aware athletes are more attuned to subtle fluctuations in the flow of the contest and can adjust that much sooner. Aware athletes can conserve vital energy by exerting no more than the needed intensity.

Learning the Basics

Awareness requires that athletes totally focus their attention on the task. This ability must be developed in practice. Coaches want their athletes to be intense and totally involved in practice because this aids in creating quality practice time. Many coaches also realize the importance of mental training for performance, but the challenge is to find time for it. For this reason, it is important to incorporate awareness training with the physical skills that are already being performed in practice. For example, coaches and sport psychology consultants should encourage athletes to develop concentration as they stretch before practice by feeling the stretch and breathing into it. This type of stretching develops concentration in that the athletes are tuned in to their body as they stretch.

With the 1984 U.S. Olympic women's field hockey team, we established a set warm-up procedure for practice to aid the athletes in mentally and physically preparing for practice. The players began by stretching, then hit the ball back and forth to work out any kinks, and finally executed **focused hitting.** Focused hitting involves hitting the ball to exact locations—for example, to the receiver's right, middle, and left. This sequence is followed for 5 minutes. These are basic field hockey skills, but there is a difference when they are done with awareness. If the player's attention is on other aspects of the day, such as a party coming up or an argument with a friend, consistency in the focused hitting drill will be impossible.

This type of drill has two major advantages for the coach. First, visible objective performance demonstrates whether or not the athlete is concentrating. More important, awareness training is incorporated into the practice of basic skills. As a result, additional practice time is not required for mental training. This sophisticated approach to basic skills allows coaches to make the most of practice time by integrating mental or awareness skills training with basic fundamentals.

During one practice, the Cal State Fullerton baseball team engaged in a focused bat and catch drill for 90 minutes because they had not been hitting exact locations consistently. This emphasis on basics was crucial because the players realized the coach was serious about executing the basics. The difference between performing the basics and focusing on the basics lies in the players' awareness. Athletes must learn to concentrate when the pressure is on, and the focal points for concentration become the task-relevant cues. Augie Garrido, Cal State Fullerton's baseball coach, gives the following example:

> We are really working on having the players clear their minds. Yesterday one player was given a bunt signal and he proceeded to pop out. His next time at the plate he was in a bunting situation and tried to bunt but missed. So I called him over and said, "You've tried two times and failed, and you are about to fail again because you still have the other two times on your mind. Give yourself the best chance to be successful by

seeing the ball and bunting the ball. You can do that. Stay right with the ingredients of bunting. You've done it a hundred times, but you have to get the other times off your mind." The player proceeded to lay down a perfect bunt. (1982)

When athletes practice physical skills and mental skills together, their confidence increases because they are ready and experienced in the subtle skill of concentration.

The days of doing sport psychology on Wednesdays from 12 to 1 must be replaced by doing it during practice as an intricate component of quality practice. This necessitates that the coach integrates it into his or her skill development. I believe that mental skills can be developed like physical skills, but they must be practiced, and awareness is the way of obtaining that quality of performance.

The All-or-None Syndrome

Awareness develops in the process of participating in sport, and this is where athletes experience self-control. Gymnasts learning new moves cannot expect to master them immediately; they must work through a series of progressions. Often, in the midst of this process, gymnasts feel they have *either* hit the move *or* missed. If they hit it, they are delighted, but if they miss, frustration begins to set in. The challenge is to maintain motivation throughout the hours of practice.

At Cal State Fullerton, we have established gradations of execution for the gymnasts to evaluate their skill development. For example, even if a move is "missed," certain aspects of the movement were probably successful, and it is important that they be identified. Similarly, in baseball a pitcher is told that he needs to raise his arm on a fastball release. The number 5 is given for the ideal release distance, and a 1 is given for a side-arm release. After each pitch the player is asked to assign a numerical value from 1 to 5 to the arm location. It is essential that the athlete reflect on the position of his arm because this requires awareness. The coach can then give an evaluation from 1 to 5. This aids the athlete in beginning to adjust his awareness to what the proper position feels like (based on a principle from Gallwey,

1974). If a video recorder is available, the performance feedback is even more specific.

When athletes gain more awareness, they can make more accurate adjustments in their performance. This ability to refine the subtle intricacies of performance is a critical skill as athletes reach for maximum performance. In addition to improving self-control, the athletes experience a feeling of growing success. Even though the outcome is not perfect, players develop a more positive attitude about the skill and will keep their motivation level where it needs to be.

Playing the Edge of Peak Performance

To reach their full sport potential, athletes must learn to play the **performance edge.** For example, they must learn to control that delicate balance between power and grace. Every sport has components that must be balanced appropriately to maximize performance. This type of control necessitates that athletes be aware. They must monitor their performance to recognize when it is at its peak. In athletic training and conditioning, athletes frequently push too hard or do not push hard enough. At such times the athletes need to relate to their movement experience with the precision of a surgeon so that they can make needed adjustments. For example, runners constantly monitor their body for subtle messages so that they can make adjustments to reach that edge of peak performance.

One awareness technique I use with runners is the blindfold run. A blindfolded runner and a partner run a specified distance together, with the partner providing physical support and removing any dangers. The blindfold alters the runner's perspective, as the runner is now totally focused on the present moment. The new perspective suspends the athlete's usual thoughts and distractions, and about 5 minutes into the run, the athlete experiences running in a more aware fashion.

Coaches and sport psychology consultants are encouraged to discuss with their athletes this idea of playing the edge so that each athlete can begin to understand and identify where that edge is for him or her. Figure 10-1 and the chapter appendix suggest ways of keeping records of the mental aspects of performance.

Awareness in Managing Performance Stress

To move consistently toward peak performance, each athlete must know and be aware of his or her own experience of optimal performance. Athletes must learn to control the excitement of the sport situation so their energy can be channeled into the performance, or to reorganize when the arousal level is too low and activate it as needed. To gain this control, athletes must learn how competitive stress affects individual performance. (See Chapter 12 for more information on this topic.) The first step is to be aware of one's **arousal level** and then to adjust it as needed. The athlete must recognize which situations or stressors tend to negatively affect his or her performance. Knowledge of stressful areas allows for the development of a strategy to prepare and cope effectively with them. For example, playing in front of a crowd or in the presence of scouts is stressful; thus, the athlete can mentally prepare to deal with the situation to avoid surprise. The athlete has time to get support from teammates and the coaching staff and also to develop his or her own strategy.

Once the athlete understands the stressors, the next step is to be aware of the way that stress is experienced since the manifestations of stress vary greatly among individuals. For example, "As the pressure mounts, my shoulders and neck tighten, my thoughts jump around, and I tend to get jittery." Changes in breathing are another bodily cue that often signals too much stress. Athletes should be trained to become sensitive to how their breathing responds to stress. For example, do they start to breathe more rapidly and shallowly? Do they hold their breath? Do they have difficulty breathing? These manifestations of stress may be perceived as problems, but they can be used as signals to provide feedback to the athlete as to whether the arousal level is appropriate. The athlete gains this personal knowledge by reflecting on previous performances and essentially using sport experiences like a biofeedback machine.

PERFORMANCE FEEDBACK SHEET

Name _____

Opponent _____

1. What were your stressors for today's game?

2. How did you experience the stress (thoughts, actions, body)?

3. How was your level of arousal for today's game? What were your feelings at these various points?

   a. Bus ride to game: _____
   b. Warm-up on field, court, etc.: _____
   c. Just before the game: _____
   d. During the game: _____

   0 ———— 5 ———— 10
   Too Low   Perfect   Too High

4. What techniques did you use to manage the stress and how effective were you in controlling it?

5. How was your self-talk? (Describe.)

6. What did you learn from today's game that will help you in your next game?

7. What mental training techniques were most effective for you?

8. Briefly describe one play or segment of the game that you enjoyed.

9. How would you rate your play? _____

10. Briefly describe how you felt about today's game.

    0 ———— 5 ———— 10
    Terrible   OK   Great

11. Anything you want to say?

Figure 10-1 Sample performance feedback sheet

To help athletes understand the concept of self-monitoring as a way to increase awareness, the coach or sport psychologist can use the analogy of a traffic signal light (Ravizza & Hanson, 1994). Sport performance is similar to driving a car. Most of the time that we are driving, we are not thinking about the mechanics or technical aspects of driving. When we come to a signal light, we must be aware of the light, or check in; if it is green, we continue. Similarly, when athletes are playing well, there is no need to think about it, but they must check in for that split second. When we are driving and the light is yellow, we have to observe the intersection in more detail to determine whether it is safe to continue as well as check our rearview mirror for a police officer. When the light is red, we must stop.

Using this analogy, the athlete must be aware of his or her signal lights and recognize the impact they have on his or her arousal level, self-talk, breathing patterns, and ability to focus. Thus, if the athlete can be aware of when he or she is shifting from a green light to a yellow light, and it is recognized early, it can be turned around more easily. When the signal light is not recognized until it is red, it is much more difficult to get it turned around. So the first use of the signal lights is to serve as an indicator of the way the athlete experiences the situation.

The second use of the signal lights is to help the athlete in preparing for consistent performance by monitoring the potential stressors that he or she may confront. For example, the field conditions may be a yellow light, the officials may be a red light, the opponent may be a red light. By acknowledging these signals, the athlete can develop contingency plans to cope effectively with them. This is part of solid mental preparation, as the athlete will be confident in handling them.

The most useful part of the signal light analogy is that it provides a vocabulary to address the awareness aspects of performance. Many times the lights are green for athletes; they have minimal awareness, and they are just playing the game when they are not in that ideal state. The traffic light analogy is useful as a symbol for how the athlete is experiencing the situation as well as the potential stressors that must be confronted in the competition.

This signal light analogy also provides a method for discussing his or her awareness level. With young athletes, this is an effective tool to have them learn to "check in" and make the needed adjustments. For example, a young tennis player is working on his serve; when the results don't happen, he works harder and faster and often his performance gets worse and his frustration rises. At this point, one has to remember the goal is to work on "quality" serves, not the quantity, or what I call "aerobic serving."

The athlete's consistent focus on his or her thoughts and feelings and use of appropriate interventions allows the athlete to maintain an optimal performance state. Interventions may include relaxation and activation techniques, concentration methods, thought control, and basic breathing techniques. (See Chapters 13–16 for specific techniques.) There are also times when the athlete must recognize that it is time just to flow with the experience and let it happen (Ravizza, 1984; Ravizza & Osborne, 1991). Once again, the sport journal described in the chapter appendix helps the athlete develop this awareness because it provides a mechanism for recording, evaluating sport performance, and processing the information learned from the act of participation.

Techniques for Developing Awareness

Many techniques are available to increase awareness. One valuable technique is keeping a sport journal. The sport journal provides a structured method to reflect on sport performances and to capitalize on the wealth of experiential knowledge gained from the performance. The journal guidelines in the appendix ask questions about stressors, manifestations of stress, and feelings associated with performance, concentration, and skill execution. After teams play a game, they can discuss what the members have learned so that, with the coach, they can establish new goals or modify earlier ones.

Following selected performances, coaches can give players feedback sheets similar to the one shown in Figure 10-1 so they can process the subjective information gained from each contest. This procedure helps the players systematically learn from the experience and bring closure to their performance so they can begin to focus on the next performance. This is particularly helpful in tournament play when the athletes have to perform many times during a short period, because it is critical to bring **closure,** or let go of one performance before beginning another.

With the athletes' permission, coaches and sport psychologists can read these journals and feedback sheets, using the information as a foundation for better understanding the athlete and what behavior or intervention might best facilitate performance and personal growth. Athletes often perceive writing feelings in a journal or on a feedback sheet as less threatening than verbal discussions. Such writing often forges an understanding that promotes discussion. (In some cases coaches have also worked with English teachers to capitalize on the athletes' interest in writing about the experiential aspects of sport performance to develop English writing skills.)

Some coaches and sport psychologists have helped athletes glean information regarding ideal psychological states for peak performance by having them fill out psychological questionnaires just before beginning performance. Ideally, this should be done prior to a number of competitions, enabling a comparison between performance and scores on the questionnaires. The intention is to find what psychological state(s) typically occurred when athletes performed at their best. The Competitive State Anxiety Inventory-2 (CSAI-2) (Martens, Vealey, & Burton, 1990) is one example of an appropriate questionnaire for this purpose. The CSAI-2 assesses the athlete's current cognitive anxiety, somatic anxiety, and self-confidence. We know from the research discussed in Chapter 11 that each of these psychological states may be relevant to performance. See some of the questionnaires discussed in other chapters for additional examples of potentially appropriate instruments. It should be noted that not all sport psychology

consultants find these questionnaires useful. It is critical that the consultant discuss the results with the athletes to determine whether the information obtained is accurate for that athlete.

Monitoring relevant physiological systems is another tool for gaining awareness regarding ideal performance states. Purportedly, Eastern European sport psychologists frequently use this procedure when working with elite athletes. Heart rate, blood pressure, brain waves, muscle tension, galvanic skin response, and catecholamine levels are all examples of types of physiological monitoring that might be appropriate for identifying an athlete's psychological state and its relationship to performance. Research and interventions in this area are still in their infancy in North America. Work by Landers and his students provides one example of what the future might hold when sophisticated technology is more common (Landers et al., 1991; Salazar et al., 1990). Even without sophisticated technology, heart rate can be monitored right before a number of critical competitions and then compared with subsequent performance to determine an optimal pulse rate. According to Dr. Alexeev of the Moscow Research Institute of Physical Culture, this is one of the best ways to discover an athlete's optimal level of anxiety (Raiport, 1988).

Athletes who are good imagers can use imagery to gain awareness of their ideal performance state. This technique is particularly effective if the athletes are in the off-season or in a situation where actual competition is not possible. Imagery is used to relive previous excellent performance, with particular attention given to identifying what feelings, arousal level, thoughts, muscle tension, attentional focus, and so forth might have occurred. There also may be merit in imaging previous bad performances in order to contrast their psychological state with what appears to be a more optimal state.

Imagery can be an effective tool as well for creating awareness when filling out performance feedback sheets after an actual performance. Athletes who are unsure of exactly what happened can replay their performance to determine what they were thinking, feeling, and attending to at any given moment.

Group discussion is another method that coaches and sport psychology consultants can use to increase athlete awareness. Coaches should provide their athletes with an opportunity to discuss a performance by encouraging but not requiring them to do so. Sport psychology consultants should do the same thing after practicing certain mental training techniques. Sometimes coaches and sport psychology consultants can foster this form of communication through one-on-one discussions. Coaches and sport psychology practitioners should share their perspective or expertise but also encourage the athletes to talk about the experience. They should ask questions about arousal and confidence levels, stressors, and manifestations. Every team is capable of this type of interaction, but such dialogue is frequently difficult to facilitate at first. As the athletes become much more aware of the needs of their teammates, team cohesion will be more likely to result. In turn, athletes gain new insights into their own sport performances. For example, if teammates understand that one athlete responds to stress by withdrawing to mentally prepare for performance, they will not think there is something wrong with the athlete who is quiet.

A good time to begin group discussions is after a positive experience because the feelings are non-threatening. For example, after a great practice, the coach can ask the athletes to discuss what made the practice so good. How was it different from a nonproductive practice session?

In regard to specific methods of increasing awareness, it is important that practitioners do what they are comfortable with. However, it is strongly suggested that coaches and sport psychology consultants slowly integrate the various methods discussed in this chapter.

Summary

Developing awareness is a critical element of peak performance because it provides athletes with the experiential knowledge to gain control of the performance. Awareness is the first step in raising self-control in sport participation. Initially, athletes need to become aware of their ideal performance state. Next, athletes need to recognize when they are no longer at that ideal state. As athletes develop awareness skills, they will recognize earlier when they are not focused or aroused appropriately. This early recognition aids athletes in gaining control before it is lost. The sooner a deviation is recognized, the easier it is to get back on course. Athletes with a range of interventions can use them to get their mental-emotional and physical states to more nearly approximate what they have found leads to peak performance. Journal keeping, performance feedback sheets, assessing precompetitive performance states through psychological questionnaires and physiological monitoring, using imagery to relive past performances, and group discussions are all effective techniques for developing awareness. Depending on the athlete's preferences and the circumstances, certain techniques may be more effective than others at any given moment.

Study Questions

1. Why is it important that athletes be aware of their ideal performance state?
2. What is the difference between merely performing skills and experiencing skills?
3. Why is it important to incorporate awareness training with the physical skills that are already being performed in practice?

4. Give an example of focused practice.

5. Describe how the all-or-none syndrome can be overcome.

6. What is meant by playing on the edge? What techniques can help an athlete become aware of this skill?

7. How can a sport journal and performance feedback sheets be used to increase awareness? Describe what might be included in a journal and feedback sheets.

8. How can psychological questionnaires and physiological monitoring be used to increase awareness of ideal performance states?

9. When might imagery and group discussion be used to increase awareness?

References

Feldenkrais, M. (1972). *Awareness through movement.* New York: Harper & Row.

Gallwey, T. (1974). *The inner game of tennis.* New York: Random House.

Garrido, A. (1982, December 7). Interview with author. Fullerton, CA.

Harris, D., & Harris, B. (1984). *The athlete's guide to sport psychology: Mental skills for physical people.* New York: Leisure Press.

Landers, D., Petruzello, S., Salazar, W., Cruz, D., Kubitz, K., Gannon, T., & Han, M. (1991). The influence of electrocortical biofeedback on performance in pre-elite archers. *Medicine and Science in Sports and Exercise, 23,* 123–129.

Martens, R., Vealey, R. S., & Burton, D. (1990). *Competitive anxiety in sport.* Champaign, IL: Human Kinetics.

McClements, J., & Botterill, C. (1979). Goal setting in shaping of future performance of athletes. In P. Klavora & J. Daniel (Eds.), *Coach, athlete and the sport psychologist.* Champaign, IL: Human Kinetics.

Raiport, G. (1988). *Red gold: Peak performance techniques of the Russian and East German Olympic victors.* Los Angeles: Tarcher.

Ravizza, K. (1984). Qualities of the peak experience in sport. In J. Silva & R. Weinberg (Eds.), *Psychological foundations for sport.* Champaign, IL: Human Kinetics.

Ravizza, K., & Hanson, T. (1994). *Heads-up baseball: Playing the game one pitch at a time.* Indianapolis: Masters Press.

Ravizza, K., & Osborne, T. (1991). Nebraska's 3R's: One play-at-a-time preperformance routine for collegiate football. *The Sport Psychologist, 5,* 256–265.

Salazar, W., Landers, D., Petruzello, S., Han, M., Cruz, D., & Kubitz, K. (1990). Hemispheric asymmetry, cardiac response, and performance in elite archers. *Research Quarterly in Exercise and Sport, 61,* 351–359.

Guidelines for Keeping a Sport Journal

The sport journal is a tool to help you further develop your mental skills for sport performance. The first step in gaining self-control is to develop an awareness of your sport performance so that you can recognize when you are pulled out of the most appropriate mental state for you. The journal provides you with an opportunity to record the different intervention strategies that you experiment with to regain control. The long-range goal is to develop various techniques that you can implement in stressful situations to perform to your utmost ability.

If you choose, the journal also can be a place to record your feelings and the personal knowledge that you are gaining about yourself, the game, your teammates, and any other factors. This is one of the few times in your life that you will ever direct so much energy toward one specific goal. There is a lot to learn from your pursuit of excellence. This journal will give you something to reflect on after your high-level participation is completed.

The journal also can serve as a place where you can express your feelings in writing and drawings. It is beneficial to get these feelings out in some way so that they don't build up and contribute to unproductive tension. The use of colored pens is often helpful to express yourself. You do not have to make an entry every day, but date the entries you do make. The journal is an informal record of your thoughts and experiences as you train for high-level performance.

If you choose to have someone read your journal, please feel free to delete any parts that you think are too personal to share. The intention of someone who is reviewing your writing should be to guide you and make *suggestions* that may facilitate your self-exploration in reaching your goals.

I would suggest that you try this technique, but it is not for everyone. If you decide not to use it, that is your choice. If you try the technique, assess the following areas with the accompanying questions/descriptors:

1. *Peak Performance.* What does it feel like when you play or practice at your best? Describe some of your most enjoyable experiences playing your sport. What have you learned from these moments when you are fully functioning?

2. *Stressors.* Outside the sport: write down your thoughts about various events outside your sport that are distracting to you—for example, parents, boy/girlfriends, peers, job hassles, financial issues, community (hometown expectations). On the field: do the same for distractions on the field, such as importance of contest, location, and spectators.

3. *Coaching Staff.* What do you need from your coaches? What can you give them in order to reach your goals? What can you do to make your relationship with your coaches more productive?

4. *Teammates.* What do you want from your teammates? What can you give them? How do you relate and work with your teammates? Write about your relationship with other teammates. Any unfinished business?

5. *Confidence.* At this time how confident are you in regard to achieving your goals? What can you do differently to feel more confident? What can you ask of yourself, coach, or teammates?

6. *Manifestations of Your Stress.* How do you experience high levels of anxiety in performance? Assess your thoughts and physiological and behavioral reactions. What did you do to intervene and keep in balance?

7. *Awareness and Concentration.* What changes do you observe in your performance when you are aware? What concentration methods are you experimenting with? What are your focal points for various skills?

8. *Relaxation Training.* How are your relaxation skills developing? Are there any parts of your body that are more difficult than others to relax? What method is best for you? How are you able to relate this to your play? How quickly can you relax?

9. *Thought Control.* How is your self-talk affecting your performance? Write out some of your negative self-talk and make it positive.

10. *Centering/Concentration Skills.* What are you doing to concentrate appropriately before

the contest and during the contest? What has been successful? Unsuccessful? Describe your preperformance routine.

11. *Imagery.* How are your imagery skills developing? Do you see a TV screen–type image or is it more of a feeling image? At what point do you notice lapses in concentration? How clear are your images? Can you control the speed and tempo of the image?

12. *Controlling Your Arousal Level.* What are you doing to control your arousal level? What are you doing to increase arousal and intensity? What are you experimenting with to reduce arousal levels? What is working for you and what is not working?

13. *Pressure Situations.* How are you handling pressure situations? What are you doing differently? What are you doing to learn to cope more effectively?

14. *Quality Practice Time.* What do you do to mentally prepare for practice? How do you keep your personal difficulties from affecting your play? What are you doing to take charge? What works for you and what hasn't worked?

15. *Anything You Want to Address.*

Goal Setting for Peak Performance

Daniel Gould, *Michigan State University*

Without goals you are like a ship without a rudder—heading in no particular direction.
—*Roy Williams, head basketball coach at the University of North Carolina*

A number of psychological strategies have been identified as ways of assisting athletes in achieving personal growth and peak performance. Goal setting is one such technique. In fact, goal setting has not only been shown to influence the performance of athletes of varied age and ability levels but also been linked to positive changes in important psychological states such as anxiety, confidence, and motivation. It is clearly a technique that coaches and sport psychologists should employ regularly.

Unfortunately, goal setting is a technique that coaches and sport psychologists do not always employ effectively. They may falsely assume, for example, that because athletes set goals on their own these goals will automatically facilitate performance. This is seldom the case, however, as many athletes set inappropriate goals or do not set goals in a systematic fashion. Similarly, coaches and sport psychologists often forget to initiate the follow-up and evaluation procedures that are necessary if goal setting is to be effective. To use goal setting effectively, coaches and sport psychologists must understand the goal-setting process and the many factors that can affect it.

This chapter has a fourfold purpose: (1) to examine psychological and sport psychological research and theory on goal setting, (2) to discuss fundamental goal-setting guidelines, (3) to present a system for effectively initiating goal-setting procedures, and (4) to identify and offer solutions for common problems that arise when setting goals. The principles and recommendations derived in this chapter are based both on research and on what sport psychologists have learned while utilizing goal-setting interventions with athletes in a variety of settings.

Goal-Setting Research and Theory

Before examining the research on goal setting and theoretical explanations for the relationships between goal setting and performance, we must first define goals and distinguish between various types of goals.

Defining Goals

Locke and Latham (2002) have generated the most widely accepted definition for the term *goal*. For these investigators, a **goal** is an "objective or aim of action" defined as attaining "a specific standard of proficiency on a task, usually within a specified time limit" (p. 705). From a practical perspective, then, goals focus on achieving some standard, whether it is increasing one's batting average by 10 percentage points, lowering one's time in the 800 meters, or losing 5 pounds. This definition also implies that such performance standards will be achieved within some specified unit of time, such as by the end of the season, within two weeks, or by the end of practice.

Even though Locke and Latham's definition provides a good general description of a goal, sport psychologists have at times found it useful to make specific distinctions between types of goals. McClements (1982), for instance, has differentiated between **subjective goals** (e.g., having fun, getting fit, or trying one's best), **general objective goals** (e.g., winning a championship or making a team), and **specific objective goals** (e.g., increasing the number of assists in basketball or decreasing a pitcher's earned run average in softball).

Similarly, Martens (1987) and Burton (1983, 1984, 1989) have made distinctions between **outcome goals,** which represent standards of performance that focus on the results of a contest between opponents or teams (e.g., beating someone), and **performance goals,** which focus on improvements relative to one's own past performance, (e.g., improving one's time in the mile). Finally, Hardy, Jones, and Gould (1996) extended the outcome-performance goal distinction to include **process goals,** which specify the procedures in which the performer will engage during performance (e.g., a skier focusing on keeping his hands in front of him during a downhill run, a tennis player on keeping her feet moving when fatigued). These distinctions are important because evidence suggests that certain types of goals are more useful in changing behavior than other types of goals.

Goal-Effectiveness Research

Extensive psychological research has been conducted on the topic of goal setting (see Locke, Shaw, Saari, & Latham, 1981; Locke & Latham, 1990, 2002; Tubbs, 1991, for extensive reviews). Typically, this research has involved a comparison of the performance of individuals who set goals or certain types of goals (e.g., specific-explicit goals) with the performance of individuals who are simply told to do their best or are given no goals. Studies sometimes manipulate other factors, such as individual characteristics (e.g., race, educational level, personality) or situational variables (e.g., the presence or absence of feedback).

Psychological research on goal setting is impressive in that it has been conducted in a variety of laboratory and field settings and has used a wide variety of tasks, ranging from truck loading to brainstorming sessions; it has employed diverse samples, including elementary school children, uneducated laborers, managers, and scientists. In addition, a clear pattern of results has emerged with ready implications for sport psychologists and coaches alike.

The most important result generated from this line of research is that goal setting clearly and consistently facilitates performance. In their excellent and comprehensive review of well over a hundred studies on goal setting, for example, Locke and colleagues (1981) concluded that "the beneficial effect of goal setting on task performance is one of the most robust and replicable findings in the psychological literature. Ninety percent of the studies showed positive or partially positive effects. Furthermore, these effects are found just as reliable in the field setting as in the laboratory" (p. 145). Thus, a review of the psychological research clearly shows that goal setting is a powerful technique for enhancing performance.

Given the abundance of research on goal setting and the consistent pattern of results found in the psychological literature in general, it is surprising that until the 1980s the topic was rarely discussed in the sport psychology literature. Nevertheless, the results of these initial investigations showed much promise. Botterill (1977), for instance, had youth ice hockey players perform an exercise endurance task under various combinations of goal difficulty, goal explicitness specificity, and goal type (group, individual, or experimenter-set) conditions. Consistent with the psychological literature, the results revealed that goal setting facilitated performance. Similarly, difficult goals were more effective in enhancing performance than easy goals, and explicit goals were more effective than general "do your best" goals. Finally, research concluded that explicit, difficult, and group-set goals were most effective in enhancing endurance task performance.

In an important field investigation, Burton (1983, 1989) examined the effects of a goal-setting training program on the performance and cognitions (e.g., levels of self-confidence, motivation, and state anxiety) of male and female intercollegiate swimmers. In a 5-month goal-setting program, performance as opposed to outcome goals were employed, and an attempt was made to explain why goal setting influences performance by relating goals to other psychological constructs such as confidence and state anxiety. The results revealed that swimmers who participated in the goal-setting training program learned to focus highest priority on performance goals and that those swimmers' high in goal-setting ability demonstrated better performance and more positive cognitions. Furthermore, a related study conducted with National Sports Festival swimmers supported these findings, demonstrating that goals were positively related to performance and positive psychological attributes (Burton, 1984).

Increased attention has been placed on goal-setting research over the last two decades. Much of this interest was spurred by a 1985 *Journal of Sport Psychology* review article written by noted goal-setting researchers Locke and Latham, which suggested that goal-setting research principles found in the general psychological literature were applicable to the sport context. This has led to a series of sport psychology studies testing Locke and Latham's proposition in the sport environment (see Burton, Naylor, & Holliday, 2002, and Burton & Weiss, 2008, for excellent reviews of these studies) and some healthy dialogue on how to study the process by which goal setting functions in sport (see Locke, 1991; Locke, 1994; Weinberg & Weigand, 1993, 1996).

More recent sport psychology goal-setting research investigations have examined such issues as whether specific goals are more effective than general "do your best" goals, the effectiveness of long-term versus short-term goals, and the relationship between goal difficulty and task performance. Results of these studies have shown that goal setting works well in sport, but not as well as in other settings such as business (Burton et al., 2002). Robert Weinberg, one of the leading sport psychology researchers in the area, has indicated that research efforts are characterized by a number of methodological problems such as spontaneous goal setting by control group participants, competition between comparison group participants, and the failure to control levels of participant motivation and commitment (Weinberg, 1994). Burton et al. (2002) also noted task complexity, the failure to use appropriate goal implementation strategies, and that athletes often operate closer to their performance potential. Hence, these problems have limited the implications that can be derived from this research and made it somewhat difficult to determine when and where goal setting works in sport. Goal setting, then, is more complex to apply in sport than it might appear on the surface.

Despite the fact that sport psychology goal-setting research has not been as fruitful as was hoped, it has shown that goal setting can and does influence performance in sport settings. In fact, in a meta-analytic statistical review of 36 independent sport and exercise goal-setting studies conducted by Kyllo and Landers (1995), it was concluded that goal setting was a successful technique for improving performance. Similarly, in the most recent review of goal setting in sport Burton and Weiss (2008) found that 70 of 88 studies (80%) showed moderate to strong effects.

Many of these studies were field rather than laboratory based. For example, Anderson, Crowell, Doman, & Howard (1988) examined goal setting along with publicly posted performance and praise on "checking" in a collegiate ice hockey team. The results of this within-subject design showed that this behavioral intervention increased checking behavior over a baseline and that the goal-setting component was associated with improved performance. Anderson and associates concluded not only that goal setting was associated with improved performance but that performance feedback moderates these effects.

In another study, Swain and Jones (1995) examined goal setting in four university basketball players over a series of games. Using a single-subject baseline design, results revealed goal setting had positive consequences on three out of four identified behaviors. Hence, goal setting was found to be effective in changing desired behaviors.

Finally, in a very well-designed single-subject multiple baseline study using four female speed skaters, Wanlin et al. (1997) had participants take part in a goal-setting package. This package involved developing an overall mission (general subjective goal), a long-term goal, subgoals and practice goals, self-talk, and goal visualization. It was taught to each skater, and performance was compared prior to and after the goal-setting package was used. Results revealed that the goal-setting package was effective in influencing the skaters to work harder and show fewer off-task behaviors. Race times also decreased. Hence, goal setting was effective in facilitating desirable behaviors and performance in the skaters and decreasing undesirable behaviors.

Taken together, these field studies support the earlier findings of Burton (1983, 1989). They also reinforce a main contention of this chapter; that is, goal setting will only be effective when a systematic approach is adopted and a knowledgeable professional customizes the goal-setting process to his or her particular setting and athletes.

In summary, although not unequivocal, the results of the psychological and sport psychology research literature provide strong support for using goal-setting procedures to facilitate athletic performance. Moreover, these findings are further strengthened by the fact that they have been demonstrated in studies using varied tasks and largely different populations in both laboratory and field settings. A survey of leading sport psychology consultants working with U.S. Olympic athletes has also shown that goal setting is the most often used psychological intervention in both individual athlete–coach and group consultations (Gould, Tammen, Murphy, & May, 1989). Data from Orlick and Partington's (1988) extensive study of Olympic athletes supports the survey results from the sport psychologists. The athletes reported daily goal setting as a part of their training program.

Examining Athletes' and Coaches' Uses of Goal Setting

A more recent development in sport psychology goal-setting research is the study of the goal-setting practices actually employed by athletes and coaches. Weinberg and his colleagues (Burton, Weinberg, Yukelson, & Weigand, 1998; Weinberg, Burton, Yukelson, & Weigand, 2000; Weinberg, Butt, Knight, & Perritt, 2001) have spearheaded this line of research. For example, Burton et al. (1998) studied 321 male and 249 female collegiate athletes representing 18 sports who were surveyed regarding their goal-setting practices. Findings revealed that most of the athletes set goals but rated them as only moderately effective, preferred moderate to very difficult goals, and more often reported problems with setting goals that were too hard versus easy.

Most interesting was the researchers' comparison between more and less effective goal setters, which found that more effective goal setters used all types of goals and implemented productive goal-setting strategies more frequently than did their less effective counterparts. Based on these results, it was concluded that coaches and athletes underutilize goal setting and need further goal-setting education. In particular, more emphasis must be placed on teaching athletes about process-oriented performance goals, the relationship between long- and short-term goals, skill and fitness goals, and implementing goals in practice and competition.

The most recent studies in this line of research showed that Olympic athletes all set some type of goals (Weinberg et al., 2000). Interviews with collegiate coaches from a variety of sports also showed that they used individual, team, practice, and competition goals (Weinberg et al., 2001), although there was some divergence in how systematic the coaches were in their use of goal setting.

Theoretical Explanations for the Relationship between Goal Setting and Performance

The old adage that there is nothing more practical than a good theory is an appropriate way to view the goal-setting process. It is important to know that goal setting influences performance, but it is equally important for coaches and sport psychologists to understand how and why goal setting is effective, especially when problems occur in goal setting and these individuals must assess the situation and make adjustments.

Several explanations have been proposed to describe how goals influence performance. More specifically, in their mechanistic theory, Locke and Latham (2002) contend that goals influence performance in four ways. First, goals direct the performer's attention and action to important aspects of the task. For example, by setting goals a basketball player will focus attention and subsequent action on improving specific skills such as blocking out under the boards or decreasing turnovers as opposed to becoming a better ball player in general. Second, goals help the performer mobilize effort. For example, by setting a series of practice goals, a swimmer will exhibit greater practice effort in attempting to achieve these objectives. Third, goals not only increase immediate effort but help prolong effort or increase persistence. As a case in point, the boredom of a long season is offset and persistence is increased when a wrestler sets a number of short-term goals throughout the year. Finally, research has shown that performers often develop and employ new learning strategies through the process of setting goals. Golfers, for instance, may learn new methods of putting in an effort to achieve putting goals that they have set in conjunction with their coach or sport psychologist.

Locke and associates' more recent writings (Locke & Latham, 1990; 2002) suggest that a number of factors mediate the goal setting–performance relationship. These include factors such as importance, self-efficacy, feedback, and task complexity. In essence, Locke has argued against a simple relationship between goals and behavior indicating that a number of factors combine to influence effective goal setting.

In contrast, Burton's cognitive theory (1983) focuses solely on how goal setting influences performance in athletic environments. Athletes' goals are linked to their levels of anxiety, motivation, and confidence. That is, when athletes focus solely on outcome or winning goals, unrealistic future expectations often result; such expectations can lead to lower levels of confidence, increased cognitive anxiety, decreased effort, and poor performance. Unlike outcome goals, performance goals are both in the athlete's control and flexible. Moreover, when properly employed, performance goals assist the athlete in forming realistic expectations. This, in turn, results in optimal levels of confidence, cognitive anxiety, and motivation, and, ultimately, in enhanced performance.

More recently, Burton and Naylor (2002) further developed his theoretical view of goal setting. The most interesting aspect of this update was the contention that an athlete's goal orientation interacts with perceived ability to produce one of three goal styles: a performance orientation where the athlete defines success based on learning and self-improvement and has high perceived ability; a success orientation where the athlete defines success on social comparison and winning and has high perceived ability; and a failure orientation where the athlete defines success on social comparison and winning but has low perceived ability. They predict that goal setting should best increase performance for the performance-oriented athlete, moderately increase performance for the success-oriented athlete, and slightly decrease performance for the failure-oriented athlete. Goal setting, then, interacts with a variety of personal and situational factors and these motivational factors must be taken into consideration in any goal-setting program. The implication is that the goal setting will work differently depending on one's goal-setting style.

When setting goals, then, coaches and sport psychologists should make every effort to become aware of the mechanisms causing performance changes to occur. Simply stated, theorists indicate that performance changes occur because of the influence of goals on such psychological attributes as anxiety, confidence, satisfaction, and motivation; directing attention to important aspects of the skill being performed; mobilizing effort; increasing persistence; and fostering the development of new learning strategies.

Life Skills Goal-Setting Programs

Goals can also be used to enhance personal development. For example, sport psychologist Steve Danish and his colleagues have used goal setting as a cornerstone of programs designed to enhance life skills, particularly in at-risk populations (Danish, Nellen, & Owens, 1996; Danish, Petitpas, & Hale, 1995). In particular, these scholars have initiated intervention programs that are designed to promote health-enhancing behaviors (such as learning how to learn, staying healthy) and decrease health-compromising behaviors (e.g., drug and alcohol use) in participants, particularly at-risk youth. Because of the importance of sport in the lives of many youth, these programs focus on identifying and then transferring valuable skills learned in the sport environment to other more general life situations. Organizers focus on effectively setting and achieving sport goals by helping athletes clarify their training and competition objectives. Efforts are then made to "teach for transfer" by helping participants apply their new goal-setting skills to other life contexts. An example of the steps followed in such a program is given in Danish et al. (1996):

> (a) the identification of positive life goals, (b) the importance of focusing on the process (not the outcome) of goal attainment, (c) the use of a general problem solving model, (d) the identification of health-comprising behaviors that can impede goal attainment, (e) the identification of health-promoting behaviors that can facilitate goal attainment, (f) the importance of seeking and creating social support, and (g) ways to transfer these skills from one life situation to another. (p. 215)

Finally, these steps are implemented in a series of 10 one-hour workshops.

Additional research on the efficacy of programs to develop life skills based on goal setting is needed, but initial reports are encouraging. Moreover, these programs clearly demonstrate the importance of looking beyond goal setting as simply an athletic performance enhancement technique to looking at it as a general skill that can positively influence all aspects of one's life. The programs also emphasize the need to teach for transfer and not assume that just because a person can effectively set goals in sport he or she will automatically use goal setting in other life contexts.

Goal-Setting Guidelines

The research clearly shows that goal setting facilitates performance. It is misleading to think, however, that all types of goals are equally effective in enhancing athletic performance. Research reviews conducted by Burton et al. (2002), Burton and Weiss (2008), Locke and Latham (1990), Weinberg (1994), and Kyllo and Landers (1995) indicate that this is not the case. Their work has produced specific guidelines concerning the most effective types of goals to use. Similarly, sport psychologists (Bell, 1983; Botterill, 1983; Carron, 1984; Gould, 1983; Harris & Harris, 1984; O'Block & Evans, 1984; Orlick, 1990) who have had extensive experience in employing goal-setting techniques with athletes have been able to derive a number of useful guidelines for those interested in utilizing such techniques, the most important of which are summarized here.

Set Specific Goals in Measurable and Behavioral Terms

Explicit, specific, and numerical goals are more effective in facilitating behavior change than general "do your best" goals or no goals at all. The research has convincingly shown that "when people are asked to do their best, they do not do so" (Locke & Latham, 2002, p. 706). Therefore, it is of the utmost importance that in the athletic environment goals be expressed in terms of specific measurable behaviors. Goals such as doing one's best, becoming better, and increasing one's strength are least effective. More effective goals include being able to high jump 6 feet 5 inches by the end of the season or increasing one's maximum lift on the bench press to 240 pounds. If athletes are to show performance improvements, specific measurable goals must be set!

Set Moderately Difficult but Realistic Goals

Locke and his associates (1981) have found a direct relationship between goal difficulty and task performance. That is, the more difficult the goal, the better the performance. It must be remembered, however, that this relationship is true only when the difficulty of the goal does not exceed the performer's ability. Unrealistic goals that exceed the ability of an athlete only lead to failure and frustration. In fact, in their meta-analysis, Kyllo and Landers (1995) found that moderately difficult (as opposed to extremely difficult) goals lead to the best performance. Thus, it is recommended that goals be set so that they are difficult enough to challenge athletes but realistic enough to be achieved (McClements, 1982).

Set Short-Range as well as Long-Range Goals

When asked to describe their goals, most athletes identify long-range objectives such as winning a particular championship, breaking a record, or making a particular team. However, a number of sport psychologists (Bell, 1983; Carron, 1984; Gould, 1983; Harris & Harris, 1984; O'Block & Evans, 1984) have emphasized the need to set more immediate short-range goals. The superiority of combining short- and long-term goals as compared to focusing only on long-term goals was also demonstrated in the Kyllo and Landers (1995) meta-analysis. Recent research has also revealed that both short- and long-range goals are needed to maintain motivation and performance (Weinberg, Butt & Knight, 2001). Short-range goals are important because they allow athletes to see immediate improvements in performance and in so doing enhance motivation.

They have been found to be especially important with complex tasks (Locke & Latham, 2002). Additionally, without short-range goals, athletes often lose sight of their long-range goals and the progression of skills needed to obtain them.

An effective way to understand the relationship between short- and long-range goals is to visualize a staircase (see Figure 11-1). The top stair represents an athlete's long-range goal or objective and the lowest stair his or her present ability. The remaining steps represent a progression of short-term goals of increasing difficulty that lead from the bottom to the top of the stairs. In essence, the performer climbs the staircase of athletic achievement by taking a step at a time, accomplishing a series of interrelated short-range goals.

Set Process and Performance Goals as well as Outcome Goals

North American society places tremendous emphasis on the outcome of athletic events. Because of this, most athletes are socialized to set only outcome goals (e.g., winning, beating a particular opponent). However, outcome goals have been shown to be less effective than performance goals (Burton, 1984, 1989; Burton et al., 2002).

Theorists suggest that focusing on outcome goals has several inherent weaknesses (Burton, 1984, 1989; Martens, 1987). First, athletes have, at best, only partial control over outcome goals. For example, a cross-country competitor can set a personal best but fail to achieve the outcome goal of winning because he or she came in second. Despite his or her superior effort, this runner could not control the behavior of the other competitors.

A second important weakness of outcome goals is that athletes who employ them usually become less flexible in their goal-adjustment practices. For example, an athlete who sets an outcome goal of winning every game but loses the initial contest will often reject goal setting altogether. However, an athlete who sets an individual performance goal such as decreasing his or her 100-meter breaststroke time by $5/10$ of a second and fails to achieve this goal is more likely to reset the goal to $1/10$ of a second.

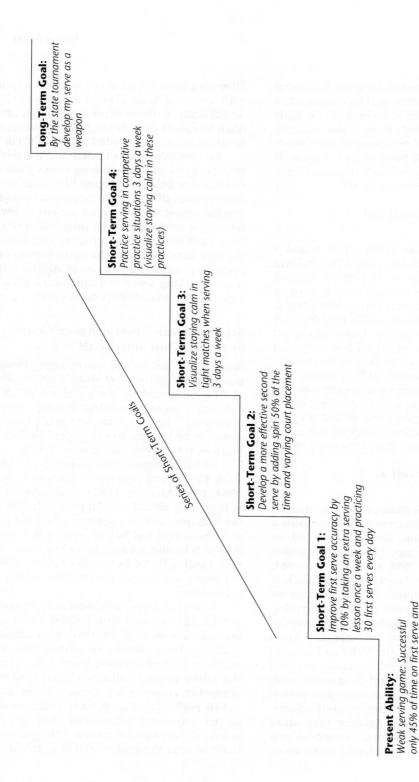

Figure 11-1 Goal Staircase example: A series of short-term goals leads to long-term goals for improved tennis serve

Finally, process goals (e.g., watch the ball longer by focusing on the pitcher's release, get back on defense) orient the athlete to focus on task-relevant strategies and procedures that need to be executed to have a good performance. Focusing on outcome goals can distract athletes, as they tend to worry about the event outcome and do not attend to task-relevant strategies (Hardy et al., 1996).

Although focusing on outcome goals, especially at the time of competition, has weaknesses, this does not mean outcome goals have no benefits. They can facilitate short-term motivation by helping athletes set long-term priorities and may be especially useful away from competition when athletes may lack the motivation to practice. Athletes with high levels of confidence may also be less affected by the negative side effects of outcome goals (Hardy et al., 1996). It is clear, however, that at or near competitions it is best to emphasize process and performance goals and that focusing exclusively on outcome goals is ineffective.

A study by Filby, Maynard, and Graydon (1999) provides additional empirical support for the idea of setting performance and process as well as outcome goals. Specifically, these investigators had physical education students perform a soccer wall volley test under one of five goal conditions: outcome goals only; outcome plus process goals; process goals only; outcome, performance, and process goals; and a control no-goal condition. Results revealed that the groups using multiple goal strategies performed best, indicating that it is important to balance outcome, process, and performance goals. Researchers concluded that the "benefits of adopting an outcome goal are realized only when the outcome goal is combined with the prioritization of a 'process orientation' immediately before, and during performance" (Filby et al., 1999, p. 242). Moreover, looking across all goals, Burton et al. (2002) reported that 9 out of 10 studies supported the notion of using a combination of process, performance, and outcome goals.

In summary, by emphasizing personal performance and process goals in an environment where outcome goals predominate, coaches create greater opportunities for meeting the success needs of all athletes. Those highly gifted competitors who easily exceed the performances of their opponents learn to compete against themselves and, in turn, reach new performance heights. Similarly, the less skilled athletes on the team are no longer doomed to failure; they learn to judge success and failure in terms of their own performance, not solely on the basis of peer comparisons. Finally, focusing on process goals directs the athlete's attention away from outcome and puts it on task-relevant cues.

Set Goals for Practice and Competition

When implementing a goal-setting program, people frequently make the mistake of only setting goals that relate to competition. This does not imply that setting competitive performance goals is inappropriate; rather, it suggests that *practice* goals should not be forgotten (Bell, 1983). In fact, Orlick and Partington (1988) found that one characteristic of highly successful Olympians was their practice of setting clear daily practice goals.

Common practice goals may include focusing 100%, making five sincere positive statements to teammates, running to and from all drills, and achieving various performance standards. These are typically not the most frequently cited goals of athletes, but they take on special significance when one considers the amount of time athletes spend in practice as opposed to competition. Moreover, most athletes report that it is easier to get "up" and motivated for a game or match, whereas additional motivation is often needed for daily practices.

Set Positive Goals as Opposed to Negative Goals

Goals can be stated in either positive terms (e.g., increase the percentage of good first serves in tennis) or negative terms (e.g., don't drop the ball). Although it is sometimes necessary for athletes to set goals in negative terms, it has been suggested that, whenever possible, goals should be stated positively (Bell, 1983). That is, identify behaviors to be exhibited as opposed to behaviors that should not be exhibited. Instead of having goal tenders in ice hockey strive to decrease the number of unblocked shots, have them set goals of increasing the number of saves they can make. This positive goal-setting procedure helps athletes focus on success instead of failure.

Identify Target Dates for Attaining Goals

Not only should goals describe the behavior of focus in specific measurable terms, but they should identify target dates for goal accomplishment. Target dates help motivate athletes by reminding them of the urgency of accomplishing their objectives in realistic lengths of time.

Identify Goal-Achievement Strategies

All too often goals are properly set but never accomplished because athletes fail to identify goal-achievement strategies. That is, the athlete fails to understand the difference between setting goals and developing and initiating effective goal-achievement strategies. In fact, it has been reported that athletes who use multiple goal-setting strategies have the best performance (Weinberg, Butt, & Knight, 2001). An important ingredient for any effective goal-setting program, then, is identification of multiple ways of achieving goals. For example, a basketball player who has set a goal of increasing her field goal percentage by 5 percentage points may want to identify a goal-achievement strategy of shooting 25 extra foul shots after every practice. Similarly, a wrestler needing to lose 10 pounds prior to the start of the season should identify an achievement strategy of cutting out a midafternoon snack and running an additional 2 miles a day.

Record Goals Once They Have Been Identified

Coaches and athletes are not consistent in writing down their goals (Weinberg, 2002). For instance, it is easy for athletes to focus attention on their goals soon after those goals have been set. Over the course of a long season, however, goals are sometimes forgotten. Therefore, it is useful for athletes to record their goals in written form and place them where they will be seen (e.g., in their lockers). In fact, the previously mentioned speed skating study (Wanlin et al., 1997), concluded that using a log book was a particularly important component of a successful goal-setting package. Additionally, Harris and Harris (1984) recommend that athletes keep notebooks recording goals, goal-achievement strategies, and goal progress on a daily or weekly basis. Finally, Botterill (1983) suggests that the coach develop a contract stating all goals and goal-achievement strategies for each athlete. Each athlete then signs his or her contract, and the coach keeps the contracts on file. Later the coach can use the contracts to remind the athletes of their goals.

Provide for Goal Evaluation

Based on their review of the research, Locke and his associates (1981) concluded that evaluative feedback is absolutely necessary if goals are to enhance performance. Therefore, athletes must receive feedback about how present performance is related to both short- and long-range goals. In many cases feedback in the form of performance statistics such as batting average, assists, goals scored, or steals made is readily available. Other goals, however, require that coaches make special efforts to provide evaluative feedback. For instance, a coach helping an athlete control his or her temper on the field may have a manager record the number of times the player loses his or her temper in practice. Similarly, a softball coach helping outfielders attain their goal of efficiently backing up one another may have an observer record the number of times players move into or fail to move into correct positions after the ball is hit. In Chapter 17, the authors suggest that sport psychologists might help athletes become more aware of negative thoughts by having them put a box of paper clips in a pocket, then transfer one paper clip at a time to another pocket for each negative thought during practice.

Provide Support for Goals

A goal-setting program will not succeed unless those individuals who are paramount in the athlete's life support it. This typically includes the coach, the athlete's family, and teammates.

Therefore, efforts must be made to educate these individuals about the types of goals the athlete sets and the importance of their support in encouraging progress toward the goals. For instance, if an athlete sets performance goals as opposed to outcome goals but significant others in the athlete's life only stress the outcome of the game or match, it is unlikely that performance goals will change behavior. Simply stated, significant others must understand the goal-setting process and support it!

Set Group Goals

Although the bulk of sport psychologists' attention has focused on individual athlete goals, Widmeyer and Ducharme (1997) emphasized the need to set group goals. A particularly important point these authors make is that understanding group goals involves more than knowing individual athletes' goals. The group task must be clearly specified along with the process for achieving group goals. When setting group goals, long-term team objectives should be identified, clear sequences of short- and long-term goals specified, team goal progress assessed, progress toward group goals rewarded, and team confidence fostered in group goals. All team members should have input into the team goal-setting process.

Dawson, Bray, and Widmeyer (2002) also have recently shown that when setting group goals, the process involves more than setting collective goals. In contrast, they found evidence for four types of goals on any team: (1) an individual member's goals for self (e.g., be the leading scorer on the team); (2) an individual's goal for the team (e.g., qualify for postseason play by finishing in the top half of the league); (3) the group's goals (e.g., win the league title); and (4) the group's goal for the individual member (e.g., lead the team in assists). They also showed that individual goals and expectations might differ from those generated by the collective. For example, one athlete might see his role as the point scorer on the team while the team sees him as an assist leader. Therefore, it is of the utmost importance that coaches and team leaders discuss and integrate individual goals with team goals. Role

clarification and definition are critical if effective team performance is to result.

A Goal-Setting System for Coaches

Goal-setting research and guidelines provide coaches with the information necessary for implementing goal-setting techniques with athletes. To be successful in implementing goal-setting procedures, however, coaches must develop and employ a goal-setting system. Botterill (1983) has outlined the essentials of such a system in detail. Of the many elements Botterill discusses, three seem paramount and can be incorporated into a three-phase goal-setting system: (1) the planning phase, (2) the meeting phase, and (3) the follow-up/evaluation phase.

The Planning Phase

Coaches will be ineffective if they attempt to set goals without first spending considerable time planning them. Before discussing goals with athletes, for instance, coaches must identify individual and team needs. These needs may focus on any number of areas such as player fitness, individual skills, team skills, playing time, sportsmanship, and enjoyment.

Following this needs analysis, coaches must identify potential team and individual goals. Most coaches can identify a large number of potential goals for their athletes, so it is important for them to consider how likely it is that their athletes will agree to and accomplish the goals. In doing so, coaches should consider the athletes' long-range goals, individual potential, commitment, and opportunity for practice. Finally, coaches must begin to consider possible strategies that they can use to help athletes achieve their goals. For example, a segment of each practice could be devoted to the accomplishment of identified goals, or extra practices could be held.

In essence, goal setting involves commitment and effort on the part of coaches as well as athletes. Therefore, coaches must be ready to initiate the goal-setting process with well-planned assessments of their athletes' abilities and established priorities.

The Meeting Phase

Once coaches have considered individual athlete and team needs, they should schedule goal-setting meetings. The first of these meetings should include the entire team. At the first meeting, coaches should convey basic goal-setting information (e.g., the value of setting goals, areas in which to set goals, types of goals to set, the importance of performance and process goals) and ask the athletes to think about their general objectives for participation, as well as specific team and individual goals. Coaches must then give the athletes time to reflect on their reasons for participation and to formulate potential goals.

A few days after the initial meeting, a second meeting should be held for the purpose of discussing some of the athletes' goals. It is especially important to examine goals in respect to their importance, specificity, and realistic nature. It is also desirable to examine possible strategies for achieving these goals.

In most cases it will be impossible to set specific goals for each athlete during these initial group meetings. Therefore, coaches must also hold a number of meetings with individual athletes and small subgroup meetings (e.g., forwards, centers, and guards in basketball). In these meetings individual goals should be recorded, specific strategies for achieving these goals identified, and goal evaluation procedures determined. Before and after practice are often the most effective times for holding such meetings.

The Follow-Up/Evaluation Phase

As previously stated, goal setting will not be effective unless evaluative feedback is provided to athletes. Moreover, recent research shows that public postings and oral feedback are critical for goal success. Unfortunately, because of the hectic nature of the season, this is often forgotten. It is therefore a good idea to schedule goal evaluation meetings throughout the season. At these meetings, subgroups of athletes should discuss their goals and progress made toward achieving them and reevaluate unrealistic goals or goals that cannot be achieved because of injury or sickness.

Finally, to facilitate goal follow-up and evaluation, coaches should develop systematic ways of providing feedback. Figure 11-2 contains such a system for the sport of basketball. Prior to the season, the coach prints goal-achievement cards that athletes complete during the preseason or seasonal meetings. These cards contain places for the athletes to rate their present skills, identify specific goals, describe goal achievement strategies, and develop goal evaluation schedules. In addition, performance evaluation cards are printed (see Figure 11-2) and used to evaluate performance on a percentage scale (0% = poor; 100% = excellent). The evaluation cards are completed after various competitions and, when combined with other available statistics, serve as feedback for weekly goal follow-up meetings. Although written in the vernacular of the coach, this goal-setting system can also be used by sport psychologists as they work with athletes on goal setting. The suggestions are equally appropriate for goals in the physical and mental skills domains, but they may need to be somewhat modified for sport psychologists working with an individual rather than the entire team.

Common Problems in Setting Goals

Goal setting is not a difficult psychological skill to use. However, it would be a misconception to think that problems do not arise when setting goals. Some of the more frequently encountered problems include attempting to set too many goals too soon, failing to recognize individual differences in athletes, setting goals that are too general, failing to modify unrealistic goals, failing to set performance and process goals as opposed to outcome goals, understanding the time and commitment needed to implement a goal-setting program, setting only technique-related goals, and failing to create a supportive goal-setting atmosphere. Each of these problems is addressed in the next sections.

Setting Too Many Goals Too Soon

A natural mistake that occurs when one first implements a goal-setting system is to set too many goals too soon. For example, it is not uncommon for coaches and athletes to set 5 or 10

Goal Achievement Card—Basketball

Name _B. Jones_____ Date _9-27-09_____

Position _Forward_____ Years Experience _2_____

Skill–Activity	Strong	Average	Needs improvement	Specific goal	Strategy	Target date
Shooting lay-ups jump shots free throws	✓	✓	✓	To correctly execute 8 out of 10 jump shots from the 8' to 10' range	Shoot 4 sets of 10 jump shots before practice every day	Oct. 27
Ball handling		✓				
Rebounding	✓					

Performance Evaluation Card—Basketball

Name _B. Jones_____ Date _12-4-09_____

Position _Forward_____ Game _3_____

Skill–Activity	Available statistics/Coach performance rating (0–100%)	Comments
Overall offensive play	80%	
Overall defensive play	94%	
Shooting lay-ups jump shots free throws	70% 2 for 2 2 for 6 3 for 4	Jump shot release ball at peak of jump
Ball handling turnovers	90% 1	
Rebounding	90%	

Figure 11-2 **Sample goal-achievement and performance evaluation cards for the sport of basketball**

specific goals. This usually has negative results. The athletes have so many individual goals that they cannot properly monitor goal progress, or if they do monitor progress, they find the record keeping overwhelming and lose interest. A more effective approach is to prioritize goals and focus on accomplishing the one or two most important ones. When these goals are achieved, the athletes then focus on the next most important prioritized goals. As the athletes become more experienced in goal setting, they also learn to handle greater numbers of goals more efficiently.

Failing to Recognize Individual Differences

Not all athletes will be excited about setting goals, and some may even have a negative attitude. Coaches and sport psychologists must expect this and not overreact. *Forcing* athletes to set goals is ineffective, for individual commitment is needed. Rather, expose all the athletes to goal setting, and then work with those who show interest. Over time, their success will convince other less committed athletes to begin setting goals.

The importance of recognizing individual differences when setting goals with athletes was demonstrated in an investigation by Lambert, Moore, and Dixon (1999). They found that the most effective type of goal setting depended on the participant's locus of control. Specifically, female gymnasts characterized by an internal locus of control (those who felt they could control what happened to them) spent more time on task when they set their own goals. In contrast, external locus of control gymnasts (those who felt they had little control over what happened to them) responded better to coach-set goals. Hence, goal-setting effectiveness was dependent on the gymnast's personality.

An especially important individual difference factor to consider when setting goals with athletes is the individual's goal perspective (Duda, 1992). High ego-oriented athletes base their success/failure competence evaluations on how they perform relative to other individuals and tend to focus on outcome goals. In contrast, high task-oriented athletes base their competence evaluations on how they perform relative to their own

previous performances and tend to focus on performance goals. Thus, athletes differing in their goal perspectives may adopt different goals. Unfortunately, Tenenbaum, Spence, & Christensen (1999) examined this issue and definitive results were not evident. Special efforts then need to be made to get ego-oriented individuals to focus on performance and process goals as opposed to outcome goals. Ego-oriented athletes with low confidence will often set unrealistically high or low goals as well.

Setting Goals That Are Too General

Throughout this chapter, the emphasis has been on the need for setting specific, measurable goals. Unfortunately, this does not always occur. Inexperienced goal setters will often set goals that are too general. Improving one's first serve in tennis, executing a better Yamashita vault in gymnastics, and lessening the frequency of negative thoughts are too vague. These goals are more effectively stated as increasing the number of good first serves from 50% to 55% in tennis, improving the Yamashita vault by sticking the landing 8 out of 10 times, and reducing negative thoughts to five or less during each practice session. When stating goals, always ask, "How can we make this goal measurable and specific?"

Failing to Modify Unrealistic Goals

In his extensive 5-month study of goal setting, Burton (1989) found that competitive collegiate swimmers had problems readjusting goals once they were set. Although the swimmers had little difficulty raising their goals once they were achieved, a number of athletes failed to lower goals that became unrealistic because of illness or injury. Coaches must recognize this problem and continually emphasize the appropriateness of lowering goals when necessary.

Failing to Set Process and Performance Goals

The work of Martens (1987), Burton (1984, 1989), and Filby et al. (1999) has demonstrated the value of setting performance and process goals as opposed to outcome goals. For too many athletes, however, winning or outcome goals are the only worthy goals. This is psychologically destructive and illogical but occurs because of the tremendous emphasis Americans place on winning. Coaches must be aware of this problem and continually emphasize the attainment of performance and process goals. For instance, coaches must continually remind athletes that great performances will typically lead to the best possible outcomes. Finally, coaches must realize that changing their athletes' perception of the importance of outcome versus performance and process goals may take a long-term effort.

Understanding the Time Commitment Needed to Implement a Goal-Setting Program

It is not uncommon for a coach to become interested in goal setting and to begin to implement a goal-setting program with his or her athletes during the preseason or early season. However, as the season progresses, less and less time is spent on goal setting. By the end of the season the goal-setting program is all but forgotten.

Like other psychological skills, goal setting takes time to implement. It must be recognized that a good deal of commitment on the part of the coach is needed. When planning your goal-setting program, think about the busiest time of your team's season and how much time is available to commit to goal setting. It is much better to devote 20 minutes a week to goal setting throughout the season and follow through on that plan than to say you will devote 20 minutes a day to goal setting and not follow through on it. Similarly, time spent in preseason planning and organization (e.g., mass-producing goal-achievement cards and goal-evaluation forms) makes the goal-setting process much more efficient and realistic to implement.

Finally, consider program efficiency when organizing your program. One collegiate basketball coach, for example, simply had her athletes write down a practice goal on index cards for the next day's practice. The coaching staff then evaluated and provided feedback relative to these practice goals during each postpractice cool-down period. This was a time-efficient yet effective program that was easy to implement for the entire season.

Setting Only Technique-Related Goals

It is very easy to focus all of one's attention on technique-related goals (e.g., shooting statistics, faster running times). However, as previously mentioned, athletes may want to use goal setting in a number of other areas. For example, a high school volleyball coach who was having trouble with his team's cohesion found it useful to have several key players set goals of giving sincere positive feedback to teammates at least five times per practice, and the team manager recorded the number of positive remarks made during practice. Similarly, an injured runner set specific goals for the number of times per week she would practice imagery. Finally, a football coach whose team seemed unenthusiastic and burned out at the end of a long season had considerable success asking the players to identify what elements of football were most fun for them (e.g., lineman throwing and catching the football) and then setting team goals to incorporate specified amounts of fun activities in every practice.

As I discussed earlier, a coach may also adopt a life skills approach by helping an athlete who has learned to set goals in the sport domain (e.g., to improve free throw shooting percentage by shooting 20 extra shots a day) to transfer this goal-setting ability to other life contexts (e.g., improve his or her math grades by setting a goal of studying 30 additional minutes a day).

Failing to Create a Supportive Goal-Setting Atmosphere

To reiterate, coaches and sport psychologists cannot set goals for their athletes or force them to participate in the goal-setting process. The athletes must be self-motivated and committed to the program. For this reason, the goal-setting leader needs to create a supportive goal-setting atmosphere, and in creating such an atmosphere, communication style is critical. Coaches and sport psychologists must act as facilitators of goal-setting discussions, not as dictators (Botterill, 1983). They must share limitations with athletes and identify unrealistic goals, while simultaneously avoiding pessimistic remarks and putdowns. In essence, the leader must adopt a positive communication style that includes good listening skills, a sincere orientation, and a positive approach.

Summary

This chapter has provided strong empirical and experiential support for the utility of using goal setting in helping athletes attain personal growth and peak performance. Goals are effective because they influence psychological states such as self-confidence, direct attention to important aspects of the task, mobilize effort, increase persistence, and foster the development of new learning strategies. A number of recognized guidelines should be followed when setting goals with athletes. These include setting behaviorally measurable goals, difficult yet realistic goals, short-range as well as long-range goals, and performance and process goals as well as outcome goals, practice and competition goals, and positive as opposed to negative goals. Equally important guidelines are identifying target dates for attaining goals, identifying goal-achievement strategies, recording goals once they have been identified, providing goal evaluation procedures, providing for goal support, and setting group goals. Lastly, common problems that arise when setting goals must be recognized. These include setting too many goals too soon, failing to recognize individual differences, setting goals that are too general, failing to modify unrealistic goals, failing to set process and performance goals, not understanding the time and commitment needed to implement a goal-setting program, setting only technique-related goals, and failing to create a supportive goal-setting atmosphere. These problems can be easily avoided or controlled if they are recognized at the onset of the goal-setting process.

Like other psychological skills, goal setting is not a magic formula that guarantees success. Goal setting is a tool, a very effective tool, that when combined with hard work and discipline can help coaches, athletes, and sport psychologists reap the fruits of personal athletic growth and peak performance. It is highly recommended, then, that coaches and sport psychologists at all levels of competition engage in goal setting with their athletes.

Study Questions

1. Define what a goal is and differentiate between the following types of goals: (a) subjective, (b) general objective, (c) specific objective, (d) outcome, (e) performance, and (f) process goals.

2. Briefly describe Locke and colleagues' (1981) mechanistic and Burton's (1983) cognitive explanations for the relationship between goal setting and performance.

3. Describe what is meant by saying life skill goal-setting programs teach for goal-setting transfer.

4. Think of your own sport and physical activity involvement and identify two goals you have set in the past. Evaluate your two goals relative to the 12 goal-setting guidelines presented in this chapter.

5. Describe the three phases of a goal-setting system for coaches and sport psychologists.

6. Indicate why failing to set performance and process goals is a common problem when setting goals with athletes.

7. Is it easier to adjust goals upward or downward? Explain.

8. Give an example of goal setting that is not technique related.

9. Four types of group goals have been set: individual group members' goals for themselves, the group's goals for individual members, the group's goals for the group, and individual members' goals for the group. Imagine that you are a member of a basketball team and provide an example of each type of goal. For your team to be effective, how best should these goals be related?

10. How can a coach create a supportive goal-setting atmosphere?

References

Anderson, D. C., Crowell, D. R., Doman, M., & Howard, G. S. (1988). Performance posting, goal setting, and activity-contingent praise as applied to a university hockey team, *Journal of Applied Psychology, 73,* 87–95.

Bell, K. F. (1983). *Championship thinking: The athlete's guide to winning performance in all sports.* Englewood Cliffs, NJ: Prentice Hall.

Botterill, C. (1977, September). *Goal setting and performance on an endurance task.* Paper presented at the Canadian Psychomotor Learning and Sport Psychology Conference, Banff, Alberta.

Botterill, C. (1983). Goal setting for athletes with examples from hockey. In G. L. Martin & D. Hrycaiko (Eds.), *Behavior modification and coaching: Principles, procedures, and research* (pp. 67–85). Springfield, IL: Thomas.

Burton, D. (1983). *Evaluation of goal setting training on selected cognitions and performance of collegiate swimmers.* Unpublished doctoral dissertation, University of Illinois, Urbana.

Burton, D. (1984, February). Goal setting: A secret to success. *Swimming World,* 25–29.

Burton, D. (1989). Winning isn't everything: Examining the impact of performance goals on collegiate swimmers' cognitions and performance. *The Sport Psychologist, 3,* 105–132.

Burton, D., & Naylor, S. (2002). The Jekyll/Hyde nature of goals: Revisiting and updating goal-setting in sport. In T. S. Horn (Ed.), *Advances in sport psychology* (2nd ed.) (pp. 459–499). Champaign, IL: Human Kinetics.

Burton, D., Naylor, S., & Holliday, B. (2002). Goal setting in sport. In R. N. Singer, H. A. Hausenblas, & C. M. Janelle (Eds.), *Handbook of sport psychology* (2nd ed.) (pp. 497–528). New York: John Wiley & Sons.

Burton, D., Weinberg, R., Yukelson, D., & Weigand, D. (1998). The goal effectiveness paradox in sport: Examining the goal practices of collegiate athletes. *The Sport Psychologist, 12,* 404–418.

Burton, D., & Weiss, C. (2008). The fundamental goal concept: The path to process and performance success. In T. Horn (ed.). *Advances in sport psychology* (3rd ed.) (pp. 339–375). Champaign, IL: Human Kinetics.

Carron, A. V. (1984). *Motivation: Implications for coaching and teaching.* London, ON: Sports Dynamics.

Danish, S. J., Mash, J. M., Howard, C. W., Curl, S. J., Meyer, A. L., Owens, S. S., & Kendall, K. (1992). *Going for the goal leader manual.* Richmond: Virginia Commonwealth University: Department of Psychology.

Danish, S. J., Nellen, V. C., & Owens, S. S. (1996). Teaching life skills through sport: Community-based programs for adolescents. In J. K. Van Raalte & B. W. Brewer (Eds.), *Exploring sport and exercise psychology* (pp. 205–225). Washington, DC: American Psychological Association.

Danish, S. J., Petitpas, A., & Hale, B. (1995). Psychological interventions: A life development model. In S. Murphy (Ed.), *Clinical sport psychology* (pp. 19–38). Champaign, IL: Human Kinetics.

Dawson, K. A., Bray, S. R., & Widmeyer, W. N. (2002). Goal setting by intercollegiate sport teams and athletes. *Avante, 8* (2), 14–23.

Duda, J. L. (1992). Motivation in sport settings: A goal perspective approach. In G. C. Roberts (Ed.), *Motivation in sport and exercise* (pp. 57–92). Champaign, IL: Human Kinetics.

Filby, W. C. D., Maynard, I. W., & Graydon, J. K. (1999). The effect of multiple-goal strategies on performance outcomes in training and competing. *Journal of Applied Sport Psychology, 11,* 230–246.

Gould, D. (1983). Developing psychological skills in young athletes. In N. L. Wood (Ed.), *Coaching science update.* Ottawa, ON: Coaching Association of Canada.

Gould, D., Tammen, V., Murphy, S., & May, J. (1989). An examination of U.S. Olympic sport psychology consultants and the services they provide. *The Sport Psychologist, 3,* 300–312.

Hardy, L., Jones, G., & Gould, D. (1996). *Understanding psychological preparation for sport: Theory and practice of elite performers.* Chichester, UK: Wiley.

Harris, D. V., & Harris, B. L. (1984). *The athlete's guide to sports psychology: Mental skills for physical people.* New York: Leisure Press.

Kingston, K., & Hardy, L. (1997). Effects of different types of goals on processes that support performance. *The Sport Psychologist, 11,* 277–289.

Kyllo, L. B., & Landers, D. M. (1995). Goal setting in sport and exercise: A research synthesis to resolve the controversy. *Journal of Sport and Exercise Psychology, 17,* 117–137.

Lambert, S. M., Moore, D. W., & Dixon, R. S. (1999). Gymnasts in training: The differential effects of self- and coach-set goals as a function of locus of control. *Journal of Applied Sport Psychology, 11,* 72–82.

Locke, E. A. (1991). Problems with goal-setting research in sports—and their solution. *Journal of Sport & Exercise Psychology, 8,* 311–316.

Locke, E. A. (1994). Comments on Weinberg and Weigand. *Journal of Sport & Exercise Psychology, 16,* 212–215.

Locke, E. A., & Latham, G. P. (1985). The application of goal setting to sports. *Journal of Sport Psychology, 7*, 205–222.

Locke, E. A., & Latham, G. P. (1990). *A theory of goal setting and task performance.* Englewood Cliffs, NJ: Prentice Hall.

Locke, E. A., & Latham, G. P. (2005). Building a practically useful theory of goal setting and task motivation: A 35-year odyssey. *American Psychologist, 57* (9), 705–717.

Locke, E. A., Shaw, K. N., Saari, L. M., & Latham, G. P. (1981). Goal setting and task performance. *Psychological Bulletin, 90*, 125–152.

Martens, R. (1987). *Coaches guide to sport psychology.* Champaign, IL: Human Kinetics.

McClements, J. (1982). Goal setting and planning for mental preparations. In L. Wankel & R. B. Wilberg (Eds.), Psychology of sport and motor behavior: Research and practice. *Proceedings of the Annual Conference of the Canadian Society for Psychomotor Learning and Sport Psychology* (pp. 165–172). Edmonton: University of Alberta.

O'Block, F. R., & Evans, F. H. (1984). Goal setting as a motivational technique. In J. M. Silva & R. S. Weinberg (Eds.), *Psychological foundations of sport* (pp. 188–196). Champaign, IL: Human Kinetics.

Orlick, T. (1990). *In pursuit of excellence* (2nd ed.). Champaign, IL: Human Kinetics.

Orlick, T., & Partington, J. (1988). Mental links to excellence. *The Sport Psychologist, 2*, 105–130.

Swain, A. B. J., & Jones, G. (1995). Goal attainment scaling: Effects of goal setting interventions on selected subcomponents on basketball performance. *Research Quarterly for Exercise & Sport, 66*, 51–63.

Tenenbaum, G., Spence, R., & Christensen, S. (1999). The effect of goal difficulty and goal orientation on running performance in young female athletes. *Australian Journal of Psychology, 51* (1), 6–11.

Tubbs, M. E. (1991). Goal setting: A meta-analytic examination of the empirical evidence. *Journal of Applied Psychology, 71*, 474–483.

Weinberg, R. S. (1994). Goal setting and performance in sport and exercise settings: A synthesis and critique. *Medicine & Science in Sport & Exercise, 26*, 469–477.

Weinberg, R. (2002). Goal setting in sport and exercise. In J. Van Raalte & B. Brewer (eds.). Exploring sport and exercise psychology. (2nd ed. pp. 25–48), Washington, DC: American Psychological Association Press.

Weinberg, R. S., Burton, D., Yukelson, D., & Weigand, D. (1993). Goal setting in competitive sport: An exploratory investigation of practices of collegiate athletes. *The Sport Psychologist, 7*, 275–289.

Weinberg, R., Burton, D., Yukelson, D., & Weigand, D. (2000). Perceived goal setting practices of Olympic athletes: An exploratory investigation. *The Sport Psychologist, 14*, 279–295.

Weinberg, R., Butt, J., & Knight, B. (2001). High school coaches' perceptions of the process of goal setting. *The Sport Psychologist, 15*, 20–47.

Weinberg, R., Butt, J., Knight, B., & Perritt, N. (2001). Collegiate coaches' perceptions of their goal-setting practices: A qualitative investigation. *Journal of Applied Sport Psychology, 13,* 374–398.

Weinberg, R. S., & Weigand, D. (1993). Goal setting in sport and exercise: A reaction to Locke. *Journal of Sport & Exercise Psychology, 15,* 88–95.

Weinberg, R. S., & Weigand, D. (1996). Let the discussions continue: A reaction to Locke's comments on Weinberg and Weigand. *Journal of Sport & Exercise Psychology, 18,* 89–93.

Widmeyer, W. N., & Ducharme, K. (1997). Team building through team goal setting. *Journal of Applied Sport Psychology, 9,* 61–72.

Arousal–Performance Relationships

Daniel M. Landers, *Arizona State University, Emeritus*
Shawn M. Arent, *Rutgers University*

Most athletes at some time or another have experienced an unexpected breakdown in their performance. Consider, for a moment, the following illustrative examples. A U.S. Olympic weight lifter in international competition surprisingly deviates from his customary preparatory routine before a clean and jerk and totally forgets to chalk his hands. As might be expected, he misses the lift. A gymnast preparing for a high flyaway dismount from the still rings suddenly focuses on self-doubts concerning his ability to perform the stunt without the presence of a spotter. These doubts, coupled with an increased fatigue level brought about by a long routine, cause him to freeze and release the rings prematurely. Finally, a sprinter who appears lackadaisical and lethargic during precompetition warm-up records one of her worst 100m times.

These are just a few examples of what athletes and coaches usually refer to as lack of concentration, "choking" under pressure, or failure to get the athlete "up" for competition. Sport competition can generate much anxiety and worry, which in turn can affect physiological and thought processes so dramatically that performance often deteriorates. In your own athletic or coaching experience, you have probably perceived a racing heartbeat, a dry mouth, butterflies in your stomach, cold and clammy hands, trembling muscles, or an inability to clearly focus thoughts. In these situations you may have told yourself that you were "too tight" or tense or that you "couldn't think straight." Common expressions like these often prompt practical questions concerning whether the athlete should be fired up as much as possible or relaxed as much as possible before an important competition. Or perhaps there is some in-between state that should be sought.

These concerns are generally related to the topic of motivation and, more specifically, to the concept of arousal. Understanding arousal and its effects on athletic performance, finding ways to estimate the arousal demands of a particular sport, and assessing arousal levels of individual athletes form the focus of this chapter. In the first section we will describe arousal and its effects and then outline a model for understanding its influence on athletic performance. In the second section we will describe the major hypotheses and research evidence for the arousal–performance relationship. Finally, in the third section we will describe a method whereby the coach or sport psychologist can estimate the optimal arousal level for a specific sport skill and for specific athletes.

The Nature of Arousal

Before considering how arousal is related to performance, it is necessary to clarify the nature of the arousal construct. This will be done by first defining arousal, followed by a discussion of its origin and how it is generated. Finally, various techniques for measuring arousal will be presented.

Defining Arousal and Related Constructs

In the psychological literature behavior is viewed as varying on only two dimensions—intensity and direction. The term *arousal* is used synonymously with the term *activation,* and these terms both refer to the intensity level of behavior (Duffy, 1957). Both of these terms also refer to a nondirective generalized bodily activation or arousal dimension. According to Malmo (1959), **arousal** consists of neural excitation on a continuum ranging from a comatose state to a state of extreme excitement as might be manifested in a panic attack. Conceptually, Duffy (1962) argues that any given point on this continuum is determined by "the extent of release of potential energy, stored in the tissues of the organism, as shown in activity or response" (p. 17). For our purposes, arousal will be viewed as an energizing function that is responsible for harnessing the body's resources for intense and vigorous activity (Sage, 1984).

Using Martens's (1974) analogy, the energy produced by increases in arousal can be likened to the engine of an automobile, which, when the car is in neutral or park, can be varied along a revolutions per minute (rpm) continuum without affecting the direction (forward or reverse) of the car. The nondirectional term *arousal* has no more positive or negative connotations than the rpm continuum described here. However, like the human, when the car is in motion and the speed is too fast for the road conditions, inappropriate levels of energy in the automobile (rpm) can disrupt efficient driving performance. The ideal rpm intensity should match the requirements for the desired task outcome (e.g., quick acceleration) to produce the greatest performance efficiency. Sometimes, however, this is not the case. The engine may be racing with the car in a forward gear but with the emergency brake on. This unnatural state is akin to what we will refer to later as a **performance disregulation,** in which extraneous influences (e.g., the brake or anxiety brought about by negative, self-defeating thought processes) interfere with the natural coordinative action of the skill being performed. The human engine refers to both the activation of the brain and the innervation of different physiological systems. Without the proper arousal athletes may simply be left "spinning their wheels."

Unlike the car engine, our human engine cannot be turned off—at least not while we are alive! Even as you sleep, there is electrical activity in your brain as well as small amounts in the muscles. Thus, arousal is a natural, ongoing state. However, when arousal levels become extremely high, you may experience unpleasant emotional reactions associated with the autonomic nervous system. This maladaptive condition is often referred to as *stress* or *state anxiety* or *distress* (Selye, 1950). Although anxiety, stress, and arousal are related concepts, they are not conceptually the same (Figure 12-1). There has been considerable confusion in the research literature resulting from these terms being used interchangeably. Recall that arousal is nondirective generalized bodily arousal-activation, and anxiety is an unpleasant emotional state.

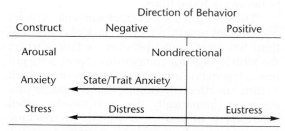

Construct	Direction of Behavior	
	Negative	Positive
Arousal	Nondirectional	
Anxiety	← State/Trait Anxiety	
Stress	← Distress	Eustress

Figure 12-1 **Direction of behavior for arousal, anxiety, and stress**

According to Spielberger (1975), the condition of anxiety is an emotional state or reaction characterized by (a) varying intensity; (b) variation over time; (c) the presence of recognizable unpleasant feelings of intensity, preoccupation, disturbance, and apprehension; and (d) a simultaneous pronounced activation of the vegetative (autonomic) nervous system. Like anxiety, stress also identifies the direction the behavior takes. Selye (1950) maintains that stress can be either positive (called *eustress*) or negative (called *distress*) in direction. In the psychological literature distress and anxiety both describe the kind of negative emotional state Spielberger (1975) is referring to in his definition. Thus, anxiety and distress can occur when arousal levels are high, but they do not have to occur at higher levels of arousal if athletes maintain control over all aspects of their performance. Thus, these terms are not conceptually and operationally the same as arousal.

Eustress is associated with one's ability to use stress in a constructive way that is beneficial to performance. Each of the theories presented here has something to say about the amount of arousal that may be conducive to producing eustress. Levels of anxiety and distress are influenced by perceptions of certainty or uncertainty and whether one can control the situation at hand. When there is total assurance of being successful, the competition is often taken for granted and the resulting underaroused state is maladaptive for effective performance. Basically, we know that some degree of uncertainty is necessary to increase arousal and motivation, but too much uncertainty can be anxiety producing. Thus, the anxiety response associated with higher states of arousal is typically related to an athlete's perceived inability to deal with the specific situation (e.g., task difficulty or demands). As we will see in a later section of this chapter, anxiety reactions to competition can result in ineffective performance, faulty decision making, and inappropriate perception. Helping athletes harness arousal so that it will not become an uncontrollable anxiety response is one of the major tasks performed by sport psychologists. It is important to bear in mind that sport psychologists do not seek to make people unemotional zombies but instead attempt to teach skills that will enable athletes to better control arousal and, thereby, more effectively cope with anxiety.

Origin of Arousal States

The structures for controlling arousal are located in the brain and primarily involve the cortex, reticular formation, the hypothalamus, and the limbic system. These centers interact with the adrenal medulla and the somatic and autonomic systems to determine overall arousal. We can demonstrate the integration of these different systems in an athletic situation by means of the following example.

A field hockey goalie sits in the dressing room minutes before an important match. She *begins to worry* about an upcoming game, which happens to be the biggest game of the season. These thoughts lead to anxiety about her performance. Her worrying may not be realistic, but to her body that does not matter. Technically speaking, as she worried, messages were being sent by a quick route to the amygdala, and another message by a longer route to the thalamus and then on to the cerebral cortex (Gorman, 2002). The amygdala, an almond-shaped cluster of cells in the midbrain, reacts quickly by activating physiological responses that are associated with fear, worry, and threat. Even before the source of the fear can be verified by higher brain centers (i.e., cerebral cortex), the amygdala activates the sympathetic nervous system causing the adrenal medulla to pump the catecholamines epinephrine and norepinephrine (also called adrenaline and noradrenaline) into the bloodstream (Gorman, 2002; Krahenbuhl, 1975). The rapid increase in these catecholamines and cortisol prepares her body and mind for an emergency "fight or flight" situation. Autonomic nervous system measures such as heart rate, blood pressure, and breathing begin to increase, and muscles in general begin to tighten. The blood supply begins to be shunted away from the digestive system and redirected to the larger muscles of the arms and legs through vasodilation. While all of these physiological reactions are already underway, the cerebral cortex begins to receive information on the worry or fear that this athlete is experiencing. The cerebral cortex analyzes this information to determine whether or not a threat exists. If analysis determines that the situation the athlete is in is not perceived to be a threat, the prefrontal cortex sends out an "all-clear signal" to the amygdala and the physiological responses described above are terminated. By contrast, if the cerebral cortex perceives the situation the athlete currently faces as a threat, then a fear label is attached to it and this is sent to the amygdala. In this case, the amygdala continues to send out a "fear alarm" and the already initiated physiological responses continue or may even increase. Having conscious awareness, she may interpret these changes as further support for her lack of ability and readiness, leading to a debilitating cycle of worry and physiological disruption of homeostasis (i.e., disregulation). The hockey goalie is now in an overly aroused or anxious state. Needless to say, we would not expect her to perform well in this condition.

How Arousal Is Generated

From the foregoing example, we can see that the athlete's fleeting self-doubt was the starting point of a chain reaction that ultimately led to

an overaroused state. This chain reaction along with the host of other factors involved in the arousal–performance relationship is outlined in Figure 12-2.

Our hockey goalie had a self-doubt that prompted physiological and subsequent cognitive appraisal that led her to conclude that her capabilities did not meet the demands of the upcoming game. This combination of an important meaningful event and doubts about her ability was responsible for generating anxiety and worry. Whether this process starts with an internal thought or an external stimulus, the amygdala triggers a physiological reaction in advance of full-fledged cognitive appraisal (Gorman, 2002). Once cognitive appraisal is initiated and the threat or doubt is confirmed, physiological reactions described in Figure 12-2 (see entries 1–4 under C) are heightened. When these physiological reactions are heightened, she begins to interpret the feelings as well (see entry 4 under D). Not knowing how to cope with the physiological reactions can create even more worry and apprehension (see entries 1–4 under D). Notice also that, once performance begins, aspects of the athlete's behavior (see entries 1–4 under E) are fed back for cognitive appraisal (see entries 1–4 under D) that may further intensify anxiety. As we will see later, this process can be influenced

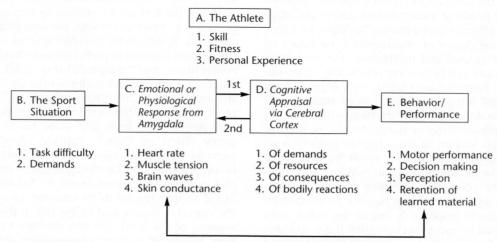

Figure 12-2 **Factors that affect the arousal–performance relationship**

by individual difference variables such as skill level, personality, physical and psychological fitness, and competitive experience.

Measurement of Arousal

Because arousal affects so many bodily functions, it appears to be an easy construct to measure. Unfortunately, this is not the case. We will discuss three types of arousal measurement and two types of anxiety measurement and highlight the advantages and disadvantages of each (Table 12-1).

Physiological measures. In sport psychology research much frustration has resulted from the lack of consistent agreement among different physiological variables and questionnaire measures. However, this poor correspondence has occurred because many investigators believed similar results would be found with a physiological arousal-activation measure and an anxiety questionnaire measure. It would not be expected that nondirective physiological measures of generalized bodily activation or arousal state would necessarily be consistent with questionnaire measures of negative emotional states like anxiety.

A more important concern is the low correlation found among physiological measures explained by Lacey, Bateman, and Van Lehn's (1953) principle of "autonomic response stereotypy." For example, in the same stressful situation, athlete A might display an elevated heart rate, and athlete B might show an increase in blood pressure. This principle suggests that averaging one physiological variable (e.g., heart rate) across the group may conceal individual arousal reactions.

To overcome this problem, Duffy (1962) has recommended the use of multiple physiological measures as an index of the arousal response. From these multiple measures, if athlete A is found to be a heart rate responder when exposed to stressors like competition, this measure would be singled out for comparison of athlete A in conditions varying in levels of perceived stress. By using each person's most responsive autonomic measure, greater differentiation can be achieved and thus more meaningful information can be gleaned.

The current view concerning physiological measures is that they are far more complex than first thought. However, with increased understanding of physiological processes and the continuing trend of cheaper, more sophisticated equipment, physiological measures have considerable potential as reliable indicators of the arousal response.

Biochemical measures. The adrenal gland is responsible for the release of epinephrine and norepinephrine into the bloodstream in times of stress. Also, a variety of corticosteroids enter the blood during high arousal. Increases in amines or cortisol have been examined primarily by analyzing either the blood or urine. Blood analysis usually involves drawing blood from the athlete by syringe or catheter. The analysis is complex and requires sophisticated equipment. Another disadvantage is that drawing blood can be traumatic or stressful to some athletes, thus confounding the results of the study. Urine analysis is less invasive but suffers from the same cost and time disadvantages as blood analysis. Furthermore, the usefulness of the analyses differs due to the speed at which the hormones of interest show up in the blood or urine. At this point it is also unclear how accurately serum measures reflect the brain's overall hormonal levels.

Questionnaires. Many questionnaires have been used to measure arousal, but unfortunately most of these are anxiety measures and not arousal measures. Only two questionnaires are specifically designed to assess nondirective generalized bodily activation, or arousal. These are the Activation-Deactivation Adjective Checklist (AD-ACL, Thayer, 1986) and the Somatic Perception Questionnaire (SPQ, Landy & Stern, 1971). The AD-ACL has been used in the exercise and sport literature. Unlike the SPQ, it contains two bipolar activation dimensions. Within the broader dimension of energetic arousal, which is generalized, nondirective bodily activation, the AD-ACL has two subscales of Energy (General Activation) and Tiredness (Deactivation-Sleep).

Table 12-1 **Some Common Physiological, Biochemical, and Questionnaire Measures of Arousal and Anxiety**

Measure and Description

I. Arousal Measures

  A. Physiological

    1. Central

      Electroencephalography (EEG). Changes occur in brain wave patterns from an alpha or relaxed state (8–14 Hz) to beta or a more aroused state (14–30 Hz).

    2. Automatic

      Electrical properties of the skin. This measure assesses either the amount of skin conductance or resistance to an electric current. Elevations in arousal cause increased perspiration, which increases the flow of the current.

      Heart rate. Increases in heart rate, the pattern of beats, and heart rate variability can all be indexes of arousal.

      Blood pressure. Increases in blood pressure are also associated with increased arousal levels and can be measured by cannulation or by the stethoscope and pressure-cuff method.

      Muscle activity. Muscle tension can be measured by electromyography (EMG), which measures the firing rate of motor units by means of surface electrodes attached to the muscle.

  B. Biochemical

    1. Epinephrine. Epinephrine is released from the adrenal medulla during times of stress. This can be measured in the urine and blood.

    2. Norepinephrine. Also elevated during stressful activities, this catecholamine can be measured by the same techniques used to analyze epinephrine.

    3. Cortisol. This steroid hormone is released from the adrenal cortex when the organism is confronted with either physical/emotional stressors or declining blood glucose levels.

  C. Questionnaires

    1. Somatic Perception Questionnaire (Landy & Stern, 1971)

    2. Activation Deactivation Adjective Checklist (Thayer, 1967)

II. Anxiety Measures

  A. Unidimensional Questionnaires

    1. State-Trait Anxiety Inventory (Spielberger, Gorsuch, & Lushene, 1970)

    2. Sport Competition Anxiety Test (Martens, 1977)

  B. Multidimensional Questionnaires

    1. Cognitive-Somatic Anxiety Questionnaire (Schwartz, Davidson, & Goleman, 1978)

    2. Competitive State Anxiety Inventory-2 (CSAI-2); (Martens, Burton, Vealey, Smith, & Bump, 1983; Martens, Burton, Vealey, Bump, & Smith, 1990)

    3. Sport Anxiety Scale (SAS; Smith, Smoll, & Schutz, 1990)

The other dimension, which is a directional measure of one's mood state, consists of the subscales of Tension (High Activation) and Calmness (General Deactivation). There is some evidence that the AD-ACL yields a better assessment of global arousal-activation than do individual physiological measures (Thayer, 1967, 1970). These questionnaire measures have broader use in a variety of sport settings. They are quick and easy to administer and are less cumbersome and intrusive than most physiological measures. However, the physiological measures are less dependent on athletes' linguistic and cultural background and are also less susceptible to behavioral artifacts (e.g., halo effects, demand characteristics, social desirability).

Anxiety Measures

The majority of sport studies published on the topic of arousal contain information derived from anxiety questionnaires. As has been pointed out earlier, it is a mistake to use the terms *arousal* and *anxiety* interchangeably. Recall that arousal is considered a nondirectional energizing function, whereas anxiety is negative in direction in that it is an emotional state or reaction characterized by unpleasant feelings of intensity, preoccupation, disturbance, and apprehension. Although the constructs of arousal and anxiety may at times be highly related, arousal is conceptually and operationally not the same as anxiety, and therefore, theories based on the construct of arousal should not be replaced by anxiety-based theories (Anderson, 1990; Neiss, 1988).

Even though anxiety measures are not appropriate for examining the arousal-performance relationship, the fact that they are so prevalent in this literature warrants some discussion of these measures. Most of these *anxiety* questionnaires focus on cognitive and physiological manifestations associated with an anxiety response. Some measure cognitive and physiological responses by differentiating between them (CSAI-2, SAS), whereas others (STAI) contain cognitively and physiologically related items, but no differentiation is made between them (see Table 12-1).

Many questionnaires are designed to assess both trait and state forms of anxiety. **Trait anxiety** is a *general* predisposition to respond across many situations with high levels of anxiety. To assess trait anxiety, individuals are asked to rate how they generally feel. **State anxiety** is much more specific, referring to an individual's anxiety at a particular moment. People who are high in trait anxiety are expected to respond with

higher levels of state anxiety, or situationally specific anxiety. The State-Trait Anxiety Inventory (Spielberger, Gorsuch, & Lushene, 1970) is a popular example of a well-researched questionnaire that assesses both dimensions of anxiety.

A more recent development in the construction of anxiety questionnaires is the trend toward multidimensional instruments. Three questionnaires, one non–sport specific (Schwartz, Davidson, & Goleman, 1978) and the others sport specific (Martens et al., 1983, 1990; Smith, Smoll, & Schutz, 1990), have subdivided anxiety into the components of somatic and cognitive aspects. The CSAI-2 (Martens et al., 1983, 1990) has somatic and cognitive state anxiety subscales plus a self-confidence scale. The SAS (Smith et al., 1990) has a somatic trait anxiety scale and two cognitive trait anxiety scales—one for worry and one for concentration disruption. Somatic or bodily anxiety is assessed by questions such as "How tense are the muscles in your body?" Cognitive anxiety would be indicated by affirmative responses to questions such as "Do you worry a lot?" By subdividing anxiety into its component parts, more will be understood about its nature and more effective therapies can thus be designed.

The Relationship between Arousal and Motor Performance

In the motor behavior literature two hypotheses have been advanced to explain the relationship between arousal and performance. We will first consider the drive theory hypothesis and then the inverted-*U* hypothesis.

Drive Theory

Although this is not a view held by all psychologists, for our purposes we will equate the term *drive* with *arousal*. In other words, drive and arousal convey what we referred to earlier as the intensity dimension of behavior.

Drive theory, as modified by Spence and Spence (1966), predicts that performance (P) is a multiplicative function of habit (H) and drive (D): P = H × D. The construct of habit in this formulation refers to the hierarchical order or dominance of correct or incorrect responses. According to this hypothesis, increases in arousal should enhance the probability of making the dominant responses. When performance errors are frequently made, as in the early stages of skill acquisition, the dominant responses are likely to be incorrect responses. Conversely, when performance errors are infrequent, the dominant response is said to be a correct response. Increases in arousal during initial skill acquisition impair performance, but as the skill becomes well learned, increases in arousal facilitate performance. This latter situation would be likened to a eustress state.

For example, a novice basketball player shooting free throws only sinks 3 shots out of 10; therefore, the incorrect response (a miss) is dominant. The drive theory hypothesis would predict that given greater pressure the novice player is likely to miss more than 7 shots out of 10. By contrast, the all-star basketball player may average 8 successful shots for every 10 attempted. In this case, because the dominant response is a correct response, an increase in arousal should enhance the player's chance of sinking more than 8 shots out of 10.

It is questionable whether a linear relationship between arousal and performance can be found for accuracy tasks such as free throw shooting. However, Oxendine (1984) argues that linear relationships, as depicted in Figure 12-3, do exist for gross motor activities involving strength and speed. These types of activities are typically overlearned, with strongly formed habit patterns. It seems likely, therefore, that a very high level of arousal is desirable for optimal performance in these types of gross motor skills. Support for this view comes from anecdotal evidence regarding superhuman feats performed in emergency situations in which unexpected physical strength and speed were required (e.g., a mother lifting a station wagon off her trapped child).

At first glance these examples seem to provide ample evidence to support a drive theory explanation for sport skills involving strength and speed. Contrary to Oxendine's analysis, however, we

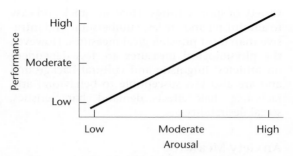

Figure 12-3 **The linear relationship between arousal and performance as suggested by drive theory**

would like to argue on conceptual grounds that the "fight or flight" arousal responses produced in these emergency situations are not appropriate comparisons to the sport situation. The sport setting is highly structured, often involving complex decision making and perceptual strategies in addition to the performance of a motor skill. The surge of adrenaline resulting from an emergency situation may enhance strength and speed in an uncontrolled manner, which may actually be detrimental to actual sport performances. For example, there are many instances of overaroused sprinters recording false starts in intense competition. Similarly, many superenergized weight lifters have forgotten to chalk up or have lifted the barbell in a biomechanically inefficient way in major competitions. Thus, on experiential grounds it appears that even among weight lifters and sprinters there are limits to the amount of arousal the athlete can tolerate without suffering performance decrements.

The drive theory has not fared much better when the experimental evidence from the motor behavior literature has been examined. For example, Freeman (1940) has shown that, with high levels of arousal, reaction times are slower than when arousal levels are in the moderate range. Furthermore, in other arousal-producing situations (e.g., audience effects) where the drive theory has received extensive support, it is now known that these effects were so small as to be of trivial practical significance (Bond & Titus, 1983;

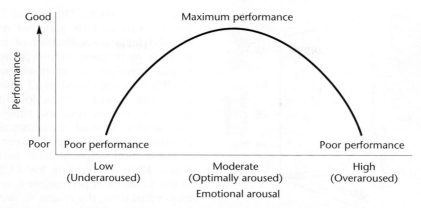

Figure 12-4 **The inverted-*U* relationship between arousal and performance**

Landers, Snyder-Bauer, & Feltz, 1978). Thus, it appears that other hypotheses, such as the inverted-*U,* need to be considered to explain the highly complex network of skills characteristic of sport performance.

Inverted-*U* Hypothesis

The inverted-*U* relationship between arousal and performance is shown in Figure 12-4. The **inverted-*U* hypothesis** predicts that as arousal increases from drowsiness to alertness there is a progressive increase in performance efficiency. However, once arousal continues to increase beyond alertness to a state of high excitement, there is a progressive decrease in task performance. Thus, the inverted-*U* hypothesis suggests that behavior is aroused and directed toward some kind of balanced or optimal state. In Selye's (1950) terms, this balanced state could also be termed *eustress.*

The idealized curve shown in Figure 12-4 is not usually seen with actual data that is based on relatively small sample sizes and only a few levels of manipulated arousal. As presented in statistics classes, most things in nature will resemble symmetrical bell-shaped curves, provided there are hundreds of cases and numerous (more than 30) levels of the independent variable. With

nearly all of the tests of the inverted-*U* hypothesis having fewer than 20 subjects and only three to five levels of arousal, it is unrealistic to expect perfectly symmetrical bell-shaped curves (i.e., idealized inverted-*U*); instead, the curve usually resembles an unsymmetrical inverted *V.* The key point is that the relationship between arousal and performance is curvilinear, with best performance occurring at an intermediate point within the range of arousal being examined.

The curvilinear relationship between arousal and performance is observed across studies with considerable regularity. This can be seen in Figure 12-5, where the curve for the difficult task looks more like an inverted *V.* This curve may have more closely resembled an inverted-*U* if 1-second increments in seconds of delay had been used. Other motor behavior laboratory studies (Martens & Landers, 1970; Wood & Hokanson, 1965) have shown support for the curvilinear relationship predicted by the inverted-*U* hypothesis. Other experiments do not show inverted-*U* curves (Murphy, 1966; Pinneo, 1961). In these studies investigators have manipulated incentive or threat to produce changes in arousal. Therefore, most of the research on this topic is limited because in most studies arousal has been examined as a dependent rather than independent variable. Anderson (1990) and Neiss (1988)

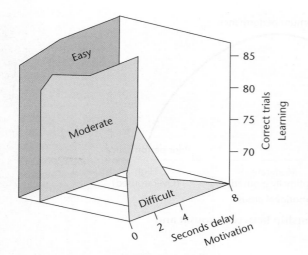

Figure 12-5   **A three-dimensional model illustrating the Yerkes-Dodson Law. Rats were held underwater and deprived of air for varying numbers of seconds, after which they were allowed to escape by selecting the correct door. The optimal level of motivation for learning depended on task difficulty**
Source: Broadhurst, 1957.

both argued that, if one wished to examine the effects of arousal on performance, data cannot be derived from anxiety or incentive manipulations. Furthermore, these arousal manipulations should be relative to arousal levels of each participant. In other words, arousal should be standardized as a percentage of a person's maximum arousal to control for baseline differences because of factors such as fitness, experience, and genetics.

Fortunately the few studies (Babin, 1966; Levitt & Gutin, 1971; Arent & Landers, 2003) that have manipulated arousal by increasing levels of physical activity have found support for the inverted-*U* hypothesis. For example, in the Arent and Landers study, participants were randomly assigned to one of eight arousal groups and they were all told they were competing for a cash prize. The eight arousal groups were 20, 30, 40, 50, 60, 70, 80, or 90% of relative heart

rate reserve (HRR). The use of HRR, which is highly correlated to maximal oxygen uptake, allowed for standardization of arousal relative to each participant. While participants rode a bicycle ergometer at their assigned percentage of HRR they responded to 12 stimulus presentations, and measures of reaction time, movement time, and overall response time were assessed. The results showed a statistically significant curvilinear relationship between arousal and reaction- and response-time performance (see Figure 12-6), accounting for 13.2% and 14.8% of the variance in performance, respectively. For movement time, the results showed a significant linear relationship between arousal and performance, accounting for 9.7% of the performance variance. Arent and Landers attributed the differences in measures of movement time to task characteristics and complexity issues that will be examined next.

Task characteristics.   From an arousal perspective, the characteristics of a skill or activity are essential determinants of performance. In the early 1900s it was known that the optimal level of arousal varied among different tasks. Using laboratory animals, Yerkes and Dodson (1908) found that, on more complex tasks, the decrement in performance under increasing arousal conditions occurred earlier than it did for less complex tasks. The interaction of task complexity with arousal level is clearly illustrated in Broadhurst's (1957) experiment (see Figure 12-5). In this study arousal was created by holding rats underwater for zero, 2, 4, or 8 seconds prior to allowing them to swim underwater to complete a two-choice maze. In one condition the choice was made easier by making the correct escape door more obvious (brightly painted lines), whereas in the more difficult condition the doors were nearly the same. As shown in Figure 12-5, decrements in time to negotiate the maze occurred much earlier (after 2 seconds of submergence) in the more complex decision-making situation. Thus, higher levels of arousal can be tolerated on simpler tasks before performance is curtailed.

What does all of this mean for the performance of sport skills? Basically, the complexity

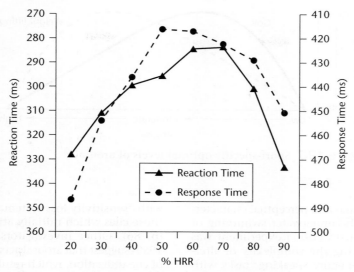

Figure 12-6 **Reaction and response time as a function of percent of maximum heart rates reserve**
Source: Arent & Landers, 2003

characteristics of the motor skill need to be analyzed to determine how much arousal is optimal. A number of factors that must be considered appear in Table 12-2. Take, for example, the precision and steadiness characteristics required for successful execution of a skill (Figure 12-7). For very precise fine motor skills that involve steadiness or control of unwanted muscle activity

(e.g., putting a golf ball), very little arousal can be tolerated without accompanying performance decrements. However, for tasks such as weight lifting that involve gross motor skills, a much higher level of arousal can be achieved before performance is impaired.

In addition to considering factors associated with the motor act itself, it is important to

Table 12-2 **The Complexity of Motor Performance**

Decision	Perception	Motor Act
Number of decisions necessary	Number of stimuli needed	Number of muscles
Number of alternatives per decision	Number of stimuli present	Amount of coordinative actions
Speed of decisions	Duration of stimuli	Precision and steadiness required
Sequence of decisions	Intensity of stimuli Conflicting stimuli	Fine motor skills required

Source: Based on Billing, 1980.

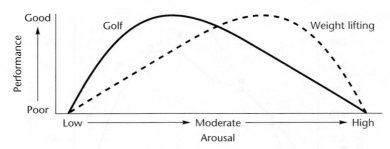

Figure 12-7 **Sport-specific optimal levels of arousal**

consider the decisional and perceptual characteristics of the task. The underwater swimming of the rats in Broadhurst's (1957) experiment was an example of varying the complexity of alternative *decisions*. Generally speaking, tasks with higher decisional demands require lower arousal levels for optimal performance compared to tasks with lower decisional demands.

The relationship of *perception* to the inverted-*U* hypothesis has been studied primarily in situations where individuals are attending to potentially conflicting stimuli. A number of studies (see Landers, 1978, 1980, for reviews) have shown that when dual tasks are performed individuals will generally allocate more attention to one of them to maintain or better their performance. This strategy is typically chosen because it is believed humans have very limited spare attentional capacity for focusing attention on task-irrelevant cues when they are performing complex motor skills.

There are many examples of attention being shifted away from secondary tasks to enhance the concentration necessary to perform the primary task. The experimental situation called the *dual-task paradigm* involves creating differing levels of arousal while subjects are performing a primary task and, at the same time, periodically reacting to a tone or a visual stimulus (Landers, Wang, & Courtet, 1985; Weltman & Egstrom, 1966).

From similar studies in which the dual-task paradigm has been used, Bacon (1974) offers the generalization that arousal effects depend on the degree of attention the stimuli attract,

with "sensitivity loss systematically occurring to those cues which initially attract less attention" (p. 86). Other investigators (e.g., Easterbrook, 1959) suggest that arousal acts to narrow the range of cue utilization, which results in the inverted-*U* function previously described. The underaroused performer, for example, has a broad perceptual range and, therefore, either through lack of effort or poor selectivity accepts irrelevant cues uncritically. Performance in this case is understandably poor. When arousal increases to a moderate or optimal level, perceptual selectivity increases correspondingly and performance improves, presumably because the performer tries harder or is more likely to eliminate task-irrelevant cues. Arousal increases beyond this optimal point result in further perceptual narrowing, and performance deteriorates in accord with the inverted-*U* hypothesis. For instance, a highly anxious football quarterback may focus attention too narrowly and therefore not be able to perceive task-relevant cues such as a cheating safety or his third receiver open downfield. The ideas of both Bacon (1974) and Easterbrook (1959) suggest that the effects of arousal impair performance through a loss of perceptual sensitivity by interfering with athletes' capacity to process information.

Individual differences. The optimal level of arousal for a particular task is also dependent on factors that are unique to the individual. Coaches who routinely give pep talks to all athletes on their team before competitions may not be aware that these arousing talks may not be beneficial for all athletes. Because of inherent personality differences and strength of dominant habits associated with the sport skill, some athletes can perform effectively at much higher levels of arousal than other athletes. People differ in the amount of prior experience with a task as well as the amount of practice they have had. As we discussed earlier, the strength of the correct habit response varies from one person to the next. The person who has greater skill—that is, has a stronger habit hierarchy—may be better able to offset the detrimental effects of increased arousal more effectively than the individual who is less skillful and possesses a weaker habit strength.

Of course, habit patterns may not always be appropriate. Landers (1985) has indicated that subtle changes in habit patterns may lead to **disregulation,** which is defined as a physiological measure of arousal that either negatively correlates with performance or creates some degree of discomfiture for the performer. For example, in our work with a world champion archer, we found that he had developed a habit of tightly squinting his nonsighting eye following the release of the arrow. At the end of several hours of shooting, this resulted in a tension headache. With the archer having to concentrate so much on the act of shooting, it was difficult for him to focus on the source of his problem. To correct this, it was necessary for us to bring the disregulation to his conscious awareness by providing an electromyographic signal of the electrical activity around his non-sighting eye. After several shots with this type of biofeedback, the squinting, which lasted for several seconds, was reduced to a blink and the headaches disappeared.

Perhaps the greatest individual difference factor is personality. The most relevant personality variables affecting optimal arousal levels are anxiety and extroversion/introversion. For instance, in the aforementioned study by Arent and Landers (2003), somatic anxiety as measured by Sport Anxiety Scale (SAS) (Smith, Smoll & Schutz, 1990), significantly contributed to the amount of reaction- and response-time variance over and above the amount of variance explained by physiological arousal alone. Neither cognitive (as measured by either the Cognitive-Somatic Anxiety Questionnaire 2 [CSAI-2] or the SAS) nor somatic anxiety (as measured by the CSAI-2) accounted for a significant amount of performance variance. Arent and Landers suggested that the failure of the CSAI-2 somatic measure to predict performance is probably related to the better psychometric characteristics of the SAS. These findings suggest that if an athlete is high-strung and intolerant of stressful situations (i.e., high perceived somatic anxiety or introverted), even a small amount of arousal can put him or her over the top an the inverted-U curve (Figure 12-8). By contrast, if the athlete is calm, cool, and collected (i.e., low perceived somatic anxiety or extroverted), he or she will be able to tolerate much higher levels of arousal without suffering a performance impairment.

Another factor emphasized by Mahoney (1979) is the ability of the individual to cope

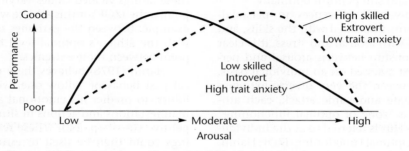

Figure 12-8 **Athlete-specific optimal levels of arousal**

with relatively high levels of arousal. This coping model emphasizes the individual's reaction to and ability to deal with arousal, since this may be "a significant determinant of its course and its effects on performance" (p. 436). For instance, if two athletes have a high absolute heart rate of 120 bpm, one athlete may be able to cope with this level of sympathetic disturbance and the other may not. With this view, there is less concern with physiological departures from normal levels and more emphasis on teaching athletes psychological skills (e.g., relaxation, imagery, self-talk). This view recognizes that a certain amount of energy (arousal) is needed for sporting activities, and a greater amount of arousal is not necessarily bad as long as the athlete can cope with it.

This point was recognized several years ago in research on rifle and pistol shooters (Landers et al., 1980). At that time some sport psychologists (Coleman, 1977; Nideffer, 1978) believed that better shooters actually decreased their heart rates below preshooting, resting levels while performing. However, research results (Landers et al., 1980; Tretilova & Rodmiki, 1979) showed that elite shooters invariably increased their heart rate above resting levels when they fired. In fact, if they did not increase heart rate at least 5 bpm above preshooting levels, they displayed poor performance (Tretilova & Rodmiki, 1979). Some elite gold medalist shooters had heart rates in excess of 50 bpm above preshooting levels and performed quite well. According to Mahoney (1979), when considering the inverted-U notion, the important factor is determining what level of arousal (usually a range) an individual athlete can cope with and still perform optimally.

Given individual differences in personality, habit patterns associated with the skills, and ability to cope with arousal and stress, it is clear that the relationship between arousal and performance is best assessed on an individual basis. Somewhere between the very diverse extremes of comatose state and panic attack, each athlete will have a "zone of optimal functioning" (Hanin, 1978). This is referred to as the Individualized Zone of Optimal Functioning (IZOF; Hanin, 2000). For some this arousal zone will be much

higher than is evident for other athletes (Landers, 1981). The trick is to know where this zone is for each athlete and then to help the athlete reproduce this arousal state more consistently from one competition to the next.

Unfortunately, in the sport psychology literature the IZOF model has only been operationalized with measures of anxiety. The questionnaires employed do not measure arousal per se, and, thus, the results of these studies should not be used to make direct inferences to the inverted-U hypothesis (Anderson, 1990; Neiss, 1988). In addition, the study by Arent and Landers (2003) shows that physiological measures of arousal explain double the amount of performance variance than measures of somatic anxiety. If performance enhancement is the desired goal, then investigators need to use either physiological measures or questionnaires that can directly measure arousal. However, the techniques presented for determining the IZOF are instructive and can be used in future research employing physiological measures or the AD-ACL. One technique, presented by Hanin (1978), had divers and gymnasts recollect and evaluate, with the aid of a retrospective anxiety scale, "how they felt before or at the time of a definite competition in the past" (Hanin 1978, p. 240). Furthermore, they were asked to recollect that state "in which they found themselves to act most effectively and achieve the highest result" (p. 242). This retrospectively determined "health anxiety" was then used to help determine an IZOF for each individual athlete. This was done by having an athlete recollect and rate his or her precompetitive anxiety prior to four favorable past competitions. If these ratings yielded values varying by only four points, the IZOF for this athlete would range, for example, between the extremes of these values, with the athlete's optimal level being the midpoint between these extremes.

Hanin (1978) believes these ratings of typical past behavior "allow one, with some credibility, to predict his emotional and behavioral manifestations and actions in situations of competitive stress" (p. 240). These retrospective ratings could then be used to estimate the level of anxiety in forthcoming competitions. If the athlete is outside his or her individually determined IZOF, the anxiety level needs to be raised or lowered by (a) altering the subjective significance of the upcoming activity; (b) increasing the athlete's confidence in his or her ability to cope with the upcoming competition; (c) limiting the number of people giving input to the athlete; and (d) creating a less stressful social environment (Hanin, 1978).

A similar approach has been used by Sonstroem and Bernardo (1982) without reliance on retrospective ratings of precompetition state anxiety. Using the State-Trait Anxiety Scale (Spielberger et al., 1970), they had athletes give ratings before each game. Over time, a pattern of ratings began to appear for each athlete, and these were then used to predict *optimal* anxiety levels from which individual IZOFs could be computed. Using a variety of different sports, Hanin (1978) and Sonstroem and Bernardo (1982) have shown that if athletes are outside their IZOFs, the outcome is typically poorer performance.

Suggested Modifications and Alternatives to the Inverted-*U* Hypothesis

The inverted-*U* hypothesis does not provide a theoretical explanation for the arousal–performance relationship; it merely posits that this relationship is curvilinear without explaining what internal state or process produces it. There are explanations for this hypothesis, but only a few have been tested in a sport context. Three of these theories/models have been presented within the confines of the inverted-*U* hypothesis—Easterbrook's cue utilization theory as a description of the interaction of task characteristics and perception, Mahoney's coping model as an explanation of individual differences in coping ability, and Hanin's IZOF model as a technique for operationally defining individual anxiety differences at the level of the individual athlete. Other theories go beyond simply clarifying certain aspects of the arousal–performance relationship predicted by the inverted-*U* hypothesis. These more recent theories have been motivated by discontent with the ability of the inverted-*U* hypothesis as a way of predicting exactly where in the expansive

range between panic attack and comatose states performance is at an optimal level. In this case, investigators have provided conceptual distinctions that, like the IZOF model, mistakenly equate anxiety with arousal and view anxiety as multidimensional. Thus, these models and theories differ dramatically from the concepts in the inverted-*U* hypothesis and were proposed as alternatives in an attempt to better explain the relationship between arousal and performance. Two of these alternative explanations, the multidimensional anxiety theory and the catastrophe cusp model, will be discussed next.

Multidimensional anxiety theory related to performance. This theory, developed by Burton (1988) and Martens et al. (1990), posits that anxiety has two different components: a cognitive component associated with fear about the consequences of failure and a somatic component reflecting perceptions of the physiological response to psychological stress. Although this theory assumes a sort of Cartesian dualism between mind and body, the authors maintain that mind and body are intertwined, but not completely. Martens et al. (1990) predicted that cognitive anxiety remains high and essentially stable prior to competition, whereas somatic anxiety peaks later (i.e., immediately prior to arrival at the site of the competition). This hypothesis has been tested in a "time to competition" paradigm and has generally been confirmed (Barnes, Sime, Dienstbier, & Plake, 1986; Burton, 1988; Gould, Petlichkoff, Simons, & Vevera, 1987; Gould, Petlichkoff, & Weinberg, 1984; Jones & Cale, 1989; Martens et al., 1990; Parfitt, 1988; Parfitt & Hardy, 1987; Speigler, Morris, & Liebert, 1968). However, this hypothesis does not deal directly with how these anxiety components influence arousal levels or the inverted-*U* relationship between arousal and performance.

To link this theory to performance, another prediction from multidimensional theory (Martens et al., 1990, pp. 123–124) is that somatic anxiety dissipates once performance begins, whereas cognitive anxiety can vary throughout performance because the subjective probability of success can change throughout performance.

Thus, Martens et al. (1990) predicted an inverted-*U* relationship between somatic anxiety and performance and a linear negative relationship between cognitive anxiety and performance. Despite the initial popularity that multidimensional theory has had in predicting performance, there are many problems with these performance predictions.

1. This theory has little relevance to the inverted-*U* relationship between arousal and performance since arousal measures have rarely been employed.

2. Multidimensional theorists have used the CSAI-2 questionnaire to measure cognitive and somatic anxiety. In an experimental study in which arousal was manipulated, Arent and Landers (2003) showed that CSAI-2 anxiety measures do not reliably predict performance. Other nonexperimental studies that have not manipulated arousal (Burton, 1988; Gould et al., 1984) have actually shown contradictory results that are not supportive of the theory. Likewise meta-analytic findings (Craft, Magyar, Becker, & Feltz, 2003) of 29 CSAI-2 studies (175 effect sizes and 2,905 participants) showed that the relationship between somatic/cognitive anxiety and performance was –.03 and .01, respectively, and these correlations were not significant from zero. Furthermore, cognitive anxiety consistently showed a positive rather than a negative performance relationship.

3. Among CSAI-2 nonexperimental studies that have tested for an inverted-*U* relationship between anxiety and performance (Burton, 1988; Gould et al., 1987; Randle & Weinberg, 1997; Woodman, Albinson, & Hardy, 1997), the only consistent relationship has been a curvilinear relationship between somatic anxiety and performance. However, an experimental arousal study (Arent & Landers, 2003) failed to find a significant CSAI-2 somatic anxiety-performance relationship, but did find a significant relationship with SAS somatic anxiety.

In summary, there is now mounting evidence that cognitive and somatic anxiety are not linearly related to sport performance. There is, however, consistent evidence that there is a curvilinear relationship between somatic anxiety and performance. In terms of the cognitive anxiety/performance relationship, research findings have not supported the hypothesized negative linear relationship derived from multidimensional anxiety theory.

Catastrophe cusp model. One problem with the multidimensional anxiety theory "is that it attempts to explain the three-dimensional relationship between cognitive anxiety, somatic anxiety and performance in terms of a series of two-dimensional relationships" (Hardy & Parfitt, 1991).

The three-dimensional model proposed by Hardy and Parfitt is derived from Zeeman's (1976) catastrophe cusp model, which was originally designed to describe ocean wave action. Hardy and Fazey (1987) suggest that the inverted-*U* relationship between physiological arousal and performance varies along another dimension defined as a *splitting factor,* which they arbitrarily identified as cognitive anxiety. They argued that this splitting factor determines whether the effects of physiological arousal (on performance) are smooth and small, large and catastrophic, or somewhere in between these extremes. According to Hardy and Fazey (1987), physiological arousal is not necessarily detrimental to performance, particularly if the skill is simple or well learned. However, when cognitive anxiety is high and dominant, "the curve is discontinuous and represents a catastrophic fall off in performance once the optimal peak is passed" (p. 29). Discontinuity, or sudden large jumps, occur along the normal factor (i.e., physiological arousal continuum) is referred to as *hysteresis.* A visual example of what this may look like can be found in Figure 12-5, where there is a sharp decline in performance under difficult conditions with relatively low levels of arousal. It is suggested that this may occur because cognitive anxiety distracts the athlete or creates doubt (consciously or unconsciously) about what is beneficial and what is detrimental physiological arousal.

A better way of addressing the catastrophe cusp theory is to experimentally examine the inverted-*U* relationship between arousal and performance and then determine if cognitive and somatic anxiety alter the shape of the curve or predict performance. Arent and Landers (2003) have done this and did not find support for the catastrophe cusp theory. When physiological arousal levels were from 70% to 90% of maximum heart rate reserve, the catastrophic fall-off in performance predicted by Hardy and Fazey was not at all evident (Figure 12-6). Analysis of the effects of anxiety on performance indicated that only SAS somatic anxiety predicted a curvilinear relationship with performance. The failure of the CSAI-2 cognitive measure to show any relationship to performance also supports the idea that Hardy and Fazey may have used an ineffectual splitting factor in their catastrophe cusp model. It may be that, for tasks of this type in which the cognitive load is relatively low, cognitive anxiety does not predict performance well.

The studies that have thus far been conducted have not supported the catastrophe cusp model. Many of these studies have had problems in the methodology employed (i.e., extremely small sample sizes and questionable statistical analyses). Furthermore, because of its complexity, Gill (1994) believes the model is of dubious value because it is difficult to test. The three-dimensional cusp catastrophe is only the second level of complexity, and Fazey and Hardy (1988) have suggested five additional higher dimensional catastrophes (i.e., swallowtail, butterfly, hyperbolic, elliptic, and parabolic). Hardy (1996) has responded to Gill's criticism with the argument that "complexity is an insufficient reason for rejecting any theory or model . . ." (p. 140). Actually, the philosophy of science offers adequate grounds for rejecting needlessly complex models and theories. The principle of parsimony maintains that given a simple and a complex description for the same phenomenon, each with empirical support, the simple description should prevail. Therefore, rather than viewing the simplicity of the inverted-*U* as a weakness (Gould & Krane, 1992), it is seen as a scientific advantage.

Estimating the Relationship between an Athlete's Optimal Arousal and Performance

As indicated previously, the optimal arousal level will depend on task characteristics as well as individual difference factors. To help athletes learn to regulate arousal during the competition, it is important that the coach or sport psychologist compare the arousal demands of the sport task to the athlete's typical competitive arousal state. We recommend the following guidelines. Select a specific task such as playing the quarterback position in football. Avoid global activities such as gymnastics, football, or basketball, and be as task specific as you can! Once you zero in on the task, answer the questions in Table 12-3. For example, high scores (3s and 4s) in the sport of archery on motor act characteristics (C1–4) would produce high total task scores. In short sprints, however, the decision/perceptual processes would in general receive low values (1s and 2s), and the gross motor nature of sprinting would keep the overall task score at a relatively low level. When using this table, bear in mind that it is only a rough guideline for estimating the complexity of your sport.

Total your scores and see where your chosen skill falls on the range in Table 12-4. If the skill has a low score, this indicates that the average athlete can be psyched up to a greater extent and still perform optimally. If an athlete performing this task is low trait anxious and typically responds to competition in a constantly laid-back way, you may need to supplement normal psych-up procedures by teaching the athlete some of the energizing techniques presented in Chapter 13. However, if the athlete scores over 32 in the specific skill you have selected, he or she will not usually be able to tolerate as much arousal. In this case it is important for the coach to extensively train the athlete in the basic skills so as to develop correct habits that are less susceptible to the debilitating effects of arousal. For those more complex skills coaches should particularly avoid implementing last-minute changes in technique; a weak habit strength for the skill

Table 12-3 **Estimating Complexity of Motor Performance**

A. Decision of Characteristics of Skill					
1. Number of decisions necessary	0 None	1 Few	2 Some	3 Several	4 Many
2. Number of alternatives per decision	0 None	1 Few	2 Some	3 Several	4 Many
3. Speed of decisions	0 Not relevant	1 Very slow	2 Slow	3 Fast	4 Very fast
4. Sequence of decisions	0 Not relevant, only one decision	1 Sequence of 2	2 Sequence of 3	3 Sequence of 4	4 Sequence of 5 or more
B. Perception Characteristics of Skill					
1. Number of stimuli needed	0 None	1 Few	2 Some	3 Several	4 Many
2. Number of stimuli present	0 Very few	1 Few	2 Some	3 Several	4 Many
3. Duration of stimuli	0 More than 20 sec	1 More than 10 sec	2 More than 5 sec	3 More than 2 sec	4 Less than 2 sec
4. Intensity of stimuli	0 Very intense	1 Intense	2 Moderately intense	3 Low intensity	4 Very low intensity
5. Clarity of correct stimulus among conflicting stimuli	0 Very obvious	1 Obvious	2 Moderately obvious	3 Subtle difference	4 Very subtle difference
C. Motor Act Characteristics of Skill					
1. Number of muscle actions to execute skill	0 1–2	1 3–4	2 5–6	3 7–8	4 9 or more
2. Amount of coordination of actions	0 Minimal	1 A little	2 Some	3 Several coordinative actions	4 A great deal
3. Precision and steadiness required	0 None	1 Minimal	2 Some	3 Considerable	4 A great deal
4. Fine motor skill required	0 None, only gross motor skill	1 Minimal	2 Some	3 Considerable	4 A great deal

will make the athlete more susceptible to the disruptive effects of arousal.

In addition to reinforcing the strength of correct habits, it is also important (in complex skills) to pay greater heed to the relaxation, imagery, and cognitive coping strategies presented in Chapters 13, 14, and 15. Athletes who display consistent, high-level performance during practice

Table 12-4 **Optimum Arousal Level and Complexity Scores for a Variety of Typical Sport Skills**

Level of Arousal	Complexity Score Range	Sport Skills
5 (extremely excited)	0–10	Football blocking, running 200 meters to 400 meters
4 (psyched up)	11–16	Short sprints, long jump
3 (medium arousal)	17–21	Basketball, boxing, judo
2 (some arousal)	22–31	Baseball, pitching, fencing, tennis
1 (slight arousal)	32 +	Archery, golf, field goal kicking

Source: Based on Oxendine, 1984, and Billing, 1980.

or unimportant competition but then fail to perform effectively in major competitions will have an even greater need to practice these coping techniques regularly.

To determine an optimal level of arousal for a given skill, athletes should be examined individually. This is most easily done by administering one of the arousal questionnaires (preferably the AD-ACL) listed in Table 12-1. By using either retrospective arousal ratings (Hanin, 1978) or ratings before each competition and noting performance levels associated with the arousal scores, a coach or sport psychologist should eventually be able to determine the athlete's IZOF. Having this as a basis, the athlete's arousal in a given competition can be compared to the arousal score associated with a personal best performance. If these arousal scores are discrepant, the coach or sport psychologist should use energizing techniques (Chapter 13) or relaxation, imagery, or other psychological skills (Chapters 13, 14, 15) to bring the athlete's arousal levels in closer alignment with the predefined IZOF.

Armed with the information in this chapter and the techniques described in Chapter 11, the athletes with whom coaches work will be better equipped to select, develop, and use the arousal self-regulation skills presented in Chapter 13. Often, coaches and sport psychologists want to identify athletes with inappropriate arousal levels for the tasks they are performing. Figure 12-2

suggests some areas that will serve as a guide in the identification process. The situation (B) of greatest interest, of course, is competition. The cognitive (C), physiological (D), and behavioral (E) response of athletes in the competitive situation can be compared to responses in noncompetitive situations (i.e., practice conditions). Marked discrepancies in these responses, accompanied by a poor competitive performance, may provide clues that the athlete is overaroused or underaroused.

At the level of cognitive appraisal (C), the coach or sport psychologist should look for signs of distraction before competition. This is usually indicated by an athlete who is not paying attention to the coach's pregame instructions. The athlete may express more concern than is normal by making statements that indicate a certain degree of self-doubt about his or her ability to meet the competitive demands. This identification process is often simplified at a cognitive appraisal level when the athlete recognizes the excessive worry and comes to the coach or sport psychologist for help.

Even without this self-disclosure, many times it is possible to detect physiological or emotional responses (D) that relate to cognitive appraisal (C) as described in Figure 12-2. Where there is a consistent shift to poor performance from practice to competition, the coach or sport psychologist should look for obvious signs of emotional reactivity (e.g., flushed face, sweaty palms, dilated pupils). Another way of getting more direct verification of the arousal mismatch is to administer various measures of arousal (e.g., AD-ACL) throughout the competitive season. Some physiological measures are also quite easy for a coach or sport psychologist to use. For instance, Landers (1981) and Tretilova and Rodmiki (1979) tracked heart rates of top U.S. and Soviet rifle shooters and found an optimal heart rate increase above resting values where best performance scores were fired.

Finally, at a behavioral level (Figure 12-2E) much can be gained from careful observation of the athlete's motor activity, actions, and speech characteristics. Hyperactivity before a performance can be gleaned from erratic behaviors such as pacing, fidgeting, and yawning. An unusually high or low energy level before or during competition may also indicate an inappropriate level of arousal. Rapid speech that sounds abnormal for a particular athlete may provide a reason for the coach or sport psychologist to inquire further into an athlete's arousal state.

The above-mentioned cognitive, physiological, and behavioral manifestations of arousal should not be the last step of the identification process. These factors are only indicators or clues that can serve as a basis for discussions with the athlete. Don't mistake fidgeting because the athlete needs to go to the bathroom as a sign of overarousal. Check out these possible signs of arousal to see what meaning the athlete gives to them. This interpretation is essential in the final determination of over-arousal. As we will see in the next three chapters, interpretation is also important for designing interventions to help bring arousal levels under control.

Summary

In this chapter we have attempted to provide a basic understanding of arousal–performance relationships. The drive theory and inverted-U hypothesis were presented, the former theory emphasizing the development of correct habits to insulate the athlete against the effects of arousal and the latter hypothesis stressing the determination and maintenance of an optimal arousal level for the task to be performed. To determine optimal arousal levels, several task characteristics as well as individual differences in state anxiety and skill must be considered.

In addition, two recent theories/models, which have been advocated as possible replacements for the inverted-U, were addressed and found to have conceptual and methodological flaws in many of the studies examining them. Although some scientific problems with tests of the inverted-U have been reported, a recent study (Arent & Landers, 2003) that has been designed to overcome these problems has still found support for the inverted-U hypothesis. Thus, the weight of the scientific evidence continues to favor the inverted-U hypothesis as the best description for how arousal affects performance.

We have provided guidelines to help coaches and sport psychologists estimate the arousal demands in reference to the complexity of the task to be performed. Finally, we have made suggestions to help identify athletes who are over- or underaroused. We anticipate that, by increasing their understanding of arousal–performance relationships, coaches and sport psychologists will be able to better assess the task demands and more accurately determine appropriate arousal levels for their athletes.

Study Questions

1. Diagram the predictions of drive theory and the inverted-*U* theory under conditions of a well-learned skill and under conditions of a novice performer learning a new skill. After diagramming, explain in words exactly where the two theories predict different performance outcomes.

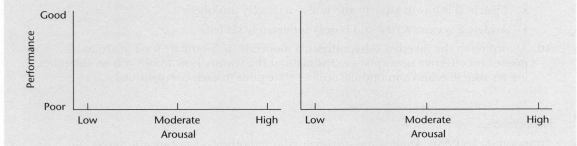

2. In 1965 Zajonc proposed a drive theory explanation for the effects of a passive audience on an individual's performance. Zajonc hypothesized that an audience produced an increase in an individual's arousal level. Assuming that Zajonc was correct and arousal is increased by an audience, how would such an increase affect the performance of a novice performer and an elite performer? According to drive theory, would you desire an audience for the novice or elite performer?

3. Describe Easterbrook's theory of cue utilization and how it provides an explanation for the inverted-*U* relationship between arousal and performance.

4. You are aware of two athletes at your school who display markedly different patterns of emotional excitement when practicing and competing. The 200-meter sprinter becomes much more emotional than the golfer. They both seem to perform well in their respective psychological states. Describe why these vastly different states may make sense in terms of the inverted-*U* hypothesis.

5. Describe what is meant by the term *arousal*. How does arousal relate to the term *anxiety?* Under what conditions might the arousal state of an individual trigger an anxiety response?

6. Describe the ways in which arousal has been measured. What do you consider to be the strengths and weaknesses of these measures?

7. What two factors are known to modify the shape of the inverted-*U* relationship?

8. How would you go about determining the complexity of motor skills such as free throw shooting in basketball versus maneuvering against three players to shoot a layup? According to the task complexity score, which task is more prone to the disruptive effects of arousal?

9. Which of the following athletes would you be most concerned about in terms of holding up under the effects of stress in an upcoming competition? Explain your choice.

- Athlete A is an outgoing individual who is relatively unskilled.
- Athlete B is an introverted person but is one of your most skilled players.
- Athlete C tends to be highly anxious and has recently made some changes in her tennis serving technique.
- Athlete D is low in anxiety and is also relatively unskilled.
- Athlete E is extroverted and is only moderately skilled.

10. According to the inverted-*U* hypothesis, a moderate or "optimal" level of arousal is needed for effective performance. Throughout the season, how would you go about helping an athlete achieve an optimal arousal state prior to each competition?

References

Anderson, K. J. (1990). Arousal and the inverted-*U* hypothesis: A critique of Neiss's "Reconceptualizing arousal." *Psychological Bulletin, 107,* 96–100.

Arent, S. M., & Landers, D. M. (2003). Arousal, anxiety, and performance. A reexamination of the inverted-*U* hypothesis. *Research Quarterly for Exercise & Sport, 74,* 436–444.

Babin, W. (1966). *The effect of various work loads on simple reaction latency as related to selected physical parameters.* Unpublished doctoral dissertation, University of Southern Mississippi, Hattiesburg.

Bacon, S. J. (1974). Arousal and the range of cue utilization. *Journal of Experimental Psychology, 103,* 81–87.

Barnes, M. W., Sime, W., Dienstbier, R., & Plake, B. (1986). A test of construct validity of the CSAI-2 questionnaire in male elite college swimmers. *Journal of Sport Psychology, 17,* 364–374.

Billing, J. (1980). An overview of task complexity. *Motor Skills: Theory Into Practice, 4,* 18–23.

Bond, C. F., & Titus, L. J. (1983). Social facilitation: A meta-analysis of 241 studies. *Psychological Bulletin, 94,* 265–292.

Broadhurst, P. L. (1957). Emotionality and the Yerkes-Dodson Law. *Journal of Experimental Psychology, 54,* 345–352.

Burton, D. (1988). Do anxious swimmers swim slower?: Reexamining the elusive anxiety–performance relationship. *Journal of Sport and Exercise Psychology, 10,* 45–61.

Coleman, J. (1977, December). Normal stress reactions in shooting. *The Rifleman,* 19–20.

Cox, R. H. (1990). *Sport psychology: Concepts and applications.* Dubuque, IA: Brown.

Craft, L. L., Magyar, T. M., Becker, B. J., & Feltz, D. L. (2003). The relationship between the Competitive State Anxiety Inventory-2 and athletic performance: A meta-analysis. *Journal of Sport & Exercise Psychology, 25,* 44–65

Duffy, E. (1957). The psychological significance of the concept of "arousal" and "activation." *Psychological Review, 64,* 265–275.

Duffy, E. (1962). *Activation and behavior.* New York: Wiley.

Easterbrook, J. A. (1959). The effect of emotion on cue utilization and the organization of behavior. *Psychological Review, 66,* 183–201.

Fazey, J. & Hardy, L. (1988). The Inverted-*U* Hypothesis: Catastrophe for sport psychology. *British Association of Sports Sciences Monograph No. 1.* Leeds, UK: The National Coaching Foundation.

Freeman, G. L. (1940). The relationship between performance level and bodily activity level. *Journal of Experimental Psychology, 26,* 602–608.

Gill, D. L. (1994). A sport and exercise psychology perspective on stress. *Quest, 44,* 20–27.

Gorman, C. (2002, June 10). The science of anxiety. *Time,* 47–54.

Gould, D., & Krane, V. (1992). The arousal–performance relationship: Current status and future directions. In T. Horn (Ed.), *Advances in sport psychology* (pp. 119–141). Champaign, IL: Human Kinetics.

Gould, D., Petlichkoff, L., Simons, J., & Vevera, M. (1987). Relationship between competitive state anxiety inventory-2 subscale scores and pistol shooting performance. *Journal of Sport Psychology, 9,* 33–42.

Gould, D., Petlichkoff, L., & Weinberg, R. (1984). Antecedents of, temporal changes in, and relationships between CSAI-2 subcomponents. *Journal of Sport Psychology, 6,* 289–304.

Hanin, Y. L. (1978). A study of anxiety in sports. In W. F. Straub (Ed.), *Sport psychology: An analysis of athlete behavior* (pp. 236–256). Ithaca, NY: Mouvement Publications.

Hanin, Y. L. (2000). Successful and poor performance and emotions. In Y. L. Hanin (Ed.), *Emotions in sport* (pp. 157–187). Champaign, IL: Human Kinetics.

Hardy, L. (1996). Testing the predictions of the cusp catastrophe model of anxiety and performance. *The Sport Psychologist, 10,* 140–156.

Hardy, J. P. L., & Fazey, J. A. (1987). *The inverted-U hypothesis—a catastrophe for sports psychology and a statement of a new hypothesis.* Paper presented at a meeting of the North American Society for the Psychology of Sport and Physical Activity, Vancouver, Canada.

Jones, J. G., & Cale, A. (1989). Relationships between multidimensional competitive state anxiety and cognitive and motor subcomponents of performance. *Journal of Sport Sciences, 7,* 129–140.

Krahenbuhl, G. S. (1975). Adrenaline, arousal and sport. *Journal of Sports Medicine, 3,* 117–121.

Lacey, J. I., Bateman, D. E., & Van Lehn, R. (1953). Heart rate feedback-assisted reduction in cardiovascular reactivity to a videogame challenge. *The Psychological Record, 39,* 365–371.

Landers, D. M. (1978). Motivation and performance: The role of arousal and attentional factors. In W. Straub (Ed.), *Sport psychology: An analysis of athletic behavior.* Ithaca, NY: Mouvement Publications.

Landers, D. M. (1980). The arousal–performance relationship revisited. *Research Quarterly, 51,* 77–90.

Landers, D. M. (1981). Reflections of sport psychology and the Olympic athlete. In J. Segrave & D. Chu (Eds.), *Olympism* (pp. 189–200). Champaign, IL.: Human Kinetics.

Landers, D. M. (1985). Psychophysiological assessment and biofeedback: Applications for athletes in closed skill sports. In J. H. Sandweis & S. Wolf (Eds.), *Biofeedback and sport science* (pp. 63–105). New York: Plenum.

Landers, D. M., Christina, R. W., Hatfield, B. D., Daniels, F. S., Wilkinson, M., & Doyle, L. A. (1980, April). Research on the shooting sports: A preliminary report. *The American Rifleman, 128* (4), 36–37, 76–77.

Landers, D. M., Snyder-Bauer, R., & Feltz, D. L. (1978). Social facilitation during the initial stage of motor learning: A reexamination of Martens's audience study. *Journal of Motor Behavior, 10,* 325–337.

Landers, D. M., Wang, M. Q., & Courtet, P. (1985). Peripheral narrowing among experienced and inexperienced rifle shooters under low- and high-stress conditions. *Research Quarterly, 56,* 57–70.

Landy, F. J., & Stern, R. M. (1971). Factor analysis of a somatic perception questionnaire. *Journal of Psychosomatic Research, 15,* 179–181.

Levitt, S., & Gutin, B. (1971). Multiple choice reaction time and movement time during physical exertion. *Research Quarterly, 42,* 405–410, 423–443.

Mahoney, M. J. (1979). Cognitive skills and athletic performance. In P. C. Kendall & S. D. Hollon (Eds.), *Cognitive-behavioral interventions: Theory, research, and procedures.* New York: Academic Press.

Malmo, R. B. (1959). Activation: A neuropsychological dimension. *Psychological Review, 66,* 367–386.

Martens, R. (1974). Arousal and motor performance. In J. H. Wilmore (Ed.), *Exercise and sport science reviews* (pp. 155–188). New York: Academic Press.

Martens, R. (1977). *Sport competitive anxiety test.* Champaign, IL: Human Kinetics.

Martens, R., Burton, D., Vealey, R. S., Bump, L. A., & Smith, D. E. (1990). Development and validation of the competitive state anxiety inventory-2. In R. Martens, R. S. Vealey, & D. Burton, *Competitive anxiety in sport* (pp. 123–124, 160). Champaign, IL: Human Kinetics.

Martens, R., Burton, D., Vealey, R., Smith, D., & Bump, L. (1983). *The development of the competitive state anxiety inventory-2 (CSAI-2).* Unpublished manuscript.

Martens, R., & Landers, D. M. (1970). Motor performance under stress: A test of the inverted-U hypothesis. *Journal of Personality and Social Psychology, 16,* 29–37.

Murphy, L. E. (1966). Muscular effort, activation level and reaction time. *Proceedings of the 74th Annual Convention of the American Psychological Association* (p. 1). Washington, DC: APA.

Neiss, R. (1988). Reconceptualizing arousal: Psychobiological states in motor performance. *Psychological Bulletin, 103,* 345–366.

Nideffer, R. M. (1978). *Predicting human behavior: A theory and test of attentional and interpersonal style.* San Diego: Enhanced Performance Associates.

Oxendine, J. B. (1984). *Psychology of motor learning.* Englewood Cliffs, NJ: Prentice Hall.

Parfitt, C. G. (1988). *Interactions between models of stress and models of motor control.* Unpublished doctoral dissertation, University College of North Wales.

Parfitt, C. G., & Hardy, L. (1987). Further evidence for the differential effects of competitive anxiety upon a number of cognitive and motor subcomponents. *Journal of Sport Sciences, 5,* 62–63.

Pinneo, L. R. (1961). The effects of induced muscle tension during tracking on level of activation and on performance. *Journal of Experimental Psychology, 62,* 523–531.

Randle, S., & Weinberg, R. (1997). Multidimensional anxiety and performance: An exploratory examination of the zone of optimal functioning hypothesis. *The Sport Psychologist, 11,* 169–174.

Sage, G. (1984). *Motor learning and control.* Dubuque, IA: Brown.

Schwartz, G. E., Davidson, R. J., & Goleman, D. (1978). Patterning of cognitive and somatic processes in the self-regulation of anxiety: Effects of meditation versus exercise. *Psychosomatic Medicine, 40,* 321–328.

Selye, H. (1950). *Stress.* Montreal: Acta.

Smith, R. E., Smoll, F. L., & Schutz, R. W. (1990). Measurement and correlates of sport-specific cognitive and somatic trait anxiety: The sport anxiety scale. *Anxiety Research, 2,* 263–280.

Sonstroem, R. J., & Bernardo, P. (1982). Intraindividual pregame state anxiety and basketball performance: A reexamination of the inverted-*U* curve. *Journal of Sport Psychology, 4,* 235–245.

Speigler, M. D., Morris, L. W., & Liebert, R. M. (1968). Cognitive and emotional components of test anxiety: Temporal factors. *Psychological Reports, 22,* 451–456.

Spence, J. T., & Spence, K. W. (1966). The motivational components of manifest anxiety: Drive and drive stimuli. In C. D. Spielberger (Ed.), *Anxiety and behavior* (pp. 291–326). New York: Academic Press.

Spielberger, C. D. (1975). Anxiety: State-trait process. In C. D. Spielberger & I. G. Sarason (Eds.), *Stress and anxiety* (Vol. 1, pp. 115–143). New York: Hemisphere.

Spielberger, C. D., Gorsuch, R. L., & Lushene, R. E. (1970). *Manual for the State-Trait Anxiety Inventory (STAI).* Palo Alto, CA: Consulting Psychologists Press.

Thayer, R. E. (1967). Measurement of activation through self-report. *Psychological Reports, 20,* 663–679.

Thayer, R. E. (1970). Activation states as assessed by verbal report and four psychophysiological variables. *Psychophysiology, 7,* 86–94.

Thayer, R. E. (1986). Activation-deactivation adjective checklist: Current overview and structural analysis. *Psychological Reports, 58,* 607–614.

Tretilova, T. A., & Rodmiki, E. M. (1979). Investigation of emotional state of rifle shooters. *Theory and Practice of Physical Culture, 5,* 28.

Weltman, A. T., & Egstrom, G. H. (1966). Perceptual narrowing in novice divers. *Human Factors, 8,* 499–505.

Wood, C. G., & Hokanson, J. E. (1965). Effects of induced muscle tension on performance and the inverted-*U*. *Journal of Personality and Social Psychology, 1,* 506–510.

Woodman, T., Albinson, J. G., & Hardy, L. (1997). An investigation of the zones of optimal functioning hypothesis within a multidimensional framework. *Journal of Sport and Exercise Psychology, 19,* 131–141.

Yerkes, R. M., & Dodson, J. D. (1908). The relation of strength of stimulus to rapidity of habit formation. *Journal of Comparative Neurology of Psychology, 18,* 459–482.

Zeeman, E. C. (1976). Catastrophe theory. *Scientific American, 234,* 65–83.

Relaxation and Energizing Techniques for Regulation of Arousal

Jean M. Williams, *University of Arizona, Emeritus*

Marty exudes calmness and never gets rattled. . . . He manages to stay relaxed under the most high-pressure situation, and that carries over to his teammates.

—Stan Fischler, NHL columnist and TV analyst, talking about Martin Brodeur, Olympic
gold medalist and three-time National Hockey League champion goalie

Somehow the misconception persists that if one practices and trains hard enough physically for a competition, everything else will magically come together. In fact, during a given competition, or between two competitions that closely follow each other, there is no marked change in an athlete's skill level, physiological capacity, or biomechanical efficiency. Fluctuation in performance is generally caused by the fluctuation in the athlete's mental control. Poorer performance comes when an athlete loses control of cognitive factors such as the ability to concentrate, to use appropriate self-talk, and to maintain optimal motivation. In the final analysis the athlete is inappropriately aroused, which we will refer to as activated, or some appropriate derivative, throughout the rest of the chapter.

Although unrealistic, wouldn't it be great if all athletes responded to competition the way Michelle Akers, a member of the 1999 U.S. World Cup soccer team, did during a game leading to the team winning the World Cup? After the semi-final game with Brazil, a reporter asked Michelle if she was nervous about being chosen to take the penalty kick with a trip to the World Cup final still hanging in the balance. Akers smiled and replied, "Nervous? I was like, 'Yeah baby, give me that.' Those are the moments you live for" (*USA Today*, July 6, 1999). Consistent high-level performance begins with the discovery of the mental and bodily states typically associated with superior performance (see Chapter 10 for suggestions on how to accomplish this goal). Athletes can then learn to consciously regulate these responses and thereby help maintain better and more consistent performance.

For example, Elmer Green and Alyce Green (1977) have studied the effects of the mental control of **autonomic functions,** including the muscular and hormonal changes that occur in sport performance. In their experiments they found that individuals can alter their brain waves, heart rate, breathing, blood pressure, body temperature, and other bodily processes that are generally regulated by the autonomic nervous system. They also discovered that the ability to voluntarily control these processes could be taught to others with ease in a relatively short period of time. The Greens concluded that each of us possesses a highly complex, sophisticated, and effectively integrated network between the mind and body and that every change in mental-emotional state is consciously or unconsciously accompanied by an appropriate change in the bodily state.

Readiness, being psyched, energized, mentally tough, activated, in the zone, or whatever you may want to call it, is an integration of the mind–body feelings and thoughts that provide the athlete with a feeling of confidence, mastery and control. The athlete can learn to reach this state voluntarily by practicing the skills and strategies included in this book; learning to regulate activation level, the subject of this chapter, is one important part of the process. Once an athlete has identified his or her optimal level of arousal for maximizing a given performance, the athlete can use appropriate relaxation or energizing techniques and strategies to reduce or increase that activation as needed (see Chapter 12 for ways of determining optimal level of activation and for a discussion of factors that influence optimal activation level).

Obviously, all athletes need a certain amount of arousal or motivation to accomplish a task, and some need more or less than others for peak performance. Because of this variability the classic "win one for the Gipper" speech can prove problematic. Some athletes will respond positively to a highly charged motivational speech, whereas others will become overactivated. Traditionally, most coaches and athletes have tended to emphasize the psyching up aspect of preparation for performance; most sport psychologists have focused on lowering activation.

As noted in the preceding chapters, a combination of physiological, psychological, and behavioral responses occurs when an athlete is worried and afraid of not performing as desired. Each athlete has to learn his or her particular pattern of overactivation resulting from worry and anxiety about performance. Learning to relax is essential to regulating these responses to avoid any detrimental effects on performance. When a muscle tenses up, as it usually does with worry and anxiety, or even with trying too hard, it contracts or is shortened. This contraction involves nerves as well. Approximately half of the nerves alert the muscles to respond to the messages from the brain, and the other half carry the messages back to the brain.

The voluntary muscles in humans (and animals) are arranged in pairs. When a muscle tightens because of perceived stress, its opposite sets up a countertension to hold the segment of the body in place. The resulting double pull can build up formidable heights of tension over much of the body, yet most people will not identify it. This double pull explains why a person can be scared stiff, become rigid with anger, be unable to move because of fright, and so forth. It also explains why an athlete shoots air balls, blows a short putt, passes with too much force, or overhits a tennis ball. The principle of the double pull, sometimes referred to as **bracing,** has great significance for the athlete. When excessive muscular tension occurs, it interferes with execution of the skill because it prevents appropriately coordinating movement. Proper form in any movement involves using just the right amount of tension at any given time in the relevant muscles. We can learn the right amount of contraction, that is, to expend only those energies necessary to accomplish our purposes without waste. This is called **differential relaxation.**

Exercise for illustrating how excessive tension disrupts speed and coordination:

Rest your dominant forearm and hand palm down on a desk or tabletop. Tense all the muscles in the hand and fingers and then try to alternately tap the index and middle fingers back and forth as quickly as possible. Relax all the muscles in the forearm and hand and repeat the exercise.

Coaches and teachers often shout "relax" to an athlete or learner whose performance is suffering because of too much muscular tension, for example, a beginning swimmer going into the deep end for the first time or a skilled athlete becoming frustrated because performance is not up to expectations. Although the instruction to relax is certainly appropriate, more often than not these performers are clueless as to how to relax, particularly when in an uptight state. To learn to avoid too much tension, athletes need to be taught to recognize unwanted tension and to relax or release that tension. The tension sensation comes from the contraction of skeletal muscle fibers. Relaxation comes from no more than stopping the contraction, thus releasing the tension from the contracted muscle. Total relaxation means letting go and doing absolutely nothing with the muscles so that no messages are traveling either to or from the brain.

You may be wondering why any athlete would want to be completely relaxed. The answer is, to learn what a **zero-activation** level feels like. In learning to train the muscles to relax totally, athletes develop a much greater sensitivity to their bodily feelings and responses and what causes their reactions. This awareness increases their sensitivity to tension levels and their ability to regulate different levels of tension to match the demands of the performance situation. In addition, once trained in deep relaxation, athletes can use this skill to remove localized tension that contributes to headaches or lower back pain or pain surrounding injuries. Complete relaxation can also facilitate recovery from fatigue, such as when athletes have only a short time between events, and it can promote the onset of sleep and reduce other insomnia problems that plague many athletes prior to competition. Probably the most important contribution that such relaxation can make to athletes is to teach them to regulate muscular tension so that nerve pathways to the muscle are never overcharged. The ability to relax completely produces a positive, pleasurable, and beneficial experience that provides the central nervous system with a rest. That, in turn, allows regeneration of physical, mental, and emotional states with the athlete in control.

Finally, the ability to relax completely provides the foundation for learning the skill of **momentary relaxation,** which can be done quickly and does not achieve as deep a relaxation state as complete relaxation. Momentary relaxation skills are extremely important for athletes because they can be used to reduce overactivation at any point during practices and competition. When the nerves are carrying worry messages instead of the stimuli for smooth, coordinated, integrated efforts, performance suffers. Momentary relaxation removes excessive muscular tension and, hopefully, worry and anxiety stimuli, resulting in enhanced kinesthetic awareness and better performance. The momentary respite also allows the athlete to return to a point of controlled balance. Every aspect of performance is enhanced: concentration, attentional focus, awareness, confidence, precision, speed, and so on.

Momentary relaxation can be used just before and during warm-up. In fact, stretching in preparation for competition is a good time to utilize the strategies of momentary relaxation and to focus on the upcoming game. The more uptight the athlete is prior to performance, the longer the session of momentary relaxation should be. After the competition, this type of relaxation can be used to return to a controlled, balanced state. During the competition, depending on the specific sport and position within it, brief periods or lapses in play allow for momentary relaxation as needed. The athlete must learn to become aware of tension and activation levels and adjust them as necessary.

In addition, learning skills and strategies for a sport can be enhanced when one is in a relaxed state, particularly if periods of learning are alternated with periods of relaxation. This is true for academic learning as well as athletic learning. Doing a quick momentary relaxation exercise also facilitates concentration and imagery practice because it eliminates or reduces other thoughts and stimulation that interfere with the needed single-minded focus.

Reviews of research findings clearly indicate the effectiveness of relaxation techniques in enhancing sport performance (Greenspan & Feltz, 1989; Meyers, Whelan, & Murphy, 1996).

For example, the Meyers et al. meta-analysis identified 25 relaxation interventions that combined for an effect size of .73 ($SD = 1.64$, $p < .01$). Little is known, however, about the relative effectiveness of different relaxation techniques. Nor do we know much about individual differences among athletes in their success at relaxing, their preferences for different relaxation techniques, and their willingness to practice the techniques.

Research with nonathlete populations does offer possible insights for teaching relaxation skills to athletes. After reviewing studies with a nonathlete population, Lehrer and Woolfolk (1993) concluded that individuals with an internal locus of control and positive expectancy for success master relaxation techniques more easily and adhere better to outside practice regimens. Their own work suggested that individuals enjoyed meditating more than practicing progressive relaxation (PR), and that they enjoyed PR more than autogenic training (AT). They cautioned, however, that these were group differences and that some individuals preferred to meditate, others to relax their muscles, others to talk about their thoughts and feelings, and so forth. These nonathlete findings suggest that for maximum effectiveness in teaching relaxation skills athletes will need exposure to several relaxation techniques and convincing that, with practice, they can learn to recognize and, at will, get rid of detrimental tension and its unwanted consequences.

When choosing the potentially most effective techniques to practice, you may want to consider matching the stress management intervention with the precise mode of the anxiety response because some evidence exists in the fields of behavioral medicine and sport psychology that greater reduction in muscular problems follows muscular interventions and that disorders that primarily involve cognitive processes tend to respond particularly well to cognitive therapies (Lehrer, Carr, Sarganaraj, & Woolfolk, 1993; Maynard, Hemmings, & Warwick-Evans, 1995; Maynard, Warwick-Evans, & Smith, 1995). More often than not, however, anxiety problems manifest themselves both cognitively and somatically. Under these circumstances, the most effective intervention will integrate physical and cognitive techniques. Even without an integrated approach, some crossover benefit often occurs; that is, reducing cognitive anxiety helps the body release physical tension and eliminating unwanted physical tension helps lessen cognitive anxiety.

This chapter primarily discusses physical stress management interventions. See Chapter 15 for a discussion of cognitive interventions that athletes can use to build confidence and manage stress resulting from self-doubt and worry. Although some overlap exists, the techniques of relaxation in this chapter can be divided into two categories. The first category includes techniques that focus on the bodily aspects, the **muscle-to-mind techniques.** Breathing exercises and Jacobson's (1930) neuromuscular relaxation or progressive relaxation (PR) fall into this category. One objective of PR is to train the muscles to become sensitive to any level of tension and to be able to release that tension. The second category of techniques works from **mind-to-muscle.** Meditation, autogenic training, and imagery all approach relaxation from the mind-to-muscle perspective. Either approach is effective; the point is to disrupt the stimulus–response pattern of half of the nerves leading to the brain or away from the brain. Learning to reduce the sensation in either half of the circuit will interrupt the stimulation necessary to produce unwanted muscular tension.

Relaxation skills must be practiced on a regular basis just like any sport skill. When teaching relaxation to athletes, it is more effective to begin the training after a workout because it is easier to release muscular tension when physically fatigued. In addition, exercise is nature's best tranquilizer and tends to lower general anxiety and tension. As previously mentioned, some athletes take longer to develop relaxation skills than others, but most should show improvement within a week or two of regular practice. Emphasize the fact that it takes time to develop the skills, and encourage athletes to continue to practice for several weeks even though they may not always detect improvement.

Muscle-to-Mind Relaxation Skills and Strategies

Most athletes respond positively to muscle-to-mind techniques, perhaps because of their more physical lifestyle. When first learning these relaxation techniques, athletes should be in a comfortable position and in a quiet, warm environment. Once athletes are trained, they can practice and should be able to relax in any environment under any condition.

Breathing Exercises[1]

You have been breathing since you were born, but are you really very good at it? Quite possibly not, according to medical experts, who blame breathing habits for ills ranging from anxiety to common physical ailments. Breathing properly is relaxing, and it facilitates performance by increasing the amount of oxygen in the blood, thereby carrying more energy to the muscles and facilitating removal of waste products. Unfortunately, many individuals have never learned deep, diaphragmatic (belly) breathing, and those who have often find their breathing patterns disrupted under stress. Athletes who get stressed out during a high-pressure performance situation find their breathing is usually affected in one of two ways—they either hold their breath or breathe rapidly and shallowly from the upper chest. Both of these adjustments create even more tension and impairment of performance.

Exercise for increasing awareness of ineffective breathing:

Raise your shoulders way up and notice what happens to your breathing. This posture forces your breathing to move into just the upper chest and to become rapid and shallow.

---

[1] Several of these exercises are adaptations from Mason (1980).

Fortunately, with practice, breathing is one of the easiest physiological systems to control. Learning to take a deep, slow, complete breath from the belly will usually trigger a relaxation response. This breath is the basis for a variety of breathing exercises. Depending on the exercise and how it is practiced, the following techniques can be used for both deep and momentary relaxation. Some coaches and sport psychologists even choreograph breaths into the performance of certain skills such as gymnastic and figure skating routines.

Complete breath.   Proper breathing comes from the *diaphragm,* the thin muscle that separates the lung and abdominal cavities. With a complete breath, the diaphragm pulls down causing the belly to expand and a vacuum to occur in the lungs, thus filling the lungs up from the bottom. To facilitate learning what this feels like, forcefully empty all the air from the lungs and notice what happens on the next inhalation. When practicing a complete breath, have the athletes imagine that their lungs are divided into three levels and that inhalation occurs in three steps. First, fill the lower section of the lungs with air by relaxing the belly and letting it gently swell out as you deeply inhale from the diaphragm. Next, fill the middle portion of the lungs by expanding the chest cavity and raising the rib cage. Finally, bring the breath (air) all the way to the top of the lungs by raising the collarbones and widening the shoulder blades. All three inhalation stages progress continuously and smoothly. Once athletes are comfortable with this sequential inhalation, emphasize taking a long, slow, deep inhalation through the nose, inhaling as much air as possible.

During the exhalation, emphasize feeling as if the air drains out of the bottom of the lungs. First empty the top of the lungs, then the rib-cage area, and finally the lower part of the lungs. To force out the last bit of air from the lungs, pull the belly in even further. The exhalation should be long, slow, and complete and result in all tension leaving the body as the air is fully exhaled. Stress to the athletes that they feel the stillness and calm at the moment directly after fully exhaling, as this is the quietest or calmest time of the breath. If athletes can feel this quietness, they are learning how to relax. Whenever athletes get too tense, they should try to recreate this moment of peace and calm by momentarily practicing this exercise.

Exercise for confirming diaphragmatic breathing:

Put one hand on your abdomen and the other on your upper chest. If you are taking a deep, complete breath from the diaphragm, the hand on your abdomen will move out with the inhalation and in with the exhalation, while the hand on the chest remains relatively still.

After learning the procedure, the athletes should take at least 30 to 40 deep breaths each day. Associating deep breathing with events that naturally occur during the day, such as answering the phone or waiting for class to begin, will facilitate practice. Some stress therapists suggest affixing a tiny colored paper disc to a person's wristwatch dial so that each time the person looks at the watch, he or she is reminded to relax by taking a deep breath. Another good time for athletes to practice this breathing exercise is when they need momentary relaxation during competition, such as before a free throw shot, tennis serve, or golf putt.

Sighing with exhalation. Sighing aids in reducing tension. Instruct the athletes as follows: "Exhale completely through the mouth, making an audible sigh. Then close the mouth and inhale quietly through the nose to a count of four. Then hold your breath for a count of seven, feeling the tension building in the throat and chest. Exhale audibly through the mouth to the count of eight as you let go of the tension in the rib cage." Repeat the cycle until the desired level of relaxation is achieved.

Rhythmic breathing. Have the athletes inhale to a count of 4, hold for a count of 4, exhale to a count of 4, and pause for a count of 4 before repeating the sequence. You can alter the rhythm of their breathing by changing the count.

1:2 ratio. Have the athletes take a deep, full breath and then exhale fully and completely. Have them breathe again, only this time to a count of 4 on the inhalation and a count of 8 on the exhalation. If the athletes run out of breath before reaching 8, suggest that next time they take a deeper breath and exhale more slowly. Emphasize awareness of a full inhalation and exhalation. With more practice and deepened relaxation on the part of the athletes, you may need to change the count to 5:10 or 6:12. This exercise creates a very powerful relaxation response if done properly.

5-to-1 count. Instruct the athletes as follows: "Say to yourself and visualize the number 5 as you take a deep, full, slow breath. Exhale fully and completely. Mentally count and visualize the number 4 with your next inhalation. During the exhalation, say to yourself, 'I am more relaxed now than I was at number 5.' Do not rush the thought. Inhale while mentally counting and visualizing the number 3. With the exhalation, say to yourself, 'I am more relaxed now than I was at number 4.' Allow yourself to feel the deepening relaxation. Continue until you reach number 1. As you approach number 1, you should feel totally calm and relaxed." The complete exercise takes 1 to 2 minutes. If done properly, it should lead to more relaxation than practicing a single complete breath. Use this exercise before or during practices and competition, depending on how much time is available and how much relaxation is needed.

Concentration breathing. Have the athletes concentrate on focusing their attention on their breathing rhythm. Tell them that if their mind wanders to some other thought between inhaling and exhaling to redirect their attention back to their next breath, letting the intruding thought disappear. Instruct them to think of becoming more relaxed with each exhalation as they continue to focus on the rhythm of their breathing. This is a good exercise for athletes to practice when they are having problems with distracting thoughts.

Progressive Relaxation Exercises[2]

Working under the assumption that an anxious mind cannot exist within a relaxed body, Jacobson (1930) developed the concept of **progressive relaxation (PR)**, another muscle-to-mind approach to relaxation. PR consists of a series of exercises that involve contracting a specific muscle group, holding the contraction for 5–7 seconds, then relaxing. The exercises progress from one muscle group to another. The contraction phase teaches an awareness and sensitivity to what muscular tension feels like. The letting go, or relaxation phase, teaches an awareness of what absence of tension feels like and that it can voluntarily be induced by passively releasing the tension in a muscle. Thus, in the learning process, one simply identifies a local state of tension, relaxes it away, and then contrasts the tension sensations with the ensuing relaxation that comes from the elimination of tension. By practicing this internal sensory observation, the athlete can become quite proficient at recognizing unwanted tension sensations wherever they may occur and can then easily release the tension. The ultimate goal of PR is for athletes to develop *automaticity,* whereby they automatically, unconsciously, and effortlessly identify and relax tensions that interfere with the smooth execution of movement skills. At a minimum, the athletes should be able to do PR on a conscious level.

The program devised by Jacobson to train relaxation was so lengthy and painstaking (e.g., first 7 days on just the left arm) that many modifications have been developed over the years. For many of the modified procedures, including the one in this chapter, initial practices require only

25–30 minutes and entail relaxing all the muscle groups. Once skill is acquired, shorter practice sessions and variations can occur.

The coach or others knowledgeable about relaxation should lead the PR exercises. Tape recordings of instructions are available, but coaches and sport psychologists can make the instructions more relevant to a particular sport and situation, plus evidence exists that live presentations are more effective than tape-recorded ones (Paul & Trimble, 1970). Encourage athletes to practice daily on their own (not within an hour after eating a meal) in order to improve skill and reap the relaxation benefits. Providing athletes with tapes or written handouts of relaxation exercises may facilitate the likelihood of practicing, but discourage reliance on tapes. With increased experience, these will not be needed.

Begin the relaxation session in a normal, conversational tone but, over the course of the session, your voice should progressively and subtly become smoother, quieter, and more monotonous while giving the relaxation phase instructions. In contrast, during the tension phase, your voice should increase slightly in volume and speed. These changes in voice will help athletes contrast the sensations of tension and relaxation.

Pace the instructions by doing the exercises with the athletes. Pause about 20 to 30 seconds after each contraction so relaxation can continue for brief periods. Tense larger muscle groups longer than the smaller ones. Repetition is the key to learning, so continue to practice until the athletes can quickly and deeply relax each muscle group without producing tension elsewhere. Before you begin, explain to the athletes why excessive physical tension occurs, how it interferes with effective movement (e.g., finger tap technique previously described), and how they can, with practice, learn to recognize and eliminate unwanted tension. Also explain that muscle twitches and spasms are to be expected as muscle fibers begin to let go. On occasion, this even happens just before one falls asleep a tremendous buildup of muscular tension has occurred and the flexor pair lets go before the extensors, resulting in a sudden jerk throughout the body.

[2] Several of these exercises are adaptations from Bernstein and Carlson (1993).

If you are working with a single athlete or a small group, you may want the participants to signal when they are fully relaxed by raising a finger. As they become proficient in relaxing, there is a tendency not to follow instructions. Emphasize the importance of following instructions passively. This is particularly essential during the relaxation phase. Just let the relaxation happen—don't force it. Relaxation requires no effort—just let go of the muscle contraction. Any effort to relax causes tension. "The process of relaxing is one in which the individual gives up the tension—just lets it go and allows the muscle fibers to elongate" (McGuigan, 1993, p. 39).

Practice PR either sitting or lying down. The latter is usually more conducive to relaxation, but athletes should sit up if they tend to fall asleep. The lying down position is on the back with the head, neck, and trunk in a straight line. The legs should be straight and 6–12 inches apart with the heels inward and the toes pointing outward. Rest the arms comfortably at the sides with the hands a little way from the thighs, palms up, and fingers comfortably bent. Put a small pillow (rolled up sweats are a good substitute) under either the knees or neck (not both) for additional comfort. If using a sitting position the athletes should sit upright, hips against the backrest, with the arms and legs uncrossed and the feet flat on the floor. The hands rest comfortably on the thighs (palms down). If no chairs are available, athletes can lean against the gymnasium wall.

Athletes wearing hard contact lenses can either remove them or keep their eyes open while practicing PR. They should also remove or loosen any constrictive clothing such as belts or shoes. The body should be completely supported by the chair, floor, mat, or whatever is being used. Regardless of which PR exercise is being practiced, the preceding protocol is a good one to follow.

Active PR.   Read the following script but keep your voice from sounding canned: "Sit or lie down in a comfortable position and try to put yourself in a relaxed state. Close your eyes and take a long, slow, deep breath through your nose, inhaling as much air as you can. Then exhale slowly and completely, feeling the tension leaving your body as you exhale. Take another deep breath and let the day's tensions and problems drain out of you with the exhalation. [Pause.] Relax as much as possible and listen to what I say. Remember not to strain to relax. Just let it happen. During the session, try not to move any more than necessary to stay comfortable. Particularly, try not to move muscles that have already been relaxed.

"As we progress through each of 12 muscle groups, you will first tense the muscle group for approximately 5 to 7 seconds and then relax for 20–30 seconds. Do not start the tensing until I say 'NOW.' Continue to tense until I say 'OKAY.' or 'RELAX,' at which time immediately let go of all the tension.

"Begin with tensing the muscles in the dominant hand and lower arm by making a tight fist and bending your hand back at the wrist NOW. Feel the tension in the hand and up into the lower arm. . . . Okay, relax by simply letting go of the tension. Notice the difference between tension and relaxation [pause 20 to 30 seconds]. . . . Make another fist NOW [pause 5 to 7 seconds]. Okay, relax. Just let the relaxation happen by stopping the contraction; don't put out any effort [pause 25 to 30 seconds].

"Next tense the muscles of the dominant upper arm by pushing your elbow down against the floor or back of the chair. Tense NOW. Feel the tension in the biceps without involving the muscles in the lower arm and hand. . . . Okay, release the tension all at once, not gradually. Just let it happen. Let it all go. . . . Tense NOW. . . .Okay, release it. Contrast the difference between tension and letting go into relaxation. Relaxation is no more than the absence of tension.

"With your nondominant hand, make a tight fist and bend your wrist back NOW. Feel the tension in your hand and lower arm, but keep the upper arm relaxed. . . . Okay, relax by simply draining all of the tension out. . . . NOW tense again. . . . Okay, relax and feel the difference between the tension and relaxation. . . . NOW push the elbow down or back to tighten the nondominant upper arm. . . . Okay, relax. . . . NOW tense the upper arm again. Note the discomfort. . . .

RELAX. Let all the tension dissolve away. . . . Enjoy the feelings of relaxation. . . . Notice the sensations you have in the muscles of both arms and hands. . . . Perhaps there is a sort of flow of relaxation—perhaps a feeling of warmth and even heaviness in these muscles. Notice and enjoy this feeling of relaxation.

"Turn your attention to the muscles in your face. Tense the muscles in your forehead by raising your eyebrows NOW. Feel the tension in your forehead and scalp. [Pause for only 3- to 5-second contractions with these smaller muscle groups.] Okay, relax and smooth it out. . . . Enjoy the spreading sensation of relaxation. . . . NOW frown again. . . . RELAX. Allow your forehead to become smooth again. . . . Your forehead should feel smooth as glass. . . .

"Next squint your eyes very tightly and at the same time pucker your lips and clinch your teeth, but not so tightly that it hurts. Tense NOW. Feel the tension. . . . Okay, relax. . . . Let the tension dissolve away. . . . NOW tense again. . . . Okay, let all the tension go. . . . Your lips may part slightly as your cheeks and jaw relax.

"Next tense the muscles of the neck and shoulders by raising your shoulders upward as high as you can while pulling your neck down into your shoulders. Tense NOW. . . . feel the discomfort. . . . RELAX. Drop your shoulders back down and feel the relaxation spreading through your neck, throat, and shoulders. . . . Let go more and more. . . . Tense NOW by raising your shoulders and sinking your neck. . . . Okay, relax. Let go more and more. Enjoy the deepening sensation of relaxation. . . . Remember relaxation is simply the absence of tension.

"Next tighten your abdomen as though you expect a punch while simultaneously squeezing the buttocks together. Tense NOW. You should feel a good deal of tightness and tension in the stomach and buttocks. . . . RELAX, release the tension, let it all drain out. Just let it happen. . . . NOW tense again. . . . Okay, relax. Feel the spreading sensation of relaxation. Let go more and more. . . .

"Turn your attention to your legs. Tighten the muscles in your thighs by simultaneously contracting all the muscles of your thighs. Tense NOW. Try to localize the tension only to your thighs. . . . Note the sensation. Okay, relax. Contrast the tension and relaxation sensations. Remember relaxation is merely the absence of tension; it takes no effort except merely releasing the tension. . . . NOW tighten the thighs again. . . . Okay, release the tension—just passively let it drain out. Enjoy the feeling of relaxation. . . .

"Next flex your ankle as though you are trying to touch your toes to your shin. Tense NOW. You should be feeling tension all through your calf, ankle, and foot. Contrast this tension with when you tensed the thigh. Okay, relax. Simply release the tension; let go of any remaining tension. . . . NOW tense again. . . . Okay, slowly release all the tension. . . .

"Next straighten your legs and point your toes downward. Tense NOW. Note the discomfort. . . . Okay, relax. Feel the spreading sensation of relaxation as you relax deeper and deeper. . . . NOW straighten your legs. . . . RELAX. Release all the tension. Let go more and more. . . .

"Relax all the muscles of your body—let them all go limp. You should be breathing slowly and deeply. Let all last traces of tension drain out of your body. You may notice a sensation of warmth and heaviness throughout your body, as though you are sinking deeper and deeper into the chair or floor. Or you may feel as though you are as light as air, as though you are floating on a cloud. Whatever feelings you have, go with them. . . . Enjoy the sensation of relaxation. . . . Relax deeper and deeper. . . . Scan your body for any places that might still feel tension. Wherever you feel tension, do an additional tense and relax.

"Before opening your eyes, take several deep breaths and feel the energy and alertness flowing back into your body. Stretch your arms and legs if you wish. Open your eyes when you are ready."

Take several minutes to discuss athletes' reactions to this PR exercise. Get them to identify what it felt like and how successful they thought they were at relaxing. For those who had difficulty relaxing, stress again the importance of the absence of efforting, of being passive and just letting it happen. Also remind them of the need to practice regularly. Just like any physical skill, PR takes practice. See if any of the athletes became aware of places in their body where they tend to hold tension. The goal is to spot this tension and release it before it leads to headaches and backaches, or performance problems. When taking an athlete or team through a PR exercise, signs to look for that indicate difficulty relaxing are frowning, darting eyes, exaggerated or rapid breathing, and habits of fidgeting (McGuigan, 1993). When too many of these occur, or they occur frequently, stop the PR exercise and discuss what is causing difficulty. When resuming practice, it may be necessary to take more time to try and learn how to relax the given muscle group.

Have the athletes practice this lengthy active PR exercise daily for several weeks or until they gain some proficiency. If less time is available, and when they become more proficient, do only one repetition of each muscle group. In successive practices, put progressively more emphasis on keeping the rest of the body totally relaxed while tensing only the muscle group in question. Once athletes have achieved some skill, have them practice the differential PR procedure described in the next section.

Differential PR.   The differential PR exercise is performed with the same sequence of muscle groups as the preceding exercise. The difference is in the amount of tension generated. Rather than doing an all-out contraction twice for each muscle group, do an initial all-out contraction followed by relaxation; then generate half as much tension and relax, and finally just enough tension to identify and let it go. Thus, differential active PR consists of studying and releasing tension of ever-decreasing intensity. Throughout the exercise, stress that tension should only occur in the muscle group being contracted and only at the predetermined level of intensity.

As noted earlier, relaxing all muscle groups as completely as one can almost never occurs in sport; neither does just total muscle contraction. Differential relaxation is far more common. **Differential relaxation** involves learning to relax all of the muscles except those that are needed for the task at hand. The muscles that are used should only be tensed to the level needed. Learning appropriate differential relaxation leads not only to better performance but also to less fatigue. With proper training in the active PR exercise, followed by practice of this exercise, athletes can better accomplish differential relaxation during practice and competition, as well as throughout the day, because they become more sensitive to the slightest unwanted tension in different muscle groups and more confident in their ability to control the level of tension.

Abbreviated active PR.   Once the athletes have learned the PR technique, you can have them use a shorter procedure to achieve deep muscle relaxation by combining some of the muscle groups. Tense each group for 5 to 10 seconds and then relax for 30 to 40 seconds. Read the following directions:

> "Make a tight fist with both hands, tighten the biceps and forearms, hold. . . and relax. . . .
>
> "Tense all of the facial and neck muscles. . . . Relax. . . .
>
> "Raise the shoulders while making the stomach hard and tightening the buttocks. HOLD. . . . Relax and let go. . . . [Give the instructions quickly so the tension buildup is continuous.]
>
> "Tighten the muscles of both legs and feet by straightening your legs and pointing your toes. HOLD. . . . Relax and let go of all the tension. . . ."

It you think the preceding procedure might require too big of a jump for the athletes, modify it by doing each arm separately and each leg separately. Once the athletes can successfully do the abbreviated exercise, which, according to Bernstein and Carlson (1993), normally takes several weeks of practice, an even shorter version is to have the athletes put as much tension as possible into the entire body. Hold this total body tension 5 to 10 seconds, and then completely release the tension, letting go into a totally relaxed state. Repeat this procedure several times, trying to deepen the relaxation state with each successive practice. Just as with the longer PR exercise, individuals will benefit from practicing the abbreviated PR exercises with the differential contraction protocol rather than just an all-out contraction.

Passive PR.   Once the athletes have learned the skill of active, deep muscle relaxation, they can relax the muscles without first tensing them. Many people find this passive form of relaxation more effective and pleasant than the active form. With passive PR, the participant merely lets go from whatever level of muscular tension is in the muscle group. There is a slow progression from one part of the body to another as the participant relaxes each body part more deeply by letting go of any remaining tension. The same sequence of complete or abbreviated body parts can be used for passive PR as for active PR.

After a general lead-in to the exercise, progress through the specific body parts with directions such as the following: "Turn your attention to your dominant hand. Just tune in to how this hand feels. Become aware of any tension that might be in it and let go of the tension—even more and more. Let go of all the muscles in your dominant hand. Allow it gradually to become looser and heavier. Think about letting go further. Now go to your nondominant hand. Think of your nondominant hand getting looser, heavier, just letting go of the muscles in your nondominant hand. Let go further, more deeply, and now feel the relaxation coming into your left and right forearms. Feel your forearms getting looser and heavier. Enjoy the relaxation that is now coming into your forearms. . . ."

Quick body scan.   The quick body scan is an abbreviated passive PR technique that is a helpful momentary muscle relaxation exercise best used during performance, such as just before serving, shooting a free throw, batting, or even while running, particularly middle or long distances. Quickly scan the body from head to toe (or toe to head). Stop only at muscle groups where the tension level is too high. Release the tension and continue the scan down (or up) the body.

Neck and shoulder check.   It is very common for athletes to carry excessive tension in the neck and shoulders when they are worried or anxious. Once they have learned to spot tension and relax, instruct your athletes to scan their neck and shoulders periodically for any undue signs of tension. If they feel tension in the neck, they should tense and relax or release it passively. Releasing excessive tension in these two areas tends to spread relaxation to the rest of the body; it may also have a calming effect on the mind.

Sport muscle check.   This momentary exercise is identical to the preceding but substitute whatever muscle group is most appropriate for the sport skill. Fox example, batters could squeeze their bat and golfers their club followed by relaxing to the appropriate level.

Mind-to-Muscle Relaxation Techniques

Other relaxation techniques and strategies focus on **efferent nerve control,** or the stimulation from the brain to the muscles. Among these techniques are meditation, visualization, and autogenic training. The techniques should be practiced initially in a comfortable position in a quiet environment. Any of the positions suggested for progressive relaxation practice can be used.

Meditation

The regular practice of meditation helps one achieve a state of deep relaxation, and it facilitates concentration by disciplining the mind. Four basic components are common to most types of meditation: a quiet environment, a comfortable position, a mental device, and a passive attitude. A mental device, such as a mantra or fixed gazing at an object, helps to quiet the mind by providing a focus of attention on something that is nonarousing and nonstimulating. A **mantra** is a nonstimulating, meaningless rhythmic sound of one or two syllables that a person regularly repeats while meditating.

It is critical that athletes not worry about how well they are performing the technique because this disrupts effective meditation. Again, emphasizing a "let it happen" attitude. The passive attitude is perhaps the most important element in learning to meditate. Distracting thoughts or mind wandering may occur, but this is to be expected and does not mean that the technique is being performed incorrectly. When these thoughts occur, simply redirect attention to the mental device, focusing on this cue and letting all other thoughts move on through consciousness with a passive attitude, making no attempt to attend to them.

The **relaxation response** developed by Herbert Benson (1975), a physician at Harvard Medical School, is an excellent meditative technique to teach athletes. This technique is a generalized version of Eastern transcendental mediation, but without reference to mysticism and unusual postures. In fact, to further eliminate any religious or cultic connotation, the technique does not even need to be called meditation. For a mental device, Benson recommended the word *one, but that* is a very stimulating word for achievement-oriented athletes. A better word might be *calm* or a word/sound of their choosing. Directions for meditation based on a variation of Benson's relaxation response follow:

1. Sit in a comfortable position in a quiet place.

2. Close your eyes.

3. Deeply relax all your muscles, beginning at the top of your head and progressing to your feet (feet to head if you prefer). Keep them relaxed.

4. Concentrate on your breathing as you breathe easily and naturally through your nose. With each breath out, say the word *calm* or some other word or nonsense sound silently to yourself.

5. When you finish, sit quietly for several minutes, at first with your eyes closed and later with your eyes open. Do not stand for a few minutes.

Do the preceding for 5 minutes initially and, with practice, build to 15–20 minutes. Do not use an alarm, but you can open your eyes to check the time. Do not worry about whether you are successful in achieving a deep level of relaxation. Try to remain passive by just letting the relaxation happen. Practice the technique once or twice daily, but not within one hour after any meal, since the digestive processes seem to interfere with the elicitation of the relaxation response.

Visualization

If athletes have imagery skills, visualizing being in a place conducive to relaxation is another successful technique for eliciting relaxation. For example, an athlete might visualize lying on a beach feeling the warm sand and sun on the body while listening to the continuous rhythm of breaking waves and smelling the salt air. Other images might be sitting in the midst of a beautiful mountain scene or lying in a grassy valley by a gentle, gurgling stream. Whatever image provides the athlete with a sense of calm and relaxation is the one he or she should use.

Autogenic training.[3] Developed in Germany in the early 1930s by Johannes Schultz, **autogenic training** has been used extensively with European athletes. The training consists of a series of exercises designed to produce two physical sensations typically associated with relaxation—warmth and heaviness. Basically, it is a technique of autohypnosis or self-hypnosis. It focuses attention on the sensations one is trying to produce. As in meditation, it is important to let the feeling happen in a very passive manner. There are six stages in the training. Learn each stage before progressing to the next stage. Some people suggest that trainees spend 2 weeks each on stages 1–3 and 1 week each on stages 4–6; however, the progression can be modified to suit athletes' learning rates as well as the training program and length of season of the sport. It usually takes several months of 10 to 40 minutes of daily practice, spread across one to six sessions, to become proficient enough to experience heaviness and warmth in the limbs and to produce the

[3] Some of these exercises have been modified from Linden (1993).

sensation of a relaxed, calm heartbeat and respiratory rate accompanied by warmth in the abdomen and coolness in the forehead. Once athletes have reached that level of training and can attain a relaxed state, they can use imagery to increase the depth of relaxation.

The first autogenic stage involves focusing attention in a passive manner on the dominant arm while silently saying: (1) "My right (left) arm is heavy" (repeat phrase six times); (2) "I am calm" (or, "I am at peace") (optional and said only once and then alternates with the first step until completing three to six cycles of these two steps). Then cancel out the effect by having the athletes bend the arm, take a deep breath, and open their eyes. The canceling out should always occur with each part of the heaviness stage, and the following stages, in order to ultimately maximize the effect. Practice just the preceding two or three sessions a day (it takes only 1 or 2 minutes each time) until the heaviness starts to spread to the opposite arm. When this occurs, replace "my right arm" with "my left arm" and, once effective, "my arms." Once the heaviness starts to generalize to the legs, replace "my arms" with "my legs are heavy" and, once effective, "my arms and legs are heavy." Ultimately, the entire body starts to feel heavy. If the mind wanders, emphasize passively redirecting attention back to the task at hand. Some athletes may be able to produce a sense of heaviness immediately; others may take 1 or 2 weeks of three or more times of practice daily to accomplish the sensation.

Once the heaviness experience has been well trained and can be induced rapidly and reliably, move on to the second stage, which is warmth and may take longer to achieve. Instructions for the warmth stage follow the same general content and format as the first stage except "heavy" is replaced with "warmth." Before practicing the warmth phrases, however, begin by repeating the final suggestion for the preceding stage:

1. "My arms and legs are heavy" (repeat six times).

2. "I am calm" (or "at peace"; say only once).

3. "My right (left) arm is warm" (and so forth, as done in stage one).

If athletes are having difficulty feeling the appropriate sensation, facilitate learning by having them first physically experience the sensation. For example, if trying to achieve heaviness in the right arm, put a pillow over the arm and, if need be, a book or two on top of the pillow. For the warmth sensation, have the athletes immerse their hands in hot water or put a heating pad or hot water bottle over the hands while they initially do the exercise.

Regulation of the heartbeat is the third stage. It consists of the autosuggestion, "My heartbeat is regular and calm" or "My heart is beating quietly and strongly." Because awareness of heart activity varies considerably among people, you may need to sensitize the trainees to their own heart activity by having them put their hand over their heart when initially doing the exercise. Again, follow the same careful and progressive procedure as that described previously, only this time begin with the phrase, "My arms and legs are heavy. My arms and legs are warm." Follow the same type of protocol for the fourth, fifth, and sixth stages, which consist of the following:

Stage 4: Breathing rate
"My breathing rate is slow, calm, and relaxed: It breathes me."

Stage 5: Warmth in the solar plexus
"My solar plexus is warm" (hand placed on upper abdominal area); or say, "Sun rays are streaming quiet and warm."

Stage 6: Coolness of the forehead
"My forehead is cool."

During Stage 4, the trainee becomes aware of the breathing rate but does not try consciously to change it. Stage 5 deals with self-regulation of the visceral organs. The trainee focuses on the area of the solar plexus because it is the most important nerve center for the inner organs. You may prefer the second phrase because it helps to depict the image that this nerve center is that of a sun from which warm rays extend into the other body areas (Linden, 1993). The well-known relaxing effect of a cool cloth on the forehead forms the basis for Stage 6. Just as warmth is associated with vasodilation, the experience of coolness on the forehead leads to a localized vasoconstriction.

Once the athlete has learned all the stages, the entire sequence can be practiced as follows:

"My arms and legs are heavy" six times; "I am calm" once.

"My arms and legs are warm" six times; "I am calm" once.

"My heartbeat is regular and calm" six times; "calm" once.

"It breathes me" six times; "calm" once.

"Sun rays are streaming quiet and warm" six times; "calm" once.

"My forehead is cool" six times; "calm" once.

Autogenic Training with Visualization

After athletes have mastered the six stages of autogenic training and can induce the desired state in a few minutes and sustain it for 30 minutes to an hour, they are ready to move to the next phase of training, which combines autogenic exercises with visualization. The progression goes from first doing the autogenic exercise to then visualizing the desired feeling or objective. For example, an athlete might build confidence by imaging some peak performance when everything went just right. An athlete might program success by imaging her- or himself performing exactly the proper execution of a skill or strategy for an upcoming competition. The visualization applications are without limit, but the athlete must first gain skill at imagery if he or she lacks it (see Chapter 14).

As indicated earlier, autogenic training takes a relatively long time to master. As a result, it is less popular in the United States. However, prior to the fall of communism, it was used extensively in many Eastern European countries where athletes were housed in sport training centers for several years working with a relatively stable staff of coaches and sports medicine personnel. Despite the time required to become proficient in autogenic training, many athletes

find it a satisfactory means of training for relaxation and imagery. This approach will be particularly appealing to those athletes who respond to autosuggestion.

When Relaxation Training Fails

Sometimes efforts to teach athletes relaxation skills will fail or the athletes may be able to relax when practicing the relaxation skill, but cannot do it when it counts most—during frustrating practices and stressful competitions. There are a number of potential sources for difficulty in learning and achieving relaxation. For example, if the individual teaching the relaxation intervention has not developed sufficient rapport with the athlete, the athlete may not be comfortable enough to consider relaxing, let alone deeply relaxing. An athlete referred by a coach may feel coerced and thus not be a willing participant. Whether from coercion or another source for lack of motivation, a failure to practice relaxation techniques sufficiently and to self-monitor frequently for the need to implement a quick relaxation intervention are common reasons for poor results. Other situations may activate personal issues for the athlete. Someone who feels a great need for personal control or fear of losing control may respond with anxiety when deepening relaxation occurs. In each of the preceding situations, more effective relaxation training would occur if strategies to overcome the difficulties were first introduced.

For athletes who know how to relax but have difficulty doing it in performance situations, more success might occur with greater practice reducing muscular tension in situations that more closely simulate the actual performance environment. An example might be a basketball player who gets really anxious when he has to shoot free throws during critical game times. Having this athlete practice his free throws using imagery that puts him on the foul line with the game on the line could create a more gamelike situation to practice staying relaxed when shooting free throws. The coach may even want to tape crowd noise and play it loudly over the PA system or invite people to watch to create more social evaluation. Teammates waiting their turn to practice could verbally harass the shooter. In this practice situation, the player should precede his shot by relaxing with a deep-breathing technique or a quick body scan followed by a brief imagery (see Chapter 14), wherein he sees himself successfully performing the skill while remaining loose and appropriately focused.

Research suggests that when some high-anxious individuals are in stressful circumstances and try to relax their effort can backfire by producing the ironic effect of intensifying anxiety and tension (Wegner, Broome, & Blumberg, 1997). In other words, just as athletes most want to relax the desire to be calm and collected may be the culprit in creating even more unwanted cognitive anxiety and somatic effects. Wegner (1994, 1997) explains these paradoxical effects with a theory he calls ironic processes of mental control. Doing the opposite of what one intends has been found for not only relaxation but also cognitions (see Chapter 15). Although the implications this theory has for sport psychology research and interventions have been discussed (e.g., see Janelle, 1999), there is no intervention research to suggest how best to deal with athletes suffering from the phenomena, but Wegner et al.'s research findings and suggestions provide some guidance. Their experimental manipulations indicated a less pronounced effect with more detailed relaxation instructions rather than the general comment, "relax." They also suggest that downplaying the importance of mental control, not providing highly motivational instructions, and even capitulating to our anxieties may be more effective than intentional relaxation.

Apter's (1989) reversal theory also offers possible insights into how best to intervene with athletes who experience ironic effects. Apter proposed that athletes in a "telic" (that is, a goal-minded, serious) motivational state are likely to perceive their high arousal as anxiety, whereas athletes in a "paratelic" (i.e., seeking fun, performing for its own sake) state are likely to perceive their high arousal as excitement, not threat. If correct, rather than focusing on trying to reduce the symptoms (e.g., physical tension) of anxiety through relaxation techniques, a better procedure might be helping these athletes put the fun back into sport. Such an approach initially entails identifying the sources of stress and disputing the underlying irrational beliefs or distortions in thinking that probably led to them. The cognitive restructuring intervention (rational emotive therapy) described in Chapter 15 is one excellent method for accomplishing the preceding (see also Kerr, 2001). Once done, the athlete should find it easier to focus on the excitement of competition, having fun, and playing for its own sake. The preceding approach is certainly worth a try but, until more is known, coaches and sport psychologists may well have to use trial and error in trying to help the athletes who need it most to relax.

Skills and Strategies for Learning How to Increase Activation and Energy

Once athletes have been taught how to slow down the heart rate and respiration rate and to increase blood flow and temperature in the extremities, they can also learn to develop skills to speed up the heart rate and respiration rate and get the physiological systems ready for action. These skills are essential for generating energy on short notice or when brief bursts of energy are needed.

Just as there are a variety of effective techniques for decreasing activation, there are many techniques for energizing or increasing activation. Such skills and strategies should be used to build appropriate activation when athletes are not psyched up enough for practice or for competition. They can also be used to reduce fatigue during practice and competition. The coach should encourage athletes to practice and develop these skills and strategies. Not only should athletes identify primary energizing techniques that tend to work for them, but they should have backup techniques for when the primary techniques fail to work. Meyers, Whelan, and Murphy's meta-analysis of sport psychology intervention studies found support for the effectiveness of psych-up procedures in enhancing performance ($n = 5$, $d = 1.23$, $SD = .73$).

First, the athletes need to identify when energizing is generally needed in their particular sport or in specific positions or situations within the sport. The coach and sport psychologist should try to become sensitive to each athlete's optimal level of activation; some athletes are much more likely than others to need energizing. The athletes also need to learn how to recognize signs and symptoms of low energy and activation and where they are located in the body. As an example, a track athlete may need to learn how to energize dead legs during a race. Or a weight lifter may want to put all available energy into the legs and arms to attain a particular lift.

We turn now to 10 specific skills and strategies athletes can use to increase their activation and energy.

Breathing

Breathing control and focus work as effectively in producing energy as in reducing tension. Instruct your athletes to focus on a regular, relaxed breathing rhythm. Now have them consciously increase that rhythm and imagine with each inhalation that they are generating more energy and activation. With each exhalation the athletes should imagine that they are getting rid of any waste products or fatigue that might prevent them from being at their best. Ask them to feel in full control, supplying sufficient oxygen and energy for any task that they have to perform. Having athletes increase their breathing rate increases their level of energy generation. Along with the accelerated breathing rate, athletes may want to say "Energy in" with each inhalation and "Fatigue out" with each exhalation.

Using Energizing Imagery

Literally hundreds of images can be conjured up as cues for generating energy: animal images, machine images, forces of nature, and so on. For example, have athletes imagine they are a train that is just beginning to move, building up steam, momentum, and power with each deep breath. Instruct the athletes to develop a supply of imagery cues that work for them in various situations encountered in their particular sport. Instruct them to establish a plan for using these cues ahead of time and to practice and prepare to use them on a regular basis. Some sports have lapses in action that are conducive to using cues for activation and energizing. Other sports enable using energizing images during actual performance. For example, the author worked with a marathon runner who found imaging herself as "the little engine that could" from a childhood story energized her when she had run out of gas. Energizing imagery is particularly effective when fatigue is beginning to set in, when a series of points have been lost, or when a sudden burst of energy is needed to finish a play.

Formulating Energizing Verbal Cues

In the midst of a performance, verbal cues can be effective energizers. Have the athletes select the word cues that are appropriate to their sport and to the tasks that they perform during competition and that they can quickly associate with energy buildup. Words such as *explode, charge, psych up, go, snap,* and the like are often effective.

Combining Energizing Cues, Images, and Breathing

Raiport (1988), a former Russian sport psychologist, described several exercises that Eastern European sport psychologists teach athletes to help them self-induce activation. Each of these exercises combines a verbal phrase with imagery and a certain breathing pattern. The breathing pattern is one of exhaling on the first part of the phrase and inhaling on the italicized part. For example, take the phrase "I've had *a good rest.*" The most meaningful part of the phrase (in italics) is combined with the inhalation, which is physiologically connected with tensing the muscles and thus facilitates energizing. When time permits, take a two-breath pause between each repetition of the phrase. The following exercises come from Raiport's 1988 book:

"I am breathing *deeper, inhaling energy*" (repeat twice). During the pauses between the phrases, visualize yourself inhaling a tiny cloud of white energy that spreads throughout your entire body. [Some athletes may prefer an energizing color such as red or yellow.]

"My body is *becoming lighter*" (repeat four times). Imagine that the white cloud of energy you inhale is a very light gas, like helium. Feel your body becoming light and energized.

"Strength is *flowing into my body*" (repeat three times). Visualize a stream of vibrating energy pouring into your body with each breath. It fills you with freshness and vigor. Feel yourself overflowing with this purifying energy; it now radiates from every pore of your body. [Some athletes may benefit from giving the stream of vibrating energy an energizing color.]

"I am *vigorous and alert*" (repeat three times). Imagine strength, power, and a keen awareness of life expanding throughout your body.

"My muscles are *quivering with energy*" (repeat four times). Feel your muscles twitching in impatient anticipation for action.

Transferring Energy

Help your athletes learn to convert energy from other sources into a positive and useful force for athletic performance. For example, activation and arousal that result from anger, frustration, or some other emotion that tends to interfere with performance can be converted into positive energy to accomplish performance goals.

Storing Excess Energy for Later Use

Many athletes have found that the strategy of storing excess energy that is frequently generated just prior to competition accomplishes two purposes: It provides them a means of transferring that energy somewhere else, and it provides a well of energy from which to draw on at some later point. If an athlete has a problem with overarousal, suggest that the athlete store away that energy and use it later when he or she feels fatigued or discouraged.

Using the Environment

Some athletes have learned how to draw energy from the spectators to use for their own performance. This type of strategy provides the home team with an advantage. Athletes need to learn how to take all types of energy available in the sport environment and put it to their own use through imagery, word cues, self-talk, and the like. They can even draw energy from their opponents, both when it appears that the opponents have the momentum going for them and when they have clearly lost it.

Listening to Music

Music is both a good relaxer and energy provider, depending on the music selected. With the availability of iPods and the like, athletes can readily select and listen to the music that works best for them. However, when loud music is played over a PA system for everyone to hear, the coach should try to ensure that it is appropriate for the optimal level of activation for all athletes.

Improving Pacing

Athletes become underactivated in some sports because of fatigue. This tiredness is often caused by inappropriate pacing and unnecessary sources of energy drain. The alert coach can spot athletes who have difficulty rationing out their energy over time. Appropriate physical practice plus teaching the athlete to become more sensitive to physical signs and symptoms can improve pacing. Pacing is also improved when unnecessary sources of energy drain are eliminated; these sources include too much muscle tension for a particular skill or situation, anger, frustration such as excessive responses to officiating calls, and anxiety or worry over one's performance or that of teammates.

Using Distraction

Another way to deal with underactivation caused by fatigue is to focus one's attention away from the state of fatigue being experienced. Most athletes do just the opposite; the more fatigued they become, the more they tune into it. This just increases the sense of fatigue as well as its detrimental effects on performance. Instead, suggest to the athletes that they apply their concentration skills and focusing ability on what is happening and about to happen within the performance setting. Remind the athletes to think about what they are doing rather than about how they are feeling. The opposite also can help, such as when long distance runners use disassociation strategies (that is, think about something completely unrelated to running).

Exercise for applying what you know about interventions:

Use the following case studies to design an optimal intervention for the particular scenario described in the case study.

1. David, a football quarterback, goes to a sport psychologist because the demands of professional football have him so stressed that he is having difficulty sleeping. During games, he is so tense that his throws are often erratic and he can't find his secondary receivers. He reports that it seems like he's "looking at the field through a roll of toilet paper." What relaxation interventions might a coach or sport psychology consultant implement to help David? Indicate how to sequence them and describe how they might be practiced.

2. Jeff, a sport psychologist, finds that his relaxation training with Jenny, a promising intercollegiate pitcher, results in ironic processing when she pitches in important games. What is happening to Jenny and how might the sport psychologist help her deal with this consequence?

3. Sue, a high school coach, finds that her team usually competes up to its potential. She is frustrated, however, with their play during practice. She feels that the team's development is not what it could be because the players often lack intensity and focus during practice. What might the coach do to try and correct this problem?

Summary

Coaches and sport psychologists have responsibility to teach athletes strategies and techniques for achieving an optimal level of activation for practice and competition. Acquiring the ability to self-regulate arousal enhances not only learning and performance of sport skills but also functioning in many nonathletic situations.

It is important for coaches to know that poor performance during competition is more frequently a consequence of overactivation than underactivation. All too often coaches assume the opposite and partially contribute to the continuation of the problem by berating athletes to try harder when some calming strategy would prove more appropriate. This chapter has described techniques for achieving total relaxation and momentary or partial relaxation. Such techniques rid the muscles of disruptive tension that interferes with performance and help quiet the rest of the body and the mind. They also promote confidence in the athlete's ability to lessen or eliminate the effects of undesirable feelings and thoughts. Energizing skills and strategies that can be used to increase activation and lessen the effects of fatigue were also described in this chapter.

No single control strategy is effective or desirable for all athletes. Consequently, coaches and sport psychologists will need to teach their athletes a variety of techniques. Athletes should be encouraged to identify and practice the primary techniques that tend to work best for them as well as backup techniques in the event that the primary ones lose their effectiveness.

Finally, although the intervention focus of this chapter has been on athletes, it is equally appropriate for coaches and sport psychologists to use these techniques because activation level also influences their performance. For example, Frey (2007) recently concluded that research and anecdotal evidence, taken together, support the importance of coaches using anxiety control—such control influences their athletes' ability to maintain confidence and control in high-pressure situations.

Study Questions

1. Discuss how relaxation skills are useful to an athlete.
2. Compare conceptually the two major types of relaxation techniques (muscle-to-mind and mind-to-muscle).
3. Give four examples of breathing relaxation techniques and describe when you might use them.
4. Compare and contrast the progressive relaxation techniques (active, passive, differential).
5. Give an example of a meditation relaxation technique.
6. How can visualization be used to achieve relaxation?
7. What is autogenic training, the premise behind it, and its six stages?
8. Briefly describe and give an example of at least six different types of techniques for increasing activation.
9. A sport psychologist is having great difficulty getting Ashley, an elite diver, to learn the skill of deep muscle relaxation. What factors might be contributing to her difficulty in relaxing?

References

Apter, M. J. (1989). *Reversal theory: Motivation, emotion, and personality.* London: Routledge.

Benson, H. (1975). *The relaxation response.* New York: Avon Books.

Bernstein, D. A., & Carlson, C. R. (1993). Progressive relaxation: Abbreviated methods. In P. M. Lehrer & R. L. Woolfolk (Eds.). *Principles and practice of stress management* (2nd ed.) (pp. 53–87). New York: The Guilford Press.

Frey, M. (2007). College coaches' experiences with stress—"problem solvers" have problems, too. *The Sport Psychologist, 21,* 38–57.

Green, E., & Green, A. (1977). *Beyond biofeedback.* New York: Dell.

Greenspan, M. J., & Feltz, D. L. (1989). Psychological interventions with athletes in competitive situations: A review. *The Sport Psychologist, 3,* 219–236.

Jacobson, E. (1930). *Progressive relaxation.* Chicago: University of Chicago Press.

Janelle, C. (1999). Ironic mental processes in sport: Implications for sport psychologists. *The Sport Psychologist, 13,* 201–220.

Kerr, J. H. (2001). *Counseling athletes: Applying reversal theory.* London: Routledge.

Lehrer, P. M., Carr, R., Sarganaraj, D., & Woolfolk, R. L. (1993). Differential effects of stress management therapies in behavioral medicine. In P. M. Lehrer & R. L. Woolfolk (Eds.), *Principles and practice of stress management* (2nd ed.) (pp. 571–605). New York: The Guilford Press.

Lehrer, P. M., & Woolfolk, R. L. (1993). Specific effects of stress management techniques. In P. M. Lehrer & R. L. Woolfolk (Eds.). *Principles and practice of stress management* (2nd ed.) (pp. 481–520). New York: The Guilford Press.

Linden, W. (1993). The autogenic training method of J. H. Schultz. In P. M. Lehrer & R. L. Woolfolk (Eds.), *Principles and practice of stress management* (2nd ed.) (pp. 205–229). New York: The Guilford Press.

Mason, L. J. (1980). *Guide to stress reduction.* Culver City, CA: Peace Press.

Maynard, I. W., Hemmings, B., & Warwick-Evans, L. (1995). The effects of a somatic intervention strategy on competitive state anxiety and performance in semiprofessional soccer players. *The Sport Psychologist, 9,* 51–64.

Maynard, I. W., Warwick-Evans, L., & Smith, M. J. (1995). The effects of a cognitive intervention strategy on competitive state anxiety and performance in semiprofessional soccer players. *Journal of Sport and Exercise Psychology, 17,* 428–446.

McGuigan, F. J. (1993). Progressive relaxation: Origins, principles, and clinical applications. In P. M. Lehrer & R. L. Woolfolk (Eds.). *Principles and practice of stress management* (2nd ed.) (pp. 17–52). New York: The Guilford Press.

Meyers, A. W., Whelan, J. P., & Murphy, S. M. (1996). Cognitive behavioral strategies in athletic performance enhancement. In M. Hersen, R. M. Eisler, & P. M. Miller (Eds.), *Progress in behavioral modification,* Vol. 30 (pp. 137–164). Pacific Grove, CA: Brooks/Cole.

Paul, G. L., & Trimble, R. W. (1970). Recorded vs. "live" relaxation training and hypnotic suggestion: Comparative effectiveness for reducing physiological arousal and inhibiting stress response. *Behavior Therapy, 1,* 285–302.

Raiport, G. (1988). *Red gold peak performance techniques of the Russian and East German Olympic victors.* Los Angeles: Tarcher.

Wegner, D. M. (1994). Ironic processes of mental control. *Psychological Review, 101,* 34–52.

Wegner, D. M. (1996). Why the mind wanders. In J. D. Cohen & J. W. Schooler (Eds.), *Scientific approaches to consciousness* (pp. 295–315), Hillsdale, NJ: Lawrence Erlbaum Associates.

Wegner, D. M., Broome, A., & Blumberg, S. J. (1997). Ironic effects of trying to relax under stress. *Behavioral Research and Therapy, 35,* 11–21.

Seeing Is Believing: Understanding and Using Imagery in Sport

Robin S. Vealey, *Miami University*
Christy A. Greenleaf, *University of North Texas*

We taped a lot of famous pictures on the locker-room door: Bobby Orr, Potvin, Beliveau, all holding the Stanley Cup. We'd stand back and look at them and envision ourselves doing it. I really believe if you visualize yourself doing something, you can make that image come true. . . . I must have rehearsed it ten thousand times. And when it came true it was like an electric jolt went up my spine.

—Wayne Gretzky (as quoted in Orlick, 1998, p. 67)

"I'll believe that when I *see* it!" Have you ever said this? Of course, we've all made this statement numerous times because it's true—seeing *is* believing. It is especially true in relation to our own accomplishments. If you've seen yourself serve well, hit strong ground strokes, and react at the net with crisp volleys in competition, then you believe you're a successful tennis player. Seeing yourself perform well in these circumstances creates positive beliefs about your ability to succeed in sport—seeing is believing.

But do we have to physically experience a skill before we believe we can do it? Absolutely not! Albert Einstein describes how he was able to conceptualize his theory of relativity by visualizing how the world would look to him as he traveled inside a beam of light. Annika Sorenstam,

the top female golfer in the world for several years, explains how she "believes by seeing." "When I'm on the golf course, I see a big green, a huge hole, just the positive things. I don't see out-of-bounds on the left or a water hazard over there. I put the ball on the ground. I see the fairway. I hit it. I just grab a club and trust it."

Tiger Woods's father recalls asking his son, then a second-grader playing in his first international tournament, what he was thinking about on the first tee as he stood with all the other nervous young golfers and prepared to hit his first shot. Tiger's answer was simple: "Where I wanted the ball to go, Daddy." Although Tiger Woods was experiencing his first major competition and could have chosen to worry about embarrassing himself or disappointing his parents, he chose instead to demonstrate exceptional mental skill and simply see himself hitting the ball perfectly.

Albert Einstein, Annika Sorenstam, and Tiger Woods took advantage of their most powerful weapon—their minds. They harnessed the power of imagery to provide the vision they needed to reach the upper limits of human potential. Imagery is simply a mental technique that programs the mind and body to respond optimally. By using imagery as a mental training tool, athletes have the capacity to see and believe, which gives them the confidence and focus to perform successfully. The purpose of this chapter is to introduce imagery as a basic mental training tool that can be used in simple and systematic ways to help athletes perform better.

What Is Imagery?

Imagery may be defined as using one's senses to re-create or create an experience in the mind. Research indicates that when individuals engage in vivid imagery, their brains interpret these images as identical to the actual stimulus situation (Jeannerod, 1994). This is what makes imagery so powerful! An Alpine skier can imagine herself skiing a downhill run, and her brain will interpret her images and fire the muscles in her legs as if she actually was skiing the course (Suinn, 1980). The power of imagery allows athletes to practice sport skills, strategies, and mental skills without physically being in the training or competitive environment.

Imagery as Re-creating or Creating

Through imagery we are able to re-create as well as to create experiences in our mind. Athletes spend a lot of time re-creating their performances in their minds. We all can remember the nights after competition when we went over and over our performances in our heads. Athletes often get stuck in this type of imagery by focusing on their mistakes and failures, and they replay these miscues without any type of planned strategy for dealing with these negative images. The key for athletes is to learn to use imagery in a productive and controlled manner to learn from performance mistakes and to program their minds and bodies to respond optimally.

Re-creating Success

Professional baseball player Todd Helton has a video iPod loaded with clips of each of the 1,509 hits he stroked in his eight major league seasons. Helton states: "It's good to watch right before a game. I can see how each [pitcher] pitched me the last time . . . and I can see my good swings, so I'll have a good feeling going in. I use it on the plane, on the bus, sitting at my locker" (Reiter, 2006, p. 36)). Helton has a career .334 batting average, so several of his teammates have followed his lead and set up their own personal iPod hitting videos.

We can also use imagery to create new experiences in our minds. Although imagery is essentially a product of memory, our brain is able to put the pieces of the internal picture together in different ways. As programmers of their own imagery programs, athletes can build images from whatever pieces of memory they choose. Nancy Kerrigan developed an imagery script to prepare for her figure skating performance in the 1994 Olympic Games. In her mind, Kerrigan created and rehearsed her ideal performance from the dressing room, through her entire routine, to the exhilarating moments after leaving the ice in which she felt intense joy and pride in her accomplishment.

Football quarterbacks may use imagery in this way to create offensive game plans based on the defensive tactics of upcoming opponents. By viewing films of the opponent's defense, a quarterback can create an offensive game plan and visualize the successful execution of this strategy without having previously played against that particular opponent. Coach Tara Van Derveer of the 1996 U.S. Olympic Women's basketball team conducted a mock medal ceremony at the Olympic basketball arena in Atlanta months before the Olympic Games so that each player experienced the gold medal being placed around her neck. Van Derveer wanted her athletes to create in their minds the emotional exhilaration of winning the gold medal to enhance their motivational drive and commitment. Of course, several months later, they all got to experience the thrill of winning the gold medal for real! Athletes should use imagery to prepare mentally for hostile crowds on the road or difficult travel conditions by creating effective responses to questions such as, "What will it be like?" and "How will you respond?" Research shows that elite athletes create mental focus plans for competition and regularly mentally practice these plans for the way they will respond productively to various competitive stressors (Greenleaf, Gould, & Dieffenbach, 2001).

Imagery as a Polysensory Experience

The second key to understanding imagery is realizing that imagery is a **polysensory** experience that should involve all relevant senses, from visual to auditory, olfactory, gustatory, tactile, and kinesthetic. Auditory refers to sound, such as hearing the crack of the bat in baseball or the sweet sound of a perfect golf drive. Olfactory refers to smell, such as a swimmer smelling chlorine in the pool. Tactile is the sensation of touch, such as feeling the grip of a golf club or the textured leather of a basketball. Gustatory refers to the sense of taste, such as tasting salty sweat in your mouth. **Kinesthetic** sense is the feel or sensation of the body as it moves in different positions. The kinesthetic sense would be important for a gymnast using imagery to practice a balance beam routine or a diver using imagery to feel the rotations before reaching for the water. The more vivid the image, the more effective it is. Let's use the example of a wide receiver in football to stress the importance of using different senses. The receiver uses his visual sense to read the defense and focus on the ball before catching it. He uses his auditory sense to listen to the snap count barked by the quarter back. He uses his tactile and kinesthetic senses to run his pattern, jump in the air, catch a hard thrown ball, and touch both feet inbounds. He might also smell freshly mown grass and the sweat of his opponent's jersey when he is tackled. He may even taste the saltiness of his own sweat. All senses should be utilized when practicing imagery to create vivid images of sport experiences.

In addition to the senses just discussed, the emotions associated with various sport experiences are also an important part of imagery. In using imagery to help control anxiety, anger, or pain, athletes must be able to re-create these emotions in their minds. For example, athletes could re-create their thoughts and feelings experienced during competition to understand how and why anxiety hurt their performance. In using imagery to re-create past outstanding performances, athletes should feel the emotions associated with those experiences such as elation, satisfaction, pride, and self-esteem.

Imagery as a Mental Training Tool

Athletes must use imagery in a continuous and systematic manner for it to qualify as mental training. Dreaming or random imagery is not systematic, and there is no evidence that these forms of imagery enhance athletes' performance. This doesn't mean that athletes have to spend numerous hours a day engaged in imagery for it to help their performance. However, they must use it in some sort of continuing, organized manner, even if in small doses, to have the desired effect on performance. This is similar to physical training, in which random, occasional physical practice won't do much to increase an athlete's skills. However, systematic, repetitive physical (and mental) practice clearly pays off in performance improvement in any sport.

Athletes must learn to control their imagery to use it effectively as a mental training tool.

Controllability is the ability of athletes to imagine exactly what they intend to imagine, and also the ability to manipulate aspects of the images that they wish to change. Dreams are for the most part uncontrollable—we simply experience them during sleep. Imagery, by contrast, must be controllable so that athletes can manipulate images in productive ways to program themselves for optimal performance. As we all remember as athletes, often our images become uncontrollable, such as when we "choke" under pressure or experience dreaded performance slumps. Thus, coaches and sport psychology consultants must help athletes gain control of their images so that imagery can be used effectively in mental training. In addition to controllability, the other key to using imagery effectively in mental training is vividness. **Vividness** refers to how clearly athletes can see an image and how detailed the image appears to them. Vividness involves such features as whether the image is in color, how many senses are being used, and the emotion or physical sensations experienced when engaging in imagery.

Overall, imagery as a mental training tool involves the systematic practice and use of imagery to engage in vivid and controllable polysensory images to enhance performance. When athletes first begin using imagery, it is typical to lack vividness and especially controllability of images. However, systematic practice has been shown to be very effective in increasing imagery ability (Evans, Jones, & Mullen, 2004; Rodgers, Hall, & Buckolz, 1991). Also, imagery has been shown to be more effective in helping athletes perform (Isaac, 1992). It is important to encourage athletes if they are not skilled in their initial attempts at imagery. Let them know that imagery is a skill that takes time to train, but it is a learnable skill that they can improve with practice. This is true even with world-class athletes, as the following example shows:

> It took me a long time to control my images and perfect my imagery, maybe a year, doing it every day. At first I couldn't see myself, I always saw everyone else, or I would see my dives wrong all the time. I would get an image of hurting myself, or tripping on the board, or I would "see" something done really bad. As I continued to work at it, I got to the point where I could see myself doing a perfect dive and the crowd yelling at the Olympics. But it took me a long time. . . . I started to see myself on the board doing my perfect dive. But some days I couldn't see it, or it was a bad dive in my head. I worked at it so much it got to the point that I could do all my dives easily. Sometimes I would even be in the middle of a conversation with someone and I would think of one of my dives and "see" it.
>
> —Olympic gold medalist, springboard diving
> (Orlick & Partington, 1988, p. 114)

Internal and External Imagery Perspectives

When you spontaneously engage in imagery, do you see yourself as if you're watching videotape or do you see yourself from behind your own eyes? This question differentiates between an external imagery perspective and an internal imagery perspective. Athletes who use an **external imagery perspective** see the image from outside their bodies as if they are viewing themselves from behind a video camera. When athletes use an **internal imagery perspective,** they see the image from inside their bodies the way their eyes normally see. Consider the different imagery perspectives used by athletes in the following examples:

> When I'm watching it on video I look visually at it and then I get this internal feeling. When I'm actually doing it I get the same feeling inside. It is a very internal feeling that is hard to explain. You have to experience it, and once you do, then you know what you are going after. I can even get a feeling for an entire program. . . . I get this internal feeling . . . and usually I'm fresh and usually it will be a perfect program.
>
> —Canadian Olympic figure skater
> (Orlick & Partington, 1988, p. 113)

Sometimes you look at it from a camera view, but most of the time I look at it as what I see from within, because that's the way it's going to be in competition. It is natural [that way] because I do the routines so many times that it's drilled in my head, what I see and how I do it. . . . I think of it as the way I've done it so many times, and that's from within my body.

—Olympic rhythmic gymnast
(Orlick & Partington, 1988, p. 114)

Research has shown that elite athletes are more likely to practice imagery from an internal perspective as compared to nonelite athletes, who are more likely to practice imagery from an external perspective (Orlick & Partington, 1988; Salmon, Hall, & Haslam, 1994). Research also supports that both imagery perspectives can enhance performance (e.g., Hardy & Callow, 1999). Thus, athletes should experiment to find the imagery perspective that is most helpful to them for specific situations.

Many athletes frequently shift back and forth between perspectives when using imagery, and they should be encouraged to practice both perspectives to be competent and comfortable with each. A suggested way to develop athletes' imagery ability is to have them actually perform the skill (e.g., serve a volleyball, noting all the sensations) and then immediately close their eyes and try to replay the serve using an internal perspective (as if from inside their body). Repeat until the athlete can discern little difference between actual and imaged performance. Do this physical-mental practice routine again, only this time with an external imagery perspective (as if seen on videotape). Once athletes are more skilled in imagery, they may prefer to keep their eyes open and may discover a preference for using one perspective more than another.

Does Imagery Work to Enhance Athletes' Performance?

Now that you have a basic understanding about imagery, your next question should be: "That's great, but does it work?" The answer is a resounding "yes!" As Figure 14-1 shows, research evidence supporting the effectiveness of imagery as a mental training tool is divided into three areas. First, imagery has been shown to enhance sport performance and learning. Second, imagery has been shown to enhance thoughts and emotions

in athletes that are critical to athletes' performance. And, third, research shows that successful athletes use imagery more extensively and systematically than less successful athletes.

Enhancing Sport Performance and Learning

Of primary interest to coaches and athletes is the effectiveness of imagery in enhancing athletes' performance. The research in this area is divided into three sections: mental practice of skill over time, preparatory imagery for competition, and imagery as part of multimodal mental training programs (see Figure 14-1).

Mental practice research. Using imagery to perform a specific sport skill repetitively in the mind is called **mental practice.** Typically, mental practice occurs across a period of time in an intermittent learning style similar to a distributed physical practice schedule. The first study of mental practice effects on motor skills took place in 1934 (Vandall, Davis, & Clugston, 1934). Since that time, a plethora of research has been conducted in this area, and comprehensive reviews have concluded that mental practice enhances performance and is better than no practice at all (Feltz & Landers, 1983; Feltz, Landers, & Becker, 1988; Martin, Moritz, & Hall, 1999). Improvement in the following sport skills has been documented through mental practice: basketball shooting, volleyball serving, tennis serving, golf, football placekicking, figure skating, swimming starts, dart throwing, alpine skiing, karate skills, diving, trampoline skills, competitive running, dance, rock climbing, field hockey, and gymnastics performance.

This research is not saying that mental practice is better than physical practice. It certainly is not, as nothing takes the place of deliberate, repetitive physical practice in refining sport skills! However, mental practice is better than no practice, and it often complements physical practice. For example, athletes can only engage in physical practice for finite periods of time, because of fatigue and attentional overload. Mental practice allows athletes to refine their sport skills without

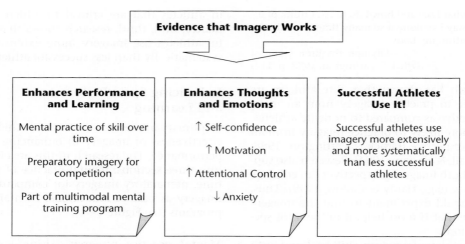

Figure 14-1 **Summary of research support for the effectiveness of imagery**

having to physically engage in the activity. A Canadian Olympic gold medalist in the bobsled emphasizes this point:

> In bobsledding, you can only do two or three runs per day. I would have liked to do 20 of them but I couldn't. The physical demands were too high. . . . So I did a lot of imagery instead and it was a real learning process. . . . Each track filled up a video-tape in my head. (Durand-Bush & Salmela, 2002)

Preparatory imagery.   Research has also shown that using imagery immediately before performance can help athletes perform better. Often, imagery is used just prior to performing to "psych up," calm down, or focus on relevant aspects of the task. Consider how Larry Bird, three-time NBA champion and MVP, used imagery during the playing of the national anthem just prior to games:

> People have noticed that during the national anthem at home games I am always looking up to the Boston Garden ceiling. . . . The thing I look at up there are our championship flags. I focus on the three championships my teams have won and I always look at them in order. I start at 1981, move to 1984 and shift over to 1986. I try to capture how I felt when we won each one and play the championship through my mind. It doesn't take very long to zip through that. (Bird, 1989)

Imagery as a preparatory strategy used prior to performance has improved performance on strength tasks (Shelton & Mahoney, 1978; Tynes & McFatter, 1987), muscular endurance tasks (Gould, Weinberg, & Jackson, 1980; Lee, 1990), and golf putting (Murphy & Woolfolk, 1987; Woolfolk, Parrish, & Murphy, 1985). Imagery also has been shown to be an effective part of athletes' pre-performance routines, which involve a planned sequence of thoughts and behaviors that lead to automatic performance execution (Lidor & Singer, 2003).

Multimodal mental training interventions.   The effects of imagery on performance and learning also have been examined within multimodal mental training interventions that are implemented with athletes over a period of time. For example, a mental training program consisting of imagery, relaxation, and self-talk training was implemented with soccer players during the season to improve three soccer-specific skills (Thelwell, Greenlees, & Weston, 2006). The program was clearly effective in enhancing the players' defensive skills in competition. Similar programs have been successful in enhancing performance in basketball (Kendall, Hrycaiko, Martin, & Kendall,

1990; Savoy, 1993), field hockey (Thomas, Maynard, & Hanton, 2007), swimming (Hanton & Jones, 1999; Sheard & Golby, 2006), gymnastics (Lee & Hewitt, 1987), figure skating (Ming & Martin, 1996; Mumford & Hall, 1985), tennis (Daw & Burton, 1994; Efran, Lesser, & Spiller, 1994; Mamassis & Doganis, 2004), golf putting (Beauchamp, Halliwell, Fournier, & Koestner, 1996), and triathlon (Thelwell & Greenlees, 2001).

Multimodal mental training intervention for a tennis player

Christy was a 14-year-old tennis player ranked in the top 25 of her age group nationally. She came to a mental trainer to improve two key aspects of her performance. First, she had a poor net game and was fearful of coming to the net for volleys. Second, she tended to "choke" on her second serve, worrying about double-faulting, even though she had the technical talent to execute a successful second serve. Thus, her mental training goals were to overcome her fear of the net game and to develop a focused and confident mental routine to allow her to execute a successful "kick" second serve.

Christy began working on her net game by physically practicing net volleys on shots that began very easy and progressed to harder. She verbalized the cue word seams out loud that made her focus her attention on the seams of the ball coming toward her and also occupied her mind to prevent negative thinking or worry. Before and after training, she mentally practiced net volleys in various situations, using her cue word to create the correct visual picture. Using imagery, she mentally practiced various net tactics for different competitive situations. A performance goal was set for her to hit at least one winner per game from the net. In training, she did not win the game or end the drill until she accomplished this goal. Her net performance improved over the course of the 25-week intervention so that she won, on average, 4 points per match from the net.

To deal with her double-fault problem, Christy developed a preservice routine using relaxation, thought-stopping, self-talk, and imagery. The routine started with bouncing the ball four times and catching it. Then she took a relaxation breath, during which she imagined air passing through her body and dissipating any tension in it. She used the cue word smooth to program a relaxed, smoothly executed serve. She then used the kinesthetic image of her racquet making contact with the ball for a perfect kick serve and a visual image of the ball "kicking" successfully within her opponent's service box. She extensively practiced thought-stopping, and used the word stop to put any irrelevant and worrisome thoughts out of her mind. This routine was developed and practiced in parts, and was completed and refined over three months of practice. Christy was able to gain fluidity and smoothness in her second serve, and to significantly decrease her double-fault percentage as the result of the mental training (modified from Mamassis & Doganis, 2004).

Enhancing Competition-Related Thoughts and Emotions

In addition to helping athletes perform better, research findings indicate that imagery enhances the competition-related thoughts and emotions of athletes. This is important because a basic objective of sport psychology is to help athletes think better—to enable them to manage their thoughts and emotions effectively to create a productive competitive focus. Imagery can enhance self-confidence (Callow, Hardy, & Hall 2001; Evans et al., 2004; Garza & Feltz, 1998; Hale & Whitehouse, 1998; Mamassis & Doganis, 2004;

McKenzie & Howe, 1997; Short, Bruggeman, Engel, Marback, Wang, Willadsen, & Short, 2002), motivation (Beauchamp et al., 1996; Martin & Hall, 1995), and attentional control (Calmels, Berthoumieux, & d'Arripe-Longueville, 2004), It also can change athletes' perceptions of anxiety from harmful and negative to facilitative and challenging (Cumming, Olphin, & Law, 2007; Evans et al., 2004; Hale & Whitehouse, 1998; Mamassis & Doganis, 2004; Page, Sime, & Nordell, 1999) and can help decrease or control precompetitive anxiety when combined with other mental training methods such as relaxation and stress inoculation training (Cogan & Petrie, 1995; Kerr & Leith, 1993; Lee & Hewitt, 1987; Ryska, 1998; Savoy, 1997). In addition, imagery can affect the self-confidence of coaches (Short, Smiley, & Ross-Stewart, 2005).

A highly successful Olympic pistol shooter states:

> As for success imagery, I would imagine to myself, "How would a champion act? How would a champion feel? How would she perform on the line?" This helped me find out about myself, what worked and didn't work for me. . . . That helped me believe that I would be the Olympic champion. (Orlick & Partington, 1988, p. 113)

Professional golfer Bob Ford, admired by peers for his ability to clear his mind for competition, describes his unique imagery practice of imagining himself on an elevator as he walks to the first tee at a tournament. When he gets to the first tee, the doors open and he envisions being on a "whole new floor." Ford explains this image allows him to leave all problems and extraneous thoughts behind on another "floor," and enables him to focus in on the "competition floor." These examples demonstrate how athletes can use imagery to identify and create the kind of thoughts, feelings, and focus that maximize chances for competitive success.

Incidence of Imagery Use

Successful elite athletes use imagery more extensively and systematically, and they have better imagery skill than less accomplished athletes (Calmels, d'Arripe-Longueville, Fournier, &

Soulard, 2003; Cumming & Hall, 2002; Gregg & Hall, 2006; Hall, Rodgers, & Barr, 1990; Salmon et al., 1994). Of 235 Canadian Olympic athletes who participated in the 1984 Olympic Games, 99% reported using imagery (Orlick & Partington, 1988). During training they engaged in pre-planned systematic imagery at least once a day, 4 days per week, for about 12 minutes each time. At the Olympic site, some reported engaging in imagery for 2 to 3 hours in preparation for their events. An analysis of the mental preparation strategies of U.S. wrestlers during the 1988 Olympics found that the wrestlers' best performances involved adherence to mental routines, including positive imagery before the matches (Gould, Eklund, & Jackson, 1992). In addition, mental training (including imagery) to develop systematic competitive routines and plans was a critical factor in the successful performance of athletes at the 1996 Olympic Games (Gould, Guinan, Greenleaf, Medbery, & Peterson, 1999). Elite gymnasts and canoeists report using imagery extensively to rehearse skills and difficult moves, to optimize concentration and quality of training, and to enhance self-confidence and motivation (White & Hardy, 1998). Eighty-six percent of the U.S. Olympic sport psychology consultants in 1988 used imagery in their mental training programs with athletes (Gould, Tammen, Murphy, & May, 1989). Coaches attending a mental skills training workshop reported using imagery with their athletes more than any other mental training technique and that it was their most useful mental technique (Hall & Rodgers, 1989).

Experiential Evidence That Imagery Works

Perhaps it would be helpful to learn firsthand from athletes themselves about how imagery works for them. Several athletes who have at one time been the best in the world at their sport advocate the use of imagery. Greg Louganis reached the pinnacle of his magnificent diving career by winning gold medals in both the springboard and platform events at the 1984 and 1988 Olympic Games. He speaks of how he used imagery to practice each dive and of his particular technique of setting his dives to music as he practiced them in his head. Chris Evert, the great tennis champion, admitted that she practiced imagery before important matches by painstakingly visualizing opponents' specific styles of play and then visualizing her successful responses to these opponents. Pat Summitt, the highly successful women's basketball coach at the University of Tennessee, described in an interview how her team uses imagery for relaxation before big games, mental practice of specific performance situations, and pregame preparation (Wrisberg, 1990). Phil Mickelson, one of the top five golfers in the world, states, "When I see a shot, I see in my mind's eye a 'window' I want the ball to pass through at the apex of its flight."

Colleen Hacker, sport psychology consultant for the U.S. women's soccer team that won the 1996 and 2004 Olympic Games and the 1999 World Cup, created individualized audio and video imagery tapes for the players prior to these competitions as well as every other major world event. The tapes are full of confidence-building trigger words, phrases, and images, all set to each player's favorite songs. The tapes became a powerful source of team chemistry when the players ended up watching them as a group. Kristine Lilly, who made a key header save in the World Cup final against China, stated: "The tapes give me that little extra confidence, remind me about who I am and what I can give. I'm inspired watching my teammates' tapes. And I'm reminded of what they do well, so I'll never second-guess them" (Lieber, 1999, p. 2c).

The following excerpt from an interview with a Canadian Olympic diver attests to this athlete's extreme commitment to and belief in imagery (Orlick & Partington, 1988):

> I did my dives in my head all the time. At night, before going to sleep, I always did my dives. Ten dives. I started with a front dive, the first one that I had to do at the Olympics, and I did everything as if I was actually there. I saw myself on the board with the same bathing suit. Everything was the same. . . . If the dive was wrong, I went back and started over again. It takes a good hour to do perfect imagery of all my dives, but for me it was better than a workout. Sometimes I would take the weekend off and do imagery five times a day.

Similarly, observe the commitment to imagery by Alex Baumann, Olympic double gold medalist in swimming:

> The best way I have learned to prepare mentally for competition is to visualize the race in my mind. . . . In my imagery I concentrate on attaining the splits I have set out to do. About 15 minutes before the race I visualize the race in my mind. I think about my own race and nothing else. I try to get those splits in my mind, and after that I am ready to go. My visualization has been refined more and more over the years. That is what really got me the world record and Olympic medals. (Orlick, 1998, p. 70)

How Does Imagery Enhance Athletes' Performance?

Many theoretical explanations for how imagery facilitates performance have been advanced in the literature (Morris, Spittle, & Watt, 2005), and it is beyond the scope of this chapter to review all of them. Three of the most contemporary and practical theoretical explanations for how imagery enhances performance are presented here.

Bioinformational Explanation

Bioinformational theory (Lang, 1977, 1979) assumes that a mental image is an organized set of propositions, or characteristics, stored in the brain's long-term memory. When individuals engage in imagery, they activate **stimulus characteristics** that describe the content of the image for them and **response characteristics** that describe what their responses are to the stimuli in that situation. For example, imagining shooting a basketball free throw in the final seconds of a close game would involve the stimulus characteristics of the feel of the ball in the hand, the sight of the basket, and the sound of the crowd. The response characteristics for this image might include muscular tension in the shooting arm, increased perspiration, feelings of anxiety, and the joyous sight of the ball swishing through the net. According to bioinformational theory, for imagery to facilitate sport performance, response characteristics must be activated so they can be modified, improved, and strengthened. Imagery enhances performance by repeatedly accessing response characteristics for a particular stimulus situation and modifying these responses to represent perfect control and execution of a skill.

Research has shown that response-oriented imagery results in greater physiological reactivity than stimulus-oriented imagery (Bakker, Boschker, & Chung, 1996; Cumming et al., 2007) and also that images of situations with which athletes have personal experience create greater physiological reactivity than less familiar images (Hecker & Kaczor, 1988). Moreover, athlete performance has been improved to a greater degree through imagery that included both stimulus and response characteristics, as opposed to imagery that just included stimulus characteristics (Smith & Collins, 2004; Smith, Holmes, Whitemore, Collins, & Devenport, 2001). Interestingly, response-oriented imagery has been shown to create more "priming" responses in the brain as measured by electroencephalographic (EEG) activity when compared to stimulus-oriented imagery (Smith & Collins, 2004).

An important implication from this is that coaches, athletes, and sport psychologists involved in imagery training should include many response characteristics when using imagery. Specifically, images should contain not only the conditions of the situation (swimming in a pool, water is rough, championship meet) but also the athlete's *behavioral* responses (swimming strongly, right on pace), *psychological* responses (feeling confident, focusing on the race), and *physiological* responses (feeling energized) to the situation. By including these positive responses, the image will be more vivid and should result in psychophysiological changes in the body and thus improved performance. (Note the positive responses to an upcoming competition described in the sample imagery script provided in Appendix A.) Also, it is important to encourage use of kinesthetic imagery to emphasize feeling the physical sensations

of performing a specific skill, which will further strengthen effective response characteristics.

Functional Equivalence Explanation

In this second theoretical explanation, imagery causes the brain to activate the same areas and processes as when the movement being imaged is actually executed. This approach has been referred to as the functional equivalence explanation for the effects of imagery on performance (Holmes & Collins, 2001; Jeannerod, 1994). Using one's imagination to simulate a movement recruits the same parts and sequences in the brain as the actual physical execution of the movement. The term *functional equivalence* means that imagery has a similar functional outcome as the actual movement.

Research has shown that more functionally equivalent imagery had a greater positive effect on both youth and adult sport performance than imagery that was less functionally equivalent (Smith, Wright, Allsopp, & Westhead, 2007). Imagery is more functionally equivalent when it

- Includes important senses and feelings associated with competition.

- Is practiced in a posture similar to one's performance posture, wearing performance clothes, holding performance implements, and in a similar environment to the performance environment.

- Is timed at the same pace as the actual timing of the skill.

- Is internal in perspective.

An interesting study found that golfers who practiced imagery by watching a video or listening to an audiotape of themselves putting successfully performed better than golfers who practiced imagery using a written script (Smith & Holmes, 2004). This finding supports the functional equivalence idea, in that the videotape and audiotape conditions stimulated the golfers' brains in more functionally equivalent ways (e.g., seeing or hearing the putt struck and falling into the cup in real time, having visual and auditory cues) than doing imagery from a written script.

Mental Readiness Explanation

The mental readiness explanation of how imagery works is not a theory but an intuitive description of the role of imagery in helping athletes to optimize arousal, attention, and confidence. Athletes commonly use imagery to psych up or calm down to meet the energy demands of a particular sport, as well as to visualize aspects of the upcoming competition to sharpen the focus they need to be successful. For example, a wrestler may use imagery before a match to psych himself up to a high energy level and to focus his attention on the specific strategies and moves he needs to use against a particular opponent.

Research has shown that imagery is effective in optimizing arousal, attention, and confidence in athletes (Calmels et al., 2004; Cumming et al., 2007; Hale & Whitehouse, 1998). A national level gymnast explains that imagery "helped her to think more clearly and 'not get all worked up,'" and an elite canoeist described imagery as helping her "feel 'switched on' and able to keep 'away from everybody'" (White & Hardy, 1998). A youth athlete stated that "Imagery helps you, like 'you can do it'" (Cumming et al., 2007), which is a great statement of self-confidence!

Can Imagery Hurt Athletes' Performance?

Often, coaches and athletes ask if imagery can ever hurt their performance. It's a good question. The answer to the question is yes, imagery *can* hurt athletes' performance *if* they focus on the *wrong* images at the *wrong* times. When individuals used negative imagery by imaging performing unsuccessful putts, their golf putting accuracy declined (Short et al., 2002; Woolfolk, Parrish, & Murphy, 1985; Woolfolk, Murphy, Gottesfeld, & Aitken, 1985). This research indicates that imagery can hurt athletes' performance if they systematically imagine bad performance. This doesn't mean that athletes should not use imagery, as the point of imagery training is to enable athletes to control their previously uncontrollable images. Athletes are going to experience images whether they engage in mental training or not, so it seems productive to enable them to

become more skillful in their use of imagery to avoid the debilitating effects of negative imagery. The point is for athletes to create a mental blueprint for perfect responses, NOT to create a mental blueprint for disastrous responses! Consider how Ken Dryden, then a 23-year-old rookie goalie for the Montreal Canadiens, created the wrong mental blueprint the night before he was to face the Boston Bruins in Game 7 of the quarterfinals at hostile Boston Garden:

> [I turned on the television in my hotel, and] the only thing I could find was *The Bruins Week in Review*. All they kept showing was the Bruins' scoring goal after goal. "Esposito scores! Orr scores! Esposito scores again!" I was already nervous, and I turned downright depressed. I went to bed and dreamed about those goals. (McCallum, 2004, p. 56)

Additional research has shown that constant attempts to suppress negative thoughts and images from conscious awareness can increase the probability that these negative thoughts and images will influence performance (Beilock, Afremow, Rabe, & Carr, 2001). In this study, individuals in a golf putting task were told, "Be careful to try not to image hitting the ball short of the target. Don't image undershooting the target!" When individuals were given "negative" image instructions (told what not to image), they performed poorly, even when they attempted to suppress these negative images. From a practical perspective, this indicates that athletes should avoid programing themselves to not do something, or constantly focus on negative images and attempt to suppress them. Likewise, coaches should refrain from "negative coaching," or giving verbal feedback such as "Don't pop up!" or "Stay away from the out-of-bounds on the left." These well-meaning, yet negative, coaching comments often create mental blueprints in athletes' heads of the exact performance the coach is suggesting that they not do.

So there is a grain of truth in the popular notion that "thinking too much" can hurt an athlete's performance. The key is to think productively and to simplify one's thinking to the point of automatic performance. This may be difficult during a performance slump, when one's controllability of images slips a bit and negative images pop up during competition. However, the goal of systematic imagery training is to develop more and more skill in controlling one's thoughts and images.

How Do You Set Up an Imagery Training Program?

Setting up the imagery program has four phases. First, sell the athletes on the use of imagery. Second, evaluate the imagery skill of the athletes so they understand their imagery abilities and areas that need improvement. Third, have athletes practice developing basic imagery skills. Fourth, implement a systematic program of imagery practice and then monitor it.

Introduce Imagery to Athletes

Imagery only works for athletes if they believe in it. Although you must convince athletes that imagery can indeed help them perform better, you should avoid unnecessary hype or unrealistic claims. Make sure they understand that imagery will not guarantee success. It is simply a mental training technique that has been shown to enhance sport performance.

An approach that we have found useful in introducing imagery to athletes is the analogy of building a machine. When athletes continuously practice a sport skill over and over, they are in essence attempting to build a machine. Divers attempt to fine-tune their body to make their muscles react flawlessly in a dive. Shot putters work hours refining their technique in order to uncoil their body in maximum thrust. Coaches and athletes spend a great deal of time using drill and repetition attempting to build a flawless, automatic machine. Why not use imagery to help? Make the point that building a machine for optimal sport performance requires mental training as well as physical training.

The introduction of imagery can take place in an informal group setting if you are working with a team. We recommend that you spend no more than 20 minutes summarizing some important points about imagery. An introduction to imagery might include the following steps.

Hook 'em. You need to grab athletes' attention right away to get them interested in imagery. You could (a) discuss the concept of building a machine, (b) ask them if they use imagery and have them describe how they use it, and (c) explain how several famous and successful athletes see and believe by using imagery. Be creative! Also, it is critical that you are enthusiastic and model your confidence and strong belief in the power of imagery.

Define and give evidence. Briefly explain what imagery is by using a definition such as "practicing in your head" or "building your mental blueprint." Without bogging them down with scientific research, provide some brief evidence that imagery does work to enhance performance. It is helpful to use testimonials from famous coaches and athletes who believe in imagery.

Explain how it works. Provide a simple and brief explanation for how imagery works to enhance performance. The amount of detail you get into here depends on the level of the athletes. We usually explain that imagery creates a mental blueprint of a particular skill and that by using imagery they are ingraining or strengthening that mental blueprint to make their skills automatic or to build a machine. Athletes are always intrigued when they learn that innervation of their brains during imagery is similar to when they are performing the skill. To emphasize the way imagery works, you may want to take your athletes through one or both of the following exercises so they can immediately experience the power of imagery.

String and bolt. Give each athlete a string approximately 14 to 16 inches long threaded through a heavy bolt (a neck chain and heavy ring also will work). Stabilizing the elbow, ideally on a table top, have each athlete lightly hold the two ends of the string between the thumb and forefinger with the weight suspended directly below. Focusing on the weight, each athlete in his or her mind's eye should imagine the weight moving right and left like the pendulum of a clock. Once most athletes have at least some movement right and left, have them change the image so the weight swings directly away from and then toward the chest. Again, once successful, change the image so the weight moves in a clockwise circle and finally in a counterclockwise circle. In discussing this exercise, you will find most athletes are impressed at how imagining the movement ultimately translates to the actual physical movement of the pendulum. Once completed, you can explain to the athletes that the subtle muscle innervation in the arm and hand created by the imagery is responsible for the movement of the pendulum.

Arm as iron bar.   Pair each athlete with a partner of similar height and strength. While directly facing each other, one partner extends his dominant arm straight out, palm up, so the back of the wrist is resting on the partner's opposite shoulder. The other partner cups both of his hands above the bend in the partner's elbow. The person whose arm is extended then maximally tightens all the muscles in the arm, trying to make it as strong as possible. Then the partner tests for strength by pushing down at the elbow with both hands, trying to see how much strength it takes to bend the arm. Then switch roles. Afterward, resume the initial position with the original partner. This time, to create strength, the partner is to close everything out of his mind and imagine that the arm is a thick steel bar. Not only is the arm a hard, steel bar, but it extends out through the opposite wall. Once the partner has created the image of an unbendable, strong steel bar, he indicates such by raising a finger on the opposite hand. This signals the partner to again test for strength. Again, switch roles. In follow-up discussion you will find that most athletes will be amazed at how much stronger their arm was with the iron bar image.

Give specifics about how imagery will be used.   At this point let the athletes know exactly how they will incorporate imagery into their training. For example, a basketball team could start by using mental practice for free throws and

imagery to mentally rehearse specific team plays. It is a mistake to try to do too much too soon. However, it is important for athletes to quickly see how imagery can be applied to meet their practical needs.

Help Athletes Evaluate Their Imagery Ability

After sparking athletes' interest in imagery, the next step is to help them evaluate their imagery abilities. One method of evaluation is to take the athletes through some of the Basic Training imagery exercises provided in this chapter. By discussing their images with them, you could determine whether certain areas need to be strengthened. Another way to evaluate imagery ability is to administer the Sport Imagery Evaluation (see Appendix B), which measures athletes' abilities to experience different senses, emotions, and perspectives during imagery. There are other inventories designed to measure imagery ability, but this evaluation seems to be most useful to the coach/practitioner.

For best results, direct athletes through the exercises in the evaluation (it takes approximately 15 minutes). Encourage athletes to answer honestly on the basis of their imagery ability. Afterward, discuss the results informally with athletes to better understand their unique imagery abilities and to target areas that can be improved through practice.

Basic Training

Basic Training is similar to a preseason physical conditioning program. By developing a foundation of strength and endurance, athletes are better equipped to fine-tune their physical skills when the season begins. By strengthening their imagery "muscles" in Basic Training, athletes are more likely to benefit from the use of imagery during the season.

Basic Training includes three types of imagery exercises. First, athletes need to develop *vivid* images. Like using a fine-tuning control on a television, increasing the vividness of images sharpens the details of the image. Second, athletes must be able to *control* their images. Controllability exercises involve learning to manipulate images by will. Third, athletes need to enhance their ability to engage in *self-awareness*. It is a skill to use imagery to become more aware of underlying thoughts and feelings that often influence our performance without our realizing it.

It is helpful for athletes to gain proficiency in all three types of imagery exercises. The example exercises purposely use vague descriptors to encourage you to develop your own imagery exercises that are tailored specifically for you or your athletes. It is also helpful to develop additional exercises in areas in which athletes are having trouble.

Vividness

Exercise 1:

Place yourself in a familiar place where you usually perform your sport (gym, pool, rink, field, track, etc.). It is empty except for you. Stand in the middle of this place and look all around. Notice the quiet emptiness. Pick out as many details as you can. What does it smell like? What are the colors, shapes, and forms that you see? Now imagine yourself in the same setting, but this time there are many spectators there. Imagine yourself getting ready to perform. Try to experience this image from inside your body. See the spectators, your teammates, your coach, and the opponents. Try to hear the sounds of the noisy crowd, your teammates' chatter, your coach yelling encouragement, and the particular sounds of your sport (e.g., ball swishing through the net, volleyball spike hitting the floor). Re-create the feelings of nervous anticipation and excitement that you have before competing. How do you feel?

Exercise 2:

Choose a piece of equipment in your sport such as a ball, pole, racket, or club. Focus on this object. Try to imagine the fine details of the object. Turn it over in your hands and examine every part of the object. Feel its outline and texture. Now imagine yourself performing with the object. First, focus on seeing yourself very clearly performing this activity. Visualize yourself repeating the skill over and over. See yourself performing from behind your own eyes. Then step outside of your body and see yourself perform as if you were watching yourself on film. Now, step back in your body and continue performing. Next, try to hear the sounds that accompany this particular movement. Listen carefully to all the sounds that are being made as you perform this skill. Now, put the sight and the sound together. Try to get a clear picture of yourself performing the skill and also hear all the sounds involved.

Exercise 3:

Pick a very simple skill in your sport. Perform the skill over and over in your mind and imagine every feeling and movement in your muscles as you perform that skill. Try to feel this image as if you were inside your own body. Concentrate on how the different parts of your body feel as you stretch and contract the various muscles associated with the skill. Think about building a machine as you perform the skill flawlessly over and over again and concentrate on the feeling of the movement.

Now try to combine all of your senses, but particularly those of feeling, seeing, and hearing yourself perform the skill over and over. Do not concentrate too hard on any one sense. Instead, try to imagine the total experience using all of your senses.

Once athletes have mastered these exercises, you might consider follow-up variations to imagine more complex skills, grouping skills together, or placing the skill in the context of competition (such as reacting to certain defenses, executing strategy, etc.).

Controllability

Exercise 1:

Choose a simple sport skill and begin practicing it. Now imagine yourself performing this skill either with a teammate or against an opponent. Imagine yourself executing successful strategies in relation to the movements of your teammate or opponent.

Exercise 2:

Choose a sport skill that you have trouble performing. Begin practicing the skill over and over. See and feel yourself doing this from inside your body. If you make a mistake or perform the skill incorrectly, stop the image and repeat it, attempting to perform perfectly every time. Re-create past experiences in which you have not performed the skill well. Take careful notice of what you are doing wrong. Now imagine yourself performing the skill correctly. Focus on how your body feels as you go through different positions in performing the skill correctly. Build a perfect machine!

Self-Awareness

Exercise 1:

Think back and choose a past performance in which you performed very well. Using all your senses, re-create that situation in your mind. See yourself as you were succeeding, hear the sounds involved, feel your body as you performed the movements, and reexperience the positive emotions. Try to pick out the characteristics that made you perform so well (e.g., intense concentration, feelings of confidence, optimal arousal). After identifying these characteristics, try

to determine why they were present in this situation. Think about the things you did in preparation for this particular event. What are some things that may have caused this great performance?

Repeat this exercise, imagining a situation in which you performed very poorly. Make sure you are very relaxed before practicing this image, as your mind will subconsciously resist your imagery attempts to re-create unpleasant thoughts, images, and feelings. Attempt to become more self-aware of how you reacted to different stimuli (e.g., coaches, opponents, officials, fear of failure, needing approval from others) and how these thoughts and feelings may have interfered with your performance.

Exercise 2:

Think back to a sport situation in which you experienced a great deal of anxiety. Re-create that situation in your head, seeing and hearing yourself. Especially re-create the feeling of anxiety. Try to feel the physical responses of your body to the emotion and also try to recall the thoughts going through your mind that may have caused the anxiety. Now attempt to let go of the anxiety and relax your body. Breathe slowly and deeply and focus on your body as you exhale. Imagine all of the tension being pulled into your lungs and exhaled from your body. Continue breathing slowly and exhaling tension until you are deeply relaxed. Now repeat this exercise imagining a situation in which you experienced a great deal of anger, and then relax yourself using the breathing and exhalation technique.

Exercise 3:

The purpose of this exercise is to help you become more aware of things that happen during competition that bother you when you perform. Think about the times when your performance suddenly went from good to bad. Re-create several of these experiences in your mind. Try to pinpoint the specific factors that negatively influenced your performance (e.g., officials, teammates, opponents' remarks, opponent started to play much better). After becoming aware of these factors that negatively affected your performance, take several minutes to re-create the situations, develop appropriate strategies to deal with the negative factors, and imagine the situations again; but this time imagine yourself using your strategies to keep the negative factors from interfering with your performance. Reinforce yourself by feeling proud and confident that you were able to control the negative factors and perform well.

Implement a Systematic Program

Athletes are now ready to begin a *systematic* program of imagery. Imagery practice must be systematic to be effective, so always follow the KISS principle (keep it simple and systematic)! The first concern is to build the imagery program into the athletes' routine. The imagery program must *not* be something extra but should instead be an integral part of training and practice.

Another key is to fit the needs of the athlete. The imagery program need not be long and complex. In fact, when first starting it is a good idea to keep it concise and simple. Initially, choose a sport skill or strategy that is easy to control, such as when the environment is stable rather than reactive. For example, in basketball you could start with free throw shooting and in racket sports with the serve. As your athletes become more proficient at and accepting of the program, you can increase its complexity.

Imagery Cookbook for Coaches and Practitioners

It is impossible to design an imagery program appropriate for all sports. For that reason, we have designed this section like a cookbook, which itemizes the necessary ingredients of an imagery program. The ingredients listed include ways to use imagery, times in which imagery may be practiced, and strategies to enhance imagery practice. It is up to you to choose which ingredients are most relevant for the needs of your athletes.

Ways to Use Imagery

Athletes can use imagery in a number of ways to enhance sport performance. These include

- Learning and practicing sport skills.
- Correcting mistakes.
- Learning and practicing performance strategies.
- Preparing a mental focus for competition.
- Automating preperformance routines.
- Building and enhancing mental skills.
- Aiding in the recovery from injuries.

Learning and practicing sport skills. One of the best places for athletes to start using imagery is mental practice, or the repetitive practice of a sport skill in their minds. They should choose one or two skills in their sport, and mentally practice these skills. Urge athletes to mentally practice on their own, but they will be more inclined to do so if mental practice is incorporated as part of their regular training. Coaches can implement a volleyball serving drill in which athletes serve 10 balls and mentally practice each serve prior to physically performing it. This also could be applied to shooting free throws, executing wrestling moves, serving in tennis, sprinting over a set of hurdles, or hitting a baseball. Mental practice is also useful to aid beginners in learning sport skills by helping them to develop a "mental blueprint for perfect responses."

Athletes can strengthen or build their mental blueprints for perfect responses by using verbal triggers and symbolic images. **Verbal triggers** are words or phrases that help athletes focus on key aspects in an image to make their mental blueprint for performance correct. Triggers are used to program the proper image. Coaches use triggers all the time in teaching skills or as points of emphasis they want athletes to think about when performing. Softball players are told to "throw their hands" and focus on a "quick bat." Volleyball serving is taught by having athletes focus on the "bow and arrow" technique. Basketball players are taught to "plant" their inside foot and "square up" for perfect jump shot form. Cross-country skiers think "quick" for their uphill technique to trigger the quick, short kick technique needed on hills. A famous golfer kept the word *oooom-PAH* written on her driver to program the image of an easy slow backswing and a strong and vigorous downswing.

Symbolic images are mental symbols or models for desired components of performance. Archers can envision a string extending from the center of the target that pulls their arrows directly into the bull's-eye. Sprinters may imagine the explosive energy in their legs as coiled springs that will catapult them from the starting blocks. U.S. biathletes have used the symbolic image *Rock of Gibraltar* to program the steady body state they need to shoot effectively. Golfers can imagine turning their body inside a barrel to ensure proper body rotation on the swing and can imagine their arms as a pendulum swinging from the shoulders for the proper putting stroke. A gymnast may visualize her back against a cold, steel wall to perfect the image and movement of a perfectly straight body during a floor exercise routine.

As you read earlier in the chapter, imagery can only hurt performance if athletes imagine the wrong responses. Triggers and symbolic images help athletes lock in the proper responses so that the imagery is "programmed" in the right way. Mental practice using triggers and symbolic images may be helpful for athletes who are mired in a slump or who are having technique problems. They should imagine themselves performing perfectly and attempt to analyze how their present technique is different from their perfect performance. It may be helpful for athletes to view videotapes of themselves performing well and then internalize that performance by using kinesthetic imagery. Coaches should help athletes identify the triggers and symbolic images that really lock in those perfect responses within a sound performance mental blueprint.

Correcting mistakes.   A very simple use of imagery for athletes is in correcting mistakes. Athletes receive constant feedback and corrections from coaches that are provided to enhance their performance. Imagery is a great tool that athletes can use to gain the most benefit from corrections provided from their coaches. Athletes should listen to their coaches' feedback or correction and then run it through their minds in a brief image of the skill now performed correctly. That is, athletes should receive the feedback, and then see it and feel it as they incorporate the information from the coach into their image and execution of the skill.

Coaches should teach and expect athletes to use imagery each time they receive feedback by requesting them to imagine the desired correction in performance in terms of seeing it and feeling it. Coaches should ask each time: Can you see it? Can you feel it? Using imagery to correct mistakes is also helpful when watching videotape of performances. When athletes and coaches identify flaws or mistakes in athletes' performance when watching tape, athletes should be cued immediately to imagine the correction by seeing it and feeling it. Coaches also can help athletes build in triggers or symbolic images to help athletes lock in the mental blueprint for perfect responses.

Coaches can help athletes "calibrate" their images by observing athletes perform and then comparing their observations with what the athletes perceive is occurring in their performance (Simons, 2000). Simons describes how a high jumper attempts to recall the image of her jump immediately after each attempt. She describes her image of her jump to her coach, who then describes her observations of the jump. In this way, the coach is calibrating the athlete's image of the jump to ensure that the athlete's perception and image of what she is doing is indeed correct in form.

Learning and practicing performance strategies.
Imagery is very useful in helping athletes learn and practice performance strategies, such as tactics, systems of play, and decision making. For example, football quarterbacks can mentally rehearse various plays in relation to specific

defenses, even imagining reacting to blitzes and changing defensive formations to audible and completing the appropriate offensive counter to this defense. When introducing a new basketball offense or out-of-bounds play, coaches can direct athletes to walk through the new pattern and then immediately follow this physical practice by imagining their movements through the patterns. Then, before competition, coaches can lead athletes in mentally rehearsing these previously learned offensive and defensive strategies and plays. Similarly, skiers may ski over a particular course in their mind to prepare for an upcoming downhill race. Softball outfielders may use imagery to practice throws from the outfield based on various situations that may arise in a game. Tennis players can mentally rehearse their planned strategy against a particular opponent.

Preparing a mental focus for competition. Imagery can be used by athletes to create and practice in their heads the strong, unshakable mental focus needed for specific competitions. Coaches should help athletes answer two questions: "What will it be like?" "How will I respond?" The first question, "What will it be like?" refers to the external factors of competition, or the physical and social environment. For each competitive situation that athletes face, they should vividly imagine what it will be like in terms of the facilities, crowd, potential distracters, officials, weather, and so on.

The second question, "How will I respond?" is by far the most important question for athletes. Athletes should plan to respond, not react. Responding requires mental skill and toughness to manage one's thoughts and emotions and performance when faced with obstacles, surprises, and disappointments. Reacting doesn't take any skill at all—it is typically a raw emission of emotion (anger, anxiety, fear) in which athletes allow the competitive environment to control them and make them reactive. Imagery is the tool athletes can use to practice over and over in their heads the ways in which they will respond to any type of competitive pressure they might face, and even those that they can't anticipate.

Think of these as "emotional fire-drills" (Lazarus, 1984), because using imagery in this way allows athletes time to practice rational and logical responses for situations that are unexpected and stressful.

Athletes should program the answers to the two questions into a short imagery routine that they practice over and over in their heads in the days and weeks leading up to a particular competition. Imagery used in this way is an attempt to help athletes gain "experience" in responding to competitive challenges. The idea is to create a sense of expectancy, so that athletes expect certain obstacles and pressures, even the unexpected. If they have been mentally trained to expect the unexpected and to respond productively to the unexpected, they will be less likely to react emotionally in ways that will hurt their performances.

Coaches should attempt to simulate competitive conditions at times in practice so that athletes can practice their mental focus plan for competition. The best coaches are masters at simulation who can create all types of situations that athletes might face in competition. These "dress rehearsals" might include wearing uniforms, using clocks and officials, and simulating environmental conditions such as noise, distractions, heat, cold, and pressure. Peter Vidmar, collegiate national champion gymnast and Olympic gold medalist, describes how he and his teammates would simulate competition during practice:

> The team did really weird things to prepare for [the Olympics]. In practice, we would turn off the radio so it was silent in the gym. We would go through the dialogues, like this next routine is the Olympic Games and it's the team finals. It's the last event, and we were neck-and-neck with the Chinese. It was only make-believe when we did it, but what if we really were neck-and-neck with the Chinese during the Games and this routine was our only chance to beat them and win the gold? We'd set the whole thing up, and my heart would be pounding and I would be imagining I was in Pauley Pavilion at the Olympic Games with all the pressure and people watching. I would get really nervous, take those few deep breaths and imagine I was there at the meet and

[Coach] was the head judge. Tim [Daggett] would be Mr. Loudspeaker. "Okay. Next up for the USA," he would say, "Mr. Peter Vidmar." We were dead serious when we were doing this.

During the Olympics, a funny thing happened. It was the last event and the USA just happened to be on the high bar and . . . I just happened to be the last up. We just happened to be neck-and-neck with the Chinese. It's the same scenario we had gone through every day for the last six months and here we were actually living it. [Coach] said, "Okay, Pete. Let's go do it just like in the gym." So I imagined I was in the UCLA gym. Consciously, I knew I was at the Olympics, but I was able to put myself in the frame of mind that I was back at the gym. I was even able to geographically orient that bar to the gym as if there was a pit over there and the wall there, etc. I did my routine and landed successfully. . . . We won the gold. (Ravizza, 1993, pp. 94–95)

Automating preperformance routines. A **preperformance routine** is a preplanned, systematic sequence of thoughts and behaviors that an athlete engages in prior to performing a specific skill. Athletes typically use preperformance routines prior to executing specific sport skills, such as a golf shot, basketball free throw, gymnastics vault, volleyball or tennis serve, field goal kick in football, start in swimming, or any of the jumping and throwing events in track and field. Research has supported preperformance routines as facilitative to athletes' performances (Lidor & Singer, 2003).

Often, imagery is included in athletes' preperformance routines (e.g., seeing the ball float softly over the front of the rim into the basket). Imagery also should be used to systematically practice preperformance routines to make them more automatic. Then, during the pressure of competition, these routines are used to lock athletes into "autopilot," where their best performances occur.

Building and enhancing mental skills. Imagery, as a mental training tool, can be used to build and enhance all types of mental skills important to an athlete's performance.

Self-confidence. Athletes should nurture a self-image of competence and success, and re-creating past successful performances and the positive feelings associated with these successes can do this. An imagery exercise called Ideal Self-Image (ISI) is useful to work on confidence. To practice the ISI exercise, athletes should imagine themselves displaying the skills and qualities that they would most like to have, such as more assertive communication skills, a confident posture after performance errors, or the ability to manage emotions during competition. Then, they should compare their ISI with their current self-image. This should enable them to understand specific behaviors and thoughts that they can actively engage in to begin to move toward their ISI. The ISI exercise should be used continuously to understand differences between their real and ideal selves. Imagery then can be used to practice new behaviors and ways of responding that move athletes toward their ISI.

Energy management. Athletes who need to increase their energy (arousal) to psych up for competition can imagine playing intensely and aggressively in front of a roaring crowd. Athletes who need to decrease their energy or arousal before competition can mentally recall their preparation and good performances in practice and previous competitions and then visualize themselves handling the pressure and performing successfully in the upcoming competition.

An imagery exercise called the Energy Room can help athletes regulate arousal from different competitive demands. The Energy Room image involves athletes walking down a dark tunnel to a door that leads them into a room that is very comfortable and pleasing. (You can create whatever type of room you wish.) The room is sealed and the idea is that special air is piped into the room that creates the type of energy that is needed for this specific athlete in his or her event. The athletes feel themselves become more energized or relaxed with each inhalation and feel increasing focus, intensity, or relaxation. The breathing continues until the athletes feel appropriately energized and walk back through the tunnel feeling relaxed, focused, intense, centered, or confident. Whatever variation is used in this image, the main objective is for athletes to have an imaginary place that they can go to create optimal energy and use any mental strategies they want to employ. The room should become comfortable and familiar so it is an easy place for athletes to go in their minds to manage and control their physical and mental arousal levels.

Stress management. Energy management is usually needed just before or during competition. Imagery may also be helpful to reduce stress that occurs because of an overload of life demands (e.g., job pressure, exams, deadlines). Coaches and athletes both should have two or three relaxing images that they can use when they need to reduce stress and help them to relax and unwind. These images might be of a favorite place or a warm beach. An example stress reduction imagery script is provided in the following box.

Sample imagery script for relaxation/ stress reduction

1. *Get into a comfortable position and close your eyes. Take several deep, cleansing breaths to relax and center yourself. Take a moment to scan your muscles. If you feel tension anywhere, gently remind yourself to "let it go." Continue to scan the muscles of your body. Wherever you feel any tension, allow yourself to consciously "let it go." As you do this, repeat the words "let it go" to yourself.*

2. *I would like you to visualize a very thick rope that is tied into a big knot. See the knot in your mind's eye. Notice the tightly intertwined pieces of the rope that are stretched taut against each other.*

Now visualize the knot slowly loosening, slowly loosening—a little bit of slack at a time until it is slack, limp, and completely uncoiled.

3. *Now visualize a candle that has burned out. Focus on the cold and hard wax that has accumulated at the base of the candle. Now visualize the wax slowly softening—becoming first gooey, then soft like butter, then totally liquid as the wax warms and melts.*

4. *Visualize yourself on a loud city corner. It's windy and cold, very busy, and very noisy. Feel people buffet you as they rush by, hear the noise of cars and trucks, and smell the fumes as buses drive by. Right beside you is a construction site, and a jack-hammer goes off without warning. It is so loud that your ears hurt and your body vibrates with the noise and concussions as it tears up the concrete. Slowly, ease yourself away so you are lying on your back on a grassy knoll by a sparkling blue lake. The sun warms your face and body, and a gentle breeze creates small ripples on the water. Listen as the jackhammer fades into a woodpecker gently rapping on a tree.*

5. *Now focus inwardly on yourself. You have released the knots and relaxed your body. You have softened and then melted the tension of your day. You have transformed the bustle and noise in your life into pleasant sounds of nature. By doing this, you have gained control over your mind and body. Remind yourself now that you have the ability to gain control of your thoughts and feelings through creative visualization. Affirm your personal power to choose to think and feel well, and to believe in your ability to transform your life in productive ways.*

6. *Refocus now on your breathing, and repeat the following affirmation each*

time you exhale: "My body is relaxed and open" (wait 30 seconds). Now change that affirmation (each time you exhale) to: "I choose to think and be well" (wait 30–50 seconds). Feel pride in yourself and your abilities, and reinforce to yourself now that you have the power each day to manage how you think and feel. Take time each day to relax your body, melt away the tension, and quiet the noise in your life.

Fanning, 1988

Increasing self-awareness. By systematically practicing imagery, athletes can become more aware of what is taking place within and around them by relaxing and paying attention to sensory details. A runner may learn much about a previously run race by vividly re-creating it in her mind. A member of the U.S. Nordic ski team was having problems sustaining the level of concentration she needed throughout her races. By imagining her past races in vivid detail, she suddenly became aware that she was shifting attention to the wrong things at the end of her races. She made a tactical correction in her race plan, and then mentally practiced her new strategy using imagery.

Aiding in the recovery from injury. Because injured athletes typically cannot participate in physical training, imagery allows them to mentally practice skills and strategies during their recovery. Injured athletes should attend team training sessions and imagine themselves running through the drills and workouts just as though they were physically performing them. Athletes should be challenged to use their time recovering from injuries to engage in mental training, and to maintain a focused, productive-thinking, strong-willed mind-set toward recovery. Among other things, athletes can set progressive rehabilitation goals and vividly imagine attaining these goals. They can also use the ISI exercise to work toward full recovery of their competitive self-image. Productive, goal-oriented imagery is essential to facilitate the critical mind–body link that has been shown to enhance the healing process. Consider the following experience of a professional (NHL) hockey goalie:

> The best example I've had . . . of the effects of positive imagery was the season with the lockout and then, being injured for eight weeks, and coming back, having to play in midseason form after a layoff of close to eight months. I came back and immediately played well that year, largely due to the visualization and my belief that I was going to be ready and I was going to play well with very little practice time. There is really no better proof than that. So I know it works . . . and if you start off slow, I know it will work for you. (Orlick, 1998, p. 74)

Times to Use Imagery

You now know some specific uses for imagery. But when is the most effective time to use it? Staying with our cookbook design, we offer three suggestions about when to use imagery.

Daily practice. To be systematic, daily imagery practice is advised. As you will see in the sample programs at the end of the chapter, this may require only 5–10 minutes per day.

First, imagery practice may be used before actual physical practice sessions. This fits imagery into the athletes' routine and may get them into the proper frame of mind for practice.

It may also be appropriate to practice imagery after actual physical practice sessions. This has been successful with groups in reaffirming the points emphasized in practice that day. Also, athletes are more relaxed at the end of practice and may be more receptive to imagery at that time.

There are certain times when imagery may be beneficial during practice. For example, if a basketball coach implements an imagery program to practice free throws, he or she may build in time for imagery practice prior to shooting free throws in practice. This is especially helpful in developing kinesthetic imagery ability.

Preperformance routine.   It is helpful for athletes to go through a preperformance imagery routine *before every contest*. This routine should be individualized for each athlete and practiced in preperformance situations. To facilitate developing a routine, it is helpful to have a quiet, comfortable room available to all athletes prior to competition. However, if no room is available, imagery can be practiced anywhere. In this case, athletes could use the Energy Room image suggested earlier to mentally prepare for competition. Suggestions about the content of these precompetitive routines are included with the sample programs at the end of the chapter.

Also, certain skills in sport are conducive to a preperformance imagery routine before actually performing the skill. Closed skills such as free throw shooting, field goal kicking, ski jumping, volleyball serving, or gymnastic vaulting are more easily practiced in this way, as opposed to open skills such as broken field running in football or executing a fast break in basketball.

Postperformance review.   Another appropriate time to use imagery is after competition. Again, this should be an individual exercise, but coaches can monitor it by having the athletes complete postcompetitive evaluation sheets based on their postperformance imagery. Using imagery at this time facilitates increased awareness of what actually happened during the competition.

Strategies to Enhance Imagery Practice

Now that you understand what athletes can use imagery for and when they can use it, this section offers some additional strategies to make their imagery more effective.

Athletes should practice imagery in many different places and positions.   Most people envision mental training as something an athlete does when lying on a couch. Athletes may want to spend time developing their imagery skills in quiet, nondistractible settings but, once they have become proficient at imagery, they should

engage in it in many different settings and positions. Athletes should be able to engage in imagery in the locker room, on the field, in the pool, during practice, during competition—in any type of setting! It helps if coaches incorporate imagery into practice sessions to make it habitual for athletes. Encourage athletes to practice imagery in many different positions. If they are mentally practicing a sport skill such as a gymnastics routine or high jump, it might be useful for them to stand up or even walk through and move their body in certain ways that match the different segments of their images. They may want to hold the bat, club, or ball in their hands to facilitate their images as they repeat their imagery triggers to themselves to cue in perfect responses.

Training the inner winner

Tony DiCicco, former coach of the U.S. Women's Soccer national team, talks about the importance of developing the "inner winner" in athletes. He describes how he attempted to boost his athletes' confidence by helping them feel themselves being successful by using imagery:

> In the middle of the day, with the sun beaming down after a hard training session, I would have the players lie down on the grass, relax and do imagery training. I had them visualize performing their unique abilities on the soccer field over and over again. I would say, 'Imagine in your mind what you do well. If you're a great header, visualize yourself winning headers. If you're a great defender, visualize yourself stripping the ball from an attacking player. If you're a great passer of the ball, visualize yourself playing balls in. If you've got great speed, visualize yourself running by players and receiving the ball.' I made a special point of saying, 'Visualize the special skills that separate you from the rest—the skills that make your team better because you possess them.' (DiCicco, Hacker, & Salzberg, 2003, p. 112)

The timing in imagery should be the same as in the actual physical execution of the skill.   Forget about slow motion and fast forward—imagery shouldn't be used for slow motion analysis nor should it be rushed. Athletes should make their images as realistic in timing as possible in relation to the actual timing of their physical performance. Timing is a critical performance factor in many sports; thus it becomes a key response characteristic that athletes want to stamp into their images. Elite swimmers and runners are typically able to imagine their races down to the fraction of a second in terms of their splits and final times.

Help athletes use technology to enhance their images.   Some athletes find it useful to buy commercially produced imagery cassette tapes or make their own imagery tapes. Sport psychology consultants can make cassette tapes for athletes that combine the practice of physical and mental skills. Imagery tapes made for athletes should be highly individualized with specific verbal triggers and symbolic images that are meaningful to each athlete.

The use of personal highlight videotapes has been shown to enhance the confidence and performance of basketball (Templin & Vernacchia, 1995), ice hockey (Halliwell, 1990), and soccer (Lieber, 1999) players. Athletes' peak performance moments are edited from competitive videotape and integrated with special effects and motivational music. These highlight videos can then be used in conjunction with imagery to enhance confidence in returning from injury or slumps.

Remember that athletes should imagine vivid mental, physiological, and behavioral responses to situations.   Athletes must load their images with vivid responses. Remember that imagery works by helping athletes build and refine mental blueprints for perfect responses (bioinformational theory). Repeatedly remind athletes that their images should include their mental, physiological, and behavioral responses to competition—not just the stimulus characteristics of the situation. That is, when they imagine a big crowd and lots of noise and distractions, make sure they imagine how they will respond (e.g., using

the energy as positive fuel, keeping focused in the "cocoon," and exuding confidence as they physically warm up for competition).

Image performance and outcome.   Tennis players should imagine executing sharply paced passing shots and then see these shots hit in the corners of their opponent's court. Baseball players should imagine a strong and compact swing, and then see the ball driven as a line-drive through the outfield. Golfers should envision and feel the swing they will use, and then "see" the trajectory the ball will take as well as exactly where it will land. Athletes should follow through on their imagery to see not only perfect performances, but also perfect outcomes.

Be specific in all uses of imagery.   Imagery should be very specifically tailored to each athlete's individual needs. For example, consider a softball pitcher who generally pitches well until there are runners on base, which seems to distract her from throwing strikes. Although it would be somewhat helpful for her to engage in the repetitive mental practice of pitching, it would be better for her to set up many different situations to practice using imagery to build her confidence and concentration to pitch effectively in changing game situations. She should repeatedly envision herself in various situations with baserunners, different counts and number of outs, and different game scores to develop strong and consistent mental and physical responses to the pressure of these situations. Athletes must consider their exact performance needs, so that their imagery practice is specific in helping them develop thoughts and behaviors that can overcome performance problems.

Using the Imagery Cookbook

You now have all the ingredients (uses, times, strategies) to cook up an effective and systematic imagery program for your athletes. Remember the KISS principle—keep it simple and systematic instead of trying to do too much at first. Carefully consider the types and methods of imagery that will work for you in your particular situation.

Sample imagery programs. Three sample imagery programs are provided next to give you a basic idea about the structure and progression of imagery programs for athletes. These program outlines are generic, and should be modified to meet the sport-specific and program-specific needs of your athletes.

Team Imagery Program

The coach or sport psychology consultant should begin the team imagery program well before the start of the competitive season so athletes are familiar with imagery and proficient in their imagery skills.

First three weeks of preseason

1. Introduce program (15–20 minutes).

2. Evaluate athletes' imagery ability (15 minutes).

3. Basic Training (three times per week for 10 minutes following practice). Begin Basic Training with the exercises suggested in this chapter, then add exercises that are appropriate for your team and sport (team tactics and strategies).

4. Provide individual imagery sessions for athletes who are interested. Also, invite athletes to meet with you individually to discuss personalized imagery training they can do on their own. Continue to provide individual sessions for athletes throughout the season if they want them.

Remainder of season (three times per week 10 minutes before, following, or during practice).

1. Repetitive practice of simple sport skills*— perform them perfectly!

2. Repetitive practice of advanced sport skills*—perform them perfectly!

3. Competitive tactics and strategies in relation to specific needs of team and upcoming opponents*

4. Re-create past successful performance

5. Goal programming for future success

Include in *all* sessions the imagery exercises marked with an asterisk. They are a warm-up for the other types of imagery. After these initial warm-up exercises, you can use any types of imagery exercises. Other suggested images might include the following:

- Confidence in fulfilling team role successfully
- Attentional focus (develop a team focus plan for different opponents)
- Using verbal triggers and symbolic images
- Energy management (Energy Room or similar image to feel control over arousal regulation)
- Correcting mistakes/practice refocusing plan
- Precompetitive routine (should be practiced at least twice a week)

Precompetitive imagery routine. The suggested practice outline (the first six steps listed under "Remainder of Season") could be incorporated into individual precompetitive routines. Encourage each athlete to develop his or her own routine, and make available a preevent imagery room or specified area in which imagery can be practiced privately.

Postgame imagery review. Devise an event evaluation sheet that athletes will complete after each game. This sheet should ask the athletes to evaluate their performance in the following areas: physical skills, strategies, fulfillment of role, achievement of goals, energy management, attentional focus, self-confidence, areas that need improvement, and strategies to improve these areas. Make the sheet concise and objective so the athletes will find it easy to complete (see Chapter 11 for a sample evaluation sheet).

Individual Imagery Program

1. Education about imagery to understand basics of imagery

2. Evaluation of imagery ability (use questionnaire)

3. Basic Training (once a day for 10 minutes).

4. Regular imagery sessions (throughout competitive season)

Prepractice (5 minutes):

Technique work

Goal programming for practice

Postpractice (10 minutes):

Re-create practice performance

Mental skills practice (according to individual need)

Practice precompetitive imagery program

5. Competition day

Preevent imagery (10–20 minutes):

Use format suggested in "Team Imagery Program"

Postevent review (10–20 minutes):

Design personal event evaluation sheet or log

Figure Skating Skill Acquisition Program

Skill acquisition exercises for an axel jump

1. Watch a skilled skater, either live or on videotape, perform an axel several times. Try to get a general idea of the timing and the movements involved. Now, close your eyes and imagine the other skater performing the axel. Next, try to put yourself in the other skater's body. Imagine what the timing and movements *feel* like.

2. Walk through the axel several times off the ice in sneakers. Notice how the jump feels. Pay attention to the timing and the rotation. Close your eyes and try to feel yourself performing the axel. Alternate between walking through the jump and imagining the jump. Try to feel balanced and in control during both activities.

3. Close your eyes and imagine yourself performing the axel. Concentrate on the feelings associated with performing the jump. Imagine yourself performing successfully

and feeling confident. Now, physically perform the axel on the ice. Focus on creating the same feelings during the physical performance as in the mental practice.

Activity.   Perform the axel 10 times, concentrating on feeling the timing, the rotation, and staying balanced.

Triggers for axel jump

1. Exhale and sit into the takeoff (proper takeoff position).

2. Kick a football and explode (bring free leg through as if you were kicking a football).

3. Step up, land backwards (shift weight to the free leg as if you were stepping up onto a step and landing on the step backwards).

4. Soft and hold (the landing motion should be soft and the landing position held).

Imagery practice with triggers.   Use the triggers in conjunction with the imagery practice and physical practice of the axel jump. Imagine performing the axel five times using the triggers as a guide for proper technique.

Routine for each jump

1. Before physically performing the jump, imagine yourself successfully performing and landing the axel. Focus on the feeling and timing of the jump, as well as the sense of control over the jump. Use the triggers to re-create the proper technique.

2. When setting up the jump, take a deep breath and exhale. Focus on feeling balanced.

3. As you enter the jump, concentrate on sitting into the entry and exploding on the takeoff.

4. On the landing, use the triggers soft and hold to achieve the proper landing position.

Case studies

Now that you've read the "cookbook" and some sample programs, let's try your hand at planning imagery training programs for athletes. In this section, three case studies are presented that describe athletes who are having performance problems. Read through each case and use your knowledge from the chapter to plan an imagery intervention to help that athlete perform better. Write your plan for each athlete down on paper, and then go on to read the hypothetical imagery interventions that we suggest for each case. Don't look ahead until you plan your own imagery interventions for each athlete!

Molly

Molly, a 13-year-old figure skater, is attempting her senior freestyle test for the third time. Molly needs to pass this test to qualify for the highest level of national competition. In practice, Molly has completed all of the elements of her freestyle program with ease, but she tends to choke during the test sessions. Her coach attempts to be patient and supportive by telling Molly that she just needs to try harder and practice more.

Mario

Mario is a collegiate ice hockey player who lacks consistency in his performance. He performs well until he becomes distracted by his anger in reaction to game events that he cannot control, such as poor officiating, rough play by opponents, or poor ice conditions. When asked about his inconsistency, Mario says, "I just can't concentrate on the game when things go wrong!" Mario's coach tells him that he'd better get a handle on his temper and focus on the game.

Dee

Dee is a gifted high school sprinter. She is in top physical condition and is expected to have a great senior season and earn a track scholarship to a major university. Dee injures her ankle before the first meet of the year, yet when she returns to competition a few weeks later, she does not perform as well as she or her coaches expected. Dee has recovered physically from the injury, but mentally she is worried about reinjury. She is not putting 100% effort into practice and her performance suffers as a result. Deep down, she is concerned that she will not make it back to her previous performance level, and she is worried that she will now fail to gain a scholarship.

Suggested Imagery Intervention Plans

Molly.   Initially we got to know Molly and talked with her about her perceived strengths and weaknesses as a figure skater. We introduced the concept of imagery to her and guided her through imagery in which she imagined her performance during practice and during a test session. After imagining each scene, she wrote down the characteristics of the performances, including how she felt during the performance, what she said to herself, how she prepared for the performances, and how she responded to mistakes. Based on an evaluation of Molly's imagery ability, we recommended some Basic Training exercises with an emphasis on arousal control and refocusing after mistakes.

We worked with Molly to develop a pretest imagery program in which she saw herself performing well, achieving her goals (goal programming), and refocusing after mistakes in her program. We developed an imagery script for Molly to use before test sessions focusing on arousal control and self-confidence. Here is an example of Molly's imagery script:

> I am calm, confident, and in control. My muscles are loose and relaxed, like flexible springs. I am breathing easily, feeling my lungs fill with energizing air. During my warm-up, I feel focused and confident. My blades cut into the ice with ease, making a crisp cutting noise. My jumps are snappy and explosive. My spins are centered and tight. My muscles are warm and elastic. As I step onto the ice for my program, I feel balanced and in control. I take my beginning position with a confident posture, feeling excited anticipation to perform my best. I know that I'm ready.

Molly practiced this pretest imagery program during simulated test sessions and during practice sessions to re-create the testing experience. Through imagery, Molly developed the mental skills to become more mentally tough and focused during pressure performances.

Mario. We first got to know Mario and talked with him about his perceived strengths and weaknesses as a hockey player. We introduced the concept of imagery to him and guided him through an imagery session in which he visualized his performance being negatively affected by anger. After the imagery, we specifically worked with Mario to identify the specific characteristics of the situation, such as what triggered his anger, his attitude before and after the trigger event, and his focus before and after the trigger. We evaluated Mario's imagery ability and recommended various Basic Training exercises, especially focusing on self-awareness and controllability.

We worked with Mario to develop a refocusing imagery program in which he saw himself refocusing after negative events, directing the anger in a productive way, and performing well after negative events. Mario imagined several different scenarios in which he typically loses his temper and his focus, such as after a poor call from an official or rough play by the opposing team. We worked with Mario to develop several imagery scripts incorporating imagery triggers, so he could mentally practice emotional control and refocusing. An excerpt from his emotional control script follows:

> [Trigger event] . . . Deep breath . . . Squeeze stick . . . Let anger swell up from the bottom of your toes, into your legs, all the way through your trunk and chest. Feel the anger flowing down out of your arms, feel the hot emotions bursting out of your fingers. Squeeze all of that anger into your stick. Take a deep breath. Relax your hands.

Mario was able to use his imagery scripts to practice emotional control and refocusing skills. He became more consistent in his ability to focus after negative events during games and continued to use imagery for refocusing.

Dee. We first got to know Dee and discussed her physical and mental approach to competition. We guided her through several imagery sessions in which she imagined her performance both before and after her injury. We asked Dee to focus on how she felt, what she said to herself, and what her mental attitude was during both situations. We had her re-create through imagery the times before her injury in which she ran well, and also had her compare her thoughts, feelings, and behaviors to times after her injury. During this time, we also had Dee practice imagery to become more skilled at controlling her images.

We worked with Dee to develop an imagery program in which she re-created the feelings of confidence and competence she experienced prior to her injury. We had her keep a log of her mental states before, during, and after practices and meets. Additionally, Dee recorded any triggers that she associated with changes in her attitude or mood toward her ability. Initially, Dee's log indicated that she questioned her running ability. After a period of systematic and consistent use of imagery, Dee's attitude began to change. She began to feel more sure of herself and thus pushed herself harder during practice. The combination of her mental and physical training helped Dee to get back to her preinjury running level. Seeing *was* believing for Dee as she went on to become a successful collegiate runner and advocate for the power of imagery.

Summary

Imagery is defined as using one's senses to re-create or create an experience in the mind. It is a mental technique that programs the human mind to respond as programmed—to see and believe. Both scientific and experiential accounts of the use of imagery to enhance sport performance report positive results. Key considerations in using imagery include developing both internal and external perspectives and understanding that imagery is a supplement to, not a replacement for, physical practice. The ability of athletes to engage in vivid and controlled images is critical to the effectiveness of imagery in enhancing performance.

Three conceptual explanations suggest how imagery may enhance performance. Bioinformational theory indicates that individuals respond to imagery with response characteristics that create psychophysiological changes in the body that positively influence performance. The functional equivalence explanation is based on the idea that imagery activates the same areas and processes in the brain as the actual physical execution of the movement. The mental readiness explanation suggests that imagery causes athletes to optimize arousal and confidence and to focus their attention on relevant cues prior to competition.

Setting up a systematic imagery program involves four steps. First, athletes are introduced to imagery. Second, athletes evaluate their imagery abilities to understand their strengths and areas that need improvement. Third, athletes should engage in Basic Training to develop and enhance their imagery skills. Finally, imagery should be integrated into a systematic program of physical and mental training.

Study Questions

1. Briefly describe some of the evidence supporting the positive influence of imagery on sport performance.

2. Describe the four phases of setting up an imagery training program.

3. Vividness, controllability, and self-awareness are three areas of Basic Training in the imagery training program. Define each of these and describe the role each plays in training an athlete to use an imagery program.

4. What are five different ways imagery can be used by athletes?

5. Identify and describe the three explanations provided in this chapter that address how imagery works to enhance sport performance.

6. Develop an imagery program for an athlete in your sport using the imagery cookbook.

7. Explain why and how imagery can be polysensory.

8. What are three different times imagery can be used optimally by athletes?

9. What is the difference between external and internal imagery, and how can athletes use each perspective?

10. Can imagery hurt athletes' performance? Explain and then identify how athletes can avoid this negative imagery effect.

References

Bakker, F. C., Boschker, M. S. J., & Chung, T. (1996). Changes in muscular activity while imagining weight lifting using stimulus or response propositions. *Journal of Sport & Exercise Psychology, 18*, 313–324.

Beauchamp, P. H., Halliwell, W. R., Fournier, J. F., & Koestner, R. (1996). Effects of cognitive-behavioral psychological skills training on the motivation, preparation, and putting performance of novice golfers. *The Sport Psychologist, 10*, 157–170.

Beilock, S. L., Afremow, J. A., Rabe, A. L., & Carr, T. H. (2001). "Don't miss!" The debilitating effects of suppressive imagery on golf putting performance. *Journal of Sport & Exercise Psychology, 23*, 200–221.

Bird, L. (1989). *Drive: The story of my life.* New York: Bantam.

Callow, N., Hardy, L., & Hall, C. (2001). The effects of a motivational general-mastery imagery intervention on the sport confidence of high-level badminton players. *Research Quarterly for Exercise and Sport, 72*, 389–400.

Calmels, C., Berthoumieux, C., & d'Arripe-Longueville, F. (2004). Effects of an imagery training program on selective attention of national softball players. *The Sport Psychologist, 18*, 272–296.

Calmels, C., d'Arripe-Longueville, F., Fournier, J. F., & Soulard, A. (2003). Competitive strategies among elite female gymnasts: An exploration of the relative influence of psychological skills training and natural learning experiences. *International Journal of Sport & Exercise Psychology, 1*, 327–352.

Cogan, K. D., & Petrie, T. A. (1995). Sport consultation: An evaluation of a season-long intervention with female collegiate gymnasts. *The Sport Psychologist, 9*, 282–296.

Cumming, J., & Hall, C. (2002). Athletes' use of imagery in the off-season. *The Sport Psychologist, 16*, 160–172.

Cumming, J., Olphin, T., & Law, M. (2007). Self-reported psychological states and physiological responses to different types of motivational general imagery. *Journal of Sport & Exercise Psychology, 29*, 629–644.

Daw, J., & Burton, D. (1994). Evaluation of a comprehensive psychological skills training program for collegiate tennis players. *The Sport Psychologist, 8*, 37–57.

DiCicco, T., Hacker, C., & Salzberg, C. (2003). *Catch them being good.* New York: Penguin.

Durand-Bush, N., & Salmela, J. H. (2002). The development and maintenance of expert athletic performance: Perceptions of world and Olympic champions. *Journal of Applied Sport Psychology, 14*, 154–171.

Efran, J. S., Lesser, G. S., & Spiller, M. J. (1994). Enhancing tennis coaching with youths using a metaphor method. *The Sport Psychologist, 8*, 349–359.

Evans, L., Jones, L., & Mullen, R. (2004). An imagery intervention during the competitive season with an elite rugby union player. *The Sport Psychologist, 18*, 252–271.

Fanning, P. (1988). *Visualization for change.* Oakland, CA: New Harbinger.

Feltz, D. L., & Landers, D. M. (1983). The effects of mental practice on motor skill learning and performance: A meta-analysis. *Journal of Sport Psychology, 5,* 25–57.

Feltz, D. L., Landers, D. M., & Becker, B. J. (1988). A revised meta-analysis of the mental practice literature on motor skill learning. In D. Druckman & J. Swets (Eds.), *Enhancing human performance: Issues, theories, and techniques* (pp. 1–65). Washington, DC: National Academy Press.

Garza, D. L., & Feltz, D. L. (1998). Effects of selected mental practice on performance, self-efficacy, and competition confidence of figure skaters. *The Sport Psychologist, 12,* 1–15.

Gould, D., Eklund, R. C., & Jackson, S. A. (1992). 1988 U.S. Olympic wrestling excellence: I. Mental preparation, precompetitive cognition, and affect. *The Sport Psychologist, 6,* 358–383.

Gould, D., Guinan, D., Greenleaf, C., Medbery, R., & Peterson, K. (1999). Factors affecting Olympic performance: Perceptions of athletes and coaches from more and less successful teams. *The Sport Psychologist, 13,* 371–394.

Gould, D., Tammen, V., Murphy, S. M., & May, J. (1989). An examination of U.S. Olympic sport psychology consultants and the services they provide. *The Sport Psychologist, 3,* 300–312.

Gould, D., Weinberg, R., & Jackson, A. (1980). Mental preparation strategies, cognitions, and strength performance. *Journal of Sport Psychology, 2,* 329–339.

Greenleaf, C. A., Gould, D., & Dieffenbach, K. (2001). Factors influencing Olympic performance: Interviews with Atlanta and Nagano U.S. Olympians. *Journal of Applied Sport Psychology, 13,* 154–184.

Gregg, M., & Hall, C. (2006). The relationship of skill level and age to the use of imagery by golfers. *Journal of Applied Sport Psychology, 18,* 363–375.

Hale, B. D., & Whitehouse, A. (1998). The effects of imagery-manipulated appraisal on intensity and direction of competitive anxiety. *The Sport Psychologist, 12,* 40–51.

Hall, C. R., & Rodgers, W. M. (1989). Enhancing coaching effectiveness in figure skating through a mental skills training program. *The Sport Psychologist, 2,* 142–154.

Hall, C. R., Rodgers, W. M., & Barr, K. A. (1990). The use of imagery by athletes in selected sports. *The Sport Psychologist, 4,* 1–10.

Halliwell, W. (1990). Providing sport psychology consulting services in professional hockey. *The Sport Psychologist, 4,* 369–377.

Hanton, S., & Jones, G. (1999). The effects of a multimodal intervention program on performers: II. Training the butterflies to fly in formation. *The Sport Psychologist, 13,* 22–41.

Hardy, L., & Callow, N. (1999). Efficacy of external and internal visual imagery perspectives for the enhancement of performance on tasks in which form is important. *Journal of Sport & Exercise Psychology, 21,* 95–112.

Hecker, J. E., & Kaczor, L. M. (1988). Application of imagery theory to sport psychology: Some preliminary findings. *Journal of Sport and Exercise Psychology, 10,* 363–373.

Hird, J. S., Landers, D. M., Thomas, J. R., & Horan, J. J. (1991). Physical practice is superior to mental practice in enhancing cognitive and motor task performance. *Journal of Sport and Exercise Psychology, 8,* 293.

Holmes, P. S., & Collins, D. J. (2001). The PETTLEP approach to motor imagery: A functional equivalence model for sport psychologists. *Journal of Applied Sport Psychology, 13,* 60–83.

Jeannerod, M. (1994). The representing brain: Neural correlates of motor intention and imagery. *Behavioral and Brain Sciences, 17,* 187–202.

Kendall, G., Hrycaiko, D., Martin, G. L., & Kendall, T. (1990). The effects of an imagery rehearsal, relaxation, and self-talk package on basketball game performance. *Journal of Sport and Exercise Psychology, 12,* 157–166.

Kerr, G., & Leith, L. (1993). Stress management and athletic performance. *The Sport Psychologist, 1,* 221–231.

Lang, P. J. (1977). Imagery in therapy: An information processing analysis of fear. *Behavior Therapy, 8,* 862–886.

Lang, P. J. (1979). A bio-informational theory of emotional imagery. *Psychophysiology, 16,* 495–512.

Lazarus, A. (1984). *In the mind's eye: The power of imagery for personal enrichment.* New York: Guilford.

Lee, A. B., & Hewitt, J. (1987). Using visual imagery in a flotation tank to improve gymnastic performance and reduce physical symptoms. *International Journal of Sport Psychology, 18,* 223–230.

Lee, C. (1990). Psyching up for a muscular endurance task: Effects of image content on performance and mood state. *Journal of Sport and Exercise Psychology, 12,* 66–73.

Lidor, R., & Singer, R. M. (2003). Preperformance routines in self-paced tasks: Developmental and educational considerations. In R. Lidor & K. P. Henschen (Eds.), *The psychology of team sports* (pp. 69–98). Morgantown, WV: Fitness Information Technology.

Lieber, J. (1999, July 6). USA won't kick habit of believing. *USA Today,* pp. 1c–2c.

Mamassis, G., & Doganis, G. (2004). The effects of a mental training program on juniors pre-competitive anxiety, self-confidence, and tennis performance. *Journal of Applied Sport Psychology, 16,* 118–137.

Martin, K. A., & Hall, C. R. (1995). Using mental imagery to enhance intrinsic motivation. *Journal of Sport and Exercise Psychology, 17,* 54–69.

Martin, K. A., Moritz, S. E., & Hall, C. R. (1999). Imagery use in sport: A literature review and applied model. *The Sport Psychologist, 13,* 245–268.

McCallum, J. (2004, May 24). It's that time again. *Sports Illustrated,* pp. 54–65.

McKenzie, A., & Howe, B. L. (1997). The effect of imagery on self-efficacy for a motor skill. *International Journal of Sport Psychology, 28,* 196–210.

Ming, S., & Martin, G. L. (1996). Single-subject evaluation of a self-talk package for improving figure skating performance. *The Sport Psychologist, 10,* 227–238.

Morris, T., Spittle, M., & Watt, A. P. (2005). *Imagery in sport.* Champaign, IL: Human Kinetics.

Mumford, P., & Hall, C. (1985). The effects of internal and external imagery on performing figures of figure skating. *Canadian Journal of Applied Sport Sciences, 10,* 171–177.

Murphy, S. M., & Woolfolk, R. (1987). The effects of cognitive interventions on competitive anxiety and performance on a fine motor skill task. *International Journal of Sport Psychology, 18,* 152–166.

Orlick, T. (1998). *Embracing your potential.* Champaign, IL: Human Kinetics.

Orlick, T., & Partington, J. (1988). Mental links to excellence. *The Sport Psychologist, 2,* 105–130.

Page, S. J., Sime, W., & Nordell, K. (1999). The effects of imagery on female college swimmers' perceptions of anxiety. *The Sport Psychologist, 13,* 458–469.

Ravizza, K. (1993). An interview with Peter Vidmar, member of the 1994 U.S. Olympic gymnastics team. *Contemporary Thought in Performance Enhancement, 2,* 93–100.

Reiter, B. (2006, July 17). Preparation. *Sports Illustrated,* p. 36.

Rodgers, W., Hall, C., & Buckolz, E. (1991). The effect of an imagery training program on imagery ability, imagery use, and figure skating performance. *Journal of Applied Sport Psychology, 3,* 109–125.

Ryska, T. A. (1998). Cognitive-behavioral strategies and precompetitive anxiety among recreational athletes. *Psychological Record, 48,* 697–708.

Salmon, J., Hall, C., & Haslam, I. (1994). The use of imagery by soccer players. *Journal of Applied Sport Psychology, 6,* 116–133.

Savoy, C. (1993). A yearly mental training program for a college basketball player. *The Sport Psychologist, 7,* 173–190.

Savoy, C. (1997). Two individual mental training programs for a team sport. *International Journal of Sport Psychology, 28,* 259–270.

Sheard, M., & Golby, J. (2006). Effect of a psychological skills training program on swimming performance and positive psychological development. *International Journal of Sport and Exercise Psychology, 4,* 149–169.

Shelton, T. O., & Mahoney, M. J. (1978). The content and effect of "psyching-up" strategies in weightlifters. *Cognitive Therapy and Research, 2,* 275–284.

Short, S. E., Bruggeman, J. M., Engel, S. G., Marback, T. L., Wang, L. J., Willadsen, A., & Short, M. W. (2002). The effect of imagery function and imagery direction on self-efficacy and performance on a golf-putting task. *The Sport Psychologist, 16,* 48–67.

Short, S.E., Smiley, M., & Ross-Stewart, L. (2005). The relationship between efficacy beliefs and imagery use in coaches. *The Sport Psychologist, 19,* 380–394.

Simons, J. (2000). Doing imagery in the field. In M. Andersen (Ed.), *Doing sport psychology* (pp. 77–92). Champaign, IL: Human Kinetics.

Smith, D., & Collins, D. (2004). Mental practice, motor performance, and the late CNV. *Journal of Sport & Exercise Psychology, 26,* 412–426.

Smith, D., & Holmes, P. (2004). The effect of imagery modality on golf putting performance. *Journal of Sport & Exercise Psychology, 26,* 385–395.

Smith, D., Holmes, P., Whitemore, L., Collins, D., & Devenport, T. (2001). The effect of theoretically-based imagery scripts on hockey penalty flick performance. *Journal of Sport Behavior, 24,* 408–419.

Smith, D., Wright, C., Allsopp, A., & Westhead, H. (2007). It's all in the mind: PETTLEP-based imagery and sports performance. *Journal of Applied Sport Psychology, 19,* 80–92.

Suinn, R. M. (1980). Psychology and sport performance: Principles and applications. In R. M. Suinn (Ed.), *Psychology in sports: Methods and applications* (pp. 26–36). Minneapolis: Burgess.

Templin, D. P., & Vernacchia, R. A. (1995). The effect of highlight music videotapes upon the game performance of intercollegiate basketball players. *The Sport Psychologist, 9,* 41–50.

Thelwell, R. C., & Greenlees, I. A. (2001). The effects of a mental skills training program on gymnasium triathlon performance. *The Sport Psychologist, 15,* 127–141.

Thelwell, R. C., Greenlees, I. A., & Weston, N. J. V. (2006). Using psychological skills training to develop soccer performance. *Journal of Applied Sport Psychology, 18,* 2006.

Thomas, O., Maynard,, I., & Hanton, S. (2007). Intervening with athletes during the time leading up to competition: Theory to practice II. *Journal of Applied Sport Psychology, 19,* 398–418.

Tynes, L. L., & McFatter, R. M. (1987). The efficacy of "psyching" strategies on a weightlifting task. *Cognitive Therapy and Research, 11,* 327–336.

Vandall, R. A., Davis, R. A., & Clugston, H. A. (1934). The function of mental practice in the acquisition of motor skills. *Journal of General Psychology, 29,* 243–250.

White, A., & Hardy, L. (1998). An in-depth analysis of the uses of imagery by high-level slalom canoeists and artistic gymnasts. *The Sport Psychologist, 12,* 387–403.

Woolfolk, R. L., Murphy, S. M., Gottesfeld, D., & Aitken, D. (1985). Effects of mental rehearsal of motor task activity and mental depiction of task outcome on motor skill performance. *Journal of Sport Psychology, 7,* 191–197.

Woolfolk, R., Parrish, W., & Murphy, S. M. (1985). The effects of positive and negative imagery on motor skill performance. *Cognitive Therapy and Research, 9,* 235–341.

Wrisberg, C. A. (1990). An interview with Pat Head Summitt. *The Sport Psychologist, 4,* 180–191.

Sample Imagery Script for Competition Preparation

Get into a comfortable position and close your eyes. Focus on the center of your body and take several slow deep breaths. With each inhalation, imagine that you are pulling all of the tension from your body into your lungs. With each exhalation, imagine that you are releasing all of your tension and negative thoughts from your body. Continue this focused breathing until your body becomes relaxed and your mind is alert and open for productive thoughts. (Pause for 30 seconds.)

Imagine it is the night before an important competition or performance. You are preparing for the next day's event. As you are preparing to go to sleep, you are focusing on feeling calm, confident, and physically and emotionally in control. (Pause for 10 seconds.) You are excited and anticipatory about performing well tomorrow. (Pause for 10 seconds.) You sleep well and awaken feeling rested, excited, and focused. (Pause for 8 seconds.) You realize that you are well prepared, both physically and mentally, for the competition. Physically, you feel balanced and ready. Mentally, you are confident and focused. (Pause for 10 seconds.)

Now imagine that you are at home preparing to leave for the competition site. (Pause for 10 seconds.) You take some time to run through your mental warm-up by visualizing several repetitions of a few basic skills in your sport, such as a warm-up drill. (Pause for 30 seconds.) Now in your mind's eye, focus on the specific goals and strategies for this particular competition. Imagine yourself performing perfectly, achieving your goals for the competition and successfully executing specific strategies for this opponent. (Pause for 60 seconds.)

Now imagine yourself arriving at the competition site feeling confident in your physical and mental preparation. (Pause for 20 seconds.) You feel the nervous anticipation of competition and remind yourself that it is exhilarating to play your sport. You love it! (Pause for 10 seconds.) Imagine your feelings as you dress and go through any precompetitive preparations. (Pause for 20 seconds.) You feel confident in your preparation and clearly focused on your upcoming performance. Your breathing is calm and controlled. Your muscles feel warm and elastic, ready to explode with intensity and precision. You are ready! (Pause for 15 seconds.) Imagine going through your competition warm-up as you have done so many times in practice. (Pause for 30 seconds.) Your warm-up goes well, yet you remind yourself that you are ready for any unexpected problem or obstacle. You are confident in your refocusing ability and remind yourself that you are mentally tough. You feel optimally energized and ready to go. Enjoy it!

Sport Imagery Evaluation

As you complete this evaluation, remember that imagery is more than just visualizing something in your mind's eye. Vivid images may include many senses, such as seeing, hearing, feeling, touching, and smelling. Vivid images also may include feeling emotions or moods.

In this exercise you will read descriptions of general sport situations. You are to imagine the situation and provide as much detail from your imagination as possible to make the image as real as you can. Then you will be asked to rate your imagery in seven areas:

a. How vividly you *saw* or visualized the image.

b. How clearly you *heard* the sounds.

c. How vividly you *felt your body movements* during the activity.

d. How clearly you were aware of your mood or *felt your emotions* of the situation.

e. Whether you could see the image from *inside your body*.

f. Whether you could see the image from *outside your body*.

g. How well you could *control* the image.

After you read each description, think of a specific example of it—the skill, the people involved, the place, the time. Then close your eyes and try to imagine the situation as vividly as you can.

There are, of course, no right or wrong images. Use your imagery skills to create the most vivid and clear image that you can. After you have completed imagining each situation, rate your imagery skills using the following scales.

For items a–f:

1 = no image present

2 = not clear or vivid, but a recognizable image

3 = moderately clear and vivid image

4 = clear and vivid image

5 = extremely clear and vivid image

For item g:

1 = no control at all of image

2 = very hard to control

3 = moderate control of image

4 = good control of image

5 = complete control of image

Practicing Alone

Select one specific skill or activity in your sport, such as shooting free throws, performing a parallel bar routine, executing a takedown, throwing a pass, hitting a ball, or swimming the butterfly. Now imagine yourself performing this activity at the place where you normally practice (gym, pool, rink, field, court) without anyone else present. Close your eyes for about 1 minute and try to see yourself at this place, hear the sounds, feel your body perform the movement, and be aware of your state of mind or mood. Try to see yourself from behind your eyes or from inside your body. Then, try to see yourself from outside your body, as if you were watching a videotape of yourself performing.

a. Rate how well you *saw* yourself doing the activity.   1   2   3   4   5

b. Rate how well you *heard* the sounds of doing the activity.   1   2   3   4   5

c. Rate how well you *felt yourself* making the movements.   1   2   3   4   5

d. Rate how well you were aware of your *mood*.   1   2   3   4   5

e. Rate how well you were able to see the image from *inside* your body.   1   2   3   4   5

f. Rate how well you were able to see the image from *outside* your body.   1   2   3   4   5

g. Rate how well you *controlled* the image.   1   2   3   4   5

Practicing with Others

You are doing the same activity, but now you are practicing the skill with your coach and teammates present. This time, however, you make a mistake that everyone notices. Close your eyes for about 1 minute to imagine making the error and the situation immediately afterward as vividly as you can. First, try to experience the feelings you have as you make the mistake. Then, quickly try to re-create the situation in your mind and imagine yourself correcting the mistake and performing perfectly. Try to see the image from behind your eyes or from inside your body as you correct the mistake. Next, try to see the image as if you were watching through a video camera as you correct the mistake.

a. Rate how well you *saw* yourself in this situation.   1   2   3   4   5

b. Rate how well you *heard* the sounds in this situation.   1   2   3   4   5

c. Rate how well you *felt yourself* making the movements.   1   2   3   4   5

d. Rate how well you *felt the emotions* of this situation.   1   2   3   4   5

e. Rate how well you were able to see the image from *inside* your body.   1   2   3   4   5

f. Rate how well you were able to see the image from *outside* your body.   1   2   3   4   5

g. Rate how well you *controlled* the image.   1   2   3   4   5

Playing in a Contest

Imagine yourself performing the same or similar activity in competition, but imagine yourself doing the activity very skillfully and the spectators and teammates showing their appreciation. As you imagine the situation, try to see the crowd and hear the noise they are making.

Imagine yourself feeling confident in your ability to perform, as well as your ability to handle the pressure. Now close your eyes for about 1 minute and imagine this situation as vividly as possible. Try to image yourself performing from inside your body, as if you were actually performing, as well as from outside your body, as if you were a spectator.

a. Rate how well you *saw* yourself in this situation. 1   2   3   4   5

b. Rate how well you *heard* the sounds in this situation. 1   2   3   4   5

c. Rate how well you *felt yourself* making the movements. 1   2   3   4   5

d. Rate how well you *felt the emotions* of this situation. 1   2   3   4   5

e. Rate how well you were able to see the image from *inside* your body. 1   2   3   4   5

f. Rate how well you were able to see the image from *outside* your body. 1   2   3   4   5

g. Rate how well you *controlled* the image. 1   2   3   4   5

Recalling a Peak Performance

Recall one of your all-time best performances—a performance in which you felt confident, in control, in the zone. Close your eyes for about 1 minute and try to see yourself in that situation,

feel your emotions, and re-create the experience. Imagine your performance and re-create the feelings you experienced, both mentally and physically, during that performance. Try to see the image from within yourself, and then try to imagine the situation from outside yourself.

a. Rate how well you *saw* yourself in this situation. 1   2   3   4   5

b. Rate how well you *heard* the sounds in this situation. 1   2   3   4   5

c. Rate how well you *felt yourself* making the movements. 1   2   3   4   5

d. Rate how well you *felt the emotions* of this situation. 1   2   3   4   5

e. Rate how well you were able to see the image from *inside* your body. 1   2   3   4   5

f. Rate how well you were able to see the image from *outside* your body. 1   2   3   4   5

g. Rate how well you *controlled* the image. 1   2   3   4   5

Scoring

Now let's determine your imagery scores and see what they mean. Sum the ratings for each category and record them below.

Directions	Dimension	Score
Sum all *a* items	Visual	_____
Sum all *b* items	Auditory	_____
Sum all *c* items	Kinesthetic	_____
Sum all *d* items	Emotion	_____
Sum all *e* items	Internal perspective	_____
Sum all *f* items	External perspective	_____
Sum all *g* items	Controllability	_____

Interpret your scores in the visual, auditory, kinesthetic, emotion, and controllability categories based on the following scale: excellent (20–18), good (17–15), average (14–12), fair (11–8), and poor (7–4). Notice the categories in which your scores were low and refer to exercises in the chapter to increase your imagery ability in those areas. All of these categories are important for imagery training, so don't just rely on your visual sense. Work to improve the others! Remember, it takes practice but you *can* increase your imagery ability. Good luck!

Cognitive Techniques for Building Confidence and Enhancing Performance

Nate Zinsser, *United States Military Academy*
Linda Bunker, *University of Virginia, Emeritus*
Jean M. Williams, *University of Arizona, Emeritus*

If you think you can do a thing or think you can't do a thing, you're right.

—Henry Ford

But with hard work, with belief, with confidence and trust in yourself and those around you, there are no limits.

—Michael Phelps, 2008, winner of 14 Olympic gold medals

The most consistent finding in peak performance literature is the direct correlation between self-confidence and success (see Chapter 9). Athletes who are truly outstanding are self-confident. Their confidence has been developed over many years and is the direct result of effective thinking and frequent experiences in which they have been successful. Because developing confidence is such a high priority for athletes and coaches who wish to become successful, understanding confidence and how to enhance it is an equally high priority for sport psychologists working in applied settings.

What we think and say to ourselves in practice and competition is critical to performance.

Confident athletes think about themselves and the action at hand in a different way than those who lack confidence. They have learned that the conscious mind is not always an ally, that it must be disciplined, just as their bodies have been disciplined, to respond effectively in the heat of competition. We all spend vast amounts of time talking to ourselves. Much of the time we are not even aware of this internal dialogue, much less its content. Nevertheless, thoughts directly affect feelings and ultimately actions:

THOUGHTS → FEELINGS → BEHAVIOR

Inappropriate or misguided thinking usually leads to negative feelings and poor performance, just

305

as appropriate or positive thinking leads to enabling feelings and good performance (Kendall, Hrycaiko, Martin, & Kendall, 1990; McPherson, 2000; Van Raalte et al., 1995).

Athletes who are truly outstanding are self-confident, and this confidence is not an accident. This chapter's central thesis is that confidence in competitive sport is the result of particular thinking habits. These thinking habits, when consistently practiced until they have become automatic and natural, enable athletes to both retain and benefit from the experiences in which they have been successful, and release or restructure the memories and feelings from the less successful experiences. The result of this selective perception is the priceless trait called confidence.

Confident athletes think they can, and *they do*. They never give up. They typically are characterized by positive self-talk, images, and dreams. They imagine themselves winning and being successful. They focus on successfully mastering a task rather than worrying about performing poorly or the negative consequences of failure. This predisposition to keep one's mind on the positive aspects of one's life and sport performance, even in the face of setbacks and disappointments, is a hallmark of the successful athlete, a trait Seligman (1991) refers to as "learned optimism." Having learned to be optimistic, these confident athletes get the most from their abilities. Their confidence programs them for successful performance.

If confidence is so critical to successful performance and personal growth, what can coaches and sport psychologists do to help promote self-confidence within their athletes? Many of the earlier chapters in this book have provided, either directly or indirectly, some answers to this question. For example, seeing improvement in physical skill and providing for a history of successful experiences builds both confidence and the expectation of future success. Coaches who observe the learning and performance guidelines outlined in Chapters 2 and 3 will be more likely to maximize successful skill development in their athletes. Effective coach–athlete interactions, as illustrated in Chapters 6, 7, and 8, are

likely to enhance each athlete's sense of self-worth and self-esteem. Practices that maximize such growth in athletes, whether the growth be in physical skills or personal development, lead to a more positive self-concept and increased self-confidence.

In this chapter we discuss techniques for improving confidence and performance by learning to use and control thoughts or cognitions appropriately. Developing and maintaining confidence for high-level competition requires that athletes recognize and then deliberately step away from many of the dysfunctional thinking habits they may have developed over the years. It is important that athletes understand how the mind works, how it affects their feelings and actions, and ultimately how it can be disciplined. Initially thoughts may appear to occur spontaneously and involuntarily—thus, beyond control. With the skills of intentional thinking, athletes can control their thoughts. They can learn to use self-talk to facilitate learning and performance. They can also learn to replace self-defeating thoughts with positive ones—thoughts that build confidence and the expectation of success. Such positive thought processes can become self-fulfilling prophecies.

Key Definitions: Confidence, Mental Toughness, Optimism, Self-Efficacy

Most dictionary definitions of *confidence* will include phrases such as "a state of assurance" and "a belief in one's powers." The image of any great athlete (e.g., Tiger Woods, Serena Williams, Tim Duncan) usually includes this assurance. Joe Morgan, the former major league baseball all-star, expressed this thought when he said, "To be a star and stay a star, I think you've got to have a *certain air of arrogance about you, a cockiness, a swagger on the field* [italics added] that says, 'I can do this and you can't stop me.' I know that I play with this air of arrogance, but I think it's lacking in a lot of guys who have the talent to be stars"

(Ferguson, 1991, p. 425). For many, confidence can be thought of as a certain level of healthy arrogance.

The idea of "mental toughness" is certainly related to the concept of confidence. Through a series of interviews with international caliber athletes, Jones, Hanton, and Connaugton (2002) arrived at a definition of mental toughness as "the natural or developed psychological edge . . . that enables you to cope better than your competitors with the demands of performance . . . and to remain more determined, focused, confident, and in control." Furthermore they identified the most important attribute of mental toughness as "an unshakable belief in your ability to achieve your competitive goals." This study reinforces the importance of belief in oneself to the concept of confidence and also emphasizes that it can be developed through time and training.

A related concept important to the understanding of confidence is optimism, defined as "a tendency to expect the best possible outcome or dwell on the most hopeful aspects of a situation." In the world of sport and competitive performance, the propensity to look for opportunities to score, to win, to excel, regardless of the circumstances, is indispensable for success. Most important, any athlete or performer can systematically cultivate and develop this optimistic tendency, as the following pages will describe.

A fourth related concept is self-efficacy (Bandura, 1977), which refers to the conviction that one can successfully execute the specific behavior required to produce the desired outcome (see Chapter 4 for a discussion of self-efficacy and its role in motivation and performance). It is useful to think of sport confidence as a relatively global concept, referring to one's overall attitude toward one's sport. Think of self-efficacy as a more specific type of confidence, referring to particular skills, techniques, and situations. Taken together, the concepts of confidence, mental toughness, optimism, and self-efficacy make up both a global and specific belief that "I can do it," which is essential for success, especially for athletic success. Without this belief, one automatically concedes an advantage to the opponent.

Perhaps the best example of the powerful impact of beliefs on performance occurred over a half century ago when Roger Bannister, a young English medical student, made history by breaking one of sport's most fabled physical and psychological barriers—running a mile in less than 4 minutes. Many today consider his run one of the defining athletic achievements of the 20th century. Until his 1954 race, it was considered physically and mentally impossible for the body to endure the punishment of such a feat. Individuals had even written treatises on why the body was physiologically incapable of running the mile in under 4 minutes. Bannister, however, believed that the mile could be run in under 4 minutes and, equally important, he was the person who would do it. He achieved the impossible not merely by physical practice but also by rehearsing in his head breaking through the 4-minute barrier so often and with so much emotional intensity that he programmed his mind and body to believe. What people do not realize, though, is that the greatest impact of his feat was on others. Within the next year, 37 runners broke the 4-minute barrier. The only thing that had changed was their belief system!

Common Misconceptions about Confidence

Misconception 1: Either You Have It or You Don't

Some people believe that confidence is an inherited disposition or trait that cannot be changed by training, practice, or experience. The truth is that the high self-confidence seen in outstanding athletes is not an accident or a random genetic occurrence over which athletes have no control. Instead, confidence is the result of a consistently constructive thinking process that allows athletes to do two things: (1) hang on to and thus benefit from their successful experiences, and (2) let go of or deemphasize their less successful experiences. Thus athletes gain confidence in the same way that they gain other skills or attributes—through practice and repetition of the proper habits.

Misconception 2: Only Positive Feedback Can Build Confidence

Although positive feedback from teammates, parents, and coaches certainly helps to build confidence, it is possible to selectively perceive and reinterpret criticism, sarcasm, and negative comments as stimulating challenges and use them to build confidence. Instead of being mentally destroyed, athletes who choose to respond by reinterpreting the comments in a constructive way or using other active strategies to combat them may actually *gain* confidence. Thus, with the right attitude and thinking skills, athletes can gain confidence even under these circumstances or when overlooked or underestimated.

Misconception 3: Success Always Builds Confidence

It is generally true that "nothing succeeds like success," but this is not the whole story. Successful high school athletes do not always make an easy transition to college competition, despite their years of previous success. Other successful athletes may lose their confidence because their past success becomes a form of pressure from which they cannot escape. Still other athletes who experience great success use their perceptual abilities to focus only on their weaknesses and to remember only their failures. Thus, successful athletes may limit their future success because they do not have the level of confidence that their accomplishments would suggest.

Logic would assert that confidence follows competence, that after having performed and accomplished at a certain level, confidence inevitably follows. Although seemingly obvious and often true, success or competence in no way guarantees confidence. Take the example of Michael Strahan, All-Pro defensive end for the New York Giants. Despite making 10 sacks and playing at his all-time best during the 1998 season, Strahan was plagued by self-doubt: "I thought I sucked, and we were losing. It was like I had no hope"

(King, 2001). How could a player of such obvious and demonstrated competence be so lacking in confidence? The answer lies in the often illogical and irrational nature of the human mind. Strahan's mind was apparently focused on his mistakes, misses, and losses, rather than on his sacks, tackles, and successes, even though he had ample successes in his immediate past to draw strength and optimism from. Only when he disciplined his thinking with regular mental training sessions that incorporated visualizations of success did Strahan's confidence come back, and with that confidence his Pro Bowl season, and his long-term dominance, were virtually assured.

Misconception 4: Confidence Equals Outspoken Arrogance

Certain confident individuals in the world of sport are outspoken and brash, but there are just as many who carry with them an equally powerful quiet confidence. Names such as Muhammad Ali, Charles Barkley, and Deion Sanders are associated with loud and often abrasive levels of confidence, but other great athletes such as Emmitt Smith, Joe Montana, and Jackie Joyner-Kersee are every bit as confident on the inside while conveying politeness and modesty on the outside. For many athletes, difficulty in separating the quiet, internal, private confidence needed for success from the noisy, external, public confidence often portrayed in athletes by the media is a serious impediment. It is crucial for athletes to realize that they can be confident without being considered conceited or arrogant.

Misconception 5: Mistakes Inevitably Destroy Confidence

The greatest difficulty in gaining confidence is the fact that sports are played by imperfect human beings who periodically make mistakes. Too many athletes respond to their mistakes with weakened or diminished confidence. Ironically, these athletes actually *lose* confidence as they gain experiences playing their sport because they selectively attend more to the mistakes and errors that are inevitable in sport. Because of this shortcoming, many athletes become more cautious, more tentative, and more fearful as they advance from the beginning to the end of their years in competitive sport. Other athletes build confidence despite repeated failures because they use their perceptual abilities to selectively attend to whatever small improvements and positive experiences occur. In fact, such positive self-monitoring and focus provide the foundation for intervention programs that have successfully enhanced performance (e.g., Kirschenbaum, Owens, & O'Connor, 1999). Thus athletes can learn to gain confidence even while making mistakes, and this is what the greatest athletes have always done.

Taken collectively, the preceding points all indicate that *confidence is a result of how one thinks, what one focuses on, and how one reacts to the events in one's life.*

Prerequisites for Gaining Confidence

Now that we have dispelled several myths about confidence and shown that confidence is within anyone's grasp, how does one gain confidence? The following four prerequisites provide a solid foundation for building confidence:

1. Understand the interaction of thought and performance.
2. Cultivate honest self-awareness.
3. Develop an optimistic explanatory style.
4. Embrace a psychology of excellence.

Understand the Interaction of Thought and Performance

The thoughts we have of our ability, of the demands we face, and of the environment we happen to be in determine to a large extent the way we feel inside at any given moment. Think "I have done this many times before," and you feel confident. Think "I am being taken advantage of," and you feel anger. Think "This practice is worthless," and you feel impatient and unmotivated.

These immediate feelings, in turn, directly affect performance, because they produce objectively verifiable changes in muscle tension, blood flow, hormone production, and attentional focus. For example, thoughts that anticipate failure lead to feelings of anxiety and, among other things, overall muscle tension and inappropriate attentional focus. When the wrong muscles are tense, or the right muscles are tense at the wrong times, coordination and timing are disrupted. The confident athlete deliberately directs his or her thoughts onto those aspects of the environment and self that produce powerful, confident feelings, so as to produce better and better performance.

Cultivate Honest Self-Awareness

Striving for control over one's thoughts and feelings is a process demanding honest self-awareness. Athletes must commit to becoming aware of what they say to themselves, what the circumstances are when the self-talk occurs, and what consequence follow from the self-talk. One must be willing to honestly pursue the question, "Am I really thinking in a way that will give me the best chance of success?" For most people who play sport the real opponent is within themselves in the form of ineffective cognitive habits. Athletes with great confidence have learned to win the battle with themselves. This is the most difficult battle that anyone will ever try to win, and it is also the challenge that makes sport such a great experience with so much potential for self-development and satisfaction.

Develop an Optimistic Explanatory Style

The term **explanatory style** refers to the way an athlete internally responds to and explains both the good and bad events that occur in his or her life. According to Seligman (1991), explanatory style is the hallmark of whether an individual is an optimist or a pessimist. This habitual style of interpreting events is developed in childhood and adolescence and "stems directly from your view of your place in the world, whether you think you are valuable and deserving, or worthless and hopeless" (Seligman, 1991, p. 98). The concept of explanatory style is especially applicable to the competitive sport environment, in that sport participation inevitably involves setbacks, obstacles, and disappointments to which an athlete must respond optimistically if he or she is to retain confidence and continue investing time and energy. In the often hostile world of sport, explanatory style is a useful tool for helping athletes maintain optimism and confidence.

Explanatory style can be broken down into three dimensions. The first is **permanence**— the degree to which one feels events will repeat themselves and continue to affect one's life either negatively or positively. An athlete with an optimistic explanatory style will usually assume that a good or positive event, such as success, will repeat itself rather than be a fluke and they respond to bad events or setbacks with the explanation that they will not continue to occur, that they are isolated and rare. In contrast, the athlete with a negative explanatory style will tend to think that good events will not repeat themselves, but that bad events or misfortune will.

The second dimension is **pervasiveness**— the degree to which one feels that a particular experience will generalize to other contexts. The optimistic athlete will tend to assume that a good event or a success in one aspect of his or her game will positively affect other aspects, but that mistakes and difficulties will remain confined to their original context. A tennis player might assume on the basis of success with the first serve that the net game and ground strokes are also going to be successful. The more pessimistic athlete will tend to assume that a breakdown in one area of the game will spread to other areas and that successes will be limited to their original context.

The third dimension of explanatory style is **personalization**—the degree to which one sees him- or herself as the primary causal agent in events. Optimistic athletes will take personal credit for successes and progress and protect their confidence by explaining misfortune as the result of outside forces beyond their control (e.g., referee's decisions, exceptional play by the opponent). More pessimistic athletes will have the opposite tendency, to see successes as functions

of luck and circumstance rather than personal actions, but to see losses and setbacks as due to personal shortcomings.

When the preceding are combined, the athlete with an optimistic explanatory style thinks, "It's just these few mistakes that I'll soon correct, they don't affect the rest of my game, and they are balanced out by all these other things I did well." Compare this with the less effective pessimistic explanatory statement, "I made tons of errors, they spoiled every part of my game, and they're going to keep on happening." An athlete's tendency to interpret events along these dimensions is learned and reinforced through experience. By learning techniques of productive self-talk and selective perception, and then employing these techniques in practice and competition, athletes can systematically cultivate optimism and gain confidence.

The preceding does not mean that one ignores mistakes or adopts a totally unrealistic view of one's ability and circumstances. Taking notice of one's errors or shortcomings is a great way to grow, as long as it is done with an eye to the bigger question, "How do I use this to help me improve?" For example, watching a game film and noting technical errors is a good idea, as long as the athlete (a) simultaneously makes note of the good points revealed on the film, (b) decides right then and there what to do about those errors, and (c) *while correcting those errors remains focused on his or her good points and bright future.* Athletes with great attitudes *do* criticize themselves occasionally, but this criticism is always constructive and kept in perspective. To summarize, an optimistic explanatory style is one in which errors are treated as temporary, specific to that one practice or game or correctable, and atypical of one's potential, whereas one looks at successes as more permanent, more general, and certainly more indicative of one's true abilities.

One caveat, however, for excessive optimism comes from a golf study by Kirchenbaum, O'Connor, and Owens (1999). They found that individuals could be overly optimistic, having such *positive illusions* about their skill and control that they make poor decisions. For example, across all skill levels, they found performance suffered on challenging holes because of too aggressive shot selection. An intervention in which golfers were taught more conservative and realistic shot selection led to better performance. A useful guideline here is the phrase "conservative strategy and cocky execution" (Rotella, 1995). This refers to setting realistic, short-term expectations and game plans, and then totally, completely, and utterly committing oneself to following them through.

Embrace a Psychology of Excellence

As has been already mentioned, confidence in competitive performance is the result of a consistently constructive thinking process, a process in which one's thoughts about oneself, one's sport, and one's experiences in that sport are all aligned to produce energy, optimism, and enthusiasm. Here are a few components of an approach, an overall psychology of excellence, that has a better chance of resulting in a pattern of constructive thinking, energy, optimism, and enthusiasm:

1. *Go for your dreams.* Get excited about doing the best that you can, even things that few people have ever done before. Believe that great things are possible.

2. *Focus on your successes.* Deliberately use your capacity for free will to dwell on and emphasize your day-by-day accomplishments, improvements, and episodes of great effort. After every practice session or competition (not just after the successful ones), file away in a training journal at least one instance of success, one instance of improvement, and one instance of great effort.

3. *Be your own best friend, biggest fan, and greatest coach.* Give yourself the same helpful advice and total support you routinely give to your very best friends. At the end of each day create the image of the most positive and helpful person you have ever known and talk to yourself the way that person would.

4. *Create your own reality.* Interpret the events in your sport in a way that opens you up to greater and greater chances for success.

If your performance early in a contest (e.g., first at bat, first field goal attempt) does not go well, take it as a signal that you are getting all the kinks out of your motion now and expect to do better as the game goes on. Conversely, if performance in the early rounds is good, take it as a signal that you are in a great groove and expect it to continue.

All athletes searching for the "mental edge" that will take their game to the next level must honestly look inside and understand the source of their thinking habits, explanatory style, emotional tendencies, and beliefs about themselves. Are those habits of mind determined by a perspective that encourages mediocrity, or are those habits of mind based on a personal perspective dedicated to success, achievement, and the realization of potential? This is an ongoing personal mental battle that each athlete must enter and win to realize their dreams. The remainder of this chapter is devoted to learning the skills that will make this possible.

Self-Talk

The key to cognitive control is **self-talk.** The frequency and content of thoughts vary from person to person and situation to situation. You engage in self-talk any time you carry on an internal dialogue with yourself, such as giving yourself instructions and reinforcement or interpreting what you are feeling or perceiving (Hackfort & Schwenkmezger, 1993). This dialogue can occur out loud (e.g., mumbling to yourself) or inside your head. Self-talk becomes an asset when it enhances self-worth and performance. Such talk can help the athlete change cognitions, regulate arousal and anxiety, stay appropriately focused, and cope with difficulties. For example, Gould, Eklund, and Jackson's (1992a, 1992b) studies of Olympic wrestlers indicated that self-talk was a technique that the wrestlers used to foster positive expectancies and appropriately focus attention. These wrestlers also reported more positive expectancies and task-specific self-talk prior to their best versus worst performances. In another qualitative study, Gould, Finch, and Jackson (1993) investigated the stress-coping strategies of U.S. national champion figure skaters and found that their two most common coping strategies were (a) rational thinking and self-talk and (b) positive focus and orientation maintenance.

Self-talk becomes a liability when it is negative, distracting to the task at hand, or so frequent that it disrupts the automatic performance of skills. For example, a study of observed self-talk and behavioral assessments with junior tennis players found that negative self-talk was associated with losing, but it failed to show a relationship of positive self-talk to better performance (Van Raalte, Brewer, Rivera, & Petitpas, 1994). The authors concluded that the tennis players may have internalized their positive self-talk and thus the researchers could not observe it as readily as negative self-talk. Other experimental studies found that positive self-talk led to better performance than negative self-talk for individuals completing fairly simple tasks (Dagrou, Gauvin, & Halliwell, 1992; Van Raalte et al., 1995) as well as complex tasks such as bowling and golfing (Johnston-O'Conner & Kirschenbaum, 1986; Kirschenbaum, Ordman, Tomarken, & Holtzbauer, 1982).

Negative self-talk becomes especially destructive when an athlete uses general labels such as *loser, choke artist,* and the like. When athletes hold these negative perceptions of themselves, they will often behave in ways that will confirm these expectations. According to prominent cognitive-behavioral psychologist, Albert Ellis, and his colleagues (Ellis, 1988; Ellis & Dryden, 1987; Grieger & Boyd, 1980), evaluating and labeling oneself this way is both destructive to one's mental health and completely irrational. Although it is possible and often desirable to rate one's *behavior* (such as test performance or execution of a sport skill), there is no logical or rational reason to label *oneself,* because what we call our "self" is a very abstract, theoretical concept and impossible to confirm with any certainty. Furthermore, even if one's self could be empirically proven, it would include so many different traits, characteristics, and performances, and would

be so ever changing, that rating and labeling it would be impossible. Ellis argues for eliminating self-rating and labeling altogether. This point will be further developed later in the discussion of irrational and distorted thinking.

The use of negative self-talk by athletes affects not only their immediate performance but also their overall self-esteem and, in extreme cases, can lead to acute depression. Seligman (1991) has described **depression** as nothing more than a disorder of conscious thought—depressed people simply think awful things about themselves and their future. Their symptom, negative self-talk, *is* their disease. Because depression results from consistently using negative thought, changing this habit to positive self-talk will help cure the disease.

Raising self-esteem through effective self-talk, however, takes time and patience. A conscientious effort to screen out negative memories and statements, to ignore so-called experts when they set limits on your abilities, and to focus the mind on present strengths and desired outcomes is required. Self-esteem and confidence begin and end in the mind of the individual, with self-talk playing the primary and most powerful role in feeding the mind. Cognitive-behavioral techniques can be effectively used for enhancing and maintaining self-esteem (Branden, 1994; McKay & Fanning, 1994). By fostering healthy self-esteem, sport psychologists can enhance the personal growth and development of athletes as well as their performance.

Before we address the matter of how specific types of self-talk can be used in different situations to help achieve excellence in learning and performance and to promote confidence and self-esteem, we want to remind you that the interview research reported in Chapter 9 found many athletes stating that their best sport performances occurred when they had no thoughts at all. The athletes were so immersed in the action that it just seemed to happen without conscious thought. Tim Gallwey, author of *The Inner Game of Tennis* (1974), Bob Rotella, author of *Golf Is a Game of Confidence* (1996), and others have stressed that peak performance does not occur when athletes are thinking about it. They emphasize learning to turn performance over to unconscious or automatic functions—functions that are free from the interference of thought.

It may be desirable to strive for such thought-free performance, but athletes usually *do* think when performing. In fact, they engage in sport related self-talk outside of practice as well as before, during, and after both practice and competition (Hardy, Gammage, & Hall, 2001). There is even evidence that more self-talk occurs in competition settings than in practice settings and that the greatest use occurs *during* competition compared to before or after performance (Hardy, Hall, & Hardy, 2004a). In addition, individual sport and skilled athletes use self-talk more frequently than team sport and less skilled athletes (Hardy, Hall, & Hardy, 2004b). This self-talk affects athletes' self-concept, self-confidence, and behavior. Therefore, it is important that coaches and sport psychologists teach athletes to recognize and control their thoughts. Once athletes can do this, they are far more likely to experience those desirable episodes of unconscious immersion. If used properly, thinking can be a great aid to performance and personal growth. The question should not be whether to think but what, when, and how to think. The rest will take care of itself.

The uses for self-talk are almost as varied as are the different types of sports. For example, effective coaches and sport psychologists can use self-talk to aid athletes in learning skills, correcting bad habits, preparing for performance, focusing attention, creating the best mood for performance, and building confidence and competence.

Self-Talk for Skill Acquisition and Performance

Researchers have found that planned, constructive self-talk can enhance skill acquisition and performance (e.g., Cutton & Landin, 2007; Hatzigeorgiadis, Zourbanos, Goltsios, Theodorakis & Perkos, 2008; Theodorakis, & Chroni, 2002) just as planned, destructive self-talk (i.e., "I will miss the bull's eye") impairs performance (Cumming, Nordin, Horton, &

Reynolds, 2006). The nature of self-talk should change as performers become more proficient. During early learning, skill acquisition is usually aided when self-instructional talk is used to remind the performer of certain key aspects of the movement. For example, cue words such as "step, swing" in tennis and "step, drop, step, kick" for a soccer punt foster cognitive associations that aid in learning proper physical execution. Even on the beginning level, self-talk should be kept as brief and minimal as possible. Oververbalization by the coach or athlete can cause paralysis by analysis. With learning, the goal is to reduce conscious control and promote the automatic execution of the skill. Thus, as skills are mastered, self-talk becomes shorter and less frequent, and it shifts from technique mechanics to strategies and optimal feelings.

The effectiveness and content of self-talk also depend on the nature of the task. Skills that are self-paced—that is, initiated by the performer when he or she is ready (e.g., pitching, shooting free throws, bowling, archery, golf, any kind of serve) provide more opportunity for preprogramming successful execution. Again, if the skills are well learned, the nature of the self-talk should focus on what the performer is trying to achieve rather than the physical mechanics of the act. For example, in the book *The Courtside Coach*, Bunker and Young (1995) suggest that a server in tennis should think or see "deep outside corner" to specify the landing area of the serve. Similarly, a pitcher might think "high and inside," or a free throw shooter might simply say, "arch and swish." With reactive, externally paced skills such as spiking in volleyball, fast breaking in basketball, or volleying in tennis, the performer needs to rely more on responding correctly automatically because there is not enough time to separately program each movement. This being the case, athletes in these sports must learn to use the naturally occurring pauses in the game (changing sides of the court, time-outs, out-of-bounds) as opportunities to control their self-talk and set themselves up for success by focusing on what they want to achieve when the action begins again.

One study, however, did find that skilled tennis players improved their volleying performance after they were taught a two-word *(split, turn)* self-talk sequence in which they separately said the words and timed each to specific reactions and movement on the court (Landin & Hebert, 1999). The players attributed the success of the self-talk to its directing their attentional focus. They also reported increased confidence. Other studies found improved competitive performance in ice hockey goaltenders who participated in a mental skills program consisting of a centering and self-talk intervention (Rogerson & Hrycaiko, 2002) and improved soccer shooting performance for elite under-14 female soccer players who received a self-talk intervention (Johnson, Hrycaiko, Johnson, & Halas, 2004). These findings suggest that self-talk enhances performance on externally paced skills as well as on self-paced skills.

Self-Talk for Changing Bad Habits

Athletes will need to use self-talk when they want to change a well-learned skill or habit. To change a bad habit, it is usually necessary to intentionally force conscious control over the previously automatic execution and to then direct attention to the replacement movement. Self-talk can facilitate this process. The more drastic the change, the more detailed the self-talk in the relearning phase. For example, if a tennis player is attempting to change from a two-hand to a one-hand backhand, considerable *self-instruction* may be required. In this case the athlete must verbally redirect the entire swing motion. However, if the change is merely to get behind the ball and hit it a little bit earlier with more weight on the front foot, then a simple cue may be all that is necessary.

When an athlete uses self-talk in this way, it is essential that the content of the statements focus on what they want to happen not on what they want to avoid. If not, the head is merely filled with the negative image, making the appropriate actions even more difficult to execute. For example, rather than saying, "Don't stay on your back foot" when hitting a backhand, use a cue

such as "step-hit." An additional bonus with this type of short but "desired action" oriented self-talk is that it reinforces the habit of making thoughts positive. Remember, "Winners say what they want to happen; losers say what they fear might happen."

Self-Talk for Attention Control

Self-talk can also help athletes control their attention (e.g., Gould et al., 1992a, 1992b; Hardy et al., 2001; Hatzigeorgiadis, Zourbanos, & Theodorakis, 2007; Landin & Hebert, 1999). It is often easy to be distracted during competition and practice. For example, when athletes allow themselves to wander into the past ("If I had only made that last putt") or focus on the future ("If I birdie the next hole, I'll be leading the field"), they will have difficulty executing the present shot. Once again, focusing the mind on what is desired *right now* ("head down, smooth") gives the athlete the best chance of making the correct shot. Several books, including *Golf Is a Game of Confidence* (Rotella, 1996), have emphasized the importance of remaining in the present tense. (For further elaboration and specific examples, see Chapter 16.)

Self-Talk for Creating Affect or Mood

Researchers have found that affective cues can enhance performance. For example, runners who say "fast" or "quick" have been found to increase their speed (Meichenbaum, 1975). Golfers who use swing thoughts such as "smooth" or "oily" produce swings that appear smoother and more controlled (Owens & Bunker, 1989). Power words such as "blast," "hit," and "go" are important aids in explosive movements, helping to create the desired mood state (Owens & Bunker, 1989). As an example, a sprinter in the starting blocks will get a faster start by saying "snap" or "explode" than by thinking about hearing the gun because the appropriate self-talk will directly trigger the desired movement when the gun sounds (Silva, 1982). Otherwise, the athlete must process the fact that the gun went off and then start. For a long-distance run, an athlete may wish to shift word cues throughout the race. During the initial portion, words that encourage consistent pace and energy conservation may be most appropriate. During the middle portion of the run, words that encourage persistence and tuning in to the body are important, whereas the finish requires speed and power. Corresponding cues might be "do it," go," and "sprint." Each word should have an emotional quality that is linked to the appropriate movement quality or content (Meichenbaum, 1975).

Self-Talk for Changing Affect or Mood

In a similar manner, the use of appropriate self-talk can help an athlete change his or her mood to achieve a desired emotional state. Golf legend Sam Snead learned in high school that simply recalling the phrase "cool-mad" helped him control his temper so that it worked for him rather than against him (Rotella, 1984). Hanton and Jones (1999a) demonstrated that competitive swimmers who perceived their precompetitive anxiety symptoms as debilitative could be taught to use self-talk interventions to reinterpret them as facilitative and thereby enhance their performance. Finn (1985) advises underaroused athletes to use a combination of self-talk and rapid breathing to reach a desired emotional state. Statements like "Come on, rev up, it's time to go all out!" alternated with rapid breathing or high-intensity running will increase the athlete's heart rate and produce a new mood state more favorable for peak performance. Use of the right affective cues can ultimately help lead to the best potential for peak performance.

Self-Talk for Controlling Effort

Self-talk can be an effective technique to help maintain energy and persistence. It may be difficult for some athletes to get started in the morning, at practice, or in the first few moments of a contest. Others may have difficulty changing tempo or maintaining effort. Phrases such as "go for it," "easy," "pace," "pick it up," "cool it," "hold onto it," "push," "stay," and so forth can be very effective in controlling effort (Harris & Harris, 1984). Athletes can use self-talk not only

to direct action but also to sustain it (Tod, Iredale, & Gill, 2003; Thellwell & Greenlee, 2003), such as during a tedious or fatiguing practice. An emphasis on effort control is essential because it helps athletes recognize the importance of hard work in achieving success. And if by chance the athletes do not succeed, they are more likely to attribute failure to insufficient effort and therefore want to work harder in the future. Coaches should note that this is a much more productive attribution strategy than blaming lack of success on factors such as luck, poor officiating, or the weather.

Self-Talk for Building Self-Efficacy

As mentioned previously, the term *self-efficacy* refers to one's expectation of succeeding at a specific task or meeting a particular challenge (Schunk, 1995) such as sinking this free throw or beating this opponent. Efficacy expectations affect performance because they determine how much effort athletes will expend on a task and how long they will maintain effort when confronted with setbacks and obstacles. Many studies have shown that athletes with high self-efficacy outperform those with lower self-efficacy on strength, endurance, and skill tasks (Kitsantas & Zimmerman, 2002; Mahoney, Gabriel, & Perkins, 1987; Weinberg, Gould, & Jackson, 1979). Research also shows that efficacy beliefs are vulnerable and need constant reinforcement when confronted with failures (Rongian, 2007) and that efficacy lowers when imaging being unconfident (Nordin & Cumming, 2005). These studies illustrate how powerful efficacy expectations are and, just as important, demonstrate that an individual's preexisting expectations of efficacy can be enhanced to improve performance.

According to Bandura (1977), self-efficacy is influenced by verbal persuasion, both from others and from self in the form of self-talk. Mahoney (1979) also states that self-talk is a useful method for building the self-efficacy expectations of athletes. For example, when Hatzigeorgiadis, et al. (2008) implemented a self-talk intervention, both self-efficacy and tennis performance improved in the experimental group compared to the control group. Hanton and Jones (1999b) found that an intervention that included cognitive restructuring strategies led to increases in confidence levels just prior to competition.

Gould and colleagues found that junior tennis coaches (Gould, Medberry, Damarjian, & Lauer, 1999) and elite college and national team coaches systematically encourage their athletes to develop positive self-talk (Gould, Hodge, Peterson, & Gianni, 1989). The coaches in the 1989 study also rated the encouragement of positive self-talk as the third most effective strategy for developing self-efficacy, ranking physical practice first and modeling confidence by the coach second. Coaches can utilize these sources of self-efficacy in two important ways. First, coaches can provide feedback to athletes on their success through highlight CDs or DVDs of actual performance. Second, coaches can actively express (model) confidence in an athlete's ability to perform well before the entire team by referring to his or her previous successes and bright future. These studies indicate how effective positive self-talk is for enhancing self-efficacy.

Self-talk also plays a crucial, self-effective role in rehabilitation from injury. Ieleva and Orlick (1991) found that athletes who recovered exceptionally fast from ankle and knee injuries had a significantly higher frequency of positive self-talk concerning the process of their recovery than did athletes who healed more slowly. It appears that positive self-talk directly influences one's belief in the body's healing power and thus in the actual healing process itself.

Self-Talk for Increasing Adoption and Maintenance of Exercise Behavior

Many studies in the area of exercise behavior have implicated self-efficacy cognitions as a significant factor in predicting adoption and adherence to an exercise program (see McAuley and Blissmer, 2000, for a review). Self-efficacy cognitions are a mediator of behavior change, that is, the mechanism by which interventions affect exercise behavior (Dishman, et al., 2004). These findings suggest that appropriately modifying self-efficacy cognitions toward exercise contribute to exercise adoption or adherence.

Identifying Self-Talk

Appropriate use of the preceding kinds of self-talk will enhance self-worth and performance. The first step in gaining control of self-talk is to become aware of what you say to yourself. Surprisingly enough, most people are not aware of their thoughts, much less the powerful impact they have on their feelings and behavior. By getting athletes to review carefully the way in which they talk to themselves in different types of situations, they and the coach or sport psychologist will identify what kind of thinking helps, what thoughts appear to be harmful, and what situations or events are associated with this talk. Once athletes develop this awareness, they usually discover that their self-talk varies from short cue words and phrases to extremely complex monologues, with the overall content ranging from self-enhancing to self-defeating. The key is to know both when and how to talk to yourself.

Successful athletes have learned to identify the type and content of thought associated with particularly good and particularly bad performances. Most athletes find different thinking during successful and unsuccessful performances. Identifying the thoughts that typically prepare an athlete to perform well and to cope successfully with problems during performance can provide a repertoire of cognitive tools for the enhancement of performance. The use of these same thoughts in future performance environments should create similar feelings of confidence and direct performance in much the same way. When an athlete can re-create these positive thoughts and bring them to the new environment, the athlete can be said to be *taking control* of his or her mind.

Most athletes discover that during an unsuccessful performance their mind actually programmed failure through self-doubt and negative statements. The body merely performed what the mind was thinking. Examples might include an athlete's thinking before a competition, "I never swim well in this pool" or "I always play poorly against this opponent" and then going on to swim or compete exactly as prophesied. Obviously, future performance would be enhanced if athletes could eliminate dysfunctional and self-defeating thoughts, but before such thoughts can be eliminated, they need to be identified. Three of the most effective tools for identifying self-talk are retrospection, imagery, and keeping a self-talk log.

Retrospection

By reflecting on situations in which they performed particularly well or particularly poorly and trying to re-create the thoughts and feelings that occurred prior to and during these performances, many athletes are able to identify typical thoughts and common themes associated with both good and bad performance. It is also beneficial to recall the specific situation, or circumstances, that led to the thoughts and resulting performance. Viewing videotapes, CDs, or DVDs of actual past performances helps the athlete recount the action by heightening the memory of the event. If this technique is used, not only should the actual performance be filmed but, ideally, the time before the contest begins, the time-outs or breaks during the contest, and even the time right after the contest ends. Thoughts during all of these times play a major role in determining the quality of one's present performance, one's expectations regarding future performance, and even one's feelings of self-esteem.

Imagery

Another technique is to have athletes relax as deeply as possible and then try reliving a past performance through imagery, recreating all relevant sensory experiences, such as how a moment felt or sounded. Obviously, this technique is more effective if athletes have been trained in imagery (see Chapter 14 for suggestions). Athletes who are effective at imagery can usually describe exactly what happened during the competition and what thoughts and feelings preceded, accompanied, and followed the performance. After athletes have relived past performances through imagery, it may be helpful to have them write down the recalled thoughts, situations, and outcomes. If it is not disruptive, the athletes may even want to talk into a tape recorder as they are imaging.

Self-Talk Log

Not all athletes can use retrospection and imagery to remember accurately how they thought and felt or what circumstances triggered their thoughts and feelings. Even athletes who are comfortable using these tools run the risk that time and personal impressions may distort the memory of actual thoughts and circumstances. Keeping a daily diary or self-talk log of thoughts and performance situations is an excellent tool for accurately creating awareness of self-talk. Thoughts should be transcribed as soon after they occur as possible. Athletes in sports such as golf, archery, rowing, and running have found it beneficial to have a recorder present while they perform so they can directly tape their thoughts and a description of the situation as they occur.

When keeping a log, the athlete should address such questions as, When I talk to myself, what do I say before, during, and following my good performances? Not only what thoughts, but how frequently am I talking to myself? When playing poorly, do I deprecate myself as a person? Do I stay in the present moment, or revert to dwelling on past performance? Do I call myself names and wish I were still sitting on the bench? Does the content of my self-talk center on how I feel about myself, or how others will feel about me, or on letting down my friends and teammates, or on how unlucky I am?

If there is a problem in thinking, the goal is to identify the problem and its boundary points in specific terms. This means that each athlete must be able to answer questions such as, When do I have negative thoughts? Do I begin doubting myself even before I have a chance to perform?

For example, when a whistle blows, do I automatically assume it is directed at me? If I have been fouled, do I start worrying from the moment the whistle blows until after I have shot the free throw, or do I begin worrying only after I walk to the free throw line? Athletes must be able to specify the initial cue that caused them to start worrying or thinking negatively to gain control over their thoughts. Also, when do they stop saying self-defeating things? Such detailed knowledge will help in planning an effective intervention. For instance, if worry begins with the referee's whistle, then this is the cue with which an alternate thought pattern should be linked.

It is also important to monitor self-talk during practice as these times play an important role in developing typical thought and behavior patterns. More specifically, the athlete should identify what is said when performing exceptionally well, after making mistakes, after teammates perform poorly, after having difficulty performing a new skill or strategy, when fatigued, and after the coach criticizes performance. Often the pattern of thoughts found during competition is merely a reflection of what occurs during practices. Learning to recognize and control the nature of self-talk during practices provides the foundation for effective thinking during competition.

Techniques for Controlling Self-Talk

Using the preceding self-monitoring tools is only the *first step* in the process necessary for producing performance-enhancing thoughts and eliminating disabling thoughts. In fact, paying too much attention to negative thoughts or thoughts associated with poor performance can be detrimental if they are not linked to some action or change process. Once awareness of negative talk and feelings is heightened, the coach or sport psychologist should immediately instruct the athlete in how to start dealing with these thoughts. Similarly, when good performance is analyzed, it should be with the intent of capitalizing on the state of mind that existed during that performance in the hope of being able to

purposefully duplicate it in the future. In this section we present techniques for controlling self-talk. The effectiveness of these techniques in enhancing sport performance has been well documented. In fact, a meta-analysis by Meyers, Whelan, and Murphy (1996) calculated a greater effect size for cognitive restructuring interventions ($n = 4$, $d = .79$, $SD = .36$) than that found for goal setting ($n = 3$, $d = .54$, $SD = .15$); mental rehearsal ($n = 28$, $d = .57$, $SD = .75$); and relaxation interventions ($n = 25$, $d = .73$, $SD = 1.65$). Techniques for controlling self-talk include:

Thought-stoppage

Changing negative thoughts to positive thoughts

Countering

Reframing

ABC cognitive restructuring

Affirmation statements

Mastery and coping tapes

Video technology

Thought Stoppage

If an athlete's self-talk is too frequent and thus distracting, or if the talk produces self-doubt, it must be terminated. Getting rid of such thoughts often makes it possible to break the link that leads to negative feelings and behaviors and an inappropriate attentional focus. The technique of **thought stoppage** provides one very effective method for eliminating negative or counterproductive thoughts (Meyers & Schleser, 1980). The technique begins with awareness of the unwanted thought and uses a trigger to interrupt or stop the undesirable thought. The trigger can be a word such as *stop* or a physical action such as snapping the fingers or clapping one hand against the thigh. Each athlete should choose the most natural trigger and use it consistently.

Thought stoppage will not work unless the athlete first recognizes undesirable thoughts and then is motivated to stop them. Developing the commitment necessary to improve the quality of an athlete's self-talk is not as easy for the coach and sport psychologist to accomplish as it sounds. This process requires athletes to invest some time in monitoring the frequency and content of their self-talk and then truly deciding to change this talk for the better. For example, even after using the typical tools for creating awareness of thoughts, one young professional golfer would not admit negative statements were affecting her golf. As a method to convince her of the severity of the problem, she was asked to empty a box of 100 paper clips into her pocket. Each time she had a negative thought, she had to move a clip to her back pocket. At the end of the golf round she had shot an 84 and had 87 paper clips in her back pocket! The process of actually counting paper clips, each of which represented a self-defeating thought, made her dramatically aware of her problem and motivated her to try thought-stoppage (Owens & Bunker, 1989).

Thought-stoppage is a skill, and, as with any other skill, it is best to first experiment and become comfortable with it during practice before using it in actual competition. An effective way to practice thought-stoppage is to combine it with imagery. Instruct the athletes to select a typical dysfunctional thought, or thought pattern, they would like to eliminate. Next they should close their eyes and as vividly as possible imagine themselves in the situation in which they usually have those thoughts. Once the situation is re-created, practice interrupting the thought with whatever trigger is selected for thought stoppage. Repeat until the athletes can effortlessly and automatically eliminate dysfunctional talk and accompanying feelings of worry and anxiety.

During the earlier stages of thought-stoppage practice, athletes may want to visibly use their trigger. Saying "stop" out loud not only makes athletes more conscious of their wish to stop excessive or negative talk but serves several additional functions. It helps the coach and sport psychologist to monitor whether athletes are doing what they were instructed to do. If an athlete's body language is showing frustration or disgust with play, his or her thoughts probably are too. The coach and sport psychologist who sees no visible thought-stoppage trigger during these circumstances should directly confront the

athlete by asking him or her what thoughts are occurring. This will serve to reinforce awareness and the need to stop negative talk immediately. The other advantage of visibly practicing the technique is that athletes realize they are not alone in their need to deal more effectively with self-talk. The technique is particularly effective when becoming more positive is a team effort and responsibility. Thus, this is a good time to encourage athletes to be supportive of one another rather than critical or sarcastic. When one high school basketball coach instituted such a program halfway through his season, he was so impressed with the outcome that he attributed turning a losing season into a winning season to his athletes' learning to control negative talk and body language and becoming supportive rather than critical of one another.

Learning to turn off negative or inappropriate thoughts takes time, particularly when negative thought patterns have become the athlete's habitual mode of response to adversity (Cautela & Wisocki, 1977). Frustration over the recurrence of negative thoughts may be lessened if the coach or sport psychologist draws the parallel to trying to unlearn some well-established error in physical technique. Old habits change slowly, whether they are physical or cognitive, and they only change with considerable motivation and practice. The more practice an athlete employs, the less likely negative thought patterns are to recur.

Even with practice it may be difficult for some to suppress an unwanted thought (e.g., "Don't think about the umpire"). In fact, studies by Wegner and his colleagues (Wegner & Erber, 1992; Wegner, Schneider, Knutson, & McMahon, 1991; Wenzlaff, Wegner, & Klein, 1991) have demonstrated that individuals deliberately trying to suppress unwanted thoughts often find themselves even more preoccupied by the thoughts they are trying to escape. Similar results have occurred within sport research (Dugdale and Ecklund, 2002; Wenzlaff & Wegner, 2000; Janelle, 1999). Wegner, Ansfield, and Pilloff (1998) also found the effect when trying to suppress action. That is, participants were more likely to overshoot the hole when putting, particularly under the stress of cognitive load, when they received instructions to *avoid* overhitting the ball. The researchers explained these failures (i.e., doing the opposite of what one intends) with the theory of ironic processes of mental control (Wegner, 1994, 1997). For an interesting discussion of the implications this theory has for sport psychology research and interventions, see Janelle (1999), Hall, Hardy, and Gammage (1999), and Taylor (1999).

These findings indicate how important it is for athletes to use negative or self-critical thoughts as the stimulus or trigger to deliberately focus the mind on a desired process or outcome. This leads to the next technique for controlling thoughts—changing self-defeating thoughts to self-enhancing thoughts.

Changing Negative Thoughts to Positive Thoughts

Although it makes sense to stop negative thoughts altogether, sometimes this cannot be accomplished. An alternative is to learn to couple any negative thought with a positive thought that either provides encouragement and support or appropriately redirects attention. The coach or sport psychologist should instruct athletes to extinguish unwanted thought as soon as it is recognized and then immediately practice switching to a positive or more appropriate thought. If, for example, a gymnast finds himself saying, "This new move is really hard—I'll never get it right!" he should learn to follow this phrase immediately with "I've learned lots of hard moves before, so I know if I'm persistent I can learn this one too."

Another advantage for teaching this technique along with thought stoppage is that it takes pressure off athletes who initially doubt their ability to control their thoughts. Although these athletes think they cannot control what thoughts first enter their head, they usually will accept their ability to control the thoughts that follow. For example, for the golfer who used the "paper clip" technique to become aware of her many self-defeating thoughts, her goal in working with cognitions was simply to reduce

the dysfunctional statements that were not followed by self-enhancing statements. Not having to worry about the occurrence of a self-defeating statement took considerable pressure off her. Each day she was able to reduce the number of paper clips that stood for negative thoughts not followed by positive thoughts, and in time she was able to get rid of the recurring pattern of dysfunctional talk.

A good way to first implement this technique is for athletes to make a list of self-defeating things they typically say and would like to change. Athletes can often generate this list from the self-talk log discussed earlier. Meichenbaum (1977) has emphasized that it is important for athletes to specify when they make these self-defeating statements and what causes them to make such statements. The goal is to recognize what the situation involved and why the negative thought occurred. Athletes should then identify a substitute positive statement. It may be helpful to make a list with each self-defeating thought on one side and the preferred self-enhancing statement directly opposite the negative thought (see Table 15-1).

Notice that the self-enhancing statements in the table always bring the athlete back to the present time and personal control of the situation. The coach or sport psychologist may also want to couple relaxation techniques with this technique as most negative thoughts occur when an individual is under stress and, therefore, usually overaroused physiologically. Instruct athletes to stop their negative thought and then take a deep breath. As they feel relaxation spreading with the long, slow exhalation, say the substitute self-enhancing thought.

There is nothing unusual about having negative thoughts, and even the greatest athletes have anxious or negative thoughts on occasion. Tennis legend Arthur Ashe once feared "he wouldn't get a single serve in the court" just before his U.S. Open championship. Bobby Jones, the famous golfer, was standing over a 2-foot putt that would allow him to win the U.S. Open when he had the thought, "What if I stub my putter into the ground and miss the ball entirely and lose the tournament?" These champions, however, did not store their negative thoughts away where

Table 15-1 Examples of Changing Negative Thoughts to Positive Thoughts

Self-Defeating Thoughts	Change to Self-Enhancing Thoughts
I can't believe it's raining. I have to play in the rain.	No one likes the rain, but I can play as well in it as anyone else.
You dumb jerk.	Ease off. Everyone makes mistakes. Sluff it off and put your mind on what you want to do.
There's no sense in practicing. I have no natural talent.	I've seen good players who had to work hard to be successful. I can get better if I practice correctly.
This officiating stinks; we'll never win.	There's nothing we can do about the officiating, so let's just concentrate on what we want to do. If we play well, the officiating won't matter.
Why did they foul me in the last minute of play—I'm so nervous, I'll probably choke and miss everything.	My heart is beating fast. That's OK, I've sunk free throws a hundred times. Just breathe and swish.
We'll win the meet only if I get a 9.0 on this routine.	Stop worrying about the score; just concentrate on how you're going to execute the routine.
The coach must think I'm hopeless. He never helps me.	That's not fair. He has a whole team to coach. Tomorrow I'll ask what he thinks I need to work on the most.
I don't want to fail.	Nothing was ever gained by being afraid to take risks. As long as I give my best, I'll never be a failure.
I'll take it easy today and go hard next workout.	The next workout will be easier if I go hard now.
Who cares how well I do anyway?	I care, and I'll be happier if I push myself.
This hurts; I don't know if it's worth it.	Of course it hurts, but the rewards are worth it.

they could build themselves into a mental block. Instead, Ashe and Jones stopped those thoughts and replaced them with positive thoughts. The key is not to give in to these negative thoughts and allow them to control and dominate the mind. Make the last thought in any string or sequence of thoughts self-enhancing. This is possible if you become aware of your negative self-talk and use it as a signal to *stop, cope,* and *take control.*

The recommendations presented above are based on research conducted with athletes and nonathletes from individualistic cultures (e.g., the United States, Western Europe). Recent research suggests that the relationship of self-talk to performance may be different for individuals from collectivist cultures (e.g., China, Singapore) and, if true, self-talk interventions such as changing negative thoughts to positive thoughts may not be appropriate for them. This concern comes from the finding by Peters and Williams (2006) that Asians had significantly more negative self-talk than European Americans during dart-throwing performance and that their negative self-talk related to better performance. Conversely, as previously found, the opposite occurred for European Americans. Additionally, cross-cultural research suggests that a self-critical versus self-enhancing orientation is a characteristic of collectivist individuals' self-concepts, and is necessary for self-improvement (Kitayama, 2002; Kashiwagi, 1986). The dart throwing findings may not replicate (Peters & Williams, 2008), nevertheless, sport psychologists and coaches should consider an athlete's culture when designing self-talk interventions.

Countering

Changing negative to positive self-statements probably will not achieve the expected behavioral outcome if the athlete still *believes* in the negative statements. For example, an athlete might change his or her talk from "I will never be able to run this offensive pattern; I'm just not quick enough" to "I can too; I'm as quick as anyone else." The athlete is merely going through the outward motions of being positive if the real belief system is still saying, "No, I can't; I really am too slow."

Athletes will rarely be able to accomplish something if they truly believe they cannot. Furthermore, the motivation even to try will be eroded if there is no belief that one's efforts will ultimately yield success. Bell (1983) proposes that in such instances merely directing one's thoughts toward desired actions may not be enough. Instead, the athlete may have to identify and build a case against the negative self-statements that are interfering with effective performance. Bell suggests using the tool of countering under these circumstances. **Countering** is an internal dialogue that uses facts and reasons to refute the underlying beliefs and assumptions that led to negative thinking. Rather than blindly accepting the negative voice in the back of the head, the athlete argues against it.

When learning to use counters, it is important that the athlete actually describe the evidence necessary to change an attitude or belief. In the preceding example, the coach or sport psychologist might try helping the athlete identify issues such as, What makes me think I am

slow? Have I ever in the past played with good speed? Am I as fast as any of the other athletes? If yes, are they successful at running this offense? What might be causing my slowness, and can I do anything to change it? If I am not quite as fast as some of my teammates, do I have any other talents that might compensate for this, such as using my good game sense to read the situation faster so I can react more quickly? What other skills do I have that might help me learn this offensive pattern?

Any or all of the preceding approaches should provide some evidence for refuting either the athlete's slowness or the importance of only speed in being successful at the offensive pattern. The more evidence and logic there is to refute the negative belief structure, the more effective the counters will be in getting the athlete to accept the positive statement; and the more firmly the athlete believes in the counters, the less time it will take to turn the thinking around. Later it may be possible for the athlete to identify the negative or irrational thought and simply dismiss it with phrases such as "No, that's not right," "Who says I can't?" or just plain "Bull."

In his discussion of countering, Bell (1983) makes another excellent point. Sometimes thoughts are neither correct nor incorrect—they cannot be verified. Bell suggests that what is more important is determining whether a given thought *helps* an athlete reach his or her goals. Encourage athletes to ask themselves, "Is this thinking in my best interest? Does this thinking help me feel the way I want to or does it make me worried and tense? Does this thinking help me perform better?" When athletes realize that thinking certain thoughts can only be detrimental, it becomes sensible, and thus easier, to stop them or change them.

Reframing

Another effective technique for dealing with negative self-talk is **reframing,** described by Gauron (1984) as the process of creating alternative frames of reference or different ways of looking at the world. Because the world is literally what we make it, reframing allows us to transform what appears at first to be a weakness or difficulty into a strength or possibility, simply by looking at it from a different point of view. Gauron encourages athletes to cultivate the skill of reframing because it helps athletes control their internal dialogue in a positive, self-enhancing manner. Almost any self-defeating statement or negative thought can be reframed, or interpreted from a different perspective, so that it aids rather than hinders the athlete.

An important element of reframing is that it does not deny or downplay what the athlete is experiencing or encourage the athlete to ignore something troublesome. Instead, by reframing, the athlete acknowledges what is happening and decides to use it to his or her best advantage. For example, if an athlete was saying, "I'm feeling tense and anxious about playing today," he can reframe the statement to "I'm feeling excited and ready." Similarly, an athlete dwelling on the *problems* of improving a skill or the *struggle* of a performance slump can turn these situations to his advantage and maintain a positive attitude by focusing on the *possibilities* of achieving a new level of skill and the *opportunity* present in each new performance.

Research support for the positive effects of reframing comes from a study that compared the mental preparation of teams who met or exceeded their goals in the 1996 Atlanta Olympics to teams that failed to meet expectations at the Games (Gould, Guinan, Greenleaf, Medbery, & Pederson, 1999). Gould et al. found that members of the more successful teams reported that they were able to "reframe negative events in a positive light." Additional support comes from research by Hanton and Jones (1999a) who improved performance in nonelite swimmers by teaching them to reframe their anxiety symptoms as facilitative rather than debilitative to performance.

Identifying Irrational and Distorted Thinking

In addition to dealing with negative self-talk and self-doubt, athletes need to realize that they may also be engaging in cognitive distortions and irrational thinking. According to Ellis (1982), athletes fail to reach their goals and perform below their ability primarily because they accept and endorse self-defeating, irrational beliefs. Ellis identifies four basic irrational beliefs that negatively affect athletes' performance. If athletes accept any of these beliefs (let alone two or three of them), or any of their variations, their progress and satisfaction will be blocked. These four irrational beliefs are (1) I *must* at all times perform outstandingly well, (2) others who are significant to me (e.g., teammates and coaches) *have to* approve and love me, (3) everyone has *got to* treat me kindly and fairly, and (4) the conditions of my life, particularly my life in sports, absolutely *must* be arranged so that I get what I want when I want.

Such thinking is counterproductive because it negatively influences self-concept, self-confidence, and performance. Once identified—a task that may take considerable soul-searching—these self-defeating types of beliefs need to be modified. Here are some irrational thoughts and cognitive distortions that are common among athletes (the first eight are from Gauron, 1984):

- Perfection is essential
- Catastrophizing
- Worth depends on achievement
- Personalization
- Fallacy of fairness
- Blaming
- Polarized thinking and labeling
- One-trial generalizations
- Shoulds
- Emotional reasoning

Let's take a look at each of these thought patterns along with some suggestions for modifying such irrational and distorted thinking.

Perfection is essential. One of the most debilitating irrational ideas for athletes (and coaches too) is that one must be thoroughly competent and successful and achieve everything attempted. No one can consistently achieve perfection. Individuals who believe they should will blame themselves for every defeat, every setback.

Their self-concept will likely suffer and they may start a fear-of-failure syndrome. Furthermore, they will put such pressures on themselves to do well that both their enjoyment and performance will likely suffer. There is always value in *striving* for perfection, but nothing is gained by *demanding* perfection.

Catastrophizing.   Catastrophizing often accompanies perfectionistic tendencies, as the athlete believes that any failure will be a humiliating disaster. Catastrophizers expect the worst possible thing to happen. Unfortunately, expecting disaster often leads to disaster! Individuals become plagued by what-ifs. "What if I lose today?" "What if my parents are embarrassed when I strike out?" Realistic evaluations of the actual situation and setting appropriate goals help combat perfectionistic thinking and catastrophizing.

Worth depends on achievement.   Too many athletes believe they are only as good as their accomplishments, what they win. Correspondingly, they think they must excel in order to please others. Try asking an athlete or coach to describe who he or she is without mentioning his or her sport or success rate! Athletes must learn to value themselves for more than what they do in sport; worth as a human being is based on factors other than achievement outcome.

Personalization.   Athletes who personalize believe they are the cause and focus of activities and actions around them. They think that everything people do or say is some kind of reaction to them. They also have a tendency to frequently compare oneself to others, trying to determine who is better, who gets more playing time, and so forth.

Fallacy of fairness and ideal conditions.   You feel resentful because you think you know what is fair but other people will not agree. "Fair" is usually a disguise for just wanting one's personal preferences. "Ideal conditions" means that coaches should carve out the easiest possible path for athletes to follow. It is irrational to think that things will come easily or that the world of

sport should somehow be fair—that each investment of time and energy should deliver an equitable level of success, or that everyone on a team or in a sport program should be treated the same. Holding these expectations will inevitably produce frustration, because in reality coaches do treat players differently; one's efforts, improvements, and achievements are not always noticed; and the breaks of the game are often unfair. Coming to grips with unfairness and learning to stay composed is one of sport's great lessons.

Blaming.   This takes two forms, you hold other people responsible for your actions and feelings, or you blame yourself for every problem or outcome. Making excuses or assigning fault to others gains nothing. Athletes must learn to replace external attributions with attributions that are within their control: "Success comes from effort and working hard to develop one's full potential, whereas failure comes from lack of effort or insufficient practice of key fundamentals." Athletes often learn their attributions from coaches. If coaches blame failure on external factors, athletes will too. This subtly leads athletes to expect failure under similar future circumstances—for example, playing in a certain arena or a weird time of the day. Coaches and sport psychologists should provide appropriate internal attributions for successes and failures. When athletes realize they are responsible for and in control of their performance, their confidence will grow after good performance and they will have more confidence in turning current failures into future successes. Accepting complete responsibility for everything, however, is equally nonproductive. For example, "We lost because I missed that last free throw." This irrational blame can lead to potential problems such as loss of confidence and the thought, "The coach and my teammates must really hate me." Instead, help athletes to be realistic and honest in evaluating performance outcome.

Polarized thinking and labeling.   Polarized thinking is the tendency to view things as black or white, good or bad, with no middle ground. This all-or-nothing thinking often leads to failing to learn from every experience and using judgmental labeling—the identification or description of something or someone with an extreme evaluative word or phrase, such as "choker," "butterfingers," "airbrain," "loser." Once established and internalized, these negative labels are difficult to erase—*labeling is disabling.* Coaches and sport psychologists should instead set a good example and stress that athletes avoid any kind of negative evaluative language, judgmentalism, and absolute thinking.

One-trial generalizations.   This cognitive distortion results from reaching a general conclusion based on a single incident or piece of evidence. For example, if something bad happens once you might expect it to happen over and over when similar circumstances present ("I can't golf well in the rain"). If these conclusions are based on only one or two experiences, then some careful analysis can usually lead athletes to negate them. If they are based on many experiences, then practicing under perceived negative conditions until success is achieved will often produce effective evidence to repudiate the initial negative generalization.

Shoulds.   These people have a list of ironclad rules about how they and other people should act. People who break the rules anger them and they feel guilty when they violate the rules. Such inflexibility and self-righteousness can cause serious problems for self and interpersonal relations.

Emotional reasoning.   You believe that what you feel must be true–automatically. If you *feel* stupid and boring, then you must *be* stupid and boring. Such people are more likely to have problems with adverse emotions because they tend to generalize them as personal characteristics versus just a transitory emotion.

Modifying Irrational and Distorted Thinking: ABC Cognitive Restructuring

Irrational beliefs often underlie much of the stress and resulting self-defeating thoughts and feelings athletes experience during athletic performance and in life in general. Unfortunately, athletes often are unaware that the culprit is maladaptive beliefs and thinking. Instead they think the circumstance or event caused the deleterious emotional reaction and behavior. For example, a basketball player misses a critical free throw in the final seconds of a game and ends up feeling worthless and fearing similar circumstance in the future. The typical athlete probably thinks his missed free throw causes thoughts and anxiety (see Figure 15-1). In actuality the *assumptions* the athlete made are the cause. In this case, irrational assumptions such as perfectionism, worth-depends-on-achievement, or personalization may have been the culprit.

The coach or sport psychologist can help athletes reduce their self-caused pressure by getting them to identify and dispute their irrational assumptions. One excellent way to do so is to use Albert Ellis's rational emotive therapy procedure (Ellis & Dryden, 1987), sometimes referred to as ABC cognitive restructuring. The process begins by getting athletes to keep a daily record in which they record not only their upsetting thoughts but also the resulting feelings and behavior and the negative events that triggered them (see Figure 15-1). In column A they briefly describe the activating event in terms of what happened, what they saw and heard. In column B they record the exact content of their dysfunctional self-talk, that is, whatever they think or say out loud that could be interpreted as debilitative. In column C they record the resulting emotional and behavioral consequences. To help determine what they should record, have the athletes use Steinmetz, Blankenship, and Brown's (1980) five criteria for deciding whether self-talk and underlying beliefs are rational or irrational, productive or unproductive.

1. Are the beliefs based on objective reality? That is, would a mixed group of people all agree that the event happened the way you perceived it, or do you exaggerate and personalize experiences?

2. Are they helpful to you? Self-destructive thoughts are usually irrational.

ABC Cognitive Restructuring

A. Activating Event	B. Beliefs or Interpretations	C. Consequences	D. Dispute
Briefly describe the actual event that led to the feelings and behavior	Record the actual dysfunctional self-talk and, if appropriate, include mental pictures	Identify feelings, bodily reactions, and behavior	Write rational response(s) to the automatic thoughts
Fouled in final ten seconds with game tied – missed free throw	"I lost the game for the team." (*personalization*) (*blaming*) "I always choke in pressure situations." (*overgeneralizations*) (*catastrophizing*)	Depressed, tensed up, blew defensive assignment after free throw	"Hey, I'm disappointed but that was just one point out of 40 minutes of play." "I missed this shot, but there are other times when I've come through under pressure. I'll put extra time into free throw practice and work on staying loose and positive."

Figure 15-1 **Example of how to use ABC cognitive restructuring to identify and modify irrational and distorted thinking**

3. Are they useful in reducing conflicts with other people, or do you set up a me-versus-them situation?

4. Do they help you reach your short- and long-term goals, or do they get in the way?

5. Do they reduce emotional conflict and help you feel the way you want to feel?

After completing the ABC steps across a designated number of days, the athletes are ready for the next critical step, which entails trying to rebut or dispute their self-criticism. The first step is to reexamine the self-talk under column B to determine the irrational beliefs or distortions in thinking that might underlie what appeared, on the surface, to be automatic dysfunctional statements. Record the underlying beliefs in column B after the self-talk statement. In many cases, more than one thinking error may have led to the self-talk. For example, see Figure 15-1 for what occurred when the athlete missed the free throw. Identifying the underlying irrational beliefs and thinking distortions helps athletes discover the erroneous or illogical aspects of their initial self-talk. Once done, the athletes are ready to substitute more rationale and productive thoughts in column D. If a particular dysfunctional thought often occurs (e.g., saying "I always screw up" or something equivalent after every disappointment), the person will want to frequently repeat the substituted rational statement until it is believed. Incorporating one of the quick relaxation techniques discussed in Chapter 13 before saying the statement may increase susceptibility to believing the statement. For example, take a deep, complete breath and with the exhalation say, "Lighten up! It's human to make mistakes. Learn from it and move on." The preceding may be difficult, but it gets easier and easier with practice. The ultimate goal is to create such awareness in the athletes that when they have dysfunctional thinking, they immediately recognize and dispute it.

Less enlightened coaches and athletes might fear that modifying irrational beliefs such as perfectionistic demands and taking excessive responsibility for performance outcome may take the edge off an athlete's competitiveness. This fear is unfounded. Reflecting back to an athlete's best moments in competition almost always reveals the opposite. Helping athletes eliminate irrational beliefs and develop more adaptive thoughts will go a long way toward improving performance and, perhaps more important, personal growth.

Constructing Affirmation Statements

Feelings of confidence, efficacy, and personal control will be enhanced if coaches and sport psychologists assist athletes in constructing personal affirmation statements. **Affirmations** are statements that reflect positive attitudes or thoughts about oneself. They are statements about what you want, *phrased as if you already had it.* For example, in 1985 Ivan Lendl had a record of 9 wins and 12 losses against John McEnroe. Lendl then started writing each day in a notebook, "I look forward to playing John McEnroe." By early 1991 his record against McEnroe had improved to 19 wins and 15 losses, and Lendl had won the last 10 straight matches (Wishful Inking, 1991).

The most effective affirmations are both believable and vivid. They are also often spontaneous and thus capture the feelings of a particularly satisfying and successful experience (Syer & Connolly, 1984). "I am as strong as a bull," "I fly down the finish line," and "I really come through under pressure" are all good examples of positive affirmations. Note that each of these expresses a personal, positive message of something that is happening in the present.

Team slogans can also serve as affirmations: "Winners think they can and they do"; "See it, think it, believe it, do it"; "Say yes to success." Each slogan can become a recipe or formula for success provided it is internalized. As just noted, a good source of affirmations is positive statements that might naturally have occurred with previous successful performance. Another way to build affirmations is to have each athlete make a self-esteem list and a success list (Gauron, 1984). The **self-esteem list** contains all of the athlete's positive attributes—all of his or her perceived assets, strengths, and positive qualities. The **success**

list contains all of the athlete's successes thus far. The goal is to use one's own personal history in an enabling way by reviewing, reexperiencing, and visualizing previous success experiences.

The self-esteem and success lists serve to remind the athlete of how capable he or she is and how deserving of being successful. This is not the time for modesty but for honest reflection on all of one's positive qualities and successes. Rushall (1979) has emphasized that once this positive frame of reference is established, the athlete should write specific affirmation statements that are *positive action-oriented* self-statements affirming capabilities and what he or she would like to do; "I play well under pressure" rather than "I know I can play well under pressure." Affirmations should be in the present tense and worded in a way that avoids perfectionist statements that may be impossible to live up to, such as "I always . . ." or "I never . . . ."

Once formulated, how can these statements be best used to foster confidence and the desired goal of the affirmation? Gauron (1984) suggests having a number-one affirmation to work on each day, especially when feeling bummed or going into a slump. An athlete may want to write the statement 10 to 20 times each day on a piece of paper or on a card that can be carried around and pulled out and read during free moments. Once the affirmation becomes so integrated into the conscious mind that it is completely believed and made automatically, the athlete can select another affirmation to work on. Other techniques for utilizing affirmations are to post them (singularly or in combination) in places such as one's bedroom, bathroom, locker, or screen saver. There is also merit in recording affirmations on cassette tapes and playing them whenever possible, such as between classes or before going to bed.

Designing Coping and Mastery Self-Talk Tapes or Files

Every individual has the capacity to program his or her mind for successful thoughts. Some athletes do it naturally; others must learn how to be effective thinkers. One very effective method for training the mind to think in a confident, success-oriented way is through the use of mastery and coping tapes or digital audio files such as an MP3 for an iPod. For a mastery tape or file the athlete records his or her own voice describing an outstanding performance in which events proceed precisely as desired, including the ideal thoughts, feelings, and emotions experienced just before, during, and after performance. Recalling a past great game or great day of competition may help the athlete get started in this process. Feedback from the coach might help in preparing the script. If the technology is available, the athletes might even want to put the voice-over on a video of their performing exactly as wanted. Combining the self-talk with a musical background that creates the desired emotions is also helpful.

The concept with the mastery tape or file is to be playing perfectly and in complete control of the situation. Speak slowly and provide pauses when recording the self-talk to allow the mind time to fully visualize each of the described or depicted scenes. Listening or watching a mastery rendition of the perfect performance over and over helps program the conscious and subconscious mind for success.

Because perfect performances are rare and because obstacles and setbacks are likely to occur in even the best of circumstances, producing and listening to a **coping tape or file** is an effective way of programming the mind to maintain confidence, control, and focus in the face of difficulties. Coping tapes or files allow the athlete to practice dealing with negative and anxious thoughts and situations, including all the potential things that could go wrong. The situation might be one in which the athlete makes a foolish mistake and loses mental or emotional control. The athlete then rehearses the strategies needed to regain control and confidence. This is an excellent opportunity to practice thought stoppage, reframing, or any of the other techniques mentioned in this chapter and in other chapters, such as the arousal control techniques in Chapter 13.

The coping tape or file includes a description of the negative situations and accompanying maladaptive self-talk and feelings followed by a description of an appropriate strategy and self-statements for dealing effectively with the situation(s), including experiencing optimal thoughts and feelings. It should be stressed that the emphasis on a coping tape or file is not on the stressful or distracting situation described but on the process by which the athlete regains control and confidence when confronted with these situations. Listening over and over to this type of self-talk will help create a sense of well-being so that if the same situation occurs in real life the athlete will already have practiced coping with it successfully. Once athletes learn the skill of imagery, they can listen to the tape or file and actually visualize successfully coping with what is described.

Use Highlight Videotapes, CDs, or DVDs to Enhance Performance

Modern video technology can also be used to help athletes gain confidence and improve skills (Ives, Straub, & Shelley, 2002). Video cameras are now so easy to use, and so common, that almost any athlete or team has access to enough raw footage from which a personal or team highlight video can be created. All that is necessary is to identify the beginning and ending points of a few scenes of peak performance. It is particularly desirable to select performances in which athletes can see themselves excelling at the skills or strategies that currently need emphasis. An audio input can add an athlete's or team's favorite musical selection to serve as the sound track to their video images. Watching well-executed play while recalling the self-talk, emotions, and sensations that accompanied the scenes serves as a form of imagery rehearsal, which can affect the body in many positive ways (see Chapter 14).

Summary

There is a direct correlation between self-confidence and success. Confident athletes think about themselves and the action at hand in a different way than those who lack confidence. The difference is that the confident athlete's self-talk and internal imagery are consistently positive and enthusiastic. The self-enhancing thinking of confident athletes is likely to lead to enabling feelings and good performance, just as the inappropriate or misguided thinking of athletes lacking in confidence is likely to lead to negative feelings and poor performance. Athletes can learn to use self-talk to build confidence and to facilitate learning and performance. The first step for an athlete in gaining control of thinking is to monitor self-talk to become aware of what kind of thinking helps, what thoughts are occurring that appear to be harmful, and what situations or events are associated with the talk. Three of the most effective tools for identifying self-talk are retrospection, imagery, and keeping a self-talk log.

Once awareness of self-talk and feelings, particularly of dysfunctional talk, is heightened the coach or sport psychologist can instruct the athlete in how to start dealing with these thoughts. Techniques such as thought stoppage, changing negative thoughts to positive thoughts, countering, reframing, ABC cognitive restructuring of irrational and distorted thinking, and constructing affirmation statements are possible tools for producing performance-enhancing thoughts and eliminating disabling thoughts. Using mastery and coping tapes or files and video technology can also enhance confidence and performance.

Using these tools will require an investment of time and faith on the part of the athlete, and there is no guarantee that immediate improvements will result. As with any other training method that truly enhances performance, the results of training the mind to think effectively will emerge gradually, in precise correlation to the athlete's persistence and commitment (Brewer & Shillinglaw, 1992). Some athletes may be hesitant to take this step, just as there are athletes who do not use recent innovations in strength, endurance, and skill training. The athletes, however, who do invest that persistence and commitment to improving their self-talk will find their efforts well rewarded.

Study Questions

1. Describe how the self-talk of a successful athlete is different from that of an unsuccessful athlete. Give five examples of the self-talk from each.

2. What is the relationship between (a) self-talk and self-esteem and (b) self-confidence and self-efficacy?

3. Compare and contrast optimistic and pessimistic explanatory styles in terms of the three dimension of explanatory style. How would you rate yourself on each of these?

4. Name and describe the six uses for self-talk. Using any sport setting, provide an example of each.

5. Susie, a varsity golfer, is concerned that her self-talk may be having an adverse effect on her play. What three techniques could she use to become more aware of her self-talk and how might she use them?

6. Describe how a coach or sport psychologist might help athletes use the techniques of thought stoppage and changing negative thoughts to positive thoughts.

7. How does countering a negative self-statement differ from reframing? Give examples of both in response to the statement "I'm always getting beaten on my opponent's first serve."

8. List and describe eight types of irrational and distorted thinking. Provide an example for how you can use the ABC cognitive restructuring intervention to help an athlete modify his or her irrational and distorted thinking.

9. When John monitors his self-talk, what five criteria should he use to determine whether his self-talk and underlying beliefs are rational or irrational?

10. What are the guidelines for writing and repeating affirmations?

11. How does a mastery tape or file help an athlete develop appropriate self-talk?

12. What is the purpose of a coping tape or file, and how is this purpose accomplished?

13. How might a videotape, CD, or DVD be designed and used to enhance an athlete's confidence and performance?

References

Bandura, A. (1977). Self efficacy: Toward a unifying theory of behavior change. *Psychological Review, 8,* 191–215.

Bell, K. E. (1983). *Championship thinking: The athlete's guide to winning performance in all sports.* Englewood Cliffs, NJ: Prentice-Hall.

Branden, N. (1994). *The six pillars of self-esteem.* New York: Bantam.

Brewer, B. S., & Shillinglaw, R. (1992). Evaluation of a psychological skills training workshop for male intercollegiate lacrosse players. *The Sport Psychologist, 6,* 139–147.

Bunker, L. K., & Young, B. (1995). *The courtside coach.* Charlottesville, VA: Links.

Cautela, J. R., & Wisocki, P. A. (1977). Thought stoppage procedure: Description, application and learning theory interpretations. *Psychological Record, 27,* 255–264.

Cumming, J., Nordin, S. M., Horton, R., & Reynolds, S. (2006). Examining the direction of imagery and self-talk on dart-throwing performance and self efficacy. *The Sport Psychologist, 20,* 257–274.

Cutton, D. M., & Landin, D. (2007). The effects of self-talk and augmented feedback on learning the tennis forehand. *Journal of Applied Sport Psychology, 19,* 288–303.

Dagrou, E., Gauvin, L., & Halliwell, W. (1992). Effets du langage positif, négatif, et neutre sur la performance motrice. [Effects of positive, negative, and neutral language on motor performance.] *Canadian Journal of Sport Sciences, 17,* 145–147.

Dishman, R. K., Motl, R. W., Saunders, R., Felton, G., Ward, D. S., Dowda, M., & Pate, R. R. (2004). Self-efficacy partially mediates the effect of a school-based physical-activity intervention among adolescent girls. *Preventive Medicine, 38,* 628–636.

Ellis, A. (1982). Self-direction in sport and life. In T. Orlick, J. Partington, & J. Salmela (Eds.), *Mental training for coaches and athletes* (pp. 10–17). Ottawa, ON: Coaching Association of Canada.

Ellis, A. (1988). Can we legitimately evaluate ourselves? *Psychotherapy Theory, Research and Practice, 25,* 314–316.

Ellis, A., & Dryden, W. (1987). *The practice of rational emotive therapy.* New York: Springer.

Ferguson, H. (1991). *The edge.* Cleveland, OH: Getting the Edge Company.

Finn, J. (1985). Competitive excellence: It's a matter of mind and body. *Physician and Sports Medicine, 13,* 61–72.

Gallwey, W. T. (1974). *The inner game of tennis.* New York: Random House.

Gauron, E. F. (1984). *Mental training for peak performance.* Lansing, NY: Sport Science Associates.

Gould, D., Eklund, R. C., & Jackson, S. A. (1992a). 1988 U.S. Olympic wrestling excellence: I. Mental preparation, precompetitive cognition, and affect. *The Sport Psychologist, 6,* 358–382.

Gould, D., Eklund. R. C., & Jackson, S. A. (1992b). 1988 U.S. Olympic wrestling excellence: II. Thoughts and affect occurring during competition. *The Sport Psychologist, 6,* 383–402.

Gould, D., Finch, L. M., & Jackson, S. A. (1993). Coping strategies used by national champion figure skaters. *Research Quarterly for Exercise and Sport, 64,* 453–468.

Gould, D., Guinan, D., Greenleaf, C., Medbery, R., & Pederson, K. (1999). Factors affecting Olympic performance perceptions of athletes and coaches from more or less successful teams. *The Sport Psychologist, 13,* 371–394.

Gould, D., Hodge, K., Peterson, K., & Gianni, J. (1989). An exploratory examination of strategies used by elite coaches to enhance self-efficacy in athletes. *Journal of Sport and Exercise Psychology, 11,* 128–140.

Gould, D., Medberry, R., Damarjian, N., & Lauer, L. (1999). A survey of mental skills training knowledge, opinions, and practices of junior tennis coaches. *Journal of Applied Sport Psychology, 11,* 28–50.

Grieger, R., & Boyd, J. (1980). *Rational emotive therapy.* New York: Van Nostrand.

Hackfort, D., & Schwenkmezger, P. (1993). In R. N. Singer, M. Murphey, and L. K. Tennant (Eds.), *Handbook of research on sport psychology* (pp. 328–364). New York: MacMillan.

Hall, C. R., Hardy, J., & Gammage, K. L. (1999). About hitting golf balls in the water: Comments on Janelle's (1999) article on ironic processes. *The Sport Psychologist, 13,* 221–224.

Hanton, S., & Jones G. (1999a) The effects of a multimodal intervention program on performers: II. Training the butterflies to fly in formation. *The Sport Psychologist, 13,* 22–41.

Hanton, S., & Jones, G. (1999b) The acquisition and development of cognitive skills and strategies: II. Training the butterflies to fly in formation. *The Sport Psychologist, 13,* 22–41.

Hardy, J., Gammage, K., & Hall, C. (2001). A descriptive study of athlete self-talk. *The Sport Psychologist, 15,* 306–318.

Hardy, J., Hall, C. R., & Hardy, L. (2004a). *Quantifying athletes' use of self-talk.* Manuscript submitted for publication.

Hardy, J., Hall, C. R., & Hardy, L. (2004b). A note on athletes' use of self-talk. *Journal of Applied Sport Psychology, 16,* 251–257.

Harris, D. V., & Harris, B. L. (1984). *The athlete's guide to sports psychology: Mental skills for physical people.* West Point, NY: Leisure Press.

Hatzigeorgiadis, A., Zourbanos, N., Theodorakis, Y. (2007). The moderating effects of self-talk content on self-talk functions. *Journal of Applied Sport Psychology, 19,* 240–251.

Hatzigeorgiadis, A., Zourbanos, N., Goltsios, C., & Theodorakis, Y. (2008). Investigating the functions of self-talk: The effects of motivational self-talk on self-efficacy and performance in young tennis players. *The Sport Psychologist, 22,* 458–471.

Ieleva, L., & Orlick, T. (1991). Mental links to enhanced healing: An exploratory study. *The Sport Psychologist, 5,* 25–40.

Ives, J. C., Straub, W. F., & Shelley, G. A. (2002). Enhancing athletic performance using digital video in consulting. *Journal of Applied Sport Psychology, 14,* 237–245.

Janelle, C. (1999). Ironic mental processes in sport: Implications for sport psychologists. *The Sport Psychologist, 13,* 201–220.

Johnson, J. J. M., Hrycaiko, D. W., Johnson, G. V., & Halas, J. M. (2004). Self-talk and female youth soccer performance. *The Sport Psychologist, 18,* 44–59.

Johnston-O'Conner, E. J., & Kirschenbaum, D. S. (1986). Something succeeds like success: Positive self-monitoring for unskilled golfers. *Cognitive Therapy and Research, 6,* 335–342.

Jones, G., Hanton, S., & Connaughton, D. (2002). What is this thing called mental toughness: An investigation of elite sport performers. *Journal of Applied Sport Psychology, 14,* 205–218

Kashiwagi, K. (1986). Personality development of adolescents. In H. W. Stevenson & H. Azuma (Eds.), *Child development and education in Japan* (pp. 167–185). New York: W. H. Freeman.

Kendall, G., Hrycaiko, D., Martin, G., & Kendall, T. (1990). Effects of an imagery rehearsal, relaxation, and self-talk package on basketball game performance. *Journal of Sport and Exercise Psychology, 12,* 157–166.

King, P. (2001, January 29). Who let this dog out? *Sports Illustrated,* 46–50.

Kirschenbaum, D. S., O'Connor, E. A., & Owens, D. (1999). Smart golf: Preliminary evaluation of a simple, yet comprehensive, approach to improving and scoring the mental game. *The Sport Psychologist, 12,* 271–282.

Kirschenbaum, D. S., Ordman, A. M., Tomarken, A. J., & Holtzbauer, R. (1982). Effects of differential self-monitoring and level of mastery on sports performance: Brain power bowling. *Cognitive Therapy and Research, 6,* 335–342.

Kirschenbaum, D. S., Owens, D., & O'Connor, E. A. (1999). Positive illusions in golf: Empirical and conceptual analyses. *Journal of Applied Sport Psychology, 11,* 1–27.

Kitayama, S. (2002). Cultural psychology of the self: A renewed look at independence and interdependence. In C. Hofsten & L. Backman (Eds.), *Psychology at the turn of the millennium* (Vol. 2, pp. 305–322). Florence, KY: Taylor & Frances/Routledge.

Kitsantas, A., & Zimmerman, B. J. (2002). Comparing self-regulatory processes among novice, non-expert, and expert volleyball players: A microanalytic study. *Journal of Applied Sport Psychology, 13,* 365–379.

Landin, D., & Hebert, E. P. (1999). The influence of self-talk on the performance of skilled female tennis players. *Journal of Applied Sport Psychology, 11,* 263–282.

Mahoney, M. J. (1979). Cognitive skills and athletic performance. In P. C. Kendall & S. D. Hollon (Eds.), *Cognitive-behavioral interventions: Theory, research and procedure.* New York: Academic Press.

Mahoney, M. J., Gabriel, T. J., & Perkins, T. S. (1987). Psychological skills and exceptional athletic performance. *The Sport Psychologist, 1,* 181–199.

McAuley, E., & Blissmer, B. (2000). Self-efficacy determinants and consequences of physical activity. *Exercise and Sport Sciences Reviews, 28,* 85–88.

McKay, M., & Fanning, P. (1994). *Self-esteem* (2nd ed.). Oakland, CA: New Harbinger.

McPherson, S. L. (2000). Expert-novice differences in planning strategies during collegiate singles tennis competition. *Journal of Sport and Exercise Psychology, 22,* 39–62.

Meichenbaum, D. (1975). Toward a cognitive theory of self-control. In G. Schwartz & D. Shapiro (Eds.), *Consciousness and self-regulation: Advances in research.* New York: Plenum.

Meichenbaum, D. (1977). *Cognitive behavior modification: An integrative approach.* New York: Plenum.

Meyers, A. W., & Schleser, R. A. (1980). A cognitive behavioral intervention for improving basketball performance. *Journal of Sport Psychology, 2,* 69–73.

Meyers, A. W., Whelan, J. P., & Murphy, S. M. (1996). Cognitive behavioral strategies in athletic performance enhancement. In M. Hersen, R. M. Eisler, & P. M. Miller (Eds.), *Progress in behavior modification* (pp. 53–65). New York: Plenum Press.

Owens, D., & Bunker, L. K. (1989). *Golf: Steps to success.* Champaign, IL: Human Kinetics.

Perkos, S., Theodorakis, Y., & Chroni, S., (2002). Enhancing performance and still acquisition in novice basketball players with instructional self-talk. *Sport Psychologist, 16,* 368–383.

Peters, H. J., & Williams, J. M. (2008). *Culture's influence on self-talk, performance, and potential moderators.* Manuscript in preparation.

Peters, H. J., & Williams, J. M. (2006). Moving cultural background to the foreground: An investigation of self-talk, performance, and persistence following feedback. *Journal of Applied Sport Psychology, 18,* 240–253.

Rogerson, L. J., & Hrycaiko, D. W. (2002). Enhancing competitive performance of ice hockey goaltenders using centering and self-talk. *Journal of Applied Sport Psychology, 14,* 14–26.

Rongian, L. T. (2007). Building and communicating collective efficacy: A season-long in-depth study of an elite sport team. *The Sport Psychologist, 21,* 8–93.

Rotella, R. (1984). Untitled manuscript. University of Virginia, Charlottesville.

Rotella, R. (1995). *Golf is not a game of perfect.* New York: Simon & Schuster.

Rotella, R. (1996). *Golf is a game of confidence.* New York: Simon & Schuster.

Rushall, B. S. (1979). *Psyching in sports.* London: Pelham.

Schunk, D. H. (1995). Self-efficacy, motivation and performance. *Journal of Applied Sport Psychology, 7,* 112–137.

Seligman, M. (1991). *Learned optimism.* New York: Knopf.

Silva, J. (1982). Performance enhancement through cognitive intervention. *Behavioral Modification, 6,* 443–463.

Steinmetz, J., Blankenship, J., & Brown, L. (1980). *Managing stress before it manages you.* Palo Alto, CA: Bull.

Syer, J., & Connolly, C. (1984). *Sporting body sporting mind: An athlete's guide to mental training.* New York: Cambridge University Press.

Taylor, J. (1999). Isn't it ironic? Or irony is in the unconscious eye of the beholder. *The Sport Psychologist, 13,* 225–230.

Thellwell, R., & Greenlee, I. (2003). Developing competitive endurance performance using mental skills training. *Sport Psychologist, 17,* 208–225.

Tod, D., Iredale, F., and Gill, N. (2003). Psyching-up and muscular force production. *Sports Medicine, 33,* 47–59.

Van Raalte, J. L., Brewer, B. W., Lewis, B. P., Linder, D. E., Wildman, G., & Kozimor, J. (1995). Cork! The effects of positive and negative self-talk on dart throwing performance. *Journal of Sport Behavior, 18,* 50–57.

Van Raalte, J. L., Brewer, B. W., Rivera, P. M., & Petitpas, A. J. (1994). The relationship between observable self-talk and competitive junior tennis players' match performance. *Journal of Sport and Exercise Psychology, 16,* 400–415.

Wegner, D. M. (1994). Ironic processes of mental control. *Psychological Review, 16,* 34–52.

Wegner, D. M. (1997). When the antidote is the poison. Ironic mental control processes. *Psychological Science, 8,* 148–150.

Wegner, D. M., Ansfield, M., & Pilloff, D. (1998). The putt and the pendulum: Ironic effects of mental control of action. *Psychological Science, 9,* 196–199.

Wegner, D. M., & Erber, R. (1992). The hyperaccessibility of suppressed thoughts. *Journal of Personality and Social Psychology, 63,* 903–912.

Wegner, D. M., Schneider, D. J., Knutson, B., & McMahon, S. R. (1991). Polluting the stream of consciousness: The effect of thought suppression on the mind's environment. *Cognitive Therapy and Research, 15,* 41–152.

Weinberg, R. S., Gould, D., & Jackson, A. (1979). Expectations and performance: An empirical test of Bandura's self-efficacy theory. *Journal of Sport Psychology, 3,* 320–331.

Wenzlaff, R. M., Wegner D. M., & Klein, S. B. (1991). The role of thought suppression in the bonding of thought and mood. *Journal of Personality and Social Psychology, 60,* 500–508.

Wenzlaff, R. M., & Wegner, D. M. (2000). Thought suppression. *Annual Review of Psychology, 51,* 39–91.

Wishful Inking. (1991, January). *Special Report: On Sports,* p. 24.

16

Concentration and Strategies for Controlling It

Jean M. Williams, *University of Arizona, Emeritus*
Robert M. Nideffer, *Enhanced Performance Systems*
Vietta E. Wilson, *York University, Senior Scholar*
Marc-Simon Sagal, *The Winning Mind*
Erik Peper, *San Francisco State University*

When I'm focused, there is not one single thing, person, anything that can stand in the way of my doing something.

—Michael Phelps, 2008, Winner of Olympic gold medals

If I had stood at the free-throw line and thought about 10 million people watching me on the other side of the camera lens, I couldn't have made anything, so I mentally tried to put myself in a familiar place. I thought about all those times I shot free throws in practice and went through the same motion, the same technique that I had used thousands of times. You forget about the outcome.

—Michael Jordan, 1998

Concentration is essential for performing one's best whether the performer is an athlete, student, surgeon, musician, or something else. According to Cox (2002), few areas in sport psychology are as important to overall performance as the area of concentration or attention.[1] Unless attention control training has occurred and concentration skills have been mastered, performance will almost always suffer.

When someone performs badly, one of the most frequently heard comments is "I couldn't concentrate" or "I lost my focus." What do we mean by good concentration? The major component of concentration is the ability to selectively attend to appropriate cues in the task at hand, such as some aspect of the environment or internal stimuli, while screening out irrelevant and distracting external and internal stimuli. External stimuli may include factors such as an audience booing, bad officiating calls, and unsportsmanlike behavior from the opponent. Internal stimuli

[1]The words *concentration* and *attention* are used interchangeably in this chapter.

336

include distracting body sensations and thoughts and feelings such as "I'm really tired," "Don't be nervous," "The pain is fierce," " My opponent is bigger and better," and "I blew it!" Although external and internal stimuli appear to be separate categories, they continually affect each other.

Under maximally demanding conditions, good concentration entails 100% attention to the task at hand. The goal is total absorption in the experience. For example, Walsh and Spelman (1983) reported that conductor Carlos Kleiber never noticed the earthquake rattling a giant chandelier when he was conducting Strauss's *Der Rosenkavalier* at La Scala. We often fail to remember someone's name upon being introduced because rather than totally focusing on the name and trying to associate it with something we can remember, we think about the impression we are making or we minimally listen because we don't care. There are exceptions to the 100% attention rule when a task does not demand maximal concentration. For example, under most conditions people can safely drive a car while also carrying on a conversation or even eating.

Optimal concentration requires being totally in the *here and now,* in the present. When our minds drift into the past or future, we are usually not as effective in present performance. To illustrate, when the University of Arizona men's basketball team was up by 15 points with only minutes to play in an NCAA tournament game that would have sent them rather than Illinois to the final four, someone brought down to the court boxes of celebratory "final four" tee shirts and caps. Obviously many factors contributed to Arizona's loss, including possibly the distraction of projecting into the future.

Optimal concentration also requires keeping an appropriate focus over an appropriate length of time as well as the ability to shift attention based upon changing performance demands. It is not enough to start with the appropriate focus; it must be maintained as long as needed. Correspondingly, for many tasks, the athlete must be able to shift his or her focus of attention in response to changing performance demands.

Based upon the preceding, we know you have lost concentration when you attend to irrelevant cues, have inappropriate divided attention, or leave the here and now. Becoming aware of gaps in experience is another sign of lost concentration. One of the best examples comes from studying. How often have you read a chapter that was boring or read when something else was on your mind only to discover that you've been turning the pages and have no idea what you read? Finally, although not always, when performance level is suffering there is a good chance you have lost optimal concentration. A first step in regaining it is to increase your awareness of these signs of lost concentration.

In what situations are we most likely to not have or to lose concentration? There are many possible answers, but the most likely ones are after mistakes, when stressed out, when not sufficiently motivated, or when overmotivated. It is impossible to perform one's best in the present moment when ruminating about a previous mistake. Instead, if there is time, quickly learn from the mistake and let it go. If there is no time to learn, let it go and deal with it later. This sounds simple, but is often difficult to do. Later, we present exercises designed to increase your ability to control focus. Motivation and stress play a major role in determining physiological arousal level and thereby affect attentional focus.

The next few sections discuss Robert Nideffer's conceptualization of concentration and his principles for attention control training. This work provides the best operational definition of concentration and foundation for training concentration, including clarifying the relationship between arousal and focus of concentration and how and why choking occurs.

Attention Control Training Principles

Attention control training (ACT) is based on a theory of attentional and interpersonal style (Nideffer, 1976). The principles underlying the application of ACT to performance enhancement are outlined here.

1. Athletes need to be able to engage in at least four different types of concentration.

2. Different sport situations will make different attentional demands on an athlete. Accordingly, the athlete must be able to shift to the appropriate type of concentration to match changing attentional demands.

3. Under optimal conditions, the average person can meet the concentration demands of a wide variety of performance situations.

4. Individual differences exist in attentional abilities; thus individual athletes have different attentional strengths and weaknesses. Attentional characteristics are at times traitlike, having predictive utility in any number of situations. At other times they are statelike, situationally determined and modifiable through training. Factors that determine the extent to which a given individual's attentional skills are traitlike include biological or genetic predispositions and alterations in arousal. As arousal moves out of the moderate range, individuals are more likely to go to their dominant attentional focus or style (Hull, 1951). Thus, the individual's dominant attentional style becomes more traitlike and more predictive of behavior when arousal levels are higher.

5. The individual's ability to perform effectively depends on two factors: (1) the appropriateness of the dominant attentional style, and (2) the level of confidence within the particular performance situation (Carver & Scheier, 1989).

6. The phenomenon of choking—of having performance progressively and uncontrollably deteriorate—occurs as physiological arousal increases well beyond the desired level, causing attention to involuntarily narrow and become more internally focused. This results in alterations in perception; time seems speeded up, which contributes to a tendency to rush (e.g., to start to throw the ball before completing the catch). Muscles antagonistic to performance begin to tighten, interfering with weight transfer, timing, and coordination.

7. Alterations in physiological arousal affect concentration. Thus, the systematic manipulation of physiological arousal is one way of gaining some control over concentration.

8. Alterations in the focus of attention will also affect physiological arousal. Thus, the systematic manipulation of concentration is one way to gain some control over arousal (e.g., muscular tension levels, heart rate, and respiration rate).

Different Types of Concentration

All too often a coach just shouts, "Concentrate!" at an athlete. The athlete is more likely to respond effectively to the instruction if the coach specifically defines the type of concentration or focus to which he or she would like the athlete to engage. To do this, it is necessary to think of attention as requiring at least two different types of focus. First, the athlete will need to control the *width* of his or her attentional focus. Certain sports, such as basketball and hockey, require a broad focus of attention. Other sports, such as sprints, diving, and shooting, require a narrow focus. The second type of focus that needs to be controlled relates to the *direction* of the athlete's attention. In some situations, attention must be directed internally to make adjustments in muscle tension or to problem solve and strategize. At other times, attention must be focused externally, on the opponent, or the flash of the starting gun. Figure 16-1 presents the four general types of concentration required by different sport situations that result when both width

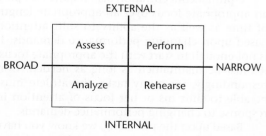

Figure 16-1   **Dimensions of attention**

and direction of attention are controlled and Figure 16-2 presents examples of each.

Shifting Attention

Recall the second principle underlying attention control training: Different sport situations make different attentional demands on athletes. Thus, a position such as quarterback in football places a greater demand on an athlete to develop a broad external focus of attention (e.g., to be aware of the entire field) than a position such as guard, which requires a narrower type of concentration (e.g., to block a particular athlete on the other team). Often there are many demands for shifting attention within a particular sport. An example from golf illustrates the point.

When golfers step up to the ball prior to hitting a shot, they need a fairly broad external type of attention in order to take in several different kinds of information. They need awareness of the placement of hazards (trees, sand traps, out-of-bounds markers, water, and the like) and course conditions (dryness of the grass, speed and direction of wind). Once they have gathered this external information, golfers shift attention to a broad internal focus to plan their shot. At this time they should recall past similar situations, remembering how they played them and what the results were. Then they must think about anything that might modify how they should

now play this similar situation (e.g., have they changed their swing, are they in a different tactical position such as needing to be conservative or to take a risk). Analyzing all of this information allows golfers to determine how they want to hit the ball and to select a particular club.

After formulating a plan, golfers shift to a narrow internal type of concentration to monitor their own tension (e.g., making sure they are not too tight or too relaxed) and mentally rehearse the shot. They may picture in their mind what they want to feel and see as they execute the shot. Finally, golfers shift attention to a narrow external focus as they address the ball and begin their backswing. At this time concentration is on the ball. To attend to other external or internal cues would only interfere with their execution of the shot.

This basic model can be applied to a great many sports. Thus, athletes are continually required to shift attention across different tasks even though some sports or positions require more of one type of attention than others. Research shows that attentional focusing can be improved with attention control training that entails drills in which athletes have to shift their attention (e.g., Ziegler, 1994).

In addition, in some sport situations coaches and other athletes can make up for attentional deficiencies of some players. As an illustration, a football coach can select the plays for the quarterback, thus limiting the need for the

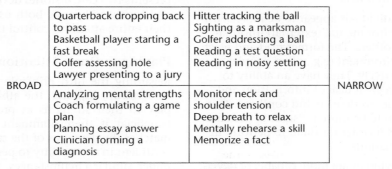

EXTERNAL

| BROAD | Quarterback dropping back to pass
Basketball player starting a fast break
Golfer assessing hole
Lawyer presenting to a jury | Hitter tracking the ball
Sighting as a marksman
Golfer addressing a ball
Reading a test question
Reading in noisy setting | NARROW |
| | Analyzing mental strengths
Coach formulating a game plan
Planning essay answer
Clinician forming a diagnosis | Monitor neck and shoulder tension
Deep breath to relax
Mentally rehearse a skill
Memorize a fact | |

INTERNAL

Figure 16-2   **Examples of dimensions of attention**

quarterback to develop a broad internal type of attention. An increasingly important role for the sport psychologist and coach is assisting athletes in recognizing the attentional demands of their sports and in assessing and developing their ability to appropriately shift from one type of attention to another.

Individual Differences

The third principle indicates that if individuals are appropriately motivated, trained in what to do (including focus), and have control over their level of arousal (so that it is neither too high nor too low), they are capable of effective concentration. They can control the width and direction of attention enough to be effective because the actual attentional demands of most sports are not so extreme that the average person cannot meet them.

At the same time, the fourth principle indicates individual differences in attentional abilities and dominant attentional style. Further, as physiological arousal begins to increase beyond an athlete's own optimal level, athletes tend to rely more heavily on their most highly developed attentional ability. Research on attentional processes suggests the following differences, among others.

1. Different individuals have different capacities for developing a broad internal type of attention. Thus, some individuals are better suited to analyzing large amounts of information than others.

2. Certain individuals appear to be more sensitive to environmental (external) information than others. The former read and react to the environment (e.g., other people) more effectively. They have an ability to deal with a great deal of information and not become overloaded and confused. This helps them to be more resistant to pressure and makes it easier for them to perform in critical situations.

3. Some individuals are more capable of developing a narrow, nondistractible type of attention. This is especially true of world

class performers in sport (Nideffer, Sagal, Lowry, & Bond, 2000). Their ability to focus narrowly makes it easier for them to be dedicated to follow through on a task, to be as selfish as they must be to make it to the top.

Thus, another important role for the sport psychologist and coach is helping athletes identify their own relative attentional strengths and weaknesses. This assessment will aid the majority of athletes in developing concentration skills and compensating for any attentional problems they may have. One of the best ways to accomplish this objective is The Attentional and Interpersonal Style (TAIS) inventory Nideffer developed and used with his colleagues in their attention control training programs (Nideffer, 1976; Nideffer & Sagal, 2001, and Nideffer, 2003). TAIS measures relevant concentration skills and interpersonal characteristics such as an athlete's attentional strengths, the types of situations likely to interfere with his or her performance, and the most likely performance errors. See Table 16-1 for a description of the attentional scales and Nideffer (1976) for the interpersonal scales. TAIS results should be used to provide a situation specific focus for an attention control training program, but TAIS is only one method for assessing the concentration and interpersonal skills required by different performance situations. Interviews, behavior rating scales, observations, and other assessment tools measuring these characteristics also may be used. McGraw-Hill's Instructor's Web site for this book presents two case histories developed by Nideffer and Sagal to illustrate both use of the TAIS and their entire attention control training processes.

Playing to One's Attentional Strength

Regarding the fifth principle underlying attention control training, the athletes' tendency to play to their strengths as pressure increases is beneficial if their dominant attentional style matches the demands of the task and if they are confident in their ability to perform. In contrast, under similar circumstances, performance may suffer with increased pressure when athletes are not attentionally suited to their sport.

Table 16-1 **Attentional Scales from the Test of Attentional and Interpersonal Style**

Scale	Scale Description
BET	*Broad External Attention:* High scores indicate good environmental awareness and assessment skills (street sense).
OET	*Overloaded by External Information:* High scores are associated with errors because attention is inappropriately focused on irrelevant external stimuli.
BIT	*Broad Internal Attention:* High scores indicate good analytical planning skills.
OIT	*Overloaded by Internal Information:* High scores are associated with errors due to distractions from irrelevant internal sources (e.g., thoughts and feelings).
NAR	*Narrow-Focused Attention:* High scores indicate the ability to remain task oriented, to avoid distractions, and to stay focused on a single job.
RED	*Reduced Attention:* High scores are associated with errors due to a failure to shift attention from an external focus to an internal one, or vice versa.

There is an unproven assumption in sport that good athletes do not make good coaches and vice versa. If this is true, one of the reasons might be that coaching makes a very heavy demand on an individual to be able to think and analyze. Coaches must be able to develop a broad internal type of attention. In contrast, many sporting situations require athletes to shut off their analyzing. If they do not, we see the paralysis by analysis that coaches are so fond of talking about. The athletes think too much and fail to react to the sport situation. They are "in their head" at an inappropriate time. Athletes who ultimately become coaches are often the ones who were continually analyzing. They are not the brilliant broken-field runners who reacted instinctively.

Take the pressure off most coaches and athletes and they can be either analytical or instinctive. Put them under pressure, however, and they play to their strengths. Analytical coaches become *too* analytical. They go inside their head and lose sensitivity to the athletes and the game situation. Often they attempt to communicate their analysis to the athletes, overloading them with information, getting them to think too much. Instinctive athletes have a tendency to react too quickly. When too pressured (i.e., physiological arousal too high), they may fail to analyze and plan when it is needed. They lose their capacity to make adjustments, getting faked out

by the same moves time and time again, not learning from their own mistakes.

Sport psychologists can help athletes and coaches *team build* and maintain effective communication under pressure. Sport psychologists do this by sensitizing coaches and athletes to their own and others' relative attentional strengths and weaknesses. Sport psychologists help coaches and athletes identify the specific situations in which communication is likely to break down and help them plan alternative ways to behave. When no sport psychologist is available to help, coaches need to be sufficiently knowledgeable and aware to do this on their own.

As an example of the team-building process, consider a situation in which a coach tends to be more analytical and more assertive than the athletes (a normally ideal situation). As pressure increases, the coach becomes more analytical and more assertive and the athletes less so. At a certain point the athletes should be confronting the coach with the fact that they are being overloaded with instructions; instead they may behave in an even more outwardly compliant way, nodding their heads to show agreement even when they are not hearing or when they are confused. The coach, thinking that he or she has a willing, even enthusiastic, audience, feels encouraged to give still more information. The sport psychologist helps the athletes recognize their feelings of confusion and provides them with the support they need to confront the coach (e.g., "Coach, I can't take all of this right now.") Then all work together to develop ways of minimizing the problem. Perhaps insight is all the coach needs to decrease the amount of information he or she gives. The sport psychologist can usually give the coach suggestions for communicating the same information in a more simplified and structured way.

Operationally Defining Choking

A perfect example of the sixth principle underlying ACT comes from a sport psychologist who worked with a football quarterback. The coach referred the player because his play was outstanding in practice, but he often blew it (choked) when under pressure in big games. The quarterback described to the sport psychologist that he became so stressed during some big games he could literally feel his heart thumping and he kept thinking he was going to blow it. Worse, when he dropped back to pass, it was like looking for the receiver through a roll of toilet paper. Before we examine the sixth principle, we must define operationally the term **choking.** (Unfortunately, there is little agreement among most coaches and athletes regarding the definition of such a critical term. Thus, when a coach tells an athlete not to choke, the athlete may have no idea of what he or she is supposed to avoid.) Given what we do know about the interaction between thought process (what we attend to) and physiological process, it is possible to come up with a definition of choking that can be very useful to coaches, athletes, sport psychology practitioners, and researchers alike.

Behaviorally, we can infer that athletes are choking when their performance seems to be progressively deteriorating and when they seem incapable of regaining control over performance on their own, that is, without some outside assistance. Examples would be that quarterback or the baseball player who follows a bobbled catch with a throwing error, or the diver or gymnast who lets an early mistake (e.g., on a dive or particular move) upset him or her to the point of making additional errors on subsequent actions. In all cases of "choking" the athlete becomes focused on the increasing pressure and physiological arousal gets too high.

Figure 16-3 illustrates the interaction that occurs between physiological and attentional processes under highly stressful conditions. The figure also shows how the changes that occur affect performance. By using Figure 16-3 and the section that follows, coaches should gain a more useful understanding of the choking process—an understanding that can help increase their ability to understand, predict, and control behavior in sport situations.

Prevention and Treatment of Choking

The seventh and eighth principles underlying attention control training suggest that by creating changes in what is going on either physiologically or attentionally athletes can break the downward spiral associated with choking. Thus, if they eliminate the physical feelings associated with excessive tension (tight muscles, pounding heart), they will reduce the number of attentional distractions and improve their ability to concentrate. Likewise, if coaches can get the athletes to either ignore or reinterpret their physical feelings (e.g., if they give a positive interpretation to being aroused, such as "I'm ready"), gradually the physical changes will be reduced and tension levels and heart rate will return to what is normal for the competitive conditions. To illustrate how important the preceding is, Abernethy (2001) and Zaichkowsky and Naylor (2004) have advocated that a foundation of psychological skills training relative to performance is increasing athletes' awareness of their arousal level as it relates to the construct of attention.

An unrealistic goal of many sport psychology programs is to prevent choking by teaching athletes some type of relaxation or rehearsal procedure. In truth, we probably can reduce the frequency of choking through better training and through some type of relaxation and rehearsal process, but we cannot eliminate it. As John McEnroe, a top professional tennis player said when he was competing, "When it comes to

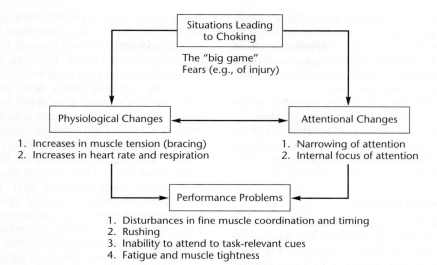

Figure 16-3   **Interaction between physiological and attentional processes under highly stressful conditions**

choking, the bottom line is that everyone does it. The question isn't whether you choke or not, but how—when you choke—you are going to handle it. Choking is a big part of every sport, and a part of being a champion is being able to cope with it better than everyone else" (cited in Goffi, 1984, pp. 61-62). When providing interventions dealing with choking, we are likely to be successful only if our program has a performance-specific focus. That is, we should teach the athletes to use relaxation and to then appropriately focus attention at a particular time (e.g., at bat one might take a deep relaxing breath or squeeze the bat tightly and then relax the muscles and then focus attention on the pitcher), and we should train them to rehearse a particular performance situation (e.g., hitting under certain conditions).

By teaching athletes to relax, to monitor their own muscle tension levels, and to use their tension levels as a signal to employ some brief type of relaxation procedure, we can help them improve the consistency of their performance. By getting them to mentally simulate anticipated performance conditions and to systematically rehearse what they will see and feel, we can begin to desensitize them to distracters

and increase the likelihood that tension will not reach a level that will cause them to choke. Later in the chapter we discuss these concepts in more detail.

With such a specific training focus we can reduce the frequency of choking and "season" athletes more quickly. Simulation and rehearsal can make up for some lack of experience. Nevertheless, there will always be unanticipated situations that we could not prepare for. If we tried to think of every contingency, we would overload ourselves and never make any progress. As a result, we must begin to train athletes to recover quickly from the unexpected. Learning to recover once tension has already gotten out of control or once a mistake has been made is even more critical than trying to eliminate choking altogether.

Developing and incorporating detailed and consistent pre-performance routines is another effective way to prevent and treat choking (Mesagno, Marchant, & Morris, 2008). In a study with bowlers predisposed to choke under pressure, they found that accuracy improved when they were taught before each delivery to use a pre-performance routine that included modifying arousal level so that it was optimal and use of behavioral steps, attention control (e.g., focusing on a target), and cue words. In addition to improving performance, use of the personalized routine led to positive psychological outcomes such as decreased conscious processing and more relevant, task-focused attention.

Next we discuss how taking a process versus outcome focus might help prevent choking or help to recover and in the sections that follow we address other concentration training exercises that have proven helpful in enhancing athletes' ability to appropriately focus and refocus if necessary.

Process versus Outcome

Once athletes have made a mistake or once they become aware of the tension and the attentional distractions that are likely to interfere with performance, what they attend to becomes critical. The prevention strategy discussed previously emphasizes training athletes to recognize and reduce physical tension, thereby improving concentration. Once they have made mistakes, however, many athletes find it difficult to directly challenge what is going on in their bodies.

Imagine a situation in which you have just double-faulted away a game in a critical tennis match. You know you are tight and you try to counter it by saying, "It's all right, just relax; the game isn't that important anyway," and a little voice inside you immediately counters with, "Oh yes it is, you blew it, you can't do it."

Your lack of confidence created by the feelings and the failure causes you to doubt your own ability. Trying to take control directly only creates more distractions and frustration. If you had a great deal of confidence in yourself you could do that. You could challenge and confront yourself, using your frustration and anger to help you concentrate on the task. When you lack confidence, however, you must focus your attention on something else. You must become process focused rather than outcome focused.

During practice, especially in sports that require a great deal of training and sacrifice on the part of the athlete, individuals motivate themselves by thinking about outcome: "If we win the championship, I'll be a hero." "I am

working this hard because I want to win a gold medal." "By making these sacrifices I can get the recognition and financial rewards I want." Once the competition begins, however, an outcome focus can become very negative.

To be thinking about how important the outcome of a contest is or about what one can win or lose during the actual competition typically generates additional physical and attentional changes that interfere with performance. One of the biggest contributors to choking is thinking about the outcome or the importance of a contest while involved in it. To help athletes break out of this thinking, sport psychologists can train them to recognize their tendency toward placing too much importance on outcome (during the competition) and to use those thoughts, when they occur, as signals to attend to the process. Coaches need to do the same thing. **Process cues** are related to the process of performing as opposed to the outcome. Later we discuss growing evidence that cues such as an external movement effect (e.g., pendulum-like motion of the golf club when pitching) are particularly beneficial. Over time, people learn that if they maintain a process focus, the outcome will take care of itself. Then, as they have success and as confidence builds, they can begin to attend to outcome to motivate themselves to try harder. Thus, the athlete who has a lot of success and who becomes a little lazy or too relaxed needs to think about outcome to get arousal levels up and to keep going.

Increasing Awareness of Types of Attention

Earlier we identified the different types of attention or concentration athletes use in athletic situations. These types were described along two dimensions: broad versus narrow and internal versus external. In concentration training, knowing what to focus on is as critical as knowing how to control one's focus. Athletes may have excellent concentration skills, but if they focus on the wrong things, the skills will not be very helpful. Additionally, they must know when to switch from one focus to another in a very short time period, sometimes even changing attentional style. Fortunately, the brain is capable of responding in milliseconds (one thousands of a second) and extremely complex skills can be done almost instantaneously if switching attention is practiced correctly.

The first step in training for better control of concentration involves coaches and sport psychologists assisting athletes in identifying the different attentional styles and when to use them (see Figures 16-1 and 16-2), including the specific application to their sport involvement. Our experience is that confusion often exists, even amongst coaches and physical educators, regarding the optimal attentional focus at any given time in the learning and performance of sport skills and strategies. Until somewhat recently, we have lacked much research to provide guidance in making these decisions. That deficit has improved, but more research is needed. We will later discuss some of the recent findings.

To familiarize athletes with the different attentional styles and to get them to experience them, a starting point might be an "expanding awareness" exercise developed by Gauron (1984). Below we present some of his exercises as well as some of our own.

1. **Narrow-external drills.** Pick some object across the room and focus on it, observing every detail and noticing just it. Once there is nothing else to observe, focus on a different object. Now pay attention to what you hear by taking each separate sound, identifying it, and then mentally labeling it, such as footsteps, voices, or a cough. Focus on only one sound at a time.

In some sports, one way to enhance a narrow external focus is for the coach to place different numbers on a ball or puck and have the athletes yell out the number as the ball or puck approaches them (e.g., receiving a served volleyball). In another version, the coach puts different colors on the balls or pucks and the players are instructed to hit with different techniques or to a different location depending on the color of the ball or puck. Because athletes have a tendency to become too aroused during these drills, we suggest that you remind them to relax the shoulder muscles and keep the knees bent so they are in a position to move quickly.

2. **Broad-external drills.** While looking straight ahead, see as much of the room and as many of the objects in the room as your peripheral vision will allow. Simultaneously observe the entire room and all the items in it.

In a team sport, a coach can enhance the experience of staying focused but open to picking up an array of important external information by making a game of FREEZE out of many sport situations. During practice the coach can randomly yell *FREEZE;* players immediately stop and close their eyes, and then the coach asks the players or a selected player where everyone was on the floor or field and where the ball or puck was.

3. **Narrow-to-broad external drills.** Extend both arms in front of you with both thumbs up approximately 4 inches apart framing some "main focus" in the distance. See the main focus in as much detail as you can. As you maintain that focus, begin to slowly move both extended arms to the side. Continue to see the main focus as well as both thumbs and everything in between. Do this in a passive manner. Relax and repeat two or three times. Many athletes report that this drill enables them to see the main focus while also clearly picking up the broader field. A variation is to ask the athletes to think of their external focus as a zoom lens; practice zooming in and out, narrowing or broadening according to your wishes. Both exercises illustrate what it is like to switch the focus from a specific to panoramic focus or vice versa, thus practicing what often occurs within athletic skills and situations.

4. **Narrow-internal drills.** Focus on your breathing for a few breaths. Notice how the abdominal region rises as the air comes in and how it gently falls as the air goes out. Now make the time to exhale longer than the time to inhale. The air comes in, pause,

then let all the air effortlessly come out for a longer time than it took to get in. It is as if the breathing is being done for you, and you are a mere spectator. Next switch the focus to any tension in your jaw (or pick another muscle group). Notice whatever tension you are feeling and, if you can, release that tension and contrast your relaxed jaw with the tense one. Attend now only to an emotion or thought. Let each thought or emotion appear gently, without being forced. Identify the nature of the thought or feeling. Remain calm no matter how pleasant or unpleasant the thoughts may be. Feel one, then another, then another. Now try to empty yourself of all thoughts and feelings. Let them go. If this is not possible, tune in to only one and hold your attention there.

Have athletes of similar height pair up and stand facing each other. One athlete will extend his or her dominant arm with the palm facing up and wrist resting on the other athlete's opposite shoulder. The athlete with the extended arm will focus his or her attention on contracting the muscles to make the arm as strong as possible while the other athlete cups his or her hands over the elbow and slowly pulls to bend the arm downward at the elbow. (Note: palm must be up to prevent elbow injury.) Begin again and this time the athlete with the extended arm focuses on staying relaxed while imagining that his or her arm is like a stiff fire hose spraying energy out of the hand against the wall or imagining a solid steel bar that extends through the wall. Once the athlete with the extended arm signals that he or she is now imagining the energy spraying or the steel bar, the other athlete will begin slowly increasing force on the elbow trying to bend it. In most cases, the arm will not bend as easily as compared to not using the imagery. This exercise demonstrates the power of a narrowly focused mind to direct energy and create great strength.

5.   Broad-internal drills. Think of some recent time when you solved a problem. What process did you go through to solve the problem? Do a quick assessment of your mental strengths and weaknesses.

Have athletes perform one of their sport skills in a low-stress environment. Instruct them to focus on every body sensation they are experiencing while simultaneously attending to what they might be feeling or thinking. Emphasize keeping a passive, open awareness. Repeat the exercise but do it when performing the skill in a high-stress environment. Contrasting these two experiences can help athletes identify the subtle changes that sometimes occur in high-stress conditions that can lead to poorer performance. It is okay if athletes, either during or after the exercise, shift to a narrow-internal focus in order to zoom in on a particularly relevant sensation.

6.   Narrow-to-broad internal drill. Now become aware of bodily sensations such as the feeling of where the chair or floor supports your body. Mentally label each sensation as you notice it. Before moving on to another sensation, let each sensation linger for a moment while you examine it; consider its quality and its source. Next, experience all these sensations simultaneously without identifying or labeling any particular one. This necessitates going into the broadest possible internal body awareness.

7.   Intention leads to attention. Intentions are psychological processes that affect our effort and attention and consequently affect our performance and physiological responses. Goal setting is one example of intention. We suggest that equally important is the intent behind *every* drill, skill, and movement. The intent is what **primes** attention. To illustrate how intention leads to attention do the following: For one minute, scan the room or court and find everything that is green. . . . Now close your eyes and describe how many things in the room are blue. You may not remember any. The same effect occurs in sport. If we are primed by our attentional focus to look for something, we are more likely to see it, and see it in more detail. Although the preceding exercise does not practice a specific attentional style, it illustrates the danger of having the wrong intention and, ergo, attention.

As we mentioned earlier, coaches should not assume that athletes automatically know where to look and how to focus when they tell them to concentrate. Instead, tell athletes specifically what to focus on, and then create drills similar to some of the preceding exercises so the athletes experience the optimal focus, if one exists. If it does not, coaches should create drills that help athletes find the focus that best suits them. For example, in football most coaches would agree that focusing on the hips (or center) rather the head of an opponent that one has to guard is better because it lessens the risk of being "faked" into the wrong movement. However, in other sports such as running or swimming where speed out of the blocks is important, the specific attentional instructions are not so clear-cut. Such athletes need to try all possible attentional strategies (e.g., focusing on the sound of the gun or "going blank," that is, no focus) while getting accurate feedback (e.g., reaction time and correct takeoff for runners and sprinters) to determine what is the best focus. Before reaching a final decision, athletes must test the attentional strategy at competitions as reactions often differ between practice and stress-filled conditions. In general, for all drills that train what to focus on, once athletes have learned the appropriate focus in a relatively stress-free environment, the coach or sport psychologist needs to add additional challenges so athletes can practice the skill in an overload situation.

The preceding sounds fairly straightforward, but the optimal attentional focus may not be what the coach and sport psychologist think. There is growing evidence that instructing individuals to focus on an external movement effect, as opposed to one's own movements or an external cue not related to the movement effect, led to the best learning and performance, probably by allowing automatic control processes to mediate movement. For example, researchers found that when learning to hit a pitch shot in golf, better results occur from focusing on the pendulum-like motion of the club (an external movement effect focus) rather than the swing of their arms (an internal focus) or the dimples on the ball (an external focus not related to the effect). In hitting a backhand cross-court shot in tennis, focusing on the trajectory of the ball and its landing point leads to greater accuracy than focusing on the backswing and the racket-ball contact point. Thus, the distance of the external movement effect also appears relevant, with best results occurring with an external focus far enough away to be easily distinguishable from body movements, but not so far that the performer cannot relate the effect to the movement technique. Although not universal, these results have been found with novices and experts and with learning a ski simulator task, basketball shooting, dart throwing, volleyball serves and soccer passes, and various balance tasks. See Wulf (2007) and Wulf and Su (2007) for a review of this literature.

In the remainder of this chapter we provide specific strategies and techniques that coaches and sport psychologists can use to train better concentration control in athletes. These strategies are divided into two sections: strategies to control distracting external factors and strategies to control internal distractions. The categorization is somewhat arbitrary because external and internal stimuli continually affect each other. Because of this interaction, strategies in one category may be equally effective in correcting apparent lack of concentration in the other category.

External Factors: Strategies to Minimize External Distractions

The novelty of the competitive environment, compared to the practice environment, tends to reduce performance. Research by Orlick and Partington (1988) found that the ability to control distractibility was closely associated with superior performance at the Olympic Games. Athletes, therefore, need to be trained not to react (orient) to irrelevant external stimuli. In a competition these stimuli are situational factors that coaches often expect the athletes to have learned to control by trial and error in previous competitive experiences. This "previous experience" strategy for developing concentration control has obvious limitations and false assumptions. Coaches need to realize that athletes can be systematically trained before a competition to be situationally independent. The concept underlying training is based on Pavlovian conditioning. Through training, the novelty of the competitive environment can be minimized when athletes practice their physical skills while being exposed to all possible external stimuli that can occur during a real competition. What follows are three strategies that reduce the competition novelty effect upon performance, but also tell athletes to expect some unusual event to occur that was not planned and prepare a "coping plan" to deal with it.

Strategy 1: Dress Rehearsal

Dress rehearsal is a particularly effective strategy for sports such as gymnastics, diving, synchronized swimming, and figure skating. Dress rehearsal is based on the concept that ease in skillful competitive performance is unconsciously conditioned by the external and internal stimuli that surround athletes during practice. The greater the number of different stimuli present during competition compared to practice, the more likely performance quality will decrease. Stimuli can include things such as the athletes' uniforms, background illumination, announcers' voices, and music and applause. Ironically, to make a good impression during the competitive event, athletes usually wear uniforms or costumes different from the ones they wear during practice. This means that an unconscious stimulus (the practice uniform) associated with the performance of the skill (response) is not elicited during the competition and also that wearing a different uniform is a new stimulus that may inhibit performance. Dress rehearsal in which the athlete wears the competition uniform and goes through the same sequence of events as in competition, including factors such as scoring and judging, needs to be conducted frequently

after athletes have mastered their skills and are practicing the whole routine for performance.

The reverse of this strategy can also be applied when an athlete is in a slump. In this case the athletes ceremoniously discard their uniforms and thereby symbolically disconnect from the slump associations while now practicing with a new uniform that has no failure associations. The athlete is metaphorically and ritualistically reborn. Athletes and coaches should not lose sight of the fact that these rituals are not the underlying reasons for nonperformance. Often it is more productive for the coach and athlete to maintain their traditional patterns with an understanding that performance is typically not linear but, rather, up and down.

Strategy 2: Rehearsal of Simulated Competition Experiences

Simulated competition experiences enable athletes to become so familiar with the stimuli associated with competition that they no longer become distracted. Athletes are trained to concentrate and dissociate from the disruptive stimuli.

In gymnastics, athletes might rehearse their routines with a loud tape recording of a previous meet played over the public address system. This tape would include another gymnast's floor exercise music, audience applause, and so on. A similar example for team sports such as football, basketball, and volleyball would be holding the week's practice before an away game with the public address system loudly playing hostile crowd noises and the opposing team's fight song. Such exercises reduce the effect of competition-induced novelty, which tends to interfere with performance. The goal is to make the practice workouts seem just like the competitive experience.

When using this strategy, coaches and sport psychologists should overtrain athletes by including simulated practice of the worst possible scenario, such as having a basketball player ready to take a free throw shot and then having to wait the length of a time-out before shooting. In football, many psychologically astute coaches turn the sprinklers on before practice and then soak the ball between plays in order to prepare for a game in which rain is likely. A similar approach is used to train pilots and astronauts. They spend a significant amount of time practicing in very realistic flight simulators in which they are presented with numerous flight and equipment problems. The simulation trains pilots to maintain their concentration and appropriate responses in the face of disruptions or emergencies. Until equivalent simulators are available for sport, wise coaches can simulate many competition situations by judiciously springing novelty situations in practice. Athletes generally look forward to these challenges as long as they provide an opportunity for learning and are not used to punish or embarrass. Just as learning a physical skill takes time, learning the mental control of concentrating on the task while not reacting to external stimuli takes many hours of training.

Strategy 3: Mental Rehearsal

Most performers report that **visualization (mental rehearsal)** is an important ingredient in their success. Scientific findings confirm that skilled performers using mental rehearsal programs perform better than control groups (see Chapter 14). Using mental rehearsal to practice competition concentration and to learn not to react to intentionally induced external distractions is another good use for imagery. Obviously, athletes can only benefit from this strategy after they have learned relaxation and imagery skills. To further enhance the effects of the imagery rehearsal, have athletes form pairs in which one member of the pair relaxes and mentally rehearses his sport while the other member attempts to distract the performer from the mental rehearsal. The distraction can be anything except touching. After this type of mental rehearsal, the coach or sport psychologist might have the athlete rate his achieved concentration on a 0–6 scale. Thereafter the athletes reverse roles.

In a study involving members of the U.S. national rhythmic gymnastic team (Schmid & Peper, 1982), the gymnasts practiced this imagery pair distraction exercise daily for 5 days. On the first and fifth days they rated their concentration. The results indicated a significant improvement from the first day to the fifth day. Through this type of exercise, athletes learn how to detach and dissociate themselves from external distractions and resulting unwanted internal reactions (stimuli) while focusing on the task of mentally rehearsing their sport. Unestahl (1983), in his Basic Mental Training program, uses dissociation and detachment exercises. He teaches athletes to screen out distractions either by building a mental wall around themselves, a wall that cannot be penetrated, or by accepting the distraction but not judging it. Let it pass by and continue on its way. These strategies can all be employed during regular physical practice sessions. Athletes are responsive to them and especially enjoy being involved in generating the distracting stimuli.

Internal Factors: Strategies to Stay Centered

The coach or sport psychologist must train the athlete's mind to exert control because concentration inhibits distraction. Lapses in concentration invite fear and self-doubt, and the resulting worry and anxiety lead to further increases in lack of concentration, thus creating a vicious cycle that ultimately leads to failure. The effect of internal factors becomes more pronounced in high-pressure situations. As an analogy, consider what would happen if someone were to ask you to walk on a board 4 inches wide, 15 feet long, and 9 inches above the ground (like a practice beam in gymnastics). You would be able to do this without hesitation just by concentrating on the task of walking across the board. In contrast, if the board were 60 feet off the ground, you might become paralyzed by the fear of falling. Such fear inhibits performance and increases the possibility of failing. Ironically, there is no difference in the physical skill required. The difference is in the psychological response to the perceived stressful event, and as a result, your attention is on trying not to fall instead of on walking across the beam. In addition, if you had previously fallen off a beam, then every time you thought about it or related the experience to someone, you might have unknowingly rehearsed all of the cognitive and motor events that led to failure.

Similar psychological processes occur during competition. For example, a field-goal kicker who normally hits his short kicks during practice may react quite differently during competition when he attempts a short field goal with only a few seconds left on the clock and his team behind by 2 points. He is even more likely to fear "blowing it" if he has recently missed a kick in similar circumstances. One professional football player, while kicking under such a high-pressure situation, described the goal posts as looking as though they had narrowed to less than a foot apart. It does not take much insight to figure out what happened to his kick!

One way to improve concentration is to reduce self-doubts and competitive anxiety and their resulting physical manifestations (e.g, increased physiological arousal). (Arousal and cognitive control techniques are discussed in Chapters 13 and 15.) Unless an athlete has control over internal dialogue, his or her focus of attention will not be congruent with good performance, let alone peak performance. In addition to the specific arousal and cognition techniques found in preceding chapters, in our work with performers we have found the following strategies helpful in controlling internal dialogue and facilitating concentration and performance.

Strategy 1: Attentional Cues and Triggers

Athletes can use visual, verbal, and kinesthetic cues to focus their concentration and to retrigger concentration once it has been lost. These cues help athletes center their attention on the most appropriate focus within the task at hand and thus help them to avoid distracting thoughts and feelings (Schmid, 1982). Similar observations have been confirmed by Nideffer (1981, 1987), who reported case histories in which athletes benefited from centering by using task-relevant cues.

Generally, it is best to find cues that focus on positives rather than negatives, the present (current or upcoming moment) rather than the past

or future, and the process (proper form or execution) rather than the score. During a television interview on September 1, 1984, Greg Louganis, the Olympic diving champion, gave some excellent examples of attentional cues that he uses to appropriately control focus. He said, "I picture my dive as the judge will see it, then as I see it." In his forward three-and-one-half somersault dive, he uses the following word cues: "Relax, see the platform, spot the water, spot the water, spot the water, kick out, spot the water again." Coaches and sport psychologists should work with athletes to help them establish effective cues for triggering optimal concentration. Such cues must be individualized because what is effective for one athlete may not be for another. Similarly, some athletes perform best with frequent cues and others with few.

Strategy 2: Centering

Centering is an excellent technique for controlling physiological arousal and for ignoring negative and task-irrelevant stimuli. It reduces arousal, stops negative or task-irrelevant focus, and shifts focus to relevant performance cues. To understand centering, you actually need to understand three terms: *center of mass, centered,* and *centering*. Draw a vertical line from your head to your toes, dividing your body into two equal parts. Next, draw a horizontal line through your body so that 50% of your weight is above the line and 50% is below it. Where those two lines intersect (somewhere behind your navel) is your **center of mass.** You are **centered** within a performance situation when your body weight is distributed about your center of mass in a way that feels comfortable (e.g., your body seems to communicate a physical readiness to perform). Exactly how your center of mass should be distributed varies from situation to situation. When you need to be more aggressive and alert, your center of mass is raised and slightly forward. The more relaxed and immovable you need to be, the lower your center of mass.

Centering is a conscious process used to adjust weight about your center of mass so you feel centered and in control. It entails directing attention inward to your center of mass and then altering breathing and tension levels in various muscle groups (e.g., breathing from your abdomen instead of up in your chest, and relaxing neck and shoulder muscle tension). The centering technique should be timed as closely as possible to the beginning of a motor sequence so that attention can be directed immediately afterward (perhaps with attentional cues) to the task at hand.

Nideffer and Sagal provide an example of centering with a baseball player in one of the case studies on the instructor's Web site. The player was instructed to use the centering technique immediately prior to each pitch when he was hitting with men on base. He was to time the end of his centering breath so that it was as close to the time the pitcher began his windup as possible. On the exhale he used two words to create the physical feelings and mental focus he wanted. He used the word *loose* to remind him of the feelings he wanted in his hands as he held the bat. He used the word *focused* to remind him to "pick up the ball on release."

Strategy 3: TIC-TOC

Another effective strategy for switching attention from nonproductive to productive thoughts, feelings, or actions is an exercise that uses the words TIC and TOC to trigger the response (Burns, 1993). Simply stated, any self-statement, thought, or idea that is irrelevant or off target to what you need to be doing right now is a TIC, and should be immediately recognized. Then you need to switch to a task relevant focus (one that focuses upon either the positive outcome or actions needed to move toward that outcome) or a TOC. In both sport and nonsport situations, become aware of TICs and immediately make them TOCs.

Strategy 4: Turning Failure into Success

Many athletes report that they commonly lose concentration after making a mistake. One way to deal with this problem is to train athletes to turn failure into success. This is a cognitive habit by which athletes mentally rehearse successful performance after a failure. Rather than dwelling on the error, as soon as possible athletes

should mentally rehearse executing the same skill perfectly. One component of successful performance is to avoid self-judgment or blaming others, which disrupts concentration, and to instead refocus on the performance, such as with imaging success.

More harmful than making a performance error is ruminating on the failed event. The verbal retelling to others or the chronic rumination on why one made a mistake is a type of global visual-motor behavior rehearsal in which the athlete conditions the mind to perform the same failure behavior again. Instead of reciting the error, athletes might ask: "What was the problem and how do I fix it?" "How could I have performed differently in the same situation?" or "What other skills do I need?" Then athletes can mentally rehearse the previous conditions leading to the error but now change their behavior so that they imagine themselves performing the skill perfectly.

The coach or sport psychologist should encourage athletes to do the same thing after an injury. When concerned friends and others ask what happened, athletes should avoid recounting the accident and instead focus on describing a perfect performance the next time. For example, after a 16-year-old downhill skier ran off the course and was seriously injured, she improved her skiing remarkably when she stopped telling people how she got injured. Whenever she was asked what happened, she described how she would now ski the race successfully. (When she felt herself going too fast, she would sink down into her skis and continue to breathe while setting the edges as she went through the gate.) As she talked, she unconsciously rehearsed how to react successfully to the conditions under which she had previously fallen (Peper & Holt, 1993).

Strategy 5: Use of Brain Biofeedback (Neurofeedback) to Enhance Attention

Previously, the influence of attention and concentration on performance has primarily depended on behavioral observations, interview data, case studies, and the self-report of performers. Ways to directly measure brain activity, using electroencephalography (EEG), are now being used to determine how athletes attend to information from the outside and attend to or process information internally, and the relationship of each of these to performance (for reviews see Hatfield, Haufler, & Spaulding, 2006, and Wilson & Gunkleman, 2000). Although simplified, a summary of the findings in these reviews indicates that efficient use of the brain occurs during elite performance, that is, as one becomes more skilled, less brain activity in the relevant brain regions is needed to produce the correct response.

This brain efficiency can be measured and trained using computerized EEG biofeedback. In short, the athlete uses his or her brain waves to control the attentional display on the computer. With practice, an athlete can improve the efficiency of the brain as noted in the research on good performance. While the cost effectiveness of the training is yet to be determined, the evidence for its positive impact is becoming widespread (see Strack, Wilson, & Linden, in press, for program examples). For sport skills where attention is paramount, such as with shooters, batters, goalies, and others, neurofeedback may be the attention training of choice in the future.

Strategy 6: Increasing Focusing and Refocusing Skills

Focus training teaches performers to gently hold their attention on a predetermined task and, if the attention wanders, to gently bring the attention back. As Landers, Boutcher, and Wang (1986) state, failure to develop refocusing skills has been the downfall of many athletes. The key to avoiding these pitfalls is to perform in the present; that is, focus awareness in the "now" rather than the past or future. One must learn how to pass quickly from negative thoughts to a constructive performance focus. The dynamics of this strategy are similar to those of meditative practices, such as Raja yoga meditation in which a person focuses on a mantra and each time the attention wanders from the mantra the person gently guides the

attention back to it. Using a similar approach, the following exercises can help performers improve their focusing skills.

Exercise A: Mindfulness. Sit quietly, close your eyes, and see how long you can focus on a single thought. For many activities this is very important. Next athletes can enhance locking in their concentration by practicing focusing in the sport location. For example, some tennis players focus only on their strings prior to a serve and then transfer this narrow focus to what they need to do in the next moment. For serve reception, tennis players might focus on the ball coming off the opponent's racket. For serving, they might focus on what is necessary for them to execute their ideal serve (such as a cue word, feeling of power, or looking at spot where ball is to go).

Exercise B: One pointing. Look at an action photo or an object from your sport. For example, if your sport is baseball, softball, or tennis, you might focus on the ball. If distracting thoughts enter your mind, bring your attention back to the ball. Don't shut out the thoughts or continue to explore the disruptive thoughts or feelings. Just gently bring your attention back to the ball. This exercise also can be done with watching a second hand or digital display on a watch "tick off" the seconds for one minute. How many times did you lose your concentration?

Have athletes practice Exercise A and B daily for 5 minutes and chart their progress. Get them to time how long they can focus their attention before becoming distracted. It is our experience that these home practices help athletes eliminate their concentration-breaking thoughts. Another similar exercise to practice focus training is Benson's relaxation response described in Chapter 13.

Exercise C: Grid exercise. Another training exercise for practicing focusing ability is the grid exercise (Harris & Harris, 1984). It requires a 10-by-10 block grid with each block containing a two-digit number ranging from 00 to 99 (see Figure 16-4 for a sample grid). The purpose of this exercise is to scan the grid and within a given time (usually 1 to 2 minutes) find and put a slash through as many numbers as possible in numerical sequence starting with number 00. The same form can be used several times by starting with a number just higher than the highest number reached on the first attempt. New grids can be developed easily by simply relocating the numbers. According to Harris and Harris, athletes who have the ability to concentrate, scan, and store relevant cues will usually score in the upper 20s and into the 30s during a 1-minute timed trial. Those who cannot disregard everything except the task at hand do poorly.

After initial practice, you can increase the difficulty of the exercise by creating distractions such as loud noises and verbal harassment by a partner. This version is an excellent vehicle for making athletes aware of when their focus breaks down by attending to irrelevant information, leaving the here and now, or not staying fully immersed in the task. Besides training focusing skills, Harris and Harris report the extensive use of this exercise in Eastern Bloc countries as a precompetition screening device to select for competition the athletes most ready to successfully compete.

Exercise D: Video games. Many video games increase reaction speed, hand–eye coordination, and concentration. For example, Michele Mitchell, the 1984 and 1988 Olympic silver medalist in women's platform diving, attributed her consistent performance to good concentration enhanced by playing computer video games. As she said: "It helped me to be in the present." The advantage of many video games is that momentary lapses in concentration result in immediate feedback—you *lose*. Most early games involved only hand movements and had little similarity to real sport, but many of the newer games involve total body movement and are sport specific. The closer the video game's reactions and movements parallel your real world demands, the more likely it will transfer to your sport setting. With boxers, for example, we have used a specific right or left

punch or a right or left block reaction time board attached to a brief time display (1/100 or 1/1000 of a second) of another boxer throwing a punch. Within a few weeks of practice, the lower-skilled boxers were almost as fast and accurate at seeing a punch as the Olympic-level boxers.

Strategy 7: Developing Pre-performance and Performance Protocols

Many athletes develop the ability to tune in to their ideal performance state by associating concentration with certain performance rituals. Preset behavioral protocols should be established for warm-ups, practice, and specific times during actual competition. These protocols should cue both body and mind. It will take time to help each athlete identify his or her own ideal preperformance concentration routine. Once a definite routine is developed, it should be practiced consistently. Over time these protocols will serve automatically to trigger the optimal arousal, thinking, and focused concentration athletes need for good performance.

Systematic precompetitive behaviors enhance performance by getting the athlete ready for the task at hand. Working with two synchronized swimmers for the 1988 Olympic competition, we initially observed that their precompetition protocol was not well thought out. For example, when one swimmer put on her nose clip, it irritated the other and triggered thoughts about non–task-related matters. After helping them analyze, plan, and carry out with minute detail their precompetition protocol, we observed that the swimmers had increased their focus on the task at hand. Similarly, Boutcher and Crews (1987) demonstrated that the use of a preshot concentration routine can improve putting performance of female golfers and, as noted previously, performance and optimal attentional focus in bowlers (Mesagno et al., 2008). Finally, if attention lapses, performers can use their personal idiosyncratic protocols to refocus their attention. The small procedural steps are the triggers for concentration on the task. A protocol for unexpected events also should be practiced.

GRID CONCENTRATION EXERCISE

Directions:
Beginning with 00, put a slash through each number in the proper sequence.

84	27	51	78	59	52	13	85	61	55
28	60	92	04	97	90	31	57	29	33
32	96	65	39	80	77	49	86	18	70
76	87	71	95	98	81	01	46	88	00
48	82	89	47	35	17	10	42	62	34
44	67	93	11	07	43	72	94	69	56
53	79	05	22	54	74	58	14	91	02
06	68	99	75	26	15	41	66	20	40
50	09	64	08	38	30	36	45	83	24
03	73	21	23	16	37	25	19	12	63

Comments:

Figure 16-4 **Sample grid exercise form for training and assessing the ability to concentrate**

Summary

Concentration is the ability to direct one's attention to appropriate cues in the present task instead of being controlled by irrelevant external or internal stimuli. The ability to control thoughts, arousal, and attentional focus is the common denominator in the concentration of winning competitors. Most top athletes have developed their own mental strategies for doing this. These strategies are often perceived as a component of natural athletic ability, but, in fact, they are primarily learned through regular practice just as any difficult physical skill is learned.

Because of genetic makeup, early life experiences, and different opportunities for training the mind and body, every athlete will have individual attentional strengths and weaknesses. These influence the ease with which the athlete can utilize the appropriate focus. They influence the types of situations that are likely to be stressful, the specific behaviors that are likely to occur under pressure, and the types of errors that occur within a performance situation (e.g., susceptible to internal versus external distractions, the tendency to become tentative when leading or to choke when under high pressure).

Nideffer's conceptualization of concentration and his principles for attention control training provide a foundation for understanding and training concentration, including clarifying the relationship between arousal and focus of attention, how and why choking occurs, and how to prevent or deal with it. Because of athlete variability concentration training should include the development of individualized, situation-specific training exercises.

The initial education phase begins with differentiating the types of concentration (width and direction of focus) required within a particular sport and recognizing when to shift from one focus to another. Next comes assessment of the athletes' strengths and weaknesses and then training. To achieve consistency in performance, athletes need to develop and practice their concentration skills in practice sessions and then practice them in competitive settings. The following is a general guideline for training:

1. Learn personal strategies to attain optimal arousal for performance.

2. Learn to practice with a positive attitude and specified intention.

3. Learn which attentional focus is best for you in given situations, how to switch focus, and when to "park" thoughts.

4. Learn and practice the attentional strategies that are best for specific situations within your particular sport.

5. Associate concentration with certain triggers such as visual, verbal, and kinesthetic cues. Practice finding TICs and making them TOCs. If arousal is an issue, learn centering and implement it according to the recommended guidelines.

6. If needed, practice the focusing and refocusing skills and desensitize yourself to the novelty effect of competition by practicing the external control strategies

7. Develop performance and preperformance protocols or rituals to focus concentration and refocus when you "lose it."

Study Questions

1. Under maximally demanding conditions, what five components are entailed in good concentration?

2. What five factors help determine if you have lost attention?

3. Under what circumstances are you most likely to lose or not have appropriate concentration?

4. Describe the eight principles that underlie attention control training.

5. Diagram the figure depicting the four different types of attentional focus, distinguish conceptually among the four (including when to use each), and give an example of each.

6. What does it mean to play to one's attentional strength and when are you most likely to do so?

7. How does arousal level influence attentional focus?

8. How is choking defined in terms of attentional focus?

9. Describe how to prevent and treat choking.

10. Explain the process versus outcome notion in regard to attentional phenomena.

11. Describe the techniques of dress rehearsal, rehearsal of simulated competition, and mental rehearsal, give an example of each, and discuss the premise behind why they are effective strategies to keep concentration.

12. How can attentional cues and triggers and the TIC-TOC exercise be used to either focus or refocus concentration?

13. What is centering, why would you use it, and how is it done?

14. Provide an example of how the technique of "turning failure into success" might be used and a brief description of why the strategy might be effective.

15. Briefly describe the four exercises under the section "Increasing Focusing and Refocusing Skills."

16. Provide two examples of when and how developing performing protocols might be used to improve concentration.

References

Abernethy, B. (2001). Attention. In R. N. Singer, H. A. Hausenblaus, and C. M. Janelle, (Eds.), *Handbook of sport psychology* (pp 53–85). New York: John Wiley & Sons.

Boutcher, S. H., & Crews, D. J. (1987). The effect of a preshot attentional routine on a well-learned skill. *International Journal of Sport Psychology, 18*, 30–39.

Burns, D. (1993). *Ten days to self esteem.* New York: William Morrow.

Carver, C. S., & Scheier, M. F. (1989). A control-process perspective on anxiety. *Anxiety Research, 1*, 17–22.

Cox, R. H. (2002). *Sport psychology: Concepts and applications.* Dubuque, IA: Brown.

Gauron, E. F. (1984). *Mental training for peak performance.* Lansing, NY: Sport Science Associates.

Goffi, C. (1984). *Tournament tough.* London: Ebury Press.

Harris, D. V., & Harris. B. L. (1984). *The athlete's guide to sports psychology: Mental skills for physical people.* New York: Leisure Press.

Hatfield, B. D., Haufler, A. J., & Spaulding, T. W. (2006). A cognitive neuroscience perspective on sport performance. In E. Acevedo & P. E. Kekakis (Eds.) *Psychobiology of physical activity* (pp. 221–240). Champaign, IL: Human Kinetics.

Hull, C. L. (1951). *Essentials of behavior.* New Haven, CT: Yale University Press.

Landers, D. M., Boutcher, S. H., & Wang, M. Q. (1986). A psychological study of archery performance. *Research Quarterly for Exercise and Sport, 57,* 236–244.

Mesagno, C., Marchant, D., & Morris, T. (2008). A pre-performance routine to alleviate choking in "choking-susceptible" athletes. The Sport Psychologist, 22, 439–457.

Nideffer, R. M. (1976). Test of attentional and inter-personal style. *Journal of Personality and Social Psychology, 34,* 394–404.

Nideffer, R. M. (1981). *The ethics and practice of applied sport psychology.* Ithaca, NY: Mouvement Publications.

Nideffer, R. M. (1987). Psychological preparation of the highly competitive athlete. *The Physician and Sports Medicine, 15*(10), 85–92.

Nideffer, R. M. (1990). Use of the test of attentional and interpersonal style in sport. *The Sport Psychologist, 4,* 285–300.

Nideffer, R. M. (2003). Theory of attentional and interpersonal style vs. Test of Attentional and Interpersonal Style (TAIS). http://www.enhanced-performance.com/articles/tais.pdf

Nideffer, R. M., & Sagal, M.S. (2001). *Assessment in sport psychology.* Morgantown, WV: Fitness Information Technology.

Nideffer, R. M., Sagal, M. S., Lowry, M., & Bond, J. (2000). Identifying and developing world class performers. In *The practice of sport and exercise psychology: International perspectives.* Morgantown, WV: Fitness Information Technology.

Orlick, T., & Partington, J. (1988). Mental links to excellence. *The Sport Psychologist, 2,* 105–130.

Peper, E., & Holt, C. F. (1993). *Creating wholeness: A self-healing workbook using dynamic relaxation, images, and thoughts.* New York: Plenum.

Phelps, M., & Abrahamson, A. (2008). *No limits: The will to succeed.* New York: Free Press.

Schmid, A. B. (1982). Coach's reaction to Dr. A. B. Frederick's coaching strategies based upon tension research. In L. D. Zaichkowsky & W. E. Sime (Eds.), *Stress management for sport* (pp. 95–100). Reston, VA: AAHPERD.

Schmid, A. B., & Peper, E. (1982). *Mental preparation for optimal performance in rhythmic gymnastics.* Paper presented at the Western Society for Physical Education of College Women Conference, Asilomar, CA.

Strack, B., Wilson, V. E., & Linden, M. (in press). *Biofeedback and neurofeedback in sport psychology.* New York: Springer Publications.

Unestahl, L. E. (1983). *Inner mental training.* Orebro, Sweden: Veje.

Walsh, M., & Spelman, F. (1983, June 13). Unvarnished symphonies. *Time,* p. 75.

Wilson, V. E., & Gunkleman, J. (2000). Practical applications of psychophysiology and neurotherapy in sport. *Journal of Neurotherapy, 12,* 14–21.

Wulf, G. (2007). *Attention and motor skill learning.* Champaign, IL: Human Kinetics.

Wulf, G., & Su, J. (2007). An external focus of attention enhances golf shot accuracy in beginners and experts. *Research Quarterly for Exercise and Sport, 78,* 384–389.

Zaichkowsky, L. D., & Naylor, A. H. (2005). Arousal in sport. *Encyclopedia of applied psychology, 1* (pp. 155–161). Elsevier, Inc.

Implementing Training Programs

Integrating and Implementing a Psychological Skills Training Program

Robert S. Weinberg, *Miami University*
Jean M. Williams, *University of Arizona*

The authors of Chapters 9 through 16 have discussed peak performance characteristics, psychological theory, and exercises for training specific psychological skills. When sport psychologists began employing psychological skills interventions in the early 1980s, not many empirical data or controlled studies were available to help guide these initial attempts to improve performance. However, the last 25 to 30 years have produced a number of field-based studies that have investigated the effectiveness of different psychological interventions to enhance performance. Although we have learned a great deal from these studies, many questions still remain. Some of the most important questions include the following: How old and skillful should athletes be before beginning psychological skills training? Who should conduct the training program—the sport psychologist or the coach? Is there an ideal time during the year for implementing a psychological skills training program? How much time is needed for psychological skills training? What specific components should be incorporated in training, and how should those components be

sequenced and integrated? What ethical considerations should one be aware of when implementing a program? In this chapter we address these questions and others, but first we must recognize that only preliminary data exist regarding some of these questions. Therefore, caution must be observed until more definitive studies are conducted.

Most comprehensive mental training programs stress the development of psychological skills and techniques such as anxiety management, imagery, goal setting, concentration, self-talk, thought stopping, routines, and confidence (just to name a few). The multitude of possibilities makes it very difficult to integrate all the components into one comprehensive mental training program. In essence, situational constraints (e.g., the athlete or team only has a few weeks to learn and implement a psychological skills training program) do not always permit the implementation of a comprehensive mental training program, and thus it is often necessary to plan an abbreviated program. Furthermore, although a number of mental training programs have been developed (e.g., Blakeslee & Goff, 2007; Ravizza & Hanson, 1995; Thelwell & Greenlees, 2001; Thelwell & Maynard, 2003), there still is no general agreement among sport psychologists on how much time should be spent learning these techniques or what techniques are best for achieving certain objectives. For example, what technique should be used for an athlete who starts thinking ahead during competition to what might happen if he or she loses or wins the game?

Unfortunately, there are no ready-made solutions to questions of how coaches and sport psychologists can integrate and implement a psychological skills training program. The database is only recently being developed, and thus new information is constantly changing the way mental training programs are implemented. Nonetheless, if a mental training program is to be effective, strategies for putting all of the different components into place must be planned and well thought out. In this chapter we offer some suggestions and practical pointers for implementing mental skills training and for integrating various psychological skill components into these programs. Unless otherwise noted, these guidelines are the same for either the coach or sport psychologist, although we will discuss the pros and cons of taking on a dual role of coach/sport psychologist. Finally, we again caution you to view these recommendations only as suggested guidelines.

Before discussing the various aspects of psychological interventions to enhance perfomance, we feel it is instructive to note that there are several other approaches to intervention in sport and exercise psychology that are different from the focus of this chapter, which is psychological skills to enhance competitive performance. In fact, many of these approaches are similar to ones developed in the counseling literature that focus more on adjustment and personal growth. Murphy (1995) discusses many of these alternative interventions, and we recommend consulting his edited text to learn more about the details of these approaches. Examples of these psychological interventions include the following: (a) a life development model focusing on

a psychoeducational-developmental approach over the life span; (b) a marital therapy model focusing on human relationships; (c) a family systems model, which makes the family central to helping athletes reach their potential; and (d) an organizational model, which focuses on how organizational dynamics influence the way psychological services are provided and received.

Are Psychological Interventions Effective in Improving Sport Performance?

Probably the most important question that sport psychology consultants need to ask themselves revolves around the effectiveness of their psychological interventions in enhancing performance and personal growth. It is the same problem that has plagued clinical psychologists and counselors over the years—demonstrating that what they do makes a difference in the behavior and well-being of their clients. Defending the effectiveness of psychological skills training programs in improving sport performance and well-being requires the accumulation of well-controlled, outcome-based intervention studies conducted in competitive sport environments. These are traditionally difficult to carry out because of time and money constraints, unwillingness of coaches and athletes to participate, and inability to adequately control the environment.

Fortunately, sport psychology researchers have been working hard to establish a database concerning the effectiveness of these psychological interventions in improving performance. Reviews by Greenspan and Feltz (1989), Vealey (1994), and Weinberg and Comar (1994) identified 45 studies employing psychological interventions in competitive sport settings, including such diverse sports as golf, karate, skiing, boxing, basketball, volleyball, gymnastics, baseball, tennis, and figure skating. Of the 45 studies, 38 (85%) found positive performance effects. Many of these studies employed a variety of psychological techniques as part of the total program package. See Meyers, Whelan, and Murphy (1996) for the most recent meta-analysis of psychological interventions to enhance sport performance. Their analysis of 90 interventions indicated moderate to large positive effects on performance for interventions such as goal setting, mental rehearsal, anxiety management, cognitive restructuring, attentional focusing, and multiple components. Had someone reviewed the intervention studies since 1996, there is every reason to assume that the findings would indicate equally strong effectiveness.

Who Will Benefit from Psychological Skills Training?

Many coaches and athletes misunderstand peak performance sport psychology. They think mental training strategies are only applicable to elite athletes or that these techniques can only fine-tune the performance of the already highly skilled. In actuality, mental skills training should be beneficial for a variety of people, although, as previously noted, we need more studies across different skill and age groups and special populations. If beginning athletes are taught to set realistic goals, increase self-confidence, visualize success, and react constructively, we can expect their performance and personal development to progress faster than the performance and personal development of athletes who do not receive similar mental training. Special adjustments may be needed, however, based on the population of athletes. For example, very young athletes may need adjustments such as fewer goals, shorter training sessions, simpler verbal instruction, and turning the exercises into games, but these athletes can still benefit from some sort of mental skills training provided they are interested in receiving it (Orlick & McCaffrey, 1991; Weiss, 1991). Furthermore, Whelan, Meyers, and Donovan (1995) present a multisystemic model for intervention with the vast amount of competitive recreational athletes. Thus psychological skills training can be applied to sport participants at all levels of skill.

The ideal time for initially implementing training may be when individuals are just beginning to participate in sport. As any experienced teacher or coach knows, it is far easier to develop proper physical technique in a beginner than it is to modify poor technique in a more experienced athlete. Although never empirically tested, the same phenomenon may be true for psychological skills. Furthermore, early implementation ensures the establishment of a psychological skills foundation that will facilitate future achievement of full athletic potential, enjoyment, and benefit.

Highly skilled athletes also can certainly benefit from systematic psychological skills training programs. As athletes get better, physical differences tend to become smaller. At this level, minute adjustments and differences can literally mean the difference between winning and losing. For example, Orlick (1986) was one of the first to provide a number of case studies of Olympic athletes who systematically employed a mental training program. The athletes report that their mental training and discipline were a critical component of their success. Their comments generally reflect the notion that everybody they were competing against was physically talented. The key difference was in their consistency of mental preparation and training. Let's look at an example of an Olympic skier in her second year of mental training:

> Last year I got angry with myself or so upset about not performing well. Initially if I didn't get angry or punish myself, I would feel guilty, as if I wasn't taking it seriously. This year I'm keeping it in perspective and reminding myself what it's for. Now I'm thinking about enjoyment as well as intensity. This year for the first time ever, I pushed during a whole training camp. I never let up. I stayed interested and motivated. When I started to coast I stopped and went free skiing. I don't want to practice skiing at low intensity. (Orlick, 1986, p. 148)

Who Should Conduct the Psychological Skills Training Program?

Ideally, a psychological skills training program should be planned, implemented, and supervised by a qualified consulting sport psychologist. The sport psychologist has the advantage of having more extensive special training and experience than a coach. Also, athletes may be more open in discussing difficulties with the psychological aspects of play because the sport psychologist does not decide who stays on the team and who gets to play. Even though it is desirable to have a sport psychologist administer the program, this is rarely feasible except perhaps at the highest levels of competition (and even here it is still a rarity for a sport psychologist to work and travel with a team throughout a season). The basic premise of this book is that it is also the responsibility of the coach to provide mental skills training and reinforce optimal psychological states; after all, who knows the athletes better and who works more closely with them? Thus, there are advantages to having mental skills training provided by the consulting sport psychologist *or* the coach.

When the mental training program is to be implemented by a sport psychologist, the selection of that person is critical. Who is qualified to be a sport psychologist? In 1991 the Association for the Applied Sport Psychology (*AASP Newsletter,* 1991) adopted criteria for certification for individuals working in the area of applied sport psychology. Basically, this certification requires individuals to have an extensive background in both the sport and psychological sciences as well as some practical supervised experience implementing psychological skills with sport and exercise participants (see Chapter 1 for a more detailed explanation of AASP certification). The USOC now requires AASP certification to become part of its sport psychology registry. Having an individual who is certified by AASP ensures a certain experience, background, and competence in applied sport psychology. However, just because an individual is certified does not necessarily mean he or she has the type of orientation or experiential background that would best meet the needs of a specific team or coach. For example, will the person's focus be on dealing with personal and emotional problems (i.e., clinical approach) or teaching mental skills for enhancing performance (performance enhancement approach)? Does the person have

experience with younger athletes or primarily elite athletes? Is he or she sufficiently knowledgeable about the sport in which the psychological skills are to be applied? How much time does the person have to spend with the team? Does the person have references from teams or individuals he or she worked with in the past developing psychological skills? These and other questions guide the selection of the sport psychologist who best suits the athletes' specific needs and goal.

If a sport psychology consultant conducts the program, we recommend that the coach, or coaching staff, attend most or all of the initial group training sessions for a number of reasons. First, the coach's presence tells the athletes that the coach thinks the sessions are important. Second, the sport psychologist will not be present during most of the physical practices and competitions; a knowledgeable coach can be a key person in ensuring the effectiveness of mental skills training by seeing that appropriate application of such training occurs. Ideally, the sport psychologist and coach should have special meetings to discuss ways for the coach to apply and reinforce whatever the sport psychologist emphasizes in mental skills training sessions. Third, misunderstandings regarding what the sport psychologist is doing will not occur because the coach will know exactly what is happening and will be providing feedback regarding what needs to be done. Ravizza (1990), in his work with professional baseball teams, notes that in the early stages a good portion of his work with coaches was done in the locker room, hotel lobby, or at meals. As the relationship progressed, they set aside mutually convenient times for formal meetings to discuss how individual players were performing, as well as any other relevant issues.

Our understanding about how to conduct psychological skills training programs with athletes has increased rapidly over the years. Along these lines, a number of sport psychologists have written about their consulting experiences with athletes and teams. In fact, as far back as 1989, separate issues of *The Sport Psychologist* (1989, #4; 1990, #4; 1991, #4) were devoted to psychological interventions with a variety of sports as well as with physically and mentally disabled athletes.

As psychological skills training programs have been developed in recent years, it has also been suggested that it is important that we understand the sport psychologist–athlete relation to maximize the effectiveness of the intervention. For example, Petitpas, Giges, and Danish (1999) have argued that the effectiveness of psychological interventions is closely tied to the quality of the relationship between athlete and sport psychologist. They draw on the counseling psychology literature, which has demonstrated that of all the techniques and variables examined the only one that has consistently related to positive therapeutic outcomes has been the counselor–client relationship (Sexton & Whitson, 1994).

In addition, certain counseling competencies have been rated as essential for sport psychologists working with athletes (Ward, Sandstedt, Cox, & Beck, 2005). These include such competencies as recognizing limits of competency or expertise, respecting confidentiality, understanding how their own values and biases may impact psychological processes, making appropriate referrals, understanding the unique athlete culture, understanding the influence of the athletic environment on athletes, and taking into consideration cultural differences when working with athletes. Thus, it would appear that sport psychologists should look closely at the counseling psychology literature to help facilitate a positive athlete–sport psychologist relationship. In fact, some sport psychology research has already indicated that the ability to build rapport, create a positive environment, and provide concrete suggestions is highly correlated with successful sport psychology interventions (e.g., Gould, Murphy, Tammen, & May, 1991; Martin, Wrisberg, Beitel, & Lounsbury, 1997). Therefore, it appears that having good counseling skills will facilitate the effectiveness of a sport psychology consultant administering mental training programs to athletes.

In addition to counseling skills, recently it also has been demonstrated that sensitivity to ethnic and racial diversity and sexual orientation (Barber & Krane, 2005) in applied sport psychology settings will enhance the quality of the relationship. Being sensitive to such multicultural concepts as identity, enculturation, generalizations, and stereotyping has been shown to be helpful in dealing with a more and more diverse clientele (Kontos & Breland-Noble, 2002). Therefore, there is probably a need for more sport psychologists of color to help with the increasing number of African American, Latino, and American Indian athletes. Along these lines, Butryn (2002) argues that there is a need for more multicultural training programs for sport psychology consultants working with diverse athlete populations.

Of course, the philosophy and implementation of mental training programs differ somewhat from one sport psychologist to the next. Each person has to understand the nature of the team or individual athletes he or she is working with and integrate that with his or her own background, training, and orientation. It's important for the sport psychologist to communicate his or her philosophy to the athletes and coaches at the outset and to make sure that everyone understands the parameters of the consultation.

It was previously noted that one of the drawbacks of having a sport psychologist conduct a psychological skills program is the difficulty in being with the athletes on a day-to-day basis. In many cases the sport psychology consultant cannot provide continuous services, either because the organization is diffused over a wide geographical area or because the consultant or athletic group cannot make the time commitment necessary to provide ongoing services. Coaches, of course, have the best access to athletes on a daily basis and are thus in a position to administer psychological interventions over the course of a season. Smith and Johnson (1990) have developed an innovative consultation model in their work with the Houston Astros minor league player development program. They call this model "organizational empowerment," and we will discuss it in some depth since it serves as an excellent prototype for sport psychology consultation.

In this model of service delivery, the sport psychology consultant trains one or more qualified individuals within the sport organization to provide psychological services to athletes and coaches. The consultant then oversees the program and provides ongoing supervision of the actual trainers. This approach thus empowers a sport organization to provide its own sport psychology services under the supervision of the consultant.

In setting up this program, one of the major challenges was to provide continuity to a major league baseball club that has minor league teams in several cities over a wide geographical area. Smith and Johnson strongly believe one-shot or occasional psychological skills training, no matter how competently carried out, cannot be as effective as that provided on a continuous basis over an extended period of time. In addition, they feel there are real advantages to having someone identified with professional baseball as the service provider, given that the trainer has the requisite background in counseling and psychological skills training. A "baseball person" may have an easier time establishing credibility within what is still a very traditional baseball establishment and may find it easier to coordinate psychological skills training with the technical aspects of player development because of the deeper knowledge of the game.

In their specific case, Smith (the sport psychology consultant) trained Johnson (a manager in the Astros organization with a Master's degree in psychology). An intensive 6-week training program was established prior to spring training. In addition, Smith accompanied Johnson to spring training for 10 days of hands-on training plus a series of orientation workshops for staff and players. Weekly and sometimes daily telephone supervision continued throughout the remainder of spring training and the regular season. Once Johnson felt comfortable with his new skills, Smith worked with him to help put together a psychological skills training program. Smith helped in overseeing the program, but it was Johnson who was in charge of implementing the day-to-day psychological exercises.

Another alternative model has been proposed for the delivery of sport psychology services to athletes and coaches (Kremer & Scully, 1998). Briefly, this model identifies the coach rather than the athlete as the primary target for psychological intervention. Thus, the sport psychologist becomes more of a management consultant who is part of the team along with the coach and support staff. This challenges the myth that sport psychologists are "shrinks" who can provide instant solutions for athletes whose problems have baffled their coaches.

When Should You Implement a Psychological Skills Training Program?

It is generally agreed that the *least* desirable time to implement a psychological skills program is after the competitive season has started, when the athlete is facing a string of competitions in quick succession. At this time, mental training often amounts to no more than a quick-fix, bandage approach and consequently is rarely, if ever, effective. One of the underlying principles of this book is that psychological skills are learned and therefore need to be practiced systematically, just like physical skills. To draw an analogy, golfers or tennis players would not change their grip on the club or racket right before a tournament without extensively using the new grip in practice for several weeks or even months. Similarly, we should not expect athletes to be able to learn new psychological skills in such a short period of time.

For these reasons, most sport psychology consultants believe the best time to initially implement psychological skills training is during the off-season or preseason. During this period there is more time to learn new skills, and it is easier to try new ideas because this is the time of year when athletes are not so pressured with winning. Some athletes have reported that it took several months to a year to fully understand and integrate their new psychological skills into actual competitions. This underscores the importance of viewing mental training as an ongoing process that needs to be integrated with physical practice.

When Should Athletes Practice Psychological Skills?

The rudiments of most psychological skills should first be taught and systematically practiced during special training sessions. The first or last 15 to 30 minutes of practice is often a good time for training. The content of the particular session will determine whether it is better held at the beginning or end of practice (see earlier chapters for suggestions on which training exercises are better practiced before or after physical workouts). Homework assignments also can be given, but unless the athletes are self-directed, it is better to have most mental training practice occur under someone's supervision.

As soon as possible the psychological skills practice should be integrated with physical skills practice. When integrating the two, the rehearsal of mental skills should have a performance-specific focus. For example, once athletes have learned the skill of relaxation and recognizing tension, they should be instructed to scan their muscles for harmful tension and practice appropriate differential relaxation while performing. Specific performance times should be identified—for example, always scan and relax before pitching, shooting a free throw, serving a tennis ball, or taking a shot in golf. Once relaxation skills have been effectively integrated into physical workouts, they should be tried during simulated or practice competition and later during actual competition. It is important not to proceed too quickly from learning to competition because the psychological skills may not be fully integrated and therefore performance decrements could occur.

This progressive method of practice is also psychologically sound from a learning standpoint because it allows athletes to gain knowledge and competence in using each mental skill as environmental demands slowly become more variable, challenging, and applicable. The ultimate goal is for the practice of mental skills to become such an integral part of all physical practices that the training program does not appear to be something extra. This type of systematic, consistent practice of mental skills is likely to achieve lasting optimal results rather than short-term placebo effects.

Let us provide some concrete illustrations of integrating psychological skills into actual physical practice. For example, let's say a tennis player is having trouble hitting the ball short, thus allowing his opponent to take the offensive. A practice drill can be set up where he has a goal to get 20 balls in a row over the net between the service line and baseline to work on his depth of shot. If he misses, he has to start over from zero. In addition, he may also use a cue word like "lift" when he swings to make sure that he follows through on the shot and lifts his racquet after impact. With this type of drill the player is practicing his concentration skills by using a concentration cue and setting the conditions of practice to require extreme concentration. In addition, this drill creates pressure. The player will typically start to get a little tight as he approaches the goal of 20 consecutive shots because he doesn't want to miss and have to start all over at that point.

Another example would be a golfer who typically gets down on herself whenever she makes a poor shot. Specifically, she uses a lot of negative self-talk to put herself down and criticize herself. First, during practice rounds she could carry a small logbook and record the type of shots she hits and then her self-talk. Keeping a log will enable her to be more aware of exactly what she is saying and under what specific conditions. Then the coach can help her come up with a number of positive self-statements that are either motivational (e.g., "hang in there, you still have nine holes to play") or informational, if there is a technique error (e.g., "bring club head straight back"). These statements can then be used in practice in place of the negative self-talk until the player feels comfortable using them in competitive matches.

How Much Time Should Be Spent in Mental Training?

By now it should be obvious that the time needed for practicing mental skills varies according to what is being practiced and how well it is learned. If a new mental skill is being introduced, special 15- to 30-minute training sessions 3 to 5 days per week may be needed. As athletes become more proficient, fewer special training sessions are necessary. However, special sessions still may be advisable for individual athletes who are experiencing difficulty learning the mental skills.

When separate times are not being designated solely for mental training, it is very important that the coaching staff or sport psychologist provide verbal reminders for integrating mental skills practice with physical skills practice. In addition, appropriate reinforcement for the use of these mental skills during practice is crucial for athletes' motivation since they are attempting to develop new habits and possibly break some old bad habits. This can be a difficult task, and a positive approach is important to keep spirits up, as well as providing informative feedback to help athletes integrate the mental skills into their physical performance.

The time frame we have just recommended may not be desirable if a sport psychology consultant is implementing the training, particularly when the sport psychologist has to spend time traveling to reach the team. Under such circumstances, fewer and longer mental training sessions are usually held unless a coach or other organization member is trained to carry out the mental training program. Most of the initial meetings should be group sessions to best use the sport psychologist's time. However, research has indicated that individual sessions and individualized training programs are needed to optimize the effectiveness of mental training programs (Seabourne, Weinberg, Jackson, & Suinn, 1985). It is particularly critical that athletes be assigned training exercises to practice during the times the sport psychologist is not with the team. The same stepwise building of competence that we described earlier should be observed here.

The traveling sport psychology consultant must design practice exercises in such a way that maximum feedback occurs from participation and that adherence to training is likely to occur. In the absence of the consultant, the coach or an individual designated by the coach can play a major role in ensuring compliance and feedback if he or she assumes responsibility for personally conducting the training exercises or at least provides the time for athletes to practice. If this is not possible, the coach or designated individual should remind athletes of their homework assignments and briefly discuss the athletes' reactions to the exercises once the homework has been completed. However, maximum effectiveness is likely only when this individual and the sport psychologist work together as a team.

A logical question that arises after a mental training program has been put in place is "When can athletes stop mental skills training?" In the truest sense, mental skills training continues as long as athletes participate in sport. In this sense, mental skills are no different from physical skills. Retention will not occur without continued practice. When we hear the names of such athletes as Peyton Manning, Roger Federer, Tiger Woods, Anika Sorenstam, Tim Duncan, Candice Parker, and Michael Phelps (just to name a few), we think of individuals who are highly skilled and great competitors. However, these same athletes are also known for their great practice habits, especially making sure that the mental aspects of their respective sports are integrated into their physical practice on an ongoing basis.

If athletes never stop mental skills training, what is the ideal length of time for their first exposure to a formal mental skills training program? Most sport psychology consultants would recommend an average of between 3 and 6 months because it takes time to learn these new mental skills, use them in practice, and then integrate them into actual competitive situations. The specific sport, time available, existing mental skills, and commitment of individuals are all factors that should be considered in determining actual length of time. For example, we have worked with athletes who simply needed

Table 17-1 **Prerace Mental Preparation Plan**

General Warm-Up	Start Preparation
Physical and Mental	*Physical and Mental*

Night Before Race

- Receive number, determine how many minutes after start I race.
- Figure out what time to awaken and leave for hill in the morning and approximately how many free runs or training course runs to have before start.
- Estimate how long to put number on, stretch inside lodge.
- Spend ideally no more than 20 to 25 minutes in start area.

Morning of Race

- Light run, exercises, begin the morning on a positive or high note.
- Wake up feeling good about myself, be optimistic, flow.
- Important for me not to project (e.g., about outcomes); just feel good about myself for myself.
- Free skiing and training courses to feel aggressive and pumped, yet calm and relaxed.
- Focused and concentrated while skiing.
- Mental imagery (to know course and feel good about myself on the course).

Start Preparation side:

- Arrive at start 20 minutes prior to my start.
- First get race skis in snow, check them to see if all is ready; see rep (equipment person).
- Begin stretching, running; think happy, relaxed thoughts.
- Apply these comments to mental imagery.

- Heavier physical preparation.
- Get into skis, binding check.
- More imagery of race focus and feeling—include correction imagery if needed.
- Quicker physical activity.
- 1 minute: Take coat, warm-ups off, intense, focused on task.
- 30 seconds: Ready myself in start, think only of course and of myself.
- Explosive start.

to change a small part of their mental approach and were able to do that in under 2 months. In contrast, Orlick (1986) has noted that many of the Canadian Olympic athletes he has consulted with developed psychological plans and mental preparation that were extremely detailed and precise, as seen in the example provided in Table 17-1 for an Olympic alpine skier (Orlick, 1986, p. 34).

Setting Up a Mental Skills Training Program

Thus far we have discussed some important questions surrounding the use of mental training programs, including who will benefit, who should conduct the program, when to implement the training program, when to actually practice the mental skills, and how much time to spend on mental training. Although this information is important in understanding mental training programs, it does not really tell us exactly what to do in setting up such a program. Therefore, we will attempt to outline some of the critical components of implementing a mental skills training program.

Self-Regulation: A Key to Effective Mental Training

One of the critical aspects of successfully implementing a mental training program is the use of self-regulation. Self-regulation can be defined as the processes by which people manage their own behaviors that are directed toward specific goals. These processes include goal setting, planning, observing, and evaluating behaviors (Kirschenbaum, 1997). Being able to regulate and control one's behavior is an essential part of any athlete's mental training plan, and this process has six specific phases.

The first phase is *problem identification.* This phase encourages you to evaluate progress in your sport thoroughly and to remain open to new suggestions about all aspects of performance. Being open to, or seeking out, suggestions for improvement in your mental skills is a step in the right direction. For example, you might become aware that you lose your concentration by thinking negatively at critical junctures during competition. This awareness is a critical first step on the road to improvement. The next step is to establish a *commitment to change.* This usually involves *developing specific plans* and *setting goals.* After problems are identified and commitments are made, *actions* must be initiated so that positive steps toward *goal attainment* can occur. This execution of self-regulated change can be viewed as a feedback loop with self-monitoring leading to self-evaluation, which in turn leads to self-consequation (Kirschenbaum, 1997). For example, you might monitor your progress toward a goal of improving your average golf score from 85 to 80. After several rounds, you could evaluate whether you achieved your goal. If you did, you might treat yourself to a great dinner; this would be an example of positive consequation. Although self-regulation implies a solitary pursuit of goals, in sport you also have to manage the environment, which might include teammates, friends, and coaches as well as specific playing and practice conditions. The long-term goal of self-regulation is to maintain behavior change over time and across different situations. This is called **generalization.** It is often difficult to achieve because it requires dedicated, consistent, systematic practice of mental skills over time.

Discuss Your Approach—What You Do and What You Don't Do

Many athletes are still fairly naive or uninformed about what sport psychology is and what sport psychologists do. Therefore, we believe it is important to spell this out right at the outset of the initial meeting. Although most athletes typically view sport psychology solely in terms of performance enhancement, they also should be made to understand its mental health aspects and potential for application outside of sport. In fact, as reflected in the title of this text, sport psychology has as much to do with personal growth issues as it does with achieving maximum performance. Therefore, these two different aspects need to be clearly communicated to athletes.

In addition to conducting a brief discussion on what sport psychology is, it is equally critical that sport psychologists spell out their specific approach in dealing with psychological problems in sport and exercise. Sport psychologists use two approaches when working with athletes: clinical and educational. Research and experience have indicated that the large majority of athletes consulting with sport psychologists require an educational approach as opposed to a clinical approach. Athletes typically need to develop a psychological skill such as improving concentration or managing anxiety rather than to deal with a deep-seated, severe psychological problem. Therefore, we will focus on the educational approach, but it should be made clear that if an educational sport psychologist or coach comes across an athlete who has such a serious psychological problem that it is beyond his or her skills to treat, then the athlete should be referred to a qualified individual or counseling center. (See Chapter 20 for a discussion of when it may be appropriate to refer athletes for counseling or psychotherapy.)

Thus, the sport psychology consultant should tell the athlete what he or she does and does not do, as many people still believe that if athletes see a sport psychologist then something must be psychologically wrong with them. This is especially true of younger athletes, who can be extra sensitive to the idea that they "have to see a shrink." Rather, we try to emphasize that if an athlete stayed after practice to work with the coach on a particular move or physical technique most people would applaud this extra effort to improve. Similarly, if an athlete realizes that he or she needs to work on some aspect of the mental game such as concentration skills, then this also should be applauded. In essence, working to improve mentally should not be looked on as a weakness but rather as simply another way for an athlete to improve performance as well as enhance personal growth.

In discussing your philosophy or approach, a contemporary way of making initial contact with athletes is through electronic methods such as e-mail or Web pages. It appears that more and more people use the Internet as a communication tool and are getting more and more comfortable using this medium. Along these lines, an interesting study by Zizzi and Perna (2002) comparing traditional versus electronic contact found that the electronic group completed more contacts and assessments compared to the traditional group 1 month after taking a workshop. In essence, results suggested that electronic contact methods are at least as good as, and in several cases superior to, traditional contact (e.g., phone, in-person contact methods regarding generating requests for service from athletes on a short-term basis).

Emphasize the Importance of Mental Training

Another important component to an initial meeting with athletes is convincing them of the need for systematic mental training. This can be done in many ways. One way to start is to have athletes identify how important their state of mind is in achieving success by having them decide what percentage of their game is mental. Then compare this percentage to the actual percentage of practice time spent training mental skills.

The disparity is usually because the mental side of sport is recognized as very important, yet little or no time is spent specifically practicing these mental aspects.

Providing anecdotes about the importance of mental preparation from relevant, well-known amateur and professional athletes is another effective way to increase receptivity. Such anecdotes are usually much more motivating than a recitation of the results of research studies on mental training. Along these lines, a study from the U.S. Olympic Training Center (Murphy, Jowdy, & Durtschi, 1990) revealed that more than 90% of Olympic athletes surveyed regularly used some sort of mental preparation and training in preparing for competition. This type of information can help athletes realize that mental training does work and is being used by many of our very best athletes, although athletes of all ability levels can benefit from such training.

Fortunately, the popularity of applied sport psychology has evolved to the point that it is becoming easier to sell a mental skills training program to most athletes. Nevertheless, some athletes still will refuse to accept mental skills training. Most sport psychologists recommend not forcing unreceptive athletes to participate. Conversely, there also can be problems with athletes who are highly enthusiastic about mental training. Occasionally this enthusiasm can lead to unreasonable expectations. Athletes, coaches, and sport psychologists must realize that no amount of mental training will substitute for poor mechanics, lack of practice, or limited physical aptitude. Also, good psychological skills cannot replace hard physical conditioning and training.

Assess Psychological Strengths and Weaknesses

Once athletes are informed of the approach the sport psychologist plans to take and are convinced of the importance of mental training, the next step is to determine the athletes' psychological strengths and weaknesses as related specifically to sport. A needs assessment helps reveal those psychological skills that are deficient or appear to have the most adverse effect on performance and personal satisfaction. In addition, it should also reveal the strong points of each athlete from a mental perspective. When something is bothering athletes or they are struggling with a specific problem, they often overlook all the things that they do well, and these should not be forgotten.

In conducting the initial evaluation of athletes' psychological strengths and weaknesses, it is important that sport psychology consultants first understand that there are factors outside the psychological realm that influence performance. These include such things as physiological conditioning, biomechanics (technique), strategy, and equipment. For example, a golfer who has a major flaw in his or her swing may attribute the resulting poor performance to ineffective concentration, whereas the underlying problem is biomechanical. A gymnast who more frequently falls off the balance beam may not have developed an anxiety problem, but she may have experienced a growth spurt to which she has yet to adjust. The important point is that one must not try to interpret all aspects of performance from a psychological perspective.

In terms of the actual psychological skills evaluation, one procedure we recommend is an oral interview as well as written psychological inventories and behavioral observation. In this way the athlete will have a chance to tell his or her story face to face as well as to respond to some objective questionnaires. This also helps the consultant in looking for consistencies (and inconsistencies) between oral and written statements.

There are various approaches to conducting an initial interview, but the one we recommend is the semi-structured interview, which Orlick (2000) outlines in detail. Some general questions provide structure to this type of interview, but there is leeway to use the athlete's responses to form other follow-up questions. For example, some key questions might include the following:

- Summarize your involvement in your sport, noting important events both positive and negative (this is a good starting point as it lets athletes talk about themselves and become more comfortable).

- Describe what you believe to be your greatest psychological strength and your biggest weakness.

- Describe the boundaries of any specific psychological problem you are currently having (i.e., when, why, how).

- What is your relationship with your coach?

It is our experience that this interview typically lasts approximately 1 hour. Of course, individual differences and time constraints can alter this time frame to some degree. The initial interview is very important not only to find out where the athlete needs help but also as a place to start building the trust that is critical for any therapeutic relationship. For a sport psychology consultant to be maximally effective, the athlete needs to feel comfortable and believe that the consultant not only is competent but cares about the athlete's particular situation. One thing that we have found important is that the consultant needs good conceptual knowledge of the sport to be effective and build credibility with the athletes.

In addition to the interview, reseach has revealed that between 63% and 75% of sport psychology consultants use paper and pencil questionnaires (O'Conner, 2004) to assess psychological skills related to sport as well as more general mood states. Although many different inventories are utilized, some of the more popular ones include the following: Sport Competition Anxiety Test (Martens, 1977), Competitive State Anxiety Inventory-2 (Martens, Vealey, & Burton, 1990), Sport Anxiety Scale (Smith, Smoll, & Schutz, 1990), Test of Attentional and Interpersonal Style (Nideffer, 1976,) Athletic Coping Skills Inventory-28 (Smith, Schutz, Smoll, & Ptacek, 1995), and Trait-State Sport Confidence Inventory (Vealey, 1986). In addition, the Ottawa Mental Skills Assessment Tool (OMSAT-3), has been developed by Durand-Bush, Salmela, and Green-Demers (2001) to assist consultants and coaches in their designing of appropriate and individualized mental training programs as well as to help researchers assess the effectiveness of interventions with sport performers.

Furthermore, a number of sport-specific inventories have been developed, such as the Tennis Test of Attentional and Interpersonal Style (Van Schoyck & Grasha, 1981) and the Anxiety Assessment for Wrestlers (Gould, Horn, & Spreeman, 1983), that provide more directed questions toward a specific sport.

It should be noted that applied sport psychology consultants should consider a number of factors before administering questionnaires or other formal assessments to athletes (Beckman & Kellmann, 2003). For example, to be used effectively, assessment instruments need to be reliable and valid for the individual athlete or sport group in question, be seen as useful by the athlete(s), and be completed honestly by the athlete(s). In addition, sport psychology consultants need to provide athletes with a clear identification of the purpose of the assessment, and make sure that the athlete and coach (if applicable) are committed to the assessment.

Once the interview and psychological inventories have been completed, we recommend that written feedback be provided to each athlete that highlights his or her psychological strengths and weaknesses as they relate to sport performance and participation. This assessment should be given to athletes in a second one-on-one meeting and athletes should be provided with an opportunity to react to it. This provides an opportunity to get consensual validation from athletes in terms of the evaluation of the sport psychology consultant. At times we have found the oral interview and written assessments to be contrary, and this is a good time to bring any discrepancy up and have the athlete resolve it. The assessment should conclude with recommendations for the type of skills and intervention program that the consultant thinks would best suit the athlete's needs.

One weakness of using interviews, questionnaires, and behavioral observation to determine an athlete's psychological strengths and weaknesses is that the athlete plays a relatively passive role in the process. This often results in the sport psychology consultant having to convince athletes that they really need to work on particular psychological skills (Butler & Hardy, 1992).

Motivation and adherence problems will occur in the psychological skills training program if the athlete does not fully accept the decisions reached in the needs assessment. Butler and Hardy propose that using performance profiling resolves this problem, and an increasing number of sport psychology consultants are using the approach and finding it very effective.

For these reasons, we recommend performance profiling as an alternative approach to assessing psychological strengths and weaknesses. When using performance profiling, the athlete, with his or her own labels and definitions, determines the psychological skills needed for success. Once done, the athlete rates him- or herself on each of the identified constructs. Butler and Hardy (1992) propose that the rating use a 0–10 scale anchored with "not at all" and "very much." The athlete's resulting constructs are then displayed in the form of performance profiles. See Figure 17-1 for one example of plotting and using a performance profile to determine psychological needs and goals.

In this particular example, an athlete client of one of the authors had the goal of making the national team. Four months before the qualifying competition, the athlete, with the help of the sport psychologist, determined what psychological skills he would need, and their relative importance, in order to make the national team (see the dark bars depicting long-term goals). The athlete then assessed his present weakness and strength specific to each of the constructs he identified (see the shaded bars). This information was displayed pictorially and together the athlete and the sport psychologist determined what progress the athlete wanted to make in the next month and exactly what he would have to do to reach each of his psychological skills goals. See the clear bars added later to represent the athlete's short-term goals. (Note: The athlete had previously received some psychological skills training and was adamant that he simultaneously work on all the constructs.)

The performance profiling sheet also has the advantage of providing one format for the athlete and sport psychology consultant to periodically assess and record the athlete's progress

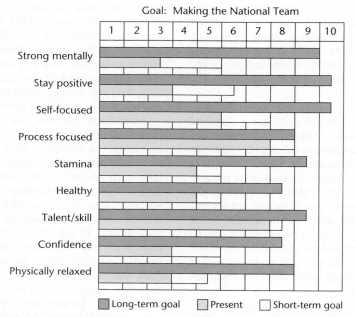

Figure 17-1 **Example of using performance profiling to determine psychological needs and goals**

in using interventions to reach his or her goals. This is done by using that same 10-point rating scale. Once done, draw a new bar to depict the rating, or you can extend or shade in the existing bar depicting starting status (labeled "present") and short-term goals. When using performance profiling in this way, we also recommend modifying the sheet in Figure 17-1 to allow sufficient room for comments after listing each construct.

The sport psychology consultant and coach can assess the psychological strengths and weakness of teams by using essentially the same procedure as that described for the individual athlete. We recommend putting the team members into groups of three to five players. Have each group take 5 to 10 minutes to identify the constructs that they perceive as important to reach the team's goal. Then have a team discussion regarding each construct identified by the groups, with the goal of reaching consensus regarding what

psychological skills to include. After identifying the resulting constructs and their relative importance, have the small groups use the 10-point scale to rate the present status of the team on each of the constructs. Also ask the groups to provide a rationale for their decision. Once finished, have all team members discuss each group's ratings and rationale until some consensus is reached regarding a final rating. One bonus of using the preceding procedure is that the discussion of the rationale for the ratings often results in a clear identification of both the attitudes and behaviors that the team members want to encourage and those that they want to discourage.

Regardless of the approach used to assess psychological strengths and weaknesses, if a sport psychology consultant is working with an entire team, it is essential that the coach be involved in the needs assessment because he or she is more likely to know the team's mental strengths and weaknesses over a period of time. This might, in turn, require different psychological approaches based on the team's history. For example, quite different psychological needs would probably be perceived for a team with a long history of losing compared to a team that climbed to the top and was currently experiencing the pressure of trying to maintain number-one status.

An obvious implication of this discussion on needs assessment is that the coach should be wary of anyone who suggests a canned mental training program that does not provide for the specific needs of a given group of athletes. Although such a program may be better than nothing, the more attention that is paid to the individual needs and the maturation and experiences of the given group, the more likely it is that the program will be successful.

Analyze Demands of the Sport

As noted in Taylor's (1995) conceptual model for integrating athletes' needs and sport demands in the development of competitive mental preparation strategies, every sport has unique physical, technical, and logistical demands that require special preparation by participating athletes. These characteristics that distinguish different sports also affect the type of mental preparation and training an athlete may employ. Thus, sport psychologists need a detailed understanding of important aspects of the sport in which they are working.

As Taylor (1995) notes, sports that involve explosiveness and anaerobic power (e.g., 100-yard dash) will differ greatly from those requiring endurance and aerobic conditioning (e.g., long-distance running and cycling). Patrick and Hrycaiko (1998) used such an approach in developing a mental training package for endurance performance. Similarly, a sport or sport skill requiring great precision (e.g., golf putting) might differ from one requiring more gross motor movements (e.g., power lifting). Furthermore, a sport or performance that lasts a very short time (figure skating) would require a different set of psychological skills than one that lasts hours (e.g., a marathon). Whether a sport or sport skill is self or externally paced influences optimal mental training interventions (e.g., see Lidor, 2007, for preparatory routines in self-paced events). Self-paced skills are ones in which the environment is relatively stable and predictable and the performer, within a few limitations, can initiate the activity when ready (e.g., free throw shot, tennis or volleyball serve, soccer penalty kick, golf). Externally paced skills typically occur when the performer has to react to an unstable and unpredictable environment (e.g., tennis and volleyball except for serving, most team sport skills). In essence, the demands of the sport or sport skill need to be carefully analyzed and considered when devising a mental skills training program.

One example of a mental training program that took into consideration the nature of the task was conducted by Terry, Mayer, and Howe (1998). Specifically, they developed a mental training package for scuba diving, basing their work on the fact that this activity can be very anxiety producing and that the ability to respond effectively under stress is crucial to survival. Therefore, their mental training program emphasized relaxation and coping skills (both cognitively and somatically oriented) such as deep rhythmic diaphragmatic breathing, guided imagery, and attentional focus. Results revealed that the mental training group exhibited lower levels of cognitive anxiety, higher levels of self-confidence, and significantly better performance than did the control group.

Determining What Skills to Include

Once the assessment is complete and all needed psychological skills have been listed, the coach or sport psychologist must decide how many of these skills to emphasize. This decision should be based on when the program is first being implemented (e.g., preseason, practice season, competitive season) and how much time the athletes and coach are willing to devote to mental skills training. Several questions are pertinent at this point:

- How much practice time will be given up on the average each week for mental skills training?

- How many weeks of practice are available?

- Will there still be time to practice mental skills after the competitive season starts, or after the first couple of losses?

- How interested are the athletes in receiving mental skills training?

The answers to these questions will help provide a realistic perspective on the commitment to mental skills training and the time available for accomplishing psychological skill objectives. When there is not adequate time or commitment for a comprehensive training program, it is better to prioritize objectives and emphasize a few to work on initially rather than work superficially on all of the needed skills. The coach or sport psychologist may even wish to develop a 2- to 3-year plan (Gould, 1983; Orlick, 1986).

Although there is certainly no definitive answer as to what a psychological skills training program should include or in what sequence these skills should be taught, Vealey (2007) provides a thoughtful analysis of the nature of psychological skills training programs. Specifically, Vealey (2007) proposes a number of skills that can and should be developed in a well-rounded psychological skills training program (see Table 17-2). It's important to note that these skills reflect areas related to personal development as well as performance enhancement.

The most basic skills, termed **foundation skills,** represent those qualities that are basic and necessary psychological skills. The first foundation skill is *achievement drive,* which is the compelling desire to overcome obstacles to accomplish something worthwhile. The second foundation skill is *self-awareness.* Before athletes can start changing some of their previous bad habits, they need to understand and become aware of exactly when and where their problem behaviors occur and what they are thinking and feeling at that time. In addition, athletes need to be aware of what they typically think and feel when performing at their best. That is, do they have an ideal performance state that is associated with peak performance? (See Chapter 9 for more detail on typical peak performance

Table 17-2 Mental Skills for Athletes

Foundation Skills:	Achievement drive
	Self-awareness
	Productive-thinking
	Self-confidence
Performance Skills:	Perceptual-cognitive skill
	Attentional focus
	Energy management
Personal Development Skills:	Identity achievement
	Interpersonal competence
Team Skills:	Leadership
	Communication
	Cohesion
	Team Confidence

Source: Vealey, 2007.

characteristics.) Keeping a sport journal is one way to increase awareness of performance states and to understand how different situations bring about different emotional reactions. (See Chapter 10 for suggestions regarding how to keep a journal and implement other techniques for increasing awareness.) If athletes are sufficiently motivated and have become aware of the relationship between their thoughts and feelings and behavior, they can begin to develop their thought processes and self-confidence. The third and fourth foundation skills are *productive thinking* and *self-confidence* which not only are critical to sport performance (see Chapters 9 and 15) but also are central to a wide array of behaviors outside the world of sport and physical activity (Bandura, 1986). Thus, it would appear inappropriate to begin other psychological skills training until individuals learn a certain level of proficiency in the foundation skills.

The **performance skills** in Vealey's (2007) model are some of the traditional psychological skills that most sport psychology consultants attempt to teach including *energy management* (e.g., arousal regulation) *attentional focus,* and *perceptual-cognitive skills* (e,g, decision-making skills). These skills are addressed in detail in various chapters throughout the text. The premise is that exceptional performance is most likely to occur when these skills are learned and integrated into an athlete's actual competitive performance.

"Personal development skills are mental skills that represent significant maturational markers of personal development, and that allow for high-level psychological functioning through clarity of self-concept, feelings of well-being, and a sense of relatedness to others" (Vealey, 2007, p. 290). Two personal development skills that Vealey (2007) feels are especially important are *identity achievement* (establishing a clear sense of identity) and *interpersonal competence* (interacting effectively with others). Taking a life skills approach is an example of a mental training intervention that focuses on personal development skills.

The final category of mental skills is **team skills,** which are collective qualities of the team that are instrumental to an effective team environment and overall team success. Team skills are made up of (a) *team confidence*—the belief that the team has the collective resources or team abilities to achieve team success, (b) *cohesion*—the team's ability to stick together and remain united in the pursuit of its goals, (c) *communication*—the process of interpersonal interaction within the team that facilitates team success and athletes' well-being, and (d) *leadership*—the ability of individuals to influence others on the team to think and act in ways that facilitate team success and the quality of the team's social-psychological environment.

Sport psychology consultants have a wide variety of methods and techniques that they can choose from to develop and enhance the preceding psychological skills. The most commonly used methods are the four traditional techniques of goal setting (Chapter 11), imagery (Chapter 14), physical relaxation and arousal regulation (Chapter 13), and thought control (Chapter 15).

Regardless of the specific skills and methods to be included in any psychological skills training program, it will be more effective if psychological objectives appropriate to the athletes are identified and if these objectives are defined in easily understood and measurable terms; Table 17-3 provides some examples. Such definitions help clarify exactly what the objective means and what outcomes are expected once it is achieved. The definitions also provide a clear foundation for planning strategies to accomplish the objectives and for assessing how effective the strategies were in achieving the objective.

Evaluation of Program Effectiveness

It is not easy to evaluate the impact of a psychology skills training program, yet evaluation is essential for improving a training program and the skills of the person in charge of the program. In fact, evaluation should be an essential feature of any organizational as well as individualized intervention. Aside from the accountability demands that ethically oblige sport psychology consultants to evaluate the effectiveness of what they do (see Smith, 1989), practical considerations are also important.

First, program evaluation provides consultants and coaches with the information needed to gauge the effectiveness of the various components of their programs and to make modifications where needed. Second, an evaluation provides consumers with an opportunity to provide feedback concerning areas that they feel weren't included or to suggest changes in the way the program was conducted. Third, evaluation is the only way we can objectively judge whether the program achieved its intended goals in changing some aspects of the individual's or team's behavior or performance.

It is important to note that evaluation should be a continuous process. Sport psychology consultants should assess the strengths and weaknesses of the content and delivery of their sessions, especially team sessions. Questions such as the following might be addressed: Did the session accomplish its objective(s)? Were explanations of psychological concepts and directions for practicing the training exercises adequate? What techniques appeared to work best? Was

Table 17-3 **A Sample of Psychological Skills Objectives and Outcomes**

Objective 1	Objective 2	Objective 3
Positive Mental Attitude	*Coping With Mistakes and Failures*	*Handling the High-Stress Situation*
Don't make negative statements at games or practices.	Accept the fact that mistakes and failures are a necessary part of the learning process.	Learn to interpret the situation as a challenge rather than a threat.
Change "I can't" statements to "I can" statements.	Don't make excuses. Appropriately accepting responsibility will help turn failures into success.	Recognize too much tension. Achieve appropriate differential relaxation.
Always give 100% effort.	Stay positive even after a stupid mistake.	Keep thoughts positive and focused on the task at hand.
Don't talk while coaches talk.	Be supportive of teammates even when they are making mistakes.	Image goal of performing well under high-stress situations.
Hustle during all plays and drills.	Keep focused concentration rather than dwelling on mistakes.	Focus concentration on appropriate cues.

time allotted appropriately during the session? Are any additions or deletions warranted? How responsive did the athletes appear to be? Writing a critique is more beneficial than simply trying to remember strengths and weaknesses. Plans for future sessions may need to be modified on the basis of the results of each session evaluation.

A more formal, total evaluation should occur at the end of the mental skills training program. This evaluation might include team and individual discussions as well as written evaluations by the athletes and coaches. The evaluation should focus on the players' assessment of the value of the program from both a psychological and performance perspective. Objective performance data should be used in addition to subjective reports from coaches and athletes. For example, one recommended objective data system entails behavioral assessment, which involves collecting and analyzing information and data to identify and describe target behaviors, identify possible causes of the behaviors, select appropriate

treatment strategies to modify the behaviors, and evaluate treatment outcomes (Tkachuk, Leslie-Toogood, & Martin, 2003). In addition, athletes should be asked how often they actually practiced their skills. When psychological skills programs don't work, one of the major reasons is simply because athletes do not systematically practice what they have learned. Information should also be obtained on different aspects of the program, such as group sessions, individual sessions, and written materials. Additional questions can be asked, such as, What did athletes see as the major strengths and weaknesses of the mental skills training? What mental skills improved the most? What exercises were the most helpful? What suggestions do athletes have to make the program even better in the future? To help out new sport psychology consultants, Partington and Orlick (1987a, 1987b) provide a sample sport psychology evaluation form as well as data on what makes a consultant effective from both the coaches' and athletes' point of view. In addition, Poczwardowski, Sherman, and Henschen (1998) provide additional suggestions on the key points when conducting programs and making evaluations.

Anderson, Miles, Mahoney, and Robinson (2002) suggest that a practitioner-administered case study approach to evaluation should be employed, which uses a number of effectiveness indicators to accommodate the constraints of a practice setting and fulfill the functional criteria for evaluating practice. More specifically, they break down effectiveness indicators into four distinct categories. These include the quality of support (e.g., consultant effectiveness), psychological skill and well-being (e.g., anxiety control, happiness), response to support (e.g., changes in knowledge and attitude), and performance (objective, subjective). This presents a more well-rounded view of evaluation than simply performance (bottom line), which is the focus of many interventions.

Practical Pointers for Teaching Mental Skills

In the preceding chapters on mental skills training the authors have presented many excellent pointers for teaching specific mental skills. The following pointers apply either to the entire psychological training program or to its components.

Provide the What, Why, When, and How of Training

For mental skills to be of maximum value, the athlete must consciously and continually choose to utilize mental training methods. This necessitates a high level of commitment, an understanding of proper execution, and ultimately the ability to be self-sufficient in mental preparation. This can be accomplished in a number of ways. Athletes who are taught the what, why, when, and how of mental skills training are much more likely to acquire the necessary knowledge base to become self-sufficient in mental training as well as the motivation to follow through with the

program. At the beginning of each special mental training session, the coach or sport psychologist should outline for the athletes the purpose, content, and approximate length of the session. The educational aspect of the program is critical to provide athletes with an understanding of what principles the program is based on and how it works. It is also a good idea to allot time for discussion and questions after practicing each exercise and at the end of each session. In addition to enhancing forthright self-examination and the learning process, the sharing that occurs in these discussions often improves communication and understanding among teammates and leads to better group support and more team cohesiveness.

Stress Personal Responsibility

When it comes to performance, some athletes have the attitude "When you're hot, you're hot, and when you're not, you're not." These athletes view peak performance as more a consequence of fate than something under their own personal control. Implementors of mental skills training should teach the opposite attitude. Peak performance is not mysterious; it is a product of the body and mind, both of which can be controlled. This is why, with the right physical and mental training, athletes can learn to repeat their best performances more consistently. This means learning to be in control of oneself instead of letting the environment or others do the controlling. The athlete must ultimately accept the fact that only he or she can take responsibility for being physically and mentally ready to compete.

Be Flexible and Individualized

When teaching mental skills to a group of athletes, the best approach is to be flexible and individualized. All athletes do not learn mental skills in the same way and at the same pace any more than they do physical skills. Within reasonable time constraints, a variety of techniques should be introduced and practiced. Do not force everyone into a fixed pattern. Instead, encourage athletes to modify or combine techniques until they derive the most effective method for them. A backup technique should also be identified and practiced for those times when the preferred one fails to accomplish its objective.

Providing handouts and cassette or CD recordings of exercises and specific concepts, including the ones in this book, is another way to ensure that athletes have a variety of exercises with which to work and the knowledge base for making modifications and application. Although many athletes like to use recordings and handouts when they practice, be sure they do not become so dependent on them that they cannot practice the mental skills without such props.

Use Goal Setting and Journal Assignments

You can also enhance and individualize the teaching of specific mental skills by using goal setting and journal assignments. This is one reason many sport psychology consultants suggest that athletes be encouraged to keep a journal (see Chapter 10) and set goals (see Chapter 11) early in a training program. The following is an example of their use.

A runner, after having been taught to recognize tension and to relax, identifies that he grimaces and his neck and shoulder muscles tighten when he is running under poor weather conditions, after experiencing the first signs of fatigue, and when a steep hill is coming up. He records this in his journal. Next, the runner sets a reasonable goal for correcting the problem: "In one week I will run a workout over hilly terrain keeping my face, neck, and shoulder muscles relaxed throughout the run." After he records the goal, he plans and records a strategy for reaching the goal: "(1) Do 5 minutes of progressive relaxation (PR) each day on just the face, neck, and shoulder muscles. (2) After PR practice, visualize running fluidly over hilly terrain. (3) When running, frequently scan the face for tension—if needed, relax the face so the forehead is smooth as glass and the jaw is slack. When the face is relaxed, scan neck and shoulders for unwanted tension. If tense, relax by slowly rolling the head and/or dropping the shoulders." Each day the runner

records his progress in achieving the goal. Once the runner feels he is consistently achieving the goal, he may want to establish a slightly more difficult goal and repeat the process.

Precompetition and Competition Plans

The ultimate goal of psychological skills training is for each athlete to learn how to create consistently at competition time the ideal performance state (thoughts, feelings, bodily responses) typically associated with peak performance. Rarely will this occur if precompetition preparation and competition behaviors are left to chance or good and bad breaks. Athletes get ready for competition in a variety of ways, but more often than not they do not have a consistent pattern of readying procedures. Performance is likely to be enhanced if an athlete's preparation becomes more systematic.

One of the objectives of precompetition planning is to arrange the external and internal world in a way that maximizes the athlete's feelings of control. The athlete's **external world** consists of the actual physical surroundings, what is happening in these surroundings, and the physical things the athlete does. The **internal world** is the athlete's physical states, thoughts, feelings, mental images, and attentional focus. The greater the familiarity, routine, and structure in the external environment, the easier it is for the athlete to be in control of his or her internal world. The external world can be stabilized in a number of ways—for example, eating similar meals the same amount of time before each competition; always arriving at the contest site with a set amount of time for precompetition preparation; establishing a set dressing ritual; and following the same equipment check, taping, and warm-up procedures.

Maintaining a constant and familiar external world is even more critical with away competitions. This is more easily accomplished when athletes diligently adhere to elaborate and consistent precompetition plans before both home and away games. The coach can also increase familiarity with the site of away games by taking the athletes to the site before the competition begins, ideally at least a day before. Some coaches and sport psychology consultants even advocate getting films of the away facility, including the locker rooms, and showing these films to their athletes well before a competition (see Chapters 14 and 16 for further elaboration on how such films can be used and why they are effective in improving performance).

The best precompetition and competition plans consist of procedures that ready the athlete physically and mentally for competition. The typical physical preparations should be supplemented with emotional and cognitive readying procedures if athletes are to maximize their chances of being ready to peak at competition time. This entails planning procedures for monitoring and controlling the task at hand as competition nears. It also means monitoring and controlling emotions so that the energy and excitement for competing build slowly.

Mental monitoring and readying procedures should be integrated with certain external markers such as waking up the morning of competition, traveling to the competition, arriving at the competition site, getting dressed, doing warm-up exercises and technique drills, and dealing with the short time between physical warm-ups and the beginning of competition. When some athletes arrive at a competition site, they like to find a quiet place where they can practice 5 to 10 minutes of relaxation exercises such as deep breathing or passive progressive relaxation. Such athletes believe these relaxation procedures have the benefit of bringing them to the same starting point prior to each competition before they begin the rest of their on-site preparation. Other athletes combine their dressing ritual with cognitive focusing techniques designed to narrow attentional focus to what the athletes want to do during the competition. Often athletes end their dressing ritual or precede their physical warm-up with a 5- to 10-minute imagery exercise of exactly what they want to feel and perform during competition. Some athletes even use *all* of these readying procedures.

The most effective readying procedure is individual; this means that the length, content, and sequencing of behavioral protocols vary greatly from one player to another—even when the players are on the same team. Such variability stems partly from different needs in creating an ideal performance state and different preferences for the mental training exercises.

Some interesting qualitative research by Gould, Eklund, and Jackson (1992) and Eklund, Gould, and Jackson (1993) on thoughts and cognitions of Olympic wrestlers highlights the importance of precompetition and competition plans as well as individual variability. First, some between-group differences among medalists and nonmedalists revealed that medalists had competition plans firmly in their minds and did not spontaneously second-guess these plans during matches, whereas nonmedalists reported that spontaneous deviations from competition plans developed for matches and often had negative consequences (i.e., poorer performance). In addition, medalists had very systematic preperformance routines that they consistently adhered to throughout the Olympics, whereas nonmedalists reported deviating from their preperformance routines, especially in matches that they considered less challenging or less important.

Despite these differences between medalists and nonmedalists, interviews revealed individual differences and variations among the medalists. For example, one medalist placed great importance on prematch focus. "I just try to think about the techniques I am going to use and what strategies I am going to do and get that into my mind before I go out on the mat so I am focused on what I am going to do" (Eklund et al., 1993, p. 43). Conversely, another medalist deemphasized preperformance routines and strategy, feeling that they made them "too programmed." This orientation is captured in the following quotation: "I don't worry about strategy and technique. I try to keep my mind clear of getting caught up in all that stuff. If I have watched a wrestler and what he does—that is all I need to know. I don't go over what I am going to do or what different strategies I am going to try to use. I just keep my mind clear and when I get out there, I just react" (Eklund et al., 1993, p. 44).

Table 17-4 Refocusing Plans for an Olympic Speedskater

Worries about Competitors before the Race

- They are human just like me. We'll see what they can do in the race, not in warm-ups or in training. I need to focus on my *own* preparation.
- All I can do is my best. Nobody can take that away from me. If my performance is good, I'll be happy. If it's not so good and I try, I shouldn't be disappointed.
- I'm racing for *me*. It's *my* max that I want.

Worry about Competitors during the Race

- If I start to think about others during the race, I'll shift my concentration to *my* race, *my* technique—"Stay low, race your race."
- "I have the potion—I have the motion."

Pre-Event Hassles

- Skate blades don't cut the ice—carry a small sharpening stone to pass over the blades.
- Delay in start—if I'm already on the ice and it's likely to be a short delay, jog around, keep moving, stay warm, do a mini warm-up with some accelerations. Follow normal prerace plan when approaching the line.
- Windy or snowy conditions—it's the same for everyone. Just go out and do what you can do.

Worries during Competition

- Poor start—no problem, it can happen. It's not the start that determines the final results. Follow your race plan. Push your max.
- Not hearing a split time—it's okay. Just skate well and race your race.
- Pain in legs—shift focus to the specifics of the task to be done, the steps in the turn, pushing the blade to the side, pushing hard to the finish line.

Source: Reprinted by permission from T. Orlick, 1986, *Psyching for Sport* (Champaign, IL: Human Kinetics Publishers), pp. 165–166.

Some excellent examples of precompetition and competition planning come from the work of Orlick (1986) with Canadian Olympic athletes. Orlick has the athletes he works with develop very specific precompetition and competition plans. However, in addition, his athletes develop precompetition and competition *refocusing* plans in case things don't go exactly as they originally planned. This is extremely important because things out of an athlete's control can throw off his or her plans at the last second. And, as Jack Donohue, Canadian Olympic basketball coach, says, "What happens to you is nowhere near as important as how you react to what happens to you." A refocusing plan is aimed at helping athletes refocus away from unwanted external distractions or internal distractions such as worries, self-doubt, and self-put-downs. Table 17-4 provides a good example of precompetition and competition refocusing plans for an Olympic speed skater.

Stress Application to Other Life Pursuits

One tremendous bonus that comes from implementing a mental training program is that the skills learned are applicable to life in general as well as to athletics, and the benefits last long after the competitive year is over. The training program can assist athletes in applying their new mental skills by suggesting relevant uses in nonathletic settings. For example, suggest that athletes learn to do their homework more quickly by using mental training concentration skills. With these skills, athletes can become more aware of when their mind is wandering and can bring their focus of attention back to the task at hand. If an athlete gets so uptight before tests that he or she cannot remember what was learned, the same relaxation and positive thinking skills that athletes are taught to control competitive anxiety can be used for test-taking anxiety and many other stressful situations people face in life. When athletic programs offer both physical and mental skills training, they provide a better argument that participating in competitive sport can also be a valuable educational experience.

A recent issue of the *Journal of Applied Sport Psychology* (2002, 4) focused on the application of psychological skills typically used in sport and exercise settings to other settings and endeavors such as business, medicine, space travel, and special forces. More and more sport psychology consultants are practicing in areas outside of sport, fueled in part by the renewed interest in the psychology of excellence. For example, Loehr and Schwartz (2001) have discussed the similarities of high performers, whether they be elite athletes or CEOs working for a Fortune 500 company. Similarly, Murphy (1996) discusses the transfer from working with elite athletes at the Olympic Training Center to working with performers in the corporate arena. Murphy reports that his clients (whether sport or nonsport) tell him that the skills they are taught help them achieve their best under pressure, allow them to stay focused during difficult tasks, and enable them to enjoy even the most challenging assignments. Thus, the transfer from sport to other areas of life seems to be a fertile ground for future practitioners and researchers.

Practice It before Teaching It

Before teaching any of the mental training exercises to athletes, sport psychology consultants and coaches should take the time to practice each technique themselves. Personally experiencing an exercise is an excellent way to increase one's ability to teach a specific technique and to answer any questions athletes may have about it. An additional bonus of practicing the exercises, particularly if the practice is systematic and long term, is that the practitioner will accrue psychological benefits similar to those the athletes receive from the practice.

Teach by Example

In regard to psychological control—or any type of behavior—good coaches and sport psychology consultants teach and lead by example. If the person leading the mental training program does not exemplify what he or she is teaching, it is highly unlikely the athletes will model it either. The coach who appears calm, confident, and in control during a competition usually has athletes who act the same way. Players are more likely to offer encouragement and support to one another when they have a leader who models encouragement (Wescott, 1980). The next time you see athletes consistently losing control and concentration after poor officiating calls, look to the bench, and you probably will see the coach behaving similarly. Watch how athletes react to poor performance. Athletes who become negative or rattled after mistakes are often led by coaches who react similarly. For psychological training to be maximally effective, the coaches and sport psychology consultants must exemplify in practice and competition the behavior they expect from athletes.

Observe Practices and Competitions Whenever Possible

As noted earlier, one of the disadvantages of sport psychology consultants conducting mental training programs with teams is their lack of day-to-day availability. Despite this limitation, it is critical that consultants attempt to attend some practices and competitions. We have found that this is particularly important at the beginning stages of the intervention. This firsthand view can provide consultants with critical information that might not be evident from an interview or paper-and-pencil measure. As noted earlier, the problem might be biomechanical or physical in nature rather than psychological, and this would not likely show up in an interview or a test. Perhaps even more important than the information gained is the trust developed when athletes know the consultants care enough about them to see them perform. In surveys evaluating the effectiveness of sport psychology consultants (Gould, Tammen, Murphy, & May, 1989; Partington & Orlick, 1987a), a critical component to the perceived effectiveness of sport psychology consultants that directly affected building trust between athletes and consultants was the amount of time the consultants spent being with and observing the athletes.

Emphasize Strengths as Competition Nears

Behavior by the coach and sport psychology consultant prior to and during competition is particularly critical. The nearer the time to competition, the more important it is that they are reassuring and complimentary toward athletes. This is not the time to be critical of technique or anything else. Besides, it is too late to change weaknesses, so there is no reason to focus on them. Instead, if at all possible, get athletes to think they are looking great and help build their confidence. In short, now is the time to build from what is positive, to play to strengths rather than weaknesses. Such behavior by the coach and sport psychology consultant will help athletes build and maintain confidence rather than self-doubt prior to competition. This usually means better performance.

The preceding recommendation is particularly critical with athletes who have higher anxiety and lower self-confidence. Williams et al. (2003) found that when these athletes perceived the coach to lose emotional control, become negative, or fail to be supportive, this was likely to lead to poorer performance and more difficulty maintaining optimal mental states and focus. Using the self-monitoring or outside monitoring described in the next section should help coaches and sport psychology consultants assess their behavior prior to and during competition.

Monitor Your Behavior

In Chapter 10, Ravizza suggests that athletes become more aware of their behavior, thoughts, and feelings through self-monitoring. The same awareness on the part of coaches and sport psychology consultants can help them become more effective in working with athletes. For example, by means of self-monitoring, coaches and sport psychology consultants can become more conscious of how they communicate with athletes during different situations. They should monitor what they say as well as what they communicate with their body language. They should ask themselves such questions as "How is my behavior likely to change in certain situations?" "Am I a good role model for the mental discipline and psychological control I wish to teach?" The awareness created by conscientious and objective self-monitoring is a necessary first step in becoming more effective in working with athletes.

There is also merit in having someone else observe and evaluate one's behavior. For example, if a coach has a sport psychology consultant working with the team, he or she would be an ideal person to observe the coach's behavior during practices and games. Coaching behaviors should be analyzed on the basis of the principles for desirable behavior elaborated in earlier chapters. Evaluation would be facilitated if special forms were employed (e.g., Smith, Smoll, & Hunt, 1977; Tharp & Gallimore, 1976). The information presented in earlier chapters can be used to help plan a specific strategy for modifying a coach's behavior in a direction that is more likely to facilitate the performance and personal growth of his or her athletes.

Ethical Considerations for the Coach and Sport Psychology Consultant

Sport psychology is a relatively young profession, and the people practicing applied sport psychology in the 1970s and early 1980s had little to guide them in terms of ethical issues. The purpose of this section is to call attention to some basic ethical concerns involved in implementing mental skills training. A more thorough discussion of these topics can be found in Moore (2003); Whelan, Meyers, and Elkin (1996); and Sachs (1993).

To better understand what specific situations and circumstances applied sport psychologists perceive as particularly difficult and possibly controversial from an ethical perspective, Petitpas, Brewer, Rivera, and Van Raalte (1994) administered surveys to individuals practicing applied sport psychology. Results revealed that four classifications of behaviors were identified as requiring the most difficult ethical judgments or were perceived as controversial. These included (a) conflicts with confidentiality (e.g., reporting recruiting violations to appropriate officials); (b) conflicts between personal values and professional ethics (e.g., working with an athlete who uses steroids); (c) conflicts with dual relationships (e.g., socializing with clients); (d) conflicts with self-presentation or advertising (e.g., including athlete testimonials in advertising). Any profession has many ethical gray areas, making decisions extremely difficult at times.

To help guide professionals working in applied sport psychology settings deal with ethical dilemmas more effectively, sport psychology associations such as the Association for Applied Sport Psychology, the North American Society for the Psychology of Sport and Physical Activity, and the Canadian Society for Psychomotor Learning and Sport Psychology have developed modifications of the American Psychological Association's Ethical Standards (1992). At the core of these standards is the general philosophy that sport psychology consultants respect the dignity and worth of the individual and honor the preservation and protection of fundamental human rights. In addition, consultants are committed to increasing the knowledge of human behavior and of people's understanding of themselves and others in sport environments. The essence of this philosophy is that the athlete's welfare must be foremost. For a more detailed discussion of ethical principles please consult the American Psychological Association's ethical guidelines (1992). In addition, McCann, Jowdy, and Van Raalte (2002) provide ethical guidelines especially for assessments.

Potential Problem Areas

Although the potential benefits of implementing a psychological skills training program are clearly demonstrable, there are of course some problems that a consultant or coach will have to deal with throughout the process. Each situation, naturally, will offer its own unique set of problems. For example, working one on one with individual athletes is quite different from working with an entire team. Working with Olympic athletes or professional athletes might present an entirely different set of problems than working with high school athletes. If the consultant or coach does not adequately deal with these problems, they can severely reduce the effectiveness of the program. Some examples of common problems include the following:

- Overcoming player reluctance about participating in a mental training program.

- Spending too little time with individual athletes in a team setting.

- Gaining the trust of the athletes.

- Making sure athletes systematically practice their skills.

- Lacking knowledge about the specific sport.

- Maintaining contact with athletes throughout a competitive season.

- Getting full cooperation from the coaching staff or organization.

A sport psychology consultant needs to be aware of these potential problem areas and ready to deal with them if necessary. It has taken most of us several years to learn many of these things by trial and error. Many of us made mistakes in our early years of consulting because we simply weren't aware of, or hadn't experienced, many of these nuances of setting up and implementing a mental training program. However, with good preparation, careful thought, and a sense of commitment, this can be a very rewarding experience. After all, helping individuals reach their potential both inside and outside the world of sport is what it's all about.

Summary

In this chapter we have addressed many general issues relating to the integration and implementation of a psychological skills training program. In summary, (1) there are advantages to having either a coach or a sport psychologist implement a psychological skills training program, (2) athletes of all types and age and skill levels can benefit from mental training, (3) mental skills training should continue for as long as an athlete participates in sport, (4) the initial mental skills training program should probably last 3 to 6 months and start in the off-season or preseason, (5) a psychological skills needs assessment should be made to determine the specific components to be incorporated in training and the psychological objectives to be achieved, (6) there is no one best way to sequence and integrate psychological components even though one was proposed, (7) once basic mental skills are acquired they should have a performance-specific focus and be integrated with practice of physical skills, and (8) real benefits from psychological skills training will only occur with long-term systematic practice.

We have also suggested practical teaching pointers that apply either to the entire psychological training program or to many of its components. Stress that athletes accept responsibility for their mental state. Be flexible, eclectic, and individualized in planning training techniques. Stress personal growth and how to use mental skills in nonathletic settings. Practice techniques before teaching them. Teach by personally exemplifying the mental skills being taught. Finally, we concluded the chapter with ethical considerations that all psychological training implementors need to be aware of and observe in their own behavior.

Study Questions

1. Discuss who will benefit most from psychological skills training.

2. Are psychological skills intervention programs effective in enhancing performance? Provide evidence to support your answer.

3. What are some advantages and disadvantages of a coach or sport psychology consultant conducting a mental training program?

4. How much time should be spent in mental training?

5. When is the best time to practice psychological skills?

6. When is the best time to implement a psychological skills training program?

7. Discuss what would be covered in a first interview with an athlete.

8. Discuss the use of psychological inventories to help assess athletes' psychological skills.

9. Discuss Vealey's distinction between psychological methods and psychological skills. What are the different categories of psychological skills? What impact does this distinction between methods and skills have on the implementation of a psychological skills training program?

10. John, a golfer, goes to a sport psychologist because his play is "erratic." One of the sport psychologist's observations is that he has no consistent preshot readying procedure. How might the sport psychologist help John develop a preshot routine, what might it include, and why should this intervention improve John's performance?

11. Discuss how a psychological skills program might be evaluated.

12. Discuss five practical pointers that may help make a psychological skills program more effective. Cite specific practical examples and research to support your points.

References

American Psychological Association. (1992). Ethical principles and code of conduct. *American Psychologist, 47*, 1597–1611.

Anderson, A., Miles, A., Mahoney, C., & Robinson, P. (2002). Evaluating the effectiveness of applied sport psychology practice: Making the case for a case study approach. *The Sport Psychologist, 16*, 432–453.

Association for the Advancement of Applied Sport Psychology Newsletter 6 (Winter 1991).

Bandura, A. (1986). *Social foundations of thought and action: A social cognitive theory.* Englewood Cliffs, NJ: Prentice Hall.

Barber, H., & Krane, V. (2005). The elephant in the lockerroom: Opening the dialogue about sexual orientation on women's sports teams. In M. Andersen (Ed.). *Sport psychology in practice.* Champaign, IL: Human Kinetics.

Beckman, J., & Kellmann, M. (2003). Procedures and principles of sport psychological assessment. *The Sport Psychologist, 17*, 338–350.

Blakeslee, M., & Goff, D. (2007). The effects of a mental skills training package on equestrians. *The Sport Psychologist,* 288–301.

Butler, R. J., & Hardy, L. (1992). The performance profile: Theory and application. *The Sport Psychologist, 6*, 253–264.

Butryn, T. (2002). Critically examining white racial identity and privilege in sport psychology consulting. *The Sport Psychologist, 16*, 316–336.

Durand-Bush, N., Salmela, J., & Green-Demers, I. (2001). The Ottawa mental skills assessment tool (OMSAT3). *The Sport Psychologist, 15*, 1–19.

Eklund, R. C., Gould, D., & Jackson, S. A. (1993). Psychological foundations of Olympic wrestling excellence: Reconciling individual differences and nomothetic characterization. *Journal of Applied Sport Psychology, 5*, 35–47.

Gould, D. (1983). Developing psychological skills in young athletes. In N. Wood (Ed.), *Coaching science update.* Ottawa, ON: Coaching Association of Canada.

Gould, D., Eklund, R. C., & Jackson, S. A. (1992). 1988 U.S. Olympic wrestling excellence I. Mental preparation, precompetition cognition, and affect. *The Sport Psychologist, 6,* 358–382.

Gould, D., Horn, T., & Spreeman, J. (1983). Competitive anxiety in junior elite wrestlers. *Journal of Sport Psychology, 5,* 58–71.

Gould, D., Murphy, S., Tammen, V., & May, J. (1991). An evaluation of Olympic sport psychology consultant effectiveness. *The Sport Psychologist, 5,* 111–127.

Gould, D., Tammen, V., Murphy, S., & May, J. (1989). An examination of the U.S. Olympic sport psychology consultants and the services they provide. *The Sport Psychologist, 3,* 300–312.

Greenspan, M. J., & Feltz, D. F. (1989). Psychological interventions with athletes in competitive situations: A review. *The Sport Psychologist, 3,* 219–236.

Kirschenbaum, D. (1997). *Mind matters: 7 steps to smarter sport performance.* Carmel, IN: Cooper Publishing.

Kontos, A., & Breland-Noble, A. (2002). Racial/ethnic diversity in applied sport psychology: A multicultural introduction to working with athletes of color. *The Sport Psychologist, 16,* 296–315.

Kremer, J., & Scully, D. (1998). What applied sport psychologists often don't ask: On empowerment and independence. In H. Sternberg, I. Cockerill, & A. Dewey (Eds.), *What sport psychologists do* (pp. 21–27). Leichester: The British Psychological Society.

Lidor, R. (2007). Preparatory routines in self-paced events. In. G. Tenenbaum & R. C. Eklund (Eds.). *Handbook of research in sport psychology* (3rd ed., pp. 445–465). Hoboken, NJ: John Wiley & Sons.

Loehr, J., & Schwartz, T. (2001, January). The making of the corporate athlete. *Harvard Business Review,* pp. 120–128.

Martens, R. (1977). *Sport competition anxiety test.* Champaign, IL: Human Kinetics.

Martens, R., Vealey, R. S., & Burton, D. (1990). *Competitive anxiety in sport.* Champaign, IL: Human Kinetics.

Martin, S. B., Wrisberg, C. A., Beitel, P. A., & Lounsbury, J. (1997). NCAA Division 1 athletes' attitudes toward seeking sport psychology consultation: The development of an objective instrument. *The Sport Psychologist, 11,* 201–218.

McCann, S., Jowdy, D., & Van Raalte, J. (2002). Assessment in sport and exercise psychology. In J. Van Raalte and B. Brewer (Eds.), *Exploring sport and exercise psychology* (2nd ed., pp. 291–305). Washington, DC: American Psychological Association.

Meyers, A. W., Whelan, J. P., & Murphy, S. M. (1996). Cognitive behavioral strategies in athletic performance enhancement. In M. Hersen, R. M. Eisler, & P. M. Miller (Eds.), *Progress in behavior modification* Vol. 30, (pp. 137–164). Pacific Grove, CA: Brooks/Cole.

Moore, Z. E. (2003). Ethical dilemmas in sport psychology: Discussion and recommendations for practice. *Professional Psychology: Research and Practice, 34,* 601–610.

Murphy, S. (1995). *Sport psychology intervention.* Champaign, IL: Human Kinetics.

Murphy, S. (1996). *The achievement zone.* New York: Putnam.

Murphy, S., Jowdy, D., & Durtschi, S. (1990). *Imagery perspective survey.* Colorado Springs, CO: U.S. Olympic Training Center.

Nideffer, R. M. (1976). Test of attentional and interpersonal style. *Journal of Personality and Social Psychology, 34,* 394–404.

Nideffer, R. M. (1989). Psychological services for the U.S. track and field team. *The Sport Psychologist, 3,* 350–357.

O'Connor, E. (2004). Which questionnaire? Assessment practices of sport psychology consultants, *The Sport Psychologist,* 18, 464–468.

Orlick, T. (1986). *In pursuit of excellence.* Champaign, IL: Human Kinetics.

Orlick, T. (2000). *In pursuit of excellence: How to win in sport and life through mental training.* (3rd ed.). Champaign, IL: Human Kinetics

Orlick, T., & McCaffrey, N. (1991). Mental training with children for sport and life. *The Sport Psychologist, 5,* 322–334.

Partington, J., & Orlick, T. (1987a). The sport psychology consultant: Olympic coaches' views. *The Sport Psychologist, 1,* 95–102.

Partington, J., & Orlick, T. (1987b). The sport psychology consultant evaluation form. *The Sport Psychologist, 1,* 309–317.

Patrick, T. D., & Hrycaiko, D. W. (1998). Effects of a mental training package on an endurance performance. *The Sport Psychologist, 12,* 283–299.

Petitpas, A., Brewer, B., Rivera, P., & Van Raalte, J. (1994). Ethical beliefs and behaviors in applied sport psychology: The AAASP ethics survey. *Journal of Applied Sport Psychology, 6,* 135–151.

Petitpas, A. J., Giges, B., & Danish, S. J. (1999). The sport psychologist–athlete relationship: Implications for training. *The Sport Psychologist, 13,* 344–357.

Poczwardowski, A., Sherman, C. P., & Henschen, K. P. (1998). A sport psychology service delivery heuristic: Building on theory and practice. *The Sport Psychologist, 12,* 191–207.

Ravizza, K. (1990). Sportpsych consultation issues in professional baseball. *The Sport Psychologist, 4,* 330–340.

Ravizza, K., & Hanson, T. (1995). *Heads up baseball: Playing the game one pitch at a time.* Indianapolis, IN: Masters Press.

Sachs, M. (1993). Professional ethics in sport psychology. In R. N. Singer, M. Murphey, & L. K. Tennant (Eds.), *Handbook of research in sport psychology* (pp. 921–932). New York: Macmillan.

Seabourne, T., Weinberg, R. S., Jackson, A., & Suinn, R. M. (1985). Effect of individualized, nonindividualized and package intervention strategies on karate performance. *Journal of Sport Psychology, 7,* 40–50

Sexton, T. L., & Whitson, S. C. (1994). The status of the counseling relationship: An empirical review, theoretical implications, and research directions. *The Counseling Psychologist, 22,* 6–78.

Smith, R. E. (1989). Applied sport psychology in the age of accountability. *Journal of Applied Sport Psychology, 1,* 166–180.

Smith, R. E., & Johnson, J. (1990). An organizational empowerment approach to consultation in professional baseball. *The Sport Psychologist, 4,* 347–357.

Smith, R. E., Schutz, R. W., Smoll, F. L., & Ptacek, J. T. (1995). Development and validation of a multi-dimensional measure of sport-specific psychological skills: The Athletic Coping Skills Inventory–28. *Journal of Sport and Exercise Psychology, 17,* 379–387.

Smith, R. E., Smoll, F. L., & Hunt, E. (1977). A system for the behavioral assessment of athletic coaches. *Research Quarterly, 48,* 401–407.

Smith, R. E., Smoll, F. L., & Schutz, R. W. (1990). Measurement and correlates of sport-specific cognitive and somatic trait anxiety: The Sport Anxiety Scale. *Anxiety Research, 2,* 263–280.

Taylor, J. (1995). A conceptual model for integrating athletes' needs and sport demands in the development of competitive mental preparation strategies. *The Sport Psychologist, 9,* 339–357.

Terry, P. C., Mayer, J. L., & Howe, B. L. (1998). Effectiveness of a mental training program for novice scuba divers. *Journal of Applied Sport Psychology, 10,* 251–267.

Tharp, R. G., & Gallimore, R. (1976, January). What a coach can teach a teacher. *Psychology Today,* 75–78.

Thelwell, R., & Greenlees, I. (2001). The effects of a mental skills training package on gymnasium triathlon performance. *The Sport Psychologist, 15,* 127–141

Thelwell, R., & Maynard, I. (2003). The effects of a mental skills training package on "repeatable" good performance in cricketers. *Psychology of Sport and Exercise, 4,* 377–386.

Tkachuk, G., Leslie-Toogood, A., & Martin, G. (2003). Behavioral assessment in sport psychology. *The Sport Psychologist, 17,* 104–117.

Van Schoyck, S. R., & Grasha, A. F. (1981). Attentional style variations and athletic ability. The advantages of a sports-specific test. *Journal of Sport Psychology, 3,* 149–165.

Vealey, R. S. (1986). Conceptualization of sport-confidence and competitive orientation: Preliminary investigation and instrument development. *Journal of Sport Psychology, 8,* 221–246.

Vealey, R. S. (1988). Future directions in psychological skills training. *The Sport Psychologist, 2,* 318–336.

Vealey, R. (1994). Current status and prominent issues in sport psychology interventions. *Medicine and Science in Sport and Exercise,* 495–502.

Vealey, R. S. (2007). Mental skills training in sport. In G. Tenenbaum & R. Eklund (Eds.). *Handbook of sport psychology* (3rd ed., pp. 287–309) New York: Wiley.

Ward, D., Sandstedt, S., Cox, R., & Beck, N. (2005). Athlete-counseling competencies for U.S. psychologists working with athletes. *The Sport Psychologist, 19,* 318–334.

Weinberg, R. S., & Comar, W. (1994). The effectiveness of psychological interventions in competitive sport. *Sports Medicine Journal, 18,* 406–418.

Weiss, M. R. (1991). Psychological skill development in children and adolescents. *The Sport Psychologist, 5,* 335–354.

Wescott, W. L. (1980). Effects of teacher modeling on children's peer encouragement behavior. *Research Quarterly, 51,* 585–587.

Whelan, J. P., Meyers, A. W., & Donovan, C. (1995). Competitive recreational athletes: A multisystemic model. In S. Murphy (Ed.), *Sport Psychology Interventions* (pp. 71–116). Champaign, IL: Human Kinetics.

Whelan, J. P., Meyers, A. W., & Elkin, D. (1996). Ethics in sport and exercise psychology. In J. L. Van Raalte and S. Brewer (Eds.), *Exploring sport and exercise psychology* (pp. 431–447). Washington, DC: American Psychological Association.

Williams, J. M., Jerome, G. J., Kenow, L. J., Rogers, T., Sartain, A., & Darland, G. (2003). Factoring structure of the coaching behavior questionnaire and its relationship to athlete variables. *The Sport Psychologist, 17,* 16–34.

Zizzi, S., & Perna, F. (2002). Integrating web pages and e-mail into sport psychology consultations. *The Sport Psychologist, 16,* 416–431.

Conducting Psychologically Oriented Coach-Training Programs: A Social-Cognitive Approach[1]

Frank L. Smoll, *University of Washington*
Ronald E. Smith, *University of Washington*

In this game, you're either a winner or a loser. Success means winning championships. Anything else is failure.

—George Allen, National Football League Hall of Fame coach

If you make winning games a life or death proposition, you're going to have problems. For one thing, you'll be dead a lot.

—Dean Smith, former University of North Carolina basketball coach

Success is peace of mind which is a direct result of self-satisfaction in knowing you made the effort to become the best you are capable of becoming.

—John Wooden, former UCLA basketball coach

The most heavily publicized area of sport psychology tends to be interventions for enhancing performance of elite athletes. However, youth sports is another domain that is equally worthy of attention. *Youth sports* refers to "adult-organized and controlled athletic programs for

[1]Preparation of this chapter was supported in part by Grant 2297 to Ronald E. Smith and Frank L. Smoll from the William T. Grant Foundation.

young people in the age range 6 to 18 years. The participants are formally organized into teams and leagues, and they attend practices and scheduled competitions under the supervision of an adult leader" (Smoll & Smith, 2002, p. xi). An estimated 41 million youngsters participate in nonschool sports, and approximately 6 to 7 million more take part in interscholastic athletics (Ewing & Seefeldt, 2002). Youth sports has seen continued growth over the past several decades, which has been accompanied by a greater degree of adult involvement as well (Martens, 1988; Weiss & Hayashi, 1996). These programs have become extremely complex social systems that have attracted the attention of researchers interested in studying the impact of competition on psychosocial development (see Brustad, Babkes, & Smith, 2001; Cahill & Pearl, 1993; Malina & Clark, 2003; Smoll & Smith, 2002; Weiss, 2004).

Youth sports are regarded as potentially important in child and adolescent development, and participation is believed to have direct relevance to the acquisition of prosocial attitudes and behaviors, such as respect for authority, cooperation, self-discipline, risk-taking, and the ability to tolerate frustration and to delay gratification (Coakley, 1993; Ewing, Seefeldt, & Brown, 1996; Martens, 1993; Scanlan, 2002; Smoll, 1989). Yet a realistic appraisal indicates that participation does not automatically result in these outcomes. The most important determinant of the effects of participation lies in the relationship between coach and athlete (Ewing, Seefeldt, & Brown, 1996; Martens, 2004; Smoll & Smith, 1989). Most coaches are fairly well versed in the technical aspects of the sport, but they rarely have had any formal training in creating a healthy psychological environment. It is here that sport psychologists are capable of making significant contributions, by developing and conducting educational programs that positively affect coaching behaviors and thereby increase the likelihood that youngsters will have positive sport experiences.

This chapter begins with an overview of the development of two interventions designed to assist coaches in relating more effectively to young athletes. Consideration is then given to cognitive-behavioral principles and techniques for implementing psychologically oriented coach-training programs. Although the focus throughout is on youth sports, the various methods and approaches are applicable to sport psychology workshops for coaches at virtually all levels of competition, including the professional ranks (Smith & Johnson, 1990).

Developing Coach-Training Programs

A crucial first step in developing training programs is to determine *what* is to be presented. In addressing this issue, our work was guided by a fundamental assumption that training programs should be based on scientific evidence rather than on intuition or what we "know" on the basis of informal observation. An empirical foundation for coaching guidelines not only enhances their validity and potential value, but also increases their credibility in the eyes of consumers.

Theoretical Model and Research Paradigm

Our approach to generating an empirical database was guided by a mediational model of coach–athlete interactions, the basic elements of which are represented as follows:

> COACH'S BEHAVIORS → ATHLETES' PERCEPTIONS AND RECALL → ATHLETES' EVALUATIVE REACTIONS

This model stipulates that the ultimate effects of coaching behaviors are mediated by the athletes' recall and the meaning they attribute to the coach's actions. In other words, what athletes remember about their coach's behaviors and how they interpret these actions affect the way athletes evaluate their sport experiences. Furthermore, a complex of cognitive and affective processes is involved at this mediational level. These processes are likely to be affected not only by the coach's behaviors but also by other factors, such as the athlete's age, what he or she expects of coaches (normative beliefs and expectations), and certain personality variables such as self-esteem and anxiety. The basic three-element model was expanded to reflect these factors (Smoll & Smith, 1989). The more comprehensive model specifies a number of situational as well as coach and athlete individual difference variables that are expected to influence coach behaviors and the perceptions and reactions of athletes to them.

In accordance with the model, we have sought to determine how observed coaching behaviors, athletes' perception and recall of the coach's behaviors, and athlete attitudes are inter-related. We have also explored the manner in which athlete and coach individual difference variables might serve as moderator variables and influence basic behavior–attitude relations.

Measurement of Coaching Behaviors

Several research groups have used behavioral assessment techniques to observe the actual behaviors of youth coaches and their effects on young athletes (see Smith, Smoll, & Christensen, 1996). To measure leadership behaviors, we developed the Coaching Behavior Assessment System (CBAS) to permit the direct observation and coding of coaches' actions during practices and games (Smith, Smoll, & Hunt, 1977). The behavioral categories, derived from content analyses of observers' verbal descriptions of coach behavior–situation units using a time-sampling procedure, are shown in Table 18-1.

The 12 CBAS categories are divided into two major classes of behaviors. *Reactive* (elicited) behaviors are responses to immediately preceding athlete or team behaviors, whereas *spontaneous* (emitted) behaviors are initiated by the coach and are not a response to a discernible preceding event. Use of the CBAS in observing and coding coaching behaviors in a variety of sports indicates that the scoring system is sufficiently comprehensive to incorporate the vast majority of overt leader behaviors, that high interrater reliability can be obtained, and that individual differences in behavioral patterns can be discerned (see Smith et al., 1996).

Coaching Behaviors and Children's Evaluative Reactions

Following development of the CBAS, a systematic program of research was carried out over a period of several years (Curtis, Smith, & Smoll, 1979; Smith & Smoll, 1990; Smith, Smoll, & Curtis, 1978; Smith, Zane, Smoll, & Coppel, 1983; Smoll, Smith, Curtis, & Hunt, 1978). This involved pursuing several questions concerning the potential impact of youth coaches on athletes' psychological welfare. For example, how frequently do coaches engage in behaviors such as encouragement, punishment, instruction, and organization, and how are observable coaching behaviors related to children's reactions to their organized athletic experiences? Answers to such questions not only were a first step in describing the behavioral ecology of one aspect of the youth sport setting, but also provided an empirical basis for the development of a psychologically oriented intervention program.

The results indicated that the typical baseball or basketball coach engages in more than 200 codable actions during an average game. We were thus able to generate behavioral profiles of up to several thousand responses over the course of a season. In large-scale observational studies, we coded more than 80,000 behaviors of some 70 male youth coaches, then interviewed and administered questionnaires after the season to nearly 1,000 children in their homes to measure their recall of their coaches' behaviors and their evaluative reactions to the coach, their sport experiences, and themselves. We also obtained coaches' postseason ratings of how frequently they engaged in each of the observed behaviors.

These data provided clear evidence for the crucial role of the coach. We found that win–loss records bore little relation to our psychosocial outcome measure (i.e., reactions to coach, enjoyment, and self-esteem); virtually all of the systematic variance was accounted for by differences in coaching behaviors. Not surprisingly, we found that the most positive outcomes occurred when children played for coaches who engaged in high levels of positive reinforcement for both desirable performance and effort, who responded to mistakes with encouragement and technical instruction, and who emphasized the importance of fun and personal improvement over winning. Not only did the children who had such coaches like their coaches more and have more fun, but they also liked their teammates more.

A recent study of 268 male and female youth basketball players yielded similar results to those discussed earlier (Cumming, Smoll, Smith, & Grossbard, 2007). The athletes' attitudes toward

Table 18-1 **Response Categories of the Coaching Behavior Assessment System**

Response Category	Behavioral Description
Class I: Reactive (Elicited) Behaviors	
Responses to desirable performance	
Reinforcement	A positive, rewarding reaction (verbal or nonverbal) to a good play or good effort
Nonreinforcement	Failure to respond to a good performance
Responses to mistakes	
Mistake-contingent encouragement	Encouragement given to an athlete following a mistake
Mistake-contingent technical instruction	Instructing or demonstrating to an athlete how to correct a mistake
Punishment	A negative reaction (verbal or nonverbal) following a mistake
Punitive technical instruction	Technical instruction following a mistake given in a punitive or hostile manner
Ignoring mistakes	Failure to respond to an athlete's mistake
Responses to misbehavior	
Keeping control	Reactions intended to restore or maintain order among team members
Class II: Spontaneous (Emitted) Behaviors	
Game related	
General technical instruction	Spontaneous instruction in the techniques and strategies of the sport (not following a mistake)
General encouragement	Spontaneous encouragement that does not follow a mistake
Organization	Administrative behavior that sets the stage for play by assigning, for example, duties, responsibilities, positions
Game irrelevant	
General communication	Interactions with athletes unrelated to the game/practice

Source: Adapted from Smith, Smoll, and Hunt, 1977.

the coach were positively associated with perceptions of a supportive, learning-oriented sport environment and negatively associated with perceptions of a coaching climate that emphasized gaining superiority over others. Win-loss percentages positively predicted players' evaluations of

their coach's knowledge and teaching ability, but accounted for far less attitudinal variance than did measures of the coaching climate. Moreover, young athletes' sport enjoyment and evaluations of their coach were more strongly related to coaching behaviors than to their team's win-loss record. Indeed, in terms of athletes' ratings of how much fun they had and how much they liked playing for their coach, our results showed that a positive coaching climate was about 10 times more influential than was the team's win-loss record.

Another important issue concerns the degree of accuracy with which coaches perceive their own behaviors. Correlations between CBAS-observed behaviors and coaches' ratings of how frequently they performed the behaviors were generally low and nonsignificant. The only actions on their self-report measure that correlated significantly (around .50) with the observational measures were the punitive behaviors. Overall, we found that children's ratings on the same perceived behavior scales correlated much more highly with CBAS measures than did the coaches' own reports! It thus appears that coaches were, for the most part, blissfully unaware of how they behaved and that athletes were more accurate perceivers of actual coach behaviors. Because behavior change requires an awareness of how one currently is behaving, this finding clearly indicated the need to increase coaches' self-awareness when developing an intervention program.

The data from one of our field studies were also used to test a hypothesis derived from a self-enhancement model of self-esteem (Smith & Smoll, 1990). This model posits that people who are low in self-esteem are particularly responsive to variations in supportiveness from others because they have a strong need for positive feedback from others (or, alternatively, because they find a lack of support to be highly aversive). This hypothesis was strongly supported by the data; the greatest difference in liking for supportive (reinforcing and encouraging) versus nonsupportive coaches was found for children who were low in self-esteem. Also consistent with a self-enhancement model, boys with low self-esteem showed the greatest difference in attraction toward (i.e., liking for) coaches who were either quite high or quite low on a behavioral dimension identified through factor analysis as instructiveness (general technical instruction and mistake-contingent technical instruction

versus general communication and general encouragement). Instructiveness should be relevant to self-enhancement because athletes are likely to perceive such behaviors as contributing to skill increments that would increase positive self-regard.

Assessing the Efficacy of a Coach-Training Program

Sweeping conclusions are often drawn about the efficacy of intervention programs in the absence of anything approximating acceptable scientific evidence. We therefore felt it was important not only to develop an empirical foundation for a coach-training program but also to measure its effects on coaches and the youngsters who play for them.

Our intervention, which is known as Coach Effectiveness Training (CET), was conceptualized within a cognitive-behavioral framework (Bandura, 1986). It was specifically designed to train coaches to provide a more positive and socially supportive athletic environment for their young athletes. In an initial field experiment (Smith, Smoll, & Curtis, 1979), 31 Little League Baseball coaches were randomly assigned either to an experimental (training) group or to a no-treatment control group. During a preseason CET workshop, behavioral guidelines derived from our earlier research were presented and modeled by the trainers. In addition to the information-modeling portion of the program, behavioral feedback and self-monitoring procedures were employed in an attempt to increase the coaches' self-awareness of their behaviors and to encourage them to comply with the coaching guidelines. To provide behavioral feedback, observers trained in the use of the CBAS observed experimental group coaches for two complete games. Behavioral profiles for each coach were derived from these observations and were then mailed to the coaches so that they were able to see the distribution of their own behaviors. Trained coaches were also given brief self-monitoring forms that they completed immediately after the first 10 games of the season.

To assess the effects of the experimental program, CBAS data were collected throughout the season, and behavioral profiles were generated for each coach in the experimental and control groups. Postseason outcome measures were obtained from 325 children in individual data collection sessions in their homes. On both observed behavior and player perception measures, the trained coaches differed from the controls in a manner consistent with the coaching guidelines. The trained coaches gave more reinforcement in response to good performance and effort, and they responded to mistakes with more encouragement and technical instruction and with fewer punitive responses. These behavioral differences were, in turn, reflected in their players' attitudes. Although the average win-loss percentages of the two groups of coaches did not differ, the trained coaches were better liked and were rated as better teachers. Additionally, players on their teams liked one another more and enjoyed their sport experiences more. These results seemingly reflect the more socially supportive environment created by the trained coaches. Perhaps most encouraging was the fact that children who played for the trained coaches exhibited a significant increase on a measure of general self-esteem compared to scores obtained a year earlier, while those who played for the untrained coaches showed no significant change.

Replication of our research on the efficacy of CET has been conducted with the inclusion of several additional outcomes measures. The study included 18 coaches and 152 children who participated in three Little League Baseball programs. Using a quasi-experimental design, one league (eight teams) was designated as the experimental group. The no-treatment control group included 10 teams from two other leagues. Prior to the season, the experimental group coaches participated in CET. The control coaches participated in a technical skills training workshop conducted by the Seattle Mariners baseball team. To assess the effects of CET, preseason and postseason data were collected for 62 and 90 children in the experimental and control groups, respectively.

The study yielded four major results. First, the CET intervention resulted in player-perceived behavioral differences between trained and untrained coaches that were consistent with the behavioral guidelines. Thus, as in previous research (Smith et al., 1979), the experimental manipulation was successful in promoting a more desirable pattern of coaching behaviors. Second, the behavioral differences resulting from the CET program were accompanied by player evaluative responses that favored the trained coaches. The trained coaches were better liked and were rated as better teachers by their players. Moreover, their players reported that they had more fun playing baseball, and a higher level of attraction among teammates was again found, despite the fact that their teams did not differ from controls in win-loss records. Third, consistent with a self-esteem enhancement model, children with low self-esteem who played for the trained coaches exhibited a significant increase in general self-esteem over the course of the season; youngsters with low self-esteem in the control group did not change (Smoll, Smith, Barnett, & Everett, 1993). Fourth, the children who played for the CET coaches manifested lower levels of performance anxiety than did the control children (Smith, Smoll, & Barnett, 1995).

An extension of the above study was completed one year after the CET intervention. At the beginning of the next baseball season, dropout rates were assessed for youngsters who had played for the two groups of coaches. The results showed a 26% dropout rate among the control group, a figure that was quite consistent with previous reports of 22% to 59% annual attrition rates in youth sport programs (Gould, 1987). In contrast, only 5% of the children who had played for the CET-trained coaches failed to return to the sport program in the next season (Barnett, Smoll, & Smith, 1992).

Other sport psychologists have utilized our research findings and CET principles in developing psychologically oriented training programs for youth sport coaches. Evaluations of the derivative interventions have shown positive changes in both observed and athlete-perceived coaching behaviors that are consistent with the interventions' behavioral guidelines. Moreover, evidence indicates that young athletes who played for trained coaches experienced beneficial effects as reflected by measures of their psychosocial development (e.g., Coatsworth & Conroy, 2006; Conroy & Coatsworth, 2004; Sousa, Cruz, Torregrosa, Vilches, & Viladrich, 2006; Sousa, Smith, & Cruz, 2008).

Achievement Goals, Motivational Climate, and Coaching

The sport environment is inherently a competence and achievement context. Consequently, motivational factors play an important role in determining the ultimate effects of participation on psychosocial development. As a theoretical framework, achievement goal theory provides an appropriate vantage point from which to explore factors (e.g., coach behaviors) that might affect motivated behavior in youth sports. Achievement goal theory (Ames, 1992a; Dweck, 1999; Nicholls, 1989) focuses on understanding the function and the meaning of goal directed actions, based on how participants define ability and how they judge whether or not they have demonstrated competence. Although a variety of variables are incorporated into achievement goal theory (e.g., goal states, attributions, fear of failure, self-perceived competence, incremental and entity implicit theories of competence), two of the central constructs have received particular attention in the sport literature namely, individual *goal orientations* that guide achievement perceptions and behavior, and the *motivational climate* created within adult-controlled achievement settings. An overview of these constructs as related to coach-athlete interactions follows. Comprehensive discussions of achievement goal theory and its implications for coaching practice appear elsewhere (e.g., Chapter 4; Duda & Balaguer, 2007; Duda & Ntoumanis, 2005; Roberts, Treasure, & Conroy, 2007).

Goal orientations.   In essence, goal orientations involve the criteria individuals use to define success. This dispositional variable is a product of

and contributes to (along with situational factors) goal involvement states in achievement situations. Achievement goal theory focuses on mastery and ego orientations and states. When an individual is in a mastery state, success is defined in a self-referenced manner and is focused on skill development, task mastery, and exerting maximum effort. In a sense, mastery-oriented people compare themselves with themselves. They can feel success and satisfaction when they have learned something new, witnessed skill improvement in themselves, or given maximum effort.

In an ego state, social comparison plays a major role in self-perceived success, and the emphasis is on outperforming others in order to attain recognition and status. Thus, ego-oriented people define success as winning or being better than others. They are always comparing themselves with others and don't feel successful unless they view themselves as performing better than others. Anything short of victory is failure and indicates to them that they are inferior.

Historically, several different labels have been attached to the two major classes of achievement goal orientations. *Mastery* and *task* have been used interchangeably by various theorists and researchers, as have *ego* and *performance* (e.g., Ames, 1992a, 1992b; Duda & Whitehead, 1998; Dweck, 1986; Midgely et al., 2000; Nicholls, 1989; Roberts, Treasure, & Kavussanu, 1997). We find the terms *mastery* and *ego* to be more semantically meaningful in relation to the underlying constructs, as well as the characteristics of the measures developed to assess them (Cumming, Smith, Smoll, Standage, & Grossbard, 2008; Smith, Cumming, & Smoll, 2008). Thus, we have chosen these labels for use in our work.

Motivational climate.   Achievement goal theory also addresses environmental factors that foster mastery or ego involvement. Because achievement behavior is influenced by interacting personal and situational factors, situational factors can predispose individuals to enter particular goal states and, over time, to acquire a disposition toward experiencing mastery or ego goal states. This is influenced, however, by the way in which relevant adults structure the situation and define success (Ames, 1992a, 1992b). A mastery climate is one in which teachers, coaches, or parents define success in terms of self-improvement, task mastery, and exhibiting maximum effort and dedication. In such a climate, students and athletes tend to adopt adaptive achievement strategies such as selecting challenging tasks, giving maximum effort, persisting in the face of setbacks, and taking pride in personal improvement. In both academic and sport settings, a wide range of salutary outcomes have been linked to a mastery-involving motivational climate, including a stronger mastery orientation on the part of participants, greater enjoyment and satisfaction, stronger intrinsic and self-determination motivation, group cohesion, and lower levels of performance anxiety.

In contrast, an ego-involving climate promotes social comparison as a basis for success judgments and tends to foster an ego achievement orientation. When coaches create an ego climate, they tend to give differential attention and concentrate positive reinforcement on athletes who are most competent and instrumental to winning, the importance of which is emphasized. Rivalry among teammates may be encouraged by comparing them openly with one another. Inadequate performance or mistakes are often punished with criticism, teaching athletes that mistakes are to be avoided at all costs and thereby building fear of failure. Another unfortunate outcome associated with ego environments is the willingness to win at all costs, even if rule-breaking is required to gain the needed advantage.

The Mastery Approach to Coaching

Inspired in part by the impressive research outcomes associated with a mastery-oriented climate, we redesigned CET to fit the framework of achievement goal theory. The new program, which is called the Mastery Approach to Coaching (MAC), incorporates content on goal orientations and motivational climate and includes specific guidelines on how to create a mastery climate. Accordingly, MAC behavioral guidelines focus on two major themes. First, it strongly emphasizes the distinction between positive versus aversive control of behavior (see Chapter 3). In a series of coaching *do's* and *don'ts* derived from the foundational research on coaching behaviors and their effects, coaches are encouraged to increase four specific behaviors—positive reinforcement, mistake-contingent encouragement, corrective instruction given in a positive and encouraging fashion, and sound technical instruction. Coaches are urged to avoid nonreinforcement of positive behaviors, punishment for mistakes, and punitive technical instruction following mistakes. They are also instructed how to establish team rules and reinforce compliance with them to avoid discipline problems, and to reinforce socially supportive behaviors among team members. These guidelines, which are summarized in Appendix A, are designed to increase positive coach-athlete interactions, enhance team solidarity, reduce fear of failure, and promote a positive atmosphere for skill development (Smith & Smoll, 2002).

The second important theme in MAC guidelines, derived from CET and also from achievement goal theory and research, is a conception of success as giving maximum effort and becoming the best one can be, rather than an emphasis on winning or outperforming others. Coaches are encouraged to emphasize and reinforce effort as well as outcome, to help their athletes become the best they can be by giving individualized attention to all athletes and by setting personalized goals for improvement, to define success as maximizing one's athletic potential, and to emphasize the importance of having fun and getting better as opposed to winning at all costs. Like the guidelines that foster positive coach-athlete relations and team solidarity, these guidelines are designed to reduce fear of failure, to foster self-esteem enhancement by allowing athletes to take personal pride in effort and improvement, and to create a more enjoyable learning environment that increases intrinsic motivation for the activity. The behavioral guidelines are thus consistent with the procedures designed by Ames (1992a, 1992b) and Epstein (1988, 1989) to create a mastery learning climate in the classroom.

In the tradition of CET, a field experiment was conducted to assess the effects of the newly evolved intervention on coaches' behaviors and on the athletes who played for them (Smith, Smoll, & Cumming, 2007; Smoll, Smith, & Cumming, 2007). Prior to the season, an experimental group of 20 basketball coaches participated in a 75-minute version of MAC. A control group of 16 coaches received no training. A total sample of 225 boys and girls, ranging in age from 10 to 14 years, responded to a variety of measures prior to and at the end of the season. Hierarchical linear modeling (multilevel modeling) analyses revealed several major findings.

- Late-season differences in athletes' reports of the coach-initiated motivational climate clearly supported the efficacy of the MAC intervention. In this regard, coaches in the experimental condition received significantly higher mastery-climate scores and lower ego-climate scores.

- In line with previous research on sport attrition (Barnett et al., 1992), youth who played for trained coaches were more likely to stay engaged on a daily basis in the program.

- Differential patterns of change occurred in achievement goal orientations over the course of the season. Athletes who played for MAC-trained coaches exhibited increases in mastery goal orientation scores and significant decreases in ego orientation scores. In contrast, athletes who played for control group coaches did not change in their goal orientations from preseason to late season.

- Paralleling a significant difference between intervention and control groups in sport-related mastery scores, a significant group difference was found on the mastery score of an academic achievement goal scale. This result suggests the importance of assessing generalization effects of sport-related interventions on athletes' functioning in other life domains.

- Young athletes who played for MAC-trained coaches showed significant decreases in both physical and mental components of sport anxiety, whereas control group youngsters increased in these measures across the season.

- The MAC intervention had equally positive effects on boys' and girls' teams.

Finally, some issues regarding experimental design deserve mention. In our initial CET field experiment, coaches were randomly assigned to the conditions (Smith et al., 1979). Fortunately, there was no difference in the mean win-loss percentages of teams coached by the experimental and control group coaches. Team success (winning) was thus ruled out as a plausible explanation for the differences obtained in the outcome variables. In the replication and extension studies, assignment to the experimental or control group was made by league rather than within leagues (Barnett et al., 1992; Smoll et al., 1993; Smith et al., 1995). Similarly, a matched quasi-experimental design was utilized in our recent evaluation of MAC (Smith et al., 2007; Smoll et al., 2007). Use of separate, intact groups helped to ensure the integrity of the intervention by reducing the possibility of contamination (communication of training guidelines to control coaches). Moreover, this procedure guaranteed that the average win-loss records of the teams in the experimental and control conditions would be an identical 50%.

Implementing Sport Psychology Workshops for Coaches

Creating a Positive Learning Environment

The most basic objectives of MAC and other sport psychology training programs are to communicate coaching principles in a way that is easy to understand and to maximize the likelihood that coaches will adopt the information. Because of this, the importance of creating a positive learning environment cannot be overemphasized.

Even the very best program is of little value if presented in a way that creates antagonism and defensiveness on the part of coaches.

There are several considerations in setting the stage for a successful session. The primary key is to convey respect for the participating coaches. They really deserve it! Indeed, without their unselfish involvement, there could be no organized youth sports.

Next, at the very outset of a training session we emphasize that the coaches themselves have a great deal to offer as a result of their own experiences and associated practical knowledge. We attempt to take advantage of their expertise by encouraging them to share it with the group. In conducting a MAC workshop as a two-way sharing of information, coaches are treated as an integral part of the session rather than a mere audience. The open atmosphere for exchange promotes active rather than passive learning, and the dialogue serves to enhance the participants' interest and involvement in the learning process.

A final key to successful program implementation is to put a considerable amount of sincere enthusiasm into leading the session. When a trainer truly enjoys his or her pedagogical role, the pleasurable feeling ultimately carries over to the coaches. In such an atmosphere, attention and audience involvement is likely to be enhanced, increasing the enjoyment of coaches and trainer alike.

In contrast to the above, three strategies are virtually guaranteed to create hostility and resistance from coaches. One is to approach coaches in a condescending manner. In other words, the thing *not* to do is communicate how much you think you know and how little they know. An associated implication concerns the way a trainer is introduced at the beginning of a session. We recommend against presenting an extensive list of credentials and professional accomplishments, which tends to convey an air of elitism. Another contraindicated approach is to intimate that your training program is designed to protect athletes from coaches. Indeed, most volunteer coaches have commendable motives for coaching (Martens & Gould, 1979; Smith et al., 1978),

and they generally make positive contributions to children's well-being. A final breach is to convey the impression that what the coaches have been doing is incorrect. Rather, we emphasize that many options are available for dealing with particular coaching situations, and although all of these tactics may work in *some* cases, certain procedures have a greater likelihood than others of being successful. By counteracting the notion of "right versus wrong," we stress the importance of flexibility and thus attempt to make coaches receptive to alternative ways of responding to specific circumstances.

Orientation to the Psychology of Coaching and a Mastery-Oriented Philosophy of Winning

In introducing the psychology of coaching, workshop participants should first be made aware of the importance of their role as coaches. Some coaches underestimate their influence, and they must be reminded of the many ways they can affect young athletes. Information and increased awareness of what they are doing can help them optimize the desirable effects they can have on young athletes.

It is generally believed that young athletes can learn from both winning and losing. But for this to occur, winning must be placed in a *healthy* perspective. We have therefore developed a four-part philosophy of winning that is taught in MAC (Smith & Smoll, 2002, pp. 16–18):

1. *Winning isn't everything, nor is it the only thing.* Young athletes cannot get the most out of sports if they think that the only objective is to beat their opponents. Although winning is an important goal, it is not the most important objective.

2. *Failure is not the same thing as losing.* It is important that athletes do not view losing as a sign of failure or as a threat to their personal value.

3. *Success is not equivalent to winning.* Neither success nor failure need depend on the outcome of a contest or on a win-loss record.

Winning and losing pertain to the outcome of a contest, whereas success and failure do not.

4. *Athletes should be taught that success is found in striving for victory (that is, success is related to commitment and effort).* Athletes should be taught that they are never "losers" if they give maximum effort.

This philosophy is designed to maximize young athletes' enjoyment of sport and their chances of deriving the benefits of participation, partly as a result of combating competitive anxiety (Smith, Smoll, & Passer, 2002). Although seeking victory is encouraged, the ultimate importance of winning is reduced relative to other participation motives. In recognition of the inverse relation between enjoyment and postcompetition stress, *fun* is highlighted as the paramount objective. The philosophy also promotes separation of the athlete's feelings of self-worth from the game's outcome, which serves to help overcome fear of failure.

Because they tend to project adult values onto children, many coaches seem to believe that how their athletes feel about them hinges on how successfully the team performs. Yet, as noted earlier, our own research has shown that differences in coaching behaviors consistently accounted for significantly more variance in player attitudes toward the coach than did win-loss records (Cumming, Smoll, et al., 2007; Smith et al., 1978). Stressing this finding to coaches tends to make them more receptive to the philosophy of winning that we espouse.

Presenting an Empirical Basis for Coach-Training Programs

We believe in the importance of establishing an empirical foundation for training guidelines, but we also feel that the ability to present supportive evidence increases the credibility of the guidelines for the coaches. A MAC workshop therefore includes a description of the differences between a mastery- and ego-oriented motivational climate. The creation of a mastery climate

is strongly recommended, and a list of salutary effects of such a climate is presented.

A number of considerations underlie our commitment to presenting empirical results. First of all, expertise (special knowledge) and trustworthiness (the quality of meriting confidence) are two critically important variables in communicating credibility (Hovland, Janis, & Kelley, 1953; Petty & Wegener, 1998). Both are enhanced when data are presented rather than intuitive beliefs. Coaches have greater confidence in a training program when they know the content is not merely composed of armchair psychology or athletic folklore. Second, the presence of empirical data arouses the curiosity and involvement of the participants. Coaches show a great deal of interest in the research, which stimulates their active involvement in the workshop. Also, presentation of unexpected results prevents either the trainer or the coaches from believing they already know all the answers. Third, the ability to demonstrate empirically that certain behaviors have positive effects on children serves to arouse the expectation that the coaches can produce similar effects if they themselves apply the behavioral guidelines. This may increase their motivation to learn and apply the information.

There are some practical points to be aware of in presenting empirical results. Trainers should use lay terms and avoid scientific jargon. It is best to present data as simply as possible and to avoid technical details. In addition, appropriate use of visual aids enhances any presentation. Diagrams and cartoons illustrating certain concepts, and tables summarizing important principles, serve to facilitate comprehension and retention.

Behavioral Guidelines and Their Presentation

The core of a MAC training session consists of a series of empirically derived behavioral guidelines. As discussed earlier, the coaching guidelines are based primarily on (a) social influence techniques that involve principles of positive control rather than aversive control, and (b) a mastery-oriented philosophy of winning.

Didactic procedures. In a MAC workshop, behavioral guidelines are presented both verbally and in a printed manual given to the coaches. The manual (Smoll & Smith, 2008) supplements the guidelines with concrete suggestions for communicating effectively with young athletes, gaining their respect, and relating effectively to their parents. The importance of sensitivity and being responsive to individual differences among athletes is also stressed. The manual eliminates the need for coaches to take notes; it facilitates their understanding of the information; and it gives coaches a tangible resource to refer to in the future.

Audiovisual aids to a presentation are necessary for providing a multisensory stimulus and for countering the potential influence of "verbalism"—the tendency to place excessive reliance on words. In MAC, animated PowerPoint slides and cartoons illustrating important points are used to present key principles and add to the organizational quality of the session. A word of caution is in order here. We have witnessed the collapse of several commendable presentations because of the failure of one or more electronic devices. Murphy's Law—if anything can go wrong it will—should be taken seriously when preparing to give a coaching workshop that includes audio or visual aids. An essential *preworkshop* procedure should thus include an operational check of each piece of equipment. (See Howell and Borman [1997] for an overview of audio and visual aids and their use.)

In introducing coaching guidelines, we emphasize that they should not be viewed as a "magic formula" and that mere knowledge of the principles is not sufficient. We stress that the challenge is not so much in learning the principles; they are relatively simple. Rather, the challenge is for the coach to integrate the guidelines into his or her own coaching style. When coaches believe that adoption of the guidelines is a result of their own dedication and effort, they are more likely to attribute behavioral changes

to themselves rather than to the trainer. This approach is supported by evidence that self-attributed behavioral changes are more enduring than those attributed to some outside causal agent (Deci & Ryan, 1987).

As noted earlier, MAC workshops are conducted with an interactive format to encourage active participatory learning (Brookfield, 2004). Efforts are made to draw coaches into a discussion of the guidelines as opposed to using an exclusively lecture-type approach. This is accomplished by directing questions to the coaches and then relating their responses to the written materials. To use this instructional style, a trainer must be well versed in the practical ramifications of the guidelines, their applicability to various kinds of coaching situations, and the kinds of questions they are likely to elicit from coaches.

A practical problem occurs when coaches ask questions that are unrelated to the topic being covered. For example, during a discussion of principles of reinforcement, a coach might inquire about formulating team rules. Our experience indicates that answering such questions disrupts the sequencing and continuity of concepts, which causes confusion for some coaches. A tactful procedure is to politely ask the coach to write down the question and to indicate when he or she should repeat the query.

What are the secrets of effective, engaging presentations? In answering this question, Chamberlin (2000) interviewed six university faculty, each of whom was known for delivering outstanding lectures. Their recommendations are presented here, along with comments by the professors.

- *Prepare, prepare, prepare.* Practicing the workshop is an excellent way to thoroughly learn the material and feel comfortable speaking and answering questions about the content. "Saying it out loud will highlight the sticky points and give you a chance to smooth those out beforehand. It feels like you run the risk of making the lecture stale, but the energy in the classroom will bring it to life and you feel like you are doing it for the first time" (p. 63). Some experienced teachers bring notes or a script to every class—even for those they have done dozens of times—and advise against trying to conduct a session cold. As one expert states, "I may never look at my typed notes, but I always have them there as a security blanket" (p. 63).

- *Find your style.* Seasoned lecturers warn about the mistake of emulating a mentor or favorite instructor. Rather, they emphasize the importance of performing in a way that reflects your own style. "Your personality is a part of your lecturing so you have to lecture in a way that is comfortable to your personality" (p. 63). In other words, do what feels right. And, as noted earlier, whatever your approach, make enthusiasm a big part of it. "Enthusiasm is infectious. If you're not excited about the material, they're not going to be either" (p. 63).

- *Spice it up.* The use of intermittent stories and anecdotes can enliven your presentation. Weaving in personal sport stories or linking coaching principles to current research and events helps keep workshop participants engaged. One trap to avoid is relying solely on computer graphics and technology to add flavor to a workshop. As a master teacher claims, "I have sat through far too many sleep-inducing PowerPoint presentations that have had a lot of power and no point" (p. 63).

- *Cover less, not more.* Another pitfall is packing too much content into a workshop because of the fear that coaches will not learn certain material if it is not included in the session. Trainers who try to cover too much inevitably end up going too fast. In this regard, "Less is more. . . . Go slowly and thoughtfully through the material" (p. 64). Additionally, one of the benefits of providing participants with a workshop manual is that they can obtain considerable information by reading on their own.

- *Make improvements.* Avoid doing the same thing over and over, even though it is not working. If your presentation style is not

effective, be committed and courageous enough to change it. An initial step toward improvement is to find out how you are doing by asking coaches for feedback, especially if you feel they are not responding well to your style or are not learning. Furthermore, do not get discouraged when you have a bad workshop. With sufficient dedication and effort, you will nail it and feel great the next time.

Credibility and persuasiveness.   A primary goal of our instructional approach is to change coaches' attitudes about some of their roles and responsibilities and about their use of certain coaching behaviors. Several aspects of the persuasion process, such as credibility, trustworthiness, likeability, and novelty, are utilized and have proven to be effective in a variety of intervention contexts (see Petty & Wegener, 1998; Taylor, Peplau, & Sears, 2005; Worchel, Cooper, & Goethals, 1991). In terms of personal characteristics, a highly *credible* communicator is more effective in changing attitudes than one with low credibility. As Galbraith (2004) emphasized, "common sense tells us that being technically proficient in the content area within the teaching and learning encounter is paramount if it is going to have some meaning and value" (p. 4). Although the best-qualified workshop presenter would be a certified sport psychologist/consultant (e.g., through the Association for Applied Sport Psychology), a well-structured "train the trainer" program should allow a youth sport administrator to present a satisfactory version. However, this hypothesis requires empirical validation.

Credibility is a multifaceted concept that seems to be a function of at least *expertise* and *trustworthiness*. As stated earlier, we endeavor to establish expertise in MAC by substantiating the content with empirical evidence from our own work and from the research of other sport psychologists as well. With respect to trusting a communicator's intentions, credibility increases when the communicator does not appear to be purposefully trying to persuade the target (i.e., coaches in this case). We therefore present information and coaching guidelines objectively, and as noted earlier, we specifically avoid a "right versus wrong" orientation. In addition, because unexpected positions are generally seen as more trustworthy, we inform coaches that although we have been studying coach–athlete interactions for more than 30 years we simply do not have all the answers, and in some cases one must be willing to say, "I don't know." The honesty of such disclosures likely contributes to credibility.

The perceived *similarity* between a communicator and the target of the message affects the power of persuasion. To increase the degree of perceived similarity with coaches, we customarily dress in a fairly casual style. More important, while leading discussions, we share examples from our own experiences as athletes and coaches, and we often phrase comments with a "we" versus "you" perspective.

The communicator's *likability* also affects the efficacy of persuasion. Because liking works by identification, we try to create a warm, friendly rapport with coaches—partly by showing enjoyment in being with them and by expressing caring for them. Empirical work from the communication studies literature suggests that teachers' behavioral cues of interpersonal warmth and students' perceptions of those behaviors are predictive of a variety of desirable learning outcomes, including students' liking for the material and their intentions to act on what they have learned (Friedrich & Douglass, 1998). Accordingly, we strive to be more persuasive agents by honestly and sincerely engaging in behaviors that are known to communicate caring for learners, such as gesturing while lecturing, modulating one's voice, making eye contact, smiling, and self-disclosing. Reciprocity is another factor that increases liking: People tend to like those who like them. We communicate our high esteem for coaches by praising their commitment to providing high-quality sport experiences for young athletes. Listening ability is yet another factor in being likable. By encouraging coaches to express themselves freely, and by listening attentively to them when they do, we are better able to conduct a MAC workshop as a mutual sharing of information.

In addition to characteristics of the communicator, several facets of the message affect its persuasiveness. Coaches are generally not opposed to the points of view advocated in MAC, so we usually present *one-sided* communications. In some instances, however, a we use *two-sided* presentation. This involves more than just acknowledging that another side exists. Rather, this approach analyzes contrary perspectives to point out their deficiencies and thus strengthen our position. For example, in discussing recommendations relative to reinforcement, the coaching guidelines are developed fully, and their beneficial effects are substantiated with empirical evidence. Then, when aversive control is considered, we proceed to point out the disadvantages of using punitive coaching behaviors. (See Chapter 3 for a discussion of the negative side effects of punishment.)

Using *rhetorical questions* is another way of influencing attitudes. We ask coaches rhetorical questions (questions to which no answer is expected) to stimulate their thinking and to make them pay closer attention to a communication. For example, "What is the best way to maintain order and teach self-discipline?"

Novelty of information also affects the message's impact. Some coaches may have had previous exposure to some of MAC's behavioral guidelines. We attempt to make the principles seem unique by using diagrams, charts, and cartoons for their presentation.

Finally, *humor* can enhance the persuasiveness of messages. If used properly, humor can loosen up a potentially tense atmosphere, make people feel good, increase their responsiveness, and reveal a more human side of the speaker (Barker & Gaut, 2002). Moreover, research suggests that humor produces psychological and physiological benefits that help students learn (Stambor, 2006). We use humorous anecdotes whenever possible—not primarily for entertainment but as an educational tool to help emphasize certain points and make concepts memorable. This objective is best accomplished by strongly establishing the link between humor and the point to be made such that coaches remember the key point, not just the good joke or story (Farrah, 2004).

Modeling. The instructional procedures described above contain many *verbal* modeling cues that essentially tell coaches what to do. Information is also transmitted through *behavioral* modeling cues (i.e., demonstrations showing coaches how to behave in desirable ways). In MAC such cues are presented by a live model (the trainer) and by symbolic models (animated coach cartoons), as many forms of modeling have been shown to be highly effective in changing behavior (Bandura, 1986; Perry & Furukawa, 1986).

Role playing. Coaches are kept actively involved in the training process through presentation of critical situations and opportunities for them to role-play appropriate ways of responding. This form of behavioral rehearsal has great promise in enhancing acquisition of desired behaviors, in providing the opportunity to practice the behaviors, and in establishing an increased level of participant involvement during the workshops.

Increasing Self-Awareness and Compliance with Coaching Guidelines

One of the striking findings from our basic research was that coaches had very limited awareness of how often they behaved in various ways (Smith et al., 1978). Thus, an important goal of MAC is to increase coaches' awareness of what they are doing, for no change is likely to occur without it. MAC coaches are taught the use of two proven behavioral-change techniques, namely, behavioral feedback and self-monitoring.

Behavioral feedback. To obtain feedback, coaches are encouraged to work with their assistants as a team and share descriptions of each other's behaviors (Edelstein & Eisler, 1976; McFall & Twentyman, 1973). They can discuss alternate ways of dealing with difficult situations and athletes and prepare themselves for dealing with similar situations in the future. Other potential feedback procedures include coaches soliciting input from athletes and provision of feedback by a league committee.

Self-monitoring. Another behavioral-change technique that has the potential for increasing coaches' awareness of their own behavioral patterns and encouraging their compliance with the guidelines is self-monitoring (observing and recording one's own behavior). This method of self-regulation has proved to be an effective behavioral-change procedure in a variety of intervention contexts (Kanfer & Gaelick-Buys, 1991; Kazdin, 1974; McFall, 1977). Because it is impractical to have coaches monitor and record their own behavior during practices or games, the workshop manual contains a brief self-monitoring form. Coaches are encouraged to complete the form immediately after practices and games (see Appendix B). Self-monitoring is restricted to desired behaviors in light of evidence that tracking undesired behaviors can be detrimental to effective self-regulation (Cavior & Marabotto, 1976; Gottman & McFall, 1972; Kirschenbaum & Karoly, 1977). Coaches are encouraged to engage in self-monitoring on a regular basis to achieve optimal results.

Additional procedures. In addition to feedback and self-monitoring, some other procedures might be valuable for increasing awareness and compliance with guidelines. For example, one or more follow-up meetings might be held with coaches during which they discuss their experiences in utilizing the guidelines and the effects that the behaviors seem to be having on their athletes. Follow-up may also occur through telephone contacts with individual coaches by the trainer. Finally, brief questionnaires may be designed and sent to coaches. Such questionnaires may be used not only to elicit information from the coaches but also to provide refresher points that will help maintain or increase compliance with coaching guidelines.

A Final Word

Given the ever-expanding nature of youth sports, the need for effective coach-training programs is obvious. Likewise, the large coach turnover from year to year creates a continuing demand for intervention. Our experience in offering workshops has shown that youth coaches are committed to providing positive experiences for youngsters. It is also reassuring to note that coaches are willing to spend time to acquire additional information, and they do take advantage of the availability of workshops. An important feature of MAC is that it is a brief program that focuses on a relatively small number of critical principles and guidelines that clearly make a difference.

In concluding this chapter, it is appropriate to restate our firm belief that extended efforts to improve the quality and value of coach-training programs are best achieved via well-conceived and properly conducted evaluation research. We agree wholeheartedly with Weiss and Hayashi (1996), who concluded that "evaluation research is essential to determine the effectiveness of . . . training programs on increasing sport science knowledge and applications" (p. 53). Future collaboration between sport psychologists and youth sport organizations not only will serve to advance understanding of the effects of competition but also will provide for enriched opportunities for children and youth in sport.

Summary

We have described the development and evaluation of an empirically supported intervention designed to assist coaches in providing a more positive and growth-inducing athletic experience for athletes. This chapter provides guidelines in how to present such a program. We describe the principles and ways we have found successful in presenting them with maximum positive impact. As noted in the chapter, there are several virtues of presenting a program that is based on scientific data rather than on "experiential knowledge" or speculation. First, you can have greater confidence in the principles you are presenting. Even more important is the approach you can take in presenting the principles. You can present your workshop as informational in nature. In other words, you can play to coaches' desire to provide the best possible experience for youngsters (the prevailing motivation for most volunteer coaches). You are not telling them what they "should do," but rather what research has shown to be effective in helping them meet their goals and how they can incorporate these findings into their own coaching style. We have always found coaches receptive to this approach. By communicating simple but sound principles and showing coaches how to implement them and become more self-aware, you provide tools that they can apply immediately. Once they begin doing so, the positive responses from athletes and the reduced need to maintain discipline through punitive means provide powerful sources of reinforcement that strengthen and maintain the new behaviors. Many a coach has reported that applying the MAC principles resulted in the most enjoyable season they had experienced in their coaching tenures, an outcome that is highly reinforcing to the trainer as well.

Study Questions

1. Describe the three basic elements of the mediational model of coach–athlete interactions that served to guide the coaching-behavior research.

2. What are the two major classes of behaviors included in the CBAS, and what is the difference between them?

3. Following development of the CBAS, field studies were conducted to establish relations between coaching behaviors and children's evaluative reactions. Describe the basic research procedures, and discuss the major findings with respect to (a) the role of winning relative to athletes' psychosocial outcome measures, (b) relations between coaching behaviors and athletes' attitudinal responses, (c) the degree of accuracy with which coaches perceived their own behaviors, and (d) the role of self-esteem as a mediator variable in coaching behavior–athlete attitude relations.

4. Describe the research design and methodology incorporated in the studies that tested the efficacy of CET. What were the results with respect to (a) behavioral differences between trained and untrained coaches, (b) win-loss records, (c) players' evaluative reactions to trained and untrained coaches, (d) self-esteem effects, (e) competitive anxiety differences between youngsters who played for trained and untrained coaches, and (f) dropout rates?

5. With respect to achievement goal theory, what are the distinctions between (a) mastery and ego goal orientations, and (b) mastery and ego motivational climates?

6. Briefly describe the (a) major behavioral guidelines (i.e., coaching *do's* and *don'ts*), and (b) mastery-oriented philosophy of winning that are emphasized in the MAC program.

7. For the field experiment that was conducted to assess the efficacy of MAC, what were the results with respect to (a) differences between the motivational climates created by trained and untrained coaches, (b) differences in sport attrition for athletes who played for trained versus untrained coaches, (c) differential patterns of change in athletes' achievement goal orientations, (d) group differences in athletes' academic achievement goals, (e) group differences in athletes' sport performance anxiety, and (f) differential effects for male and female athletes?

8. In implementing sport psychology workshops for coaches, the trainer should create a positive learning environment. What are some ways to foster a receptive and cooperative attitude on the part of coaches? What approaches should be avoided?

9. Describe the components of the healthy philosophy of winning that is taught in MAC, and indicate how this orientation is designed to combat competitive anxiety.

10. In conducting a MAC workshop, what is the rationale/justification for presenting empirical results to coaches?

11. What are the advantages of conducting coach-training programs with an interactive format, and how might this be accomplished?

12. Discuss the key points associated with the following recommendations for making effective presentations: (a) prepare, prepare, prepare; (b) find your style; (c) spice it up; (d) cover less, not more; and (e) make improvements.

13. With respect to changing coaches' attitudes during a training program, explain how the following aspects of the persuasion process might be taken into account: (a) credibility (expertise and trustworthiness) of the trainer, (b) perceived similarity between the trainer

and the coaches, (c) likability of the trainer, (d) one-sided versus two-sided communications, (e) use of rhetorical questions, (f) novelty of information, and (g) use of humor.

14. Describe the procedures that can be utilized to increase coaches' self-awareness and their compliance with coaching guidelines.

References

Ames, C. (1992a). Classrooms: Goals, structures, and student motivation. *Journal of Educational Psychology, 84,* 261–271.

Ames, C. (1992b). Achievement goals and adaptive motivational patterns: The role of the environment. In G. C. Roberts (Ed.), *Motivation in sport and exercise* (pp. 161–176). Champaign, IL: Human Kinetics.

Bandura, A. (1986). *Social foundations of thought and action: A social cognitive theory.* Englewood Cliffs, NJ: Prentice Hall.

Barker, L. L., & Gaut, D. A. (2002). *Communication* (8th ed.). Boston: Allyn and Bacon.

Barnett, N. P., Smoll, F. L., & Smith, R. E. (1992). Effects of enhancing coach–athlete relationships on youth sport attrition. *The Sport Psychologist, 6,* 111–127.

Brookfield, S. D. (2004). Discussion. In M. W. Galbraith (Ed.). *Adult learning methods: A guide for effective instruction* (3rd ed., pp. 209–226). Malabar, FL: Krieger.

Brustad, R. J., Babkes, M. L., & Smith, A. L. (2001). Youth in sport: Psychosocial considerations. In R. N. Singer, H. A. Hausenblas, & C. M. Janelle (Eds.), *Handbook of sport psychology* (2nd ed., pp. 604–635). New York: John Wiley & Sons.

Cahill, B. R., & Pearl, A. J. (Eds.). (1993). *Intensive participation in children's sports.* Champaign, IL: Human Kinetics.

Cavior, N., & Marabotto, C. M. (1976). Monitoring verbal behaviors in a dyadic interaction. *Journal of Consulting and Clinical Psychology, 44,* 68–76.

Chamberlin, J. (2000, December). Stand and deliver. *Monitor on Psychology, 31,* 62–64.

Coakley, J. (1993). Social dimensions of intensive training and participation in youth sports. In B. R. Cahill & A. J. Pearl (Eds.), *Intensive participation in children's sports* (pp. 77–94). Champaign, IL: Human Kinetics.

Coatsworth, J. D., & Conroy, D. E. (2006). Enhancing the self-esteem of youth swimmers through coach training: Gender and age effects. *Psychology of Sport and Exercise, 7,* 173–192.

Conroy, D. E., & Coatsworth, J. D. (2004). The effects of coach training on fear of failure in youth swimmers: A latent growth curve analysis from a randomized, controlled trial. *Journal of Applied Developmental Psychology, 25,* 193–214.

Cumming, S. P., Smith, R. E., Smoll, F. L., Standage, M., & Grossbard, J. R. (2008). Development and validation of the Achievement Goal Scale for Youth Sports. *Psychology of Sport and Exercise, 9,* 686–703.

Cumming, S. P., Smoll, F. L., Smith, R. E., & Grossbard, J. R. (2007). Is winning everything? The relative contributions of motivational climate and won-lost percentage in youth sports. *Journal of Applied Sport Psychology, 19,* 322–336.

Curtis, B., Smith, R. E., & Smoll, F. L. (1979). Scrutinizing the skipper: A study of leadership behaviors in the dugout. *Journal of Applied Psychology, 64,* 391–400.

Deci, E. L., & Ryan, R. M. (1987). The support of autonomy and the control of behavior. *Journal of Personality and Social Psychology, 53,* 1024–1037.

Duda, J. L., & Balaguer, I. (2007). Coach-created motivational climate. In S. Jowett & D Lavallee (Eds.), *Social psychology in sport* (pp. 117–130). Champaign, IL: Human Kinetics.

Duda, J. L., & Ntoumanis, N. (2005). After-school sport for children: Implications of task-involving motivational climate. In J. L. Mahoney, R. W. Larson, & J. S. Eccles (Eds.), *Organized activities as contexts of development: Extracurricular activities, after school, and community programs* (pp. 311–330). Mahwah, NJ: Erlbaum.

Duda J. L., & Whitehead, J. (1998). Measurement of goal perspectives in the physical domain. In J. L. Duda (Ed.), *Advances in sport and exercise psychology measurement* (pp. 21–48). Morgantown, WV: Fitness Information Technology.

Dweck, C. S. (1986). Motivational processes affecting leaning. *American Psychologist, 41,* 1040–1048.

Dweck, C. S. (1999). *Self-theories and goals: Their role in motivation, personality, and development.* Philadelphia: Taylor & Francis.

Edelstein, B. A., & Eisler, R. M. (1976). Effects of modeling and modeling with instructions and feedback on the behavioral components of social skills. *Behavior Therapy, 7,* 382–389.

Epstein, J. (1988). Effective schools or effective students? Dealing with diversity. In R. Haskins & B. MacRae (Eds.), *Policies for America's schools* (pp. 89–126). Norwood, NJ: Ablex.

Epstein, J. (1989). Family structures and students motivation: A developmental perspective. In C. Ames & R. Ames (Eds.), *Research on motivation in education: Vol. 3. Goals and cognitions* (pp. 259–295). New York: Academic Press.

Ewing, M. E., & Seefeldt, V. (2002). Patterns of participation in American agency-sponsored youth sports. In F. L. Smoll & R. E. Smith (Eds.), *Children and youth in sport: A biopsychosocial perspective* (2nd ed., pp. 39–56). Dubuque, IA: Kendall/Hunt.

Ewing, M. E., Seefeldt, V. D., & Brown, T. P. (1996). Role of organized sport in the education and health of American children and youth. In A. Poinsett (Ed.), *The role of sports in youth development* (pp. i–157). New York: Carnegie Corporation.

Farrah, S. J. (2004). Lecture. In M. W. Galbraith (Ed.), *Adult learning methods: A guide for effective instruction* (3rd ed., pp. 227–271). Malabar, FL: Krieger.

Friedrich, J., & Douglass, D. (1998). Ethics and the persuasive enterprise of teaching psychology. *American Psychologist, 53,* 549–562.

Galbraith, M. W. (2004). The teacher of adults. In M. W. Galbraith (Ed.), *Adult learning methods: A guide for effective instruction* (3rd ed., pp. 3–21). Malabar, FL: Krieger.

Gottman, J. M., & McFall, R. M. (1972). Self-monitoring effects in a program for potential high school dropouts: A time series analysis. *Journal of Consulting and Clinical Psychology, 39,* 273–281.

Gould, D. (1987). Understanding attrition in children's sport. In D. Gould & M. R. Weiss (Eds.), *Advances in pediatric sport sciences: Vol. 2. Behavioral issues* (pp. 61–85). Champaign, IL: Human Kinetics.

Hovland, C. I., Janis, I. L., & Kelley, H. H. (1953). *Communication and persuasion.* New Haven, CT: Yale University Press.

Howell. W. S., & Borman, E. G. (1997). *The process of presentational speaking* (2nd ed.), Boston: Allyn and Bacon.

Kanfer, F. H., & Gaelick-Buys, L. (1991). Self-management methods. In F. H. Kanfer & A. P. Goldstein (Eds.), *Helping people change: A textbook of methods* (4th ed., pp. 305–360). Boston: Allyn and Bacon.

Kazdin, A. E. (1974). Self-monitoring and behavior change. In M. J. Mahoney & C. E. Thoresen (Eds.), *Self-control: Power to the person* (pp. 218–246). Pacific Grove, CA: Brooks/Cole.

Kirschenbaum. D. S., & Karoly, P. (1977). When self-regulation fails: Tests of some preliminary hypotheses. *Journal of Consulting and Clinical Psychology, 45,* 1116–1125.

Malina, R. M., & Clark, M. A. (Eds.). (2003). *Youth sports: Perspectives for a new century.* Monterey, CA: Coaches Choice.

Martens, R. (1988). Youth sport in the USA. In F. L. Smoll, R. A. Magill, & M. J. Ash (Eds.), *Children in sport* (3rd ed., pp. 17–23). Champaign, IL: Human Kinetics.

Martens, R. (1993). Psychological perspectives. In B. R. Cahill & A. J. Pearl (Eds.), *Intensive participation in children's sports* (pp. 9–17). Champaign, IL: Human Kinetics.

Martens, R. (2004). *Successful coaching* (3rd ed.). Champaign, IL: Human Kinetics.

Martens, R., & Gould, D. (1979). Why do adults volunteer to coach children's sports? In G. C. Roberts & K. M. Newell (Eds.), *Psychology of motor behavior and sport, 1978* (pp. 79–89). Champaign, IL: Human Kinetics.

McFall, R. M. (1977). Parameters of self-monitoring. In R. B. Stuart (Ed.), *Behavioral self-management: Strategies, techniques and outcomes* (pp. 196–214). New York: Brunner/Mazel.

McFall, R. M., & Twentyman. C. T. (1973). Four experiments on the relative contributions of rehearsal, modeling, and coaching to assertion training. *Journal of Abnormal Psychology, 81,* 199–218.

Midgley, C., Maehr, M. M., Hruda, L. M., Anderman, E., Anderman, L., Freeman, K. E., et al. (2000). *Manual for the Patterns of Adaptive Learning Scales.* Ann Arbor, MI: University of Michigan School of Education. Retrieved February 2, 2004, from http://www.umich.edu/~pals/pals

Nicholls, J. G. (1989). *The competitive ethos and democratic education.* Cambidge, MA: Harvard University Press.

Perry, M. A., & Furukawa, M. J. (1986). Modeling methods. In F. H. Kanfer & A. P. Goldstein (Eds.), *Helping people change: A textbook of methods* (3rd ed., pp. 66–110). New York: Pergamon.

Petty, R. E., & Wegener, D. T. (1998). Attitude change: Multiple roles for persuasion variables. In D. T. Gilbert, S. T. Fiske, & G. Lindzey (Eds.), *The handbook of social psychology, Vol. I* (4th ed., pp. 323–390). Boston: McGraw-Hill.

Roberts, G. C., Treasure, D. C., & Conroy, D. (2007). Understanding the dynamics of motivation in sport and physical activity: An achievement goal interpretation. In G. Tenenbaum & R. C. Eklund (Eds.), Handbook of sport psychology (3rd ed., pp. 3–30). Hoboken, NJ: Wiley.

Roberts, G. C., Treasure, D. C., & Kavussanu, M. (1997). Motivation in physical activity contexts: An achievement goal perspective. In M. L. Maehr & P. R. Pintrich (Eds.), *Advances in motivation and achievement* (Vol. 10, pp. 413–447). Greenwich, CT: JAI Press.

Scanlan, T. K. (2002). Social evaluation and the competition process: A developmental perspective. In F. L. Smoll & R. E. Smith (Eds.), *Children and youth in sport: A biopsychosocial perspective* (2nd ed., pp. 393–407). Dubuque, IA: Kendall/Hunt.

Smith, R. E., Cumming, S. P., & Smoll, F. L., (2008). Development and validation of the Motivational Climate Scale for Youth Sports. *Journal of Applied Sport Psychology, 20,*116–136.

Smith, R. E., & Johnson, J. (1990). An organizational empowerment approach to consultation in professional baseball. *The Sport Psychologist, 4,* 347–357.

Smith, R. E., & Smoll, F. L. (1990). Self-esteem and children's reactions to youth sport coaching behaviors: A field study of self-enhancement processes. *Developmental Psychology, 26,* 987–993.

Smith, R. E., & Smoll, F. L. (2002). *Way to go, coach! A scientifically-proven approach to coaching effectiveness* (2nd ed.). Portola Valley, CA: Warde.

Smith, R. E., Smoll, F. L., & Barnett, N. P. (1995). Reduction of children's sport performance anxiety through social support and stress-reduction training for coaches. *Journal of Applied Developmental Psychology, 16,* 125–142.

Smith, R. E., Smoll. F. L., & Christensen, D. S. (1996). Behavioral assessment and interventions in youth sports. *Behavior Modification, 20,* 3–44.

Smith, R. E., Smoll, F. L., Cumming, S. P., & Grossbard, J. R. (2006). Measurement of multidimensional sport performance anxiety in children and adults: The Sport Anxiety Scale-2. *Journal of Sport & Exercise Psychology, 28,* 479–501.

Smith, R. E., Smoll, F. L., & Cumming, S. P. (2007). Effects of a motivational climate intervention for coaches on young athletes' sport performance anxiety. *Journal of Sport & Exercise Psychology, 29,* 39–59.

Smith, R. E., Smoll, F. L., & Curtis, B. (1978). Coaching behaviors in Little League Baseball. In F. L. Smoll & R. E. Smith (Eds.), *Psychological perspectives in youth sports* (pp. 173–201). Washington, DC: Hemisphere.

Smith, R. E., Smoll, F. L., & Curtis, B. (1979). Coach effectiveness training: A cognitive-behavioral approach to enhancing relationship skills in youth sport coaches. *Journal of Sport Psychology, 1,* 59–75.

Smith, R. E., Smoll, F. L., & Hunt, E. B. (1977). A system for the behavioral assessment of athletic coaches. *Research Quarterly, 48,* 401–407.

Smith, R. E., Smoll, F. L., & Passer, M. P. (2002). Sport performance anxiety in young athletes. In F. L. Smoll & R. E. Smith (Eds.), *Children and youth in sport: A biopsychosocial perspective* (2nd ed., pp. 501–536). Dubuque, IA: Kendall/Hunt.

Smith, R. E., Zane, N. W. S., Smoll, F. L., & Coppel, D. B. (1983). Behavioral assessment in youth sports: Coaching behaviors and children's attitudes. *Medicine and Science in Sports and Exercise, 15,* 208–214.

Smoll, F. L. (1989). Sports and the preadolescent: "Little league" sports. In N. J. Smith (Ed.), *Common problems in pediatric sports medicine* (pp. 3–15). Chicago: Year Book Medical Publishers.

Smoll, F. L., & Smith. R. E. (1989). Leadership behaviors in sport: A theoretical model and research paradigm. *Journal of Applied Social Psychology, 19,* 1522–1551.

Smoll, F. L., & Smith, R. E. (Eds.). (2002). *Children and youth in sport: A biopsychosocial perspective* (2nd ed.). Dubuque, IA: Kendall/Hunt.

Smoll, F. L., & Smith, R. E. (2008). *Coaches who never lose: Making sure athletes win, no matter what the score* (3rd ed.). Palo Alto, CA: Warde.

Smoll, F. L., Smith, R. E., Barnett. N. P., & Everett, J. J. (1993). Enhancement of children's self-esteem through social support training for youth sport coaches. *Journal of Applied Psychology, 78,* 602–610.

Smoll, F. L., Smith, R. E., & Cumming, S. P. (2007). Effects of a motivational climate intervention for coaches on changes in young athletes' achievement goal orientations. *Journal of Clinical Sport Psychology, 1,* 23–46.

Smoll, F. L., Smith, R. E., Curtis, B., & Hunt, E. (1978). Toward a mediational model of coach–player relationships. *Research Quarterly, 49,* 528–541.

Sousa, C., Cruz, J., Torregrosa, M., Vilches, D., & Viladrich, C. (2006). Behavioral assessment and individual counseling programme for coaches of young athletes. *Revista de Psicologia del Deporte, 15,* 263–278.

Sousa, C., Smith, R.E., & Cruz, J. (2008). An individualized behavioral goal-setting program for coaches: Impact on observed, athlete-perceived, and coach-perceived behaviors. *Journal of Clinical Sport Psychology, 2,* 258–277.

Stambor, Z. (2006, June). How laughing leads to learning. *Monitor on Psychology, 37,* 62–64.

Taylor, S. E., Peplau, L. A., & Sears, D. O. (2005). *Social psychology* (12th ed.). Upper Saddle River, NJ: Prentice Hall.

Weiss, M. (Ed.). (2004). *Developmental sport and exercise psychology: A lifespan perspective.* Morgantown, WV: Fitness Information Technology.

Weiss, M. R., & Hayashi, C. T. (1996). The United States. In P. De Knop, L-M. Engstrom, B. Skirstad, & M. R. Weiss (Eds.), *Worldwide trends in youth sport* (pp. 43–57). Champaign, IL: Human Kinetics.

Worchel, S., Cooper, J., & Goethals, G. R. (1991). *Understanding social psychology* (5th ed.). Pacific Grove, CA: Brooks/Cole.

Summary of Coaching Guidelines

I. Reacting to Athlete Behaviors and Game Situations

A. Good plays

Do: Provide *reinforcement!* Do so immediately. Let the athletes know that you appreciate and value their efforts. Reinforce effort as much as you do results. Look for positive things, reinforce them, and you will see them increase. Remember, whether athletes show it or not, the positive things you say and do remain with them.

Don't: Take their efforts for granted.

B. Mistakes

Do: Give *encouragement* immediately after mistakes. That's when the youngster needs your support the most. If you are sure the athlete knows how to correct the mistake, then encouragement alone is sufficient. When appropriate, give *corrective instruction,* but always do so in an encouraging manner. Do this by emphasizing not the bad things that just happened but the good things that will happen if the athlete follows your instruction (the "why" of it). This will make the athlete positively self-motivated to correct the mistakes rather than negatively motivated to avoid failure and your disapproval.

Don't: *Punish* when things are going wrong! Punishment isn't just yelling. It can be tone of voice, action, or any indication of disapproval.

Athletes respond much better to a positive approach. Fear of failure is reduced if you work to reduce fear of punishment. Indications of displeasure should be limited to clear cases of lack of effort; but, even here, criticize the lack of effort rather than the athlete as a person.

Don't: Give corrective instruction in a hostile, demeaning, or harsh manner. That is, avoid *punitive instruction.* This is more likely to increase frustration and create resentment than to improve performance. Don't let your good intentions in giving instruction be self-defeating.

C. Misbehaviors, lack of attention

Do Maintain order by establishing clear expectations. Emphasize that during a game all members of the team are part of the activity, even those on the bench. Use reinforcement to strengthen team participation. In other words, try to prevent misbehaviors by using the positive approach to strengthen their opposites.

Don't: Get into the position of having to constantly nag or threaten athletes to prevent chaos. Don't be a drill sergeant. If an athlete refuses to cooperate, deprive him or her of something valued. Don't use physical measures, such as running laps. The idea here is that if you establish clear behavioral guidelines early and work to build team spirit in achieving them, you can avoid having to repeatedly *keep control*. Youngsters want clear guidelines and expectations, but they don't want to be regimented. Try to achieve a healthy balance.

II. Getting Positive Things to Happen and Creating a Good Learning Atmosphere

Do: Give *technical instruction*. Establish your role as a caring and competent teacher. Try to structure participation as a learning experience in which you are going to help the athletes become the best they can be. Always give instruction in a positive way. Satisfy your athletes' desire to improve their skills. Give instruction in a clear, concise manner and, if possible, demonstrate how to do skills correctly.

Do: Give encouragement. Encourage effort, don't demand results. Use encouragement selectively so that it is meaningful. Be supportive without acting like a cheerleader.

Do: Concentrate on the activity. Be "in the game" with the athletes. Set a good example for team unity.

Don't: Give either instruction or encouragement in a sarcastic or degrading manner. Make a point, then leave it. Don't let "encouragement" become irritating to the athletes.

Note: These guidelines were excerpted from the manual that is given to MAC workshop participants (Smoll & Smith, 2008).

Coach Self-Report Form

Complete this form as soon as possible after a practice or game. Think about what you did, but also about the kinds of situations in which the actions occurred and the kinds of athletes who were involved.

1. When athletes made good plays, approximately what percent of the time did you respond with REINFORCEMENT? _____%

2. When athletes gave good effort (regardless of the outcome), what percent of the time did you respond with REINFORCEMENT? _____%

3. About how many times did you reinforce athletes for displaying good sportsmanship, supporting teammates, and complying with team rules? _____

4. When athletes made mistakes, approximately what percent of the time did you respond with:

   A. Encouragement only _____%

   B. Corrective instruction given in an encouraging manner _____%

   (Sum of A and B should not exceed 100%)

5. When mistakes were made, did you stress the importance of learning from them? _____Yes _____No

6. Did you emphasize the importance of having fun while practicing or competing? _____Yes _____No

7. Did you tell your athletes that doing their best is all you expect of them? _____Yes _____No

8. Did you communicate that winning is important, but working to improve skills is even more important? _____Yes _____No

9. Did you do or say anything to help your athletes apply what they learned today to other parts of their life (for example, doing the right things in school, family, or social life)? _____Yes _____No

10. Something to think about: Is there anything you might do differently if you had a chance to coach this practice or game again?

This form was excerpted from the manual that is given to MAC workshop participants (Smoll & Smith, 2008).

CHAPTER

19

Gender and Cultural Considerations

Diane L. Gill, Ph.D., *University of North Carolina at Greensboro*

Cindra S. Kamphoff, Ph.D., *Minnesota State University, Mankato*

How many goodly creatures are there here! How beauteous mankind is! O brave new world that has such people in it!

—From William Shakespeare's The Tempest, V, 1, 182

One size does NOT fit all!

Both our larger world and our sport world do indeed include a wondrous diversity of people. Just as clearly—one size does NOT fit all—whether we are considering clothing, policies, institutions or applied sport psychology. Gender and cultural diversity issues are real and powerful, and as the quotes suggest, diversity may well constrain behavior and opportunity. As applied sport psychologists, whether in teaching, research or consulting with athletes, it is imperative that we recognize the possibilities and constraints of cultural diversity and keep reminding ourselves that one size does not fit all. Attention to gender and cultural diversity is vital to our scholarship, and cultural competence is essential to professional practice. We hope the inclusion of this chapter will encourage more scholarship

on diversity issues and greater emphasis on cultural competencies in professional practice.

Overview and Framework

This chapter begins with a guiding multicultural framework, examines gender and cultural diversity in sport, and then focuses on applied sport psychology research and professional practice (for more detail on related research, see Gill, 2007). Throughout the chapter we include examples and quotes, as well as suggestions for promoting cultural competence in applied sport psychology. We interpret sport broadly, including all levels and forms of sport, and we intentionally advocate *sport for all*. That is, applied sport psychology can best address gender and

417

cultural diversity by promoting safe, inclusive physical activity and by highlighting cultural competence in professional practice.

Multicultural Psychology

Although gender and cultural diversity are seldom central themes in applied sport psychology, the larger field of psychology, and particularly the American Psychological Association (APA), has developed a scholarly base and professional resources on multicultural psychology. The continuing work in gender psychology and the rapidly growing multicultural psychology scholarship provide a framework for this chapter, help clarify terminology, and provide guidelines for professional practice. First, we will adopt an encompassing definition of culture and multicultural psychology, and then clarify the relevant terminology using the APA's guidelines and publications.

In one representative current text, *multicultural psychology* is defined as the *"systematic study of behavior, cognition, and affect in many cultures"* (Mio, Barker-Hackett, & Tumambing, 2006, p. 3). *Culture,* however, is complex and not easily defined. As Mio et al. note, narrow definitions emphasize ethnicity, but a broader definition refers to *shared values, beliefs, and practices of an identifiable group of people.* Thus, culture includes race/ethnicity, language, spirituality, sexuality, and of particular relevance here, *physicality* (physical abilities and characteristics).

This chapter draws from that expanding multicultural psychology scholarship along with the feminist and cultural sport studies literatures. These sources converge on the following common themes that form the guiding framework for this chapter:

> *Multiple, intersecting cultural identities.* We all have gender, race/ethnicity and multiple cultural identities, with the mix varying across individuals, time, and contexts.

> *Power relations.* Gender and culture relations involve power and privilege. Who makes the rules? Who is *left out?*

> *Action and advocacy.* Multicultural perspectives demand action for social justice.

Culturally competent applied sport psychology professionals develop their own multicultural competencies and also advocate sport for all.

Gender and Multiple Identities

The APA and psychology in general have addressed gender issues in both research and practice for some time. More recently, recognizing the diversity among women, and noting that disparities still persist despite tremendous gains for women in many areas, the APA (2007) developed and approved Guidelines for Psychological Practice with Girls and Women. Specifically, these guidelines "will enhance gender- and culture-sensitive psychological practice with women and girls from all social classes, ethnic and racial groups, sexual orientations, and ability/disability statuses in the United States" (APA, 2007, p. 950). These guidelines draw from similar APA guidelines related to lesbian, gay, and bisexual clients (APA, 2000), older adults (APA, 2004), and multicultural education, research, practice, and organizational change (APA, 2003).

These guidelines (APA, 2007) clearly take a multicultural perspective and also include definitions that are relevant to this chapter. First, the guidelines clarify the distinction between sex and gender, with *sex* referring to biological aspects of being male or female, and *gender* referring to psychological, social, and cultural experiences and characteristics associated with being male or female. Rather than defining culture, the guidelines define the broader term, *social identities* as encompassing personal and group definitions embedded in social groups and statuses including gender, race, ability level, culture, ethnicity, geographic location, intellectual ability, sexual orientation, gender identity, class, age, body size, religious affiliation, acculturation status, socioeconomic status, and other sociodemographic variables. The guidelines explicitly note the complex and dynamic interactions of identities.

Exercise 1: Identify Your Own Multiple Identities

List as many as you can of your own social identities (gender, race/ethnicity, social class, sexuality, spirituality/religion, physicality, etc.). You should have a long list. Try to mark three identities that are especially salient or influential for you (that won't be easy, as different identities are more or less salient in different situations). In what ways do you experience power and privilege? Now, select a profession in which you might be working with sport participants such as sport psychology consultant, athletic trainer, coach, or fitness leader. How will your own multiple, intersecting identities impact your work and interactions with participants?

The APA (2007) guidelines define *oppression* as discrimination against and/or systematic denial of resources to members of groups who are identified as different, inferior, or less deserving than others. *Privilege* refers to social status, power or institutionalized advantage gained by virtue of valued social identities. The APA (2007) guidelines clearly recognize connections and interactions of multiple identities and power relations, and they emphasize social justice and advocacy in the specific guidelines for psychological practice.

By adopting the approach of the APA (2007) guidelines, and the multicultural framework of this chapter, applied sport psychology can advance our understanding of gender and cultural diversity, and promote cultural competence in professional practice—but that's no easy task. Sport psychology is explicitly context dependent, and sport culture is unique in many ways. As multicultural psychologists advocate, applied sport psychologists must pay attention to power relations and social context in sport, but they also must retain concern for the individual. The combined focus on the individual and cultural relations is the essence of cultural competence in

applied sport psychology—and promoting inclusive and empowering sport for all.

The Cultural Context of Sport

Before examining the scholarship on gender and cultural diversity, consider the cultural context of sport. Specifically consider gender and culture in the following exercise.

Exercise 2: Gender and Culture Influence in Sport

Chris, the most talented 12-year old soccer player on the team, often loses focus and has angry outbursts on the field. The coach wants to help Chris develop emotional control and game skills and asks your advice. Before moving into a psychological skills training program, consider how gender and culture might affect Chris, the coach, and your advice. Specifically, would you expect different behaviors or reactions from Christine and Christopher? Do you think others (parents, teammates) would react the same way to both of them? What if Chris's parents were immigrants from a non-Western culture? What if Chris were not so talented?

Gender and culture are embedded in sport. If you try to be nonsexist or nonracist and treat everyone the same, you will have difficulty. Moreover, power and privilege are involved; trying to treat everyone the same may well do a disservice to participants. Our world is shaped by gender and culture. Gender influence is particularly powerful in sport, with some unique features.

Sport participants are diverse, but not as diverse as the broader population. Until the 1970s, athlete meant male athlete, and those male athletes were not very culturally diverse. Elite sport programs clearly reflect gender and cultural restrictions.

Exercise 3: Treating Everyone the Same

As a physical educator or coach, you likely want to be fair and treat all of your students and athletes the same. How may that be problematic? How might treating everyone the same do a disservice to athletes? How might considering gender, social class, or race help you better understand a student?

Gender and Sport

Society and social institutions are clearly gendered, and sport has a unique gender context. Early women's physical education provided a women-oriented environment for sport long before the women's movement of the 1970s. Early women leaders advocated putting athletes first, preventing exploitation, downplaying competition while emphasizing enjoyment and sportsmanship, and promoting activity for all rather than an elite few, as expressed in the classic statement, *"A game for every girl and every girl in a game"* (National Amateur Athletic Federation [NAAF], 1930, p. 41). The 1972 passage of Title IX of the Educational Amendments Act marked the beginning of the move away from that model toward today's competitive women's sport programs. Indeed, female athletic participation has exploded in the last generation. Still, the numbers of female and male participants are not equal. More important, female athletes are not the same as male athletes. To understand gender and sport we must look beyond biological sex differences to the social context. *Citius, Altius, Fortius*—the Olympic motto—translates as "swifter, higher, stronger," underscoring that sport is competitive and hierarchical as well as physical. The average male may be taller, faster, and stronger than the average female, but biological sex is only part of the gender mix. All the meanings, social roles, and expectations related to gender are constructed in the sport context.

Cultural Diversity in Sport

In considering cultural diversity, we must go beyond numbers to consider power and privilege—*"who makes the rules."* Derald Wing Sue (2004)

illustrates the power differential in noting that while white males make up just 33% of the U.S. population, they hold 80% of tenured faculty positions, 92% of Forbes 400 CEO-level positions, 80% of the House of Representatives and 84% of the Senate, and of special interest here, *99% of the athletic team owners.* As Sue (2004) noted, privileged people are often unaware of power relations, and "color blindness" often denies opportunity to others. Sue argued that psychology must make the invisible visible— it must recognize white privilege and the culture-bound nature of our scholarship and practice to advance psychology's mission and enhance the health and well-being of all people. As Sue noted, most of us do not recognize our own privilege. The following quote from Muhammad Ali clearly illustrates that white privilege is clear and obvious to those who are not so privileged:

> *We were taught when we were little children that Mary had a little lamb, its fleece was white as snow. Then we heard about Snow White, White Owl cigars. White Swan soap. White Cloud tissue. White Rain hair rings. White Tornado floor wax. White Plus toothpaste. All the good cowboys ride white horses and wear white hats. The President lives in the White House. Jesus was White. The Last Supper was White. The angels is White. Miss America is White. Even, Tarzan, the King of the Jungle in Africa is White.*
>
> —Muhammad Ali, 1967. (cited in Hauser, 1996, p. 76; McDonald, 2005, p. 245)

Richard Lapchick's annual *Racial and Gender Report Cards* clearly show racial and gender inequities in sport, with little progress. In the 2005 report card (Lapchick, 2006) African Americans were 24.8% of the male athletes and 15.4% of the female athletes in Division I, a higher percentage than in the overall U.S. population, but Latino, Asian American, and Native American athletes were underrepresented at very low percentages.

When we consider the "power" positions, diversity is nonexistent. Before Title IX (1972), over 90% of women's athletic teams were coached by women and had a woman athletic director. Vivian Acosta and Linda Carpenter (Carpenter & Acosta, 2008) have clearly documented the continuous decline in the number of women coaches since then. In their most recent 2008 update (available at: http://www.acostacarpenter.org) they report that participation in female athletics is at the highest level ever, but the representation of females as coaches remains low at 42.8%. The proportion of female athletic directors (21.3%), head athletic trainers (27.3%), and sports information directors (11.3%) has risen, but remain far below male numbers. White men dominate coaching, even of women's teams. The 2005 Racial and Gender Report Card indicated that whites dominate collegiate coaching, holding approximately 90% of the head coaching positions at all divisions. The number of African American men coaching Division I basketball reached an all time high of 25.2%, and the number of African American women coaches increased to 9.3%, but that is still far below the proportion of African American women basketball players (43.7%). Coaches of other racial/ethnic identities hardly can be counted, and administration remains solidly white male. Clearly, elite sport is culturally elite.

Gender bias and white male privilege may not totally explain the declining numbers of women coaches, but Kamphoff's (2006) dissertation research clearly shows that women coaches within collegiate athletics experience marginalization, devaluation, and homophobia. The former women coaches that she interviewed suggested they received fewer resources, lower salaries, more responsibilities, and less administrative support than their male counterparts. For example, here are quotes from two of those coaches:

> The women's basketball coach, the male, hadn't even set foot on campus and he's given double what some of us that have already proven to be good coaches, to be successful coaches . . . that's hard to swallow. (A former collegiate coach, Kamphoff, 2006, p. 123)
> . . .the thing that aggravates me to this day is there is a double standard. I watch _____ on the sidelines and [he] rips them up and down. And what do the announcers' say, "Look at the passion that he coaches with." . . . If I did that, I need to calm down . . . there is a double standard there and I hate it. I resent it. You see how the guys sometimes treat their players. If a woman would do that, it's not the same. (A former collegiate coach, Kamphoff, 2006, p. 131)

The women she interviewed also had difficulty balancing work and family, and they reported that others saw them "distracted by motherhood" if they had children. As one commented:

> When I resigned, I remember [the athletic director] telling me, "You know, I often wondered how you could juggle being a wife, and having two kids." . . . Are you kidding me? He wouldn't say that to a man. (A former collegiate coach, Kamphoff, 2006, p. 134)

Cultural Diversity in Exercise and Physical Activity

Perhaps exercise and physical activity are more diverse than elite sport—or perhaps not. Census data and public health reports indicate that physical activity is limited by gender, race, class, and especially by physical attributes. Physical activity decreases across the adult lifespan, with men more active than women, racial/ethnic minorities less active across all age groups (Pratt, Macera, & Blanton, 1999; USDHHS, 2000). For example, Kimm et al. (2002) used a large national data base to track girls' physical activity levels across adolescence. Physical activity declined dramatically—100% for black girls and 64% for white girls—so that at age 18–19, 56% of black girls and 31% of white girls reported no regular physical activity. Crespo, Ainsworth, Keteyian, Heath, and Smit (1999), in one of the few studies to look at social class, found greater inactivity in less privileged social classes, with females more inactive in all social class groups. Crespo (2005) called for professionals to consider unique needs and cultural constraints when giving advice on exercise.

Gender and Cultural Diversity in Sport Psychology

Despite the diversity of participants and need for cultural competence, sport psychology has not adopted multicultural perspectives. Research does not address diversity issues, professional practice focuses on elite sport, and educational programs do not incorporate multicultural competencies. Gender scholarship has not followed psychology's move to more multicultural perspectives, and research on cultural diversity is virtually nonexistent.

Duda and Allison (1990) first identified the lack of research on race/ethnicity, reporting that only 1 of 13 published theoretical papers, and 7 of 186 empirical papers (less than 4%) considered race/ethnicity, and most of those were sample descriptions. Ram, Starek, and Johnson (2004) updated that report by reviewing articles in sport and exercise psychology research journals between 1987 and 2000 for both race/ethnicity and sexual orientation content. They confirmed the persistent void in the scholarly literature, finding that only 20% of the articles made reference to race/ethnicity and 1.2% to sexual orientation. More important, those few articles provided few insights to advance our understanding. Ram et al. concluded that there is no systematic attempt to include the experiences of marginalized groups.

Exercise 4: Lack of Research on Cultural Diversity

Research reviews (Duda & Allison, 1990; Kamphoff, Araki & Gill, 2004; Ram et al., 2004) demonstrate a lack of culturally diverse samples in sport psychology research. Assume that you want to study psychological skills and motivation in sport. How might you design a study to include a more culturally diverse sample? Which specific aspects of diversity will you include in your study? How and why? What research questions will the study address?

Cindra Kamphoff and colleagues (Kamphoff, Araki, & Gill, 2004) surveyed the Association for Applied Sport Psychology (AASP) conference programs from the first conference in 1986 to 2003 and found little attention to multicultural issues. From 1986 to 1995, the percentage of abstracts addressing diversity issues increased slightly, with no further change from 1995 to 2003. However, most of those few abstracts on diversity issues were mainly sample comparisons of gender differences with few analyses that extend beyond group differences. AASP program content extends beyond the research to professional issues, but our investigation of program abstracts suggests that sport settings, educational programs, and professional practice are culturally elite with little attention to the wider range of participants or multicultural issues.

Butryn (2002), taking a critical perspective, examined white privilege in sport psychology consulting. Like Sue (2004), Butryn called attention to "invisible" white privilege and specifically argued that "confronting the invisible knapsack of white privilege" is essential for effective sport psychology consulting. Butryn further reminded us that race is not just black and white, and that we must expand the discourse on race and privilege to the wider range of racial/ethnic identities.

To expand our worldview, sport psychology must expand the research base on gender and cultural diversity, and adopt multicultural competencies for professional practice. To get started, we can draw from related gender and multicultural psychology scholarship.

Exercise 5: White Privilege in Sport Psychology

Sue discussed "invisible whiteness" and Butryn (2002) examined white privilege in sport psychology, arguing that we should confront the often "taken for granted" notion of race. Check the Association of Applied Sport Psychology's Web site, and specifically the Certified Consultants link (http://appliedsportpsych.org/consultants/consultant-websites) and http://appliedsportpsych.org/consultants). What do these Web sites and the consultant's bios and pictures tell you about cultural diversity in applied sport psychology? Do these Web sites help us to examine white privilege in applied sport psychology?

Gender and Sexuality

Gender Scholarship

Gender is a clear and powerful influence in society, and a particularly powerful and persistent influence in sport. Gender scholarship in sport psychology largely follows gender scholarship within psychology, which has shifted from sex differences, to gender role as personality, to social context and processes. As noted earlier, gender scholarship in psychology has recently moved to a multicultural perspective, and sport psychology would do well to follow that model. This section highlights the scholarship that has most influenced applied sport psychology (see Gill, 2007 for a more detailed discussion).

In their classic review Maccoby and Jacklin (1974) stated that few conclusions could be drawn from the literature on sex differences. Despite many claims to the contrary, continuing psychological research confirms that main conclusion. Hyde (2005) recently reviewed 46 meta-analyses of the extensive sex differences literature and concluded that results support the *gender similarities hypothesis*. That is, males and females are more alike than different, and overstated claims of gender differences cause harm and limit opportunities.

Much of the sport psychology research on gender issues emphasizes personality, following Bem's (1978) lead and using her *Bem Sex Role Inventory* (BSRI), which suggested that both males and females can have masculine or feminine personalities, or both (androgynous). More recently, the masculine and feminine categories and measures have fallen out of favor, and even Bem (1993) moved to a more encompassing gender perspective. Still, most sport psychology gender research is based on that early work. For example, Spence and Helmreich (1978) reported that most female collegiate athletes were either androgynous or masculine, in contrast to nonathlete college females who were most often classified as feminine, and several studies in the sport psychology literature yielded similar findings (e.g., Harris & Jennings, 1977). One recent study (Koca & Asci, 2005) expands our cultural perspective by surveying a large Turkish sample. As with Western samples, Turkish female athletes scored higher on masculinity, and the authors suggested that both female and male athletes must be competitive, assertive, independent, and willing to take risks. Overall, this research suggests that female athletes possess more masculine personality characteristics than do female nonathletes, but this is not particularly enlightening.

Psychology research has moved beyond the male-female and masculine-feminine dichotomies to more complex developmental, social, and multicultural models. Psychological research confirms that how people *think* males and females differ is more important than how they actually differ. For example, in the United States, dance is considered a feminine activity, but in many cultures, dance is part of masculine rituals. If children think that dance is for girls, boys will stand aside while girls dance.

Gender Stereotypes

Gender stereotypes are pervasive, and particularly so in sport. In her classic analysis Eleanor Metheny (1965) identified gender stereotypes and concluded that it is not socially appropriate for women to engage in contests in which the resistance of the opponent is overcome by bodily contact, the resistance of a heavy object is overcome by direct application of bodily force, or the body is projected into or through space over long distances or for extended periods of time.

Gender stereotypes did not fade away with the implementation of Title IX. Kane and Snyder (1989) confirmed gender stereotyping of sports, and identified physicality—an emphasis on physical muscularity, strength, and power—as the key feature. Research (e.g., Kane & Parks, 1992; Messner, Duncan, & Jensen, 1993) indicates that media coverage reflects gender bias. Female athletes receive much less coverage than males, and different coverage, with the emphasis on athletic ability and accomplishments for men, but on femininity and physical attractiveness for women.

Stereotypes are a concern because we act on them, exaggerating minimal gender differences and restricting opportunities for everyone. Both girls and boys can participate in gymnastics or baseball, and at early ages physical capabilities are similar. Yet children see female gymnasts and male baseball players as role models; peers gravitate to sex-segregated activities; and parents, teachers, and coaches support gender-appropriate activities of children.

Fredericks and Eccles' (2004) review of the literature on parental influence and youth sport involvement revealed that parents held gender-stereotyped beliefs about athletics and were gender-typed in their behaviors, providing more opportunities and encouragement to sons than to daughters. Fredericks and Eccles (2005) later confirmed that boys had higher perceived competence, value, and participation, despite the absence of gender differences in motor proficiency.

Exercise 6: Gender Stereotyping in the Media

Follow the coverage of both men's and women's intercollegiate basketball for a week in a newspaper, television news sport report, sport magazine, or sport Web site. Do men and women receive different amounts of time or space? Does the type of coverage differ (e.g., references to accomplishments, appearance, personal lives)? Do you find gender stereotyping or bias?

Body image

Body perceptions are particularly relevant to sport psychology, and body image is clearly gender related. Research on body image in sport psychology focuses on gender ideals and unhealthy eating behaviors with female participants. Some researchers find positive relationships between participation in sport and body perceptions (Hausenblas & Mack, 1999), but others find negative relationships (Davis, 1992). Reel and colleagues (Reel, SooHoo, Jamieson, & Gill, 2005) found that social physique anxiety and eating disorder scores were moderate, but college female dancers overwhelmingly reported pressures to lose weight with unique pressures related to mirrors, performance advantages, and landing roles. Krane, Waldron, Michalenok and Stiles-Shipley (2001) found that athletes reported positive affect and body image within the athletic context, but more negative body image and maladaptive behaviors (disordered eating)

in other social contexts. Cox and Thompson (2000) similarly reported that elite female soccer players were confident in their athletic bodies, although generally dissatisfied with their overall body image, while Greenleaf (2002) found that competitive female athletes recognized conflict between their athletic bodies and social ideals.

In a unique study, Conception and Ebbeck (2005) explored the role of physical activity with domestic abuse survivors and reported that physical activity provided a sense of accomplishment, enhanced mental and physical states, and offered more of a sense of being "normal." Overall, research suggests that body image concerns in sport are powerful and gender related, and they vary with the activity and cultural context. Sport professionals who understand the role of gender and culture in body perceptions can better promote healthy sport and exercise behaviors.

Gender and Social Development

Several researchers and community service professionals have promoted sport and physical activity programs for youth development, and some research confirms benefits for both girls and boys, with gender and cultural variations. Miller, Sabo, Farrell, Barnes, and Melnick (1999) used data from a large national survey of white, African-American, and Hispanic adolescents to address the practical question: Does sport reduce the risk of teen pregnancy? Girls who participated in sport were indeed at less risk for teen pregnancy, reporting lower rates of sexual experience, fewer partners, later age of first intercourse, higher rates of contraception use, and lower rates of past pregnancies. Boys in sport also reported higher contraceptive use, but on other measures reported more sexual experience. In addition to the main results on sport and sexual behaviors, Miller et al. (1999) reported that males had higher sport participation rates than did females, and whites had the highest participation of the three race/ethnic groups, with Hispanic youth reporting the lowest rates.

Erkut, Fields, Sing, and Marx (1996) explored experiences (including sport) that influence urban girls representing five ethnic backgrounds

(Native American, African American, Anglo-European American, Asian Pacific Islander, and Latina). One somewhat surprising result was that athletics was the most common response when girls were asked "what activities make you feel good about yourself?" When asked why, the most common response was mastery or competence (e.g., "I'm good at it") followed by enjoyment. Erkut et al.'s large, diverse sample and the many variations in findings highlight the importance of cultural contexts in the lives of these girls and suggest exciting directions for sport psychology.

The Tucker Center (2007) recently released a 10-year update on their influential 1997 report on girls and physical activity. The 2007 report provides updated research summaries on the psychological, sociocultural and physiological dimensions of girls' physical activity. The report includes tables that list specific recommendations for best practices in programs, policies, and future research (available at www.tuckercenter .org). The recommendations in the psychosocial category highlight supportive practices that promote intrinsic motivation, mastery orientation, positive self-perceptions, social development, coping skills and mental health, and they generally emphasize engagement and empowerment. Sociocultural best practices emphasize positive gender confirmation and challenge limiting and unhealthy stereotypes. Physiological practices emphasize regular moderate to vigorous physical activity in fostering lifestyle activity.

Sexuality

Sexuality and sexual orientation are clearly linked with gender, but clarification of terminology is in order before reviewing the scholarship. Discrimination and prejudice on the basis of sexual orientation is often described as homophobia, but Herek (2000), a leading psychology scholar on lesbian/gay/bisexual (LGB) issues, prefers *sexual prejudice*. As Herek notes, sexual prejudice is an attitude (evaluation), directed at a social group, involving hostility or dislike. *Homophobia* is typically understood as an irrational fear, and the term implies psychopathology or mental

illness. *Heterosexism* refers to the institutionalized oppression of nonheterosexual people. Sexual prejudice is used here, but related scholarship also refers to homophobia and heterosexism.

Messner (1992) argues that homophobia is particularly powerful in sport and leads all boys and men (gay or straight) to conform to a narrow definition of masculinity; real men compete and avoid anything feminine that might lead them to be branded a sissy. Still, homophobia in sport is typically discussed in relation to women's athletics. Despite the visibility of a few prominent lesbian athletes, many women athletes go out of their way to avoid any appearance of lesbianism. We stereotypically assume that sport attracts lesbians (of course, not gay men), but no research or logic supports any inherent relationship between sexual orientation and sport. No doubt, homophobia has kept more heterosexual women than lesbians out of sports, and homophobia restricts the behavior of both women and men in sport. The former women coaches that Kamphoff interviewed provided examples of rampant homophobia in U.S. collegiate coaching, and they clearly felt pressure to act in a heterosexual way to fit into the collegiate system.

> I know a specific case of a lesbian coach that was asked to leave and they [administrators] said, "We want to change the face of the coaching staff." So, what does that mean? A lesbian coach, of course, is going to take that as you want a straight coach . . . . You are saying it without saying it. (A former collegiate coach, Kamphoff, 2006, p. 148)

Vikki Krane (2001; Krane & Barber, 2003) is the leading scholar on sexuality and heterosexism in sport psychology. Krane and colleagues draw connections among gender, sexism, and heterosexism using social identity as a theoretical framework (e.g., Krane & Barber, 2003). Barber and Krane (2005) have taken the feminist approach of moving to social action, and offer suggestions for considering gender and sexuality in sport psychology practice.

Sport psychology scholarship on sexual orientation focuses on competitive athletics, with little research on sexual prejudice in other physical activity settings. Although research is limited, reports from the National Gay and Lesbian Task Force Policy Institute (Rankin, 2003) and Human Rights Watch (2001) suggest that organized sport is a particularly hostile environment for LGB youth. In one of the few empirical studies, Morrow and Gill (2003) reported that both physical education teachers and students witnessed high levels of homophobic and heterosexist behaviors in public schools, but teachers failed to confront those behaviors. Gill, Morrow, Collins, Lucey, and Schultz (2006) examined attitudes toward racial/ethnic minorities, older adults and persons with disabilities, as well as perceptions of sexual minorities, and found that attitudes of our preprofessional students were markedly more negative for both gay men and lesbians than for other minority groups, with males especially negative toward gay men.

Sexual Harassment

Considerable research (e.g., Koss, 1990) demonstrates the prevalence of sexual harassment, in all types of settings but the sport psychology literature, which is silent on this topic. Lenskyj (1992) linked sexual harassment to power relations and ideology of male sports, noting unique concerns for female athletes. At the 2001 International Society of Sport Psychology Congress, Kari Fasting of Norway and Celia Brackenridge of the United Kingdom (2001) organized a symposium on related issues. Those reports indicate that the sport climate fosters sexual harassment and abuse; that young, elite female athletes are particularly vulnerable; that neither athletes nor coaches have education or training about the issues; and that both research and professional development are needed in sport and exercise psychology to address the issues (Brackenridge, 1997; Bringer, Brackenridge, & Johnston, 2001; Kirby & Wintrup, 2001; Leahy, Pretty, & Tenenbaum, 2001; Volkwein, 2001).

Sport psychology professionals who are aware of gender and cultural dynamics might be quicker to recognize sexual harassment and help athletes deal with the situation; similarly, coaches and others who have this awareness might be less likely to sexually prey on their young athletes. Both females and males must be aware of issues, and administrators can support educational efforts.

Gender and sexuality are particularly salient in the ever-changing cultural context of sport. Race/ethnicity is just as important, but has received far less attention in the sport psychology literature.

Race, Ethnicity, and Social Class

Race/ethnicity is just as salient as gender and sexuality in the ever-changing cultural context of sport, but it has received far less attention in the sport psychology literature. As noted earlier, Ram, Starek, and Johnson (2004) confirmed that the striking void in sport psychology research on race and ethnicity persists despite the increased multicultural diversity in society and in sport. Research on social class is even more limited, and thus, this section focuses on race/ethnicity, and largely comes from psychology and sport studies.

The psychology scholarship on race/ethnicity is growing and beginning to take a multicultural perspective. Much of that work addresses health disparities, which are well documented (USD-HHS, 2003) and relevant for sport psychology. Contrada et al. (2000) summarized research indicating that racial/ethnic minorities face stress based on discrimination, stereotypes, and conformity pressures and that these stresses affect health and well-being. As Yali and Revenson (2004) suggest, with the changing population demographics, socioeconomic disparities are likely to have an even greater impact on health and mental health in the near future. Given that physical activity is a key health behavior, sport psychology professionals who are aware of health disparities research are in better position to provide guidance on promoting physical activity for health and well-being.

Steele's (1997; Steele, Spencer, & Aronson, 2002) extensive research on gender and racial/ethnic stereotypes and *stereotype threat*—the influence of negative stereotypes on performance—indicates that stereotypes affect all of us. That research, largely in academic settings, indicates that the most devastating effects are on those minority group members who have abilities and are motivated to succeed. On the positive side, Steele's research also suggests that even simple manipulations that take away the stereotype threat (e.g., telling students the test is not related to race or gender) can help. Beilock and McConnell (2004) reviewed the related sport psychology literature, concluding that negative stereotypes are common in sport and lead to performance decrements.

The prevalence of negative stereotypes for racial/ethnic minorities, particularly African American athletes, is well-documented. The stereotypes are clearly illustrated in a section from a commentary by Ruth Hall (2001) that includes a quote by Isiah Thomas:

> We aren't recognized for using intelligence in our game. We're not thinkers, we're doers. As basketball great Isiah Thomas stated, "It's like I came dribbling out of my mother's womb" (Berkow, 1987). The reality is that we excel because we package our intellect with our skill. (Hall, 2001, p. 387).

Research confirms the prevalence of those stereotypes. Devine and Baker (1991) found "unintelligent" and "ostentatious" associated with the category "black athlete," and Krueger (1996) found that both black and white participants perceived black men to be more athletic than white men. Stone, Perry, and Darley (1997) had individuals listen to a college basketball game and found that black players were rated more athletic whereas white players were perceived as having more basketball intelligence. Stone and colleagues (1999) later confirmed stereotype threat in a study in which black participants did worse when told a test was of sports intelligence, while white participants performed worse when told the test was of natural ability.

As Beilock and McConnell concluded, we know less about stereotype threat in physical domains than in cognitive areas, and clearly this is a relevant issue for sport psychology. Beilock and McConnell also pointed out that people are members of multiple groups, and how they think about their group membership is critical. Ruth Hall, who is particularly eloquent on

intersections of gender, race and class in sport and exercise, began a discussion of women of color in sport (Hall, 2001) with a commentary in "She Got Game: A Celebration of Women's Sports" that claimed.

> Race and gender are firecrackers that ignite America's social conscience, rattle the cages that bind us—cages that block our passage to equality. It's a double whammy for African American female athletes since we aren't the dominant norm—we're not white. Race and racism loom large and throw a level playing field off kilter.
>
> Many of us don't fit the Anglo mold. We stretch the parameters of gender roles by our presence, our physical appearance, and sometimes unorthodox style. We aren't "feminine" they say. Commentators describe figure skaters Debbie Thomas and Surya Bonaly and the tennis star Venus Williams as "athletic" "muscular" meaning not feminine. We create dissonance with our skin color, body type, and facial features. We are the other. . . . (Hall, 2001, p. 386-387)

Physicality and Cultural Diversity

Sport psychology professionals deal with physical activities, and thus, physical abilities and characteristics are prominent. Moreover, opportunity is limited by physical abilities, physical skills, physical size, physical fitness, and physical appearance—collectively referred to here as *physicality*. Elite sport implies physically elite performers. Persons with disabilities certainly are among the "left-outs" in sport and exercise settings, and the increasing public attention on obesity has created a negative culture for overweight and obese persons. Indeed, exclusion on the basis of physicality is nearly universal in sport and exercise, and this exclusion is a public health issue. Rimmer (2005) notes that people with physical disabilities are among the most inactive segments of the population; he further argues that rather than physical barriers, organizational policies, discrimination, and social attitudes are the real barriers.

As part of a larger study on sexual prejudice, we (Gill, Morrow, Collins, Lucey, & Schultz, 2005) examined the climate for minority groups (racial and ethnic minorities; gay, lesbian, and bisexual people; older adults; and people with disabilities) in organized sport, exercise settings, and recreational settings. Notably, they found the climate most exclusionary for those with disabilities. Testimony from those who have faced discrimination because of physicality speaks clearly. Pain and Wiles (2006) conducted in-depth interviews with obese and disabled individuals, and their participants clearly cited barriers and challenges in their daily lives. For example, consider these quotes from three of the participants:

> *I am frightened to go back about this wheelchair because they're always going on about my weight.*

> *They think that because you are in a wheelchair you haven't got a brain.*

> *I have got to say that actually every time you go outside your front door, life's really difficult . . . . Barriers all the way along, really.*

(each of these quotes is from an obese and disabled person, Pain & Wiles, 2006, p. 4)

Considerable research within the adapted physical education and therapeutic recreation areas confirms such testimony, and the scholarly and professional literatures in those areas emphasize inclusion in all ways. Notably much of the work on inclusion in physical education and activity settings has moved away from the medical model, which assumes disability is a biological condition calling for treatment or intervention, to a social model more in line with a multicultural framework (e.g., An & Hodge, 2008; Block & Obrusnikova, 2007; Tripp & Rizzo, 2006). Research and professional resources focus on social conditions, context, and social-psychological factors such as support, perceptions, and social interactions. Block and Obrusnikova's (2007) review suggests that inclusion has positive benefits for students with disabilities and their peers, but the evidence is less convincing for teacher awareness programs. As with other cultural diversity issues, we have far to go to identify best practices and resources for professionals.

Physicality is particularly relevant to applied sport psychology. Physical skill, strength, and fitness are key sources of restrictions and

stereotyping. Physical appearance influences outcomes in subjectively judged sports such as gymnastics—and perhaps in some that are not so subjectively judged. Physical size, particularly obesity, is a clear source of social stigma and oppression, and a particular concern in physical activity and health promotion.

A recent report released by the U.S. Bureau or Labor Statistics (Lempert, 2007; available at http://www.bls.gov/ore) documented an increase in the "wage penalty" for obese and overweight persons, a trend that was most pronounced for white women. That is, the difference in wages for obese individuals and their thinner counterparts has increased from 1981 to 2000, demonstrating increasing antifat bias. In a review, Puhl and Brownell (2001) documented clear and consistent stigmatization of obese individuals in employment, education, and health care.

Sport and physical activity professionals are just as likely as others to hold negative stereotypes and biases. Greenleaf and Weiller (2005) found that physical education teachers held moderate antifat bias and strong personal weight control beliefs (obese individuals are responsible for their obesity). Similarly, Chambliss, Finley, and Blair (2004) found a strong antifat bias with implicit measures among exercise science students (see Exercise 7 to test your own implicit attitudes). As they concluded, antifat bias and weight discrimination among professionals have important implications for health promotion. Research confirms that obese individuals are targets for teasing, are more likely to engage in unhealthy eating behaviors, and are less likely to engage in physical activity (Faith, Leone, Ayers, Heo, & Pietrobelli, 2002; Puhl & Wharton, 2007; Storch, Milsom, DeBranganza, Lewin, Geffken, & Silverstein, 2007).

Exercise 7: Test your Implicit Biases

Go to the Project Implicit Web site at Harvard University (https://implicit.harvard.edu/implicit/) and take the IAT on weight demonstration test to assess your own implicit attitudes about obesity.

Most likely you will find that you have some implicit bias. Implicit bias does not necessarily suggest that you are prejudiced, but it does indicate the power of the negative stereotypes and associations that are so prevalent that we don't recognize them. Think about those implicit assumptions and cultural biases that may affect your behaviors and interactions in sport. Specifically, how might you counter that implicit bias to make a youth sport program more welcoming for youth who are overweight or not physically skilled? Check information on the Project Implicit site and Puhl and Wharton's (2007) article for ideas.

Cultural Competence in Sport Psychology

Cultural competence takes gender and cultural diversity directly into professional practice. Culturally competent professionals act to empower participants, challenge restrictions, and advocate for social justice. Indeed, cultural competence is a professional competency required in psychology and many health professions, and applied sport psychology might well follow that lead. In a widely cited report, the Joint Commission on Health Education and Promotion Terminology (2002) described cultural competence as: "the ability of an individual to understand and respect values, attitudes, beliefs, and mores that differ across cultures, and to consider and respond appropriately to these differences in planning, implementing and evaluating health education and promotion programs and interventions." By simply changing "health education and promotion" to "sport psychology," we have a guide for our field.

Psychology actively promotes multicultural competencies, providing a model for sport psychology. As Mio, Barker-Hackett, and Tumambing (2006) discuss, *multicultural competence* refers to *the ability to work effectively with individuals who are of a different culture.* Multicultural competencies include three general

areas: (1) awareness of one's own cultural values and biases, (2) understanding of the client's worldviews, and (3) development of culturally appropriate intervention strategies.

Exercise 8: Becoming Aware of Your Own Worldview

Becoming aware of your own limited worldviews is the first step to becoming culturally competent. Consider your own perceptions and stereotypes about one specific marginalized group (e.g., women, Asians, gay athletes). Be sure to check for implicit biases. For each perception or stereotype consider (a) why do you believe this? And, (b) how might this perception influence a client–consultant relationship and/or one's research?

The American Psychological Association (APA) has recognized the key role of multicultural competencies in fulfilling psychology's mission to promote health and well-being and social justice. Sport psychology can move toward the goal of sport for the health and well-being of all by following these APA (2003) Multicultural Guidelines:

Guideline 1: Psychologists are encouraged to recognize that, as cultural beings, they may hold attitudes and beliefs that can detrimentally influence their perceptions of and interactions with individuals who are ethnically and racially different from themselves.

Guideline 2: Psychologists are encouraged to recognize the importance of multicultural sensitivity and responsiveness, knowledge, and understanding about ethnically and racially different individuals.

Guideline 3: As educators, psychologists are encouraged to employ the constructs of multiculturalism and diversity in psychological education.

Guideline 4: Culturally sensitive psychological researchers are encouraged to recognize the importance of conducting culturally centered and ethical psychological research among persons from ethnic, linguistic, and racial minority backgrounds.

Guideline 5: Psychologists strive to apply culturally appropriate skills in clinical and other applied psychological practices.

Guideline 6: Psychologists are encouraged to use organizational change processes to support culturally informed organizational (policy) development and practices.

Not only does the APA provide multicultural guidelines, but APA Division 47 (Exercise and Sport Psychology) has adopted its own *Affirmation of Diversity,* which states as follows:

> *Division 47 of the American Psychological Association strongly endorses the position of the APA respecting the fundamental rights, dignity, and worth of all people. Psychologists have an ethical responsibility to be aware of cultural, individual, and role differences, including those relating to age, gender, race, ethnicity, national origin, religion, sexual orientation, language, and socioeconomic status. The Division opposes participation in discrimination based on any of these factors, or the condoning of such discrimination.* (Heyman, 1993; in APA-47 newsletter)

Also, the AASP Ethical Guidelines, Principle D (Respect for People's Rights and Dignity) clearly call for cultural competence within applied sport psychology in stating "AASP members are aware of cultural, individual, and role differences, including those due to age, gender, race, ethnicity, national origin, religion, sexual orientation, disability, language, and socioeconomic status. AASP members try to eliminate the effect on their work of biases based on those factors, and they do not knowingly participate in or condone unfair discriminatory practices" (AASP, 2006; available at: http://appliedsportpsych.org).

William Parham (2005), a leader in APA's multicultural efforts as well as an active sport psychology professional, provides a nice overview of psychology's legacy with race, ethnicity, and culture. He then offers useful guidelines

based on his professional practice, including the following three guiding premises:

Context is everything. First, context is key when providing consultation services to diverse athletes. When working with diverse individuals (and all sport psychology professionals work with diverse individuals) history, economics, family, and social context are all relevant.

Culture, race, and ethnicity as separate indexes do little to inform us. Parham reminds us that cultural groups are not homogenous, and every individual has a unique mix of cultural identities.

Using paradigms reflecting differing worldviews. People from culturally diverse backgrounds may have developed sources of resiliency and strength in dealing with power relations. The typical U.S. worldview emphasizes independence, competitiveness, and individual striving. Emphasis on connectedness rather than separation, deference to higher power, mind–body interrelatedness rather than control, and a sense of "spirit-driven energy" may be more prominent in another's worldview.

Hazel Markus and colleagues (Markus, Uchida, Omoregie, Townsend, & Kitayama, 2006) provided evidence for diverse worldviews with their study of Japanese and American explanations of Olympic performances. They found that in Japanese contexts, agency (and performance) is construed as jointly due to athletes' personal attributes, background and social-emotional experience. In American contexts, agency is construed as disjoint, separate from background or social-emotional experience; performance is primarily due to personal characteristics. They further note that these differing explanations are reflected and fostered in the culture, particularly television reports. As Markus et al. (2006) suggest, we may all "go for the gold" but we go for it in different ways, and we value gold in different ways. We all live, act, and engage in sport within a cultural context, and that context affects our perceptions and interpretations (our worldview) as well as our performance.

Exercise 9: Working with Diverse Clients

Assume that you are a professional sport psychology consultant. You begin working with a client from a culture about which you have limited knowledge (e.g., an Australian indigenous athlete, a Muslim athlete, an athlete from China). What could you do to increase your understanding and work more effectively with this client? List three ways you can learn more about the athlete's culture and enhance your cultural competence. Why or when might you need to refer this client based on differing cultures?

Cultural Competence for Sport and Physical Activity Professionals

Cultural competence is integral to quality programs and effective practice, not only for sport psychology but for all sport and physical activity professionals. Sport psychology specialists can play an important role in helping all sport professionals develop multicultural competencies.

As part of a project to develop more inclusive physical activity programs, we (Gill, Jamieson, & Kamphoff, 2005) first collected survey and focus group data from professionals and adolescent girls in physical activity settings. Both groups rated the climate as inclusive, particularly for racial and ethnic minority youth; but youth with physical or mental disabilities and gay or lesbian youth were most often excluded. Focus group responses from adolescent girls, however, suggested that programs cater to boys and the physically skilled. Professionals rated their ability to deal with students of other cultural backgrounds as good, but they seldom took any proactive steps to promote inclusion. Our preliminary results suggest that professionals and participants see the need for cultural competence

resources and programs, but the work has barely begun.

In our project, we provided a working definition and resources on cultural competence to the professionals. We drew from several sources, all of which view cultural competence as a developmental process. Specifically, Cross, Bazron, Dennis, and Isaacs (1999) describe a continuum of cultural competence moving from the lowest level of cultural destructiveness to the highest level of cultural proficiency:

Cultural destructiveness—characterized by policies, actions, and beliefs that are damaging to cultures.

Cultural incapacity—not intending to be culturally destructive, but lack ability to respond effectively to diverse people (e.g., bias in hiring practices, lowered expectations).

Cultural blindness—philosophy of being unbiased and that all people are the same (e.g., encouraging assimilation, blaming individuals for not "fitting in").

Cultural precompetence—desire but no clear plan to achieve cultural competence.

Cultural competence—respect and recognition for diversity, genuine understanding of cultural differences (e.g., seek training and knowledge to prevent biases from affecting work, collaboration with diverse communities, willingness to make adaptations, continued training, and commitment to work effectively with diverse groups).

Cultural proficiency—culture held in high esteem and it is understood to be an integral part of who we are (e.g., conducting research to add to knowledge base, disseminating information on proven practices and interventions, engage in advocacy with diverse groups that support the culturally competent system).

Cross, et al. (1999) also describe several conditions that help individuals and agencies move along this continuum: (1) diversity is valued, (2) cultural biases are understood and acknowledged, (3) an unbiased consciousness of the dynamics when cultures interact is sought, (4) development of cultural knowledge occurs, and (5) the ability to adapt is cultivated. Although the emphasis is on health services rather than psychology, the Cross et al. (1999) model and APA multicultural guidelines reflect similar themes. That is, professionals recognize and value cultural diversity, continually seek to develop their multicultural knowledge and skills, translate those understandings into practice, and extend their efforts to advocacy by promoting organizational change and social justice.

Exercise 10: Consider Your Own Cultural Competence

How culturally, competent are you? Review the six points on the continuum of cultural competence and think about your current or possible applied sport psychology activities. Are you culturally proficient or competent? How so? Are any of your activities culturally destructive or incapacitating? Where does your school, agency, or program fit on this continuum? How could you move "up" the cultural competence continuum? List two specific things you could do.

The health professions are far ahead of sport psychology in recognizing the essential role of multicultural competencies. For example, Luquis, Perez, and Young (2006) found that most health education programs address cultural competence in their curricula. You might consult with health education colleagues for ideas and resources you might use in your own sport psychology practice. For example, you might check the following online resources to help you move up the cultural competence continuum. For example, the Office of Minority Health Web site includes terminology and resources on assessing cultural competence, and the National Center for Cultural Competence (NCCC) has a wealth of resources related to developing and assessing cultural and linguistic competence.

National Center for Cultural Competence (http://www.georgetown.edu/research/gucdc/nccc/) The National Center for Cultural Competence at the Georgetown University Center for Child and Human Development offers many online resources on cultural and linguistic competence.

Anti-Defamation League (http://www.adl.org) ADL's A World Of Difference Institute is the leading provider of diversity and antibias training and resources.

Office of Minority Health (U.S. Dept. of Health and Human Services) (http://www.omhrc.gov/) The office of Minority Health provides information on various initiatives, programs, health statistics, and resources relevant to minority health in the United States. It includes a section on cultural competency.

Bureau of Health Professions (Diversity link) (http://bhpr.hrsa.gov/diversity/default.htm) This site is sponsored by the U.S. Department of Health and Human Services aimed at professional training programs for underrepresented groups.

Summary

Gender and cultural diversity characterize sport and influence all sport participants. Culturally competent applied sport psychology professionals cannot simply treat everyone the same. However, we cannot go to the other extreme and assume that males and females are dichotomous opposites and treat all males one way and all females another way. Gender and culture are dynamic social influences best understood within a multicultural framework that recognizes multiple, intersecting identities, power relations, and the need for social action. Sport psychology has barely begun to address multicultural issues in research and professional practice. To date most scholarship focuses on gender issues, with few truly multicultural frameworks. Multicultural perspectives and cultural competence are especially needed for sport psychology in the real world. To advance sport psychology research and professional practice, we must develop our multicultural competencies, expand our reach to the marginalized "leftouts" and promote sport for all.

Study Questions

1. Identify and briefly explain the three themes in the multicultural framework for this chapter.

2. Describe the impact of Title IX on girls' and women's participation in athletics and in coaching and administration positions.

3. Explain the terms *invisible whiteness* and *white privilege*. Give two specific examples to demonstrate white privilege in sport.

4. Define the terms *sexual prejudice, heterosexism,* and *homophobia,* and explain how sexual prejudice might affect sport participants.

5. Define stereotype threat and explain how stereotype threat might operate in sport.

6. Describe the research on stereotypes and biases related to obesity, and explain how such bias might affect participants and professionals in physical activity programs.

7. Define *cultural competence* and identify the three general areas of multicultural competencies.

8. Identify the steps or levels on the cultural competence continuum. Give two specific things a sport psychology professional could do to move up to a higher level of cultural competence. Describe how sport psychology professionals might promote organizational change and social justice in sport.

References

American Psychological Association (2000). Guidelines on for psychotherapy with gay, lesbian and bisexual clients. *American Psychologist, 55,* 1440–1451.

American Psychological Association (2003). Guidelines on multicultural education, training, research, practice and organizational change for psychologists. *American Psychologist, 58,* 377–402. (available online at APA PI directorate: http://www.apa.org/pi).

American Psychological Association (2004). Guidelines for psychological practice with older adults. *American Psychologist, 59,* 236–260.

American Psychological Association (2007). Guidelines for psychological practice with girls and women. *American Psychologist, 62,* 949–979 (available online at APA PI directorate women's programs office: http://www.apa.org/pi/wpo).

An, J., & Hodge, S. R. (2008, Feb.). Conceptualization of disability knowledge in physical education teacher preparation. *NAKPEHE Chronicle of Kinesiology and Physical Education in Higher Education,* 19 (1), 8–9, 18.

Barber, H., & Krane, V. (2005). The elephant in the locker room: Opening the dialogue about sexual orientation on women's sport teams. In M.B. Anderson (Ed.), *Sport psychology in practice* (pp. 265–285). Champaign, IL: Human Kinetics.

Beilock, S. L., & McConnell, A. R. (2004). Stereotype threat and sport: Can athletic performance be threatened? *Journal of Sport and Exercise Psychology, 26,* 597–609.

Bem, S. L. (1978). Beyond androgyny: Some presumptuous prescriptions for a liberated sexual identity. In J. Sherman & F. Denmark (Eds.), *Psychology of women: Future directions for research* (pp. 1–23). New York: Psychological Dimensions.

Bem, S. L. (1993). *The lenses of gender.* New Haven: Yale University Press.

Berman, E., DeSouza, M. J., & Kerr, G. (2005). A qualitative examination of weight concerns, eating and exercise behaviors in recreational exercisers. *Women in Sport and Physical Activity Journal, 14,* 24–38.

Block, M. E., & Obrusnikova, I. (2007). Inclusion in physical education: A review of the literature from 1995–2005. *Adapted Physical Activity Quarterly, 24,* 103–124.

Brackenridge, C. (1997). Playing safe: Assessing the risk of sexual abuse to elite child athletes. *International Review for the Sociology of Sport, 32,* 407–418.

Bringer, J. D., Brackenridge, C. H., & Johnston, L. H. (2001). A qualitative study of swimming coaches' attitudes towards sexual relationships in sport. In A. Papaioannou, M. Goudas, & Y. Theodorkis (Eds.), *International Society of Sport Psychology 10th World Congress of Sport Psychology: Programme & Proceeding* (Vol. 4, pp. 187–189). Thessaloniki, Greece: Christodoulidi Publications.

Butryn, T. M. (2002). Critically examining white racial identity and privilege in sport psychology consulting. *The Sport Psychologist, 16,* 316–336.

Carpenter, L. J. & Acosta, R. V. (2008). *Women in intercollegiate sport: A longitudinal, national study thirty-one year update 1977–2008.* Retrieved 3/20/08 from http://www.acostacarpenter.org.

Chambliss, H. O., Finley, C. E. & Blair, S. N. (2004). Attitudes toward obese individuals among exercise science students. *Medicine and Science in Sports & Exercise, 36,* 468–474.

Conception, R. Y. & Ebbeck, V. (2005). Examining the physical activity experience of survivors of domestic violence in relation to self-views. *Journal of Sport and Exercise Psychology, 27,* 197–211.

Contrada, R. J., Ashmore, R. D., Gary, M. L., Coups, E., Egeth, J. D., Sewell, A., Ewell, K., Goyal, T., & Chasse, V. (2000). Ethnicity-related sources of stress and their effects on well-being. *Current Directions in Psychological Science, 9,* 136–139.

Cox, B., & Thompson, S. (2000). Multiple bodies: Sportswomen, soccer and sexuality. *International Review for the Sociology of Sport, 35,* 5–20.

Crespo, C. J. (2005, June). Physical activity in minority populations: Overcoming a public health challenge. *The President's Council on Physical Fitness and Sports Research Digest, series 6 No. 2.*

Crespo, C. J., Ainsworth, B. E., Keteyian, S. J., Heath, G. W., & Smit, E. (1999). Prevalence of physical inactivity and its relations to social class in U.S. adults: Results from the Third National Health and Nutrition Examination Survey, 1988–1994. *Medicine & Science in Sports & Exercise, 31,* 1821–1827.

Cross, T., Bazron, B., Dennis, K., & Isaacs, M. (1999). *Towards a culturally competent system of care.* Washington, D.C. National Institute of Mental Health, Child and Adolescent Service System Program Technical Assistance Center, Georgetown University Child Development Center.

Davis, C. (1992). Body image, dieting behaviors, and personality factors: A study of high-performance female athletes. *International Journal of Sport Psychology, 23,* 179–192.

Devine, P. G. & Baker, S. M. (1991). Measurement of racial stereotype subtyping. *Personality and Social Psychology Bulletin, 17* (1), 44–50.

Duda, J. L., & Allison, M. T. (1990). Cross-cultural analysis in exercise and sport psychology: A void in the field. *Journal of Sport & Exercise Psychology, 12,* 114–131.

Erkut, S., Fields, J. P., Sing, R., & Marx, F. (1996). Diversity in girls' experiences: Feeling good about who you are. In B. J. Ross Leadbeater & N. Way (Eds.), *Urban girls: Resisting stereotypes, creating identities* (pp. 53–64). New York: New York University Press.

Faith, M. S., Leone, M. A., Ayers, T. S., Heo, M., & Pietrobelli, A. (2002). Weight criticism during physical activity, coping skills, and reported physical activity in children. *Pediatrics, 110* (2), e23.

Fasting, K., & Brackenridge, C. (2001, June). *Sexual harassment and abuse in sport—Challenges for sport psychology in the new millennium.* Symposium presented at the International Society of Sport Psychology 10th World Congress of Sport Psychology, Skiathos, Greece.

Fredericks, J. A. & Eccles, J. S. (2004). Parental influences on youth involvement in sports. In M. R. Weiss (Ed.), *Developmental sport and exercise psychology: A lifespan perspective.* (pp. 145–164). Morgantown, WV: Fitness Information Technology, Inc.

Fredericks, J. A. & Eccles, J. S. (2005). Family socialization, gender and sport motivation and involvement. *Journal of Sport & Exercise Psychology, 27,* 3–31.

Gill, D. L. (2007). Gender and cultural diversity. In G. Tenenbaum & R. C. Eklund (Eds.), *Handbook of Sport Psychology* (3rd ed., pp. 823–844). Hoboken, NJ: Wiley.

Gill, D. L., Jamieson, K. M. & Kamphoff, C. (2005). *Final report: Promoting cultural competence among physical activity professionals.* American Association of University Women Scholar-in-Residence award, 2003–2004.

Gill, D. L., Morrow, R. G., Collins, K. E., Lucey, A. B. & Schultz, A. M. (2005). Climate for minorities in exercise and sport settings. *Journal of Sport & Exercise Psychology, 27,* Suppl., S68.

Gill, D. L., Morrow, R. G., Collins, K. E., Lucey, A. B. & Schultz, A. M. (2006). Attitudes and sexual prejudice in sport and physical activity. *Journal of Sport Management, 20,* 554–564.

Greenleaf, C. (2002). Athletic body image: Exploratory interviews with former competitive female athletes. *Women in Sport and Physical Activity Journal, 11,* 63–74.

Greenleaf, C., & Weiller, K. (2005). Perceptions of youth obesity among physical educators. *Social Psychology of Education, 8,* 407–423.

Griffin, P. S. (1998). *Strong women, deep closets: Lesbians and homophobia in sport.* Champaign, IL: Human Kinetics.

Hall, R. L. (2001). Shaking the foundation: Women of color in sport. *The Sport Psychologist, 15,* 386–400.

Harris, D. V., & Jennings, S. E. (1977). Self-perceptions of female distance runners. *Annals of the New York Academy of Sciences, 301,* 808–815.

Harris, O. (2000). African American predominance in sport. In D. Brooks & R. Althouse (Eds.). *Racism in college athletics: The African-American athlete's experience* (2nd ed., pp. 37–51). Morgantown, WV: Fitness Information Technology.

Hausenblas, H., & Mack, D. E. (1999). Social physique anxiety and eating disorders among female athletic and nonathletic populations. *Journal of Sport Behavior, 22,* 502–512.

Herek, G. M. (2000). Psychology of sexual prejudice. *Current directions in psychological science, 9,* 19–22.

Heyman, S. R. (1993, Spring). Affirmation of diversity. *ESPN: Exercise and Sport Psychology Newsletter, 7,* p. 2.

Human Rights Watch (2001). Hatred in the hallways: Violence and discrimination against lesbian, gay, bisexual, and transgender students in U.S. schools. *American Journal of Health Education, 32,* 302–306. Full report retrieved August 6, 2006 from http://www.hrw.org/reports/2001/uslgbt/toc.htm.

Hyde, J. S. (2005). The gender similarities hypothesis. *American Psychologist, 60,* 581–592.

Joint Terminology Committee (2002). Report of the 2000 joint committee on health education and promotion terminology. *Journal of School Health, 72*(1), 3–7.

Kamphoff, C. (2006). *Bargaining with patriarchy: Former women coaches' experiences and their decision to leave collegiate coaching.* Dissertation completed at the University of North Carolina at Greensboro.

Kamphoff, C., Araki, K., & Gill, D. (2004, Fall) Diversity issues in AAASP. *AAASP Newsletter, 19* (3), pp. 26–27.

Kane, M. J., & Parks, J. B. (1992). The social construction of gender difference and hierarchy in sport journalism—A few new twists on very old themes. *Women in Sport and Physical Activity Journal, 1,* 49–83.

Kimm, S. Y. S., et al. (2002). Decline in physical activity in black girls and white girls during adolescence. *New England Journal of Medicine, 347,* 709–715.

Kirby, S. L., & Wintrup. G. (2001). Running the gauntlet: An examination of initiation/ hazing and sexual abuse in sport. In A. Papaioannou, M. Goudas, & Y. Theodorkis (Eds.), *International Society of Sport Psychology 10th World Congress of Sport Psychology: Programme & Proceedings*, Vol. 4 (p. 186). Thessaloniki, Greece: Christodoulidi Publications.

Koca, C., & Asci, F. H. (2005). Gender role orientation in Turkish female athletes and nonathletes. *Women in Sport and Physical Activity Journal, 14,* 86–94.

Koss, M. P. (1990). The women's mental health research agenda. *American Psychologist,* 45, 374–380.

Krane, V. (2001). We can be athletic and feminine, but do we want to? Challenging hegemonic femininity in women's sport. *Quest, 53,* 115–133.

Krane, V. & Barber, H. (2003). Lesbian experiences in sport: A social identity perspective. *Quest, 55,* 328–346.

Krane, V., Waldron, J., Michalenok, J., & Stiles-Shipley, J. (2001). Body image concerns in female exercisers and athletes. *Women in Sport and Physical Activity Journal, 10,* 17–54.

Krueger, J. (1996). Personal beliefs and cultural stereotypes about racial characteristics. *Journal of Personality and Social Psychology, 71,* 536–548.

Lapchick, R. (2006). *The 2005 Racial and Gender Report Card.* Retrieved March 2008 from http://www.bus.ucf.edu/sport.

Leahy, T., Pretty, G., & Tenenbaum, G. (2001). "Once I got into the elite squad, it was a lot easier for him to get me" Sexual abuse in organised sport, a comparison of elite and club athletes' experiences. In A. Papaioannou, M. Goudas, & Y. Theodorkis (Eds.), *International Society of Sport Psychology 10th World Congress of Sport Psychology: Programme & Proceedings* (Vol. 4, pp. 190–192). Thessaloniki, Greece: Christodoulidi Publications.

Lempert, D. (2007). Women's increasing wage penalties from being overweight and obese. U.S. Bureau of Labor Statistics. Retrieved 3/19/08 from http://www.bls.gov.ore.

Lenskyj, H. (1992). Unsafe at home base: Women's experiences of sexual harassment in university sport and physical education. *Women in Sport & Physical Activity Journal, 1,* 19–33.

Luquis, R., Perez, M., & Young, K. (2006). Cultural competence development in health education professional preparation programs. *American Journal of Health Education, 37* (4), 233–240.

Maccoby, E., & Jacklin, C. (1974). *The psychology of sex differences.* Stanford, CA: Stanford University Press.

Markus, H. R., Uchido, Y. Omoregie, H., Townsend, S. S. M. & Kitayama, S. (2006). Going for gold: Models of agency in Japanese and American context. *Psychological Science, 17,* 103–112.

McAuley, E., Bane, S., & Mihalko, S. (1995). Exercise in middle-aged adults: Self-efficacy and self-presentational outcomes. *Preventive Medicine, 24,* 319–328.

McDonald, M. G. (2005). Mapping whiteness and sport: An introduction. *Sociology of Sport Journal, 22,* 245–255.

Messner, M. A. (1992). *Power at play: Sports and the problem of masculinity.* Boston: Beacon Press.

Messner, M. A., Duncan, M. C., & Jensen, K. (1993). Separating the men from the girls: The gendered language of televised sports. In D. S. Eitzen (Ed.), *Sport in contemporary society: An anthology* (4th ed., pp. 219–233). New York: St. Martin's Press.

Metheny, E. (1965). Symbolic forms of movement: The feminine image in sports. In E. Metheny, *Connotations of movement in sport and dance* (pp. 43–56). Dubuque, IA: W. C. Brown.

Miller, K. E., Sabo, D. F., Farrell, M. P., Barnes, G. M., & Melnick, M. J. (1999). Sports, sexual behavior, contraceptive use, and pregnancy among female and male high school students: Testing cultural resource theory. *Sociology of Sport Journal, 16*, 366–387.

Mio, J. S., Barker-Hackett, L., & Tumambing, J. (2006). *Multicultural psychology: Understanding our diverse communities*. Boston: McGraw-Hill.

Morrow, R. G. & Gill, D. L. (2003). Perceptions of homophobia and heterosexism in physical education. *Research Quarterly for Exercise and Sport, 74*, 205–214.

National Amateur Athletic Federation. Women's Division (1930). *Women and athletics*. Compiled and edited by the Women's Division, National Amateur Athletic Federation. New York: A. S. Barnes.

Parham, W. D. (2005). Raising the bar: Developing an understanding of athletes from racially, culturally, and ethnically diverse backgrounds. In M.B. Anderson (Ed.), *Sport psychology in practice.* (pp. 201–215). Champaign, IL: Human Kinetics.

Pain, H. & Wiles, R. (2006). The experience of being disabled and obese. *Disability and Rehabilitation, 28* (19), 1211–1220.

Pratt, M., Macera, C. A., & Blanton, C. (1999). Levels of physical activity and inactivity in children and adults in the United States: current evidence and research issues. *Medicine and Science in Sport and Exercise, 31*, 526–533.

Puhl, R., & Brownell, K. D. (2001). Bias, discrimination, and obesity. *Obesity Research, 9*, 788–805.

Puhl, R. M. & Wharton, C. M. (2007). Weight bias: A primer for the fitness Industry. *ACSM's Health & Fitness Journal, 11* (3), 7–11.

Ram, N., Starek, J., & Johnson, J. (2004). Race, ethnicity, and sexual orientation: Still a void in sport and exercise psychology. *Journal of Sport & Exercise Psychology, 26*, 250–268.

Rankin, S. R. (2003). *Campus climate for gay, lesbian, bisexual, and transgender people: A national perspective*. New York: The National Gay and Lesbian Task Force Policy Institute.Retrieved August 6, 2006 from: http://www.thetaskforce.org/reslibrary/list.cfm? pubTypeID=2#pub112.

Reel, J. J., Soottoo, Jamieson, K. M., & Gill, D. L. (2005). Femininity to the extreme: Body image concerns among college female dancers. *Women in Sport and Physical Activity Journal, 14*, 39–51.

Rimmer, J. H. (2005). The conspicuous absence of people with disabilities in public fitness and recreation facilities: Lack of interest or lack of access? *American Journal of Health Promotion, 19*, 327–329.

Smith, T. B., Constantine, M. G., Dunn, T. W., Dinehart, J. M., & Montoya, J. A. (2006). Multicultural education in the mental health professions: A meta-analytic review. *Journal of Counseling Psychology, 53,* 132–145.

Spence, J. T., & Helmreich, R. L. (1978). *Masculinity and femininity.* Austin, TX: University of Texas Press.

Steele, C. M. (1997). A threat in the air: How stereotypes shape intellectual identity and performance. *American Psychologist, 52,* 613–629.

Steele, C. M., Spencer, S. J., & Aronson, J. (2002). Contending with group image: The psychology of stereotype and social identity threat. *Advances in Experimental Social Psychology, 34* (pp. 379–440). New York: Academic Press.

Stone, J., Lynch, C. I., Sjomeling, M., & Darley, J. M. (1999). Stereotype threat effects on black and white athletic performance. *Journal of Personality and Social Psychology, 77,* 1213–1227.

Stone, J., Perry, Z. W., & Darley, J. M. (1997). White men can't jump": Evidence for the perceptual confirmation of racial stereotypes following a basketball game. *Basic and Applied Social Psychology, 19,* 291–306.

Storch, E. A., Milsom, V. A., DeBranganza, N., Lewis, A. B., Geffken, G. R., & Silverstein, J. H. (2007). Peer victimization, psychosocial adjustment, and physical activity in overweight and at-risk-for-overweight youth. *Journal of Pediatric Psychology, 32* (1), 80–89.

Sue, D. W. (2004). Whiteness and ethnocentric monoculturalism: making the "invisible" visible. *American Psychologist, 59,* 761–769.

Tripp, A. & Rizzo, T. (2006). Disability labels affect physical educators. *Adapted Physical Activity Quarterly, 23,* 310–326.

Tucker Center for Research on Girls and Women in Sport. (2007). *The 2007 Tucker Center Research Report, Developing physically active girls: An evidence-based multidisciplinary approach.* Retrieved 3/19/08 from Tucker Center for Research on Girls & Women in Sport, University of Minnesota Web site: http://www.tuckercenter.org/projects/tcrr/default.html.

U.S. Department of Health and Human Services (2000). *Healthy people 2010.* Washington, DC: DHHS.

U.S. Department of Health and Human Services (2003). *National healthcare disparities report.* Washington, DC: DHHS.

Volkwein, K. A. E. (2001). Sexual harassment of women in athletics vs academia. In A. Papaioannou, M. Goudas, & Y. Theodorkis (Eds.), *International Society of Sport Psychology 10th World Congress of Sport Psychology: Programme & Proceedings* (Vol. 4, p. 183). Thessaloniki, Greece: Christodoulidi Publications.

Yali, A. M. & Revenson, T. A. (2004). How changes in population demographics will impact health psychology: Incorporating a broader notion of cultural competence into the field. *Health Psychology, 23,* 147–155.

Enhancing Health and Well-Being

When to Refer Athletes for Counseling or Psychotherapy

David Tod, *Aberystwyth University*
Mark B. Andersen, *Victoria University*

Canst thou not minister to a mind diseas'd, Pluck from the memory a rooted sorrow, Raze out the written troubles of the brain, And with some sweet oblivious antidote Cleanse the stuff'd bosom of that perilous stuff Which weighs upon the heart?

—*Macbeth, act V, scene iii*

A sport psychology practitioner had been working with a gifted collegiate male hammer thrower for about 3 months. A close trusting relationship had formed, and together they had addressed a number of performance and communication issues. Recently, however, the thrower started to miss sessions, although he always contacted the consultant and rescheduled. The consultant was concerned beçause he also had noticed the athlete had been losing weight. One day when the young man failed to attend a session and did not call, the practitioner tried to contact him and left a message. After not hearing from the thrower for 2 days, the sport psychology practitioner attended practice and found out from the coach (who knew the athlete had been seeing the consultant) that the thrower had missed the last 2 days of training because of the flu. Later that evening the practitioner finally made contact with the athlete via the telephone. The thrower was very apologetic and also scared because he had not had the flu but had lied to his coach. On further discussion, the athlete admitted that he had not been able to train, go to school, or even bring himself to eat. He had fallen into a dark place, and he wanted to go to sleep without waking up. The consultant, recognizing the signs of depression and realizing the associated risk of suicide, managed to convince the athlete to come to his office straight away.

Depression is "the common cold" of mental health disorders among the general population (Andersen, 2004a), and sport psychology consultants will invariably come across athletes displaying some signs and symptoms, such as those in the previous example. Athletes often experience depressed moods following a loss or a failure to perform as hoped or expected. If depressed moods are particularly severe or seem to last longer than usual, athletes may need help to get through the sense of loss or disappointment. In many cases, individuals hide their depression from others or may self-medicate through the use of alcohol or other substances. Individuals experiencing depression may show personal or social withdrawal, hopelessness, or loss of self-esteem. Lethargy is also a common symptom and may prevent sports participants from training (Faulkner & Biddle, 2004). Verbalizations indicating depression, hopelessness, or poor self-esteem should be red flags for coaches and sport psychology consultants alike. Overt and covert signs may signal a call for help. With depression there is often the possibility of suicide, which may take the form of unusual risk-taking (see Barney & Andersen, 2000, and Cogan, 2000, for examples of working with suicidal athletes). Treatment may include psychotherapy and anti-depressant medication, and unless the sport psychology consultant is competent and qualified to deal with depressed athletes, a referral to another professional is needed. Referral is a sensitive issue, and consultants need to show compassion and care (see Andersen & Van Raalte, 2005, for how the above case example was successfully resolved through the sport psychology practitioner referring the athlete to a licensed clinical psychologist with expertise in depression).

Most athletes' requests for assistance with performance issues, such as help with goal setting or prerace anxieties, will not necessitate referral to professionals trained to help individuals with clinical, deep-seated, or severe emotional difficulties. On occasion, however, some sport psychology consultants, particularly those who label themselves as educational practitioners, and coaches may come into contact with athletes they are not equipped to help, and in these situations referral is the ethical path to follow. The goal of this chapter is to provide a set of guidelines that people working with athletes and exercise participants can use for referring individuals for professional counseling or psychotherapy. We also will provide suggestions about making suitable referrals for varying circumstances, and we will present dialogue from a referral session. Referring athletes to mental health practitioners does not mean sport psychology consultants

need to stop working with their clients. There are no ethical violations or professional problems when a performance enhancement sport psychology practitioner and a clinical or counseling psychologist work with an athlete at the same time, as long as all parties are informed with the client's consent. In many cases, a team approach can be the optimal way to deliver services. In the space of a chapter it is impossible to describe the symptoms, methods for assessment, and suitable interventions for the many possible mental health issues athletes may present. Such information already exists, and readers are referred to the American Psychiatric Association's (2000) *Diagnostic and Statistical Manual for Mental Disorders: Text Revision* (DSM-IV-TR) for information on specific issues. Instead, we provide some information on many of the more common issues for referral to clinical and counseling practitioners that might arise in the sport setting.

Counseling and Sport Psychology

The fields of counseling, clinical, and applied sport psychology are becoming closer as practitioners begin to recognize the extensive overlap of sport performance and mental health. Recent examples show just how blurry and artificial the lines between sport and exercise psychology and clinical practice are (Brown & Cogan, 2006; Hays, 2002; Hays & Smith, 2002; Lesyk, 1998; Marchant & Gibbs, 2004; Robertson & Newton, 2001). Over the last 2 decades, increased attention in sport psychology literature has been paid to the psychosocial and mental health issues affecting sport participants (Andersen, Denson, Brewer, & Van Raalte, 1994; Brewer & Petrie, 2002; Carr & Murphy, 1995; Grove, Lavallee, Gordon, & Harvey, 1998; Thompson & Sherman, 1993; Tricker & Cook, 1990). This emphasis is also reflected in the strong clinical and counseling themes found in edited books (Andersen, 2000, 2005; Etzel, Ferrante, & Pinkney, 1996; Lavallee & Cockerill, 2002; Murphy, 1995; Ray & Wiese-Bjornstal, 1999; Van Raalte & Brewer, 2002) and in the writings of authors showing the overlap between sport, counseling, and clinical psychology (see Lent, 1993; Petrie, Diehl, & Watkins, 1995; Petrie & Watkins, 1994; Tod, 2007a). Poczwardowski, Sherman, and Henschen's (1998) model for sport psychology service is solidly grounded in counseling psychology principles. An emerging area in applied sport psychology emphasizes the relationships between sport psychology practitioners and athletes (Andersen, 2000, 2006; Petitpas, Giges, & Danish, 1999; Strean & Strean, 1998; Tod & Andersen, 2005), a core feature of clinical and counseling psychology practice. In addition, in 2007 a new journal focused on clinical psychology issues in sport (the *Journal of Clinical Sport Psychology*) emerged. Also, the categorization of athlete concerns into "performance" and "personal" issues seems increasingly like a false dichotomy. Andersen (2006) commented that success or failure on the playing field may be tied to a host of personal issues such as self-worth, self-concept, identity, family dynamics, and the relationships between coaches and athletes. Counseling athletes on performance touches areas that may go to the core of the individual's being.

Even though the gap between performance enhancement sport psychology practitioners and those more interested in athletes' clinical or counseling issues is decreasing, it still exists and can create some difficulties. In North America, for example, there is great diversity in training students in applied sport psychology, with the majority of individuals having received their graduate degrees from kinesiology/exercise science programs (e.g., Williams & Scherzer, 2003). As a result, individuals vary greatly in their range of competencies. With respect to mental health issues, persons with limited mental health training may not be sensitive to signs and symptoms that indicate when athletes need additional help. A similar situation may exist in other countries such as the United Kingdom, where individuals may be accredited by the British Association for Sports and Exercise Sciences or charted as psychologists by the British Psychological Society (Niven & Owens, 2007). In other countries, such as Australia and Flanders (Belgium), sport psychology training has come under the umbrella of the mainstream discipline (i.e. psychology) and qualified individuals might possess greater uniformity of skills and knowledge. Complicating the situation further, practitioners may market themselves under a variety of labels, such as mental skills coach, therapist, or counselor, and it may be difficult for athletes and coaches to readily determine if the practitioner they have approached is suitable for their issues. It is likely that ethical practitioners engage in continuous self-examination to determine whether they have the necessary skills and knowledge to competently help athletes with their issues or to begin referral processes in caring and sensitive ways.

Differentiating Performance Enhancement from More Problematic Personal Issues

In many instances it may not be possible to disentangle performance from personal issues, and sometimes they may be one and the same. Imagine, for example, that a performance enhancement consultant has worked with an athlete for several months and the client's skill level has improved to the point that making an international team is now a realistic possibility. The athlete's life may have changed considerably; she is now living her dream, her self-worth has risen, and her relationships with her coach, parents, and siblings have improved. She has become a happier person. The false performance versus personal issues dichotomy overlooks the important question: "How does performance fit in the rest of the athlete's life?" Performance enhancement techniques, such as goal setting and self-talk, may be of limited value if the athlete's life is a jumble of confusion and conflict. For an athlete experiencing prerace anxiety that is intimately tied to parental love and acceptance, or feelings of worthiness as a human being, then relaxation may prove to be an inadequate Band-Aid for what are deeper issues than prerace nerves.

In much of the performance enhancement literature, problems in performance are related to issues such as competition anxiety, motivational problems, poor self-talk, and lapses in concentration (Meyers, Whelan, & Murphy, 1996; see also Weinberg & Williams, this volume). Determining whether other factors might be involved requires understanding a number of interrelated issues.

An athlete coming to a coach or sport psychology practitioner may be uncomfortable if an interview probes personal areas. Likewise, the practitioner may be reluctant to ask highly personal questions. It is possible, however, to get at least a feel for some of the salient issues in typical discussions of sport performance factors. It is natural for the sport psychology consultant or coach to build rapport by asking athletes about themselves. Getting athletes to talk about their lives can lead not only to understanding their performance or motivational problems but also to an understanding of the whole person.

Fortunately, most requests for assistance with performance enhancement will be just what they appear to be and practitioners with supervised experience and adequate sport psychology training will be able to assist the majority of the athletes with whom they interact. In some cases, however, athletes will present with issues outside the realm of practitioners' expertise, and sometimes those concerns will emerge after the consultant and athlete have worked together for a while. The next few paragraphs provide some guidelines to help practitioners decide if an issue warrants additional professional assistance to help the athlete grow and develop.

First, how long a problem has existed, its severity, and its relationship to other issues in the person's life become important. A problem that is more recent, that is not severe in its emotional implications, and that does not have substantial overlap with other aspects of a person's life is less likely to require professional assistance. For example, an athlete who is facing a tough competitive situation and who experiences mild to moderate anxiety and negative self-talk is not likely to require referral. A person for whom each athletic competition becomes an all-or-nothing battle for a sense of self, whose emotional state is dependent on performance outcomes, and where strong anxiety, depressive states, or substance abuse may also be involved is more likely

to need a referral, although performance-related issues can still be addressed by the performance enhancement sport psychology consultant.

Second, unusual emotional reactions may also need to be considered. Anxiety that generalizes to situations beyond the athletic arena may signal that other issues are present and that interventions may be needed to help deal with other areas of the person's life. Anger or aggression is likely to be an issue presented by an athlete only if it has become a problem to others. Unfortunately, it may take the form of fights with strangers, which sometimes involve legal complications, as well as familial abuse issues. In other cases, an athlete may lose control within the competitive context. This emotional reaction may inhibit otherwise good performance or be a performance threat in that the person becomes a liability in terms of penalties or ejections from the game.

Third, it may also be important to examine the effectiveness of more traditional performance enhancement interventions. For example, perhaps an athlete has not disclosed the full extent of the issue or is not aware of it. It may be that the person working with the athlete did not come to understand the nature and extent of the problem. If more traditional interventions, such as working on self-talk and imagery, do not seem to be working, there are several possibilities to consider. Perhaps the athlete did not respond to the particular intervention—for example, not all individuals can visualize. It may also be that the sport-related problem was not accurately assessed or was stronger than initially assumed. It may also be, however, that the sport-related issue is intimately tied to other issues in the person's life and may have deeper, stronger, or more chronic patterns. These possibilities should be investigated.

How to Start the Referral Process

The referral process is not always a straightforward one. If trust and rapport have been built between the sport psychology consultant and the athlete, sending the athlete directly to someone else when material comes up that the practitioner does not feel competent to handle may not be the optimal choice. Instead of referring out, referring in may be the better choice (see Van Raalte & Andersen, 2002). Bringing in a qualified professional and having all three parties sit down and discuss a plan may be less threatening to the athlete and help ease the individual into the therapeutic process. Referring in may be the best way to keep that therapeutic process going.

Most articles on referring athletes to other practitioners (e.g., Andersen & Van Raalte, 2005; Van Raalte & Andersen, 2002) focus on what to do (and what not to do), and what should happen. The question of many students is, "how do you do it?" There is probably no better way (except for a live role play) to demonstrate how to do a referral than through dialogue and commentary. The second author's (Mark Anderson's) experiences when he knew he was not qualified to work with an athlete with an eating disorder illustrate the issue.

I had been seeing a swimmer, Angela, for about 2 months, working with her primarily on self-talk and arousal regulation. When she arrived at our eighth meeting, I could see something was wrong. We had built a strong working alliance, so when she answered my question about how things were going with a very flat "Okay, I guess," I jumped in:

Mark (M): From over here, it doesn't look like things are okay. It looks like something not very good is going on.

Angela (A): I don't know Doc, I'm just kind of worried. [I kept silent to see if she would go on, but she just sighed.]

M: So, what's troubling you, Angela?

A: [beginning to have tears in her eyes] I am just outta control [now full tears flowing].

M: I can see that this is really painful; tell me what's going on.

A: You'd be disgusted with me.

M: We've worked together for about 2 months, and I think we've built up a good relationship.

I don't know everything about you, but what I know is that you are a fine person. I can't imagine that anything you could tell me would put me off. So let's look at what's going on and see if we can figure out what to do.

At this point, I know something big is coming. Angela is having trouble talking to me about the problem for a variety of reasons. First, she is disgusted with herself and thinks I will be disgusted too. Because of our strong working alliance and her positive transference to me, she does not want to say anything that will disappoint me (see Andersen, 2004c, for a discussion on transference and countertransference). I am trying to reassure her of my unconditional positive regard and to remind her that we are in this endeavor together and that we will look for solutions. Angela then began to tell me of being stressed with swimming, her weight, and school pressures and how her long-standing once a week binge–purge episodes had turned into an almost daily occurrence.

A: How can I do that to myself? Don't you think it's terrible?

M: No, I don't think it's terrible. In fact, right now I am feeling really proud of you for having the courage to talk about all this. I know it's gotta be one of the harder things you've done. . . . I want to do everything I can to help, but Angela, to tell you the truth, I am not trained in eating problems. I think we need to talk to an expert.

A: But I don't want to talk to anyone else. I want to talk to you. Those people over in Student Health don't understand athletes.

M: I know what you mean, but I know a great psychologist over there who is a runner herself and competed in college. She is a major sweetheart and really understands eating problems and weight concerns in sport.

A: I just hate going over there, and I don't want to go to sports medicine. If I did that, I know it would get back to the coach.

M: Nothing is going to get back to the coach unless you want it to. I have an idea. How about if I ask Dr. Kerstner [the expert] to come over here and you and she and I all sit down together? We could meet right here in my office just like our usual appointment. How's that sound?

A: I guess that would be okay. I just feel comfortable with you.

M: I'll be there with you all the way, and I know you and Dr. Kerstner will hit it off.

A: Can I still keep seeing you?

M: Of course! I am your sport psychologist as long as you want me to be. We can keep working on your swimming, and I'll be checking in with you and Dr. Kerstner occasionally on how things are going. How's that?

A: Okay, ask her to come over.

M: I'll get hold of her right after our session.

A: Doc, could we do a nice long autogenic thing today? I'm kind of frazzled.

M: You bet, you know the drill. All right, get yourself in a comfortable position and take a nice deep breath. . . .

This interchange contains many different processes, all directed at making the referral an acceptable option. First, I assure Angela that instead of seeing her problem as terrible (and disgusting) I am proud of her. I am letting her know that my opinion of her has only changed for the better because of what she has told me. Next, I introduce the idea of referral, but she is quite resistant. Athletes at large North American universities (from my experience) often feel that services on "main campus" are not geared for their needs. I attempt to overcome the resistance by telling her a little bit about the psychologist's sport background and by letting her know that I think quite highly of Dr. Kerstner. This last point illustrates the importance of having a referral network of health care professionals who are sensitive to athletes' issues. Angela is coming around, but she still wants to stay with me. Her reaction is understandable; our relationship has been built to this intimate point, a point where she is able to talk about truly painful issues in

her life. Getting here was a long process, and she may not want to tell her problems to a stranger. I address her lingering resistance by suggesting that we refer Dr. Kerstner *in* to familiar turf (my office) and by letting her know I will be with her all the way.

At the end of this emotionally draining session (for athlete and psychologist both), Angela wants to return to the familiar and the soothing, so we do something together that we have done several times before—we relax. In time, other professionals (e.g., a physician or nutritionist) would be called in to help Angela (see Petrie & Sherman, 2000, for a description of a team approach to eating disorders). This first, and largest, referral step helped Angela get on the path of treatment. No two referrals are alike, and some referrals are easier than others. But almost all referrals are complex and sensitive in nature.

When Referrals Don't Go Smoothly

Athletes may not always follow their sport psychology consultants' advice to seek assistance from other professionals. Van Raalte and Andersen (2002) presented a list of *dos* and *don'ts* for the referral process that provide some indications of why athletes do not always follow their consultants' suggestions. First, consultants and athletes may not have a sound working alliance. In the absence of close relationships, athletes may not trust that their sport psychologists have their best interests at heart. Consultants' recommendations, for example, might be interpreted as attempts to rid themselves of their athletes and pass them onto other professionals. From such interpretations, athletes might infer they are damaged goods and possibly unworthy.

Second, if handled insensitively, athletes might feel unsupported and believe their trepidations regarding referral have been ignored. One fear might be that the mental health practitioners will take away from athletes what made them high achievers in sports. Confidentiality is important as well; if word gets around that athletes are seeing other practitioners, they might feel they have lost some of their dignity. Although society has become more psychologically aware in recent years, there are those who still stigmatize people seeking counseling.

Third, consultants may not have prepared athletes adequately for the referral process. Consultants need to educate athletes about what referrals involve, whom the other helpers include, why they might help, and what the implications are for the existing sport psychologist–athlete relationships. Practitioners can begin preparation right from the start by signaling to athletes in their first sessions together that referral might be a possibility in the future. Athletes poorly prepared for referral may have unrealistic expectations about how helpful the new practitioners might be, particularly if sport psychology practitioners have oversold the benefits to convince athletes to seek help.

Fourth, in the absence of any follow-up or facilitation, athletes might never contact the recommended practitioners or may not persist after the initial meetings. The match between the athlete and the helper may not be close enough for benefits to accrue. Also, it may have been a huge step for athletes to share sensitive material with their sport psychology practitioners, who may be among the few trusted people in their lives. Athletes may not be ready to establish new relationships with other strangers.

When faced with referrals that do not appear to be working well, consultants can still keep in contact with athletes. To maintain a close relationship, the perception that the sport psychology practitioner's continued help is conditional on the athlete meeting with the external helper needs to be avoided. It is probably inadvisable, and impractical, to force athletes to meet with other professionals if they are uncomfortable, except in situations where there is a threat of harm to self or others. Then consultants have legal obligations to consider. Sport psychologists who maintain their relationships with their athletes can continue to provide performance enhancement assistance and can still initiate referral process in the future if athletes change their minds.

More Specific Athlete-Related Issues

Sometimes, in addition to performance issues, or related to them, other issues confronting athletes may surface. Insights into depression were presented at the start of this chapter; let's now look at some other issues in more detail.

Identity Issues

One of the most problematic issues for many athletes is that their whole sense of self has revolved around their roles as athletes (Balague, 1999). This overidentification may be particularly salient for competitors at elite levels or in more glamorous sports, but it can occur for any person in any sport. Often the athlete's hopes for the future, and social support from others, may revolve around the sport and the athlete's success. For someone working with these issues, attempts at performance enhancement may take on an extreme urgency, as the athlete's sense of self may well be riding on the outcome. When athletes identify with the role of athlete exclusively, they are said to have *foreclosed* their identities (Miller & Kerr, 2003). Petitpas and Danish (1995) have discussed psychological identity foreclosure:

> In psychological foreclosure people rigidly adhere to their identities to maintain security or to cope with intrapsychic anxiety. This might be seen in athletes who are adult children of an alcoholic parent. They may be resistant to change and more vulnerable to threats of identity loss because their method of coping with their life situations is to seek approval through their athletic successes. The loss of their athletic role would compromise their entire defensive structure. (p. 263)

Major threats to identity can come through athletic injury (Brewer, 1994; Brewer, Van Raalte, & Linder, 1991, 1993; Kolt, 2004; Chapter 23 of this text) and through career terminations (Baillie & Danish, 1992; Grove et al., 1998; Lavallee & Andersen, 2000; Chapter 24 of this text). Brewer and Petrie (2002) have reported that 5% to 24% of athletes who sustain an injury experience clinically significant levels of psychological distress. For a more thorough discussion of issues in athletic injury, refer to Chapter 23 in this book, Udry and Andersen (2008), and Brewer and Petitpas (2005). The last reference contains an in-depth case study about an international skier who had experienced repeated knee injuries.

Negative Identities

Although we normally think of the identity of athletes as something both individuals and peer groups see as positive, valuable, and rewarding, there are also versions that become negative identities (Balague, 1999; Erikson, 1968). In essence, a *negative identity* is the acceptance and valuing of an identity that is generally disapproved of by society. For example, the dumb jock is one such negative identity. Individuals and subgroups may determine that athletes shouldn't care about school or shouldn't do well, and so forth. This negative identity, although disapproved of by many, may become important to an individual or subgroup.

Similarly, the tough jock identity is problematic. For many, being an athlete—most commonly for men but increasingly so for women—means being tough, and it often involves intimidating others verbally or physically.

Substance abuse issues also can become part of negative identity patterns. To be a successful jock one may need to be able to consume a great deal of alcohol or other drugs. In some cases such activity is done covertly, with an eye to the clean-cut image that has to be maintained for public relations purposes.

As with many other human affairs, unless individuals see these identity issues as areas that are problematic and that they would like to change, it may only be possible for coaches or educational sport psychologists to communicate concern for these areas and to point athletes in the direction of those who can help them work on these difficulties.

Sexual Orientation and Homophobia

Athletes' sexual orientation, particularly for gay men, has only received a smattering of attention in the sport psychology literature (Andersen, Butki, & Heyman, 1997; Anderson, 2005; Cogan & Petrie, 2002; Gough, 2007; Krane, 1995; Martens, & Mobley, 2005; McConnell, 1995; Ram, Starek, & Johnson, 2004), and one must go to sociological and popular writings to learn about the experiences of gay male athletes and the culture of homophobia in sport (Louganis & Marcus, 1996; Plummer, 2006). Although gay and lesbian athletes may struggle with the "coming out" process, for most of these sports participants their sexuality is not their primary issue. The homophobia present in the sporting world is usually a far more serious concern, and it raises fears in athletes about getting less playing time, being kicked off teams, being harassed, and being physically abused if their orientations were made public (Martens & Mobley, 2005). Reactions to the homophobic environment of sport may manifest in anxiety disorders, relationship problems, depression, and even suicidal ideation. All of these potential problems may require referral to clinical professionals. If sport psychology practitioners are uncomfortable interacting with gay and lesbian athletes or are not sensitive to the homophobic environments and issues these athletes experience, then referral may be the optimal and ethical decision. Gay and lesbian athletes are likely to feel more comfortable talking with professionals who can empathize with them and offer specific assistance.

Sex-and Health-Related Issues

Most athletic careers start seriously sometime during adolescence and usually end somewhere in the mid-20s to late 30s. In Eriksonian terms (Erikson, 1968) many athletes are in the middle of the challenges of either "identity versus role confusion" or "intimacy versus isolation." Both these times are periods of experimentation, exploration, and finding out about oneself. For some athletes the exploration of self and intimate relationships may involve risk-taking behavior, especially in the realm of sex. The number of sexually transmitted diseases (STDs) is overwhelming. HIV is only the most obvious. Other potentially lethal or debilitating STDs include hepatitis B and C, gonorrhea, and syphilis (making a comeback in many urban centers).

Athletes may approach sport psychology practitioners to talk about risky sexual behaviors they have engaged in that have made them quite anxious about their health status. If a consultant is uncomfortable discussing intimate behavior or is just not knowledgeable about STDs, referral to a counselor with expertise in sexual health is most appropriate.

A study by Butki, Andersen, and Heyman (1996) revealed that collegiate athletes and non-athletes alike use condoms irregularly, but athletes in general engage in sexual behavior more frequently and have more partners than their nonathlete peers. Student athletes may be at greater risk for a variety of sexually transmitted diseases than students in general. At the same time, it must be understood that sharing needles, in addition to sexual behaviors, is a high-risk factor for hepatitis B and C and HIV infection. Steroids can be injected, and often in gyms or locker rooms several athletes may use the same syringe. Again, athletes or sport participants may need to talk with someone about their behaviors and their fears. This person should be knowledgeable and should also be able to make referrals for more specific issues.

Eating Disorders

Because of the complexities of eating disorders and the psychological, physical, and physiological effects that accompany them, referral to a variety of health care professionals (e.g., dieticians, gastroenterologists, psychologists, and team doctors) is becoming the norm. Eating disorders among athletes have received much attention in the sports medicine and sport psychology fields (Brewer & Petrie, 2002; Martin & Hausenblaus, 1998; Papathomas & Lavallee, 2006; Petrie & Greenleaf, 2007; Petrie & Sherman, 2000; Swoap & Murphy, 1995). Reported prevalence rates for eating disorders among athletes vary considerably depending on the sport and who is doing the study. For example, Sundgot-Borgen (1994) found that 8% of elite female Norwegian athletes were diagnosable as having eating disorders, but Burckes-Miller and Black (1988) found a huge prevalence rate—39%—for female collegiate athletes.

Although estimates of eating disorder incidence in men vary greatly, from 0.2% to 20% depending on the study cited, the rate may be increasing (Braun, Sunday, Huang, & Halmi, 1999). Eating disorders historically have been considered a "female" concern, and so there is probably significant underreporting of the prevalence and incidence in males (Baum, 2006). Compared to women, however, men may have a higher age of onset (Braun et al., 1999; Carlat, Camargo, & Herzog, 1997), seek therapeutic help less often (Olivardia, Pope, Mangweth, & Hudson, 1995), and have less chance of successful outcomes (Oyebode, Boodhoo, & Schapira, 1988). In controlling weight, men may be more likely to use saunas, steam baths, and exercise (Johnson, Powers, & Dick, 1999), whereas women may resort to purging, diet pills, and laxatives (Braun et al., 1999; Johnson et al., 1999).

A central feature of eating disorders is often a disturbance in body image, and over the last 2 decades interest in the ways men view their physiques has grown. Increasingly, men are feeling as if they need to attain a highly muscular mesomorphic body shape (Leone, Sedory, & Gray, 2005; Lilleaas, 2007; Pope, Phillips, & Olivardia, 2000). In addition to eating disorders, body dissatisfaction has been related with body dysmorphia, some forms of somatic delusional disorders, poor self-esteem, depression, social anxiety, inhibition, sexual dysfunction, and a variety of health-risk behaviors, such as excessive exercise and steroid use (Blouin & Goldfield, 1995; Brower, 1992; Cash & Grant, 1996; Cash & Szymanski, 1995; McMurray, Bell, & Shircore, 1995).

The etiologies for eating disorders and body dissatisfaction in the general public and in athletes are probably, in some cases, dissimilar. Andersen and Fawkner (2005) identified a number of reasons why athletes may experience disturbed eating and body dissatisfaction. First, although poor body image might motivate exercise and sports participation, there may be no changes in some anatomical features, and, hence, the source of the dissatisfaction may not be alleviated. Second, some sports and types of exercise may not produce desired body changes. Third, participation in sport and exercise may raise expectations beyond what is realistically or genetically possible. Fourth, comparing oneself against others may result in a negative evaluation. The chance of dissatisfaction may be heightened in sports where comparisons are part of the competitive process, especially in sports such as diving or gymnastics. Fifth, participants may be reinforced for developing an excessive preoccupation with their weight and physique, notably those athletes whose coaches dwell on body appearance. Disturbed body image may continue past an athletic career into retirement (Stephan & Bilard 2003). Sixth, individual, psychosocial, and cultural factors also need consideration. For example, men with stronger affiliations to the gay community experience greater body dissatisfaction compared to those with weaker affiliations (Beren, Hayden, Wifley, & Grilo, 1996). Andersen and Fawkner suggested that individual, psychosocial, and cultural factors need more empirical and clinical examination if a better understanding of the relationships between exercise participation, sports involvement, body dissatisfaction, and eating disorders is to be achieved.

Athletes with eating disorders should be referred for treatment if the sport psychology consultant is not knowledgeable regarding eating disorders and how best to treat them. A more important question in sports, however, is whether the pathogenic sport environment should be the object of treatment. I (Mark Andersen) worked with a collegiate gymnast whose disordered eating was essentially environmentally dependent. When she was away from school and away from the coach and the gym, her bulimic behavior dropped to zero. After returning from semester break, she said, "I was just fine at home; it didn't happen, not even once. But as soon as I get back here—Blam!—it's starting all over again." I met this gymnast in her senior year and we worked together on some cognitive-behavioral interventions to decrease the frequency of her bulimic behavior. She was successful at reducing the frequency of the bulimic behaviors, but the eating disorder did not go into full remission until she finished her competitive career and left the sport at the end of her senior year.

Eating disorders are difficult to treat, and eating disorders among athletes, more than many

other referrals, bring up the question of whom or what is really in need of referral. Stimulated by the previously mentioned case (and others), the Eating Disorders Team at my (Mark Andersen) university (composed of general practitioners, a psychiatrist, psychologists, a dietician, and a sport psychologist from the student mental health center) ran educational seminars in the athletics department. These seminars were aimed at increasing the awareness of coaches, administrators, and sports medicine personnel to the signs and symptoms of eating disorders and helping them make referrals to appropriate services. The athletics department was receptive to these interventions, in part, because they and the university were facing litigation from a former student athlete who claimed she arrived at the university healthy and left with an eating disorder directly related to her sport.

Some warning signs of eating disorders to watch for include a marked loss in weight, preoccupation with weight, avoidance of team and other socially related functions involving food, eating very little at such functions, visits to the bathroom after meals, bloodshot eyes after bathroom visits, a decrease in energy level and ability to concentrate, chronic gastrointestinal complaints, and increased mood swings. Eating disorders among athletes is a topic deserving an entire chapter on its own, and entire books have been written on the subject (see Black, 1991; Dosil, 2008; Thompson & Sherman, 1993). For further information also consult the following: Swoap and Murphy (1995), Petrie and Sherman (2000), and Seime and Damer (1991).

Alcohol and Substance Abuse Issues

Due to the public attention to celebrities' problems with alcohol and drugs, this domain is one in which athletes' problems have received extensive attention (see Stainback & Taylor, 2005, for an in-depth case study of a college football player). Authors in this book (Anshel, Chapter 21) and in other volumes (Martens, Dams-O'Connor, & Kilmer, 2007; Carr & Murphy, 1995; Tricker & Cook, 1989) have considered these areas. The association in the United States and other Western countries between masculinity and drinking (as well as the ability to consume large amounts of other substances) may make some athletes more vulnerable to developing problems in this area. Research suggests that student-athletes consume more alcohol, start drinking earlier, and engage more frequently in alcohol-related risk behaviors (e.g., driving after drinking) than their nonsporting counterparts (Hildebrand, Johnson, & Bogle, 2001). Research also indicates that athletes' alcohol consumption may vary with different sports and at various times during the competitive year (Doumas, Turrisi, & Wright, 2006; Martens Dams-O'Connor, & Duffy-Paiement, 2006; Martens, Watson, & Beck, 2006). In addition, individuals inclined to take risks, or "sensation seekers," as Zuckerman (1979) has called them, are also likely to indulge in greater amounts of alcohol and drug use. Certain sports may disproportionately attract sensation seekers.

Someone working with athletes should recognize the general symptoms of excessive alcohol or drug use. Most commonly these signs involve chronic use or binges, centering on major events around drug and alcohol usage, personality changes during usage, and usage interfering with other life activities or relationships. Unfortunately, high school and college life in general, and often the athletic environment, will cloak problem usage with different forms of social acceptability. Given denial and defensiveness around alcohol and drug use, coaches or sport psychology practitioners concerned about these issues can note their concerns, but not in lecturing or threatening ways. It is important to have sources for referral available, particularly if athletes become concerned about their usage and would like to seek help.

Anger and Aggression Control

In many competitive sports we encourage psychological attributes of toughness and competitiveness and see the opponent as an enemy to be defeated. In contact sports in particular, but in other sports as well, physical aggression is sanctioned. Most athletes are able to control their anger and aggression both on the field and off,

although some require a little time after competition for the behavioral controls to reset.

For some individuals, however, who experience difficulty with anger or aggression control, a referral might be appropriate. Some individuals may have always had a reputation for conflict. For men, this tendency may have a negative identity component that cloaks the problem in an acceptable way for a peer group. The athlete may be tough on and off the field, someone "not to mess with." Unfortunately, the frequency and severity of conflicts may escalate to harmful levels.

In other cases, someone going through a personally difficult time may be less able to control anger or aggression. This difficulty may be expressed either on or off the field. Particularly when anger and aggression have not been issues for a person before, they might be discussed with the athlete and a referral made.

Alcohol and drug use may also be related to such behaviors. In general, when people are intoxicated, bottled-up anger or rage may be expressed more easily. In recent years, in addition, *roid rages,* or violent reactions in some individuals who are taking steroids, have been noted (Choi & Pope, 1994; Gregg & Rejeski, 1990; Hartgens & Kuipers, 2004).

There are ways to help individuals deal with anger (e.g., Novaco, 1975) as well as with aggression (Heyman, 1987). It is easier to help individuals resolve conflicts and reestablish controls if they have had a reasonably good history of anger and aggression control. Helping athletes with more problematic histories is possible, but it may be a slower process.

Relationship Issues

Athletes and sport participants are likely to have relationship problems similar to those of others in their peer groups. Some problems, however, might be unique to athletes, although similar to others who are celebrities or who are dedicated to demanding activities in which their partners may not be involved.

Many athletes have to be away from friends or family for extended periods of time. This absence can cause loneliness, anxiety, and depression, for both the athlete and the family members. There may be conflicts in the relationship, or fears or suspicions, and these problems can manifest themselves in decreased performance, increased anger and aggression, or a number of other ways.

At the same time, practice and competition place demands on the athlete's time at home, and this pressure, too, may be problematic for the partner. For many marathoners, who may not be elite or competitive athletes, for example, the months taken to train may disrupt family or relationship patterns. Someone who spends years involved in training and competition may need a very understanding or mutually involved partner.

The glamour and celebrity status that can surround athletes, as well as long travels away from home, offer opportunities for infidelity. Even when an athlete is not unfaithful, the partner may have fears about straying when the athlete is away, or the athlete may have anxiety about the partner left behind.

It is not always easy to identify these issues. In some cases, when performance becomes problematic, the athlete will indicate that the source is an interpersonal or relationship problem. In other cases, a relationship problem may manifest itself in changes in mood; the expression of anger, depression, or anxiety; or increases in alcohol or drug use. Often teammates will be told of the situation, and they may discuss it with a coach or others.

The athlete or sport participant may need to talk with someone individually to understand personal reactions better and to make decisions about commitments and behaviors. In other cases, marital, relationship, or family counseling or therapy might be the best referrals.

Professional Development Tasks for Practitioners and Students

Practitioners and students can engage in professional development in a number of ways to make referral processes more likely to occur smoothly and to ensure that athletes feel accepted and supported. Becoming familiar with the psychopathology of various mental health problems is a valuable first step, particularly for those individuals without clinical backgrounds. Practitioners with knowledge about the origins and manifestations of mental and behavioral disorders will be better placed to recognize when athletes are experiencing serious difficulties and be able to direct them to suitable professionals. Knowledge of psychopharmacology is also relevant because practitioners need to be familiar with what drugs are prescribed for various disorders and the typical side effects. For example, some anxiolytic drugs may lower blood pressure, and if relaxation treatment is also being used, blood pressure may drop to unhealthy levels. Also, sport psychology practitioners, coaches, and athletes need to be aware of what medications are prohibited by national and international sport governing agencies (e.g., the World Anti-Doping Agency, WADA, at http://www.wada-ama.org/en/). Sport psychology consultants, well informed about psychopathology and pharmacology, may have greater appreciation of what life is like for people with mental health concerns, and they may be able to use that empathic understanding to maintain helpful working relationships with their athletes. Being able to talk knowledgeably and nonjudgmentally about mental disorders with athletes will help practitioners better support their clients and prepare them for referrals to recommended mental health professionals. Texts and chapters, such as the *DSM-IV-TR* (American Psychiatric Association, 2000) and Andersen (2004a, 2004b), contain useful information for practitioner continuing education, and sport psychologists can supplement their technical knowledge by reading biographies of athletes who have experienced mental health issues such as depression or drug dependency (Fussell, 1991; Hadlee & Francis, 1985; Louganis & Marcus, 1996; Shea, 2005). Many NCAA institutions in the United States are seeking licensed clinical sport psychologists who can assist athletes with performance enhancement and address a range of clinical issues (Gardner, 2007). If such a trend continues, then individuals who are trained in sport and exercise science departments may find it worthwhile considering further training to become licensed psychologists.

Another way students and practitioners can prepare themselves for future referrals is by identifying professionals they know and trust. Sport psychologists can select from a range of suitable individuals, depending on athletes' needs. These professionals include psychiatrists, clinical and counseling psychologists, social workers, pastoral care providers, marriage and family therapists, substance abuse counselors, and career guidance experts. Athletes' concerns may not always be related to mental health, but instead to other domains such as nutrition or physical well-being. Sport psychologists' networks could include nutritionists, biomechanists, sports medicine specialists, and exercise physiologists. Understanding the sporting backgrounds of the individuals in sport psychologists' professional networks will help practitioners suggest experts who are best suited to helping and forming working alliances with athletes. For example, a clinical psychologist who has participated in track and field events may be a good choice for the depressed hammer thrower mentioned at the start of this chapter.

Sport psychology practitioners and students also can engage in role-plays to prepare themselves for making referrals. By rehearsing the referral process, sport psychologists can practice ways to interact with athletes in a caring and compassionate manner. For example, an athlete may feel threatened by meeting a clinical or counseling psychologist, and role-playing helping the athlete overcome those anxieties adds another dimension to the sport psychologist's repertoire. Peer-group supervision is an ideal place to conduct role-plays because fellow practitioners can receive feedback from their colleagues in a safe, problem-solving environment (see Tod, 2007b, about how role plays may contribute to professional development).

Supervision, generally, can be an ideal place for practitioners to seek guidance from senior practitioners and colleagues about specific athletes whom they are unsure if they can help. Seeking advice and guidance from others may be instrumental in deciding if referral is suitable and how best to handle such instances. Supervision is also a place where practitioners can self-reflect and develop their skills. For example, sport psychology consultants need to be comfortable when interacting with gay and lesbian athletes (see the case vignette in Martens and Mobley, 2005, for how a student consultant, receiving effective supervision, was able to help a gay male athlete). In supervision, practitioners can engage in self-examination to determine their own levels of homophobia and identify ways to address any homophobic tendencies. Practitioners who do not examine their own attitudes and behaviors may not be in a position to help others. A person who is open and accepting of others, however, will convey an important message to athletes and will increase the likelihood of the athlete agreeing to referral procedures.

Summary

Throughout this chapter, we have tried to address a variety of issues involved in deciding when to refer an athlete for professional counseling or psychotherapy. We hope that this chapter has provided helpful information for recognizing when athletes present issues beyond the scope of the usual performance enhancement realm. It is also important, however, for individuals working on performance-enhancement issues to recognize the need for sensitivity to the athlete's personal issues in making appropriate referrals. These helping individuals should also be cognizant of their own issues and values because they might affect their ability to work with and to be sensitive to the issues others might have.

This chapter has been a difficult one to write (and rewrite) because referral involves many complex issues that should be discussed, or at least acknowledged. Many of these topics could easily merit chapters on their own. For example, referral for career termination counseling issues (Lavallee & Wylleman, 2000; Lavallee & Andersen, 2000; Chapter 24) or for psychological treatment during injury rehabilitation (e.g., Kolt, 2000, 2004; Chapter 23) have not been discussed. This chapter has explored ways to help those not trained in counseling or psychotherapy to recognize these issues and to facilitate sensitive and caring referrals.

Study Questions

1. From the dialogue in the chapter, what are some important issues to be sensitive to when making a referral?

2. What are three patterns someone might note as indicating more serious problems when working with an athlete on performance enhancement?

3. What are some reasons why the hammer thrower presented at the beginning of this chapter may not meet with a mental health practitioner?

4. How does homophobia in society and in the sport world contribute to problems for athletes that may manifest in mental and behavioral disorders?

5. How might a concern with food or making weight reflect more serious eating disorder problems?

6. What can sport psychologists do to prepare themselves for making referrals?

7. What are some signs that aggressiveness in an athlete has become problematic? Is it likely that an athlete who has been driven by anger will become less successful if underlying conflicts are resolved?

8. What factors related to sport can cause or exacerbate relationship problems for athletes?

9. How might a coach or sport psychologist find professionals to whom to refer athletes for counseling or psychotherapy?

10. What might you do if an athlete currently does not want to take your referral advice?

References

American Psychiatric Association. (2000). *Diagnostic and statistical manual of mental disorders: Text revision* (4th ed.). Washington, DC: Author.

Andersen, M. B. (Ed.). (2000). *Doing sport psychology.* Champaign, IL: Human Kinetics.

Andersen, M. B. (2004a). Recognizing psychopathology. In G. S. Kolt, & M. B. Andersen (Eds.), *Psychology in the physical and manual therapies* (pp. 81–92). Edinburgh, Scotland: Churchill Livingstone.

Andersen, M. B. (2004b). Personality disorders. In G. S. Kolt, & M. B. Andersen (Eds.), *Psychology in the physical and manual therapies* (pp. 321–332). Edinburgh, Scotland: Churchill Livingstone.

Andersen, M. B. (2004c). Transference and countertransference. In G. S. Kolt, & M. B. Andersen (Eds.), *Psychology in the physical and manual therapies* (pp. 71–80). Edinburgh, Scotland: Churchill Livingstone.

Andersen, M. B. (Ed.). (2005). *Sport psychology in practice.* Champaign, IL: Human Kinetics.

Andersen, M. B. (2006). It's all about sports performance . . . and something else. In J. Dosil (Ed.), *The sport psychologist's handbook: A guide for sport-specific performance enhancement* (pp. 687–698). Chichester, England: Wiley.

Andersen, M. B., Butki, B. D., & Heyman, S. R. (1997). Homophobia and sport experience: A survey of college students. *Academic Athletic Journal, 12* (1), 27–38.

Andersen, M. B., Denson, E. L., Brewer, B. W., & Van Raalte, J. L. (1994). Disorders of personality and mood in athletes: Recognition and referral. *Journal of Applied Sport Psychology, 6,* 168–184.

Andersen, M. B., & Fawkner, H. J. (2005). The skin game: Extra points for looking good. In M. B. Andersen (Ed.), *Sport psychology in practice* (pp. 77–92). Champaign, IL: Human Kinetics.

Andersen, M. B., & Van Raalte, J. L. (2005). Over one's head: Referral processes. In M. B. Andersen (Ed.), *Sport psychology in practice* (pp. 159–169). Champaign, IL: Human Kinetics.

Anderson, E. (2005). *In the game: Gay athletes and the cult of masculinity.* Albany, NY: State University of New York Press.

Baillie, P. H. F., & Danish, S. J. (1992). Understanding the career transitions of athletes. *The Sport Psychologist, 6,* 77–98.

Balague, G. (1999). Understanding identity, value, and meaning when working with elite athletes. *The Sport Psychologist, 13,* 89–98.

Barney, S. T., & Andersen, M. B. (2000). Looking for help, grieving love lost: The case of C. In M. B. Andersen (Ed.), *Doing sport psychology* (pp. 139–150). Champaign, IL: Human Kinetics.

Baum, A. (2006). Eating disorders in the male athlete. *Sports Medicine, 36,* 1–6.

Beren, S. E., Hayden, H. A., Wilfley, D. E., & Grilo, C. M. (1996). The influence of sexual orientation on body dissatisfaction in adult men and women. *International Journal of Eating Disorders, 20,* 135–141.

Black, D. R. (Ed.). (1991). *Eating disorders among athletes: Theory, issues, and research.* Reston, VA: American Alliance for Health, Physical Education, Recreation, & Dance.

Blouin, A. G., & Goldfield, G. S. (1995). Body image and steroid use in male bodybuilders. *International Journal of Eating Disorders, 18,* 159–165.

Braun, D. L., Sunday, S. R., Huang, A., & Halmi, K. A.(1999). More males seek treatment for eating disorders. *International Journal of Eating Disorders, 25,* 415–424.

Brewer, B. W. (1994). Review and critique of models of psychological adjustment to athletic injury. *Journal of Applied Sport Psychology, 6,* 87–100.

Brewer, B. W., & Petitpas, A. J. (2005). Returning to self: The anxieties of coming back after injury. In M. B. Andersen (Ed.), *Sport psychology in practice* (pp. 93–108). Champaign, IL: Human Kinetics.

Brewer, B. W., & Petrie, T. A. (2002). Psychopathology in sport and exercise. In J. L. Van Raalte, & B. W. Brewer (Eds.), *Exploring sport and exercise psychology* (2nd ed. pp. 307–323). Washington, DC: American Psychological Association.

Brewer, B. W., Van Raalte, J. L., & Linder, D. E. (1991). Role of the sport psychologist in treating injured athletes: A survey of sports medicine providers. *Journal of Applied Sport Psychology, 3,* 183–190.

Brewer, B. W., Van Raalte, J. L., & Linder, D. E. (1993). Athletic identity: Hercules' muscles or Achilles heel. *International Journal of Sport Psychology, 24,* 237–254.

Brower, K. J. (1992). Addictive potential of anabolic steroids. *Psychiatric Annals, 22,* 30–34.

Brown, J. L., & Cogan, K. D. (2006). Ethical clinical practice and sport psychology: When two worlds collide. *Ethics & Behavior, 16,* 15–23.

Burckes-Miller, M. E., & Black, D. R.(1988). Male and female college athletes: Prevalence of anorexia nervosa and bulimia nervosa. *Athletic Training, 23,* 137–140.

Butki, B. D., Andersen, M. B., & Heyman, S. R. (1996). Knowledge of AIDS and risky sexual behavior among athletes. *Academic Athletic Journal, 11* (1), 29–36.

Carlat, D. J., Camargo, C. A. Jr., & Herzog, D. B. (1997). Eating disorders in males: A report on 135 patients. *American Journal of Psychiatry, 154,* 1127–1132.

Carr, C. M., & Murphy, S. M. (1995). Alcohol and drugs in sport. In S. M. Murphy (Ed.), *Sport psychology interventions* (pp. 283–306). Champaign, IL: Human Kinetics.

Cash, T. F., & Grant, J. R. (1996). Cognitive-behavioral treatment of body-image disturbances. In V. B. Van Hasselt & M. Hersen (Eds.), *Sourcebook of psychological treatment manuals for adults disorders* (pp. 567–614). New York: Plenum.

Cash, T. F., & Szymanski, M. L. (1995). The development and validation of the Body-Ideals Questionnaire. *Journal of Personality Assessment, 64,* 466–477.

Choi, P. Y. L., & Pope, H. G., Jr. (1994). Violence toward women and illicit androgenic-anabolic steroid use. *Annals of Clinical Psychiatry, 6,* 21–25.

Cogan, K. D. (2000). The sadness in sport: Working with a depressed and suicidal athlete. In M. B. Andersen (Ed.), *Doing sport psychology* (pp. 107–119). Champaign, IL: Human Kinetics.

Cogan, K. D., & Petrie, T. A. (2002). Diversity in sport. In J. L. Van Raalte & B. W. Brewer (Eds.), *Exploring sport and exercise psychology* (2nd ed., pp. 417–436). Washington, DC: American Psychological Association.

Dosil, J. (Ed.). (2008). *Eating disorders in athletes.* Chichester, England: Wiley.

Doumas, D. M., Turrisi, R., Wright, D. A. (2006). Risk factors for heavy drinking in college freshmen: Athletic status and adult attachment. *The Sport Psychologist, 20,* 419–434.

Erikson, E. (1968). *Identity: Youth and crisis.* New York: Norton.

Etzel, E. F., Ferrante, A. P., & Pinkney, J. W. (Eds.). (1996). *Counseling college student-athletes: Issues and interventions* (2nd ed.). Morgantown, WV: Fitness Information Technology.

Faulkner, G., & Biddle, S. J. H. (2004). Exercise and depression: Considering variability and contextuality. *Journal of Sport & Exercise Psychology, 26,* 3–18.

Fussell, S. W. (1991). *Muscle: Confessions of an unlikely bodybuilder.* New York: Avon Books.

Gardner, F. L. (2007). Introduction to the special issue: Clinical sport psychology in American intercollegiate athletics. *Journal of Clinical Sport Psychology, 1,* 207–209.

Gough, B. (2007). Coming out in the heterosexist world of sport: A qualitative analysis of web postings by gay athletes. In E. Peel, V. Clarke, & J. Drescher (Eds.), *British Lesbian, Gay, and Bisexual psychologies: Theory, research and practice* (pp. 153–174). New York: Haworth Press.

Gregg, E., & Rejeski, W. J. (1990). Social psychobiologic dysfunction associated with anabolic steroid abuse: A review. *The Sport Psychologist, 4,* 275–284.

Grove, J. R., Lavallee, D., Gordon, S., & Harvey, J. H. (1998). Account-making: A model for understanding and resolving distressful reactions to retirement from sport. *The Sport Psychologist, 12,* 52–67.

Hadlee, R., & Francis, T. (1985). *At the double: The story of cricket's pacemaker.* Auckland, New Zealand: Stanley Paul.

Hartgens, F., & Kuipers, H. (2004). Effects of androgenic-anabolic steroids in athletes. *Sports Medicine, 34,* 513–554.

Hays, K. F. (2002). *Move your body, tone your mood: The workout therapy workbook.* Oakland, CA: New Harbinger.

Hays, K. F., & Smith, R. J. (2002). Incorporating sport and exercise psychology into clinical practice. In J. L. Van Raalte, & B. W. Brewer (Eds.), *Exploring sport and exercise psychology* (2nd ed., pp. 479–502). Washington, DC: American Psychological Association.

Heyman, S. R. (1987). Counseling and psychotherapy with athletes: Special considerations. In J. R. May & M. J. Asken (Eds.), *Sport psychology: The psychological health of the athlete.* New York: PMA.

Hildebrand, K. M., Johnson, D. J., & Bogle, K. (2001). Comparison of patterns of alcohol use between high school and college athletes and non-athletes. *College Student Journal, 35,* 358–365.

Johnson, C., Powers, P. S., & Dick, R. (1999). Athletes and eating disorders: The National Collegiate Athletic Association study. *International Journal of Eating Disorders, 26,* 179–188.

Kolt, G. S. (2004). Injury from sport, exercise, and physical activity. In G. S. Kolt, & M. B. Andersen (Eds.), *Psychology in the physical and manual therapies* (pp. 247–267). Edinburgh, Scotland: Churchill Livingstone.

Kolt, G. S. (2000). Doing sport psychology with injured athletes. In M. B. Andersen (Ed.), *Doing sport psychology* (pp. 223–236). Champaign, IL: Human Kinetics.

Krane, V. (1995). Performance related outcomes experienced by lesbian athletes. *Journal of Applied Sport Psychology, 7* (Suppl.), S83.

Lavallee, D., & Andersen, M. B. (2000). Leaving sport: Easing career transitions. In M. B. Andersen (Ed.), *Doing sport psychology* (pp. 249–260). Champaign, IL: Human Kinetics.

Lavallee, D., & Cockerill, I. (Eds.). (2002). *Counselling in sport and exercise contexts.* Leicester, England: British Psychological Society.

Lavallee, D., & Wylleman, P. (Eds.). (2000). *Career transitions in sport: International perspectives.* Morgantown, WV: Fitness Information Technology.

Lent, R. W. (1993). Sports psychology and counseling psychology: Players in the same ball park? *The Counseling Psychologist, 21,* 430–435.

Leone, J. E., Sedory, E. J., & Gray, K. A. (2005). Recognition and treatment of muscle dysmorphia and related body image disorders. *Journal of Athletic Training, 40,* 352–359.

Lesyk, J. L. (1998). *Developing sport psychology within your clinical practice: A practical guide for mental health professionals.* San Francisco: Jossey-Bass.

Lilleaas, U-B. (2007). Masculinities, sport, and emotions. *Men and Masculinities, 10,* 39–53.

Louganis, G., & Marcus, E. (1996). *Breaking the surface.* New York: Penguin Putnam.

Marchant, D., & Gibbs, P. (2004). Ethical considerations in treating borderline personality in sport: A case example. *The Sport Psychologist, 18,* 317–323.

Martens, M. P., Dams-O'Connor, K., & Duffy-Paiement, C. (2006). Comparing off-season with in-season alcohol consumption among intercollegiate athletes. *Journal of Sport & Exercise Psychology, 28,* 502–510.

Martens, M. P., Dams-O'Connor, K., & Kilmer, J. R. (2007). Alcohol and drug use among athletes: Prevalence, etiology, and interventions. In. G. Tenenbaum & R. C. Eklund (Eds.). *Handbook of research in sport psychology* (3rd ed., pp. 859–878). Hoboken, NJ: Wiley.

Martens, M. P., & Mobley, M. (2005). Straight guys working with gay guys: Homophobia and sport psychology service delivery. In M. B. Andersen (Ed.), *Sport psychology in practice* (pp. 249–263). Champaign, IL: Human Kinetics.

Martens, M. P., Watson, J. C., II., & Beck, N. C. (2006). Sport-type differences in alcohol use among intercollegiate athletes. *Journal of Applied Sport Psychology, 18,* 136–150.

Martin, K. A., & Hausenblas, H. A. (1998). Psychological commitment to exercise and eating disorder symptomatology among female aerobic instructors. *The Sport Psychologist, 12,* 180–190.

McConnell, K. E. (1995). Homophobia in women's intercollegiate athletics: A case study. *Journal of Applied Sport Psychology, 7* (Suppl.), S89.

McMurray, N. E., Bell, R., & Shircore, J. (1995, July). *Psychological factors influencing positive and negative health behaviors in a community sample of men and women.* Paper presented at the 9th European Congress of Psychology, Athens, Greece.

Meyers, A. W., Whelan, J. P., & Murphy, S. M. (1996). Cognitive behavioral strategies in athletic performance enhancement. In M. Hersen, R. M. Eisler, & P. M. Miller (Eds.), *Progress in behavior modification* (Vol. 30, pp. 137–164). Pacific Grove, CA: Brooks/Cole.

Miller, P. S., & Kerr, G. A. (2003). The role experimentation of intercollegiate student athletes. *The Sport Psychologist, 17,* 196–219.

Murphy, S. M. (Ed.). (1995). *Sport psychology interventions.* Champaign, IL: Human Kinetics.

Niven, A. G., & Owens, A. (2007). Qualification and training routes to becoming a practicing sport and exercise psychologist in the UK. *Sport & Exercise Psychology Review, 3* (2), 47–50.

Novaco, R. W. (1975). *Anger control: The development and evaluation of an experimental treatment.* Lexington, MA: Heath.

Olivardia, R., Pope, H. G., Jr., Mangweth, B., & Hudson, J. I. (1995). Eating disorders in college men. *American Journal of Psychiatry, 152,* 1279–1285.

Oyebode, F., Boodhoo, J. A., & Schapira, K. (1988). Anorexia nervosa in males: Clinical features and outcome. *International Journal of Eating Disorders, 7,* 121–124.

Papathomas, A., & Lavallee, D. (2006). A life history analysis of a male athlete with an eating disorder. *Journal of Loss and Trauma, 11,* 143–179.

Petitpas, A., & Danish, S. J. (1995). Caring for injured athletes. In S. M. Murphy (Ed.), *Sport psychology interventions* (pp. 255–281). Champaign, IL: Human Kinetics.

Petitpas, A. J., Giges, B. & Danish, S. J., (1999). The sport psychologist–athlete relationship: Implications for training. *The Sport Psychologist, 13,* 344–357.

Petrie, T. A., Diehl, N. S., & Watkins, C. E., Jr. (1995). Sport psychology: An emerging domain in the counseling psychology profession? *The Counseling Psychologist, 23,* 535–545.

Petrie, T. A., & Greenleaf, C. A. (2007). Eating disorders in sport: From theory to research to intervention. In G. Tenenbaum & R. C. Eklund (Eds.). *Handbook of sport psychology* (3rd ed., pp. 352–378). Hoboken, NJ: Wiley.

Petrie, T. A., & Sherman, R. T. (2000). Counseling athletes with eating disorders: A case example. In M. B. Andersen (Ed.), *Doing sport psychology* (pp. 121–137). Champaign, IL: Human Kinetics.

Petrie, T. A., & Watkins, C. E., Jr. (1994). Sport psychology training in counseling psychology programs: Is there room at the inn? *The Counseling Psychologist, 22,* 335–341.

Plummer, D. (2006). Sportophobia: Why do some men avoid sport? *Journal of Sport & Social Issues, 30,* 122–137.

Poczwardowski, A., Sherman, C. P., & Henschen, K. P. (1998). A sport psychology service delivery heuristic: Building on theory and practice. *The Sport Psychologist, 12,* 191–207.

Pope, H. G., Jr., Phillips, K. A., & Olivardia, R. (2000). *The Adonis complex: The secret crisis of male body obsession.* New York: Free Press.

Ram, N., Starek, J., & Johnson, J. (2004). Race, ethnicity, and sexual orientation: Still a void in sport and exercise psychology? *Journal of Sport & Exercise Psychology, 26,* 250–268.

Ray, R., & Wiese-Bjornstal, D. M. (Eds.). (1999). *Counseling in sports medicine.* Champaign, IL: Human Kinetics.

Robertson, J. M., & Newton, F. B. (2001). Working with men in sports settings. In G. R. Brooks & G. E. Good (Eds.), *The new handbook of psychotherapy and counseling with men: A comprehensive guide to settings, problems, and treatment approaches* (Vol. 1, pp. 92–125). San Francisco: Jossey-Bass.

Seime, R., & Damer, D. (1991). Identification and treatment of the athlete with an eating disorder. In E. F. Etzel, A. P. Ferrante, & J. W. Pinkney (Eds.), *Counseling college student-athletes: Issues and interventions* (pp. 175–198). Morgantown, WV: Fitness Information Technology.

Shea, A. (2005). *Petria Thomas: Swimming against the tide.* Sydney, Australia: ABC Books.

Stainback, R. D., & Taylor, R. E. (2005). Facilitating change: Alcohol and violence among athletes. In M. B. Andersen (Ed.), *Sport psychology in practice* (pp. 135–158). Champaign, IL: Human Kinetics.

Stephan, Y., & Bilard, J. (2003). Repercussions of transition out of elite sport on body image. *Perceptual and Motor Skills, 96,* 95–104.

Strean, W. B., & Strean, H. S. (1998). Applying psychodynamic concepts to sport psychology practice. *The Sport Psychologist, 12,* 208–222.

Sundgot-Borgen, J. (1994). Risk and trigger factors for the development of eating disorders in female elite athletes. *Medicine and Science in Sports and Exercise, 26,* 414–419.

Swoap, R. A., & Murphy, S. M. (1995). Eating disorders and weight management in athletes. In S. M. Murphy (Ed.), *Sport psychology interventions* (pp. 307–329). Champaign, IL: Human Kinetics.

Thompson, R. A., & Sherman, R. T. (1993) *Helping athletes with eating disorders*. Champaign, IL: Human Kinetics.

Tod, D. (2007a). Reflections on collaborating with a professional rugby league player. *Sport & Exercise Psychology Review, 3* (1), 4–10.

Tod, D. (2007b). The long and winding road: Professional development in sport psychology. *The Sport Psychologist, 21,* 94–108.

Tod, D., & Andersen, M. (2005). Success in sport psychology: Effective sport psychologists. In S. Murphy (Ed.), *The sport psych handbook* (pp. 305–314). Champaign, IL: Human Kinetics.

Tricker, R., & Cook, D. L. (Eds.). (1990). *Drugs and sport: Athletes at risk*. Dubuque, IA: Brown.

Udry, E., & Andersen, M. B. (2008). Psychological Aspects of athletic injury and sport behavior. In T. S. Horn (Ed.), *Advances in sport psychology* (3rd ed., pp. 401–422). Champaign, IL: Human Kinetics.

Van Raalte, J. L., & Andersen, M. B. (2002). Referral processes in sport psychology. In J. L. Van Raalte & B. W. Brewer (Eds.), *Exploring sport and exercise psychology* (2nd ed., pp. 325–337). Washington, DC: American Psychological Association.

Van Raalte, J. L., & Brewer, B. W. (Eds.). (2002). *Exploring sport and exercise psychology* (2nd ed.). Washington, DC: American Psychological Association.

Williams, J. M., & Scherzer, C. B. (2003). Tracking the training and careers of graduates of advanced degree programs in sport psychology, 1994–1999. *Journal of Applied Sport Psychology, 15,* 335–353.

Zuckerman, M. (1979). *Sensation seeking: Beyond the optimal level of arousal*. Hillsdale, NJ: Erlbaum.

Drug Abuse in Sport: Causes and Cures

Mark H. Anshel, *Middle Tennessee State University*

Athletes who think they're immortal are playing Russian roulette with their health by toying with drugs. Experts warn of heart disease and tumors. Ask the friends of former NFL stud Lyle Alzado, who blamed his death from cancer at 42 on steroids.

—Sandy Grady, USA Today

The use of banned substances in elite sport—both professional and amateur—has received more media attention than ever in recent years. For example, baseball home run king Barry Bonds, U.S. Olympic gold medal winner Marianne Jones, and deceased professional wrestler Chris Benoit have all been implicated in the inappropriate use of anabolic steroids. Jones had to forfeit her medals after admitting to steroid use leading up to the 2000 Olympic games, and she was sentenced to six months in prison for lying under oath in U.S. District Court about her drug use (*USA Today*, January 14, 2008, p. 18C). Benoit committed suicide after first murdering his wife and son, a crime that has been linked to at least one known effect of prolonged steroid use, heightened aggression, commonly called "roid rage." Perhaps it is incidents like these that are compelling sport organizations and governing bodies to pay even closer attention to drug use by competitors, and why those who support and follow organized sport should care about drug-taking behaviors.

The use of drugs in sport is not new. Greek athletes in the third century B.C. ingested substances to improve their performance. In the 1970s performance-enhancing drugs were used among medal winners from the Soviet Union and other Eastern European countries, most notably East Germany, but it was not until the 1976 Olympic Games held in Montreal that the International Olympic Committee (IOC) started widespread drug testing and penalized athletes for testing positive. Two gold medal winners and one silver medal winner were disqualified. At the 1988 Olympic games in Seoul, the Canadian world-class sprinter Ben Johnson tested positive for steroids, and 2.9% urine specimens tested positive for illegal drug use. Even with more rigorous testing for banned substances at the Olympics, the problem of ingesting banned substances and engaging in other inappropriate behaviors continue among both the world's best and less elite athletes.

Perhaps engaging in unethical actions in sport is not surprising, even if it means facing severe penalties if tests confirm the use of banned substances that provide a performance edge. Considering the emphasis put on winning, and that winning is often tied to an athlete's self-esteem, it is not surprising that some athletes will do whatever it takes to succeed. The sport community must not let that happen, and this chapter explains the reasons for rules and the need for tough enforcement of those rules because drug education, alone, is ineffective in preventing drug abuse among sports competitors. In particular, this chapter will (1) present the different types of drugs that athletes are taking and other forms of banned behaviors (e.g., blood doping) in which athletes are engaging to gain a performance edge, (2) describe the reasons these substances and actions are banned, including the negative, even possibly fatal, effects on the athlete's physical and mental health, and (3) suggest strategies that coaches, sports administrators, and sport psychology consultants may use to reduce the likelihood of drug-taking in sport.

Why are certain substances banned from competitive sport, and why should sport administrators, coaches, parents of athletes, and athletes themselves be concerned about the use of drugs categorized as "performance-enhancing"? Yesalis and Cowart (1998) state that the use of steroids by athletes (a) may cause physical and psychological harm, (b) violates state and federal laws if used for nonmedical purposes, (c) is cheating and violates the team rules and organizational policies of almost every sport, and (d) contaminates performance results, which are obtained by unnatural means. The same can be said for most other banned substances or procedures. Only when causes for drug usage are identified can we devise cognitive and behavioral strategies to help prevent and perhaps eliminate this problem.

The word *drug* means different things to different people. The two most common categories of drug use among competitive athletes are performance-enhancing drugs, such as anabolic steroids, and drugs referred to as "recreational" or "mind-altering," such as cocaine, heroin, or marijuana. The objective of recreational drug users is to alter the state of mind, with no intention of improving performance. The different rationales

for ingesting performance-enhancing and recreational drugs must be taken into account when developing strategies to reduce or eliminate such behaviors.

How prevalent is taking recreational drugs among competitive athletes? In their review of related literature, Martens, Dams-O'Connor, and Kilmer (2007) concluded that drug use among athletes and nonathletes is comparable. In most studies, for example, marijuana usage rates of college male athletes the 30 days prior to responding to a survey is slightly higher among nonathletes (16%) compared to athletes (12%). Usage rates were similar for female nonathletes (11%) and athletes (10%).

A National Collegiate Athletic Association (NCAA, 2001) study of the prevalence of steroid use among college athletes found that "only" 1.6%, 1.3%, and 1.4% of athletes competing in Divisions I, II, and III, respectively, reported using steroids in the previous 12 months. Sport type, however, was an important moderating variable in determining the extent of steroid use. Athletes competing in football, baseball, and water polo reported far higher steroid usage rates than those in tennis, lacrosse, swimming, and track and field. In a classic case of possible underreporting, only .06% of track and field college athletes reported steroid use, and yet, evidence reported in the media has been mounting in recent years about repeated positive drug tests for elite track and field athletes. Underreporting is an inherent limitation of any self-report study that requires acknowledging one's behavior that may be considered undesirable or illegal (Anshel, 1993). Relatively few athletes will admit to engaging in a behavior that they know is either illegal or unethical. One approach to overcoming this problem is to ask athletes about the behaviors of "others" rather than themselves (e.g., Anshel, 1990); however, this approach has been rarely used.

Yesalis and Cowart (1998) contend that steroid use in middle schools has increased significantly due, primarily, to the well-known steroid habits of elite athletes. Steroid use is now ubiquitous in the school system, from college to middle school. A study by the University of Michigan in

2003 indicated that 3.5% of high school seniors, all nonathletes, had used illegal steroids, a 2% increase from 10 years earlier. The primary reason for ingesting steroids, particularly by young male nonathletes, is to enhance one's musculature and physique. Thus, adolescent males' use of steroids to improve physical appearance is expanding (Ringhofer & Harding, 1996). Apparently, failing to control the availability of performance-enhancing drugs is taking a toll on society beyond competitive sport.

Review of Drugs Banned in Sport

The IOC refers to the act of ingesting banned drugs as "doping" (Prokop, 1990). **Doping** has been defined as "the administering or use of substances in any form alien to the body or of physiological substances in abnormal amounts and with abnormal methods by healthy persons with the exclusive aim of attaining an artificial and unfair increase of performance in competition" (p. 5). Williams (1994) cites IOC doping legislation that stipulates that any physiologic substance taken in abnormal quantities with the intention of artificially and unfairly increasing performance should be construed as doping, violating the ethics of sport performance. The IOC has classified five doping categories that are banned from international competition: anabolic androgenic steroids, stimulants (including hallucinogens), narcotic analgesics, beta-adrenergic blockers, and diuretics (Lennehan, 2003). Local anesthetics and corticosteroids (anti-inflammatory drugs that relieve pain) are not on the IOC list but selected international competitions test for them (Chappel, 1987). Typically, these substances are considered illegal. In addition, as an ergogenic aid, the technique of blood doping is also banned. The reasons for banning such drugs in sport are understandable given their psychophysiological effects (Weinhold, 1991; Williams, 1998).

Not banned by the IOC and, therefore, not against policies of national and international sport organizations, at least for mature-age athletes, are alcohol, nicotine (e.g., tobacco products), diet regimens (e.g., carbohydrate loading or any other food-ingestion habits), amino acids, caffeine (within limits), antidepressants, and vitamins (Lennehan, 2003; Williams, 1998). In recent years, additional supplements such as creatine, human growth hormone (HGH), and tetra-hydrogestrinone (THG) have been banned from certain professional sports, such as Major League Baseball. The results of additional research may result in banning other nutritional supplements.

Anabolic Steroids

Anabolic steroids are the best-known category of performance-enhancing drug. Of course, any potential benefit of steroid use to sport performance depends on the type of skills and physical demands required of that sport. Perhaps the most salient advantage of steroid use on sport performance is improved strength and power (Yesalis & Cowart, 1998), thus aiding performance in sports such as football and track and field. This is because the function of anabolic steroids is to increase the male hormone androgen and decrease the female hormone estrogen. Increased strength occurs because steroids promote the synthesis of proteins that are used to build skeletal muscle tissue (Yesalis & Cowart, 1998). Anabolic steroids also are used for medicinal purposes, most notably, to promote muscle growth and tissue repair as part of injury rehabilitation.

The harmful side-effects of prolonged steroid use are extensive (see Lubell, 1989; Mottram, Reilly, & Chester, 1997; Yesalis & Cowart, 1998). High testosterone levels have a masculinizing effect for females (e.g., increased facial and body hair, lowered voice, increased muscular bulk and strength, interference with reproductive function). When testosterone levels become too high, the hypothalamus in the brain starts to shut down the body processes involving the hormone. These processes include stimulation and maintenance of the sex organs for males, leading to increased feminine characteristics (e.g., reduced facial and body hair, reduced sperm production and impotence). Both genders may experience temporary or permanent sterility (Ringhofer & Harding, 1996). In addition, tendons and ligaments may not strengthen at the same rate as muscle tissue, thus increasing risk of injury (Wright & Cowart, 1990). The negative side effects of prolonged steroid use are even greater for individuals who have not yet reached physiological maturity. For example, adolescent abusers may incur reduced bone growth because of premature fusion of the epiphysis of long bones. The result is permanently stunted growth. (Miller, Barnes, Sabo, Melnick, & Farrell, 2002).

More ominously, prolonged heavy steroid users risk cancerous liver cell tumors, high blood pressure (i.e., hypertension), premature heart disease, myocardial infarction (heart attack), and stroke. Another undesirable effect of prolonged steroid use is heightened, uncontrolled aggression and temper, often referred to as "roid rage." Roid rage is a condition in which a behavioral manifestation of chronic steroid users is increased aggressiveness, and concomitant high-risk behaviors (e.g., drinking and driving, unsafe sex, nonuse of seat belts, attempted suicide) (Branch, 2002). Related behavioral outcomes include child abuse, domestic violence, suicide, and attempted murder or death. When chronic steroid use is suddenly stopped, clinical depression often results.

Another concern about steroid use is its addictive properties, both psychologically and physiologically (Weinhold, 1991). From a psychological perspective, the individual may feel dependent on steroids for maintaining a sense of well-being, perceived strength and musculature, and a performance edge. Failing to maintain the steroid regimen may result in lost confidence, fear of failure, and depression. Physiological addiction may reflect the body's dependence on molecular substances for protein synthesis, which builds skeletal tissue. Symptoms of sudden withdrawal of prolonged steroid ingestion include changes in heart rate, blood pressure, tension, and fatigue (Leccese, 1991).

According to Schlaadt and Shannon (1994), athletes may attempt to overcome these problems by taking "drug holidays" between periods of use by "pyramiding" or "stacking." Pyramiding consists of beginning with a lower dose, then increasing the amount progressively until the maximum dose is reached, then tapering the dosage until the drug is completely withdrawn.

Stacking consists of using numerous drugs and varying the dosage throughout the cycle. The authors conclude, however, that "no scientific evidence supports the idea that 'stacking' or 'pyramiding' the drugs is more effective than other methods of using them or that it minimizes the harmful side effects of steroid use" (p. 50).

To find detailed information about steroids and their effects, read the National Institute on Drug Abuse Research Report Series, which is sponsored by the National Institutes of Health and can be obtained at http://www.nida.nig.gov/ResearchReports/Steroids/anabolicsteroids3.html.

Stimulants

Stimulant drugs increase the rate and, hence, the work capacity of the heart, central nervous system, and respiratory system. Stimulants are divided into four groups: **psychomotor** (e.g., amphetamines, cocaine, and most diet suppressants); **sympathomimetic amines,** which stimulate the sympathetic and autonomic nervous systems; **hallucinogens,** often referred to as recreational, mind-altering, or street drugs (Martens et al., 2007); and miscellaneous **central nervous system (CNS) stimulants** such as ephedrine that are found in many prescription and over-the-counter cold remedies. Ostensibly these drugs improve athletic performance by increasing alertness through inhibition of mental and physical fatigue. However, on the minus—and very dangerous—side, some stimulants (e.g., cocaine) may result in death due to seizures, damage to the heart muscle, or stroke (Doweiko, 1996).

Hallucinogens, often referred to as "recreational" or "mind-altering" drugs, influence the individual's perceptions of incoming stimuli by slowing response and decision-making time, and inhibiting attentional focusing. Hallucinogens are categorized as either stimulants (e.g., cocaine), which increase somatic arousal (e.g., heart or respiration rate), or narcotic analgesics (e.g., marijuana, LSD, PCP), which can reduce pain (as an anti-inflammatory) and anxiety (as a sedative). Not surprisingly, this category of drug actually impairs, not promotes, sport performance. The IOC bans all types of hallucinogens. The use of these drugs is also against the laws of most countries.

Narcotic Analgesics (Anti-Inflammatories)

Narcotic analgesics, discussed briefly in the previous paragraph, are used by athletes for their pain-killing properties, to slow or stop the inflammation and swelling of tissue, to reduce fever, and to produce feelings of well-being or invincibility (Thornton, 1997). As pain suppressants, these drugs enable an injured competitor to continue playing despite tissue damage and injury. Anti-inflammatories can reduce performance effectiveness in some sports due to their sedative effect. All analgesics are toxic and addictive in large doses (Doweiko, 1996). Examples of narcotic analgesics include codeine, heroin, morphine, and opium. Harmful effects of analgesics include gastrointestinal disturbances, physical and psychological dependence, and depressed respiration, including respiratory arrest. Nonnarcotic analgesics such as aspirin and acetaminophen, which are not habit forming, do not affect the central nervous system and are not banned.

Beta-Adrenergic Blockers

Perhaps best known for the treatment of high blood pressure and some forms of heart disease, **beta-blockers** are among the few drugs banned by the IOC that do not induce dependence. They aid performance by slowing the heart rate, decreasing anxiety, and steadying natural body tremors. These are desirable outcomes in sports such as rifle and pistol shooting, archery, bowling, and golf, which are why their use creates an unfair advantage. Adverse effects of beta-blockers include bronchospasms, CNS disturbances, hypotension, and impotence. In addition, beta-blockers may negatively affect high-intensity, longer endurance tasks.

Diuretics

Diuretics increase the rate at which water and salts leave the body as urine. Athletes such as jockeys, wrestlers, and boxers use diuretics to make weight for a competition. Other athletes use diuretics to overcome fluid retention—often to modify the excretion rate of urine in order to alter the urinary concentrations of banned drugs such as anabolic steroids. The rapid depletion of body fluids in general and of potassium in particular can produce heart arrhythmias. Nausea, heat exhaustion or stroke from impaired thermoregulatory control, blood clotting, reduced blood volume, and muscle cramps are other possible outcomes (Russell, 1990).

Additional Banned Performance Aids

Caffeine is another type of central nervous system (CNS) stimulant that is banned by the IOC if ingested beyond moderation. How much caffeine intake is too much? Moderate caffeine intake commensurate with less than 18 ounces of coffee is not prohibited by the IOC. Caffeine increases alertness and arousal, thereby preventing or overcoming mental and physical fatigue. These effects may improve forms of athletic performance that depend on heightened CNS activity. Excessive amounts of caffeine can prolong endurance performance and high-intensity short-duration exercise, creating an unfair advantage in competitive sport. However, excessive caffeine may also adversely affect thermoregulation (i.e., internal body temperature). As a diuretic, caffeine increases urination. Combined with insufficient water intake, the athlete's internal body temperature rises, inducing premature fatigue and, at dangerous levels, heat-related illnesses.

Blood Doping

Blood doping is unethical and falls under the IOC's ban on ingesting a substance in an abnormal quantity or using an improper route of entry into the body for the purpose of artificially fostering physical performance. Blood doping involves removing approximately one liter (about two units) of the athlete's blood one to two months before the competition and appropriately freezing and storing it. The athlete's frozen red blood cells are then infused back into the competitor shortly before competition, thus producing increased red cell mass and hemoglobin of up to 15%. The effect may last as long as 2 weeks. This technique increases oxygen uptake—the blood's oxygen-carrying capacity—thereby improving aerobic (endurance) performance. Blood doping has few medical dangers if a careful and knowledgeable physician performs it. Still, an ominous sign of the times in which we live concerns the possible contamination of blood with hepatitis B, hepatitis C, and HIV (AIDS) infection if samples are mixed up. Equally serious is the occasional mishandling or mislabeling of blood products. As Williams (1998) indicates, "an incompatible blood transfusion could be fatal" (p. 143).

Erythropoietin (Epo)

Another form of blood doping may occur by ingesting the hormone erythropoietin, or Epo. Epo is a hormone secreted by the kidneys in response to hypoxia—a lack of oxygen in the blood—that stimulates production of red blood cells (hemoglobin). As Branch explained (2002), "an increase in hemoglobin and the circulating red blood cell mass by doping would increase the oxygen content of oxygen in arterial blood and enhance the body's ability to transport oxygen to peripheral exercising muscle (p. 61). Typically, Epo is used clinically to treat anemia in hemodialysis patients; however, world-class endurance athletes also have been known to ingest Epo. For example, selected world class cyclists who competed in the Tour de France were thought to ingest Epo (Abt, 1998). Epo reduces the onset of muscular fatigue and may improve regulation of the internal body temperature, thus providing an unfair advantage to endurance athletes who use Epo. The American College of Sports Medicine (ACSM) considers blood doping unethical, and sports-governing bodies have banned its use. Readers are referred to Sawka et al. (1996) for the ACSM's position paper on the use of blood doping.

Creatine

Creatine has become increasingly popular since St. Louis Cardinals' home run slugger Mark McGuire admitted using it during the 1998 season in which he hit 70 home runs (he has since discontinued using creatine, according to media reports). Creatine is classified as a physiological sports ergogenic, although it is also regarded as a nutritional sports ergogenic (Williams, 1998; Williams et al., 1999). Ostensibly, its function is to increase muscular power and speed

in sports events (Williams, 1998). It is a popular substance for three reasons: (1) it is not considered an anabolic steroid; (2) it is not, at this writing and in the absence of scientific research on its long-term effects, considered unsafe in reasonable amounts; and (3) it is legally available in drug and health food stores and fitness clubs around the world. Although banned by the National Football League and Major League Baseball, creatine is still allowed by the IOC, and many athletes at virtually all levels of competition use it. One estimate is that 80% of the athletes at the 1996 Summer Olympics in Atlanta used creatine (Williams et al., 1999, p. 7).

How effective is it? The results of studies are equivocal. Williams et al. (1999) has concluded that "short-term creatine supplementation may contribute to increased total body mass, at least in males, although much of the increase in body mass may be attributed to water retention rather than increased contractile protein. Chronic creatine supplementation, combined with resistance training, may increase lean body mass, but more supportive research is desirable to determine efficacy and the possible underlying mechanism" (p. 194). Williams (1998), however, also reports that "creatine supplementation might be detrimental to performance in events dependent primarily on the oxygen energy system. Creatine phosphate is not a very important energy source for prolonged aerobic exercise" (p. 180). Williams concludes that creatine supplementation may have a beneficial effect only in certain types of performance (e.g., repetitive, high-intensity, very short-term tasks with brief recovery periods).

Human Growth Hormone and Gamma-Hydroxybutyrate

Human Growth Hormone (HGH), banned by the IOC, is naturally secreted by the pituitary gland. More recently, it has been created by recombinant DNA technology, but it remains very expensive. Clinically, HGH is prescribed to overcome pituitary deficiency in children. In adults, HGH increases lean body mass and decreases fat mass. It was the primary steroid used by the late professional football player, Lyle Alzado, discussed earlier, who died at age 42 of two brain tumors.

Banned by the IOC, HGH is medically used to treat dwarfism by stimulating growth (Goldberg, 1998). In addition, the U.S. national media reported in 2004 that HGH has been taken by 20,000 to 30,000 nonathletes in the United States to prevent aging at a cost of $1,000 per month (*The Tennessean*, January 16, 2007, p. A3). Although this anabolic outcome may appear to have a beneficial effect related to sport performance, the results of past studies have indicated that the use of HGH for 6 months produces less than 5 pounds of muscle mass and a similar decrease in fat. This outcome is similar following resistance training, but without the use of HGH. Thus, the effect of HGH on physical performance seems negligible in contrast to regular exercise. It can also cause the skull to thicken and the forehead and eyebrow ridge to become especially prominent; the hands and feet grow out of proportion with the rest of the body, causing a condition called acromegaly. If a patient is young enough that his or her bones are still growing, exposure to excessive HGH will result in gigantism.

A related hormone that ostensibly has an ergogenic effect is *gamma-hydroxybutyrate (GHB)*. Although the body produces this substance naturally, too much can lead to distorted physical characteristics, which is why it is referred to as "Frankenstein's syndrome." GHB stimulates the release of human growth hormone and can lead to a coma and death. The IOC also bans GHB.

Rationale for an Antidrug Policy in Sport

There are several reasons for controlling drug intake in competitive sport. These are categorized as legal, ethical, and medical. **Legal** considerations reflect federal and state laws that ban the use or sale of selected substances, such as hallucinogenic drugs, and the illegal use of steroids, narcotic analgesics, and beta-blockers. **Ethical** issues form the core reason for banning drug use in sport: it's cheating, thus creating an unfair advantage. This issue is best expressed by Thomas H. Murray, Ph.D., director of the Center for Biomedical Ethics at the School of Medicine at Case Western Reserve University, who asserts: "The use of performance-enhancing drugs is a form of cheating, counter to the quest for physical excellence that sport is supposed to honor . . . the purpose of sport is the encouragement and reward of excellence" (p. 144). In addition, most reasonable persons would agree that allowing athletes to ruin their health for short-term gain is immoral. **Medical** factors that include the long-term harmful effects of prolonged drug use among athletes are severe and well-known (e.g., Appleby, Fisher, & Martin, 1994; Martens et al., 2007; Wemyss-Holden, Hamdy, & Hastie, 1994). These outcomes include dehydration, heatstroke, cardiac arrest, liver cancer, lymphoma, cardiovascular disease, kidney stones, irregular heartbeat, sterility, and hypertension. Psychological problems include heightened anxiety, suicidal tendencies, short attention span, depression, aggression, and schizophrenia (Pope & Katz, 1994; Weinhold, 1991). Finally, most drugs are addictive.

How Widespread Is Drug Abuse in Sport?

It is impossible to determine the exact extent of drug abuse in sport. The two primary sources of information about drug usage, anecdotal evidence and scientific research studies, have serious limitations. Anecdotal reports, among other serious shortcomings, fail to provide concrete evidence documenting the usage of drugs. Scientific studies suffer from underreporting because ethical and legal considerations make drug taking a largely clandestine behavior. Keep these limitations in mind when examining the following information.

Anecdotal Evidence

Anecdotal evidence consists of information provided by individuals based on their own experiences or perceptions. For example, former U.S. Olympic gold medal hurdler Edwin Moses (1988) asserted that "at least 50 percent of the athletes in high-performance sports such as track and field, cycling, and rowing would be disqualified if they weren't so adept at beating the tests" (p. 57).

Not surprisingly, steroid abuse has been traditionally rampant in professional (U.S.) football. Testimony given to the Committee on the Judiciary in amending the Controlled Substances Act (Steroid Trafficking Act of 1990) included the following: "Recognized as a sport plagued by alarming levels of steroid use, football has always favored those players that are bigger, bulkier and more aggressive than their opponents." The National Football League now has a policy of random periodic testing. The first violation results in a four-game suspension (see Table 21-2).

Other anecdotal evidence exists to show that some coaches actually sanction drug use, either *passively* by failing to warn their athletes against drug use, or *actively* by encouraging athletes to use steroids and ways to avoid positive drug tests. Other forms of encouragement to take banned substances were direct (e.g., advising, "Taking steroids is the only way to stay competitive") or indirect (e.g., requiring that the participant reach an unrealistic body weight by a certain time, requiring a particularly demanding performance goal, or ignoring drug-taking behavior and thus sanctioning its use). For example, Canadian world-class sprinter Ben Johnson, after having his gold medal taken away, strongly asserted to a Canadian government inquiry that his coach knowingly gave him a substance that was banned by international sport organizations (*Time*, 1989). "Charlie [Francis] was my coach. . . . If Charlie gave me something to take, I took it" (p. 57). In fact, this coach's testimony at the same inquiry supported Johnson's contention. Francis told Johnson (and other sprinters) that "drugs marked the only route to international success and admitted that he provided such chemicals to his charges" (*Time*, June 26, 1989, p. 57).

Anecdotal evidence indicates team physicians also have contributed to drug abuse among athletes. For example, Ye Qiaobo, a Chinese speed skater, was sent home in disgrace from the 1988 Olympics after testing positive for steroids. A later inquiry revealed that she unknowingly had been taking steroids prescribed by the team

doctor. Television's coverage of the 1992 (Madrid), 1996 (Atlanta), and 2000 (Sydney) Olympics revealed the extensiveness, as far back as preparation for the 1976 Olympics, of experimentation with steroids by many countries. In the former East Germany, for example, team doctors, under orders from the highest political powers, prescribed steroids for athletes, even 13-year-old girls, and then kept careful records regarding the effects of different dosages on performance and the length of time needed to test clean.

The president of the World Anti-Doping Agency, Mr. Dick Pound, suspects that as many as one-third of National Hockey League's 700 players use some form of performance enhancing substances (*The Tennessean*, November 25, 2005, p. C2). Not surprisingly, NHL commissioner, Gary Bettman, disagrees with this assessment as indicated by his response, "We don't have the (steroid) problem in hockey."

Perhaps the highest profiled case is that of former San Francisco Giants home run king, Barry Bonds. At this writing, Bonds had been indicted by a U.S. federal grand jury on perjury and obstruction of justice in his denial of knowingly using performance-enhancing drugs (*USA Today*, November 16, 2007, p. C1). Despite a plethora of circumstantial evidence, Bonds has denied using steroids—at least "knowingly." Federal investigators feel otherwise; not only that he used steroids, but that he lied about it to a grand jury. This does not necessarily mean that Bonds is formally charged or convicted of a crime, but that a jury felt that sufficient evidence exists to pursue the case in court. The report of a full investigation on the use of performance-enhancing drugs in Major League Baseball, headed by former U.S. Senator George Mitchell, was presented to a U.S. Congressional Committee December 13, 2007 (Mitchell, 2007). Selected content of this 409-page report will be discussed later.

Barry Bonds is only one of many athletes (e.g., track stars Michelle Collins, Marion Jones, Regina Jacobs, Justin Gatlin, Calvin Harrison, and Tim Montgomery, among many others) who have been tainted by obtaining performance-enhancing drugs supplied by a company based in San Francisco, California, called BALCO, based on the records of company owner and founder

Victor Conte, who spent three months in prison for pleading guilty for steroids distribution (*USA Today,* November 16, 2007, pp. 1A, 2A). Bond's alleged extensive and prolonged use of steroids was chronicled in the book *Game of Shadows,* released in March 2006.

Scientific Evidence

Scientific research on drug use in sport has centered primarily on performance-enhancing drugs, particularly anabolic steroids. Studies of specific sport populations, particularly ones involving strength or endurance, report higher drug usage. In an example of possible underreporting, Pope, Katz, and Champoux (1988) found that only 17 of 1,010 (1.7%) U.S. college male athletes reported using anabolic steroids. The motive for using steroids of all but four of these men was to improve sport performance. In another study, Yesalis et al. (1988) distributed surveys about steroid use to 60 elite U.S. male bodybuilders. Of the 45 competitors who returned the survey, 15 (33%) admitted to anabolic steroid use. Perhaps no sport has experienced greater use of anabolic steroids than weight lifting.

Grogan et al. (2006) conducted in-depth interviews with five male and six adult female body builders to examine their motives for steroid use and the subsequent effects of prolonged steroid use. They found that users believed steroids used in moderation were safe, and that serious side effects were not significant disincentives. Perhaps not surprisingly, the researchers found that competitors deemphasized serious side effects relative to short-term gains. This result has widespread implications for athletes in other sports in which more immediate concerns about performance enhancement is more important than possible long-term risks. While the use of so-called "performance-enhancing drugs" is not going away any time soon, what is unknown at this time is the extent to which these drugs, and others, are used at various levels of competitive sport.

The seriousness of ingesting steroids in sport is apparently a concern to coaches. BlueCross BlueShield of Tennessee and the Tennessee Secondary School Athletic Association surveyed 462 high school coaches in Tennessee (*Daily News*

Journal, November 18, 2005, p. C2). They found that 90% of the coaches perceive performance-enhancing drugs as a problem among high school athletes, with 18% concluding it is a "serious" problem. In addition, while 98% of the coaches believe that educating students about performance-enhancing drugs is important, 54% of the coaches do not believe students understand the long-term effects of using such drugs, and 65% said they have warned the athletes against using them. These data, if accurate and generalizable to other samples, represents a turning point for coaches to finally acknowledge the seriousness and pervasiveness of drug usage in sport. Clearly, more research is needed to examine the extent of drug use among athletes at all levels of competition in order to determine the proper strategies to at least minimize, if not eliminate, its use.

In one study, Anshel (1991a) examined the evidence of drug use on a college football team located in the southwest U.S. He conducted personal interviews with U.S. university athletes, 94 males and 32 females, competing in nine sports. To overcome the inherent dangers of underreporting found in related literature, information about the participants' personal use of drugs was not solicited. Of the 126 athletes surveyed, 81 (64%) revealed "known" drug use on their team. More specifically, 68 (72%) of the 94 males and 13 (40%) of the 32 females contended that teammates took a drug the user knew was illegal or banned from their sport. Forty-three percent (494 of the athletes' 1,156 responses) acknowledged that athletes use drugs for the purpose of enhancing performance as opposed to recreational use.

Sadly, researchers also report widespread use of steroids well beyond the sport venue. For example, in an early study, Taylor (1987) reported that at least 1 million Americans have used or are currently using steroids for nonmedical purposes, to either increase athletic performance or improve physical appearance. His data revealed that steroid use among high school students is nearly as common as the use of crack cocaine. A brief review of this literature in the United States Steroid Trafficking Act of 1990 report concluded that "up to 500,000 male high school students use, or have used, steroids (with) more than one-third of the users (starting) at the age of 15 or younger; two-thirds had started by the age of 16" (p. 4). Similarly disturbing is a study by White-head, Chillag, and Elliott (1992), who examined the use of steroids among 3,900 male high school students in a rural (U.S.) state. The most common reason for using steroids, among 205 students (5.3%) who admitted to drug use, was to *improve physical appearance* (43%). In addition, steroid use was closely associated with illicit drug and ciga-rette use. Apparently, the abuse of anabolic ste-roids is not restricted to metropolitan areas.

Melia, Pipe, and Greenberg (1996) attempted to determine the prevalence of use of anabolic steroids and other performance-enhancing drugs among 16,119 Canadian students from grades 6–12 representing five regions of Canada. They found that 2.8% of this sample ($N = 4,513$) ingested these banned substances in attempts to improve sport performance or to improve body build. To some extent, there appears to be a gen-der gap in drug taking among athletes. Doweiko (1996), supporting earlier findings by Anshel (1991a), concluded from his review of literature that more males than females abuse anabolic steroids.

Despite numerous attempts to ascertain the prevalence of drug taking among competitive ath-letes, the results of these studies must be viewed cautiously. Asking athletes to acknowledge their own unethical behavior is very difficult, if not impossible. This is one reason well-publicized antidrug policies by sports organizations and coaches, a strong drug testing program that has consequences, continuous drug education, and close monitoring of athlete behavior by coaches and parents are of extreme importance, issues that will be addressed later.

Likely Causes of Drug Abuse in Sport

Based on a review of the anecdotal and scientific literature the causes of drug use lie within three categories: physical (performance enhancement), psychological and emotional, and social.

Physical Causes

Enhance sport performance. The most com-mon physical cause for ingesting drugs is attempting to enhance sport performance. As indicated earlier, coaches and sponsors can and often do contribute to the competitors' dilemma by reinforcing the need to win at any cost. The expectations of parents, media, teammates, and peers only fuel the pressure to maximize perfor-mance, even if by ingesting banned substances (Lamb, 1984; Williams, 1989). Depending on the drug being taken, the athlete may be seeking benefits such as increased strength, endurance, alertness, and aggression, or decreased fatigue, anxiety, and muscle tremor.

For example, in a rare study in this area, Laure and Reinsberger (1995) attempted to identify the reasons for using anabolic steroids among elite race walkers. Improving performance, the wish—and pressure—to win, and financial incentives (e.g., commercial contracts and product endorse-ments) were the three principal motives to use banned performance-enhancing drugs. Forty-one percent of these athletes had heard of endurance walkers using such drugs. Apparently, the pres-sure of performing well in international events only exacerbates the problem.

Cope with pain and injury rehabilitation. Ath-letes also ingest drugs to cope psychologi-cally with physical discomfort and to expedite recovery from injury (English, 1987; Goldman, Bush, & Katz, 1984). For example, athletes may feel that medical treatment is not sufficient to eliminate pain. They will take drugs to atten-uate pain with no prescription and without the coach's knowledge, usually to avoid dis-appointing the coach or losing starting status (a tendency more typical of the male athletes) (Anshel, 1991a).

Weight control. Amphetamines are often used to control appetite, while diuretics reduce fluid weight. This allows the athlete to com-pete in a lower weight group, which the athlete feels is more likely to lead to success (Donald, 1983).

Psychological Causes

By far the most common rationale for using recreational drugs among athletes is psychological and emotional (Anshel, 1991a, 1995). Several psychological reasons promote taking banned drugs.

Stress and anxiety.   Emotions such as stress, tension, and anxiety may be antecedent causes of ingesting drugs, particularly hallucinogens and beta-blockers. The need to control anxiety and other undesirable emotions in sport is widely known, but artificial means provide an unfair advantage. Recreational drug use has also been used to help athletes managing stress and anxiety, which is both unethical and illegal (Anshel, 1991a). Instead, athletes should be taught mental skills for controlling emotions.

Boredom.   Recreational drugs, which, of course, are illegal, might be ingested to help overcome boredom (Julien, 1981), which is more prevalent on weekends, when teams travel, or when team-related activities are unplanned (Anshel, 1991b; Egger, 1981).

Personal problems.   Clinical sport psychologists deal with pathological issues that may lead to drug taking in sport, perhaps in response to a personal problem independent of the athlete's sport involvement. The athlete's personal life may be in turmoil (e.g., poor school grades, an unhappy or dysfunctional home life). Drugs, then, may be a coping mechanism or a means of escape in dealing with personal difficulties away from the sport venue (Gardner & Moore, 2006).

Low self-confidence and self-esteem.   Athletes may use drugs, either performance-enhancing to build self-confidence or recreational, due to a lack of self-confidence (Anshel, 1991a; Nardo, 1992). Perhaps the athlete doubts his or her skills or is worried about the perceived superior skills of an opponent (e.g., "They make me feel better about my ability," "I'm sure 'so and so' is taking them," "If I'm going to perform at 'X' speed, I have to take these"). These feelings may reflect a personality trait called low *self-esteem*, which

is a person's evaluation of the picture they hold about themselves (Sonstroem, 1997). Athletes with low self-esteem or chronic low confidence would benefit from therapy by a licensed clinical sport psychologist.

The Superman (Adonis) Complex.   The Superman, or Adonis, Complex is a condition in which some athletes feel impervious to the known harmful effects of drugs, even after obtaining valid information about possible detrimental effects to their health (Anshel, 1993; Collins, Pippenger, & Janesz, 1984). According to Don Weiss, executive director of the National Football League: "It is not easy to convince pro football players that they are vulnerable to the negative health effects of steroids. Some of these young men are such great physical specimens with such great athletic ability that they think they'll be like that forever" (Shroyer, 1990, p. 115). Also worrisome is that the Superman/Adonis Complex can prompt adolescent *nonathletes* to use steroids improve their physique (Pope, 2002).

What may change these perceptions of invincibility are the publicized stories of high-profile athletes whose health has significantly deteriorated or who have died because of the prolonged use of anabolic steroids. This was the exact reaction to the death of former Denver Broncos football player Lyle Alzado in 1989 at age 42. Alzado died from cancer that he (and his doctors) attributed to prolonged, extensive use of steroids and human growth hormone (HGH). In an article published in *Sports Illustrated* (July 8, 1991) entitled, "I'm sick and I'm scared," Alzado asserted, "If I had known that I would be this sick now, I would have tried to make it in football on my own—naturally. Whoever is doing this stuff, if you stay on it too long or maybe if you get on it at all, you're going to get something bad from it. . . . It is a wrong thing to do" (*Sports Illustrated*, 1991, p. 25).

Negative perfectionism.   Some individuals are never pleased with their accomplishments, even with the appropriate recognition and adulation of others. For these people, "good" is never quite good enough. A **perfectionist** is someone who has trouble discriminating between realistic and idealized standards (Flett & Hewitt, 2002). He or she bypasses attainable excellence in pursuit of unattainable perfection. Using performance-enhancing drugs provides a means to overcome the self-doubt and anxiety associated with failing to meet excessively high standards, a condition called neurotic perfectionism (Hewitt & Flett, 2002). Although researchers have increased their attention to perfectionism in recent years (Stoll, Lau, & Stoeber, 2007), additional research is needed to determine its connection to drug use in sport.

Social Causes

Perhaps there is no greater cause of succumbing to drug ingestion than response to social—and societal—pressures.

Peer pressure and acceptance. Pressure from peers, the need to gain group acceptance, or the natural need to be accepted and admired by others all form likely causes of drug taking, especially among younger sports participants (Wragg, 1990). In their eagerness to attain social acceptance, adolescents become aware of the types of approval-earning behaviors—the need to please other people—that will facilitate popularity. Newman (1994) concluded, in his study of Canadian adolescents, that the lure of steroids is too strong for many teens due to extreme demands on conformity, particularly among males. This is why a rigorous drug-taking policy is needed to protect younger athletes from the pressures of taking banned substances to gain acceptance, respect, or popularity from their peers.

Models. If sports stars are known to ingest steroids, will younger, less skilled athletes be copycats? Modeling occurs when we learn by demonstration or change our behavior to imitate behaviors we have observed (Chu, 1982). Modeling has a particularly influential effect during adolescence. Accordingly, the development of appropriate (e.g., training and effort) and inappropriate (e.g., cheating, drug taking) behavior of young athletes is often derived from the

modeling of older, more experienced counterparts. The modeling effect is reinforced by media reports that publicize incidences of drug abuse by professional athletes (Collins et al., 1984). More recently, the Mitchell Report (2007) on steroid use in major league baseball highlighted the increased proliferation of steroid use by adolescents, both athletes and nonathletes, and partly attributed the problem to the perception that professional athletes are also taking these drugs.

Strategies for Controlling Drug Abuse

The effectiveness of strategies to prevent or eliminate drug-taking in sport is often a function of factors such as the individual's perceived needs for using drugs (e.g., gaining self-confidence, overcoming pain, improving strength or performance); the type of drug usage (e.g., performance-enhancing versus mind-altering); the sport's physical demands (e.g., those requiring improved aerobic capacity, strength, or steadiness); and situational factors (e.g., boredom, stress, endorsements, the high expectations of others). However, because athletes share similar psychological demands and performance requirements, many of the issues described here can be applied to competitors from various sports, skill levels, genders, and cultures.

An array of techniques is available in the antidrug arsenal (see Anshel, 1991b, 1993, 2005, for extensive reviews of drug prevention and control strategies). Strategies for eliminating the intake of banned substances are only as effective as the policy makers, sports organizations, coaches, consultants, and parents who help implement them. Strict policies by sports organizations to which the athlete belongs form a formidable obstacle to drug abuse in sport, as evidenced by organizations representing elite sports (e.g., IOC, USOC, professional sporting organizations). Regulating drug use, therefore, starts with organizational policy. The coach, however, is the one person who has the most credibility with the athlete and who is the most important agent in preventing drug use on the team (Anshel, 1986, 1990a, 1993; Smith, 1983) yet coaches, and the organizations that employ them, have traditionally seemed disconnected from the seriousness of this problem. This has been especially apparent in the relatively recent *Mitchell Report* (Mitchell, 2007) in which Major League Baseball is accused of having its "head in the sand" over ignoring an apparent proliferation of anabolic steroid use by players.

The two approaches taken in this chapter for combating drug use center on cognitive and behavioral strategies. **Cognitive** strategies deal with influencing the athlete's behaviors and attitudes intellectually and psychologically through verbal and nonverbal communication. **Behavioral** techniques involve two components: (1) setting up situations that foster certain desirable responses from the athletes, including instituting organization and team policies that prohibit drug use, and (2) using verbal and nonverbal techniques that reinforce favorable behaviors or performance outcomes (Martin & Lumsden, 1987). The following suggestions were derived from anecdotal and scientific literature, media reports, and my own experiences as a sport psychology consultant.

Cognitive Approaches

Provide education. Education is the most widely used strategy for preventing drug abuse. Traditionally, the primary objective of drug education programs was to disseminate accurate information about the negative consequences of drug taking. Two underlying factors may explain the limited success of educational programs in controlling drug use. First, education is based on the tenet that people use drugs because they have little knowledge of its deleterious effects (Nicholson & Agnew, 1989). Supposedly, after being educated about these deleterious effects, the individual is expected to develop a negative attitude toward drug use that, in turn, will dictate desirable behavior. However, the effectiveness of drug education programs on drug-taking behaviors has been less than optimum. For example, Heitzinger and Associates (1986) indicated that "drug education deterred [only] about 5% of the

regular users from experimenting with drugs; drug testing and knowledge of punishment deterred 5% of the social users" (p. 158). Numerous studies have shown that increased knowledge about the harmful effects of drugs and drug education programs do not lead to reduced drug use (Anshel & Russell, 1997; Hanson, 1980; Kinder, Pope, & Walfish, 1980; Marcello, Danish, & Stolberg, 1989; Stuart, 1974). This could be due to poor judgments about drug use by most drug users (Perko et al., 1995). Yesalis and Cowart (1998), however, contend that providing information about the potential *benefits* of anabolic steroids provides greater credibility for disclosing its harmful effects. More research awaits this somewhat unusual approach to drug education.

Discuss ethical issues. It is generally known that drug taking has three effects on compromising the integrity of sport competition: (1) The athlete will never know his or her real full potential, (2) drug use has a health risk, and (3) athletes who use drugs are quitting on themselves; they are relying on a foreign substance to reach peak performance rather than on their own physical and mental training and nutritional habits. Sports administrators, coaches, and parents must send a joint message that drug taking is cheating, and this dishonesty deprives athletes and others of knowing the true victor at the risk of one's health. Ethical concerns may not be a primary motive that influences drug-taking behavior in sport, however. For example, Martin and Anshel (1991) found that Australian athletes were more likely to use a banned performance-enhancing drug if drug testing could not detect it than if the athlete thought it could be detected. More effective communication and education strategies appear to be needed that address ethical considerations of drug use in sport.

Recognize the athletes' use of drugs. To think "it can't happen on my team (or to me)" is not only naive but also irresponsible. To be effective, coaches and parents must detect signs and symptoms of drug ingestion—even legal drugs that are against team rules, such as alcohol and tobacco—before it becomes addictive and has long-lasting negative consequences to good health. Unfortunately, according to at least one study (Hanson & Gould, 1988), parents and coaches cannot always detect athletes' thoughts, emotions, and signals of certain behavioral patterns. Coaches and team consultants (e.g., athletic trainers, sport psychology consultants, academic tutors) should be sensitive to various aspects of athletes' lives. Examples include a newly divorced or deceased parent, poor school grades, high absentee rate, a personal crisis, frequent illnesses, short-term change in physical features, heightened aggression, frequent bouts of anger, and unwarranted challenges to authority (Damm, 1991).

According to Damm, "when drug abuse is suspected in the student-athlete, referral should be made to a trained professional (e.g., physician, psychologist, drug counselor) who can confirm or deny its existence" (p. 159). Attempts to stop the drug-taking behavior must be enacted immediately. While sensitivity toward the athlete's condition is needed at this time, strict limit-setting about the offending—and perhaps illegal—behavior is also required. This is why organizational and team policy on drug taking (discussed later in the chapter) is so necessary. Physical, emotional, behavioral, and cognitive signs of drug use are listed in Table 21-1.

Build confidence and self-esteem. According to Tobler's (1986) personal development program model, low self-esteem and low self-confidence are other reasons for drug ingestion. Athletes who doubt their ability to succeed are more susceptible to performance-enhancing drugs than their more confident counterparts. Athletes should be encouraged to believe in their ability to perform to their capability by continually learning new skills and strategies, and through hard physical and mental training. Sport psychologists can help athletes with low self-esteem and self-confidence by teaching them the cognitive techniques found in Chapter 17.

Professional counseling. An athlete's decision to ingest steroids, particularly over a prolonged period of time, usually has a psychological explanation. Low self-esteem, irrational thinking,

Table 21-1 Physical, Behavioral, Emotional, and Cognitive Signs of Drug Use

Physical Signs

- Bloodshot eyes
- Dark circles under eyes
- Profuse sweating
- Heightened sensitivity to touch, smell, and sound
- Chronic fatigue
- Trouble maintaining normal body temperature (always feeling too hot or cold)

Behavioral Signs

- Unusually secretive behavior
- Increased tardiness to practice and school
- Apathetic attitude about school
- Poor school performance
- Social isolation
- Often broke or out of money
- Irresponsible
- High risk-taking behaviors
- Change in dress style
- New circle of friends
- Marked changes in usual or normal ways of behaving (e.g., unwarranted challenges to authority, isolation, increased arguments, new friends)

Emotional Signs

- Extreme mood swings
- Irritability
- Highly reactive
- Less affectionate
- Chronic physical fatigue
- Heightened aggression/hostility
- Recurrent depressive episodes

Cognitive Signs

- Decreased mental capabilities
- Disordered thinking
- Increased forgetfulness
- Paranoid thoughts that others are out to get him or her
- Denial of problems
- Superman complex (i.e., sense of invulnerability)
- Shortened attention span
- Thoughts of suicide

depression, pressure to meet abnormally high expectations (both their own and those of others, a condition associated with neurotic perfectionism), chronic anxiety, pressure to achieve, need for peer approval and acceptance by others, or feelings of helplessness and low personal control are all reasons for athletes to obtain professional counseling. Possible reasons for an athlete's drug-taking habit must be addressed immediately (Ringhofer & Harding, 1996).

Coaches do not typically have training in counseling, but the coach is often the first—and most important—person to whom an athlete comes to discuss personal or team-related concerns (Anshel, 1990b; Rosenfeld et al., 1989). Team members need private and confidential access to their coach. The sport psychology consultant, who should have training in at least basic counseling skills, can be another effective confidant and facilitator in helping athletes deal with their pressures and problems. Addressing the issues surrounding drug-taking behavior may warrant referral to a licensed mental health professional (see Chapter 20 for guidelines on referral).

Motivational Interviewing (MI). Miller and Rollnick (2002) have developed a client-centered directive method to increase a client's intrinsic motivation for health behavior change by exploring and resolving ambivalence. MI could perform three essential functions with respect to reducing or eliminating drug use in sport: (a) collaborating with the athlete to create a safe, supportive, and nonjudgmental environment within which to influence the athlete to avoid drug use, (b) exploring with the athlete reasons for and against drug use, the goal of which is to resolve ambivalence, and (c) developing the athlete's sense of autonomy, or responsibility, for changing the decision to take drugs. While there is an apparent absence of research examining the effectiveness of MI on drug-taking attitudes and behaviors in competitive sport, one study using MI on health behavior change indicated significant improvements in fitness, exercise adherence, and blood lipids (i.e., changes in diet) among Tennessee police officers (Anshel & Kang, 2008).

Behavioral Strategies

As indicated earlier, the primary objective of a behavioral approach is to shape the environment to control and influence subsequent behavior, a system referred to as "contingency management" (see Martin & Lumsden, 1987, and Rushall & Siedentop, 1972, for explanations and guidelines). Specifically, behavioral techniques involve (1) setting up situations that foster certain desirable responses from the athletes, and (2) using verbal or nonverbal techniques that reinforce favorable behaviors or performance outcomes.

Teach sport skills and offer positive feedback. Athletes, perhaps more than most other individuals, are driven to achieve the virtually impossible task of performing consistent and error-free skilled movements. Experiencing improved performance will give the athletes fewer reasons to take banned substances. Offer high quality, proper conditioning programs so they associate improved performance with better training. Good coaches are good teachers (Anshel, 2003). The key objectives for the coach are to make skill and conditioning improvement apparent to the athlete, and to positively reinforce desirable performance changes by verbally and nonverbally communicating approval of competent performance (Martin & Lumsden, 1987).

Develop and implement a drug policy and plan of action. This strategy is of particular importance, especially given the recent drug scandal that has engulfed Major League Baseball (see the Mitchell Report, 2007). Sports organizations at all levels of competition starting in preadolescent competition should include widespread information about the dangers of drugs in sport. Teams and sport organizations must develop a drug policy, including consequences for taking them, and a vehicle to inform athletes about banned drugs the drug policy. Failure to do so, in effect, actually sanctions drug use—or gives the impression that sport leaders do not care. For example, a study conducted by *USA Today* (February 1, 1990) showed that "only 54 percent of coaches said their school has an anti-steroids drug policy" (p. 1B). Although this study is not new, there is reason to believe, according to the Mitchell Report's (2007) conclusions about performance-enhancing drug use in sport and among adolescents in the United States, that the problem persists.

The results of research support this contention. Fields, Lange, Kreiter, and Fudala (1994) examined current and proposed drug testing policies from 288 athletic directors across the United States. Of the 245 respondents, 29% reported drug testing of their student athletes, mostly conducted on a random basis. Surprisingly, however, most of the tests covered cocaine (85%) and amphetamines (83%), with only 56% of tests for using performance-enhancing drugs such as anabolic steroids. Referral for treatment rather than immediate termination from the team or school was the most common consequence for testing positive.

Athletes need to know the boundaries between acceptable and unacceptable behaviors. The coach and parents must jointly assert that taking drugs is not allowed. Strict limit setting is equally important for responding effectively to an infringement of the team's policy. This is especially relevant following a positive drug test. The team's response to breaking team rules is the most important element in protecting each player and maintaining the coach's (and organization's) integrity.

A strict sport organization and team drug policy also relieves athletes of feeling pressured to engage in behaviors that are illegal, unethical, and detrimental to their physical and mental health. Drug policies have become more stringent at the professional level as well. The drug policy of the National Basketball Association (NBA), according to *Sports Illustrated* (June 3, 1991, p. 83), is this: "If a player who used drugs came forward voluntarily, the NBA would quietly help him find treatment, without recrimination. The league, however, had the right to administer random drug tests to players if there was "reasonable cause." Table 21-2 lists the most recent policies of elite sports organizations for steroid use based on media reports (e.g., *USA Today,* January 25, 2007, p. C1; *The Tennessean,* December 14, 2007, p. 15A). These policies remain current at publication of this chapter.

If a drug-taking incident occurs, coaches should know whom to call—physicians, school administrative personnel, a counselor, a legal advisor, perhaps a religious leader, and so on. For example, should parents be notified if their son or daughter is involved in taking banned substances of any kind? All team leaders and athletes should know *in advance* the necessary steps in responding to a player's drug problem or the results of a positive drug test. This policy should be an integral part of an overall crisis management plan. Medical and psychological support services should be in place and ready to respond in an emergency 24 hours a day. A management-by-crisis approach must be avoided.

Respecting the competitor's confidentiality and privacy is another important ingredient to an effective plan of action. Cases of drug abuse need not be publicized or handled publicly. The objective of an effective response to drug abuse is to extinguish the probability of future undesirable behaviors by responding efficiently to an emergency. Effective crisis management consists of anticipating the likelihood of a drug problem and being ready to react accordingly (Wilkerson, 1995).

Have a continuous random drug-testing program. Drug policies and educational programs should also emphasize drug testing. Drug-testing programs in sports have become a more common reality for intercollegiate and elite athletes—probably so much so that, in some settings, drug-testing programs and sanctions now contribute to the effective prevention of drug use. Drug testing, especially if used randomly so the athletes do not anticipate it, can be a particularly powerful behavioral controller when the threat of dismissal or some other serious penalty accompanies a positive drug test. This is especially the case if evidence of drug taking occurs more than once.

The results of studies show that drug testing effectively reduces the likelihood of drug abuse among athletes. For example, Albrecht, Anderson, McGrew, McKeag, and Hough (1992a) found, in their study of 2,282 college athletes, that "among those athletes participating at

Table 21-2 **Policies for Steroid Use Among Elite Sports Organizations**

Organization	Policy	Penalty
Olympics (USOC)	Regular testing year-round.	A violation brings a 2-year ban.
NCAA	Year-round testing in football and track and field; testing at postseason championships in all sports.	Violators lose a year of eligibility.
NFL	Year-round, random testing for all performance-enhancing drugs, including HGH, up to three times a season.	First violation brings a 20-game suspension and automatic forfeiture of a prorated portion of a player's signing bonus.
NBA	Urine tests for performance-enhancing drugs and amphetamines four times a season.	10-game, 25-game, and 1-year suspensions for first, second, and third positive tests, respectively. Lifetime ban for a fourth positive test.
PGA Tour	Random drug-testing begins in July for anabolic steroids, HGH, and narcotics.	Warning, 1-year, and lifetime suspensions for first, second, and third offenses, respectively.
NASCAR	Drivers are tested in the preseason and randomly the rest of the season based on suspicion.	At NASCAR's discretion.
MLB	Year-round urine (no blood) test for performance-enhancing drugs, not including HGH (policy currently under review).	First-time detection of steroids is a 50-game suspension. 100 games and lifetime suspensions for second and third positive tests, respectively.
NHL	Two random urine (no blood) tests for performance-enhancing drugs, one of which is a team-wide test.	One positive test results in a 20-game suspension without pay and mandatory evaluation and education program; possible treatment. 60-game suspension for second offense. Lifetime ban for third offense.
(WWE)	World Wrestling Entertainment	No current drug-testing policy.

college and universities with institutionally based drug-testing programs, individuals who are aware of the fact they are susceptible to periodic testing are more inclined to view such procedures as an effective deterrent to drug use" (p. 245). These results can be generalized to adolescent athletes as well (Martin & Anshel, 1991).

Perhaps nowhere has drug testing become more expected, persistent, and sophisticated than at the Olympic Games. Drug-testing programs at the Olympics include short- or no-notice testing during training periods, testing at qualifying competitions, and testing at the Olympic Games. In their review of these procedures, Catlin and Murray (1996) report that the 1996 Games in Atlanta included testing urine samples for stimulants, narcotics, anabolic agents (particularly steroids), diuretics, peptides, and glycoprotein hormones, as well as prohibited methods of enhancing performance, including blood doping and pharmacological, chemical, and physical manipulation of urine. Also on the banned substance list of the U.S. Olympic Committee is a drug called **clenbuterol**, a popular drug used by athletes for its purported tissue-building, fat-reducing effects (Prather, Brown, North, & Wilson, 1995). Animal research shows the drug will inhibit the storage of fat and increase the deposit of lean body mass. To date, no human data are available.

Four principles contribute to an effective drug-testing program.

1. *Announce the policy in advance.* All team personnel should become aware of the team's or league's rules and guidelines from the first day of participation. Only in this way can participants effectively be held accountable for their actions. However, the actual testing procedure should *not* be announced in advance. To reduce costs, **random testing**—in which only a percentage of the team's athletes, rather than all players, are selected—has been shown to deter, though not necessarily eliminate, drug-abuse (Martens et al., 2007).

2. *Be consistent in implementing the policy.* The least effective approach to enacting a drug policy is responding to one athlete differently than to others. Unfortunately, group members will likely test team rules. If the coach or league officials are serious about drug abuse prevention and control, they must react vigorously and consistently to the team's most and least talented players. Otherwise, any credibility the policy has will be destroyed (National Collegiate Athletic Association, 2001).

3. *Have an independent organization responsible for testing.* The Mitchell Report (2007), which addresses future drug-testing in Major League Baseball (MLB), recommended that antidoping tests be conducted by an external agency, such as the World Anti Doping Agency (WADA). MLB, however, prefers to conduct its antidoping testing in-house, setting up a contentious

debate between MLB, WADA, and the U.S. Congress on who should control future testing (*USA Today*, January, 17, 2008, p. 7C).

4. *Link test results to sanctions.* The coach's and league's responses to positive drug tests can be very restrictive (e.g., the player is dismissed from the team) or more flexible (e.g., counseling and monitoring). However, the least appropriate response is to have a policy that includes sanctions that are not implemented or used inconsistently. Athletes, not unlike others in a subordinate position, need to realize that behaviors that are illegal, unethical, and medically unsafe cannot be tolerated.

Use behavioral contracting. A **contract system,** often called a performance contract, is among the most sophisticated forms of contingency management. It is a preplanned agreement between two parties (the coach or administrative unit and athlete in this case) that a specified reinforcement will occur to the athlete following the occurrence of a particular action (Martin & Lumsden, 1987; Rushall & Siedentop, 1972). Contracts can be verbal or, perhaps more effectively, in written form and signed by the parties involved. Of course, in professional sports in the United States, player unions and team contracts stipulate drug-testing procedures and penalties.

Use a support group. Results of research on the effectiveness of educational programs on drug (Palmer, 1989) and alcohol prevention (Werch, Carlson, Pappas, Edemon, & DiClemente, 2000) revealed that high school seniors serve as excellent peer educators and role models in drug prevention among fellow student athletes and nonathletes. Among the first structured attempts at dealing with drug abuse on a sports team, particularly at the elite level, was one conducted by the Cleveland Browns football team (Collins et al., 1984). In addition to medical and psychological treatment programs, the team owner hired a psychiatrist to conduct group and individual therapies and to establish self-help meetings for players and their wives. The core of the program consisted of a subgroup called The Inner Circle, which included of a group of identified drug-involved players. According to Collins et al.:

> Group discussions typically dealt with who was relapsing and why and the need for changes in the individual's lifestyle to support staying "clean." . . . Rather than participating in cover-ups and deceptions, the players saw that relapses were "contagious," and that when one member was in trouble, others would soon follow. . . . The group eventually became responsible for much of its own therapeutic work in keeping its individual members away from drugs (p. 490).

Invite guest speakers. Sometimes athletes become *coach deaf*—they are so accustomed to the voice of their coach (or, for that matter, their parents) that they tune him or her out. Guest speakers bring to the team a renewed sense of authority, expertise, credibility, and respect. Examples of guest speakers include pharmacists, retired athletes, former coaches, physicians, lawyers, religious leaders, and individuals whose personal history may benefit the listeners (e.g., the medical problems of a former steroid abuser, former champion athletes who can reveal their commitment and dedication to become successful).

Finally, in response to the recent (December 2007) Mitchell Report on steroid use in Major League Baseball, *USA Today* (January 8, 2008, p. 13C) reported that baseball commissioner, Bud Selig, "is expected to implement all of former senator George Mitchell's recommendations in his steroid report." Specifically, MLB must (a) inform clubs they no longer will be given advance notice to drug tests; (b) have designated areas available at all times for drug tests, with credentials readily available for testers; (c) perform mandatory background checks on all existing clubhouse personnel, including random drug tests; (d) maintain a log of all packages sent to club houses; (e) distribute baseball's policy on "Disclosing Information Relating to the Use, Possession, or Distribution of Prohibited Substances" to all employees; and finally, (f) post the policy in the clubhouse. Indeed, things are changing regarding attempts to control drug abuse in professional sport. According to media reports by numerous members of the U.S. Congress, if MLB does not clean their own house, the U.S. Congress will.

Two Intervention Models for Regulating Drug Use in Sport

Two relatively recent models, which have similar components, have been published that have direct implications for reducing or eliminating drug use in sport. Briefly, the Drugs in Sport Deterrence Model (DSDM; Strelan & Boeckman, 2003) applies deterrence theory to help athletes conclude that taking banned substances has serious legal, social, psychological, and health-related costs. Anshel and Kang's (2007) Disconnected Values Model consists of an intervention in which the athlete concludes that the action of taking banned substances is inconsistent with his or her values and that this misalignment is unacceptable, given its costs and consequences. Both models warrant additional research related to drug-taking behaviors in sport.

Drugs in Sport Deterrence Model (DSDM). The DSDM provides a rare attempt at influencing the athlete's decision about using banned substances using deterrence theory by providing athletes with extensive information about the possible—even likely—consequences of engaging in a behavior pattern, in this case, using banned substances. Ostensibly, the athlete's acknowledgement of consequences will provide an adequate deterrent to drug-taking. Identifying the downside of a behavior pattern has more credibility to the client, however, if the advantages, or benefits, of the inappropriate behavior are also determined.

The authors contend that the DSDM provides "a theoretical framework for some much-needed systematic research into understanding performance-enhancing drug use decisions by elite athletes. . .and have important implications for the way in which future drug deterrence policies are framed and funded" (p. 181). To date, studies are needed to examine the efficacy of this model on influencing the decision-making process on using banned substances in sport.

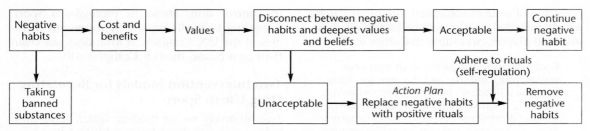

Figure 21-1   **The disconnected values intervention model for drug use in sport**

Disconnected Values Model. The pressures to succeed in sport, especially at elite levels, are too great to expect athletes to regulate their own personal behavior. And, as indicated earlier, frequently the athletes' self-esteem is dependent on their sport success—at virtually any cost. In addition, typical of human nature, most athletes do not associate a negative, unhealthy habit with longer-term harmful outcomes. Short-term benefits prevail over long-term consequences. A unique approach to behavioral change among athletes and nonathletes that appeals to the very core of the athletes' reasons for competing—their deepest values and beliefs—is the *Disconnected Values Model* (Anshel & Kang, 2007).

The primary purpose of the model is to assist athletes in acknowledging that taking drugs, whether it is for performance-enhancing or recreational purposes, is a negative habit that has benefits, but also dire costs and long-term consequences, similar to Strelan and Boeckman's (2003) DSDM. The model is driven by the athletes' willingness to become aware of the "disconnect," or contradiction, between their deepest values and beliefs and their actions—negative

habits—in this case, taking banned substances. For example, athletes may acknowledge a disconnect, or inconsistency, between their values of competitiveness, integrity, fairness, health, honesty, and faith and their conscious decision to ingest substances they know to be illegal in society, unhealthy to long-term health, or against the team's or sport organization's rules. Does the athlete find this disconnect acceptable? If the athlete acknowledges the disconnect, yet deems it acceptable, for whatever reason, the negative habit (i.e., drug-taking) will continue. The ability to act in a way that is consistent with one's deepest values and beliefs is referred to as expanding spiritual capacity (Loehr & Schwartz, 2003). The model, presented in Figure 21-1, depicts the intervention stages. Research findings have indicated that, used as an intervention, the DVM significantly improved cardiovascular and strength fitness, exercise adherence, and blood lipids profile of university faculty (Anshel & Kang, 2007) and police officers (Anshel & Kang, 2008). Investigation on the model's effectiveness in changing attitudes and behaviors related to drug use in sport, in particular, is needed.

Summary

The causes of drug taking among athletes are multidimensional and lead to taking different performance-enhancing and recreational drugs. Although personal characteristics play a relevant role in drug taking, situational and environmental issues also contribute by exacerbating the pressures placed on athletes to achieve sport success. Examples include unreasonable expectations by others, particularly the coach; defining success as a function of outcome rather than performance improvement; peer pressure; the perception of social acceptance through media reports of high-profile athletes who take drugs; and, at the elite level, the financial incentives for success. Given the extent and persistence of pressures to be competitive, or win, perhaps it is not surprising that education, threatening team and sport organization policies, and even drug testing alone are not always efficient means of eliminating drugs in sport.

Winning should not be at the expense of the athletes' health and psychological well-being. It is true that athletes, rather than their coaches and other sport leaders, must take the primary responsibility for their actions, particularly when those actions are illegal and unethical. However, athletes also need protection and a support network to help cope with sport-related pressure and stress (Rosenfeld et al., 1989). When athletes attach too much of their self-esteem to sport success, the probability of using drugs increases. Athletes must stop viewing drug taking as a key to their performance success and return to relying on hard training, continued skill development, proper nutrition, and the correct use of mental skills to reach and maintain their optimal performance. Many players need help, especially at the elite level, because they often do not have the personal resources to cope with the pressure to win and thus withstand the allure of illegal performance enhancing substances or behaviors. Protection from this pressure must come from their coach, sport organizational policies, sport psychology consultants whose expertise includes teaching effective mental skills, and licensed psychologists who are trained to deal with pathological issues related to the athlete's irrational thinking, various disorders, addictions, and personal traits and characteristics that make the athlete vulnerable to drug use. It is unrealistic to expect athletes to eliminate the problem of drug abuse without external support.

The various national and international sporting organizations have to show a high degree of consistency and unanimity in fighting drugs in sport. The IOC seems to be leading the pack. In addition to stripping the gold medal from U.S. sprinter, Marion Jones, the IOC decided not to give the medals to second place winner, Katerina Thanou because she was caught in a doping scandal at the 2004 Athens Games (*USA Today,* November 16, 2007, p. C15). In addition, IOC President, Jacque Rogge, said the fight against performance-enhancing drugs was being hampered by the slow pace of implementation of the World Anti-Doping Agency's code of ethics. He urged Olympic sports bodies to achieve compliance by January 1, 2009. Any sport that does not comply with the code can be kicked out of the Olympics. In addition, professional sports, especially Major League Baseball and the National Hockey League, have to become more vigilant in their pursuit of athletes who ingest banned substances. As reported in the U.S. media (e.g., Christine Brennan, *USA Today,* May 3, 2007, p. 2C), professional sports need to adopt an independent testing body whose actions would be transparent, and would act as "police, judge, and executioner" with respect to coordinating drug testing and enforcement. Based on its current testing policy, Major League Baseball is about 15–20 years behind the IOC in drug testing policy.

Clearly, additional research is needed on the effectiveness of various cognitive and behavioral interventions on changing the attitudes and actions of athletes, coaches, and sports organizations about drug use in sport. Two models were reviewed, the Drugs in Sport Deterrence Model and the Disconnected Values Model, that are intended to deter athletes from ingesting banned substances. Further research is needed to examine the efficacy of these models on influencing drug-taking behavior in sport. The fight against illegal and unethical drug use in sport must be aggressive to protect the integrity and future of competitive sport.

Study Questions

1. How does the IOC define doping?

2. List the five doping categories banned by the IOC. Give an example of drugs under each category and indicate why athletes might take such a drug.

3. Identify the different health concerns for ingesting drugs from the different doping categories.

4. What is the rationale for an antidrug policy in sport?

5. Using both anecdotal reports and evidence from scientific studies, give some indication of the extensiveness of drug abuse in sport.

6. Discuss the physical, psychological and emotional, and social causes of drug abuse in sport.

7. Distinguish between cognitive approaches and behavioral strategies in controlling drug abuse in athletes. Provide examples of both types of interventions.

8. If you were the team's head coach, describe the cognitive and behavioral strategies you would use with your team to prevent and respond to the use of anabolic steroids.

9. Discuss the three main components of an effective drug-testing program and how to help ensure an effective testing program.

10. Should sports administrators and coaches institute drug-taking policies? Why not simply allow athletes to take any substance they wish, if they thought it would help their performance? There is, after all, a case in favor of allowing drug taking (stated in this chapter) and to ignore an athlete's behaviors away from the sports venue.

11. Why should sports' administrators and coaches at all levels of competition institute and rigidly enforce strong policies against drug use by athletes? How would these policies be carried out and enforced?

12. What strategies can *parents* of athletes use to reduce the chance their child athlete will use anabolic steroids and other banned substances?

References

Abt, S. (1998). Top team expelled by Tour de France over drug charges. *The New York Times,* July 18, pp. A1, C2.

Albrecht, R. R., Anderson, W. A., McGrew, C. A., McKeag, D. B., & Hough, D. O. (1992a). NCAA institutionally based drug testing: Do our athletes know the rules of *this* game? *Medicine and Science in Sport and Exercise, 24,* 242–246.

Albrecht, R. R., Anderson, W. A., & McKeag, D. B. (1992b). Drug testing of college athletes: The issues. *Sports Medicine, 14,* 349–352.

Alzado, L. (1991, July 8). I'm sick and I'm scared. *Sports Illustrated, 75,* 21–25.

Anshel, M. H. (1986, May/June). The coach's role in preventing drug abuse by athletes. *Coaching Review, 9,* 29–32, 34–35.

Anshel, M. H. (1987, November 15). *Coaching strategies for managing drug abuse in sport.* Presentation to coaches of the United States Olympic Ski Team, Colorado Springs, CO.

Anshel, M. H. (1990a). Commentary on the national drugs in sport conference—1989. Testing the causes and symptoms. *Australian Journal of Science and Medicine in Sport, 22,* 49–56.

Anshel, M. H. (1991a). Causes for drug abuse in sport: A survey of intercollegiate athletes. *Journal of Sport Behavior, 14,* 283–307.

Anshel, M. H. (1991b). Cognitive and behavioral strategies for combating drug abuse in sport: Implications for coaches and sport psychology consultants. *Sport Psychologist, 5,* 152–166.

Anshel, M. H. (1993). Psychology of drug use in sport. In R. N. Singer, M. Murphey, & L. K. Tennant (Eds.), *Handbook of research on sport psychology* (pp. 851–876). New York: Macmillan.

Anshel, M. H. (2003). *Sport psychology: From theory to practice* (4th ed.). San Francisco: Benjamin-Cummings.

Anshel, M. H. (2005). Substance use: Chemical roulette in sport. In S. Murphy (Ed.), *The sport psych handbook* (pp. 255–276). Champaign, IL: Human Kinetics.

Anshel, M.H., & Kang, M. (2007). Effect of an intervention on replacing negative habits with positive routines for improving full engagement at work: A test of the Disconnected Values Model. *Journal of Consulting Psychology: Practice and Research, 59,* 110–125.

Anshel, M. H., & Kang, M. (2008). Effectiveness of motivational interviewing techniques on changes in fitness, blood lipids, and exercise adherence of police officers: An outcome-based action study. *Journal of Correctional Health Care, 14,* 48–62.

Anshel, M. H., & Russell, K. (1997). Effect of an educational program on knowledge and attitudes toward ingesting anabolic steroids among track and field athletes. *Journal of Drug Education, 27,* 172–187.

Appleby, M., Fisher, M., & Martin, M. (1994). Myocardial infarction, hyperkalaemia and ventricular tachycardia in a young male body-builder. *International Journal of Cardiology, 44,* 171–174.

Australian Sports Medicine Federation. (1989, October). *Survey of drug use in Australian sport* (2nd ed.). Canberra, A.C.T. (Australia): Australian Sports Drug Agency.

Bell, J. A., & Doege, T. C. (1987). Athletes' use and abuse of drugs. *The Physician and Sportsmedicine, 15,* 99–106, 108.

Branch, J. D. (2002). Performance-enhancing drugs and ergogenic aids. In L. L. Mostofsky & L. D. Zaichkowsky (Eds.), *Medical and psychological aspects of sport and exercise* (pp. 55–71). Morgantown, WV: Fitness Information Technology.

Buckley, W. E., Yesalis, C. E., Friedl, K. E., Anderson, W. A., Streit, A. L., & Wright, J. E. (1988). Estimated prevalence of anabolic steroid use among male high school seniors. *Journal of the American Medical Association, 260,* 3441–3445.

Catlin, D. H., & Murray, T. H. (1996, July 17). Performance-enhancing drugs, fair competition, and Olympic sport. *Journal of the American Medical Association, 276,* 231–237.

Chaikin, T., & Telander, R. (1988, October 24). The nightmare of steroids. *Sports Illustrated,* pp. 84–93, 97–98, 100–102.

Chappel, J. N. (1987). Drug use and abuse in the athlete. In J. R. May & M. J. Asken (Eds.), *Sport psychology: The psychological health of the athlete* (pp. 187–212). New York: PMA.

Chu, D. (1982). *Dimensions of sport studies*. New York: Wiley.

Cohen, J. C., Noakes, T. D., & Benade, A. J. S. (1988). Hypercholesterolemia in male power lifters using anabolic-androgenic steroids. *The Physician and Sportsmedicine, 16*, 49–50, 53–54, 56.

Cohen, S. (1979). Doping: Drugs in sport. *Drug Abuse and Alcoholism Newsletter, 8* (1), pp. 2–4.

Collins, G. B., Pippenger, C. E., & Janesz, J. W. (1984). Links in the chain: An approach to the treatment of drug abuse on a professional football team. *Cleveland Clinic Quarterly, 51*, 485–492.

Corrigan, B. (1988, October–December). Doping in sport. *Sports Coach, 12*, 11–17.

Damm, J. (1991). Drugs and the college student-athlete. In E. F. Etzel, A. B. Ferraute, & J. W. Pinkney (Eds.), *Counseling college student-athletes: Issues and interventions* (pp. 151–174). Morgantown, WV: Fitness Information Technology.

Delbeke, F. T., Desmet, N., & Debackere, M. (1995). The abuse of doping agents in competing body builders in Flanders (1988–1993). *International Journal of Sportsmedicine, 16*, 66–70.

Dezelsky, T. L., Toohey, J. V., & Shaw, R. S. (1985). Non-medical drug use behavior at five United States universities: A 15-year study. *Bulletin of Narcotics, 37*, 49–53.

Donald, K. (1983). *The doping game*. Brisbane, Australia: Boolarang.

Doweiko, H. E. (1996). *Concepts of chemical dependency* (3rd ed.). Pacific Grove, CA: Brooks/Cole.

Drugs in sport: Second report of the Senate Standing Committee on Environment, Recreation and the Arts. (1990, May). Canberra, ACT: Australian Government Publishing Service.

Egger, G. (1981). *The sport drug*. Boston: George, Allen & Unwin.

English, G. (1987). A theoretical explanation of why athletes choose to use steroids, and the role of the coach in influencing behavior. *National Strength and Conditioning Association Journal, 9*, 53–56.

Fields, L., Lange, W. R., Kreiter, N. A., & Fudala, P. J. (1994). *Medicine and Science in Sports and Exercise, 26*, 682–686.

Fisher, A. C., Mancini, V. H., Hirsch, R. L., Proulx, T. J., & Staurowsky, E. J. (1982). Coach–athlete interactions and team climate. *Journal of Sport Psychology, 4*, 388–404.

Flett, G. L., & Hewitt, P. L. (2002). Perfectionism and maladjustment: An overview of theoretical, definitional, and treatment issues. In G. L. Flett & P. L. Hewitt (Eds.), *Perfectionism: Theory, research, and treatment* (pp. 5–32). Washington, DC: American Psychological Association.

Forman, S. G. (1997). *Coping skills interventions for children and adolescents*. San Francisco: Jossey-Bass.

Galper, D. I. (1996, March). *Anabolic steroid beliefs and attitudes: Differences between users and non-users*. Paper presented at the 17th Annual Society of Behavioral Medicine Conference, Washington, DC.

Gardner, F., & Moore, Z. (2006). *Clinical sport psychology*. Champaign, IL: Human Kinetics.

Gerslick, K., Grady, K., Sexton, E., & Lyons, M. (1981). Personality and sociodemographic factors in adolescent drugs use. In D. J. Lettiers & J. P. Ludford (Eds.), *Drug abuse and the American adolescent* (pp. 81–116). Rockville, MD: U.S. Department of Health and Human Services, National Institute on Drug Abuse, Research Monograph No. 38.

Gill, D. (1986). *Psychological dynamics of sport.* Champaign, IL: Human Kinetics.

Goldberg, R. (1998). *Taking sides: Clashing views on controversial issues in drugs and society* (3rd ed.). New York: McGraw-Hill.

Goldman, B., Bush, P., & Katz, R. (1984). *Death in the locker room: Steroids and sports.* South Bend, IN: Icarus Press.

Grogan, S., Shepherd, S., Evans, R., Wright, S., & Hunter, G. (2006). Experiences of anabolic steroid use: In-depth interviews with men and women body builders. *Journal of Health Psychology, 11,* 845–856.

Hanson, D. (1980). Drugs education, does it work? In F. Scarpitti & S. Datesman (Eds.), *Drugs and youth culture: Annual reviews of drug and alcohol abuse* (Vol. 4, pp. 212–236), Beverly Hills, CA: Sage.

Hanson, T. W., & Gould, D. (1988). Factors affecting the ability of coaches to estimate their athletes' trait and state anxiety levels. *Sport Psychologist, 2,* 298–313.

Harris, R. C., Soderlund, K., & Hultman, E. (1992). Elevation of creatine in resting and exercised muscle of normal subjects by creatine supplementation. *Clinical Science, 83,* 367–374.

Heitzinger & Associates. (1986). *1981–1986 data collection and analysis: High school, college, professional athletes alcohol/drug survey.* 333 W. Mifflin, Madison, WI.

Hewitt, P. L., & Flett, G. L. (2002). Perfectionism and stress processes in psychopathology. In G. L. Flett & P. L. Hewitt (Eds.), *Perfectionism: Theory, research, and treatment* (pp. 255–284). Washington, DC: American Psychological Association.

Hughes, R., & Coakley, J. J. (1991). Positive deviance among athletes. *Sociology of Sport Journal, 8,* 307–325.

Julien, R. M. (1981). *A primer of drug action* (3rd ed.). San Francisco: Freeman.

Kandel, D. B. (1978). *Longitudinal research on drug use: Empirical findings and methodological issues.* Washington, DC: Hemisphere-Wiley.

Kennedy, M. C., & Lawrence, C. (1993). Anabolic steroid abuse and cardiac death. *Medical Journal of Australia, 158,* 346–348.

Kinder, B. N., Pope, N. E., & Walfish, S. (1980). Drug and alcohol education programs: A review of outcome studies. *International Journal of the Addictions, 15,* 1035–1054.

Lamb, D. R. (1984). Anabolic steroids in athletics: How well do they work and how dangerous are they? *American Journal of Sports Medicine, 12,* 31–38.

Laure, P., & Reinsberger, H. (1995). Doping and high-level endurance walkers—knowledge and representation: A prohibited practice. *Journal of Sports Medicine & Physical Fitness, 35,* 228–231.

Leccese, A. P. (1991). *Drugs and society: Behavioral medicines and abusable drugs.* Upper Saddle River, NJ: Prentice Hall.

Lennehan, P. (2003). *Anabolic steroids.* London: Taylor & Francis.

Loehr, J., & Schwartz, T. (2003). *The power of full engagement.* New York: Free Press.

Lombardo, J. (1993). The efficacy and mechanisms of action of anabolic steroids. In C. E. Yesalis (Ed.), *Anabolic steroids in sport and exercise* (pp. 89–106). Champaign, IL: Human Kinetics.

Lubell, A. (1989). Does steroid abuse cause—or excuse—violence? *The Physician and Sportsmedicine, 17,* 176, 178–180, 185.

Marcello, R. J., Danish, S. J., & Stolberg, A. L. (1989). An evaluation of strategies developed to prevent substance abuse among student-athletes. *The Sport Psychologist, 3,* 196–211.

Martens, M., Dams-O'Connor, K., & Kilmer, J. R. (2007). Alcohol and drug abuse among athletes. In G. Tenenbaum & R. C. Eklund (Eds.). *Handbook of research in sport psychology* (3rd ed., pp. 859-878). Hoboken, NJ: John Wiley & Sons.

Martin, M. B., & Anshel, M. H. (1991). Attitudes of elite junior athletes on drug-taking behaviors: Implications for drug prevention programs. *Drug Education Journal of Australia, 5,* 223–238.

Martin, M. B., & Anshel, M. H. (1999). Attitudes of elite adolescent Australian athletes toward drug taking: Implications for effective drug prevent programs. *Drug Education Journal of Australia, 5,* 223–238.

Martin, G. L., & Lumsden, J. A. (1987). *Coaching: An effective behavioral approach.* St. Louis, MO: Times Mirror/Mosby.

Meilman, P. W., Crace, R. K., Presley, C. A., & Lyerla, R. (1995). Beyond performance enhancement: Polypharmacy among collegiate users of steroids. *Journal of American College Health, 44,* 98–104.

Melia, P., Pipe, A., & Greenberg, L. (1996). The use of anabolic-androgenic steroids by Canadian students. *Clinical Journal of Sport Medicine, 6,* 9–14.

Miller, K. E., Barnes, G. M., Sabo, D., Melnick, M. J., & Farrell, M. P. (2002). Anabolic-androgenic steroid use and other adolescent problem behaviors: Rethinking the male athlete assumption. *Sociological Perspectives, 45,* 467–489.

Miller, W. R., & Rollnick, S. (2002). *Motivational interviewing: Preparing people for change* (2nd ed.). New York: Guilford Press.

Mitchell, G. J. (December 13, 2007). *Report to the Commissioner of baseball of an independent investigation into the illegal use of steroids and other performance enhancing substances by players in major league baseball.* Presented to the Commissioner of Major League Baseball.

Moses, E. (1988, October 10). An athlete's Rx for the drug problem. *Newsweek,* p. 57.

Mottram, D. R. (1999). Banned drugs in sport: Does the International Olympic Committee (IOC) List need updating? *Sports Medicine, 27,* 1–10.

Mottram, D. R., Reilly, T., & Chester, N. (1997). Doping in sport: The extent of the problem. In R. Reilly & M. Orne (Eds.), *The clinical pharmacology of sport and exercise* (pp. 3–12). Amsterdam: Excerpta Medica.

Mottram, D. R. (Ed.). (1988). *Drugs in sport.* London: Spon.

Nakatani, Y., & Udagawa, M. (1995). Anabolic steroid abuse and mental disorder. *ArukoruKenkyuto-Yakubutsu, 30,* 333–347.

Nardo, D. (1992). *Drugs and sports.* San Diego, CA: Lucent Books, Inc.

National Collegiate Athletic Association (2001). *NCAA study of substance use habits of college student-athletes.* Indianapolis: IN

Newman, S. (1994). Despite warnings, lure of steroids too strong for some young Canadians. *Canadian Medical Association Journal, 151,* 844–846.

Nicholson, N., (1989, July). The role of drug education. In S. Haynes & M. H. Anshel (Eds.), *Proceedings of the 1989 National Drugs in Sport Conference—Treating the causes and symptoms.* University of Wollongong, Wollongong, NSW, Australia.

Nicholson, N., & Agnew, M. (1989). *Education strategies to reduce drug use in sport.* Canberra, ACT: Australian Sports Drug Agency.

Orlick, T. (1990). *In pursuit of excellence* (2nd ed.). Champaign, IL: Human Kinetics.

Palmer, J. (1989, Fall). High school senior athletes as peer educators and role models: An innovative approach to drug prevention. *Journal of Alcohol and Drug Education, 35,* 23–27.

Park, J. (1990). Analytical methods to detect dope agents. In J. Park (Ed.), *Proceedings of the International Symposium on Drug Abuse in Sports (doping)* (pp. 51–70). Seoul: Korea Institute of Science and Technology.

Perko, M. A., Cowdery, J., Wang, M. Q., & Yesalis, C. S. (1995). Associations between academic performance of Division I college athletes and their perceptions of the effects of anabolic steroids. *Perceptual Motor Skills, 80,* 284–286.

Polich, J., Ellickson, P., Reuter, P., & Kahan, P. (1984). *Strategies for controlling adolescent drug use.* Santa Monica, CA: The Rand Corporation.

Pope, H. G., & Katz, D. L. (1994). Psychiatric and medical effects of anabolic-androgenic steroid use. A controlled study of 160 athletes. *Archives of General Psychiatry, 51,* 375–382.

Pope, H. G., Katz, D. L., & Champoux, R. (1988, July). Anabolic-androgenic steroid use among 1,010 college men. *The Physician and Sportsmedicine, 16,* 75–77, 80–81.

Pope, H. G., Jr. (2002). *The Adonis complex: How to identify, treat, and prevent body obsession in men and boys.* New York: Free Press.

Potteiger, J. A., & Stilger, V. G. (1994). Anabolic steroid use in the adolescent athlete. *Journal of Athletic Training, 29,* 60–62, 64.

Prather, I. D., Brown, D. E., North, P., & Wilson, J. R. (1995). Clenbuterol: A substitute for anabolic steroids? *Medicine and Science in Sports and Exercise, 27,* 1118–1121.

Prokop, L. (1990). The history of doping. In J. Park (Ed.), *Proceedings of the International Symposium on Drug Abuse in Sport (doping)* (pp. 1–9). Seoul: Korea institute of Science and Technology.

Radakovich, J., Broderick, P., & Pickell, G. (1993). Rate of anabolic-androgenic steroid use among students in junior high school. *Journal of American Board of Family Practice, 6,* 341–345.

Reilly, C. (1988). *An evaluation of the peer support program.* (Report No. A 88/5). Sydney, NSW (Australia): NSW Department of Health.

Ringhofer, K. R., & Harding, M. E. (1996). *Coaches guide to drugs and sport.* Champaign, IL: Human Kinetics.

Rosenfeld, L. B., Richman, J. M., & Hardy, C. J. (1989). Examining social support networks among athletes: Description and relationship to stress. *Sport Psychologist, 3,* 23–33.

Rushall, B. S., & Siedentop, D. (1972). *The development and control of behavior in sport and physical education.* Philadelphia: Lea & Febiger.

Russell, D. G. (1990). *Drugs and medicines in sport.* Wellington, NZ: Royal Society of New Zealand.

Ryan, A. J. (1982). Advantage, drug-free athletes. *The Physician and Sportsmedicine, 10,* 50.

Sawka, M. N., Joyner, M. J., Miles, D. S., Roberson, R. J., Spriet, L. L., & Young, A. J. (1996). American College of Sports Medicine position stand: The use of blood doping as an ergogenic aid. *Medicine and Science in Sports and Exercise, 28,* i–viii.

Schlaadt, R. G., & Shannon, P. T. (1994). *Drugs: Use, misuse, and abuse.* Upper Saddle River, NJ: Prentice Hall.

Shroyer, J. (1990). Getting tough on anabolic steroids. Can we win the battle? *The Physician and Sportsmedicine, 18,* 106, 108–110, 115, 118.

Smith, G. (1983). Recreational drugs in sport. *The Physician and Sportsmedicine, 11,* 75–76, 79, 82.

Sonstroem, R. J. (1997). Physical activity and self-esteem. In W. P. Morgan (Ed.), *Physical activity and mental health* (pp. 127–143). Washington, DC: Taylor & Francis.

Steroid Trafficking Act of 1990 (1990, August 30). Committee of the Judiciary, 101st Congress, 2nd Session, Report No. 101–433.

Stoll, O., Lau, A., & Stoeber, J. (2007). Perfectionism and performance in a new basketball training task: Does striving for perfections enhance or undermine performance? *Psychology of Sport and Exercise, 9,* 111–129.

Strauss, R. H. (1987). Anabolic steroids. In R. H. Strauss (Ed.), *Drugs and performance in sports* (pp. 59–68). Philadelphia: Saunders.

Strauss, R. H. (1988, October–December). Drug abuse in sports: A three-pronged response. *Sports Coach,* pp. 12, 23.

Strelan, P., & Boeckman, R. J. (2003). A new model for understanding performance-enhancing drug use by elite athletes. *Journal of Applied Sport Psychology, 15,* 176–183.

Stuart, R. (1974). Teaching facts about drugs: Pushing or preventing? *Journal of Educational Psychology, 66,* 189–201.

Taylor, W. N. (1987). Synthetic anabolic-androgenic steroids: A plea for controlled substance status. *The Physician and Sportsmedicine, 15,* 140–150.

Thornton, J. S. (1997). Pain relief for acute soft-tissue injuries. *Physician and Sportsmedicine, 25,* 108.

Tobler, N. (1986). Meta-analysis of 143 adolescent drug prevention programs: Quantitative outcome results of program participants compared to a control or comparison group. *Journal of Drug Issues, 16,* 537–567.

Uzych, L. (1991). Drug testing of athletes. *British Journal of Addictions, 86,* 5–8.

Wagner, J. C. (1991). Enhancement of athletic performance with drugs. An overview. *Sports Medicine, 12,* 250–265.

Weinhold, L. L. (1991). Steroid and drug use by athletes. In L. Diamant (Ed.), *Psychology of sport, exercise, and fitness: Social and personal issues.* New York: Hemisphere.

Wemyss-Holden, S. A., Hamdy, F. C., & Hastie, K. J. (1994). *British Journal of Urology, 74,* 476–478.

Werch, C. E., Carlson, J. M., Pappas, D. M., Edemon, P., & DiClemente, C. C. (2000). Effects of a brief alcohol preventive intervention for youth attending school sports physical examinations. *Substance Use and Misuse, 35,* 421–432.

Whitehead, R., Chillag, S., & Elliott, D. (1992). Anabolic steroid use among adolescents in a rural state. *Journal of Family Practice, 35,* 401–405.

Wilkerson, L. A. (1995). Taking a strong stance against anabolic steroid use [editorial]. *Journal of the American Osteopathic Association, 95,* 468–470.

Williams, M. H. (1989). *Beyond training: How athletes enhance performance legally and illegally.* Champaign, IL: Leisure Press.

Williams, M. H. (1994). The use of nutritional ergogenic aids in sports: Is it an ethical issue? *International Journal of Sport Nutrition, 4,* 120–131.

Williams, M. H. (1998). *The ergogenics edge: Pushing the limits of sports performance.* Champaign, IL: Human Kinetics.

Williams, M. H., Kreider, R. B., & Branch, J. D. (1999). *Creatine: The power supplement.* Champaign, IL: Human Kinetics.

Wright, J. E., & Cowart, V. S. (1990). *Anabolic steroids: Altered states.* Carmel, IN: Cooper Publishing Group.

Yesalis, C. E., & Bahrke, M. S. (1995). Anabolic-androgenic steroids. Current issues. *Sports Medicine, 19,* 326–340.

Yesalis, C. E., & Cowart, V. S. (1998). *The steroids game.* Champaign, IL: Human Kinetics.

Yesalis, C. E., Herrick, R. T., Buckley, W. E., Friedl, K. E., Brannon, D., & Wright, J. E. (1988). Self-reported use of anabolic-androgenic steroids by elite power-lifters. *The Physician and Sportsmedicine, 16,* 91–94; 96–98.

Burnout in Sport: Understanding the Process—From Early Warning Signs to Individualized Intervention

Kate Goodger, *English Institute of Sport*,
David Lavallee, *Aberystwyth University*,
Trish Gorely, *Loughborough University*,
Chris Harwood, *Loughborough University*

Maybe 14 is too young to handle everything emotionally and I needed to escape from the expectation of being able to win every tournament I entered. I was always expected to be at the top and if I didn't win, to me that meant I was a loser. If I played terrible I thought I could handle it, but really I couldn't. I felt no one liked me as a person. I was depressed and sad and lonely and guilty. . . . I burned out. After the U.S. Open I spent a week in bed in darkness, just hating everything. When I looked in the mirror I saw this distorted image. I just wanted to kill myself. I'm not addicted to drugs, but you could say I was an addict to my own pain. I had this sarcasm about everything. I was depressed and sad and lonely and guilty.

—Jennifer Capriati, in 2001, reflecting on an earlier time in her tennis career

Introduction

Burnout as an academic construct within the field of sport psychology, and burnout framed in the anecdotal accounts of athletes, coaches, parents, athletic directors, and trainers, presents something of a paradox. Media and sport organizations popularized the term, and early research interest grew from media accounts documenting the negative experiences of a series of high-profile athletes (Cresswell & Eklund, 2006a). Much concern exists regarding the impact of burnout on performance and athlete welfare (Cresswell & Eklund, 2005a), and this interest has led to the term burnout becoming a buzzword (Raedeke, 1997) within the sport community. As such, burnout appears readily identifiable and well understood, yet in research terms, and the applied practice which research informs, this is not in fact the case. The paucity of burnout research leaves the concept poorly understood, with much still to explore. This chapter provides an overview of what we know about burnout. We begin with the historical development of the term and then define *burnout* in comparison to the related concepts of dropout, overtraining, and staleness. Next, we examine the signs, symptoms, and consequences of burnout, along with traditional theories and models of burnout in sport. We then review key research conducted on both athletes and coaches, highlight tools for monitoring burnout, and discuss potential intervention strategies. The chapter closes with a case study.

The Historical Development of Burnout

The first appearance of burnout within academic literature focused on job-related stress (Freudenberger, 1974) and later extended to encompass human services and helping professions (Maslach, 1976). It was not long before individuals made the observation that stressors in the competitive sport context were similar to those reported in the work setting (Dale & Weinberg, 1990), and research examining coaching burnout began (Caccese & Mayerberg, 1984; Kelley & Gill, 1993; Vealey, Udry, Zimmerman, & Soliday, 1992). More recently, attention has shifted to the exploration of burnout in athlete populations (e.g., Cresswell & Eklund, 2005a, 2005b, 2007; Gould, Tuffey, Udry, & Loehr, 1996a, 1996b, 1997; Harlick & McKenzie, 2000; Lemyre, Treasure & Roberts, 2006; Raedeke & Smith, 2004).

A significant challenge to applied practice and the advancement of empirical research into burnout has been the attainment of a universal definition. The lack of agreement stems from conceptual confusion centering upon two longstanding points of conjecture. First is the question of what comprises burnout. Second, how does burnout differ from closely associated conditions with which it shares key characteristics? With regard to the former, early research produced such an all-encompassing definition of *burnout* that the term was almost meaningless (Schaufeli & Buunk, 2003). In the latter case, within the professional context burnout has shown considerable overlap with conditions such as depression, fatigue and job stress, and in the sport domain, dropout, overtraining, and

staleness. These problems have led to the question of whether burnout actually represents a new and distinct psychological phenomenon (Schaufeli & Buunk). This conceptual confusion not only concerns how to define burnout, but also how the concept is operationalized through measurement and assessment. Cresswell and Eklund (2006a) suggest that because of the lack of conceptual clarity, the people often apply the term *burnout* inaccurately.

Within the work-related context, one definition has emerged as the most accepted and instrumental in shaping the field (Schaufeli & Buunk, 2003). Maslach and Jackson (1984) describe *burnout* as a "psychological syndrome of emotional exhaustion, depersonalization, and reduced sense of performance accomplishment that can occur among individuals who work with people in some capacity" (p. 134). Their definition soon broadened for utilization across a range of occupations outside the helping professions. Emotional exhaustion refers to emotional depletion and extreme fatigue and is the central of the three dimensions (Schaufeli & Taris, 2005). Depersonalization is now known as *cynicism,* denoted by a distant and indifferent attitude toward others at work, and is a proposed defensive coping strategy (Schaufeli & Taris). Researchers now describe the third dimension of performance accomplishment as *professional efficacy.* This incorporates social and nonsocial aspects of occupational accomplishment (Schaufeli & Buunk, 2003). This dimension is the least well understood but is a possible consequence of burnout (Schaufeli & Taris, 2005).

Defining Burnout in Sport

Burnout in the sport context as in the work domain, is marked by a lack of consensus about how to define it. Research studies by Raedeke and colleagues (Raedeke, 1997; Raedeke et al., 2002; Raedeke & Smith, 2001) have provided a foundation for future agreement through an athlete-specific definition framed within Maslach and Jackson's (1984) tri-dimensional conceptualization. Earlier research employed a similar coach-based definition (e.g., Kelley,

1994; Quigley, Slack & Smith, 1987), but Raedeke (1997) did not view it as valid for athlete populations. To facilitate use with athletes, Raedeke (1997) modified the original three dimensions based upon an examination of contextual differences and the components that are central to the athletic experience. Subsequently, Raedeke identified the dimensions as physical and emotional exhaustion (associated with intense training and competition) and reduced sense of accomplishment (in terms of skills and abilities and the inability to achieve personal goals or to perform up to expectations). In addition, *sport devaluation* (characterized by a loss of interest, "don't care" attitude, and resentment) replaced depersonalization because it was not a salient dimension in athlete burnout (Raedeke & Smith, 2001). Through research among swimmers Raedeke et al. (2002) offer the following definition of athlete burnout: "A withdrawal. . . noted by a reduced sense of accomplishment, devaluation/resentment of sport, and physical/psychological exhaustion" (p. 181).

Burnout, Dropout, Overtraining, and Staleness

Researchers and practitioners have used *burnout* interchangeably with the concepts of dropout, overtraining, and staleness. Although these conditions are related, they are separate concepts. The association between them has led to confusion as to where each begins and ends, but recent research efforts offer clearer differentiation between them (e.g. Cresswell & Eklund, 2006c; Kellmann & Kallus, 2000; Kentta & Hassmen, 1998).We discuss this research in more detail in the section, "Theories and Models of Burnout in Sport" later in the chapter.

The product of burnout, if not managed effectively, is withdrawal or dropout from the activity. However, not every dropout in sport is the result of burnout (Gould & Dieffenbach, 2002). Individuals may simply want to try something new, or aspects of their life change and other priorities emerge. Gould (1997) explains that athletes who discontinue sport as a result

of burnout do so because of prolonged, excessive stress. Other athletes who drop out have not experienced this prolonged stress.

In a review of overtraining, Raglin and Wilson (2000) comment that the use of terminology within the literature has been inconsistent. They explain that existing research defines overtraining in both positive and negative terms and as a stimulus, response, or process. Raglin and Wilson also identify a distinction between the use of the term by European coaches and sport scientists and those in North America. In Europe, overtraining reflects the detrimental effects of excessive training, whereas in North America it is considered a beneficial, prescribed period of training that sometimes results in reduced performance. More recently, a specially convened U.S. Olympic Committee has established a consensus definition of *overtraining* (Gould and Dieffenbach, 2002). This task force defines *overtraining* as "a syndrome that results when excessive, usually physical, overload on an athlete occurs without adequate rest" (p. 25). In other words, the athlete is unable to recover sufficiently from the overload. The consequences of this overload are performance decrements, an inability to train, and potentially staleness and even burnout.

Staleness is generally associated with a negative outcome of overtraining that is the result of the athlete's failure to adapt to the prescribed training regimen (Raglin & Wilson, 2000). Raglin, Sawamura, Alexiou, Hassmen, and Kentta (2000) explain that staleness "is an unexpected and long-term loss of performance that cannot be attributed to factors such as illness or injury" (p. 61). An operational definition that has been employed to help identify incidences of staleness is the "[experience of] a significant performance decrement that [has] persisted for at least two weeks, and that without doubt was caused by physical training (i.e., not by illness or injury)" (Kentta, Hassmen, & Raglin, 2001, p. 461). A range of symptoms is associated with staleness, but the most consistent include loss of appetite, mood disturbance, depression, and increased perceptions of effort (Kentta et al.).

Distinguishing burnout from related conditions such as overtraining and staleness is difficult, but two key aspects appear to differentiate them. The first is that overtraining and staleness are both associated with physical overload that is largely training based, whereas burnout may also result from stress that is not training related (e.g., coach interactions, parental influence, restrictions on other activities). Secondly, as demonstrated in a study of staleness in Swedish age-group athletes, Kentta and colleagues (2001) found that overtrained and stale athletes are distinguishable from those with burnout through an observable motivational shift and associated subsequent motivational consequences. These consequences included most notably a lack of desire to train. The authors argued that athletes who are overtrained and experience staleness typically retain the motivation to train, whilst in cases of burnout, athletes lose interest in continuing participation in their sport and motivation to train or compete.

Signs, Symptoms, and Consequences of Burnout

Burnout is described as a multidimensional psycho-social syndrome (Cresswell & Eklund, 2006a). A syndrome refers to a group of signs and symptoms that occur together and characterise a particular abnormality (Shirom, 2005). Symptoms of burnout are well documented but are also problematic on a number of levels (Schaufeli & Buunk, 2003). The challenges to the symptomatology of burnout include a broad spectrum of identified symptoms, a shared symptomatology with related conditions (i.e. anxiety, depression, and overtraining), the unique and personal nature of burnout (Gould, Tuffey, Udry, & Loehr, 1997), and finally the difficulty researchers have found in distinguishing between a symptom and a consequence. For example, fatigue could be either.

In an attempt to provide an overview of burnout for practitioners, Cresswell and Eklund (2003) present a model of the athlete burnout syndrome stemming from their work with professional rugby players. They offer a summary of early signs, symptoms, and potential consequences of athlete burnout, as well as potential intervention strategies. The early signs are indicative of athletes who are *at risk* for experiencing burnout, and include enduring negative mood shifts, a struggle to meet professional and personal obligations, feelings of disappointment and frustration, feeling physically tired, difficulty in communicating or unhappiness with social life, and a feeling of insufficient support from staff. Cresswell and Eklund (2003) make the important distinction that these early warning signs may be subjective signs (relating to the athletes' own perceptions) or objective signs (observable by others). They explain that the athletes' own perceptions determine if elements actually indicate burnout, although signs observable by others also may aid those who are responsible for the athletes' welfare. Identification of these early warning signs permits the implementation of proactive management strategies to prevent or reduce the incidence of burnout.

According to Cresswell and Eklund (2003), the types of symptoms burned-out athletes display include mental and physical exhaustion, feelings of isolation, low confidence, difficulty in concentrating during performance, and feelings that their career is not moving forward and that their own contribution to the team is small or not valued by others. The authors acknowledge, however, that such clear examples of symptoms are rare because of the variations that exist among individuals' stress perceptions and personal experiences of burnout.

In their review of 25 years of burnout research within the work domain, Schaufeli and Buunk (2003) classify the consequences of burnout into five categories. The categories are consequences associated with (1) affective (e.g., feeling gloomy, tearful, and depressed); (2) cognitive (e.g., helplessness, hopelessness, and powerlessness); (3) physical (e.g., emotional exhaustion, and somatic complaints); (4) behavioral (e.g., smoking, consumption of medication, impaired performance, and absenteeism); and (5) motivational (e.g., lack of zeal, enthusiasm, and interest) aspects. Within the sport context, the impact of burnout echoes much of what has been experienced in the work domain. Referring again to Cresswell and Eklund's (2003) model, potential consequences include decreased commitment to the sport. Loss of enthusiasm for preparation and competition, or reluctance or lack of motivation to self-initiate work in training sessions; performance decrements that affect selection, potential funding, and athlete confidence; increased susceptibility to injury and illness; and the requirement of extended recovery periods to return to fitness reflect these potential consequences. The burned-out individual also may experience mood changes that affect social consequences in that they are difficult to be around or prefer to distance themselves from others. The social distancing behavior may ultimately end in withdrawal from the sport. Cresswell and Eklund (2003) also discuss the wider implications of burnout to significant others within the athlete's social network. Burnout may lead to relationship problems and family or marital issues. Antisocial behaviors in the form of drug and alcohol abuse may occur in cases of burnout that are more progressive.

From other research, further significant consequences associated with athlete burnout include lack of fulfilment of human potential and curtailment of athletic development (Feigley, 1984), physical and psychological decrements in performance (Gould et al., 1996b; Cresswell & Eklund; 2006a), lowered performance standards (Feigley, 1984), anxiety (Vealey, Armstrong, Comar, & Greenleaf, 1998), mood disturbance (Tenebaum, Jones, Kitsantas, Sacks, & Berwick, 2003) interpersonal difficulties (Cresswell & Eklund, 2007; Udry et al., 1997), and debilitating effects on general health and well-being (Coakley, 1992; Harlick & McKenzie, 2000). Situation Study 1 highlights the chronic nature of burnout and the accumulative effects of the signs, symptoms, and consequences of the syndrome.

Theories and Models of Burnout in Sport

Within the burnout literature, four *traditional* theories explain what causes burnout and how it develops in sport. These theories offer frameworks through which to understand how burnout manifests and to inform intervention strategies to prevent and/or manage burnout.

Silva's (1990) Negative Training Stress Response Model

Silva (1990) was among the first to attempt to distinguish burnout from overtraining and staleness. The model proposes that burnout is a negative product of excessive training. Physical training places stresses on the athlete that can be both positive and negative. Although positive stress results in positive adaptations and training gains, negative stresses such as too much training lead to negative adaptation and negative training responses. Silva states that these responses include staleness ("an initial failure of the body's adaptive mechanisms to cope with psycho-physiological stress," p. 10), overtraining ("detectable psycho-physiological malfunctions characterized by easily observed changes in the athletes' mental orientation and physical performance," p. 10), and burnout ("an exhaustive psycho-physiological response exhibited as a result of frequent, sometimes extreme, but generally ineffective efforts to meet excessive training and sometimes competitive demands," p. 11). Silva hypothesizes that these responses lie on a continuum from staleness experienced because of overtraining, which if unmanaged, progress to the more severe state of burnout (Gould & Dieffenbach, 2002).

Smith's (1986) Cognitive–Affective Stress Model

Smith (1986) offered a four-stage cognitive-affective stress model to explain stress-induced burnout. The model proposes that burnout is a process that involves physical, psychological, and behavioral components. An overarching feature of this model is that motivation and personality factors influence these components. The first stage of the model refers to situational demands the athlete experiences, and may include such factors as intense training schedules. The second stage involves cognitive appraisal of the situation. Some athletes may perceive the situation as threatening and that the demands

Situation Study 1

The Problem Kid or the Kid with the Problem?

Mark had been swimming his whole life. He could not remember a time when he had not been in the water. He loved it; it was that simple. From early on, Mark's talent and natural ability for swimming also were apparent. He was enthusiastic to join a swimming club when a coach approached his parents at the local pool; swimming fast and faster still became his drive. At age 14, he secured his place on the national team, and he had been representing his country ever since.

At age 18, Mark elected to take a year or two out of education to train full time, and swimming become a very different place for him. His life was swimming. Everyone knew Mark as "Mark the swimmer." People had high hopes of him and they expected that an Olympic campaign was to figure prominently in his future career. Mark, however, no longer felt the same about swimming. The sport he had loved he had now grown to hate. Each day was the same routine and his coach constantly pushed him. He would wake up exhausted and go to sleep exhausted. He had not felt like the old Mark for more months than he could remember. Where he once had found solitude in the water, a place to forget about the rest of the world, he now found the sound of the water against him deafening and was desperate for each session to be over. He no longer attacked his races, and even when he tried to put all that he had left into the race, the results failed to come. The passion and hunger had died. He was left with anger, hurt, and frustration. Swimming was eating away at him and he was becoming the "problem athlete" that he had always despised. This was the kind of athlete who strode around poolside with an "I do not care" and "I cannot be bothered" attitude. Coaches did not like them, and teammates resented them. He withdrew from people and found it easier to disappear. Things had gone from a few almost unbearable days to a procession of them, rolling from one long week into the next. There was no escape. His coping strategy was to spend as little time as possible around swimming and other swimmers. He was now last in and first out, and absent when possible. Happiness only came when he was away from the pool. The hardest part of all, however, was the realization that he wanted out, and that no one could hear or see that this was what he wanted and desperately needed.

outweigh their resources to cope with them. This appraisal governs the nature and intensity of emotional responses, and negative appraisal may lead to stress. In the third stage of physiological responses, if an individual perceives the situation as threatening, physiological changes occur such as increased tension and fatigue, insomnia, lethargy, and illness. Types of coping and task behavior such as performance decrements and withdrawal that result from the physiological responses characterize the fourth and final stage. An additional feature of this model considers the burnout process circular and continuous, where behavioral responses feed back into the situational demands stage. Gould et al. (1996a) hypothesize reciprocal relationships between the four stages (Gould et al., 1996a).

Smith (1986) asserted, however, that not all withdrawal from sport is burnout related. In an attempt to differentiate between burnout-induced withdrawal and other-determinant withdrawal (i.e., dropout), Smith applied Thibaut and Kelley's (1959) social exchange theory as a framework. The principles of this theory propose that the desire to maximize positive experiences and to minimize negative ones govern human behavior. Individuals participate in activities as long as they are favorable. The balance of costs and rewards, and how these compare to the outcomes of alternative activities, determine this favorability (Weinberg & Gould, 2003). If activities fall below the comparison level for alternatives, individuals are likely to withdraw in the hope of pursuing alternative activities. Smith (1986) reported that the most prevalent reason for dropout in youth sport is the attraction of alternative activities. The individual perceives these alternatives to be above the outcomes of participation in their current sport. For the individual who experiences burnout, however, withdrawal results from an increase in stress-induced costs from the present activity. The previously enjoyed activity becomes an aversive source of stress.

Coakley's (1992) Unidimensional Identity Development and External Control Model

Although stress-induced perspectives such as Smith's (1986) model have dominated the literature, alternative approaches have also been advanced and supported. Coakley's (1992) Unidimensional Identity Development and External Control Model postulates that stress is a symptom of burnout rather than a cause. Through a sociological perspective, this model asserts that burnout is a social problem that is the product of the organization of sport. Specifically, organizational constraints prevent the development of a multifaceted identity. Exclusive involvement in sport means that young performers are unable to explore and develop other aspects of their identity. Others identify and recognize them through sport, and their identity becomes hinged upon success in sport. Furthermore, the organization of the sport results in limited autonomy for the young person because decision making is in the hands of others. According to the model, burnout in athletes results from a sport organization associated with the creation of a unidimensional identity and a lack of control over one's own life.

Schmidt and Stein's (1991) Sport Commitment Model

Another divergent approach to the stress-induced perspective of burnout is Schmidt and Stein's (1991) sport commitment model of burnout. This model suggests that burnout is more than a simple reaction to stress, and that, although everyone can experience stress, not everyone who experiences stress burns out (Raedeke, 1997). Schmidt and Stein propose that three primary determinants influence athlete commitment, and athletes who experience burnout are committed to sport for reasons that differ from those who do not experience burnout. The determinants of athlete commitment are satisfaction based on rewards and costs associated with sport, attractiveness of alternative options, and resources athletes have invested in sport. The model proposes that burnout is likely to occur in athletes who display an entrapment profile, where they are participating in the sport because they have to rather than want to. This occurs when athletes experiences high costs and low rewards but remains in the sport because they feel that they have invested a lot in terms of resources, and perceive a lack of attractive alternatives. This contrasts with the dropout athlete who is not committed to the sport. The perspective has received recent attention through the work of Raedeke and colleagues (e.g., Raedeke, 1997; Raedeke & Smith 2001). These authors highlight different commitment profiles, which may predispose individuals to burnout. To illustrate, Raedeke (1997) describes entrapped swimmers who are participating in their sport because they "have to" as opposed to "wanting to." These athletes are more susceptible to burnout.

Theories of Coach Burnout

At present, there is only one published model of coach burnout (Kelley, 1994). In testing this model, Kelley hypothesized that the personal and situational variables of coaching issues, social support, hardiness, gender, and win–loss record would predict stress appraisal. Types of coaching issues include budget management, coach–athlete relationships, and role conflict. Stress appraisal would then predict burnout. The model adopts basic tenants of Smith's (1986) model but focuses specifically on burnout in coaches. Research findings have reported partial support for the model in that both coaching issues and hardiness predict stress appraisal in both male and female coaches. Social support predicts perceived stress in males but not in females, and winning percentage does not predict burnout in either gender. Perceived stress is a predictor of all three dimensions of burnout (emotional exhaustion, depersonalization, and reduced performance accomplishment).

Examining Burnout in Sport

Research interest in burnout in sport really began in earnest during the early 1980s through the work of Caccese and Mayerberg (1984) focusing on burnout in coaches. This early work drew comparisons between the role of the coach and that of individuals in helping professions. Human relationships were a central feature of the coaching profession, and this, together with the stressful and volatile nature of the coaching environment, made coaches a prime candidate for burnout just as research had shown in the helping professions. Research within the sport domain has extended to other individuals, including athletic trainers, athletic directors, officials, and athletes. Since the 1990s, growth in research conducted on athlete populations has fueled contemporary research. This stems in part from the growing concern that demands placed on young athletes have intensified considerably in recent years, and that the competitive pressures these athletes experience may lead to discontinued sport involvement and increased incidence of athletic burnout (Gould, 1997; Gould & Dieffenbach, 2002). Much of this concern stems from shared beliefs that young athletes train too much, take part in too many competitions, focus entirely on one sport at too young an age, and continually have to learn to cope with pressure from parents and coaches (Coakley, 1992; Gould et al., 1996a; Harlick & McKenzie, 2000).

Research on Athletes

Research examining burnout in athlete populations has sought largely to understand more about the factors that cause burnout and its subsequent consequences. Goodger, Lavallee, Gorely, and Harwood (2007) conducted an extensive search of the literature regarding burnout in sport (up to 2005) to provide an up-to-date summary of the field. Through a systematic review approach, the authors found no causal relationships, but they identified a number of factors as potential correlates of burnout. These correlates can be divided into two broad categories: psychological (e.g., trait anxiety and commitment) and demographic or situational (e.g., age and training loads). In athlete populations, researchers have tended to focus more on psychological than demographic or situational factors, and hence this represents the category about which most is known. Goodger et al. report that burnout has been positively associated with the following variables: amotivation, anxiety, training stress/under recovery and failure adaptation, mood disturbance, and staleness. Motivation, intrinsic motivation, enjoyment, coping, and social support are all negatively associated with burnout. Research has shown that athletes who experience burnout are lower in intrinsic motivation or are amotivated, perceive less enjoyment or fail to enjoy their involvement in sport, possess ineffective coping strategies, have low or negative social support, and may exhibit signs of stress and anxiety that can be the result of intense physical training or insufficient recovery. The association between burnout and extrinsic motivation and parental involvement is indeterminate at this time as findings are conflicting. In studies of parental involvement in burnout among junior tennis players, Udry et al. (1997) and Harlick and McKenzie (2000) report both positive and negative effects of parents. That is, parents may contribute to feelings of being burned out through acting as an additional stressor, or conversely they may take on the role of a buffer or mediator who helps to reduce their son or daughter's exposure to stress.

The first studies of burnout conducted on an athlete sample group were by Cohn (1990) and Silva (1990). Cohn examined sources of stress and perceived causes of burnout in high school golfers and identified too much playing or practice, lack of fun and enjoyment, no new goals to strive for, going into a slump, and pressure to do well from self, coaches, and parents as the primary causes of burnout. Silva examined burnout in relation to physical training and resultant findings led to the advancement of the Negative Training Stress Response Model (discussed earlier in the chapter). Shortly after these studies, Coakley (1992) undertook a further study from a sociological perspective that proposed the Unidimensional Identity Development and External Control Model of burnout.

A landmark study of athlete burnout in elite junior tennis players by Gould and colleagues (Gould, Tuffey, Udry, & Loehr, 1996a, 1996b, & 1997) (commissioned by the U.S Tennis Association) remains one of the most in-depth explorations within the literature. Arising from considerable debate concerning the competitive pressures placed upon junior players, and the consequences of such pressure, the purpose of the study was to identify and describe in psychological terms players who had experienced burnout, in contrast to equivalent players who had not. In so doing, the authors intended to learn more about the burnout experience from those who had actually lived with it, together with gathering information to inform future preventative and management strategies. The study was divided into two phases. Phase one consisted of the completion of a battery of psychological and social psychological inventories. The authors then sought to contrast results with the comparative samples in the first article (Gould, et al., 1996a). In addition, a subsample (*n* = 10) of burned-out players was selected from phase one to participate in in-depth interviews during the second phase (Gould, et al., 1996b). This part of the study reported physical characteristics (e.g., injuries or illness) and mental characteristics (e.g., lacking energy/motivation, negative feelings, feelings of isolation, concentration

problems, and high and low mood), recommendations for prevention of burnout, and examination of three existing models of athlete burnout. The article also promoted the novel suggestion of the existence of different strains of burnout. The authors proposed that two major strains were *physically driven* and *social-psychologically driven*. Physically driven burnout is essentially the result of overtraining and heavy training and competition loads. Social-psychologically driven burnout is the result of athlete perfectionism and situation pressure such as parental or coach pressure. The identification of these different strains suggests the need to consider carefully the structure and nature of interventions for individuals affected by burnout. A final article in the series (Gould et al., 1997) presented examples of the different strains of burnout through three case studies of the experiences of individual players.

More recently, three major themes of enquiry have emerged in athlete-based research. First, increasing attention has begun to focus on the exploration of athlete burnout conceptualized as the three dimensions that Raedeke advanced (1997) (i.e. physical and emotional exhaustion, sport devaluation, and reduced athletic accomplishment). This research has examined these dimensions with regard to the development and validation of a self-report measure (Cresswell & Eklund, 2006c; Raedeke & Smith, 2001), potential attributions of burnout (Cresswell & Eklund, 2006a), motivation and self-determination (Cresswell & Eklund, 2005a, 2005b; Lemyre, Treasure, & Roberts, 2006), and characteristics of each dimension (Cresswell & Eklund, 2006a, 2007; Raedeke, et al., 2002). See Situation Study 2 for a sample of the characteristics associated with each dimension reported within the existent literature. Second, a perspective from Europe aims to explain the complex relationships among staleness, overtraining, recovery, stress, burnout, coping, and mood through psychological, sociological, and physiological frameworks. This approach by Kellmann and Kallus (2000) proposes that conditions such overtraining, staleness, and eventually burnout are the product of accumulating stress (training and nontraining based) without appropriate recovery. See *Enhancing Recovery: Preventing*

Situation Study 2

Some of the typical characteristics associated with Raedeke's (1997) three dimensions of athlete burnout are outlined in Table 22-1.

Table 22-1

Physical and Emotional Exhaustion	Reduced Athletic Accomplishment	Sport Devaluation
Tired	Up and down performances	Doubts and disbelief about career—"why am I doing this?"
Lethargic	Downward spiral of performance	
Too tired to do things outside sport	Loss of control over performance	Mental desire for competition slipping away
Wanting a break from the sport	Not playing to potential	Sport not enjoyable any more
Feeling emotionally low	Going backwards	Don't care about sport participation
		Sick of playing

Underperformance in Athletes (Kellmann, 2002) for a key overview of this work. Finally, Gould et al. (1996b) originally proposed that Self-Determination Theory (SDT) (Deci & Ryan, 1985) may provide a useful framework through which to explore burnout among athletes, but it is through the work of Cresswell and Eklund (2005a and 2005b) in particular that this perspective has begun to be applied to empirical enquiry. Ryan and Deci (2000) assert that the basis of human well-being is the satisfaction of three basic needs (i.e., autonomy, competence, and relatedness), and conversely, a state of ill-being (e.g., depression) is the result of chronic failure to meet these needs. In the context of athlete burnout, Cresswell and Eklund (2006a), suggest that burnout may result from a perception of chronically unfulfilled needs. Burnout is believed to possess a "motivational signature" (i.e., the prominence of motivation, or a lack of motivation) (Cresswell and Eklund, 2005a), and as such motivational theories could play an important role in advancing future

understanding of the syndrome. Empirical evidence has begun to emerge supporting a relationship between self-determination and burnout (Cresswell & Eklund, 2005a, 2005b; Lemyre, Treasure, & Roberts, 2006).

Research on Coaches

Goodger et al's. (2007) systematic review of coach burnout research found that perceived stress (Kelley, 1994), coaching issues (Kelley & Gill, 1993), role conflict (Capel, Sisley, & Desertrain, 1987), role ambiguity (Quigley, Slack, & Smith, 1987), and gender (Pastore & Judd, 1993) have all been associated positively with burnout. Coaches who experienced coaching issues such as budget considerations, coach–athlete relationships, and role conflict experience higher perceived stress, which in turn predicts burnout (Kelley, 1994). In studies reporting gender differences, females have higher levels of emotional exhaustion and a greater sense of reduced performance accomplishment compared to males (Kelley & Gill, 1993; Pastore & Judd, 1992). An explanation for this observed trend is that female coaches feel overloaded with work, often experience role conflict between home life and coaching (Drake & Herbert, 2002), must cope with the tendency for female sport to be marginalized in sport programs, and feel undervalued in their job. Male coaches are, however, higher generally in depersonalization than females (Dale & Weinberg, 1989). The socialization effect of the "win orientated" culture endemic within modern sport causes male coaches to be more impersonal toward their athletes (Vealey et al., 1998), which results in higher depersonalization. In contrast to athlete research, much of what we understand about coach burnout is through factors associated with the coaching environment, rather than individual difference or psychological factors. Demands of the coaching environment, the time-intensive nature of the coaching role, and intense internal and external pressure to produce results create a climate in which coaches are potentially highly vulnerable to burnout. The case of Simon in Situation Study 3 highlights these demands.

As performance standards become higher, together with the mass spectatorship of modern sport, demands on coaches are likely to increase as they have with athletes. It is important that governing bodies of sport consider helping coaches to develop appropriate skills through coach education, continued professional development, and mentoring schemes in order to develop effective coping strategies to reduce the incidence of coach burnout. Furthermore, a secondary effect of coach burnout is the potential impact on the development and performance of their athletes. Two studies examining how coach burnout affects athlete burnout and psychological responses of athletes support this concern (e.g., Price & Weiss, 2000; Vealey, et al. In a sample of female soccer players and head coaches, Price and Weiss (2000) reported that players perceived coaches higher in emotional exhaustion as providing less training and instruction and social support, while making fewer autocratic (and more democratic) decisions (depersonalization and reduced personal accomplishment were not significantly related). Lower perceived competence and enjoyment, and higher anxiety and burnout among players, were associated with coaches who exhibited less frequent training and instruction, social support, and positive feedback. These were generally characteristics of coaches experiencing high levels of burnout. Vealey et al. (1998) examined the influence of perceived coaching behavior and burnout and competitive anxiety in female college athletes. Findings suggest that coach burnout relates significantly to perceived coaching behaviors, perceived coaching behavior was predictive of athletes' burnout, and athletes' anxiety and athlete burnout are significantly related. What emerges from this research is that not only do coaches have a role to play in safeguarding athletes from burnout, but also that they must be mindful of their own vulnerability.

Monitoring Burnout

Traditionally, self-report measures have been the popular research tool for measuring burnout. In coach-based research, the Maslach Burnout Inventory (MBI) (Maslach & Jackson, 1986) has usually been used. A stumbling block to the study of athlete burnout was the failure to develop valid measurement tools for use with athletes until 2001.

Raedeke and Smith (2001) developed their Athlete Burnout Questionnaire (ABQ) by employing modified dimensions of Maslach and Jackson's (1984) original three dimensions of burnout. The ABQ consists of 15 items relating to three subscales of physical and emotional exhaustion, performance accomplishment, and sport devaluation. Respondents rate their responses using a 5-point Likert scale from *almost never* to *almost always*. Use of the ABQ in empirical research is limited, but in a study comparing the construct

Situation Study 3

Pressure in basketball—it is not just the players

Simon is an experienced and much respected collegiate basketball coach. Positions in the program are highly competitive and each year new recruits are keen to make an impression on the head coach. Simon's coaching and squad are well supported by a committed support staff of assistant coach, athletic trainer, sports science staff, and a consultant sport psychologist. Going into the new season, both the assistant coach and athletic trainer noticed that Simon does not quite appear to be himself. Usually a measured speaker known to turn a player's game around through a few well-chosen words, Simon had begun yelling at players in training for what appeared to be mild misdemeanors or errors. The team had not performed as expected in the previous season and there was a level of pressure from the dean and the university to reinstate the team's reputation as a tough opponent. In addition, some of the players expected to matriculate as freshmen had either failed to enroll or were injured. The team dynamic had changed with the new players and the loss of some key players to graduation, and the team had been struggling to find its feet through preseason training. Concerned, the assistant coach talked to Simon over lunch one day and asked how things were going. Simon expressed concerns about the team this season and let slip that he was having some problems at home. The competitive season was intense and his wife complained about the time he spent away from her and the kids and that when he was home he never switched off from work. The assistant coach suggested Simon talk to the sport psychologist but Simon refused, saying he did not need it. The first half of the season saw a number of mediocre performances from the team which seemed plagued by injury. Simon appeared to be becoming increasingly agitated and expressed frustration routinely with players during practice. His frustration was also edging into games, where his players had previously seen him as a rock for the team, motivating while also calming and supporting them. Players loved to play for him. On the bus journey back from an away game the sport psychologist chatted with Simon about some player issues and voiced his observations that Simon appeared to be under some stress. Simon talked about the pressure from home and from the university and additional responsibilities he had been forced to take on. He said he felt tired all the time but could not sleep. He could no longer switch off and became really stressed before games, which he had never experienced before. Worst of all for him he was waking up some days dreading going to the job. He had always been a driven coach and this change scared him. He felt he could not tell anyone and just had to get on with it as everyone relied on him—his family, his players, his staff. He was the coach; he was meant to be in charge.

validity of the ABQ with the more widely known *Maslach Burnout Inventory* (MBI-GS), Cresswell and Eklund (2006c) reported acceptable validity and satisfactory divergence, and advocate the ABQ as the instrument of choice in assessing sport burnout. The ABQ also has implications for interventions in that the three subscales enable practitioners to develop more tailored interventions for individuals at risk of or already suffering from burnout. For example, one athlete at the early stages of burnout may appear to be experiencing greater emotional exhaustion, and hence may be in need of effective recovery strategies or physical rest, whereas another may be experiencing a significant sense of reduced accomplishment and, in turn, low self-confidence.

In an attempt to monitor the relationship between stress and recovery and facilitate early identification of cases of imbalance between them where overtraining, staleness, or burnout may become an issue, Kellmann and Kallus (2001) developed the Recovery Stress Questionnaire (RESTQ). The instrument assesses the recovery state of individuals, which indicates the extent that they are physically or mentally stressed, whether or not they are capable of using individual strategies for recovery, as well as which strategies are used. Versions exist for athletes (RESTQ-Sport; Kellmann & Kallus, 2001) and coaches (RESTQ-Coach; Kallus & Kellmann, 1995). Two subscales within the instrument refer specifically to burnout; these are emotional exhaustion and personal accomplishment. Applications of the RESTQ-Sport have been used successfully to identify incidences of stress and under recovery in the lead-up to and during major competitions (Kellmann & Gunther, 2000), to assess the effects of a yearly improved training schedule, and to provide concrete recommendations for interventions (Kellmann & Gunther, 2000). The development of such a tool has created an excellent opportunity to bring together multidisciplinary support services to work collaboratively to support athletes and coaches.

Interventions

An interesting feature of the burnout in sport literature is the absence of any published intervention studies. Web-based searches using *burnout* as a keyword will produce hundreds of hits that advise the top ten ways to beat burnout, and periodicals and magazines provide further strategies for athletes, coaches, and parents. Despite this information being readily available there is no empirical base to support existing intervention approaches. There is still much that we do not know and understand about burnout, including effective prevention and management approaches. Furthermore, it must be remembered the challenge that such approaches face in a social context in which the mindset "more is better," "winning is everything" is endemic. In addition, within professional sport where athletes often are the assets of the sports club business, Cresswell and Eklund (2006a and 2007) reported players' concerns for job security and contractual issues if they took time off to recover.

One study that sought advice on how to help athletes with burnout and how to reduce the incidence of burnout is that by Gould et al. (1996b). In this study, the authors asked junior tennis players who had experienced burnout for their recommendations on how to prevent burnout. Their results appear in three sections: Advice for Other Players, Advice for Parents, and Advice for Coaches.

Advice for Other Players

- Play for your own reasons.
- Balance tennis with other things.
- No fun—no play.
- Try to make it fun.
- Relax.
- Take time off.

Advice for Parents

- Recognize the optimal amount of "pushing" needed.
- Lessen involvement.
- Reduce the importance of the outcome.
- Show support amd empathy.
- Separate and clarify the parent–coach role.
- Solicit player input.
- Find ways to deal with stress.

- Talk things over with someone.
- Try a new approach to increase enjoyment.

Advice for Coaches

- Cultivate personal involvement with the player.
- Have two-way communication with the player.
- Utilize player input.
- Understand player feelings.

This advice is also helpful in identifying key individuals within the athlete's social network who may play an important role in potential prevention and intervention strategies. Parents and coaches have an important role to play, and, as such, intervention should look at developing awareness among these individuals, possibly through the delivery of athlete, parent, and coach education sessions.

Another useful publication that specifically addressed intervention issues was the Practitioner's Model by Cresswell and Eklund (2003) that we reviewed earlier. In the last tier of this model, the authors highlight a range of potential strategies, including the following:

- Time-off training.
- Time away from rugby.
- Relaxation.
- Life and career counseling (i.e., to attain more balance).
- Player rotation (scheduled rest from training and games).
- Increased involvement in decision making.
- Specialized counseling (e.g., relationship counselor).
- Social support—teammates and family.

The authors distinguish between intervention strategies that can have a preventative or management approach in order to tailor interventions to the needs of the individual. Furthermore, and building on the notion of tackling burnout

from a range of levels through different key persons (i.e., coach, athlete, and parent), Cresswell and Eklund (2003) suggest that prevention and management of burnout may happen at the personal level (e.g., skills and relaxation training) or the organizational level (e.g., player rotation, increased involvement in decision making). The authors make the valid point, however, that there is an assumption that individuals experiencing characteristics of burnout are motivated enough to learn and are able to implement new strategies. This may be a key determining factor influencing the relative success of an intervention.

Although research on interventions is limited, the extant literature suggests a number of common themes that may serve to prevent and manage burnout in sport, including the following:

- *Identify early warning signs—prevention is better than cure.* Coaches, parents, and athletes need to become aware and monitor periods of underperformance. It is more common that individuals will experience performance slumps than burnout, but the process of burnout has to start somewhere. Look out for the early warning signs.

- *Involve athletes in decision making.* This not only aids motivation but also provides a sense of ownership, which can raise confidence.

- *Schedule time-outs.* Doing too much too soon, or not resting enough, can become a fast track to burnout if not handled effectively. Time-outs give athletes the opportunity to have time away from the sport, experience quality recovery, and return fresh and ready to go.

- *Quality recovery and management of training regimes.* Athletes who are driven to succeed (or driven by others) may not rest enough to satisfy the needs of their body. They are desperate to get better and improve, and feel that time off may set them back in training. By failing to rest and enable the body to recover more fully, they gradually become more fatigued and performance starts to slip. Initially, overtraining may occur in a bid to return their performance to its original standards, but staleness and burnout can be the result.

- *Utilize athlete input—listen.* The athlete is the expert in knowing himself or herself and they should feel comfortable enough with the coach and support staff to be open about how they feel they are performing or responding to competition and training. A more open dialogue could enable coaches and support staff to identify the warning signs sooner.

- *Coach and parent support.* Social support is a key vehicle in both the prevention and management of burnout. By educating significant others within the athlete's social network (such as the parent or coach), these individuals may become effective buffers, able to mediate potential causes of burnout, as well as to support an athlete who is experiencing burnout. The burned-out athlete may not always be an easy individual to deal with, or be around, and this can influence the quality of support (or the athletes' perception of it).

- *Make it fun—enjoyment is crucial.* Athletes that experience burnout probably once started out as athletes who loved their sport. By making training and competition fun and motivating, the love of the sport is more likely to continue. Equally, unhappy athletes are unlikely to produce their best performances. The variability principle of training is particularly important in endurance sports such as swimming where the mundane nature of trudging up and down the training pool may easily become boring and tiresome. Variety is the spice of life.

- *Time and lifestyle management.* Burnout is the result of exposure to chronic stress and this stress may be training or nontraining related. It is essential that athletes maintain a healthy balance in their life between work and play and have time away from the sport environment. They come back revitalized and more eager to train and compete. This balance in lifestyle is not just a preventative measure for burnout but also ensures that the enjoyment continues and that young performers move into adulthood with varied life experiences.

Case Study

Within the positive drive to help a normal, healthy, and talented athlete reach his or her potential, it might be understandable that the rather negative topic of burnout is rarely the main or natural focus of a sport psychology consultant's work. Clearly, the sport psychology practitioner has a role in providing informational support and advice to coaches on psychological dimensions of the training and coaching environment, as well as a means to monitor and support athletes as they move through their career, and the various transitional stages along the way (Wylleman & Lavallee, 2004).

An actual case example may illustrate the potential roles of the practitioner more clearly. Sarah is a 15-year-old British tennis prodigy. The physical demands of training are often intense, and they combine with the grind of a tournament schedule that takes her away from home for long periods. Sarah has little freedom away from the court, and her training and competitive program lie under the control of her national governing body. Furthermore the intensity of the program, in keeping up with world-class standards in the women's game, has resulted in diminished schooling, and Sarah sees a private tutor outside of a normal educational environment. Her contact with other teenagers outside tennis circles is limited, therefore, and although her parents are supportive, Sarah feels that the coach heavily guides them and they often seem more interested in her tennis than anything else. There is also great media interest in Sarah and agents have been interested in signing her up as a prospective British champion.

Within this case lie many of the potential antecedents to burnout that have been discussed in this chapter, and with them the opportunity for early intervention to prevent burnout. From a psychological perspective, there is much to explore for Sarah in terms of motivation, internal (personal expectations) and external pressure (expectations of the coach, parents, and sport), personal development, social support, and identity. The consultant may help Sarah develop her own monitoring and management strategies for keeping her motivation healthy and coping with the pressures of expectation. In addition, from a social perspective, there are education opportunities for parents and coaches to provide an effective social support network and positive motivational climate and to foster greater lifestyle balance and the development of a more multidimensional identity. This may include planning a structure in which Sarah can gain some benefit from spending time as a normal teenager and developing valued friendships both within and outside of the sport, and using facilities such as the Internet to stay in contact with friends while on tour. This approach can help her become more than just "Sarah the tennis player," and as suggested by the construct of relatedness in self-determination theory (Deci &

Ryan, 1985), it can help her establish a sense of belonging with the constant support of others. Parents and coaches may also check their own behavior on and off the court, and in other environments such as in the car journey to matches and training and at home. From a physiological perspective, a consultant (with the support of coaches) might encourage Sarah to self-monitor certain lifestyle parameters, including sleep, waking heart rate, diet, illness, mood, and training stress as potential indicators of overtraining. This also will help Sarah develop a high level of responsibility and autonomy.

In sum, proactive work exists for the sport psychology consultant to put preventative burnout strategies in place. Practitioners need to consider the assessment of the psychological demands and sources of stress placed on the athlete, the motivational characteristics of the athlete, and the quality of the support environment available to the athlete. Assimilating this information should aid practitioners in developing a well-considered and integrated plan for monitoring and preventing the symptoms of burnout.

Summary

The term *burnout* within sporting contexts stems from the professional literature where it originated. A significant challenge to professional practice and the advancement of empirical research into burnout has been the lack of agreement on a universal definition. Within the sport context recent research efforts (Raedeke, 1997) have advanced an athlete-specific definition of burnout based upon a popular conceptualization by Maslach and Jackson (1984) from the professional literature. Based upon their approach, burnout within sport is characterized by a withdrawal from an activity denoted by a reduced sense of accomplishment, devaluation or resentment of sport, and physical and/or psychological exhaustion. The similarity of the symptoms it shares with the related concepts of overtraining, staleness, and dropout confounds the debate surrounding the agreement of a universal definition of burnout in sport.

Within the sport psychology literature, there are four *traditional* theories of burnout. These, together with recent theoretical perspectives, comprise two broad categories: stress-induced burnout and non-stress-induced burnout. The stress-induced perspectives have tended to dominate and continue to do so, but approaches that are more recent have advanced the field by offering more multidimensional conceptualizations of burnout across physiological, social, and psychological subsystems.

From Caccese and Mayerberg's (1984) initial research on coach burnout, empirical research has expanded to incorporate work-examining burnout among athletic trainers, athletic directors, officials, and athletes. Research on coaches and athletes has received the majority of the research attention. In addition to the difficulties in establishing a universal definition of burnout, the development of valid and reliable research tools has also been problematic. A breakthrough has occurred, however, with the advent of the Athlete Burnout Questionnaire by Raedeke and Smith (2001), which assesses perceived burnout across the three dimensions of physical and emotional exhaustion, sport devaluation, and reduced performance accomplishments.

Despite the popularity of burnout and its use as a colloquial term within the everyday sport context, there remains much to understand about the construct. One of the areas in which our lack of knowledge and understanding is most significant is in the development of effective intervention strategies. To date, there remains a significant gap in the literature in terms of intervention studies. What little is known relies upon the recall of individuals who have previously experienced burnout (Gould et al., 1996b), and therefore intervention approaches must be addressed as an important area for future research efforts.

Study Questions

1. List the three dimensions of athlete burnout proposed by Raedeke (1997) and identify key symptoms associated with each dimension.

2. With reference to Situation Study 1 and Mark's story describe the principal tenets of Coakley's (1992) Unidimensional Identity Development and External Control Model and Schmidt and Stein's (1991) Sport Commitment Model.

3. Explain the impact recovery has on the potential incidences of overtraining, staleness, and burnout with reference to the Stress and Recovery Model (Kellmann & Kallus, 2000) and Overtraining and Recovery Model (Kentta & Hassmen, 1998).

4. Describe the differences between staleness, overtraining, and burnout.

5. Give an account of the contribution of Gould et al.'s (1996a, 1996b, and 1997) research to the athlete burnout literature.

6. How can practitioners monitor burnout?

7. Describe an athlete who is at risk of burnout and design an intervention program that will prevent burnout in the athlete.

References

Caccese, T. M., & Mayerberg, C. K. (1984). Gender differences in perceived burnout of college coaches. *Journal of Sport and Exercise Psychology, 6,* 279–288.

Capel, S. A., Sisley, B. L., & Desertrain, G. S. (1987). The relationship of role conflict and role ambiguity to burnout in high school basketball coaches. *Journal of Sport Psychology, 9,* 106–117.

Coakley, J. A. (1992). Burnout amongst adolescent athletes: A personal failure or social problem? *Sociology of Sport Journal, 9,* 271–285.

Cohn, P. (1990). An exploratory study on sources of stress and athlete burnout in youth golf. *The Sport Psychologist, 4,* 95–106.

Cresswell, S. L., & Eklund, R. C. (2003). The athlete burnout syndrome: A practitioner's guide. *New Zealand Journal of Sports Medicine, 31* (1), 4–9.

Cresswell, S. L., & Eklund, R. C. (2005a). Motivation and burnout among top amateur rugby players. *Medicine and Science in Sports and Exercise, 37* (3), 469–477.

Cresswell, S. L., & Eklund, R. C. (2005b). Changes in athlete burnout and motivation over a 12-week league tournament. *Medicine and Science in Sports and Exercise, 37* (11), 1957–1966.

Cresswell, S. L., & Eklund, R. C. (2006a). The nature of athlete burnout: Key characteristics and attributions. *Journal of Applied Sport Psychology, 18,* 219–239.

Cresswell, S. L., & Eklund, R. C. (2006b). The convergent and discriminant validity of burnout measures in sport: A multi-method multi-trait analysis. *Journal of Sports Sciences, 24,* 209–212.

Cresswell, S. L., & Eklund, R. C. (2006c). Athlete burnout: Conceptual confusion, current research, and future directions. In S. Hanton & S. D. Mellalieu (Eds.) *Literature Reviews in Sport Psychology* (pp. 91–126). New York: Nova Science Publishers.

Cresswell, S. L., & Eklund, R. C. (2007). Athlete burnout: A longitudinal study. *The Sport Psychologist, 21,* 1–20.

Dale, J., & Weinberg, R. S. (1989). The relationship between coaches leadership style and burnout. *The Sport Psychologist, 3,* 1–13.

Dale, J., & Weinberg, R. S. (1990). Burnout in sport: A review and critique. *Journal of Applied Sport Psychology, 2,* 67–83.

Deci, E. L., & Ryan, R. M. (1985). The general causality orientations scale: Self-determination in personality. *Journal of Research in Personality, 19,* 109–134.

Drake, D., & Herbert, E. P. (2002). Perceptions of occupational stress and strategies for avoiding burnout: Case studies of two female teacher coaches. *The Physical Educator, 59* (4), 170–183.

Feigely, D. A. (1984). Psychological burnout in high-level athletes. *The Physician and Sports-medicine, 12,* 109–119.

Freudenberger, H. J. (1974). Staff burnout. *Journal of Social Issues, 30,* 159–165.

Goodger, K. I., Lavallee, D. E., Gorely, P. J., & Harwood, C. G. (2007). Burnout in sport: A systematic review. *The Sport Psychologist, 21,* 127–151.

Gould, D. (1997). Burnout: Personal motivation gone awry. *Journal of Applied Sport Psychology, 7,* 176–189.

Gould, D., & Dieffenbach, K. (2002). Overtaining, underrecovery, and burnout in sport. In M. Kellman (Ed.), *Enhancing recovery: Preventing underperformance in athletes* (pp. 25–35). Champaign IL: Human Kinetics.

Gould, D., Tuffey, S., Udry, E., & Loehr, J. (1996a). Burnout in competitive junior tennis players: Quantitative psychological assessment. *The Sport Psychologist, 10,* 322–340.

Gould, D., Tuffey, S., Udry, E., & Loehr, J. (1996b). Burnout in competitive junior tennis players: II. Qualitative analysis. *The Sport Psychologist, 10,* 341–366.

Gould, D., Tuffey, S., Udry, E., & Loehr, J. (1997). Burnout in competitive junior tennis players: III. Individual differences in the burnout experience. *The Sport Psychologist, 11,* 257–276.

Harlick, M., & McKenzie, A. (2000). Burnout in junior tennis: A research report. *New Zealand Journal of Sport Medicine, 28,* 36–39.

Lemyre, P. N., Treasure, D. C., & Roberts, G. C. (2006). Influence of variability in motivation and affect on elite athlete burnout susceptibility. *Journal of Sport and Exercise Psychology, 28,* 32–48.

Kallus, K. W., & Kellmann, M. (1995). The Recovery-Stress-Questionnaire for coaches. In R. Vanfraechem-Raway & Y. Vanden Auweele (Eds.), *Integrating laboratory and field studies* (pp. 26–33). Brussels, Belgium: European Federation of Sports Psychology.

Kallus, K. W., & Kellmann, M. (2000). Burnout in athletes and coaches. In Y. L. Hanin (Ed.), *Emotions in sport* (pp. 209–230). Champaign IL: Human Kinetics.

Kelley, B. C. (1994). A model of stress and burnout in collegiate coaches: Effects of gender and time of season. *Research Quarterly for Exercise and Sport, 65,* 48–58.

Kelley, B. C., & Gill, D. L. (1993). An examination of personal and situational variables, stress appraisal, and burnout in collegiate teacher–coaches. *Research Quarterly for Exercise and Sport, 64,* 94–102.

Kellmann, M. (Ed.). (2002). *Enhancing recovery: Preventing underperformance in athletes.* Champaign, IL: Human Kinetics.

Kellmann, M., & Gunther, K. (2000). Changes in stress and recovery in elite rowers during preparation for the Olympic Games. *Medicine and Science in Sport and Exercise, 32,* 676–683.

Kellmann, M., & Kallus, K. W. (2001). *Recovery-Stress Questionnaire for athletes: User manual.* Champaign, IL: Human Kinetics.

Kentta, G. (2001). *Overtraining, staleness and burnout in sports.* Unpublished Ph.D. thesis, Stockholm Universitet, Psykologiska Institutionen.

Kentta, G., & Hassmen, P. (1998). Overtraining and recovery: A conceptual model. *Sports Medicine, 26,* 1–16.

Kentta, G., Hassmen, P., & Raglin, J. S. (2001). Training practices and overtraining syndrome in Swedish age-group athletes. *International Journal of Sports Medicine, 22,* 460–465.

Maslach, C. (1976). Burn-out. *Human Behavior, 5,* 16–22.

Maslach, C., & Jackson, S. E. (1984). Burnout in organizational settings. In S. Oskamp (Ed.), *Applied social psychology annual: Applications in organizational settings* (Vol. 5, pp. 133–153). Beverly Hills, CA: Sage.

Pastore, D. L., & Judd, M. R. (1992). Burnout in two-year college coaches of women's team sports. *Journal of Physical Education, Recreation, and Dance, 63,* 74–79.

Pastore, D. L., & Judd, M. R. (1993). Burnout and gender differences in two year college coaches of women's athletic teams. *Sociology of Sport Journal, 10,* 205–212.

Price, M. S., & Weiss, M. R. (2000). Relationships among coach burnout, coach behaviors, and athletes psychological responses. *The Sport Psychologist, 14,* 391–409.

Quigley, T. A., Slack, T., & Smith, G. J. (1987). Burnout in secondary school teacher-coaches. *The Alberta Journal of Educational Research, 33,* 260–274.

Raedeke, T. D. (1997). Is athlete burnout more than just stress? A sport commitment perspective. *Journal of Sport & Exercise Psychology, 19,* 396–417.

Raedeke, T. D., Lunney, K., & Venables, K. (2002). Understanding athlete burnout: Coach perspectives. *Journal of Sport Behavior, 25,* 181–201.

Raedeke, T. D., & Smith, A. L. (2001). Development and preliminary validation of an athlete burnout measure. *Journal of Sport & Exercise Psychology, 23,* 281–306.

Raglin, J., Sawamura, S., Alexiou, S., Hassmen, P., & Kentta, G. (2000). Training practices and staleness in age-group swimmers: A cross-cultural study. *Pediatric Exercise Science, 12,* 61–70.

Raglin, J. S., & Wilson, G. S. (2000). Overtraining in athletes. In Y. L. Hanin (Ed.), *Emotions in sport* (pp. 191–207). Champaign, IL: Human Kinetics.

Ryan, R. M., & Deci, E. L. (2000). The darker and brighter sides of human existence: Basic psychological needs as a unifying concept. *Psychological Inquiry, 11,* 319–338.

Schaufeli, W. B., & Buunk, B. P. (2003). Burnout: An overview of 25 years of research and theorizing. In M. J. Schabracq, J. A. M. Winnubst, & C. L. Cooper (Eds.), *The handbook of work and health psychology* (2nd ed., pp. 383–425). London: John Wiley and Sons.

Schaufeli, W. B., & Taris, T. W. (2005). Commentary: The conceptualisation and measurement of burnout: Common ground and worlds apart. *Work & Stress, 19,* 256–262.

Schmidt, G. W., & Stein, G. L. (1991). Sport commitment: A model integrating enjoyment, dropout, and burnout. *Journal of Sport & Exercise Psychology, 8,* 254–265.

Shirom, A. (2005). Reflections on the study of burnout. *Work & Stress, 19,* 263–270.

Silva, J. M. (1990). An analysis of the training stress syndrome in competitive athletics. *Journal of Applied Sport Psychology, 2,* 5–20.

Smith, R. E. (1986). Toward a cognitive-affective model of athlete burnout. *Journal of Sport Psychology, 8,* 36–50.

Tenebaum, G., Jones, C. M., Kitsantas, A., Sacks, D. N., & Berwick, J. P. (2003). Failure adaptation: An investigation of the stress response process in sport. *International Journal of Sport Psychology, 34,* 27–62.

Thibaut, J. W., & Kelley, H. H. (1959). *The social psychology of groups.* New York: Wiley.

Udry, E., Gould, D., Bridges, D., & Tuffey, S. (1997). People helping people? Examining the social ties of athletes coping with burnout and injury stress. *Journal of Sport & Exercise Psychology, 19,* 368–395.

Vealey, R. S., Armstrong, L., Comar, W., & Greenleaf, C. A. (1998). Influence of perceived coaching behaviors on burnout and competitive anxiety in female college athletes. *Journal of Applied Sport Psychology, 10,* 297–318.

Weinberg, R. S., & Gould, D. (2003). *Foundations of sport and exercise psychology* (3rd ed.). Champaign, IL: Human Kinetics.

Wylleman, P., & Lavallee, D. (2004). A developmental perspective on transitions faced by athletes. In M. R. Weiss (Ed.), *Developmental sport and exercise psychology: A lifespan perspective* (pp. 503–524). Morgantown, WV: Fitness Information Technology.

CHAPTER

23

Injury Risk and Rehabilitation: Psychological Considerations

Jean M. Williams, *University of Arizona*, Emeritus
Carrie B. Scherzer, *State University of New York College at Potsdam*

I knew I was in trouble when I heard snap, crackle and pop, and I wasn't having a bowl of cereal.
—Nick Kypreos, Toronto Maple Leaf player (in McDonell, 2004, p. 96)

Although many of the causes for injury are undoubtedly physical in nature (e.g., level of conditioning, equipment failure, poor playing surface, faulty biomechanics) or just plain bad luck, psychosocial factors also play a role. When the original draft of this chapter was completed in 1986, relatively few studies had tried to identify psychological factors that might predispose athletes to injury (e.g., Bramwell, Masuda, Wagner, & Holmes, 1975; Coddington & Troxell, 1980; Passer & Seese, 1983) and researchers had not attempted to integrate them in a meaningful way for the athlete, coach, sport psychologist, or athletic trainer. In the intervening years, more than 50 studies have been completed and models have been generated (e.g., Andersen & Williams, 1988) and even revised (Williams & Andersen, 1998) to counter the narrow scope and atheoretical nature of early research.

Also, although some clinical articles appeared before 1986 discussing athletes' psychological reactions to injury (e.g., Nideffer, 1983; Yaffe, 1983), the practical implications were not clear. Knowledge has expanded considerably regarding psychological reactions to injury, how to facilitate psychological adjustment once injured, and the role of psychological interventions in enhancing physical healing and rehabilitation.

This chapter reviews the research on psychology of injury and provides examples of how to implement psychological interventions to reduce injury risk and to enhance the physical and psychological recovery of the injured athlete. It is beyond the scope of this chapter to discuss the psychological issues involved when injuries are so severe or permanent that return to sport is impossible, but the reader is directed to Chapter 24 in this volume and to injury books edited by Heil (1993) and Pargman (1999).

Factors That Predispose Athletes to Injury

Research with recreational and nonelite to elite competitive athletes has found that certain psychosocial factors predispose individuals to injury, whereas other psychosocial factors help protect them from injury. Andersen and Williams (1988) proposed that most psychosocial variables, if they influence injury outcome at all, probably do so through a linkage with stress and a resulting stress response. The central hypothesis of their stress-injury model is that individuals with a history of many stressors, personality characteristics that exacerbate the stress response, and few coping resources will, when placed in a stressful situation such as a demanding practice or crucial competition, be more likely to appraise the situation as stressful and to exhibit greater physiological activation and attentional disruptions (see Figure 23-1). The severity of the resulting stress response, caused by the increased stress reactivity, is what predisposes the athletes to injury. Considerable support exists for all facets of the stress-injury model (see Williams and Andersen, 1998 and 2007, for a more thorough review of research testing the model).

The central core of the stress-injury model, the stress response, is a bidirectional relationship between the person's cognitive appraisal of a potentially stressful external situation and the physiological and attention aspects of stress. In terms of sport participation, the individual makes some cognitive appraisal of the demands of the practice or competitive situation, the adequacy of his or her ability to meet those demands, and the consequences of failure/success in meeting the demands. For example, if an athlete views competition as challenging, exciting, and fun, the resulting "good" stress (eustress) may help the athlete stay focused and successfully "flow" with the competition. Injury risk in this situation would be lower than when the athlete feels "bad" stress (distress), such as appraising the competition as ego threatening or anxiety producing. This interpretation most likely occurs when athletes perceive that they do not have the resources to meet the demands of the situation and it is important to do so because failure will result in dire consequences.

Whether the cognitive appraisal is accurate or distorted by irrational beliefs or other maladaptive thought patterns (see Chapter 15) is unimportant. If the athlete perceives inadequate resources to meet the demands of the situation, and it is important to succeed, the stress response manifests itself physiologically, attentionally, and in the perception of higher state anxiety.

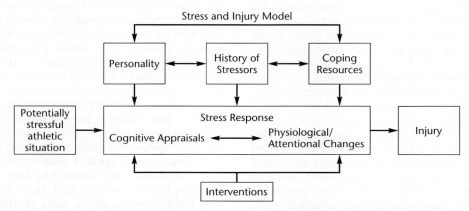

Figure 23-1   **Revised version of the stress and injury model. From Williams and Andersen (1998)**

Correspondingly, these cognitive appraisals and physiological and attentional responses to stress constantly modify and remodify each other. For example, a relaxed body can help calm the mind just as anxious thoughts can activate the physical stress response. The resulting individual differences in stress responsivity due to differences in psychosocial variables may either help inoculate the athlete against injury or exacerbate his or her risk.

Of the myriad physiological and attentional changes that occur during the stress response, Andersen and Williams (1988) hypothesized that increases in generalized muscle tension, narrowing of the visual field (the revised model added auditory cues, Williams and Andersen, 1998), and increased distractibility were the primary culprits in the stress–injury relationship. For example, generalized muscle tension can lead to fatigue and reduced flexibility, motor coordination difficulties, and muscle inefficiency, thereby creating a greater risk for incurring injuries such as sprains, strains, and other musculoskeletal injuries. Narrowing of peripheral vision could lead to not picking up or responding in time to dangerous cues in the periphery such as a defensive player running in to tackle the quarterback. Attention disruptions, often due to attention to task-irrelevant cues, may also result in failure to detect or respond quickly enough to relevant cues in the central field of vision such as when a batter with a high-risk psychosocial profile fails to avoid a pitch coming directly at his head.

When comparing performance under stressful and nonstressful laboratory conditions, considerable support (five studies) exists for athletes with a high-risk psychosocial profile experiencing greater peripheral narrowing when performing under stress compared to athletes with a low-risk profile. Only one study (Williams & Andersen, 1997) examined central field of vision (e.g., missing or delayed response to important visual cues, responding to irrelevant cues), and it too found a greater susceptibility to attention disruptions for athletes with a high injury risk profile when they performed under higher stress. The one study that examined the connection between psychosocial factors and muscle tension

found increased muscle tension during the stress condition for the total group, but failed to support the hypothesis of even greater muscle tension for individuals with a high-risk profile. The failure to do so may have resulted from Andersen studying the general population rather than a high-risk subpopulation.

Before addressing the implications of these findings for designing interventions to decrease injuries due to psychosocial factors, we will discuss how history of stressors, personality factors, and coping resources influence stress and injury. These variables may contribute interactively or in isolation in influencing the stress response and, ultimately, injury occurrence and severity. The original stress-injury model hypothesized that an athlete's history of stressors contributes directly to the stress response, whereas personality factors and coping resources act on the stress response either directly or through a moderating influence on the effects of the history of stressors. Ten years later, when Williams and Andersen (1998) critiqued and revised their stress-injury model, they proposed bidirectional arrows between each of the three predictor categories.

History of Stressors

This category of injury risk variables includes major life change events, daily hassles, and previous injury. Of these, the most support exists for the detrimental effects of experiencing major life events—typically assessed as the amount of change and upset that athletes experienced in the year prior to a competitive season. Examples of general life events are incidents such as the breakup of a relationship, change in residence, and death of a loved one, whereas major events related to sports include eligibility difficulties, trouble with coaches, and change in playing status.

A review by Williams (2001) reported that 30 out of 35 studies that assessed life events found at least some type of positive relationship between high life stress and injury. The best evidence involves football (six studies), but similar findings have occurred across other physical activities as diverse as Alpine skiing, race walking, figure skating, baseball, gymnastics, soccer, field hockey, wrestling, track and field, and ballet. The new studies supported an earlier review by Williams and Roepke (1993) that reported injuries tended to occur 2 to 5 times more frequently in athletes with high compared to low life stress and that the risk of injury tended to increase in direct proportion to the level of life stress.

Most research efforts failed to support daily hassles (e.g., minor daily problems, irritations, or changes) as a contributor to injury risk (Blackwell & McCullagh, 1990; Hanson, McCullagh, & Tonymon, 1992; Smith, Smoll, & Ptacek, 1990; Van Mechelen et al., 1996), but the results are suspect because of assessing hassles only once. In contrast, a study that measured hassles on a weekly basis (the more appropriate methodological approach) found that injured athletes had a significant increase in hassles for the week prior to injury compared to no significant increases for the noninjured athletes (Fawkner, McMurray, & Summers, 1999).

Personality and Coping Resources

The presence of desirable personality attributes and coping resources may buffer individuals from stress and injury by helping them to perceive fewer situations and events as stressful or by helping them cope more effectively with their history of stressors. Conversely, the lack of desirable personality characteristics and coping resources, or the presence of undesirable ones, may leave individuals vulnerable to higher stress (acute and chronic) and, presumably, greater injury risk.

It would be very useful to have a specific personality test that predicts injury-prone athletes, but none exists. From those studies that have used measures of more basic, stable personality patterns (with instruments such as Cattel's 16 Personality Factors Questionnaire or the California Personality Inventory) no consistent results have emerged. Still, some support does exist for selected personality variables possibly influencing injury risk.

Fields, Delaney, and Hinkle (1990) reported that runners scoring high (e.g., more aggressive, hard-driving) on Type A behavior experienced significantly more injuries, especially multiple injuries, compared to runners with lower scores. Similar results occurred in Japan with a large sample of college athletes ($N = 2,164$) (Nigorikawa et al., 2003). Wittig and Schurr (1994) determined that being tough-minded (i.e., more assertive, independent, and self-assured) predicted the likelihood of more severe injuries but not the occurrence of injury, and Thompson and Morris (1994) found that high anger directed outward, but not inward, increased injury risk.

Mixed results occurred when researchers examined locus of control and trait anxiety. **Locus of control** is a concept that deals with the degree to which individuals view their lives and environment as under their personal control. **Trait anxiety** is a general disposition or tendency to perceive situations as threatening and to react with an anxiety response. Pargman and Lunt (1989) reported that a higher injury rate correlated with an external locus of control in a sample of freshman college football players. In contrast, Kolt and Kirkby (1996) found a more internal locus of control predicted injury in elite gymnasts, but not with nonelite gymnasts. Other researchers who used nonsport tools to assess locus of control (Blackwell & McCullagh, 1990; Hanson, McCullagh, & Tonymon, 1992; Kerr & Minden, 1988; McLeod & Kirkby, 1995) and trait anxiety (Kerr & Minden, 1988; Lysens, Auweele, & Ostyn, 1986; Passer & Seese, 1983) found no relationship between these variables and the incidence of injury. When researchers used sport-specific tools, athletes who scored high on either external locus of control (Dalhauser & Thomas, 1979), competitive trait anxiety (Blackwell & McCullagh, 1990; Hanson et al., 1992; Passer & Seese, 1983; Petrie, 1993), or somatic trait anxiety (Smith, Ptacek, & Patterson, 2000) had more injuries, more severe injuries, or more time-loss due to injury than athletes with the opposite profile.

In Petrie's (1993) study, the finding occurred for football starters but not nonstarters. Petrie also found that competitive trait anxiety moderated the effects of positive life stress such that higher levels of anxiety and stress were associated with more days missed because of injury.

He conjectured that the combination of starting and having high life stress and competitive trait anxiety "may have negatively influenced these athletes' appraisals such that they either viewed practices and competitions as threatening or uncontrollable or believed they did not have the resources to cope. Such appraisals may have corresponded with attentional and physiological disruptions that would have increased the starters' vulnerability to injury" (p. 272).

Other researchers also have tested whether personality variables might interact with history of stressors or with other personality and coping variables in influencing injury risk. Smith et al. (2000) found that the combination of high daily life stress and high cognitive or somatic anxiety predicted high injury time-loss in ballet dancers affiliated with a major ballet company. In another study (Smith, Ptacek, & Smoll, 1992), only athletes who scored low in sensation seeking had a significant positive relationship between major negative life events and subsequent injury time-loss. According to Zuckerman (1979), sensation avoiders, unlike sensation seekers, have a lower tolerance for arousal and, therefore, do not care for change, avoid the unfamiliar, and stay away from risky activities. Smith and his colleagues found no support for a competing hypothesis that the risk-taking characteristics of high sensation seeking would constitute an injury vulnerability factor. Also, although they found that sensation avoiders reported poorer stress management coping skills, no support existed for differences in coping skills mediating the injury vulnerability differences.

In other promising personality research, defensive pessimism, dispositional optimism, and hardiness influenced injury risk. Perna and McDowell (1993) found that athletes who scored high on defensive pessimism, and who also experienced a high degree of life stress, experienced more illness or injury symptoms than did athletes scoring low on defensive pessimism and having fewer stressful life events. Meyer (1995), however, failed to replicate their results, but Ford, Eklund, and Gordon (2000) found that athletes high in optimism and hardiness experienced less injury time-loss when positive life

change increased, compared to athletes low in optimism or hardiness.

In addition to the preceding findings for personality traits, mood states also influence injury risk. For example, Williams, Hogan, and Andersen (1993) concluded that intercollegiate football, volleyball, and cross-country athletes who experienced positive states of mind (e.g., ability to stay focused, keep relaxed, share with others) early in the season incurred significantly fewer injuries during their athletic season compared to athletes who had less positive states of mind. Whereas positive states of mind might buffer the effects of potentially stressful sport situations, thereby creating less stress and fewer injuries, the presence of negative states might do the opposite. Fawkner (1995) reached the same conclusion when she assessed team and individual sport athletes' mood states (five negative and one positive) over the course of the competitive season. She noted significant increases in mood disturbance in the measurement immediately prior to injury. Kleinert (2007) reported similar results for risk of serious injuries with assessment of mood disturbance three hours to three days before tournament play. Lavallee and Flint (1996) also reported a relationship of negative mood states to injury vulnerability. A higher degree of tension/anxiety correlated with a higher rate of injury and a higher degree of tension/anxiety, anger/hostility, and total negative mood state correlated with higher severity of injury. In a related study, Van Mechelen et al. (1996) stated that persons who reported vital exhaustion, which represented more feelings of depression, malfunctioning, apathy, and anxiety, were more likely to sustain an injury.

Compared to research on personality factors, coping resources have received less attention but more consistent results. An athlete's coping resources, particularly social support, appear to influence injury outcome directly and by lessening the negative effects of high life-event stress (e.g., Hardy, O'Connor, & Geisler, 1990; Petrie, 1992; Williams, Tonymon, & Wadsworth, 1986). These findings suggest that increasing social support from family, friends, and significant others—a group likely to include coaches and teammates—is one way to reduce injury risk. Richman, Hardy, Rosenfeld, and Callahan (1989) offer an excellent source for a variety of strategies coaches and sport psychologists could implement to enhance social support in student-athletes.

Although a greater number of supportive relationships may be desired, the *quality* of such relationships is also important. For example, on one football team a young man with fairly strong religious values felt he had to go out, drink, and chase women with his teammates to receive their support and friendship. Although he achieved an external measure of support, the relationships were unfulfilling for him and added to his level of stress. It was, in fact, through a classroom discussion of stress that the athlete sought someone with whom to discuss his conflicts. Both his coach and his teammates were unaware of the nature and range of his stress. The athlete successfully resolved the conflicts, and may well have been an accident that *did not* happen.

In addition to the merits of increasing social support, the findings of Smith, Smoll, and Ptacek (1990) and Andersen and Williams (1999) suggest that increasing psychological coping skills (e.g., the ability to stay focused under pressure, to be confident, to self-regulate activation) might also decrease injury risk. Smith and colleagues found that most injuries occurred in athletes who experienced high negative life events and who lacked both social support and psychological coping skills (see Situation Study 1). Andersen and Williams found that the high-risk profile of scoring low in social support and high in life stress and attentional disruptions—more specifically, peripheral narrowing under stress—accounted for 25% of the injury variance. Also, Kerr and Goss (1996) found less injury time-loss for gymnasts taught psychological coping skills.

Interventions to Reduce Injury Vulnerability

The stress-injury model proposes a two-pronged approach to prevent injuries from the increased stress reactivity of individuals at risk of injury due to their psychosocial profile. One set of interventions aims to change the cognitive appraisal of potentially stressful events (see Chapter 15 for techniques to eliminate or modify cognitions that cause stress) and the second set to modify the physiological/attentional aspects of the stress response. Chapter 13 describes relaxation techniques such as progressive muscle relaxation, meditation, autogenics, and breathing exercises, and Chapter 16 explains techniques to decrease distractibility and to keep an appropriate attentional focus. Also included on the cognitive appraisal side of the stress response are interventions for fostering realistic expectations, a sense of belonging (e.g., team cohesiveness), and optimal coach–athlete communication. For example, if coaches communicate effective with their athletes regarding their capabilities and potential, athletes will have a more realistic appraisal of the demands and resources available in potentially stressful athletic situations (see Chapter 8 and 11 for suggestions to enhance coach–athlete communication and realistic goal setting). In addition, the interventions presented in these chapters can be used to directly influence some of the variables under coping resources and personality factors.

Considerable support exists, both direct and indirect, for the interventions portion of the model. DeWitt (1980) found that her basketball and football players detected a noticeable decrease in minor injuries after participation in a cognitive and physiological (biofeedback) training program. Murphy (1988) describes another psychological intervention program in which injuries were not the specific focus, but there may have been injury benefits. He conducted relaxation sessions after every workout until competition with 12 members of a team at the 1987 Olympic Sports Festival. At the start, 5 athletes had minor injuries and 2 serious injuries, but all 12 athletes were able to compete.

Davis (1991) reported an archival review of injury data collected by athletic trainers before and after two university teams practiced progressive relaxation and technique/strategy imagery during team workouts. A 52% reduction in injuries to the swimmers and a 33% reduction to the football players occurred during the athletic season

Situation Study 1

Athlete at Risk of Injury

John is in his second season as the starting quarterback for his university's football team. He is under a lot of pressure because of a new coaching staff and many changes in the offensive plays. In addition, he is very worried about his mother who just began treatment for breast cancer. Both his academics and football performance are suffering because he is so stressed out. Normally he talks his troubles out with his girlfriend, but she broke up with him over the summer. He used to love game days, but now he dreads them because he has so much anxiety about playing well. He fears losing his starting position and, more important, letting his teammates down. Although normally an upbeat person, he's become very moody and pessimistic.

in which they practiced relaxation and imagery skills. Another favorable intervention study comes from May and Brown (1989) who used techniques such as attention control, imagery, and other mental practice skills in their delivery of interventions to individuals, pairs, and groups of U.S. alpine skiers in the Calgary Olympics. In addition to their mental skills training, they also employed team building, communication, relationship orientations, and crisis interventions. May and Brown reported that their interventions led to reduced injuries, increased self-confidence, and enhanced self-control.

Kerr and Goss (1996) offer more experimentally sound support for reducing life stress and injuries through a stress management program. Participants included 24 gymnasts who competed on the national and international level. They were matched in pairs according to sex, age, and performance and then randomly assigned to a control or experimental group. Across an 8-month time period, each gymnast in the experimental group met individually with one of the experimenters for 16 one-hour, biweekly stress management sessions. Meichenbaum's stress inoculation training program provided the framework for the stress management program, which included skills such as cognitive restructuring, thought control,

imagery, and simulations. The stress management group reported less negative athletic stress, less total negative stress, and half the amount of time injured (5 versus 10 days) compared to the participants in the control group. In a similar randomized, single-blind clinical trial with collegiate athletes, a seven-session cognitive behavioral stress management program that used a stress-inoculation training format found that athletes assigned to the intervention group experienced significant reductions in the number of injury and illness days compared to athletes in the control group (Perna, Antoni, Baum, Gordon, & Schneiderman, 2003).

The injury benefits from the preceding intervention programs are even more impressive considering that none of them targeted athletes at risk of injury (they targeted athletes in general) and many of the programs did not include cognitive or concentration training interventions. Two more recent studies, however, did identify and target at-risk athletes and then employed an intervention-control group design. Johnson, Ekengren, and Andersen (2005) offered six intervention sessions and two telephone contacts consisting of treatments such as stress management skills, somatic and cognitive relaxation, goal-setting skills, and attribution and self-confidence training. The results showed that 10 of 13 in the experimental group remained injury free, in contrast to only 3 of 16 in the control group. Maddison and Prapavessis (2005) also found less time-loss due to injury for rugby players in their cognitive behavioral stress management group. In addition, these athletes reported an increase in coping resources and a decrease in worry following the intervention program.

The success of these interventions in reducing injuries suggests that coaches, sport psychologists, and athletic trainers may want to implement them with athletes they suspect are predisposed to injury due to psychosocial variables. Recognize, however, that it would be most egregious to think that all individuals in an at-risk group will experience an injury or that no individuals in a low-risk group will experience injury. Identifying athletes most predisposed to injury simply allows us to target specific interventions to those most likely to benefit from them and also enables us to watch for the earliest signs of injury risk.

To identify at-risk athletes, coaches and others must be aware of what is happening in athletes' lives and the presence of personal characteristics identified in the at-risk profile. Sport psychologists or others trained in the use of psychological tests may even want to employ the questionnaires used in injury research as screening instruments. Coaches also should consider reducing exposure to high-risk activities, such as learning a new and potentially dangerous vault or dive, with athletes who meet the high-risk profile and who appear to be in a stressed or distracted state. Where levels of stress appear to be extreme and coping skills minimal, professional counseling may be necessary (see Chapter 20).

Athletes' Reactions to Injury

Regardless of the best efforts of athletes, coaches, and athletic trainers, injuries still occur, and the resulting consequences are both physical and mental. For example, when injury keeps athletes from performing at their best (or at all), it may be difficult for some athletes to see themselves as worthwhile people. Historically, sport medicine specialists have been most concerned with the physical aspects of injury rehabilitation, assuming that completing physical rehabilitation prepared the athlete for a safe and successful return to competition.

But some athletes, despite physical readiness, are not psychologically ready to return to competition. To them even the suggestion of returning creates unmanageable stress from fears such as reinjury and embarrassing performance. As a result, optimal injury rehabilitation often requires both physical and psychological components. When done well, injuries often heal faster, psychological adjustment is healthier, and higher levels of performance occur more quickly. Such an approach entails gaining an understanding and appreciation of the psychology of injury rehabilitation, which is the focus of the remainder of this chapter.

Psychological Reactions to Injury

Athletes perceive injury in various ways. Some view it as a disaster; some as an opportunity to display courage; others welcome it as a relief from the drudgery of practice or the embarrassment and frustration of poor performance or lack of playing time; and still others see it as an opportunity to focus on other aspects of their life. It is not uncommon for injured athletes to feel concerned about whether they will ever completely recover and return to their previous form. Understanding the emotional response of injured athletes can lead to more effective interventions. Injured athletes are often uncertain if they will be facing a quick return to action, a long rehabilitation process, or the end of their career. Athletes may also underestimate the seriousness of their injury initially, which may impact their emotional response (de Heredia, Munoz, & Artaza, 2004). Athletes have good reason to be upset when injured but, as one athletic trainer stated, "I know it's frustrating for athletes to be injured, but I found that those who have the negative attitudes or poor mood state, that they are the ones who are continuously in rehab, and having problems making it to rehab" (Granito, 2001, p. 78). A positive and enthusiastic response will ensure the best possible chance of complete rehabilitation both physically and mentally.

A study by Mainwaring et al. (2004) sheds some light on athletes' reactions to injury. Following concussion, athletes experienced increased ratings of depression, confusion, and overall total mood disturbance. The authors postulate that the mood changes are due to the injury itself and not just the removal from sport, as they experienced a normalization of mood before their return to sport. De Heredia et al. (2004) also found support for the normalization of mood prior to reentry—their athletes' mood states rebounded by the midway point in recovery.

Others also notice changes in injured athletes. According to a survey of 482 certified athletic trainers, 47% believed that every injured athlete suffers negative psychological effects (Larson, Starkey, & Zaichkowsky, 1996) such as stress and anxiety, anger, treatment compliance problems, depression, problems with concentration/attention, and exercise addiction. In addition, 24% of their trainers referred an athlete for counseling for situations related to their injury, and 25% reported having a sport psychologist on their sports medicine team. Unfortunately, 75% of athletic trainers in the United States do not have access to a sport psychologist (Cramer Roh & Perna, 2000).

Initially, sport psychologists (e.g., Pederson, 1986; Rotella, 1984) believed that, following injury, athletes experienced a sequence of predictable psychological reactions like those outlined by Kubler-Ross in *On Death and Dying* (1969). These reactions include (1) disbelief, denial, and isolation; (2) anger; (3) bargaining; (4) depression; and (5) acceptance and resignation while remaining hopeful about the eventual return to competition. Grief models, in which injured athletes proceed sequentially through a series of stages on the way to recovery, have not been empirically supported (Brewer, 1994). Quinn and Fallon (1999) found that athletes experience many emotions (e.g., tension, depression, anger) postinjury, and all of these improve

as rehabilitation progresses. Brewer posited that cognitive appraisal models provide a better conceptualization of the process of coping with athletic injury. For individuals still inclined toward a grief approach, Evans and Hardy's (1995) article provides a better understanding of grief models and suggestions on better empirical assessments of the application of this concept.

Cognitive Appraisal Models

Brewer (1994) identified five cognitive appraisal models relevant to psychological responses to athletic injury. Each model (Figure 23-2) is rooted in the literature on stress and coping; athletic injury is conceptualized as a stressor to the athlete, who then evaluates or *appraises* the stressor in accordance with personal and situational factors. Cognitive appraisal models account for individual differences in response to athletic injury. The response to injury comes from how the athlete interprets or perceives the injury. This cognitive appraisal determines the emotional response (e.g., anger, depression, relief), which determines the behavioral response to injury rehabilitation (e.g., adherence to rehabilitation regimens).

Personal factors. Personal factors contribute to cognitive appraisal and emotional and behavioral responses to athletic injury. For example, Brewer (1994) reported that Shaffer (1992) found that a history of successful rehabilitation positively affected assessments of ability to manage a subsequent injury. This rehabilitation self-efficacy, in turn, related positively to physical recovery. Grove, Stewart, and Gordon (1990) documented a positive relationship between pessimistic explanatory style and depression and anger for the first month of knee rehabilitation. In contrast, hardiness was negatively associated with total mood disturbance. Brewer (1993) found that physical self-esteem may buffer the negative effects of athletic injury on mood. Brewer (1994) reported that adherence to injury rehabilitation programs was linked to personal factors such as self-motivation (Duda, Smart, & Tappe, 1989; Fisher, Domm, & Wuest, 1988), task involvement (Duda et al., 1989), pain tolerance,

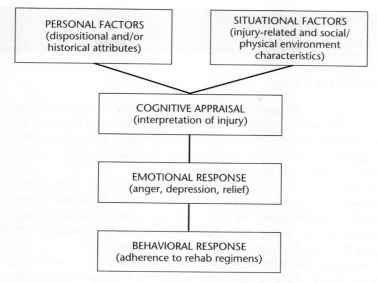

Figure 23-2   **Cognitive appraisal model of psychological adjustment to athletic injury**
Source: B. W. Brewer, 1994. *Journal of Applied Sport Psychology,*
6, 87–100. Used with permission of the publisher.

and perceived exertion (Fisher et al., 1988). In addition, Daly, Brewer, Van Raalte, Petitpas, and Sklar (1995) found that when athletes have negative emotional responses they may be less motivated to work at rehabilitation.

Tracy (2003) examined the emotional response of athletes to moderate to severe injuries. She found that at the onset of injury, the type and severity did not matter as much as the injury itself and that athletes experienced a myriad of emotions. Frustration was the primary negative affect one week postinjury. Three weeks postinjury, emotions were more positive as some athletes had resumed sport participation and others were close to return, and those who weren't reported a positive outlook with regard to returning to sport. Four main themes describe the interplay of cognitions on the emotional response: (1) internal thoughts, (2) injury and rehabilitation concerns, (3) concern for and comparison to others, and (4) looking ahead to the future (Tracy, 2003). Overall, the athletes focused on healing and return to sport, not the

possibility of reinjury, and they also saw their injury as a learning opportunity. These findings reinforce the importance of cognitive appraisal of the injury and rehabilitation process.

One of the most supported personal factors is the influence an athlete's psychological investment in sport has on his or her adjustment to athletic injury (e.g., Brewer, 1993; Brewer, Van Raalte, & Linder, 1993). For many athletes, particularly those who are intensely involved with their sport and/or achieve notable success, the whole focus of their identity may be as an athlete (see Situation Study 2). Many of the issues athletes face with injury parallel those that occur with career termination or retirement (see Chapter 24).

The more narrowly focused an injured athlete's sense of self is, the more threatened the athlete will be. Such a person appears more likely to appraise his or her injury in terms of threat or loss (Brewer et al., 1993) and to experience feelings of anxiety, depression, or hopelessness (Brewer, 1993; Smith, Scott, O'Fallon, & Young, 1990). Athletes who are more involved in sport

Situation Study 2

An Athlete Reacting to Injury

Beth was a two-time all-state performer who had already accepted a full athletic scholarship to a major college soccer powerhouse. During the winter months, Beth was a starter on the varsity basketball team. During the third game of the season she severely injured her right knee diving for a loose ball. The injury required surgery to repair torn ligaments, and the doctors told Beth that with hard work she would be as good as new in a few months.

This was Beth's first major injury. She was afraid, and she was angry at herself for getting injured because she felt it was a stupid play on her part. She also felt that she had let her parents and friends down because of what might happen if she didn't fully recover. She asked herself many of the same questions she heard her friends asking: Would she lose her scholarship? Would she be able to play as well as before? Did she make a mistake by playing basketball this year?

Up to this point, it seemed that the anger, guilt, and other feelings that resulted from the injury caused Beth to doubt herself and her ability to cope with the situation. She found it easier to be alone than to deal with family and friends. Although withdrawing from people brought her temporary relief from her feelings, it also kept her away from the support she needed to get through this unexpected transition.

During her rehabilitation, Beth refused to go to basketball games or social events that she normally attended. She was very moody and seemed to become angry at the smallest thing. Her boyfriend would come over to visit, but these meetings usually ended in a fight because Beth would say he didn't know what she was going through. She was becoming frustrated at her progress in physical therapy, even though she was reaching her therapist's treatment goals. She would be particularly demanding of her therapist if her strength or range of motion had not improved from day to day. Her frustration led her to ignore her therapist's recommendations. She pushed her exercises so hard that she cried from the pain and then became angry at herself for not being tough enough. Instead of getting better, Beth suffered a setback.

Although Beth was trying to deal with her feelings, she found herself pushing away the people who were trying to help her. At the same time her fear caused her to make some poor decisions about her rehabilitation program. Fortunately, Beth was able to get the support she needed to work through her feelings.

Beth's physical therapist introduced her to a counselor who was working in the training room. The counselor listened to Beth's story and tried to understand what she was going through. For the first time Beth was able to voice her anger and sadness. After this, the counselor helped Beth identify the skills that she had used to become a good athlete and showed her how to use them to deal with her injury. Beth had not been prepared for her injury, and her emotions kept her from using the goal-setting and imagery techniques that she used to improve her sport skills.

Beth had also failed to seek help from others. Before her injury, she had always sought out the best coaches for advice and had often talked with players she admired to learn more about game strategies and techniques. She withdrew from this type of support while she was injured. Once Beth learned to use her skills and the support of others, she made better decisions about her rehabilitation and made a quick recovery.

Reprinted by permission from Petitpas, Champagne, Chartrand, Danish, & Murphy, 1997, Athlete's Guide to Career Planning. Champaign, IL: Human Kinetics, 11–12.

before injury may be confused during rehabilitation and may perceive a lesser degree of recovery at the end of rehabilitation (Johnston & Carroll, 2000). He or she might be more motivated to return to sport, possibly prematurely. Eric Lindros, a former player in the national hockey league (NHL), is a prime example. He was a standout player in juniors and, when he played in the NHL for the Philadelphia Flyers, he was a dominant force who was named the league's most valuable player in 1994–1995. Lindros's career was marred with injuries, though, concussions in particular. In January 2004, playing for the New York Rangers, he suffered his eighth concussion. Rather than taking a cue from his younger brother Brett, who retired from the NHL because of multiple concussions, Eric has repeatedly returned to the game. Lindros played in a career low 33 games for the Toronto Maple Leafs in the 2005–2006 season, then played one more season (2006–2007) with the Dallas Stars (ESPN.com, 2007a). In November 2007, after failing to sign with a team for the season, Lindros announced his retirement (ESPN.com, 2007b). He had public feuds with the Flyers over the treatment he received and pressure to return to the game. The coach, athletic trainer, or others involved during rehabilitation should be sensitive to these issues. It may be appropriate to help the athlete see himself or herself more fully as a person, with many potentials, and to explore other possibilities— not to replace the sport or athlete identity, but to complement it. The development of the NCAA CHAMPS/Life Skills program and books to help athletes plan for careers, such as the one by Petitpas, Champagne, Chartrand, Danish, and Murphy (1997), are helping athletes develop in other realms. Highlighting past athletes' success in establishing careers after sport may be helpful. For example, Tim Horton, a former NHL player, opened one doughnut shop that has expanded into one of the most recognized chains in Canada. Other athletes have gone on to careers in sport broadcasting (e.g., Bill Walton, Sean Elliot), owning a business (e.g., ex–Cleveland Brown Clay Matthews's Ford dealership), and law and federal politics (e.g., ex-NHL player Ken Dryden).

Although referral for counseling or therapy may not be necessary as part of reframing the athlete's understanding of and reaction to injury (Smith, Scott, & Wiese, 1990), it may offer the opportunity to discover *positive* implications of the injury (Ermler & Thomas, 1990), not in a Pollyannaish way but as a source of self-understanding, self-growth, and discovery. Ermler and Thomas note that individuals who develop positive meanings from injury adjust and cope better than those who do not.

A study by Udry, Gould, Beck, and Bridges (1997) assessed the possible benefits of season-ending injuries in elite skiers. Four general dimensions were identified: personal growth, psychologically based performance, physical and technical development, and none (Udry et al., 1997). Examples of these included clarified priorities, increased mental toughness, better or smarter technical skiing, and nothing, respectively. The authors concluded that individual athletes grew in positive ways from their injury experiences. The implication for working with injured athletes is that a silver lining exists for every cloud.

The question of referral for counseling can be problematic (see Chapter 20 for when to refer). Not all sport psychologists are trained as counselors, and not all counselors will be sensitive to the particular issues confronting athletes. One alternative to referring athletes for counseling is having athletic trainers take a more active role in providing sport psychology in the athletic training room. Several authors have suggested that athletic trainers are in a perfect position to train athletes to use psychological skills (e.g., goal-setting, imagery), as they are in frequent contact with injured athletes and possess a wealth of knowledge about injuries (e.g., Cramer Roh & Perna, 2000; Ford & Gordon, 1997; Misasi, Redmond, & Kemler, 1998; Tuffey, 1991). In fact, Misasi et al. (1998) point out that "the athletic therapist cannot avoid the need to be an effective counselor or helper" (p. 36). Scherzer and Williams (2008) found that when athletic trainers are given additional training in sport psychology, they perceive themselves as more skilled at using the various techniques and they think that they use the skills more.

Situational factors.   Many potential situational factors influence cognitive appraisal and emotional and behavioral responses to injury. For example, Wiese-Bjornstal, Smith, Shaffer, and Morrey (1998) enumerated three types of situational factors: (1) sport factors (e.g., time in season, playing status); (2) social factors (e.g., coach and sports medicine team influences); and (3) environmental factors (e.g., accessibility to rehabilitation). Granito (2001) sought to provide empirical support for Wiese-Bjornstal et al.'s (1998) model. He conducted focus groups with injured athletes and found that athletes' responses and reactions to injury fell into seven categories: (1) personal factors (e.g., athlete's personality, role on team); (2) effects on relationships (e.g., with coaches, parents, teammates); (3) sociological aspects (i.e., gender differences, athletic subculture); (4) physical factors (e.g., pain and use of painkillers); (5) daily hassles (i.e., stress); (6) feelings associated with injury (e.g., frustration, depression, tension); and (7) rehabilitation (i.e., adherence, ease of receiving treatment). Granito's investigation provides support that many factors contribute to an athlete's response to injury, including the personal and situational factors that are part of the cognitive appraisal model of psychological adjustment to athletic injury.

Combined with grief model.   Considerable research support exists for the cognitive appraisal models (see Brewer, 1994; Wiese-Bjornstal et al., 1998). Other researchers (Striegel, Hedgpeth, & Sowa, 1996) have proposed a model that incorporates both the grief stage model by Kubler-Ross (1969) and the individual nature of the stress response as encompassed in cognitive appraisal models. Striegel and colleagues' model has three levels: (1) short-term rehabilitation (i.e., first 2 weeks of recovery); (2) long-term rehabilitation (i.e., any duration of rehabilitation longer than 2 weeks but less than permanent withdrawal from sport); and (3) termination of participation (i.e., withdrawal from sport). Cognitive appraisal is incorporated in levels one and two, and the Kubler-Ross model (1969) is incorporated in level

three, indicating that there may be differences in the psychological reaction of athletes who will be injured for 2 weeks versus athletes who will never compete again (Striegel et al., 1996). At present, support for this model is theoretical rather than empirical.

Harris (2003) proposed that integrating the Kubler-Ross stage model and the Chickering and Reisser psychosocial developmental theory may provide insight for working with injured collegiate athletes. This theory enables athletic trainers to relate to and better understand collegiate athletes, who are in the midst of developmental growth. In addition, Junge (2000) proposed an integrative theoretical model based on stress theory to explain the relationship between psychological factors and sports injuries. This model is based on that of Andersen and Williams (1988); however, it requires empirical support.

Other models.   Another model, which extends cognitive-appraisal models, has been proposed by Hagger, Chatzisarantis, Griffin, and Thatcher (2005). They proposed that self-regulation theory, in which people form a representation of their injury on the basis of (1) general information available about the injury, (2) information obtained from expert sources (e.g., athletic trainer, physician), and (3) current and past experiences with injury, may explain the reactions of injured athletes. In their study of 220 injured athletes, they found that emotional representations were a significant factor in predicting both positive and negative affect and that some cognitive representations were predictors of physical function, while others predicted sports function. The authors note that this is the first study to examine the applicability of self-regulation theory on emotional and functional outcomes of athletic injury. For a more thorough description of self-regulation theory and its applicability to athletic injury, we recommend the Hagger et al. (2005) article or Hagger, Chatzisarantis, and Griffin's (2004) chapter on the same model.

Brewer, Andersen, and Van Raalte (2002) put forward a biopsychosocial model to explain the way seven components occur in concert and influence each other through the rehabilitation process. They suggest that psychological factors play a key role, particularly in terms of reciprocal interaction with biological and social/contextual factors. The other factors in this model are injury, sociodemographic factors, biological factors, intermediate biopsychological outcomes, and sport injury rehabilitation outcomes (Brewer et al., 2002).

Potentially Dangerous Attitudes

To help athletes develop into successful competitors, many coaches and athletic trainers have unknowingly fostered erroneous attitudes concerning successful injury rehabilitation. Understanding these potentially dangerous attitudes is crucial to appreciating the psychological aspects of injury and rehabilitation.

Act tough and always give 110%. Athletes have been systematically taught that mental toughness and giving 110% all the time are necessary for success in sports. Although mental toughness and giving one's best are important to success, we must realize that when taken to *extremes* these actions can foster injury and failure. Curt Schilling's performance in the 2004 World Series epitomizes these beliefs. Schilling suffered an ankle injury during the opening game of the American League Division Series. The extent of the injury was apparent in his subpar performance in Game 1 of the league's championship series against the New York Yankees. Rather than succumbing to his injury, the Boston Red Sox medical team devised a method to stabilize his tendon that allowed him to pitch again in Game 6 of the series, which he won. On the morning of his scheduled start in Game 2 of the World Series, Schilling awoke to numbness in his foot and was prepared to tell the team he couldn't pitch. Again, the medical staff found a solution that enabled Schilling to take to the mound (MacMullan, 2004). In both outings in which his tendon was stabilized by stitches, Schilling truly wore a red sock for the Red Sox— his socks turned red from blood oozing from his injury. Schilling needed ankle surgery during the

off-season and in 2005 began the season on the disabled list. He has since rebounded and helped lead the Red Sox to a second World Championship in 2007 ("Curt Schilling," 2007).

Athletes must be capable of "playing through" some kinds of pain. Seldom, however, do we educate athletes about which kinds of pain to ignore and which kinds of pain to listen and respond to appropriately. Both the Schilling example and research findings indicate that sports medicine practitioners can be complicit in this culture of risk. Safai (2003) interviewed physicians, physiotherapists, and intercollegiate athletes at a Canadian university and found that sports medicine practitioners seem to understand why athletes endorse the sport ethic of playing through pain and they help them return to sport as quickly as possible, even if it is before an injury is healed.

How is this sport ethic learned, and is it pervasive at less competitive levels of sport? Malcom (2006) observed girls aged 11–16 who played in a softball league over three years. Most of the injuries she observed tended to be minor, but how the girls learned to react to them was fascinating. Some girls would initially react to the injuries in order to gain attention, while others would try to move out of harm's way to avoid injury. As the season(s) wore on, coaches and other players taught the girls to play through the injuries by ignoring complaints of injuries, teasing girls about injuries, or modeling acting tough when injured (e.g., a coach would catch a line drive without a glove and not react). Malcom demonstrated that the sport ethic is learned through participation in sport, though it is not directly taught. Other researchers (Liston, Reacher, Smith, & Waddington, 2006) were curious whether the sport ethic would be found in nonelite rugby, reasoning that professional athletes might be more willing to play through pain due to financial and commercial pressures. They found that the sport ethic was present and identified two codes in rugby: (1) a willingness to be hurt, and (2) playing when hurt for the good of the team. It seems as though the sport ethic of playing in pain permeates every strata of athletics.

Reacting to Injured Athletes

Others' reactions to an injured athlete can play a role in the athlete's interpretation of the injury. Reaction to an injured athlete can spring thoughtlessly from old-school attitudes about toughness in sport or can proceed naturally from a philosophy that embraces the concept of the athlete as a whole person, not just a sport participant. The first reaction not only can impede an athlete's recuperation from injury; it can arguably *predispose* an athlete to sport accidents. The second reaction deals with short- and long-term aspects of an injury situation in a way that greatly increases the chances of an athlete's return to healthy sport participation.

The well-intentioned appearance of dedication and commitment to sport develops into the projection of a false image of invulnerability. Eventually, athletes begin to believe they only deserve to feel proud if they give 110%. No one points out to them that giving 110% is impossible or that trying to do so can lead to performing at 50% of optimal ability. This belief persists despite the fact that most athletes who adhere to these attitudes are unable to perform at their best. Athletes become extremely vulnerable and totally unprepared for the incapacitating injury or lifelong pain that may follow. A major change in attitude is required to ensure a healthy adaptation to injury and life. Sport professionals must realize the hazards of these mistaken attitudes of the past before they can fully use the psychological strategies that we present later in this chapter.

Injured athletes are worthless

Some coaches believe that the best way to foster a rapid recovery from injury is to make injured athletes feel unimportant. Coaches who hold this view communicate to their athletes that they only care for them as performers. Leaders in sport must realize that the time when athletes are recovering from injury is crucial for either developing or destroying trust. It is during this time that leaders have a chance to demonstrate care and concern and show that they are as committed to their athletes as they ask their athletes to be to them.

Successful leaders of athletes must help them realize that attitudes such as desire, pride, and commitment are beneficial at the right time and place but that these attitudes may also be hazardous to present and future health if taken to the extreme. The key is for leaders to do what is in the *best interest* of injured athletes. When this approach is followed, athletes, coaches, athletic trainers, and teams alike will have the best possible chance of attaining their fullest potential.

Whole-Person Philosophy

"Listen," said Rose, "I know a guy who fought the whole organization because he didn't want to jeopardize his health—Johnny Bench. He told them, 'I will not catch anymore, period. I don't plan to be a cripple when I'm through.'"

Rose paused . . . "And I'm not gonna sit here and tell you that someone who says that is wrong. I mean, hell, when you finish playing this game, you've still got half your life in front of you."

Harry Stein, "Brought to His Knees,"
Sport, September 1984, p. 63

Danish (1986) makes an excellent point when he reminds us to respond to athletes as people, not just injuries. An athlete with an injury is no less of an athlete, no less of a person than before the injury. As such, it is unwise to treat the athlete as the injury. Danish describes a helping skill model that can be of use to those working with athletes.

Social support. Social support is critical in the rehabilitation process, particularly with moderate to severe injuries. If athletic identification has been strong, family and friends may respond to the athletes primarily as athletes. In many cases friendships are based exclusively along these lines, particularly with teammates or other athletes. Suddenly these important ties may be ruptured. Injured athletes may no longer be seen and may no longer see themselves as athletes. Activities around which their lives centered now move along without them. No one quite knows how to relate to these athletes except perhaps in terms of their past glory or possible future—but not to the injured people in the present.

Too often, when athletes are kept away because of injury, they feel that their teammates and time have marched on. There are new jokes, new alignments—in essence a new situation that excludes injured athletes and into which they must try to reintegrate themselves. By being there, other athletes have grown and developed with the situation.

We would go so far as to say that as soon as athletes can rejoin a team—even if on crutches or bandaged—they should do so. It is sometimes too much to ask someone to get back on a horse after being thrown, but a modified approach allows a gradual remount while preventing the consolidation of fears of overwhelming obstacles. Asking an injured athlete to help the coaching staff or to mentor younger players provides ways in which an injured athlete can still be a contributing member of the team. But it is important to consider that attending practice while injured may have a negative impact on an athlete's emotional state. Some of the athletes Tracy (2003) interviewed explained that it was really difficult to be at practice while injured; in fact, 6 of the 10 participants chose not to attend practice, while 4 either chose to or were told to by their coaches. Giving athletes the option to rejoin the team when injured might be a good starting point.

Coaches and sport psychologists must help ensure that normal contacts are maintained. They should be reassuringly optimistic about recovery of past abilities, and they should encourage injured athletes to discover other bases of support. Athletes do need support from their coaches as they move toward recovery (Peterson, 2001). In particular, athletes will benefit from informational support (i.e., information about the injury) and emotional support (i.e., helping the athlete express emotions and feel understood) from coaches and athletic trainers throughout the injury and recovery processes.

With athletes whose rehabilitation will take longer than 2 weeks, Striegel, Hedgpeth, and Sowa (1996) suggest two additional forms of social support: peer mentors and injury support groups. Peer mentor relationships are opportunities for an injured athlete to talk with an athlete who has successfully rehabilitated a similar injury. Injury support groups provide injured athletes with a forum to talk about their injury, rehabilitation, and anything else with others who are in the same position. Both of these forms of support may help motivate injured athletes as rehabilitation continues and give athletes a sense that they are not alone.

Athletic trainers and medical staff can also be valuable sources of support for injured athletes. The athletes interviewed by Tracy (2003) indicated that interactions with medical and training staff could "make or break" their days. Athletes used their athletic trainers' facial expressions (e.g., grimacing when examining the injury) to guide their mood for the day. Further illustrating the role athletic trainers play, Bone and Fry (2006) examined the influence of their support on athletes' beliefs about the rehabilitation process. They found that injured athletes look to their athletic trainers for support, particularly listening support, and that athletes' beliefs about rehabilitation are somewhat explained by the support they receive from their athletic trainers.

Although social support and the reintegration of the injured athlete are important parts of the rehabilitation process, there are two problems with this "double-edged crutch." First, an injured athlete may present a conscious or unconscious threat to others: "If it could happen to them, it could happen to me." This fear may evoke anything from a mild feeling of discomfort to an almost phobic avoidance of the injured player. This effect may even be exacerbated when a physical disfigurement or highly visible disability is present. When this type of situation develops, it is important for sport personnel to show that the injured person should not be feared and relay the message that the injured athlete will recover and rejoin the team.

Second, although cooperation and cohesion are part of teamwork, so is competition. An athlete's injury may present an opportunity to another person. The second-string player, for example, may have a chance for glory. This is what happened in the New England Patriots organization. Early in the 2000–2001 football season, the Patriots' starting quarterback, Drew Bledsoe, was injured. The starting job was turned over to an unknown, Tom Brady. With Brady as quarterback, the Patriots won seven games and were in contention for the playoffs. When Bledsoe was cleared to play, Coach Bill Belichick decided to keep Brady as the starter. When Brady got hurt in the AFC championship game, Bledsoe stepped in and carried the team to victory. With only the Super Bowl left, Belichick had a tough decision on his hands. Should he start his high-profile, high-salary quarterback or his young breakout star who had been great all season? Brady was deemed healthy to play, got the start, and the Patriots won the first of what would be three NFL championships in four years, all with Brady as quarterback ("New England Patriots," 2007). Bledsoe was traded to the Buffalo Bills after the 2001 season, then played with the Dallas Cowboys, and retired in 2007 (Smith, 2007).

Where possible, this type of competition should be appropriately focused on the athletic situation and not personalized. Tensions within the system (a polarization of teammates into factions around the competing athletes) should be brought to the surface and discussed. One cannot ignore the realities of competition. One can, however, try to maintain as positive a climate as possible.

> To treat a knee and ignore the brain and emotions that direct the choreography of that knee is not consistent with total care of the patient.
>
> G. J. Faris, "Psychological Aspects of Athletic Rehabilitation," Clinics in Sports Medicine, 4, 1985, p. 546

Addressing the whole person. When dealing with an injured athlete, one of the most crucial aspects entails understanding what the athlete is experiencing before trying to "fix" him or her (Petitpas & Danish, 1995). An injured athlete may experience all, some, or none of a range of effects including grief, identity loss, separation and loneliness, fear, loss of confidence, and performance decrements. If you try to address all of these issues, or some of them, without assessing what the individual athlete is experiencing, you risk frustrating the athlete. It can sometimes be difficult to remember that the injured athlete is a person and not just a broken leg. As Andersen (2000) put it, "We do not treat knees; we treat people" (p. 46). Thus, it is important to talk to the athlete about him or herself and not only about the injury.

Petitpas and Danish suggest a series of steps to follow when working with an injured athlete. First, build rapport with the athlete. This allows you to develop a clear understanding of what the athlete is experiencing with his or her injury. Education is next, when the athlete learns about the actual injury and the rehabilitation process. This helps the athlete become more active in the rehabilitation process. The phases of skill development and practice and evaluation follow the general education phase. The opportunity to learn and use skills (e.g., goal setting, imagery) helps athletes with rehabilitation and with performance once they are "back in the game."

Two recent case studies highlight the importance of treating the whole person. Davis and Sime (2005) documented their work with a collegiate baseball player struggling to regain his form following an eye injury. He had lingering effects after his injury had healed medically; he was not hitting effectively, reported feeling anxious when he had two strikes during an at-bat, and felt as though his vision was not 100%. Davis and Sime used a mix of traditional (e.g., breathing and relaxation training, imagery) and nontraditional strategies (i.e., electroencephalograph biofeedback) to great success—the athlete had his most successful season following the interventions. This blended intervention demonstrates the possibilities created when considering the whole picture (that is, both psychological and physiological aspects), and the whole person (i.e., his psychological fears and perceived visual losses). Vergeer (2006) took a different approach; she tried to more thoroughly understand the way an injured athlete processes injury-relevant information. As a result of eight interviews over a 20-week period following his injury and a chance encounter with him three years later to gather follow-up information, Vergeer (2006) proposed that we should conceptualize injury recovery as a multitrack process; that is, as athletes progress in rehabilitation and recovery, changes occur on many levels that need to be attended to. By spending extensive amounts of time with one injured athlete, Vergeer was able to propose a thorough conceptualization; however empirical support is now needed.

Heil, Wakefield, and Reed (1998) suggest that conceptualizing rehabilitation as an athletic challenge may help athletes through the rehabilitation process. By using this metaphor, the rehabilitation process encompasses familiar skills and rehabilitation becomes just another part of training for excellence rather than a setback in achieving athletic goals.

Teaching Specific Psychological Rehabilitation Strategies

Increasingly, coaches and athletes recognize the mental aspects of sport performance and rehabilitation. The same mental skills and techniques that help athletes succeed in sport (e.g., goal-setting, mental imagery) can play a role in successful rehabilitation from injury. Coaches, sport psychologists, and athletic trainers may need to teach athletes that it is reasonable and appropriate to think the injury is unfortunate, untimely, and inconvenient and to feel irritated, frustrated, and disappointed when one occurs. It is *unreasonable* for athletes to convince themselves that the situation is hopeless, that injuries are a sign of weakness and should be hidden, or that their season or career is over.

Part of the learning is about the injury itself and the rehabilitation process. It is difficult, if not impossible, for intelligent athletes to be positive and relaxed if they lack knowledge, are anxious, and wonder why they are doing what they are doing in the athletic training room. Athletes who realize the purpose of rehabilitation are more likely to work hard and to provide useful information about their progress.

When athletes are experiencing depressed mood, coaches or sport consultants must not negate disturbing feelings by urging athletes to "pick their spirits up." They should explain to athletes that these feelings are normal and a sign of progress toward recovery. To help overcome these feelings, athletes may benefit from sharing experiences with other athletes who have successfully recovered from similar injuries and returned to competition. For more seriously injured athletes, support groups for sharing and discussing concerns, fears, and difficulties may be helpful (Granito, 2001; Silva & Hardy, 1991; Striegel et al., 1996; Wiese & Weiss, 1987). If prolonged detachment, lack of spontaneity, and disinterest in activities and people persist, professional counseling or therapy may be necessary (Wehlage, 1980).

Two studies that examined psychosocial factors possibly related to sports injury rehabilitation found that athletes who possess certain mental attributes and who use certain mental skills may recover faster from injury. In the first study by Ievleva and Orlick (1991), athletes who used more goal setting, healing mental imagery, and positive self-talk recovered faster than athletes who did not. A follow-up study by Loundagin and Fisher (1993) revealed a similar pattern of results and also that focus of attention and stress reduction significantly enhanced recovery time. In contrast, a study by Scherzer (1999) failed to find any correlation between using mental skills and recovery from knee surgery except for goal setting predicting one outcome measure. In a review of research on both preventive and rehabilitative psychological interventions for sport injury, Cupal (1998) concluded that psychological interventions significantly altered the rehabilitation outcome for injured athletes in terms of earlier gains in strength, increases in functional ability, and reduction of pain, state anxiety, and reinjury anxiety. Both research and extensive anecdotal information from consulting experiences offer support for teaching the following psychological interventions to injured athletes.

Thought-Stoppage and Cognitive Restructuring. What athletes say to themselves following an injury helps determine their subsequent behavior. Athletes can be taught coping skills to control their inner thoughts. Then, when self-defeating internal dialogues occur, athletes can use an intervention strategy such as thought-stoppage or cognitive restructuring. (See Chapter 15 for more information on these and other techniques for controlling thoughts.) Thought-stoppage and cognitive restructuring can be conceptualized as "self-talk" or how we speak to ourselves. Positive self-talk is thought to contribute to personal well-being and the enhancement of healing (Ievleva & Orlick, 1991), possibly because such self-statements are under athletes' control or because the statements enhance motivation.

As an example of the importance of inner dialogue, consider an injury-related situation in which an athlete is going through rehabilitation exercises while experiencing pain and little apparent improvement in the injured area. If her inner dialogue becomes self-defeating, the athlete worries and questions the benefit of treatment and exercise:

> This is awful. This hurts too much to be beneficial. These exercises will probably cause me more harm. Besides, I've been doing this for three days now, and I can't see any progress. It would be a lot easier to just let the injury heal on its own. I don't think I'll come tomorrow. If it's really important, the coach will call me. If she doesn't, it will mean I was right. It really doesn't matter if I get treatment.

The athlete does not get much out of today's treatment and begins to develop excuses for not continuing therapy.

On the other hand, if the athlete's inner dialogue is self-enhancing, she worries and questions the benefits of treatment and exercise but then thinks:

> Stop. These exercises hurt, but it's okay— they'll pay off. I'm lucky to have knowledgeable people helping me. I'll be competing soon because I'm doing these exercises. If the pain gets too severe, I'll ask my rehabilitation trainer if I am doing it

right and, if I am, I'll live with it and think about how happy I'll be to be competing again.

The athlete has a good treatment session and prepares herself to continue for as long as necessary. She develops rapport with her athletic trainer and coach, both of whom feel good about the athlete. By using cognitive techniques that promote positive self-talk and attitude, athletes can often shorten the time period they need to rehabilitate from injury (Ievleva & Orlick, 1991; Loundagin & Fisher, 1993).

Imagery

> *In his second at bat since coming off the disabled list, Matuszek cracked a leadoff, pinch-hit home run in the seventh inning to give the Phillies a 3–2 victory over the Cubs. He hit the first pitch into the right-field bull pen. "That was all I had on my mind during my time on the disabled list. I kept envisioning some ways to help this team win a game. Even with the injury, my attitude has been good."*
>
> "Phillie Unloads Frustration on Cubs," *The Daily Progress*, July 24, 1984, p. D3

Athletes' imaginations can greatly influence their response to injury. Many imagine the worst that could happen. Athletes can learn to control their visual images and to direct them productively to reduce anxiety and to aid in rehabilitation and successful return to sport. See Chapter 14 for more detailed information on what imagery is and techniques that can be used to teach and enhance imagery skills.

Mastery imagery can be used to foster motivation for rehabilitation and confidence on return to competition. While disabled, athletes may visually rehearse returning to competition and performing effectively. For athletes who experience difficulty viewing themselves vividly in their mind, relaxation exercises should precede the imagery session. Some athletes visualize better with the aid of recordings or video replays of their most effective game performances. Injured athletes also can use coping rehearsal to visually rehearse anticipated problematic situations or obstacles that may stand in the way of their successful return to competition and then rehearse effectively overcoming these obstacles. Such visual rehearsal methods can effectively prepare injured athletes for any number of competitive or practice situations, helping them maintain physical skills, retain confidence in their ability, and dissipate any lingering fears they may have of reinjury on return to competition (Ievleva & Orlick, 1993).

Injured athletes can use emotive imagery to help feel secure and confident that rehabilitation will be successful. The athletes rehearse various scenes that produce positive self-enhancing feelings such as enthusiasm, self-pride, and confidence. Athletes may, for instance, rehearse feeling excited about their first game following injury or rehearse thoughts of the admiration coaches, teammates, and friends will have for them on their return. Athletes can also be instructed to think of other athletes like themselves who have overcome similar injuries and then generate other scenes that produce positive feelings.

Athletes can use healing imagery to vividly envision what is happening to the injury internally during the rehabilitation process. To do this, athletes must receive a detailed explanation of their injury and how it will heal physiologically. Color pictures should be used to help athletes develop a mental picture of the injury. The healing process and purpose of the rehabilitation techniques are then explained. After visualizing the healing process, athletes are asked to imagine in vivid color the healing occurring during treatment sessions and at intervals during the day. For example, athletes can imagine increased blood flow and warmth going to the injured area, or they can imagine the stretching necessary for enhancing range of motion. In addition to healing imagery, research supports the effectiveness of using imagery for pain management (Driediger, Hall, & Callow, 2006).

Despite research findings that imagery can help with recovery (e.g., Ievleva & Orlick, 1991), many athletes do not use imagery extensively during rehabilitation (Driediger et al., 2006; Sordoni, Hall, & Forwell, 2000). Milne, Hall, and Forwell (2005) sought to extend Sordoni et al.'s

results (2000) and found that injured athletes used more motivational and cognitive imagery than healing imagery while rehabilitating. They suggest that athletes may need additional instruction in healing imagery if they are to use it. This concern is echoed by Evans, Hare, and Mullen (2006), who interviewed four injured athletes about their use of imagery in performance contexts, during injury rehabilitation, and any other uses of imagery. They found that the athletes used imagery to control pain and enhance healing, but were more familiar with performance-related imagery.

With regard to specific injuries, Cupal and Brewer (2001) found that for people recovering from ACL reconstruction, practicing mental imagery was associated with gains in strength and less reinjury, anxiety, and pain. These benefits were observed despite participants practicing visualization less often than expected. When imagery was added to the rehabilitation protocol for athletes recovering from ankle sprains, Christakou, Zervas, and Lavallee (2007) found that the athletes developed strong imagery abilities and showed greater improvements in muscular endurance and balance stability than athletes rehabbing the same injury without imagery instruction. These studies demonstrate the valuable role imagery can play in injury rehabilitation.

Goal-Setting

It is helpful for the rehabilitation team to work with the injured athlete at setting specific short- and long-term goals for recovery, return to practice and competition, and day-to-day rehabilitation throughout the rehabilitation process (DePalma & DePalma, 1989). Athletes should be actively involved in this process, with more seriously injured athletes more actively involved. (See Chapter 11 for specific suggestions on how to effectively set goals and implement a goal-setting program.)

The following example of a college pitcher who needed surgery on his throwing arm highlights the effective use of goals in a rehabilitation process designed to physically and psychologically prepare him for return to practice the following spring. He was reminded of how excited he would be on the first day of practice to be back on the field with his teammates and to see if he still "had it." He also was told that he would feel great and have an almost overpowering urge to try all his pitches and overthrow on the first day his arm felt good, but he would overcome the urges by being smart, disciplined, and emotionally controlled. The desire to help his teammates be successful and the thrill of getting back on stage and becoming a star again would be highly motivating.

Together, this athlete, his coaches, and his athletic trainers outlined a specific goal plan. They decided on a set number of throws each day, the distance of the throws, the approximate speed of the throws, and the kinds of throws. For the first 3 weeks the athlete's catcher and a coach would help make sure that the plan was adhered to on a daily basis. Short- and long-term goals were detailed so that by the fifth game of the year the athlete would be ready to return to the pitching mound for three innings of relief pitching. It is essential that these goals are important to the athlete (Danish, 1986), and this is best accomplished if time is taken to explain to the athlete the relationship between staying focused on and committed to agreed-upon goals and successful rehabilitation and return to competition.

A similar plan was detailed for physical treatments. Both plans were reinforced by coaches, athletic trainers, and teammates, as well as by daily visualization of the good feelings and results that would occur from sticking to the plan. Despite many days of questioning, doubt, and uncertainty, the athlete generally remained positive, stayed with the plan, and made a highly successful return to competition one week later than planned.

As with many other athletes, the process from injury to return to competition was a challenge to this athlete's mind and body. Because the process was managed properly, it allowed for a positive and bright future. Research by Filby, Maynard, and Graydon (1999) found support for the notion that setting multiple goals (e.g., outcome, process, and performance goals) improved task performance. Wayda, Armenth-Brothers, and Boyce (1998) further explain that if the injured athlete feels that he or she is part of the process (i.e., by taking an active role in goal-setting), he or she is more likely to be committed to the rehabilitation program.

Relaxation

Practicing any of the relaxation techniques (see Chapter 13) can play a role in reducing stress and speeding injury rehabilitation and recovery (Loundagin & Fisher, 1993). These results may occur for a number of reasons. Relaxation helps open the mind–body channels that regulate the body, enabling inner control over the body (Botterill, Flint, & Ievleva, 1996). Tension levels often increase in the injured area owing to the stress of being injured (Brewer, Van Raalte, & Linder, 1991). This tension can increase pain and work against the effectiveness of the rehabilitation exercises by, for example, reducing blood flow and range of motion. Practicing a relaxation routine can relieve the tension and enhance blood circulation. The greater the blood flow, the faster injured tissues are repaired (Ievleva & Orlick, 1993). Injured athletes who participated in stress inoculation training (i.e., deep breathing, progressive muscular relaxation, imagery) experienced less anxiety, less pain, and fewer days to recovery than counterparts who received only physical therapy, demonstrating the effectiveness of adding relaxation training to physical rehabilitation protocols (Ross & Berger, 1996).

Summary

Sport psychologists have made great advances in understanding the psychological rehabilitation of athletes and the psychological factors that put athletes at risk of injury. Although some athletes have effective psychological responses, others do not. This chapter focuses on factors that may predispose athletes to injuries, patterns of negative reactions to injuries, and ways in which coaches and sport psychologists can help athletes respond psychologically to injuries in positive, growth-oriented ways.

Although no clear injury-prone personality has been identified, some factors such as high life stress and low social support and psychological coping skills are predictive of injury. Possible preventive interventions are available for these and other factors related to injury. Athletes can respond to injury in more and less adaptive ways. Using a cognitive appraisal model, we identify personal and situational factors that might influence an athlete's cognitive appraisal of the injury and his or her resulting emotional and behavioral responses to both the injury and injury rehabilitation. We agree with Brewer's (1994) conclusion that cognitive appraisal models offer a useful framework to guide both future empirical efforts and rehabilitation practice. Systems of social support, treatment of the whole person, and cognitive-behavioral interventions are ways to help injured athletes respond to injury in a more positive way.

Study Questions

1. What are key factors that may predispose some athletes to injury? How can the athlete and the sport or team environment be modified to reduce risk factors and enhance buffering factors?

2. List five responses that may occur as a result of anxiety and tension associated with an injury on an athlete's initial return to competition.

3. How and why might personal growth possibilities become an important part of the psychological rehabilitation of the injured athlete?

4. List five problematic results of an athlete returning to competition following an injury if not psychologically prepared.

5. Diagram the cognitive appraisal model of psychological adjustment to athletic injury and discuss the different components.

6. Explain the differences among mastery imagery, coping rehearsal, emotive imagery, and healing imagery.

7. Describe what other psychological strategies might be used to hasten rehabilitation and to prepare for returning to competition.

References

Andersen, M. B. (2000). Supervision of athletic trainers; counseling encounters. *Athletic Therapy Today, 5,* 46–47.

Andersen, M. B., & Williams, J. M. (1988). A model of stress and athletic injury: Prediction and prevention. *Journal of Sport and Exercise Psychology, 10,* 294–306.

Andersen, M. B., & Williams, J. M. (1999). Athletic injury, psychosocial factors, and perceptual changes during stress. *Journal of Sports Sciences, 17,* 735–741.

AskMen.com. (2004). *Eric Lindros.* Retrieved September 29, 2004, from http://www.askmen.com/men/sports/45_eric_lindros.html.

Blackwell, B., & McCullagh, P. (1990). The relationship of athletic injury to life stress, competitive anxiety and coping resources. *Athletic Training, 25,* 23–27.

Bone, J. B., & Fry, M. D. (2006). The influence of injured athletes' perceptions of social support from ATCs on their beliefs about rehabilitation. *Journal of Sport Rehabilitation, 15,* 156–167.

Botterill, C., Flint, F. A., & Ievleva, L. (1996). Psychology of the injured athlete. In J. E. Zachazewski, D. J. Magee, & W. S. Quillen (Eds.), *Athletic injuries and rehabilitation* (pp. 791–805). Philadelphia: W. B. Saunders.

Bramwell, S. T., Masuda, M., Wagner, N. N., & Holmes, T. H. (1975). Psychosocial factors in athletic injuries. *Journal of Human Stress, 2,* 6–20.

Brewer, B. W. (1993). Self-identity and specific vulnerability to depressed mood. *Journal of Personality, 61,* 343–364.

Brewer, B. W. (1994). Review and critique of models of psychological adjustment to athletic injury. *Journal of Applied Sport Psychology, 6,* 87–100.

Brewer, B. W., Andersen, M. B., & Van Raalte, J. L. (2002). Psychological aspects of sport injury rehabilitation: Toward a biopsychosocial approach. In D. L. Mostofsky & L. D. Zaichkowsky (Eds.), *Medical and psychological aspects of sport and exercise* (pp. 41–54). Morgantown, WV: Fitness Information Technology.

Brewer, B. W., Van Raalte, J. L., & Linder, D. E. (1991). Role of the sport psychologist in treating injured athletes: A survey of sport medicine providers. *Journal of Applied Sport Psychology, 3,* 183–190.

Brewer, B. W., Van Raalte, J. L., & Linder, D. E. (1993). Athletic identity: Hercules' muscles or Achilles heel? *International Journal of Sport Psychology, 24,* 237–254.

Christakou, A., Zervas, Y., & Lavallee, D. (2007). The adjunctive role of imagery on the functional rehabilitation of a grade II ankle sprain. *Human Movement Science, 26,* 141–154.

Coddington, R. D., & Troxell, J. R. (1980). The effects of emotional factors on football injury rates—a pilot study. *Journal of Human Stress, 7,* 3–5.

Cramer Roh, J. L., & Perna, F. M. (2000). Psychology/counseling: A universal competency in athletic training. *Journal of Athletic Training, 35,* 458–465.

Crossman, J., & Jamieson, J. (1985). Differences in perceptions of seriousness and disrupting effects of athletic injury as viewed by athletes and their trainer. *Perceptual and Motor Skills, 61,* 1131–1134.

Cupal, D. D. (1998). Psychological interventions in sport injury prevention and rehabilitation. *Journal of Applied Sport Psychology, 10,* 103–123.

Cupal, D. D., & Brewer, B. W. (2001). Effects of relaxation and guided imagery on knee strength, reinjury anxiety, and pain following anterior cruciate ligament reconstruction. *Rehabilitation Psychology, 46,* 28–43.

Curt Schilling. (2007, November 4). In *Wikipedia, The Free Encyclopedia*. Retrieved November 4, 2007, from http://en.wikipedia.org/wiki/Curt_Schilling.

Dalhauser, M., & Thomas, M. D. (1979). Visual disembedding and locus of control as variables associated with high school football injuries. *Perceptual and Motor Skills, 49,* 254.

Daly, J. M., Brewer, B. W., Van Raalte, J. L., Petitpas, A. J., & Sklar, J. H. (1995). Cognitive appraisal, emotional adjustment, and adherence to rehabilitation following knee surgery. *Journal of Sport Rehabilitation, 4,* 23–30.

Danish, S. J. (1986). Psychological aspects in the care and treatment of athletic injuries. In P. E. Vinger & E. F. Hoerner (Eds.), *Sports injuries: The unthwarted epidemic* (pp. 345–353). Littleton, MA: PSG.

Davis, J. O. (1991). Sports injuries and stress management: An opportunity for research. *The Sport Psychologist, 5,* 175–182.

Davis, P. A., & Sime, W. E. (2005). Toward a psychophysiology of performance: Sport psychology principles dealing with anxiety. *International Journal of Stress Management, 12,* 363–378.

de Heredia, R. A. S., Munoz, A. R., & Artaza, J. L. (2004). The effect of psychological response on recovery of sport injury. *Research in Sports Medicine, 12,* 15–31.

DePalma, M. T., & DePalma, B. (1989). The use of instruction and the behavioral approach to facilitate injury rehabilitation. *Athletic Training, 24,* 217–219.

DeWitt, D. J. (1980). Cognitive and biofeedback training for stress reduction with university athletes. *Journal of Sport Psychology, 2,* 288–294.

Driediger, M., Hall, C., & Callow, N. (2006). Imagery use by injured athletes: A qualitative analysis. *Journal of Sport Sciences, 24,* 261–271.

Duda, J. L., Smart, A. E., & Tappe, M. K. (1989). Predictors of adherence in the rehabilitation of athletic injuries: An application of personal investment theory. *Journal of Sport Psychology, 11,* 367–381.

Ermler, K. L., & Thomas, C. E. (1990). Interventions for the alienating effect of injury. *Athletic Training, 25,* 269–271.

ESPN.com (2007a). *Eric Lindros.* Retrieved November 3, 2007, from http://sports.espn.go.com/nhl/players/stats?playerId=543.

ESPN.com (2007b). *Former MVP Lindros Announces Retirement After 13 NHL Seasons.* Retrieved November 16, 2007, from http://sports.espn.go.com/espn/wire?section=nhl&id=3100724.

Evans, L., & Hardy, L. (1995). Sport injury and grief responses. A review. *Journal of Sport & Exercise Psychology, 17,* 227–245.

Evans, L., Hare, R., & Mullen, R. (2006). Imagery use during rehabilitation from injury. *Journal of Imagery Research in Sport and Physical Activity, 1,* 1–19.

Faris, G. J. (1985). Psychologic aspects of athletic rehabilitation. *Clinics in Sports Medicine, 4,* 545–551.

Fawkner, H. J. (1995). *Predisposition to injury in athletes: The role of psychosocial factors.* Unpublished master's thesis, University of Melbourne, Australia.

Fawkner, J. J., McMurray, N. E., & Summers, J. J. (1999). Athletic injury and minor life events: A prospective study. *Journal of Science and Medicine in Sport, 2,* 117–124.

Fields, K. B., Delaney, M., & Hinkle, S. (1990). A prospective study of type A behavior and running injuries. *Journal of Family Practice, 30,* 425–429.

Filby, W. C. D., Maynard, I. W., & Graydon, J. K. (1999). The effect of multiple-goal strategies on performance outcomes in training and competition. *Journal of Applied Sport Psychology, 11,* 230–246.

Fisher, A. C., Domm, M. A., & Wuest, D. A. (1988). Adherence to sports-injury rehabilitation programs. *The Physician and Sportsmedicine, 16,* 47–52.

Ford, I. A., Eklund, R. C., & Gordon, S. (2000). An examination of psychosocial variables moderating the relationship between life stress and injury time-loss among athletes of a high standard. *Journal of Sports Sciences, 18,* 301–312.

Ford, I., & Gordon, S. (1997). Perspectives of sport physiotherapists on the frequency and significance of psychological factors in professional practice: Implications for curriculum design in professional training. *Australian Journal of Science and Medicine in Sport, 29,* 34–40.

Granito, V. J. (2001). Athletic injury experience: A qualitative focus group approach. *Journal of Sport Behavior, 24,* 63–82.

Green, S. L., & Weinberg, R. S. (2001). Relationships among athletic identity, coping skills, social support, and the psychological impact of injury in recreational participants. *Journal of Applied Sport Psychology, 31,* 40–59.

Grove, J. R., Stewart, R. M. L., & Gordon, S. (1990, October). *Emotional reactions of athletes to knee rehabilitation.* Paper presented at the annual meeting of the Australian Sports Medicine Federation, Alice Springs, Australia.

Hagger, M. S., Chatzisarantis, N. L. D., & Griffin, M. (2004). Coping with sports injury: Testing a model of self-regulation in a sports setting. In D. Lavallee, J. Thatcher, & M. V. Jones (Eds.) *Coping and emotion in sport* (pp. 105–130). Hauppauge, NY: Nova Science Publishers.

Hagger, M. S., Chatzisarantis, N. L. D., Griffin, M., & Thatcher, J. (2005). Injury representations, coping, emotions, and functional outcomes in athletes with sports-related injuries: A test of self-regulation theory. *Journal of Applied Social Psychology, 35,* 2345–2374.

Hanson, S. J., McCullagh, P., & Tonymon, P. (1992). The relationship of personality characteristics, life stress, and coping resources to athletic injury. *Journal of Sport and Exercise Psychology, 14,* 262–272.

Hardy, C. J., O'Connor, K. A., & Geisler, P. R. (1990). The role of gender and social support in the life stress injury relationship. *Proceedings of the Association for the Advancement of Applied Sport Psychology, Fifth Annual Conference (Abstract),* 51.

Harris, L. L. (2003). Integrating and analyzing psychosocial and stage theories to challenge the development of the injured collegiate athlete. *Journal of Athletic Training, 38,* 75–82.

Heil, J. (Ed.). (1993). *Psychology of sport injury.* Champaign, IL: Human Kinetics.

Heil, J., Wakefield, C., & Reed, C. (1998). Patient as athlete: A metaphor for injury rehabilitation. In K. F. Hays (Ed.), *Integrating exercise, sports, movement and mind: Therapeutic unity.* Binghamton, NY: Haworth Press.

Ievleva, L., & Orlick, T. (1991). Mental links to enhanced healing: An exploratory study. *Sport Psychologist, 5,* 25–40.

Ievleva, L., & Orlick, T. (1993). Mental paths to enhanced recovery from a sports injury. In D. Pargman (Ed.), *Psychological bases of sport injuries* (pp. 219–245). Morgantown, WV: Fitness information Technology.

Johnson, U., Ekengren, J., & Andersen, M. B. (2005). Injury prevention in Sweden: Helping soccer players at risk. *Journal of Sport and Exercise Psychology, 27.*

Johnston, L. H., & Carroll, D. (2000). The psychological impact of injury: Effects of prior sport and exercise involvement. *British Journal of Sports Medicine, 34,* 436–439.

Junge, A. (2000). The influence of psychological factors on sports injuries. *American Journal of Sports Medicine, 28,* S10–S15.

Kerr, G., & Goss, J. (1996). The effects of a stress management program on injuries and stress levels. *Journal of Applied Sport Psychology, 8 ,* 109–117.

Kerr, G., & Minden, H. (1988). Psychological factors related to the occurrence of athletic injuries. *Journal of Sport and Exercise Physiology, 37,* 1–11.

Kleinert, J. (2007). Mood states and perceived physical states as short term predictors of sport injuries: Two prospective studies. *International Journal of Sport and Exercise Psychology, 5,* 340–351.

Kolt, G. S., Hume, P. A., Smith, P., & Williams, M. M. (2004). Effects of a stress-management program on injury and stress of competitive gymnasts. *Perceptual and Motor Skills, 99,* 195–207.

Kolt, G., & Kirkby, R. (1996). Injury in Australian female competitive gymnasts: A psychological perspective. *Australian Physiotherapy, 42,* 121–126.

Kubler-Ross, E. (1969). *On death and dying.* New York: Macmillan.

Larson, G. A., Starkey, C., & Zaichkowsky, L. D. (1996). Psychological aspects of athletic injuries as perceived by athletic trainers. *Sport Psychologist, 10,* 37–47.

Lavallee, L., & Flint, F. (1996). The relationship of stress, competitive anxiety, mood state, and social support to athletic injury. *Journal of Athletic Training, 31,* 296–299.

Liston, K., Reacher, D., Smith, A., & Waddington, I. (2006). Managing pain and injury in nonelite rugby union and rugby league: A case study of players at a British university. *Sport in Society, 9,* 388–402.

Loundagin, C., & Fisher, L. (1993, October). *The relationship between mental skills and enhanced injury rehabilitation.* Paper presented at the annual meeting of the Association for the Advancement of Applied Sport Psychology, Montreal, Quebec.

Lysens, R., Auweele, Y. V., & Ostyn, M. (1986). The relationship between psychosocial factors and sports injuries. *Journal of Sports Medicine and Physical Fitness, 26,* 77–84.

MacMullen, J. (2004, October 31). Schilling talked a good game—and was a man of his word. *Boston Globe.* Retrieved November 4, 2007, from http://www.boston.com.

Maddison, R., & Prapavessis, H. (2005). A psychological approach to the prediction and prevention of athletic injury. *Journal of Sport and Exercise Psychology, 27,* 289–310.

Mainwaring, L. M., Bisschop, S. M., Green, R. E. A., Antoniazzi, M., Comper, P., Kristman, V., et al. (2004). Emotional reaction of varsity athletes to sport-related concussion. *Journal of Sport and Exercise Psychology, 26,* 119–135.

Malcom, N. L. (2006). "Shaking it off" and "toughing it out." Socialization to pain and injury in girls' softball. *Journal of Contemporary Ethnography, 35,* 495–525.

May, J. R., & Brown, L. (1989). Delivery of psychological services to the U.S. alpine ski team prior to and during the Olympics in Calgary. *Sport Psychologist, 3,* 320–329.

McDonald, S. A., & Hardy, C. J. (1990). Affective response patterns of the injured athlete: An exploratory analysis. *Sport Psychologist, 4,* 261–274.

McDonell, C. (2004). *Shooting from the lip.* Buffalo, NY: Firefly Books.

McLeod, S., & Kirkby, R. J. (1995). Locus of control as a predictor of injury in elite basketball players. *Sports Medicine, Training and Rehabilitation, 6,* 201–206.

Meyer, K. N. (1995). *The influence of personality factors, life stress, and coping strategies on the incidence of injury in long-distance runners.* Unpublished master's thesis, University of Colorado, Boulder.

Milne, M., Hall, C., & Forwell, L. (2005). Self-efficacy, imagery use, and adherence to rehabilitation by injured athletes. *Journal of Sport Rehabilitation, 14,* 150–167.

Misasi, S. P., Redmond, C. J., & Kemler, D. S. (1998). Counseling skills and the athletic therapist. *Athletic Therapy Today, 3,* 35–38.

Murphy, S. M. (1988). The on-site provision of sport psychology services at the U.S. Olympic Festival. *Sport Psychologist, 2,* 337–350.

New England Patriots. (2007, November 3). In *Wikipedia, The Free Encyclopedia.* Retrieved November 3, 2007, from http://en.wikipedia.org/wiki/New_England_Patriots.

Nideffer, R. M. (1983). The injured athlete: Psychological factors in treatment. *Orthopedic Clinics of North America, 14,* 374–385.

Nigorikawa, T., Oishi, E., Yasukawa, M., Kamimura, M., Murayama, J., & Tanaka, N. (2003). Type A behavior pattern and sports injuries. *Japanese Journal of Physical Fitness and Sports Medicine, 52,* 359–367.

Pargman, D., (Ed.). (1999). *Psychological bases of sports injuries* (2nd ed.). Morgantown, WV: Fitness Information Technology.

Pargman, D., & Lunt, S. D. (1989). The relationship of self-concept and locus of control to the severity of injury in freshman collegiate football players. *Sports Medicine, Training and Rehabilitation, 1,* 201–208.

Passer, M. W., & Seese, M. D. (1983). Life stress and athletic injury: Examination of positive versus negative events and three moderator variables. *Journal of Human Stress, 10,* 11–16.

Pedersen, P. (1986). The grief response and injury: A special challenge for athletes and athletic trainers. *Athletic Training, 21,* 312–314.

Perna, F. M., Antoni, M. H., Baum, A., Gordon, P., & Schneiderman, N. (2003). Cognitive behavioral stress management effects on injury and illness among competitive athletes: A randomized clinical trial. *Annals of Behavioral Medicine, 25,* 66–73.

Perna, F., & McDowell, S. (1993, October). *The association of stress and coping with illness and injury among elite athletes*. Paper presented at the annual meeting of the Association for the Advancement of Applied Sport Psychology, Montreal, Quebec.

Peterson, K. (2001). Supporting athletes during injury rehab. *Olympic Coach, 11,* 7–9.

Petitpas, A., Champagne, D., Chartrand, J., Danish, S., & Murphy, S. (1997). *Athlete's guide to career planning*. Champaign, IL: Human Kinetics.

Petitpas, A., & Danish, S. J. (1995). Caring for injured athletes. In S. M. Murphy (Ed.), *Sport psychology interventions* (pp. 255–281). Champaign, IL: Human Kinetics.

Petrie, T. A. (1992). Psychosocial antecedents of athletic injury: The effects of life stress and social support on female collegiate gymnasts. *Behavioral Medicine, 18,* 127–138.

Petrie, T. A. (1993). Coping skills, competitive trait anxiety, and playing status: Moderating effects of the life stress-injury relationship. *Journal of Sport and Exercise Psychology, 15,* 261–274.

Quinn, A. M., & Fallon, B. J. (1999). The changes in psychological characteristics and reactions of elite athletes from injury onset until full recovery. *Journal of Applied Sport Psychology, 11,* 210–229.

Richman, J. M., Hardy, C. J., Rosenfeld, L. B., & Callahan, A. E. (1989). Strategies for enhancing social support networks in sport: A brainstorming experience. *Journal of Applied Sport Psychology, 1,* 150–159.

Ross, M. J., & Berger, R. S. (1996). Effects of stress inoculation training on athletes' postsurgical pain and rehabilitation after orthopedic injury. *Journal of Consulting and Clinical Psychology, 64,* 406–410.

Rotella, R. (1984). Psychological care of the injured athlete. In L. Bunker, R. J. Rotella, & A. S. Reilly (Eds.), *Sport psychology: Psychological considerations in maximizing sport performance*. Ithaca, NY: Mouvement Publications.

Safai, P. (2003). Healing the body in the "Culture of Risk": Examining the negotiation of treatment between sport medicine clinicians and injured athletes from Canadian intercollegiate sport. *Sociology of Sport Journal, 20,* 127–146.

Scherzer, C. B. (1999). *Using psychological skills in rehabilitation following knee surgery*. Unpublished master's thesis, Springfield College, Springfield, MA.

Scherzer, C. B., & Williams, J. M. (2008). Bringing sport psychology into the athletic training room. *Athletic Therapy Today, 13,* 15–17.

Shaffer, S. M. (1992). *Attributions and self-efficacy as predictors of rehabilitative success*. Unpublished master's thesis, University of Illinois, Champaign.

Silva, J. M., & Hardy, C. J. (1991). The sport psychologist: Psychological aspects of injury in sport. In F. O. Mueller & A. Ryan (Eds.), *The sport medicine team and athletic injury prevention* (pp. 114–132). Philadelphia: Davis.

Smith, M. (2007). *Bledsoe retires, ends 14-year career*. Retrieved November 3, 2007, from http://sports.espn.go.com/nfl/news/story?id=2834191.

Smith, R. E., Ptacek, J. T., & Patterson, E. (2000). Moderator effects of cognitive and somatic trait anxiety on the relation between life stress and physical injuries. *Anxiety, Stress & Coping, 13,* 269–288.

Smith, A. M., Scott, S. G., O'Fallon, W. M., & Young, M. L. (1990). Emotional responses of athletes to injury. *Mayo Clinic Proceedings, 65,* 38–50.

Smith, A. M., Scott, S. G., & Wiese, D. M. (1990). The psychological effects of sports injuries. *Sports Medicine, 9,* 352–369.

Smith, R. E., Ptacek, J. T., & Smoll, F. L. (1992). Sensation seeking, stress, and adolescent injuries: A test of stress-buffering, risk-taking, and coping skills hypotheses. *Journal of Personality and Social Psychology, 62,* 1016–1024.

Smith, R. E., Smoll, F. L., & Ptacek, J. T. (1990). Conjunctive moderator variables in vulnerability and resiliency research: Life stress, social support and coping skills, and adolescent sport injuries. *Journal of Personality and Social Psychology, 58,* 360–369.

Sordoni, C., Hall, C., & Forwell, L. (2000). The use of imagery by athletes during injury rehabilitation. *Journal of Sport Rehabilitation, 9,* 329–338.

Stein, H. (1984, September). Brought to his knees. *Sport,* 63–66.

Striegel, D. A., Hedgpeth, E. G., & Sowa, C. J. (1996). Differential psychological treatment of injured athletes based on length of rehabilitation. *Journal of Sport Rehabilitation, 5,* 330–335.

Thompson, N. J., & Morris, R. D. (1994). Predicting injury risk in adolescent football players: The importance of psychological variables. *Journal of Pediatric Psychology, 19,* 415–429.

Tracy, J. (2003). The emotional response to the injury and rehabilitation process. *Journal of Applied Sport Psychology, 15,* 279–293.

Tuffey, S. (1991). The role of athletic trainers in facilitating psychological recovery from athletic injury. *Athletic Training, 26,* 346–351.

Udry, E., Gould, D., Bridges, D., & Beck, L. (1997). Down but not out: Athlete responses to season-ending injuries. *Journal of Sport and Exercise Psychology, 19,* 229–248.

Van Mechelen, W., Twisk, J., Molendijk, A., Blom, B., Snel, J., & Kemper, H. C. G. (1996). Subject-related risk factors for sports injuries: A 1-yr prospective study in young adults. *Medicine and Science in Sports and Exercise, 28,* 1171–1179.

Vergeer, I. (2006). Exploring the mental representation of athletic injury: A longitudinal case study. *Psychology of Sport and Exercise, 7,* 99–114.

Wayda, V. K., Armenth-Brothers, F., & Boyce, B. A. (1998). Goal setting: A key to injury rehabilitation. *Athletic Therapy Today, 3,* 21–25.

Wehlage, D. F. (1980). Managing the emotional reaction to loss in athletics. *Athletic Training, 15,* 144–146.

Wiese-Bjornstal, D. M., Smith, A. M., Shaffer, S. M., & Morrey, M. A. (1998). An integrated model of response to sport injury: Psychological and sociological dynamics. *Journal of Applied Sport Psychology, 10,* 46–69.

Wiese, D. M., & Weiss, M. R. (1987). Psychological rehabilitation and physical injury: Implications for the sport medicine team. *Sport Psychologist, 1,* 318–330.

Williams, J. M. (2001). Psychology of injury risk and prevention. In R. N. Singer, H. A. Hausenblas, & C. M. Janelle (Eds.), *Handbook of research in sport psychology* (2nd ed., pp. 766–786). New York: Wiley.

Williams, J. M., & Andersen, M. B. (1997). Psychosocial influences on central and peripheral vision and reaction time during demanding tasks. *Behavioral Medicine, 26,* 160–167.

Williams, J. M., & Andersen, M. B. (1998). Psychosocial antecedents of sport injury: Review and critique of the stress and injury model. *Journal of Applied Sport Psychology, 10,* 5–25.

Williams, J. M., & Andersen, M. B. (2007). Psychosocial antecedents of sport injury and interventions for risk reduction. In. G. Tenenbaum & R. C. Eklund (Eds.). *Handbook of research in sport psychology* (3rd ed., pp. 379–403), Hoboken, NJ: John Wiley & Sons.

Williams, J. M., Hogan, T. D., & Andersen, M. B. (1993). Positive states of mind and athletic injury risk. *Psychosomatic Medicine, 55,* 468–472.

Williams, J. M., & Roepke, N. (1993). Psychology of injury and injury rehabilitation. In R. N. Singer, M. Murphy, & K. Tennant (Eds.), *Handbook of research in sport psychology* (pp. 815–839). New York: Macmillan.

Williams, J., Tonymon, P., & Wadsworth, W. A. (1986). Relationship of stress to injury in intercollegiate volleyball. *Journal of Human Stress, 12,* 38–43.

Wittig, A. F., & Schurr, K. T. (1994). Psychological characteristics of women volleyball players: Relationships with injuries, rehabilitation, and team success. *Personality and Social Psychology Bulletin, 20,* 322–330.

Yaffe, M. (1983). Sports injuries: Psychological aspects. *British Journal of Hospital Medicine, 27,* 224–232.

Zuckerman, M. (1979). *Sensation seeking: Beyond the optimal level of arousal.* Hillsdale, NJ: Erlbaum.

CHAPTER

24

Career Transition among Athletes: Is There Life after Sports?

Jim Taylor, *San Francisco*
David Lavallee, *Aberystwyth University*

I can't do it physically anymore, and that's really hard for me to say. It's hard to walk away. I can't explain in words how much everyone has meant to me. I'll never be able to fill the void of playing a football game. I don't look at it as a retirement. I look on it as graduation. You graduate from high school and you graduate from college. I'm graduating from pro football.

—John Elway, two-time Super Bowl–winning quarterback

During the course of athletes' careers, the primary focus of most sports administrators, coaches, and sport psychologists is on assisting athletes to maximize their competitive performances. This emphasis is expected, as athletes are their responsibilities during their competitive tenures and, when the athletes leave the team or sport organization, their attention has to turn to the current athletes under their charge. This system, unfortunately, tends to neglect what happens to athletes when they retire and must make the transition to another career and lifestyle.

Fortunately, interest is growing at many levels of sport and among many groups involved in sport in the issue of what has become known as "career transition" (Baillie & Danish, 1992). Popular accounts of this issue over the years have provided anecdotal depictions of professional athletes adjusting to life after sport (Hoffer,

1990). These have most often recounted difficulties that athletes have had following the conclusions of their careers (Bradley, 1976) with a few exceptions of athletes who have had successful transitions (Batten, 1979). These accounts also have suggested that athlete retirement is a pervasive problem, but the accuracy of these observations comes into question because these writings lack empirical rigor and the ability to generalize to the larger population of athletes experiencing the end of their sports careers.

History and Background

The issue of career transition gained the attention of sport psychologists just four decades ago. Leading professionals in the field in Europe such as Miroslav Vanek, Paul Kunath, Ferruccio Antonelli,

Lars-Erik Unestahl, and John Kane, who were consultants for various national teams, began to discuss this issue, describe experiences they had in their work with athletes, and express concern about the athletes' adjustment to a life after sport. Additionally, the media (e.g., Bradley, 1976) and early scholarly, although anecdotal, writings (McPherson, 1980; Ogilvie & Howe, 1982) brought to light some of the significant concerns associated with career transition among athletes. Soon after these preliminary discussions began, research emerged investigating the issues raised by these professionals (e.g., Haerle, 1975; Hill & Lowe, 1974). This research studied the impact of career transition on athletes in different sports and at various levels of competition.

Over time the opportunity to study and address career transition needs of elite athletes has proven to be difficult for a variety of reasons. Typically, trained professionals such as sport psychologists and career counselors have had limited contact with athletes during their competitive careers, much less after they leave their sport. Until recently, sport administrators had little concern for athletes after they retire and sport psychologists rarely had the occasion to evaluate the need for such services to elite athletes. Additionally, the contact time that professionals had with athletes was not conducive to exploration of postcareer concerns. For example, sport psychologists usually work with elite athletes at training camps and competitions, neither of which provide opportunities for discussion of career transition issues.

The divergent perspectives of administrators and coaches with respect to career transition also may have hindered further exploration of these concerns. For example, administrators either didn't see the need for career-transition services for their athletes or were limited because of budgetary constraints. Head coaches may have sabotaged career counseling programs because they interpreted them as distracting the athletes from their primary focus of winning. During the last 20 years, however, national sports federations in countries around the world have been establishing career transition programs for elite athletes (Anderson & Morris, 2000; Sinclair & Hackfort,

2000; Wylleman, Lavallee, & Aflermann, 1999). For example, the Olympic Athlete Career Centre was launched in Canada in 1985 to assist their elite-level athletes in preparing for their life after sport. The United States Olympic Committee initiated the Career Assistance Program for Athletes in 1988 to provide support to retiring athletes during the career transition process. In addition, the Lifeskills for Elite Athletes Program was launched in Australia in 1989, and later merged with the Athlete Career and Education (ACE) Program to provide a consistent career and education service for Australia's elite athletes. Although there is a dearth of research examining the value of these programs, one recent evaluation of the Australian ACE Program has shown that it is effective in assisting active athletes in the areas of career planning and professional development (Gorely, Lavallee, Bruce, Teale, 2001).

Professional sports teams also appear to be responding to these concerns. The players' associations of the National Football League (NFL) and the National Basketball Association (NBA) have recently offered career counseling services to their members. However, the extent to which athletes use these services is unclear. In fact, research indicates that relatively few elite athlete consider postathletic career concerns (Allison & Meyer, 1988; McInally, Cavin-Stice, & Knoth, 1992). It may be that the high salaries accorded these athletes may provide them with a false sense of security.

In recent years, the academic interest in career transitions has expanded. An international special-interest group of the European Federation of Sport Psychology (FEPSAC) has been initiated to exchange information on applied and investigative work in the area, and this organization has published Position Statements on Sports Career Termination and Sports Career Transitions as well as a monograph on the topic (Wylleman et al., 1999). A literature search in 2000 by Lavallee, Wylleman, and Sinclair identified 270 references related to sports career transition, compared with 20 references reported by McPherson in 1980. Although the focus of this chapter is on life after sport for athletes, it is interesting to note that research has also been conducted on the career transitions experiences of coaches (e.g., Lavallee, 2007) and within-career transitions of athletes (e.g., Pummell, Harwood, & Lavallee, in press).

Theoretical Perspectives on Career Transition

Since the onset of interest in the area of career transition for elite athletes, attempts have been made to provide a formal conceptualization of this process. Most investigators have drawn on retirement research outside of sport and tried to apply these models to the concerns of athletes.

Thanatology

Rosenberg (1982) originally suggested that retirement from sports is akin to social death, which is characterized as social isolation and rejection from the former in-group. This explanation has received support from anecdotal and fictitious accounts of athletes who have experienced similar reactions on retirement (Deford, 1981). However, the concept of social death also has been widely criticized and there has been little empirical support for this position (Blinde & Greendorfer, 1985; Blinde & Stratta, 1992).

Social gerontology

This view focuses on aging and considers life satisfaction as being dependent upon characteristics of the sports experience. Six social gerontological perspectives have been offered as the most applicable to sports retirement (Greendorfer & Blinde, 1985; Rosenberg, 1982). Disengagement theory (Cummings, Dean, Newell, & McCaffrey, 1960) posits that the person and society withdraw for the good of both, enabling younger people to enter the workforce and for the retired individuals to enjoy their remaining years. Subculture theory (Rose, 1962) asserts that people can be less active and well-adjusted during retirement even if the situation is different from overall social norms. Activity theory (Havighurst & Albrecht, 1953) suggests that lost roles are replaced by new ones, so that people may maintain their overall level of activity. Continuity theory (Atchley, 1980) states

that, if people have different roles, the time and energy from the earlier role may be reallocated to the remaining roles. Exchange theory (Homans, 1961) was developed to explain how aging individuals rearrange their activities so that their remaining energy generates maximum return. Finally, social breakdown theory (Kuypers & Bengston, 1973) proposes that retirement becomes associated with negative evaluation, which causes individuals to withdraw from the activity and internalize the negative evaluation.

Despite their intuitive appeal, these views have been criticized as inadequate when applied to athletic retirement. Specifically, early research by Arviko (1976), Greendorfer and Blinde (1985), and Lerch (1982) provided little support for any of the social gerontological approaches.

Retirement as transition

A criticism of both thanatology and social gerontology theories is that they view retirement as a singular, abrupt event (Blinde & Greendorfer, 1985). In contrast, other researchers characterize retirement as a transition or process that involves development through life (Stambulova, 1994). Greendorfer and Blinde (1985) suggest that the focus should be on the continuation rather than cessation of behaviors, the gradual alteration rather than relinquishment of goals and interests, and the emergence of few difficulties in adjustment. Data collected from former collegiate athletes support their view of retirement as transition (Blinde & Greendorfer, 1985; Greendorfer & Blinde, 1985).

Building on this perspective, theorists have offered models of career transition considering the specific needs and concerns of the athletic population. Hill and Lowe (1974) applied Sussman's (1971) analytic model to sport, which stressed the roles that personal, social, and environmental factors have in the transition process. Schlossberg (1981) offered a similar model that emphasized athletes' perceptions of the transition, characteristics of the pre- and posttransition environments, and the attributes of the individuals in their roles in the adaptation to the transition. Research by Sinclair and Orlick

(1993) and Swain (1991) have supported this model. Both Hopson and Adams (1977) and Kubler-Ross (1969) also offer models that can help describe the steps through which athletes progress after leaving their sport with a particular emphasis on the emotional implications of career transition.

The Conceptual Model of Career Transition

To continue the evolutionary process in our understanding of career transition among elite athletes, Taylor and Ogilvie (1994) developed a conceptual model that attempted to integrate the theoretical and empirical investigations to date by incorporating aspects of earlier theorizing, taking into account the findings of previous empirical research, and considering their own applied work with athletes in career transition. What emerged was a model that addresses all relevant concerns from the initiation of career transition to its ultimate consequences (see Figure 24-1).

Stage 1: Causes of Career Termination

The causes for termination of an athletic career are found most frequently to be a function of four factors: age, deselection, the consequences of an injury, and free choice. These factors influence a variety of psychological, social, and physical issues that contribute to the likelihood of distress because of career transition.

Age

Age or, more specifically, the decline in performance because of advancing age is a primary cause of retirement. Although anecdotal accounts of former elite athletes underscore the importance of age in retirement, empirical evidence also has shown that a substantial proportion of elite athletes retire because of decreased performance associated with age (e.g., Alfermann, 1995).

The influence of age on career termination is a function of physiological, psychological, and social factors and has significant ramifications for both young and older athletes. For athletes competing in sports in which high-level performance occurs during adolescence, career termination may result when they are still teenagers. This will be particularly evident for those sports such as gymnastics in which puberty, and the accompanying physical changes, can restrict rather than contribute to motor development and performance.

Similar difficulties with older athletes also are evident in sports such as baseball, football, and tennis that require size, strength, and precise motor skills. Athletes' ability to continue to perform at an elite level depends on whether they can maintain their physical capabilities at a competitive level.

Age also has psychological influences on retirement. As athletes become older, they may lose their motivation to train and compete, and they may conclude that they have reached their competitive goals (Werthner & Orlick, 1986). Athletes' values may also change. In an early study, Svoboda and Vanek (1982) found that Czechoslovakian world-class athletes shifted their priorities away from a self-focus involving winning and traveling toward an other-focus with an emphasis on family and friends.

Finally, age possesses a social element. "Aging" athletes, particularly those whose performances begin to diminish, can be devalued by fans, management, media, and other athletes. Sinclair and Orlick (1993) reported that elite-amateur athletes who retired because of declining competitive performance tended to have the most difficulties with loss of status and a lack of self-confidence.

Deselection

One of the most significant contributors to career termination is the nature of the selection process that occurs at every level of competitive sports (Munroe & Albinson, 1996). This process, which follows a Darwinian "survival of the fittest" philosophy, selects only those athletes capable of progressing to the next level of competition and

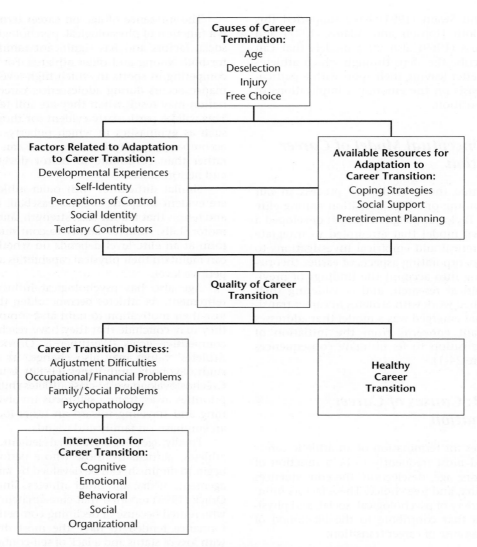

Figure 24-1 **Conceptual model of adaptation to career transition**

disregards those who do not meet the necessary performance criteria. Organized youth programs still place the highest priority on winning and this same philosophy predominates throughout high school, university, and professional sport. Data indicates that only one in 10,000 scholastic athletes receives college scholarships and only 1% of those play professionally. Moreover, the typical career length of a professional player in sports such as football, basketball, and baseball is only 4 to 5 years (National Collegiate Athletic Association, 2003).

Injury

Research has shown that the occurrence of serious or chronic injury often forces athletes to end their athletic careers prematurely (e.g., Allison & Meyer, 1988; Werthner & Orlick, 1986). Furthermore, it has been suggested that severe injuries may result in a variety of psychological difficulties including fear, anxiety, loss of self-esteem, depression, and substance abuse (Ogilvie & Howe, 1982).

Injury also has significant ramifications as retired athletes consider postsport careers. It is not uncommon for elite athletes to leave their sport permanently disabled to varying degrees. These physical disabilities can influence retired athletes negatively, producing a range of psychological and emotional problems. Injuries sustained during their athletic careers also may limit them in their choices of new careers.

Free Choice

An often neglected cause of career termination is that of the free choice of the athlete (Coakley, 1983). Research has indicated that it is a common cause of retirement among elite amateur and professional athletes (Alfermann & Gross, 1997). The impetus to end a career by choice is the most desirable of causes of retirement, because the decision resides wholly within the control of the athlete. Athletes choose to end their careers voluntarily for a variety of personal, social, and sport reasons. Athletes may choose to embark on a new direction in their lives (Lavallee, Grove, & Gordon, 1997). They may experience a change in values, motivations, and the desire to pursue new interests and goals (Greendorfer & Blinde, 1985).

Athletes in career transition may wish to spend more time with family and friends or seek out a new social milieu in which to immerse themselves (Schmid & Schilling, 1997). Lastly, their relationship with their sport also may change, for example, when athletes may have reached their sport-related goals (Sinclair & Orlick, 1993) or found that their sports participation was no longer enjoyable and rewarding (Werthner & Orlick, 1986).

Athletic careers that end voluntarily do not necessarily preclude athletes from having transition difficulties. Kerr and Dacyshyn (2000) reported that some athletes who chose to retire described their retirement as difficult. They also suggested that "voluntary" retirement is not always truly voluntary. Although athletes may decide to retire of their own volition, their decision may be in response to a difficult situation such as conflict with a coach or the high stress of competition.

A similar issue was raised in a study of Australian elite-amateur athletes in which nine causes of retirement emerged: work or study commitments, lost motivation, politics of sport, decrease in performance, finance, decrease in enjoyment, age, injury, and deselection (Lavallee et al., 1997). Although the authors suggested that only the latter three causes were involuntary, all of the causes could be interpreted as outside of the control of the athletes. For example, the athletes retired because of dissatisfaction (the politics of sport), a forced change in priorities (work or study commitments, finance), or a decline in competitiveness (a decrease in performance). The athletes who seemed to have retired voluntarily may be more appropriately characterized as "reluctant dropouts" (Kerr & Dacyshyn, 2000).

Other Causes of Career Termination

Other factors have been either suggested or report-ed to contribute to career termination. These causes include family reasons (Mihovilovic, 1968), problems with coaches or the sports organization (Werthner & Orlick, 1986), and financial difficulties (Lavallee et al., 1997).

Stage 2: Factors Related to Adaptation to Career Transition

Athletes experiencing career transition may face a wide range of psychological, social, financial, and occupational changes. The extent of these changes and how athletes perceive them may dictate the quality of the adaptation they experience as a function of their retirement.

Developmental contributors.   The presence and quality of adaptation to career transition may depend on developmental experiences that occurred since the inception of their athletic careers. The nature of these experiences will affect the emergence of self-perceptions and interpersonal skills that will influence how athletes adapt to retirement.

The often single-minded pursuit of excellence that accompanies elite sports participation has potential psychological and social dangers, and this quest is rooted in the earliest experiences athletes have in their youth sports participation. The personal investment in and the pursuit of elite athletic success, although a worthy goal, may lead to a restricted development.

Although there is substantial evidence demonstrating the debilitating effects of deselection self-esteem among young athletes (e.g., Alfermann,1995; Webb, Nasco, Riley, & Headrick, 1998), little consideration has been given to changing this process in a healthier direction. Most organized youth programs still appear to place the highest priority on winning with less concern for the positive development of young athletes.

To alleviate these difficulties at their source, the adoption of a more holistic approach to sports development can be beneficial early in the lives of athletes (Pearson & Petitpas, 1990; Petitpas & Champagne, 2000). This perspective relies on a primary prevention model that emphasizes preventing problems prior to their occurrence (Conyne, 1987). The first step in the prevention process is to engender in parents and coaches involved in youth sport a belief that long-term personal and social development is more important than short-term athletic success (Ogilvie, 1987).

Self-identity.   Most fundamental of the psychological issues that influence adaptation to career transition is the degree to which athletes define their self-worth in terms of their participation and achievement in sports (Blinde & Greendorfer, 1985; Svoboda & Vanek, 1982). Athletes who have been immersed in their sport to the exclusion of other activities will have a self-identity that is composed almost exclusively of their sports involvement (Brewer, Van Raalte, &

Petitpas, 2000). Without the input from their sport, retired athletes have little to support their sense of self-worth (Pearson & Petitpas, 1990).

Athletes who are disproportionately invested in their sports participation may be characterized as "unidimensional" people, in which their self-concept does not extend far beyond the limits of their sport (Coakley, 1983; Ogilvie & Howe, 1982). These athletes often have few options in which they can gain meaning and fulfillment from activities outside their sport (McPherson, 1980). A one-year longitudinal study by Stephen and colleagues (Stephen, Bilard, Ninot, & Dilignieres, 2003) found that perceieved physical condition, physical self-worth, and global self-esteem decreased during the first six months of transition out of elite sport. This was subsequently followed by a period of increase in these dimensions, as well as in perceived sports competence and physical strength.

It has been suggested that athletes with overly developed athletic identities are less prepared for postsport careers (Baillie & Danish, 1992), have restricted career and educational plans (Blann, 1985), and typically experience retirement from sport as something very important that is lost and can never be recovered (Werthner & Orlick, 1986).

Grove, Lavallee, and Gordon (1997) found that athletes who overly identified with their sports careers were most vulnerable to transition distress. Finally, how effectively athletes adapted their identities in a healthy way following retirement is necessary to a positive reaction to distress over career termination (Lavallee et al., 1997).

Kerr and Dacyshyn (2000) suggest that the demands athletic retirement places on adolescent athletes can be excessive and destructive. Instead of adolescence being a time of identity formation (Erikson, 1963), it can actually be deconstructed, which may slow the identity-formation process. They further assert that transition of young female athletes can be particularly difficult. Retirement at an early age, which is common among female athletes such as gymnasts, figure skaters, and swimmers, inhibits their ability to try out different roles and relationships, interferes with the development of autonomy and decision-making skills (Chickering & Reisser,

1993), and can distort perceptions related to body weight, body image, and eating habits (Piphers, 1994). They conclude that these issues have the cumulative effect of interfering with the healthy development of a mature self-identity in young female athletes.

Perceived control.   Central to the issue of perceived control in career transition is whether athletes chose to leave their sport or were forced to retire (Kerr & Dacyshyn, 2000; Lavallee et al., 1997). The degree of perceived control that the athletes have with respect to the end of their careers also can impact how they respond to career transition (McPherson, 1980). Of the four primary causes of athletic retirement discussed earlier, namely, age, deselection, injury, and free choice, the first three are predominantly outside the control of the individual athlete (Lavallee et al., 1997). This absence of control related to an event so intrinsically connected to athletes' self-identities may create a situation that is highly aversive and threatening (Lavallee & Robinson, 2007).

Both early and contemporary research examining Olympic-caliber and professional athletes has indicated that the causes of retirement for many athletes were beyond their control and that they experienced a decrease in their sense of personal control following retirement (Mihovilovic, 1968; Svoboda & Vanek, 1982; Webb et al., 1998). Although this issue has not been addressed extensively in the sports literature, there is considerable research from the areas of clinical, social, and physiological psychology demonstrating that perceived control is related to many areas of human functioning including a sense of self-competence and the interpretation of self and other information. In addition, perceptions of control may influence individuals' feelings of helplessness, motivation, physiological changes, and self-confidence. Loss of control has been associated with a variety of pathologies including depression, anxiety, substance abuse, and dissociative disorders.

Social identity.   The diversity of athletes' social identities can affect their adaptation to career transition (Gorbett, 1985). Researchers have associated retirement with a loss of status and social identity (Tuckman & Lorge, 1953). McPherson (1980) suggests that many athletes define themselves in terms of their popular status, although this recognition is typically short-lived. As a result, retired athletes may question their self-worth and feel the need to regain the lost public esteem (Webb et al., 1998).

In addition, athletes whose socialization process occurred primarily in the sports environment may be characterized as "role restricted" (Ogilvie & Howe, 1982). That is, these athletes have only learned to assume certain social roles specific to the athletic setting and are only able to interact with others within the narrow context of sports. As a result, their ability to assume other roles following retirement may be severely inhibited (Blinde & Greendorfer, 1985). Studies by Chamalidis (1997), Haerle (1975), Mihovilovic (1968), and Werthner and Orlick (1986) indicate that athletes with a broad-based social identity that includes family, friendship, and educational and occupational components demonstrated better adaptation following sports career termination. Recent research examining the career transition process for teams (Danish, Owens, Green, & Brunelle, 1997; Zaichkowsky, King, & McCarthy, 2000) also highlights similar issues with regard to social identity.

Tertiary contributors.   In addition to the above intrapersonal factors, personal, social, and environmental variables may influence athletes' adaptation to retirement. These factors may be viewed as potential stressors whose presence will likely exacerbate the primary adaptive factors just discussed (Coakley, 1983).

Socioeconomic status may influence the adaptation process (Menkehorst & van den Berg, 1997). Athletes who are financially dependent on their sports participation and possess few skills to earn a living outside of sport or have limited financial resources to fall back on may perceive retirement as more threatening and, as a result, may evidence distress (Lerch, 1982; McPherson, 1980; Werthner & Orlick, 1986).

It also has been argued that minority status (Blinde & Greendorfer, 1985; Hill & Lowe, 1974) and gender (Coakley, 1983) will affect the adaptation process because of what are perceived as fewer postathletic career opportunities (Haerle, 1975). These factors are likely to be most significant when interacting with socioeconomic status and preretirement planning. The health of athletes at the time of retirement will further affect the quality of the adaptation (Gorbett, 1985; Hill & Lowe, 1974). Athletes with chronic disabilities incurred during athletic careers may, as a result of the injuries, have limited choices in their postathletic careers. Also, marital status, as an aspect of social support, will influence the adaptation process (Curtis & Ennis, 1988). Athlete characteristics including age, years competing, and level of attainment also will influence adaptation in the retirement process.

Stage 3: Available Resources for Adaptation to Career Transition

Athletes' adaptation to career transition depends largely on the resources they have available to surmount the difficulties that arise. Two of the most important factors that can influence people's ability to respond effectively to these problems include coping skills (Lazarus & Folkman, 1984; Meichenbaum, 1996) and social support (Sarason & Sarason, 1986). In addition, research indicates that another valuable resource, preretirement planning, may significantly influence adaptation to career transition (Parker, 1994; Pearson & Petitpas, 1990).

Coping strategies. During the course of retirement, athletes are faced with dramatic changes in their personal, social, and occupational lives. These changes will affect them cognitively, emotionally, and behaviorally. The quality of the adaptation to career transition athletes experience will depend on the manner in which they respond to these changes. The availability of effective coping strategies may facilitate this process and reduce the likelihood of difficulties. Sinclair and Orlick (1993) reported that finding another focus of interest to replace their sports participation, keeping busy, maintaining their training and exercise regimens, talking with

someone who listens, and staying in touch with their sport and friends in their sport were effective coping strategies for facilitating the transition process.

Cognitively, retiring athletes must alter their perceptions related to the career transition process, specifically with respect to self-identity, perceived control, and social identity (Williams-Rice, 1996). Athletes can use cognitive restructuring (Lazarus, 1972) and mental imagery (Smith, 1980) to reorient their thinking in a more positive direction, self-instructional training (Meichenbaum, 1996) to improve attention and problem solving, and goal setting to provide direction and motivation in their postathletic careers (Bruning & Frew, 1987). These techniques have been used successfully to enhance adaptation in a variety of populations and activities (Meichenbaum & Cameron, 1973).

Similarly, relevant techniques could be used for emotional and physiological stressors. Specifically, athletes in transition could employ anger and anxiety strategies such as time-out (Browning, 1983), relaxation training (May, House, & Kovacs, 1982), and health, exercise, and nutritional counseling (Bruning & Frew, 1987) to alleviate these difficulties. Finally, a regimen of behavior modification could deal with overt manifestations of distress associated with career transition. Techniques such as assertiveness training (Lange & Jakubowski, 1976), time management training (Bruning & Frew, 1987), and skills assessment and development (Taylor, 1987) could be effective in overcoming behavioral difficulties caused by retirement.

One study of elite athletes reported that commonly used coping strategies included acceptance, positive reinterpretation, planning, active coping, and seeking social support (Grove et al., 1997). These researchers also found that athletes who had strong athletic identities tended to use avoidance-based coping strategies such as denial, mental and behavioral disengagement, and venting of emotions rather than more problem-focused techniques. Lally (2007) has also found that athletes who proactively dimished their athletic identity prior to retirement were able to adjust better following their career termination.

This evidence, suggesting that athletes in transitions may employ various coping strategies as a function of their self-identity, provides a link between Step 2 and Step 3 of the present model.

Social support.   Because of athletes' total psychological and social immersion in the sports world, the majority of their friends, acquaintances, and other associations are found in the sports environment and their social activities often revolve around their athletic lives (Petitpas & Champagne, 2000). Thus, athletes' primary social support system often will be derived from their athletic involvement (Coakley, 1983; Rosenfeld, Richman, & Hardy, 1989).

When the athletes' careers end, they are no longer an integral part of the team or organization. Consequently, the social support that they received previously may no longer be present. In a sample of athletes with international competitive experience, Sinclair and Orlick (1993) reported that missing the social aspects of their sport was a frequently reported difficulty during career transition. Moreover, because of their restricted social identity and the absence of alternative social support systems, they may become isolated, lonely, and unsustained socially, thus leading to significant distress (Alfermann, 1995; Blinde & Greendorfer, 1985; Schmid & Schilling, 1997).

Ungerleider (1997) reported that ex-Olympic athletes received support from coaches, parents, and significant others. In addition, the 20% of athletes who reported experiencing serious difficulties following career termination received help from a mental health professional. Another study of retired world-class athletes indicated that they received considerable support from family and friends and little institutional support from the national governing body or their former coaches (Sinclair & Orlick, 1993). In a study of retiring disabled athletes, Wheeler, Malone, Van Vlack, and Nelson (1996) found that retirement was facilitated by having family interests outside of sport.

Preretirement planning. Of the available resources that are being discussed, preretirement planning appears to have the broadest influence on the quality of the career transition process (Murphy, 1995). Preretirement planning may include a variety of activities including continuing education, occupational and investment opportunities, and social networking. As a result, preretirement planning may significantly affect most of the factors previously discussed that are related to the adaptation process. For example, preretirement planning has been found to broaden an athlete's self-identity, enhance perceptions of control, and diversify his or her social identity (Lavallee & Robinson, 2007). As for the tertiary contributors, socioeconomic status, financial dependency on the sport, and postathletic occupational potential would all be positively influenced. Substantial research involving both elite-amateur and professional athletes supports this position (e.g., Haerle, 1975; Sinclair & Orlick, 1993).

Perna, Ahlgren, and Zaichkowsky (1999) found that collegiate athletes who could state a postcollegiate occupational plan indicated significantly more life satisfaction that those who did not have such a plan. Similarly, disabled athletes have indicated that their retirement was easier if they had job interests outside of sport (Martin, 1996; Wheeler et al., 1996).

Despite these benefits, a common theme that emerges from the literature on retirement outside of sports is the resistance on the part of individuals to plan for their lives after the end of their careers (Petitpas & Champagne, 2000). Gorely et al. (2001) found that athletes often do not consider their career termination until it draws near. Yet, it is likely that this denial of the inevitable will have serious, potentially negative, and long-term implications for the athletes. A wide range of difficulties have been reported because of athletes' resistance to preretirement planning.

Structured preretirement planning that involves reading materials and workshops (Anderson & Morris, 2000) is a valuable opportunity for athletes to plan for and work toward meaningful lives following retirement. In addition, effective money management and long-term financial planning can provide athletes with financial stability following the conclusion of their careers (Menkehorst & van den Berg, 1997).

Increasingly, the incorporation of preretirement planning is becoming a part of collegiate, elite-amateur, and professional organizations (Sinclair & Hackfort, 2000). The research clarifying the extent to which elite athletes use these services indicates that only a small proportion take advantage of them (Gorely et al., 2001; Sinclair & Orlick, 1993). There is also still no empirical evidence of how effective these programs are for athletes in career transition.

Stage 4: Quality of Career Transition

Based on the present model to this point, it may be concluded that career transition from sports will not necessarily cause a distressful reaction on the part of athletes (Coakley, 1983). Rather, the quality of athletes' adaptation to career transition will depend on the previous steps of the retirement process. It is at the point of retiring that the athlete's reaction to career transition will become evident. A variety of psychological, social, and environmental factors will determine the nature of the athlete's response. Specifically, the presence or absence of the contributing variables described in the early steps of the model will dictate whether athletes undergo a healthy transition following retirement or experience distress in response to the end of their competitive career.

The question is often raised as to the incidence of those individual athletes who exhibit some form of distress when forced from their sport. In fact, the extant literature has not produced widespread evidence of transition difficulties at all levels of sports participation. Notably, there is little evidence of distress in athletes concluding their scholastic and collegiate careers (Williams-Rice, 1996). This may be because of the fact that the completion of high school and college athletic careers as dictated by eligibility restrictions may be seen as a natural part of the transition to entering college or the workforce, respectively (Coakley, 1983).

At the same time, another group of researchers assert that career transition may cause distress that manifests itself in a wide variety of disruptive ways. Sinclair and Orlick (1993), for example, reported that about one-third of a sample of elite-amateur athletes experienced fair to serious problems with missing the social aspects of their sport, job-school pressures, and finances. In addition, 11% felt dissatisfied with their lives since retirement and 15% felt that they did not handle the transition well.

Kerr and Dacyshyn (2000) reported that 70% of their sample of elite female gymnasts experienced distress when their careers ended. These athletes described feelings of disorientation, void, and frustration, and struggled with issues such as self-identity, personal control, and body image. A review of 12 studies, which included 2,665 athletes representing a wide range of sports and participation levels, also has reported that 20% of the athletes studied required considerable psychological adjustment on their career termination (Lavallee, Nesti, Borkoles, Cockerill, & Edge, 2000).

Other researchers over the years also have reported more serious manifestations of transition difficulties consisting of incidences of alcohol and drug abuse, participation in criminal activities, and significant anxiety, acute depression, and other emotional problems following retirement (e.g., Chamalidis, 1997; Mihovilovic, 1968). The emergence of distress among elite-amateur and professional athletes is likely because of the significantly greater life investment in their sports and their commitment to their sports participation as a career into adulthood.

Stage 5: Intervention for Career Transition

Career transition may be characterized as a complex interaction of stressors. Whether the stressors are financial, social, psychological, or physical, their effects may produce some form of distress when athletes are confronted with the end of their careers. Despite the best efforts made in the prevention of career transition distress, difficulties may still arise when the reality of the end of an athletic career is recognized. The experience of career transition crises may adversely affect athletes cognitively, emotionally, behaviorally, and socially. As a result, it is important to address each of these areas in an active and constructive manner.

Unfortunately, as discussed earlier, there are significant organizational obstacles to the proper treatment of career transition difficulties (Sinclair & Hackfort, 2000; Thomas & Ermler, 1988). In particular, the limited involvement of sport psychologists at the elite level, where problems are most likely to occur, inhibits their ability to provide for the career transition needs of athletes. Also, the team psychologists typically associated with national governing bodies, collegiate teams, or professional organizations rarely have the opportunity to develop an extended relationship with team members. This limited contact rarely presents an opportunity to discuss issues related to career transition. Also, because retired athletes are no longer a part of a sports organization, treatment of the athletes may not be seen as being within the purview of the organization's psychologist (Sinclair & Hackfort, 2000).

The retiring athletes themselves also may present their own obstacles to intervention. Surveys of former world-class amateur athletes indicate that they do not perceive personal counseling as a useful coping strategy during the career transition process (e.g., Sinclair & Orlick, 1993).

The treatment of distress related to career transition may occur at a variety of levels. As discussed earlier, the changes that result from retirement may detrimentally impact a person psychologically, emotionally, behaviorally, and socially. As a consequence, it is necessary for the sport psychologist to address each of these areas in the intervention process.

Perhaps the most important task in the transition process is to assist athletes in maintaining their sense of self-worth when establishing a new self-identity. The goal of this process is to adapt their perceptions about themselves and their world to their new roles in a way that will be maximally functional. The sport psychologist can assist them in identifying desirable nonsport identities and experiencing feelings of value and self-worth in this new personal conception. Van Raalte and Andersen (2007) have explained that people intimately involved in sport (sport psychologists included) may have a prejudice toward sport relative to other possible activities or goals. Because this bias may influence how sport psychologists listen to, interpret, and formulate athlete cases, they suggest that practitioners need to carefully manage bias.

Also, sport psychologists can aid athletes in working through any emotional distress they may experience during retirement (Grove, Lavallee, Gordon, & Harvey, 1998). Specifically, they can provide the athletes with the opportunity to express feelings of doubt, concern, or frustration relative to the end of their careers (Gorbett, 1985). Constantine (1995) reported that a group counseling experience comprised of supportive counseling techniques and psychoeducational exercises for retired female collegiate athletes who were experiencing adjustment difficulties indicated higher levels of satisfaction from participation in the group. Lavallee (2005) also has evaluated the effectiveness of a life development intervention on career transition adjustment in retired professional athletes. Intervention and control groups were recruited for this study, both of which contained recently retired male professional soccer players. Results revealed significant post-intervention treatment group differences on career transition adjustment in favor of the life development intervention.

On a manifest level, the sport psychologist can help the athletes cope with the stress of the transition process (Gorbett, 1985). Traditional therapeutic strategies such as cognitive restructuring (Garfield & Bergin, 1978), stress management (Meichenbaum & Jaremko, 1983), and emotional expression (Yalom, 1980) can be used in this process. It also has been recommended that Shapiro's (1995) eye movement desensitization and reprocessing (EMDR) can be employed as a psychomotor technique to ameliorate undesirable beliefs and images associated with career-ending injuries (Sime, 1998). Also, athletes can be shown that the skills they used to master their sport can be used as effectively in overcoming the challenges of a new career and lifestyle (Meichenbaum & Jaremko, 1983).

Grove et al. (1998) have adapted Horowitz's (1986) model of coping with loss to retirement from sport. This perspective stresses a working-through process in the form of the construction of a narrative about the career termination experience, termed *account-making*. This account enables athletes to better understand their career transition, allows them to gain closure on their athletic careers, and encourages the adoption of an evolving self- and social identity that will foster growth in their postathletic lives. Preliminary research indicates that account-making was directly related to athletes' success in coping with career termination (Lavallee et al., 1997).

Finally, the professional can help athletes at a social level. This goal may be accomplished by having athletes explore ways of broadening their social identity and role repertoire (Brewer et al., 2000). Additionally, athletes can be encouraged to expand their social support system to individuals and groups outside of the sports arena. The use of group therapy and the articulation of the athletes' potential social networks can be especially useful in aiding them in this process. Wolff and Lester (1989) propose a three-stage therapeutic process comprised of listening and confrontation, cognitive therapy, and vocational guidance to aid athletes in coping with their loss of self-identity and assist them in establishing a new identity.

Little empirical research has examined the significant factors in this process. Outside of sport, Roskin (1982) found that implementing a package of cognitive, affective, and social support interventions within didactic and small-group settings significantly reduced depression and anxiety among a high-stress group of individuals composed partly of retirees. Advances in the measurement of career transitions in sport in recent years, however, can assist practitioners, including the development of the *Athletes' Retirement Decision Inventory* (Fernandez, Stephen, & Fouquereau, 2006), *Retirement Sports Survey* (Alfermann, Stambulova, & Zemaityte 2004), *British Athletes Lifestyle Assessment Needs in Career and Education* (BALANCE) *Scale, Athlete Retirement Questionnaire* (Sinclair & Orlick, 1993), *Australian Athletes Career Transition Inventory* (Hawkins & Blann, 1993), and *Professional Athletes Career Transition Inventory* (Blann & Zaichkowsky, 1989).

Intervention at the organizational level also can be a useful means of facilitating the career transition process. As indicated earlier, many elite-amateur and professional organizations offer some form of preretirement and career transition assistance. Reece, Wilder, and Mahanes (1996) suggest that such programs should emphasize the transferability of skills from sport to a new career. They further highlight the importance of identifying specific transferable skills and successful role models, and clarifying interests, values, and goals that will promote an effective career transition.

Sinclair and Orlick (1993) also support intervention at the organizational level as having a positive impact on career transitions of elite athletes. They recommend that sports organizations can facilitate the transition process by continuing financial support for a short time following retirement, encourage sports organizations to stay in contact with retired athletes, offer seminars on career transition issues, and establish a resource center for athletes in transition. Additionally, sports organizations should provide retired athletes with opportunities to stay involved in their sport and show them how mental skills training can be used in their new pursuits (Sinclair & Hackfort, 2000).

Summary

This chapter has reviewed the relevant literature pertaining to career transition among athletes. From this overview, several conclusions can be drawn. First, the extant research suggests that career transition difficulties are more likely to emerge with elite-amateur and professional athletes than with scholastic or collegiate athletes. This finding appears to be because of the greater ego-involvement and personal investment of the former group of athletes and because transition from world-class and professional sports participation typically occurs outside of the normal developmental process. Second, distress because of career transition will not necessarily occur. Rather, problems emerge because of a variety of developmental, psychological, and social factors including early life experiences, coping strategies, perceptions of control, self and social identities, social support, and preretirement planning. Third, addressing career transition issues can begin at the earliest stages of sports participation. This process involves having parents, coaches, and youth sports administrators create an environment that will enable young athletes' sports involvement to be a meaningful vehicle that will engender healthy personal and social development. Finally, despite the best efforts to eliminate distress that may arise because of career transition, it may still occur when athletes fully recognize that their sports careers are over. This distress can manifest itself psychologically, emotionally, behaviorally, and socially. It is important that each of these areas is addressed directly and constructively by a trained professional.

Study Questions

1. Compare the Eastern European and Western methods of athlete development and their implications for career transition.

2. Briefly describe the causes of career termination and indicate how each factor would affect athletes' adaptation to career transition.

3. Discuss the most prevalent factors to adaptation to career transition.

4. Discuss the interpersonal factors that affect athletes' reactions to career transition and how they are related to the athletes' adaptation.

5. Indicate the role that early development has on athletes' reactions to career transition and give an example of an ideal upbringing for healthy transition.

6. Describe the three primary resources available to athletes to help them during the career transition process and give examples of how they influence retiring athletes.

7. Discuss the difficulties that retiring athletes most often experience and what types of athletes are most likely to have these difficulties.

8. Provide the primary areas that sport psychologists must address in working with a retiring athlete and describe some of the techniques that could be used.

Situation Study

Sarah is a 25-year-old softball player who was informed earlier in the week that she was not selected for the Olympic Team. In terms of her deselection, she does not think that it is fair that the selectors suddenly decided that she could no longer do what she had trained so long and hard for. Sarah feels very frustrated and angry because this was going to be her first Olympics, and she is also disappointed that she will not compete alongside her teammates, who are some of her best friends. She also is concerned about what she is going to do next, as her philosophy has always been that she shouldn't concentrate on anything other than softball if she wanted to be the best and retain her place on the team.

1. *Based on the model presented in this chapter, what kind of reaction might you expect from her and why?*
2. *What are the primary issues that might affect the quality of her retirement?*
3. *What could she have done to alter her reaction?*
4. *Create an intervention plan to help Sarah through her transition.*

References

Alfermann, D. (1995). Career transitions of elite athletes: Drop-out and retirement. In R. Vanfraechem-Raway & Y. Vanden Auweele (Eds.), *Proceedings of the 9th European Congress of Sport Psychology* (pp. 828–833). Brussels: European Federation of Sports Psychology.

Alfermann, D., & Gross, A. (1997). Coping with career termination: It all depends on freedom of choice. In R. Lidor & M. Bar-Eli (Eds.), *Proceedings of the IX World Congress on Sport Psychology* (pp. 65–67). Netanya, Israel: International Society of Sport Psychology.

Alfermann, D., Stambulova, N., & Zemaityte, A. (2004). Reactions to sports career termination: A cross-cultural comparison of German, Lithuanian, and Russian athletes. *Psychology of Sport and Exercise, 5,* 61–75.

Allison, M. T., & Meyer, C. (1988). Career problems and retirement among elite athletes: The female tennis professional. *Sociology of Sport Journal, 5,* 212–222.

Anderson, D., & Morris, T. (2000) Athlete lifestyle programs. In D. Lavallee and P. Wylleman (Eds.), *Career transitions in sport: International perspectives* (pp. 59–81). Morgantown, WV: Fitness Information Technology.

Arviko, I. (1976). *Factors influencing the job and life satisfaction of retired baseball players.* Unpublished master's thesis, University of Waterloo, Ontario.

Atchley, R. C. (1980). *The social forces in later life.* Belmont, CA: Wadsworth.

Baillie, P. H. F., & Danish, S. J. (1992). Understanding the career transition of athletes. *The Sport Psychologist, 6,* 77–98.

Bandura, A. (1977). Self-efficacy: Toward a unifying theory of behavior change. *Psychological Review, 84*, 191–215.

Batten, J. (1979, April). After the cheering stops can athletes create new life in the business world? *Financial Post Magazine*, pp. 14–20.

Blann, F. W. (1985). Intercollegiate athletic competition and students' educational and career plans. *Journal of College Student Personnel, 26*, 115–119.

Blann, F. W., & Zaichkowsky, L. (1989). *National Hockey League and Major League Baseball players' post sports career transition surveys*. Final report prepared for the National Hockey League Players' Association, USA.

Blinde, E. M., & Greendorfer, S. L. (1985). A reconceptualization of the process of leaving the role of competitive athlete. *International Review of Sport Sociology, 20*, 87–94.

Blinde, E. M., & Stratta, T. M. (1992). The "sport career death" of college athletes: Involuntary and unanticipated sports exits. *Journal of Sport Behavior, 15*, 3–20.

Bradley, B. (1976). *Life on the run*. New York: Quadrangle/The New York Times.

Brewer, B. W., Van Raalte, J. L., & Petitpas, A. J. (2000) Self-identity issues in sport career transitions. In D. Lavallee & P. Wylleman (Eds.), *Career transitions in sport: International perspectives* (pp. 29–43). Morgantown, WV: Fitness Information Technology.

Browning, E. R. (1983). A memory pacer for improving stimulus generalization. *Journal of Autism and Developmental Disorders, 13*, 427–432.

Bruning, N. S., & Frew, D. R. (1987). Effects of exercise, relaxation, and management skills on physiological stress indicators: A field experiment. *Journal of Applied Psychology, 72*, 515–521.

Chamalidis, P. (1997). Identity conflicts during and after retirement from top-level sports. In R. Lidor & M. Bar-Eli (Eds.), *Proceedings of the IX World Congress of Sport Psychology* (pp. 191–193). Netanya, Israel: International Society of Sport Psychology.

Chartrand, J. M., & Lent, R. W. (1987). Sports counselling: Enhancing the development of the student-athlete. *Journal of Counseling and Development, 66*, 164–167.

Chickering, A., & Reisser, L. (1993). *Education and identity* (2nd ed.). San Francisco: Jossey-Bass.

Coakley, J. J. (1983). Leaving competitive sport: Retirement or rebirth. *Quest, 35*, 1–11.

Curtis, J., & Ennis, R. (1988). Negative consequences of leaving competitive sport? Comparison findings for former elite-level hockey players. *Sociology of Sport Journal, 5*, 87–106.

Danish, S. J., Owens, S. S., Green, S. L., & Brunelle, J. P. (1997). Building bridges for disengagement: The transition process for individuals and teams. *Journal of Applied Sport Psychology, 9*, 154–167.

Deford, F. (1981). *Everybody's All-American*. New York: The Viking Press.

Erikson. E. (1963). *Childhood and society*. New York: Norton.

Fernandez, A., Stephan, Y., & Fouquereau, E. (2006). Assessing reasons for sports career termination: Developing the Athletes' Retirement Decision Inventory. *Psychology of Sport and Exercise, 7*, 407–421.

Garfield, S., & Bergin, A. (1978). *Handbook of psychotherapy and behavior change: An empirical analysis* (2nd ed.). New York: Wiley.

Gorbett, F. J. (1985). Psycho-social adjustment of athletes to retirement. In L. K. Bunker, R. J. Rotella, & A. Reilly (Eds.), *Sport psychology: Psychological considerations in maximizing sport performance* (pp. 288–294). Ithaca, NY: Mouvement Publications.

Gorely, T., Lavallee, D., Bruce, D., & Teale, B. (2001). An Evaluation of the Athlete Career and Education Program. *Athletic Academic Journal, 15,* 11–21.

Greendorfer, S. L., & Blinde, E. M. (1985). "Retirement" from intercollegiate sport: Theoretical and empirical considerations. *Sociology of Sport Journal, 2,* 101–110.

Grove, J. R., Lavallee, D., & Gordon, S. (1997). Coping with retirement from sport: The influence of athletic identity. *Journal of Applied Sport Psychology, 9,* 191–203.

Grove, J. R., Lavallee, D., Gordon, S., & Harvey, J. H. (1998). Account-making: A model of understanding and resolving distressful reactions to retirement from sport. *The Sport Psychologist, 12,* 52–67.

Haerle, R. K., Jr. (1975). Career patterns and career contingencies of professional baseball players: An occupational analysis. In D. Ball & J. Loy (Eds.), *Sport and social order* (pp. 461–519). Reading, MA: Addison-Wesley.

Havighurst, R. J., & Albrecht, R. (1953). *Older people.* New York: Longmans, Green.

Hawkins, K., & Blann, F. W. (1993). *Athlete/coach career development and transition.* Canberra: Australian Sports Commission.

Hill, P., & Lowe, B. (1974). The inevitable metathesis of the retiring athlete. *International Review of Sport Sociology, 4,* 5–29.

Hoffer, R. (1990, December 3). Magic's kingdom. *Sports Illustrated,* 106–110.

Homans, G. (1961). *Social behavior: Its elementary forms.* New York: Harcourt Brace Javanovich.

Hopson, B., & Adams, J. (1977). Toward an understanding of transition: Defining some boundaries of transition. In J. Adams & B. Hopson (Eds.), *Transition: Understanding and managing personal change* (pp. 3–25). Montclair, NJ: Allenhald & Osmund.

Horowitz, M. J. (1986). *Stress response syndromes* (2nd ed.). Northvale, NJ: Jason Aronson.

Kerr, G., & Dacyshyn, A. (2000). The retirement experiences of elite, female gymnasts. *Journal of Applied Sport Psychology, 12,* 115–133.

Kubler-Ross, E. (1969). *On death and dying.* New York: Macmillan.

Kuypers, J. A., & Bengston, V. L. (1973). Social breakdown and competence: A model of normal aging. *Human Development, 16,* 181–120.

Lally, P. (2007). Identity and athletic retirement: A prospective study. *Psychology of Sport and Exercise, 8,* 85–99.

Lange, A. J., & Jakubowski, P. (1976). *Responsible assertive behavior.* Champaign, IL: Research Press.

Lavallee, D., Gordon, S., & Grove, J. R. (1997). Retirement from sport and the loss of athletic identity. *Journal of Personal and Interpersonal Loss, 2,* 129–147.

Lavallee, D., Grove, J. R., & Gordon, S. (1997). The causes of career termination from sport and their relationship to post-retirement adjustment among elite-amateur athletes in Australia. *Australian Psychologist, 32,* 131–135.

Lavallee, D., Nesti, M., Borkoles, E., Cockerill, I., & Edge, A. (2000). Intervention strategies for athletes in transition. In D. Lavallee & P. Wylleman (Eds.), *Career transitions in sport: International perspectives* (pp. 111–130). Morgantown, WV: Fitness Information Technology.

Lavallee, D., & Robinson, H. (2007). In pursuit of an identity: A qualitative exploration of retirement from women's artistic gymnastics. *Psychology of Sport and Exercise, 8,* 119–141.

Lavallee, D., & Wylleman, P. (1999). Toward an instrument to assess the quality of adjustment to career transitions in sport: The British Athlete Lifestyle Assessment Needs in Career and Education (BALANCE) Scale. In V. Hosek, P. Tilinger, & L.Bilek (Eds.), *Psychology of sport and exercise: Enhancing the quality of life* (pp. 322–324). Prague: Charles University.

Lavallee, D., Wylleman, P., & Sinclair, D. A. (2000). Career transitions in sport: An annotated bibliography. In D. Lavallee & P. Wylleman (Eds.), *Career transitions in sport: International perspectives* (pp. 207–258). Morgantown, WV: Fitness Information Technology.

Lazarus, A. A. (1972). *Clinical behavior therapy.* New York: Brunner/Mazel.

Lazarus, A. (1972). *Behavior theory and beyond.* New York: McGraw-Hill.

Lazarus, R. S. (1975). The self-regulation of emotion. In L. Levi (Ed.), *Emotions—Their parameters and measurement* (pp. 47–68). New York: Ravel.

Lazarus, R. S., & Folkman, S. (1984). *Stress, appraisal, and coping.* New York: Springer.

Lerch, S. H. (1982). Athletic retirement as social death: An overview. In N. Theberge & P. Donnelly (Eds.), *Sport and the sociological imagination* (pp. 259–272). Fort Worth: Texas Christian University Press.

Manion, U. V. (1976). Preretirement counseling: The need for a new approach, *Personnel and Guidance Journal, 55,* 119–121.

Martin, J. J. (1996). Transitions out of competitive sport for athletes with disabilities. *Therapeutic Recreation Journal, 30,* 128–136.

May, E., House, W. C., & Kovacs, K. V. (1982). Group relaxation therapy to improve coping with stress. *Psychotherapy: Theory, research and practice, 19,* 102–109.

McInally, L., Cavin-Stice, J., & Knoth, R. L. (1992, August). *Adjustment following retirement from professional football.* Paper presented at the annual meeting of the American Psychological Association, Washington DC.

McPherson, B. P. (1980). Retirement from professional sport: The process and problems of occupational and psychological adjustment. *Sociological Symposium, 30,* 126–143.

Meichenbaum, D. (1996). Stress inoculation training for coping with stressors. *Clinical Psychologist, 49,* 4–7.

Meichenbaum, D., & Jaremko, M. (1983). *Stress reduction and prevention.* New York: Plenum.

Meichenbaum, D. H., & Cameron, R. (1973). Training schizophrenics to talk to themselves: A means of delivering attentional controls. *Behavior Therapy, 4,* 515–534.

Menkehorst, G. A. B. M., & van den Berg, F. J. (1997). Retirement from high-level competition: A new start. In R. Lidor & M. Bar-Eli (Eds.), *Proceedings of the IX World Congress on Sport Psychology* (pp. 487–489). Netanya, Israel: International Society of Sport Psychology.

Mihovilovic, M. (1968). The status of former sportsman. *International Review of Sport Sociology, 3*, 73–96.

Munroe, K. J., & Albinson, J. G., (1996, April). *Athletes' reactions immediately after and four months following involuntary disengagement at the varsity level.* Paper presented at the Joint Conference of the North American Society for the Psychology of Sport and Physical Activity and the Canadian Society for Psychomotor Learning and Sport Psychology, Ontario, Canada.

Murphy, S. M. (1995). Transition in competitive sport: Maximizing individual potential. In S. M. Murphy (Ed.), *Sport psychology interventions* (pp. 331–346). Champaign, IL: Human Kinetics.

National Collegiate Athletic Association (2003). *1981–2002 Sponsorship and participation report.* Indianapolis, IN: Author.

Ogilvie, B. C. (1987). Traumatic effects of sports career termination. *Proceedings of the National Conference of Sport Psychology, U.S. Olympic Committee.* Washington: DC.

Ogilvie, B. C., & Howe, M. (1982). Career crisis in sport. In T. Orlick, J. T. Partington, & J. H. Salmela (Eds.), *Proceedings of the Fifth World Congress of Sport Psychology* (pp. 176–183). Ottawa: Coaching Association of Canada.

Parker, K. B. (1994). "Has-beens" and "wanna-bes": Transition experiences of former major college football players. *Sport Psychologist, 8*, 287–304.

Pearson, R., & Petitpas, A. (1990). Transition of athletes: Pitfalls and prevention. *Journal of Counseling and Development, 69*, 7–10.

Perna, F. M., Ahlgren, R. L., & Zaichkowsky, L. (1999). The influence of career planning, race, and athletic injury on life satisfaction among recently retired collegiate male athletes. *Sport Psychologist, 13*, 144–156.

Petitpas, A., & Champagne, D. (2000). Practical considerations in implementing sport career transition programs. In D. Lavallee & P. Wylleman (Eds.), *Career transitions in sport: International perspectives* (pp. 81–93). Morgantown, WV: Fitness Information Technology.

Piphers, M. (1994). *Reviving Ophelia: Saving the selves of adolescent girls.* New York: Ballantine Books.

Pummell, B., Harwood, C., & Lavallee, D. (in press). Jumping to the next level: A qualitative examination of within-career transition in adolescent event riders. *Psychology of Sport and Exercise.*

Reece, S. D., Wilder, K. C., & Mahanes, J. R. (1996, October). *Program for athlete career transition.* Paper presented at Association for the Advancement of Applied Sport Psychology annual meetings, Williamsburg, Virginia.

Rose, A. M. (1962). The subculture of aging: A topic for sociological research. *Gerontologist, 2*, 123–127.

Rosenberg, E. (1982). Athletic retirement as social death: Concepts and perspectives. In N. Theberge & P. Donnelly (Eds.), *Sport and the sociological imagination* (pp. 245–258). Fort Worth: Texas Christian University Press.

Rosenfeld, L. B., Richman, J. M., & Hardy, C. J. (1989). Examining social support networks among athletes: Description and relationship to stress. *Sport Psychologist, 3*, 23–33.

Roskin, M. (1082). Coping with life changes: A preventive social work approach. *American Journal of Community Psychology, 10*, 331–340.

Schlossberg, N. (1981). A model for analyzing human adaptation to transition. *Counseling Psychologist, 9*, 2–18.

Schmid, J., & Schilling, G. (1997). Self-identity and adjustment to the transition out of sports. In R. Lidor & M. Bar-Eli (Eds.), *Proceedings of the IX World Congress on Sport Psychology* (pp. 608–610). Netanya, Israel: International Society of Sport Psychology.

Shapiro, F. (1995). *Eye movement desensitization and reprocessing: Basic principles, protocols, and procedures.* New York: Guilford Press.

Sime, W. E. (1998). Injury and career termination issues. In M. A. Thompson, R. A. Vernacchia, & W. E. Moore (Eds.), *Case studies in applied sport psychology: An educational approach* (pp. 195–226). Dubuque, IA: Kendall/Hunt.

Sinclair, D. A., & Hackfort, O. (2000). The role of the sport organization in the career transition process. In D. Lavallee & P. Wylleman (Eds.), *Career transitions in sport: International perspectives* (pp. 131–142). Morgantown, WV: Fitness Information Technology.

Sinclair, D. A., & Orlick, T. (1993). Positive transitions from high-performance sport. *Sport Psychologist, 7*, 138–150.

Smith, R. E. (1980). A cognitive-affective approach to stress management training for athletes. In C. Dadeau, W. Halliwell, K. Newell, & G. Roberts (Eds.), *Psychology of motor behavior and sports* (pp. 55–71). Champaign, IL: Human Kinetics.

Stambulova, N. B. (1994). Developmental sports career investigations in Russia: A post-perestroika analysis. *Sport Psychologist, 8*, 221–237.

Stephan, Y., Bilard, J., Ninot, G., & Delignieres, D. (2003). Epercussions of transition out of elite sport on subjective well being: A one-year study. *Journal of Applied Sport Psychology, 15*, 354–371.

Sussman, M. B. (1971). An analytical model for the sociological study of retirement. In F. M. Carp (Ed.), *Retirement* (pp. 29–73). New York: Behavioral Publications.

Svoboda, B., & Vanek, M. (1982). Retirement from high level competition. In T. Orlick, J. T. Partington, & J. H. Salmela (Eds.), *Proceedings of the Fifth World Congress of Sport Psychology* (pp. 166–175). Ottawa, Canada: Coaching Association of Canada.

Swain, D. A. (1991). Withdrawal from sport and Schlossberg's model of transitions. *Sociology of Sport Journal, 8*, 152–160.

Taylor, J. (1987, September). *The application of psychological skills for the enhancement of coaching effectiveness.* Presented at the Association for the Advancement of Applied Sport Psychology annual meetings, Newport Beach, California.

Taylor, J., & Ogilvie, B. C. (1994). A conceptual model of adaptation to retirement among athletes. *Journal of Applied Sport Psychology, 6*, 1–20.

Thomas, C. E., & Ermler, K. L. (1988). Institutional obligations in the athletic retirement process. *Quest, 40*, 137–150.

Tuckman, J., & Lorge, I. (1953). *Retirement and the industrial worker.* New York: Macmillan.

Ungerleider, S. (1997). Olympic athletes' termination from sport to workplace. *Perceptual and Motor Skills, 84,* 1287–1295.

Webb, W. M., Nasco, S. A., Riley, S., & Headrick, B. (1998). *Journal of Sport Behavior, 21,* 338–362.

Werthner, P., & Orlick, T. (1986). Retirement experiences of successful Olympic athletes. *International Journal of Sport Psychology, 17,* 337–363.

Wheeler, G. D., Malone, L. A., Van Vlack, S., & Nelson, E. R. (1996). Retirement from disability sport: A pilot study. *Adapted Physical Activity Quarterly, 13,* 382–399.

Williams-Rice, B. T. (1996). After the final snap: Cognitive appraisal, coping, and life satisfaction among former collegiate athletes. *Academic Athletic Journal,* Spring, 30–39.

Wolff, R., & Lester, D. (1989). A theoretical basis for counseling the retired professional athlete. *Psychological Reports, 64,* 1043–1046.

Wylleman, P., Lavallee, D., & Aflermann, D. (Eds). (1999). *Career transitions in competitive sports.* Biel, Switzerland: European Federation of Sport Psychology Monograph Series.

Yalom, I. D. (1980). *Existential psychotherapy.* New York: Harper/Collins.

Zaichkowsky, L., King, E., & McCarthy, J. (2000). The end of an era: The case of forced transition involving Boston University football. In D. Lavallee & P. Wylleman (Eds.), *Career transitions in sport: International perspectives* (pp. 195–205). Morgantown, WV: Fitness Information Technology.

Exercise Psychology

Rod K. Dishman, *The University of Georgia*
Heather O. Chambliss, *Collaborating Scientist*, *The Cooper Institute*, *Dallas*, *Texas*

Muscular vigor will . . . always be needed to furnish the background of sanity, serenity, and cheerfulness to life, . . . to round off the wiry edge of our fretfulness, and make us good-humored and easy of approach.

—William James, 1899

Physical inactivity is a public health burden in the United States and many other nations (Allender et al., 2007; Bauman & Craig, 2005; Joubert et al., 2007; U.S. Department of Health & Human Services, 2000). Although chronic diseases (e.g., cardiovascular disease, diabetes, cancer) and obesity have received most of the attention in public health, interest in physical activity for promotion of mental health continues to grow. Depression and dementia were among the 10 leading risk factors of disability-adjusted life expectancy in high-income nations worldwide during 2001 (Lopez et al., 2001), and they are projected to rank first and third by the year 2030 (Mathers & Loncar, 2006). In the United States, dementia and other disorders of the central nervous system are a leading cause of death, and mental disorders account for more than 40% of years lost to disability (Michaud et al., 2006). Evidence continues to accumulate supports that physical activity reduces odds of disorders such as depression, anxiety, and cognitive decline associated with

aging, while promoting better sleep and feelings of energy and well-being.

Despite the potential benefits of being physically active, 25% to 40% of adults in the United States are sedentary during their leisure time, and another 20% to 25% are not active enough to meet the levels recommended for health and fitness (Barnes, 2007; Centers for Disease Control and Prevention, 2005; 2007). About a third of adolescents do not meet recommended levels of physical activity (Grunbaum et al., 2004). Hence, understanding what motivates people to exercise is a high priority for public health.

The primary focus of exercise psychology has been to explain the social-cognitive antecedents of leisure-time physical activity and the psychological consequences of being physically active (Buckworth & Dishman, 2002; Dishman, 2000). To describe key aspects of the accumulated knowledge in those areas, we have organized this chapter into two sections in which we describe the evidence for positive effects on mental health and address issues in physical activity behavior change and exercise adherence.

Research in these areas has implications for public health. First, evidence suggests that physical activity positively affects depression, anxiety, distress, well-being, energy, fatigue, sleep, self-esteem, and cognitive performance, and it can be an effective adjuvant to traditional interventions used in counseling, clinical psychology, or psychiatry. In addition, understanding the dynamics of physical activity behavior over time is critical to the development of successful interventions to increase the initiation and maintenance of a physically active lifestyle.

Exercise and Mental Health

Anxiety and Depression

The potential for exercise to have a positive effect on mental health has been addressed in many reviews (e.g., Dishman, 1998; Dunn, Trivedi, & O'Neal,,2001; Ekeland et al., 2005; Faulkner & Taylor, 2005; Laurin et al., 2007; O'Connor, Raglin, & Martinsen, 2000; O'Neal, Dunn, & Martinsen, 2000; Sonstroem, 1998). Nearly 15 years ago, exercise scientists reached an international consensus that acute exercise is associated with reduced state anxiety and that chronic exercise and physical fitness are associated with reduced trait anxiety (Landers & Petruzzello, 1994), reduced depression (Morgan, 1994), and increased self-esteem and well-being (McAuley, 1994). Anxiety and depression are serious, prevalent diseases in the United States. Annually, they each affect 6–10% of the adult population and cost about $85 billion. These disorders not only affect quality of life, but also increase the risks for other chronic diseases, such as coronary heart disease (Stansfield & Marmot, 2002). Table 25-1 outlines the symptoms of generalized anxiety disorder, and Table 25-2 lists symptoms of major depressive disorder.

Population-based cross-sectional studies show that regular physical activity is associated with lower odds of experiencing anxiety symptoms (DeMoor et al., 2006; Strine, 2005; Taylor, 2004; Thorsen et al., 2005) and also diagnosis of an anxiety disorder (i.e., specific phobia, social

Table 25-1 Symptoms of Generalized Anxiety Disorder (GAD)

- Feeling persistently and excessively anxious and worried about routine life events
- Feeling restless, keyed up, or on edge
- Being easily tired
- Having difficulty thinking or concentrating
- Feeling irritabile
- Experiencing muscle tension
- Having difficulty falling or staying asleep

Symptoms of sympathetic nervous system activation are common in anxiety disorders and may include trembling, being easily startled, agitation, vigilance, gastrointestinal distress, dry mouth, and increased heart rate.

American Psychiatric Association (1994). *Diagnostic and statistical manual of mental disorders* (4th ed).

phobia, generalized anxiety, panic, and agoraphobia) by an average of about 40% (Goodwin, 2003). The odds remained nearly 30% lower after adjustments were made for other risk factors including sociodemographic factors and chronic health conditions. At least two studies used a prospective cohort design, which reduces the likelihood that the association is explainable by people becoming less active after they experience anxiety symptoms. The studies reported that the odds of developing any anxiety disorder were reduced by about half among physically active Australian adults (Beard et al., 2007) and adolescents and young adults in Munich, Germany (Ströhle et al., 2007) when compared with inactive people.

In a meta-analysis of exercise and anxiety, Landers and Petruzzello (1994) found a nearly one-half SD average effect size for decreases in state anxiety; effects were a little larger when exercise lasted from 20 to 30 minutes. An effect of one SD is comparable to increasing a grade from a C to a B in a course graded using a normal or bell-shaped curve. Although vigorous, acute exercise can temporarily increase state anxiety (O'Connor, Petruzzello, Kubitz, & Robinson, 1995), moderate intensities of exercise lasting

Table 25-2 **Symptoms of Major Depressive Disorder (MDD)**

- Persistent depressed mood, sadness, or irritability
- Loss of interest or pleasure in previously enjoyed activities
- Changes in weight and/or appetite
- Sleep disturbances including insomnia or hypersomnia
- Psychomotor agitation or retardation
- Fatigue or loss of energy
- Feelings of guilt or worthlessness
- Difficulty thinking or concentrating; indecisiveness
- Thoughts of death or suicide

American Psychiatric Association. (1994). *Diagnostic and statistical manual of mental disorders* (4th ed.).

at least 30 minutes are generally associated with the largest reductions in self-rated state anxiety.

Long and van Stavel (1995) reported a mean effect of .40 SD for decreases in trait anxiety after exercise training in 40 quasi-experimental and experimental studies of healthy adults. Since 1995, about 50 randomized controlled trials of exercise training have been reported. The cumulative mean reduction in anxiety ratings in those newer studies also approximated .40 SD in healthy adults and nonpsychiatric medical patients (Herring, O'Connor, Dishman, unpublished observations, 2009). Two randomized controlled trials have shown a reduction in anxiety after exercise training among people who have an anxiety disorder (e.g., Broocks et al., 1998; Merom et al., 2007).

Exercise has been recommended as helpful in treating depression for many centuries. Hippocrates prescribed exercise for depression, and clinical reports about using exercise in the psychiatric treatment of depression appeared as early as 1905. However, the first research efforts to discover the potential impact of exercise on depression did not begin until the early 1960s, led by William P. Morgan. Since then, a number of correlational, quasi-experimental, and experimental studies have been conducted.

A meta-analysis of a dozen studies by Lawlor & Hopker (2001) found that exercise groups decreased depression scores 1 SD more than comparison groups, but the authors noted several methodological limitations of the studies that have prevented clear interpretations of the results. A recent analysis of 13 randomized controlled trials of depressed patients conducted since their review yielded a virtually identical result of a 1 SD reduction in symptoms (Dishman & Dunn, unpublished observations, 2008). Generally, the newer studies were methodologically superior to the earlier studies. Four studies reported that reductions in symptoms met criteria for a clinically meaningful drop in symptoms (50%) or remission (Blumenthal et al., 2007; Dunn et al., 2005; Pinchasov et al., 2000, Singh et al. 2005).

At least 120 population-based, observational studies of physical activity and depression symptoms have been published worldwide since 1995 (Dishman, Puetz, & Chambliss, unpublished observations, 2008). Approximately 30 used a prospective cohort design. Few studied adolescents (e.g., Motl et al., 2004) or the transition from adolescence to young adulthood (Ströhle et al., 2007) when depression risk is highest. The average odds of experiencing symptoms were about 25% to 40% lower among active people compared with inactive people. After adjustment for risk factors such as age, gender, race, education, income, smoking, alcohol use, chronic health conditions, and other social and psychological variables, the odds remained nearly 15% to 25% lower among active people. Only seven cohort studies examined whether the protective effects of physical activity vary according to the amount of physical activity. The adjusted odds were reduced by about 15% in the lowest level of physical activity and by about 25% in each of the next two levels of physical activity. Thus, the highest level of activity did not confer more protective benefits than did the more moderate level, and each was more protective than the lowest levels.

Randomized controlled trials in humans diagnosed with depression (e.g., Blumenthal et al., 1999; 2007; Brenes et al., 2007) and experimental studies with rats (Dishman et al., 1997; Yoo, Bunnell, Crabbe, Kalish, & Dishman, 2000) have demonstrated that exercise training can reduce signs or symptoms of depression to a degree comparable to antidepressant drugs. There is no consensus, however, on the exercise prescription that is most effective for treating depression or anxiety (Dunn, Trivedi, & O'Neal, 2001). We know of only two controlled studies that addressed the dose response issue in depressed individuals. Dunn, Trivedi, Kampert, Clark, and Chambliss (2005) found that greater weekly energy expenditure (17.5 kcal/kg/wk) produced greater decreases in depressive symptoms after 12 weeks of aerobic training compared to a lower dose (7.0 kcal/kg/wk) and to an equal contact control. However, there was no difference in depression scores for exercise frequency (3 days/week versus 5 days/week). Singh et al. (2005) reported greater symptom reduction after resistance exercise at an intensity of 80% one repetition maximum (RM) compared to an intensity of 20% 1 RM 3 days per week for 8 weeks.

Distress and Well-Being

Psychological distress is a risk factor for psychiatric disorders and coronary heart disease (Stansfield & Marmot, 2002), and it is negatively associated with quality of life. Also, exaggerated physiological responses to mental stress are believed to play a role in the development of coronary heart disease and hypertension. Conversely, a feeling of well-being can reduce psychiatric risk and is an important feature of high life quality and health (Pressman & Cohen, 2005).

During the past decade, at least 15 prospective cohort studies and 30 randomized controlled trials of physical activity and feelings of distress or well-being have been published worldwide (Dishman and Müeller, unpublished observations, 2008). In the cohort studies, the odds favored active people by nearly 20% after adjustment for risk factors such as age, gender, socioeconomic status, smoking, alcohol or substance use, chronic health conditions, life events, job stress, and social support. The effects of exercise training were small, about .25 SD, and weren't

better than a placebo in many of the randomized controlled trials.

For the most part, the evidence for altered physiological responses during mental stress after exercise training is also ambiguous. Crews and Landers's (1987) meta-analytical review reported a significant effect size of one-half SD, implying that aerobically fit subjects had a reduced response to psychosocial stress response. A more recent meta-analysis of the cumulative evidence published from 1965 to 2004 found that cardiorespiratory fitness was weakly associated with increased physiological reactivity, but quicker recovery, from laboratory stress. Also, responses such as heart rate and blood pressure to laboratory stress were not affected in randomized exercise training studies that increased cardiorespiratory fitness (Jackson & Dishman, 2006). Notwithstanding those negative findings, vascular and blood flow responses, as well as their modulation by the autonomic nervous system, may be more important to health than gross measures of heart rate and blood pressure. However, those factors have been understudied (e.g., Dishman, Nakamura, Jackson, & Ray, 2003) especially in people with elevated risk of cardiovascular disease (e.g., Jackson & Dishman, 2002).

Sleep

According to reports from the National Institutes of Health's conference on sleep and sleep disorders (*Frontiers of Knowledge in Sleep & Sleep Disorders: Opportunities for Improving Health and Quality of Life*, March 2004), each year 50 to 70 million Americans experience some effects on their health from sleep disorders, sleep deprivation, and excessive daytime sleepiness. The annual prevalence of insomnia is nearly one-third of the adult population in the United States. The financial cost is approximately $65 billion, 50 billion of that in costs to industry from lost productivity. Only about 5% to 20% of people who suffer sleep disturbances will seek help from a primary care physician, and many will purchase over-the-counter sleep aids.

A meta-analysis of English-language literature on the acute effects of physical activity on sleep (Youngstedt, O'Connor, & Dishman, 1997) found statistically significant increases in total sleep time, slow wave sleep, and REM latency (the time before REM onset), with a decrease in REM, after an exercise session. The changes in REM sleep may be important for treating or preventing depression. Many people with typical major depression have reduced REM latency and increased REM and respond with reduced depression after REM deprivation therapy. However, the effects in the meta-analysis ranged from about .20 to .50 *SD,* which are small-to-moderately large effects statistically, but that equate to only a few minutes of sleep in each case, well within normal night-to-night variation. The subjects studied were good sleepers, so the effects may be underestimates of the potential efficacy of exercise among people with sleep disorders.

About a dozen epidemiological studies have reported an association between physical activity and good sleep based on questionnaires administered to population samples, but few studies have examined the long-term effects of exercise on sleep among people with sleep disorders (Youngstedt & Kline, 2006). There is some evidence that higher levels of usual physical activity appear to be protective against incident and chronic insomnia in older adults (Morgan, 2003), and a few randomized controlled trials have found that both aerobic (King et al., 1997) and resistance (Singh et al., 1997) exercise training led to improvements in self-rated sleep among older adults who had sleep problems. The long-term effects of exercise on polysomnographic measures of sleep among poor sleepers are not known.

Feelings of Fatigue or Low Energy

Feelings of low energy and fatigue are a public health problem in the United States. Although less than 1% of the population suffers from "chronic fatigue syndrome," about 20% of adults say they have persistent feelings of fatigue (Wessely, Hotopf, & Sharp, 1998). Feelings of fatigue or low energy are common reasons for doctor visits, yet treatment is often inadequate (Lange,Cook & Natelson, 2005). A dozen

population-based observational studies, including four prospective cohorts published since 1995, suggest a protective effect of physical activity against feelings of fatigue or low energy (OR = 0.61, 95% CI = 0.52 to 0.72) (Puetz, 2006), and randomized controlled trials of groups of medical patients and other adults show a moderate reduction in symptoms of fatigue (Puetz, O'Connor, Dishman, 2006). A few small, randomized controlled trials have reported positive effects of exercise training on symptoms of chronic fatigue syndrome (Fulcher and White, 1997; Moss-Morris et al., 2005; Powell et al., 2001; Wallman et al., 2004; Weardon et al., 1998).

Self-Esteem

Enhanced self-esteem is important for mental health because it provides a feeling of value or worth and it is a general indicator of psychological adjustment (Pressman & Cohen, 2005). Symptoms of anxiety and depression often are associated with low self-esteem, and physical activities including sports may favorably mediate the association between self-esteem and depression (e.g., Dishman et al., 2006; Motl et al., 2005). Positive changes in physical self-concept after exercise training are more likely to be observed than changes in self-esteem, but increased physical self-concept may contribute to enhanced self-esteem (Fox, 2000; Sonstroem & Morgan, 1989). Changes in self-esteem with exercise are also more likely in children than adults, for whom self-esteem is more multidimensional.

A meta-analysis of eight randomized controlled trials of children and youths indicated a moderate (one-half *SD*) effect of physical activity (Ekeland et al., 2004). However, the small number of diverse studies yielded little regarding the modifying influences of different types of exercise or settings. A recent meta-analysis of about 50, mostly small, randomized controlled trials reported an average increase in self-esteem of about .25 *SD* among adults (Spence et al., 2005). Self-esteem is increased among adults (Spence et al., 2005) and youths (Strong et al., 2005) when physical fitness is increased, more so than when the physical activity setting and study outcomes are focused on motor skills. However, the study designs used have not clarified the importance of the social context of the physical activity settings relative to features of physical activity, exercise, and fitness. Thus, it remains unclear whether it is exercise itself that increases self-esteem, or something in the social context of the exercise setting, including people's expectations of benefits (Desharnais, Jobin, Cote, Levesque, & Godin, 1993). The greatest gains in self-esteem can be expected for individuals with low initial levels, and for whom physical attributes have a relatively high value as a part of global self-concept.

Cognitive Function

Cognition involves the selection, manipulation, and storage of information and the use of that information to guide behavior. Cognitive function generally matures in childhood, peaks during young adulthood and declines after middle age. Hence, there has been an interest in whether exercise or physical fitness moderates cognitive function during the lifespan. Early studies yielded mixed evidence about the benefits of regular exercise or cardiorespiratory fitness on cognitive functioning (e.g., Tomporowski & Ellis, 1986). Reevaluation of that evidence and more recent research suggest some positive effects of both acute and chronic exercise on selected features of cognitive function in children (Davis et al., 2007; Tomporowski, 2003) and older adults (McAuley, Kramer, & Colcombe, 2004). First, the influence of fitness on cognitive performance among older adults seems to depend on features of the cognitive tasks. Fitness is more related to performance on tasks that are novel, complex, and require attention and fast processing speed (Chodzko-Zajko & Moore, 1994). Second, recent studies have shown that cardiorespiratory fitness and chronic aerobic exercise training facilitate executive control functions of cognition among older adults (Colcombe et al., 2004).

The evaluation of the results of 18 experiments reviewed by Colcombe and Kramer (2003) indicated that aerobic exercise training produced a .48 *SD* benefit for all cognitive tasks, with the greatest effect (.68 *SD*) for executive control tasks

that measured goal-oriented decision-making behavior. Executive control includes response inhibition, attentional control, working memory, and rule discovery and is mainly regulated by neural activity in the prefrontal cortexes of the brain, areas that are further modulated by activity in the temporal and parietal cortexes, the hippocampus, and several other brain areas involved with motivated behavior (Royall et al., 2002). The cumulative evidence has indicated a small positive effect of about one-third to one-half *SD* of both acute and chronic exercise on several indicators of cognitive performance (Etnier et al., 1997; Sibley & Etnier, 2003). Whether those effects depend directly upon physical fitness remains unclear (Etnier et al., 2007).

At least 17 prospective population-based cohort studies assessed the relation between individuals' level of physical activity and the onset of age-related decline in cognitive functioning or incident cases of dementia or against cognitive decline in healthy aging adults (Tomporowski & Dishman, unpublished observations, 2008). Of the 11 studies of dementia, 7 reported a protective effect of physical activity. The average risk reduction in the onset of dementia was nearly 40%. A meta-analytic review of randomized controlled studies of older adults with Alzheimer's disease or other dementia (Heyn, Abreu, & Ottenbacher, 2004) concluded that physical activity interventions benefit the cognitive function of older adults who have dementia.

Plausible Mediators or Mechanisms

Mood and Emotion

The explanations of how physical activity improves mental health are largely unknown. However, the precise mechanisms for the therapeutic effect of psychotherapy and medications are also unclear. Cognitively based explanations for a beneficial effect of exercise on mental health include distractions from worries or symptoms, increased sense of mastery, or improved perceptions of the self, including self-esteem. Exercise also may decrease anxiety by redefining the subjective meaning of arousal or by offering a way to manage symptoms of anxiety. Improvements in mental health also may stem from increased opportunities for social interaction, meeting and reaching goals, or an enhanced sense of control or purpose.

Hypotheses about biological mechanisms for explaining reduced anxiety and depression after exercise include increased body temperature and brain blood flow, increased endorphins, altered autonomic, endocrine, and brain monoamine systems, and several neuropeptides that function as neuromodulators or neuronal growth factors. However, biologically oriented hypotheses have been incompletely developed largely due to a lack of training in related fields of study (e.g., biological psychology, neuroscience, or psychiatry) and resources (e.g., access to brain imaging or molecular biology techniques).

The thermogenic hypothesis that reduced anxiety after exercise is dependent on the increased body temperature typical of moderate-to-heavy exertion seems plausible but has received little support (Koltyn & Morgan, 1992; Petruzzello, Landers, & Salazar, 1993; Youngstedt, Dishman, Cureton, & Peacock, 1993). The hypothesis that increased brain blood flow during acute exercise can explain changes in mood or anxiety has not been developed in a way consistent with current evidence. Brain blood flow and metabolism are increased by various stressors, but the effects of exercise seem mainly limited to regions involved with motor, sensory, and cardiovascular regulation, rather than emotional responses (Nybo & Secher, 2004; Secher et al., 2008). Although both acute and chronic exercise has influenced blood flow in the anterior cingulate and insular cortexes (areas that are involved with emotional processing and cardiovascular control) (Colcombe et al., 2004; Williamson, McColl, & Mathews, 2003), it remains to be determined whether such responses to exercise reflect emotional responding to exercise or sensory and cardiovascular responses to increased arousal.

The hypothesis that endorphins are responsible for changes in mood or anxiety following exercise remains plausible, but it has been perpetuated with little evidence. Endorphins play a role in modulating dopamine neurons in parts of the brain involved with motivation and pleasure and could thus indirectly influence positive moods. Plasma-endorphin is reliably elevated during intense exercise, but a plausible link between peripheral-endorphin or enkephalins and mood or hypoalgesic responses to acute exercise has not been established. In nearly all studies, opioid antagonists, which block the effects of endorphins, have not blocked mood changes after exercise. The influence of blood-endorphin on the brain is probably limited by the blood brain barrier. Studies with rats and mice show increased levels of endorphins or enkephalin receptor binding in the brain after acute exercise, but the effects of the levels on behavior, emotion, or physiology were not demonstrated and remain unknown. Although opioid-mediated hypoalgesia (Cook & Koltyn, 2000) could indirectly influence mood, peripheral opioid responses to acute exercise apparently inhibit catecholamine influences on cardiovascular, respiratory, and endocrine responses during exercise. A direct influence by peripheral opioid levels on mood is implausible at present. Notwithstanding the limitations of past evidence, a recent uncontrolled study reported a correlation between self-reports of euphoria and brain opioid binding measured by positron emission tomography in 10 experienced distance runners (Boecker et al., 2008). This is the first and only evidence that brain opioids are influenced by exercise in humans in a way that may help explain mood changes associated with running (Dishman & O'Conner, 2009).

Evidence from animal models of depression and anxiety points to exercise-induced changes in brain norepinephrine (NE) and serotonin as potential mechanisms for the positive effects on mood. NE and serotonin are major modulators of brain neural activity. In rats, chronic physical activity induces positive alterations in brain levels of NE and serotonin and major metabolites in regions known to be involved in integrating behavioral and endocrine responses to stressors other than exercise (Chaouloff, 1997; Dishman et al., 1997; Dunn, Reigle, Youngstedt, Armstrong, & Dishman, 1996; Soares, Holmes, Renner, Edwards, Bunnell, & Dishman, 1999). Human studies indicate that exercise training does not alter plasma levels of NE or muscle sympathetic nerve activity (which releases NE) measured at rest.

It is also important to consider the effects of exercise training on the hypothalamic-pituitary-adrenal (HPA) cortical axis because it is involved in models of the pathogenesis of cardiovascular disease, anxiety disorders, and major depression. Moderate exercise training results in a diminished HPA response during the same absolute exercise intensity, but heavy exercise training can be associated with either a suppressed or elevated HPA response under resting conditions in humans or after stress in animals, which can interact with reproductive hormones, suggesting gender differences (White-Welkley, Bunnell, Mougey, Meyer-hoff, & Dishman, 1995; White-Welkley et al., 1996). Limited correlational evidence suggests that altered HPA cortical responses that can accompany increases in negative moods after overtraining in athletes are consistent with those typically observed in patients diagnosed with major depression (O'Connor, Morgan, Raglin, Barksdale, & Kalin, 1989).

The spinal Hoffmann reflex (H-reflex) has been studied in respect to exercise to locate evidence for effects of exercise on central nervous system aspects of self-reported anxiety. The H-reflex is a monosynptic reflex, but, ascending and descending supraspinal tracts exist that would permit it to be modulated by the central nervous system. A series of studies conducted by deVries (deVries, Simard, Wiswell, Heckathorne, & Carabetta, 1982) and others (Bulbulian & Darabos, 1986) showed a reduction in the H-reflex after exercise and hypothesized that the reduction was indicative of a tranquilizing effect of exercise. Recent research, however, has found that changes in the H-reflex are not correlated with changes in self-reports of anxiety after exercise (Motl & Dishman, 2004; Motl, O'Connor, & Dishman, 2004), and it appears that the reduction of the H-reflex after exercise does not extend beyond the specific spinal segments involved with the limbs involved in the exercise (Motl & Dishman, 2003).

Hemispheric asymmetry in brain electroencephalographic (EEG) responses measured at anterior brain recording sites has been hypothesized as a correlate or possible mechanism for mood changes in response to acute exercise (e.g., Petruzzello, Hall, & Ekkekakis, 2001). However, the cumulative evidence testing that idea has been mixed (e.g., Crabbe, Smith, & Dishman, 2007) and studies of acute exercise and EEG activity indicate that activity in all frequency bands increases in response to exercise regardless of hemispheric site (Crabbe & Dishman, 2004). However, the studies were limited to just a few recording sites and did not use dense-array electrode mapping. The evidence suggests that acute exercise increases EEG activity in a general way consistent with increased arousal, possibly from increased sensory and cardiovascular neural traffic to the thalamus processed through the brain stem.

New areas of research implicate other potential biological mechanisms for positive effects of exercise on mental health. For example, neurotrophic proteins such as brain-derived neurotrophic factor (BDNF) and VGF enhance the growth and maintenance of several neuronal systems, and might have an important role in the neuropathology and treatment of depression (Hunsberger et al., 2007; Russo-Neustadt, 2003). Animal studies of chronic exercise have demonstrated increased gene expression for VGF and BDNF in the hippocampus, which is involved with contextual memories (e.g., Adlard & Cotman, 2004), and the ventral tegmental area of the meso-limbic system, which helps modulate appetitive or hedonic behaviors (Van Hoomissen, O'Neal, Holmes, & Dishman, 2003).

Cognition

Some evidence suggests that exercise training might slow declines in brain volume associated with aging (Colcombe et al., 2006). Animal studies also indicate that exercise has a beneficial, moderately strong effect on some aspects of learning and memory, such as contextual conditioning (Van Hoomissen et al., 2004) and spatial memory (e.g., Fordyce & Farrar, 1991; Van Praag et al., 1999; Anderson et al., 2000), which depend largely on hippocampal function. Plausible mechanisms that might explain enhanced cognitive function in response to exercise include enhancements in brain blood flow, neurotransmitter systems, and neuronal plasticity (Chodzko-Zajko & Moore, 1994). For example, a brain neuroimaging study demonstrated decreased blood flow in the anterior cingulate cortex among fit older adults during an executive function task requiring error detection, which was associated with their better performance (Colcombe et al., 2004). However, the altered blood flow could be the result of improved neural function rather than its cause. Most studies of brain blood flow during acute exercise were conducted under extreme conditions to understand limits to performance and central fatigue rather than cognitive function (Nybo & Secher, 2004; Secher et al., 2008). Animal studies have shown that acute increases in blood flow during exercise (Vissing, Andersen, & Diemer, 1996) and adaptations in oxidative capacity after chronic exercise (McCloskey, Adamo, & Anderson, 2001) are mainly restricted to brain regions involved with sensory processing and motor control than with cognition.

A large animal literature shows a strong effect of both acute and chronic physical activity on neural plasticity and the expression of neurotrophic growth factors in the hippocampal formation (Cotman & Berchtold, 2002), especially BDNF, which appears dependent on noradrenergic function (Garcia et al., 2003; Ivy et al., 2003). Galanin, a neuropeptide that serves as both a neurotrophin and a neurotransmitter and is responsive to chronic exercise (O'Neal, Van Hoomissen, Holmes, & Dishman, 2001), has been hypothesized to be more important than BDNF for some types of learning (Van Hoomissen et al., 2004).

Research Issues in Exercise and Mental Health

Some of the inconsistency in links between exercise and mental health can be traced to the quality of the research. Many studies did not quantify physical activity and exertion adequately, examine clearly defined clinical groups, control for subject expectancy or social interaction effects, or

consider health and activity history of the participants (Tieman, Peacock, Cureton, & Dishman, 2001). Most studies of exercise and anxiety or depression have not used clinical diagnostic criteria or concomitantly measured biological signs that are common features of standard clinical diagnosis. Theoretically based studies of how changes in mood after exercise might affect negative and positive emotional responding have received little study (Crabbe, Smith, & Dishman, 2007; Smith & Crabbe, 2000; Smith, O'Connor, Crabbe, & Dishman, 2002).

Current knowledge about dose-response relationships and biological plausibility for effects of exercise on mental health remains limited (Dunn et al., 2001). Difficulties in defining a dose–response relationship also come from inconsistencies in mode, intensity, and duration of exercise treatment. The effects of different types of exercise haven't been fully studied. More studies of resistance training are needed, as are studies other types of exercise, including milder forms such as Eastern health practices (e.g.,Tai Chi and Qigong). Although evidence does not indicate that the mental health benefits of physical activity depend upon changes in aerobic fitness, recommendations by the American College of Sports Medicine (ACSM) for exercise that increases or maintains fitness among healthy adults offer prudent guidelines for a graduated exercise program that can enhance mental health among people who have no other medical contraindications for physical exertion. People who do not desire to exercise for the purpose of marked gains in fitness may benefit from the complementary recommendation by the ACSM and the American Heart Association that people engage in moderate-intensity physical activity (e.g., brisk walking) for at least 30 minutes each day, possibly accumulated in multiple sessions, 5 or more days each week. However, whether meeting that recommendation provides similar mental health benefits as does meeting recommendations for more vigorous physical activity remains untested by experimental methods. Table 25-3 lists several practical applications of physical activity to improve mental health.

Table 25-3 **Coaching Points for Mental Health**

- **General Well-Being**—Improved mental health is a short-term benefit that can be used to reinforce exercise training. Motivate clients and athletes by having them pay attention to benefits such as increased energy levels, lower stress, and improved mood after exercise. If an athlete shows a decline in psychological functioning with training, it may be useful to review the regimen to ensure that the athlete is not becoming stale.

- **Mood Disorders**—Anxiety and depression are common clinical disorders. Know the signs and symptoms, and have local referral resources available. If a client or athlete has a history of a mood disorder, exercise can be a useful adjunctive treatment. Don't encourage a person to discontinue medication or other prescribed treatment, but provide education on the mental health benefits of exercise.

- **Sleep**—Exercise may help regulate sleep patterns for some people. If a client or athlete complains of sleep problems, suggest that he or she experiment with the timing of the exercise routine to see what works best. In addition, light exposure from exercising outdoors may provide additional benefit.

- **Self-Esteem**—Exercise may improve self-esteem and physical self-concept, particularly among children and individuals with low initial self esteem. Help individuals by setting realistic goals and establishing an environment that promotes feelings of mastery, competence of new sport skills, and a positive body image.

- **Cognitive Function**—Exercising the body is good for the mind too. Even walking has been shown to reduce cognitive decline in older adults. Remind clients and athletes of this important benefit, and maximize the potential impact of exercise by creating stimulating learning environments. Create a brain and body workout—maximize the mental complexity of physical tasks, change up the exercise environment, or even pair athletic drills with memory tasks.

Physical Activity Behavior Change

Increased physical activity and cardiorespiratory fitness can make significant contributions to public health, but efforts to increase adoption and maintenance of an active lifestyle have yielded modest results. The proportion of adults who participated in regular moderate or vigorous physical activity stayed at 30% from 1997 to 2002, and it remains below the Healthy People 2010 goal of 50% (Centers for Disease Control, 2005a; 2005b). Although there was a small but significant decline from 1994 to 2002 in the proportion of adults reporting no leisure-time physical activity (30% to 25%) (Grunbaum et al., 2004), this is still above the Healthy People 2010 goal of 20%. In addition, rates of overweight and obesity are steadily increasing to epidemic proportions.

Physical activity decreases significantly in late adolescence after high school and college, and the participation rate continues to decrease with increasing age. Traditional interventions have not addressed the cyclical or dynamic nature of exercise behavior, and the dropout rate from structured exercise programs has remained at roughly 50% for the past 20 years (Dishman, 1994a). Therefore, it is important to study the dynamics of exercise behavior and the factors necessary to increase physical activity and exercise adherence.

Theories of Exercise Behavior

Several theories have been used to predict and explain exercise behavior (see Biddle & Nigg, 2000, for a review). Many studies of exercise determinants and interventions have been based on social cognitive theories, including planned behavior and self-efficacy; self-determination theory; behavior modification; and cognitive behavior modification. The transtheoretical model, or the stages of change model, has been applied to exercise behavior over the past 20 years or so and has been used successfully to guide intervention development. The ecological model is gaining support through efforts to implement multilevel multidimensional interventions with a focus on environmental influences.

Social cognitive. Social cognitive theories conceptualize cognition, affect, and value-related variables as mediators in the choice of goals, intentions to act, and thus exercise behavior. The theories assume that personal factors, environmental events, and behavior function as interacting and reciprocal determinants of each other (Bandura, 1991; 2004).

The *Theory of Planned Behavior* (Ajzen, 2002) proposes that the direct cause of behavior is intention, which is determined by perceived behavioral control, attitude, and subjective norm. Perceived behavioral control also has a direct effect on behavior independently of intention. The cumulative evidence from nonexperimental studies has supported those relations for understanding adults' and adolescents' intentions to be physically active and the relation of those intentions with physical activity (see Dishman et al., 2006; Godin, 1994 for reviews). However, those studies used correlational analyses that failed to identify the functional network of direct and indirect relations of the variables with physical activity, or they failed to model change in both physical activity and its predictors across time.

Self-efficacy conceptualizes a belief in personal capabilities to organize and execute the courses of action required to attain a behavioral goal (Bandura, 1997a). Like self-efficacy, perceived behavioral control includes efficacy beliefs about internal factors (e.g., skills, abilities, and willpower) and external factors (e.g., time, opportunity, obstacles, and dependence on other people) that are imposed on behavior. Although both variables represent personal efficacy judgments about the ease or difficulty of performing a behavior, perceived behavioral control also emphasizes beliefs about personal control over performance of the behavior (Rodgers & Murray, 2007). Each factor is distinguishable from *outcome expectancy*, which is the perceived likelihood that performing a behavior will result in a

specific outcome. Bandura (1997) proposed that self-change operates through self-initiated reactions. For example, individuals dissatisfied with their current exercise or fitness who adopt challenging goals and are confident (i.e., have high self-efficacy) that they can attain their goals would have strong intentions and optimal motivation for maintaining exercise (Dishman et al., 2006). Past studies of physical activity usually did not assess the influence of social- and physical-environmental contexts on social-cognitive variables and affective responses to physically active and sedentary choices. For example, correlational studies suggest that family support is associated with physical activity in youths (Gustafson & Rhodes, 2006), but how self-efficacy influences, is influenced by, or interacts with family support has received little study (e.g., Dowda et al., 2007).

Self-Determination. Self-determination theory is complementary to social-cognitive theory and offers ideas about how intrinsic motives for physical activity develop and how they interact with physical and social-environments to influence physical activity. Self-determination is concerned with the development and functioning of personality within social contexts (Ryan & Deci, 2000). The theory assumes that people have innate drives to master ongoing challenges and to integrate their experiences into a coherent sense of self. However, the natural tendency to strive toward self-determination requires ongoing prompts and supports from the social environment, which can either facilitate or impede the development of people's motives for personal growth. For example, whether people develop extrinsic motives for physical activity (such as social affiliation and appearance) or intrinsic motives (such as physical competence and enjoyment) can be shaped by reinforcement history in different social contexts.

Behavior modification. Behavior modification is the planned, systematic application of principles of learning to the modification of behavior. According to behavior modification theory, changes in behavior result from associations between external stimuli and the consequences of a specific behavior. This theory minimizes the role of thoughts, motives, and perceptions. What precedes and what follows a behavior will influence the frequency of that behavior—that is, behavior is cued and reinforced. According to behavior modification, the key to behavior change lies in the identification of the target behavior (e.g., walking at lunch or doing aerobics when the children take gymnastics) and effective cues and reinforcers. Behavioral approaches, such as written agreements, behavioral contracts, lotteries, and stimulus and reinforcement control, have been successful in exercise intervention studies.

Cognitive-behavior modification. Cognitive behavior modification is based on the assumption that psychological variables are the mediators of behavior. A wide range of dysfunctional or maladaptive behaviors results from the individual's irrational, unproductive thoughts and incompletely formed cognitions. Learning or insight can serve to restructure, augment, or replace faulty thoughts with behaviorally effective beliefs and cognitive skills. Simply put, cognitions moderate or mediate behavior, and cognitions can be changed. Clients are educated about the relationship between cognitions, feelings, and behaviors and are taught skills to identify and control antecedents and consequences that prompt and reinforce behavior. Cognitive-behavioral approaches, including self-monitoring, goal setting, feedback, and decision making, have been effective in increasing exercise adherence when used alone or when combined in intervention packages.

Transtheoretical model. The transtheoretical model, also known as the stages of change model, has been used to describe the processes of health behavior change and has been applied to exercise (Marcus, Pinto, Simkin, Audrain, & Taylor, 1994; Marshall & Biddle, 2001). Behavior change is seen as a dynamic process that occurs through a series of five interrelated stages: precontemplation, contemplation, preparation, action and maintenance (Marcus & Simkin, 1994;

Prochaska & Marcus, 1994). People in precontemplation are not thinking about starting an exercise program. Those in the contemplation stage are considering starting an exercise program. During the preparation stage, a plan has been made but not implemented. People in the action stage have started regular exercise within the past 6 months but are at greater risk of not adhering than someone in the maintenance stage, for whom exercise behavior is more established. Three components of the transtheoretical model that are proposed mediators of behavior change are self-efficacy, decisional balance (i.e., pros and cons), and processes of change. The processes of change include application of both cognitive strategies (e.g., self-reevaluation) and behavioral strategies (e.g., stimulus control, reinforcement management) to different degrees depending on the stage of change.

Ecological Models. Some scholars contend that the lack of progress in increasing physical activity may be a consequence of only targeting people's knowledge and personal motivation. Ecological models acknowledge that behavior can be influenced by intrapersonal, social environment, physical environment, and public policy variables. Sallis and Owen (1999) applied this model to physical activity and defined the *behavioral setting* to describe environmental factors that can facilitate the decisions to be more active and support that behavior. Social environmental factors are supportive behaviors, social climate, culture, policies governing incentives for activity and inactivity, and policies governing resources and infrastructures related to activity and inactivity. Physical environmental factors are divided into natural and constructed environment. Natural environmental factors are weather and geography. Constructed environment includes information, level of urbanization, architecture, transportation environments, and the entertainment and recreation infrastructures. Using this model, physical activity is targeted through changing the environmental and public policies. For example, administrators at the Centers for Disease Control and Prevention have begun to address physical activity behavior change through establishing relationships with a variety of nontraditional partners, including city planners, architects, environmental psychologists, and specialists in transportation and recreation.

Correlates of Physical Activity

The known correlates of physical activity, which might mediate the effects of interventions or modify their effects, can be categorized as personal attributes, environmental influences, and aspects of physical activity itself (Dishman & Sallis, 1994). Mediators are variables in a causal sequence that transmit the relation or effect of an independent variable on a dependent variable. Effect modifiers or moderators are variables not in a causal sequence but which modify the relation or effect between an independent variable and a dependent variable (MacKinnon, Fairchild, & Fritz, 2007).

Personal attributes include cognitions, beliefs, attitudes, emotions, and values that can interact with environmental variables, such as social support and the weather. For example, someone who values physical fitness and is self-motivated may be less influenced by the weather and thus more likely to exercise when it is cold than someone whose fitness is less important and needs more external support and prompts.

Personal attributes. Identifying factors associated with physical activity and exercise that reside in the individual is important because researchers can identify population segments that may be responsive or resistive to physical activity interventions. Personal attributes such as smoking, education, income, and ethnicity can be markers of underlying habits or circumstances that reinforce sedentary living. Demographics such as low education and income, age, smoking, and female gender are consistent correlates of physical inactivity. There is no experimental evidence, however, that those factors cause inactivity. Obviously there are many women, smokers, and older people who are very active physically.

Most studies of physical activity have targeted social and psychological variables, but biological characteristics of individuals also can play a critical role in decisions and habits, and may interact significantly with social-cognitive variables (Trost, Owen, Bauman, Sallis, & Brown, 2002). For example, body mass index, obesity, and physical discomfort have been negatively correlated with self-reported physical activity (Trost et al., 2002), and those who perceive their health as poor are less likely to adopt and adhere to an exercise program (Dishman & Sallis, 1994). Physiological influences on physical activity may be more basic, as proposed by Rowland (1998), whereby the amount of daily physical activity may be regulated by analogous brain centers that also control biological processes such as feeding behavior (Dishman 2008).

Being active in the recent past predicts present and future participation, but playing sports when young has not influenced adult physical activity patterns in reported studies, especially among males. No prospective study has shown a relationship between interscholastic or intercollegiate athletics and free-living physical activity in adults, and there is mixed evidence that activity patterns in childhood are predictive of later physical activity (Barnekow-Bergkvist, Hedberg, Janlert, & Jansson, 1998; Seefeldt, Malina, & Clark, 2002). As mentioned earlier, vigorous physical activity significantly decreases during adolescence and young adulthood. However, participation in moderate-intensity activity seems to be stable with increasing age.

The cognitive variable with the most support as a determinant is self-efficacy, accounting for 25–35% of the variation in physical activity in most studies. It is difficult to determine if self-efficacy causes physical activity. Active people may report a high self-efficacy because of past success in physical activity, but other factors may have actually caused the exercise habit. Other cognitive variables positively associated with physical activity are self-schemata (in which one sees oneself as an exerciser) (Kendzierski, 1994), expectations of benefits, self-motivation, enjoyment, and behavioral intentions (Trost et al., 2002). Like self-efficacy, attitudes and intentions commonly account for about 25% of variations in people's self-ratings of their physical activity

(Dzewaltowski, 1994; Godin, 1994), but past physical activity habits can be more strongly related to contemporary exercise behavior (Trost et al., 2002). Mood disorders are negatively associated with physical activity. There has been little research on personality traits and exercise adherence (Rhodes & Smith, 2006), although there is some promise in linking personality variables, such as extroversion, with exercise behavior, motives, barriers, and preferences (Courneya & Hellsten, 1998).

Environmental influences.   Social influences in the form of social support (i.e., encouragement or help from someone) and prompting (e.g., images of exercise) appear to be strong correlates of physical activity. Climate or season has a consistent relationship with physical activity in adults, whereas there is weak or contradictory evidence of association between cost and access to home exercise equipment with physical activity (Trost et al., 2002). Objectively measured access to facilities is a reliable predictor of physical activity (Dowda et al., 2009), but evidence on perceived access is mixed (Dishman, 1994c; Dowda et al., 2009; Motl et al., 2007). The reason most often given for dropping out of a supervised exercise program is lack of time, but it is not clear if this represents a true determinant, a perceived determinant, poor time-management skills, or a rationalization for lack of motivation to exercise (Dishman & Buckworth, 1996). Identifying environmental factors in exercise behavior demonstrates the need to look beyond the individual and small group in developing interventions. The target of interventions should include policy and facility planning at the international, national, and community level and should include educational-behavioral applications in schools, churches, and health care and recreational settings (Blair et al., 1996; Dishman & Sallis, 1994).

Physical activity characteristics.   Identifying specific aspects of physical activity that enhance adoption and adherence is especially important to practitioners prescribing exercise in a variety of settings (Buckworth, 2003; Dishman & Buckworth, 1996; Kahn et al., 2002). It is not known if there are different determinants for different types of exercise. Some studies have examined the influence of different frequencies and durations, or accumulating a public health dose of physical, on adherence. Jakicic, Winters, Lang, and Wing (1999) randomized 148 sedentary, overweight women to three interventions: long-bout exercise (LB), multiple short-bout exercise (SB), or multiple short-bout exercise with home exercise equipment (SBEQ) using a treadmill. After 18 months, women in the SBEQ group demonstrated better adherence that those in the LB and SB groups, but there were no group differences in weight loss or improvements in cardiorespiratory fitness.

Both adoption and maintenance of exercise programs are inversely associated with exercise intensity (Dishman & Buckworth, 1996; Pollock et al., 1991; Trost et al., 2002). Although adherence was similar in a 1-year randomized exercise trial with middle-aged adults in groups assigned to low or high intensities based on percentage peak heart rate, each group selected intensities during the year that regressed toward a moderate intensity level (King, Haskell, Taylor, & DeBusk, 1991). Perceived effort has a strong negative association with physical activity, so it is possible that prescriptions based on preferred intensities might increase adherence to exercise programs (Dishman, 1994b).

Interventions

Physical activity is a health behavior that encompasses complex behavioral demands. Physical activity is also perceived as requiring more time and effort than other health behaviors (Turk, Rudy, & Salovey, 1984). However, interventions, particularly those based on behavior modification, can be effective in changing exercise behavior at least in the short term. Planning for participation, initial adoption of physical activity, continued participation or maintenance, and overall periodicity of participation (e.g., relapse, resuming activity, and seasonal variation) are characteristics of physical activity that can involve different mediators and may warrant different interventions.

To clarify the early literature in this area, we conducted a quantitative meta-analysis of

127 studies that examined the efficacy of interventions for increasing physical activity among 130,000 people in community, worksite, school, home, and health care settings (Dishman & Buckworth, 1996). The estimated population effect, weighted by sample size, was about three-fourths of a standard deviation, which is comparable to increasing adherence from 50%, the rate typically observed in exercise programs without a behavior change component, to a success rate of about 85% with the intervention. We examined moderators to establish practical information about which interventions worked, with whom, and under what conditions. The largest effects were found when interventions employed the principles of behavior modification and were delivered to healthy people in a community, particularly when the interventions were delivered to groups using media (e.g., telecommunication, print mailings, motivating signage), rather than face-to-face counseling by a professional. The best effect was for unsupervised, low-intensity, leisure-time physical activity. Sustained benefits weren't shown or examined in most studies, though.

Studies using behavioral economics have demonstrated the strong influence of environmental context on sedentary choices made by children and adolescents (Epstein & Roemmich, 2001; Epstein et al., 2004). An emerging focus promotes environmental manipulations that increase opportunities and decrease barriers to physical activity. Informational interventions (e.g., "point-of-decision" prompts to encourage stair use and communitywide campaigns), school-based physical education (e.g., Pate et al., 2005; 2007), social support in community settings, and environmental or policy intervention to create or enhance access to places for physical activity have had some short-term success (Kahn et al. 2002).

Self efficacy. Consistent evidence indicates that self-efficacy is a mediator of behavior change, that is, the mechanism by which an intervention has its effect (e.g., Dishman et al., 2004). There is some longitudinal evidence that exercise self-efficacy increases as one moves from an established sedentary lifestyle to long-term maintenance of regular exercise (Dishman, Motl

et al., 2004; McAuley & Blissmer, 2000). Four sources of efficacy information can be manipulated in interventions: performance accomplishments, vicarious experiences, verbal persuasion, and physiological/psychological states. *Performance accomplishments* refer to mastering a difficult or previously feared task and are the most potent strategy for increasing self-efficacy (Bandura, 1991). Breaking the target behavior into components that are easy to manage (i.e., shaping) helps individuals to develop and refine skills and develop coping mechanisms. Someone who is successful meeting a reasonable but challenging short-term exercise goal will have a sense of accomplishment and increased efficacy. *Vicarious experiences* enable learning via observation of events or other people. Modeling is an effective strategy if the model is similar to the participant and the model succeeds through effort with clear rewarding outcomes. For example, an overweight teenager will develop more confidence for playing soccer if he sees another overweight teen score a goal. *Verbal persuasion* entails encouragement or support to reinforce progress toward reaching the target behavior and fosters the attribution of accomplishments to the person's own behavior. Finally, the *physiological* response to exercise may appear to be negative feedback about performance to sedentary people. Because high arousal impairs performance and decreases efficacy expectations, understanding that heavy breathing, increased heart rate, fatigue, and muscle discomfort are normal responses to exercise can help manage *psychological* arousal during exercise. Teaching individuals to reframe physical symptoms in a positive interpretation and notice positive psychological states with exercise (e.g., increased energy, lower stress) can foster immediate confidence in the person's ability to complete a physical activity task.

Stage-specific interventions. Researchers are beginning to study the mediators of stage transitions in physical activity (Wallace & Buckworth, 2003), which may differ from other health behaviors (Rosen, 2000). Most interventions try to fit the participant to an exercise program or behavioral intervention, rather than fit a program to the characteristics and needs of the participant. A major contribution of the transtheoretical model lies in the assertion that interventions should be targeted or matched to an individual according to his or her activity history and readiness for change (Prochaska & Marcus, 1994). For example, the goal in working with people in the precontemplation stage is to get them to begin thinking about changing. The personal benefits and barriers of exercise should be identified, and ways to overcome the barriers should be addressed. Strategies that help precontemplators develop a personal value for exercise and understand the importance of exercise in a healthy lifestyle are useful in helping them consider exercise (Marcus & Forsyth, 2003; Gorely & Gordon, 1995). Health-risk appraisals and fitness testing don't directly increase sustained physical activity, but they can prompt contemplation and enhance motivation to become more active (King, 1994).

The goal with contemplators is to help them take action. Marketing and media campaigns promoting exercise, as well as accurate, easy-to-understand information about how to start an exercise program, can help move people into the action stage. Other elements that can affect the intention to start exercising are role models, perceived barriers and benefits, and social-cognitive variables such as self-efficacy. Integrating decision theories with social marketing strategies may be helpful for increasing knowledge, attitudes, and intentions to adopt physical activity (Donovan & Owen, 1994; Kahn et al., 2002).

Examples of behavioral strategies

Stimulus control involves manipulating antecedent conditions, or cues, that can prompt a behavior. Prompts can be verbal, physical, or symbolic. The goal is to increase cues for the desired behavior and decrease cues for competing sedentary behaviors. Examples of cues to increase exercise behavior are posters, slogans, posted notes, placement of exercise equipment in visible places, recruitment of social support, and performance of exercise at the same time and place every day (Knapp, 1988). Exercising first thing in the

morning is an example of timing exercise when the risk of distracting cues is less.

Reinforcement control involves understanding and controling the consequences of target behavior to increase or decrease its occurrence. An example of positive reinforcement is an aerobics instructor praising a participant for finishing an especially hard routine. In other words something positive (praise) is added during or immediately after the target behavior to increase its frequency. Contracts with consequences, positive feedback, tokens, participation-based prizes, and group lotteries are other examples of reinforcement control.

Goal setting is used to attain a specific task in a prescribed period of time. Goals can be as simple and time limited as doing a 10-minute walk 3 times in the upcoming week or as complex as participating in a triathlon. Goals serve as immediate regulators of human behavior, providing direction, mobilizing effort, and fostering persistence in completing a task. Specific, measurable and time-limited goals make it easier to monitor progress, make adjustments, and know when the goal has been accomplished. Goals must be reasonable and realistic. A goal might be achievable, but personal and situational constraints can make it unrealistic. For example, losing 2 pounds (1 kg) a week through diet and exercise is reasonable, but almost impossible for the working mother of three who has minimal time for exercise and cooking. Unrealistic goals set the participant up to fail, which can damage self-efficacy and adherence to the behavior-change program.

Manageable short- and long-term goals that are consistent with capabilities, values, resources, and needs should be set. Self-efficacy predicts adoption and maintenance of exercise, and can be increased with mastery experiences. Initial goals should thus be challenging but realistic in order to foster increases in exercise self-efficacy. Environmental and social supports and barriers also should be evaluated and modified to promote the new behaviors.

Social support and relapse prevention can help keep individuals in the action phase from dropping out of an exercise program. Social support is critical in this stage. Instruction in self-regulatory skills, such as stimulus control, reinforcement management, and self-monitoring of progress, and relapse prevention are also useful strategies. Relapse prevention is based on the premises that the impact of interruptions and life events on exercise can be diminished if the individual anticipates and plans for their occurrence, recognizes them as only temporary obstructions, and develops self-regulatory skills for preventing relapses to inactivity (Knapp, 1988).

Movement from the action phase to the maintenance phase follows a decrease in the risk of relapse and an increase in self-efficacy. Interventions will be more effective if they involve reevaluation of rewards and goals and promote strategies to cope with potential lapses from relocation, travel, or medical events. Social support, self-motivation, self-regulatory skills, and interventions such as relapse prevention seem necessary to maintain or resume exercise. Table 25-4 summarizes these tools.

Research Issues in Exercise Behavior

Over 50 different correlates of physical activity have been reported among youths and adults. Our understanding of how these factors operate to influence physical activity continues to behindered by (1) the frequent use of cross-sectional, correlational designs, (2) poorly validated measures of the moderators and mediators, (3) self-report, rather than objective, measures of physical activity, and (4) limited use of statistical procedures that permit multilevel (i.e., personal and group level variables) modeling of direct, indirect (i.e., mediated), and moderated (i.e., interactions of mediators with external factors) relations of physical activity with theoretical networks of determinants.

Mediation Studies. Previous physical activity interventions have been weakly effective in the long term, in part because they didn't focus the intervention on theoretically based mediators of physical activity (e.g., Dishman et al., 2005).

Perceived and Real Environments. Both the perception of living near physical activity facilities and the objective measure of facilities are related to physical activity. Cross-sectional studies have found that self-reports of the social and built environments (e.g., neighborhood safety and facility accessibility) are correlates of physical activity in population-based samples. Studies are needed to determine whether perceived access and actual proximity to facilities have direct relations with physical activity and/or indirect relations moderated or mediated by social-cognitive factors such as social support and efficacy beliefs about overcoming barriers to physical activity. (e.g., Dowda et al., 2009).

Table 25-4 **Applying Behavioral Skills for Physical Activity Promotion**

- **Self-Monitoring**—Have individuals keep a tangible record of progress; use exercise logs to set goals, review progress, and identify areas for improvement.

- **Stimulus Control**—Use cues and prompts to promote exercise behaviors; identify and control psychosocial and environmental cues that have a negative impact on physical activity.

- **Goal Setting**—Have individuals set specific, realistic, but challenging, and measurable short- and long-term goals; use appropriate reward strategies when goals are achieved.

- **Problem Solving**—Identify potential barriers and apply stepwise problem-solving strategies to overcome them; encourage clients to write down their barriers and brainstorm solutions before selecting the best solution to apply.

- **Social Support**—Few goals in life are achieved in isolation; encourage individuals to identify where they need support and identify specific people who can help

- **Cognitive Restructuring and Relapse Prevention**—Recognize unhelpful thought patterns such as negative or all-or-nothing thinking; plan ahead for high risk times and prepare for potential lapses.

Measurement Properties of Scales Used.

Measurement properties of the instruments used to assess mediators usually have not been verified according to high standards using available methods such as confirmatory factor analysis and item response modeling to establish the factorial validity and measurement equivalence or invariance of the measures between different types of people and across time.

Measurement of Physical Activity.   Most studies have used self-reports of physical activity. Fewer, more recent studies have used standardized observational systems or objective monitoring by accelerometry or global positioning devices. Although some self-report measures have been validated by demonstrating correlations with objective measures, those correlations are typically modest, accounting for less than 30% common variance. Studies of moderators and mediators of physical activity should increasingly compare results using both subjective and objective measures to enhance convergence of methods.

Validity of Stages.   Despite its appeal as a model for exercise behavior change and its application in several intervention studies (Spencer et al., 2006), uncertainty remains about whether the transtheoretical model has stages and processes that are applicable to understanding physical activity change, especially adherence after the adoption of an exercise program (Adams & White, 2005; Dishman 1991; Godin et al., 2004; Rosen 2000; Weinstein et al 1998). Bandura (1997b) raised several concerns and criticisms of the transtheoretical model in general, such as a lack of adherence to basic tenants of traditional stage theory (i.e., qualitative transformations across stages and invariant sequence of change). A recent meta-analysis of the transtheoretical model literature concluded that experiential and behavioral processes of change were applied sequentially across stage transitions for smoking cessation, but were employed simultaneously by people trying to adopt regular exercise. This conclusion suggests that readiness for exercise is not a discrete variable (Rosen 2000). The usefulness of the transtheoretical model for exercise interventions has

also been mixed. No longitudinal studies demonstrate that a change in a person's stage accurately predicts a change in physical activity, and the instruments to measure stage (e.g., Godin et al., 2004; Reed, Velicer, Prochaska, Rossi, and Marcus 1997) and processes of change have been poorly validated for exercise (Dishman 1991; Dishman 1994a; Paxton et al., 2008; Rosen 2000).

Measurement of Change using Multilevel Models.   Conceptual models should include variables measured at the individual level (e.g., personal motivation), including the family and home environment, but also measured at the community level (e.g., neighborhoods, churches, schools). Complex models are needed to describe the independent and interactive contributions of key variables at each level to change in physical activity. Advanced techniques such as structural equation modeling and latent growth modeling provide optimal precision for multilevel, theoretically derived analysis of change in physical activity. Three or more measurement periods are needed to examine change and to assess inter-individual variation in initial status (i.e., baseline) and inter- and intra-individual variation in change

Gene-Environment Interactions.   Little is known about how genes, the environment, and their interactions influence the brain's regulation of physical activity behavior or mental health outcomes of physical activity (De Moor, Boomsma, Stubbe, Willemsen, & de Geus, 2008). Family and twin studies have reported that 30–70% of the variation in human physical activity is inherited (e.g., Stubbe et al., 2006), and a few studies have implicated candidate genes that might explain small, but significant, portions of that variation (e.g., Rankinen et al., 2006). Most candidate genes for physical activity suggested by correlational studies were selected for study based on understanding of energy intake pathways that influence energy balance more so than models of otherwise motivated behavior (Simonen et al., 2003). However, some genes that have been studied (e.g., those related to dopamine, serotonin, and Orexin A) might be involved in regulation of motivation systems for both feeding and physical activity (Dishman, 2008).

Summary

Population studies using prospective epidemiological designs have reported that self-rated symptoms of depression, anxiety, and feelings of distress and fatigue are lower among people who are physically active regardless of gender, age, and race, although minority groups have been understudied. Randomized controlled trials of varying quality show that small-to-moderate decreases in self-rated anxiety and depression and improvements in sleep quality accompany both acute and chronic exercise. A few good studies were on patients diagnosed with depression and anxiety disorders. Prospective cohort studies and randomized controlled trials also suggest that physical activity is useful for enhancing cognitive performance in children, slowing cognitive decline associated with adult aging, and slowing the onset of dementia. More application of methodologies from behavioral and cognitive neuroscience is needed to help explain how physical activity and exercise affect the brain. Most of the exercise training programs lasted about 4 to 5 months, but without behavior modification nearly 25–50% of people drop out of an exercise program within that time period. So, much of the potential benefits of exercise are lost because people quit.

Clarifying the factors that affect physical activity habits over time is a major focus in exercise psychology. A lot of research has been conducted over the past 25 years to identify determinants of exercise adoption and adherence and to apply interventions to increase physical activity. However, effects have been modest for sustaining increases in physical activity. Recent research has focused on environmental factors that may be associated with physical activity in children and adults, such as the impact of the built environment on transportation and access to physical activity settings.

The modest success in sustaining increases in physical activity within the U.S. population can be attributed to the complexity of physical activity and gaps and weaknesses in the research discussed earlier. Experimental evidence verifying how interventions change putative mediators of physical activity (e.g., goals, intentions and efficacy beliefs about overcoming barriers to physical activity) or how environmental or social factors (e.g., access and social support) modify the effectiveness of interventions are needed. Also, research must consider multilevel (i.e., personal and group) influences within dynamic theories that explain the interaction of personal motivation with social and physical environments. The origin and time course for intrinsic reinforcement of physical activity remain unknown, so persistent interventions at the personal and population level, including community, school, worksite, and clinical settings, are required along with national policy initiatives that provide better social and environmental infrastructures to promote and support physical activity.

Study Questions

1. What is meant when we talk about the dose-response for decreases in depression after exercise?

2. List and discuss three plausible explanations or mechanisms for changes in mental health with exercise training.

3. What is executive control function and what evidence suggests that regular exercise affects it?

4. What are potential public health benefits from exercise-induced decreases in responses to mental stress?

5. List the three major research areas in exercise psychology, and discuss public health implications of each.

6. List the primary factors involved in behavior change according to social-cognitive, behavior modification, and cognitive-behavior modification theories.

7. Describe the major components of transtheoretical model and their weaknesses for understanding maintenance of physical activity change.

8. What are the three general categories of physical activity correlates? Give examples of moderators or mediators in each category. Discuss why it is important to consider how different correlates might interact.

9. A sedentary friend wants to "get in shape" and started walking after work 2 weeks ago. He missed walking for the past 3 days and asked for your help to restart his program and keep it going. What exercise stage is he in? How could relapse prevention theory help?

10. Describe cues that prompt you to exercise and some of the ways your exercise is reinforced.

References

Adams J, White M. (2005). *Why don't stage-based activity promotion interventions work?* Health Education Research. 20(2), 237–243

Adlard, P. A., & Cotman, C. W. (2004). Voluntary exercise protects against stress-induced decreases in brain-derived neurotrophic factor protein expression. *Neuroscience, 124,* 985–992.

Ajzen, I. (2002). Perceived behavioral control, self-efficacy, locus of control, and the theory of planned behavior. *Journal of Applied Social Psychology, 32,* 1–20.

Allender S., Foster C., Scarborough P., & Rayner, M. (2007). The burden of physical activity–related ill health in the UK. *Journal of Epidemiology and Community Health, 4,* 344–348.

American Psychiatric Association. (1994). *Diagnostic and statistical manual of mental disorders* (4th ed.). Washington, DC: American Psychiatric Association.

Anderson, B. J., Rapp, D. N., Baek, D. H., McCloskey, D. P., Coburn-Litvak, P. S., & Robinson, J. K. (2000). Exercise influences spatial learning in the radial arm maze. *Physiology and Behavior, 70,* 425–429.

Bandura A. (1994). Health promotion by social cognitive means. *Health Education and Behavior, 31,* 143–164.

Bandura, A. (1991). Social cognitive theory of self-regulation. *Organizational Behavior and Human Decision Processes, 50,* 248–287.

Bandura A. (1997a). *Self-efficacy: The exercise of control.* New York: W.H. Freeman and Company, 1997.

Bandura, A. (1997b). The anatomy of stages of change [Editorial]. *American Journal of Health Promotion, 12*, 8–10.

Baranowski, T., Anderson, C., & Carmack, C. (1998). Mediating variable framework in physical activity interventions: How are we doing? How might we do better? *American Journal of Preventive Medicine, 15*, 266–297.

Barnekow-Bergkvist, M., Hedberg, G., Janlert, U., & Jansson, E. (1998). Prediction of physical fitness and physical activity level in adulthood by physical performance and physical activity in adolescence—An 18-year follow-up study. *Scandinavian Journal of Medicine and Science in Sports, 8*, 299–308.

Barnes, P. (2007). *Physical activity among adults: United States, 2000 and 2005*. Hyattsville, MD: US Department of Heath and Human Services, CDC. Available at http://www.cdc.gov/nchs/products/pubs/pubd/hestats/physicalactivity/physicalactivity.htm.

Bauman, A. & Craig, C.L. (2005). The place of physical activity in the WHO Global Strategy on Diet and Physical Activity. *International Journal of Behavioral Nutrition and Physical Activity, 2*, 10.

Beard, J.R., Heathcote, K., Brooks, R., Earnest A., & Kelly, B. (2007). Predictors of mental disorders and their outcome in a community based cohort. *Social Psychiatry and Psychiatric Epidemiology, 42* (8), 623–630.

Biddle, S.J.H., & Nigg, C. R. (2000). Theories of exercise behavior. *International Journal of Sport Psychology, 31*, 290–304.

Blair, S. N., Booth, M., Gyarfas, I., Iwane, H., Marti, B., Matsudo, V., Morrow, M. S., Noakes, T., & Shephard, R. (1996). Development of public policy and physical activity initiatives internationally. *Sports Medicine, 21*, 157–163.

Blumenthal, J.A., Babyak, M.A., Doraiswamy, P.M., et al., (2007). Exercise and pharmacology in the treatment of major depressive disorder. *Psychosomatic Medicine, 69*, 587–596.

Blumenthal, J. A., Babyak, M. A., Moore, K. A., Craighead, W. E., Herman, S., Khatri, P., Waugh, R., Napolitano, M. A., Forman, L. M., Appelbaum, M., Doraiswamy, P. M., & Krishnan, K. R. (1999). Effects of exercise training on older patients with major depression. *Archives of Internal Medicine, 159*, 2349–2356.

Boecker H., Sprenger T., Spilker M. E., Henriksen G., Koppenhoefer M., Wagner K. J., Valet M., Berthele A., Tolle T. R. (2008, February 21). The runner's high: Opioidergic mechanisms in the human brain. *Cerebral Cortex*. 18(11), 2523–2531.

Brenes, G. A., Williamson, J. D., Messier, S. P., Rejeski, W. J., Pahor, M., Ip, E., & Penninx W. J. H. (2007). Treatment of minor depression in older adults: a pilot study comparing sertraline and exercise. *Aging & Mental Health, 11*, 61–68.

Broocks, A., Bandelow, B., Pekrun, G., George, A., Meyer, T., Bartmann, U., et al. (1998). Comparison of aerobic exercise, clomipramine, and placebo in the treatment of panic disorder. *American Journal of Psychiatry, 155*, 603–609.

Buckworth, J. (2003). Behavior modification. In E. T. Howley & B. D. Franks (Eds.), *Health fitness instructor's handbook* (4th ed.). Champaign, IL: Human Kinetics.

Buckworth, J., & Dishman, R. K. (2002). *Exercise Psychology.* Champaign, IL: Human Kinetics.

Bulbulian, R., & Darabos, B. L. (1986). Motor neuron excitability: The Hoffmann reflex following exercise of low and high intensity. *Medicine and Science in Sports and Exercise, 18,* 697–702.

Centers for Disease Control and Prevention (2005). Trends in leisure-time physical inactivity by age, sex, and race/ethnicity—United States, 1994–2004. *Morbidity and Mortality Weekly Report, 54* (39), 991–994.

Centers for Disease Control and Prevention. (2007). Prevalence of regular physical activity among adults—United States, 2001 and 2005. *Morbidity and Mortality Weekly Report, 56,* 1209–1212.

Chaouloff, F. (1997). Effects of acute physical exercise on central serotonergic systems. *Medicine and Science in Sports and Exercise, 29,* 58–62.

Chodzko-Zajko, W. J., & Moore, K. A. (1994). Physical fitness and cognitive functioning in aging. *Exercise and Sport Sciences Reviews, 22,* 195–220.

Colcombe, S. J., Kramer, A. F., Erickson, K. I., Scalf, P., McAuley, E., Cohen, N. J., Webb, A., Jerome, G. J., Marquez, D. X., & Elavsky, S. (2004). Cardiovascular fitness, cortical plasticity, and aging. *Proceedings National Academy of Sciences U S A, 101* (9), 3316–3321.

Colcombe, S. J., Erickson, K. I., Scalf, P. E., Kim, J. S., Prakash, R., McAuley, E., Elavsky, S., Marquez, D. X., Hu, L., & Kramer, A. F. (2006). Aerobic exercise training increases brain volume in aging humans. *The Journals of Gerontology. Series A, Biological Sciences and Medical Sciences, 61* (11), 1166–1170.

Cook, D. B., & Koltyn, K. F. (2000). Pain and exercise. *International Journal of Sport Psychology, 31,* 256–277.

Cotman C. W., & Berchtold N. C. (2002). Exercise: A behavioral intervention to enhance brain health and plasticity. *Trends in Neuroscience, 25* (6), 295–301.

Courneya, K. S., & Hellsten, L. M. (1998). Personality correlates of exercise behavior, motives, barriers, and preferences: An application of the five-factor model. *Personality and Individual Differences, 24,* 625–633.

Crabbe, J. B., & Dishman, R. K. (2004). Brain electrocortical activity during and after exercise: A quantitative synthesis. *Psychophysiology, 41,* 563–574.

Crabbe, J. B., Smith, J. C., & Dishman, R. K. (2007). Emotional & electroencephalographic responses during affective picture viewing after exercise. *Physiology & Behavior, 90* (2–3), 394–404.

Crews, D. J., & Landers, D. M. (1987). A metaanalytic review of aerobic fitness and re-activity to psychosocial stressors. *Medicine and Science in Sports and Exercise, 19* (Suppl.), S114–S120.

Davis, C. L., Tomporowski P. D., Boyle, C. A., Waller, J. L., Miller, P. H., Naglieri, J. A., & Gregoski, M. (2007). Effects of aerobic exercise on overweight children's cognitive functioning: a randomized controlled trial. *Research Quarterly for Exercise and Sport, 78,* 1–10.

De Moor, M. H. M., Beem, A. L., Stubbe, J. H., Boomsma, D. I., & de Geus, E. J. C. (2006). Regular exercise, anxiety, depression and personality: A population-based study. *Preventive Medicine, 42,* 273–279.

De Moor, M. H., Boomsma, D. I., Stubbe, J. H., Willemsen, G., & de Geus, E. J. (2008). Testing causality in the association between regular exercise and symptoms of anxiety and depression. *Archives of General Psychiatry*, 65 (8), 897–905.

Desharnais, R., Jobin, J., Cote, C., Levesque, L., & Godin, G. (1993). Aerobic exercise and the placebo effect: A controlled study. *Psychosomatic Medicine, 55,* 149–154.

Dishman, R. K. (Ed.). (1994a). *Advances in exercise adherence.* Champaign, IL: Human Kinetics.

Dishman, R. K. (1997). Brain monoamines, exercise and behavioral stress: Animal models. *Medicine and Science in Sports and Exercise, 29,* 63–67.

Dishman, R.K. (2008). Gene-physical activity interactions in the etiology of obesity: Behavioral considerations. *Obesity,* 16 Suppl 3, 560–565.

Dishman, R. K. (1991). Increasing and maintaining exercise and physical activity. *Behavior Therapy, 22,* 345–378.

Dishman, R. K. (2000). Introduction: Special issue on exercise psychology. *International Journal of Sport Psychology, 31,* 103–109.

Dishman, R. K. (1998). Physical activity and mental health. In H. S. Friedman (Ed.), *Encyclopedia of Mental Health* (Vol. 3, pp. 171–188). San Diego, CA: Academic Press.

Dishman, R. K. (1994b). Prescribing exercise intensity for healthy adults using perceived exertion. *Medicine and Science in Sports and Exercise, 26,* 1087–1094.

Dishman, R. K. (1994c). The measurement conundrum in exercise adherence research. *Medicine and Science in Sports and Exercise, 26,* 1382–1390.

Dishman, R. K., Berthoud, H. R., Booth, F. W., Cotman, C. W., Edgerton, V. R., Fleshner, M. R., Gandevia, S. C., Gomez-Pinilla, F., Greenwood, B. N., Hillman, C. H., Kramer, A. F., Levin, B. E, Moran, T. H., Russo-Neustadt, A. A., Salamone, J. D., Van Hoomissen, J. D., Wade, C. E., York, D. A., & Zigmond, M. J. (2006). Neurobiology of exercise. *Obesity (Silver Spring), 14* (3), 345–56.

Dishman, R. K., & Buckworth, J. (1996). Increasing physical activity: A quantitative synthesis. *Medicine and Science in Sports and Exercise, 28,* 706–719.

Dishman, R. K., Hales, D., Pfeiffer, K., Felton, G., Saunders, R., Ward, D. S., Dowda, M., & Pate R. R. (2006). Physical self-concept and self-esteem mediate the association of physical activity with depression symptoms in adolescent girls: a cross-sectional study. *Health Psychology, 25* (3), 396–407.

Dishman, R. K., & Jackson, E. M. (2000). Exercise, fitness, and stress. *International Journal of Sport Psychology, 31,* 175–203.

Dishman, R. K., Motl, R. W., Saunders, R., Felton, G., Ward, D. S., Dowda, M., & Pate, R. R. (2004). Self-efficacy partially mediates the effect of a school-based physical-activity intervention among adolescent girls. *Preventive Medicine, 38,* 628–636.

Dishman, R. K., Nakamura, Y., Jackson, E. M., & Ray, C. A. (2003). Blood pressure and sympathetic nerve activity during cold pressor stress: Fitness and gender. *Psychophysiology, 40,* 370–380.

Dishman, R. K., & O'Connor, P. J. (2009). Lessons in exercise neurobiology: the case of endorphins. Mental Health and Physical Activity, published online, 31 January 2009. *doi: 10.1016/j.mhpa.2009.01.002*

Dishman, R. K., Renner, K. J., Youngstedt, S. D., Reigle, T. G., Bunnell, B. N., Burke, K. A., Yoo, H. S., Mougey, E. H., & Meyerhoff, J. L. (1997). Activity wheel running reduces escape latency and alters brain monoamine levels after footshock. *Brain Research Bulletin, 42* (5), 399–406.

Dishman, R. K., & Sallis, J. F. (1994). Determinants and interventions for physical activity and exercise. In C. Bouchard, R. J. Shephard, & T. Stephens (Eds.), *Physical activity, fitness and health: International proceedings and consensus statement* (pp. 214–238). Champaign, IL: Human Kinetics.

Dishman, R. K., Saunders, R., Dowda, M., Felton, G., Ward, D., & Pate, R. R. (2006). Goals and intentions mediate efficacy beliefs and declining physical activity in girls. *American Journal of Preventive Medicine, 31* (6), 475–483.

Dowda, M., Dishman, R. K., Pfeiffer, K. A., & Pate, R. R. (2007). Family support for physical activity in girls from 8th to 12th grade in South Carolina. *Preventive Medicine, 44* (2):153–159.

Dowda, M., Dishman, R. K., Porter, D., Saunders, R. P., & Pate, R. R. (2009). Commercial facilities, social cognitive variables, and physical activity of 12th grade girls. Annals of Behavioral Medicine, published online 20 February 2009 DOI 10.1007/s12160-009-9080-0

Dunn, A. L., Reigle, T. G., Youngstedt, S. D., Armstrong, R. B., & Dishman, R. K. (1996). Brain norepinephrine and metabolites after treadmill training and wheel running in rats. *Medicine and Science in Sports and Exercise, 28,* 204–209.

Dunn, A. L., Trivedi, M. H., Kampert, J. B., Clark, C. G., & Chambliss, H. O. (2005). Exercise treatment for depression efficacy and dose response. *American Journal of Preventive Medicine, 28,* 1–8.

Dunn, A. L., Trivedi, M. H., & O'Neal, H. A. (2001). Physical activity dose-response effects on outcomes of depression and anxiety. *Medicine and Science in Sports and Exercise, 33,* S587–S597.

Dzewaltowski, D. A. (1994). Physical activity determinants: A social cognitive approach. *Medicine and Science in Sports and Exercise, 26,* 1395–1399.

Ekeland, E., Heian, F., Hagen, K. B., Abbott, J., & Nordheim, L. (2004). Exercise to improve self-esteem in children and young people. *Cochrane Database of Systematic Reviews, 1:* CD003683.

Epstein, L. H. & Roemmich, J. N. (2001). Reducing sedentary behavior: Role in modifying physical activity. *Exercise and Sport Sciences Reviews, 29* (3), 103–108.

Epstein, L. H., Roemmich, J. N., Saad, F. G., & Handley, E. A. (2004). The value of sedentary alternatives influences child physical activity choice. *International Journal of Behavioral Medicine, 11* (4), 236–242.

Etnier, J. L., Nowell, P. M., Landers, D. M., & Sibley, B. A. (2006). A meta-regression to examine the relationship between aerobic fitness and cognitive performance. *Brain Research Reviews, 52* (1), 119–30.

Etnier, J. L., Salazar, W., Landers, D. M., Petruzzello, S. J., Han, M., & Nowell, P. (1997). The influence of physical fitness and exercise upon cognitive functioning: A meta-analysis. *Journal of Sport and Exercise Psychology, 19*, 249–277.

Faulkner, G. E. J. & Taylor, A. H. (2005). *Exercise, health and mental health.* New York: Routledge, pp. 1-233.

Fordyce, D. E., & Farrar, R. P. (1991). Enhancement of spatial learning in F344 rats by physical activity and related learning-associated alterations in hippocampal and cortical cholinergic functioning. *Behavioral Brain Research, 46*, 123–133.

Fox, K. R. (2000). Self-esteem, self-perceptions and exercise. *International Journal of Sport Psychology, 31*, 228–240.

Fulcher, K. Y. & White, P. D. (1997). Randomised controlled trial of graded exercise in patients with the chronic fatigue syndrome. *BMJ, 314* (7095), 1647–1652.

Garcia, C., Chen, M. J., Garza, A. A., Cotman, C. W., Russo-Neustadt, A. (2003). The influence of specific noradrenergic and serotonergic lesions on the expression of hippocampal brain-derived neurotrophic factor transcripts following voluntary physical activity. *Neuroscience, 119*, 721–732.

Godin, G. (1994). Social-cognitive models. In R. K. Dishman (Ed.), *Advances in exercise adherence* (pp. 113–136). Champaign, IL: Human Kinetics.

Godin, G., Lambert, L. D., Owen, N., Nolin, B., & Prud'homme, D. (2004). Stages of motivational readiness for physical activity: a comparison of different algorithms of classification. *British Journal of Health Psychology, 9* (Pt. 2), 253–67.

Goodwin, R. D. (2003). Association between physical activity and mental disorders among adults in the United States. *Preventive Medicine, 36* (6), 698–703.

Gorely, T., & Gordon, S. (1995). An examination of the transtheoretical model of exercise behavior in older adults. *Journal of Sport and Exercise Psychology, 17*, 312–324.

Grunbaum, J. A., Kann, L., Kinchen, S., Ross, J., Hawkins, J., Lowry, R., Harris, W. A., McManus, T., Chyen, D., & Collins, J. (2004). Youth risk behavior surveillance—United States, 2003. *Morbidity and Mortality Weekly Reports: Surveillance Summaries, 53* (2), 1–96.

Gustafson, S. L. & Rhodes, R. E. (2006). Parental correlates of physical activity in children and early adolescents. *Sports Medicine, 36* (1), 79–97.

Heyn, P., Abreu, B. C., & Ottenbacher, K. J. (2004). The effects of exercise training on elderly persons with cognitive impairment and dementia: a meta-analysis. *Archives of Physical Medicine and Rehabilitation, 85* (10), 1694–1704.

Hunsberger, J. G., Newton, S. S., Bennett, A. H., Duman, C. H., Russell, D. S., Salton, S. R., & Duman, R. S. (2007). Antidepressant actions of the exercise-regulated gene VGF. *Nature Medicine, 13* (12), 1476–1482.

Ivy, A. S., Rodriguez, F. G., Garcia, C., Chen, M. J., & Russo-Neustadt, A. A. (2003). Noradrenergic and serotonergic blockade inhibits BDNF mRNA activation following exercise and antidepressant. *Pharmacology, Biochemistry, and Behavior, 75,* 81–88.

Jackson, E. M. & Dishman, R. K. (2002). Hemodynamic responses to stress among black women: Fitness and parental hypertension. *Medicine and Science in Sports and Exercise, 34,* 1097–1104.

Jackson, E. M. & Dishman, R. K. (2006). Cardiorespiratory fitness and laboratory stress: a meta-regression analysis. *Psychophysiology, 43* (1), 57–72. Erratum in: *Psychophysiology, 43* (1) (2006, January), 126.

Jakicic, J. M., Winters, C., Lang, W., & Wing, R. R. (1999). Effects of intermittent exercise and use of home exercise equipment on adherence, weight loss, and fitness in over-weight women: A randomized trial. *Journal of the American Medical Association, 282,* 1554–1560.

Joubert, J., Norman, R., Lambert, E. V., Groenewald, P., Schneider, M., Bull, F., & Bradshaw, D.; South African Comparative Risk Assessment Collaborating Group. (2007). Estimating the burden of disease attributable to physical inactivity in South Africa in 2000. *South African Medical Journal, 97* (8, Pt. 2), 725–731.

Kahn, E. B., Ramsey, L. T., Brownson, R. C., Heath, G. W., Howze, E. H., Powell, K. E., et al. (2002). The effectiveness of interventions to increase physical activity. A systematic review. *American Journal of Preventive Medicine, 22,* 73–107.

Kendzierski, D. (1994). Schema theory: An information processing focus. In R. K. Dishman (Ed.), *Advances in exercise adherence* (pp. 137–159). Champaign, IL: Human Kinetics.

Kessler, R. C., McGonagle, K. A., Zhao, S., Nelson, C. B., Hughes, M., Eshleman, S., Wittchen, H., & Kendler, K. S. (1994). Lifetime and 12 month prevalence of DSM-III-R psychiatric disorders in the United States. *Archives of General Psychiatry, 51,* 8–19.

King, A. C. (1994). Community and public health approaches to the promotion of physical activity. *Medicine and Science in Sports and Exercise, 26,* 1405–1412.

King, A. C., Haskell, W. L., Taylor, H. C., & DeBusk, R. F. (1991). Group- vs. home-based exercise training in healthy older men and women. *Journal of the American Medical Association, 266,* 1535–1542.

King, A. C., Oman, R. F., Brassington, G. S., Bliwise, D. L., & Haskell, W. L. (1997). Moderate-intensity exercise and self-rated quality of sleep in older adults. A randomized controlled trial. *Journal of the American Medical Association, 277,* 32–37.

Knapp, D. N. (1988). Behavioral management techniques and exercise promotion. In R. K. Dishman (Ed.), *Exercise adherence: Its impact on public health* (pp. 203–236), Champaign, IL: Human Kinetics.

Koltyn, K. F., & Morgan, W. P. (1992). Influence of underwater exercise on anxiety and body temperature. *Scandinavian Journal of Medicine, Science and Sports, 2,* S41.

Landers, D. M., & Petruzzello, S. J. (1994). Physical activity, fitness, and anxiety. In C. Bouchard, R. J. Shephard, & T. Stephens (Eds.), *Physical activity, fitness and health: Proceedings and consensus statement* (pp. 868–882). Champaign, IL: Human Kinetics.

Lange, G. Cook, D. B., & Natelson. B. H. (2005). Rehabilitation and treatment of fatigue. In J. DeLuca (Ed.) *Fatigue as a Window to the Brain*. Cambridge, MA, MIT Press.

Lawlor, D. A., & Hopker, S. W. (2001). The effectiveness of exercise as an intervention in the management of depression: Systematic review and meta-regression analysis of randomized trials. *British Medical Journal, 322*, 1–8.

Lopez, A. D., Mathers, C. D., Ezzati, M., Jamison, D. T., & Murray, C. J. (2006). Global and regional burden of disease and risk factors, 2001: Systematic analysis of population health data. *Lancet, 367* (9524), 1747–1757.

MacKinnon D. P., Fairchild A. J., Fritz M. S. (2007). Mediation analysis. *Annual Review of Psychology, 58*, 593–614.

Marcus, B. H., & Forsyth, L. H. (2003). *Motivating people to be physically active*. Champaign, IL: Human Kinetics.

Marcus, B. H., Pinto, B. M., Simkin, L. R., Audrain, J. E., & Taylor, E. R. (1994). Application of theoretical models to exercise behavior among employed women. *American Journal of Health Promotion, 9*, 49–55.

Marcus, B. H., & Simkin, L. R. (1994). The transtheoretical model: Applications to exercise behavior. *Medicine and Science in Sports and Exercise, 26*, 1400–1404.

Marshall, S. J., & Biddle, S. J. H. (2001). The transtheoretical model of behavior change: A meta-analysis of applications to physical activity and exercise. *Annals of Behavioral Medicine, 23*, 229–246.

Mathers, C. D., & Loncar, D. (2006). Projections of global mortality and burden of disease from 2002 to 2030. *PLoS Medicine, 3* (11), e442.

McAuley, E. (1994). Physical activity and psychosocial outcomes. In C. Bouchard & R. J. Shephard (Eds.), *Physical activity, fitness, and health: International proceedings and consensus statement* (pp. 551–568). Champaign, IL: Human Kinetics.

McAuley, E., & Blissmer, B. (2000). Self-efficacy determinants and consequences of physical activity. *Exercise and Sport Sciences Reviews, 28*, 85–88.

McAuley, E., Kramer, A. F., & Colcombe, S. J. (2004). Cardiovascular fitness and neurocognitive function in older adults: A brief review. *Brain Behavior and Immunity, 18* (3), 214–220.

McCloskey, D. P., Adamo, D. S., & Anderson, B. J. (2001). Exercise increases metabolic capacity in the motor cortex and striatum, but not in the hippocampus. *Brain Research, 891*, 168–175.

Merom, D., Phongsavan, P., Wagner, R., Chey, T., Marnane, C., Steel, Z., Silove, D., & Bauman, A. (2007). Promoting walking as an adjunct intervention to group cognitive behavioral therapy for anxiety disorders—A pilot group randomized trial. *Journal of Anxiety Disorders*. doi:10.1016/j.janxdis.2007.09.010.

Michaud, C. M., McKenna, M. T., Begg, S., Tomijima, N., Majmudar, M., Bulzacchelli, M. T., Ebrahim, S., Ezzati, M., Salomon, J. A., Kreiser, J. G., Hogan, M., & Murray, C. J. (2006). The burden of disease and injury in the United States 1996. *Population Health Metrics, 4*, 11.

Morgan, K. (2003). Daytime activity and risk factors for late-life insomnia. *Journal of Sleep Research, 12,* 231–238.

Morgan, W. P. (1994). Physical activity, fitness, and depression. In C. Bouchard, R. J. Shephard, & T. Stephens (Eds.), *Physical activity, fitness and health: International proceedings and consensus statement* (pp. 851–867). Champaign, IL: Human Kinetics.

Moss-Morris, R., Sharon, C., Tobin, R., & Baldi, J. C. (2005). A randomized controlled graded exercise trial for chronic fatigue syndrome: outcomes and mechanisms of change. *Journal of Health Psychology, 10*(2), 245–259.

Motl, R. W., Birnbaum, A., Kubik, M., & Dishman, R. K. (2004). Naturally occurring changes in physical activity are inversely related to depressive symptoms during early adolescence. *Psychosomatic Medicine, 66* (3), 336–342.

Motl, R. W., & Dishman, R. K. (2003). Acute leg-cycling exercise attenuates the H-reflex recorded in soleus but not flexor carpi radialis. *Muscle & Nerve, 28,* 609–614.

Motl, R. W., & Dishman, R. K. (2004). Effects of acute exercise on the soleus H-reflex and self-reported anxiety after caffeine ingestion. *Physiology & Behavior, 80,* 577–585.

Motl, R. W., Dishman, R. K., Saunders, R. P., Dowda M., & Pate, R. R. (2007). Perceptions of physical and social environment variables and self-efficacy as correlates of self-reported physical activity among adolescent girls. *Journal of Pediatric Psychology, 32* (1), 6–12.

Motl, R. W., Konopack, J. F., McAuley, E., Elavsky, S., Jerome, G. J., & Marquez, D. X. (2005). Depressive symptoms among older adults: long-term reduction after a physical activity intervention. *Journal of Behavioral Medicine, 28,* 385–394.

Motl, R. W., O'Connor, P. J., & Dishman, R. K. (2004). Effects of cycling exercise on the soleus H-reflex and state anxiety among men with low or high trait anxiety. *Psychophysiology, 41,* 96–105.

Nybo, L., & Secher, N. H. (2004). Cerebral perturbations provoked by prolonged exercise. *Progress in Neurobiology, 72,* 223–261.

O'Connor, P. J., Morgan, W. P., Raglin, J. S., Barksdale, C. N., & Kalin, N. H. (1989). Mood state and salivary cortisol levels following overtraining in female swimmers. *Psychoneuroendocrinology, 14,* 303–310.

O'Connor, P. J., Petruzzello, S. J., Kubitz, K. A., & Robinson, T. L. (1995). Anxiety responses to maximal exercise testing. *British Journal of Sports Medicine, 29,* 97–102.

O'Connor, P. J., Raglin, J. S., & Martinsen, E. W. (2000). Physical activity, anxiety and anxiety disorders. *International Journal of Sport Psychology, 31,* 136–155.

O'Neal, H. A., Dunn, A. L., & Martinsen, E. W. (2000). Depression and exercise. *International Journal of Sport Psychology, 31,* 110–135.

O'Neal, H. A., Van Hoomissen, J. D., Holmes, P. V., & Dishman, R. K. (2001). Prepro-galanin messenger RNA levels are increased in rat locus coeruleus after treadmill exercise training. *Neuroscience Letters, 299* (1–2), 69–72.

Pate, R. R., Saunders, R., Dishman, R. K., Addy, C., Dowda, M., & Ward, D. S. (2007). Long-term effects of a physical activity intervention in high school girls. *American Journal of Preventive Medicine, 33* (4), 276–280.

Pate, R. R., Ward, D. S., Saunders, R. P., Felton, G., Dishman, R. K., & Dowda, M. (2005). Promotion of physical activity among high-school girls: a randomized controlled trial. *American Journal of Public Health, 95* (9), 1582–1587.

Paxton, R. J., Nigg, C. R., Motl, R. W., McGee, K. A., McCurdy, D. K., Horwath, C. C., & Dishman, R. K. (2008). Are constructs of the Transtheoretical Model for physical activity measured equivalently between sexes, age groups, and ethnicities? *Annals of Behavioral Medicine, 32,* in press.

Petruzzello, S. J., Hall, E. E., & Ekkekakis, P. (2001). Regional brain activation as a biological marker of affective responsivity to acute exercise: Influence of fitness. *Psychophysiology, 38* (1), 99–106.

Petruzzello, S. J., Landers, D. M., & Salazar, W. (1993). Exercise and anxiety reduction: Examination of temperature as an explanation for affective change. *Journal of Sport and Exercise Psychology, 15,* 63–76.

Pinchasov, B. B., Shurgaja, A. M., Grischin, O. V., & Putilov, A. A. (2000). Mood and energy regulation in seasonal and non-seasonal depression before and after midday treatment with physical exercise or bright light. *Psychiatry Research, 94* (1), 29–42.

Pollock, M. L., Carroll, J. F., Graves, J. E., Leggett, S. H., Braith, R. W., Limacher, M., & Hagberg, J. M. (1991). Injuries and adherence to walk/jog and resistance programs in the elderly. *Medicine and Science in Sports and Exercise, 23,* 1194–1200.

Powell, P., Bentall, R. P., Nye, F. J., & Edwards, R. H. (2004). Patient education to encourage graded exercise in chronic fatigue syndrome. 2-year follow-up of randomised controlled trial. *British Journal of Psychiatry, 184,* 142–146.

Pressman, S. D. & Cohen, S. (2005). Does positive affect influence health? *Psychological Bulletin, 131,* 925–971.

Prochaska, J. O. & Marcus, B. H. (1994). The transtheoretical model: Applications to exercise. In R. K. Dishman (Ed.), *Advances in exercise adherence* (pp. 161–180). Champaign, IL: Human Kinetics.

Puetz, T. W. (2006). Physical activity and feelings of energy and fatigue: epidemiological evidence. *Sports Medicine, 36* (9), 767–80.

Puetz, T., O'Connor, P. J., & Dishman, R. K. (2006). Effects of exercise on feelings of energy and fatigue: a quantitative synthesis. *Psychological Bulletin, 132* (6), 866–876.

Rankinen, T., Bray, M. S., Hagberg, J. M., Perusse, L., Roth, S. M., Wolfarth, B., & Bouchard, C. (2006). The human gene map for performance and health-related fitness phenotypes: the 2005 update. *Medicine and Science in Sports and Exercise, 38* (11), 1863–1888.

Reed, G. R., Velicer, W. F., Prochaska, J. O., Rossi, J. S. & Marcus, B. H. (1997). What makes a good staging algorithm: Examples from regular exercise. *American Journal of Health Promotion, 12* (1), 57–66.

Rhodes R. E., Smith N. E. (2006). Personality correlates of physical activity: a review and meta-analysis. *British Journal of Sports Medicine, 40* (12), 958–965.

Rodgers, W. M. & Murray, T. C. (2007, October 17). Distinguishing among perceived control, perceived difficulty, and self-efficacy as determinants of intentions and behaviours. *British Journal of Social Psychology, 47(*4), 607–630.

Rosen, C. S. (2000). Is the sequencing of change processes by stage consistent across health problems? A meta-analysis. *Health Psychology, 19,* 593–604.

Rowland, T. W. (1998). The biological basis of physical activity. *Medicine and Science in Sports and Exercise, 30,* 392–399.

Royall, D. R., Lauterbach, E. C., Cummings, J. L., Reeve, A., Rummans, T. A., Kaufer, D. I., LaFrance, W. C., Jr., & Coffey, C. E. (2002). Executive control function: A review of its promise and challenges for clinical research. A report from the Committee on Research of the American Neuropsychiatric Association. *Journal of Neuropsychiatry and Clinical Neuroscience, 14* (4), 377–405.

Russo-Neustadt, A. (2003). Brain-derived neurotrophic factor, behavior, and new directions for the treatment of mental disorders. *Seminar in Clinical Neuropsychiatry, 8,* 109–118.

Ryan, R. M. & Deci, E. L. (2000). Self-determination theory and the facilitation of intrinsic motivation, social development, and well-being. *American Psychologist, 55* (1), 68–78.

Sallis, J. F., & Owen, N. (1999). *Physical activity and behavioral medicine.* Thousand Oaks, CA: Sage Publications.

Secher, N. H., Seifert, T., & Van Lieshout, J. J. (2008). Cerebral blood flow and metabolism during exercise: implications for fatigue. *Journal of Applied Physiology, 104* (1), 306–314.

Seefeldt, V., Malina, R. M., & Clark, M. A. (2002). Factors affecting levels of physical activity in adults. *Sports Medicine, 32,* 143–168.

Sibley, B. A., & Etnier, J. L. (2003). The relationship between physical activity and cognition in children: A meta-analysis. *Pediatric Exercise Science, 15,* 243–256.

Simonen, R. L., Rankinen, T., Perusse, L., Leon, A. S., Skinner, J. S., Wilmore, J. H., Rao, D. C., & Bouchard, C. (2003). A dopamine D2 receptor gene polymorphism and physical activity in two family studies. *Physiology & Behavior, 78,* 751–757.

Singh, N. A., Clements, K. M., & Fiatrone, M. A. (1997). A randomized controlled trial of the effect of exercise on sleep. *Sleep, 20,* 95–101.

Singh, N. A., Stavrinos, T. M., Scarbek, Y., Galambos, G., Liber, C., & Singh, M. A. (2005). A randomized controlled trial of high versus low intensity weight training versus general practitioner care for clinical depression in older adults. *Journals of Gerontology Series A: Biological and Medical Sciences, 60* (6), 768–776.

Smith, J. C., & Crabbe, J. B. (2000). Emotion and exercise. *International Journal of Sport Psychology, 31,* 156–174.

Smith, J. C., O'Connor, P. J., Crabbe, J. B., & Dishman, R. K. (2002). Emotional responsiveness after low- and moderate-intensity exercise and seated rest. *Medicine and Science in Sports and Exercise, 34* (7), 1158–1167.

Soares, J., Holmes, P. V., Renner, K., Edward, G., Bunnell, B. N., & Dishman, R. K. (1999). Brain noradrenergic responses to footshock after chronic activity wheel running. *Behavioral Neuroscience, 113,* 558–566.

Sonstroem, R. J. (1998). Physical self-concept: Assessment and external validity. *Exercise and Sport Sciences Reviews, 26,* 133–164.

Sonstroem, R. J. & Morgan, W. P. (1989). Exercise and self-esteem: rationale and model. *Medicine and Science in Sports and Exercise, 21* (3), 329–337.

Spence, J. C., McGannon, K. R., & Poon, P. (2005). The effect of exercise on global self-esteem: a quantitative review. *Journal of Sport & Exercise Psychology, 27,* 311–334.

Spencer, L., Adams, T. B., Malone, S., Roy, L., & Yost, E. (2006). Applying the transtheoretical model to exercise: a systematic and comprehensive review of the literature. *Health Promotion Practice, 7,* 428–443.

Stansfield, S. A. & Marmot, M. G. (eds.). (2002). *Stress and the heart: Psychosocial pathways to coronary heart disease.* London: BMJ Books.

Ströhle, A., Hofler, M., Pfister, H., Muller, A. G., Hoyer, J., Wittchen, H. U., & Lieb R.. (2007). Physical activity and prevalence and incidence of mental disorders in adolescents and young adults. *Psychological Medicine, 37* (11), 1657–1666.

Strine, T. W., Chapman, D. P., Kobau, R., & Balluz, L. (2005). Associations of self-reported anxiety symptoms with health-related quality of life and health behaviors. *Social Psychiatry and Psychiatric Epidemiology, 40,* 432–438.

Strong, W. B., Malina, R. M., Blimkie, C. J., Daniels, S. R., Dishman, R. K., Gutin, B., Hergenroeder, A. C., Must, A., Nixon, P. A., Pivarnik, J. M., Rowland, T., Trost, S., & Trudeau, F. (2005). Evidence based physical activity for school-age youth. *Journal of Pediatrics, 146* (6), 732–737.

Stubbe, J. H., Boomsma, D. I., Vink, J. M., Cornes, B. K., Martin, N. G., Skytthe, A., Kyvik, K. O., Rose, R. J., Kujala, U. M., Kaprio, J., Harris, J. R., Pedersen, N. L., Hunkin, J., Spector, T. D., & de Geus, E. J. (2006). Genetic influences on exercise participation in 37,051 twin pairs from seven countries. *PLoS ONE, 1,* e22.

Taylor, M. K., Pietrobon, R., Pan, D., Huff, M., & Higgins, L. D. (2004). Healthy people 2010 physical activity guidelines and psychological symptoms: Evidence from a large nationwide database. *Journal of Physical Activity and Health, 1,* 114–130.

Thorsen, L., Nystad, W., Stigum, H., Dahl, O., Klepp, O., Bremnes, R. M., Wist, E. & Fosså, S. D. (2005). The association between self-reported physical activity and prevalence of depression and anxiety disorder in long-term survivors of testicular cancer and men in a general population sample. *Supportive Care in Cancer, 13,* 637–646.

Tieman, J. G., Peacock, L. J., Cureton, K. J., & Dishman, R. K. (2001). Acoustic startle eyeblink response after acute exercise. *International Journal of Neuroscience, 106,* 21–33.

Tomporowski, P. D. (2003). Cognitive and behavioral responses to acute exercise in youths: A review. *Pediatric Exercise Science, 15,* 348–359.

Tomporowski, P. D., & Ellis, N. R. (1986). The effects of exercise on cognitive processes: A review. *Psychological Bulletin, 99,* 338–346.

Trost, S. G., Owen, N., Bauman, A., Sallis, J. F., & Brown, W. J. (2002). Correlates of adults' participation in physical activity: Review and update. *Medicine and Science in Sports and Exercise, 34,* 1996–2001.

Turk, D. C., Rudy, T. E., & Salovey, P. (1984). Health protection: Attitudes and behaviors of LPNs, teachers, and college students. *Health Psychology, 3,* 189–210.

U.S. Department of Health and Human Services. (2000). *Healthy people 2010: Understanding and improving health.* Washington, DC: U.S. Government Printing Office.

Van Hoomissen, J. D., Chambliss, H. O., Holmes, P. V., & Dishman, R. K. (2003). Effects of chronic exercise and imipramine on mRNA for BDNF after olfactory bulbectomy in rat. *Brain Research, 974,* 228–235.

Van Hoomissen, J. D., Holmes, P. V., Zellner, A. S., Poudevigne, A., & Dishman, R. K. (2004). Effects of beta-adrenoreceptor blockade during chronic exercise on contextual fear conditioning and mRNA for galanin and brain-derived neurotrophic factor. *Behavioral Neuroscience, 118,* 1378–1390.

Van Praag, H., Christie, B. R., Sejnowski, T. J., & Gage, F. H. (1999). Running enhances neurogenesis, learning, and long-term potentiation. *Proceedings of the National Academy of Sciences, 96* (23), 13427–13231.

Vissing, J., Andersen, M., & Diemer, N. H. (1996). Exercise-induced changes in local cerebral glucose utilization in the rat. *Journal of Cerebral Blood Flow and Metabolism: Official Journal of the International Society of Cerebral Blood Flow and Metabolism, 16,* 729–736.

Wallace, L. S., & Buckworth, J. (2003). Longitudinal shifts in exercise stages of change in college students. *Journal of Sports Medicine and Physical Fitness, 43,* 209–212.

Wallman, K. E., Morton, A. R., Goodman, C., Grove, R., & Guilfoyle, A. M. (2004). Randomised controlled trial of graded exercise in chronic fatigue syndrome. *Medical Journal of Australia, 180* (9), 444–448.

Wearden, A. J., Morriss, R. K., Mullis, R., Strickland, P. L., Pearson, D. J., Appleby, L., Campbell, I. T., & Morris, J. A. (1998). Randomised, double-blind, placebo-controlled treatment trial of fluoxetine and graded exercise for chronic fatigue syndrome. *British Journal of Psychiatry, 172,* 485–490. Erratum in: *British Journal of Psychiatry; 173* (1998 July), 89.

Weinstein, N. D., Rothman, A. J., & Sutton, S. R. (1998). Stage theories of health behavior: Conceptual and methodological issues. *Health Psychology, 17* (3), 290–299.

Wessely, S., Hotopf, M., & Sharpe, M. (1998). *Chronic fatigue and its syndromes.* Oxford: Oxford University Press.

White-Welkley, J. E., Bunnell, B. N., Mougey, E. H., Meyerhoff J. L., & Dishman, R. K. (1995). Treadmill exercise training and estradiol differentially modulate hypothalamic-pituitary adrenal cortical responses to acute running and immobilization. *Physiology & Behavior, 57,* 533–540.

White-Welkley, J. E., Warren, G. L., Bunnell, B. N., Mougey, E. H., Meyerhoff, J. L., & Dishman, R. K. (1996). Treadmill exercise training and estradiol increase plasma ACTH and prolactin after novel footshock. *Journal of Applied Physiology, 80,* 931–939.

Williamson, J. W., McColl, R., & Mathews, D. (2003). Evidence for central command activation of the human insular cortex during exercise. *Journal of Applied Physiology, 94* (5), 1726–1734.

Yoo, H. S., Bunnell, B. N., Crabbe, J. B., Kalish, L. R., & Dishman, R. K. (2000). Failure of neonatal clomipramine treatment to alter forced swim immobility: Chronic treadmill or activity-wheel running and imipramine. *Physiology and Behavior, 70,* 407–411.

Yoo, H. S., Tackett, R. L., & Dishman, R. K. (1996). Brain-adrenergic responses to wheel running. *Medicine and Science in Sports and Exercise, 28* (5, Suppl.), S109.

Youngstedt, S. D., Dishman, R. K., Cureton, K. J., & Peacock, L. J. (1993). Does body temperature mediate anxiolytic effects of acute exercise? *Journal of Applied Physiology, 74,* 825–831.

Youngstedt, S. D. & Kline, C. E. (2006). Epidemiology of exercise and sleep. *Sleep and Biological Rhythms, 4* (3), 215–221.

Youngstedt, S. D., O'Connor, P. J., & Dishman, R. K. (1997). The effects of acute exercise on sleep: A quantitative synthesis. *Sleep, 20,* 203–214.

Youngstedt, S. D., O'Connor, P., Crabbe, J. B., & Dishman, R. K. (2000). Effects of acute exercise on caffeine-induced insomnia. *Physiology & Behavior, 68,* 563–570.

SUBJECT INDEX

Note: Figures and tables are indicated by *f* or *t*, respectively, following the page number.